London

THE ROUGH GUIDE

There are more than sixty Rough Guide titles covering destinations from Amsterdam to Zimbabwe

Forthcoming titles include
Bali • Costa Rica • Goa • Hawaii • Majorca • Rhodes
Singapore • Vietnam

Rough Guide Reference Series
Classical Music • World Music

Rough Guide Phrasebooks
Czech • French • German • Greek • Italian • Spanish

Rough Guide Credits

Text Editors:	Jonathan Buckley and Mark Ellingham
Series Editor:	Mark Ellingham
Editorial:	Martin Dunford, Jules Brown, Graham Parker, Samantha Cook, Jo Mead, Alison Cowan, Amanda Tomlin, Annie Shaw, Lemisse al-Hafidh, Catherine McHale
Production:	Susanne Hillen, Andy Hilliard, Alan Spicer, Judy Pang, Link Hall, Nicola Williamson
Cartography	Melissa Flack
Finance:	John Fisher, Celia Crowley, Simon Carloss
Marketing and Publicity:	Richard Trillo (UK), Jean-Marie Kelly, Jeff Kaye (US)
Administration:	Tania Hummel

Acknowledgements

Rob Humphreys would like to thank the following for their help in the preparation of this guide: Kate, Stan, Joshua, Nat, Gren and Juliet Middleton, David Charap, Dan Richardson, Bert Spicer, Bill Fishmann, Sam Doty, Tania Smith, Pol Ferguson-Thompson, Val and Gordon Humphreys, Pat Yale, Mark Ellingham, Jonathan Buckley, Martin Dunford, Alan Spicer and Melissa Flack.

This first edition published in 1995 and reprinted in July 1995 by Rough Guides Ltd, 1 Mercer Street, London WC2H 9QJ.

Distributed by the Penguin Group:

Penguin Books Ltd, 27 Wrights Lane, London W8 5TZ.

Penguin Books USA Inc, 375 Hudson Street, New York 10014, USA.

Penguin Books Australia Ltd, 487 Maroondah Highway, PO Box 257, Ringwood, Victoria 3134, Australia.

Penguin Books Canada Ltd, 10 Alcorn Avenue, Toronto, Ontario, Canada M4V 1E4.

Penguin Books (NZ) Ltd, 182–190 Wairau Road, Auckland 10, New Zealand.

Printed in the United Kingdom by Cox & Wyman Ltd (Reading).

Typography and **original design** by Jonathan Dear and The Crowd Roars.

Illustrations throughout by Edward Briant.

Mapping is based upon the Ordnance Survey maps with the permission of the Controller of Her Majesty's Stationery Office, © Crown copyright.

LRT Registered User N° 95/2165, London Underground Map and Bus Map.

608pp. Includes index.

British Library Cataloguing in Publication Data

A catalogue record for this book is available from the British Library.

ISBN 1-85828-117-2

London

THE ROUGH GUIDE

Written and researched by
Rob Humphreys

With additional accounts by
Guy Barefoot, Jules Brown, Jonathan Buckley,
Samantha Cook, Michelle de Larrabeiti,
Mark Ellingham, Chris Scott and Annie Shaw

THE ROUGH GUIDES

Contents

Maps

MAP SYMBOLS

	Road		Stately Home
	Passageway		Public Gardens
	Railway		Building
	River/canal		Church
	Ferry route		Synagogue
	Chapter division boundary		Mosque
	Underground station		Christian cemetery
	Train station		Park
	Tourist Office		Building site

Introduction

What strikes visitors more than anything about London is the sheer size of the place. The population – currently around seven million – may be declining, but it is still by far Europe's largest city, spreading across an area of more than 620 square miles from its core on the River Thames. Londoners tend to cope with this by compartmentalizing the city, identifying with the neighbourhoods in which they work or live, and making occasional forays into the "centre of town" – the West End, London's shopping and entertainment heartland.

Those without local roots can find the place bafflingly diverse. With around two hundred languages spoken within its confines and all the major religions represented, London can seem more like an entire country than a single city, and it is Europe's most multi-ethnic metropolis. Over thirty percent of the population is made up of first-, second- and third-generation immigrants, while some claim as many as seventy-five percent of white Londoners are in fact descended from French Huguenot refugees.

Whatever its exact make-up, London has a pre-eminent status in Britain: it's where the country's news and money are made, it's where the central government resides, and as far as its inhabitants are concerned, provincial life begins beyond the circuit of the city's orbital motorway. Londoners' sense of superiority causes enormous resentment in the regions, yet it's undeniable that the capital has a unique aura of excitement and success – in most walks of British life, if you want to get on, you've got to do so in London.

For a run-down on London's highlights, see "Introducing the City" (p.27).

Despite its dominant role, however, London is the only capital city in Europe that lacks it own governing body, a symptom of more than a decade's political indifference from the Conservative government. This neglect, compounded by a political culture that penalizes the unfortunate, has resulted in a city of spiralling extremes – ostentatious private affluence and increasing public squalor. At night, the West End is packed with theatregoers, while the doorways and shopfronts serve as dormitories for the growing band of London's dispossessed. The city's problems come into further high relief in

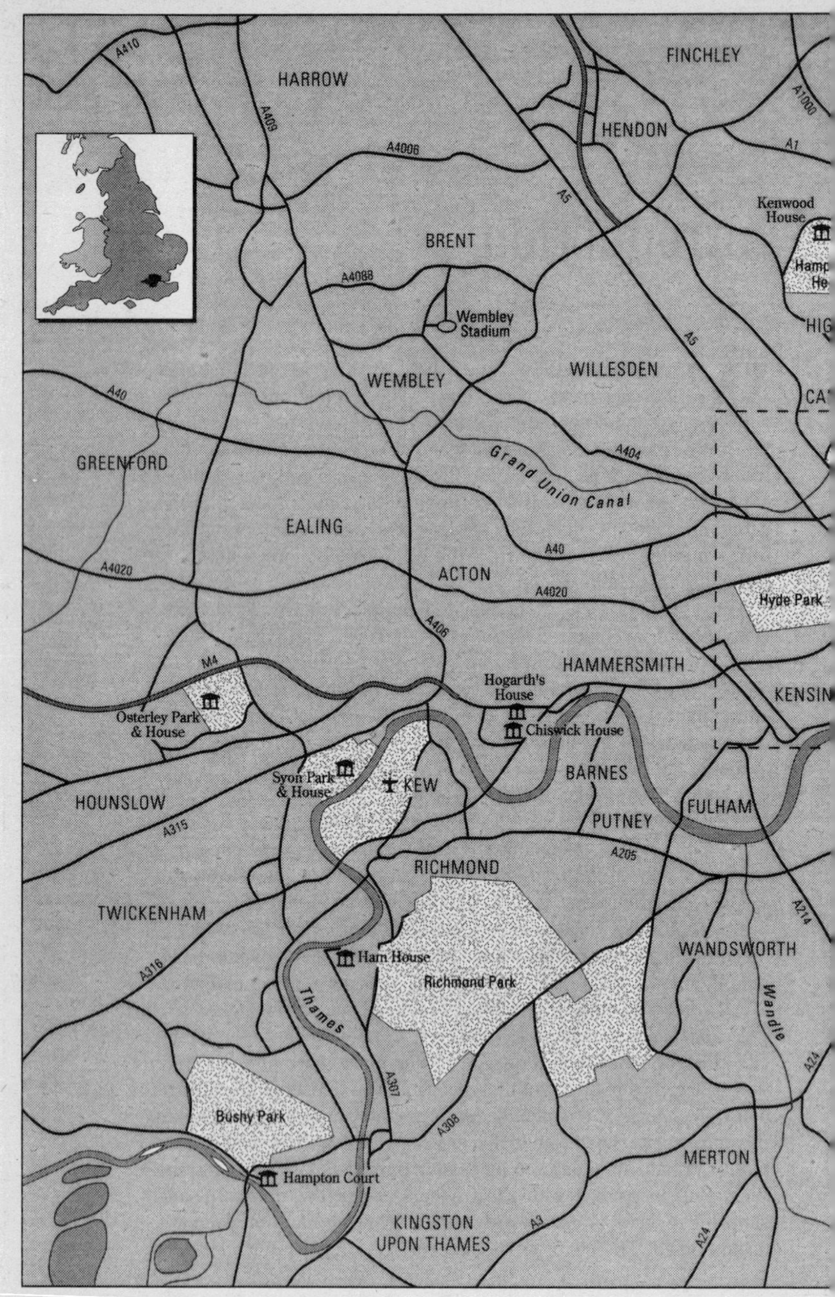

HARROW
FINCHLEY
HENDON
A410
A409
A4006
A1000
A1
A5
Kenwood House
BRENT
A4088
Wembley Stadium
WEMBLEY
WILLESDEN
A40
GREENFORD
A404
Grand Union Canal
EALING
A40
A4020
ACTON
A4020
Hyde Park
A406
M4
HAMMERSMITH
Hogarth's House
Chiswick House
Osterley Park & House
KENSIN
Syon Park & House
KEW
BARNES
HOUNSLOW
A315
PUTNEY
FULHAM
A205
RICHMOND
TWICKENHAM
A214
Ham House
WANDSWORTH
Richmond Park
A316
Thames
Wandle
A307
A24
Bushy Park
A308
Hampton Court
MERTON
KINGSTON UPON THAMES
A3
A24

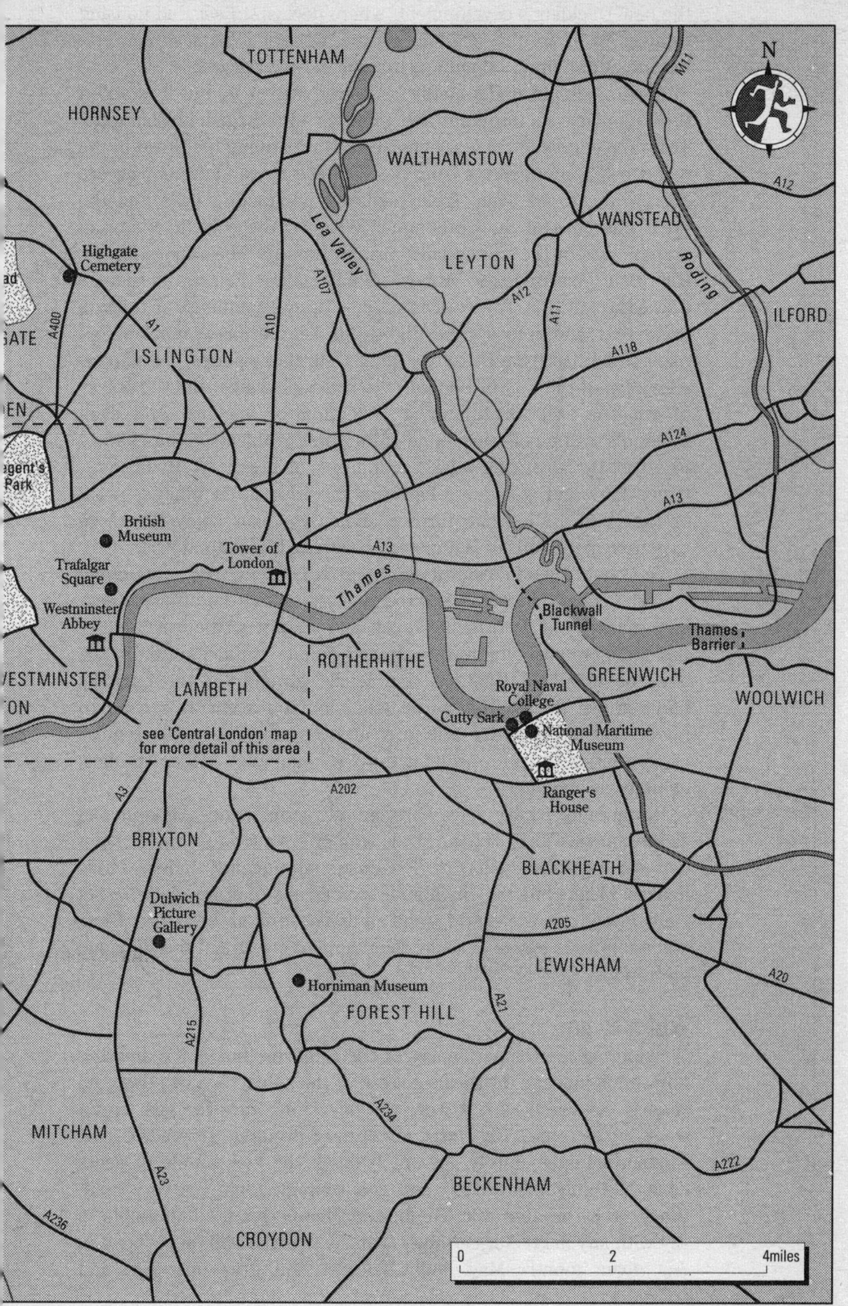

TOTTENHAM
HORNSEY
WALTHAMSTOW
N
M11
A12
WANSTEAD
Lea Valley
Highgate
Cemetery
LEYTON
Roding
A107
A12
A11
ILFORD
A400
A1
A10
ISLINGTON
A118
A124
A13
British
Museum
Tower of
London
A13
Trafalgar
Square
Thames
Westminster
Abbey
Blackwall
Tunnel
Thames
Barrier
ROTHERHITHE
GREENWICH
LAMBETH
Royal Naval
College
WOOLWICH
Cutty Sark
National Maritime
Museum
see 'Central London' map
for more detail of this area
A202
A3
Ranger's
House
BRIXTON
BLACKHEATH
Dulwich
Picture
Gallery
A205
LEWISHAM
A20
Horniman Museum
FOREST HILL
A21
A215
A234
MITCHAM
A222
A23
BECKENHAM
A236
CROYDON
0
2
4miles

the new Docklands development, where decaying East End housing estates stand in the shadow of the Canary Wharf skyscraper, harbinger of a financial miracle that never materialized.

London should undoubtedly be better than it is, but it is still a thrilling place. Its museums and galleries – the British Museum, the Tate, and scores of smaller specialists – are among the finest in the world, while monuments from the capital's more glorious past are everywhere to be seen, from medieval banqueting halls and the great churches of Sir Christopher Wren to the eclectic Victorian architecture of the triumphalist British Empire. The major sights – Big Ben, Westminster Abbey, Buckingham Palace, St Paul's Cathedral and the Tower of London – draw in millions of tourists every year, and in most cases rightly so. Yet there is as much enjoyment to be had from the city's quiet Georgian squares, the narrow alleyways of the City of London, the riverside walks, and the quirks of what is still identifiably a collection of villages. And even London's traffic pollution – one of its worst problems in the 1990s – is offset by surprisingly large expanses of greenery: Hyde Park, Green Park and St James's Park are all within a few minutes' walk of the West End, while further afield, you can enjoy the more expansive parklands of Hampstead Heath and Richmond Park.

You could spend days just shopping in London, too, hobnobbing with the ruling classes in *Harrod's*, or sampling the offbeat weekend markets of Portobello Road and Camden, the seedbed of London's famously innovative street fashion – an inspiration to the likes of Jean-Paul Gaultier, and fertile ground for the capital's home-grown talent. The music and clubbing scene is second to none, and mainstream arts are no less exciting, with regular opportunities to catch brilliant theatre companies, dance troupes, exhibitions and opera.

Restaurants, these days, are an attraction, too. London has caught up with its European rivals, and offers a range from Michelin two-star establishments to low-cost, high-quality Indian curry houses. Meanwhile the city's pubs have heaps of atmosphere, especially away from the centre – and an exploration of the farther-flung communities is essential to get the complete picture of this dynamic metropolis.

When to go

Considering the temperateness of the English climate, it's amazing how much mileage the locals get out of the subject – a two-day cold snap is discussed as if it were the onset of a new Ice Age, and a week in the upper 70s starts rumours of drought. The fact is that English summers rarely get hot (though the last couple of years have had July heatwaves) and the winters don't get very cold, though they're often wet. The bottom line is that it's impossible to say with any degree of certainty that the weather will be pleasant in any given month. May might be wet and grey one year and gloriously sunny the next, and the same goes for the autumnal months – November stands an equal chance of being crisp and clear or foggy and grim.

As far as crowds go, tourists stream into London pretty much all-year round, with peak season from Easter to October, and the biggest crush in July and August, when you'll need to book your accommodation well in advance. Costs, however, are pretty uniform year-round.

Average daily temperatures in London

	Jan	Feb	Mar	Apr	May	Jun	Jul	Aug	Sep	Oct	Nov	Dec
°F	42	43	46	51	56	62	65	65	60	54	48	44
°C	5	6	8	11	14	17	18	18	16	12	9	6

Average monthly rainfall in London

	Jan	Feb	Mar	Apr	May	Jun	Jul	Aug	Sep	Oct	Nov	Dec
inches	2.1	1.6	1.5	1.5	1.8	1.8	2.2	2.3	1.9	2.2	2.5	1.9
mm	54	40	37	37	46	45	57	59	49	57	64	48

The Basics

Getting There from North America

All the major US and Canadian airlines run direct services from North America to London, England's busiest gateway city. Two of London's airports – Heathrow and Gatwick – handle transatlantic flights, and in terms of convenience they are about equal (see p.31)

Figure on six and a half hours' **flying time** from New York; it's an hour extra going the other way, due to headwinds. Most eastbound flights cross the Atlantic overnight, depositing you at your destination the next morning without much sleep, but if you can manage to stay awake until after dinner that night, you should be over the worst of jet lag by the next morning. Some flights from the East Coast depart early in the morning, arriving late the same evening, but this lands you in London just as the city is shutting down – a recipe for a disorienting and expensive first night.

Shopping for Tickets

Given the enormous volume of air traffic crossing the Atlantic, you should have no problem finding a seat – the problem will be sifting through all the possibilities. Basic fares are kept very reasonable by intense competition, and discounts by bulk agents and periodic special offers by the airlines themselves can drive prices still lower. Any local **travel agent** should be able to access airlines' up-to-the-minute fares, although in practice they may not have time to research all the possibilities – you might want to call a few **airlines** directly (see p.4).

The least expensive tickets widely available from the airlines are **Apex** (Advance Purchase Excursion) tickets, which carry certain restrictions: you have to book – and pay – at least 21 days before departure, spend at least seven days abroad (maximum stay three months), and tend to get penalized if you change your schedule. There are also winter **Super Apex** tickets, which are slightly less expensive than an ordinary Apex, but limiting your stay to between 7 and 21 days. Some airlines also issue **Special Apex** tickets to those under 24, often extending the maximum stay to a year.

Whatever the airlines are offering, however, any number of specialist travel companies should be able to beat it. These are the outfits you'll see advertising in the Sunday newspaper travel sections, and they come in several forms. **Consolidators** buy up large blocks of tickets that airlines don't think they'll be able to sell at their published fares, and sell them at a discount. Besides being inexpensive, consolidators normally don't impose advance purchase requirements (although in busy times you'll want to book ahead just to be sure of getting a ticket), but they do often charge very stiff fees for date changes. Also, these companies' margins are pretty tiny, so they make their money by dealing in volume – don't expect them to entertain lots of questions. Some agencies specialize in **charter flights**, which may be even cheaper than anything available on a scheduled flight, but again there's a trade-off: departure dates are fixed and withdrawal penalties are high. **Discount travel clubs** are another option for those who travel a lot – most charge an annual membership fee, which may be worth it for discounts on air tickets, car rental and the like.

Incidentally, don't automatically assume that tickets purchased through a travel specialist will be the least expensive on offer – once you get a quote, check with the airlines and you may turn up an even cheaper promotion. Be advised also that the pool of travel companies is swimming with sharks – exercise caution with any outfit that sounds shifty or impermanent, and never deal with a company that demands cash up front or refuses to accept payment by credit card.

Regardless of where you buy your ticket, the **fare** will depend on season. Fares to London are highest from June to September, when everyone wants to travel; they drop during the "shoulder" seasons, March/April and October, and you'll get the best deals during the low season, November through to March (excluding Christmas). The Christmas–New Year holiday period is a thing unto itself – if you want to travel at this time, book at least two or three months ahead, and be prepared for fares even higher than those in summer. Note that flying on weekends ordinarily adds $20–60 to the round-trip fare; price ranges quoted in the sections below assume midweek travel.

Flights from the US

Dozens of airlines fly from New York to London, and a few fly direct from other East Coast and Midwestern hubs. The best low-season fares from **New York** to London hover around $400 round-trip, with peak-season prices likely to run $150–250 higher. To give an idea of low-season fares to London from other cities, several carriers fly from **Boston** for as little as $400, **Washington DC** from $450 or **Chicago** from $520; *Delta* flies from **Atlanta** for about $500 and from **Miami** for $540; *Virgin* from **Orlando** for $560; *TWA* from **St Louis** for $525; *American* from **Dallas/Fort Worth** for about $600; and *Continental* from **Denver** for $590.

Don't assume you'll have to change planes when flying from the **West Coast** – it might be worth paying extra to fly nonstop (*American*, *BA* and *United* all do so from LA), though you'll have to decide just how much that luxury is worth to you. Several carriers fly or connect with flights to London from **Los Angeles** or **San Francisco**, with low-season midweek fares from both cities starting at around $620. From **Seattle** the price will be more in the region of $550. High-season fares will be at least $200 higher.

Flights from Canada

In Canada, you'll get the best deal flying to London from the big gateway cities of Toronto and Montréal, where competition between *Air Canada*, *Canadian Airlines*, *British Airways* and others drive off-season midweek fares as low as Can$550 round-trip; direct flights from Ottawa and Halifax will probably cost only slightly more. From Vancouver, Edmonton and Calgary, London flights start at Can$750 off-season. High-season

MAJOR AIRLINES IN NORTH AMERICA

Aer Lingus ☎800/223-6537. Flights from New York and Boston to London, via Dublin or Shannon.

Air Canada ☎800/776-3000. Flights from Ottawa, Vancouver, Toronto, Montréal, Halifax and St John (Newfoundland) to London.

Air India ☎800/223-7776. New York and Toronto to London.

American Airlines ☎800/433-7300. Serves London from half a dozen American gateway cities (Dallas-Fort Worth is its hub)

British Airways ☎800/247-9297. Flights from major North American cities to London.

Canadian Airlines ☎800/426-7000. Flights from Vancouver, Edmonton, Calgary and Toronto to London.

Continental Airlines ☎800/231-0856. Flights to London from Newark, Houston and Denver, with other routes feeding into these gateway cities.

Delta Airlines ☎800/241-4141. Atlanta, Cincinnatti, Miami and Orlando to London.

Kuwait Airways ☎800/458-9248. New York to London.

Northwest Airlines ☎800/225-2525. Minneapolis and Boston to London.

TWA ☎800/221-2000. St Louis to London.

United Airlines ☎800/538-2929) Flights from New York, Washington, Los Angeles, San Francisco and Seattle to London; many other routings possible via these gateways.

US Air ☎800/622-1015. New York to London.

Virgin Atlantic Airways ☎800/862-8621. Flights to London from Newark, JFK, Boston, LA, Miami, Orlando and San Francisco.

DISCOUNT AGENTS, CONSOLIDATORS AND TRAVEL CLUBS

Air Brokers International, 323 Geary St, Suite 411, San Francisco, CA 94102 ☎800/883-3273. Consolidator.

Council Charter, 205 East 42nd St, New York, NY 10017 ☎800/223-7402. Youth-oriented charter broker.

Council Travel, 205 East 42nd St, New York, NY 10017 ☎800/743-1823 or 212/661-1450; 312 Sutter St, San Francisco, CA 94108 ☎415/421-3473; and many other regional outlets. Youth-oriented discount agent.

Discount Travel International, Ives Building, 114 Forrest Ave, Suite 205, Narberth, PA 19072 ☎215/668-7184. Discount travel club, membership $45.

Moment's Notice, 425 Madison Ave, New York, NY ☎212/486-0503. Travel club.

Nouvelles Frontières, 12 East 33rd St, New York, NY 10016 ☎212/779-0600; 1001 Sherbrooke Est, Suite 720, Montréal, H2L IL3 ☎514/526-8444; and other US and Canadian locations. Discount travel agent.

STA Travel, 48 East 11th St, New York, NY 10003 ☎800/777-0112 or 212/477-7166; 106 Geary St, San Francisco, CA 94108 ☎415/391-8407; and other East and West Coast offices. Big discount agent specializing in student and youth deals.

Stand Buys, 311 W Superior St, Chicago, IL 60610 ☎800/548-1116. Travel club.

Travel Cuts, 187 College St, Toronto, Ont, M5T 1P7 ☎416/979-2406; and outlets on most Canadian university campuses. Student/youth discount agency.

UniTravel, 1177 North Warson Rd, St Louis, MO 63132 ☎800/325-2222. Consolidator.

travel will add a premium of $300–400 to all these fares.

Packages and Organized Tours

Although you'll want to see London at your own speed, don't dismiss the idea of a **package deal** out of hand. Many agents and airlines put together very flexible packages, sometimes amounting to nothing more restrictive than a flight plus accommodation, and these can work out cheaper – and less stressful – than the same arrangements made independently.

There are plenty of **tour** operators specializing in travel to London, and they can be contacted either directly or through travel agents – the cost is the same. Choose only an operator that is a member of the *United States Tour Operator Association* (*USTOA*) or has been approved by the *American Society of Travel Agents* (*ASTA*). What follows is a survey of some of the most popular deals, while the box below contains useful addresses; for a full but uncritical listing, contact the *British Tourist Authority* (see p.17). The prices quoted below are for packages from New York; for West Coast flights you'll pay around $200–350 extra, for Chicago it's around $200 extra, and for Miami you should add around $100.

British Airways Holidays offers a spread of tours departing from various cities, as the airline has a lot of US gateways and agreements with other airlines to connect those gateways with airports not served by *BA*. The *BA* selection includes "A Taste of London", a four-day/three-night (or six-day/seven-night) tour for between $499 and $1109 including airfare, airport transfers, hotel accommodation, one pub lunch, daily continental breakfast, $25 toward sightseeing excursions, and a Travelcard for unlimited travel on London's public transport system. Other value-minded options include "London on Stage", a package which offers one ticket to *Sunset Boulevard*, another ticket to a show of your choice, and a backstage theatre pass, for $699–1049; and "London Shop Till You Drop", with extras including £25 vouchers for *Harrods* and *Marks & Spencer*, afternoon tea at *Fortnum & Mason*, and a Sunday morning tour of some of London's street markets for $599–949. *BA* also offers apartments in London for prices ranging from $83 to $1164 depending on location, size, etc. (Short-stay apartments in London can also be arranged through *Keith Prowse*, 234 West 44th St, New York, NY 10036; ☎ 212/398-1430 or 800/669-8687. Rates range from $553 to $2000 per week.).

TWA Getaway Vacations offers London city, theatre and shopping packages similar to the *BA* ones for prices in the $300–1100 range. *Virgin Vacations*, another good airline-run package company, offers numerous options including "London Lite", a three-day/two-night plan from

$399, providing air fare, breakfasts, and choice of three-day Travelcard or theatre pass. *Virgin*'s "Luxury in London" is a six-night plan from $1259; and "West End Weekend" is a three-night theatre extravaganza costing from $479.

Travel Bound offers the "London Weekend", three-days/two nights or four days/three nights from $349 including round-trip airfare, hotel accommodation, daily breakfast and a welcome pack with maps and information; "Introducing London" is a seven-day/six-night package which includes round-trip air fare, accommodation, breakfast, airport transfers, city sightseeing tour, afternoon tea at *Selfridge's*, half-day excursion to Windsor and Hampton Court, one theatre pass of your choice, a seven-day Travelcard, and an entrance pass to Madame Tussaud's, starting at $709.

BritTours provides seven- and fourteen-night vacations which allow you to explore London and one or two other British cities for $999–$1899. If it's just the capital you're interested in, you might take the "Exclusively London" package, ranging from $569 (for two nights) to £1079 (seven nights).

NORTH AMERICAN TOUR OPERATORS TO ENGLAND

American Airlines Fly Away Vacations, c/o *American Airlines*, PO Box 619616, Dallas Fort Worth Airport 75261-9616 ☎ 800/321-2121. Independent and group itineraries.

BA Tours, 5728 Major Blvd, Suite 750, Orlando, FL 32819 ☎ 800/359 8722. BA package tour agents.

British Travel International, PO Box 299, Elkton, VA 22827 ☎ 800/327-6097. Agent for made-to-measure packages: air tickets, rail and bus passes, hotels, and a comprehensive B&B reservation service.

BritRail Travel International Inc., 1500 Broadway, New York, NY 10036 ☎ 800/677-8585 or 212/575-2667. *British Rail*' s tour agents offering flight and accommodation deals.

Contiki Holidays, 300 Plaza Alicante, Suite 900, Garden Grove, CA 92640 ☎ 800/466-0610. Specific tours for groups between the ages of eighteen and thirty-five.

Sterling Tours, 2707 Congress St, Suite 2-G, San Diego, CA 92110 ☎ 800/727-4359. Offers a variety of independent itineraries and packages.

STS Travel, 795 Franklin Ave, Franklin Lakes, NJ 07417 ☎ 800/752-6787. Customized history, literature, theatre and horticulture tours.

Trafalgar Tours, 212 East 26th St, New York, NY 10010 ☎ 800/854-0103 or 212/689-8977. Independent and group tours to London.

Travel Bound, 599 Broadway, New York, NY 10012 ☎ 800/456-8656. A variety of London deals, including Virgin packages.

TWA Getaway Vacations, 10 East Stowe Rd, Marlton, NJ 08053 ☎ 800-GETAWAY. General interest tour operator offering similar deals to *BA*.

Virgin Vacations, 599 Broadway, New York, NY 10012 ☎ 800/364 6466 or 212/843-9797. *Virgin*'s package division.

Getting There from Australia and New Zealand

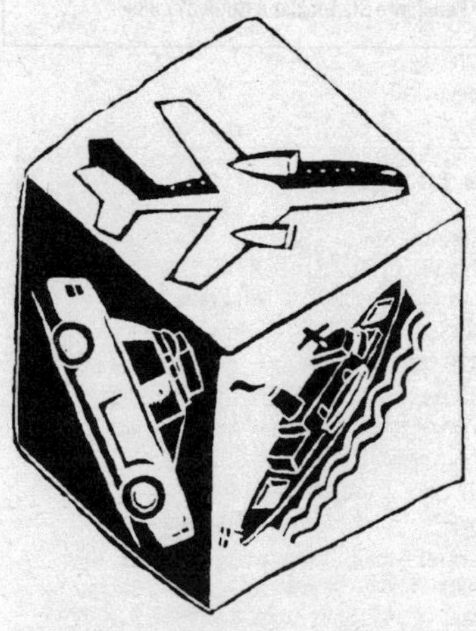

There are daily **flights** to London from Melbourne, Sydney, Brisbane and Perth, with no great difference in the fares from these departure points. With *Garuda*, the least expensive airline, a return ticket from Sydney to London should be available for around Aus$1600 in the low season – mid-November to mid-December. With *BA*, *Thai* or *Malaysian* airlines add at least another hundred dollars. From Auckland, expect to pay around NZ$1170 single or NZ$2050 return in the low season – October to November – with *Qantas*.

For these and other low-price tickets, the most reliable operator is *STA* (*STS* in New Zealand), who also supply packages with companies such as *Contiki* and *Top Deck*. *STA* can also advise on **visa regulations** for Australian and New Zealand citizens – and for a fee will do all the paperwork for you.

TRAVEL AGENTS

Accent on Travel, 545 Queen St, Brisbane ☎07/832 1777.

Adventure World, 73 Walker St, North Sydney ☎02/956 7766; 8 Victoria Ave, Perth ☎09/221 2300.

Anywhere Travel, 345 Anzac Parade, Kingsford, Sydney ☎02/663 0411.

Brisbane Discount Travel, 360 Queen St, Brisbane ☎07/229 9211.

Budget Travel, PO Box 505, Auckland ☎09/309 4313.

Discount Travel Specialists, Shop 53, Forrest Chase, Perth ☎09/221 1400.

Flight Centres

Australia: Circular Quay, Sydney ☎02/241 2422; Bourke St, Melbourne ☎03/650 2899; plus other branches nationwide.

New Zealand: National Bank Towers, 205–225 Queen St, Auckland ☎09/309 6171; Shop 1M, National Mutual Arcade, 152 Hereford St, Christchurch ☎09/379 7145; 50–52 Willis St, Wellington ☎04/472 8101; other branches nationwide.

STA Travel, 732 Harris St, Ultimo, Sydney ☎02/212 1255 or 281 9866; 256 Flinders St, Melbourne ☎03/347 4711; 100 James St, Northbridge, Perth WA 6003 ☎09/227 7299; other offices in Townsville, Cairns and state capitals.

STA Travel, Traveller's Centre, 10 High St, Auckland ☎09/309 9995; 233 Cuba St, Wellington ☎04/385 0561; 223 High St, Christchurch ☎03/379 9098; other offices in Dunedin, Palmerston North and Hamilton.

Topdeck Travel, 45 Grenfell St, Adelaide ☎08/410 1110.

Tymtro Travel, Suite G12, Wallaceway Shopping Centre, Chatswood, Sydney ☎02/413 1219.

Passport Travel, 320b Glenferrie Rd, Malvern, Melbourne ☎03/824 7183.

AIRLINES

British Airways, 64 Castlereagh St, Sydney ☎02/258 3300; Dilworth Building, cnr. Queen and Customs streets, Auckland ☎09/367 7500.

Garuda, 175 Clarence St, Sydney ☎02/334 9900; 120 Albert St, Auckland ☎09/366 1855.

MAS, 388 George St, Sydney ☎02/231 5066 or ☎008/269 998; Floor 12, Swanson Centre, 12–26 Swanson St, Auckland ☎09/373 2741.

Qantas, International Square, Jamison St, Sydney ☎02/957 0111/236 3636; Qantas House, 154 Queen St, Auckland ☎09/303 2506.

Thai 75–77 Pitt St, Sydney ☎02/844 0999 or 008 221 320); Kensington Swan Building, 22 Fanshawe St, Auckland ☎09/377 3886.

Getting There from Ireland and the Continent

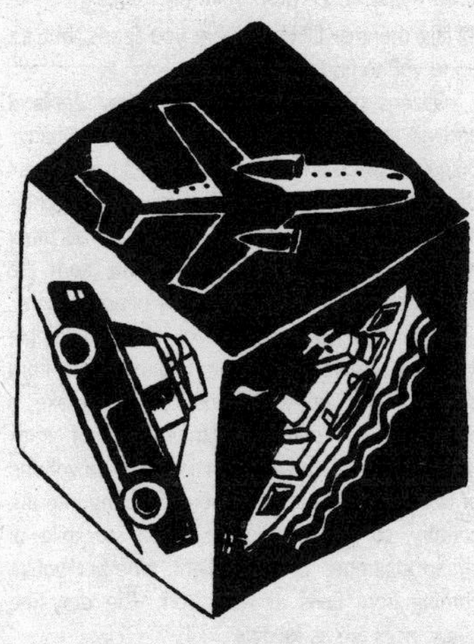

The only foot passengers likely to find ferries a cost-effective way of getting to London are students or under-26s coming from Ireland – and even then, the extra cost of a flight is so little that it's probably worth paying for the added convenience. A Super Apex return flight with *Aer Lingus* (☎01/844 4777) *Ryanair* (☎01/844 4400) or *British Midland* (☎01/283 8833) from **Dublin to London** should cost in the region of IR£80, as against an average of IR£70 for a return rail plus ferry ticket. *British Airways* (☎01232/899 131) fly **Belfast to London** for around £95 return, subject to availability; *British Midland* (☎01232/241 188) is slightly cheaper at £90 return peak season, £75 off season.

With the Channel Tunnel finally operational, **drivers from Europe** now have the option of missing out on the view across the water and taking *Le Shuttle*, as the freight trains carrying coaches, cars and motorbikes are known. Prices for *Le Shuttle* are almost identical to the shortest ferry routes, but tariff rates are bewilderingly complex: prices vary with the month, day or even hour at certain times of the year, not to mention how long you're staying and the size of your car. Travellers contemplating one of the longer ferry routes should bear in mind that some kind of sleeping accommodation is often obligatory on night crossings, pushing the price way above the basic rate. As an indication of cost, two people driving in a small car from Calais, Boulogne, Dieppe, Zeebrugge or Ostend to one of the English Channel ports could expect to pay the equivalent of £90–130 one-way (a return ticket is usually just twice the price of a one-way)

For foot passengers there are now ***Eurostar* trains** running through the tunnel, connecting London with Paris and Brussels (and various major European cities); these are operated by British, French and Belgian rail companies. Trains between Paris and London take just three and a half hours, with the cheapest tickets currently around £95 return.

Visas, Customs Regulations And Tax

Citizens of the **US** can travel in England for up to six months without a visa. For longer stays, apply to the British Embassy (see box below). Full-time, bona fide college students can get temporary work or study permits through the Council on International Education Exchange (CIEE), 205 East 42nd St, New York, NY 10017 (☎212/661-1414). Work permits cost $125 to arrange and are good for six months; CIEE will give you leads, but it's up to you to find the work.

Citizens of **Canada**, **Australia**, **New Zealand** and all the countries of **Europe** except Albania, Bulgaria, Poland and the states of the former Soviet Union can enter Britain with just a passport, generally for up to three months. Citizens of all other nationalities require a visa, obtainable from the British Consular office in the country of application.

Since the inauguration of the EU Single Market, travellers coming into Britain directly from another EU country do not have to make a declaration to **Customs** at their place of entry. However, there are still restrictions on the volume of **tax- or duty-free** goods you can bring into the country, so you can't invest in a stockpile of cheap cigarettes on your flight, whether you're coming from Paris or New York. The duty-free allowances are as follows:

- **Tobacco**: 200 cigarettes; or 100 cigarillos; or 50 cigars; or 250 grammes of loose tobacco.
- **Alcohol**: 2 litres of still wine **plus** one litre of drink over 22 percent alcohol, or two litres of alcoholic drinks not over 22 percent, or another 2 litres of still wine.

BRITISH EMBASSIES ABROAD

Australia Commonwealth Ave, Yarralumla, Canberra, ACT 2600 ☎062/270-6666.

Canada 80 Elgin St, Ottawa, ON K1P 5K7 ☎613/237-1530.

Ireland 31–33 Merrion Rd, Dublin 4 ☎01/695211.

New Zealand Reserve Bank Bldg, 2 The Terrace, PO Box 1812, Wellington ☎04/726-049.

USA 3100 Massachusetts Ave, NW, Washington, DC 20008 ☎202/462-1340.

OVERSEAS EMBASSIES IN BRITAIN

American Embassy, 5 Upper Grosvenor Street, London W1 ☎0171/499 9000.

Australian High Commission, Australia House, The Strand, London WC2 ☎0171/379 4334.

Canadian High Commission, 1 Grosvenor Square, London W1 ☎0171/258 6600.

Irish Embassy, 17 Grosvenor Place, London SW1 ☎0171/235 2171.

New Zealand High Commission, New Zealand House, 80 Haymarket, London SW1 ☎0171/930 8422.

• **Perfumes**: 60cc of perfume plus 250cc of toilet water.
Plus other goods to the value of £32.

There are **import restrictions** on a variety of articles and substances, from firearms to furs derived from endangered species, none of which should bother the normal tourist. However, if you need any clarification on British import regulations, you should contact HM Customs and Excise, New Kings Beam House, 22 Upper Ground, London SE1 9PJ ☎0171/620 1313). You are not allowed to bring **pets** into Britain.

Most goods in Britain, with the chief exceptions of books and food, are subject to **Value Added Tax** (VAT), which increases the cost of an item by 17.5 percent. Visitors from non-EU countries can save a lot of money through the Retail Export Scheme, that allows a refund of VAT on goods to be taken out of the country. (Savings will usually be minimal for EU nationals, because of the rates at which the goods will be taxed upon import to the home country.) Note that not all shops participate in this scheme (those doing so will display a sign to this effect) and that you cannot reclaim VAT charged on hotel bills or other services.

Money, Banks and Costs

The easiest and safest way to carry your money is in travellers' cheques, available for a small commission (normally one percent) from any major bank. The most commonly accepted travellers' cheques are American Express, followed by Visa and Thomas Cook – most cheques issued by banks will be one of these three brands. You'll usually pay commission again when you cash each cheque, normally another one percent or so, or a flat rate – though no commission is payable on Amex cheques exchanged at Amex branches. Keep a record of the cheques as you cash them, and you can get the value of all uncashed cheques refunded immediately if you lose them.

You'll find that most hotels, shops and restaurants in London accept the major **credit cards** – *Access/MasterCard, Visa/Barclaycard, American Express* and *Diners Club.* You can also get cash advances from selected banks and bureaux de change on credit cards, though there will invariably be a minimum amount you can draw. *Visa* cards can be used in *Barclays* cashpoint machines, while *MasterCard* can be used at *Lloyds, Midland* and *National Westminster* banks. Travellers' cheques are accepted by some of the larger stores but it's not common practice, and you won't be able to use them at restaurants. It's best to cash them as you go.

Every area of London has a branch of at least one of the big four high-street **banks**: *National Westminster, Barclays, Lloyds* and *Midland* (listed in descending order of their number of branches). Basic **opening hours** are Mon–Fri 9.30am–3.30pm, though some branches are also open an hour later on Thursday and Friday (sometimes even Mon–Fri) and on Saturday morning.

Almost everywhere banks are the best places to **change money and cheques**; outside banking hours you're best advised to go to a **bureau de change**, which are to be found at train stations or airports and all over central London; try to avoid changing money or cheques in hotels, where the rates are normally the poorest on offer.

If, as a foreign visitor, you run out of money or there is some kind of emergency, the quickest way to get **money sent out** is to contact your bank at home and have them wire the cash to the nearest bank. You can do the same thing through *Thomas Cook* or *American Express.* Americans and Canadians can have cash sent out through *Western Union* (☎0800/833 833) to a nearby bank or post office. Make sure you know when it's likely to arrive, since you won't be notified by the receiving office. Remember you'll need some form of identification when you pick up the money.

There are no exchange controls in Britain, so you can bring in as much cash as you like and change travellers' cheques up to any amount.

Currency

The British **pound sterling** (£) is a decimal currency, divided into 100 pence (p). Coins come in denominations of 1p, 2p, 5p, 10p, 20p, 50p and £1. Notes come in denominations of £5, £10, £20 and £50; shopkeepers will carefully scrutinize any £20 or £50 notes, as forgeries are widespread, and you'd be well advised to do the same. The quickest test is to hold the note up to the light to make sure there's a thin wire filament running from top to bottom; this is by no means foolproof, but it will catch most fakes. Very occasionally you may receive Scottish banknotes from £1 upwards: they're legal tender throughout Britain, but if you have any problems go to the nearest bank and get them changed for English currency.

Costs

London is a very expensive place to visit., chiefly because of the cost of accommodation. The minimum expenditure, for a couple staying in a budget hotel and grabbing takeaway meals, pizzas or other such basic fare, would be in the region of £35–40 per person per day. You only have to add the odd better-quality meal, plus some major tourist attractions, plus a few films or other shows, and you're looking at **around £60** as a daily budget, even in decidedly average accommodation. Single travellers should budget on spending around 60 percent of what a couple would spend (single rooms cost more than half a double). For more detail on the costs of accommodation, transport and eating, see "Introducing the City" (p.27) and Chapters 13, 14 and 15.

Insurance and Emergencies

All visitors to London would be well advised to have some kind of **travel insurance** to cover for loss or theft of possessions, and visitors from outside the EU should have cover for the cost of medical and dental treatment. British visitors should check any household insurance policies they hold, as they might already be covered against theft and loss. If not, take out a travel insurance policy from a company such as *Endsleigh*, who provide one month's cover for around £12. *Endsleigh* policies are available from most youth/student travel specialists or direct from their offices at 97–107 Southampton Row, London WC1 (☎0171/436 4451).

In the **US and Canada** you should check the insurance policies you already have carefully before taking out a new one, as you may discover that you're covered already for medical costs and other losses while abroad. Canadians are usually covered by their provincial health plans, and holders of ISIC cards are entitled (outside the USA) to be reimbursed for $3000-worth of accident coverage and 60 days of in-patient benefits up to $100 a day for the period the card is valid. Students may also find their health coverage extends during vacations, and many bank and charge accounts include some form of travel cover; insurance is also sometimes included if you pay for your trip with a credit card.

If you do want a specific travel insurance policy, there are numerous kinds to choose from: short-term combination policies covering everything from baggage loss to broken legs are the best bet and cost around $50 for fifteen days, $80 for a month, $150 for two months, for $190 for three months. One thing to bear in mind is that none of the currently available policies covers theft; they only cover loss while in the custody of an identifiable person – though even then you must make a report to the police and get their written statement. Two companies you might try are *Travel Guard*, 110 Centrepoint Drive, Steven Point, WI 54480 ☎715/345-0505 or 800/826-1300), or *Access America International*, 600 Third Ave, New York, NY 10163 (☎212/949-5960 or 800/284-8300)

In **Australia**, your best bet, *CIC Insurance*, has some of the widest cover available (from AUS$140 for 31 days) and can be arranged through most travel agents or direct from *Cover-More Insurance Services* (Level 9, 32 Walker St, North Sydney ☎02/202 8000), plus branches in Victoria and Queensland.

Whatever your policy, if you have anything stolen, get a copy of the police report of the incident, as this is essential to substantiate your claim.

Medical Matters

No vaccinations are required for entry into Britain. Citizens of all EU countries are entitled to free medical treatment at National Health Service hospitals; citizens of other countries will be charged for all medical services except those administered by accident and emergency units at NHS hospitals. Thus a US citizen who has been hit by a car would not be charged if the injuries simply require stitching and setting in the emergency unit, but would be charged if admission to a hospital ward were necessary. Health insurance is therefore extremely advisable for all non-EU nationals

Pharmacists can dispense only a limited range of drugs without a doctor's prescription. Most pharmacies are open standard shop hours, though some stay open later; in emergencies, every police station keeps a list of all the pharmacies in its area.

HELPLINES

Aids Helpline ☎0800/567 123 (24hrs; free).

Alcoholics Anonymous ☎0171/352 3001 (Mon–Fri 10am–10pm).

Dental Emergency Care Service ☎0171/955 5000 (24hrs).

Pregnancy Advisory Service ☎0171/637 8962 (Mon–Fri 8.30am–6pm; Sat 9.30am–12.30pm).

Rape Crisis Centre ☎0171/837 1600 (24hrs).

Samaritans ☎0171/734 2800 (24hrs).

HOSPITALS

The most central hospitals with 24-hr emergency units are:

Guys, St Thomas St, SE1 ☎0171/955 5000.

St Bartholomews, West Smithfield, EC1 ☎0171/601 8888.

St Thomas's, Lambeth Palace Rd ☎0171/928 9292.

University College, Gower St, W1 ☎0171/387 9300.

Westminster Hospital, Dean Ryle St, SW1 ☎0181/746 8000.

Doctor's surgeries tend to be open from about 9am to noon and then for a couple of hours in the evenings; outside surgery hours, you can turn up at the casualty department of the local hospital for complaints that require immediate attention – unless it's an emergency, in which case ring for an ambulance, ☎999.

Police

Although the traditional image of the friendly British "Bobby" has become increasingly tarnished by stories of corruption and crooked dealings, in the normal run of events the **police** continue to be approachable and helpful. If you're lost in London, asking a police officer is generally the quickest way to pinpoint your destination – alternatively, you could ask a **traffic warden**, a species of law-enforcer much maligned in car-loving England. Traffic wardens wear a variety of uniforms, but are generally distinguishable by their flat caps and satchels; police officers on street duty wear a distinctive domed hat with a silver tip.

As with any capital city, London has its dangerous spots, but these tend to be around housing estates where no tourist has any reason to be. The chief risk on London's streets is pick-pocketing, and there are some virtuoso villains at work, especially on the big shopping streets and the Underground (tube). Carry only as much money as you need for the day, and keep all bags and pockets fastened. Should you have anything stolen or be involved in some incident that requires reporting, go to the local police station; the ☎999 number should only be used in emergencies.

EMERGENCY SERVICES

For Police, Fire Brigade and Ambulance dial ☎999.

Information and Maps

If you want to do a bit of research before arriving in London, you could contact the **British Tourist Authority** (BTA) in your home country – the addresses are given in the box below. The BTA will send you a wealth of free literature, some of it just rosy-tinted advertising copy, but much of it extremely useful, especially the maps, guides and event calendars. You can also pick up maps and information at the tourist posts at the airports, ports, and in central London.

Maps

The *Geographers'* A–Z map series produces a whole range of street-by-street maps of London from pocket-size foldouts to giant atlases, and the *Nicholson Streetfinder* series is similarly comprehensive. The maps in this book should be adequate for holiday purposes, but if you want something more detailed the best investment is one of the spiral-bound notebook-sized atlases produced by *Geographers'* and *Nicholson*, costing around £5. These books mark and index every street in the city, down to the narrowest alleyway. Virtually every main newsagent in London stocks one or other of them, or you could pick them up from one of the shops listed below. Free maps of the Underground and bus networks can be picked up at tourist offices and London Transport information offices – see p.33.

MAP OUTLETS

LONDON

London *Daunt Books*, 83 Marylebone High St, W1 ☎0171/224 2295; *National Map Centre*, 22–24 Caxton St, SW1 ☎0171/222 4945; *Stanfords*, 12–14 Long Acre, WC2 ☎0171/836 1321; *The Travellers Bookshop*, 25 Cecil Court, WC2 ☎0171/836 9132.

NORTH AMERICA

Chicago *Rand McNally*, 444 North Michigan Ave, IL 60611 ☎312/321 1751.

New York *British Travel Bookshop*, 551 5th Ave, NY ☎800/448-3039 or ☎212/490-6688; *The Complete Traveler Bookstore*, 199 Madison Ave, NY 10016 ☎212/685 9007; *Rand McNally*, 150 East 52nd St, NY 10022 ☎212/758 7488; *Traveler's Bookstore*, 22 West 52nd St, NY 10019 ☎212/664 0995.

San Francisco *The Complete Traveler Bookstore*, 3207 Filmore St, CA 92123; *Rand McNally*, 595 Market St, CA 94105 ☎415/777 3131.

Seattle *Elliot Bay Book Company*, 101 South Main St, WA 98104 ☎206/624 6600.

Toronto *Open Air Books and Maps*, 25 Toronto St, M5R 2C1 ☎416/363 0719.

Vancouver *World Wide Books and Maps*, 1247 Granville St ☎604/687 3320.

AUSTRALIA

Adelaide *The Map Shop*, 16a Peel St, Adelaide, SA 5000 ☎08/231 2033.

Brisbane *Hema*, 239 George St, Brisbane, QLD 4000 ☎07/ 221 4330.

Melbourne *Bowyangs*, 372 Little Bourke St, Melbourne, VIC 3000 ☎03/670 4383.

Sydney *Travel Bookshop*, 20 Bridge St, Sydney, NSW 2000 ☎02/241 3554.

Perth *Perth Map Centre*, 891 Hay St, Perth, WA 6000 ☎09/322 5733.

BRITISH TOURIST AUTHORITY HEAD OFFICES

Australia: 210 Clarence St, 4th Floor, Sydney, NSW 2000 ☎02/267 4555.

Canada: 111 Avenue Rd, Suite 450, Toronto, Ontario M5R 3J8 ☎416/925-2175.

Ireland: BTA, 123 Lower Bagot St, Dublin 2 ☎1/661 4188.

New Zealand: BTA, Suite 305, 3rd Floor, Dilworth Building, corner of Customs and Queen streets, Auckland ☎649/303 1446.

US: 2580 Cumberland Pkwy, Suite 470, Atlanta, GA ☎404/432-9641;

625 North Michigan Ave, Suite 1510, Chicago, IL ☎312/787-0490;

World Trade Center, Suite 450, 350 S Figueroa St, Los Angeles, CA ☎213/628-3525;

551 5th Ave, Suite 701, New York, NY 10176 ☎212/986-2200.

MAIN TOURIST OFFICES IN LONDON

British Travel Centre, 12 Regent St, London SW1Y 4PQ (no telephone enquiries).

London Tourist Board, 26 Grosvenor Gardens, Victoria, London SW1 (no telephone enquiries).

For listings of all London's information offices, see p.32.

Post and Phones

London **post offices** are open Mon–Fri 9am–5.30pm and Sat 9am–12.30 or 1pm, with the exception of the Trafalgar Square Post Office, 24–28 William IV St, WC2N 4DL (☎0171/930 9580), which is open Mon–Sat 8am–8pm. It's to this office that Post Restante mail should be sent (mark the envelope "Hold"). In the suburbs you'll find sub-post offices operating out of shops, but these are open the same hours as regular post offices, even if the shop itself is open for longer.

Stamps can be bought at post office counters, from vending machines outside post offices, or from an increasing number of newsagents, although they usually only sell books of four or ten stamps. A first-class letter to anywhere in the British Isles costs 25p and should arrive the next day; second class letters cost 19p, taking two to four days. Airmail letters of less than 20g (0.7oz) to EU countries also cost 25p, to non-EU European countries 28p and elsewhere overseas from 41p (US, Canada, Australia and New Zealand). Pre-stamped aerogrammes conforming to overseas airmail weight limits of under 10g cost 39p from post offices only.

Public **payphones** are operated by *British Telecom* (*BT*) and there should be one within ten minutes' walk of wherever you're standing. Most pubs have a public phone too. Many *BT* payphones take all coins from 10p upwards, but an increasing proportion accept only **phonecards**, available from post offices and newsagents which display *BT*'s green logo. These cards come in denominations of £1, £2, £5 and £10. Some *BT* phones accept credit cards too. Resist the temptation to use the phone in your **hotel** room – a recent survey of phone surcharges in European hotels showed that London was the most extortionate city on the continent, with hoteliers imposing a mark-up of around 800 percent in many instances.

Inland calls are cheapest between 6pm and 8am and at weekends. **Reduced rate periods** for most **international calls** are 8pm–8am from Monday to Friday and all day on Saturday and Sunday, though for Australia and New Zealand it's midnight–7am & 2.30–7.30pm daily.

Throughout this guide, every telephone number is prefixed by the area code – 0171 for inner London, 0181 for outer London – separated from the subscriber number by an oblique slash. You don't have to dial the prefix if you're in the same area code. Any number with the prefix ☎0800 is free to the caller. For advice on international calls, see the box below.

OPERATOR SERVICES

Domestic operator ☎100 (free service)

International operator ☎155 (free service)

Domestic directory assistance ☎192

Overseas directory assistance ☎153

INTERNATIONAL CALLS

To **call England** from overseas dial the international access code (☎011 from the US and Canada, ☎0011 from Australia and ☎00 from New Zealand) followed by 44, then the area code minus its initial zero, and then the number. To dial **out of England** it's ☎00 followed by the country code, area code (without the zero if there is one) and subscriber number. Country codes are as follows:

US and Canada ☎ 1

Ireland☎353

Australia ☎61

New Zealand ☎64

Opening Hours, Holidays and Entrance Charges

General **shop hours** are Mon–Sat 9am–5.30 or 6pm, although there's a lot of Sunday and late-night shopping in London, particularly on Thursday or Friday evenings. The big supermarkets also tend to stay open until 8 or 9pm from Monday to Saturday, and from 10am to 4pm on Sundays, as do many of the stores in the suburban shopping complexes. Note that many service stations (gas/petrol stations) in London are open for 24 hours and have small shops.

Fee-charging attractions and state museums are open typically Mon–Sat 9.30am–6pm, with shorter hours (often 10am or noon to 5pm) on Sundays and so-called Bank Holidays (marked * in the list in the box below). Individual opening hours are given for all attractions in the margins of this guide.

A few of London's historic properties come under the control of the private **National Trust**, 36 Queen Anne's Gate, London SW1H 9AS (☎0171/222 9251) or the state-run **English Heritage**, Keysign House, 429 Oxford St, London W1R 2HD (☎0171/973 3000), whose properties are denoted in the guide with "NT" or "EH" after the opening hours.

Both these organizations charge an entry fee for the majority of their sites, and these can be quite high (around £5), especially for the more grandiose National Trust sights. **Annual membership** (NT £24, EH £17.50) allows free entry to their respective properties, though if you're only visiting London, it's hardly worth it. Many other old buildings, albeit rarely the most momentous structures, are owned by the local authorities, which are generally more lenient with their admission charges, sometimes allowing free access.

Many of London's great galleries and museums, notably the British Museum, the Tate and the National Gallery, are free, but some of these cash-strapped institutions are requesting "voluntary donations" with increasing insistence – the Victoria & Albert Museum technically has no entrance charge, but they make you feel like a deviant if you don't make the suggested contribution. Some religious institutions have also adopted strong-arm tactics to raise money – St Paul's charges you just to set foot inside the door, and at Westminster Abbey you have to pay a lot of money to see the most interesting sections.

As for sights run by the private sector, the trend towards the use of interactive displays, dark rides, animatronics and other expensive trickery has pushed prices into the region of £8, and expense is not necessarily an indication of quality. Madame Tussaud's and the London Planetarium, for example, now charge nearly £10 admission.

The majority of fee-charging attractions in London have **reductions** for senior citizens, the unemployed, full-time students and children under 16, with under-5s being admitted free almost everywhere. Proof of eligibility will be required in most cases, though even the flintiest desk clerk will probably take on trust the age of a babe-in-arms. The entry charges given in the guide are the full adult charges – as a rule, adult reductions are in the range of 25–35 percent, while reductions for children are around 50 percent.

PUBLIC HOLIDAYS

January 1

Good Friday – late March to early April

Easter Monday – as above

First Monday in May* (this public holiday may soon be replaced by a date in October)

Last Monday in May*

Last Monday in August*

December 25

December 26

Note that if January 1, December 25 or December 26 falls on a Saturday or Sunday, the next weekday becomes a public holiday.

The Media

Most visitors will want to make use of the English press chiefly for its listings of events. The mainstay in this market is the weekly magazine, *Time Out*, whose listings cover just about everything going. The "serious", news-sheet, daily national papers also have events listings, as does London's only daily paper, the *Evening Standard*. Another useful publication is *The Big Issue*, a weekly magazine (published Monday) which has detailed listings as well as focusing on homelessness, the issue of the title; a large proportion of the cover price goes to the vendors, who are themselves homeless.

American and **European** newspapers are on fairly wide sale in the West End, with well-stocked newsstands in Leicester Square and Piccadilly Circus, and specialist newsagents in Soho and Covent Garden. Australasians can get a free résumé of the news from home, as well as information about jobs, accommodation and events in the capital, through the weekly free magazine, *TNT*, distributed outside main tube stations.

The English Press

Daily newspapers divide into two breeds: news-sheets, which have extensive foreign coverage, as well as home news, and tabloids, which concentrate (in some cases exclusively) on sex, sport, scandal and the royals (ideally in combination). Politically, almost all of the national papers are right wing, and come election time they proclaim out-and-out allegiance to the Conservative Party.

Of the news-sheets, the two most worth your time are the *Independent*, which strives to live up to its self-righteous name, and the *Guardian*, which inhabits a niche just to the left of centre and has the best listings in its handy little Saturday "The Guide" supplement. *The Times* is part of the Murdoch stable, not as dull as it used to be but not very sympa. *The Telegraph*, which tries hard to shake off its old fogey image, is best for sport. All of the tabloids are crap, though the *Sun* (rabidly right wing) and *Daily Mirror* (vaguely on the left) have some great headlines ("Freddie Starr ate my hamster").

The scene is a little more varied on a Sunday, when the Guardian-owned *Observer*, England's oldest **Sunday newspaper**, supplements the Sunday editions of the dailies, whose ranks are also swelled by the amazingly popular *News of the World*, a smutty rag known to all as "The News of the Screws".

London's *Evening Standard*, which comes out in several separate editions every weekday, is good for events in the city, and saves commuters the trouble of having to talk to one another. In addition, each of the London boroughs has its own paper, usually printed twice weekly, covering local issues, but filled mostly with adverts. The most useful London-based publication for visitors is, as mentioned above, ***Time Out***, which comes out every Wednesday. It carries critical appraisals of all the week's theatre, film, music, exhibitions, children's events and much more besides.

When it comes to **specialist periodicals**, London newsagents can offer a range covering just about every subject, the one noticeably poor area being current events. The only high-selling weekly commentary magazine is the right-leaning *Economist*, essential reading in the boardrooms of England; the socialist alternative, the *New Statesman and New Society*, has so few readers that it's stuck with the nickname "The Staggers". The satirical bi-weekly *Private Eye* is a much-loved institution that prides itself on printing the stories the rest of the press won't touch, and on riding the consequent stream of libel suits. And if you feel you can stomach a descent into the scatalogical pit of the male English psyche, take a look at *Viz*, a fortnightly comic which has managed to lodge its caricatures (Johnny Fartpants, Spoilt Bastard, etc) in the collective consciousness.

Television and Radio

England has three terrestrial television stations: the state-owned **BBC** (with two public service channels), and the independent commercial channels, **ITV** and **Channel Four**. Though assailed by critics in the Conservative party, who think that a nationalized anything is a Leninist throwback, the BBC is just about maintaining its worldwide reputation for in-house quality productions, ranging from expensive costume dramas to intelligent documentaries. BBC 2 is the more offbeat and heavyweight BBC channel; BBC 1 is avowedly mainstream. Various regional companies together form the ITV network, but they are united by a more tabloid approach to programme-making – necessarily so, because if they don't get the advertising they don't survive. The London stations are Carlton (weekdays) and London Weekend (weekends); the latter is a bit more adventurous. Channel Four, a partly subsidized institution, is the most progressive of the bunch, with a reputation for broadcasting an eclectic spread of "arty" and minority-pleasing programmes, and for supporting small-budget movies.

Rupert Murdoch's multi-channel **Sky** has a monopoly of the satellite business, presenting a blend of movies, news, sport (including a monopoly on Premier League live football), re-runs and overseas soaps. It has an increasing number of rivals in the form of **cable** TV companies, which are making big inroads in London. Within a few years these commercial stations will probably be making life uncomfortable for the BBC and ITV networks, but for the time being the old terrestrial stations still attract the majority of viewers.

Market forces are eating away rather more quickly at the BBC's **radio** network, which has five stations: Radio One is almost exclusively pap music, with a chart-biased view of the rock world; Two is even more bland, mostly easy-listening; Three is predominantly classical music; Four a blend of current affairs, arts and drama; and Five Live, a mix of live sport and news. Radio One has rivals on all fronts, with *Virgin* running a youth-oriented nationwide commercial network, and a plethora of local commercial stations – like London's *Capital Radio* and the *Kiss FM* soul, dance and reggae station – attracting large sections of Radio One's target audience. *Melody Radio* has whittled away at the *Radio Two* easy listening market, as has *Jazz FM*, while *Classic FM* has lured people away from Radio Three, by offering a "Greatest Hits" view of the greats. The BBC also operates a local station, imaginatively entitled *Radio London*; it's mainly chat, with a few documentary items.

Disabled Travellers

English attitudes towards travellers with disablilities are often begrudging and guilt-ridden, and London is not an easy city for disabled travellers – public transport systems are devised with almost no thought for people with mobility problems, and access to many public buildings remains problematic, despite the improvements of recent years. Accommodation is the same story, with modified suites for people with disabilities found only at higher-priced establishments and an occasional B&B.

In view of this situation, you might consider approaching one of the growing number of **tour operators** catering for physically handicapped travellers. For more information on these operators and on facilities for the disabled traveller, get in touch with the *Royal Association for Disability and Rehabilitation* (*RADAR*), 25 Mortimer St, London W1N 8AB (☎0171/637 5400), a good source of all kinds of information and advice. There's also *Mobility International*, 228 Borough High St, London SE1 1JX (☎0171/403 5688), who put out a quarterly newsletter, among other things, that keeps up-to-date with developments in disabled travel; and the *Holiday Care Service*, 2 Old Bank Chambers, Station Rd, Horley, Surrey GU9 8RW (☎01293/774 535), who publish numerous fact sheets on disabled travel abroad and deal with all sorts of queries – they also run a useful "Holiday Helpers" service. Another useful and more local service is *Tripscope* (☎0181/994 9294; Mon–Fri 9.30am–5pm), a free information line for travellers with disabilities.

Mobility International have a **North American office** and are contactable at PO Box 3551, Eugene, OR 97403 (☎503/343-1284). In **Australia** contact *ACROD*, PO Box 60, Curtain, ACT 2605 (☎06/682 4333) or *Barrier Free Travel*, 36 Wheatley St, North Bellingen, NSW 2454 (☎066/551 1733); in **New Zealand**, try the *Disabled Persons Assembly*, PO Box 10–138, The Terrace, Wellington (☎04/472 2626).

Directory and Services

Airlines *American Airlines*, 421 Oxford St, W1 ☎0171/572 5555; *British Airways*, 156 Regent St, W1 ☎0181/897 4000; *Lufthansa*, 23 Piccadilly, W1 ☎0171/408 0322; *TWA*, 200 Piccadilly, W1 ☎0171/439 0707; *Virgin Atlantic*, Virgin Megastore, 14 Oxford St, W1 ☎0293/562 000.

Airport enquiries Gatwick ☎0293/535 353; Heathrow ☎0181/759 4321; Stansted ☎0279/680 500.

American Express 6 Haymarket, SW1 ☎071/930 4411.

Bicycle rental *On Your Bike*, 22 Duke St Hill, London Bridge, SE1 ☎0171/378 6669; *Evans*, The Cut, Waterloo, SE1 ☎0171/928 4785.

Bus stations Long-distance coach services depart from Victoria Coach Station, Buckingham Palace Rd (Victoria tube). *National Express* have ticket offices here and at 13 Regent St (timetable info ☎0171/730 0202). European services are operated by *Eurolines*, 52 Grosvenor Gardens SW1 ☎0171/730 8235.

Car rental Best rates are at *Holiday Autos*, 25 Savile Row, W1 ☎0171/491 1111. The big firms have outlets all over London; ring their central offices to find the nearest one: *Avis* ☎0181/848 8733; *Hertz* ☎0181/679 1799; *Europcar* ☎0181/950 5050.

Cigarettes The last decade has seen a dramatic change in attitudes towards smoking and a significant reduction in the consumption of cigarettes. Smoking is now outlawed from just about all public buildings and on public transport, and some restaurants and hotels have become non-smoking establishments. Smokers are advised to check before booking a table or a room.

Drugs Likely-looking visitors coming to England from Holland or Spain can expect scrutiny from customs officers on the lookout for hashish. Being caught with possession of a small amount of hashish or marijuana will lead to a fine, but possession of larger quantities or of "harder" narcotics could lead to imprisonment or deportation.

Electricity Throughout England the current is 240V AC. North American appliances will need a transformer and adaptor; Australasian appliances will need only an adaptor.

Information The *Capital Helpline* ☎0171/388 7575 (Mon–Fri 9.30am–5.30pm) can fill you in on most aspects of London life.

Laundry Coin-operated laundries (launderettes) are to be found all over London and are open from around 8am–8pm from Monday to Friday, 9am–6pm at weekends. A wash followed by a spin or tumble dry costs about £2.50, with "service washes" (your laundry done for you in a few hours) about £1–2 more. Dry-cleaners in central London usually offer a same day cleaning and mending service.

Left luggage facilities are available at London train stations: Charing Cross daily 6.30am–10.30pm; Euston daily 24hr; Paddington daily 7am–midnight; Victoria daily 7.15am–10pm; Waterloo Mon–Sat 6.30am–11pm.

Lost property London transport buses and tube ☎0171/486 2496 (Mon–Fri 9.30am–2pm). Gatwick airport ☎0923/503 162. Heathrow airport ☎0181/745 7727. At the train stations: Charing Cross ☎0171/922 6061; Euston ☎0171/922 6477; King's Cross ☎0171/922 9081; Liverpool St ☎0171/922 9189; Marylebone ☎0171/922 9543; Paddington ☎0171/922 6773; St Pancras ☎0171/922 6478; Victoria ☎0171/922 6216; Waterloo ☎0171/922 6135.

Pharmacies Every police station keeps a list of emergency pharmacies in its area.

Photography Major pharmacies are the best places to buy film, and most of them offfer a photo-developing service, usually with a range of charges reflecting the speed of the process (one-hour, 24-hour and so on). Photography is not allowed in most museums and galleries unless you've paid a permissions fee.

Police HQ is New Scotland Yard, Broadway ☎0171/230 1212. The station at 10 Vine St ☎0171/434 5212, just off Regent St, is most convenient for the West End.

Public toilets are few and far between in much of London, and the standards of maintenance are often dreadful. The toilets at main line train stations are tolerable, usually charging a fee of 20p. All premises licensed to serve alcohol must by law have toilets, so if you're desperate you could pop into the nearest pub, though it might be advisable to buy a drink before using the facilities – publicans can turn nasty with people using their establishment as a public convenience.

Time Greenwich Mean Time (GMT) is used from late October to late March, when the clocks go forward an hour for British Summer Time (BST). GMT is five hours ahead of the US Eastern Standard Time and ten hours behind Australian Eastern Standard Time.

Tipping and service charges In restaurants a service charge is usually included in the bill; if it isn't, leave a tip of 10–15 percent. Some restaurants are in the habit of leaving the total box blank on credit-card counterfoils, to encourage customers to add another few percent on top of the service charge – if you're paying by credit card, check that the total box is filled in before you sign. Taxi drivers expect a tip in the region of 10 percent. You do not tip bar staff – if you want to show your appreciation, offer to buy them a drink.

Train stations and information As a broad guide, Euston handles services to the northwest and Glasgow; King's Cross the northeast and Edinburgh; Liverpool St eastern England; Paddington western England; Victoria and Waterloo southeast England. For information, call ☎0171/928 5100 for services to eastern and southern England, and eastern and southern London; ☎0171/262 6767 for the south Midlands, west England, west London and south Wales; ☎0171/387 7070 for north Midlands, north Wales, northwest England and northwest London; and ☎0171/287 2477 for northeast England and eastern Scotland.

Videos Visitors from North America planning to use their video cameras in Britain should note that Betamax video cassettes are less easy to obtain in England, where VHS is the commonly used format.

The City

Introducing the City

With a population of just under eight million, and stretching more than thirty miles at its broadest point, **London** is by far the largest city in Europe. It is also far more diffuse than the great cities of the Continent, such as Rome or Paris. The majority of London's sights are situated to the north of the River Thames, which loops through the centre of the city from west to east, but there is no single predominant focus of interest, for London has grown not through centralized planning but by a process of agglomeration – villages and urban developments that once surrounded the core are now lost within the amorphous mass of Greater London. Thus London's highlights are widely spread, and visitors should make mastering the public transport system, particularly the underground (tube), a top priority.

One of the few areas which is manageable on foot is **Whitehall and Westminster** (Chapter 1), the city's royal, political and ecclesiastical powerbase for several hundred years. It's here you'll find the adjacent National Gallery and National Portrait Gallery, and a host of other London landmarks: Buckingham Palace, Nelson's Column, Downing Street, the Houses of Parliament and Westminster Abbey. From Westminster it's a manageable walk upriver to the Tate Gallery, repository of the nation's largest collection of modern art as well as the main assemblage of British art. The grand streets and squares of **Piccadilly, St James's, Mayfair and Marylebone** (Chapter 2), to the north of Westminster, have been the playground of the rich since the Restoration, and now contain the city's busiest shopping zones: Piccadilly itself, Bond Street, Regent Street and, most frenetic of the lot, Oxford Street.

East of Piccadilly Circus, **Soho and Covent Garden** (Chapter 3) form the heart of the **West End** entertainment district, where you'll find the largest concentration of theatres, cinemas, clubs, flashy shops, cafés and restaurants. Adjoining Covent Garden to the north, the university quarter of **Bloomsbury** (Chapter 4) is the traditional home of the publishing industry and location of the **British Museum**, a stupendous treasure house that attracts more than five

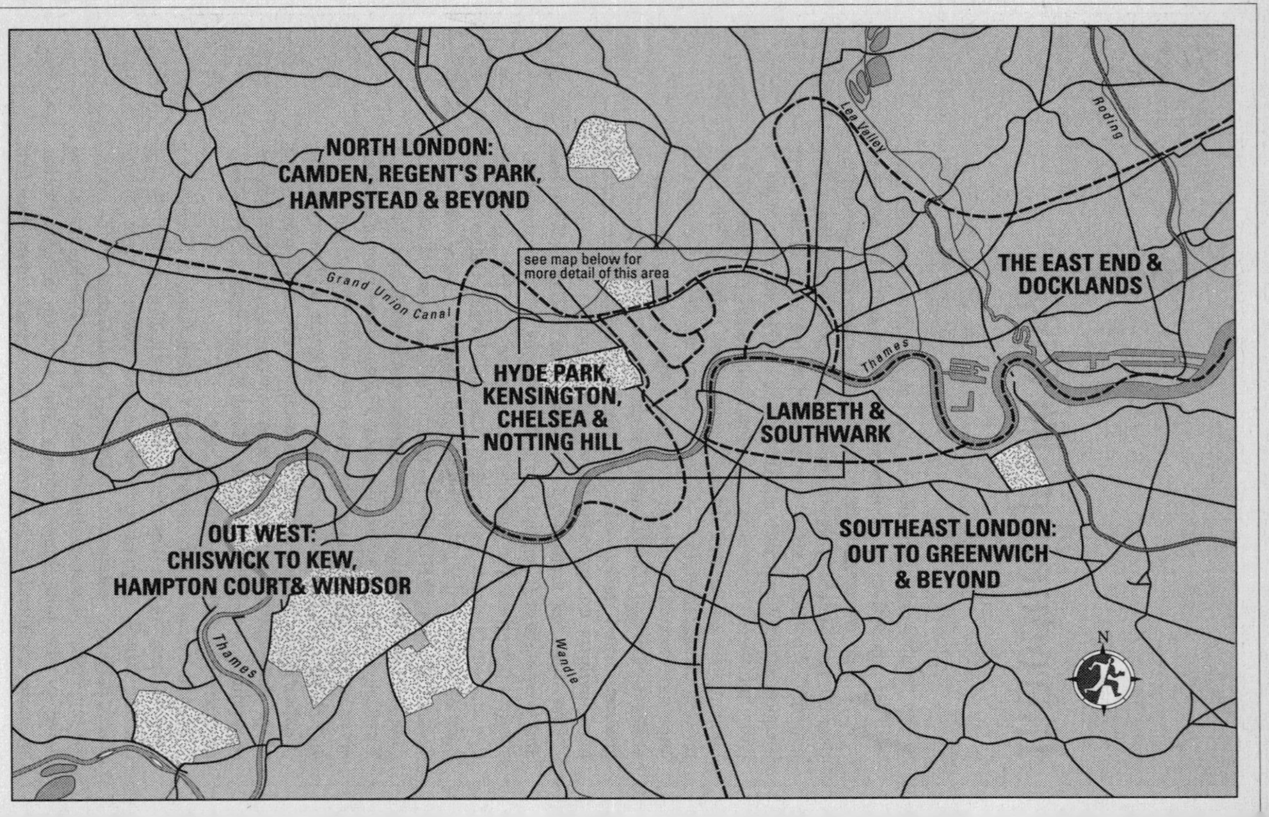

NORTH LONDON:
CAMDEN, REGENT'S PARK,
HAMPSTEAD & BEYOND
see map below for
more detail of this area
Grand Union Canal
Lea Valley
Roding
THE EAST END &
DOCKLANDS
HYDE PARK,
KENSINGTON,
CHELSEA &
NOTTING HILL
Thames
LAMBETH &
SOUTHWARK
OUT WEST:
CHISWICK TO KEW,
HAMPTON COURT& WINDSOR
SOUTHEAST LONDON:
OUT TO GREENWICH
& BEYOND
Thames
Wandle
N

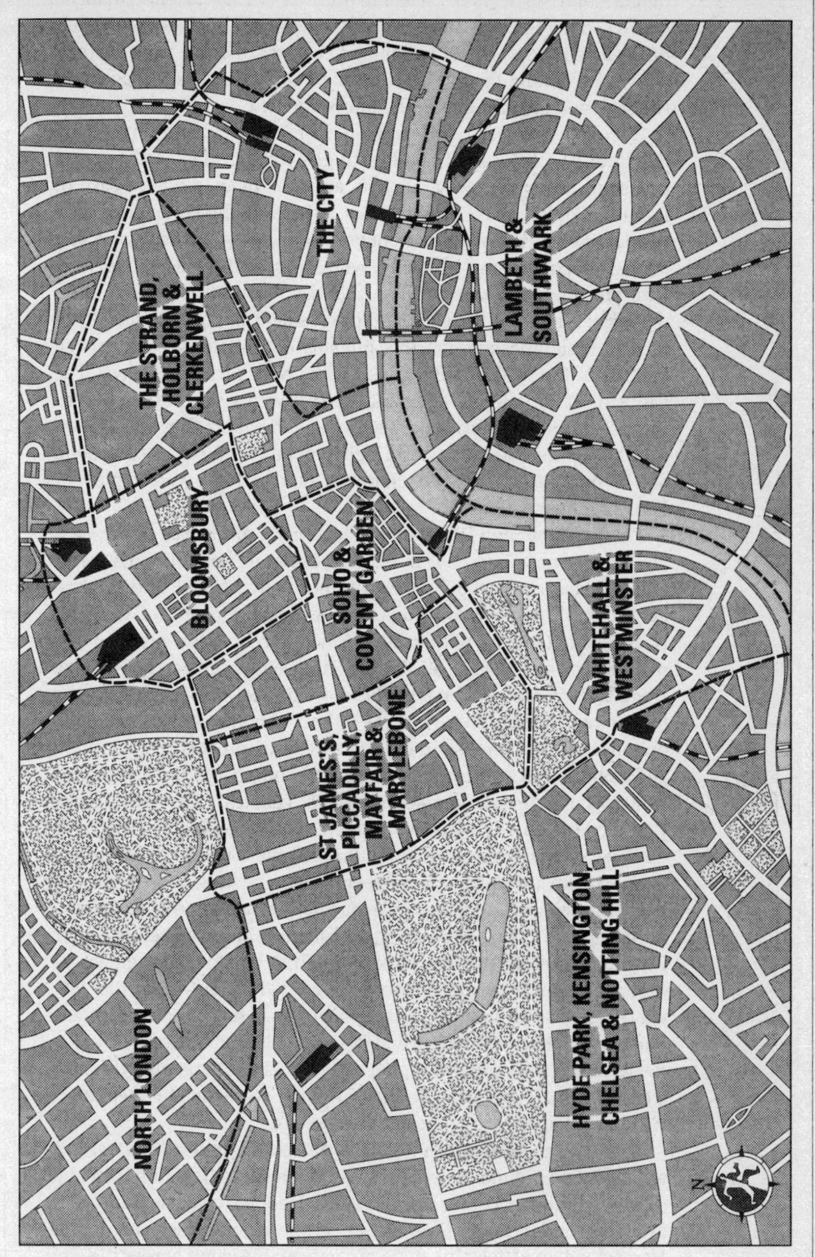
THE STRAND, HOLBORN & CLERKENWELL
THE CITY
LAMBETH & SOUTHWARK
BLOOMSBURY
SOHO & COVENT GARDEN
WHITEHALL & WESTMINSTER
ST JAMES'S, PICCADILLY, MAYFAIR & MARYLEBONE
NORTH LONDON
HYDE PARK, KENSINGTON, CHELSEA & NOTTING HILL
N

million tourists a year. Welding the West End to the financial district, **The Strand, Holborn and Clerkenwell** (Chapter 5) are little-visited areas, but offer some of central London's most surprising treats, among them the eccentric Sir John Soane's Museum and the secluded quadrangles of the Inns of Court.

A couple of miles downstream from Westminster, **The City** (Chapter 6) – the City of London, to give its full title – is at one and the same time the most ancient and the most modern part of London. Settled since Roman times, it became the commercial and residential heart of medieval London, with its own Lord Mayor and its own peculiar form of local government, both of which survive, with considerable pageantry, to this day. The Great Fire of 1666 obliterated most of the City, and the resident population has dwindled to insignificance, yet this remains one of the great financial centres of the world, ranking just below New York and Tokyo. The City's most prominent landmarks nowadays are the hi-tech offices of the legions of banks and insurance companies, but the Square Mile boasts its share of historic sights, notably the Tower of London and a fine cache of Wren churches that includes the mighty St Paul's Cathedral.

The **East End and Docklands** (Chapter 7), to the east of the City, are equally notorious, but in entirely different ways. Impoverished and working-class, the East End is not conventional tourist territory, but to ignore it is to miss out a crucial element of the real, multi-ethnic London. With its abandoned warehouses converted into overpriced apartment blocks for the city's upwardly mobile, Docklands is the converse of the down-at-heel East End, with the half-empty Canary Wharf tower, the country's tallest building, epitomizing the pretensions of the Thatcherite dream.

Lambeth and Southwark (Chapter 8) comprise the small slice of central London that lies south of the Thames. The South Bank Centre, London's little-loved concrete culture bunker, is the most obvious starting point, while Southwark, the city's low-life district from Roman times to the eighteenth century, is less well known, except to the gore-addicts who queue up for the London Dungeon.

In the districts of **Hyde Park, Kensington and Chelsea** (Chapter 9) you'll find the largest park in central London, a segment of greenery which separates wealthy West London from the city centre. The museums of South Kensington – the Victoria & Albert Museum, Science Museum and Natural History Museum – are a must, and if you have shopping on your London agenda you may well want to investigate the hive of plush stores in the vicinity of *Harrod's*, superstore to the upper echelons.

Some of the most appealing parts of **North London** (Chapter 10) are clustered around Regent's Canal, which skirts Regent's Park and serves as the focus for the capital's trendiest weekend market, around Camden Lock. Further out, in the chic literary suburbs of Hampstead and Highgate, there are unbeatable views across the city

Boroughs, districts and addresses

Greater London is divided into thirty-one **boroughs**, plus the City of Westminster and the City of London. Each borough has a population of between 150,000 and 300,000, making them too unwieldy to use as divisions for the purposes of this guide. Instead, we've generally used the **district** names by which **Londoners** designate the areas in which they live and work. Most of these districts take their names either from smaller boroughs which disappeared in the boundary changes of 1965, or from parishes or villages which have now been subsumed into the fabric of the city. Thus when we refer to Camden or to Greenwich, we are talking not about the present-day London boroughs of Camden or Greenwich, but about the core areas from which these districts take their names.

London is further divided into **postal areas**, which do not coincide with any of the above boundaries. Each street name is followed by a letter giving the geographical location of the street in relation to the City (E for "east", WC for "west central" and so on) and a number that specifies its location more precisely. Be warned that to the uninitiated this number is not a reliable indication of distance from the centre – SE5, for example, is closer to the centre of town than SE3, and W5 lies beyond the remote-sounding NW10. Full postal addresses end with a digit and two letters, which specify the individual block, but these are only used in correspondence.

from half-wild Hampstead Heath, the favourite parkland of thousands of Londoners. The glory of **Southeast London** (Chapter 11) is Greenwich, with its nautical associations, royal park and observatory. Finally, there are plenty of rewarding day trips along the Thames from **Chiswick to Windsor** (Chapter 12), a region in which the royalty and aristocracy have traditionally built their homes, the most famous being Hampton Court Palace and Windsor Castle.

Arriving in London

Flying into London, you'll arrive at one of the capital's three main **international airports**, Heathrow, Gatwick or Stansted, each of which is less than an hour from the city centre. (London's fourth airport, City, is used only by business shuttle flights to Brussels, Paris, Amsterdam and a few other European commercial centres.)

Getting into London from **Heathrow**, twelve miles west of the city, couldn't be easier. The **Piccadilly Underground line** connects the airport to central London in under an hour, with one station serving terminals 1, 2 and 3, and another serving terminal 4; trains depart every few minutes, cost £3 and run between 5am and midnight, taking about thirty to forty minutes to reach the centre. If you plan to spend the rest of your arrival day sightseeing, buy a multi-zone one-day travelcard for £3.70 (see "Getting around the city", below). There are also **Airbuses** which run from outside all four Heathrow terminals to several destinations in the city: *Airbus*

A1 (every 20–45 minutes daily 5.50am–8.30pm) drops passengers at designated points in Earl's Court, South Kensington, Knightsbridge and Victoria; *Airbus* **A2** (same frequency daily 5.40am–9.45pm) goes to Notting Hill, Paddington, Lancaster Gate, Marble Arch, Baker Street, Euston and Russell Square. Both routes take about an hour and cost £5, but can be worth the money if you have a lot of luggage to haul. *National Express* also run a service to Victoria for £5.50 (every 30min daily 8am–11.30pm). After midnight, the night bus #N97 runs hourly from Heathrow to Trafalgar Square. **Taxis** are plentiful, but will set you back around £35 to central London.

Gatwick Airport is thirty miles to the south; the non-stop *Gatwick Express* **trains** run between the airport's South Terminal and Victoria, taking thirty minutes and costing £8.60; trains depart every fifteen minutes throughout the day and night except between 2am and 5am, when they're hourly. *British Rail* also run scheduled train services to King's Cross Thameslink, costing £9.50 and taking fifty minutes; these are better if you're heading for north London, as they save you from having to cross London by tube (Mon–Sat every 15min 4am–11pm; Sun every 30min 7am–midnight). *Flightline 777* **coaches** depart Gatwick's North and South Terminals once an hour between 6.30am and 11.30pm, arriving at Victoria Coach Station approximately eighty to ninety minutes later; the journey costs £7.50.

Stansted, newest and smallest of the London international airports, lies 34 miles northeast of the capital and is served by trains to Liverpool Street (Mon–Sat every 30min 6am–11pm, Sun hourly 7am–11pm), which take 45 minutes and cost £10.

Coming into London from abroad by **coach or train**, you're most likely to arrive at Victoria – either at the train station, which serves the English Channel ports, or at the coach station, a couple of hundred yards south down Buckingham Palace Road. Trains using the **Channel Tunnel** come in at Waterloo's new international terminal. Arriving by train from elsewhere in Britain, you'll come into one of London's numerous mainline British Rail stations, all of which have adjacent Underground stations that link into the city centre's tube network.

Information

The **London Tourist Board** (LTB) has a desk at Heathrow Airport in the Underground station concourse for terminals 1, 2 and 3 (daily 8.30am–6.30pm), but the **main central office** is in the forecourt of Victoria station (daily 8am–7pm). Other centrally located offices can be found near Piccadilly Circus in the British Travel Centre, 12 Regent St (Mon–Fri 9am–6.30pm, Sat & Sun 10am–4pm), in Liverpool Street Underground station (Mon–Sat 9am–4.30pm, Sun 8.30am–3.30pm), and at 35–36 Woburn Place in Bloomsbury (daily 7.30am–7.30pm). There are also LTB information counters in the basement of *Selfridge's* on Oxford Street, in Greenwich at 46 Greenwich Church St (daily 10am–1pm & 2–5pm; ☎0181/858 6376), and in Richmond, inside the Old Town Hall on Whittaker Avenue (Mon–Fri 10am–6pm, Sat 10am–5pm, plus Sun 10.15–4.15pm in summer; ☎0181/940 7970). Finally, there's an information office run by the Corporation of London opposite the south side of St Paul's Cathedral (April–Sept daily 9.30am–5pm; Oct–March Mon–Fri 9.30am–5pm, Sat 9.30am–12.30pm; ☎0171/332 1456).

The Greenwich, Richmond and St Paul's offices are the only ones that will accept enquiries by phone. The best that the LTB can offer is a spread of pre-recorded phone announcements – these are a very poor service indeed, and the calls are charged at an exorbitant rate. Rather more useful are the LTB's daily menu of events on ☎0171/730 3488 and the Capital Helpline ☎0171/388 7575, which can fill you in on most aspects of London life.

Most of the above offices hand out a useful quick reference **map** of central London, plus plans of the public transport systems, but to find your way around every cranny of the city you need to invest in either an *A–Z Atlas* or a *Nicholson Streetfinder*, both of which have a street index covering every street in the capital; you can get them at most bookshops and newsagents for around £4. The only comprehensive and critical weekly **listings** magazine is *Time Out*, which costs £1.70 and comes out every Tuesday afternoon. In it you'll find details of all the latest exhibitions, shows, guided walks and events in and around the capital.

Getting around the city

London's network of **buses** is very dense, but you will soon find that the Underground – or tube, as it's known to all Londoners – is generally quicker, since much of central London is a permanent log-jam. An essential investment is a London Transport **travelcard**, which is available from machines and booths at all tube and train stations and at some newsagents as well (look for the London Transport sticker), and is valid for the bus, tube and suburban rail networks. One-day travelcards, valid on weekdays from 9.30am and all day at weekends, cost £2.70 for the central zones 1 and 2, rising to £3.70 for all six London Transport zones (which includes Heathrow). Weekly travelcards are even more economical, beginning at £13 for zones 1 and 2; these cards can only be bought by carriers of a **photocard**, which you can get, free of charge, from tube and train station ticket booths on presentation of a passport photo.

The principal **London Transport information office**, providing excellent free maps and details of bus and tube services, is at **Piccadilly Circus tube station** (daily 9am–6pm); there are other desks at Euston, King's Cross, Liverpool Street, Oxford Circus, St James's Park and Victoria stations. There's also a 24-hour phone line for information on all bus and tube services (☎0171/222 1234).

The tube

The eleven different tube lines cross much of the metropolis, although London south of the river is not well covered – an extension to the Jubilee Line will soon connect Greenwich to the network, but the majority of south Londoners will still be a long way from the nearest tube station. Services operate from around 5.30am until shortly after midnight, and you will rarely have to wait more than five minutes for a train between central stations. However, the reliability of connections to farther-flung stations, especially on the notorious Northern Line, is not what it should be, due to the endemic British problem of underfunded public services. Tickets are bought from automatic machines or from a ticket booth in the station entrance hall; the minimum for a single journey is currently 90p.

Buses

Bus journeys cost a minimum of 50p, but the average trip in the centre costs around 80p; normally you pay the driver on entering, although some routes – especially those which traverse the West End – are covered by older Routemaster buses, which are staffed by a conductor and have an open rear platform. A lot of bus stops are request stops, so if you don't stick your arm out to hail the bus you want, it will pass you by. While the majority of London's buses are still the distinctive London Transport red double-deckers, some routes are served by different-coloured private buses: prices on these have remained about the same as their red counterparts and the great majority will accept travelcards (private buses accepting travelcards display the London Transport logo on the windscreen or door). Regular buses operate between about 6am and midnight, and a network of **night buses** (prefixed with the letter "N") operates outside this period. Night bus routes radiate out from Trafalgar Square at approximately hourly intervals, more frequently on some lines, and on Friday and Saturday nights. Fares are twice as expensive on night buses; one-day travelcards aren't valid on them, but weekly ones are.

Suburban trains

Large areas of London's suburbs, particularly in the southeast, are not served by the tube and are impractical to reach by bus. The only way to reach these parts of London is by the **suburban train** network (travelcards valid), which fans out from the main termini. Wherever a sight can only be reached by overground train, we've indicated the nearest train station and the central terminus from which you must depart.

A couple of useful train lines which actually cross the capital are the **North London Line**, which runs between Richmond and North Woolwich via Hampstead and Camden (Mon–Sat every 15min; Sun every 30min), and the **Thameslink** service which runs north-south via King's Cross, Blackfriars and London Bridge.

Taxis

If you're in a group of three or more, London's metered **black cabs** can be an economical way of getting around the centre – a ride from Euston to Victoria, for example, should cost around £10. A yellow light over the windscreen tells you if the cab is available – just stick your arm out to hail it. (If you want to book one in advance, call ☎0171/272 0272.) London's cabbies are the best trained in Europe; every one of them knows the shortest route between any two points in the capital, and they won't rip you off by taking another route. They are, however, a blunt and forthright breed, renowned for their generally reactionary opinions.

Minicabs are less reliable than black cabs, as their drivers are just private individuals rather than trained professionals; however, they are often considerably cheaper, so you might want to take one back from a late-night club. There are hundreds of minicab firms in the phone book, but the best way to pick is to take the advice of the place you're at, unless you want to be certain of a woman driver, in which case call *Ladycabs* (☎0171/254 3501). Most minicabs are not metered, so always establish the fare beforehand.

Guided Tours and Walks

Standard **bus tours** are run by *London Transport Sightseeing Tours* and dozens of rival companies, their open-top double-deckers setting off every thirty minutes from Victoria station, Trafalgar Square, Piccadilly, and other conspicuous spots. Most tours take approximately ninety minutes and cost around £8. Alternatively, you can save yourself the money and the inane commentary by hopping on a real London bus – the #11 will take you past the Houses of Parliament, up Whitehall, along the Strand and on to St Paul's.

Walking tours are infinitely more appealing, covering a relatively small area in much greater detail, mixing solid historical facts with juicy anecdotes in the company of a local specialist. Walks on offer range from a literary pub crawl round Bloomsbury to a roam around the remains of the Jewish East End. You'll find most of them detailed, week by week, in *Time Out* (in the "Around Town" section); as you'd imagine, there's more variety on offer in the summer months. Tours tend to cost £3–4 and take around two hours; normally you can show up at the starting point and join a tour, though guides prefer you to phone ahead.

If you want to plan – or book – walks rather more in advance, you might contact one of the following companies direct:

Original London Walks ☎0171/624 3978. The widest range of walks, including a **Beatles tour** that takes you to such famous places as the Abbey Road pedestrian crossing near the EMI studios – and sometimes into the very studio in which the Fabs laid down most of their tracks.

Angel Walks ☎0171/226 8333. Concentrates on the north London suburb of Islington, visiting the haunts of Joe Orton, George Orwell and Charles Dickens among others.

Historical Tours ☎0181/668 4019. Focuses on the City and Westminster, and also offers evening pub walks.

Museums, monuments and sights

The opening hours and prices listed below (and in the text of the guide) are the latest available, though bear in mind that some of the sights are prone to raising their charges dramatically from year to year. A concessionary rate is available at each of these sights for holders of a student card, senior citizens, under-eighteens, and the registered unemployed. Under-fives usually get in free, and many attractions offer discount family tickets, though these are only really worthwhile if you have at least two adults and two children over five years old in your family unit. The South Kensington museums, the museums at Greenwich and the royal palaces operate special tickets which allow you entry into a group of sights at a discount, and an increasing number of places now offer good-value season tickets for those wishing to make several visits to a particular sight.

British Museum Mon–Sat 10am–5pm, Sun 2.30–6pm; free; ☎0171/636 1555.

Buckingham Palace Aug & Sept daily 9.30am–5.30pm; £8; ☎0171/930 4832.

Courtauld Institute Mon–Sat 10am–6pm, Sun 2–6pm; £3; ☎0171/873 2526.

Cutty Sark April–Sept 10am–6pm, Sun noon–6pm; Oct–March closes 5pm; £3.25; ☎0181/858 3445.

Hampton Court Palace March–Oct Mon 10.15am–6pm, Tues–Sun 9.30am–6pm; Oct–March closes 4.30pm; £7; ☎0181/781 9500.

HMS Belfast March–Oct daily 10am–6pm; Nov–Feb closes 5pm; £4; ☎0171/407 6434.

Houses of Parliament mid-Jan to mid-July & mid-Oct to mid-Dec; Mon–Thurs 4.30–10.30pm or later, Fri 10am–3pm; free; ☎0171/219 4272.

Imperial War Museum daily 10am–6pm; £3.90; ☎0171/416 5000.

Kensington Palace Mon–Sat 9am–5pm, Sun 11am–5pm; £4.50; ☎0171/937 9561.

Kenwood House April–Sept daily 10am–6pm; Oct–March closes 4pm; free; ☎0181/348 1286.

Kew Gardens April–Aug Mon–Sat 9.30am–6.30pm, Sun 9.30am–8pm; Sept–March closes around dusk; £4; ☎0181/332 5000.

London Dungeon April–Sept daily 10am–6.30pm; Oct–March daily 10am–5.30pm; £6.95; ☎0171/403 7221.

London Zoo April–Oct 10am–5.30pm; Nov–March closes 4pm; £6.95; ☎0171/722 3333.

Madame Tussaud's May–Sept daily 9.30am–5.30pm; Oct–April opens 10am Mon–Fri; £8.25; ☎0171/935 6861.

Monument April–Sept Mon–Fri 9am–6pm, Sat & Sun 2–6pm; Oct–March Mon–Sat 9am–4pm; £1; ☎0171/626 2717.

Museum of London Tues–Sat 10am–5.50pm, Sun noon–5.50pm; £3.50; ☎0171/600 3699.

Museum of Mankind Mon–Sat 10am–5pm, Sun 2.30–6pm; free; ☎0171/437 2224.

Museum of the Moving Image (MOMI) daily 10am–6pm; £5.50; ☎0171/928 3232.

National Gallery Mon–Sat 10am–6pm, Sun 2–6pm; free; ☎0171/ 839 3321.

National Maritime Museum March–Oct daily 10am–6pm; Nov–Feb Mon–Sat 10am–5pm, Sun noon–5pm; £4.95; ☎0181/858 4422.

Natural History Museum Mon–Sat 10am–5.50pm, Sun 11am–5.50pm; £5; ☎0171/938 9123.

National Portrait Gallery Mon–Sat 10am–6pm, Sun noon–6pm; free; ☎0171/ 306 0055.

RAF Museum daily 10am–6pm; £5.20; ☎0181/205 2266.

Science Museum Mon–Sat 10am–6pm, Sun 11am–6pm; £4.50; ☎0171/938 8008.

St Paul's Cathedral Mon–Sat 8.30am–4.15pm; £3; ☎0171/248 2705.

Tate Gallery Mon–Sat 10am–5.50pm, Sun 2–5.50pm; free; ☎0171/887 8000.

Tower Bridge April–Oct daily 10am–6.30pm; Nov–March closes 5.15pm; £5; ☎0171/407 0922.

Tower of London March–Oct Mon–Sat 9am–6pm, Sun 10am–6pm; Oct–March closes 5pm; £7.95; ☎0171/709 0765.

Victoria & Albert Museum Mon noon–5.50pm, Tues–Sun 10am–5.50pm; free, but £4.50 donation requested; ☎0171/938 8500.

Westminster Abbey Royal Chapels Mon–Fri 9am–4pm, Wed 6–7.45pm, Sat 9am–2pm & 3.45–5pm; £4, free Wed 6–7.45pm; ☎0171/222 5152.

Windsor Castle March–Oct daily 10.30am–5pm; Nov–Feb 10am–3pm; £8; ☎0753/868 286.

Whitehall and Westminster

Political, religious and regal power has emanated from **WHITEHALL** and **WESTMINSTER** for almost a millennium. It was Edward the Confessor who first established Westminster as London's royal and ecclesiastical power base, some three miles west of the real, commercial City of London. The embryonic English parliament met in the abbey in the fourteenth century and eventually took over the old royal palace when Henry VIII moved out to Whitehall. In the nineteenth century, Whitehall became the "heart of Empire", its ministries ruling over a quarter of the world's population. Even now, though the UK's world status has diminished, and its royalty and clergy no longer wield much real power or respect, the institutions that run the country inhabit roughly the same geographical area: Whitehall for the civil servants, Westminster for the politicans.

The monuments and buildings covered in this chapter also span the millennium, and include some of London's most famous landmarks – **Nelson's Column**, **Big Ben** and the **Houses of Parliament**, **Westminster Abbey** and **Buckingham Palace**, plus the city's two finest permanent art collections, the **National Gallery** and the **Tate**. It's a well-trodden tourist circuit for the most part – hence the council's decision to reinstate the old red phone boxes – with few shops or cafés and little street life to distract you, but it's also one of the easiest parts of London to walk round, with all the major sights within a mere half mile of each other, linked by two of London's most triumphant avenues, **Whitehall** and **The Mall**.

Nearby Soho and Covent Garden are far better areas for pubs, cafés and restaurants, though you'll find good cafés in the National Gallery, St Martin-in-the-Fields church, and the ICA on the Mall.

Until the westward expansion of the City of London in the seventeenth century, Westminster was a more or less separate city. Today, the modern borough of Westminster encompasses a much wider area than that covered in this chapter, including most of the West End and parts of the well-to-do districts of Mayfair and Belgravia, making it one of the richest councils in the country. In the 1980s this was one of the Thatcher government's flagship

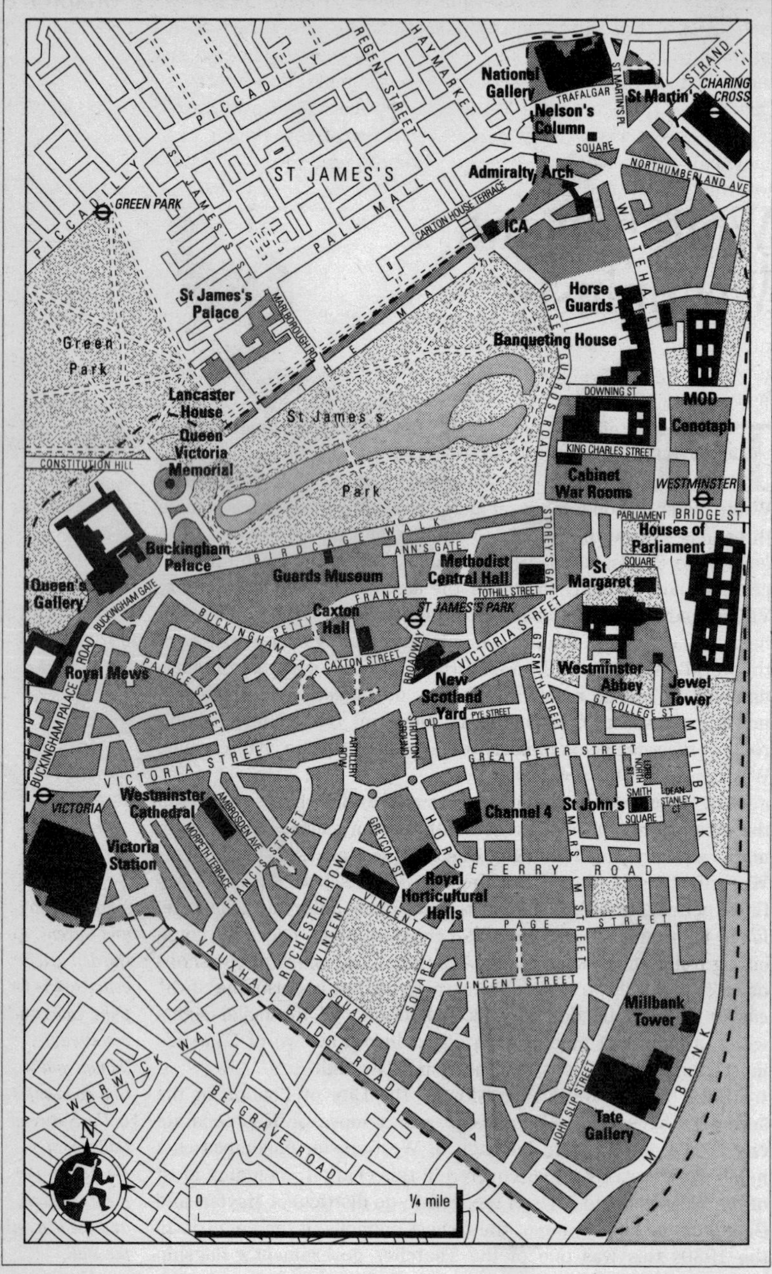

National Gallery
Nelson's Column
St Martin's
CHARING CROSS
STRAND
TRAFALGAR SQUARE
NORTHUMBERLAND AVE
PICCADILLY
REGENT STREET
HAYMARKET
ST JAMES'S
Admiralty Arch
GREEN PARK
PALL MALL
CARLTON HOUSE TERRACE
ICA
THE MALL
WHITEHALL
Horse Guards
St James's Palace
MARLBOROUGH RD
Green Park
Banqueting House
HORSE GUARDS ROAD
DOWNING ST
MOD
Lancaster House
St James's Park
Queen Victoria Memorial
Cenotaph
KING CHARLES STREET
CONSTITUTION HILL
Cabinet War Rooms
WESTMINSTER
PARLIAMENT
BRIDGE ST
BIRDCAGE WALK
STOREY'S GATE
Houses of Parliament
Buckingham Palace
ANN'S GATE
Methodist Central Hall
St Margaret
Guards Museum
Queen's Gallery
BUCKINGHAM GATE
FRANCE
TOTHILL STREET
Caxton Hall
ST JAMES'S PARK
PETTY
VICTORIA STREET
CAXTON STREET
BROADWAY
GT SMITH STREET
Royal Mews
PALACE STREET
New Scotland Yard
Westminster Abbey
Jewel Tower
PYE STREET
GT COLLEGE ST
BUCKINGHAM PALACE ROAD
ARTILLERY ROW
STRUTTON GROUND
GREAT PETER STREET
MILLBANK
VICTORIA
Westminster Cathedral
AMBROSDEN AVE
Channel 4
St John's
SMITH SQUARE
DEAN STANLEY ST
Victoria Station
MORPETH TERRACE
GREYCOAT ST
HORSEFERRY ROAD
MARSHAM STREET
FRANCIS STREET
ROCHESTER ROW
Royal Horticultural Halls
VINCENT
PAGE STREET
VINCENT SQUARE
VINCENT STREET
VAUXHALL BRIDGE ROAD
Millbank Tower
WARWICK WAY
BELGRAVE ROAD
JOHN SLIP STREET
Tate Gallery
N
0
¼ mile

right-wing councils, at the forefront of immoral and – so it now seems – illegal privatization campaigns, closing down its hostels for the homeless, selling off its housing stock, even its cemeteries, and reducing spending and services to a minimum. Its leader was Lady Porter, heiress of the Tesco supermarket chain, who, with her colleagues, is currently facing allegations of vote-rigging and financial corruption on a scale hitherto unknown in local government.

Trafalgar Square

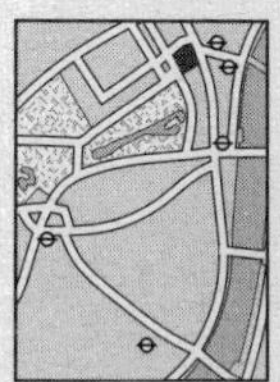

Trafalgar Square is a major terminus for day and (usefully) night buses. The nearest tube stops are Charing Cross and Leicester Square.

Despite being little more than a glorified, sunken traffic island, infested with scruffy urban pigeons, **Trafalgar Square** is still one of London's grandest architectural set-pieces. John Nash designed the basic layout in the 1820s, but died long before the square took its present form. The Neoclassical National Gallery filled up the northern side of the square in 1838, followed shortly afterwards by the square's central focal point, Nelson's Column; the famous bronze lions didn't arrive until 1868, and the fountains – a real rarity in a London square – didn't take their present shape until the eve of World War II. The development of the rest of the square was equally haphazard, though the overall effect is unified by the safe Neoclassical styles and Portland Stone facades of the buildings.

As one of the few large public squares in London, Trafalgar Square has been both a tourist attraction and the main focus for **political demonstrations** for over a century. It was here in 1848 that the Chartists assembled before marching to Kennington Common. Countless demos and rallies were held over the next hundred years, including huge turns outs for nuclear disarmament, and a non-stop vigil outside the South African embassy during the 1980s and early 90s, maintained despite police harassment until the release of Nelson Mandela. More recently, violence erupted again during a demonstration against the Poll Tax in March 1990, when police baton-charged demonstrators and sparked off rioting and looting round the neighbouring West End. All of which would seem to justify the provision of a police phonebox purpose-built into one of the stone bollards in the southeast corner of the square, which once had a direct link to Scotland Yard.

On a more festive note, the square is also graced each December with a giant Christmas tree covered in fairy lights, donated by Norway in thanks for liberation from the Nazis. And on **New Year's Eve**, thousands of inebriates sing in the New Year, though injuries and fatalities in recent years have meant that, as of 1993, just about everything traditionally associated with the event – drinking, dancing and indiscriminate kissing of police officers – is now strictly forbidden.

Trafalgar Square

The column and the square

Nelson's Column, raised in 1843 and now one of London's best-loved monuments, commemorates the one-armed, one-eyed admiral who defeated Napoleon at the Battle of Trafalgar in 1805, but paid for it with his life. The statue which surmounts the granite column is triple life-size but still manages to appear minuscule, and is coated in anti-pigeon gel to try and stem the build-up of guano. The acanthus leaves of the capital are cast from British cannon, while bas-reliefs around the base – depicting three of Nelson's victories as well as his death aboard HMS Victory – are from captured French armaments. Edwin Landseer's four gargantuan bronze lions guard the column and provide a climbing frame for kids (and demonstrators) to clamber over. If you can, get here before the crowds and watch the pigeons take to the air as Edwin Lutyens' fountains jet into action at 9am.

Keeping Nelson company at ground level is an equestrian statue of George IV (bareback, stirrupless and in Roman garb), which he himself commissioned for the top of Marble Arch, over at the north-east corner of Hyde Park, but which was later erected "temporarily" in the northeastern corner of the square. Either side of the column are bronze statues of Napier and Havelock, major-generals who helped keep India British, and, against the north wall, busts of later military leaders: Beatty, Jellicoe and Cunningham. Predating the entire square is the **equestrian statue of Charles I**, stranded on a traffic island to the south of the column. This was completed in 1633 only to be confiscated and sold off during the Civil War to a local brazier, with strict instructions for it to be melted down. The said brazier made a small fortune selling bronze mementoes, allegedly from the metal, while all the time concealing the statue in the vaults of St Paul's Church in Covent Garden. After the Restoration the brazier resold the statue, and it was placed on the very spot where those who had signed the king's death warrant were executed in 1660, and within sight of the Banqueting House in Whitehall where Charles himself was beheaded (see below).

Charles' statue also marks the original site of **Charing Cross**, from where all distances from the capital are measured. The original thirteenth-century cross was the last of twelve erected by Edward I to mark the overnight stops on the funeral procession of his wife Eleanor, from Nottinghamshire to Westminster Abbey in 1290. The cross was pulled down during the Civil War, though a Victorian imitation now stands amidst the taxis outside Charing Cross station, at the beginning of the Strand, to the east.

St Martin-in-the-Fields

In the northeastern corner of Trafalgar Square stands James Gibbs' church of **St Martin-in-the-Fields**, fronted by a magnificent Corinthian portico and topped by an elaborate, and distinctly unclassical, tower and steeple. The first church on this site was indeed built "in the fields", outside the city perimeters, while the present building, completed in 1726, was hemmed in on all sides for more than a century before the surrounding houses were demolished to make way for Trafalgar Square, giving the church a much grander setting. The interior is purposefully simple, though the Italian plasterwork on the barrel vaulting is exceptionally rich; it's best appreciated while listening to one of the church's free lunchtime concerts. St Martin's witnessed the christening of Charles II, its now defunct graveyard held the body of his mistress, Nell Gwynne, and George I was a churchwarden (though he seldom turned up for duties); the present church maintains strong royal and naval connections – there's a royal box on the left of the high altar, and one for the admiralty on the right.

The St Martin's crypt café is a good value sanctuary on Trafalgar Square.

The touristy souvenir market along the north wall of the church is just one of St Martin's many money-spinning exercises; more usefully there's a licensed café in the roomy **crypt**, accessible via steps on the southern exterior, not to mention a shop, gallery and brass rubbing centre (Mon–Sat 10am–6pm, Sun noon–6pm). The set of steps by the market leads down to a subterranean "social care centre" and soup kitchen serving the burgeoning ranks of the West End homeless, for whom the church has consistently cared since the pioneering work of one of its vicars, Dick Sheppard, among the parish's homeless ex-soldiers after World War I. St Martin's is also the venue for the annual **Costermongers' Harvest Festival** held in early October. Since Victorian times, Cockney market stallholders and their families have converged on the church from all over London dressed up in aid of charity as "Pearly Kings and Queens", their clothes studded with hundreds of pearly buttons.

The National Gallery

The National Gallery is open Mon–Sat 10am–6pm, Sun 2–6pm; admission is free. It is quietest on weekday mornings.

Taking up the entire north side of Trafalgar Square, the vast, but dull, Neoclassical hulk of the **National Gallery** houses one of the world's greatest art collections. Unlike the Louvre or the Hermitage, the National Gallery is not based on a former royal collection, but was begun as late as 1824 when the government reluctantly agreed to purchase 38 paintings belonging to a Russian emigré banker, John Julius Angerstein. Further paintings were bought by the gallery's wily directors or bequeathed by private individuals in lieu of Estate Duty – in other words to help the rich avoid paying taxes. These days the gallery's budget can do little to compete with the private endowments of the Getty and other American galleries, though in times of emergency (for example when a painting is put up for sale by a stately home) the government has been known to step in with a one-off financial package.

The gallery's hundred and seventy years of canny acquisition has produced a collection of more than 2200 paintings, but the collection's virtue is not so much its size, but the range, depth and sheer quality of its contents. A quick tally of the National's Italian masterpieces, for example, includes works by Piero della Francesca, Raphael, Botticelli, Uccello, Michelangelo, Caravaggio, Titian, Paolo Veronese and Mantegna. From Spain there are dazzling pieces by Velázquez, El Greco and Goya; from the Low Countries, Memlinc, van Eyck, van der Weyden and Rubens, and an array of Rembrandt paintings that features some of his most searching portraits. Poussin, Claude, Watteau, and the only David paintings in the country are the early highlights of a French contingent that has a particularly strong showing of Cézanne and other Impressionists. British art is also represented, with important works by Turner, Gainsborough, Stubbs and Hogarth, though for twentieth-century British art – and many more Turners – you'll need to carry on to the Tate.

Some gallery highlights . . .

The National Gallery's original collection was put on public display at Angerstein's old residence at 100 Pall Mall, until this purpose-built building on Trafalgar Square was completed in 1838. A hostile press dubbed the gallery's diminutive dome and cupolas "pepperpots", and poured abuse on the Greek Revivalist architect, William Wilkins, who went into early retirement, and died a year later. Subsequent additions to the rear of the building over the next hundred and fifty years provoked little comment, but a similar barrage of abuse broke out in the mid-1980s over plans for the new **Sainsbury Wing**, endowed by the supermarket dynasty. The winning design, by Ahrends, Burton and Koralek, elicited the oft-quoted remark from Prince Charles about "a monstrous carbuncle on the face of a much-loved and elegant friend". Planning permission was, of course, not granted. Instead, backed by money from the supermarket giants, the American husband and wife team, Robert Venturi and Denise Scott-Brown, were commissioned to produce a softly-softly, post-modern adjunct, which playfully imitates elements of Wilkins' Neoclassicism and even Nelson's Column, and, most importantly, got the approval of Prince Charles, who laid the foundation stone in 1988.

Visiting the gallery

There are three entrances to the National Gallery: Wilkins' original elevated entrance on Trafalgar Square, the back entrance on Orange Street, and the new entrance on the ground floor of the Sainsbury Wing. All three entrances have cloakrooms, and both the Trafalgar Square and Sainsbury Wing entrances have a shop, a café/restaurant and an information desk, which hands out free plans.

The Sainsbury wing café is an elegant, modest-priced lunch or coffee stop.

The Sainsbury Wing also features the innovative **micro gallery** on the first floor, an early multimedia exploration. A range of computer consoles allow you to plan – and print out – your own personalized tour; it is good for locating particular favourites, learning more about specific paintings and painters and for generally playing around on, but by no means essential if this is your first visit.

Although virtually the entire collection is now on permanent display, you'll need visual endurance to see everything in one day. If you want to view the collection chronologically, begin with the Sainsbury Wing. If you're after the twentieth–century rooms, go through the main, central entrance and head for rooms 43–46. Another possibility is to join up with one of the gallery's free **guided tours** (Mon–Fri 11.30am & 2.30pm, Sat 2 & 3.30pm) which set off from the Sainsbury Wing foyer. The guides vary enormously in the politics and style of their art criticism, and their choice of paintings, but all try and give you a representative sample. In addition, there are free lectures and films in the gallery's three theatres, all listed in the monthly newsletter available from the information desks.

On any one visit, you're likely to discover at least one or two rooms which are in the process of being rehung. If so, you might find the missing paintings lurking in rooms B–F of the little-visited **Lower Floor Collection**, accessible from the stairs in room 13 and directly from the Orange Street entrance, though it's often closed due to staff shortages. The gallery's reserve collection is also on permanently cramped display in Room A.

Temporary exhibitions take place in the basement of the Sainsbury Wing but compare unfavourably with those in London's other public art galleries: the rooms are small, have no natural light, and there is often an entrance fee. The temporary displays in the Sunley Room in the main building, however, are always free; they often focus on the background to one of the gallery's works, or feature an annual exhibition by the gallery's artist-in-residence.

Leonardo da Vinci

A chronological tour, starting in Room 51, in the Sainsbury Wing . . .

The first room you enter in the Sainsbury Wing (room 51) contains the earliest works in the collection, but also boasts **Leonardo da Vinci**'s melancholic *Virgin on the Rocks* (the more famous version hangs in the Louvre), and behind it, in a separate dimly-lit shrine of its own, the "Leonardo Cartoon" – a preparatory drawing of *The Virgin and Child with Saint Anne and John the Baptist* for a painting which, like so many of Leonardo's projects, was never completed.

Before the 1960s, the cartoon was known only to scholars – that is, until an American tried to buy the picture for £2,500,000. In 1987, it gained further notoriety when an ex-soldier blasted the work with a sawn-off shotgun in protest at the political status quo – hence the bullet-proof glass behind which it now hides.

Giotto to Uccello

Appropriately enough the early works in room 51 include one by **Giotto**, considered, even by his contemporaries, to be "the father of modern painting". He was one of the first painters to develop a softer, more three-dimensional approach to painting after the flat, Byzantine-style paintings which had gone before. **Duccio**, a Sienese contemporary of Giotto, maintained a more iconic approach, but also introduced a new sense of movement and space to his narrative paintings, several of which hang in room 52. The panels are taken from his *Maestà* (a Sienese invention depicting the Madonna enthroned as Queen of Heaven) which was carried in triumph from the artist's studio to the cathedral in 1311 with virtually the whole of Siena looking on.

Rooms 53–55

Room 53 features the extraordinarily vivid **Wilton Diptych**, a portable altarpiece painted by an unknown fourteenth-century artist for the boy king Richard II, who is depicted being presented by his patron saints to the Virgin, Child and assorted angels. During recent restoration a minuscule map was discovered in the orb atop the banner, showing a green island, a white castle and a boat in full sail, symbolizing Richard's island kingdom. Also in this room is a vast altarpiece by **Jacopo di Cione**, whose canvases are like richly patterned, gilded jewels, with the figures of Christ and Mary just discernible in their white and gold robes.

Paolo Uccello's blood-free *Battle of San Romano*, which dominates room 55, once decorated a Medici bedroom, as part of a three-panel frieze on the same theme. First and foremost, it's a commemoration of a recent Florentine victory over her bitter Sienese rivals, but it's also an early essay in perspective: a foreshortened body, broken lances and pieces of armour are strewn across the foreground to persuade the viewer that the picture is, in fact, three-dimensional. The bucking white charger at the centre of the battle also appears in Uccello's much smaller *St George and the Dragon*, one of the earliest surviving canvas paintings.

Jan van Eyck

Room 56

Room 56 switches to the beginnings of oil painting, which did away with the painstaking overpainting of egg-based tempera, and allowed the artist to blend infinite gradations of pigment in the palette. The possibilities of depicting the minutiae of life with oils were explored by the likes of **Rogier van der Weyden** in *The Magdalen Reading*, where even the nails in the floor are carefully picked out. But the master of early oil painting was **Jan van Eyck**, whose *Arnolfini Marriage* is an immensely sophisticated painting despite its seemingly mundane domestic setting. Under fifteenth-century Flemish law a couple could enter into marriage without employing the services of a priest, and the appearance of van Eyck's signature in Latin on the back wall suggests that the picture itself served as a marriage certificate. Van Eyck and another figure appear as witnesses in the mirror on the back wall (though the dog alone acknowledges their presence); note, too, the Passion sequence picked out in the smaller surrounding mirrors. Such a marriage was only valid if the couple produced a child within a year, which may account for the seemingly pregnant bride.

Bellini, Mantegna and Botticelli

National Gallery

The art returns to Italy in room 57, where one of **Andrea Mantegna**'s early works, *The Agony in the Garden*, demonstrates a convincing use of perspective, with one of the earliest successful renditions of middle distance; nearby, the dazzling dawn sky in the painting on the same theme by his brother-in-law **Giovanni Bellini**, shows the artist's celebrated mastery of natural light. One of the most accomplished perspectivist paintings of the period was **Carlo Crivelli**'s *Annunciation*, an exercise in ornamentation and geometry, its single focal point the red hat of the man in the background standing before the window.

Room 57

Botticelli's elongated *Venus and Mars* dominates room 58, with a naked and replete Mars in a deep post-coital sleep, watched over by a beautifully calm Venus, fully clothed and somewhat less overcome. His rondo painting of the *Adoration of the Magi* hangs opposite, with the painter himself the best-dressed man at the nativity, resplendent in bright red stockings, giving the audience a knowing look. The **Pollaiuolo** brothers' *Martyrdom of St Sebastian*, in room 59, reads like an anatomical textbook with the three pairs of archers surrounding the saint all striking different poses. Before moving on, don't miss the bloody excesses of Piero di Cosimo's *Fight between the Lapiths and Centaurs*, apparently considered an entertaining subject for a marriage gift.

Room 58–59

Room 60 contains the first batch of the National's nine works by **Raphael**, the *Ansidei Madonna*, painted when the artist was a mere twenty-one years of age. In Room 61 are some fine examples of **Mantegna**'s "cameo" paintings, which imitate the effect of classical stone reliefs, reflecting the craze amongst fashionable Venetian society for collecting antique engraved marbles and gems. The largest of them (painted to be viewed from below), *The Introduction of the Cult of Cybele*, was the artist's last work, and was commissioned by Francesco Cornaro, a Venetian nobleman who claimed descent from one of the greatest Roman families. The Venetian theme is continued with **Bellini**'s *Doge Leonardo Loredan*, one of the artist's greatest portraits.

Rooms 60–61

Bosch, Dürer, Memlinc and della Francesca

Rooms 62–64

The next three rooms, 62 to 64, take you away from Italy with a jolt; four manic tormenters (one wearing a dog's collar) bear down on Jesus in the National's one and only work by **Hieronymus Bosch**, *Christ Mocked*. Gerard David's *Christ Nailed to the Cross* is unusual in that Jesus (who shows no outward signs of pain) is been hammered onto his crucifix whilst flat on the ground. Look out, too, for **Albrecht Dürer**'s sympathetic portrait of his father (a goldsmith in Nuremberg) which was presented to Charles I in 1636 by Dürer's home town. A new acquisition is **Hans Memlinc**'s perfectly poised *Donne Triptych*, a portable altarpiece which features Memlinc himself peering from behind a pillar in the left-hand shutter.

National Gallery

Room 66

At the far end of the wing in room 66, it's back to Italy once more for **Piero della Francesca**'s monumental religious paintings: *The Nativity* and *The Baptism of Christ*, the latter one of Piero's earliest surviving pictures, dating from the 1450s, and a brilliant example of his immaculate compositional technique. Blindness forced Piero to stop painting some twenty years before his death, after which he concentrated on his equally innovative work as a mathematician.

Into the main gallery: rooms 9–11

Veronese and Titian

The first main building room you come to from the Sainsbury Wing is the vast Wohl Room (room 9) containing mainly large-scale Venetian work. The largest of the lot is **Paolo Veronese**'s lustrous *Family of Darius before Alexander*, its array of colourfully clad figures revealing the painter's remarkable skill in juxtaposing virtually the entire colour spectrum in a single canvas. **Titian**'s colourful early masterpiece *Bacchus and Ariadne* and his very late, much gloomier *Death of Actaeon*, separated by some fifty years, hang on either side of the far doorway amply demonstrating the painter's artistic development and longevity. His consummate skill is already apparent in *La Schiavona*, a precisely executed portrait within a portrait; *The Virgin and Child*, by contrast, is a typical late work, with paint jabbed on and rubbed in.

There are more Venetian works in room 10 and in room 11, an octagonal room hung with all four canvases of Veronese's *Allegories of Love*.

From Bronzino to El Greco

Room 8

Next door, in room 8, **Agnolo Bronzino**'s strangely disturbing *Venus, Cupid, Folly and Time* is a classic piece of Mannerist eroticism, which suitably enough made its way into the hands of François I, the decadent, womanizing, sixteenth-century French king. It depicts Cupid about to embrace Venus as she, in turn, attempts to disarm him; above them Father Time tries to reveal the face of Fraud as nothing but a mask, while the cherub of Folly gets ready to shower the couple with roses; weirdest of all is the half-animal, half-human Pleasure, whose double-edged quality is symbolized by her honeycomb and the sting in her tail.

In the same room, **Raphael**'s trenchant *Pope Julius II* – his (and Michelangelo's) patron – is masterfully percipient, though the gallery's curators thought it was no more than a copy until it was cleaned in 1970. Here too is the gallery's only work by **Michelangelo** – his early unfinished *Entombment*. Unlike earlier, static depictions this painting shows Christ's body being hauled into the tomb, and has no fixed iconography by which to identify the figures – either of the women could be Mary Magdalene, for example, and it is arguable whether the man in red is John the Evangelist or Nicodemus.

National Gallery

Michelangelo also provided drawings for the *Raising of Lazarus* by **Sebastiano del Piombo**, the largest painting in the room, which was planned as the altarpiece for Narbonne Cathedral.

Rooms 7 and 6

For the next few rooms it pays to keep your focus selective. The small, adjacent room 7 contains one great masterpiece by the Cretan painter **El Greco**, *Christ Driving Traders from the Temple*, its acidic colouring and angular composition typical of his highly individual work. The striking use of colour and composition in **Lorenzo Lotto**'s *Lady as Lucretia* stands out among the crowd of portraits which line the walls of room 6.

Room 2

In room 2 the standouts are **Correggio**'s *School of Love*, with Mercury teaching Cupid to read (though it's the sensuous Venus who's the picture's real subject), and the *Madonna of the Basket*, a scene of domestic bliss, with Christ being dressed by Mary while the breadwinner Joseph keeps himself busy with his carpentry.

Holbein and Cranach

Room 5

Room 5 contains several masterpieces by **Hans Holbein**, among them his intriguing portrait *A Lady with a Squirrel and a Starling*, painted in 1527 during the artist's first visit to England. In Holbein's masterfully detailed double portrait *The Ambassadors*, the French duo flank an open cabinet piled high with various objects: instruments for studying the heavenly realm on the upper shelf, those for contemplating the earthly life on the lower. The painting clearly demonstrates the subjects' wealth, power and intelligence, but also serves as an elaborate *memento mori*, a message underlined by the distorted skull in the foreground.

The striking portrait of the sixteen-year-old *Christina of Denmark* was part of a series of portraits commissioned by Henry VIII when he was looking for a potential fourth wife. The king eventually plumped for Anne of Cleves on the basis of Holbein's flattering portrait (now in the Louvre), though when he saw her in the flesh he was distinctly unimpressed with his "Flanders mare", after which Holbein fell from royal favour.

Holbein's contemporary **Lucas Cranach the Elder** made his name from erotic slender nudes such as the model used for *Cupid Complaining to Venus*, a none too subtle message about dangerous romantic liaisons. Venus' enormous headgear only emphasises her nakedness, while the German landscape, to the right, serves to gives this mythological morality tale a distinctly "contemporary" edge.

Vermeer, Lorrain and Poussin

Rooms 16 and 18

The Dutch collection begins in room 16 with **de Hooch**'s classic *Courtyard in Delft* and **Vermeer**'s serene *Young Woman Standing at a Virginal*, whose subject is now thought to be Vermeer's eldest daughter Maria, though nobody is quite sure of the relevance of the picture of Cupid that hangs above her. The darkened interior of room 18 is given over entirely to the seventeenth-century **Hoogstraten**

National Gallery

Peepshow, a box of tricks which reveals the Dutch obsession of the time with perspectival and optical devices.

Rooms 19, 20 and 15

The dreamy classical landscapes and seascapes of **Lorrain**, and the mythological scenes of **Poussin** were favourites of aristocrats on the Grand Tour, and made both artists very famous in their time; nowadays, though Poussin has a strong academic following, they strike many people as empty and dull.

Hardly surprising then that rooms 19 and 20, which are given over entirely to these two French artists, are among the quietest in the gallery. Claude's *Enchanted Castle* caught the imagination of the Romantics, supposedly inspiring Keats' *Ode to a Nightingale*, while **Turner** left specific instructions in his will for two of his Claude-influenced paintings to be hung alongside a couple of the French painter's landscapes. All four now hang in room 15, and were slashed by a homeless teenager in 1982 in an attempt to draw attention to his plight.

Van Dyck, Rubens and Dutch landscapes

Rooms 21–26

The Flemish artist, **Anthony Van Dyck**, was court painter for Charles I for many years, though few of the works in room 21 actually derive from his stay here. The one Englishman whose portrait hangs here, George Cage, sat for Van Dyck whilst on a visit to Rome. Also from Van Dyck's trip to Italy is the Titian-influenced colouring of *Charity*, while the most familiar portrait is of *Cornelius van der Geest*, a wealthy merchant from the painter's home town of Antwerp.

Room 22, in the northwest corner of the North Wing, is full of the expansive fleshy canvases of **Peter Paul Rubens**, another Flemish painter whom Charles I summoned to the English court. The one woman with her clothes on is the artist's future sister-in-law, Susanna Fourment, whose delightful portrait became known as *Le Chapeau de Paille* (The Straw Hat) – though the hat is actually made of black felt and decorated with white feathers. At the age of fifty-four Rubens married Susanna's younger sister, Helena (she was just sixteen), the model for all three goddesses posing in the later version of *The Judgement of Paris*, painted in the 1630s.

Across the way in room 23, Rubens' rather more subdued landscapes are displayed, one of which, the *Castle of Steen*, shows off the very fine view from the country mansion Rubens bought in 1635, earning himself the title Lord of Steen.

In room 24, your eye is drawn to the back wall, to one of the finest of all Dutch landscapes, **Meyndert Hobbema**'s *Avenue, Middleharnis*. The market for such landscapes at the time was limited and Hobbema quit painting at the age of just thirty. **Jacob von Ruisdael**, Hobbema's teacher, whose works are on display nearby, also went hungry for most of his life.

The only sure way to make good money was to do portraiture, hence the success of **Frans Hals**, whose *Family Group*, can be seen in room 26.

Rembrandt

Room 27

Having waded through several rooms of genre paintings, pause in room 27, where two of **Rembrandt**'s self-portraits, painted thirty years apart, regard each other – the melancholic *Self Portrait Aged 63*, from the last year of his life, making a strong contrast with the sprightly early work. Similarly, the joyful portrait of *Saskia*, Rembrandt's wife, from the most successful period of his life, contrasts with his more contemplative depiction of his mistress, *Hendrickje*, who was hauled up in front of the city authorities for living "like a whore" with Rembrandt. The largest Rembrandt picture in the room is the highly theatrical *Belshazzar's Feast*, painted for a rich Jewish patron.

Velázquez, Caravaggio and David

Room 29

The cream of the National Gallery's Spanish works are displayed in room 29, among them **Diego Velázquez**' *Kitchen Scene with Christ in the House of Martha and Mary*, where Mary's choice of the contemplative life is held up for approval, though the sensuous pleasure of the painting, which focuses on moody Martha's domestic chores, might suggest the opposite. A less ambivalent sensuality pervades the startling *Rokeby Venus*, one of the gallery's most famous pictures, painted when Velázquez was court painter to Philip IV, himself the subject of two portraits displayed here. Despite the fact that Philip was something of a religious fanatic, he owned several paintings of nudes, though with the Inquisition at its height, they were considered a highly immoral subject for a Spanish artist. Velázquez nonetheless is known to have painted at least four in his lifetime, of which only the *Rokeby Venus* survives, an ambiguously narcissistic image that was slashed in 1914 by suffragette Mary Richardson, who loved the picture but was revolted by the way it was leered at.

Rooms 30 and 32

Next door, among the dull state portraits in room 30, is **Van Dyck**'s *Portrait of Charles I*, a fine example of the work that made him the favourite of the Stuart court, romanticizing the monarch as a dashing horseman. In the adjacent room (32), **Caravaggio**'s art is represented by the typically salacious *Boy Bitten by Lizard*, and the melodramatic *Christ at Emmaus*. The latter was a highly influential painting: never before had biblical scenes been depicted with such naturalism – a beardless and halo-less Christ surrounded by scruffy disciples. At the time it was deemed to be blasphemous, and, like many of Caravaggio's religious commissions, was eventually rejected by the customers.

Rooms 35–40

Rooms 35–40 feature **Canaletto**'s *Stonemason's Yard*, an unusual portrayal of everyday Venetian life compared to his usual glittery vistas of Venice (of which there are also several examples). Here, too, standing in contrast to Canaletto's rather static art, are examples of the airy draughtsmanship of **Tiepolo**, father and son, seen to best effect in the *Allegory with Venus and Time*, commissioned for the ceiling of a Venetian palazzo.

National Gallery

British art from Hogarth to Turner

Room 34

When the Tate opened in 1897 the vast bulk of the National's British art section was transferred there, leaving a small but highly prized core of works behind in room 34 (The Sackler Room). These include a trio of superb late masterpieces by Turner, two of them heralding the new age of steam: *Rain, Steam and Speed*, and *The "Fighting Temeraire"*, in which a ghostly apparition of the veteran battleship from Trafalgar is pulled into harbour by a youthful, fire-snorting tug.

There are also several works by **Thomas Gainsborough** – landscapes, as well as the portraits at which this quintessentially British artist excelled. The painting of the actress Sarah Siddons is one of his finest "grand ladies", and his feathery, light technique is seen to superb effect in *Morning Walk*, a double portrait of a pair of newlyweds. Where Gainsborough excelled in his "grand ladies", his rival **Joshua Reynolds** was at his best with male sitters – as in the extraordinarily effeminate *General Tarleton*.

Here, too, is **Constable**'s *Hay Wain*, probably the most famous British painting of all time, though it was just one of a series of landscapes that he painted in and around his father's mill in Suffolk.

Room 39

Room 39, just off the Central Hall, houses all six paintings from **William Hogarth**'s *Marriage à la Mode*, a witty, moral tale which allowed Hogarth to give vent to his pet hates: bourgeois hypocrisy, snobbery and bad (ie continental) taste.

From David to Picasso

Room 41 features the only two paintings in Britain by the supreme Neoclassicist **Jacques-Louis David**, and the dapper self-portrait by **Louise Vigée le Brun**, one of only three women artists in the whole National Gallery collection.

Boris Anrep's Floor Mosaics

One of the most overlooked features of the National Gallery are the mind-boggling **floor mosaics** executed by Russian-born Boris Anrep between 1927 and 1952 on the landings of the main staircase leading to the Central Hall. The *Awakening of the Muses*, on the halfway landing, features a bizarre collection of famous figures from the 1930s – Virginia Woolf appears as Clio (Muse of History), Greta Garbo plays Melpomema (Muse of Tragedy). The mosaic on the landing closest to the central hall is made up of fifteen small scenes illustrating the *Modern Virtues*: Anna Akhmatova is saved by an angel from the Leningrad Blockade in *Compassion*; T. S. Eliot contemplates the Loch Ness Monster and Einstein's Theory of Relativity in *Leisure*; Bertrand Russell gazes on a naked woman in *Lucidity*; Edith Sitwell, book in hand, glides across a monster-infested chasm on a twig in *Sixth Sense*; and in the largest composition, *Defiance*, Churchill appears in combat gear on the white cliffs of Dover, raising two fingers to a monster in the shape of a swastika.

Here too hangs **Francisco de Goya**'s gloomy portrait of the Duke of Wellington alongside works by **Eugène Delacroix**, who was profoundly impressed by Constable's dappled application of paint. **Ingres**' elegant portrait of the wealthy banker's wife, *Madame Moitessier*, was completed when the artist had reached the age of 76, having taken twelve years to finish. Also in this room, **Géricault**'s galvanic *Horse Frightened by Lightning* demonstrates why Géricault abandoned his teacher, Carle Vernet, claiming "one of my horses would have devoured six of his". But the most popular of all the paintings in the room is **Paul Delaroche**'s slick and phoney *Execution of Lady Jane Grey*, in which the blindfolded, white-robed, seventeen-year old queen stoically awaits her fate.

National Gallery

Room 41

Four magnificent rooms of Impressionist and early twentieth-century paintings close the proceedings, starring, in room 43, **Manet**'s unfinished *Execution of Maximilian*. This was one of three versions Manet painted of the subject and was cut into pieces during the artist's lifetime, then bought and reassembled by Degas after Manet's death. Other major Impressionist works here include **Renoir**'s *Umbrellas*, **Monet**'s *Gare St Lazare* and several works from **Pisarro**'s period of exile, when he lived in south London.

Room 43–46

A comprehensive showing of **Cézanne**, with works taken from every period of the great artist's long life, is gradually revealed over the course of the next three rooms. *The Painter's Father* is one of Cézanne's earliest extant works, originally painted on to the walls of his father's house outside Aix. *The Bathers*, by contrast, is one of Cézanne's very late works, whose angular geometry exercised an enormous influence on the Cubism of Picasso and Braque.

Seurat's *Bathers at Asnières* is one of the most reproduced paintings in room 44, which also contains **Degas**' *La Coiffure*, and several late works by **van Gogh**, including his dazzling *Sunflowers*, just one of seven versions he painted, one of which became the most expensive picture ever sold when it was bought for over £24,000,000 in 1987 by a Japanese insurance company. van Gogh himself sold only one painting in his lifetime, and used to dream of finding someone who would pay just £25 for his work.

Rooms 44 to 45

In room 45, there's an eclectic mix including *Portrait of Hermione Gallia* by **Klimt**, Redon's *Ophelia*, a vast canvas of waterlilies by Monet, and **Picasso**'s sentimental Blue Period *Child with a Dove*. Much of the wall space in rooms 45 and 46 has been given over to paintings on loan from the **Berggruen Collection** of Impressionist paintings and sketches which will be here until April 1996. Among the works permanently here is **Matisse**'s vaguely arabesque *Greta Moll* after Veronese.

For a more comprehensive display of modern and Impressionist art, see the Tate Gallery, p.77. The Courtauld Institute (p.164) also has a collection of Impressionists.

National Portrait Gallery

The National Portrait Gallery is open Mon–Sat 10am–6pm, Sun noon–6pm; free admission.

The National Portrait Gallery

Around the east side of the National Gallery lurks the **National Portrait Gallery**, which was founded in 1856 to house uplifting depictions of the good and the great. Though it has some fine works among its collection of 10,000 portraits, many of the studies are of less interest than their subjects, and the overall impression is of an overstuffed shrine to famous Brits rather than a museum offering any insight into the history of portraiture. However, it is fascinating to trace who has been deemed worthy of admiration at any moment: warmongers and imperialists in the early decades, writers and poets in the 1930s and 40s, and, latterly, retired footballers and pop stars.

The special exhibitions, too, are well worth seeing – and the photography shows, in particular, are often excellent.

Tudors and Stuarts

For some sense of the development of portraiture, and Britain, the place to start is **Level 4**, a mezzanine floor where **Henry VIII** and his predecessors preside. Holbein's larger-than-life cartoon, a preparatory drawing for a much larger fresco in Whitehall Palace, shows the king as a macho buck against a modish Renaissance background. The most eye-catching portrait, however, is the anamorphic painting of the syphilitic **Edward VI**, Henry's only male heir. An illusionistic device – similar to that used on the skull in Holbein's *Ambassadors* in the National Gallery – the painting must be looked at from the side to be viewed properly.

Level 5 starts at the next landing with the intriguing *Allegory of the Reformation under Edward VI*, who is depicted casting down the Pope and burning religious images. The sixteenth-century rooms that follow are filled with Tudor royalty, dour prelates, hanged traitors and the only known painting of **Shakespeare** from life, a subdued image in which the Bard sports a gold-hoop earring – appropriately enough, the first picture acquired by the gallery. Among the seventeenth-century personalities there's a dashing portrait of the red-headed Prince Rupert, and a more effeminate rendering of George Villiers, James I's favourite. **Oliver Cromwell** looks dishevelled but resolute in a miniature painted four years before he became Lord Protector. Further on, an overdressed, haggard **Charles II** presides over a room crammed full of his mistresses, including Frances Teresa Stuart, upon whom, according to the caption, the King was "mighty hot", and a louche Nell Gwynne, the orange-seller turned actress.

The Georgian period

The next series of rooms spans the eighteenth century, starting with the jowly "Butcher" Cumberland, scourge of the Jacobites, alongside a petite Flora MacDonald, Bonnie Prince Charlie's lover. One whole room is filled with members of the **Kit-Kat Club**, a group of Whig patriots – including Robert Walpole – who met in a pub run by one Christopher Cat. The club was formed to ensure the Protestant succession at the end of William's reign and painted by one of its members, Geoffrey Kneller, a naturalized German artist.

Among the various artists and musicians are several fine self-portraits: an energetic, determined **William Hogarth**, a perplexed **Sir Joshua Reynolds**, a relaxed **Thomas Gainsborough** and **George Stubbs** painted onto a Wedgwood plate. Politicians begin to dominate with the death of **Pitt the Elder**, who collapsed in the House of Lords having struggled in to denounce American Independence; at the same time the first caricatures begin to creep into the collection, led by Gilray. **Captain Cook** can be seen posing with his Tahitian lover, Omai, and there's a bold likeness of **Lord Nelson**, along with one of the many idealized portraits the smitten George Romney painted of Nelson's mistress, **Lady Emma Hamilton**.

The Romantics are represented by **Lord Byron** in Albanian garb, the ailing **John Keats**, an open-collared **Shelley**, with his wife, **Mary Wollstonecroft**, above, and a moody image of **Wordsworth** by the history painter Benjamin Haydon. This portrait, painted in response to Wordsworth's sonnet on another of Haydon's pictures, itself became the subject of Elizabeth Barrett Browning's sonnet *Wordsworth on Helvellyn*. In the final room on this level there's a picture of **George IV** and the twice-widowed Catholic woman, Maria Fitzherbert, whom he married without the consent of his father. His official wife, **Queen Caroline**, is depicted in the House of Lords at her adultery trial at which she was acquitted.

The Victorians and Edwardians

Downstairs on **Level 3** are the Victorians and Edwardians: mostly stuffy royalty, dour men of science and engineering and stern statesmen. One deteriorated and oddly affecting group, however, shows the **Brontë sisters** as seen by their disturbed brother Branwell; you can still see where he has painted himself out, leaving a ghostly blur between Charlotte and Emily. Also notable on this floor are two great Victorian photographs: one, by Julia Margaret Cameron showing the historian **Thomas Carlyle**, the other, engineer **Isambard Kingdom Brunel** perkily posed in front of colossal iron chains.

The twentieth century

The twentieth-century collection is rearranged more often than any other, according to the whims and tastes of the day, making it difficult to predict what exactly will be on show. That said, the three rooms on **Level 2** change less than the rest, so you can be fairly sure of glimpsing Wyndham Lewis' self-portrait, Jacob Epstein's vigorously sculpted busts of George Bernard Shaw and Sybil Thorndike, plus a parade of faces from the **Bloomsbury circle**.

Level 1 is by far the most popular section of the collection, concentrating as it does on post-war personalities. There are some

National Portrait Gallery

pretty uninspired paintings here, epitomized by Rodrigo Moynihan's reverential portrait of Margaret Thatcher, and Bryan Organ's obsequious renderings of the royals. It's all a bit like the thinking person's Madame Tussaud's, with several merciless political caricatures by Gerald Scarfe, a gimmicky video gallery on swimmer Duncan Goodhew, and homages to Bobby Charlton and Lady Di. You half expect to see Take That. One of the more diverting pieces is a copper sheet and plastic sculpture of ballerina Lynn Seymour by the high priest of British camp, Andrew Logan, hanging from the ceiling of the central hall.

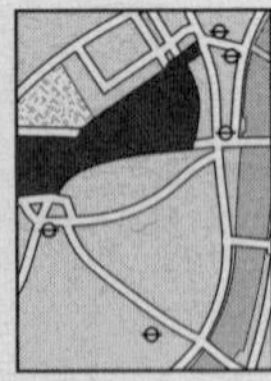

The Mall

The best time to view the Mall is on Sundays when it is closed to traffic.

The tree-lined sweep of **The Mall** – London's nearest equivalent to a Parisian boulevard – was laid out early this century as a memorial to Queen Victoria, and runs along the northern edge of St James's Park. The bombastic **Admiralty Arch** marks the entrance at the Trafalgar Square end, over half a mile from Buckingham Palace and the ludicrous **Victoria Memorial**, Edward VII's overblown tribute to his mother: Truth, Motherhood and Justice keep Victoria company around the plinth, which is topped by a gilded statue of Victory, while the six outlying bronze groups confidently proclaim the great achievements of her reign.

There has been a thoroughfare on the site of The Mall since the Restoration, though its most distinctive building, Carlton House Terrace, is by Regency architect John Nash. This graceful cream-coloured terrace, just beyond Admiralty Arch, is the unlikely home of the **Institute of Contemporary Arts**, or ICA (Mon–Sat noon–1am, Sun noon–10.30pm; day pass £1.50), headquarters of the official avant-garde, as it were, with a regular programme of exhibitions, films, writers' talks, and performances. Many people pay the day membership simply for admission to the bar, which stays open till 1am most nights and has the unusual distinction of being a trendy gathering point with no style arbiters or bouncers on the door. There's also a good Italian-run café-restaurant and an arts bookshop with cutting-edge stock.

St James's Park

St James's Park is open daily, dawn to dusk.

St James's Park, on the south side of the Mall, is the oldest of the royal parks, having been drained for hunting purposes by Henry VIII and opened to the public by Charles II, who used to stroll through the grounds with his mistresses, and even take a dip in the canal. By the eighteenth century, when some 6500 people had access to night keys for the gates, the park had become something of a byword for prostitution: Boswell was, of course, among those who went there specifically to be accosted "by several ladies of the town". The park was finally landscaped by Nash into its present elegant appearance in 1828, in a style that established the trend for Victorian city parks.

Today the pretty tree-lined lake is a favourite picnic spot for the civil servants of Whitehall and an inner-city reserve for wildfowl. James I's two crocodiles have left no descendants, alas, and even the pelicans (related to a pair presented to Charles II by the Russian Ambassador) have been banished to London Zoo as punishment for preying on London's beloved pigeons, but there are ducks and Canada geese aplenty. From the bridge across the lake there's a fine view over to Westminster and the jumble of domes and pinnacles along Whitehall. Even the dull facade of Buckingham Palace looks majestic from here.

For more on Carlton House Terrace and the grand houses to the north of the park, see p.88.

Buckingham Palace

Buckingham Palace is open in Aug & Sept only, daily from 9.30am to 5.30pm; £8. The nearest tube is Green Park.

The graceless colossus of **Buckingham Palace**, popularly known as "Buck House", has served as the monarch's permanent London residence since the accession of Victoria. It began its days in 1702 as the Duke of Buckingham's city residence, built on the site of a notorious brothel, and was sold by the Duke's son to George III in 1762. The building was overhauled for the Prince Regent in 1812 by Nash and again in 1913, producing a palace that's about as bland as it's possible to be.

For ten months of the year there's little to do here, with the Queen in residence and the palace closed to visitors – not that this deters the crowds who mill around the railings all day, and gather in some force to watch the **Changing of the Guard**, (see p.61), in which a detachment of the Queen's Foot Guards marches to appropriate martial music from St James's Palace (unless it rains, that is).

The interior

Her Majesty is not at home in public visiting months.

Until recently, unless you were one of the select 30,000 invited to attend one of the Queen's three annual garden parties – the replacements for the society débutantes' "coming out" parties, which ceased to be royally sanctioned in 1958 – you had little chance of seeing inside Buckingham Palace. Since August 1993, however, the hallowed portals have been grudgingly nudged open for two months of the year. **Tickets** are sold from the tent-like box office in Green Park at the western end of The Mall; queues vary enormously, but can be over two hours long, after which there's a further wait until your allocated visiting time. Once inside, it's all a bit of an anticlimax, despite the voyeuristic pleasure of a glimpse behind those forbidding walls: of the palace's 660 rooms you're permitted to see just eighteen, and there's little sign of life, as the Queen and her family decamp to Scotland every summer.

The Royal Family

Tourists may still flock to see London's five royal palaces – Buckingham Palace, Windsor Castle, St James's Palace, Kensington Palace and Clarence House – but the British public are becoming less and less happy about footing the huge tax bill which goes to support the **Royal Family** in the style to which they are accustomed. This creeping republicanism can be traced back to 1992, which the Queen herself, in one of her few memorable Christmas Day speeches, accurately described as her *annus horribilis* ("One's Bum Year" as a *Sun* headline pithily put it). This was the year that saw the marriage break-ups of Charles and Di, and Andrew and Fergie, and the second marriage of divorcee Princess Anne.

Matters came to a head, though, over who should pay the estimated £50 million costs of the fire at Windsor Castle (p.389). Misjudging the public mood, the Tories immediately offered taxpayers' money to foot the bill. After a furore, it was agreed that at least some of the cost would be raised from the astronomical admission charges to Windsor Castle and to Buckingham Palace, a few rooms of which were grudgingly opened to public view when the royals were safely ensconced in their summer retreat in Scotland.

In addition, under pressure from public opinion polls, the media and even some Tory backbenchers, the Queen also offered to reduce the number of royals paid for out of the Civil List, and, for the first time in her life, pay taxes on her personal fortune. Estimates of the Queen's wealth range from a modest £50 million to £6.5 billion, a calculation dismissed by Prince Edward as "absolute crap". Whatever the truth, she's certainly not hard up, and public subsidy of the richest woman in the world doesn't stop at the Civil List; millions more is spent by government departments on the Royal Yacht, the Royal Train, the Queen's Flight and the upkeep of the palaces. Only Princess Anne has captured the public mood: she performs more official duties per year than any other royal, lives in her own house with a minimal amount of officialdom, and insisted on a modest spread of sandwiches at the reception of her second marriage.

Despite public disenchantment with the Royal Family, none of the political parties currently advocate abolishing the monarchy. The nearest to it are the Labour Party, who favour a cut-price bicycling monarchy, along Scandinavian lines: their Heritage spokesperson, Mo Mowlam, recently provoked outrage by suggesting selling off Buck House and building a new modern palace. The debate will doubtless run and run, along with the ever-more entertaining soap opera of royal life – arguably, the royals' main modern function, pulling in *Hello!* magazine readers from all corners of the old empire.

The public entrance is via the **Ambassadors' Court** on Buckingham Palace Road, which lets you into the enormous **Quadrangle**, from where you can see the Nash portico, built in warm Bath Stone, that looked over St James's Park until it was closed off by Queen Victoria. Through the courtyard, you hit the **Grand Hall**, site of the Duke of Buckingham's original entrance hall and now a frenzy of red carpets, gold and marble, decorated to the taste of Edward VII.

From the hall, Nash's winding, curlicued **Grand Staircase**, with its floral gilt bronze balustrade, leads past a range of dull royal portraits, all beautifully lit by Nash's glass dome. Beyond, the small Guard Room, decorated with Gobelin tapestries and nineteenth-century sculpture, is a mere formality which leads into the **Green Drawing Room**, a blaze of unusually bright green silk walls, framed by lattice-patterned pilasters, and a heavily gilded coved ceiling. In the scarlet and gold **Throne Room**, there's an unusual Neoclassical plaster frieze, depicting the War of the Roses, two winged figures holding up the proscenium arch, but disappointingly, no regal throne, just two pink his 'n' hers chairs initialled ER and P.

Nash's vaulted **Picture Gallery**, stretching right down the centre of the palace, is more impressive, though the original spectacular hammerbeam ceiling was replaced by a rather dull glazed arched ceiling in 1914. On show here is a selection of the Royal Collection (see below) – among them several Van Dycks, two Rembrandts and an excellent Vermeer. It's hard to imagine Prince Charles disco dancing among all the Old Masters, but it was here that he celebrated his fortieth birthday, with music from the Three Degrees (his long-time favourite pop group) and the room decked out like a harem. The gallery continues through several more smaller rooms until you reach the stultifyingly scarlet and gilt **State Dining Room**, and, beyond, Nash's **Blue Drawing Room**, with thirty fake onyx columns, flock wallpaper, yet more gilt coving and an extraordinary Sèvres porcelain table made for Napoleon.

The best place from which to view the palace grounds is the enormous semi-circular bow window of the domed **Music Room**, where Anne, Charles and Andrew were all baptised with water brought from the River Jordan. The frothy gold and white Nash ceiling and priceless French antiques of the **White Drawing Room** form the incongruous setting for an annual royal prank: when hosting the reception for the diplomatic corps, the Queen and family emerge from a secret door behind the fireplace to greet the ambassadors – nobody seems clear why.

Before you leave the palace, be sure to check out the Canova sculptures, *Fountain Nymph* at the bottom of the Ministers' Staircase, and *Mars and Venus* in the Marble Hall. These are the principal art treasures on display in the palace.

The Queen's Gallery and the Royal Mews

You can see a further small selection of the monarch's art collection at the **Queen's Picture Gallery**, a couple of meanly-proportioned rooms with no natural light, round the south side of the palace on Buckingham Palace Road. The Royal Collection is more than three times larger than the National Gallery's, indefensibly so since so little

The Queen's Gallery is open Tues–Sat 10am–5pm, Sun 2–5pm; £2.50. The nearest tube is Victoria.

is shown at any one time. The exhibitions change annually but usually include some works by Reynolds, Gainsborough, Vermeer, Rubens, Rembrandt and Canaletto, which make up the bulk of the collection.

Whilst on the subject of the Royal Collection, it's worth recalling that the Surveyor of the Queen's Pictures until 1979 was an ex-Russian spy, Anthony Blunt, KGB talent-spotter at Cambridge for many years in the 1930s. This fact was known to the British intelligence service, MI6, since 1964, when Blunt told all in a "keep it secret" deal with the Establishment, and it was not until fifteen years later that parliament was informed. The press subsequently hounded Blunt, dwelling as much on his homosexuality ("the Queen's queen") as his espionage. He died shortly afterwards.

The Royal Mews are open summer Tues–Thurs noon–4pm; winter Wed only; £2.

There's more pageantry on show at the **Royal Mews**, further south on Buckingham Palace Road, built by Nash in the 1820s after the old mews were demolished to make way for Trafalgar Square. The horses – or at least their backsides – can be viewed in the stables, along with an exhibition of equine accoutrements, but it's the royal carriages, lined up under a glass canopy in the courtyard, that are the main attraction. The most ornate is the Gold Carriage, made for George III in 1762, smothered in 22-carat gilding and weighing four tons, its axles supporting four life-size figures. Eight horses are needed to pull it and the whole experience made Queen Victoria feel quite sick; since then it has only been used for coronations and jubilees.

The Wellington Barracks

The Guards Museum is open daily except Fri 10am–6pm; £2. The nearest tube is St James's Park.

Birdcage Walk – named for James I's aviary which once stood here – runs along the south side of St James's Park, with the **Wellington Barracks** occupying more than half its length. Of the various building here, it's the modernist lines of the **Guards Chapel** which comes as the biggest surprise; its rebuilding was necessary after the old chapel was hit by a V-1 rocket bomb, on June 18, 1944, killing over one hundred worshippers. In a bunker opposite is the **Guards Museum**, which displays the various uniforms of the Queen's Household Regiments (see below), and generally glamorizes war through the ages.

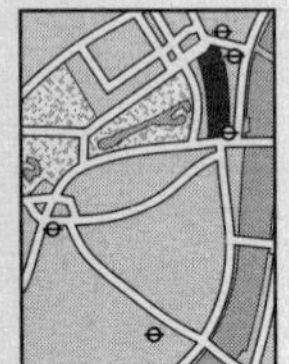

Whitehall

Whitehall, the broad avenue connecting Trafalgar Square to Parliament Square, is synonymous with the faceless, pin-striped bureaucracy charged with the day-to-day running of the country. Since the seventeenth century, nearly all the key governmental ministries and offices have migrated here, re-housing themselves on an ever-increasing scale, a process which reached its apogee with the grimly bland **Ministry of Defence** building, the largest office

The Changing of the Guards and royal parades

The Queen is colonel-in-chief of the seven **Household Regiments**: the Life Guards (who dress in red and white) and the Blues and Royals (who dress in blue and red) are the two Household Cavalry regiments; while the Grenadier, Coldstream, Scots, Irish and Welsh Guards make up the Foot Guards. The Foot Guards can only be told apart by the plumes (or lack of them) in their busbies, and by the arrangement of their tunic buttons. Mostly dating back to the seventeeth century, these regiments form part of the modern army (the Coldstream Guards were among the British troops sent to Bosnia) as well as performing ceremonial functions such as the Changing of the Guard.

The **Changing of the Guard** takes place at three locations: the two Household Cavalry regiments take it in turns to stand guard at the Horse Guards building on Whitehall (Mon–Sat 11am, Sun 10am); the Foot Guards take care of Buckingham Palace (May–Aug daily 11.30am; Sept–April alternate days; no ceremony if it rains) and the Tower of London.

A considerably grander – and, if you're trying to move around this part of London, disruptive – ceremony is the **Trooping of the Colour**, when one of the Household battalions presents its colour (flag) for inspection to the Queen. This takes place on the Saturday nearest the Queen's official birthday, June 6, with rehearsals (minus Her Majesty) on the two preceding Saturdays. The other spot of marching is the floodlit **Beating of the Retreat**, which takes place on three evenings in May/June.

Both ceremonies culminate in Horse Guards Parade, though you can watch them march to their destination along The Mall. If you want tickets for a seat in the stands around the parade ground, you'll need to book tickets well in advance; phone ☎0171/930 4466 for exact dates and details.

block in London when it was completed in 1959. The statues dotted about Whitehall recall the days when this street stood at the centre of an empire on which the sun never set. Nowadays – or for the time being at least – it's just the heart of the United Kingdom: the Scots are ruled from the cute little Dover House, the Welsh are run from Gwydyr House opposite, while Northern Ireland still receives most attention from the Ministry of Defence.

During the sixteenth and seventeenth centuries Whitehall was synonymous with royalty, since it was the permanent residence of the kings and queens of England. The original **Whitehall Palace** was built for Henry VIII after a fire at Westminster forced him to find alternative accommodation; it was here that he celebrated his marriage to Anne Boleyn in 1533, and here that he died fourteen years later. Described by one contemporary chronicler as nothing but "a heap of houses erected at diverse times and of different models, made continuous", it boasted some two thousand rooms and stretched for half a mile along the Thames. Little survived the fire of 1698, after which, partly due to the dank conditions in this part of town, the royal residence shifted to St James's.

Banqueting House

The Banqueting House is open Mon–Sat 10am–5pm; £2.75.

The one part of the palace which survived the fire is the **Banqueting House**, the first Palladian building to be built in England, begun by Inigo Jones in 1619.

The house opened in 1622 with a performance of Ben Jonson's *Masque of Anger*, with Jones providing the scenery and costumes; the entertainment took place in the main banqueting hall, which is still used for state occasions.

Other plays and masques were performed here until Charles I banned such shows in 1634 to prevent candle smoke damaging the ceiling paintings he had commissioned from Rubens, glorifying the Stuart dynasty. Sixteen years later Charles walked through the room for the last time and stepped onto the executioner's scaffold from one of its windows. He wore several shirts in case he shivered in the cold, which the crowd would take to be fear; once his head was chopped off, it was then sewn back on again for burial in Windsor – a very British touch. The execution is still commemorated here on the last Sunday in January with a parade by the Royalist wing of the Civil War Society.

Cromwell moved into the palace in 1654, having declared himself Lord Protector, and kept open table for the officers of his New Model Army; he died here in 1658. Two years later Charles II was welcomed here by the Lords and Commons for the Restoration, and kept open house for his adoring public – Pepys recalls seeing the underwear of one of his mistresses, Lady Castlemaine, hanging out to dry in the palace's Privy Garden. (Charles housed two mistresses and his wife here, with a back entrance onto the river for courtesans.) The weathervane on the north side of the roof was erected in 1686 by James II to warn of the foul "Protestant wind" that might propel William of Orange over the seas from Holland; it did little to protect James from the Glorious Revolution, however, and, after taking the throne in 1689, William and Mary came to live here until William's asthma forced them to move to Kensington.

Inside, the one room open to the public has no original furnishings but is well worth seeing for the **Rubens** ceiling paintings. The information boards posted in the room explain everything you need to know to appreciate the paintings; the video and the acoustaphone commentary are not worth bothering with unless your English history's a bit thin and you want a rather formal remedy.

Horse Guards

Across the road, where Henry VIII had the palace cock-fighting pit, tennis courts and a tiltyard for bear-baiting, two mounted sentries of the Queen's Household Cavalry and two horseless colleagues, all in ceremonial uniform, are posted daily from 10am to 4pm. Ostensibly they are protecting the **Horse Guards** building, a modestly proportioned edifice by William Kent, originally built as the old palace guard house, but now guarding nothing in particular. The mounted guards are changed hourly; those standing have to remain motionless and impassive for two hours before being replaced.

Try to time your visit to coincide with the **Changing of the Guard** (see box on previous page), when a squad of twelve mounted troops in full livery arrive from Hyde Park Barracks via Hyde Park Corner, Constitution Hill. The main action takes place at the rear of the building in the small section of Horse Guards Parade, most of which is used as a car park for top civil servants.

Downing Street and the Cenotaph

Farther down this west side of Whitehall is London's most famous address, **Number 10 Downing Street**, the terraced house that has been the residence of the prime minister since it was presented to Sir Robert Walpole, Britain's first prime minister, by George II in 1732. With No. 11 – home of the Chancellor of the Exchequer – and No. 12, it's the only remaining bit of the original seventeenth-century cul-de-sac, though all three are now interconnecting and, having been greatly modernized over the years, house much larger complexes than might appear from the outside. The public have been kept at bay since 1990 when Margaret Thatcher ordered a pair of iron gates to be installed at the junction with Whitehall, an act more symbolic than effective – a year later the IRA lobbed a mortar into the street from Horse Guards Parade, coming within a whisker of wiping out the entire Tory cabinet.

Just beyond the Downing Street gates, in the middle of the road, stands Edwin Lutyens' **Cenotaph**, built in wood and plaster for the first anniversary of the Armistice in 1919, and rebuilt, by popular request, in Portland stone the following year. The stark monument, which eschews any kind of Christian imagery, is inscribed simply with the words "The Glorious Dead" – the lost of World War I, who, it was once calculated, would take three and a half days to pass by the Cenotaph marching four abreast. The memorial remains the focus of the Remembrance Sunday ceremony in November, with its "great awful silence", a two-minute silence once observed throughout the entire British Empire.

The Cabinet War Rooms

The Cabinet War Rooms are open daily 10am–6pm; £3.80.

In 1938, in anticipation of Nazi air raids, the basement of the civil service buildings on the south side of King Charles Street were converted into the **Cabinet War Rooms**. Though these claustrophobic suites were fragile in comparison with Hitler's bunker in Berlin (the Führer's refuge was fifty feet below ground, whereas Churchill's was protected only by a concrete slab), it was here that Winston Churchill directed operations and held cabinet meetings for the duration of World War II. By 1945 the warren had expanded to cover more than three acres, including a hospital, canteen and shooting range, as well as sleeping quarters for officers. Churchill had an emergency bedroom, though he rarely stayed there, preferring to watch the air raids from the roof of the building, or rest his head at the Savoy Hotel.

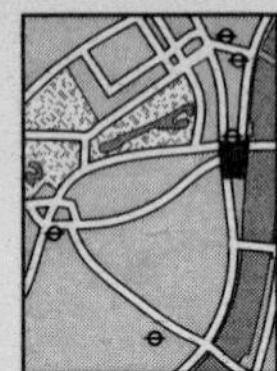

Parliament Square

Parliament Square was laid out in the mid-nineteenth century to give the new Houses of Parliament and the adjacent Westminster Abbey a grander setting, and has the dubious privilege of being one of the city's first traffic roundabouts. Statues of notables – Abraham Lincoln, Benjamin Disraeli and Jan Smuts to name but a few – are scattered amid the swirling cars and buses. Winston Churchill stoops determinedly in the northeast corner of the central green.

Parliament's nearest tube is Westminster.

The other noteworthy statue is on the corner of Westminster Bridge, where Boudicca (Boadicea) can be seen keeping her horses and daughters under control without the use of reins; Cowper's boast – "regions Caesar never knew, thy posterity shall sway" – adorns the plinth. Incidentally Wordsworth's poem, *Lines Written Upon Westminster Bridge* – "Earth has not anything to show more fair . . ." and so on – were addressed to the bridge's predecessor. The current one was opened in 1862.

The Houses of Parliament

The Palace of Westminster, better known as the **Houses of Parliament**, is London's best-known monument. The "mother of all parliaments" and the "world's largest building" – or so it was claimed at the time – it is also the city's finest Victorian building, the symbol of a nation once confident of its place at the centre of the world. Best viewed from the south side of the river, where the likes of Monet and Turner set up their easels, the building is distinguished above all by the ornate, gilded clock tower popularly known

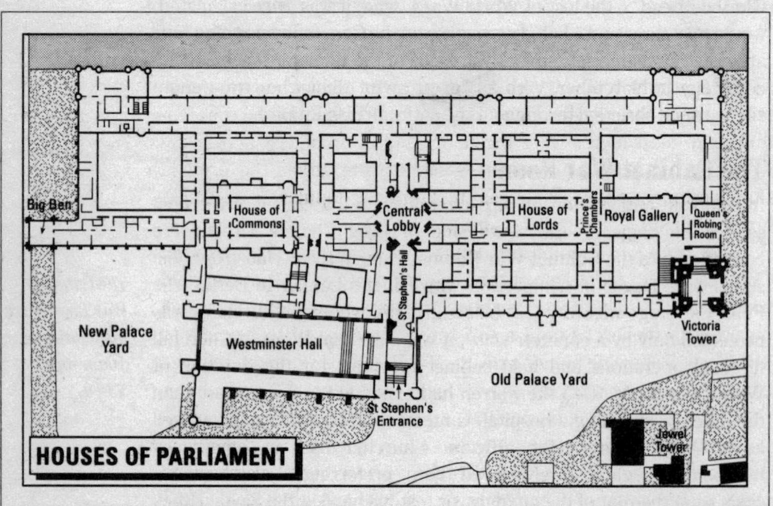

Visiting the Houses of Parliament

Debates in the Commons – the livelier House – begin at 2.30pm and end no earlier than 10.30pm each weekday except Friday, when they start at 9.30am and finish at 3pm. Question Time – when the House is at its most raucous and entertaining – lasts from 2.30pm until about 3.30pm from Monday to Thursday; Prime Minister's Question Time is on Tuesday and Thursday from 3.15pm until 3.30pm. To attend either Question Time you need a special ticket (see below). Recesses (holiday closures) of both Houses occur at Christmas, Easter, and from August to the middle of October. If parliament is in session a flag flies from the southernmost tower, the Victoria Tower, and at night there is a light above the clock face on Big Ben.

To watch the proceedings in either the House of Commons or the Lords, simply join the queue for the **public galleries** (known as Strangers' Galleries) outside St Stephen's Gate. The public are let in slowly from about 4.30pm onwards from Monday to Thursday, and 10am on Fridays; the security checks are very tight, and the whole procedure can take an hour or more. If you want to avoid the queues, turn up an hour or two later when the crowds have usually thinned. If you just want to sit in on one of the select committee meetings, which take place throughout the day, you can usually jump the queue; phone ☎0171/219 4272 for more information. Full explanatory notes on the procedures (and warnings about joining in or causing a disruption) are supplied to all visitors.

To see Question Time, you need to book a **ticket** several weeks in advance from your local MP (if you're a UK citizen) or your embassy in London (if you're not). To contact your MP, simply phone ☎0171/219 3000 and ask to be put through.

MPs and embassies can also arrange **guided tours** which take place in the morning from Monday to Thursday and on Friday afternoons. The full price of a tour is £15–20, but individuals can ask to join up with a pre-booked group, thus cutting the costs to around £2–3. If you want to climb **Big Ben** before or after your tour, say so and this can be arranged.

Parliament Square

as **Big Ben**, which is at its most impressive at night when the clock-face is lit up. Strictly speaking, "Big Ben" refers only to the thirteen-ton main bell which strikes the hour (and is broadcast across the world by the BBC), and takes its name from either the original Commissioner of Works, Benjamin Hall, or a popular heavyweight boxer of the time, Benjamin Caunt.

The original Westminster Palace was built by **Edward the Confessor** in the first half of the eleventh century, so that he could watch over the building of his abbey. It then served as the seat of all the English monarchs until a fire forced Henry VIII to decamp to Whitehall. Following Henry's death, the House of Commons moved from the abbey's Chapter House into the palace's St Stephen's Chapel, thus beginning the building's associations with parliament.

In 1834 the old palace burned down. Save for a few pieces of the old structure buried deep within the interior, everything you see today is the work of **Charles Barry**, whose design had won the competition to create something that expressed national greatness through the use of Gothic and Elizabethan styles. The resulting orgy of honey-coloured pinnacles, turrets and tracery, somewhat restrained by the building's classical symmetry, is the greatest achievement of the Gothic Revival. Inside, the Victorian love of mock-Gothic detail is evident in the maze of over one thousand committee rooms and offices, the fittings of which were largely the responsibility of Barry's assistant, **Augustus Pugin**.

Westminster Hall is accessible only on a guided tour (see box above). It can be glimpsed from St Stephen's Porch en route to see a session in Parliament.

Westminster Hall

Virtually the only relic of the medieval palace is the bare expanse of **Westminster Hall**, on the north side of the complex. First built by William Rufus in 1099, it was saved from the 1834 fire by the timely intervention of the Prime Minister, Lord Melbourne, who had the fire engines brought into the hall itself, and personally took charge of the fire fighting. The sheer scale of the hall – 240ft by 60ft – and its huge oak hammerbeam roof, added by Richard II in the late fourteenth century, make it one of the most magnificent secular halls in Europe.

Unless you're on a guided tour, you can only peer down from St Stephen's Porch at the bare expanse which has witnessed some nine hundred years of English history. Nowadays, the hall is only used for the lying-in-state of members of the royal family and a select few non-royals, but until 1821 every royal coronation banquet was held here, a ceremony during which the Royal Champion would ride into the hall in full armour to challenge any who dared dispute the sovereign's right to the throne.

From the thirteenth to the nineteenth centuries the hall was used as the country's highest court of law: among the many tried here was **Guy Fawkes**, the Catholic caught in the cellars trying to blow up the House of Lords on November 5, 1605; he was later hanged, drawn and quartered in Old Palace Yard. **Charles I** was also tried in the hall, but refused to take his hat off, since he did not accept the court's legitimacy. **Oliver Cromwell**, whose statue now stands outside the hall, was sworn in here as Lord Protector in 1653, only to have his head stuck on a spike above the hall after the Restoration – it remained there for several decades until a storm dislodged it. It now resides in a secret location in Cromwell's old college in Cambridge.

St Stephen's Hall and the Central Lobby

From St Stephen's Porch the route to the parliamentary chambers passes into **St Stephen's Hall**, designed by Barry as a replica of the chapel built by Edward I, where the Commons met for nearly three hundred years until 1834. The ersatz vaulted ceilings, faded murals, statuary and huge wooden doors create a rather sterile atmosphere, doing nothing to conjure up the dramatic events which have unfolded here. It was into this chamber that Charles I entered with an armed guard in 1642 in a vain attempt to arrest five MPs – "I see my birds have flown", he is supposed to have said. Shortly afterwards the Civil War began, and no monarch has entered the Commons since. St Stephen's also witnessed the only assassination of a prime minister, when in 1812 Spencer Perceval was shot by a merchant whose business had been ruined by the Napoleonic Wars.

After a further wait the doorkeeper shepherds you through the bustling, octagonal **Central Lobby**, where constituents "lobby" their MPs. In the tiling of the lobby Pugin inscribed in Latin the motto "Except the Lord keep the house, they labour in vain that build it". In view of what happened to the architects, the sentiment seems like an indictment of Parliamentary morality – Pugin ended up in Bedlam mental hospital and Barry died from overwork within months of completing the job.

The House of Commons

The Commons chamber.

If you're heading for the **House of Commons**, you'll be ushered into a small room where all visitors sign a form vowing not to cause a disturbance; long institutional staircases and corridors then lead to the Strangers' Gallery, rising steeply above the chamber. Everyone is given a guide to the House, which includes explanatory diagrams and notes on procedure, and a Points of Order sheet to help unravel the matters discussed. Protests from the Strangers' Gallery were once a fairly regular occurrence: suffragettes have poured flour, farmers have dumped dung, Irish Nationalists have lobbed tear gas, and gay women have abseiled down into the chamber. Rigorous security arrangements have unfortunately put paid to such antics.

Since an incendiary bomb in May 1941 destroyed Barry's original chamber, what you see now is a rather lifeless reconstruction by Giles Gilbert Scott, completed in 1950. Barry's design was itself modelled on St Stephen's Chapel (see above), hence the choirstall arrangement of the MPs' benches. Members of the cabinet (and the opposition's shadow cabinet) occupy the two "front benches"; the rest are "back benchers". To avoid debates degenerating into physical combat, MPs are not allowed to cross the red lines – which are exactly two swords' length apart – on the floor of the chamber during a debate, hence the expression "toeing the party line".

The House of Lords

On the other side of the Central Lobby a corridor leads to the **House of Lords** (or Upper House), a far dozier establishment, peopled by unelected Lords and Ladies, both hereditary and appointed by successive PMs, and a smattering of bishops. Their home boasts a much grander decor than the Commons, full of regal gold and scarlet, and dominated by a canopied gold throne where the Queen sits for the state opening of parliament in November. Directly in front of the throne, the Lord Chancellor runs the proceedings from the scarlet Woolsack, an enormous cushion stuffed with wool, which harks back to the time when it was England's principal export. Once again, before ascending to the Strangers' Gallery here, you will be given a guide to the House, with explanatory diagrams and notes on procedure.

Nowadays, the Lords have little real power – they can only advise and review pariamentary bills, although a handful act as the country's final court of appeal. During the 1980s, however, they proved themselves to be a good deal more progressive than the Thatcher government, which suffered several deeply embarrassing defeats in the House. That said, its 1000-plus members are dominated by solidly conservative members of the Establishment (over a quarter went to Eton College), and in emergencies, such as the May 1988 vote on the Poll Tax, the Conservatives generally wheel in enough "backwoodsmen" (hereditary Lords who rarely leave their country estates) to give themselves an easy majority.

The royal apartments

If the House of Lords takes your fancy, you can see more pomp and glitter by joining up with a guided tour. You'll be asked to meet at the **Norman Porch entrance** below Victoria Tower, where the Queen arrives in her coach for the state opening. Then, after the usual security checks, you'll be taken up the Royal Staircase to the Norman Porch itself, every nook of which is stuffed with busts of eminent statesmen.

Next door is the **Queen's Robing Chamber**, which boasts a superb coffered ceiling and lacklustre Arthurian frescoes. As its name suggests, this is the room where the monarch dons the crown jewels before entering the Lords for the opening of parliament. Beyond here you enter the **Royal Gallery**, a cavernous writing room for the House of Lords, hung with portraits of the royals past and present, and two forty-five-foot-long frescoes of Trafalgar and Waterloo. Before entering the House of Lords itself, you pass through the **Prince's Chamber**, commonly known as the Tudor Room after the numerous portraits that line the room, including Henry VIII and all six of his wives.

The guides then take you through both Houses, St Stephen's Hall and finally Westminster Hall (all described above), before ejecting you into New Palace Yard. Sadly, the fourteenth-century crypt known as St Mary Undercroft, and the cloister beyond, are no longer open to the public.

The Jewel Tower is open April–Sept daily 10am–1pm & 2–6pm; Oct–March Tues–Sun closes 4pm; EH; £2.

Jewel Tower and the Victoria Tower Gardens

The **Jewel Tower**, across the road from parliament, is a remnant of the medieval palace. The tower formed the southwestern corner of the exterior fortifications (there's a bit of moat left, too), and was constructed by Edward III as a giant strong-box for the crown jewels. Nowadays, its three floors house an excellent exhibition on the history of parliament, ending with a twenty-five minute video on the procedural rigmarole which still persists there.

Alongside the Jewel Tower, the small stretch of lawn sporting a Henry Moore sculpture is a prime spot for TV interviews with MPs, with the Houses of Parliament as a backdrop. On the other side of the road are the rather more attractive and leafy **Victoria Tower Gardens**, which look out onto the Thames. A replica of Rodin's famous statue, *The Burghers of Calais*, makes a surprising appearance here, whilst nearby stands **Emmeline Pankhurst**, leader of the suffragette movement, who died in 1928, the same year that women finally got the vote on equal terms with men.

Westminster Abbey

The Houses of Parliament dwarf their much older neighbour, **Westminster Abbey**, which squats uncomfortably on the western edge of Parliament Square. Yet this single building embodies much of the history of England: it has been the venue for all but two coronations since the time of William the Conqueror, and the site of more or less every royal burial for some five hundred years between the reigns of Henry III and George II. Scores of the nation's most famous citizens are honoured here, too – though many of the stones commemorate people buried elsewhere – and the interior is cluttered with hundreds of monuments, reliefs and statues.

Legend has it that the first church on the site was consecrated by Saint Peter himself, who came down from heaven and was rowed across the Thames by a fisherman named Edric. More verifiable is that there was a small Benedictine monastery here by the end of the tenth century, for which **Edward the Confessor** built an enormous church. Nothing much remains of Edward's church, which was consecrated on December 28, 1065, just ten days before his own death, though the ground plan is his, as is the crypt.

Less than a year later, William the Conqueror rode up the aisle on horseback and, in an attempt to cement his rather tenuous claim to the throne, established the tradition of royal coronation within the Confessor's church. In 1161 there was a ceremony here to canonize Edward the Confessor, and it was again in Edward's honour that **Henry III** began to rebuild the abbey in 1245, in the style of the recently completed Rheims cathedral. Over the next twenty-five years the entire east end, both transepts and four bays of the nave were constructed, Henry bankrupting the royal coffers in the process.

Nothing more was done to the church for another hundred years until Richard II came to the throne; the vaulting had to wait until the reign of **Henry VII**, who contributed the single most significant addition to the church, the late Gothic masterpiece of the rebuilt Lady Chapel at the east end. The monks were kicked out during the Reformation, but the church's status as the nation's royal mausoleum saved it from anything worse. Finally, in the early eighteenth century Nicholas Hawksmoor gave the church its quasi-Gothic twin towers and west front.

Westminster Abbey

Admission to the nave is free.

The nave

With over three thousand people buried beneath its flagstones and countless others commemorated here, the abbey is in essence a giant mausoleum. It has long ceased to be primarily a working church and admission charges are nothing new: Charles Lamb complained about them back in 1823. Less than a century later, so few people used the abbey as a church that, according to George Bernard Shaw, one foreign visitor who knelt down to pray was promptly arrested because the verger thought he was acting suspiciously. Despite attempts to prove otherwise – like the current policy of broadcasting prayers every hour – the abbey is now more a mass tourist attraction than a House of God.

The **nave** is narrow, light and, at over a hundred feet in height, by far the tallest in the country. However, your eyes are immediately drawn away from the building to the statues and monuments which line the interior. The first one to head for is the **Tomb of the Unknown Soldier**, with its garland of red poppies commemorating the one million British soldiers who died in World War I. Close by is a large floor slab to **Churchill**, though he chose to be buried in his family plot in Bladon; Neville Chamberlain, his prime ministerial predecessor, lies forgotten in the south aisle.

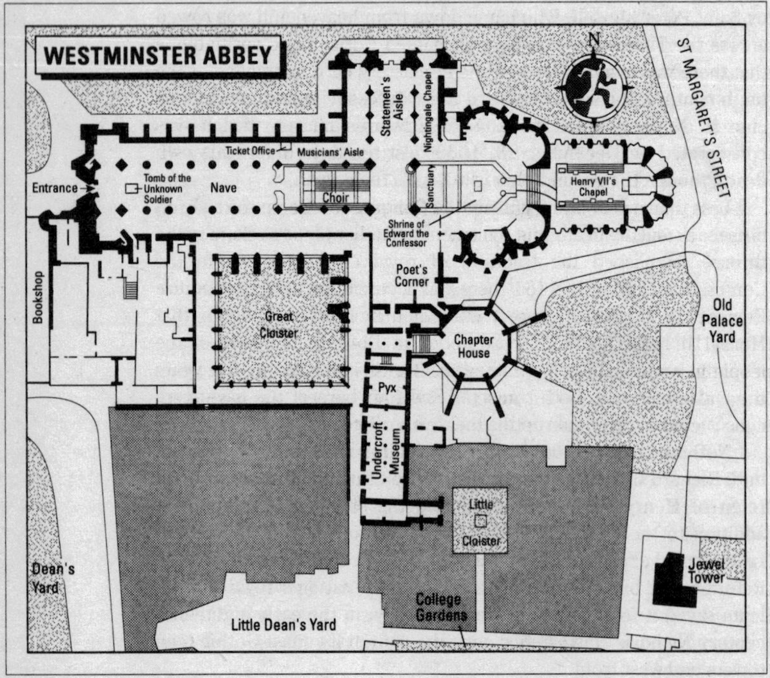

Visiting the Abbey

The abbey is open Mon–Sat 8am–6pm, Sun between services. Entry to the main nave (and to all services) is free, but to see the best of the monuments, the royal tombs or Poets' Corner, you have to pass through the north choir aisle, which is open Mon–Fri 9am–4.45pm, Sat 9.45am–2.45pm & 3.45–5.45pm; this costs £3, except on Wednesday 6–7.45pm when admission is free. You have to pay again to visit the Chapter House or the Pyx Chamber which are run by English Heritage (for times, see below).

On the first right-hand pillar is a doleful fourteenth-century portrait of **Richard II**, the oldest known image of an English monarch painted from life. Above the west door, **William Pitt the Younger**, prime minister at just 23, teaches Anarchy a thing or two, while History takes notes.

Back by the Unknown Soldier is a tablet in the floor marking the spot where **George Peabody**, the nineteenth-century philanthropist whose housing estates in London still provide homes for the poor, was buried for a month before being exhumed and removed to his home town in Massachusetts; he remains the only American to have received the privilege of burial in the abbey.

In the north aisle is the florid tomb of Pitt's great rival, the hard-drinking, hard-gambling **Charles James Fox**, who lies in the arms of Liberty, a black American at his feet thanking him for his anti-slavery campaigning. **Clement Atlee**, the great prime minister of the post-war Labour government, is buried a short distance away, close to **Sidney and Beatrice Webb**, Fabians and founders of the left-wing journal *The New Statesman*. Further along the north wall is the grave of poet and playwright **Ben Jonson**, who, despite being a double murderer, was granted permission to be buried here, upright to save space; his epitaph reads simply, "O Rare Ben Jonson".

The dried and salted body of the explorer and missionary **David Livingstone** is buried in the centre of the nave – except for his internal organs, which, according to the beliefs of the African people in whose village he died, were buried in a box under a tree. In an alcove of the gilded neo-Gothic choir screen is a statue of **Isaac Newton**, who, although a Unitarian by faith, was no doubt happy enough to be buried in such a prominent position.

Other scientists' graves cluster nearby, including that of **Lord Rutherford**, who, when asked if electrons really existed, replied, "Not exist? Not exist! Why, I can see the little buggers as plain as I can see that spoon in front of me!" Last, but not least, despite being at loggerheads with the church for most of his life over *On the Origin of Species*, **Charles Darwin** was given a religious burial and lies underneath your feet as you queue for tickets to enter the rest of the abbey.

Westminster Abbey

Admission to all the sights beyond the Musicians' Aisle costs £4.

The Musicians' and Statesmen's Aisle and Sanctuary

Once you've paid your admission charge, you enter the so-called **Musicians' Aisle**, though just two musicians of great note are buried here: Ralph Vaughan Williams and Henry Purcell, who served as the abbey's organist. Of the statues lining the aisle, only the tireless anti-slavery campaigner, William Wilberforce, slouching in his chair, is actually buried in the abbey.

The north transept is littered with overblown monuments to long-forgotten empire builders, but the central section, traditionally known as **Statesmen's Aisle**, features more familiar nineteenth-century politicians. One of the few to be buried here is the great Liberal leader, **William Ewart Gladstone**, who despite being prime minister a record four times, is best known for his penchant for "saving" prostitutes. At the far end, **Pitt the Elder** stands high above his extravagantly expensive tomb, lording it over Britannia and Neptune.

Far superior funereal art, however, can be found in the side chapels on the east side of the north transept, often known as the **Nightingale Chapel**, after its most prominent grave, in which Elizabeth Nightingale, who died from a miscarriage, collapses in her husband's arms while he tries to fight off the skeletal figure of Death, who is climbing out of the tomb. Nearby is another remarkable monument, to **Sir Francis Vere**, made out of two slabs of black marble, between which lies Sir Francis; on the upper slab, supported by four knights, his armour is laid out, to show that he died away from the field of battle.

The central **Sanctuary**, before the High Altar, is the site of the coronations. On its north side are three wonderful fourteenth-century gabled tombs featuring "weepers" around their base, the last of them that of Edmund Crouchback, founder of the House of Lancaster. But the most precious work of art here is the **Cosmati floor mosaic**, which was constructed in the thirteenth century by Italian craftsmen. It depicts the universe with interwoven circles and squares of marble, glass and porphyry, but remains covered by carpet except on state occasions. Behind the High Altar lies the shrine of Edward the Confessor; to get to it you must first pass along the north ambulatory and through the chapel of Henry VII.

Henry VII's Chapel

Before you enter the main body of **Henry VII's Chapel**, signs direct you into the chapel's north aisle, which is virtually cut off from the chancel. Here James I erected a huge ten-poster tomb to his predecessor, **Elizabeth I**. Unless you read the plaque on the floor, you'd never know that Elizabeth's Catholic half-sister, "Bloody Mary", is also buried here, in an unusual act of reconciliation. The far end of the north aisle, where James I's two infant daughters lie, is known as **Innocents' Corner**: Princess Sophia, who died aged three days, lies in an alabaster cradle, her face peeping over the covers, just about visible in the mirror on the wall; while Princess Mary, who died the following year at the age of two, is clearly visible, casually leaning on a cushion. Set into the wall between the two is the tomb of the murdered princes, Edward V and his brother, whose remains were discovered under a staircase in the Tower of London during Charles II's reign.

The **main nave** of the chapel is the most dazzling architectural set-piece in the abbey. Built by Henry VII in 1503 as his future resting place, it represents the final gasp of the English Perpendicular style, with its intricately carved vaulting, fan-shaped pendants and statues of nearly one hundred saints, installed high above the choir stalls. The stalls themselves are decorated with the banners and emblems of the Knights of the Order of the Bath, to whom the chapel was dedicated by George I. **George II**, the last king to be buried in the abbey, lies in the burial vault under your feet, along with Queen Caroline – their coffins were fitted with removable sides so that their remains could mingle. Close by lies the son they both hated, **Frederick Louis**, who died after being hit in the throat by a cricket ball.

Beneath the altar is the grave of Edward VI, the single, sickly son of Henry VIII, while behind lies the chapel's *raison d'être*, the black marble sarcophagus containing **Henry VII** and his spouse – their gilded effigies are obscured by an ornate Renaissance grille, designed by Torrigiano, who fled from Italy after breaking Michelangelo's nose in a fight. **James I** is also interred within Henry's tomb, while the first of the apse-chapels, to the north, hosts a grand monument to James's lover, George Villiers, the first non-royal to be buried in this part of the abbey, who was killed by one of his own soldiers. The easternmost chapel is dedicated to the RAF, and sports a modern stained glass window depicting airmen and angels in the Battle of Britain. Beneath it, a plaque marks the spot where Oliver Cromwell rested until the Restoration, whereupon his body was disinterred, hanged at Tyburn and beheaded.

Confusingly, visitors are channelled back through the nave, through the shrine of Edward the Confessor (see below), before being allowing into the south aisle of Henry VII's chapel. The first red-robed effigy belongs to the Countess of Lennox, James I's grandmother, followed by James's mother, **Mary Queen of Scots**, whom Elizabeth I beheaded. James had Mary's remains brought from Peterborough cathedral in 1612 and paid out significantly more for her extravagant eight-postered tomb than he had done for Elizabeth's (see above); the twenty-seven hangers-on who are buried with her are listed on the nearby wooden screen. The last of the tombs here is that of **Lady Margaret Beaufort**, Henry VII's mother, her face and hands depicted wrinkles and all. Below the altar, commemorated by simple modern plaques, lie yet more royals: **William and Mary**, **Queen Anne** and **Charles II**.

The Shrine of Edward the Confessor

Before reaching the south aisle of Henry VII's Chapel, the one-way system sends you across a reinforced glass bridge and past the tomb of **Henry V**. His plain oak effigy was originally covered with silver-gilt plates and topped by a solid silver head, all subsequently stolen; above is the highly decorative chantry he asked for in his will, containing the body of his wife, Catherine of Valois.

The chantry acts now as a sort of gatehouse for the **Shrine of Edward the Confessor**, the most sacred heart of the building since his abbey was consecrated. The tomb's green wooden canopy, made after the original was destroyed in the Reformation, detracts a little from the battered beauty of the marble casket itself (on which you can still spot traces of mosaic) and the niches in which pilgrims would kneel, praying for a cure from the saint.

Proximity to the shrine was of paramount importance in medieval times, hence the parade of royal tombs, surmounted by some of the abbey's oldest effigies, around the shrine. To the north, the bronze-gilt images of **Henry III** and Edward I's queen **Eleanor** are two of the most striking, both protected by Gothic wooden canopies; **Edward I** himself is interred in an unadorned, effigy-less tomb, as he requested. On the south side, **Richard II** and Anne of Bohemia lie hand in hand, their images, cast during the king's lifetime, represent the earliest accurate portraiture in English sculpture. Next along, the outer recesses of **Edward III**'s tomb are decorated with gleaming bronze figures of his children – of the original fourteen only six remain, visible from the south ambulatory.

Beyond the Confessor's tomb, in front of a fifteenth-century stone screen portraying scenes from his life, is Edward I's **Coronation Chair**, a decrepit oak throne dating from around 1300. The chair, used in every coronation since, was custom-built to incorporate the **Stone of Scone** – a great slab of red sandstone which acted as the Scottish coronation stone for centuries before Edward pilfered it in 1297, in a demonstration of his mastery of the north. In the 1950s some enterprising Scottish nationalists managed to steal it back, though the stone (or something like it) was eventually returned.

Poets' Corner

Nowadays, the royal tombs have been upstaged by **Poets' Corner**, in the south transept, accessible via the south ambulatory. The first occupant, **Geoffrey Chaucer**, was buried here in 1400, not because he was a poet, but because he lived nearby. His battered tomb, on the east wall, wasn't built for another hunded and fifty-odd years. When **Edmund Spenser** was buried here in 1599, his fellow poets – Shakespeare may well have been among them – threw their own works and quills into the grave. But it wasn't until the eighteenth century that this zone became an artistic Pantheon, since when the transept has been filled with tributes to all shades of talent.

Among those who are actually buried here, you'll find – after much searching – grave slabs or memorials for John Dryden, Samuel Johnson, Robert Browning, Lord Tennyson, Charles Dickens, Rudyard Kipling and Thomas Hardy (though his heart was buried in Dorset). Among the merely commemorated is the dandyish figure of William Shakespeare, erected in 1740 on one of the east walls, and starting a trend that has continued well into this century, with the maverick William Blake only receiving official recognition in 1957 with a sculpture by Jacob Epstein.

Among the non-poets buried here is the German composer, **George Frideric Handel**, who spent most of his life at the English court; he is depicted in similar dandyish mode by Roubiliac directly opposite Shakepeare. Further along the same wall, the great eighteenth-century actor **David Garrick** is seen parting the curtains for a final bow. The one illiterate is old Thomas Parr, who died in 1635 at the alleged age of 152, whose remains were brought here by Charles II. The place is now so overcrowded that the abbey authorities claim to have called a stop to all burials here, the last one being that of the actor, **Laurence Olivier**, who died in 1989.

The south choir aisle

As you leave Poets' Corner and the south transept, there are a few memorials which deserve closer inspection in the south choir aisle – ask a verger to let you through to see them. The court portrait painter **Godfrey Kneller**, who declared, "By God, I will not be buried in Westminster . . . they do bury fools there", is nevertheless commemorated in the abbey; his epitaph is by Pope, who admitted it was the worst thing he ever wrote. Close by lies **Admiral Clowdisley Shovell**, with his shirt unbuttoned and a roll of hairy flab hanging out. He was washed up alive on a beach in the Scilly Isles, after his crew got drunk and wrecked his ship, only to be killed by a fisherwoman for his emerald ring.

Returning to the south wall, there's a monument to **John André**, who was hung as a spy by the Americans despite his plea to George Washington to be shot as a soldier; it was forty years before his body was brought back from America and given a proper funeral. Further along the wall are two huge marble memorials with statues by Roubiliac, one of which – **General Hargrave**'s – has the deceased rising from the grave in response to the Last Trumpet; at the time there was a public outcry that such an undistinguished man should receive such a vast memorial.

The cloisters

Doors in the south choir aisle lead to the **Great Cloister**, rebuilt after a fire in 1298 and paved with yet more funerary slabs, including that of the proto-feminist writer **Aphra Behn**, at the bottom of the ramp. There's a shop and brass rubbing centre in the northern cloisters, while at the eastern end of the cloisters lies the octagonal

Westminster Abbey

The Chapter House, Pyx Chamber and Undercroft Museum are open daily 10.30am–4pm; EH; £2.

Chapter House, where the House of Commons met from 1257 until Henry VIII's reign, though the monks were none too happy about it, complaining that the shuffling and stamping wore out the expensive tiled floor. Despite their whingeing, the thirteenth-century decorative paving stones and wall-paintings have survived.

The nearby **Pyx Chamber**, entered from the east of the cloister, was the sacristy of Edward the Confessor's church and subsequently the royal treasury – hence the mighty double doors and panoply of locks. It now displays the abbey's plate, and boasts the oldest altar in the building.

Housed in one of the few surviving Norman sections of the abbey is the **Undercroft Museum**, filled with generations of bald royal death masks, including those of Edward III and Henry VII. Wax funeral effigies include representations of Charles II, William III and Mary (the King on a stool to make him as tall as his wife), and Lady Frances Stuart, model for Britannia on the old penny coin, complete with her pet parrot, who died a few days after her.

The College Gardens are open Thurs April–Sept 10am–6pm; Oct–March 10am–4pm; free.

If you happen to be here on a Thursday, make your way via Little Cloister to the little known **College Gardens**, a stretch of green that provides a quiet retreat and a croquet lawn for pupils of Westminster School (see below); brass band concerts take place here at 12.30 and 2pm in August and September.

Around the abbey

Sitting in the shadow of the abbey is **St Margaret's Church**, which has been the unofficial parliamentary church since the entire Commons tipped up here in 1614 to unmask religious Dissenters among the MPs. The interior is plain, light and remarkably uncluttered after the abbey. There's not much to see here, though buried beneath its stones are Sir Walter Ralegh, who was beheaded in Old Palace Yard, Václav Hollar, the Czech engraver, and William Caxton, who set up the country's first printing press in the abbey close in 1476. This has also long been a fashionable church to get married in – Pepys, Milton and Shakespeare were followed this century by Churchill and Mountbatten.

On the other side of the Abbey lies **Westminster School**, one of the country's top public (in other words, private) schools, with alumni ranging from Ben Jonson and John Dryden to A. A. Milne and Peter Ustinov. Dean's Yard is open to the public via the archway on Broad Sanctuary, but you can only peek at Little Dean's Yard – the prettier of the school's two courtyards – whose buildings date back as far the eleventh century. In Broad Sanctuary itself, outside the abbey's main entrance, is a modest column to old boys who lost their lives in the Crimean War.

In an attempt to avoid the Gothic of the abbey, and the Byzantine style of the Catholic cathedral, the Methodists opted for the Edwardian Beaux Arts style of architecture for their national headquarters, the **Methodist Central Hall**, situated to the northwest of the abbey on Storey's Gate. It's an unusual building for London, looking something like a giant casino, and hardly appropriate given the Methodists views on gambling and alcohol. It is used these days for political meetings – being handy for the MPs across the square.

Millbank and the Tate Gallery

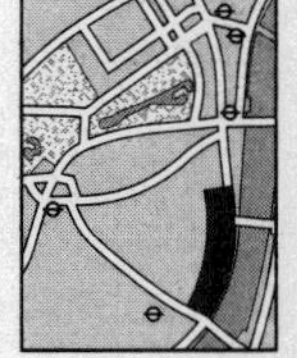

Running south, from midway along the Victoria Tower Gardens, **Millbank** is dominated by the unprepossessing 1960s Millbank tower. Behind and to the south of it, the Tate Gallery occupies the site of the Millbank prison, built in the shape of a six-pointed star in 1821 according to the ideas of Jeremy Bentham. The prisoners were kept under constant surveillance, forbidden to communicate with each other for the first half of their sentence, and put to work making mail bags and shoes – for its day an extremely liberal regime. Nevertheless, very little natural light penetrated the three miles of labyrinthine passages, and epidemics of cholera and scurvy were commonplace. The prison closed down in 1890.

The multicoloured post-modernist ziggurat across the water is the indiscreet new headquarters of the British Secret Intelligence Service, **MI6**. Designed by Terry Farrell at a cost of £230m, it was no sooner completed than a huge refurbishment was started, allegedly costing a further £85 million, a large slice of which went on a tunnel under the river to Whitehall. It's a far cry from the days when MI6 were ensconced in a building whose unmarked front door was in the tasteful and terribly English terrace of houses on Queen Anne's Gate.

The Tate Gallery

Founded in 1897 with money from Sir Henry Tate, inventor of the sugar cube, the **Tate Gallery** does its best to perform a difficult dual function as both the nation's chief collection of British art and its primary gallery for international modern art. The British stuff remains pretty much the same from year to year, whereas the international twentieth-century collection – which, with the outstanding Turner collection, is the reason most people come here – is re-hung on an almost yearly basis, with much of it being farmed out to the Tate's two regional subsidiaries in Liverpool and St Ives. Even so, there only enough room to hang a fraction of the five thousand works the Tate owns, hence the recent acquisition of the Bankside power station, which, it is hoped, will become a permanent home for the Tate's modern art collection.

The Tate is open Mon–Sat 10am–5.50pm, Sun 2–5.50pm; free. The nearest tube is Pimlico.

The Tate hosts some of London's best **art exhibitions** and every autumn sponsors the **Turner Prize**, the country's most prestigious modern art prize. Works by the short list of four artists, which can be in any medium, are displayed in the gallery a month or two prior to the prize-giving. The competition is nothing if not controversial, since it tends to rake up all the usual arguments about the value and accessibility of modern art, but it's the machinations behind the scenes which are, in fact, more suspect. In particular, the role of the Saatchis, the advertising magnates who sit on the Tate's committee of patrons, has been called into question. Prime movers in the art world, they are in a position to manipulate the art market, through the Tate and their own gallery of modern art (p.307), thus wielding undue influence over the promotion of certain artists for their own financial benefit.

The modern collection

Over half the gallery space in the Tate is given over to its crowd-pulling **modern collection**, which contains first-rate pieces from most of this century's major western art movements – Constructivism, Surrealism, Minimalism, Cubism, Pop Art, Dada and Expressionism (Abstract and Germanic), as well as a respectable showing of the Impressionists and Post-Impressionists who preceded them.

It's difficult to predict what will be on display at any one time, but you're unlikely to go away disappointed. Certain names survive every rearrangement: the central sculpture hall normally features at least one work by **Rodin**, usually *The Kiss*, and it's a pretty safe bet that the major Surrealists – **Ernst**, **Dalí**, **Magritte** and **Mirò** – will be on show. The Tate owns works, too, from all the key periods of **Picasso**'s life, and a fine array of works by **Matisse**, from his Fauve paintings through to the jaunty paper collages of his final years.

The Tate has never shied away from controversy, and few works have caused quite so much infamy as Carl André's famous pile of bricks, gnomically entitled *Equivalent VIII*, first displayed in 1972. Another of the Tate's controversial acquisitions is the series of abstract paintings commissioned by the swanky *Four Seasons* restaurant in New York, but withheld by the artist, **Mark Rothko**, who decided he didn't wish his art to be a mere backdrop to the recreation of the wealthy.

In addition to its international collection, the Tate owns a huge catalogue of twentieth-century works by British artists. The sculptors Barbara Hepworth and **Henry Moore**, and painters Stanley Spencer, Lucien Freud and **Francis Bacon** are just some of the better-known artists in the collection, but there's also a good selection of work by living artists such as David Hockney, R. B. Kitaj, Aselm Kiefer, Sean Scully and Gilbert and George.

British art

The native section kicks off with the art of the Tudor and Stuart periods, beginnning with *Man in a Black Cap*, by John Bettes, an English follower of Henry VIII's court painter, Hans Holbein. Richly bejewelled portraits of the Elizabethan nobility predominate, the most striking being the *Cholmondeley Sisters*; there's also a rare full-size portrait by the native-born miniaturist, **Nicholas Hilliard**. Despite a smattering of English talent, such as **William Dobson**, whose *Endymion Porter* is displayed here, the Stuarts continued to rely heavily on imported talent such as Van Dyck, Peter Lely and Godfrey Kneller, or "Pictor Regis" as he used to sign himself – he painted ten royal portraits, enjoying his greatest success under William and Mary.

Room 2 is given over almost entirely to **William Hogarth**, the first great British artist. The Tate owns none of the series of moralistic paintings for which he is best known, but it does have a series of six wonderfully spontaneous portraits of his servants, as well as *The Roast Beef of Old England*, a particularly vicious visual dig at the French. Hogarth despised Britain's continental neighbours, even more so when, on one of his rare visits abroad, he was arrested and deported from Calais on suspicion of being a spy.

In the next room the two great portrait artists **Thomas Gainsborough** and **Joshua Reynolds** battle it out. Of the two, Reynolds, first president of the Royal Academy, was by far the more successful, elevating portraiture to pole position among the genres and flattering his sitters by surrounding them in classical trappings, as in *Three Ladies Adorning a Term of Hymen*. Gainsborough was equally adept at flattery, but rarely used classical imagery, preferring instead more informal settings, and concentrating on colour and light, as in the vivacious portrait of the ballerina, *Giovanna Baccelli*.

At the outset of his career Gainsborough was also a landscape artist, often painting his native Stour valley in Suffolk. The same area was to produce **John Constable**, perhaps the most famous of all British artists, thanks to the *The Hay Wain*, which hangs in the National Gallery, though the same location features in *Flatford Mill* in room 8. Constable was also the first British artist to work *al fresco*, as witnessed by his many sketches, cloud studies and smaller works in room 5.

There's a larger collection of works by Constable in the V & A Museum, *see p.276.*

Next door, in room 4, is a sprinkling of works by **George Stubbs**, for whom "nature was and always is superior to art", and who portrayed animals – horses in particular – with a hitherto unknown anatomical precision.

The visionary strand in English art begins in room 7 with a sublime collection of works by the poet **William Blake**, who was considered something of a freak by his contemporaries. He rejected oil painting in favour of watercolours, and often chose unusual subject matter which matched his highly personal form of Christianity. He earned a pittance producing illuminated books written and printed entirely by himself, and painted purely from his own visions; "Imagination is My World; this world of Dross is beneath my notice", as he wrote. From illuminated books he moved on to do a series of twelve large colour prints on the myth of the Creation, now considered among his finest works, ten examples of which are on display in the Tate.

Perennially popular are the **Pre-Raphaelites** who formed their Brotherhood in 1848 in an attempt to re-create the humble, pre-humanist, pre-Renaissance world. The origins of the name lay in their artistic gripe against the slavish imitation of the late style of Raphael – prevalent in English art at the time – epitomized by William Etty's works (there are examples in room 6). The movement's first batch of paintings, among them **Rossetti**'s *Girlhood of Mary Virgin*, were well received, but the following year **Millais**' *Christ in the House of His Parents* caused considerable outrage. Dickens described the figure of Jesus as "a hideous, wry-necked, blubbering, red-headed boy in a bed-gown". Millais also got into trouble for *Ophelia*, after his model, Elizabeth Siddal, caught a chill from lying in the bath to pose for the picture, prompting threats of lawsuits from her father. Siddal later married Rossetti, and is also the model in his *Beata Beatrix*, painted shortly after she died of an opium overdose in 1862. Other classics in the collection are Hunt's *Awakening Conscience*, **Burne-Jones**' *King Cophetua and the Beggar Maid* and and Waterhouse's *The Lady of Shalott*, the last two both inspired by Tennyson poems.

At this point the exclusively British section ends, though **twentieth-century British artists** are well represented in the modern art section on the other side of the main sculpture hall (see above).

The Clore Gallery: the Turner Bequest

J. M. W. Turner (1775–1851), possibly the greatest artist Britain has ever produced, bequeathed over a hundred oil paintings to the nation, and by the time his relatives had finished bequeathing their share of the spoils the total came to three hundred, plus a staggering nineteen thousand watercolours and drawings. The world's largest Turner collection is housed here, in the adjoining Clore Gallery, a surprisingly institutional and inadequate building designed by arch-postmodernist James Stirling, and opened in 1987. Although you can reach the Clore from the main galleries of the Tate, the rooms are arranged chronologically from the Clore Gallery's own entrance. The rooms are nearly always crowded, but be sure to avoid the Sunday afternoon crush.

Two of Turner's major early paintings are hung in the National Gallery, see p.50.

Turner was an extremely successful artist, exhibiting his first watercolours in the window of his father's barber shop in Maiden Lane, Covent Garden while still a boy, and at the Royal Academy when he was just fifteen, becoming a full member in his twenties. Marine scenes appealed to Turner throughout his life, beginning with his earliest oil painting, *Fishermen at Sea*, which is displayed in room 107 along with other **early works**. Natural cataclysms feature strongly, either for their own sake, as in *Deluge*, or as part of a grand historical painting like *Snow Storm: Hannibal and his Army Crossing the Alps*.

From 1810 onwards, the influence of the French painter Claude Lorrain became more and more important for Turner, a theme explored in room 106, through works ranging from direct imitations such as *The Decline of Carthage* to *Crossing the Brook*, in which a traditional English landscape is given the Claude treatment. In room 105 Turner pays less slavish tribute to another of his heroes, Canaletto – pictures like *Venetian Festival* have only their geographical location in common with the earlier master.

Room 103 contains Turner's only known self-portrait (he had no pretensions as a portraitist and was rather ashamed of his ruddy complexion), alongside belongings such as his pocket watercolour kit and fishing rod, and his toothless death mask. In later life Turner painted at the country mansions of two devoted patrons: the architect John Nash, who had a neo-Gothic pile on the Isle of Wight; and the Earl of Egremont, who owned Petworth House, which inspired *Interior at Petworth*, an astonishing light-filled picture painted in 1835.

Turner's great late works are housed in room 101, the first room you enter if you're coming from the main Tate building. Great smudges of colour, they seem to anticipate Monet in their almost total abandonment of linear representation. *Snow Storm* is a classic late Turner, a symbolic battle between the steam age and nature's primeval force. It was criticised at the time as "soapsuds and white-wash", though Turner himself claimed he merely painted what he saw, having been "lashed to a mast" for four hours.

A whole room is given over to watercolours, a medium the artist never abandoned. The rest of the bequest is displayed floor to ceiling in the **reserve galleries** on the second floor, where there is also a study room (Wed 10.30am–1pm & 2–4.30pm) with monographs and books on all aspects of Turner's works and influences.

From Millbank to Queen Anne's Gate

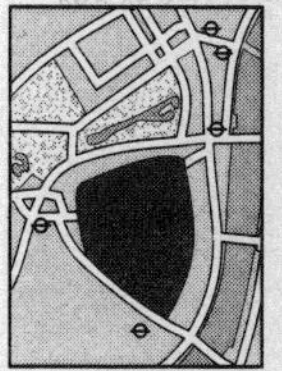

The area to the south and west of Westminster Abbey – bounded by Millbank to the east and St James's Park to the north – is cut off from the noise and pollution which disfigures Parliament Square. Property prices are high, due partly to the area's proximity to Parliament, which makes it a favourite place for MPs to have their London bases – many of the restaurants and pubs in the area have "division bells", which ring eight minutes before the members are needed for a vote in the House of Commons. In addition, various governmental ministries have spread their departmental tentacles across the area, some 3600 civil servants occupying the triple tower blocks on Marsham Street alone. As for landmarks, the area boasts two of London's most unusual churches: the Baroque fancy of **St John's, Smith Square**, and the exotic **Westminster Cathedral**, the capital's principal Catholic church.

Smith Square, Page Street and the RHS Halls

Two blocks south of the abbey precinct, **Smith Square** was at the heart of British politics until Labour moved their headquarters to the more proletarian surroundings of Southwark in the 1970s. The Tory headquarters remain here, however, as do the transport workers' union (TGWU).

St John's has lunchtime classical music concerts and a good crypt restaurant.

The fine early Georgian architectural ensemble is almost overwhelmed by the church of **St John**, a slice of full-blown Baroque rare in London. With its four distinctive towers topped by pineapples, it has been dubbed the "footstool church" – the story being that Queen Anne, when asked by the architect how she would like the church to look, kicked over her footstool. Gutted in the last war, it has since been restored as a concert venue, best known for its BBC lunchtime recitals; there's a licensed restaurant, *The Footstool*, in the crypt and if the church is not being used for rehearsals or performances, you can have a peek at the bare interior. To complete the Georgian experience, approach the square from Lord North Street, to the north, an almost perfect early eighteenth-century terrace, built at the same time as the church and square.

Before heading west to Westminster Cathedral, continue two more blocks south and pick up **Page Street**, flanked by Edwin Lutyens' chequerboard council flats, erected in the 1920s – walking between the five-storey blocks is a surreal experience. Page Street brings you, almost, to the playing fields of Vincent Square, where the **Royal Horticultural Society** has one of its two exhibition halls (the second is round the corner down Elverton Street). Flower shows are still held here regularly, supplemented by exhibitions on model railways, vintage cars, stamps and so on. While you're in these parts, be sure to pass by Richard Rogers' new **Channel 4 TV headquarters** on Horseferry Road, a mass of shiny neo-industrial tubes and webbing, its most striking innovation being the glazed pool that forms the roof of an underground studio, and the vast concave glass curtain. The TV offices and studios are part of a bold new development, including a hundred apartments and a garden square, which should bring new life to these backstreets.

The Cathedral is open Mon–Fri 7am–7pm/8pm (winter/summer), Sat & Sun 7am–8.30pm; its tower can be climbed from mid-March to Oct daily 9am–5pm; £2. The nearest tube is Victoria.

Westminster Cathedral

To the west of Vincent Square, just off Victoria Street, you'll find one of London's most surprising churches, the stripey neo-Byzantine concoction of the Roman Catholic **Westminster Cathedral**. Begun in 1895, it is one of the last and wildest monuments to the Victorian era: constructed from more than twelve million terracotta-coloured bricks, decorated with hoops of Portland Stone, it culminates in a magnificent tapered campanile which rises to 274 feet.

A small piazza has been laid out to the north, from where you can admire the cathedral and the neighbouring mansions on Ambrosden Avenue, whose brickwork echoes the cathedral's.

The **interior** is only half finished, and the domed ceiling of the nave – the widest in the country – remains an indistinct blackened mass, free of all decoration. To get an idea of what the place will look like when it's finally completed, explore the series of **side chapels** – in particular the All Souls Chapel in the north aisle – whose rich, multicoloured decor makes use of over one hundred different marbles from around the world. Before leaving, be sure to check out the outrageous baldacchino (the canopy above the High Altar), and the Stations of the Cross sculpted by Eric Gill during World War I.

North of Victoria Street

In the 1860s, Victorian planners ploughed their way through the slums of Westminster to create **Victoria Street**, a direct link between Parliament and the newly built Victoria train station. The bland 1960s blocks which now line the street give you some idea of what the rest of London might have looked like if the developers had got it all their own way in that iconoclastic decade. One tower-block that deserves mention, however, is **New Scotland Yard**, the headquarters of the Metropolitan Police, opposite the Strutten Ground market, if only for its revolving sign on Broadway, familiar to Brits from countless TV detective serials and news reports.

Further down Broadway, at no. 55, is the austere **Broadway House**, home to London Transport and St James's Park tube station, and the tallest building in London when it was built in 1929. It gained a certain notoriety at the time for its nude statues by Jacob Epstein, in particular the boy figure in *Day*, whose penis had to be shortened to appease public opinion. Round the corner in Caxton Street is the old **Blewcoat School**, built in 1709 as a charity school for the poor but now a National Trust shop; a statue of a blue-coated charity boy stands above the doorway.

There's more Queen Anne architecture just to the north in **Queen Anne's Gate**, an amalgamation of two exquisite streets, originally separated by a wall whose position is indicated by a weathered statue of Queen Anne. The western half is the older and more interesting of the two, each of its doorways surmounted by a rustic wooden canopy with pendants in the shape of acorns. It's worth walking round the back of the houses on the north side to appreciate the procession of elegant bow windows which look out onto St James's Park.

Chapter 2

St James's, Piccadilly, Mayfair and Marylebone

St James's, **Mayfair** and **Marylebone** emerged in the late seventeenth century as London's first real suburbs. Sheep and cattle were driven off the land as small farms made way for London's first major planned development: a web of brick and stucco terraces and grid-plan streets feeding into grand, formal squares, with mews and stables round the back. This expansion set the westward trend for middle-class migration, which gradually extended to Kensington and Chelsea, and as London's wealthier consumers moved west, so too did a large section of the city's commerce, particularly the more upmarket shops and luxury hotels, which are still a feature of the area.

Aristocratic **St James's**, the rectangle of land to the north of St James's Park, was one of the first areas to be developed, and remains the preserve of the seriously rich. **Piccadilly** – at the centre of this area – is no longer the fashionable promenade it once was, but a whiff of exclusivity still pervades **Bond Street** and its tributaries, whose windows display the wares of top couturiers, art dealers and jewellers. **Regent Street** was created as a new "Royal Mile", a tangible borderline to shore up these new fashionable suburbs against the chaotic maze of Soho and the City, where the working population still lived. Now, along with **Oxford Street**, it has become London's busiest shopping district, drawing in thousands of shoppers from all over the world, particularly during the Christmas rush.

Away from the shops, the streets of **Mayfair** are quieter and more residential in flavour, with pockets of well-preserved Georgian architecture here and there, particularly around **Shepherd Market** and Hanover Square. **Marylebone**, which lies to the north of Oxford Street, is another grid-plan Georgian development, elegant in parts, though several social and real estate leagues below Mayfair. It preserves much of its original village high street, while nearby Manchester Square boasts one of the city's best art galleries, the **Wallace Collection**.

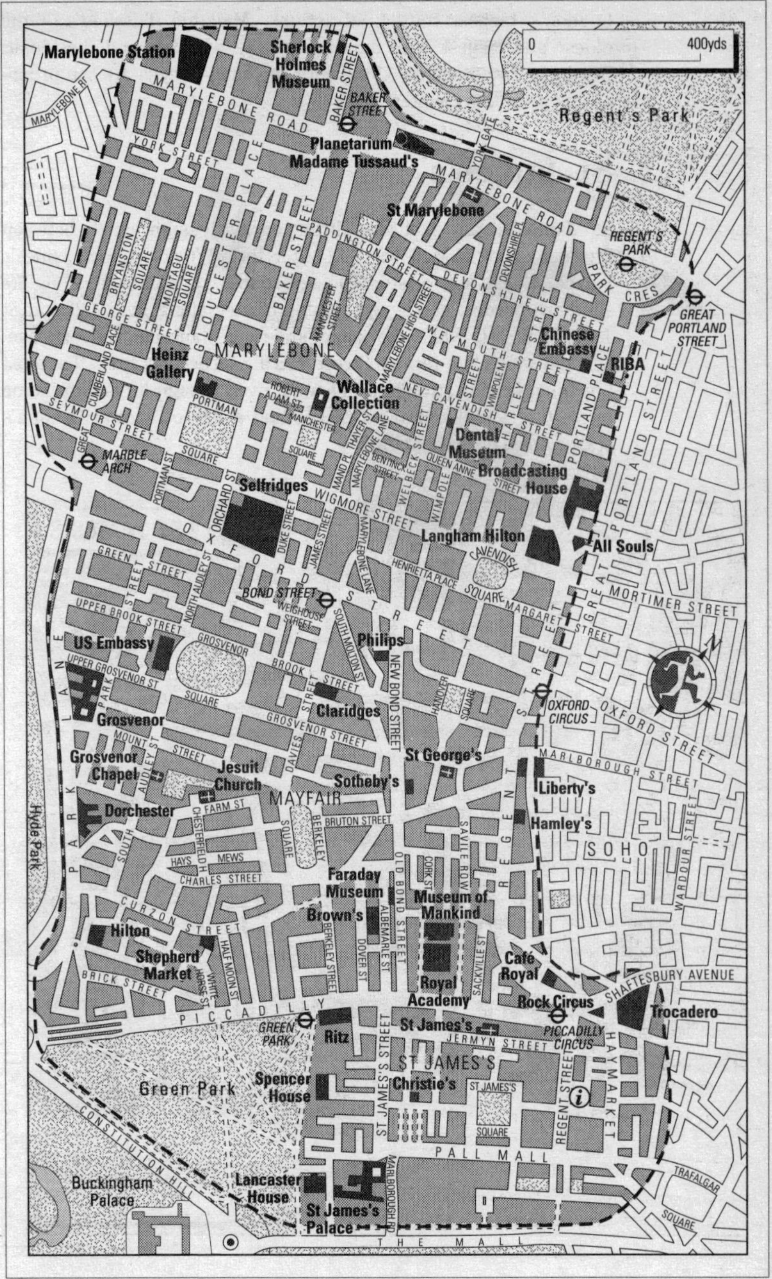

In the northern fringes of Marylebone, you'll also find one of London's biggest tourist attractions, **Madame Tussaud's** – the oldest and largest wax museum in the world – and, beside it, London's **Planetarium**. Along with the shops, these are the principal sights of this chapter.

St James's

St James's, an exclusive little enclave sandwiched between Piccadilly and the Mall, was laid out in the 1670s close to St James's Palace. Royal and aristocratic residences predominate along its southern border, gentlemen's clubs cluster along Pall Mall and St James's Street, while the jacket-and-tie restaurants and expense-account shops line Jermyn Street. Hardly surprising, then, that most Londoners rarely stray into this area, even though it contains some interesting architectural set-pieces and a few of central London's scarce areas of real tranquillity.

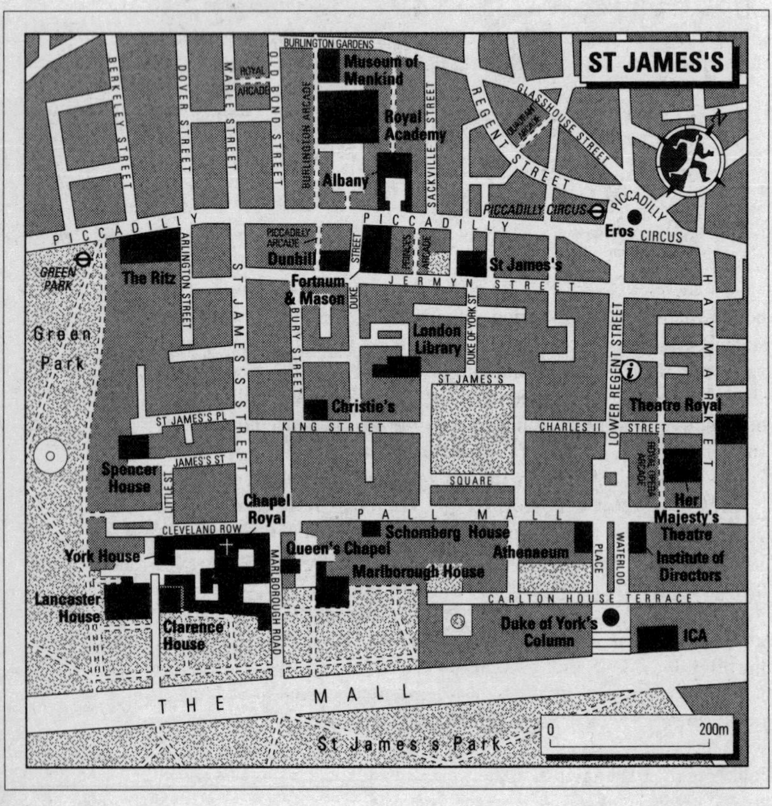

If you're not here for the shops, the best time to visit is on a Sunday, when the traffic is quieter, and the royal chapels plus the one accessible Palladian mansion open their doors to the public.

Haymarket

No prizes for guessing what **Haymarket**, which connects Piccadilly Circus with Pall Mall, was until 1830, despite numerous attempts to close it down and get rid of the smell. It was also, until early this century, an area where, in Dostoyevsky's words, "thousands of whores swarm through the dark" servicing the wealthy gentlemen who frequented the street's two historic theatres, both of which survive to this day.

The nearest tube is Piccadilly Circus.

The Nash-built **Theatre Royal**, on the east side, with its handsome Corinthian portico and gilded acanthus leaves, is the more impressive, but **Her Majesty's Theatre**, opposite, has the finer pedigree, having played a leading part in London's musical life for over two centuries. It was the venue for numerous Handel premières between 1711 and 1736, when the composer was joint-manager, and was effectively the city's royal opera house until Covent Garden rose to prominence this century. The present building, constructed in 1897, is only half the size of its predecessors, which were built on a scale with La Scala, Milan. Their scale is still suggested by the **Royal Opera Arcade**, which Nash placed round the back of the opera house, a short distance down Charles II Street on the left.

Clubland: Lower Regent Street and Waterloo Place

The rest of Regent Street is described on p.94.

Lower Regent Street, which runs parallel with Haymarket, was the first stage in John Nash's ambitious plan to link George IV's magnificent Carlton House with Regent's Park, though few of today's houses date from that period. Like so many of Nash's grandiose schemes, it never quite came to fruition, as George IV, soon after ascending the throne, decided that Carlton House – the most expensive palace ever to have been built in London – wasn't quite luxurious enough, and had it pulled down. Its Corinthian columns now support the main portico of the National Gallery.

Lower Regent Street now opens up into **Waterloo Place**, which Nash was able to extend beyond Pall Mall once Carlton House had been demolished. At the centre of the square stands the Guards' Crimean Memorial, fashioned from captured Russian cannon, and commemorating the 2,162 Foot Guards who died during the war – its horrors were witnessed by Florence Nightingale, whose statue graces one of the monument's pedestals. Having dodged the traffic hurtling down Pall Mall and cutting the square in two, you come face to face with the two grandest **gentlemen's clubs** in St James's (see box below). Their almost identical Neoclassical designs are the work of Nash's protégé, Decimus Burton: of the two, the better looker is the **Athenaeum**, to the west, whose portico sports a garish

For more on Florence Nightingale, see p.251.

gilded statue of the goddess Athena, and above, a Wedgwood-type frieze based on the Elgin marbles, which had just arrived in London from Athens.

The Duke of Wellington was a regular at the United Service Club, now the **Institute of Directors**, over the road, and the horseblocks – confusingly positioned outside the Athenaeum – were designed so the duke could mount his steed more easily. Another inveterate club man, Edward VII – the "Gentleman of Europe" as he was known – sits permanently on his horse between the two clubs, while more statuary hides in the railings of the Waterloo Gardens, including one of Captain Scott, sculpted by the widow he left behind after failing to complete the return journey from the South Pole. Beyond, overlooking St James's Park, is the "Grand Old" **Duke of York's Column**, erected in 1833 and paid for by stopping one day's wages for every soldier in the army he marched "up the hill and down again", in the famous doggerel verse.

Having pulled his old palace down, George IV had Nash build **Carlton House Terrace**, whose monumental facade looks out onto St James's Park, but whose rear is built on a much more human scale. It has long been a sought-after address: the **Royal Society**,

The Gentlemen's Clubs

The gentlemen's clubs of Pall Mall and St James's Street remain the final bastions of the male chauvinism and public-school snobbery for which England is famous. Their origins lie in the coffee and chocolate houses of the eighteenth century, though the majority were founded in the post-Napoleonic peace of the early nineteenth century, by those who yearned for the life of the all-male officers' mess. Drinking, whoring and gambling were the major features of early club life. **White's** – the oldest of the lot with a list of members that still includes numerous royalty (Prince Charles held his stag party here), prime ministers and admirals – was renowned for its high stakes. Bets were wagered over the most trivial of things to relieve the boredom – "a thousand meadows and cornfields were staked at every throw" – and in 1755 one MP, Sir John Bland, shot himself after losing £32,000 in one night.

The clubs were also, in their day, the battle ground of sartorial elegance, where the dandies-in-chief, led by Beau Brummell, set the fashion trends for the London upper class and provided endless fuel for gossip. It was said that Brummell's greatest achievement in life was his starched neckcloth, and that the Prince Regent himself wept openly when Brummell criticized the line of his cravat or the cut of his coat. More serious political disputes were played out in clubland, too. When the Whigs founded **Brooks'**, the Tories, led by Wellington, countered by starting up the **Carlton Club**, still the leading Conservative club, still men-only (Mrs Thatcher had to be made a special member) and still sufficiently important to be targeted by an IRA bomb attack in 1990. The **Reform Club**, from which Phileas Fogg set off on his trip "Around the World in 80 Days", was the gathering place of the liberals behind the 1832 Reform Act, and remains one of the more "progressive" – it's one of the few to admit women as members.

the scientific body set up by, among others, Wren, occupies no. 6; De Gaulle was given no. 4, by the exquisitely tranquil Carlton Gardens, for the headquarters of the Free French during the last war; while no. 7–9, by the Duke of York steps, was the site of the German embassy from 1849 (when it was the Prussian legation) until the outbreak of World War II. Albert Speer redesigned the interior but the only external reminder of this period is a tiny grave for *Ein Treuer Begleiter* (a true friend) behind the railings near the column. It commemorates **Giro**, the Nazi ambassador's pet alsatian, accidentally electrocuted in February 1934.

Pall Mall and St James's Square

Running west from Trafalgar Square across Waterloo Place, **Pall Mall** is again renowned for its clubs, whose dull Italianate and Neoclassical facades still punctuate the street, fronted by cast-iron torches. It gets its bizarre name from the game of *paglio a maglio* (literally "ball and mallet") – something like modern croquet – popularized by Charles II and played here and on The Mall. Crowds gathered here in 1807 when it became London's first gas-lit street – the original closely spaced lamp-posts (erected to reduce the opportunities for crime and prostitution) are still standing – but the heavy traffic which now pounds down it makes it no fun to explore.

Instead, once you've passed Waterloo Place, head one block north to **St James's Square**, which had considerable cachet as a fashionable address when it was first laid out in the 1670s. Around the time of George III's birth at no. 31, the square could boast no fewer than six dukes and seven earls, and over the decades it has maintained its exclusive air: no. 10 was occupied in turn by prime ministers Pitt the Elder, Lord Derby and Gladstone, while no. 4 was the home of Nancy Astor, the first woman MP to sit in the House of Commons, in 1919. The narrowest house on the square (no. 14) is home to the **London Library**, the oldest and grandest private library in the country, founded in 1841 by Thomas Carlyle, who got sick of waiting up to two hours for books to be retrieved from the British Library shelves only to find he couldn't borrow them (he used to steal them instead). It's open only to fee-paying members.

St James's Square gardens are open to all.

Architecturally, the square is no longer quite the period piece it once was but its proportions remain intact, as do the central **gardens**, which feature an equestrian statue of William III, depicted tripping over on the molehill that killed him at Hampton Court Palace. In the northeastern corner, across the road from the Astors' pad, there's a small memorial marking the spot where WPC Yvonne Fletcher was shot dead during the 1984 siege of the now-abandoned Libyan Embassy, at no. 5. It has a quiet dignity lacking in most of London's public statuary to the great and (rarely) good.

Back on Pall Mall, the unusual seventeenth-century facade of **Schomberg House** is one of the few to stand out, thanks to its

Dutch-style red brickwork and its elongated caryatids; it was here that Gainsborough spent the last years of his life. Next door, at no. 79 (now the *P&O* headquarters), Charles II housed Nell Gwynne, so the two of them could chat over the garden wall, which once backed onto the grounds of St James's Palace. It was from one of the windows overlooking the garden that Nell is alleged to have dangled the six-year old future Earl of Burford, threatening to drop him if Charles didn't acknowledge paternity and give the boy a title; another more tabloid version of the story alleges that Charles was persuaded only after overhearing Nell saying "Come here, you little bastard", then excusing herself on the grounds that she had no other name by which to call him.

St James's Palace

The nearest tube is Green Park.

At the western end of Pall Mall stands **St James's Palace**, built on the site of a lepers' hospital which Henry VIII bought and demolished in 1532. It was here that Charles I chose to sleep the night before his execution, so as not to have to listen to his scaffold being erected, and when Whitehall Palace burned down in 1698, St James's became the principal royal residence. In keeping with tradition, an ambassador to the UK is still known as Ambassador to the Court of St James, even though the court moved down the road to Buck House when Queen Victoria came to the throne.

The main red-brick gate-tower, which looks out onto St James's Street, is the most conspicuous reminder of Tudor times, but the rest of the rambling, crenellated complex is the result of Nash's restoration and remodelling, and now provides a bachelor pad for Prince Charles and a home for the Duke and Duchess of Kent, as well as offices for various royals and the Lord Chamberlain. Nash was also responsible for **Clarence House**, connected to the palace's south-west wing and barely visible from Cleveland Row. Built for William IV when he was the Duke of Clarence, it was the royal residence for the seven years of his reign and is currently home to the Queen Mother, widow of George VI, and a nonagerian star in the royal soap.

The Chapel Royal is open Oct to Good Friday, Sunday 8.30 & 11.15am services only.

The palace is off limits to the public, with the exception of the **Chapel Royal**, where Charles I took holy communion on the morning of his execution, and which also saw the marriages of William and Mary, George III and Queen Charlotte, Victoria and Albert, and George V and Queen Mary. One of the few remaining sections of Henry VIII's palace, it was redecorated in the 1830s, though the painted roof matches the original Tudor ceiling which commemorated the brief marriage of Henry and Anne of Cleves (thought to have been the work of Hans Holbein). The only other part of the palace you can explore is the partly arcaded **Friary Court**, on Marlborough Road, assembly point for the Foot Guards marching to the Changing of the Guard ceremony at Buckingham Palace (p.57).

The Queen's Chapel and Marlborough House

On the other side of Marlborough Road is the **Queen's Chapel**, once part of St James's Palace but now in the grounds of Marlborough House. A perfectly proportioned classical church, it was designed by Inigo Jones for the Infanta of Spain, the intended child bride of Charles I, and later completed for his French wife, Henrietta Maria, who was also a practising Catholic. A little further down Marlborough Road, looking thoroughly forgotten, is the glorious Art Nouveau memorial to **Queen Alexandra** (wife of Edward VII), comprising a bronze fountain crammed with allegorical figures and flanked by robust lamp-posts.

The Queen's Chapel is open Easter–July Sun 8.30 & 11.15am services only.

Marlborough House is hidden from Marlborough Road by a high spiked brick wall, and is only partly visible from The Mall. Queen Anne sacrificed half her garden in granting this land to her confidante, the Duchess of Marlborough, in 1709. The duchess in turn told Wren to build her a "strong, plain and convenient" palace, and from the outside that's all it is; the interior, however, includes frescoes depicting the duke's famous victories at Blenheim, Ramillies and Malplaquet, along with ceiling paintings transferred from the Queen's House in Greenwich. The royals took over in 1817, though the last one to live here was Queen Mary, wife of George V, who died in 1953. The current residents are the Commonwealth Secretariat.

Marlborough House is closed to the public except by written permission.

Green Park and Spencer House

To the west of St James's Palace lies **Green Park**, laid out on the burial ground of the old lepers' hospital; it was left more or less flowerless – hence its name. Nowadays, it's a moderately peaceful grassy spot, dominated by graceful London plane trees, but in its time it was a popular spot for duels (banned from neighbouring St James's Park), ballooning and fireworks displays. The most famous was the one immortalized by Handel's *Music for the Royal Fireworks*, performed here on April 27, 1749, to celebrate the Peace of Aix-la-Chapelle – over 10,000 fireworks were let off, setting fire to the custom-built Temple of Peace, and causing three fatalities. The music was a great success, however.

Green Park extends from St James's Park and connects, via a subway, with Hyde Park. You can thus walk entirely over parkland to Notting Hill.

Along the east side of the park runs the wide, pedestrian-only **Queen's Walk**, laid out for Queen Caroline, wife of George II, who had a little pavilion built nearby. At its southern end, there is a good view of **Lancaster House** (closed to the public), a grand Neoclassical palace now used for government receptions and conferences; it was here that the end of white rule in Rhodesia was negotiated.

Two doors up is Princess Di's ancestral home, **Spencer House**, one of London's finest Palladian mansions, completed in 1756, and the only one regularly open to the public. Its best-looking facade looks out onto Queen's Walk, though access is from St James's

Spencer House is open Feb–July & Sept–Dec, Sun only 11am–5.30pm; £6.

Place. Inside, tour guides take you through nine rooms, recently returned to something like their original state by their current owners, the Rothschilds. The Great Room features a stunning coved and coffered ceiling in green, white and gold, while the adjacent Painted Room is a feast of Neoclassicism, decorated with murals in the "Pompeian manner". The most outrageous decor, though, is to be found in Lord Spencer's Room with its astonishing gilded palm-tree columns.

Jermyn Street

Jermyn Street (pronounced like "German"), which runs parallel with Piccadilly, has been the spiritual home of English gentlemen's fashion, along with Savile Row, since the advent of the clubs, and its window displays and wooden panelled interiors still evoke an age when mass consumerism was unthinkable. The kind of pukka Englishmen for whom these shops originally catered are now a dying breed, and nowadays Americans and Japanese tend to make up the bulk of the customers.

The Pipe Smokers' Museum is open Mon–Sat 10am–4pm; free. The second part of the museum is by appointment only (☎0171/499 9566).

The endurance of the cigar as a status symbol is celebrated at *Davidoff*, on the corner of St James's and Jermyn Street, with nothing so vulgar as a cigarette in sight. If pipes are more your thing, head for the *Dunhill* shop on the corner with Duke Street, which runs a **Pipe Smokers' Museum**. The first part of the museum is within the shop itself, which contains the sea chest in which Sir Walter Ralegh first imported the evil substance into this country, plus photos of those gents who have followed his example and won themselves the accolade of Pipe Smoker of the Year. The range of pipes in the first-floor gallery is as nothing, though, to the second (appointment only) part of the museum, on the other side of Piccadilly above the *Mont Blanc* pen shop in Burlington Arcade, where you can inspect Mr Dunhill's greatest cigarette inventions, such as the in-car hookah and the motorist's pipe with a windshield for open-top toking.

Back on Jermyn Street, on the corner with Bury Street, is *Turnbull & Asser*, who have placed shirts on the backs of VIPs from David Bowie to Ronald Reagan. *Wilton's*, at no. 55, is a truly Edwardian English restaurant where the main course alone costs £25 and ties and jackets are required Monday to Saturday (men can leave the tie home on a Sunday); while *Floris*, at no. 89, covers up the royal family's body odour with their ever so English fragrances. Of more general interest is *Paxton & Whitfield*, at no. 93, a shop boasting an unrivalled selection of English and foreign cheeses. Lastly, at no. 21A there's *Bates* the hatters, not quite as famous as *Lock's* on St James's Street, where the bowler hat was invented in 1850, but more memorable thanks to Binks, the stray cat who entered the shop in 1921 and never left, having been stuffed in a glass cabinet inside the shop, sporting a cigar and top hat. The shop has never had anything so vulgar as a sale.

Piccadilly Circus and Regent Street

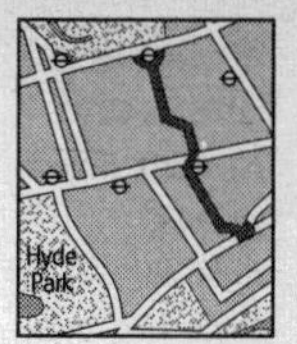

The nearest tube is Piccadilly Circus.

Anonymous and congested it may be, but **Piccadilly Circus** is, for many Londoners, the nearest their city comes to having a centre. A much-altered product of Nash's grand 1812 Regent Street plan, and now a major traffic bottleneck, it is by no means a picturesque place, despite a major clean-up in recent years. It's probably best seen at night when the spread of illuminated signs (a feature since the Edwardian era) gives it a touch of Las Vegas dazzle, and when the human traffic flow is at its most frenetic.

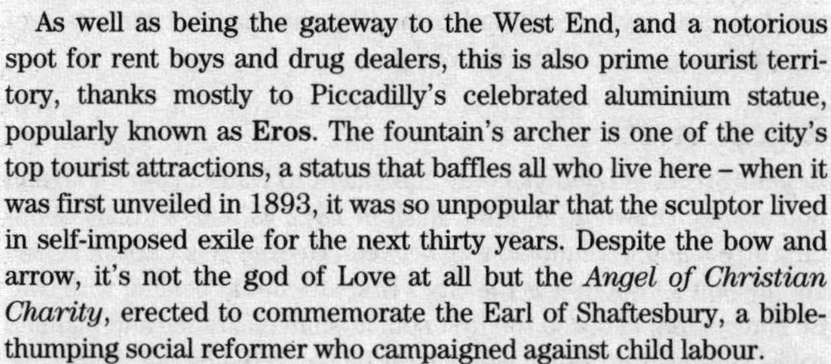

As well as being the gateway to the West End, and a notorious spot for rent boys and drug dealers, this is also prime tourist territory, thanks mostly to Piccadilly's celebrated aluminium statue, popularly known as **Eros**. The fountain's archer is one of the city's top tourist attractions, a status that baffles all who live here – when it was first unveiled in 1893, it was so unpopular that the sculptor lived in self-imposed exile for the next thirty years. Despite the bow and arrow, it's not the god of Love at all but the *Angel of Christian Charity*, erected to commemorate the Earl of Shaftesbury, a bible-thumping social reformer who campaigned against child labour.

Eros' plinth stands in front of the **Criterion**, one of London's more elegant theatres, with a sumptuous restaurant adjoining. This Art Nouveau building, with its ceiling of glittering gold mosaics, was, incredibly, covered over by plastic pizza chain decor from the 1960s to the mid-1980s but it is now back to its former glory. On the other side of the Criterion theatre is *Lillywhites*, a long-established emporium for all things sporting, while another megastore – *Tower Records* flagship UK outlet, open and crowded to midnight daily – fronts the west side of the Circus.

The London Pavilion and Trocadero

The Rock Circus is open Mon, Wed, Thurs & Sun 11am–9pm, Tues noon–9pm, Fri & Sat 11am–10pm; £6.50.

If Eros' fame remains a mystery, the constant queue outside the nearby **Rock Circus**, in the old London Pavilion music hall, across the Circus from the Criterion, is a good deal more perplexing. Billed as an all-singing extravaganza, it's little more than an array of Madame Tussaud's waxen rock legends accompanied by snippets of their hits on malfunctioning headphones. The *pièce de résistance*, the "circus" of the title, is a twenty-minute show of jerky animatronic "classic rock" performances: Phil Collins, swathed in dry ice, simulates a crashing drum solo by feebly tapping a cymbal; Madonna, bearing an uncanny resemblance to Bette Davis, pitifully shakes a tambourine behind a net curtain; Janis Joplin blinks a lot and offers a poignant narration.

The Trocadero is open daily 10am–10pm; passport for all sights £14.95.

Continuing in the same seaside resort spirit is the **Trocadero**, site of another great nineteenth-century music hall, transformed in the 1980s into a tacky, three-storey shopping, amusements and food complex, which gets even more congested than the streets outside but has yet to pay its way for the developers. The new plan is to turn it into a state-of-the-art games and multimedia centre. At present, the main attraction is the *Emaginator*, an "interactive" cinema showing continuous performances of 70mm shorts (£3 each) designed to make the most of the four-person moveable bob-sleighs in which the audience are strapped. Other attractions include the terrifying *Alien War*, in which you get to act out one of the scenes from the film, *Quasar*, the laser-gun war game, and the *Guinness World of Records*, cataloguing the biggest, smallest, fattest, and so on.

Aptly situated next door to the Trocadero is *Planet Hollywood*, the American-style restaurant owned by the macho triumvirate of Schwarzenegger, Stallone and Willis.

Regent Street

Regent Street is London's only equivalent to Haussmann's Parisian boulevards. Drawn up by John Nash in 1812 as both a luxury shopping street and a triumphal way between George IV's Carlton House and Regent's Park, it was the city's first attempt at dealing with traffic congestion, and also the first stab at slum clearance and planned social segregation, which would later be perfected by the Victorians. Several unsavoury neighbourhoods were wiped off the map and the completed street acted as a barrier separating the disreputable, immigrant Soho from the bourgeois quarters of Mayfair, St James's and Marylebone.

Despite the subsequent destruction of much of Nash's work and its replacement by what one critic has described as "neo-fascist Art Deco", it's still possible to admire the stately intentions of his original Regent Street plan, in particular the curve of the **Quadrant**, which swerves north from Piccadilly Circus. Sadly the Victorians, many of whom thought Nash's architecture monotonous, tore down the Quadrant's graceful colonnades in 1848 – shopkeepers claimed they obscured their window displays and encouraged prostitution.

Regent Street enjoyed eighty years as Bond Street's nearest rival, a place where "elegantly attired pedestrians evince the opulence and taste of our magnificent metropolis" as one Victorian observer put it. Redevelopment this century coincided with an increase in the purchasing power of the city's middle classes, bringing the tone of the street "down" and ushering in several heavyweight stores catering for the masses. The only truly bourgeois survivor in the Quadrant itself is the **Café Royal**, at no. 68, focus of the *beau monde* from the 1890s to the outbreak of World War I, when Oscar Wilde and Aubrey Beardsley presided, along with Sickert, Beerbohm, Augustus John and George Bernard Shaw; later Edward VIII and George VI hung out there (in their days as princes), though already it was a shadow of its former self. The present Grill Room, built in the 1920s, preserves some of the flavour of the café's halcyon days.

Continuing en route to Oxford Circus, the big stores are mostly on the right: recent recruits such as *Gap*, followed by more firmly established giants like *Hamley's*, the world's largest toy shop, and *Liberty's*, the department store that popularised Arts and Crafts designs at the beginning of this century. The latter store is divided into two: the older part, which looks onto Regent Street features a traditional, central rooflit well, surrounded by wooden galleries carved from the timbers of two old naval battleships; an overhead walkway leads to the eye-catching mock-Tudor extension, added in the 1920s and stretching back as far as Carnaby Street (p.123). Opposite is a very different 1920s' structure, Palladium House, an elegant cigarette box of black granite which culminates in a quasi-Egyptian Art Deco cornice.

For a run-down on department store shopping, see p.507.

From All Souls to Park Crescent

North of Oxford Circus, the shops stop abruptly at **All Souls**, Nash's simple and ingenious little Bath stone church which provides a visual full stop to Regent Street and a pivot for the awkward twist in the triumphal route to Regent's Park. The conical spire, which caused outrage in its day, now sits in the shadow of **Broadcasting House**, the BBC's headquarters. Given the organisation's long line of despotic chiefs, it's a suitably totalitarian building – Orwell, a one-time employee, modelled *1984*'s Ministry of Truth on it. The figures of Prospero and Ariel (pun intended) above the entrance are by Eric Gill, who caused outrage by sculpting Ariel with over-large testicles, and, like Epstein a few years earlier at Broadway House (p.83), was forced in the end to cut the organs down to size.

BBC land: north of Oxford Circus tube.

Opposite Broadcasting House stands the **Langham Hilton**, built in heavy Italianate style in the 1860s, badly bombed in the last war, and recently refurbished at a cost of millions. It features in several Sherlock Holmes mysteries and its former guests have included Dvořák (who courted controversy by ordering a double room for himself and his daughter to save money), exiled emperors Napoleon III and Haile Selassie, and the once-famous Ouida, who threw outrageous parties for young Guards officers and wrote many of her best-selling romances in her dimly lit hotel boudoir.

After the chicane around All Souls, Regent Street opens out into **Portland Place**, laid out by the Adam brothers in the 1770s, and incorporated by Nash in his grand route. Once the widest street in London, lined exclusively with Adam-style houses, it's still a majestic avenue, boasting several embassies, including the Chinese legation at no. 49. The exiled republican leader **Sun Yat Sen** was kidnapped and held incognito here for several days in 1896, on the express orders of the Chinese emperor. Eventually Sun managed to send a note to one of his British friends saying "I am certain to be beheaded. Oh woe is me!", though it was only when the press got hold of the story that Sun was finally released; he went on to found the Chinese Nationalist Party and became the first president of China in 1911.

RIBA bookshop opens Mon–Fri 9.30am–5.30pm Sat 10.30am–1pm.

Arguably the finest of all the buildings on Portland Place is the sleek Portland Stone facade of **RIBA** (Royal Institute of British Architects), built in the 1930s amidst the remaining Adam houses. The highlight of the building is the interior, which you can view en route to the institute's ground floor bookshop, or during one of the frequent exhibitions and Tuesday evening lectures held here. The main staircase remains a wonderful period piece, with two large black marble columns rising up on either side of the stairs, etched glass balustrades and walnut veneer.

Regent's Park is covered on p.310; for Marylebone and Madame Tussauds see p.105–10.

At the far end of Portland Place, Nash originally planned a giant "circus" as a formal entrance to Regent's Park. Only the southern half – two graceful arcs of creamy terraces known collectively as **Park Crescent** – was eventually completed, and they are now cut off from the park by the busy thoroughfare of Marylebone Road.

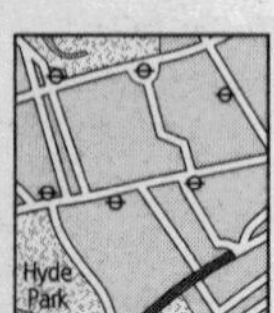

Piccadilly

Piccadilly apparently got its name from the ruffs or "pickadills" worn by the dandies who used to promenade here in the late seventeenth century. Despite its fashionable pedigree, it is no place for promenading in its current state, with traffic careering down it nose to tail most of the day and night. Infinitely more pleasant places to window-shop are the **nineteenth-century arcades**, originally built to protect shoppers from the mud and horse-dung on the streets, but now equally useful for escaping exhaust fumes.

From Simpson's to the Ritz

With the exception of the modernist 1930s facade of *Simpson's* department store, there's nothing much to distract the eye along the south side of Piccadilly until you reach **St James's**, Wren's favourite parish church (he built it himself). As so often with London churches, the contents are less interesting than the historical associations – Pitt the Elder and William Blake were baptised here – and the contemporary politics of the place.

St James's is another London church with a decent café and lunchtime concerts.

St James's is a traditional venue for big society weddings, yet, like St Martin-in-the-Fields on Trafalgar Square, it also ministers to the homeless (the church's heated interior is an unofficial daytime refuge) and the memorial garden currently contains a bread oven, with free flour provided for "home-baking", and a rather less useful "cloud chamber", a willow and sandstone wigwam for "contemplating the clouds passing overhead". In addition, to generate some extra income, the church runs a daily craft market in the churchyard, and a vegetarian café at the west end of the church; it also puts on top-class free lunchtime concerts.

Piccadilly

Piccadilly may not be the shopping heaven it once was, but there are still several old firms which proudly display their royal warrants. **Hatchard's Bookshop**, at no. 187, was founded in 1797, when it functioned like a cross between a gentlemen's club and a library, with benches outside for customers' servants, and daily papers for the gentlemen inside to peruse. Today, *Hatchard's* is the prestige branch of the *Dillons* group, elegant still, but with its old traditions marked most overtly by a large section on royalty.

An even older institution, and a favourite with the twin-set and pearls contingent, is **Fortnum & Mason**, the food emporium at no. 181, which was established in the 1770s by one of George III's footmen, Charles Fortnum. Fortnum's intimate knowledge of the needs of a royal household, together with his partner, Hugh Mason's, previous work at nearby St James's Market (now defunct), helped make the shop an instant success. Fortnums has been serving delicacies to the royal family and slightly less exalted mortals ever since, watched over by the figures of its founders, who bow to each other on the hour as the clock clanks out the Eton school anthem – a rather kitsch addition which dates only to 1964.

Afternoon tea at Fortnum's 4th floor restaurant competes with hotels like the Ritz, and a full "high tea" (£12.25) is also on offer – ol: English comfort food to set you up for the evening.

The store is most famous for its picnic hampers, an upper-class institution, first introduced as "concentrated lunches" for hunting and shooting parties, and now *de rigueur* for Ascot, Glyndebourne,

Afternoon tea in Mayfair

Only the horribly rich can afford to stay in Mayfair's top hotels, but anyone – provided they are suitably attired – can enjoy their sumptuous decor by partaking in the ritual of a "traditional" afternoon tea (usually served between 3 and 6pm). At a cost of £12–15 a head, this is no quick cuppa, but a high-cholesterol feast that kicks off with sandwiches, moves on to scones festooned with clotted cream and jam, and finishes up with assorted cakes, all washed down with innumerable pots of tea.

Tea in the (no-smoking) Palm Court at the *Ritz* is to most people's minds the ultimate in extravagance, and is consequently oversubscribed. For a more intimate, specifically English ambience, you might prefer the leather sofas and wooden panelling of *Brown's*, on Abermarle Street, or *Fortnum and Mason* on Piccadilly (see above). Other grand hotel tea options in Mayfair include *Claridge's*, the Art Deco masterpiece on Brook Street, which has the most obsequious waiters, assisted by liveried footmen and a string quartet; the *Dorchester*, on Park Lane, built in the 1930s and now owned by the Sultan of Brunei, which has recently been refurbished at a cost of millions and is rather more vulgar in its opulence; and the *Park Lane Hotel* on Piccadilly, again extravagantly revamped but featuring a wonderful grey and silver Jazz Age foyer from the 1920s.

Other grand hotels for a central London tea include the *Savoy* and *Waldorf Astoria* on the Strand (p.162). And keep in mind that any of these hotels will do you a traditional **English breakfast**, wheeling out kippers, eggs, bacon and all manner of offal on silver platters, again for around £15 a head for the works. The *Savoy*, in particular, excels at this.

Henley and other society events. They are, of course, ludicrously priced, but the food hall (there are upper floors for clothes and accessories) has more affordable and individual treats to incite most visitors into opening their wallets, and there is a tea room and restaurant, too.

Further along Piccadilly, is the **Piccadilly Arcade**, an Edwardian extension to the much earlier Burlington Arcade (see below), lined with squeaky clean bow windows, displaying, among other items, Wedgwood porcelain, Russian icons and Etonian collars. On the corner of St James's Street, **Barclay's Bank** occupies a building that was built as a car show room in the 1920s. The interior has been left pretty much intact, with zig-zag inlaid marble flooring, Chinese-style painted woodwork and giant red lacquer columns among the most striking features.

Across St James's Street, with its best rooms overlooking Green Park, stands the **Ritz**, a byword for decadence since it first wowed Edwardian society in 1906; the hotel's design, with its mansard roof and long arcade, was based on the buildings of Paris's Rue de Rivoli. For a prolonged look inside, you'll need to be in good appetite for the famous afternoon tea (see box on p.97).

The Royal Academy and Burlington Arcade

The Royal Academy (RA) hosts some of London's major art exhibitions – as well as its own infamous summer show.

Across the road from Fortnum & Mason, the **Royal Academy of Arts** occupies the enormous Burlington House, one of the few survivors from the ranks of aristocratic mansions that once lined the north side of Piccadilly. Rebuilding in the nineteenth century destroyed the original curved colonnades beyond the main gateway, but the complex has kept much of its Palladian *palazzo* design from the early eighteenth century; it's a shame you can't see it better, with the central courtyard used as a car park. The Academy itself was the country's first-ever formal art school, founded in 1768 by a group of English painters including Gainsborough and Reynolds.

The Academy's roll call of past members ranges from Turner and Constable to Elizabeth Frink, though the college has always had a conservative reputation for its teaching and, until recently, most of its shows. These days, the avant garde does get an occasional look-in at the Academy's big temporary exhibitions, although you wouldn't guess it from the **Summer Exhibition**, which opens in June each year. It is an odd event: a stop on the social calendar of upper middle class England, who are catered for, as at Wimbledon and Ascot, with a *Pimms* bar (*Pimms* is the classic English summer cocktail). And yet the show itself is, more or less, egalitarian. Anyone can enter paintings in any style, and the lucky winners get hung, in rather close proximity, and sold. Supposed gravitas is added by the RA "Academicians", who are allowed to display six of their own works – no matter how awful. The result is a bewildering display, which gets panned annually by the critics.

As well as hosting exhibitions, the RA has a small **permanent collection**, featuring the heavyweights of its formative decades (free guided tours 1pm Tues–Fri), plus the gallery's most valuable asset, Michelangelo's marble relief, the *Taddei Tondo*, displayed in the glass atrium of Norman Foster's new Sackler Galleries.

Piccadilly

Another palatial Piccadilly residence which has avoided redevelopment is the **Albany**, a plain, H-shaped Georgian mansion, neatly recessed behind its own iron railings and courtyard to the east of the Royal Academy. It was originally built for Lord Melbourne, but was divided in 1802 into a series of self-contained bachelor apartments. These are a classic address and have been occupied over the years by such literary figures as Byron, Priestley, Aldous Huxley and Graham Greene; women have only recently been allowed to lease flats at the Albany in their own right.

The other side of the Royal Academy is flanked by the **Burlington Arcade**, built in 1819 for Lord Cavendish, then owner of Burlington House, to prevent commoners throwing rubbish into his garden. Today it's London's longest and most expensive nineteenth-century arcade, lined with mahogany-fronted jewellers, gentlemen's outfitters and the like. Upholding Regency decorum, it is still illegal to whistle, sing, hum, hurry or carry large packages or open umbrellas on this small stretch, and the arcade's two beadles (known as Burlington Berties), in their Edwardian frock-coats and gold-braided top hats, take the prevention of such criminality very seriously.

Mayfair and the West End shops

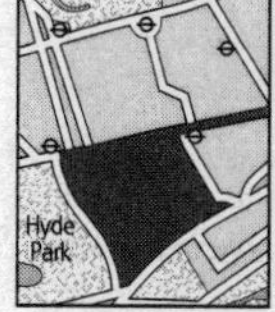

Mayfair (the district north of Piccadilly) and Park Lane (its western border) are the most expensive properties on the Monopoly board, and still among the most monied addresses in central London. Mayfair's rise to fame originated in the eighteenth century, when it began to attract aristocratic London away from hitherto fashionable Covent Garden and Soho. Across rolling fields north of Piccadilly, the two big landowners, the Grosvenors and the Berkeleys, laid out magnificent squares, which remained at the heart of London's high society from the 1720s onwards. Offices, embassies and luxury hotels now outnumber aristocratic *pieds à terre* – a process accelerated by the last war which forced many businesses to re-locate here away from the bomb-damaged City – though the social fabric has remained much the same.

On the borders of Mayfair are London's prime shopping streets – catering to all classes and all purses. It's here that Londoners talk of "going shopping up the West End": to Picadilly and Regent Street (described above), Bond Street, and Oxford Street. Piccadilly was already a fashionable place to shop by the eighteenth century, as was Bond Street, which runs through Mayfair. Regent Street was created in 1812 and took a while to catch on, while Oxford Street, to the north, didn't really come into its own until early this century, though it now surpasses the lot in the sheer mass of people who fight their way down it.

Bond Street

Bond Street runs more or less parallel with Regent Street, extending right the way from Piccadilly to Oxford Street. It is, in fact, two streets rolled into one: the southern half, laid out in the 1680s, is known as Old Bond Street; its northern extension, which followed less than fifty years later, is known as New Bond Street. In contrast to their international rivals – Rue de Rivoli or Fifth Avenue – they are both pretty unassuming streets architecturally; the shops which line them, however, are among the flashiest in London.

For a consumers' guide to London's fashion shops, see p.510. For art gallery listings, p.500.

Unlike its purely masculine counterpart, Jermyn Street (p.92), Bond Street caters for both sexes, and though it also has its fair share of old established names, it's now dominated by foreign *haute couture* outlets like *Cerruti*, *Versace*, *YSL* and so on. *Versace*'s palatial premises are a sight worthy of any guidebook – the Versailles of consumerist London, spread over four floors (though two are closed amid rumours of bad times for Gianni), adapted from already opulent banking premises at a cost of over £12m. Another grand emporium, and a rare British-based success story in the fashion world, is the new *Nicole Farhi* store at 158 New Bond Street – 10,000 square feet of minimalist design and elegant wearable clothes.

Pedestrianized **South Molton Street**, northwest off New Bond Street and surfacing on Oxford Street just behind Bond Street tube, again specializes in fashion, with representation from the likes of

Auction houses

A very Mayfair-style entertainment lies in visiting its trio of **auction houses**: *Christie's*, on King Street in St James's, which has attracted high society since the days of Garrick, Reynolds and Boswell; *Sotheby's*, at 34–35 New Bond Street, the oldest of the three, having been founded in 1745, though its pre-eminence only really dates from the last war; and *Phillips*, a little more modest, around the corner in Blenheim Street.

Viewing at all three houses takes place daily except Saturday, and the galleries are open free of charge, though without a catalogue (£10–12) the only information you'll glean is the lot number. Thousands of the works that pass through the rooms are of museum quality, and, if you're lucky, you might catch a glimpse of a masterpiece in transit between private collections, and therefore only ever on public display in the auction house galleries. And of course anyone can attend the auctions themselves, though remember to keep your hands firmly out of view.

Sotheby's also offers free valuations, if you have an heirloom of your own to check out. There is always a line of people unwrapping plastic bags under the polite gaze of valuation staff, who call in the experts if they see something that sniffs of real money.

Romeo Gigli and *Adolfo Dominguez*. The largest retailer is *Browns*, a honeypot of the trendier labels, spread over half a dozen or so shops. Outside of the sales, it is geared firmly to rich and committed fashion victims; Madonna calls in with her bodyguards when she is in town.

In addition to fashion, Bond Street is renowned for its **auction houses** and for its **fine art galleries**. Visiting the auction houses is free and can be fun (see box), but even if you don't venture in, take a look at the doorway of *Sotheby's*, topped by an Egyptian statue, dating from 1600 BC and thus the oldest outdoor sculpture in London. Bond Street's art galleries – exclusive mainstays of the street – are actually outnumbered by those on neighbouring **Cork Street**. The main difference between the two locations is that the Bond Street dealers are basically heirloom offloaders, whereas Cork Street galleries sell largely contemporary art. Both have impeccably presented and somewhat intimidating staff, but if you're interested, walk in and look around. They're only shops, after all.

The Museum of Mankind

East off Old Bond Street, along Burlington Gardens, is an imposing nineteenth-century Italianate pile, built to house London University's administration, but currently home to the excellent **Museum of Mankind**. Run by the ethnographic department of the British Museum, the collection comprises a superb array of domestic, religious and figurative objects from every corner of the globe – there are supposedly so many good spirits here that people send in jinxed and evil items to be exorcised.

The Museum of Mankind is open Mon–Sat 10am–5pm, Sun 2.30–6pm; free. The nearest tube is Green Park.

The only items on more or less permanent display are those in the "Introduction to the Galleries" in room 5 – across the foyer, past the heavy-browed Easter Island statue. These exhibits give a quick idea of the museum's range: shrunken human heads from Ecuador; an impossibly delicate Botswanan hat made from spiders' webs; a mask from the Côte d'Ivoire bristling with gun cartridges; chunky Polynesian and Hawaiian temple images; a Kazakh's silken robes; rough-hewn Native American totem poles; skinny Tibetan trumpets.

The rest of the building is given over to a variety of specialized displays, though certain favourite exhibits – such as the rock-crystal Aztec skull (which some suspect is a fake) – are nearly always exhibited somewhere in the galleries. The museum also puts on superb "temporary" shows which can last a couple of years – the most recent one focused on the mixed-up world of contemporary Papua New Guinea.

The Royal Arcade and the Faraday Museum

On the west side of Old Bond Street, a garish orange and white plasterwork entrance announces the **Royal Arcade**, a full-blown High Victorian shopping mall with tall arched bays and an elegant glass roof, designed so that the wealthy guests of **Brown's** hotel in Albermarle Street could have a sheltered and suitably elegant approach to the shops on Bond Street. Apart from being a posh hotel (see "Tea" box on p.97), *Brown's* was where the country's first telephone call was placed by Alexander Graham Bell in 1848, though initially he got a crossed line with a private telegraph wire, before finally getting through at around 3am to the hotel manager, at his home in Hammersmith. Also in Albermarle Street, still in their original premises at no. 50, are the officers of *John Murray*, the publishers of Byron and of the oldest British travel guides. It was here in 1824 that Byron's memoirs were tragically destroyed, after Murray managed to persuade Tom Moore, to whom they had been bequeathed, that they were too scurrilous to publish.

Brown's hotel is another good tea locale – see p.97.

Further up Albermarle Street at no. 21 is the Neoclassical facade of the **Royal Institution**, a scientific body founded in 1799 "for teaching by courses of philosophical lectures and experiments the application of science to the common purposes of life"; its professors have included Humphrey Davy (inventor of the miners' lamp), Michael Faraday and Lord Rutherford.

The building's basement has since been converted into a small **Faraday Museum**, featuring his original notebooks, equipment and a mock-up of the lab in which the "father of electricity" discovered the laws of electro-magnetics. Faraday (who features on the current £20 note) was also instrumental in inaugurating the Royal Institution's six Christmas Lectures, a continuing tradition designed to popularize science among school children.

The Faraday Museum is open Mon–Fri 1–4pm; £1.

Savile Row and Hanover Square

Running parallel with the Bond Streets, three blocks east, is another classic address in sartorial matters, **Savile Row**, still considered *the* place for made-to-measure suits, for those with the requisite £1400 or so to spare. In recent years, as property developers have started buying up whole tranches of the street, the number of bespoke tailors has declined, but one business is a permanent fixture: *Gieves & Hawkes*, at no. 1. They were the first tailors to establish themselves here back in 1785, with Nelson and Wellington among their first customers, and today their wares are still an exhibition of upper class taste, both for business and for country.

Savile Row has a further connection with the pop world at no. 3, where the Beatles' record label, *Apple*, had their offices and recording studio from 1968 until the building's near physical collapse in 1972. In February 1969 the Beatles gave their last live gig on the roof here, stopping the traffic and eventually attracting the attentions of the local police – as captured on film in *Let It Be*.

The nearest tube is Oxford Circus or Piccadilly Circus.

The Row terminates at Conduit Street, where the funnel-shaped St George's Street splays into **Hanover Square**, site of the old Hanover Square Rooms where Bach, Liszt, Haydn and Paganini all performed before the building's demolition in 1900. Halfway up St

George Frideric Handel

Born **Georg Friedrich Händel** (1685–1759) to a barber-surgeon in Halle, Saxony, Handel paid his first visit to London in 1711, where he marked his arrival by the composition of *Rinaldo*, which he wrote in fifteen days flat. The furore it produced – not least when Handel released a flock of sparrows for one aria – made him a household name. On his return in 1712 he was commissioned to write several works for Queen Anne, before becoming the court composer to George I, his one-time patron in Hanover.

London became Handel's spiritual home: he changed his name and nationality and lived out the rest of his life here, producing all the work for which he is now best known, including the *Water Music* and *Fireworks Music*, and his *Messiah*, which was composed in less than a month, failed to enthrall its first audiences, but is now one of the great set-pieces of Protestant culture. George III was so moved by the grandeur of the Hallelujah Chorus that he leapt to his feet and remained standing for the entire performance. Handel himself fainted during a performance of the work in 1759, and died shortly afterwards in his home at 25 Brook Street; he is buried in Westminster Abbey. His birthday is celebrated with a concert of his music given at the Coram Foundation, site of the old Foundling Hospital (p.154) which he helped to finance.

George's Street, and contemporaneous with the square, is the sooty Corinthian portico of **St George's Church**, much copied since, but the first of its kind in London when it was built in the 1720s. Nicknamed "London's Temple of Hymen", it has long been Mayfair's most fashionable church for weddings: among those who tied the knot here are the Shelleys, George Eliot, Disraeli and Teddy Roosevelt; Handel, a confirmed bachelor, was a churchwarden here for many years (see box).

Shepherd Market

Strictly speaking, Mayfair is the area bordered by Regent Street, Piccadilly, Oxford Street and Park Lane but its residential heart has been pushed further west towards Hyde Park. If you're coming from Green Park tube, head west down Piccadilly until you get to Half Moon Street, where the fictional Jeeves and his faithful valet Wooster of P. G. Wodehouse's novels lived, and where in 1763 the real James Boswell, newly arrived from Edinburgh, took lodgings and wrote his scurrilous diary.

At the end of the street turn left into Curzon Street, site of **Crewe House**, now a company headquarters, and one of the few eighteenth-century Mayfair mansions still standing. It was originally constructed by local builder, Edward Shepherd, who also laid out **Shepherd Market**, a little warren of alleyways and passages now occupied by swanky cafés and restaurants, plus a couple of Victorian pubs, all extremely popular in summer. It was here that the infamous May Fair – which gives the area its name – took place until it was suppressed in the mid-eighteenth century because of "drunkenness, fornication, gaming and lewdness". Appropriately enough, the market is still a well-known haunt for high-class prostitutes, popular with politicians and media folk.

Around Grosvenor Square

Grosvenor Square, to the northwest, is the largest of the three Mayfair squares, and was known during World War II as "Little America" – General Eisenhower, whose statue now stands here, ran the D-Day campaign from no. 20. The American presence is still pretty strong, thanks to the Roosevelt Memorial, which overlooks the square's central park, and to the monstrously ugly **American Embassy**, which occupies the entire west side of the square. Completed in 1960 to designs by Eero Saarinen, the embassy is watched over by a giant gilded eagle plus a small posse of police, as most weeks there's some demonstration or other against US foreign policy – albeit nothing to rank with 1968's violent protests against US involvement in Vietnam.

Tea at Claridges? See p.97.

Eisenhower's initial *pied à terre* was a room painted "whorehouse pink" in **Claridge's**, the hotel for the rich and royal one block east of Grosvenor Square on Brook Street. *Claridge's* also served as the wartime hang-out of the OSS, forerunner of the CIA, one of whose representatives held a historic meeting here in 1943 with Samuel Zygelbojm from the Jewish Board of the Polish government-in-exile. Zygelbojm was told that Roosevelt had refused his request to bomb the rail lines leading to Auschwitz; the following day he committed suicide.

American troops stationed over here used to worship at the **Grosvenor Chapel** on South Audley Street, a building reminiscent of early settlers' churches in New England. It's still a favourite with the American community in London, though its most illustrious occupant is radical MP John Wilkes ("Wilkes and Liberty" was the battle cry of many a riot in the mid-eighteenth century). Behind the chapel are the beautifully secluded **Mount Street Gardens**, dotted with two-hundred-year-old plane trees and enclosed by nineteenth-century red-brick mansions. At the far eastern end of the gardens is the back entrance to the **Church of the Immaculate Conception**, on Farm Street, the Jesuits' London stronghold, built in ostentatious neo-Gothic style in the 1840s.

Oxford Street

As wealthy Londoners began to move out of the City in the eighteenth century in favour of the newly developed West End, so **Oxford Street** – the old Roman road to Oxford – gradually replaced Cheapside (p.202) as London's main shopping street. Today, despite successive recessions and sky-high rents, this scruffy, two-mile hotchpotch of shops is still one of the world's busiest streets, its Christmas lights are still switched on by esteemed public figures such as Princess Di and gameshow host Nicholas Parsons, and its traffic wardens have to be equipped with loud hailers to prevent the hordes of Christmas shoppers from taking their lives at the busy road junctions.

East of Oxford Circus, the street is littered with booths selling cheap gifts and policemen's hats, and auctioneers selling liquidated stock out of short-lease shops. There's a fair number of nationwide giants here as well, including the main *HMV* record store, the *Virgin Megastore*, and *Marks and Spencer* – the great British success story, which opened in 1912 under the slogan "Don't ask the price – it's a penny".

Oxford Street has four tube stations along its length, from west to east: Marble Arch, Bond St, Oxford Circus and Tottenham Court Rd.

The west end of the street is dominated by more upmarket chain stores, including the street's one great landmark, **Selfridge's**, a huge Edwardian pile fronted by giant Ionic columns, with the Queen of Time riding the ship of commerce and supporting an Art Deco clock above the main entrance. The store was opened in 1909 by Chicago millionaire Gordon Selfridge, who flaunted its 130 departments under the slogan, "Why not spend a day at Selfridge's?", but was later pensioned off after running into trouble with the Inland Revenue. We have Selfridge's to thank for the concept of the "bargain basement", the irritating "only ten more shopping days to Christmas" countdown, and the bouquet of perfumes from the women's cosmetics counters, strategically placed at the entrance to all department stores to entice customers in.

The nearest tube for Selfridge's is Bond Street.

Marylebone

Hyde Park

To the north of Oxford Street lies **Marylebone**, once the outlying village of St Mary-by-the-Bourne. Samuel Pepys walked through open countryside to reach its pleasure gardens in 1668 and declared it a "pretty place". During the course of the next century, the gardens were closed and the village was swallowed up as its chief landowners – among them the Portlands and the Portmans – laid out a mesh of uniform Georgian streets and squares, much of which has been left unaltered.

Sights in this part of town include the massively touristed Madame Tussauds and the Planetarium, on Marylebone Road, the low-key galleries of the Wallace Collection, and Sherlock Holmes' old stamping grounds around Baker Street. There is a pleasure, though, in just wandering the Marylebone streets, especially the village-like quarter around Marylebone High Street.

Doctors and dentists

The northwest corner of Cavendish Square marks the beginning of **Harley Street**, where doctors, dentists and medical specialists opened up shop in the mid-nineteenth century to serve the area's wealthy citizens. Private medicine survived the threat of the post-war NHS, and the most expensive specialists and hospitals are still to be found in the streets around here.

The Dental Museum is open Mon–Fri 9am–5pm; free.

For the dentorially-inclined, the national dental body, the BDA, run a **Dental Museum** at 64 Wimpole Street. Though dentistry is traditionally associated with pain, it was, in fact, a dentist who discovered the first anaesthetic, without which you wouldn't go anywhere near the hideous contraptions displayed here. The upstairs gallery contains the most gruesome exhibits, an array of historical tools, fillings, crowns and dentures accompanied by old prints of agonising extractions.

The Wallace Collection

The Wallace Collection is open Mon–Sat 10am–5pm, Sun 2–5pm; free. The nearest tube is Bond Street.

Of the three squares immediately north of Oxford Street, only Manchester Square has kept its peaceful Georgian appearance thanks to its position away from the main traffic arteries. At its head is Hertford House, a miniature eighteenth-century French château transplanted to central London, which holds the splendid **Wallace Collection**, a museum-gallery best known for its eighteenth-century French paintings and decorative art. The collection was bequeathed to the nation in 1897 by Lady Wallace, widow of Sir Richard Wallace, an art collector who, as the illegitimate son of the fourth Marquess of Hertford, also inherited this elegant mansion and the family treasures.

The Wallace Collection is an old-fashioned institution, with exhibits piled high in glass cabinets and paintings covering every inch of wall space. It is the combined effect of the exhibits set amidst the period fittings – and a bloody great armoury – which makes the place so remarkable. That said, the quality of the exhibits is uneven, so the best advice is to take in the overall effect and then head for the first floor (room 22 in particular) where the best of the paintings are hung.

The ground floor

The **ground floor** rooms, set around an open-air courtyard, kick off with a group of fine nineteenth-century pictures, including several translucent watercolours by **Richard Parkes Bonington**, who spent most of his brief life in France, where he exhibited alongside his close friend, Delacroix, who also features here. Several other rooms contain interesting medieval and Renaissance pieces, ranging from majolica to Limoges porcelain and Venetian glass. On the walls are several mildly distracting paintings by Reynolds and Lawrence's typically sensuous portrait of the author and society beauty, the Countess of Blessington.

In the Smoking Room (room 7), only a small alcove at the far end survives to give an idea of the effect of the original Minton-tiled decor Wallace chose for this room. The next three rooms house the extensive armoury bought *en bloc* by Wallace around the time of the

Franco-Prussian War, while a fourth room houses Oriental arms and armour, collected by the fourth Marquess of Hertford.

The first floor

The most famous paintings in the collection are on the first floor, the tone of which is set by **Boucher**'s sumptuous mythological scenes over the main staircase. In rooms 13–16 you'll find furniture from the courts of Louis XV and XVI, decorative gold snuff boxes and fine Sèvres porcelain – including mighty wine and ice-cream coolers made for Empress Catherine II of Russia. Portraits here include **Reynolds**' doe-eyed moppets and **Greuze**'s winsome kids, and two by **Louise Vigée le Brun**, one of the most successful portraitists of pre-revolutionary France.

Among the Rococo delights in rooms 23–25 are some elegiac scenes by **Watteau**, such as *Halt During the Chase* and *Music Party;* **Fragonard**'s coquettes, one of whom flaunts herself to a smitten beau in *The Swing*; and Boucher's gloriously florid portrait of Madame de Pompadour, Louis XV's mistress and patron of many of the great French artists of the period. In addition to all this French finery there's a good collection from the Dutch and Venetian schools in rooms 19–21: **de Hooch**'s *Women Peeling Apples*, oil sketches by **Rubens**, landscapes by **Ruisdael**, plus contrasting vistas by **Canaletto** and **Guardi**, whose works were more or less souvenirs for eighteenth-century Brits doing the Grand Tour.

Room 22, the largest room in the house, was specifically built by Wallace to display what he considered to be his finest paintings – including **Frans Hals**' arrogant *Laughing Cavalier*. Here, too, are **Titian**'s *Perseus and Andromeda*, **Velázquez**'s *Lady with a Fan* and **Rembrandt**'s affectionate portrait of his teenage son, Titus, who was helping administer his father's estate after bankruptcy charges, and who died at the age of just twenty-eight. At the far end of the room are four portraits of the actress Mary Robinson: two by Romney, one by Reynolds and, best of the lot, **Gainsborough**'s deceptively innocent portrayal, in which she insouciantly holds a miniature of her lover, the nineteen-year old Prince of Wales (later George IV).

Marylebone High Street and Baker Street

Baker St is the nearest tube for Marylebone High Street – and for Baker Street!

Marylebone High Street, which starts near Manchester Square and finishes at Marylebone Road, is all that's left of the village street that once ran along the banks of the Tyburn stream. It has become considerably more cosmopolitan and upmarket since those bucolic days – witness the Rolls Royce showroom at the northern end – though the pace of the street is leisurely by central London standards, and its shops and cafés are mostly small, independent ventures, a pleasant contrast to the big stores on nearby Oxford Street. One or two shops in particular deserve mention: *Maison Sagne*, the patisserie at no. 105, is decorated with the same mock-

Pompeian frescoes that adorned it when it was founded in the 1920s by a Swiss pastry-cook; *Villandry*, at no. 89, is a more recent, but equally stylish *charcuterie* and *fromagerie*; while at no. 83 is *Daunt*, a purpose-built bookshop with long glass-roofed galleried hall from 1910, which specializes in travel books.

St Marylebone Church

At the north edge of Marylebone High Street is **Marylebone Road**, an extension of Euston Road, built in the 1750s to provide London with its first bypass. The traffic which pounds down its six lanes cuts off **St Marylebone Church** from Nash's York Gate, designed as an alternative gateway to Regent's Park. The church crypt is now a counselling and healing centre with a vegetarian café attached, but the main interior is only fitfully open to the public; in any case, its most attractive feature – the gilded caryatids of the cupola – are visible from outside.

St Marylebone church has a café.

It was here in 1846 that Elizabeth Barrett and Robert Browning were secretly married; a facsimile of the certificate is displayed outside the church. Elizabeth – forty years old, an invalid and a virtual prisoner in her father's house on Wimpole Street – returned home and acted as if nothing had happened. A week later the couple eloped to Italy, where they spent most of their married life.

The Sherlock Holmes Museum

The Sherlock Holmes Museum is open daily 9.30am–6pm; £5. Devotees may also want to visit the Sherlock Holmes pub, off Northumberland Avenue.

Czech writer Karel Čapek was disappointed to find no trace of Sherlock Holmes on **Baker Street**, which cuts across Marylebone Road – "if we briefly touch upon its underground station, we have exhausted everything including our patience" he wrote in the 1930s. Happily, for those on the trail of English literature's languid super-sleuth, who lived at 221b Baker Street, London's tourist industry has rectified all that with the **Sherlock Holmes Museum** at no. 239 (the sign on the door says 221b). It's a competent excercise in period reconstruction but the building has no proven connection with Holmes or his creator, Sir Arthur Conan Doyle. There's no attempt to impart any insights, or even basic facts about Holmes or Doyle, yet the narrow staircases are crowded every day with fans from all over the world. The ground floor is given over to Hudson's Restaurant (Hudson was Holmes' and Watson's opium-tolerant landlady), a little over-themed but not a bad spot for tea.

One last curiosity in this area is **Marylebone Station**, hidden in the backstreets to the north of Marylebone Road on Melcombe Street, where a delicate and extremely elegant wrought-iron canopy links the station to the former *Great Central Hotel*. The last and most modest of the Victorian terminals, this was intended to be the terminal for the Channel tunnel of the 1880s, a scheme abandoned after only a mile or so of digging, when Queen Victoria got nervous about foreign invasions. Marylebone now serves the commuter belt in Buckinghamshire.

Madame Tussaud's and the Planetarium

Madame Tussaud's wax models have been pulling in the crowds ever since the good lady arrived in London in 1802 bearing the sculpted heads of guillotined aristocrats (she herself only just managed to escape the same fate – her uncle who started the family business was less fortunate). The entrance fee might be extortionate, the likenesses occasionally dubious and the automated dummies inept by *Jurassic Park* standards, but you can still rely on finding London's biggest queues here – an hour's wait is the summertime minimum.

Madame Tussaud's Mon–Fri 10am–5.30pm, Sat & Sun 9.30am–5.30pm; £8.25. The nearest tube is Baker Street.

The best photo opportunities come in the first section, an all-star Garden Party peppered with contemporary politicians, TV and sports personalities (many of them unknown to non-British visitors). The next section, called **200 Years**, is more off-beat, beginning with the very first Tussaud figure, Madame du Barry, Louis XV's mistress, who gently respires as Sleeping Beauty – in reality she was beheaded in the French Revolution. Close by, the dismembered heads and limbs of outdated personalities – Muhammad Ali, Sophia Loren, Nikita Khrushchev – are ranged on a shelf as in a butcher's shop, along with a fire-damaged model of George IV with a melted eye.

A dull array of international screen stars leads down to the **Grand Hall**, lined with oil paintings and hung with chandeliers to lend a regal air to this po-faced gathering of statesmen, clerics, generals and British royalty stretching back to medieval times. The collection of past US presidents look like the bunch of crooks several of them undoubtedly were and Lenin looks diminutive enough, but elsewhere the veracity is a bit suspect – Princess Di is somehow shorter than Prince Charles, Margaret Thatcher looks like a kindly aunt and the Beatles are virtually unrecognizable.

The **Chamber of Horrors**, the most popular section of all, is irredeemably tasteless, including a reconstruction of a foggy East End street strewn with one of Jack the Ripper's mutilated victims. Press clippings gratuitously detail the exploits of all the "great" British serial killers, as well as Charles Manson and his "family". It is the murderer's greatest honour to be included here: one bequeathed his suit the day before his execution, while Dennis Nilsen, a gruesome killer of young gay men in the 1980s, begged to be allowed to pose for Tussaud's whilst in prison – his unfulfilled ambition was to have an entire section to himself, as does John Christie.

The tour of Tussaud's ends with its newest show, the **Spirit of London**, a manic five-minute romp through the history of London in miniaturized taxi cabs. It begins well, dropping witty visual jokes as it careers through Elizabethan times, the Great Plague, the Great Fire, Wren and Dickens through to Swinging London, ending in a postmodern heritage nightmare (not unlike much of London today) with a cacophany of punks and beefeaters, before shuddering to a halt by a slobbering Benny Hill.

The Planetarium is open the same hours as Madame Tussaud's, with shows every 40mins; £4.

The Planetarium

The adjoining and equally crowded **London Planetarium** has an excellent permanent display featuring a giant revolving Earth circled by satellites, live weather satellite transmissions, images from a space telescope, touch-screen computers and information on the rest of the planets in the solar system.

All this is just a taster, however, for the trippy, thirty-minute *Star Show*, upstairs in the circular auditorium, in which images collected by satellite and space probes are projected onto a vast dome – the pictures are stunning and the narration lucidly informative and ecologically sound.

Chapter 3

Soho and Covent Garden

SOHO and **COVENT GARDEN** are very much the heart of London – and the centre's most characterful areas. It's here you'll find the city's street fashion on display, its more oddball shops, its opera houses, theatres, mega-cinemas, and the widest variety of restaurants and cafés – where, whatever hour you wander through, there's always something going on. There always was a life to these neighbourhoods, of course, but their aspect today is very different to the recent past. The two neighbourhoods started out as wealthy residential developments, then sunk into legendary squalor, until their revival, over the past twenty years. Soho, uniquely, retains an unorthodox and slightly raffish air born of an immigrant history as rich as that of the East End; while Covent Garden's transformation from a fruit and veg market into a fashion-conscious *quartier* is one of the most miraculous and enduring developments of the 1980s. Both districts are worth making time for well beyond their ostensible "sights", both by day, and, for Soho especially, by night.

Soho and Covent Garden form a generous core of our pub and restaurant listings – see chapters 15 and 16.

Soho gives you the best and worst of London. The porn joints that made the district notorious in the 1970s are still strongly in evidence, especially to the west of Wardour Street, as are the yuppies who pushed up the rents in the 1980s. Nevertheless, the area continues to boast a lively fruit and veg market on Berwick Street, and a nightlife which has attracted writers and ravers to the place since the eighteenth century. The big movie houses on Leicester Square always attract crowds of punters, and the tiny enclave of **Chinatown** continues to double as a focus for the Chinese community and a popular place for inexpensive Chinese restaurants. And in the last three or four years, Soho has transformed itself again, this time into one of Europe's leading gay centres, with bars and cafés bursting out from the Old Compton Street area.

A little more sanitized and unashamedly commercial, **Covent Garden** today is a far cry from its heyday when the piazza was the great playground (and red-light district) of eighteenth-century London. The buskers in front of St Paul's, the theatres round about,

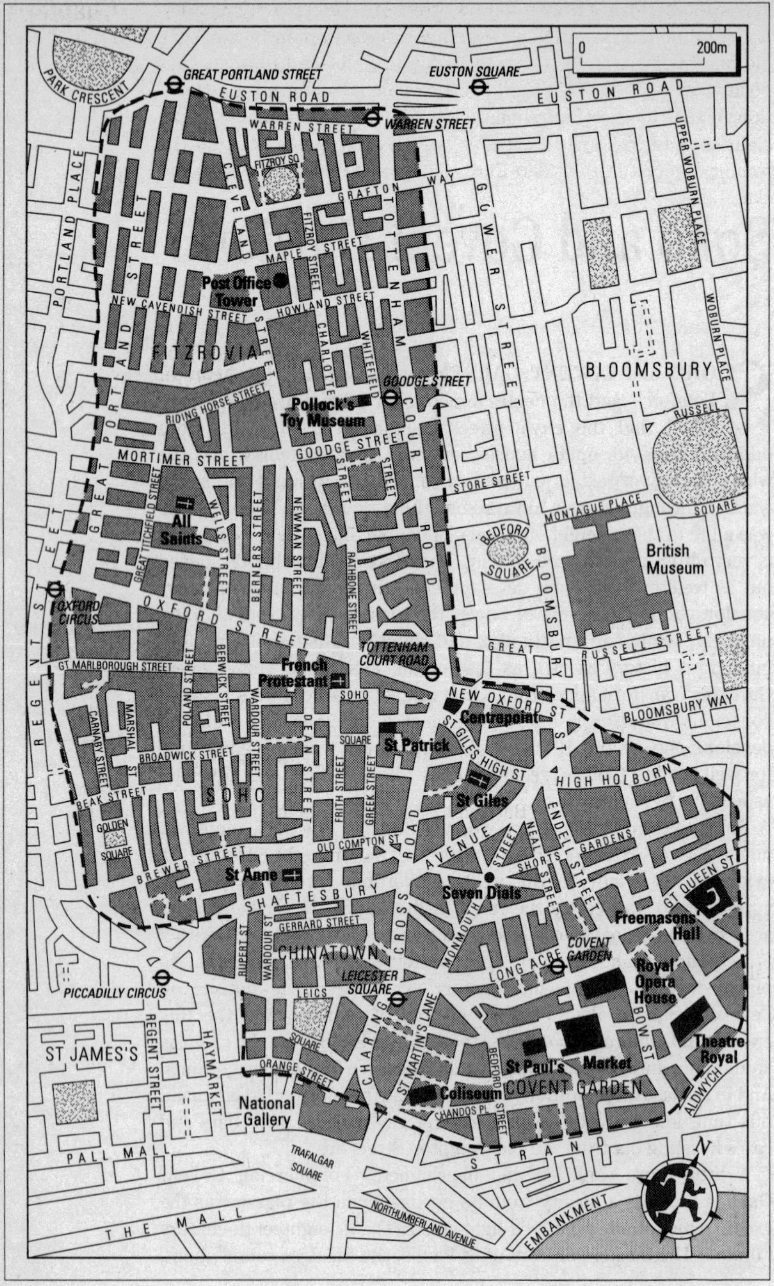

0
200m
PARK CRESCENT
GREAT PORTLAND STREET
EUSTON SQUARE
EUSTON ROAD
EUSTON ROAD
WARREN STREET
WARREN STREET
FITZROY SQ
UPPER WOBURN PLACE
GRAFTON WAY
CLEVELAND
PORTLAND PLACE
STREET
FITZROY STREET
MAPLE STREET
TOTTENHAM
GOWER STREET
Post Office Tower
NEW CAVENDISH STREET
HOWLAND STREET
CHARLOTTE
WHITEFIELD
WOBURN PLACE
FITZROVIA
GOODGE STREET
BLOOMSBURY
RIDING HORSE STREET
Pollock's Toy Museum
COURT
RUSSELL
GREAT PORTLAND
MORTIMER STREET
GOODGE STREET
STREET
STREET
STORE STREET
GREAT TITCHFIELD STREET
All Saints
WELLS STREET
BERNERS STREET
NEWMAN STREET
RATHBONE STREET
ROAD
MONTAGUE PLACE
SQUARE
BEDFORD SQUARE
BLOOMSBURY
British Museum
OXFORD CIRCUS
OXFORD STREET
REGENT STREET
TOTTENHAM COURT ROAD
GREAT RUSSELL STREET
ST MARLBOROUGH STREET
French Protestant
SOHO
BERWICK STREET
WARDOUR STREET
NEW OXFORD ST
BLOOMSBURY WAY
Centrepoint
MARSHAL ST
POLAND STREET
CARNABY STREET
DEAN STREET
SQUARE
St Patrick
ST GILES HIGH ST
BROADWICK STREET
HIGH HOLBORN
BEAK STREET
SOHO
FRITH STREET
GREEK STREET
St Giles
GOLDEN SQUARE
ENDELL STREET
NEAL STREET
OLD COMPTON ST
AVENUE
GARDENS
BREWER STREET
St Anne
SHORTS
GT QUEEN ST
SHAFTESBURY
Seven Dials
CROSS ROAD
GERRARD STREET
Freemasons' Hall
RUPERT ST
WARDOUR STREET
CHINATOWN
MONMOUTH
COVENT GARDEN
LONG ACRE
PICCADILLY CIRCUS
LEICESTER SQUARE
Royal Opera House
LEICS SQUARE
CHARING
ST MARTIN'S LANE
BOW ST
ST JAMES'S
REGENT STREET
HAYMARKET
ORANGE STREET
St Paul's
Market
Theatre Royal
Coliseum
COVENT GARDEN
BEDFORD STREET
National Gallery
CHANDOS PL
ALDWYCH
PALL MALL
TRAFALGAR SQUARE
STRAND
N
THE MALL
NORTHUMBERLAND AVENUE
EMBANKMENT

and the Royal Opera House on Bow Street are survivors in this tradition, and on a balmy summer evening, Covent Garden Piazza – the old marketplace – is still an undeniably lively place to be. Another positive side-effect of the market development has been the renovation of the run-down warehouses to the north of the piazza, especially around the Neal Street area, which now boasts some of the trendiest shops in the West End, selling everything from shoes to skateboards.

Soho

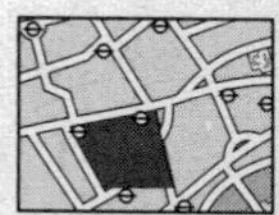

When **Soho** – named for the cry that resounded through the district when it was a hunting ground – was first built over in the seventeenth century, its streets were among the most sought-after addresses in the capital. Princes, dukes and earls built their mansions around Soho and Leicester squares, which became the centre of high society nightlife, epitomized by Viennese *prima donna* Theresa Cornelys' wild masquerades, which drew "a riotous assembly of fashionable people of both sexes", a traffic jam of hackney chairs and a huge crowd of onlookers. By the end of the eighteenth century, however, the party was over, the rich moved west to Mayfair, and Soho began its inexorable descent into poverty and overcrowding.

Soho can look a bit rough but the streets are well peopled – making it one of London's safer areas, day or night.

Even before the last aristocrats left, Soho had become, along with the East End, the city's main dumping ground for immigrants, a place caricatured (albeit much later) by Galsworthy as "untidy, full of Greeks, Ishmaelites, cats, Italians, tomatoes, restaurants, organs, coloured stuffs, queer names, people looking out of upper windows". The first wave of refugees were the French Huguenots who settled in Bateman Street after fleeing from Louis XIV's intolerant regime, followed later by more French, Italians, Irish and Jews. More recently, Asians, particularly the Chinese, took advantage of Soho's post-war cheap rents for their workshops and restaurants.

For a long time Soho had also been a favourite haunt of the capital's creative bohos and literati. It was at the *Turk's Head* in 1764, in what is now Chinatown, that Joshua Reynolds founded "The Club", to give Dr Johnson unlimited opportunities for talking with the likes of Goldsmith, Burke and Boswell. Thomas de Quincey turned up in Soho in 1802, having run away from school, and was saved from starvation by a local prostitute, an incident later recalled in his *Confessions of an English Opium Eater*. Wagner arrived destitute in the neighbourhood in 1839, Marx ended up here after the failure of the upheavals of 1848, and Rimbaud and Verlaine escaped here after the fall of the Paris Commune.

For listings of Soho's music clubs, see p.473.

Soho's reputation for tolerance made it an obvious place of refuge from dour, post-war Britain, too. Jazz and skiffle clubs

Soho

proliferated in the 1950s, folk and rock clubs in the 1960s, and punk rock venues at the end of the 1970s. Throughout this period, the *Colony Club*, one of many private drinking clubs, catered for Soho's artistic (and alcoholic) clique, under the helm of Muriel Belcher, who, according to *Colony* stalwart, Daniel Farson, "presided over its shabby bamboo-clad bar like a monarch over a small, tightly knit kingdom, her strong Sephardic profile reminiscent of a canny, watchful hawk". Other pubs and clubs provided – and provide – focal points for other political, literary and cultural circles: the satirical magazine *Private Eye* is based in Carlisle Street and drinks at the *Coach and Horses* pub, while writers, publishers and budding movie producers hold court at the members-only *Groucho Club* in Dean Street.

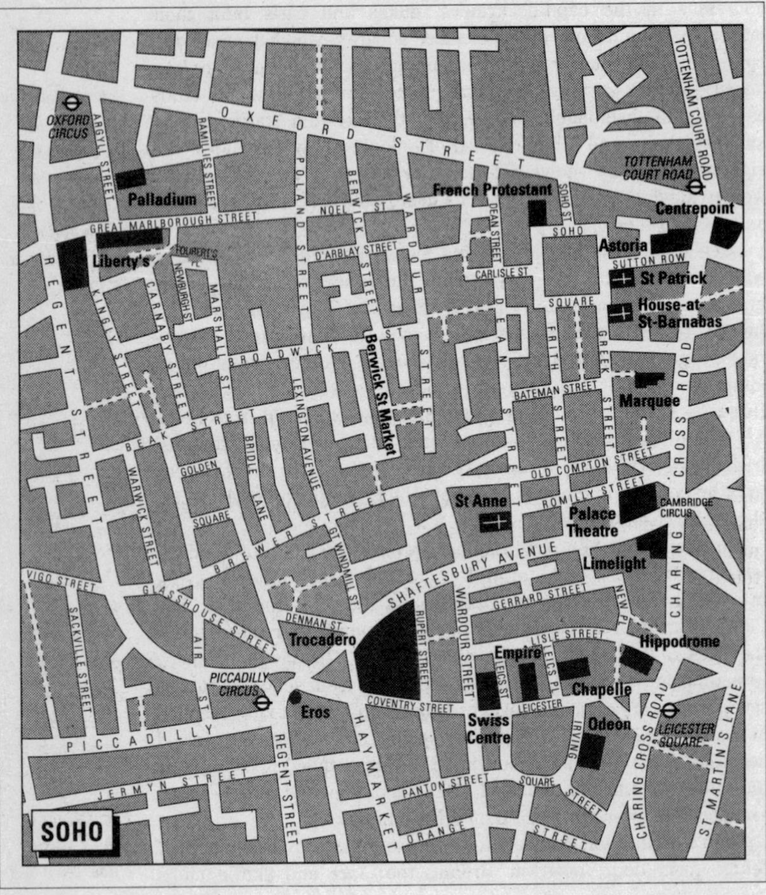

The area's creative energy is perhaps best expressed in its clubs – both public and private – and the presence of Wardour Street, core of the movie and advertising business in Britain, provides a clientele on the doorstep. The attraction, though, remains in the unique mix of Soho people. There's nowhere else in the city where such a diverse slice of London comes face to face with each other: businessmen, clubbers, drunks, theatregoers, fashion victims, market stallholders, pimps and prostitutes, politicians. Take it all in, and enjoy – for most of London is not like this!

Leicester Square

A short hop east of Piccadilly Circus, **Leicester Square** was a total sleaze pit until Westminster Council stepped in with a long-overdue restoration in 1993. Overhauled, it is safe and popular again, with the big cinemas and discos here doing good business, and buskers entertaining the crowds. By night it is one of the most crowded places in London, particularly on a Friday or Saturday when huge numbers of tourists and half the youth of the suburbs seem to congregate here. By day, the Society of West End Theatres booth pulls the queues for its half-price deals, while touts haggle with tourists over the price of dodgy tickets for the top shows, and clubbers hand out flyers to likely-looking punters.

The nearest tube is Leicester Square – which is actually on Charing Cross Road.

Before the clean-up, the small patch of grass at the centre of the square was once London's own "Needle Park", but it is now closed at night, and the junkies have moved on. At its centre is a copy of the Shakespeare memorial in Westminster Abbey's Poets' Corner and a statue of Charlie Chaplin (neither of whom has any connection with the square); around the edge are busts of Sir Isaac Newton, William Hogarth, Joshua Reynolds and a Scottish surgeon, John Hunter – all of whom lived hereabouts in the eighteenth century.

See p.492 for the low-down on buying theatre tickets.

At that time, the square was a kind of court for the fashionable "Leicester House set", headed by successive Princes of Wales who didn't get on with their fathers at St James's. It wasn't until the mid-nineteenth century that the square began to emerge as an entertainment zone, with Turkish baths, accommodation houses (for prostitutes and their clients), oyster rooms and music halls such as the grandiose *Empire* and the *Hippodrome* (just off the square), edifices which survive today as cinemas and discos. Cinema moved in during the 1930s, a golden age evoked by the sleek black lines of the *Odeon* on the east side, and maintains its grip on the area. The *Empire*, at the top end of the square, is the favourite for the big royal premières, and, in a rather half-hearted imitation of the Hollywood (and Cannes) tradition, there are hand prints visible in the pavement by the southwestern corner of the garden railings.

For listings of discos, see p.477; for cinemas, p.498.

There are no sights as such on the square, though some unsuspecting tourists take advantage of the benches provided by the monumentally ugly Swiss Centre, only to find themselves assaulted

– on the hour, every hour – by a five-minute medley played by the Centre's alpine peasants on a wall-mounted glockenspiel-clock.

One little known sight, just off the north end of the square, hidden away in Leicester Place, is the modern **Notre-Dame de France** Catholic church. The church's unusual circular plan is derived from the Panorama, a rotunda 90ft in diameter originally built here by the Irish artist Robert Barker in 1796. The main point of interest, however, is the Chapelle du Saint-Sacrement which contains a series of simple frescoes by Jean Cocteau from 1960.

Chinatown

Chinatown, hemmed in between Leicester Square and Shaftesbury Avenue, is a self-contained jumble of shops, cafés and restaurants that makes up one of London's most distinct and popular ethnic enclaves. Gerrard Street, Chinatown's main drag, has been endowed with ersatz touches – telephone kiosks rigged out as pagodas and fake oriental gates – and few of London's 60,000 Chinese actually live in the three small blocks of Chinatown. Nonetheless, it remains a focus for the community, a place to do business or the weekly shop, celebrate a wedding, or just meet up for meals, particularly on Sundays, when the restaurants overflow with Chinese families tucking into *dim sum*.

If you're in the city for Chinese New Year, check Time Out *for details of events.*

The **Chinese New Year** celebrations, instigated here in 1973, are a community-based affair, drawing in thousands of Chinese for the Sunday nearest to New Year's Day (late Jan or early Feb). Huge papier maché lions dance through the streets to a cacophony of firecrackers, devouring cabbages hung from the upper floors by strings pinned with money. The noise is deafening, and if you want to see anything other than the backs of people's heads, you'll need to position yourself close to one of the cabbages around noon and stand your ground.

See p.429 for reviews of Chinese restaurants.

For the rest of the year, most Londoners come to Chinatown simply to eat – easy and inexpensive enough to do, though the choice is somewhat overwhelming, especially on Gerrard Street itself. Cantonese cuisine predominates, though there's a smattering of Shanghainese and spicey Szechuan outlets. You're unlikely to be disappointed wherever you go – watch where the Chinese themselves eat is the most obvious policy, and if you get offered local advice on what to eat where, take it.

In addition to the restaurants, most of the shops in Chinatown are geared towards Chinese trade. If the mood take you, you can while away several hours sorting through the trinkets, ceramics and ornaments in the various arts and crafts shops, like *Guanghua*, on Newport Place, which is also the biggest Chinese bookshop in the city and a good place to pick up eastern newspapers in English or Cantonese. If you know what you're looking for, you can amass the right ingredients for a demon stir-fry – with exotic fruits to finish – in the supermarkets on Newport Place.

London's Chinese

London's first Chinese immigrants were sailors who arrived here in the late eighteenth and early nineteenth centuries on the ships of the East India Company. A small number settled permanently around the docks at Limehouse (see p.241), which became London's first Chinatown, boasting over thirty Chinese shops and restaurants by the turn of the century. Predominantly male, this closed community achieved a quasi-mythical status in Edwardian minds as a hotbed of criminal dives and opium dens, a reputation further enhanced by Sax Rohmer's novels (later made into films), featuring the evil Doctor Fu Manchu.

Wartime bomb damage, post-war demolition and protectionist union laws all but destroyed Limehouse Chinatown. At the same time, following the Communist takeover in China, a new wave of predominantly Cantonese refugees arrived via Hong Kong, and began to buy up the cheap and run-down property around Gerrard Street. Western interest in Chinese food provided the impetus for the boom in the catering industry, which to this day remains inexpensive, since it continues to provide for the Chinese community itself.

This community is now struggling to absorb a fresh wave of immigration from Hong Kong, fleeing the colony before it passes into the hands of Communist China in 1997. Hong Kong's uncertain future also looks likely to strengthen the hand of the Triads, organized crime societies who have long been involved in drug dealing, gambling, protection rackets and other misdemeanours, and who are keen to get out of Hong Kong before the Chinese takeover. Needless to say, as an outsider, it's easy to remain happily oblivious to all of this.

Charing Cross Road and Shaftesbury Avenue

The creation of **Charing Cross Road**, Soho's eastern border and a thoroughfare from Trafalgar Square to Oxford Street, was less disruptive than other Victorian "improvements", though slum clearance was part of its design. The street now boasts the highest concentration of **bookshops** anywhere in London, one of the first to open here being the chaotic *Foyles* at no. 119, where De Valera, George Bernard Shaw, Walt Disney and Conan Doyle were all once regular customers. The street was later immortalized in Helene Hanff's biographical novel *84 Charing Cross Road*, based on her correspondence with the now defunct bookshop at that address, *Marks & Co*. The radical bookshop, *Colletts*, founded by lefties in the 1920s, was equally well known in its day, but finally folded in 1992, giving way to an expansion of *Waterstone's* at no. 121, whose stock – like that of *Books Etc* across the road (and with its own café) at no. 120 – now rivals that of Foyles. Apart from these two flagship chain shops, the main concentration of shops lies south of Cambridge Circus: here you'll find the capital's main feminist bookshop, the newly expanded *Silver Moon*, along with a cluster of ramshackle second-hand bookshops, and swankier outfits like *Zwemmer*, who have a shop on Charing Cross Road, an art books' branch on

London's bookshops are detailed on p.518.

Litchfield Street, and an exceptionally good Russian and East European specialist branch at the far end of Denmark Street (see below).

One of of the nicest places for second-hand book browsing is **Cecil Court**, the alleyway between the southern end of Charing Cross Road and St Martin's Lane, which boasts specialist bookshops devoted to travel, dance, Italy, new age philosophies and the like, plus various antiquarian dealers selling modern first editions, old theatre posters, maps and stamps. Another place you shouldn't miss, just off Charing Cross Road, is the **Photographers' Gallery** (Tues–Sat 11am–7pm; free) on Great Newport Street, established in 1971 as the first of its kind in London, and hosting free temporary exhibitions that are invariably worth a browse.

The Photographer's Gallery also has a fine café and bookshop.

As well as being prime bookworm territory, Charing Cross Road is one of the main drags through the West End, flanked by **theatres, clubs and rock venues**. At the southern end is the *Garrick Theatre* where *No Sex Please We're British* played for 23 years too long, rivalling Agatha Christie's *Mousetrap*, at nearby *St Martin's*, which has been on since 1952; further up is the high-tech *Hippodrome* nightclub, where queues of eager punters begin to gather early in the evening. On Cambridge Circus, the huge terracotta *Palace Theatre* opened in 1891 as the Royal English Opera House, but folded the following year and is now owned by Andrew Lloyd Webber; *Les Misérables* are long-term residents.

See p.474 for details of the music clubs.

There is more of a club scene across Shaftesbury Avenue, where you'll find the *Limelight*, one of London's most extravagant nightclubs, converted from a Welsh Presbyterian Chapel. Further north still, is the *Marquee*, a rock venue which continues to live off the reputation it forged at its old premises on Wardour Street in the 1960s when the likes of the Rolling Stones strutted their stuff and Phil Collins worked as a cloakroom attendant. Across the street are the guitar shops of Denmark Street, London's tame version of New York's Tin Pan Alley, and round the corner in Oxford Street is another classic music venue, the *100 Club*, where Siouxsie, The Clash, the Sex Pistols, The Damned and the Vibrators all played during the heyday of punk in 1976, though nowadays it's returned more to its jazz roots.

See p.491 for more on the city's theatres.

Sweeping northeast towards Bloomsbury from Piccadilly Circus, and separating Soho proper from Chinatown, is the gentle curve of **Shaftesbury Avenue**, the heart of mainstream Theatreland, with five theatres and two cinemas along its length. Like Charing Cross Road, it was conceived in the late 1870s, ostensibly to relieve traffic congestion but with the dual purpose of destroying the slums which lay in its path. Ironically, it was then named after Lord Shaftesbury (of Eros fame), whose life had been spent trying to help the likes of those dispossessed by the road scheme.

Central Soho

If Soho has a main drag, it has to be **Old Compton Street**, which runs parallel with Shaftesbury Avenue, linking Charing Cross Road and Wardour Street. The corner shops, sex shops, boutiques and trendy cafés here are typical of the area and a good barometer of the latest Soho fads. One of the few places which has survived the vicissitudes of fashion on this short stretch is the original *Patisserie Valerie* (there are now several branches elsewhere), opened by Madame Valerie in 1926 and long a favourite with art students and other bohemian life. *Valerie's* is now vastly outnumbered by mock-continental cafés whose pavement tables provide maximum posing potential, with the *Soho Brasserie*, the cutting edge of yuppiedom in the 1980s, almost entirely open to the street.

The liberal atmosphere of Soho has made it a permanent fixture on the **gay scene** for much of this century: gay servicemen frequented the *Golden Lion* from the last war until the end of National Service, while a succession of gay artists found refuge here (and in neighbouring Fitzrovia) during the Fifties and Sixties. Nowadays the scene is much more upfront, with bars, clubs and cafés jostling for position on Old Compton Street, and round the corner in Wardour Street. And it doesn't stop there: there's now a gay travel agency, a gay financial adviser and, even more convenient, a gay taxi service.

Full gay and lesbian listings are to be found on p.480.

Greek Street, Frith Street and Soho Square

The streets off Old Compton Street are lined with Soho institutions old and new, starting in the east with **Greek Street**, named after the Greek church which once stood nearby. This and parallel **Frith Street** both lead north to Soho Square.

On Romilly Street, which runs between the two, just south of Old Compton Street, is one of London's landmark restaurant, *Kettner's*, founded back in the 1860s by Napoleon III's personal chef and favoured by Oscar Wilde. It's now part of the excellent *Pizza Express* chain, but the decor retains a smidgeon of faded Edwardian elegance – and a pianist in its champagne bar. Only a little younger is *Maison Bertaux* opposite, at 28 Greek St, which was founded in 1871; its windows are still piled high with patisseries, and its owners resolutely refuse to serve any type of coffee other than *café au lait*. It has more room than it looks, with a wonderful little salon upstairs.

One of Soho's nicest pubs, the old Dog and Duck Hotel, is a couple of doors up from Ronnie Scott's. For more Soho pub listings, see p.463

Close by, on Greek Street, is the *Coach and Horses*, an ordinary sort of pub that was for years lorded over by the boozy gang of writer Jeffrey Bernard, painter Francis Bacon and jazz man George Melly, as well as the *Private Eye* crew. Jazz connections are in evidence on Frith Street, too, where *Ronnie Scott's*, London's longest-running jazz club, was founded in 1958 and still pulls in the big names. Opposite is the *Bar Italia*, an Italian café with a big screen for satellite TV transmissions of Italian football games, and late-night hours that ensure its place as an espresso stop on every self-respecting clubber's itinerary. It was in this building, in pre-café days, but appropriately enough for such a media-saturated area, that John Logie Baird made the world's first public television transmission in 1926. Next door, a plaque recalls that the seven-year-old Mozart stayed here in 1763, having wowed George III and London society by performing a duet with his four-year-old sister.

Soho Square is virtually the only patch of green amid the neighbourhood's labyrinth of streets and alleys. It began life as a smart address, surrounded by the houses of the nobility and centred on an elaborate fountain topped by a statue of Charles II. Charles survives, if a little worse for wear, and stands on one of the pathways, but the fountain has made way for an octagonal, mock-Tudor garden shed, installed as a ventilation shaft for the tube. As for the buildings around the square, they are a typical Soho mix: *20th Century Fox* occupies one corner; the *Hospital for Sick Women*, close by, still serves as a health clinic; Paul McCartney has his corporate headquarters, *mpl*, in another corner; and no. 2 belongs to the literary publishers *Bloomsbury*, noted for their blockbuster, *A Princess in Love*, the kiss-and-tell memoir of Princess Di's lover. There are also two square, red-brick churches: the Italianate **St Patrick's Church**, which serves the Irish, Italian and Chinese communities, and the **French Protestant Church**, sole survivor of London's twenty-three Huguenot churches, concealed on the north side of the square.

St Barnabas is open Wed 2.30–4.15pm & Thurs 11am –12.30pm; donation requested. The nearest tube is Tottenham Court Road.

If you're finding it difficult to imagine Soho ever having been an aristocratic haunt, pay a visit to the **House of St Barnabas-in-Soho**, a Georgian mansion, just south of the square on Greek Street. Built in the 1740s, this retains some exquisite Rococo plasterwork on the main staircase and in the Council Chamber, which has a lovely view onto Soho Square. Since 1861 the building has been a Christian charity house for the destitute, so the rest of the interior is much altered and closed off. You can, however, visit the paved garden, whose plane trees inspired Dickens, and whose twisted and gnarled mulberry tree was planted by some silk-weaving Hugeunots. On the south side of the garden is a cute little Byzantine-style chapel, built for the residents and used by the Serbs during World War I.

Dean and Wardour streets

One block further west of Frith Street runs **Dean Street**, home of the *Colony Club*, the heart of the post-war bohemian drinking scene, and of the *Groucho Club*, where London's literati and media types preen themselves. Neither is especially exclusive but you need to find a member to sign you in. If your interest doesn't extend that far, there's an open-to-all bohemian landmark nearby in the form of *The French House*, at no. 49. This was just the plain old *York Minster* pub when it was bought by a Belgian, Victor Berlemont in

1914 and transformed into a French emigré haunt. It was frequented by De Gaulle and the Free French forces during the last war, and has long had a reputation for attracing artists (Salvador Dalí, among others) and writers.

Soho's once-strong Jewish presence is now confined to the modern Jewish cultural complex at 21 Dean St, housing the West London Synagogue and, on the top floor, the **Ben Uri Art Gallery**, which provides a showcase for contemporary Jewish artists and once a year (around May/June) exhibits a selection of its permanent collection. The most famous Jewish immigrant to live in Soho was **Karl Marx**, who in 1851 moved into two "evil, frightful rooms" across the street from here, on the top floor of no. 28, with his wife and maid (both of whom were pregnant by him) and four children, having been evicted from his first two addresses for failing to pay the rent. There's a plaque commemorating his stay, and the waiters at *Leoni's Quo Vadis* restaurant, the current occupants, will happily show diners round the rooms on request.

The Ben Uri Art Gallery is open Mon–Thurs 10am–5pm, Sun 2–5pm; free.

West again is **Wardour Street** – Soho's longest street, stretching from Coventry Street to Oxford Street, and a kind of dividing line between the trendier, eastern half of Soho and the muckier western zone. Its southern end is now part of Chinatown (see above); north of Shaftesbury Avenue, there's a small park laid out on what used to be **St Anne's Church**, bombed in the last war, with only its tower now standing, soon to be opened as a Soho museum. The rest of the street is largely given over to the film industry – *Warner Brothers* is based here, along with numerous smaller companies. Many of the film industry workers drink in the *Intrepid Fox* on the corner of Peter Street, a pub named after Charles James Fox, who used it as a base for his notorious 1784 election campaign, during which the beautiful Duchess of Devonshire is alleged to have offered kisses for votes.

West of Wardour Street

Despite the council's best efforts, the **vice and prostitution** rackets still have the area immediately west of Wardour Street well staked out. Straight prostitution in fact makes up a small proportion of what gets sold here (King's Cross and Mayfair are the places for that), and has been since Paul Raymond – Britain's richest man – set up his Folies-Bérgère style *Revue Bar* in the late 1950s off Brewer Street, now complemented by the transvestite floor show next door at *Madame Jo-Jo's*. These last two are paragons of virtue compared with the dodgy videos, short con outfits and rip-off joints that operate in the neighbouring streets.

From Berwick Street to Poland Street

In amongst the video shops and triple-X-rated cinemas is **Berwick Street Market**, one of the capital's finest (and cheapest) fruit and veg markets, whose barrow displays are works of art in themselves.

Soho vice

Prostitution is nothing new to Soho. Way back in the seventeenth and eighteenth centuries, prince and prole alike used to come here (and to Covent Garden) for paid sex. Several prominent courtesans were residents of Soho, their profession recorded as "player and mistress to several persons", or, lower down on the social scale, "generally slut and drunkard; occasionally whore and thief". *Hooper's Hotel*, a high-class Soho brothel which the Prince of Wales frequented, even got a mention in a popular book of the late eighteenth century, *The Mysteries of Flagellation*. By Victorian times, the area was described as "a reeking home of filthy vice" where "the grosser immorality flourishes unabashed from every age downwards to mere children". And it was in Soho that Gladstone used to conduct his crusade to save prostitutes – managing "to combine his missionary meddling with a keen appreciation of a pretty face", as one perceptive critic observed.

By World War II, organized gangs like the notorious Messina Brothers from Malta controlled a huge vice empire in Soho, later taken over by one of their erstwhile henchmen, Bernie Silver, Soho's self-styled "Godfather". In the Sixties and Seventies, the sex trade threatened to take over the whole of Soho, aided and abetted by the police themselves, who were involved in a massive protection racket. The complicity between the gangs and the police was finally exposed in 1976, when ten top-ranking Scotland Yard officers were charged with taking bribes and corruption on a massive scale and sentenced to prison for up to twelve years (Silver himself was put inside in 1974). Since then, the combined efforts of the Soho Society and, more recently, Westminster Council, have reduced the number of sex establishments. Soho's vice days are by no means over – the sex shops and peep shows still dominate large parts of the neighbourhood – but they are well down on their all-time high of the mid-1970s.

See p.521 for a full guide to London's record stores.

On either side of the marketholders are some of London's best specialist pop record shops: *Selectadisc* and *Sister Ray* cater for the indie crowd, *Daddy Kool* supplies reggae and rap deejays, while *Reckless Records* trade in second-hand rock, soul and jazz.

The market stops at the crossroads with Broadwick Street, which features a replica of the waterpump which caused the deaths of some five hundred Soho residents in the **cholera epidemic** of 1854. Doctor John Snow traced the outbreak to the pump, thereby proving that the disease was waterborne rather than airborne as previously thought. No one believed him, however, until he removed the pump handle and effectively stopped the epidemic. The original pump stood outside the pub now called the *John Snow*, beside which there's a plaque and a red granite kerbstone as further commemoration.

This part of Soho has its fair share of **artistic associations** too. It was on Broadwick Street that William Blake was born in 1757, above his father's hosiery shop, and where from the age of nine he had visions of "messengers from heaven, daily and nightly". He opened a print shop of his own next door to the family home, and later moved to nearby Poland Street, where he lived six years with his "beloved Kate" and wrote perhaps his most profound work, *The Marriage of Heaven and Hell*, among other poems. Poland Street was also Shelley's first halt after having been kicked out of Oxford in 1811 for distributing *The Necessity of Atheism*, while Canaletto ran a studio on Beak Street for a couple of years, as he sat out the Seven Years' War in exile in London.

Carnaby Street and around

Until the 1950s, **Carnaby Street** was a backstreet on Soho's western fringe, occupied, for the most part, by sweat-shop tailors who used to make up the suits for Savile Row. Then, sometime in the mid-1950s, Bill Green opened a shop called *Vince* selling outrageous clothes for the gay men who were hanging out at the local baths. He was followed by John Stephen, a Glaswegian grocer's son, who, within a couple of years, owned a string of trendy boutiques which catered for the new market for flamboyant men's clothing. By 1964 – the year of the offical birth of the Carnaby Street myth – Mods, West Indian Rude Boys and other "switched-on people", as the *Daily Telegraph* noted, began to hang out in Carnaby Street, which became the epicentre of Swinging Sixties' London, and its street sign London's most popular postcard.

A victim of its own hype, Carnaby Street quickly declined into an avenue of overpriced tack, and so it remained for the next twenty odd years. Despite a recent facelift, it remains pretty tacky, lined with cheap leather and jeans shops. The streets feeding into and parallel to it, however, are beginning to show signs of improvement. *Muji*, the Japanese no-label store, has moved onto the top end of Carnaby Street itself, Foubert's Place is bristling with new shops, and **Newburgh Street** has become a showcase for some of the wilder spirits of London fashion: *John Richmond*, *Helen Storey* and the outrageously sexy *Pam Hogg* are the main players.

For fashion listings, see p.509

Fitzrovia

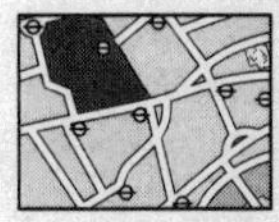

Bounded by Gower Street to the east, Great Portland Street to the west and the shabby eastern half of Oxford Street to the south, **Fitzrovia** is a northern extension of Soho. Like Soho, it has a raffish, cosmopolitan reputation, and has attracted its fair share of writers and bohemians over the last hundred years or so, including the Pre-Raphaelites and members of the Bloomsbury Group (for more on whom, see p.152). That said, there's a lot less going on here than in Soho and just two real sights – the Victorian church on Margaret Street and Pollock's Toy Museum – now that the landmark Post Office Tower is closed to the public.

The best tube to start a tour of Fitzrovia is Goodge Street.

All Saints, Margaret Street

Few London churches are as atmospheric as **All Saints**, built by William Butterfield in the 1850s two blocks north of Oxford Street on Margaret Street. Patterned brickwork characterizes the entire ensemble of clergy house, choir school (Laurence Olivier sang here as a boy) and church, set around a small court that's entered from the street through a pointed arch. The interior, one of London's gloomiest, is best visited on a sunny afternoon when the light pours in through the west window, illuminating the fantastic variety of coloured marble and stone which decorates the place from floor to ceiling. Several of the walls are also adorned with Pre-Raphaelite Minton tile paintings, the east window is a quasi-Byzantine iconostasis with saintly images nestling in gilded niches, and the elaborate pulpit is like the entire church in miniature.

Surrounded by such iconographical clutter, you would be forgiven for thinking you were in a Catholic church – but then that was the whole idea of the High Church movement, which sought to re-Catholicize the Church of England, without actually returning it to the Roman fold.

Charlotte Street

Charlotte Street's Greek restaurants are reviewed on p.437.

After All Saints, the place to head for in Fitzrovia is **Charlotte Street**, where inexpensive Greek-Cypriot restaurants compete for space with some very designer-conscious French places. Two restaurants here trade on their literary associations: *The White Tower*, where Wyndham Lewis and Ezra Pound launched the Vorticist magazine *Blast*; and *L'Etoile*, which the likes of Dylan Thomas and T. S. Eliot used to patronize. The same crowd used to get plastered in the nearby *Fitzroy Tavern* – from which the area got its sobriquet in the 1930s – along with rather more outrageous bohemians, like the hard-drinking Nina Hamnett, the self-styled "Queen of Bohemia", who used to boast that Modigliani once told her she had the best tits in Europe.

The Toy Museum is open Mon–Sat 10am–5pm; £2.

One block east, on Scala Street, is **Pollock's Toy Museum**, housed above a toyshop. Its collections include a fine example of the Victorian paper theatres popularized by Benjamin Pollock, who sold them under the slogan "a penny plain, twopence coloured". The other exhibits range from vintage teddy bears to rod and glove puppets, Red Army soldiers to wax dolls, filling every nook and cranny of the museum's six tiny, rickety rooms. There are occasionally Pollock Theatre performances in the basement; if you're seriously interested, it's best to ring ahead.

Exploring Fitzrovia, it's impossible to ignore the looming presence of the **Post Office Tower** (these days the privatized British Telecom Tower), a glass-clad pylon designed in the early 1960s by a team of bureaucrats in the Ministry of Works, one block west of Fitzroy Street, the extension of Charlotte Street. It was the city's tallest building until the NatWest Tower topped it in 1981, and is still one of the most obvious landmarks north of the river. Sadly, following an anonymous bomb attack in 1971, the tower and its revolving restaurant have been closed to the public.

Fitzroy Square and around

At the top of Fitzroy Street is **Fitzroy Square**, the only formal square in Fitzrovia, begun by the Adam brothers in the 1790s and faced, unusually, with light Portland Stone rather than the ubiquitous dark Georgian brickwork. Traffic has recently been excluded, but few pedestrians come here either, leaving the place pretty much deserted. It's a square with both Bloomsbury and Soho associations. Virginia Woolf's blue plaque is here: her Bloomsbury chums considered it a disreputable neighbourhood but she moved here with her brother in 1907, after taking the precaution of checking with the police. It had enjoyed an even dodgier reputation in the 1890s when the square was home to the International Anarchist School for children run by sixty-year old French anarchist, Louise Michel. The police eventually raided the building and closed down the school after finding bombs hidden in the basement.

The nearest tube is Warren Street.

For more on the Bloomsbury Group, see p.152.

Fitzrovia's radical pedigree has a further presence in **Marie Stopes House** (now renamed the *Well Woman Clinic*) on nearby Whitfield Street, originally opened as the pioneering *Mother's Clinic for Constructive Birth Control* in 1921 and kept functioning in the face of numerous legal battles. A qualified palaeobotanist, Stopes courted controversy by advocating birth control as an aid to women's sexual pleasure, after her first marriage failed to be consummated in five years. However, her espousal of eugenics – she was keen to reduce the size of working-class families in order to improve the nation's stock and even invented her own cervical cap called "Pro-racial" – has left a cloud over her reputation.

Tottenham Court Road

For the record, it's been centuries since there was a stately mansion – the original Tottenham Court – at the end of **Tottenham Court Road**, which now makes a strong challenge for London's least prepossessing street. A rash of shops at the southern end flogging discount-priced stereos, CD players, computers and all sorts of electrical equipment has pushed out the furniture makers, the street's original vendors, though a few shops – notably *Habitat* and the old-fashioned *Heal's* – survive at its northern end. The London listings magazine, *Time Out*, has its new base here, too, after years of residence in Covent Garden.

Unless you're desperate for a Sega Megadrive or a pine bed base, however, you won't lose much by giving this whole street a miss.

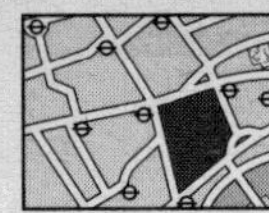

Covent Garden

Covent Garden has come full circle: what started out in the seventeenth century as London's first luxury neighbourhood is once more a highly desirable place to live, work and shop. Based around Inigo Jones' piazza – London's oldest planned square – the area had for years been a market centre for fruit and vegetables. But that closed in 1974 and for a while it looked as if the developers would move in on this prime central real estate and demolish it all for unwanted new office blocks. As luck would have it, these plans collapsed and, instead, the elegant old market hall and its environs were restored to house shops, restaurants and arty-crafty stalls.

Covent Garden tube takes you to the heart of the area. Leicester Square is also close by.

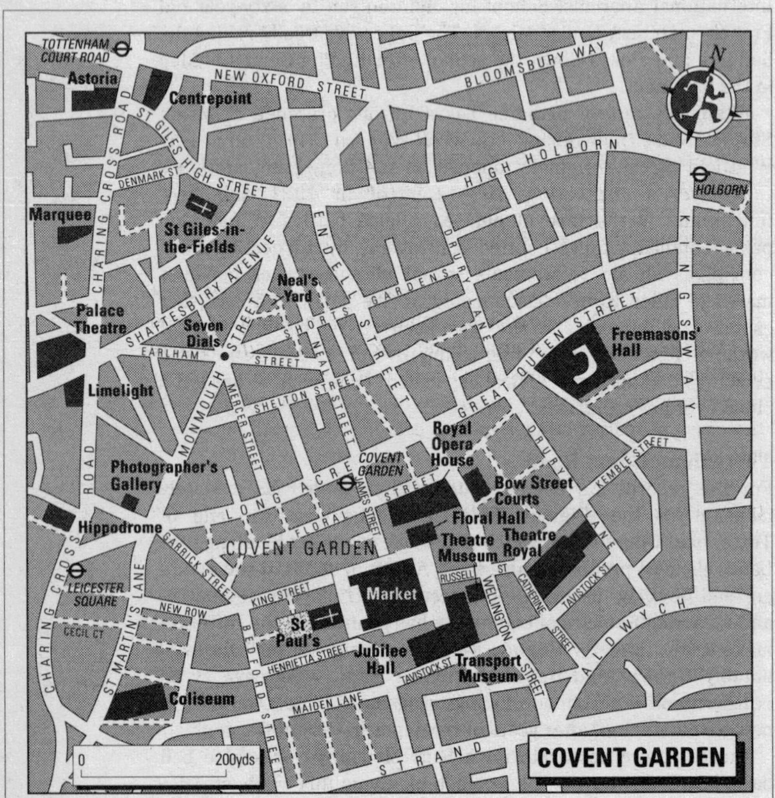

Boosted by buskers and street entertainers, it has become one of London's major tourist attractions, prompting in its wake a wholesale gentrification of the streets to the north of the market, which now boast some of the trendiest clothes shops, cafés and restaurants in London. Alongside them – and saving the area from being too twee and over-commercial – are a few odd pockets of mid-70s "alternative" culture, which established itself here, in squats and cheap rentals, when the whole area was threatened with destruction. London's tourism revenues owe them a considerable debt – it was only their demonstrations, and mass squats, that saved the area.

The intervening three hundred and fifty years had been rather less salubrious – if perhaps a lot more fun – but little or no trace of those bacchanalian days survive in the pricey bars and cafés around the piazza. The most enduring feature of Covent Garden has been its theatres and, of course, the internationally famous Royal Opera House, or "The Garden" as it's known amongst the cogniscenti.

The Piazza

Covent Garden's **Piazza** was laid out in the 1630s, when the Earl of Bedford commissioned Inigo Jones to design a series of graceful Palladian-style arcades, based on the main square in Livorno, where Jones had helped build the cathedral. Initially the development was a great success, its novelty value alone attracting a rich and aristocratic clientele, but over the next century the tone of the place fell as the fruit and vegetable market, set up in the Earl's back garden, expanded, and theatres and coffeehouses began to take over the peripheral buildings. Macaulay evoked the following scene: "fruit women screamed, carters fought, cabbage stalks and rotten apples accumulated in heaps at the thresholds of the Countess of Berkshire and the Bishop of Durham".

By the early eighteenth century the area was known as "the great square of Venus", with dozens of gambling dens, bawdy houses and so-called *bagnios* in and around the piazza. Some *bagnios* were plain Turkish baths but most doubled as brothels, where courtesans would stand in the window and, according to one contemporary, "in the most impudent manner invited passengers from the theatres into the houses".

Some of London's most famous coffee houses were concentrated here, too, attracting writers such as Sheridan, Dryden and Aphra Behn. The rich and famous frequented places like the *Shakespeare's Head*, whose cook made the best turtle soup in town, and whose head waiter, John Harris, even produced a kind of "Who's Who of Whores", revised annually. London's great man of letters, Samuel Johnson, and his future biographer, James Boswell, bumped into one another by chance at *Davies's* bookshop on Russell Street in 1763. Boswell thought Johnson "very slovenly and most uncouth", but resolved to "mark what I remember of his conversation", which is precisely what he did for the next twenty years, thus compiling the material for his famous *Life of Johnson*.

Russell Street, which leads east from the piazza, was one of the most notorious streets in Covent Garden, and housed the infamous *Rose Tavern*, immortalized in a scene from Hogarth's *Rake's Progress*. It was one of the oldest brothels in Covent Garden – Pepys mentions "frigging with Doll Lane" at the *Rose* in his diary of 1667 – and specialized in "Posture Molls", who engaged in flagellation and strip-tease, and were deemed a cut above the average whore. Food at the *Rose* was apparently excellent, too, and despite the frequent brawls, men of all classes from royalty to ruffians made their way there.

The piazza's status as a centre of entertainment declined with the approach of the nineteenth century. The theatres still drew crowds but the market now occupied most of the area, and the few remaining taverns had become dangerous. In the 1830s the piazza was cleaned up, slums were torn down and a proper market hall built in Greek Revival style. A glass roof was added in the late Victorian era, but otherwise the building stayed unaltered until the closure of the market in 1974, when trade moved to Nine Elms in Vauxhall, and its early 1980s renovation as a shopping arcade.

St Paul's

Of Jones' original piazza, the only remaining parts are a tiny section of north-side arcading (rebuilt by the Victorians) and the church of **St Paul's**, facing the west side of the market building. In a now famous exchange, the Earl of Bedford told Jones to make St Paul's no fancier than a barn, to which the architect replied, "Sire, you shall have the handsomest barn in England". The proximity of so many theatres has made it known as the "Actors' Church", and it's filled with memorials to international thespians from Boris Karloff to Gracie Fields.

The space in front of the church's Tuscan portico – where Eliza Doolittle was discovered selling violets by Henry Higgins in Shaw's *Pygmalion* – is now a legalized venue for buskers and street performers, who must audition for a slot months in advance. Despite the vetting, the standard of the acts varies enormously, though comedy is the ultimate aim.

The piazza's history of entertainment actually goes back to May 1662, when the first recorded performance of Punch and Judy in England was staged by Italian puppeteer, Pietro Gimonde, and witnessed by Pepys. This historic event is now commemorated every second Sunday in May by a **Punch and Judy Festival**, held in the churchyard, in which numerous booths compete for audiences in the overgrown churchyard; for the rest of the year the churchyard provides a tranquil respite from the activity outside (access is from either King Street or Henrietta Street).

The Piazza's markets and shops

The market stalls in the Piazza are a victim of their own success, with a captive tourist market all too likely to pick up novelties and "craft" items. However, among the back massage tools, the jokey duvet cases, and the ceramic flying nuns, there are always a few worthwhile stalls – even the odd clothing designer (knitwear, especially) with imagination and style. And stallholders alternate, often operating on only one or two days, so if you come more than once, you may find a different scene.

Covent Garden

The market stalls are open 10am–7pm daily, later in summer.

There are in fact three separate market areas: the "Apple Market", inside the old market building; the Opera House market, on your left coming from Covent Garden tube station; and the tackier Jubilee Hall market, on the far side of the piazza. The first two specialize in arts and crafts, the latter in clothes, though all three are given over largely to antiques on Mondays.

As for the shops in the Piazza complex, increased rents have edged out many of the odder and more interesting outlets of the early days, in favour of blander fare, including a number of chain stores – exactly the reverse of the original development plans. A couple of more interesting, smaller outlets, in keeping with the idea of the place, are the *Museum Shop*, which stocks goods and reproductions from museums across Europe and America, and *Mullins and Westley*, a snuff and tobacco parlour, with its own brands and mighty selections of Cuban cigars.

The London Transport Museum

The London Transport Museum is open daily 10am–6pm; £3.95.

An original flower-market shed on the piazza's east side is now occupied by the **London Transport Museum**, which re-opened in 1993 after a lengthy refurbishment. A herd of old buses, trains and trams make up the bulk of the exhibits, though there's enough interactive fun – touch-screen computers, videos and so forth – to keep most children amused. The layout is pretty confusing, but the museum's survey begins with the 1820s, when the Thames was finally abandoned as the city's main thoroughfare.

The "oldest" exhibit (it's actually a reconstruction) is the 1829 *Shillibeer* Horse Omnibus, which provided the city's first regular (albeit unsuccessful) horse bus service. Despite having the oldest underground system in the world, begun in 1863, London was still heavily reliant on horse power at the turn of the century – 50,000 animals worked in the transport system, producing 1000 tonnes of dung a day. You can clamber aboard several of the electric trams on display here, which, by the 1930s, formed part of the largest electric tram system in the world. By 1952 the whole network had been dismantled; trolleybuses bit the dust in the following decade.

The contemporary section quite rightly rails against recent government policy: some 50,000 people are killed or injured on the roads each year, while the average speed of traffic through central London has now slowed to just 8mph, and the public transport system has been allowed to run down.

London Transport's stylish maps and posters, many commissioned from well-known artists, are now displayed in their very own gallery, and you can buy reproductions, plus countless other LT paraphernalia, at the shop on the way out.

The Theatre and Mechanical Theatre museums

The Theatre Museum is open Tues–Sun 11am–7pm; £3.

The rest of the old flower market now houses the **Theatre Museum**, displaying three centuries of memorabilia from every conceivable area of the performing arts in the West (the entrance is on Russell Street) The corridors of glass cases cluttered with props, programmes and costumes are not especially exciting, and the portrait collection is dull – far better to head for the **study room**, which is flanked by pull-out panels of engravings, photographs and letters. Among the hundreds of papers are a cable from Sarah Bernhardt cheerfully announcing the imminent amputation of her leg; eighteenth-century cartoons, including one of an overcrowded theatre, a chaos of fainting, vomiting and discarded clothing; and Victorian advertisements for "dog dramas", melodramas with canine heroes.

In addition to the permanent exhibits, two special areas host long-term temporary shows – "Slap", a history of stage make-up, is a lot of fun, with videos of the creation of Lloyd Webber's *Phantom of the Opera* and a make-up artist on hand to give you a hideous bullet wound or scar. As well as offering a **booking service** for West End shows and an unusually good selection of cards and posters, the museum is also a resource centre, with a theatre hosting performances, lectures and debates.

The Cabaret Mechanical Theatre is open summer Mon–Sat 10am–7pm, Sun 11am–7pm; winter closes 6.30pm; £1.75.

Not strictly a museum, but more than just a shop, the **Cabaret Mechanical Theatre** on the lower floor of the market building, is a quirky permanent collection of fifty-odd, eccentric inventions, handmade gadgets and witty automata, many of which are for sale. Jokes, from the slapstick to the erudite, are plentiful and the devices within the museum function at the touch of a button.

Bow Street

The area's high crime rate was no doubt the reason behind the opening of a new magistrates office in **Bow Street** in 1748. The first two magistrates were Henry Fielding, author of *Tom Jones*, and his blind half-brother John – nicknamed the "Blind Beak" – who seem to have been exceptional in their honesty and the infrequency with which they accepted bribes (the only income a magistrate could rely on). Finding "lewd women enough to fill a mighty colony", Fielding also set about creating the city's first police force, known as the **Bow Street Runners**. Never numbering more than a dozen, they were employed primarily to combat prostitution, and they continued to exist a good ten years after the establishment of the uniformed Metropolitian Police in 1829. Before it was finally closed in 1989, Bow Street police station had the honour of incarcerating Oscar Wilde after he was arrested for "commiting indecent acts" in 1895 – he was eventually sentenced to two years' hard labour. And in 1928,

Radclyffe Hall's lesbian novel, *Well of Loneliness*, was deemed obscene by magistrates at Bow Street and remained banned in this country until 1949.

The Royal Opera House

The Corinthian portico of the **Royal Opera House** stands opposite Bow Street magistrates court. First built as the *Covent Garden Theatre* in 1732, in a backstreet behind a fruit and veg market, it witnessed premières of Goldsmith's *She Stoops to Conquer* and Sheridan's *The Rivals* before being destroyed by fire in 1809. To offset the cost of building the new theatre, ticket prices were increased; riots ensued for 61 consecutive performances until the manager finally backed down. However, it was only after *Her Majesty's* on Haymarket burned down in 1847 that the venue became the city's main opera house; royal patronage ensured its success, and since the last war it has been home to both the Royal Ballet and Royal Opera.

For details of Opera tickets, see p.489.

Theatre Royal, Drury Lane

One block east of Bow Street runs **Drury Lane**, nothing to write home about in its present condition, but a permanent fixture in London's theatrical and social life since the time of Charles II, when the first **Theatre Royal** was built in 1663. (The current one dates from 1812 and faces onto Catherine Street). It was here that women were first permitted to appear on stage in England (their parts having previously been played by boys), but critics were sceptical about their abilities to portray their own gender, and thought their profession little better than prostitution – and indeed, most had to work at both to make ends meet (as the actress said to the bishop). The women who sold oranges to the audience were even less virtuous, **Nell Gwynne** being the most famous, though she also trod the boards in comic roles. Eventually she became Charles II's mistress, the first in a long line of Drury Lane actresses who made it into royal beds. Sarah Siddons' success brought a degree of respectability to the female acting profession for the first time; the majority of eighteenth-century actresses, however, were more in the vein of Nancy Dawson, who "danced the jigg to smutty songs" here.

It was at the *Theatre Royal* that **David Garrick**, as actor, manager and part-owner from 1747, revolutionized the English theatre. Garrick treated his texts with a great deal more reverence than had been customary, insisting on rehearsals and cutting down on improvisations. The rich and privileged, who had previously occupied seats on the stage itself, were confined to the auditorium, and the practice of refunding those who wished to leave at the first interval was stopped. However, an attempt to prevent half-price tickets being sold at the beginning of the third act provoked a riot by disgruntled punters and was eventually withdrawn. Despite Garrick's reforms, the theatre remained a boisterous and often dangerous place of entertainment: George II and George III both narrowly escaped attempts on their lives whilst in the *Theatre Royal*, and the orchestra often had good cause to be grateful for the cage under which they were forced to play.

The building is soon to undergo a £55 million development (due to be completed in 1996), which will affect the whole of the northeast side of the square: the green wrought-iron Floral Hall on the piazza will become the main entrance. Funds permitting, there are further plans for Inigo Jones' arcade and loggia to be rebuilt from James Street eastwards, and – controversially – for the Georgian terrace on the north side of Russell Street to be demolished to make way for an office block. A long-standing mural proclaims local opposition.

Floral Street, Long Acre and Neal Street

The area to the north of Covent Garden piazza is, on the whole, more interesting in terms of its shops, pubs and eating places than the market place. Floral Street, Long Acre, Shelton Street and especially Neal Street are all good shopping locales.

Floral Street, Long Acre and the Masonic Temple

The western half of **Floral Street** is dominated by top-selling British designer Paul Smith, who runs three adjoining shops, with outposts for jeans and workwear – marketed as *R. Newbold* – on adjoining Langley Court. Keeping him company are branches of *Nicole Farhi* and *Jones*, the ultimate fashion-victim bazaar, plus a few quirkier outlets, like a shop dedicated purely to Tintin, the boy detective.

Long Acre, parallel to Floral Street, was Covent Garden's main shopping street long before the market was converted into a glorified shopping mall, though it originally specialized in coach manufacture. Nowadays, it is dominated by branches of the main clothing chains, continental-style cafés and bistros, but there are some survivors of earlier times – notably *Flip*, a second-hand American clothes store which was among the Covent Garden pioneers, and *Stanford's*, the world's oldest and largest map shop.

Free guided tours of the Freemasons' Hall Mon–Fri 11am & 4pm.

Looking east down the gentle curve of Long Acre, it's difficult to miss the austere, pharaonic mass of the **Freemasons' Hall**, built as a memorial to all the masons who died in World War I. Whatever you may think of this reactionary, male-only secretive organization, which enjoys a virtual stranglehold over institutions like the police and judiciary, the interior is worth a peek for its pompous, bombastic decor, laden with heavy symbolism. Under pressure from the media, the Freemasons recently decided to become more open in their activities and since 1993 have offered tours. The Masonically- curious might also take a look at the shops opposite the temple which sell Mason merchandise: aprons, rings, and all the essential accoutrements and souvenirs of the art.

Neal Street and Seven Dials

North from Long Acre runs **Neal Street**, currently the most sought-after commercial address in Covent Garden, and featuring some fine Victorian warehouses, complete with stair towers for loading and shifting goods between floors. The Neal Street landlords have attempted to discriminate in their leases, favouring single theme shops like *The Kite Shop* and *The Bead Shop*, *Neal Street East*, an Oriental goods emporium, and trendy fashion stores like *Red or Dead*, *Michiko Koshino* and *Christopher New*.

A decade ago, the feel of the street was a lot less monied and more alternative, but that ambience only really survives in *Food for Thought*, the veggie café that's been here since 1971, *The Ecology Centre*, one block east on Shelton Street, which showcases green technology and includes an art gallery and café, and **Neal's Yard**, a wholefood haven set in a tiny little courtyard off Shorts Gardens, prettily festooned with flower boxes and ivy. Here, you'll find the excellent Neal's Yard co-op bakery, several vegetarian cafés and take-away outlets, a superb cheese shop, a herbalist, and even a bit of therapy. The complex was set up in the early 1970s by Nick Saunders, one of the leading lights of "alternative London" and the rescue of Covent Garden, and is endowed with a splendid water clock (above the *Neal's Yard Wholefood Warehouse*), which gave the unwary a soaking on the hour, every hour, until the staff, tired of the joke, put up a canopy.

Still, there's enough in and around Neal's Yard to divert most visitors. Skateboarders pick their way through the wholefood to get to *Slam City Skates*, one of a number of cult shops in the area whose popularity is impenetrable to outsiders – its shop front "tagged" to death, its basement home to *Rough Trade* records, haven of obscure indie produce. Fruitcakes flock to *The Astrology Shop* on Neal Street and *Mysteries* round the corner on Monmouth Street, while boys (rarely girls) who haven't grown up head for *Comic Showcase* at the top of Neal Street. Coffee addicts have a treat in store, too, in *Monmouth Street Coffee Shop*, another Saunders initiative, which roasts on the premises.

Specialist and oddball shops are reviewed on p.517.

Inevitably, amid all this innovative consumerism, there are one or two blemishes: the new **Thomas Neal Centre**, a sanitized shopping mall that resounds to musak, and the **Comyn Ching Triangle**, an old ironmongers' yard hidden off Shelton Street, which postmodern architect Terry Farrell has converted into a totally useless piece of public space.

West of Neal Street is **Seven Dials**, the meeting point of seven streets which make up a little circus centred on a slender column topped by six tiny blue sundials (the seventh dial is formed by the column itself and the surrounding road). The column has had a chequered history: erected in 1693, it was torn down in 1773 when a rumour went about that treasure was hidden beneath it; it was re-erected in Weybridge fifty years later, and a replica was placed here in 1988, only to be obscured by advertising hoardings, supposedly raising money for a renovation that was completed in 1994.

Earlham Street, which runs from Seven Dials into Charing Cross Road, was once a flourishing market street, though only a handful of stalls remain. They include, however, one of London's very best cut flower stalls – a visual treat at any time of year.

St Giles

> *"Women with scarcely the articles of apparel which common decency requires, with forms bloated by disease, and faces rendered hideous by habitual drunkenness – men reeling and staggering along – children in rags and filth – whole streets of squalid and miserable appearance whose inhabitants are lounging in the public road, fighting, screaming and swearing . . . ".*

Thus Dickens described the old **St Giles rookery**, the predominantly Irish slum area, north of Covent Garden, which, less than a hundred years earlier, had provided the setting for Hogarth's *Gin Lane*. Even at its height, St Giles was by no means the most dangerous slum in London – parts of the East End were far worse. But it was the rookery's position at the heart of the West End that scared the daylights out of wealthy Londoners. Here were ten to twelve acres of densely populated hovels which provided "a convenient asylum for the offscourings of the night-world" – Dickens again. Even after the establishment of the police, few officers could expect to emerge from the maze of brothels and gin shops unscathed; on one occasion a foolhardy evangelist was ejected from the slums stripped and bound, his mouth stuffed with powdered mustard.

In the end, the wide new roads of the Metropolitan Board of Works did what no police force or charity organization could manage, by "shovelling out the poor" as one critic put it. Virtually the only reminder is the early eighteenth-century church of **St Giles-in-the-Fields**, on the south side of the old St Giles High Street; the rest of the slums were demolished to make way for New Oxford Street and the busy interchange of Shaftesbury Avenue, High Holborn and St Giles High Street at the top of Neal Street.

At the eastern end of the old high street is St Giles Circus, now a godforsaken spot skewered by the hideous skyscraper called **Centrepoint**. Designed by Richard Seifert (who was also responsible for the NatWest Tower on Bishopsgate), it was built by property tycoon Harry Hyams who kept it famously empty for more than a decade, a profit-making venture whose cynicism transcended even the London norms of the time. Plans to add lifts to the side of the building and turn the top floor into a viewing platform have been thwarted by the tower's recently acquired status as a listed building.

Chapter 4

Bloomsbury

Bloomsbury gets its name from the medieval landowners, the Blemunds, who were probably given the estate – described in the *Domesday Book* as having vineyards and "wood for 100 pigs" – by William the Conqueror. Nothing was built here, though, until, in the 1660s, the Earl of Southampton laid out Bloomsbury Square , which John Evelyn thought "a noble square or piazza – a little towne". Through marriage, the Russell family, the earls and later dukes of Bedford, acquired much of the area, and established the many formal, bourgeois squares which are the main distinguishing feature of Bloomsbury. The Russells named the grid-plan streets after their various titles and estates, and kept the pubs and shops to a minimum to maintain the tone of the neighbourhood.

This century, Bloomsbury acquired a reputation as the city's most learned quarter, dominated by the dual institutions of the British Museum and London University, home to many of the London's chief book publishers, but perhaps best known for its literary inhabitants. Today, the **British Museum** is clearly the star attraction – it takes up half the chapter, and could occupy you for several days or more – but there are other sights, such as the **Dickens Museum**, that are high on many people's itineraries.

In its northern fringes, the character of the area changes dramatically, becoming steadily more seedy as you near the two big mainline train stations of **Euston** and **King's Cross**, where cheap B&Bs and run-down council estates provide fertile territory for prostitutes and drug dealers.

The British Museum

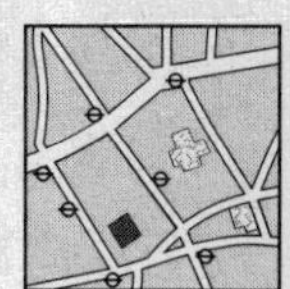

The **British Museum** is one of the great museums of the world and, after Blackpool Beach, is Britain's most popular tourist attraction (5.8m visitors a year). With over four million exhibits – a number increasing daily with the stream of new acquisitions, discoveries and bequests – ranged over two and a half miles of galleries, this is one of the largest and most comprehensive collections of antiquities,

The British Museum

The area south of the BM is good for bookshops, cafés and pubs. The museum's own café isn't up to much.

prints, drawings and books to be housed under one roof. Its collection of Roman and Greek art is unparalleled, its Egyptian collection is the most significant outside Egypt, and, in addition, there are fabulous treasures from Anglo-Saxon and Roman Britain, from China, Japan, India and Mesopotamia – not to mention an enormous collection of prints and drawings, only a fraction of which can be displayed at any one time.

The origins of the BM (as regular users call it) lie in the collection of over 80,000 curios – from plants and fossils to coins and medals – belonging to Sir Hans Sloane, a wealthy Chelsea doctor who bequeathed them in 1753, in return for £20,000. His collection

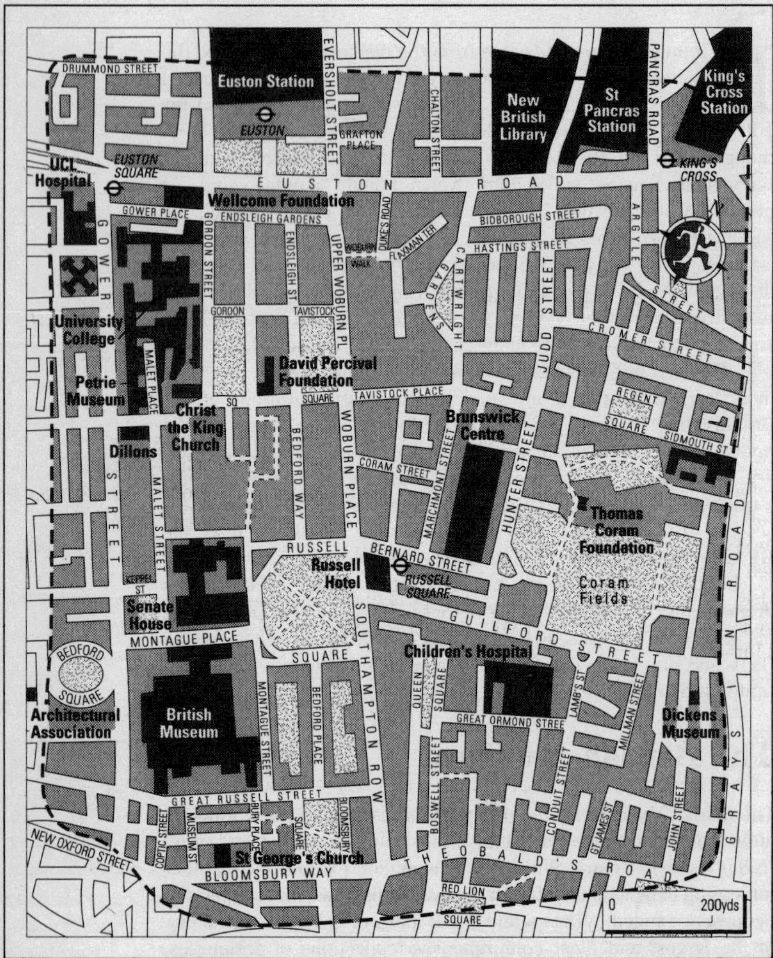

was purchased by an unenthusiastic government to form the kernel of the world's first public museum, housed in a building bought with the proceeds of a dubiously conducted public lottery. Soon afterwards the BM began to acquire the antiquities which have given it a modern reputation as the world's largest museum of stolen goods. The "robberies" of Lord Elgin are only the best known; countless others engaged in sporadic looting throughout the Empire – the Napoleonic Wars provided the victorious Brits with heaps of antiquities pilfered by the French in Egypt and the BM itself sent out its own archeologists to strip Classical sites bare.

As early as 1820 it was clear that more space was needed for all this loot, hence the present structure, built piecemeal over the course of the next thirty years. The overall design was by Sir Robert Smirke, whose giant Ionian colonnade and portico, complete with a pediment frieze, make this the grandest of London's Greek Revival buildings. Lack of space has, however, continued to be a problem: the natural history collections were transferred to South Kensington in the 1880s (p.285), the ethnographical department was rehoused near Piccadilly to become the Museum of Mankind (see p.101), and the British Library will eventually move to new premises when the long-awaited building at St Pancras is completed (p.158). There are also £100 million redevelopment plans afoot to bring the ethnographical department back to the BM, and to open up Smirke's Great Court around the central Reading Room of the British Library, which will feature a glass roof designed by Norman Foster.

Visiting the British Museum

The British Museum is open Mon–Sat 10am–5pm, Sun 2.30–6pm; free. The nearest tube is Tottenham Court Road.

The BM's fourteen-acre site is enough to tire even the most ardent museum lover. J. B. Priestley, for one, wished "there was a little room somewhere in the British Museum that contained only about twenty exhibits and good lighting, easy chairs, and a notice imploring you to smoke". Short of such a place, the best advice is either to see the highlights (see the box below) and leave the rest for another visit, or to concentrate on one or two sections. Alternatively, you might consider one of the BM's **guided tours** (Mon–Sat 10.30am, 11am, 1.30pm & 2pm, Sun 3, 3.20 & 3.45pm; £6), which cover the highlights in around one and a half hours.

There are **two entrances** (both have cloakrooms): the main one, on Great Russell Street, brings you to the information desk and bookshop, while the smaller doorway on the north side of the building in Montague Place opens onto the Oriental galleries. The information desk will furnish you with a free museum plan, and the noticeboard close by announces which rooms are currently closed. Even equipped with a plan, it's easy enough to get confused – the room numbering is complicated and many sections are spread over more than one floor. It can get crowded, too, and if you're heading for the major sights, try to get here as early in the day as possible, and avoid the weekends if you can, when the popular galleries are overrun. It's a far cry from the museum's beginnings in 1759 when it was open for just three hours a day, entry was by written application only, and tickets for "any person of decent appearance" were limited to ten per hour.

Temporary displays and exhibitions

Because of the sheer volume of the BM's hoard of **prints and drawings**, everything from Botticelli to Bonnard, there is only space for temporary exhibitions in room 90, which change every three to four months. The same is true of the BM's collection of 500,000 **coins and medals**, of which only a fraction can be shown at any one time in room 69a. The sensitive materials used in Japanese art mean that the **Japanese Galleries** in rooms 91 to 94 also host only temporary shows. And finally, the BM puts on regular **temporary exhibitions** (Tutankhamun was the most famous) on a wide range of themes in rooms 27 and 28, for which there is usually an entrance charge.

Greek and Roman antiquities

Greek and Roman antiquities make up the largest section in the museum, spread over three floors. The ground floor (rooms 1–15) is laid out along broadly chronological lines, starting with the

Where to Find What in the British Museum

This check list gives the floor and room numbers of the main permanent exhibitions:

Books and manuscripts – *Ground floor 29–32*
Coins and medals – *First floor 69a*
Egyptian antiquities – *Ground floor 25, First floor 60–66*
Greek and Roman antiquities – *Ground floor 1–15, Basement 77–89, First floor* 68–73
Medieval, Renaissance and Modern collections – *First floor 41–50*
Oriental collections – *Ground floor 33–34, First floor 91–94*
Prehistoric and Romano-British collections – *First floor 36–40*
Prints and drawings – *First floor 90*
Western Asiatic antiquities – *Ground floor 16–26, Basement 88 & 89, First floor 51–59*

This check list gives the floor and room number of the museum's most popular items:

Elgin Marbles *Ground floor 8*
Egyptian mummies *First floor 60, 61*
Lewis chessmen *First floor 42*
Lindisfarne Gospels *Ground floor 30a*
Oxus Treasure *First floor 51*
Portland Vase *First floor 70*
Rosetta Stone *Ground floor 25*
Sutton Hoo treasure *First floor 41*
Lindow Man *First floor 37*

Bronze Age and finishing up in late Roman times; highlights include the Elgin Marbles and the Nereid Monument. The basement (rooms 77–85) houses the chaotic Townley collection, while the first floor (rooms 68–73) houses generally less spectacular finds, the exception being the Portland Vase.

From Prehistoric to Classical Greece

Rooms 1 and 2

From the foyer, pass through the bookshop, ignore the alluring Assyrian sculpture to your right, and enter through the twin half-columns taken from one of the bee-hive tombs at Mycenae. Room 1 kicks off with Cycladic figures, from the Aegean islands, whose significance is still disputed, while room 2 contains Minoan artefacts (mainly from Knossos on Crete), the Aegina treasure of gold jewellery, and a small selection of Mycenaean finds.

Greek vases

The BM boasts an exhausting array of **Greek vases**, starting with the Geometric and early pictorial-style period (ninth and eight century BC) in room 2, and moving on through the unusual Corinthian hybrid-animal vases to more familiar Athenian black-figure vases of the Archaic period (seventh and sixth century BC) in room 3, and the later red-figured vases from Greece's Classical age (fifth century BC) in rooms 4 and 5. There are further hoards of early Greek vases in the basement of room 3 and later, mostly red-figure ones in room 9 and the mezzanine room 11, not to mention the various examples dotted about rooms 68–73 on the first floor.

The Harpy Tomb, Bassae sculpture and Nereid Monument

Room 5

From room 5 onwards, the real highlights of the Classical section begin, starting with the marble relief from the **Harpy Tomb**, a huge imposing funerary pillar from Xanthos, which originally rose to a height of nearly 30ft. Its name derives from the pairs of strange bird-women which appear on two sides of the relief, carrying children in their arms.

Room 6

In the purpose-built mezzanine room 6 is the fifth-century BC marble frieze from the **Temple of Apollo at Bassae**, which would orginally have been lodged fifty feet up by the roof of the temple, barely visible and poorly lit. Here, you come face to face with naked Greeks battling it out with half-clad Amazons, and inebriated Centaurs misbehaving at a Lapith wedding feast, all depicted vigorously in high relief.

Back down the stairs, your eyes are drawn to the reconstructed fourth-century BC **Nereid monument**, a mighty temple-like tomb of a Lycian chieftain, fronted with Ionic columns interspersed with figures once identified as Nereids (sea nymphs), now thought to be Aurae or wind goddesses. The monument was the most important construction at Xanthos – in western Turkey – until 1842, when it was carried off by Charles Fellows on the *HMS Beacon*, along with the greater part of the site's moveable art (including the aforementioned Harpy Tomb relief).

The Elgin Marbles

Room 8: the Duveen gallery

A large, purpose-built hall (room 8) is devoted to the museum's most famous relics, the **Parthenon sculptures**, better known as the **Elgin Marbles**, after Lord Elgin, who removed them from the Parthenon in Athens 1801. As British ambassador to Constantinople, Lord Elgin was able to wangle permission from the Turkish Porte (which then ruled Greece) to remove "any pieces of stone with figures and inscriptions". He interpreted this as a licence to make off with almost all of the bas-reliefs of the Parthenon frieze and most of its pedimental structure, which he displayed in a shed in his Pall Mall garden until he eventually sold them to the BM in 1816 for £35,000.

There were justifications for Elgin's actions – the Turks' tendency to use Parthenon stones in their lime kilns, and the fact that the building had already been partially wrecked by a missile that landed on the pile of gunpowder the Turks had thoughtfully stored there – though it was controversial even then and opposed notably by Byron. The Greek government has repeatedly requested the sculptures be returned, and has commissioned a special museum to house them near the Acropolis itself, though for the time being the BM shows no signs of relenting.

Despite their grand setting (and partly due to all the hype), first impressions of the marble friezes, carved between 447 and 432 BC under the supervision of the great sculptor Pheidias, can be a little disappointing. After the vigorous high relief of the Bassae frieze, the Parthenon's sculptures seem flat and lifeless, made up of long, repetitive queues of worshippers. If that is your reaction – and it must be said, other visitors are moved to tears – head for the traffic jam of horsemen on the north frieze, which is better preserved and exhibits more compositional variety.

As for the subject of the frieze, there is currently no agreement over what it actually depicts: the Panathenaic festival held every four years to glorify the goddess Athena, or the victory parade after the Battle of Marathon. At each end of the room are the metopes and pedimental sculptures; the figures from the east pediment are the most impressive, though most are headless; the surrounding metopes, which vary enormously in quality, depict the struggle between Centaurs and Lapiths in high relief.

The Tomb of Payava and the Mausoleum of Halicarnassus

Room 9

Beyond the Nereid monument, in room 9, you come to two of Lord Elgin's less defensible appropriations, looking particularly forlorn and meaningless: a single column and one of the six caryatids from the portico of the **Erechtheion** on the Acropolis.

Room 11

Further on, in room 11, is another large relic from Xanthos, the **Tomb of Payava**, built during the incumbent's lifetime; the reliefs on the tomb's steep roof (particular to Lycia) would have been out of view of earthbound mortals, and are best viewed from the gallery containing the reserve collection of Greek vases.

Room 12 contains fragments from two of the Seven Wonders of the Ancient World: two huge figures, a frieze and a marble horse the size of an elephant from the self-aggrandizing tomb of **King Mausolus at Halicarnassus** (source of the word "mausoleum"); and a column base from the colossal Temple of Artemis at **Ephesus**.

Room 12

The basement galleries: Greek and Roman sculpture

Rooms 77–85

From room 12 steps lead down to the basement galleries. The architecture gallery in room 77 is rather like a Classical builder's yard, piled high with bits of columns, architraves, entablatures and capitals. Next comes a room full of Classical inscriptions, followed by room after room of Greek and Roman sculpture, arranged in the whimsical manner preferred by the eighteenth-century English collectors who amassed the stuff.

The best selection is in the final room (84), which houses the **Townley Collection**, bought from dealers in Rome and London between 1768 and 1791 by Charles Townley for his house in Queen Anne's Gate. Among the bewildering array of sculpture – much of it modified to Townley's own tastes – you'll find two curiously gentle marble greyhounds, a claw-footed sphinx, a chariot-shaped latrine, and one of Townley's last purchases, a Roman copy of the famous Classical Greek bronze of Discobolus (the discus thrower).

Elsewhere, in room 85 there are dozens of portrait busts of emperors and mythological heroes, and in room 83 a monumental marble foot from a statue of Zeus in Alexandria.

The first floor galleries

Rooms 68–73

The remainder of the Greek and Roman collection is situated on the first floor (rooms 68–73), which you can either approach from the main stairs, or from the west stairs, which are lined with mosaic pavements from Halicarnassus. From the main stairs, turn immediately right and right again to get to room 68, which is lined with miniature statuary. The "Daily Life" exhibition in room 69 is one of the most user-friendly in the whole collection, with a variety of objects grouped under specific themes such as gladiators, music, women and so on.

Room 69a hosts temporary exhibitions drawn from the BM's collection of over 500,000 coins and medals.

The highlight of these first-floor rooms, though, is the **Portland Vase** (room 70), made from cobalt-blue, blown glass around the beginning of the first millennium, and decorated with opaque white cameos. The vase was smashed into over 200 separate pieces by a young Irishman in 1845, but is perhaps best known as the inspiration for Keats' *Ode on a Grecian Urn*. Nearby, and equally arresting in its own way, is the warty crocodile-skin suit of armour worn by a Roman follower of the Egyptian crocodile cult.

Room 70

The last three rooms (rooms 71–73) of Etruscan artefacts, Cypriot antiquities and Apulian red-figure vases, which round off the Classical section, are of minor interest only.

Western Asiatic antiquities

The collections of the department of **Western Asiatic Antiquities** cover all the lands east of Egypt and west of Afghanistan. The majority of exhibits on the ground floor come from the Assyrian empire; upstairs you'll find the Nimrud ivories, rich pickings from Mesopotamia and the Oxus Treasure from ancient Persia.

Assyrian sculpture and reliefs

Assyrian halls

Through the bookshop, before you enter the Greek and Roman antiquities section, two attendant gods, their robes smothered in inscriptions, fix their gaze on you, signalling the beginning of the BM's remarkable collection of **Assyrian sculptures and reliefs**. Ahead of you lies the Egyptian Hall (room 25; see below), but to continue with Assyria, turn left and pass between the two awesome five-legged, human-headed winged bulls which once guarded the temple of Ashurnasirpal II (two larger ones stand in room 16). Beyond is a full-scale reconstruction of the colossal wooden **Balawat Gates** from the palace of Shalmaneser III (858–824 BC), which are bound together with bronze strips decorated with low-relief friezes (the originals are displayed close by) depicting the defeat and execution of Shalmaneser's enemies.

Rooms 19–21

All the above serves as a prelude to the Assyrian finds which are ranged in rooms 19–21, parallel to the Egyptian Hall. At the centre of room 20 stands a small black obelisk carved with images of foreign rulers paying tribute to Shalmaneser III, interspersed with cuneiform inscriptions whose discovery in 1846 helped significantly in the decoding of this early form of writing. The finest of the **Nineveh reliefs** in room 21 record the stupendous effort involved in transporting the aforementioned winged bulls from their quarry to the palace; they should be read from left to right, so start at the far end of the room. Evidently the Assyrians moved these huge carved beasts in one piece; not so the British, who cut the two largest winged bulls in the BM into six pieces before transporting them – the joins are still visible on the pair in room 16, round the corner from room 20.

Room 17

The partitioned galleries known collectively as room 17 are lined with even more splendid friezes from Nineveh. On one side is an almost continuous band portraying the chaos and carnage of the Assyrian capture of the Judaean city of Lachish; the Assyrian king Sennacherib's face was smashed by Babylonian soldiers when the Assyrian capital finally fell to its southern neighbours in 612 BC. On the other side are the **royal lion hunts** of Ashurbanipal (668–627 BC), which involved rounding up the beasts before letting them loose in an enclosed arena for the king's sport, a practice which effectively eradicated the species in Assyria; the succession of graphic death scenes features one in which the king slaughters the cats with his bare hands.

Mesopotamia, the Nimrud ivories and the Oxus Treasure

Room 89

From room 17, it's a convenient trot down into the basement (room 89), where **Mesopotamian friezes** and domestic objects include an iron bathtub-cum-coffin from the Mesopotamian capital of Ur, thought to be the first great city on earth, dating from 2500 BC (there are more finds from Ur on the first floor; see below).

Room 24

Before heading back to the west stairs which will take you up to the rest of the collection, check out the gruesome reconstruction of a subterranean tomb in the **Ancient Palestine** gallery (room 24) by the stairs. Originally intended for one man, six others joined him when they were convicted of grave-robbing and, according to Islamic law, had their hands cut off before being executed. Up the west stairs from room 24, you leap forward again chronologically, in room 58, to the superb **Nimrud ivories**, which include miniature figures, low-relief panels and a whole set of crouching calves, much of it brought to Assyria as war booty or tribute between 900 and 700 BC.

Room 58

Ur treasures: room 56

Further on, in room 56, are some of the BM's oldest artefacts, dating from Mesopotamia in the third millennium BC. The most extraordinary treasures hail from Ur: the enigmatic **Ram in the Thicket**, a deep blue lapis lazuli and white shell statuette of a goat on its hind legs, peering through gold-leaf branches; the equally mysterious **Standard of Ur**, a small hollow box showing scenes of battle on one side, with peace and banqueting on the other, all fashioned in shell, red limestone and lapis lazuli, set in bitumen; and the **Royal Game of Ur**, one of the earliest known board games. A selection of tablets scratched with infinitesimal cuneiform script includes the **Flood Tablet**, a fragment of the Epic of Gilgamesh, perhaps the world's oldest story.

Room 49: the Oxus Treasure

Finally, there's the **Oxus Treasure**, a hoard of goldwork which appears to have passed from one band of robbers to another until eventually being bought from the bazaar at Rawalpindi by British collectors. The pieces date from the seventh to the fourth century BC and hail from Persepolis, once capital of the Persian Empire. The most celebrated are the miniature four-horse chariot and the amulet sprouting a pair of fantastical bird-headed creatures sporting horns. At the time of writing, the Oxus Treasure was displayed in room 49, accessible only from room 41, on the south side of the first floor.

Egyptian antiquities

There are more Egyptian antiquities in the nearby Petrie Museum, *p.156*

The BM's collection of **Egyptian antiquities**, ranging from Predynastic times to Coptic Egypt, is one of the finest in the world, rivalled only by Cairo's and the New York Met's; the highlights are the Rosetta Stone, the vast hall of Egyptian sculpture and the large collection of mummies.

The British Museum

The Egyptian Hall

Beyond the bookshop on the ground floor, just past the entrance to the Assyrian section (see above), two black granite statues of Amenophis III guard the entrance to the **Egyptian Hall** (room 25), where the cream of the BM's Egyptian antiquities are on display. The name "Belzoni", scratched under the left heel of the larger statue, was carved by the Italian circus strongman responsible for dragging some of the heftiest Egyptian treasures to the banks of the Nile, prior to their export to England.

Rooms 25 and 25a

Beyond, a crowd usually hovers around the **Rosetta Stone**, a black basalt slab found in the Nile delta in 1799 by French soldiers. It was surrendered to the Brits in 1801, but nevertheless it was a French professor who finally unlocked the secret of Egyptian hieroglyphs, by comparing the stone's three different scripts – ancient hieroglyphs, demotic Egyptian and Greek.

Beyond the stone are a series of **false doors** richly decorated with hieroglyphs and figures of the deceased, through which, it was believed, the dead person's *ra* (soul) could pass to receive the food offerings laid outside burial chamber. A long, dimly lit side gallery (room 25a) is the tomb-like setting for the brightly painted sandstone head of Mentuhotep II, and, completely different in style, the head of Queen Hatshepsut (or her daughter), formed from smooth green schist that bears an uncanny resemblance to the texture of human skin. A naturalistic and oddly touching **tomb painting** at the end of the room shows a nobleman hunting wildfowl with his wife and daughter – the sky full of birds, fat fish floating in the river, and an excited tabby cat clutching three dead birds in its claws.

Back in the main hall, a sombre trio of life-sized granite statues of Sesotris III make a doleful counterpoint to the colossal pink-speckled granite head of **Amenophis III**, whose enormous dislocated arm lies next to him. Glass cases in the central atrium display a fascinating array of smaller objects from signet rings to eye-paint containers in the shape of hedgehogs, as well as figurines and religious objects, including a bronze of the cat goddess **Bastet**, with gold nose- and ear-rings – the subject of the museum's most popular reproduction. Further on still, another giant head and shoulders, made of two pieces of differently coloured granite, still bears the hole drilled by French soldiers in an unsuccessful attempt to remove it from the Ramesseum, the mortuary temple of Ramesses II.

More evidence of the Egyptian **animal cults** appears in the small avenue of animal statues: a ram, a baboon, several falcons and Theoris, the goddess of women in childbirth, who's depicted as a hippopotamus standing on her hindlegs with a swollen belly. There are further animal statues in the second side gallery (room 25b), whose gilded wooden sarcophagus is of a richness comparable with the Tutankhamun treasures whose display at the BM in 1972 (the first time they had been seen outside Egypt) drew in a record one and a half million visitors.

The mummies and other funerary art

Rooms 60 and 61

Climbing the west stairs brings you to the **Egyptian mummy** collection in rooms 60 and 61. The sheer number of exhibits here is overwhelming, and, beautiful though many individual pieces are, it's frustrating that there's little in the way of explanation (hence the box below). One display cabinet to make for, though, is that containing the mummies of various animals, including cats, apes, crocodiles and falcons, along with their highly ornate coffins – there's even an eel, whose bronze coffin depicts the deceased as a cobra with a human head.

Rooms 62–65

Room 62 contains funerary papyruses and tomb paintings showing scenes from the Book of the Dead, and a whole cabinet of wood or wax *shabti* alongside their little *shabti* boxes (see box below). Aside from rather academic displays of alabaster vases, room 63 features numerous crude wooden model boats which were placed in the tomb so that the deceased's *ka* would have some form of transport in the afterlife; other figures engaged in brewing beer and baking bread were added in order to provide further sustenance for the *ka*. The last few rooms are less interesting, though the Nubian finds in room 65 are much more thoughtfully laid out, and the five-thousand-year-old sand-preserved corpse in room 64 always comes in for ghoulish scrutiny.

Egyptian burials

To attain the afterlife it was necessary, according to ancient Egyptian beliefs, that the deceased's name and body continued to exist, in order to sustain the *ka* or cosmic double that was born with every person. By the New Kingdom (1567–1085 BC) embalmers were offering three categories of **mummification**. The de luxe version entailed removing the brain (which was discarded) and the viscera (which were preserved in jars); dehydrating the cadaver in salts for about forty days; packing it to reproduce lifelike contours; inserting artificial eyes and painting the face or entire body either red (for men) or yellow (for women); wrapping it in gum-coated linen bandages; and finally cocooning it in mummy-shaped coffins. On the chest of the mummy and its coffin were placed heart scarabs, designed to prevent the deceased's heart from bearing witness against him or her during the judgement of Osiris.

Royal burials were elaborate affairs. As the mummy's coffin was lowered into its sarcophagus, priests slashed the forelegs of sacrificial animals, whose limbs were burned as the tomb was walled up. The tomb's contents (intended to satisfy the needs of the pharoah's *ka* in the afterlife) included food, drink, clothing, furniture, weapons and dozens of **shabti figures** to perform any task that the gods might require. At this point the *ka* had to undertake a journey through the underworld, followed by the **judgement of Osiris**, episodes which dominate the funerary artwork which smothers the tombs. During the latter, the deceased's heart (believed to be the seat of intelligence) was weighed against Maat's feather of Truth. The hearts of the guilty were devoured by crocodile-headed Ammut, while the righteous were led into the presence of Osiris to begin their resurrection.

Prehistoric and Romano-British collections

Rooms 36–40

The BM fulfils its less controversial role as national treasure house in the (rather loosely defined) Prehistoric and Romano-British collections on the first floor (rooms 36–40), though even here there have been calls for the items to be shared more with the regional museums. At the top of the main stairs, forming the centrepiece to room 35, is the BM's largest **Roman mosaic** centred on the earliest-known mosaic representation of Christ. Close by is a hologram of the most sensational of the BM's recent finds, the **Lindow Man**, whose leathery half-corpse is displayed on the other side of the hologram. Clubbed and garotted during a sacrificial Druid ceremony (or so it's reckoned), he lay in a hide-preserving Cheshire bog for some 2000 years.

Brilliant displays of **Celtic craftwork** follow in room 38, where two of the most distinctive objects are the French Basse-Yutz wine flagons, made from bronze and inlaid with coral. Showing Persian and Etruscan influences, they are supreme examples of Celtic art, with happy little ducks on the lip and rangy dogs for handles. From England there are fabulous heavy golden necklaces, a horned bronze helmet, and fine decorative mirrors and shields. Best of all is the **Snettisham Treasure** at the far end of room 39, made up mostly of gold and silver torcs (neck-rings), the finest of which is made of eight strands of gold twisted together, each of which is in turn made of eight wires.

Next door in room 40 is a gathering of domestic objects from Roman Britain, the most famous of these being the 28 pieces of silver tableware known as the **Mildenhall Treasure** – the Great Dish is an outstanding late Roman work, weighing over eight kilos and decorated with a mixture of pagan and Christian images in low relief.

Medieval, Renaissance and Modern collections

The medieval and modern collections cover more than a millennium from the Dark Ages to the inter-war period. The first gallery (room 41) houses finds from all over Europe, but most visitors come here to see the Anglo-Saxon **Sutton Hoo treasure**, which includes silver bowls, gold jewellery decorated with inset enamel, and an iron helmet bejewelled with gilded bronze and garnets, all buried along with a forty-oar open ship in East Anglia around 625 AD. Discovered by accident in 1939, this enormous haul is by far the richest single archeological find ever made in Britain.

Room 41: the Sutton Hoo treasure

Rooms 42–45

In the next room (42) are the thick-set **Lewis chessmen**, wild-eyed twelfth-century Scandinavian figures carved from walrus ivory, which were discovered in 1831 by a Gaelic crofter in the Outer Hebrides. There are more walrus ivories – mostly chess pieces and religious plaques – from France and Germany elsewhere in the room. At the far end of the room is the richly enamelled, fourteenth-century French **Royal Gold Cup**, given by James I to the Constable of Castille, only to find its way back to this country in later life.

Clocks

Room 43 displays tile mosaics and the largest tile pavement in the country, but you're likely to get more joy out of the adjacent room (44), which resounds to the tick-tocks and chimes of a hundred or more **clocks**, from pocket watches to grandfather clocks. These range in design from the very simple to the highly ornate, like the sixteenth-century gilded copper and brass clock from Strasbourg based on the one which used to reside in the cathedral there; the series of moving figures includes the Four Ages of Man who each strike one of the quarter hours.

The purple-carpeted chamber beyond (room 45) contains the **Waddesdon Bequest**, amassed by Baron Rothschild in the nineteenth century: a mixed bag of silver gilt, enamelwork, glassware and hunting rifles. The two finest works are a Flemish sixteenth-century boxwood altarpiece which stands only six inches high and is carved with staggering attention to detail, and the Lyte Jewel, which contains a miniature of James I by Hilliard.

Rooms 46–47

Renaissance and Baroque art fills the long gallery of room 46, with a bafflingly wide range of works from all over Europe (though much of it is of British origin). Highlights to look out for are the Tudor silver dining service, two pure gold ice pails which used to belong to Princess Di's family, the magic mirror used by Elizabethan alchemist, John Dee and the collection of Huguenot silver. Room 47 brings you into the **nineteenth century**, and reflects the era's eclectic tastes, with almost every previously existing style – Chinese, Japanese, medieval Gothic, Classical and so on – being rehashed.

Room 48: the 20th century

Before you leave, however, you must pay a visit to room 48, whose small number of **early twentieth-century exhibits** are of the highest quality. There are stunning examples of Tiffany glass and Liberty pewter, a copper vase by Frank Lloyd Wright and even some Russian Suprematist porcelain, including one dish celebrating the first anniversary of the October Revolution. Perhaps the finest exhibit of all, though, is the chequered oak clock with mother-of-pearl face, designed by the Scottish architect and designer, Charles Rennie Mackintosh.

Oriental collections

The **Oriental collections** cover some of the same geographical area as the museum's Ethnography Department (now the Museum of Mankind), and also overlap with material in the V&A. The Chinese collection is, however, unrivalled in the West, and the Indian sculpture is easily as good as anything at the V&A. The easiest way to approach the Oriental galleries (rooms 33–34 & 91–94) is from the Montague Place entrance; from the Great Russell Street entrance, walk through the British Library section, continue up the stairs past the eleven-metre totem pole and pass along the temporary displays in room 33a.

Chinese collection

Room 33: the Hotung Gallery

The Chinese collection occupies the eastern half of the recently opened Hotung Gallery (room 33), which is centred on a wonderful marble well which allows you to look down onto the Montague Place foyer. The garish **"three-colour" statuary** occupying the centre and far end of the room is the most striking, particularly the central cabinet of horses and grotesque figures, but it's the smaller pieces that hold the attention the longest. For example, the cabinet of miniature landscapes popular amongst bored Chinese bureaucrats during the Manchu Empire, or the incredible array of **snuffboxes** in different materials – lapis lazuli, jade, crystal, tortoiseshell, quartz and amber.

There's more Chinese porcelain on display in the Percival David Foundation, see p.157.

The Chinese invented **porcelain** long before anyone else, and it was highly prized both in China and abroad. The polychrome Ming and the blue and white Yuan porcelain became popular in the West from the fifteenth century onwards, as did the brightly-coloured cloisonné enamelware, but it's the much earlier unadorned porcelain which steals the show, with its austere beauty and subtle pastel colours, as in the grey-green Ru porcelain and blue-green celadons from the Song dynasty.

South East Asian antiquities

The other half of room 33 starts with a beautiful gilt-bronze statue of the Bodhisattva Tara, who was born from one of the tears wept by Avalokitesvara, a companion of the Buddha. She heralds the beginning of the **South East Asian** antiquities, a bewildering array of artefacts from as far apart as India and Indonesia. There are so many cultures and countries covered (albeit briefly) in this section that it's impossible to do more than list some of the highlights: a cabinet of **Tibetan musical instruments** with a conch shell trumpet decorated with gilt and precious stones; two fearsome *dakinis*, malevolent goddesses with skull tiaras; a Nepalese altar screen with filigree work inset with bone shell and semi-precious stones; and a jackfruit wooden door from a Balinese temple.

The classic Hindu image of **Shiva as Lord of the Dance**, trampling on the dwarf of ignorance, occupies centre stage halfway along the hall. Beyond are larger scale **Indian stone sculptures**, featuring a bevy of intimidating goddesses such as Durga, depicted killing a buffalo demon with her eight hands. The showpiece of the collection, however, lies behind a glass screen in room 33a, a climatically controlled room of dazzling limestone reliefs, drum slabs and dome sculptures purloined from **Amaravati**, one of the finest second-century Buddhist stupas in southern India. The display is somewhat chaotic and you'll have to consult the accompanying illustrations to get any idea of how it might have looked.

Room 33a

The Islamic gallery

Room 34

The museum's **Islamic** antiquities, ranging from Moorish Spain to southern Asia, are displayed in room 34, adjacent to the Montague Place entrance. The bulk of the collection is made up of thirteenth- to fifteenth-century **Syrian brass** objects, inlaid with silver and gold and richly engraved with arabesques and calligraphy (figural representation being forbidden under Islamic law), and **Iznik ceramics** in pure blues, greens and tomato-reds.

The best stuff is at the far end of the room, where Moorish lustre pottery resides alongside thirteenth-century astrolabes and celestial globes, scimitars and sabres, and a couple of Mughal hookahs encrusted with lapis lazuli and rubies set in gold. Most unusual of all is a naturalistic **jade terrapin**, discovered in Allahabad in 1600. Other curiosities include a falcon's perch, a back scratcher, a Dervish begging bowl and a Russian-influenced lacquered papier-mâché stationery set.

The British Library

The museum building is still the home of the **British Library**, currently in the throes of a much-delayed move to a site near St Pancras.

Free guided tours of the Round Reading Room take place Mon–Fri 2.15pm & 4.15pm. To study in the library you must apply for membership, with reasons why you need to use the collections.

By law the BL must preserve a copy of every book, magazine and newspaper printed in Britain, so it's hardly surprising that conditions here are now too cramped, with literally thousands of books kept in outhouse stacks all over London. In its infancy the BL could be happily accommodated in the copper-domed **Round Reading Room**, which lies to the north of the main foyer. It was built over Smirke's Great Court in the 1850s, boasts one of the largest domes in the world and is surrounded by bookstacks thirty feet high. Its padded leather desks have accommodated the likes of Karl Marx, who penned *Das Kapital* here, and Lenin, who worked here under his pseudonym of Jacob Richter in 1902. Once the move to St Pancras is completed, there are plans to restore the splendid domed room and to create wider public access to the room, while retaining its character as a library.

Room 30: manuscripts and maps

A small part of the library in the east wing, lined with tall, glass-protected bookshelves, is used as exhibition space. From the main foyer, pass through the Grenville Library (now the BL shop) to get to the **Manuscript Saloon** (room 30), where a selection of ancient manuscripts and precious books are displayed. They include a selection of the library's **classic literary manuscripts**, among them James Joyce's manically scribbled *Finnegans Wake* – a chaotic contrast to Coleridge's fastidious *Kubla Khan* and the touchingly beautiful hand-written and illustrated copies of Lewis Carroll's *Alice in Wonderland*. **Musical texts** range from the Beatles to Brahms, while **historical documents** include the **Magna Carta**, a desperate plea from Charles I to the Earl of Newcastle, begging for troops to defend the monarchy in the Civil War, and the last – unfinished –

letter from Lord Nelson to Emma Hamilton during the Battle of Trafalgar. Close by are a host of old **maps**: a tiny little plan of New York from 1695 showing Broadway and Battery Park, a map of Britain from 1250 and an Anglo-Saxon world map from 1000 AD with the words "here lions abound" for the Far East.

Room 30a

The Middle Room (30a) displays a wealth of illuminated manuscripts, with the richly illustrated **Lindisfarne Gospels**, from the 690s AD – seen by many as the apotheosis of Celtic art – always on show at the entrance.

Room 32: the King's Library

On the other side of the manuscript saloon lies the long hall of the **King's Library** (room 32), built to house the 10,500 volumes donated to the museum by George II in 1757. Manuscripts and books from Persia to ancient China via Germany are displayed here; at the centre stands Roubiliac's statue of Shakespeare, whose collected works from 1623 are on view nearby. Just beyond lies the **Gutenberg Bible**, the first Bible printed using moveable type (and therefore capable of being mass-produced), opposite much earlier examples of printing from eighth-century China. Finally, there are various pull-out panels on either side of the room used to mount highlights of the BL's gargantuan stamp collection.

Stamps

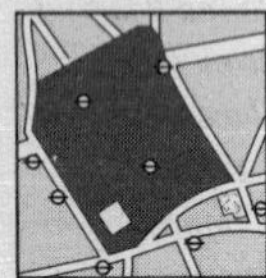

The rest of Bloomsbury

In comparison with the BM, the other sundry attractions of **Bloomsbury** are pretty lightweight, though no less enjoyable for that. The **Dickens Museum** in Doughty Street, on the edge of Holborn, is the most popular; the less well-known **Wellcome Foundation**, who fund a high-tech science museum in the unlikely surroundings of the Euston Road, is of more specialist appeal. Then of course, there are Bloomsbury's leafy squares, which, though no longer the set-pieces of Georgian architecture they once were, still provide some of the nicest picnic spots in central London.

South of the British Museum

For details of the cafés and restaurants in the area, see Chapter 15.

The grid of streets south of the BM has been threatened with demolition more than once, in order to make space for a more monumental approach to the museum. The future of this mostly Georgian "museum quarter" seems secure for the moment – in fact the parallel streets of Museum Street and Bury Place are currently thriving on a mixture of antiquarian and second-hand bookshops and an increasing number of foodie cafés.

The church is open Mon–Fri 9am–3.30pm.

Set back from busy Bloomsbury Way, three blocks south of the BM, is the church of **St George's, Bloomsbury**, the westernmost of Hawksmoor's six London churches, built so that Bloomsbury's respectable residents wouldn't have to cross the St Giles rookery (p.134) in order to attend services. Its main point of interest is the unusual steeple – a stepped pyramid based on Pliny's description of the tomb of Mausolus at Halicarnassos, fragments of which subsequently made their way to the BM – which is topped by London's only outdoor statue of the unpopular, German-speaking monarch, George I, dressed, for reasons now obscure, in a Roman toga.

The Bloomsbury squares

A little further down Bloomsbury Way, past St George's, is **Bloomsbury Square**, dating from 1665 and the first of the city's open spaces to be called a "square". Little remains of its original or later Georgian appearance, and the only reason to venture down Bloomsbury Way is to see the **Sicilian Avenue**, an unusually continental promenade sliced diagonally across the slums on the corner of Bloomsbury Way and Southampton Row. Separated from the main roads by slender Ionic screens, this simple but effective piece of town planning was created in 1910. It houses a couple of restaurants and one of the city's largest second-hand bookshops, the palindromic *Skoob Books*.

The most handsome of the Bloomsbury squares is **Bedford Square**, to the west of the BM, up Bloomsbury Street. What you see now is pretty much as it was built in the 1770s by the Russells (who still own the square), though the gates which sealed the square from traffic have unfortunately been removed, as have all but one of the mews which used to accommodate the coaches and servants of the square's wealthy inhabitants. It is a perfect example of eighteenth-century symmetery and uniformity: each doorway arch is decorated with rusticated Coade stones, each facade is broken only by the white stuccoed centre houses. The best way to get a look inside one of these Georgian mansions is to head for the **Architectural Association (AA)** at no. 34–36, which puts on occasional exhibitions, and has a bookshop in the basement and a café-bar on the first floor.

Look inside a Bloomsbury mansion at the AA bar; open term time 9.30am–9pm.

The largest Bloomsbury square – indeed one of the largest in London – is **Russell Square**, to the northeast of the BM. Apart from its monumental scale, little remains of the Georgian scheme, though the gardens, with their gargantuan plane trees and defunct 1960s fountains, are good for a picnic or a hot drink at the café. The figure most closely associated with this square is T. S. Eliot, who worked at no. 24, then the offices of *Faber & Faber*, from 1925 until his death. The only architectural curiosity is the *Russell Hotel*, on the eastern side; twice as high as everything around it, it's a no-holes-barred Victorian fancy, concocted in a bewildering mixture of styles in 1898. The hotel's wood-panelled *King's Bar* is worth closer inspection, as is the main foyer and ballroom (the latter hosts book-fairs on Mon & Tues in the second week of each month) – though the nicest touch is the wonderfully incongruous *Virginia Woolf* burgers, pasta and grills restaurant.

Woolf Burgers and a good-looking bar at the Bloomsbury Hotel.

The Rest of Bloomsbury

The Bloomsbury Group

The **Bloomsbury Group** were essentially a bevy of upper middle-class friends, who lived in and around Bloomsbury, at that time "an antiquated, ex-fashionable area", in the words of Henry James. The Group revolved around Virginia, Vanessa, Thoby and Adrian Stephen, who moved into 46 Gordon Square in 1904, shortly after the death of their father, Sir Leslie Stephen, editor of the *Dictionary of National Biography*. Thoby's Thursday evening gatherings and Vanessa's Friday Club for painters attracted a whole host of Cambridge-educated snobs who subscribed to Oscar Wilde's theory that "aesthetics are higher than ethics". Their diet of "human intercourse and the enjoyment of beautiful things" was hardly revolutionary, but their behaviour, particularly that of the two sisters (unmarried, unchaperoned, intellectual and artistic), succeeded in shocking London society, especially through their louche sexual practices (most of the group swung both ways).

All this, though interesting, would be forgotten were it not for their individual work. In 1922 Virginia declared, without too much exaggeration, "Everyone in Gordon Square has become famous": Lytton Strachey had been the first to make his name with *Eminent Victorians*, a series of unprecedently frank biographies; Vanessa, now married to the art critic Clive Bell, had become involved in Roger Fry's prolific design firm, Omega Workshop; and the economist John Maynard Keynes had become an adviser to the Treasury (he later went on to become the leading economic theorist of his day). The Group's most celebrated figure, Virginia, now married to Leonard Woolf and living in Tavistock Square, had become an established novelist; she and Leonard had also founded the Hogarth Press, which published T. S. Eliot's *Waste Land* in 1922.

Eliot was just one of a number of writers, such as Aldous Huxley, Bertrand Russell and E. M. Forster, who were drawn to the inter-war Bloomsbury set, but others, notably D. H. Lawrence, were repelled by the clan's narcissism and snobbish narrow-mindedness. (Virginia Woolf once compared *Ulysses* to a "bell-boy at Claridges" scratching his pimples.) Whatever their limitations, the Bloomsbury Group were Britain's most influential intellectual coterie of the inter-war years, and their appeal shows little sign of waning – even now scarcely a year goes by without the publication of the biography and or memoirs of some Bloomsbury peripheral.

Gordon Square, once the centre of the Bloomsbury Group (see box above), remains a quiet sanctuary, used by students from the university departments round about. Its one building of note is the strangely towerless neo-Gothic **University Church**, built in 1853 and looking like a miniature cathedral in the southwest corner of the square – the unbuilt tower was to have been nearly three hundred feet high. On the east side, where the Georgian houses stand intact, plaques mark the residences of Lytton Strachey (no. 51) and Keynes (no. 46), while another (at no. 50) commemorates the Bloomsbury Group as a whole. At the centre of the square is a statue of Mahatma Ghandi, staring towards the copper birch tree planted by his compatriot Jawaharlal Nehru in 1953. At no. 53 is the Percival David Foundation of Chinese art (see p.157).

Bloomsbury plaques on Gordon Square; the nearest tube is Russell Square.

One block east, and exhibiting almost identical proportions Gordon Square, is **Tavistock Square**, laid out by Thomas Cubitt in the early part of the nineteenth century. Though the west side of the square survives intact, the house at no. 52 where the Woolfs lived from 1924 until shortly before Virginia's suicide in 1941 is no longer standing. It was here that Woolf wrote her most famous novels – *To the Lighthouse*, *Mrs Dalloway*, *Orlando* and *The Waves* – in a little studio decorated by her sister Vanessa and Duncan Grant.

A short distance up Upper Woburn Place, to the northeast of the square, is the beautifully preserved Georgian terrace of **Woburn Walk**, designed in 1822 by Cubitt as London's first pedestrianized shopping street. W. B. Yeats lived at no. 5 from 1895 to 1919, writing some of his greatest poetry while hobnobbing with the likes of Ezra Pound, T. S. Eliot and Rabindranath Tagore. The same address was later occupied by the unrequited love of Yeats' life, Irish nationalist Maud Gonne, reputedly the most beautiful woman in Ireland, with, in Yeats' own words, "the carriage and features of a goddess".

The Foundling Hospital and Coram Fields

The nearest tube is Russell Square.

Halfway along Guilford Street, east off Russell Square, is the old entrance to the **Foundling Hospital**, founded in 1756 by Thomas Coram, a retired sea captain. Coram campaigned for seventeen years to obtain a royal charter for the hospital, having been shocked by the number of dead or dying babies left by the wayside on the streets of London. Papers in the archives of the Old Bailey relate the typical story of a mother who "fetched her child from the workhouse, where it had just been 'new-clothed', for the afternoon. She strangled it and left it in a ditch in Bethnal Green in order to sell its clothes. The money was spent on gin".

As soon as it was opened, the hospital was beseiged – you can still see the alcove between the main gates on Guilford Street where the infants used to be left for collection. Children were brought along half-dead just so they could be buried at the expense of the hospital, which soon became more like a graveyard than a hospital. After less than four years, funding was cut off, since the open-door policy was deemed to encourage prostitution, and the hospital was forced to drastically reduce its admissions. After 1801 only illegitimate children were admitted, and even then only after the mother had filled in a questionnaire and given a verbal statement confirming that "her good faith had been betrayed, that she had given way to carnal passion only after a promise of marriage or against her will; that she therefore had no other children; and that her conduct has always been irreproachable in every other respect."

All that remains of the original eighteenth-century building – which was demolished when the foundation moved to the Home Counties in the 1920s – is the whitewashed loggia which now forms

A kid's park.

the borders to a wonderful inner-city **park for children**, with swings, slides, hens and horses, plus a whole host of sheep, pigs and rabbits. Adults are not allowed into the grounds unless accompanied by a child.

The Thomas Coram Foundation is open Mon & Fri 1.30–4.30pm; £1.

Just to the north of the fields, on Brunswick Square, are the offices of the **Thomas Coram Foundation**. This contains a few remnants saved from the old hospital, though its main attraction is the collection of paintings donated by artists such as Gainsborough and Reynolds, on the suggestion of Hogarth, who was a governor of the institution and even fostered two of the foundlings; Hogarth's own *March of the Guards to Finchley* remains the finest of the pictures on show. Handel was another of the hospital's early benefactors, giving annual charity performances of the *Messiah* and donating an organ for the chapel, only the keyboard of which survives. Lastly, the Court Room, with all its fine stuccowork, has been faithfully reconstructed to give some idea of the eighteenth-century ambience; the governors still hold their meetings here.

To the south of Coram Fields is the **Hospital for Sick Children** on Great Ormond Street, which was founded a hundred years after the Coram Foundation by Charles West, who like Coram was appalled by the infant mortality rate in London. Just as Handel had helped out Coram, so Great Ormond Street Hospital was assisted by J. M. Barrie, who donated the copyright of *Peter Pan* to the hospital in 1929. With another four hospitals in close proximity, nearby **Queen Square** is more popularly known as "hospital square".

Dickens' House

Dickens' House is open daily 10am–5pm; £3.

Despite the plethora of blue plaques marking the residences of local luminaries, **Dickens' House**, southeast of Coram Fields at 48 Doughty St, is Bloomsbury's only literary or house museum. Dickens moved here in 1837 – when it was practically on the northern outskirts of town – shortly after his marriage to Catherine Hogarth, and they lived here for two years, during which time he wrote *Nicholas Nickleby* and *Oliver Twist*. This is the only one of Dickens' fifteen London addresses to survive intact, but only the drawing room, in which Dickens entertained his literary friends, has been restored to its original Regency style. The letters, manuscripts and first editions, the earliest known portrait (a miniature painted by his aunt in 1830) and the annotated books he used during extensive lecture tours in Britain and the States are the rewards for those with more than a passing interest in the novelist.

The University

London has more students than any other city in the world (over half a million at the last count), which isn't bad going for a city that only organized its own **University** in 1828, more than six hundred years after the likes of Oxford and Cambridge. The university

Charles Dickens

Few cities are as closely associated with one writer as London is with **Charles Dickens** (1812–70). Though not born in London, Dickens spent much of his life here, and the recurrent motifs in his novels have become the clichés of Victorian London – the fog, the slums and alleys, the prisons and workhouses, and of course the stinking river. Drawing on his own personal experience, he was able to describe the workings of the law and the conditions of the poor, with an unrivalled accuracy. He also lived through a time of great social change, during which London more than doubled in size, yet in his writing, London remains a surprisingly compact place: only rarely do his characters venture east of the Tower, or west of St James's, with the centre of the city hovering somewhere around the Inns of Court, described in detail in *Bleak House*.

Born in Portsmouth to a clerk in the naval pay office, Dickens spent a happy early childhood in London and Chatham, on the Kent coast. This was cut short at the age of twelve when his father was imprisoned in Marshalsea debtors' prison, and Charles was forced to work in a rat-infested factory in the old Hungerford Market. The experience, though brief, scarred him for life – he was hurt further by his mother's attempt to force him to keep the job rather than return to school, even after his father's release. After two years as a solicitor's clerk at Gray's Inn, Dickens became a parliamentary reporter, during which time he wrote *Sketches by Boz* (Boz was Dickens' journalistic pen-name). The publication of this propelled him to local fame and comparative fortune in 1836, and in the same year he married Elizabeth Hogarth and moved to the bourgeois neighbourhood of Doughty Street.

There followed nine children – "the largest family ever known with the smallest disposition to do anything for themselves" as Dickens later described them – and sixteen novels, each published in monthly instalments, which were awaited with bated breath by the Victorian public. Then in 1857, at the peak of his career, Dickens fell in love with an eighteen-year-old actress, Ellen Ternan. His subsequent separation from his wife, and his insistence that she leave the family house (while her sister Georgina stayed), scandalized society and forced the author to retreat to his country house in Rochester.

In the last decade of his life, Dickens found an outlet for his theatrical aspirations, and a way of supporting the three households for which he was now responsible, by touring Britain and America giving dramatic readings of his works. He died at his desk at the age of 58, while working on *The Mystery of Edwin Drood*. According to his wishes, there was no public announcement of his burial, though he was interred in Westminster Abbey (at Queen Victoria's insistence) rather than in Rochester (as he had requested). The twelve people present at the early morning service were asked not to wear a black bow, long hat-band or any other accessories of the "revolting absurdity" of mourning.

started life in Bloomsbury but it wasn't until after World War I that the institution really began to take over the area. Nowadays, its various colleges and departments have spread their tentacles to form an almost continuous wedge from the British Museum all the way to Euston Road, with plenty more outside this area. Despite this, the university's piecemeal development has left the place with no real focus, just a couple of landmarks in the form of Senate House and University College, plus two specialist art museums.

Senate House and University College

Looming behind the British Museum is the skyscraper of **Senate House**, a "bleak, blank, hideous" building according to Max Beerbohm. Completed by Charles Holden in 1932 and austerely clad in Portland stone, it's best viewed from Malet Street, at the end of which is *Dillons*, the excellent university bookshop, now flagship branch of a chain, strategically placed opposite the students' union.

The university's oldest building is William Wilkins' Neoclassical **University College** near the top of Gower Street, nicknamed the "godless college" because it was founded for non-Anglican students, who were at the time excluded from both Oxford and Cambridge. In 1878 it also became the first university to accept women as equals. UCL is also home to the most famous of London's art schools, the **Slade**, which has a small collection of early works by former students, including Stanley Spencer and Augustus John (term time Mon–Fri 1–2.30pm; free).

To view Bentham, ask at the Porters' Lodge, just inside the entrance gate on Gower St.

Also on display at UCL is the philosopher **Jeremy Bentham**, one of the university's founders, who bequeathed his fully-clothed skeleton so that he could be posthumously present at board meetings of the University College Hospital governors, where he was duly recorded as "present, but not voting". The skeleton, topped by wax head and wide-brimmed hat, is in "thinking and writing" pose as Bentham requested, and can be seen in a hermetically sealed mahogany booth in the north cloister of the main building, close to the pair of watchful Egyptian lions, reconstructed from several thousand fragments belonging to the Petrie Museum (see below).

On the other side of Gower Street stands **University College Hospital** (UCH) a typically striking terracotta and red-brick jumble built by Alfred Waterhouse at the turn of the century. Waterhouse designed the hospital with strictly segregated wards so as to prevent the miasma or "foul air" from passing from ward to ward – despite the fact that the discovery of bacterial infection in 1867 had made such precautions redundant.

The university museums

The Petrie Museum is open Mon–Fri 10am–noon & 1.15–5pm; free. The nearest tube is Goodge Street.

Two university departments have collections well worth dipping into if you've a particular interest in Egyptology or Chinese art. The **Petrie Museum of Egyptian Archeology**, on the first floor of the Watson building, down Malet Place, has two rooms jam-packed with antiquities, the bulk of them from excavations carried out by Sir Flinders Petrie in the 1880s. The first room is little more than broken bits of pottery to the non-specialist, but the second includes the Langton collection of miniatures of the cat-goddess Bastet (some less than one centimetre high), and several cabinets of smaller objects, ivories, *shabti*, toys and jewellery, not to mention the world's oldest dress.

Tucked away in the southeast corner of Gordon Square, at no. 53, is the **Percival David Foundation of Chinese Art**, three floors of ceramics based around the collection of Sir Percival David, bequeathed to the university in 1950. Since the best stuff is on the top two floors, you might as well head straight for the first floor, which features delicate, pastel-coloured, unadorned Ru, Ding and Yue ware, striking purple and blue Jun ware, and Guan ware, with its distinctive heavily cracked glaze. The most famous pieces are on the second floor – the vivid blue-and-white "David" vases made in Jingdezhen in the fourteenth century that have so influenced Western tastes in crockery, and the red and blue enamel Ming vases – along with more colourful works in cobalt blue, coffee brown and copper red and a whole spectrum of primary colours.

The Percival David Foundation is open Mon–Fri 10.30am–5pm; free. Nearest tube is Russell Square.

Euston and King's Cross

The northern boundary of Bloomsbury is defined by the **Euston Road**, laid out in 1756 as the city's first traffic bypass, now a six-lane traffic jam moving west into Marylebone Road and east towards the Angel. Euston Road marked the northern limit of the city until the mid-nineteenth century, and it was here that the rival railway companies built Euston, King's Cross and St Pancras stations, the termini of the lines serving the industrial boom towns of the north of England. Since those days, Euston Road has had some of the city's worst office architecture foisted on it, which, combined with the volume of traffic and King's Cross' reputation as a centre of prostitution and drugs, makes this an area for selective viewing.

Euston

Euston Road's oldest edifice is **St Pancras new church**, built in the 1820s on the corner of Upper Woburn Place. Designed in Greek Revival style, it is notable for the caryatids tacked onto the north facade which are modelled on the Erechtheion on the Acropolis, and for its octagonal tower, based on another Athenian structure, the Tower of the Winds. The best time to visit the interior, which features a dramatically lit Ionic colonnade in the apse, is during one of the free Thursday lunchtime recitals.

The nearest tubes are Euston and Euston Square.

The evergreen-tinted high-rise directly opposite the church is the headquarters of the pharmaceutical giants *Wellcome*, who fund a scientific museum and research centre further up the road (see below). Easy to miss amidst all the hubbub of Euston Road is the depressing modernist hulk of **Euston Station**, descendant of the first of London's great railway termini, which was built way back in 1840. All that remain of Philip Hardwick's original Neoclassical ensemble are the sad-looking lodge-houses, part of the Euston Arch, a much-loved landmark demolished in the face of fierce protests in

Euston's main appeal lies in some very good curry houses in Drummond Street – see p.439.

the 1960s – British Rail claimed they needed the space in order to lengthen the platforms, which they never did.

On the other side of the road from Euston is the **Wellcome Building** (Mon–Fri 9.45am–5pm, Sat 9.45am–1pm; free), a Neoclassical block from the 1930s. The grandiloquent foyer has been stylishly renovated by the pharmaceutical company who also fund the hi-tech exhibition on medicine, "Science for Life". Interactive videos and hands-on models of the human body all make for an enjoyable, gore-free way of learning about human biology. There's a giant space-age mock-up of a human cell which you can walk through and, inevitably, a section plugging the triumphs of modern medicines (the discredited AIDS drug AZT is currently given a glowing reference). Temporary exhibitions take place on the fourth floor, while in the basement there's a brief display on the history of the company, which was the first to receive permission to conduct animal experiments, a practice they are still engaged in.

Still more obscure is the **Cartoon Museum**, 183 Eversholt Street (Mon–Fri noon–6pm, Sat & Sun 2–6pm; £2.50 donation suggested), which features temporary exhibitions of international cartoonists' art.

King's Cross

A couple of blocks to the east of Euston, the new **British Library** is at last approaching completion. A standard exercise in red-brick brutalism, it has received more state investment than any previous UK building (over £450 million so far) and taken over twenty years to build. One can but pity the architect, Colin St John Wilson, who has spent the best part of his career on a project that will be a good thirty years out of vogue by the time it opens. More critically, the shelving space is already inadequate, thus destroying the original purpose of housing the entire British Library stock in one place.

The British Library also has the misfortune of standing in the shadow of one of the most glorious of London's Victorian edifices, the majestic sweep of lancets, dormers and chimneypots of Gilbert Scott's *Midland Grand* hotel, which languished as under-used British Rail offices until the government nominated **St Pancras Station**, which lies behind it, as a future Channel Tunnel terminal north of the river. The hotel and station have been cleaned and renovated, though as yet no buyer has been found for the hotel.

Compared to St Pancras, **King's Cross Station** is a mere shed, though it was simple and graceful enough until British Rail added the modern forecourt. Opened in 1850 as the terminus for the Great Northern Railway, it is now set to return to its private origins (as are the other stations) thanks to the Conservatives' myopic rail privatization plans. By day, the station is no more seedy than any other mainline station, but as the night wears on, the drunks, druggies and prostitutes who have made the area notorious begin to take over. Until recently, King's Cross and the surrounding area were set to be massively redeveloped, but with the onset of recession, the goverment switched to the cheaper option of making St Pancras the Chunnel terminal, and the whole plan has now been shelved for the foreseeable future.

The Strand, Holborn and Clerkenwell

The area covered in this chapter – the **Strand**, **Holborn** and **Clerkenwell** – lies on the periphery of the entertainment zone of the West End and the financial district of the City. The **Strand**, as its name suggests, once lay along the riverbank: it achieved its present-day form when the Victorians shored up the banks of the Thames to create the Embankment. **Holborn**, to the northeast, has long been associated with the law. Even today, every aspiring barrister must study at one of the four **Inns of Court** here in order to qualify. Secretive, and typically old-fashioned (not to say reactionary) institutions, the Inns make for a interesting stroll, their archaic, cobbled precincts exuding the rarefied atmosphere of an Oxbridge college, and sheltering one of the city's oldest churches, the twelfth-century **Temple church**. Close by the Inns, in Lincoln's Inn Fields, is the added attraction of **Sir John Soane's Museum**, one of the most memorable and enjoyable of London's small museums, packed with architectural illusions and an eclectic array of curios.

Clerkenwell, further to the northeast, is off the tourist trail, and not much known to Londoners either, but it contains a host of unusual sights including vestiges of two pre-Fire of London priories, an old prison house, London's own "Little Italy" and the **Marx Memorial Library**, where the exiled Lenin plotted revolution. Clerkenwell's origins as a village are visible on Clerkenwell Green, and its long history as an artisanal adjunct to the City continues among the jewellers of Hatton Garden and the clockmakers of Clerkenwell Road.

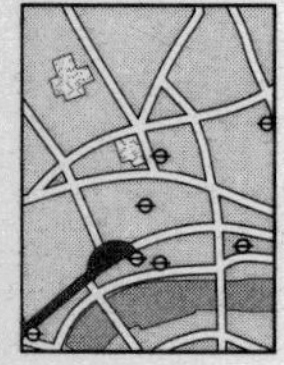

The Strand

The Strand – the main road connecting Westminster to the City – is a shadow of its former self. From the thirteenth century onwards, the street was famous for its riverside mansions, owned by bishops,

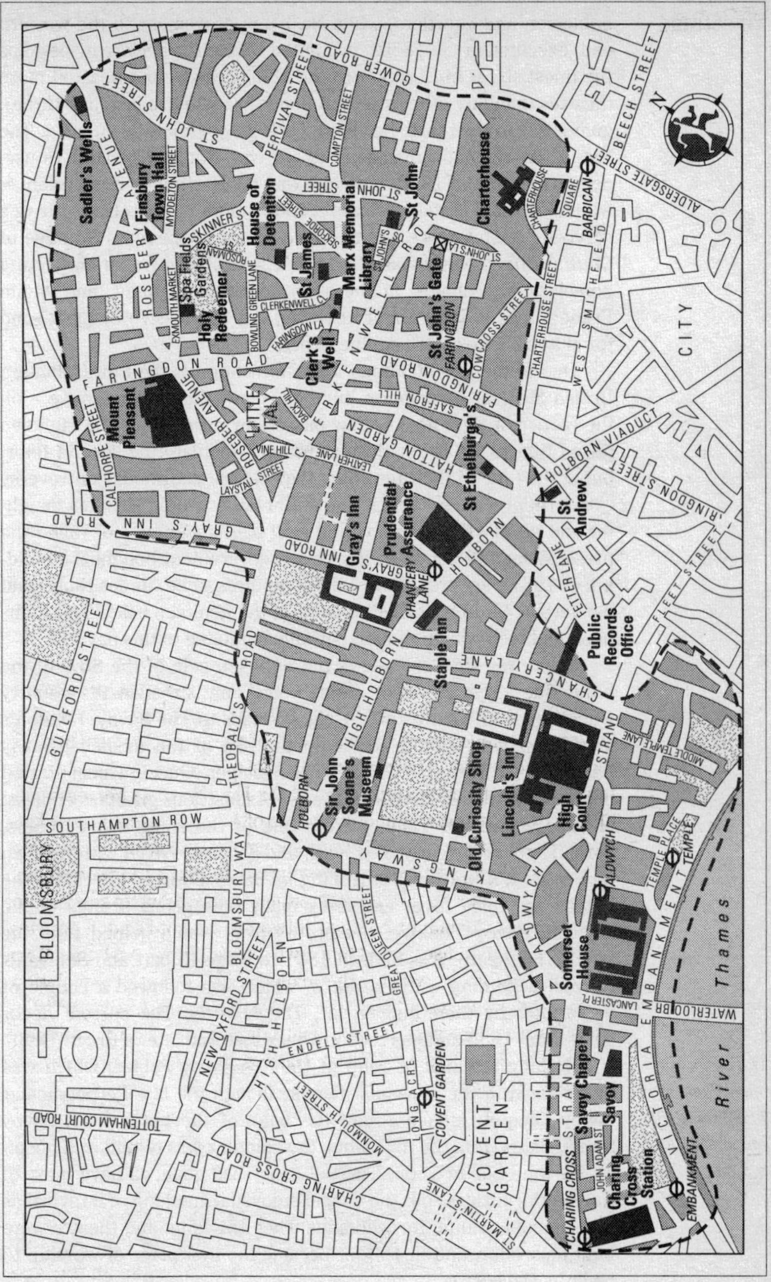

Sadler's Wells
Finsbury Town Hall
House of Detention
Marx Memorial Library
St John
Charterhouse
Spa Fields
Holy Redeemer
St James
St John's Gate
Clerk's Well
Mount Pleasant
LITTLE ITALY
St Etheldburga's
Gray's Inn
Prudential Assurance
St Andrew
Staple Inn
Public Records Office
Sir John Soane's Museum
Old Curiosity Shop
Lincoln's Inn
High Court
Somerset House
Savoy Chapel
Savoy
Charing Cross Station
COVENT GARDEN
BLOOMSBURY
CITY
River Thames
ST JOHN STREET
GOWER ROAD
PERCIVAL STREET
COMPTON STREET
ROSEBERY AVENUE
FARINGDON ROAD
CLERKENWELL ROAD
CHARTERHOUSE SQUARE
ALDERSGATE STREET
BEECH STREET
BARBICAN
WEST SMITHFIELD
CHARTERHOUSE STREET
COWCROSS STREET
FARINGDON
HOLBORN VIADUCT
HATTON GARDEN
SAFFRON HILL
GRAY'S INN ROAD
CALTHORPE STREET
HOLBORN
CHANCERY LANE
FETTER LANE
FLEET STREET
STRAND
MIDDLE TEMPLE LANE
TEMPLE PLACE
TEMPLE
HIGH HOLBORN
THEOBALD'S ROAD
GUILFORD STREET
SOUTHAMPTON ROW
BLOOMSBURY WAY
KINGSWAY
ALDWYCH
LANCASTER PL
WATERLOO BR
EMBANKMENT
VICTORIA
NEW OXFORD STREET
ENDELL STREET
GREAT QUEEN STREET
LONG ACRE
MONMOUTH STREET
CHARING CROSS ROAD
TOTTENHAM COURT ROAD
ST MARTIN'S LANE
CHARING CROSS
JOHN ADAM ST

noblemen and courtiers, while Nash's improvement to the western end, executed in the 1830s, prompted Disraeli to declare it "perhaps the finest street in Europe". In the 1890s, the Strand boasted more theatres than any other street in London (there are now just three), giving rise to the music hall song *Let's all go down the Strand*. The last of its riverside mansions to go was Northumberland House, demolished in the 1870s to make way for Northumberland Avenue, which leads off Trafalgar Sqaure, and a hundred years later, the one surviving Nash terrace was chopped in two by the glass frontage of *Coutts' Bank*. Nowadays the Strand is best known for the young homeless who shelter in the shop doorways at night, and whom Prime Minister John Major criticized for "aggressive begging" and for cluttering up this once fine street.

One of the few buildings worth a mention is the Edwardian-era British Medical Association building – now **Zimbabwe House** – on the corner of Agar Street. Few passers-by even notice the eighteen naked figures by Jacob Epstein which punctuate the second floor, but at the time of their unveiling they caused enormous controversy – "a form of statuary which no careful father would wish his daughter and no discriminating young man his fiancée to see" railed the press. When the Southern Rhodesian government bought the building in 1937 they pronounced the sculptures to be "undesirable" and dangerous, and proceeded to hack at the genitals, heads and limbs of all eighteen, which remain partially mutilated to this day.

Some way further east on the opposite side of the Strand, the blind side street of Savoy Court – the only street in the country where the traffic drives on the right – leads to **The Savoy**, London's grandest hotel, built in 1889 on the site of the medieval Savoy Palace. César Ritz was the original manager, Guccio Gucci started out as a dishwasher here, and the list of illustrious guests is endless: Monet painted the Thames from one of the south-facing rooms, Sarah Bernhardt nearly died here, and Strauss arrived with his own orchestra. It's worthwhile strolling up Savoy Court to check out the hotel's Art Deco foyer and the equally outrageous fittings of the adjacent **Savoy Theatre**, the profits from which helped fund the hotel. The theatre was built in 1881 to stage Gilbert and Sullivan's operas, beginning with *Patience*, which was followed a couple of years later by their biggest hit, *The Mikado*. The current decor dates from 1930 and has recently been restored after a fire in 1990.

The chapel is open Tues–Fri 11.30am–3.30 pm; closed Aug & Sept.

Nothing remains of John of Gaunt's Savoy Palace, which was burnt down in the Peasants' Revolt, though the late Perpendicular **Savoy Chapel**, hidden round the back of the hotel down Savoy Street, dates from the time when the complex was rebuilt as a hospital for the poor in 1505. The tall belfry has gone, as have most of the interior fittings, but the chapel enjoyed something of a revival as a fashionable venue for weddings when the hotel and theatre were built next door, and in 1890 it became the first place of worship to be lit by electricity.

Victoria Embankment

To get to the **Victoria Embankment**, head down Villiers Street, which slopes sharply down the flank of Charing Cross Station. The street marks the site of the old Hungerford Market, where Dickens was employed filling jars with boot polish, from the age of 11, while his father began his slow descent to the debtors' prison. More recently, this whole area was the domain of the city's homeless, though the council moved them on to make way for central London's biggest development of the 1990s – Terry Farrell's **Embankment Place**, suspended in part above the railway tracks. The corporate headquarters of accountants *Coopers Lybrand*, this is a deeply undistinguished building, with jokey Classical references doing little to relieve the repro-jukebox design.

The Victoria Embankment itself was the inspiration of French engineer Joseph Bazalgette, whose project simultaneously relieved congestion along the Strand, provided an extension to the underground railway and sewage systems, and created a new stretch of parkland with a riverside walk – no longer much fun due to the volume of traffic. The 1626 **York Watergate**, in the Victoria Embankment Gardens to the east of Villiers Street, gives you an idea of where the banks of the Thames used to be; the steps through the gateway once led down to the river.

Less evidence remains of the Adam brothers' magnificent riverside development, known as the **Adelphi**, from the Greek for "brothers". Built between 1768 and 1772, this featured a terrace of eleven houses supported by massive arches and vaults which opened out onto a newly constructed wharf. The scheme was by no means a success – the houses wouldn't sell (despite having the actor David Garrick among their first residents), the wharf was prone to flooding, and the brothers ended up practically bankrupt – but it was a distinctive feature of the waterfront until 1936, when it was thoughtlessly demolished. The only surviving Adam houses are between the Victoria Embankment Gardens and the Strand: 1–3 Robert Street and 7 Adam Street, both of which retain the Adams' innovative stucco decoration on their pilasters, and – most elaborate of all – nos. 6–8 John Adam Street, home to the Royal Society for Arts.

London's oldest monument, **Cleopatra's Needle**, languishes little-noticed on the Thames' side of the busy Victoria Embankment, guarded by two Victorian sphinxes. The sixty-foot-high stick of granite in fact has nothing to do with Cleopatra – it's one of a pair erected in Heliopolis in 1475 BC and taken to Alexandria fifteen years after Cleopatra's suicide by the Emperor Augustus. This obelisk was presented to Britain in 1819 by Mohammed Ali, ruler of Egypt, but nearly sixty years passed before it finally made its way to London; the other one is in New York's Central Park.

The **Benjamin Franklin House** at 36 Craven St, on the other side of Charing Cross Station, is likely to attract more visitors, when it finally opens (1996 is the tentative projected date if the required £3m is found). Born in 1706, the tenth son of a candlemaker, Franklin spent nearly twenty years of his life in London, espousing the cause of the British colonies (as the US then was), before returning to America to help draft the Declaration of Independence, negotiate the peace treaty with Britain and frame the Constitution.

Aldwych

Aldwych tube is now closed; the nearest station is Temple.

The wide crescent of **Aldwych**, forming a neat "D" with the eastern part of the Strand, was driven through the slums of this zone in the last throes of the Victorian era. A confident ensemble occupies the centre, with the enormous **Australia House** and **India House** sandwiching **Bush House**, home of the BBC's World Service since 1940. Despite its thoroughly British associations, Bush House was built by the American speculator Irving T. Bush, whose planned trade centre flopped in the 1930s. The giant figures on the north facade and the inscription, "To the Eternal Friendship of English-speaking Nations", thus refer to the friendship between the US and Britain, and are not, as many people assume, the declaratory manifesto of the current occupants.

Not far from these former bastions of Empire, up Hough Street, lurks that erstwhile hotbed of left-wing agitation, the **London School of Economics**. Founded in 1895 by, among others, the proto-socialists Sidney and Beatrice Webb, the LSE gained a radical reputation in 1968, when a student sit-in ended in violent confrontations which were the closest London came to the heady events in Paris that year. Alumni include Carlos the Jackal, Cherie Booth, wife of Labour leader Tony Blair, and Mick Jagger but the place has been pretty quiet for the last two decades.

Somerset House: the Courtauld Institute

South of Aldwych and the Strand stands **Somerset House**, sole survivor of the grandiose edifices which once lined this stretch of the riverfront, its four wings enclosing a large courtyard rather like a Parisian *hôtel*. The original sixteenth-century palace, occupied intermittently by Elizabeth I and other royals, was demolished to make way for the present building, which was begun in 1776 by William Chambers as a purpose-built development for governmental offices. Instead, it became home to the Royal Academy of Arts from 1780 to 1836, then offices for the General Register of Births, Deaths and Marriages until 1973. Part of the north wing has recently become the gallery of the **Courtauld Institute**, though the majority of the building remains in the hands of the distinctly unaesthetic Inland Revenue, who use the graceful forecourt as a car park.

The Courtauld Institute is open Mon–Sat 10am–6pm, Sun 2–6pm; £3.

The Courtauld was founded in 1931 as part of the University of London, and was the first body in Britain to award degrees for art history as an academic subject. Its priceless collection is chiefly known for its Impressionists and Post-Impressionists, but there are a few masterpieces among the earlier works: **Cranach the Elder**'s *Adam and Eve*, **Botticelli**'s *Holy Trinity with Saints John and Mary*, plus a large collection of **early Rubens** canvases. **Gainsborough**'s portrait of his wife and Beechley's *Queen Caroline* stand out among the early Brits, who are occasionally joined by a smattering of later works from the collection by the likes of Walter Sickert, Ivon Hitchins, Ben Nicholson and Oskar Kokoschka.

Most visitors, however, head straight for the pink and turquoise room that holds the collection's most famous paintings, amongst them **Degas**' *Two Dancers*, **Renoir**'s *La Loge*, a small-scale version of **Manet**'s bold *Déjeuner sur l'herbe*, and the same artist's atmospheric *Bar at the Folies-Bergère*, a nostalgic celebration of bohemian Montmartre, painted two years before his death. **Cézanne** gets a room practically to himself, featuring one of his series of *Card Players* and several magnificent landscapes, geometrical but lush. **Gauguin**'s Breton peasants *Haymaking* contrasts with his later Tahitian works, while the most popular **van Gogh** is his *Self Portrait with Bandaged Ear*, painted shortly after his remorseful self-mutilation, following an attack on his flat-mate Gauguin. A classic **Modigliani** nude and works by Seurat and Toulouse-Lautrec round off the show.

King's College to St Clement Danes

Next door to Somerset House, the ugly concrete facade of **King's College** conceals Smirke's much older buildings, which date from its foundation in 1829. If you enter the college and follow the signs down Surrey Steps to the so-called **Roman Bath** (Wed 1–4pm; NT), you'll discover a fifteen-foot-long tub (probably dating from Tudor times) with a natural spring belching out two thousand gallons a day. Further east along the Strand are two more architectural curiosities. **Twinings** tea shop was founded in 1710 by Thomas Twining, tea supplier to Queen Anne; its slender Neoclassical portico features two reclining Chinamen, dating from the time when all tea came from China. Several doors beyond, **Lloyds Bank**'s Law Courts branch retains the extravagant turquoise majolica foyer of the *Palsgrave Head Tavern*, which stood here in 1883.

Two historic churches survived the Aldwych development, and are now stranded amid the traffic of the Strand. The first is James Gibbs' **St Mary-le-Strand**, his first commission, built in Baroque style and topped by a delicately tiered tower. Even in the eighteenth century parishioners complained of the noise from the roads, and it's incredible that recitals are still given here.

In allusion to his own St Mary's, Gibbs placed a 115-foot tower on top of Christopher Wren's nearby **St Clement Danes**, whose bells play out the tune of the nursery rhyme *Oranges and Lemons*

– though St Clement's Eastcheap is more likely to be the one referred to in the rhyme. Reduced to a smouldering shell during the Blitz, the church was handed over to the RAF in the 1950s and is now a very well-kept memorial to those killed in the air battles of the last war. The nave and aisles are studded with over 700 squadron and unit badges, while heavy tomes set in glass cabinets record the 120,000 who died.

In front of the church, Gladstone and his four female allegorical companions are flanked by two air chiefs: to the right, Lord Dowding, the man who oversaw the Battle of Britain; to the left, **Sir Arthur Harris**, better known as "Bomber Harris", architect of the saturation bombing of Germany, which resulted in the slaughter of thousands of German civilians (and over 55,000 Allied airmen now commemorated on the plinth). Although Churchill was ultimately responsible, most of the opprobrium was left to fall on Harris, who was denied the peerage all other service chiefs received, while his forces were refused a campaign medal. The decision to honour Harris with this privately funded statue, unveiled by the Queen Mother in May 31, 1992 (the anniversary of the bombing of Cologne), drew widespread protests in Britain and from Germany.

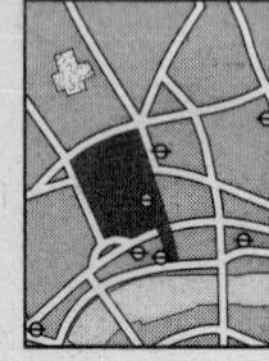

Holborn and the Inns of Court

Bounded by Kingsway to the west, the City to the east, the Strand to the south and Theobalds Road to the north, **Holborn** (pronounced "Ho-burn") is a fascinating area to explore. Strategically placed between the royal and political centre of Westminster and the mercantile and financial might of the City, this wedge of land became the hub of the English legal system in the early thirteenth century. Hostels, known as **Inns of Court**, were established where lawyers could eat, sleep and study English Common Law (which was not taught at the universities at the time).

Even today every barrister in England must study (and eat a required number of dinners) at one of the four Inns – Inner Temple, Middle Temple, Lincoln's Inn and Gray's Inn – before being called to the Bar. It's an old-fashioned system of patronage (you need contacts to get accepted at one of the Inns) and one that has done much to keep the judiciary overwhelmingly white, male and Oxbridge-educated.

Temple

Temple is the largest and most complex of the Inns of Court, comprising an amalgamation of two Inns – Middle Temple and Inner Temple – both of which lie to the south of the Strand and Fleet Street, just within the boundaries of the City of London. The

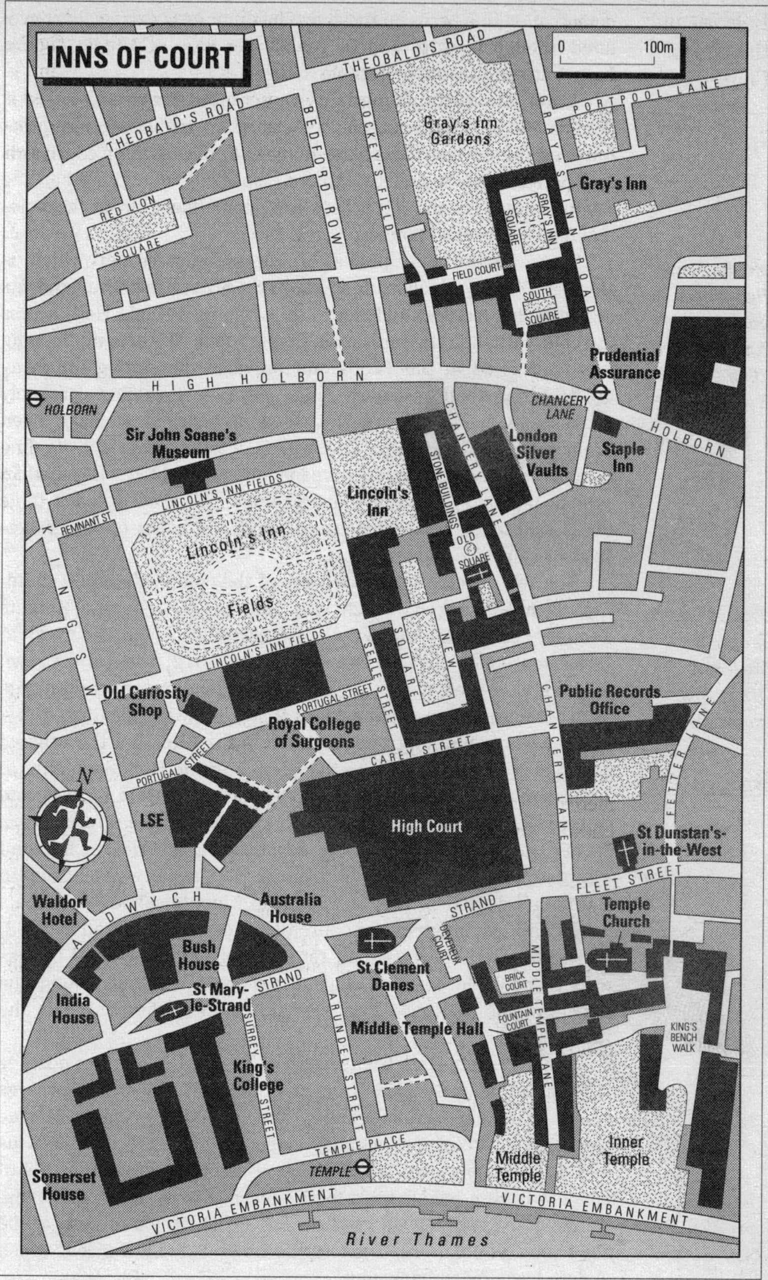
INNS OF COURT
0 100m
THEOBALD'S ROAD
PORTPOOL LANE
BEDFORD ROW
JOCKEY'S FIELD
Gray's Inn Gardens
GRAY'S INN ROAD
Gray's Inn
GRAY'S INN SQUARE
RED LION SQUARE
FIELD COURT
SOUTH SQUARE
Prudential Assurance
HIGH HOLBORN
HOLBORN
CHANCERY LANE
HOLBORN
Sir John Soane's Museum
London Silver Vaults
Staple Inn
LINCOLN'S INN FIELDS
Lincoln's Inn
STONE BUILDINGS
REMNANT ST
KINGSWAY
Lincoln's Inn Fields
OLD SQUARE
NEW SQUARE
SERLE STREET
Old Curiosity Shop
PORTUGAL STREET
Royal College of Surgeons
Public Records Office
FETTER LANE
CAREY STREET
PORTUGAL STREET
LSE
High Court
St Dunstan's-in-the-West
N
FLEET STREET
ALDWYCH
Waldorf Hotel
Australia House
STRAND
Temple Church
Bush House
DEVEREUX COURT
St Clement Danes
BRICK COURT
MIDDLE TEMPLE LANE
India House
St Mary-le-Strand
STRAND
SURREY STREET
ARUNDEL STREET
Middle Temple Hall
FOUNTAIN COURT
KING'S BENCH WALK
King's College
TEMPLE PLACE
TEMPLE
Middle Temple
Inner Temple
Somerset House
VICTORIA EMBANKMENT
VICTORIA EMBANKMENT
River Thames

demarcation line between these two institutions is extremely convoluted, though most of Middle Temple lies west of Middle Temple Lane, with most of Inner Temple to the east.

A few very old buildings survive here, but the overall scene is dominated by the soulless neo-Georgian reconstructions that followed the devastation of the Blitz. Still, the maze of courtyards and passageways is fun to explore, especially at night, when the Temple is gas-lit, and it's always a welcome haven from the noise and fumes of central London.

Middle Temple Hall is open during term time Mon–Fri 10am–noon & 3–4.30pm.

There are several points of access, simplest of which is Devereux Court, which leads south off the Strand. Medieval students ate, attended lectures and slept in the **Middle Temple Hall**, across the courtyard, still the Inn's main dining room. The present building was contructed in the 1560s and provided the setting for many great Elizabethan masques and plays – including probably Shakespeare's *Twelfth Night*, which is believed to have been premiered here in 1602. The hall is worth a visit for its fine hammerbeam roof, wooden panelling, decorative Elizabethan screen, portraits of Tudor monarchs, and the small wooden table that's said to be have been carved from the hatch of Sir Francis Drake's ship, *The Golden Hind*.

Temple Church is open Wed–Sun 10am–4pm; closed Aug.

The two Temple Inns share use of the complex's oldest building, **Temple Church**, which was built in 1185 by the Knights Templar, an order founded to protect pilgrims on the road to Jerusalem which had its base here until 1312, when the Crown took fright at their power and handed the land over to the Knights of St John. An oblong chancel was added in the thirteenth century, and the whole building was damaged in the Blitz, but the original round church – modelled on the Church of the Holy Sepulchre in Jerusalem – still stands, with its recumbent marble effigies and tortured grotesques grimacing in every arch. At the northwestern corner of the choir, behind the decorative altar tomb to Edmund Plowden, builder of the Middle Temple Hall, a stairwell leads up to a tiny cell, less than five feet long, in which disobedient knights were confined. Much of the church was restored by Wren in 1682, although only his carved oak reredos remains today, and he was also responsible for the elegant red-brick buildings along the northern side of King's Bench Walk, south of the church in the Inner Temple Court.

The garden is open Mon–Fri noon–2.30pm.

Inner Temple Hall, to the south of Temple Church, is a postwar reconstruction, as is clear from the brickwork. Inner Temple was where Mahatma Gandhi studied law in 1888, living as a true Englishman, dressing as a dandy, dancing, taking elocution lessons and playing the violin, while his close associate Jawaharlal Nehru spent two even wilder years here a decade or so later, gambling, drinking and running up considerable debts. If you're here at the right time, you can also explore the **Inner Temple Garden**, which slopes down the embankment.

Temple Bar and the Royal Courts of Justice

If you walk to the top of Middle Temple Lane, you'll hit the Strand right at **Temple Bar**, the latest in a long line of structures marking the boundary between Westminster and the City of London. Wren's triumphal arch was removed in 1878 to ease traffic congestion and now moulders away in Waltham Cross, though there are plans to restore it and bring it back to London. The heads of executed traitors (boiled in salt so the birds wouldn't eat them) were displayed on the arch until the mid-eighteenth century – one could even hire out a telescope for a closer look. The monument which replaced the arch marks the spot where the sovereign must ask for the Lord Mayor's permission to enter the City, at the annual Lord Mayor's Show, but it is an uninteresting object.

Occupying the north side of the last stretch of the Strand before it hits Temple Bar are the **Royal Courts of Justice**, better known as the High Court, where the most important civil cases are tried (criminal cases are heard at the Old Bailey, see p.194). The main portal and steps of this daunting Gothic Revival complex are familiar from innumerable news reports, since this is where many major appeals and libel suits are heard – it was where the Guildford Four and Birmingham Six walked to freedom, and countless pop and soap stars have battled it out with the tabloids here. Though they do their best to conceal the fact, the fifty-odd courtrooms are, in fact, open to the public. There are stringent security checks, but once through those you're into the intimidating Great Hall, where you can study the day's business or ask at the information desk for directions to the nearest court in session.

The Courts are open Mon–Fri 10am–4.30pm.

Lincoln's Inn Fields

On the north side of the Law Courts lies **Lincoln's Inn Fields**, London's largest square, laid out in the early 1640s; no. 59–60, on the west side, is the sole survivor from that period – it's possibly the work of Inigo Jones. The gardens were used as a more or less permanent campsite by the city's homeless for much of the last decade; the recent lengthy renovation moved them on. To the north is a statue of Margaret MacDonald – wife of the first Labour prime minister, Ramsay MacDonald, who lived for a time at no. 3 – amid a brood of nine children, commemorating her social work among the young. Much of the south side of the square is occupied by the gigantic **Royal College of Surgeons**, containing the Hunterian Collection of pickled bits and bobs, a fascinating museum but only open to those with genuine medical interests (you need to apply in writing). On a different scale, to the west, is one of London's few surviving timber-framed buildings, the seventeenth-century **Old Curiosity Shop**, which claims to be the inspiration for Dickens' cloyingly sentimental tale of the same name. This seems unlikely but it is certainly London's oldest shop building.

Holborn and the Inns of Court

The Soane Museum is open Tues–Sat 10am–5pm; free; there is an excellent tour on Saturdays at 2.30pm.

Sir John Soane's Museum

A group of buildings on the north side of Lincoln's Inn Fields house **Sir John Soane's Museum**, an unsung glory which many people consider their favourite museum in London – bar none. Soane, a bricklayer's son who rose to be architect of the Bank of England, gradually bought up three adjoining Georgian properties here, altering them to serve not only as a home and office, but also as a place to stash his large collection of art and antiquities. Number 13, the central house with the stone loggia, is arranged much as it was in his lifetime, with an ingenious ground plan and an informal, treasure-hunt atmosphere, with surprises in every alcove. Few of Soane's projects were actually built, and his home remains the best example of what he dubbed his "poetry of architecture", using mirrors, domes and skylights to create wonderful spatial ambiguities.

To the right of the hallway, you enter the **dining room**, which adjoins the **library**, bedecked in Pompeiian red and green to give it a Roman feel. Through Soane's tiny study and dressing room, little more than a corridor crammed with fragments of Roman marble and loads of cameos and miniatures, and you find yourself in the main colonnaded display hall, built over the former stables: all around are busts and more masonry; below you is the Egyptian sarcophagus (see below); above your head is the wooden chamber on stilts from which Soane used to supervise his students into other rooms and floors. To your right is the **picture room** whose false walls swing back to reveal another wall of pictures (including original Piranesi studies of the temples at Paestum and architectural drawings of Soane's projects), which itself opens to reveal a window and a balcony looking down onto the basement. The star paintings are **Hogarth**'s satirical *Election* series and his merciless morality tale *The Rake's Progress*.

A narrow staircase leads down into the flagstoned **crypt**, which features the "monk's parlour", a Gothic folly dedicated to a make-believe padre, Giovanni, complete with tomb, cloister and eerie medieval casts and gargoyles. The hushed sepulchral chamber continues the morbid theme with its wooden mummy case, a model of an Etruscan tomb (complete with skeleton), and the tombstones of Soane's wife and son. You then emerge into another colonnaded atrium, where the alabaster **sarcophagus of Seti I**, rejected by the British Museum and bought by Soane, is watched over by rows and rows of antique statuary.

Soane's mausoleum lies in Old St Pancras graveyard, *see p.316.*

Back on the ground floor, make your way to the **breakfast parlour**, which features all of Soane's favourite architectural features: coloured skylights, a canopied dome and ranks of tiny convex mirrors. A short stroll up the beautiful cantilevered staircase brings you to the first-floor **drawing rooms**, whose airiness and bright colour scheme come as a relief after the ancient clutter of the downstairs rooms; there's also a startling view of the ground floor's numerous and varied skylights from the north drawing room.

At 2.30pm every Saturday, a fascinating, hour-long **free guided tour** takes you round the museum and next door to no. 12, which holds an enormous research library of architectural drawings and books, and a room crammed with cork and wood models of Pompeiian and Paestum temples (some of these are also displayed in the basement).

Lincoln's Inn

Lincoln's Inn is open Mon–Fri 9am–5pm; the chapel and gardens are open Mon–Fri noon–2.30pm.

East of Lincoln's Inn Fields lies **Lincoln's Inn**, the first and in many ways the prettiest Inn of Court, having miraculously escaped the ravages of the Blitz; famous alumni include Thomas More, Oliver Cromwell and Margaret Thatcher. As you might guess, the oldest buildings are in the Old Buildings courtyard, starting chronologically with the fifteenth-century **Old Hall**, where the lawyers used to live and where Dickens set the case Jarndyce versus Jarndyce in *Bleak House*. To get inside, go to the porter's lodge at the entrance by Lincoln Inn's Fields.

Beyond the Old Hall is the sixteenth-century **gatehouse**, impressive for its age and bulk, not to mention its faded diaper-patterned brickwork, a decoration repeated elsewhere in the Inn. Finally there's the early seventeenth-century **chapel**, with its unusual fan-vaulted open undercroft, and, on the first floor, its late Gothic nave, hit by a Zeppelin in World War I and much restored since. To the north of the chapel, on the other side of Old Square lie the Palladian **Stone Buildings**, very different in style to the rest of the Inn and best appreciated from the manicured lawns of the Inn's garden; the strange miniature castle near the garden entrance is the gardeners' tool shed, a creation of Sir George Gilbert Scott, designer of the old red telephone boxes.

Chancery Lane and Gray's Inn

Running along the eastern edge of Lincoln's Inn is legal London's main thoroughfare, **Chancery Lane**, home of the Law Society (the solicitors' regulatory body) and lined with shops where barristers, solicitors and clerks can buy their wigs, gowns, legal tomes, stationery and champagne. A confident piece of Victorian municipal architecture, opposite Lincoln's Inn's Tudor gateway, houses the **Public Records Office**, whose research library is full of historians consulting primary source material, and whose **museum** (Mon–Fri 10am–5pm; free) contains the Domesday Book, Guy Fawkes' confession and Shakespeare's will, amongst many other fascinating manuscripts. A little further up on the same side of the street are the **London Silver Vaults** (Mon–Fri 9am–5.30pm, Sat 9am–1pm; free), a claustrophobic lair of subterranean shops selling every kind of silverware – occasionally antique, mostly tasteless.

Gray's Inn is open Mon–Fri 10am–4pm; the gardens are open Mon–fri noon–2.30pm.

The last of the four Inns of Court, **Gray's Inn**, lies hidden to the north of High Holborn, at the top of Chancery Lane; the entrance is through an anonymous cream-coloured building next door to the

Cittie of Yorke pub. Established in the fourteenth century, the inn took its name from the de Grey family, who owned the original mansion used as student lodgings; many more buildings were added during the sixteenth century, but most of what you see today was rebuilt after the Blitz. The **Hall** (open by appointment only; ☎071/405 8164), with its fabulous Tudor screen and stained glass, is thought to have witnessed the première of Shakespeare's *Comedy of Errors* in 1594. Unlike the south side, the north side of the Inn, taken up by the wide green expanse of **Gray's Inn Gardens**, is entirely and impressively visible through its wrought-iron railings from Theobald's Road.

Holborn Circus

Heading east towards Holborn Circus, it's worth pausing to admire two remarkable buildings. The first, on the right, is **Staple Inn**, not one of the Inns of Court, but one of the now defunct Inns of Chancery, which used to provide a sort of foundation course for those aspiring to the Bar. Its overhanging half-timbered facade and gables date from the sixteenth century and are the most extensive in the whole of London; they survived the Fire, which stopped just short of Holborn Circus, but had to be extensively rebuilt after the Blitz. The second building is the terracotta red palace on the opposite side of Holborn, begun in 1879 by Alfred Waterhouse for the **Prudential Assurance Company**. You need to penetrate the inner courtyard to appreciate the magnificent scale of this fortress of Victorian capitalism – you can peek through the windows at the original Doulton tiled interior.

St Andrew's Church is now owned by the Royal College of Organists and closed to the public.

At **Holborn Circus** the traffic swirls around London's politest statue, a cheerful equestrian figure of Prince Albert doffing his hat to passers-by. The nearby church of **St Andrew**, Wren's largest parish church, where Disraeli was baptized, marks the beginning of the City, which lies to the south and east, over the Holborn Viaduct. Across the way is the 1950s-functional **Daily Mirror** building, one-time headquarters of the late robber-baron Robert Maxwell, who installed a heliport to fly in and bully his minions.

Take the first left off Charterhouse Street, which runs northeast from the Circus, and you'll come to **Ely Place**, named after the Bishop of Ely, whose London residence used to stand here. Guarded by a beadle, lodge and wrought-iron gates, this patch is technically still outside the jurisdiction of the London authorities, but all that remains of the bishop's palace is its plain Gothic chapel, now **St Ethelreda's Church**, hidden halfway down this dead-end street on the left. Since 1874 this has been an exclusive Catholic stronghold, attracting a fair number of worshippers from the City during the week (there are no papist shrines in the Square Mile), and foreign diplomats at the weekend. The gloomy crypt has recently been restored and contains a model of the pre-Reformation complex.

Clerkenwell

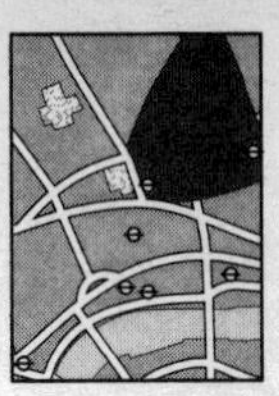

The hushed collegiate atmosphere of the Inns of Court comes to an abrupt end in **Clerkenwell**, one of inner London's little-known quarters, which lies north and slightly uphill from the City. Clerkenwell began life in the twelfth century as a village serving the local monastic foundations (two of which survive). Following the Great Fire and the Great Plague, the area was settled by craftsmen, including newly arrived Huguenots, excluded by the restrictive practices of the City guilds. At the same time, the springs which give the place its name were rediscovered and Clerkenwell became a fashionable spa resort for a century or so.

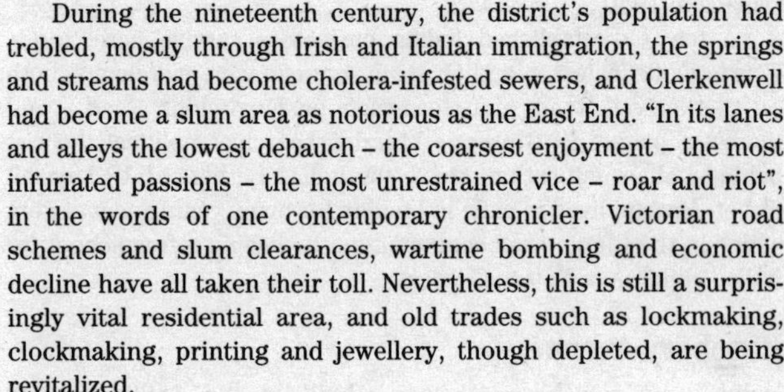

During the nineteenth century, the district's population had trebled, mostly through Irish and Italian immigration, the springs and streams had become cholera-infested sewers, and Clerkenwell had become a slum area as notorious as the East End. "In its lanes and alleys the lowest debauch – the coarsest enjoyment – the most infuriated passions – the most unrestrained vice – roar and riot", in the words of one contemporary chronicler. Victorian road schemes and slum clearances, wartime bombing and economic decline have all taken their toll. Nevertheless, this is still a surprisingly vital residential area, and old trades such as lockmaking, clockmaking, printing and jewellery, though depleted, are being revitalized.

Hatton Garden and Leather Lane

No one would try to pretend that **Hatton Garden**, which connects Holborn Circus with Little Italy, is an attractive spot, but as the centre of the city's diamond and jewellery business it's a fascinating place to visit during the week. As in Amsterdam and New York, ultra-Orthodox Hassidic Jews – easily discernible by their frock coats, black hats, flowing beards and sidelocks – control much of the trade. They are catered for by a couple of kosher cafés on nearby Granville Street.

For more on London's Hassidic Jewish community, see p.235.

While you're here, be sure to take a wander through the **Leather Lane market** (Mon–Fri; lunchtimes), an old Cockney market running parallel to Hatton Garden, now revitalized thanks to the new office developments around Holborn, and selling everything from fruit and veg to clothes and electrical gear.

Little Italy

In the latter half of the nineteenth century, London experienced a huge influx of Italian immigrants who created their own **Little Italy** in the triangle of land now bounded by Clerkenwell Road, Rosebery Avenue and Farringdon Road. Craftsmen, artisans, street performers and musicians were later joined by ice-cream vendors, restaurateurs and political refugees. Between the wars the population peaked at around 10,000 Italians, crammed into overcrowded, insanitary slums. The old streets have long been demolished to make way for council and other low-rent housing, and few Italians live here these days; nevertheless, the area remains a focus for a community that's now spread right across the capital.

St Peter's is the starting point of the annual Italian Procession (or Festival of Our Lady of Mount Carmel), begun in 1883 and now a permanent fixture on the Sunday nearest July 16.

The main point of reference is **St Peter's Italian Church**, built in 1863 and still the favourite venue for Italian weddings and christenings, as well as for Sunday mass. It is rarely open outside of services, though you can view the memorial, situated in the main porch, to the seven hundred Anglo-Italian internees who died aboard the *Arandora Star*, a POW ship which sank en route to Canada in 1940.

A few old-established Italian businesses survive here, too – *Terroni's* delicatessen and *Cantina Augusto* wine merchants, both on Clerkenwell Road, and *Gazzano's* on Farringdon Road – and there's a plaque to **Giuseppe Mazzini**, the chief political theorist behind Italian unification, above the Italian barbers at 10 Laystall Street. Mazzini lived in exile in London for many years and was very active in the Clerkenwell community, establishing a free school for Italian children in Hatton Garden.

Rosebery Avenue

Halfway up Rosebery Avenue – built in the 1890s to link Clerkenwell Road with Islington – stands the **Mount Pleasant Post Office**, the country's largest sorting office, built on the site of the Coldbath Fields prison. Over a third of all inland mail passes through this building, much of it brought by the post office's own underground railway network. Built between the wars and similar in design to the Tube, the railway is fully automatic, sending driverless trucks between sorting offices at speeds of up to 35mph. It's an intriguing sight and one which you can witness if you write to the Post Office Controller, Mail Rail, 148–164 Old Street EC1.

Opposite Mount Pleasant is **Exmouth Market**, a raggle-taggle of tatty stalls (Mon–Sat 9.30am–4.30pm) which survives on the local office workers as much as the residents. The Grimaldi family of clowns lived in Exmouth Market in the nineteenth century, so it's appropriate that the street's church of the **Holy Redeemer** should boast such an unusual Italianate campanile and Roman Catholic interior. At the end of the market, the Spa Field Gardens recall Clerkenwell's days as a fashionable spa, which began in 1683 when Thomas Sadler re-discovered a medicinal well in his garden and established a music house to entertain visitors. The well has long since dried up, but the musical tradition lives on at **Sadler's Wells Theatre**, further up Rosebery Avenue, now one of the city's main venues for visiting opera and ballet companies.

Clerkenwell Green and around

Izaak Walton lived on **Clerkenwell Green** while he wrote *The Compleat Angler*, but by the eighteenth century the green had already lost its grass, and by the nineteenth century poverty and overcrowding were the main feature of Clerkenwell – Oliver Twist learnt the tricks of the trade here in Dickens' tale. At this time the green was known in the press as "the headquarters of republicanism, revolution and ultra-non-conformity" and became a popular spot for demonstrations. The most violent of these was the "Clerkenwell Riot" of 1832, when a policeman was stabbed to death during a clash between unemployed demonstrators and the newly formed Metropolitan police force; the "blue devils", as they were known, were at the height of their unpopularity, and the coroner reached a verdict of justifiable homicide.

The largest building on the green is the Middlesex Sessions House, once the scene of many a political trial, now in the hands of the freemasons. The oldest building, at no. 37a, is the former Welsh Charity School, now the **Marx Memorial Library**, headquarters of the left-wing London Patriotic Club from 1872, and later the Social Democratic Federation press, where **Lenin** edited seventeen editions of the Bolshevik paper *Iskra* in 1902–03 (see box below). The library was founded in 1933 in response to the book burnings taking place in Nazi Germany, and the poky little back room where Lenin worked is maintained as it was then, as a kind of shrine (ask the librarian for permission to see it); to consult the library's unrivalled collection of books and pamphlets on the labour movement, you need to become a member.

The Marx Memorial Library is open Mon 1–6pm, Tues–Thurs 1–8pm, Sat 10am–1pm.

Clerkenwell's connections with **radical politics** have continued into this century: the modern-day Labour Party was founded at a meeting of socialists and trade unionists on Farringdon Road; the Communist Party had its headquarters at St John Street for many years, and the Party paper, the *Daily Worker* (later the *Morning Star*) was printed on Farringdon Road, currently home to *The Guardian*, the country's only left-leaning broadsheet daily with a mass readership.

The area north of the Green was once occupied by the Benedictine convent of St Mary, founded in the twelfth century. The buildings have long since vanished, though the late eighteenth-century church of **St James** on Clerkenwell Close is the descendant of the convent church. The original **Clerk's Well**, which gives the area its name, flowed through the west wall of the nunnery and was "excellently clear, sweet and well tasted" even in 1720, and still in use until the mid-nineteenth century, by which time it had become polluted. It was rediscovered in 1924 and is now visible through the window of 14–16 Farringdon Lane; to get inside, you need to arrange a visit with the Finsbury Library on St John's Street (Mon & Thurs 9am–8pm, Tues & Sat 9am–8pm, Fri 9am–1pm; free).

The House of Detention is open daily 10am–6pm; £3.

Long before Clerkenwell became known for its "thieves' houses", it had been blessed with no fewer than four prison houses to take the overspill from the City gaols. All have since been torn down, but the basement of the **House of Detention**, built in 1846 and demolished in 1890, has recently been excavated and opened as a museum on Clerkenwell Close, just north of St James's church. Tickets are sold from the plush former warder's residence above ground; underground the place has been left authentically dark and dank, enhanced by a theatrical use of sound and light. There's a fifteen-minute guided tour, followed by a Walkman commentary compiled from prisoners' accounts of conditions here, at a time when the emphasis was on religious conversion through sensory deprivation – prisoners were made to wear masks and forbidden to talk, the penalty for which was three days and nights in the "dark cells". The prison's greatest claim to fame, however, was the Irish Fenian bomb attack of 1867, which destroyed much of the prison and killed several people, marking the beginning of modern terrorism in the capital.

Lenin in Clerkenwell

Virtually every Bolshevik leader spent at least some time in exile in London at the beginning of this century, to avoid the attentions of the Tsarist secret police. Lenin and his wife Krupskaya arrived in London in April 1902 and found unfurnished lodgings at 30 Holford Square, off Great Percy Street, under the pseudonyms of Mr and Mrs Jacob Richter (the house was destroyed in the war). The couple entertained numerous other exiles – including Trotsky, whom Lenin met for the first time at Holford Square in October 1902 – but the most important aspect of Lenin's life here was his editing of *Iskra* with Yuli Martov (later the Menshevik leader) and Vera Zasulich (one-time revolutionary assassin). The paper was set in Cyrillic script at a Jewish printer's in the East End and run off the presses at the SDF press on Clerkenwell Green.

In May 1903, Lenin and Krupskaya left to join other exiles in Geneva, but over the next eight years Lenin visited London on five more occasions, twice for research purposes, three times for party congresses. The first two congresses (the 2nd and 3rd overall) were held at secret locations, but the 5th, attended by 330 delegates including Trotsky, Gorky and Stalin, was held openly in the Brotherhood Church on Southgate Road in Islington (since destroyed).

The nearest tubes are Farringdon and Barbican.

St John's and Charterhouse

Of Clerkenwell's three medieval religious establishments, remnants of two – St John's Priory and Charterhouse – survive, hidden away to the southeast of Clerkenwell Green.

St John's Gate museum is open Mon–Fri 10am–5pm, Sat 10am–4pm; £1.

St John's Gate

The oldest of the three foundations was the priory of the Order of St John of Jerusalem, whose Knights Hospitaller, along with the Knights Templar, were responsible for the defence of the Holy Land against the heathens. The sixteenth-century **St John's Gate**, built in

Kentish ragstone on the south side of Clerkenwell Road and originally forming the southern entrance to the complex, is the most visible survivor of the foundation. The twelfth-century priory was sacked by Wat Tyler's poll tax rebels in 1381, when the prior was dragged out and beheaded on Tower Hill.

The gatehouse now forms part of a **museum**, which traces the development of the order prior to its dissolution by Henry VIII, and its re-establishment in 1831, after which it became involved with the nursing and ambulance work that it continues today. Guided tours at 11am and 2.30pm take you into the Gatehouse and Chapter Hall, both of which were re-designed in Victorian mock-medieval style, and over the road into the Grand Priory Church, whose crypt is the only surviving element from the original complex. The priory church was circular, just like the Temple church (see p.168), but all that remains is the curve of its walls, traced out in the cobblestones of St John's Square.

Charterhouse

A little further to the southeast lies **Charterhouse**, founded in 1371 as a Carthusian monastery. The public school, with which the foundation is now most closely associated, left here in 1872 and moved out to Surrey, but forty-odd pensioners – known as "brothers" – are cared for here. The Carthusians were one of the few religious bodies in London to put up any resistance during the Reformation, for which the prior was hanged, drawn and quartered at Tyburn, after which his severed arm was nailed to the gatehouse as a warning to the rest of the community, fifteen more of whom were later martyred. This gatehouse on Charterhouse Square, which retains its fourteenth-century oak doors, is the starting point for exhaustive two-hour **guided tours** that are the only way to visit the site.

There are guided tours of Charterhouse April–July Wed 2.15pm; £3.

In the Tudor period the monastery was rebuilt as a private mansion, which is why its architecture is reminiscent of an Oxbridge college rather than a religious institution. Very little remains of the original monastic buildings, which featured a large cloister surrounded by individual monks' cells, each with its own garden. The monks lived on a diet of fish and home-grown vegetables, and were only allowed to speak to one another on Sundays; three of their tiny self-contained cells can still be seen in the west wall of **Preachers' Court**.

The larger of the two enclosed courtyards, **Masters' Court**, which was badly gutted in the last war, retains the wonderful Great Hall, which boasts a fine carved Renaissance screen and a largely reconstructed hammerbeam roof, and the Great Chamber where Elizabeth I and James I were entertained. The **Chapel**, with its geometrical plasterwork ceiling, is half-Tudor and half-Jacobean, and contains the marble and alabaster tomb of **Thomas Sutton**, whose greyhound-head emblem crops up throughout the building. It was Sutton, deemed "the richest commoner in England" at the time, who bought the place in 1611 and converted it into a charity school for boys and an almshouse for gentlemen.

The City

THE CITY is where London begun. Long established as the financial district, it stretches from Temple Bar in the west to the Tower of London in the east – administrative boundaries that are only a slightly larger than those marked by the Roman walls and their medieval successors. In this Square Mile (as the City is sometimes referred to), you'll find precious few leftovers of London's early days, however, since four-fifths of the area burnt down in the Great Fire of 1666. Rebuilt in brick and stone, the City gradually lost its centrality as London swelled westwards, though it has maintained its position as Britain's financial heartland, home to banking, insurance and other services. What you see on the ground is mostly the product of three fairly recent phases: the Victorian building boom of the latter half of the nineteenth century; the over-zealous post-war reconstruction following the Blitz; and the money-grabbing frenzy of the Thatcherite 1980s, in which nearly fifty percent of the City's office space was rebuilt, regardless of the lack of potential occupants. Much of the City now comprises impressive-looking but redundant real estate.

When you consider what has happened here, it's amazing that so much has survived to pay witness to the City's two-thousand-year history. Wren's spires still punctuate the skyline here and there, and his masterpiece, **St Paul's Cathedral**, remains one of London's geographical and tourist pivots. At the eastern edge of the City, the **Tower of London**, begun shortly after the Norman Conquest, still stands protected by some of the best preserved medieval fortifications in Europe. Other lesser relics, such as Wren's **Monument** to the Great Fire, and the city's oldest synagogue and church, are less conspicuous, and even Londoners have problems finding the more modern attractions of the **Museum of London** and the **Barbican** arts complex.

It's also worth checking out some of the new architecture that has shot up within the Square Mile since the mid-1980s, most famously the **Lloyds Building**, London's most adventurous modern building, designed by Richard Rogers. There are obvious parallels between new City projects and the benighted Docklands development (see Chapter 7), but creations such as the vast **Broadgate** complex, up by Liverpool Street Station, have been more successful on the whole.

Perhaps the biggest change of all, though, has been in the City's population. Up until the eighteenth century the vast majority of Londoners lived and worked in or around the City; nowadays while more than 300,000 commuters spend the best part of Monday to Friday here, only 5000 people remain at night and at weekends, most of them cooped up in the upmarket apartments of the Barbican complex. The result of this demographic shift is that the City is fully alive only during office hours, and the installation of police roadblocks in 1993, after a couple of vastly destructive IRA bombs, has done little to add to its charm.

The time to visit the City is during the week, since many pubs, restaurants and even some tube stations and tourist sights close when the workers go home.

The one unchanging aspect of the City is its special status, conferred on it by William the Conqueror and extended and reaffirmed by successive monarchs and governments ever since. Nowadays, with its Lord Mayor, its Beadles, Sheriffs and Aldermen, its separate police force and its select electorate of freemen and liverymen, the City is an anachronism of the worst kind. The Corporation, which runs the City like a one-party mini-state, is an

The City churches

The City of London is now over-endowed with churches – thirty-six at the last count, the majority of them built or re-built by Wren. Prompted by the decline in the City's population, the Victorians demolished a fair few; but there are still far to many to be supported by the tiny resident population. In 1994 the Templeman Commission recommended leaving only twelve open for worship, and although it seems unlikely that this plan will be implemented in full, the threat of closure hangs over even the six choice buildings listed below.

St Bartholomew-the-Great, Cloth Fair. The oldest surviving church in the City and by far the most atmospheric; a fascinating building. St Paul's aside, if you visit just one church in the City, it should be this one (see p.195).

St Mary Abchurch, Cannon Street. Uniquely for Wren's City churches, the interior features a huge painted domed ceiling, plus the only authenticated Gibbons' reredos (see p.205).

St Mary Aldermary, Queen Victoria Street. Wren's most successful stab at Gothic, with fan vaulting in the aisles and a panelled ceiling in the nave (see p.202).

St Mary Woolnoth, Lombard Street. Hawksmoor's only City church, sporting an unusually broad, bulky tower and a Baroque clerestory that floods the church with light from its semicircular windows (see p.204).

St Olave, Hart Street. Built in the fifteenth century, and one of the few pre-Fire Gothic churches in the City (see p.211).

St Stephen Walbrook, Walbrook. Wren's dress-rehearsal for St Paul's, with a wonderful central dome, and plenty of wood carving by Gibbons (see p.204).

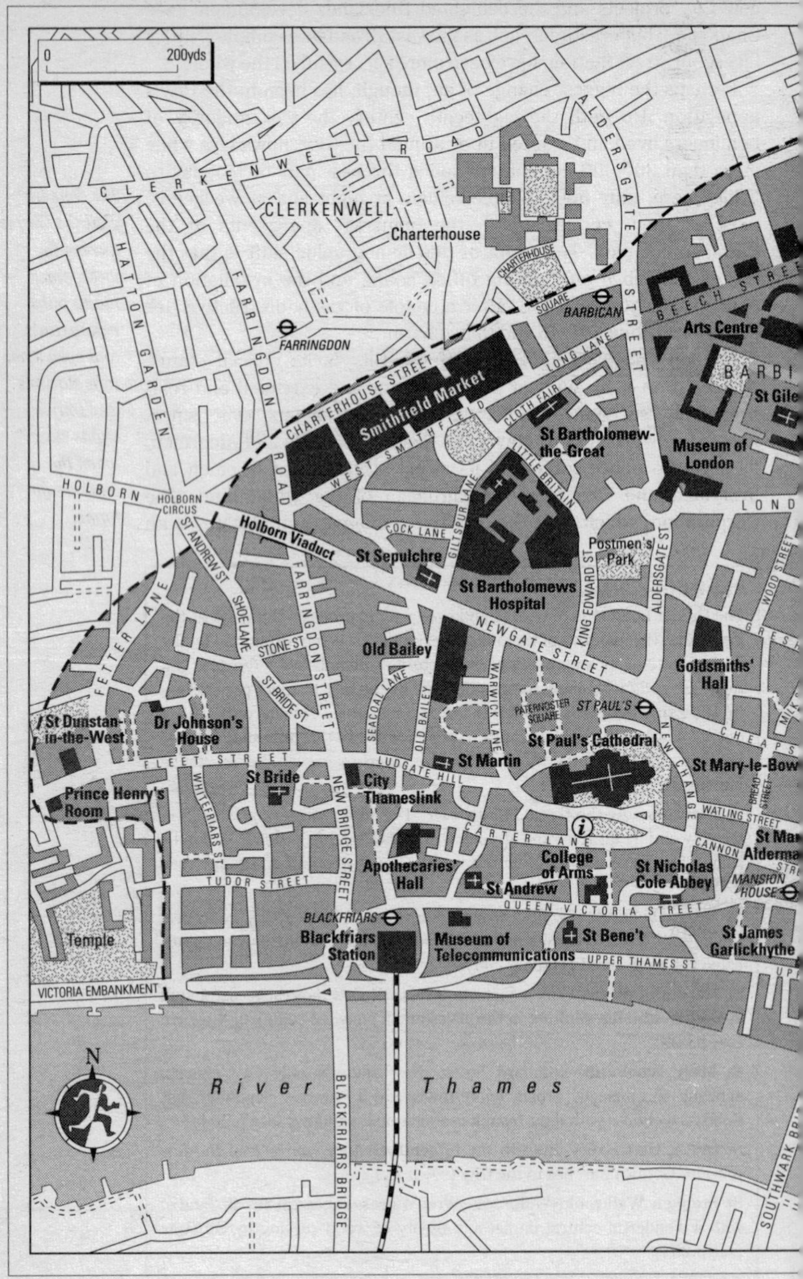
0
200yds
CLERKENWELL ROAD
CLERKENWELL
Charterhouse
CHARTERHOUSE SQUARE
ALDERSGATE STREET
HATTON GARDEN
FARRINGDON ROAD
FARRINGDON
BARBICAN
BEECH STREET
Arts Centre
BARBI
St Gile
LONG LANE
CHARTERHOUSE STREET
Smithfield Market
WEST SMITHFIELD
CLOTH FAIR
St Bartholomew-the-Great
LITTLE BRITAIN
Museum of London
LOND
HOLBORN
HOLBORN CIRCUS
Holborn Viaduct
COCK LANE
GILTSPUR LANE
St Sepulchre
Postmen's Park
St Bartholomews Hospital
KING EDWARD ST
ALDERSGATE ST
WOOD STREET
ST ANDREW ST
SHOE LANE
FETTER LANE
FARRINGDON STREET
NEWGATE STREET
GRESH
STONE ST
Old Bailey
ST BRIDE ST
Goldsmiths' Hall
SEACOAL LANE
OLD BAILEY
WARWICK LANE
PATERNOSTER SQUARE
ST PAUL'S
St Dunstan-in-the-West
Dr Johnson's House
St Paul's Cathedral
NEW CHANGE
CHEAPS
FLEET STREET
LUDGATE HILL
St Martin
St Mary-le-Bow
St Bride
City Thameslink
NEW BRIDGE STREET
BREAD STREET
WATLING STREET
Prince Henry's Room
WHITEFRIARS ST
CARTER LANE
CANNON
St Ma
Alderma
College of Arms
Apothecaries' Hall
St Nicholas Cole Abbey
St Andrew
MANSION HOUSE
TUDOR STREET
QUEEN VICTORIA STREET
BLACKFRIARS
Blackfriars Station
Museum of Telecommunications
St Bene't
St James Garlickhythe
Temple
UPPER THAMES ST
VICTORIA EMBANKMENT
N
River Thames
BLACKFRIARS BRIDGE
SOUTHWARK BR

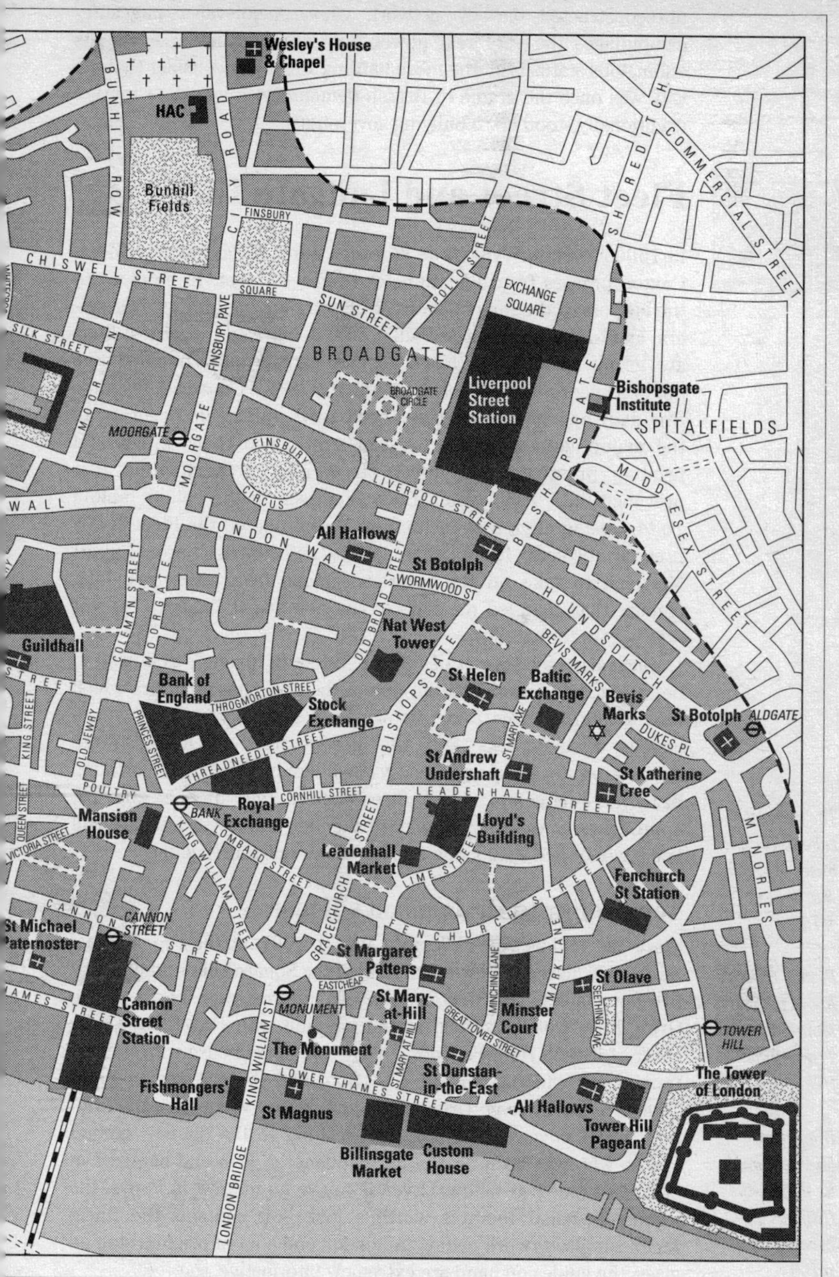

Wesley's House & Chapel
HAC
BUNHILL ROW
Bunhill Fields
CITY ROAD
FINSBURY SQUARE
SHOREDITCH
COMMERCIAL STREET
CHISWELL STREET
SILK STREET
MOOR LANE
FINSBURY PAVE
SUN STREET
APOLLO STREET
EXCHANGE SQUARE
BROADGATE
BROADGATE CIRCLE
Liverpool Street Station
Bishopsgate Institute
SPITALFIELDS
MOORGATE
FINSBURY CIRCUS
LIVERPOOL STREET
MIDDLESEX STREET
WALL
LONDON WALL
All Hallows
St Botolph
WORMWOOD ST
OLD BROAD STREET
COLEMAN STREET
MOORGATE
BISHOPSGATE
HOUNDSDITCH
Guildhall
Nat West Tower
BEVIS MARKS
Bank of England
THROGMORTON STREET
Stock Exchange
St Helen
Baltic Exchange
Bevis Marks
St Botolph
ALDGATE
DUKES PL
KING STREET
OLD JEWRY
PRINCES STREET
THREADNEEDLE STREET
St Andrew Undershaft
ST MARY AXE
St Katherine Cree
POULTRY
BANK
CORNHILL STREET
LEADENHALL STREET
QUEEN STREET
Mansion House
Royal Exchange
Lloyd's Building
MINORIES
VICTORIA STREET
KING WILLIAM STREET
LOMBARD STREET
Leadenhall Market
LIME STREET
Fenchurch St Station
CANNON STREET
St Michael Paternoster
GRACECHURCH STREET
FENCHURCH STREET
St Margaret Pattens
MINCHING LANE
MARK LANE
St Olave
SEETHING LANE
EASTCHEAP
St Mary-at-Hill
THAMES STREET
Cannon Street Station
MONUMENT
Minster Court
GREAT TOWER STREET
TOWER HILL
KING WILLIAM ST
The Monument
ST MARY AT HILL
St Dunstan-in-the-East
The Tower of London
Fishmongers' Hall
LOWER THAMES STREET
St Magnus
All Hallows
Tower Hill Pageant
LONDON BRIDGE
Billinsgate Market
Custom House

unreconstructed old-boy network whose medievalist pageantry camouflages the very real power and wealth which it holds. Its anomalous status is all the more baffling when you consider that the City was once the cradle of British democracy: it was the City that traditionally stood up to bullying sovereigns.

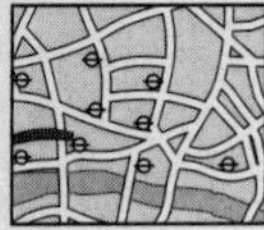

Fleet Street and Ludgate Hill

In 1500 a certain Wynkyn de Worde, a pupil of Caxton, moved the Caxton presses from Westminster to **Fleet Street**, to be close to the lawyers of the Inns of Court, who were among his best customers, and to the clergy of St Paul's, who comprised the largest literate group in the city. However, the street really boomed two hundred years later, when in 1702 the *Daily Courant*, Britain's first daily paper, was published here. By the nineteenth century all the major national and provincial dailies had their offices and printing presses in the Fleet Street district, a situation that prevailed until 1985, when Eddy Shah set up the colour tabloid *Today*, using computer technology that rendered the Fleet Street presses obsolete. It was then left to gutter-press baron Rupert Murdoch to take on the printers' unions in a bitter year-long dispute that changed the face of the newspaper industry forever (see p.240, for details).

These days the "Street of Ink" or "Street of Shame", as it used to be known, is no more. All but one of the press headquarters which once dominated this part of town have now relocated, leaving a couple of landmarks and the headquarters of Reuters/Press Association to testify to nearly five hundred years of printing history. Nonetheless, Fleet Street offers one of the grandest approaches to the City, thanks to the view across to Ludgate Hill and beyond to St Paul's, the City's number one tourist sight.

The nearest tube is Temple; buses #4, #6, #9, #11 or #15.

Temple Bar to Dr Johnson's House

Since the Middle Ages, **Temple Bar** (p.169), at the top of Fleet Street, has marked the western limit of the Square Mile's administrative boundaries. This western part of the street was spared by the Great Fire, which stopped at the junction with Fetter Lane, just short of **Prince Henry's Room**, a fine Jacobean house with timber-framed bay windows on the first floor and the gateway to Inner Temple at street level. Originally a pub, later a waxworks, the first-floor room now contains material relating to the diarist, **Samuel Pepys**, who was born nearby in Southampton Row and baptized in St Bride's (see box below). Even if you've no interest in Pepys, the wooden-panelled room is worth a look – it contains the finest Jacobean plasterwork ceiling in London and a lot of original stained glass; the guides on hand are extremely informative, too.

Prince Henry's Room is open Mon–Sat 11am–2pm; free.

Inner and Middle Temple lie within the City but are covered on p.166.

Opposite stands the church of **St Dunstan-in-the-West**, whose distinctive octagonal tower and lantern, built in neo-Gothic style, dominate this top end of the street. To the side of the tower is the much earlier clock temple, erected by the parishoners in thanks for escaping the Great Fire; within the temple, Gog and Magog, in gilded loincloths, nod their heads and clang their bells on the hour.

Numerous narrow alleyways lead off the north side of Fleet Street beyond Fetter Lane, concealing legal chambers and offices. Two such alleys – Bolt Court and Hind Court – eventually open out into **Gough Square**, a newly cobbled courtyard surrounded, for the most part, by neo-Georgian buildings.

Dr Johnson's House

Dr Johnson's House is open May–Sept Mon–Sat 11am–5.30pm; Oct–April closes 5pm; £3.

Gough Square's one seventeenth-century building is **Dr Johnson's House**, where the great *savant*, writer and lexicographer lived from 1747 to 1759, whilst compiling the 41,000 entries for the first dictionary of the English language. Johnson came to London from Lichfield with David Garrick, the pair taking it in turns to ride the one horse they could afford; Garrick had three halfpennies in his pocket, Johnson was richer by a penny. For several years Johnson lived on little more than bread and water in a garret on Exeter Street, before he finally rented the house on Gough Square, paid for with the £1500 advance he received for the dictionary. Despite his subsequent fame, though, Johnson remained in and out of debt all his life – his famous philosophical romance, *Rasselas*, was written in less than a week to raise funds for his mother's funeral.

For details of Fleet Street's pubs, see Chapter 16.

The grey-panelled rooms of the house are peppered with period furniture and lined with portraits and etchings of Johnson, as well as pictures of Boswell, his biographer, and other members of their circle, including Johnson's black servant Francis Barber. Quirky memorabilia include Boswell's coffee cup, two first edition copies of the great *Dictionary*, and Johnson's gout chair from the *Old Cock Tavern*, a pub still standing on Fleet Street. The open-plan attic, in which Johnson and his six helpers put together the *Dictionary*, now looks a bit like a classroom, lined with explanatory panels on lexicography.

The press buildings and St Bride's

Two outstanding pieces of architecture bear witness to Fleet Street's heyday. First off, at no. 135, is the old HQ of the **Daily Telegraph** (dubbed the "Torygraph" for its entrenched conservatism), now occupied by the *Credit Agricole* bank. An adventurous building for such a conservative newspaper, it was one of London's first (and few) truly Art Deco edifices. It was upstaged three years later, however, by the sleek black **Daily Express** building, the city's first glass curtain-wall construction, with its remarkable chrome and gold foyer. You can glimpse this from outside but it has been closed for redevelopment since the paper's departure from the street in

Fleet Street and Ludgate Hill

St Bride's is open Mon–Sat 8.30am–5pm, Sun 9am–7.30 pm; choral services take place Sun 11am & 6.30pm.

1989. Across the way, **Reuters/Press Association** are the sole survivors of the old Fleet Street, still occupying the Portland stone fortress designed in 1935 by Lutyens.

The best source of information about the old-style Fleet Street is the so-called "journalists' and printers' cathedral", the church of **St Bride's**, situated behind the Reuters building on the site of Wynkyn de Worde's sixteenth-century press. The church boasts Wren's tallest and most exquisite spire (said to be the inspiration for the traditional tiered wedding cake), but was extensively damaged in the Blitz. The Nazis' bombs did, however, reveal a crypt containing remains of Roman mosaics, medieval walls and seven churches. Nestled amongst these relics, a little **museum of Fleet Street history** includes a print of the front page of the first *Daily Courant* and a 1785 issue of the *Universal Daily Register*, which was to become *The Times*, claiming to be "the faithful recorder of every species of intelligence . . . circulated for a particular set of readers only".

Samuel Pepys

Born to a tailor and a washmaid in Salisbury Court, off Fleet Street, **Samuel Pepys** (1633–1703) was baptized in St Bride's and buried in St Olave's, having spent virtually his entire life in London. Family connections ensured an education at St Paul's and Cambridge, followed by a rapid rise through the ranks of the civil service. He served as an MP, rose to the position of Secretary to the Admiralty, and was largely responsible for the establishment of a professional British Navy. In 1679 he was imprisoned for six weeks in the Tower on suspicion of treason but returned to office only to be forced out again in 1689, following the overthrow of James II, after which he withdrew from public life.

Pepys' career achievements are well documented in official archives, but it is his diaries which have immortalized him. The diaries' million-plus words record one of the most eventful decades in English history. Written between 1660 and 1669, this rollicking journal includes eyewitness accounts of the Restoration of the monarchy, the Great Plague of 1665 and the Great Fire of 1666, giving an unparalleled insight into life in mid-seventeenth-century London. Ultimately, Pepys emerges, warts and all, from the pages as a eminently likeable character, who seems almost imperturbable – he gives as much space to details of his pub meals as he does to the Great Fire, and finishes each day with his catch phrase "and so to bed".

Pepys was also a notorious womanizer, detailing his philanderings in his diary in Spanish, so as to avoid detection by his French Huguenot wife. Nevertheless he was caught *in flagrante* with one of his wife's best friends, and his slow reconciliation with his wife is recorded in a novelist's detail, the diary ending in 1669 as they sail off to the Continent to patch things up. In the event his wife died later that year and he never remarried. Pepys' later years were largely taken up with compiling his vast library, which he bequeathed along with his manuscripts to his old college in Cambridge. There his diaries lay undiscovered until the nineteenth century, when they were finally transcribed from their shorthand (with the erotic passages omitted) and published for the first time in 1825.

Ludgate Circus and Ludgate Hill

Fleet Street and Ludgate Hill

Fleet Street terminates at **Ludgate Circus**, which has held onto three of its four original segments dating from the 1870s, when it replaced the bridge crossing the Fleet River, which joins the Thames at Blackfriars Bridge. Buried under the roads in the 1760s after a drunken butcher got stuck in the mud and froze to death, the Fleet marked the western boundary of the Roman city, and was an unmissable feature of the landscape, as the tanneries and slaughterhouses of Smithfield (p.196) used to turn the Fleet red with entrails. The western bank of the Fleet was the site of the notoriously inhumane **Fleet Prison**, whose famous incumbents included the poet John Donne, imprisoned here for marrying without his father-in-law's consent. Until the Marriage Act of 1754, Fleet Prison was famous for its clandestine "**Fleet Marriages**", performed by priests (or imposters) who were imprisoned there for debt. These marriages, which attracted men of all classes, took place in the prison chapel until 1710 when they were banished to the neighbouring taverns, the fee being split between clergyman and innkeeper.

The nearest tube is Blackfriars.

Beyond the Circus, **Ludgate Hill** curves up to St Paul's, the view of the dome punctuated by the lead spire of the church of **St Martin-within-Ludgate**, which still rises above the housetops just as Wren intended. It was originally the church of Ludgate, one of the six city gates, which according to tradition was built by King Lud in the first century BC; the gate was eventually torn down in 1760. The cruciform interior of the church is crisply maintained by several city guilds and masonic lodges, including the secretive Knights of the Round Table.

St Paul's Cathedral

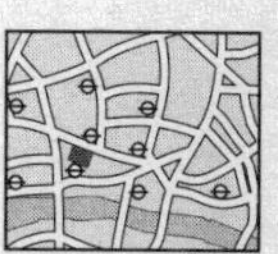

St Paul's Cathedral, topped by an enormous lead-covered dome that's second in size only to St Peter's in Rome, has been a London icon since the Blitz, when it stood defiantly unscathed amid the carnage (or so it appeared on the famous wartime propaganda photo). It remains a dominating presence in the City despite the encroaching tower blocks of the financial sector – its showpiece west facade is particularly magnificent, fronted by a wide flights of steps, a double-storey portico and two of London's most Baroque towers, at its most impressive at night bathed in sea-green arc lights. Westminster Abbey, St Paul's long-standing rival, has the edge when it comes to celebrity corpses, pre-Reformation sculpture, royal connections and sheer atmosphere. St Paul's, by contrast, is a soulless but perfectly calculated architectural set-piece, a burial place for captains rather than kings, though it does continue to serve as a popular wedding church for the privileged few of the upper stratosphere. Charles and Di exchanged their vows here.

St Paul's is open Mon–Sat 8.30am–4.15pm; £3, combination ticket with the galleries £5; the nearest tube is St Paul's.

St Paul's Cathedral

Excluding the temple to Apollo which may have stood here in Roman times, the current building is the fifth church on this site, its immediate predecessor being Old St Paul's, a huge cathedral whose 489-foot spire was one of the wonders of medieval Europe. By all accounts, Old St Paul's was an unruly place, and home to obscure cults devoted to the likes of the fictitious St Uncumber, a bearded virgin who could rid women of unwanted husbands in return for pecks of oats. Horse-fairs took place here, ball-games had to be banned in 1385, and by the close of the sixteenth century it had become a "common passage and thoroughfare . . . a daily receptacle for rogues and beggars however diseased, to the great offence of religious-minded people". During the Commonwealth, the nave became a cavalry barracks, with both men and horses living in the church, and shops were set up in the portico. By the Restoration things had become so bad that St Paul's was dubbed "a loathsome Golgotha" – and on one memorable occasion a circus horse named Morocco performed tricks here, including a quick trot up the stairs to the top of the belltower.

The Great Fire caused irreparable damage to this unlikely centre of iniquity, and Christopher Wren was given the task of building a replacement – just one of over fifty church commissions he received in the wake of the blaze. The final design was a compromise solution after several more radical, European-style plans were rejected by the conservative clergy. Hassles over money plagued the project throughout; at one point Parliament withheld half of Wren's salary because they felt the work was proceeding too slowly. Wren remained unruffled and rose to the challenge of building what was, in effect, the world's first Protestant cathedral, completing the commission in 1711 during the reign of Queen Anne, whose statue still stands in front of the west facade.

The interior

St Paul's is now a major tourist business, with visitors funnelled towards the ticket booth through revolving doors. Before reaching the till you pass the **Chapel of All Souls**, containing a memorial to Lord Kitchener, the moustachioed figure on the First World War "Your Country Needs You" posters.

Once through the turnstiles, you can take in the main body of the church for the first time. Queen Victoria thought it "dirty, dark and undevotional", though since the destruction of the stained glass in the Blitz it is once again light and airy as Wren intended. The place to start a tour is under the **dome**, which was decorated (against Wren's wishes) by Thornhill's *trompe l'oeil* frescoes, rather insipid but built on a scale that can't fail to impress.

Churchill lay in state here in 1965, and a memorial plaque beneath the dome indicates where his catafalque stood, while several million paid their respects. St Paul's permanent funerary monuments are disappointing, however, commemorating for the most part nineteenth-century military and political figures. Burials are actually confined to the crypt; the memorials in the main body of the church are just that. The best of the bunch are Flaxman's **Nelson memorial**, in the south transept, with its sea-sick lion, and, in the north aisle, Alfred Steven's bombastic bronze and marble **Duke of Wellington monument**, begun in 1857 but only topped by the statue of the duke astride his faithful steed, Copenhagen, in 1925. On the opposite side of the nave hangs St Paul's most famous work of art, the crushingly symbolic *Light of the World* by the Pre-Raphaelite painter Holman Hunt, depicting Christ knocking at the handleless, bramble-strewn door of the human soul, which must be opened from within.

The commercialism of the various souvenir stalls (soon to be confined to the crypt) is as nothing compared to the exhibition sponsored by one of the privatized electricity companies in the north choir aisle – supposedly telling "The History of St Paul's", it's little more than a self-congratulatory gathering of Royal photographs, somewhat inappropriately in the case of Chas and Di. With the one-way system, you have to walk past all this in order to admire the intricately carved choir stalls and organ casing, possibly the work of Grinling Gibbons, who worked with Wren on many of his commissions. To leave the chancel, you pass through the south choir aisle, where the upstanding shroud of **John Donne**, poet, preacher and one-time Dean of St Paul's, now resides, the only complete effigy to have survived from the previous cathedral.

The crypt

The staircase to the **crypt** – reputedly the largest in Europe – is immediately on your left as you leave the south choir aisle. The whitewashed walls and bright lighting, however, make this one of the least atmospheric mausoleums you could imagine – a far cry from the last century, when visitors were shown around the tombs by candlelight.

Immediately to the left as you enter is a new memorial to the hundreds of British soldiers who died in the **Falklands War**, listed aphabetically without rank, in an unusually egalitarian gesture. The two star tombs are those of **Nelson** and **Wellington**, both occupying centre stage and both with more fanciful monuments upstairs. Nelson's embalmed body lies in a black marble sarcophagus originally designed for Cardinal Wolsey and later intended for Henry VIII and his third wife, Jane Seymour; Wellington's porphyry and granite monstrosity is set in its own mini-chapel surrounded by other illustrious British field marshals, including Admiral Beatty, who in 1936 became the last person to be buried in St Paul's.

At the eastern end of the crypt is St Faith's Chapel, named after the parish church which disappeared when the choir of Old St Paul's was enlarged in the fourteenth century. It's now the most modern part of the cathedral, having been redesigned on and off since the 1960s, when it was designated the OBE Chapel, commemorating the state-honoured. The southern aisle is popularly known as **Artists' Corner**, and boasts as many painters and architects as Westminster Abbey has poets. It became a popular resting place with the arrival of Wren himself; his son composed the inscription on his tomb – *lector, si monumentum requiris, circumspice* (reader, if you seek his monument, look around). Close to Wren are the graveslabs of Reynolds, Turner, Millais, Holman Hunt, Lord Leighton and Alma-Tadema; nearby there's a bust of Van Dyck, whose monument perished along with Old St Paul's. In the north aisle are a modern plaque to the great church reformer John Wycliffe, and the grave of Alexander Fleming, the discoverer of penicillin.

The **treasury**, situated at the west end of the crypt, displays church plate, richly embroidered copes and mitres, and bejewelled altar crosses. More interesting is the exhibition on the previous churches on the site, including a model of Old St Paul's, Wren's early plans for the cathedral, and his "Great Model", a wooden replica of the architect's favoured design, which was to have had a dome even larger than the present structure. Nearby there are a couple of damaged marble effigies from the previous cathedral, including the mutilated half torso of Francis Bacon.

The dome

It'll cost you an extra £2.50 to climb up into the dome's galleries if you haven't bought a combination ticket at the entrance.

A series of stairs, begining in the south transept, lead to the dome's three **galleries**, none are which are much fun for anyone with a fear of heights.

The initial 250-odd steps are relatively painless and take you as far as the internal **Whispering Gallery**, so-called because of its acoustic properties – words whispered to the wall on one side are distinctly audible over one hundred feet away on the other. Another 118 steps up, the broad exterior **Stone Gallery**, around the balustrade at the base of the dome, offers a great view of the City and along the Thames where you should be able to identify the distinctive white facade of Wren's London house from which he could contemplate his masterpiece.

The final leg of the climb – 153 fire-escape-type steps – takes you inside the dome's very complicated structure: the inner painted cupola is separated from the wooden, lead-covered outer dome by a funnel-shaped brick cone which acts as a support for the lantern, with its **Golden Gallery**, and ultimately the golden ball and cross which tops the cathedral. The view from the Golden Gallery is unbeatable, but before you ascend the last flight of stairs, be sure to take a look through the peephole in the floor, which looks down onto the monochrome marble floor beneath the dome, a truly terrifying sight.

The Blitz

The **Blitz** bombing of London in World War II began on September 7, 1940 and continued for 57 consecutive nights, then intermittently until the final and most devastating attack on the night of May 10, 1941, when 550 Luftwaffe planes dropped over 100,000 incendiaries and hundreds of explosive bombs in a matter of hours. The death toll that night was over 1400, bringing the total killed during the Blitz to between 20,000 and 30,000, with some 230,000 homes wrecked. Along with the East End, the City was particularly badly hit: in a single raid on December 29 (dubbed the "Second Fire of London"), 1400 fires broke out across the Square Mile. Some say the Luftwaffe left St Paul's standing as a navigation aid, but it came close to destruction when a bomb landed near the southwest tower; luckily this didn't go off, and was successfully removed to the Hackney marshes, where its detonation left a crater 100 feet wide.

The authorities were ready to build mass graves, but unable to provide adequate air-raid shelters. The corrugated steel "Anderson" shelters were only of use for one in four London households – those with gardens in which to bury them. Around 180,000 made use of the Tube, despite initial government reluctance, by simply buying a ticket and staying below ground. The cheery photos of singing and dancing in the Underground which the censors allowed to be published tell nothing of the stale air, rats and lice that folk had to contend with. And even the Tube stations couldn't withstand a direct hit, as occurred at Bank, when over 100 died. In the end, the vast majority of Londoners – some 60 percent – simply hid under the sheets and prayed.

The churchyard

The City of London Information Centre (April–Sept daily 9.30am–5pm; Oct–March Mon–Fri 9.30am–5pm, Sat 9.30am–12.30pm) is situated to the south of St Paul's.

St Paul's itself may have survived the war relatively unscathed, but the area immediately surrounding it, still known as **St Paul's Churchyard**, was obliterated. From 1500 until World War II this district was the centre of the London book trade; Wynkyn de Worde was among the first to set up shop here, though his main office was on Fleet Street. Another feature of the churchyard was **St Paul's Cross** – also known as "Pol's Stump" – where proclamations and political speeches were made from a wooden pulpit. Heretics were regularly executed on this spot, and in 1519 Luther's works were publicly burned here, before Henry VIII changed sides and demanded the "preaching down" of papal authority from the same spot. The cross was finally destroyed by Cromwell and his followers, and a memorial to the cross erected to the northeast of the cathedral in 1910.

Blackfriars to Southwark Bridge

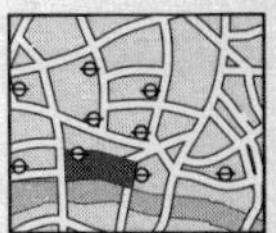

The combination of Victorian town planning, which created Queen Victoria Street, and post-war traffic schemes, which are responsible for the thundering dual carriageway and underpass of Upper Thames Street, are enough to put most people off venturing into

Blackfriars to Southwark Bridge

this part of the City, to the south of St Paul's. Despite these handicaps, however, there are several fine Wren churches to explore in the backstreets and alleyways, and attempts are under way to reclaim the riverfront for pedestrians, now that the old wharves are no longer in use. So far, the riverside walk extends from Blackfriars Bridge as far as Broken Wharf, beyond which there are still several derelict sites waiting to be redeveloped.

Blackfriars area

The area around **Blackfriars**, where a Dominican monastery stood until the Dissolution, sees few tourists nowadays, yet in the seventeenth century it was a fashionable district – Ben Jonson had a house here as did Shakespeare and later Van Dyck. Thoroughly destroyed in the Great Fire, the area suffered only peripheral damage from wartime bombing, leaving a warren of alleyways, courtyards and narrow streets, which, while holding few specific sights, manage to convey something of the look of the City before the Victorians, the German bombers and the Sixties' brutalists did their worst. To give some structure to your wanderings, head down

The Black Friar, *London's most ornate Arts and Crafts pub, stands near the site of the old monastery.*

The City Livery Companies

The ninety or so City **Livery Companies** are descended from the craft guilds of the Middle Ages, whose medieval purpose was to administer apprenticeships and take charge of quality control, in return for which they were granted monopolies. As their powers and wealth grew, the guilds advertised their success by staging lavish banquets and building ever more opulent halls for their meetings and ceremonies. The wealthiest members of each company wore elaborate "livery" or uniforms on such occasions, and automatically received the Freedom of the City, entitling them to take part in the election of the Lord Mayor and his Sheriffs and stand for the Court of Common Council, the Corporation's ruling body.

Despite various attempts to introduce democracy over the centuries, the organization of the Livery Companies remains deeply undemocratic, but their prodigious wealth has enabled them to fund almshouses, schools and a wide range of other charities, all of which has helped pacify their critics. As in masonic lodges (to which most liverymen belong), the elaborate ceremonies are used to hide the very real power which these companies still hold. For, in spite of the fact that many of the old trades associated with the Livery Companies have died out, liverymen still dominate the Court of Common Council.

Anyone visiting the City can't fail to notice the numerous signs directing you to the livery company halls, many with enticing names such as the Wax Chandlers and Cordwainers. Few medieval halls survived the Great Fire, fewer still the Blitz, but they are worth a look nonetheless. The problem is gaining admission. Some have limited free entry but most allow only holders of advance tickets, which are dispensed by the City of London Information Centre (☎0171/606 3030; £2.50 per hall). It's not really something you can do on the spur of the moment, since most tickets are valid for a specific afternoon two weeks or more in advance.

Creed Lane and St Andrew's Hill, backstreets to the south of Ludgate Hill, to the least costly of Wren's churches, **St Andrew-by-the-Wardrobe**, so called because the royal depot for furniture and armour was situated here before the Great Fire. To the north, off **Carter Lane**, you'll find various unexpected little streets and courtyards – like Wardrobe Place – that present a slice of the pre-Blitz City. At the end of Carter Lane you come to Ludgate Broadway and the cobbles of Blackfriars Lane. Ahead is the wedding-cake spire of St Bride's (p.184), viewed across bomb sites that are only now being redeveloped; to the south is the **Apothecaries' Hall**, one of the prettiest of the City livery companies (see box below), with a tiny doorway leading to a pastel-shaded seventeenth-century court.

Queen Victoria Street

South of St Andrew-by-the-Wardrobe, on Queen Victoria Street, is British Telecom's **Story of Telecommunications** museum, housed in a pebbledash carbuncle that looks like a multi-storey car park. The exhibition inside is interesting enough, though unless you've a passionate interest in optic fibre cables or suchlike, you'll find some

The BT Museum is open Mon–Fri 10am–5pm; free.

If you're determined, below is a selection of the most interesting of the City Livery halls.

Apothecaries' Hall, Blackfriars' Lane (☎071/236 1180). This seventeenth-century courtyard is open to the public but to view the magnificent staircase and the Great Hall, with its musicians' gallery, portrait by Reynolds and collection of pharmaceutical gear, entry is by written application only.

Fishmongers' Hall, London Bridge (☎0171/626 3531). A prominent Greek Revival building on the riverfront, with a grand staircase and the dagger that killed Wat Tyler (see p.196); limited tickets occasionally available from the tourist office.

Goldsmiths' Hall, Foster Lane (☎0171/606 8971). Features a sumptuous central staircase built in the 1830s. One of the easiest to visit: there are occasional public exhibitions; at other times, limited tickets are available from the tourist office.

Merchant Taylors' Hall, 30 Threadneedle Street (☎0171/588 7606). Contains more medieval masonry than any other livery hall in the fourteenth-century crypt chapel; entry by written application only.

Skinners' Hall, Dowgate Hill (☎0171/236 5629). Seventeenth-century courtroom and hall containing a splendid Russian chandelier; limited tickets are available from the tourist office.

Tallow Chandlers' Hall, Dowgate Hill (☎0171/248 4726). Retains its seventeeth-century courtroom; limited tickets are available from the tourist office in June only.

Vintners' Hall, Upper Thames Street (☎0171/236 1863). The oldest hall in the City, dating from 1676, with magnificent staircase; limited tickets are available from the tourist office.

of it hard going. The top floor takes you from the early telegraph system to the present day. BT's privatization is mentioned in passing, though oddly enough there's no mention of the company's outrageous profits, the management's unbelievable pay rises, nor the fortune spent on the new prancing Pan logo. The museum continues downstairs with more interactive displays on various themes; you can also have go at the latest gadget set to hit the market, a videophone.

The College of Arms is open Mon–Fri 10am–4pm; free.

Further along Queen Victoria Street stands the surprising little red-brick mansion of the **College of Arms**, which was built round a courtyard in the 1670s, but subsequently opened up to the south with the building of the new road. The Earl Marshal's Court – featuring a gallery, copious wooden panelling and a modest throne – is the only one open to the public, unless you apply to trace your family or study heraldry in the college library. Wren's Dutch-looking church of **St Benet**, opposite, completes this vignette of seventeenth-century London, but like his church of St Nicholas Cole Abbey, further east, it is usually closed.

St James Garlickhythe and Dick Whittington

Just down Lambeth Hill, is the tower of St Mary Somerset, looking very forlorn, its main body having been destroyed in 1871. Further east still, along Upper Thames Street, is the elegant three-tiered steeple of yet another Wren church, **St James Garlickhythe**, hit in the Blitz and again in 1991 by a nearby crane which fell through the south rose window into the nave. The accident occurred on a weekday morning, and given the volume of traffic on Upper Thames Street, it's a miracle there were no injuries. The interior, on which three and a half million pounds was recently spent, remains much as Wren designed it, with the highest roof in the City apart from St Paul's, generously lit by clear arched windows in the clerestory, an arrangement which earned it the nickname of "Wren's Lantern".

Continuing eastwards, along Skinner's Lane, is **St Michael Paternoster Royal**, another Wren church badly damaged in the war, less remarkable for its architecture than for its modern stained glass window of the pantomine character **Dick Whittington** with his knapsack and cat. Whittington, the only Mayor of London anyone has ever heard of, was buried in the church and lived next door on College Hill, still an evocative little cobbled street even today. The third son of a wealthy Gloucestershire family, he rose to become one of the richest men in the city by the age of twenty-one. He was, an early philanthropist and on his deathbed in 1423 he left money to pay half the costs of the Guildhall library, to repair St Bartholomew's Hospital, to refurbish Newgate Prison and to build various almshouses and a college of priests adjacent to the church who would pray for his soul.

The pantomime story appeared for the first time some two hundred years after Whittington's death, though quite how the wealthy Whittington became the fictional raggamuffin who comes to London after hearing the streets are paved with gold, no one seems to know. In the story, Whittington is on the point of leaving London with his knapsack and cat, when he hears the Bow bells ring out "Turn again, Whittington, thrice Lord Mayor of London" (he was, in fact, mayor on four occasions and was never knighted as the story also claims). The theory on the cat is that it was a common name for a coal barge at the time, and Whittington is known to have made much of his fortune in the coal trade.

Newgate to Smithfield

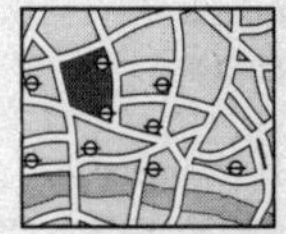

The area to the **north of St Paul's** is one of the most interesting parts of the City. The finanical and business sectors play only a minor role here, the three most important institutions being the criminal court at the Old Bailey, which stands on the site of the old Newgate Prison, the hospital of St Bart's, the only medieval hospital which occupies its original site to the present day, and the meat market at Smithfield, one of the last of the ancient London markets within the City.

Paternoster Square and Postman's Park

The Blitz destroyed the area immediately to the north of St Paul's, incinerating all the booksellers' shops and around six million books. In their place the City authorities built the brazenly modernist **Paternoster Square**, a grim pedestrianized piazza, surrounded by concrete office blocks. This became the subject of much heated debate in the 1980s when it was decided to pull the buildings down and start again. The new proposals, including one from Richard Rogers, architect of the Lloyds Building, provoked the first in a long line of architectural interventions from Prince Charles, who blamed planners and architects for having "wrecked the London skyline and desecrated the dome of St Paul's with a jostling scrum of office buildings". The Corporation took fright and new Neoclassical plans by John Simpson, one of the prince's favourite architects, were accepted. Demolition is due to start in 1995; meanwhile Paternoster Square, emptied of businesses, looks more forlorn than ever.

To the north of Paternoster Square, on Newgate Street is the hollowed-out shell of Wren's **Christ Church**, bombed out in the last war and restored as a rose garden, with only the tower standing entirely intact, now converted into an architect's office. Further north still is **Postman's Park**, one of the most curious and little-visited corners of the City, situated diagonally opposite what used to be London's Central Post Office on King Edward Street. Here, in 1900, in the churchyard of another Wren church, **St Botolph-without-Aldersgate**, the painter and sculptor George Frederick

Watts paid for a national memorial to "heroes of everyday life", a patchwork of tiles inscribed with the names of ordinary folk who had died in the course of some act of heroism. It exhibits the classic Victorian sentimental fascination with death, and makes for macabre but compelling reading: "Drowned in attempting to save his brother after he himself had just been rescued" or "Saved a lunatic woman from suicide at Woolwich Arsenal, but was himself run over by the train".

The Old Bailey, Newgate and St Sepulchre's

The nearest tube is St Paul's.

You can watch courtroom dramas from the visitors' gallery; Mon–Fri 10.15am & 1.45pm; closed Aug. Note that no bags or cameras are allowed, and there is no bag check.

A short distance along Newgate Street you'll find the Central Criminal Court, more popularly known as the **Old Bailey**, after the street on which it stands, which used to form the outer wall of the medieval city. The building itself is undistinguished but for its green dome, surmounted by a gilded statue of Justice holding the sword and scales. Its fame rests upon the fact that since 1834 virtually all the country's most serious criminal court cases have taken place here, including the trials of the Nazi propagandist "Lord Haw-Haw", the wrongly convicted Guildford Four and Birmingham Six "IRA bombers", and all Britain's multiple murderers.

Until 1902 the Old Bailey was also the site of **Newgate Prison**, which began life as one of the prisons above the medieval gateways into the City and was burned down during the Gordon Riots of 1780, only to be rebuilt as "a veritable Hell, worthy of the imagination of Dante", as one of its more famous inmates, Casanova, put it. Earlier well-known temporary residents included Sir Thomas Malory, who wrote *La Morte d'Arthur* while imprisoned here for murder (among other things), Daniel Defoe, who was put inside for his *The Shortest Way with Dissenters*, Christopher Marlowe, Ben Jonson and the murderer Major Strangeways, who was "pressed" to death with piles of weights in the courtyard in 1658.

St Bartholomew's hospital and churches

Directly opposite Pie Corner (see *Bodysnatchers* box opposite) stands the main building of **St Bartholomew's Hospital** – affectionately known as Bart's. This is the oldest hospital in London, and arguably the most respected, though it is now in danger of closure under the Tories' "health policies". Its departments spread their tentacles across the surrounding area, creating a kind of open-plan medical village. With a couple of notable exceptions (detailed below) the buildings themselves are unremarkable, but the history of the place is fascinating. It began as an Augustinian priory and hospice in 1123, founded by Rahere, court jester to Henry I, on the orders of Saint Bartholomew, who appeared to him in a vision while he was in malarial delirium on a pilgrimage to Rome. The priory was dissolved by Henry VIII, though in 1546, as a sick old man with just two weeks to live, Henry agreed to refound the hospital.

Public executions and bodysnatchers

After 1783, when hangings at Tyburn were stopped, **public executions** drew the crowds to Newgate, with more than 100,000 turning up on some occasions. The last public beheading took place here in 1820, when the five Cato Street conspirators, who had planned to assassinate the Cabinet, were decapitated with a surgeon's knife. It was in hanging, however, that Newgate excelled, and its most efficient gallows could dispatch twenty criminals simultaneously. Public unease over the "robbery and violence, loud laughing, oaths, fighting, obscene conduct and still more filthy language" that accompanied public hangings drove the executions inside the prison walls in 1868. Henceforth, a black flag and tolling of the bell of Old Bailey were the only signs that an execution had taken place.

The night before an execution, a handbell was tolled outside the condemned cell, while the gaoler recited the Newgate verse, bellowing the last two lines: "And when St Sepulchre's bell tomorrow tolls/The Lord have mercy on your souls". The reference was to the "Great Bell of Old Bailey" in the church of **St Sepulchre-without-Newgate**, diagonally opposite the Old Bailey, which tolled the condemned to the scaffold at eight in the morning. The handbell and verse are now displayed inside the church.

The bodies of the executed were handed over to the surgeons of St Bartholomew's for dissection, but **body snatchers** also preyed on those buried in the St Sepulchre churchyard. Such was the demand for corpses that relatives were forced to pay a nightwatchman to guard over the graveyard in a specially built watch-house that still stands to the north of the church – in order to prevent the "Ressurection Men" from retrieving their quarry. The stolen stiffs would then be taken up Giltspur Street to the *Fortune of War* tavern, on Pie Corner, at the junction of Cock Lane, where the bodies were laid out for the surgeons. The pub has now gone, but Pie Corner is still marked by a gilded over-fed cherub known as **Fat Boy**. He commemorates the "staying of the Great Fire", which, when it wasn't blamed on the Catholics, was ascribed to the sin of gluttony, since it had begun in Pudding Lane and ended at Pie Corner.

There's a statue of Henry in the main gateway, built in 1702 looking out over Smithfield Market; a lame man and a melancholic man sit above the broken pediment. Immediately on your left as you pass through the gateway stands the church of **St Bartholomew-the-Less**, sole survivor of the priory's four chapels, where Inigo Jones was baptized. The tower is fifteenth-century but the interior was largely rebuilt in nineteenth-century neo-Gothic and reconstructed after the last war. Beyond the church lies three-quarters of the courtyard created for the hospital by Gibbs in the mid-eighteenth century, including the **Great Hall** and the **staircase**, its walls decorated with Biblical murals which were painted free of charge by Hogarth, who was born and baptized nearby, and served as one of the hospital's governors.

The Great Hall and staircase of Bart's can only be visited as part of a guided tour (which takes in Smithfield and surrounding area too); April–Nov Fri 2pm; £4.

St Bartholomew-the-Great, hidden away in the backstreets to the north of the hospital, is London's oldest and most exquisite parish church. Begun in 1123 as the priory's main church, it was partly demolished in the Reformation, and gradually fell into ruins: the cloisters were used as a stable, there was a non-conformist boys' school in the triforium, a coal and wine cellar in the crypt, a blacksmith's in the north transept, and a printing press (where Benjamin Franklin worked for while) in the Lady Chapel. From 1887 the architect Aston Webb set about restoring what was left of the old church, patching up the chequered patterning and adding the flintwork that now characterizes the exterior.

To get an idea of the scale of the original church, approach it through the half-timbered Tudor **gatehouse**, on Little Britain Street, which was discovered after a Zeppelin raid in World War I. A wooden statue of Bartholomew stands in a niche, holding the knife with which he was flayed; below is the thirteenth-century arch which once formed the entrance to the nave – where the nave once stood is now the churchyard. The remains of the old priory church are a confusion of elements including one side of the cloisters, portions of the transepts and, most impressively, the **chancel**, where thick Norman pillars separate the main body from the ambulatory. There are various pre-Fire monuments, the most prominent being Rahere's tomb, which shelters under a fifteenth-century canopy to the north of the altar, with an angel at his feet and two canons kneeling beside him reading from the prophets. Beyond the ambulatory lies the **Lady Chapel**, mostly Webb's work though with original stonework here and there; it's now dedicated to the City of London Squadron, hence the RAF standard.

It's also worth taking a while to wander the narrow network of streets around the church, particularly along **Cloth Fair**, where several new houses feature oriel windows, echoing the two rare pre-Fire examples at no. 41, which date from the early seventeenth century and were restored by the architects who now occupy them.

Smithfield

The nearest tube is Farringdon.

Blood and guts were regularly spilled at **Smithfield** long before the meat market was legally sanctioned here in the seventeenth century. This patch of open ground outside the City walls (its name is a corruption of "Smooth Field") was used as a horsefair in Norman times, and later for jousts and tournaments. In 1381 the poll tax rebels under **Wat Tyler** assembled here to negotiate with the boy king Richard II. Tyler's lack of respect towards the king gave Mayor Walworth the excuse to pull Tyler from his horse and stab him, after which he was bustled into Bart's for treatment, only to be dragged out by the king's men and beheaded on the spot.

Smithfield subsequently became a venue for **public executions**. There were hangings, and the Bishop of Rochester's cook was boiled alive here in 1531, but the local speciality was burnings. These reached a peak during the reign of "Bloody" Mary when hundreds of Protestants were burned at the stake for their beliefs, in revenge for the Catholics who had suffered a similar fate under her father; a plaque on the side of St Bartholomew's Hospital commemorates some of those who died.

Even more popular than the public executions was the **St Bartholomew's Fair**, a cloth fair established by Rahere in the twelfth century in order to fund Bart's, and held over two weeks every August until the Victorians closed it down to protect public morals. It was, of course, much more than just a cloth fair, with every kind of debauchery and theatrical entertainment laid on: Rahere himself used to perform juggling tricks, while Pepys reports seeing a horse counting sixpences and, more reliably, a puppet show of Ben Jonson's play *Bartholomew Fair*.

The **meat market** with which Smithfield is now synonymous grew up as a kind of adjunct to the fair. Live cattle continued to be herded into central London and slaughtered here until 1855, when the fair was suppressed and the abbatoirs moved out to Islington. A new covered market hall (currently being restored) was erected in 1867, along with the "Winkle", a spiral ramp at the centre of West Smithfield, linked to the market's very own underground station (now a car park). Smithfield remains London's main market for TK (town-killed) meat, but it's living on borrowed time. In January 1996 new European Union hygiene regulations come into force, making redundant the markets' pitchers, who carry the carcasses into the market; the bummarees, who carry the meat out into waiting vans, will stay, but their traditional wooden barrows must go. Before then, the traders are being forced to move into the newly revamped section of Smithfield, at around four times the rent. If you want to see what little is left of Smithfield in action, you'll need to get here soon, and early – the action starts around 4am and is all over by 9 or 10am. The compensation for getting up at this ungodly hour is the early licensing laws which apply to certain local pubs, where you can get a hearty breakfast and an early morning pint.

North of London Wall

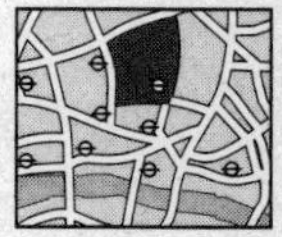

London Wall, a highway driven through the bomb sites in the north of the City and lined by a phalanx of post-war architectural errors, forms the southern boundary of the Barbican complex, extending east as far as Bishopsgate. As the name suggests, it follows the line of the **Roman wall**, portions of which still stand on the north side in St Alphage's Garden and by the Barber Surgeons' Hall; these surviving sections formed part of the Roman fort which was incorporated into the wall system at Cripplegate. If you're interested in tracing the line of the old city walls, you can follow a trail that begins outside the nearby Museum of London and extends a mile and a half to the Tower of London, with explanatory panels displayed at intervals along the way.

North of London Wall

The museum is open Tues–Sat 10am–5.50pm, Sun 2–5.50pm; £3.50, tickets valid for 3 months, free after 4.30pm.

Museum of London

Despite London's long pedigree, very few of its ancient structures are now standing, thanks to the Great Fire, the Blitz and the post-war developers. However, numerous Roman, Saxon and Elizabethan remains have been discovered during the City's various rebuildings and many of these finds are now displayed at the **Museum of London**, hidden above the western end of London Wall, in the southwestern corner of the Barbican complex. The museum's permanent exhibition is basically an educational trot through London's history from prehistory to the Blitz. This is interesting enough (and attracts a lot of school groups), but the real strength of the museum lies in the excellent temporary exhibitions, lectures, walks and videos it organizes throughout the year.

The permanent displays start on the **upper floor** with "London as it might have appeared in early winter about 130,000 years ago", moving swiftly on to the **Roman** relics. These include marble busts from the Temple of Mithras (p.204), a richly coloured second-century wall painting unearthed in Southwark, and the Bucklersbury pavement, a mosaic discovered during the Victorian road-building projects and now displayed in a mock-up of a wealthy Roman house. The **medieval section** contains some excellent models of the great buildings of pre-Fire London: Old St Paul's, the Royal Exchange, London Bridge, Whitehall Palace and the Rose Theatre. At the end of the upper floor there's a diorama accompanied by a loop-tape of Pepys' first-hand account of the Great Fire.

From here a ramp leads to the post-Fire section on the **lower floor**, set around a nursery garden, filled with plants and flowers typical of various epochs. The most eye-catching item here is the **Lord Mayor's coach**, which rivals the Queen's in sheer weight of gold decoration. Maps of the expanding capital and replicas of a late Stuart interior and a Newgate prison cell are followed by several reconstructed offices, pubs and shops from the **Victorian** era, when London became the largest city in the world. The highlight of the twentieth-century gallery is undoubtedly the **Art Deco lift** from *Selfridge's*, which precedes the museum's account of the Blitz.

The nearest tube is Barbican.

The Barbican

The City's only large residential complex is the **Barbican**, a phenomenally ugly and expensive concrete ghetto built on the heavily bombed Cripplegate area. It's an upmarket urban dystopia, comprising a maze of pedestrian walkways and underground car parks, pinioned by three 400-foot, 42-storey tower blocks – the tallest residential accommodation in Europe when it was built in the 1970s. The great footballer and drinker George Best, a resident in the following decade, described it as "like living in Colditz. If I came home the worse for wear it was an achievement to find my own front door in that concrete wasteland and in all the months we were there I never even saw a neighbour, never mind spoke to one." Be warned.

The zone's solitary pre-war building is the heavily restored sixteenth-century church of **St Giles Cripplegate**, where Oliver Cromwell was married in 1620 and John Milton was buried. St Giles is now bracketed between a pair of artificial lakes, opposite the only reason to venture into this depressing complex – the **Barbican Arts Centre**, the "City's Gift to the Nation", which was formally opened in 1982, nearly thirty years after the first plans were drawn up.

North of London Wall

For details of Barbican events, see p.492 (theatre) and p.487 (music). Free jazz and classical concerts are held most days in the various foyers.

Even the arts centre has its drawbacks, not least an obtusely confusing layout which has proved so user-repellent that it's about to be restructured. Just finding the main entrance on Silk Street is quite a feat for most Londoners, and the new glass canopy, surmounted by gilded Oscar-like figures, is unlikely to alleviate the problem. Built on nine levels, three of them subterranean, the complex contains a huge concert hall (home of the London Symphony Orchestra), two theatres for the London chapter of the Royal Shakespeare Company, a good repertory three-screen cinema, a public library and a poorly designed exhibition space, as well as housing the Guildhall School of Music and Drama.

Bunhill Fields and Wesley's Chapel

The nearest tube is Old Street.

Some way to the northeast of the Barbican, and strictly speaking outside the administrative boundaries of the City, lie **Bunhill Fields**, once a plague pit and later the main burial ground for Dissenters or non-Conformists (practising Christians who were not members of the Church of England). Following bomb damage in the last war, most of the graveyard was fenced off from the public, though you can still stroll through on the public footpaths. The three most famous graves have been placed in the central paved area: William Blake's simple tombstone stands next to a replica of Daniel Defoe's, while opposite lies John Bunyan's recumbent statue. The cricket field to the south, belongs to the **Honourable Artillery Corps** (HAC), whose quasi-medieval barracks face onto City Road. The HAC is a volunteer unit formed by Henry VIII in 1537, and now performs ceremonial duties in the City, including the gun salutes which take place outside the Tower of London on Tower Wharf.

Directly opposite the entrance to Bunhill Fields, the largely Georgian ensemble of **Wesley's Chapel and House** strikes an unusual note of calm on City Road. A place of pilgrimage for Methodists, the chapel was built in 1777 and heralded the coming of age of Wesley's sect, which had started out in a small foundry to the east of the present building. The name "Methodist" was first coined as a term of abuse by Wesley's fellow Oxford students, but it wasn't until his "conversion" at a prayer meeting in Aldersgate (marked by a plaque outside the Museum of London) in 1738, and later expulsion from the Anglican church, that he decided to become an independent field preacher. More verbal and even physical abuse followed – Wesley was accused of being a papist spy and an illegal gin distiller – but by the time of his death there were more than 350 Methodist chapels serving over 130,000 worshippers.

The chapel forms the centrepiece of the complex, though it is uncharacteristically ornate for a Methodist place of worship and has often attracted well-heeled weddings; one Margaret Hilda Roberts got married to divorcé Dennis Thatcher here in 1951. The museum in the basement tells the strictly orthodox story of Wesley and Methodism, with no mention, for instance, of the insanely jealous forty-year-old widow he married, and who eventually left him. Wesley himself lived his last two years in the Georgian house to the right of the main gates, and inside you can see bits of his furniture, his death bed, plus an early shock therapy machine he was particularly keen on; his grave is round the back of the chapel, under the shadow of a modern office block.

The museum is open Mon–Sat 10am–4pm; £3.

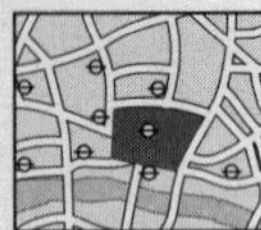

From Guildhall to Bank

The City has been London's financial centre since the Middle Ages when business was conducted in the local streets, courtyards and coffee shops. In 1570, prompted by England's persistently bad weather and Antwerp's brand new stock exchange, Thomas Gresham, financial adviser to Elizabeth I, founded the Royal Exchange. Nevertheless, it wasn't until 1694 that the Bank of England came into existence – until then all of London's financial institutions were dominated by the accounting skills of the Italians, who inhabited nearby Lombard Street.

Today all the key money markets and the City's five hundred foreign banks continue to be concentrated around Bank, as this area is known. By virtue of its position between New York and Tokyo, and the employment of a highly skilled workforce whose native tongue is the international language of finance, the City has remained in the triumvirate of top money markets. The financial sector employs over 120,000 people in the City, dominates the European share and foreign-exchange markets, and leads the world in futures and options. Whether the City will maintain its hegemony into the next century, however, is open to debate. Office space in the Square Mile is currently cheap, but there are several blots on the City's copybook: the shoddy public transport system, the scandals – Maxwell, Polly Peck, BCCI, and Lloyd's – and last, but not least, the IRA bomb scares which caused the Corporation to throw its "ring of steel" around the financial centre in the summer 1993.

The Guildhall is the civic focus of the City, just as the Bank of England is its financial focus, making the area around and between these two institutions very much the City's hub. The architecture here is typical of much of the City: a mixture of the old and very new, scattered with Wren churches, Livery Halls and post-war towerblocks. Apart from the Guildhall and Bank of England themselves, the only really specific sights are the churches, in particular Wren's St Mary Aldermary and St Stephen Walbrook, and Hawksmoor's St Mary Woolnoth.

From Guildhall to Bank

Guildhall

Situated at the geographical centre of the City, **Guildhall** has been the ancient seat of the City administration for over eight hundred years. It remains the headquarters of the Corporation of London, and is still used for many of the City's formal civic occasions. Architecturally, however, it no longer exudes the municipal wealth it once did, having been badly damaged in both the Great Fire and the Blitz, and scarred by the addition of a grotesque zig-zag concrete cloister and wing in the early 1970s.

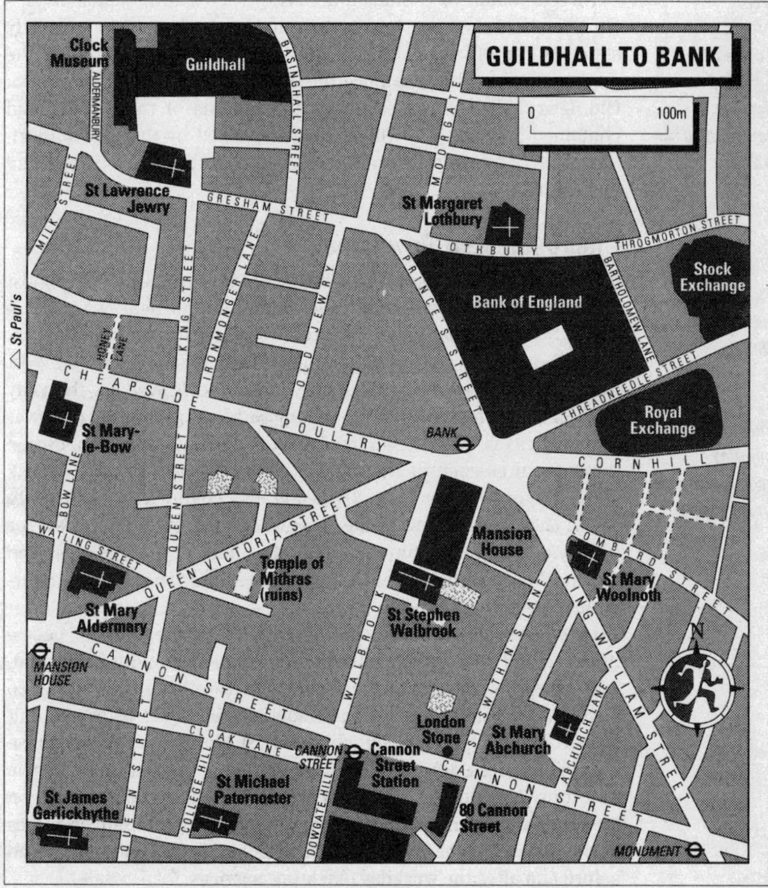

From Guildhall to Bank

The Guildhall's Great Hall is open daily 10am–5pm, unless it's being used; free. The Clock Museum is open Mon–Fri 9.30am–4.45pm; free.

Nonetheless the **Great Hall** is worth a visit and is more accessible than it looks – it's entered through the hideous modern extension, not the quasi-Indian porch, which was tacked on in the eighteenth century and is the most striking aspect of the exterior. The interior of the hall is basically a post-war reconstruction of a Victorian reconstruction of the fifteenth-century original; for the real thing, you have to descend into the **crypt**, which dates from the thirteenth to the fifteenth centuries.

The Guildhall owns an impressive art collection, currently stashed away but due to be put on public display sometime in 1996. In the meantime, visitors must content themselves with the **Clock Museum**, a collection of over six hundred timepieces rather unimaginatively displayed by the Clockmakers' Company in a room by the Guildhall library and bookshop on Aldermanbury.

For more on London's Jewish community see p.224.

Directly south of Guildhall, across the courtyard, stands Wren's church of **St Lawrence Jewry**, the splendour of its interior perfectly suited to the official church of the Corporation of London. As the name indicates, this was once the site of London's **Jewish ghetto**. Old Jewry, two blocks east, was the nucleus of the quarter and contained a synagogue which was confiscated by the City authorities in 1272, shortly before the expulsion of the entire community by Edward I.

Cheapside and Bow Lane

The nearest tube is Mansion House.

It's difficult to believe that **Cheapside** was the City's foremost medieval market place. Only the names of the nearby streets – Bread Street, Honey Lane, Poultry – recall its former prominence, which faded when the shops and their customers moved to the West End from the seventeenth century onwards. Nowadays the only distinguishing feature on this otherwise bleak parade of post-war office blocks is Wren's church of **St Mary-le-Bow**, whose handsome tower features each of the five Classical orders, a granite obelisk and a dragon weather vane. The tower also contains post-war replicas of the famous "Bow Bells", which sounded the 9pm curfew for Londoners from the fourteenth to the nineteenth centuries, and within whose earshot all true Cockneys are born. The church's interior itself is nothing special.

There's a popular vegetarian café in the crypt.

Down the side of St Mary-le-Bow runs **Bow Lane**, narrow, pedestrianized and jam-packed with office workers heading for the sandwich bars, but also featuring a butcher's and fishmonger's, not to mention several good pubs. At its southern end, just before you hit Queen Victoria Street, is the church of **St Mary Aldermary**, whose pinnacled spire suggests a pre-Fire edifice, though it is, in fact, a rare foray into the Perpendicular style by Wren, no doubt based on the original church. The plasterwork fan vaulting and saucer domes in the aisles are the highlight, but the church can only be viewed before and after the weekday lunchtime services.

Bank

From Guildhall to Bank

The nearest tube is Bank.

Established by William III to raise funds for his costly war against France, the **Bank of England**, the so-called "Grand Old Lady of Threadneedle Street", wasn't erected on its present site until 1734. Fifty years later a colonnaded facade was added by Sir John Soane, but nowadays there's little to see of Soane's work, on which he spent the best part of his career, as much of the windowless hulk was rebuilt between the wars by Herbert Baker. However, you can view reconstructions of both architects' work – Soane's Bank Stock Office and Baker's rotunda (wrecked in the Blitz) – in the Bank's **museum**, which is entered from Bartholomew Lane. The models are exhibited along with various bank notes, a brain-straining computer on which you can play at wheeling and dealing on the stock market, and a Victorian-style diorama of the attack on the Bank during the Gordon Riots of 1780.

The museum is open Mon–Fri 10am–5pm; free.

The Bank is the only City institution which still admits the public, all the others having been scared off by the IRA. The modern **Stock Exchange**, a little further up Threadneedle Street, closed its public gallery after a bombing in 1990, and in any case the human scrum has now been largely replaced by computerized dealing. Even the **Royal Exchange**, the most graceful of the trio of Neoclassical buildings around Bank, and headquarters of the futures market, is now only offices; what little dealing survives, now goes on at the Exchange's building on Cannon Street, where the public gallery is open only to pre-booked groups. The arcaded inner courtyard no longer buzzes with the polyglot sound of Dutch, Spanish, Scottish, Irish and Jewish traders, as it once did, and the dozens of shops once ranged above the surrounding portico have been replaced by a scattered few on the ground floor of the building.

Mansion House, the Lord Mayor's sumptuous Neoclassical lodgings during his or – on only one occasion so far – her term of office, is open only for group tours (Tues–Thurs 11am & 2pm; apply by letter) and these are booked up months in advance. The tour lasts around forty-five minutes and the highlights are the opulent

London's first public convenience

Down gleaming walls of porc'lain flows the sluice
That out of sight decants the kidney juice
Thus pleasuring those gents for miles around
Who, crying for relief, once piped the sound
Of wind in alleyways.....

This celebratory ode was composed by Josiah Feable for the opening, in 1855, of the first public lavatories, which were situated outside the Royal Exchange. The toilets were gents only – there was a charge of one penny (hence the old euphemism) – and ladies had to hold theirs in until 1911 when new lavatories were built. A plaque used to record their significance, and quoted some of the Feable verse; the new ones, alas, are silent on this small piss of history.

Egyptian Hall, the Lord Mayor's insignia, and the vast collection of gold and silver plate.

Sadly, one of the ever-decreasing number of Victorian buildings in the vicinity has recently bitten the dust: after years of wrangling, the Mappin & Webb building on the corner of **Poultry** has been demolished to make way for a much less remarkable building, ruining this historically-rich part of the City. The first plans to redevelop the site were drawn up way back in 1968 when a twenty-storey tower by Mies van der Rohe was put forward as a proposal, dubbed by Prince Charles as "yet another glass stump". Instead, a building by the late James Stirling, popularly known as the "wireless set", is to take its place, thanks to the persistent campaigning of Lord Palumbo, one-time head of the Arts Council.

Walbrook

Along the west wall of Mansion House runs Walbrook, named after the shallow stream which used to provide Roman London with its fresh water. On the eastern side of Walbrook, behind Mansion House, stands the church of **St Stephen Walbrook**, the Lord Mayor's official church and Wren's most spectacular after St Paul's. Faced with a fairly cramped site, Wren created a church of great space and light, with sixteen Corinthian columns arranged around a central dome, which many regard as a practice run for the cathedral. The modern beech-wood pews don't fit well with Grinling Gibbons' dark-wood furnishings, but Henry Moore's altar, an amorphous blob of stone, works rather better. The Samaritans were founded here in 1953 and their first helpline telephone now rests on a plinth in the southwest corner as a memorial.

Remains of a **Temple to Mithras**, which once stood on the river's western bank, were discovered in 1954 during the laying of the foundations for Bucklersbury House, the monstrosity set back from Queen Victoria Street. Mithraism was a male-only cult popular amongst the Roman legions before the advent of Christianity. Its deity, Mithras, is always depicted slaying a cosmic bull, while a scorpion grasps its genitals and a dog licks its wounds – the bull's blood was seen as life-giving, and initiates to the cult had to bathe in the stuff in subterranean tombs. The foundations of the temple, which have been reassembled in the shadow of the office block, give very little impression of what the building would have been like – the rich finds and more substantial reconstruction in the Museum of London give a slightly better idea.

St Mary Woolnoth to the London Stone

Hidden from the bustle of Bank itself, a short distance down King William Street, stands **St Mary Woolnoth**, one of Nicholas Hawksmoor's six idiosyncratic London churches. It's the west front which really sets it apart, with its twin turrets, Doric pillars and heavy rustication. As the only City church to come through the war unscathed, there are plenty of Hawksmoor's furnishings left inside; these will soon be seen in their in their original, more prominent sites, once the restoration programme aimed at removing the Victorian "improvements" is completed.

From Guildhall to Bank

Running east, to the north of St Mary Woolnoth is **Lombard Street**, focus of London's financial community before the Royal Exchange was built, named after the region of Italy from which most of the bankers and merchants originated. The street contains the head office of Lloyd's Bank and also the sign of the golden grasshopper, emblem of Thomas Gresham, who used to live on the site of the oldest bank in the city, **Martin's**, founded in 1563. Lombard Street also boasts several old trade signs re-hung for the coronation of Edward VII in 1902. Framed in iron and often as thick as paving stones, these were previously a feature of every commercial street in London, but were banned in 1762 after one fell down and killed four passers-by.

A complete contrast to Hawskmoor's church is provided by Wren's **St Mary Abchurch**, set in its own courtyard (the paved-over former graveyard) on Abchurch Lane, south off King William Street. Nothing about the dour red-brick exterior prepares you for the interior – dominated by a vast dome painted by a local parishioner and lit by oval lunettes. The limewood reredos, festooned with swags, is the only authenticated work by Gibbons in the City.

The nearest tube is Cannon Street.

A brief diversion will take you to one of London's most esoteric sights, the **London Stone**, a small block of limestone lodged behind an iron grille within the exterior wall of the Overseas Chinese Banking Corporation on the north side of Cannon Street, at the corner of St Swithin's Lane. To some it is London's omphalos, its geomantic centre; to the uninitiated, it looks more like a lump of Roman masonry. Whatever your reaction to this bizarre relic, it has been around for some considerable time, certainly since the 1450 peasants' revolt, when the Kentish rebel, Jack Cade, struck it, declaring himself "Lord of the City".

Bishopsgate to the Tower

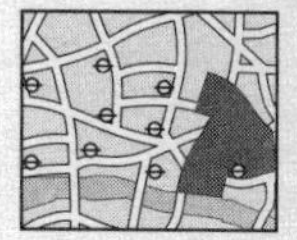

The brashest of the City's new architecture and the largest number of pre-Fire churches are concentrated in the easterly section of the Square Mile between Bishopsgate and the Tower. Neither genre of building was spared in the IRA bombs attacks of April 1992 and April 1993, and the repair work necessitated by those blasts is still going on. Financial institutions predominate here, and provide the two most obvious landmarks: the controversial Lloyd's Building and the generally disliked NatWest Tower. These, plus the Victorian splendour of Leadenhall Market and the oldest synagogue in the country, make for an especially interesting sector of the City to explore.

Broadgate

The **Broadgate complex**, to the north of Bank and west of Bishopsgate, is by far the largest and most ambitious of the "Big Bang" office developments of the late 1980s, and one of the most successful. The take-up of the new offices has been much quicker than at Canary Wharf in Docklands – thanks to their proximity to Liverpool Street Station – and the new traffic-free piazzas have proved popular with City workers. This relative success story didn't prevent the developers from going bankrupt, as at Canary Wharf, but at least the project was up and running. The architecture is in the bland US corporate style, replete with security cameras and guards, but on the plus side Broadgate is adorned with a substantial crop of outdoor sculpture, which succeeds in heightening the tone a bit. Another positive note has been the renovation of the City's busiest train terminal, **Liverpool Street**, which has been transformed from a blackened hull into a bright and airy station, with vibrantly painted Victorian wrought-iron arches.

The easiest way to reach the Broadgate complex is to head west from the main station concourse until you come face to face with the rusting steel sheets of *Fulcrum*, an immense sculpture by Richard Serra. To the north lies **Broadgate Square**, with its circular arena, used as an open-air ice-rink in winter and as a performance space in summer. Cascading foliage thankfully obscures much of the architecture in this square, which is probably the most popular of all the piazzas. To the east, **Finsbury Avenue** is disappointing – only the sculptural commuters of *Rush Hour* are at all memorable.

Exchange Square, built above the rail tracks to the north of the station, is the most impressive of the new piazzas, but also the most remote – you're unlikely to come across it by chance. It's dominated by the hi-tech Exchange House, which floats on eight piers spanned by giant arches, but the sculpture here has thrust itself onto the public consciousness more than the buildings, in particular the hefty *Broadgate Venus* by Fernando Botero, and Xavier Corbero's *Broad Family* of obelisks, one of whose "children" reveals a shoe. The last word goes to the European Bank for Economic Development, on the east side of the square. Set up to provide assistance to the old Eastern Bloc countries, it squandered much of its budget on Italian marble and other luxury fittings for this headquarters.

Bishopsgate

The final and most visible stage of the Broadgate development is the thirteen-floor office block which occupies a huge chunk of land on the west side of **Bishopsgate**. It's an unoriginal and undistinguished muddle of orders and motifs, and looks all the more so by contrast with the faience facade of the diminuitive **Bishopsgate Institute** across the road, a rare Art Nouveau building by Harrison Townsend.

Back on the south side of the train station, the church of **St Botolph-without-Bishopsgate**, where John Keats was christened, marks the northernmost extent of the bomb damage caused by the IRA's Bishopsgate bomb of April 1993, which left one dead and forty injured and caused an estimated billion pounds worth of damage. It's currently clad in scaffolding and looks unlikely to open again; the churchyard, with a fountain and tennis court, is a favourite picnic spot for City workers and contains a small Turkish bathhouse.

Further south down Bishopsgate, the devastation caused by the IRA bombs becomes apparent in the swathes of hoardings and scaffolding still in place. The **NatWest Tower**, Britain's tallest building until the completion of Canary Wharf, was damaged in both blasts; this was regarded as one of the few positive outcomes of the bombing campaign by those who see Seifert's colossus as the nadir of post-war City development, but money has been found to give it a facelift which will take it into the next century. Alas, no such money has been found to rebuild the tiny pre-Fire church of **St Ethelburga**, hemmed in by office blocks on the opposite side of Bishopsgate, which was all but totally destroyed in the 1992 Baltic Exchange bomb, which left three dead, ninety-one injured and caused some £800 million worth of damage.

Two other pre-Fire churches to the east of Bishopsgate are both closed for repairs, but will eventually reopen. The late-Gothic church of **St Helen** is the most interesting, with its undulating crenellations and Baroque bell-turret. It incorporates the original Benedictine nuns' church and contains five grand pre-Fire tombs including that of Thomas Gresham, the Elizabethan merchant who founded the Royal Exchange. **St Andrew Undershaft**, on the other side of the giant P&O towerblock on St Mary Axe, is less remarkable, though it does contain the tomb erected by the widow of John Stow, a humble tailor who wrote the first detailed account of the City in 1598. A memorial service is held here annually, during which the Lord Mayor replaces the quill pen in the tailor's hand.

Lloyd's and Leadenhall Market

To the south of the the P&O building stands Richard Rogers' glitzy **Lloyd's Building**, on Leadenhall Street. Thought to have been the IRA's real target, it's the one building in the vicinity which came away relatively unscathed. A startling array of glass and blue steel pipes – a vertical version of Rogers' own Pompidou Centre – this is easily the most popular of the new City buildings, at least with the general public. Its claims of ergonomic and environmental efficiency have, however, proved to be false, and the open-plan trading floor is extremely unpopular with the workers themselves. It came as something of a surprise that one of the most conservative of all the City's institutions should have decided to build such an avant-garde edifice, which is still guarded by porters in waiters' livery, in recognition of the company's modest origins as a coffee house.

Lloyd's started out in shipping (where it still has major interests) and is now the largest insurance market in the world. The company's famous Lutine Bell, brought here from a captured French frigate in 1799, is still struck – once for bad news, twice for good. Members of Lloyd's syndicates (known as "Names") pledge their personal fortunes in return for handsome and consistent premiums – that is until recently when Lloyd's suffered record losses of over a billion pounds, the result of a sequence of disasters including the 1988 Piper Alpha oil rig explosion, Hurricane Hugo in the US, the Exxon Valdez oil spill and the European storms of 1990. Many Names (including numerous Tory MPs) have found themselves with bills of over a million pounds, and costly litigation is currently underway to try and force Lloyd's to take responsibility for its underwriters.

Lloyd's is no longer open to the public.

Just south of the Lloyd's building you'll find the picturesque **Leadenhall Market**, whose trading traditions reach back to its days as the centre of the Roman forum. The graceful Victorian cast-ironwork is richly painted in cream and maroon, and each of the four entrances to the covered arcade is topped by an elaborate stone arch. Inside, the traders cater mostly for the lunchtime City crowd, their barrows laden with exotic seafood and game, fine wines, champagne and caviar. The shops and bars remain open until the evening, but it is best to get here at breakfast or lunchtime to catch the atmosphere.

The market is open Mon–Fri 7am–3pm.

Bevis Marks, St Katherine Cree and Aldgate

Another victim of the Baltic Exchange bomb (but since restored) was the **Bevis Marks Synagogue**, hidden away behind a modern red-brick office block in a little courtyard off Bevis Marks, at the north end of St Mary Axe. Built in 1701 by Sephardic Jews who fled the Inquisition in Spain and Portugal, this is the country's oldest surviving synagogue, and its roomy, rich interior gives an idea of just how wealthy the community was at the time. Although it seats over six hundred, it is only a third of the size of its prototype, the Esnoga in Amsterdam, where many Sephardic Jews initially settled. Past congregations have included some of the most successful Anglo-Jews, including the Disraeli family and Sir Moses Montefiore, whose family still has a special seat reserved for it in the front pew. Nowadays the Sephardic community has dispersed across London, and the congregation has dwindled, though the magnificent array of chandeliers makes it very popular for candle-lit Jewish weddings.

There are guided tours of the synagogue Mon, Wed & Fri noon, Tues & Sun 11.30am; £1.

Close by, just past Creechurch Lane, stood the even larger Great Synagogue of the Ashkenazi Jews, founded in 1690 but bombed out of existence in 1941, and recalled now only by a plaque. At the southern end of Creechurch Lane is the church of **St Katherine Cree**, where Holbein is supposed to have been buried after dying of the plague in 1543. Holbein's grave is now lost but the church, which was rebuilt in the 1620s, survived the Great Fire, and remains a rare example of its period. It's a transitional building with Classical elements, such as the Tuscan columns topped by Corinthian capitals, supporting Gothic lierne vaulting.

St Botolph's Aldgate is another unusual church, designed in 1741 by George Dance, and with a bizarre interior, remodelled last century, featuring blue-grey paintwork, gilding on top of white plasterwork, some dodgy modern art, a batik reredos, and a stunning stained glass rendition of Rubens' *Descent from the Cross* on a deep purple background. At the very edge of the East End, this is a famous campaigning church, active on issues like gay priests, headquarters of the society for promoting Jewish-Christian understanding, and with a crypt used as a day centre for homeless men.

Saint Botolph was an Anglo-Saxon abbot who cared for travellers, hence his churches on the City's gates.

London Bridge and the Monument

The nearest tube is Monument.

Until 1750 **London Bridge** was the only bridge across the Thames. The Romans were the first to build a permanent crossing here, a structure succeeded by a Saxon version pulled down by the Danes in 1014, an event which gave rise to the popular nursery rhyme "London Bridge is falling down". It was the medieval bridge, however, that achieved world fame: built of stone and crowded with timber-framed houses, it became one of the great attractions of London. At the Southwark end was the richly ornate Nonsuch House, decorated with onion domes and Dutch gables; at the City end was the Great Gatehouse, on which the heads of the traitors were displayed, dipped in tar to preserve them; and at the centre stood a chapel dedicated to Thomas à Becket. The houses were finally removed in the mid-eighteenth century, and a new stone bridge erected in 1831; that one now stands in the middle of the Arizona desert, having been bought for $2.4 million in the late 1960s by a gentleman who, so the story goes, was under the impression he had purchased Tower Bridge. The present concrete structure, without doubt the ugliest yet, dates from 1972.

The Monument is open April–Sept Mon–Fri 9am–6pm, Sat–Sun 2–6pm, Oct–March Mon–Sat 9am–4pm; £1.

The only reason to go anywhere near London Bridge is to see the **Monument**, which was designed by Wren to commemorate the Great Fire of 1666 (see box below). Crowned with spiky gilded flames, this plain Doric column stands 202 feet high, making it the tallest isolated stone column in the world; if it were laid out flat it would touch the bakery where the Fire started, east of Monument. The bas-relief on the base, now in very bad shape, depicts Charles II and the Duke of York in Roman garb conducting the emergency relief operation. The 311 steps to the gallery at the top – a favourite place for suicides until a cage was built around it in 1842 – once guaranteed an incredible view; nowadays it is dwarfed by the buildings around it.

From Monument to the Tower

Signs from the Monument will point you in the right direction for another Wren edifice, the church of **St Magnus the Martyr**, whose octagonal spire used to greet travellers arriving across old London

The Great Fire

In the early hours of September 2, 1666, the **Great Fire** broke out at *Farriner's*, the king's bakery in Pudding Lane. The Lord Mayor refused to lose any sleep over it, dismissing it with the line "Pish! A woman might piss it out". Pepys was also roused from his bed, but saw no cause for alarm. Four days and four nights later, the Lord Mayor was found crying "like a fainting woman", and Pepys had fled: the Fire had destroyed some four-fifths of London, including 87 churches, 44 livery halls and 13,200 houses. The medieval city was no more.

Miraculously there were only nine recorded fatalities, but 100,000 people were made homeless. "The hand of God upon us, a great wind and a season so very dry" was the verdict of the parliamentary report on the Fire; Londoners preferred to blame Catholics and foreigners. The poor baker eventually "confessed" to being an agent of the Pope and was executed, after which the following words, "but Popish frenzy, which wrought such horrors, is not yet quenched", were added to the Latin inscription on the Monument. (The lines were erased in 1831).

Bridge. Now it stands forlorn and battered by the heavy traffic hurtling down Lower Thames Street, and is closed for restoration. Access to the Thames from here is via Midland Bank, which stands alongside the striking, titanium-blue glass cubes of Montague House.

Beyond is the old **Billingsgate Market**, London's chief wholesale fish market from Roman times until 1982, when it was moved out to Docklands. It's hard now to imagine the noise and smell of old Billingsgate, whose porters used to carry the fish in towers of baskets on their heads, and whose wives were renowned for their bad language even in Shakespeare's day: "as bad a tongue...as any oyster-wife at Billingsgate" (*King Lear*). The Victorian hall was successfully renovated in 1990 by Richard Rogers, but remained empty until the Bishopsgate bomb forced NatWest to re-locate temporarily.

From Billingsgate you can walk along the riverside to the gates of the **Custom House**, which has been collecting duties from incoming ships since around 1275; the present undistinguished Neoclassical structure dates from 1825.

As an alternative to the riverside walk you could cut north from Lower Thames Street up **Lovat Lane**, one of the City's most atmospheric cobbled streets; once renowned for its brothels and known as Love Lane until 1939. For a different scale of architecture, cross over Eastcheap – site of the medieval meat market – and head down Mincing Lane. Occupying a vast site between here and Mark Lane is **Minster Court**, the new London Underwriting Centre, nicknamed "Munster Court" for its haunted, hammer-horror Gothicisms, one of the three quasi-cathedrals that surround the main courtyard burned to the ground in 1991 (it's since been rebuilt), which can only make you wonder about the success of the new working practices and "building regulations" foisted on the construction industry during the late 1980s. A stroll under the vast glass atrium guarded by three giant horses will bring you to Dunster Court, and then to **Fenchurch Street Station**, a modest little terminal with a scalloped canopy.

To the south of the station, down New London Street, is the ragstone Gothic church of **St Olave's**, or "St Ghastly Grim", as Dickens called it for the skulls and crossbones and vicious-looking spikes adorning the entrance to the graveyard on Seething Lane. Only the outside walls made it through the Blitz, though there are interesting pre-Fire brasses and monuments. Pepys lived in Seething Lane for much of his life, and had his own seat in the church's Navy Office pew in the now demolished galleries; he and his wife, Elizabeth, are both buried here – Elizabeth's monument was raised by Pepys himself, Pepys' own is Victorian.

All Hallows is open Mon, Wed & Fri 9am–6pm, Tues 8am–5pm, Thurs 9am–7pm, Sat & Sun 10am–5pm.

At the bottom of Seething Lane, on the other side of the noisy highway of Lower Thames Street, stands another pre-Fire church, **All-Hallows-by-the-Tower**. It too was reduced to a burnt-out shell by the Blitz, with only the red-brick tower (from which Pepys watched the Great Fire) remaining intact; the needle-sharp copper spire is a post-war addition. The rest of the church is a personal reinterpretation of the Gothic style by the post-war architect Lord Mottistone. Don't miss the exquisitely carved Gibbons' limewood font cover, sealed in a private chapel in the southwest corner of the church. Close by is an arch from the original church on this site, founded in 675 AD; even older remains of two Roman pavements can be found in the claustrophobic little crypt.

The Tower area

The area around the Tower of London is choked with tourists, traffic and office workers. Souvenir stalls, Tower Hill Pageant and the dominating presence of London's most famous landmark, Tower Bridge, add further bustle to the scene, and also make this an expensive part of the City to visit – entry to all three sights will cost you nearly £20. Yet despite all the hype and heritage claptrap, the Tower remains one of London's most remarkable buildings, site of some of some of the goriest events in the nation's history and somewhere all visitors and Londoners should explore at least once.

Tower of London

The nearest tube is Tower Hill.

The **Tower of London**, one of London's main tourist attractions, overlooks the river at the eastern boundary of the old city walls. Chiefly famous as a place of imprisonment and death, it has variously been used as a royal residence, armoury, mint, menagerie, observatory and – a function it still serves – a safe-deposit box for the Crown Jewels. Yet amidst the crush of tourists and the weight of history surrounding the place, it's easy to forget that the Tower is, above all, the most perfectly preserved medieval fortress in the country.

The Tower area

Although you can explore the Tower complex independently, it's a good idea to get your bearings by joining up with one of the **guided tours**, given every thirty minutes by one of the forty-odd, eminently photographable **Beefeaters**. These ex-servicemen are best known for their scarlet and gold Tudor costumes, but unless it's a special occasion you're more likely to see them in dark-blue Victorian garb. The nickname "Beefeaters" – officially they're known as Yeoman Warders – was coined in the seventeenth century, when it was a common term of abuse for a well-fed domestic servant.

A brief history

Beginning simply as a watchtower built by William the Conqueror to keep an eye on the City, by 1100 the Tower had evolved into a palace-fortress. The inner curtain wall, with its numerous towers, was built in the time of Henry III, and a further line of outer fortifi

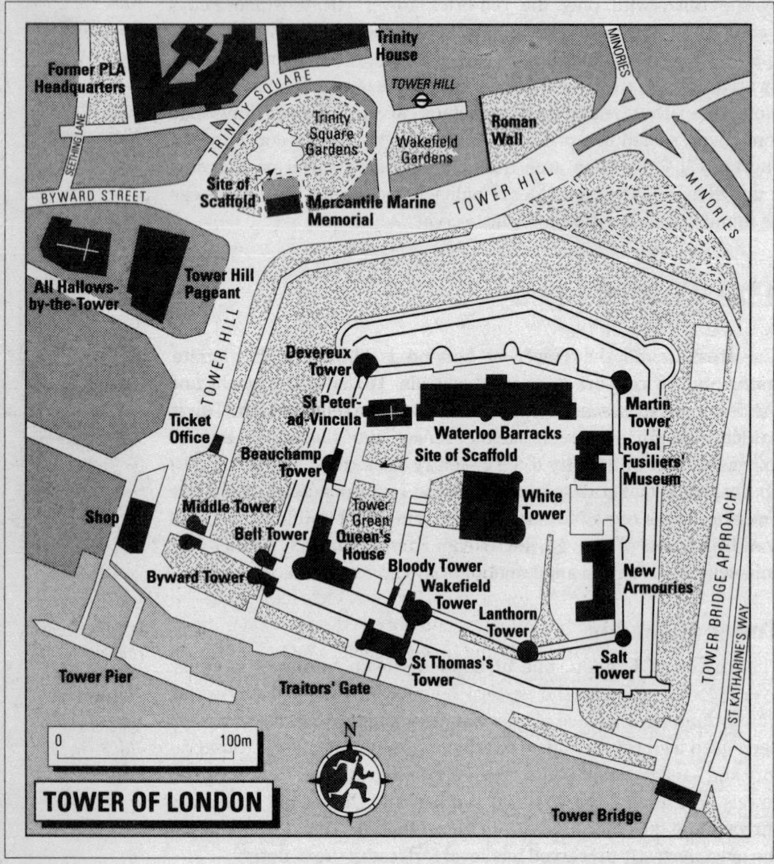

cations, plus an even wider moat, were added by Edward I, which means that most of what's visible today was already in place by 1307, the year of Edward's death.

The Tower area

The Tower's first prisoner, the Bishop of Durham, arrived in 1101 and escaped from the window of his cell by a rope, having got the guards drunk. Gruffyd, the last Welshman to be Prince of Wales, attempted a similar feat in 1244, with less success: "his head and neck were crushed between his shoulders . . . a most horrid spectacle". The most famous escapee from the Tower was the Earl of Nithsdale, imprisoned for his part in the 1715 Jacobite rebellion, who, despite his red beard, managed to get past the guards dressed as a woman, and lived on in exile for another thirty years. Richard II was the first king to be imprisoned here, though like the vast majority of prisoners to the Tower, he was later set free.

The Tower is open April–May & Sept–Oct Mon–Sat 9am–6pm, Sun 10am–6pm; June–Aug closes 6.30pm; Nov–March Mon–Sat 9.30am–5pm, Sun 10am–5pm; £7.95. Arrive early to get a look at the Crown Jewels.

Following the Restoration, guns were placed along the walls and a permanent garrison stationed in the Tower, which continued to be used as a state prison, the royal mint and an arsenal. At the same time, the general public were admitted for the first time to view the coronation regalia and the impressive displays of arms and armour. Under the Duke of Wellington, who was convinced revolution was around the corner, the Tower returned to a more military role and the public was excluded. Even long after its military obsolescence, it was used to hold German spies during both world wars; the last execution took place in the Tower on August 14, 1941, when a German spy, who had broken his ankle on landing by parachute, was given the privilege of being seated during his execution.

The White Tower

William the Conqueror's central hall-keep, known as the **White Tower**, is the original "Tower", begun in 1076 by the Bishop of Rochester. Whitewashed (hence its name) in the reign of Henry III, it was later returned to its Kentish ragstone exterior by Wren, who added the large windows. Of the tower's four turrets, topped by stylish Tudor cupolas, only three are square; the fourth is rounded in order to encase the main spiral staircase, and for a short while was used by Charles II's astronomer royal, Flamsteed, before he moved to Greenwich to escape the attentions of the Tower's ravens.

There's nowhere to get anything to eat or drink within the Tower. The best local spot for a snack is the branch of Pret à Manger underneath Tower Bridge. You can obtain a re-entry pass as you leave the Tower.

The main entrance to the tower is the original one, high up in the south wall, out of reach of the enemy, and accessed by a wooden staircase which could be removed during times of siege. The tower houses part of the **Royal Armouries**, a huge array that has been on almost permanent display since the time of Charles II. Jousting costumes, lances, seven-foot long hunting guns, Henry VIII's giant suit of armour and a stupendous suit for an elephant are just some of the more unusual exhibits. On the ground floor, on the way out, there's a small collection of torture instruments, the block and axe by which Lord Lovat lost his head, and a display of bald, severed heads – discarded wooden effigies from a 1680s' museum of English royalty.

Even if you've no interest in military paraphernalia, you should at least pay a visit to the **Chapel of St John**, on the second floor of the White Tower, a beautiful Norman structure completed in 1080, making it the oldest intact church building in London. It was here that Henry VI's body was buried following his murder in 1471, that Henry VII's queen, Elizabeth of York, lay in state surrounded by eight hundred candles, after dying in childbirth, that Lady Jane Grey came to pray on the night before her execution, and that "Bloody Mary" was betrothed by proxy to King Philip of Spain. Today, the once highly decorated blocks of honey-coloured Caen limestone are free of all ecclesiastical excrescences, leaving the chapel's smooth curves and rounded apse perfectly unencumbered.

Tower Green

Being beheaded at Tower Hill (as opposed to being hanged, drawn and quartered) was a privilege of the nobility; being beheaded on **Tower Green**, the stretch of lawn to the west of the White Tower, was an honour conferred on just seven people, whose names are recorded on a brass plate at the centre of the green. It was an arrangement that suited both parties: the victim was spared the jeering crowds and rotten apples of Tower Hill (see below), and the monarch was spared bad publicity. The seven privileged victims were: Lord Hastings, executed immediately after his arrest on the orders of Richard III, who swore he wouldn't go to dinner until Hastings was beheaded; Anne Boleyn (Henry VIII's second wife), accused of incest and adultery, who was dispatched cleanly and swiftly with a French longsword rather than the traditional axe, at

The Royal Menagerie and the ravens

The **Royal Menagerie** began in 1235 when the Holy Roman Emperor presented three leopards to Henry III; the leopard keeper was initially paid sixpence a day for the sustenance of the beasts, one penny for himself. They were put on public display and joined three years later by an elephant from the King of France and a polar bear from the King of Norway. James I was particularly keen on the menagerie, which by then included eleven lions, two leopards, three eagles, two owls, two mountain cats and a jackal. He used to stage regular animal fights on the green, but the practice was stopped in 1609 when one of the bears killed a child. Even in the eighteenth century, visitors were still advised not to "play tricks" after an orang-utang threw a cannonball at one and killed him.

The menagerie was transferred to the newly founded London Zoo in 1831, leaving the Tower with just its **ravens**, descendants of early scavengers attracted by waste from the palace kitchens. They have been protected by royal decree since the reign of Charles II, and have their wings clipped so they can't fly away – legend says that the Tower (and therefore the kingdom) will fall if they do. The ravens may appear harmless but are in fact vicious, territorial creatures best given a wide berth. They live in coops in the south wall of the Inner Ward, have individual names, and even have their own graveyard in the moat near the ticket barrier.

her own insistence; Katherine Howard (Henry VIII's fifth wife and Anne's cousin), convicted of adultery and beheaded along with her lady-in-waiting, who was deemed an accomplice; the seventy-year-old Countess of Salisbury; the seventeen-year-old Lady Jane Grey; and the Earl of Essex, one-time favourite of Elizabeth I. The bloody, headless corpses of these "traitors", and those of many other noble victims, including Sir Thomas More, were all hastily buried in the plain Tudor **Chapel of St Peter-ad-Vincula**, to the north of the scaffold site and accessible only on the Beefeaters' tours.

On the far side of the green is the **Queen's House** (closed to the public), built in the last years of Henry VIII's reign and distinguished by its swirling timber frames. These were the most luxurious cells in the Tower, and were used to incarcerate the likes of Katherine Howard and Anne Boleyn, who had also stayed there shortly before her coronation. Lady Jane Grey was cooped up here in 1554 after just nine days as queen, and from here watched her husband, Lord Dudley, being led from the nearby Beauchamp Tower to his death on Tower Hill, only hours before her own execution. The last VIP inmate at the Queen's House was **Rudolf Hess**, Hitler's deputy, who flew secretly into Britain to sue for peace in 1941, was held here for four days, and died in Spandau prison in post-war Berlin in 1987.

The Crown Jewels

The castellated Waterloo Barracks, built to the north of the White Tower during the Duke of Wellington's term as Constable of the Tower, now holds the **Crown Jewels**, perhaps the major reason so many people flock to the Tower. At least some of the Crown Jewels have been kept in the Tower since 1327, and have been on display since Charles II let the public have a look at them (there was a steep entrance charge even then). These days, the displays are efficient and disappointingly swift. In March 1994 the jewels were moved from the barracks' stuffy basement, where they had been since 1967, to more spacious, bomb-proof premises. Whilst queuing, giant video screens inflict a three-minute loop of footage from the last coronation, plus close-up photos of the baubles. Finally, you get to view the actual jewels, sped along on moving walkways which allow just 28 seconds' viewing – and there's no going back for a second look.

The vast majority of exhibits postdate the Commonwealth (1649–60) when many of the royal riches were melted down for coinage or sold off. The oldest piece of regalia is the twelfth-century **Anointing Spoon**; the most famous is the **Imperial State Crown**, sparkling with a 317-carat diamond, a sapphire from a ring said to have been buried with Edward the Confessor, and assorted emeralds, rubies and pearls. All in all, it's a stunning ensemble, though only a few of the exhibits – Queen Victoria's small diamond crown, for example – could be described as beautiful. Assertion of status and wealth are more important considerations, and the jewels include the world's three largest cut diamonds in the world, including the legendary

Koh-i-Noor, set into the Queen Mother's Crown in 1937, displayed separately near the exit.

Martin Tower to the New Armouries

When the Crown Jewels were first put on show during the reign of Charles II, they were housed in the **Martin Tower**, to the northeast of the Waterloo Barracks. Shortly after their installation, "Colonel" Thomas Blood, an Irish adventurer, made an attempt to make off with the lot, dressed as a parson. He was caught on the point of escape with the crown under his habit, the orb in one of his accomplices' breeches and the sceptre on the point of being filed in half. Charles, good-humoured as ever, pardoned the felon, and even restored him to his estate in Ireland.

Previously the tower had been the home of Henry Percy, the Earl of Northumberland, who moved in here in 1605 having rejected another suite of cells because of their smell and lack of shade. He had good reason to be choosy, since he was serving a sentence of life imprisonment in the Tower for failing to inform the king of the Gunpowder Plot. One of the richest men in the country, Percy employed his own cook, and paid for a bowling alley as well as for the walls near his cell to be paved for his daily stroll. Like Sir Walter Ralegh (held at the same time in the Bloody Tower – see over), Percy brought a library with him, plus three eminent scholars to assist him with his astrological and alchemical studies. When he was finally released in 1621 he was given a royal salute from the Tower guns.

The **Royal Fusiliers Museum**, in the small, castellated building to the south of the Martin Tower, requires a very small additional entrance fee, but is hardly worth even that. To the south, the **New Armouries** building contains the nineteenth- and twentieth-century sections of the Royal Armouries, but is currently closed.

Bloody Tower

The main entrance to the Inner Ward is beneath a three-and-a-half ton, seven-hundred-year-old portcullis, which forms part of the **Bloody Tower**. Here the twelve-year-old Edward V and his ten-year-old brother were accommodated "for their own safety" in 1483 by their uncle, Richard of Gloucester (later to be Richard III) after the death of their father, Edward IV. Of all the Tower's many inhabitants, few have so captured the public imagination as the "**Princes in the Tower**", due in part to Sir Thomas More's detailed account of their murder. According to More, they were smothered in their beds, and buried naked at the foot of the White Tower. In 1674, during repair work, the skeletons of two young children were discovered one on top of the other close to the tower; they were subsequently buried in Innocents' Corner in Westminster Abbey. Some have contended that Richard III has been the victim of Tudor propaganda, and that several other people in high places were equally keen to dispose of the little dears; the jury is still out on this one.

The Bloody Tower's other illustrious inmate – even more famous in his time than the princes – was **Sir Walter Ralegh**, who spent three separate periods in the Tower. His first stay was in 1592, when he incurred the displeasure of Elizabeth I for impregnating one of her ladies-in-waiting; his second and longest spell began in 1603 when his death sentence for suspected involvement in the Gunpowder Plot was commuted to life imprisonment. In the end, he spent thirteen years here smoking tobacco (his most famous discovery), writing poetry, concocting various dubious potions in his distillery, and completing the first volume of his *History of the World*, which in its day outsold even Shakespeare, despite being banned by James I for being "too saucy in censuring princes". Ralegh's study is re-created on the ground floor, while his sleeping quarters, built especially to accommodate his wife, children and three servants, are upstairs. Ralegh was eventually released in 1616 and sent off to Guyana to discover gold, on condition that he didn't attack the Spanish. He broke his word and was sent straight back to the Tower on his return in 1618. For six weeks he was imprisoned in "one of the most cold and direful dungeons", before being beheaded at Westminster.

Traitors' Gate to the Bell Tower

Prisoners were delivered through **Traitors' Gate**, on the waterfront to the south of the Bloody Tower, having been ferried down the Thames from the courts at Westminster Hall. The gate forms part of St Thomas's Tower, which, along with the Wakefield Tower, has been reconstructed to recreate the atmosphere of Edward I's **Medieval**

> **Tower ceremonies**
>
> The **Changing of the Guard** is the Tower ceremony you're most likely to witness, as it takes place daily at 11am on Tower Green.
>
> The **Ceremony of the Keys** is a seven-hundred-year-old, seven-minute floodlit ceremony which commences at 9.53pm daily: the Chief Yeoman Warder, accompanied by the Tower Guard, locks the Tower gates, and the following exchange then takes place – "Halt. Who comes there?" "The Keys." "Whose Keys?" "Queen Elizabeth's Keys" "Pass, Queen Elizabeth's Keys. All's well". To obtain tickets to witness this long-running drama you must write several months in advance to the Resident Governor and Keeper of the Jewel House, Queen's House, HM Tower of London EC3.
>
> **Royal Gun Salutes** are fired by the Honorable Artillery Company at 1pm at Tower Wharf on royal birthdays and other special occasions.
>
> **May 21**, the anniversary of the murder of King Henry VI, is remembered by students from Eton and King's College, Cambridge, who place white lilies and roses in the Wakefield Tower.
>
> The **Beating of the Bounds** ceremony takes place once every three years on Ascension Day (forty days after Easter), outside the walls of the Tower. The twenty-nine stones which mark the limits of the Tower's jurisdiction are beaten with white willow wands by the Beefeaters, while the Chief Yeoman Warder gives the order "whack it boys! whack it!".

Palace, with period-clad actors on hand to answer questions. The Aula, where the king ate and relaxed, has a beautiful little oratory in one of the turrets, while the Throne Room, in the Wakefield Tower, contains a gilded and colourful replica of the Coronation Chair (the battered original is in Westminster Abbey), and a huge crown-shaped candelabra depicting the twelve gates of the New Jerusalem. It was in the Throne Room's oratory that the "saintly but slightly daft" Henry VI was murdered at prayer on the orders of Edward IV in 1471.

Two of the first victims of the Reformation – Sir Thomas More and John Fisher – were incarcerated in the **Bell Tower**, near the main entrance and exit. More was initially allowed writing materials, but later they were withdrawn; Fisher was kept in even worse conditions ("I decay forthwith, and fall into coughs and diseases of my body, and cannot keep myself in health") and was so weak by the end that he had to be carried to the scaffold on Tower Hill. The twenty-year-old future Elizabeth I arrived here via Traitors' Gate in 1554, while her sister Queen Mary tried to find incriminating evidence against her. Mass was performed daily in her cell for the two months of her imprisonment, but she refused to be converted.

Tower Hill

Perhaps it's fitting that traffic-blighted **Tower Hill** should be such a godawful place, for it was here that over one hundred "traitors" were executed after being held in the Tower. The first beheading took place in 1388; Sir Thomas More, the Earl of Stafford, Lord Dudley, the Duke of Monmouth and the eighty-year-old Jacobite Lord Lovat, were among those who subsequently met their end here. The Duke of Monmouth is credited with the most botched execution: it took five blows of the axe to sever his head, and even then the executioner had to finish the job off with a surgeon's knife. Lord Lovat – the last man to be beheaded in England, in 1747 – drew such a crowd that one of the spectators' stands close to the scaffold collapsed killing several bystanders, at which Lovat is said to have exclaimed: "the more mischief, the better sport". Hangings continued on this spot for another thirty-odd years, ending with the execution of two prostitutes and a one-armed soldier arrested for attacking a Catholic-run pub in the Gordon Riots of 1780.

The actual spot for the executions, at what was the country's first permanent scaffold, is marked by a plaque in **Trinity Square Gardens**, to the northeast of the Tower. Close by stands the **Mercantile Marine Memorial**, a temple designed by Lutyens and smothered with the names of those who died at sea in World War I, and subsequently enlarged to commemorate the victims of the last war in a zig-zagging sunken section to the north. The marine theme is continued in the buildings overlooking the gardens: the gargantuan temple-like former headquarters of the **Port of London Authority**, with Neptune adorning the main tower; and, to the east, the elegant Neoclassical **Trinity House**, which oversees the upkeep of the country's lighthouses. Continuing east, you'll find perhaps the most impressive remaining section of the **old Roman walls** in **Wakefield Gardens**, close to Tower Hill tube station.

Tower Hill Pageant

The **Tower Hill Pageant**, situated behind All Hallows church, sounds like some ersatz medieval revelry, but is in fact a rather unlikely cross between Madame Tussaud's and an archeological museum. It all starts with a subterranean "dark ride" aboard a ghost train, which trundles through various animatronic tableaux, with sound effects and smells (particularly unpleasant at the mass grave of plague victims), making for an enjoyable romp through London's history.

Tower Hill Pageant is open April–Sept daily 9.30am–5.30pm; Nov–March closes 4.30pm; £5.45.

You then clamber out and head upstairs to the museum proper, a small but thoughtful arrangement of archeological finds that struggles to hold your attention after the more immediate thrills of the train ride. Exhibits range from Saxon pottery, medieval earpicks and pilgrims' souvenirs to a preserved Roman quay. Look out, too, for the minutes of the medieval equivalent of a local council meeting, which reports perilously uncovered wells and dirty streets, and also charges one Mawde Sheppyster of being "a strumpet to more than one and a bawd also". The exhibition closes with a section on disease and death, including an odd selection of medieval shoes worn out by hammer toes and nasty bunions.

Tower Bridge

Tower Bridge is only just one hundred years' old, yet it ranks with Big Ben as the most famous of all London landmarks. Its neo-Gothic towers, clad in granite and Portland Stone, conceal a steel frame, which, at the time, represented a considerable engineering achievement, inventing a road crossing that could be raised to allow tall ships access to the upper reaches of the Thames. The raising of the bascules (from the French for "see-saw") remains an impressive sight, though one which now occurs infrequently (ask at the bridge for the next scheduled opening). The elevated walkways, linking the summits of the towers (intended for public use), were closed from 1909 to 1982 due to their popularity with suicides and prostitutes; you can visit them now as part of the guided tour described below.

Tower Bridge is open April–Oct daily 10am–6.30pm; Nov–March closes 5.15pm; £5.

Exploiting the glut of people looking for things to do after leaving the Tower, the City of London Corporation has installed a touristy exhibition called *The Celebration Story*, which employs videos and an animatronic chirpy Cockney to tell the story of the bridge's construction in the 1890s. The guided tour takes around an hour, which is about twice as long as it need be, leaving many visitors so wearied that they don't bother with the Engine Room, where you can see the giant coal-fired boilers which drove the hydraulic system until 1976, and play some inter-active engineering games. Whatever you do, skip the *Royal Opening* video at the end of the tour.

Chapter 7

The East End and Docklands

The East End of London is the hell of poverty. Like an enormous, black, motionless, giant kracken, the poverty of London lies there in lurking silence and encircles with its mighty tentacles the life and wealth of the City and of the West End...

J. H. Mackay *The Anarchists* (1891)

Few places in London have engendered so many myths as the **EAST END** (a catch-all title which covers just about everywhere east of the City, but has its heart closest to the latter). Its name is synonymous with slums, sweatshops and crime, as epitomized by anti-heroes such as Jack the Ripper and the Kray Twins, but also with the rags-to-riches careers of the likes of Harold Pinter and Vidal Sassoon, and whole generations of Jews who were born in the most notorious of London's cholera-ridden quarters and have now moved to wealthier pastures. Old East Enders will tell you that the area's not what it was – and it's true, as it always has been. The East End is constantly changing as newly arrived immigrants assimilate and move out.

The East End's first immigrants were French Protestant Huguenots, fleeing from religious persecution in the late seventeenth century – the word "refugee", from *réfugié*, entered the English language at this time. With anti-Catholic feeling running high in London, they were welcomed with open arms by all except the apprentice weavers whose work they undercut, and who attacked them on more than one occasion. Some settled in Soho but the vast majority settled in Spitalfields, where they were operating an estimated 12,000 silk looms by the end of the eighteenth century

Within three generations the Huguenots were entirely assimilated, and the Irish became the new immigrant population. Traditionally engaged in the construction industry, Irish labourers, ironically enough, played a major role in building the area's many

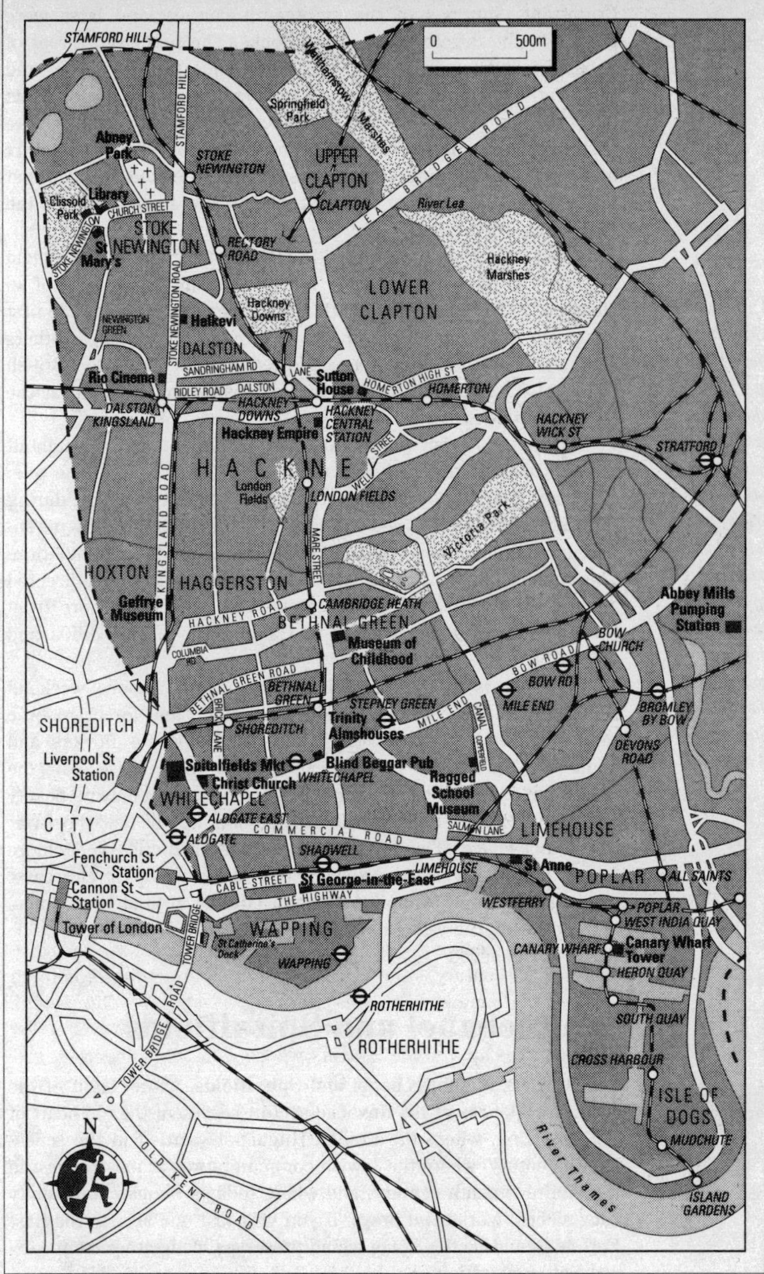

STAMFORD HILL
0
500m
Walthamstow Marshes
Springfield Park
Abney Park
STAMFORD HILL
STOKE NEWINGTON
UPPER CLAPTON
LEA BRIDGE ROAD
Clissold Park
Library
CHURCH STREET
CLAPTON
River Lea
STOKE NEWINGTON
St Mary's
RECTORY ROAD
Hackney Marshes
STOKE NEWINGTON ROAD
LOWER CLAPTON
Hackney Downs
Halkevi
NEWINGTON GREEN
DALSTON
SANDRINGHAM RD
LANE
Sutton House
HOMERTON HIGH ST
HOMERTON
Rio Cinema
RIDLEY ROAD
DALSTON
DALSTON KINGSLAND
HACKNEY DOWNS
HACKNEY CENTRAL STATION
Hackney Empire
HACKNEY WICK ST
STRATFORD
HACKNEY
London Fields
LONDON FIELDS
WELL STREET
Victoria Park
MARE STREET
KINGSLAND ROAD
HOXTON
HAGGERSTON
Geffrye Museum
CAMBRIDGE HEATH
Abbey Mills Pumping Station
HACKNEY ROAD
BETHNAL GREEN
Museum of Childhood
COLUMBIA RD
BOW CHURCH
BOW ROAD
BOW RD
BETHNAL GREEN ROAD
BETHNAL GREEN
MILE END
STEPNEY GREEN
BRICK LANE
CANAL
BROMLEY BY BOW
SHOREDITCH
SHOREDITCH
Trinity Almshouses
MILE END
DEVONS ROAD
Liverpool St Station
Spitalfields Mkt
Blind Beggar Pub
Christ Church
WHITECHAPEL
Ragged School Museum
WHITECHAPEL
CITY
ALDGATE EAST
SALMON LANE
LIMEHOUSE
ALDGATE
COMMERCIAL ROAD
Fenchurch St Station
SHADWELL
LIMEHOUSE
St Anne
POPLAR
ALL SAINTS
Cannon St Station
CABLE STREET
St George-in-the-East
THE HIGHWAY
WESTFERRY
POPLAR
WEST INDIA QUAY
Tower of London
WAPPING
St Catherine's Dock
TOWER BRIDGE
CANARY WHARF
Canary Wharf Tower
WAPPING
HERON QUAY
TOWER BRIDGE ROAD
ROTHERHITHE
SOUTH QUAY
ROTHERHITHE
CROSS HARBOUR
ISLE OF DOGS
N
MUDCHUTE
River Thames
OLD KENT ROAD
ISLAND GARDENS

Protestant churches of the eighteenth century and later were crucial to the development of the docks. The perceived threat of cheap Irish labour provoked the Spitalfields riots of 1736, and their Catholicism made them easy targets during the Gordon Riots of 1780. Famine and disease in Ireland brought thousands more Irish over to London in the 1840s and 1850s, but it was the influx of Jews escaping pogroms in eastern Europe and Russia, that defined the character of the East End in the second half of the nineteenth century.

Jewish immigration prompted the Bishop of Stepney to complain in 1901 that his churches were "left like islands in the midst of an alien sea". The same year the MP for Stepney helped found the first organized racist movement in the East End, the British Brothers League, whose ideology foreshadowed that of the later British Union of Fascists, led by Sir Oswald Mosley and defeated at the Battle of Cable Street (see p.224).

It's best to visit Whitechapel and Spitalfields on a Sunday, when the markets of Petticoat Lane, Spitalfields, Brick Lane and Columbia Road are buzzing. By contrast, Docklands is a Monday to Friday place, ghostly quiet after dark and at weekends.

The area's Jewish population has now dispersed throughout London, though the East End remains at the bottom of the pile; even the millions poured into the Docklands development during the last decade have failed to make any impression on the perennial unemployment and housing problems of the local population. The current spate of racist attacks in the East End are directed against the extensive Bengali community, who came here from the poor rural area of Sylhet in Bangladesh in the 1960s and 1970s.

Most visitors to the East End come for its famous weekend **markets**: **Petticoat Lane** for clothing, **Brick Lane** for bric-a-brac (and wonderful curry houses), **Columbia Road** for flowers and plants, and **Spitalfields** for crafts and organic food. These apart, the area is not an obvious place for sightseeing, and certainly no beauty spot – Victorian slum clearances, Hitler's bombs and post-war towerblocks have all made their mark. However, there's plenty more to get out of a visit, including a trio of **Hawksmoor churches**, **waterside pubs** in Wapping, **Bengali culture** around Brick Lane, and, not least, the vast **Docklands** redevelopment, which has to be seen to be believed.

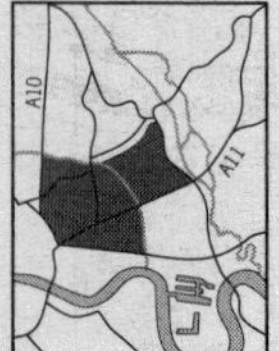

Whitechapel and Spitalfields

The districts of **Whitechapel** and **Spitalfields**, within sight of the sleek towerblocks of the financial sector, represent the old heart of the East End, where the French Huguenots settled in the seventeenth century, where the Jewish community was at its strongest in the late nineteenth century, and where today's Bengali community eats, sleeps, works and prays. If you visit just one area in the East End, it should be this zone, which preserves mementoes from each wave of immigration.

Petticoat Lane (Middlesex Street)

Petticoat Lane is London's most famous street market, and has been trading every Sunday for more than two hundred years. The Huguenots sold the petticoats that gave the market and the street its name; the authorities renamed the street Middlesex Street in 1830 to avoid the mention of ladies' underwear (though the name has stuck) and tried to prevent Sunday trading here until it was finally sanctioned by law in 1936. In the Victorian era the market grew into one of the largest in London, and by the turn of the century it stood at the heart of the Jewish East End, a "stronghold of hard-sell Judaism . . . into which no missionary dared to set foot" according

Whitechapel and Spitalfields

The nearest tubes are Liverpool Street and Aldgate.

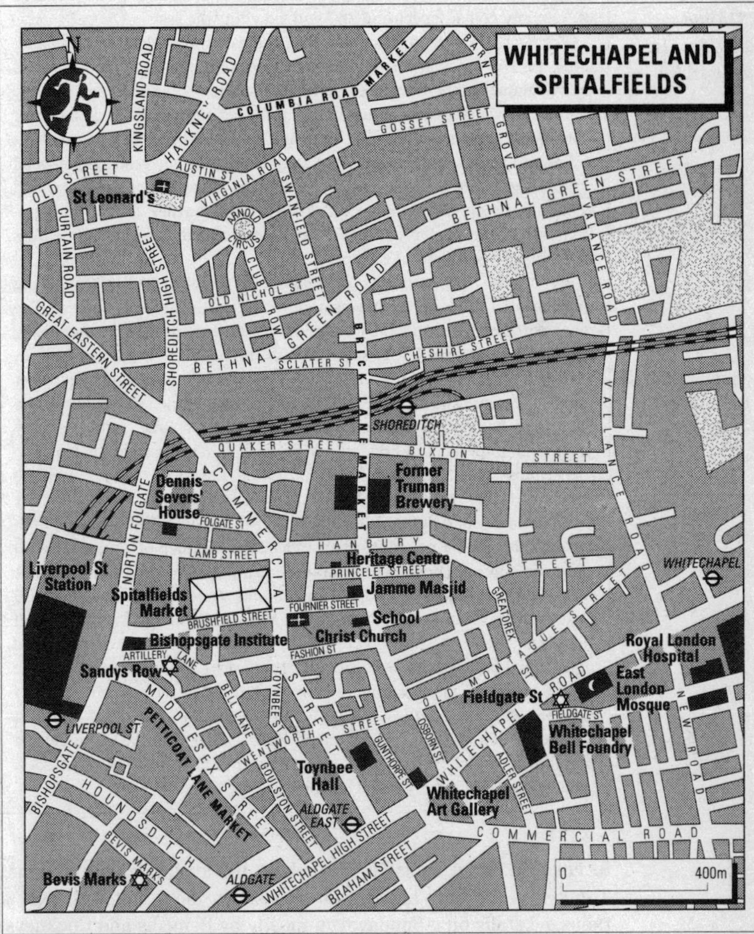

London's two Jewish museums are covered on p.315 and p.333. See also Stamford Hill, p.235.

London's Jews

It was William the Conqueror who invited the first **Jews** to England in 1066. Regarded with suspicion because of their finanical astuteness, yet exploited for these very qualities, Jews were banned from numerous professions, but actively encouraged to pursue others, such as money-lending (Christians themselves were banned from lending money for interest, a practice considered sinful by the church). After a period of relatively peaceful co-existence and prosperity, the small community increasingly found itself under attack, milked by successive monarchs, and forced eventually to wear the distinguishing mark of the *tabula* on their clothing. The Crusades whipped up further religious intolerance, the worst recorded incident taking place in 1189, when thirty Jews were killed by a mob during the coronation of Richard I. In 1278 Edward I imprisoned the entire community of around six hundred Jews on a charge of "clipping coins", executing 267 and expelling the rest.

For nearly four centuries thereafter, Judaism was outlawed in England, until, in 1656, Cromwell readmitted Jews to England. The Jews who arrived immediately following this **Readmission** were in the main wealthy merchants, bankers and other businessmen of Sephardic (ie Spanish or Portuguese) origin. In contrast to conditions in the rest of Europe, Jews in London were self-governing and subject to the same restrictions as all other religious dissenters and foreigners. As a beacon of tolerance and economic prosperity, London quickly attracted further Jewish immigration by poorer Sephardi families and, increasingly, Ashkenazi settlers from Eastern and Central Europe.

By far the largest influx of **Ashkenazi Jews** arrived after fleeing pogroms that followed the assassination of Tsar Alexander II in 1881. The more fortunate were met by relatives at the Irongate Stairs by Tower Bridge; the rest were left to the mercy of the boarding-house keepers or, after 1885, found shelter in the Jewish Temporary Shelter in Leman Street (later moved to Mansell Street). They found work in the sweatshops of the East End: cabinet-making, shoe-making and, of course, tailoring – by 1901 over 45 percent of London's Jews worked in the garment industry.

Perhaps the greatest moment in Jewish East End history was the **Battle of Cable Street**, which took place on October 4, 1936 when Sir Oswald Mosley and 3000 of his black-shirted fascists attempted to march through the East End. More than twice that number of police tried to clear the way for Mosley with baton charges and mounted patrols, but they were met with a barrage of bricks and stones from some 100,000 East Enders chanting the slogan of the Spanish Republicans, "They Shall Not Pass". Barriers were erected along Cable Street and eventually the police chief halted the march – and another East End legend was born.

After the war, more and more Jews moved out to the suburbs of north London, where the largest Jewish communities are now to be found in Golders Green (p.333) and Stamford Hill (p.235). The East End Jewish population, which had peaked at around 130,000 in 1914, was soon reduced to a handful of Jewish businesses.

to novelist, Israel Zangwill. Nowadays, the kosher take-away joint, *Taboon*, is the only high-profile Jewish business, but with over a thousand stalls on a Sunday, run mostly by Bengalis and Cockneys, this is still the city's number-one bargain-basement clothes market. A smaller lunchtime version runs throughout the week on neighbouring Wentworth Street.

Petticoat Lane market runs throughout the week, but is at its busiest on Sundays.

To the **north of Petticoat Lane** are further reminders of the old Jewish community: the Soup Kitchen for the Jewish Poor, on Brune Street, which opened in 1902 and finally closed in 1992 (the undulating stone lettering is still clearly visible); the Jewish Free School, which functioned on the corner of Frying Pan Alley from 1821 to 1939, and boasted 4300 pupils at the turn of the century, making it the largest school in the country; and the **Sandys Row synagogue**, which now struggles to maintain a *minyan* (the minimum of ten male adults needed to perform a service).

The network of narrow streets around Sandy Row is fascinating to walk around – unique survivors which give a strong impression of the old East End. From Sandys Row, walk down Artillery Passage, a mixture of Bengali shops and new, City-type businesses, and on into Artillery Row, which boasts a superb eighteenth-century Huguenot shop front at no. 56. Incidentally, the ballistic connection dates from the reign of Henry VIII, when the Royal Artillery used to hold gunnery practice here.

Spitalfields Market and Christ Church

To the north of Petticoat Lane lies **Spitalfields Market**, until recently the capital's premier wholesale fruit and vegetable market. The old fruiterers' shops can still be seen throughout the area but they have been boarded up since the market moved out to Stratford in 1991; only the strange-looking red-brick and green gabled **market halls**, built in 1893 by rags-to-riches speculator Robert Horner, remain open. Various plans have been put forward for the future use of these – mostly along a Covent Garden model of retail and office space – but nothing has yet been decided and the current leasees are a temporary bunch of shops and sports facilities. The best time to visit is on Sundays when an organic food market shares space with clothes, jewellery and food stalls, and for kids a miniature railway and even a troupe of animals from the local city farm.

The nearest tube is Liverpool Street.

The dominant architectural presence in Spitalfields, facing the market halls, is **Christ Church**, a characteristically bold design by Nicholas Hawksmoor. Best viewed from Brushfield Street, the church's main features are its huge 225ft-high broached spire and a giant Tuscan portico, raised on steps and shaped like a Venetian window (a central arched opening flanked by two smaller rectangles), a motif repeated in the tower and doors. For years the place lay derelict and under threat of demolition, but a recent restoration progamme has stopped the rot. One of the most important archeological projects in post-war London has been the excavation of the crypt – a completely undisturbed grave site, complete with records of burials, that has resulted in reappraisal of the way remains are

Christ Church concerts are among the finest in the capital and the church is the focus of the Spitalfields Festival, held in June.

dated. That said, it was not a job for those with weak stomachs; workers had to don gas-masks and protective clothing because of still-live bacilli and viruses in semi-decomposed corpses.

The church hall, next door, was host in spring 1888 to meetings of the **Bryant & May match girls**, who personified the Dickensian stereotype of the downtrodden East End girl. Some 672 of them went on strike against their miserable wages and work conditions, which gave no protection against "phossy jaw", a deterioration of the jawbone caused by prolonged exposure to yellow phosphorus. Feminist Annie Besant organized a strike committee and galvanized public opinion, and within a fortnight the firm had backed down.

An outstanding feature of the Spitalfields area is its early Georgian terraced housing. First occupied by Huguenot silk-weavers and merchants, many of the houses in the streets around the market retain their weaving attics, identifiable by their long windows. The best examples are to be seen on **Fournier Street**, most of which have been restored by a fairly well-heeled wave of 1970s and 1980s immigrants – a mix of artists, academics and, latterly, city workers. You can, on occasion, visit **18 Folgate Street**, to the north of the market, which has been impeccably restored by the American Dennis Severs. Severs conducts a theatrical tour of the house, evoking its (fictitious) Georgian era residents, Mr and Mrs Jervis, who are waited on by a (real) butler in full eighteenth-century livery. The house is entirely candle-lit and log-fired, and decked out as it would have been two hundred years ago.

Dennis Severs' house is open the first Sun of each month 2–5pm; £5; ☎0171/247 4013 for details of the evening performances.

Brick Lane and Columbia Road markets

Crossing the eastern end of Fournier Street, **Brick Lane**, as its name suggests, was once the main location for the brick kilns which helped rebuild the City after the Great Fire. At the turn of the last century, many of the streets around here were one hundred percent Jewish, making this the high street of the ghetto. Nowadays, Brick Lane lies at the heart of the Bengali community, and each step is accompanied by the smell of spices from the numerous cafés and restaurants, the bright colours of the fabrics which line the clothes' shop windows, and the heavy beat of Bhangra music from passing cars and music shops. For the outsider, it's a compelling scene, glimpsed en route to a cheap curry house; hidden behind this facade, though, are overcrowded flats and sweatshops, which would not look out of place in Victorian times, and a history of racism that stretches back centuries.

In the 1970s, Brick Lane emerged as a kind of "front line" of defence against racist attacks on the Bengali community. The most publicized eruption of violence occurred during the Sunday market in the summer of 1978, when 150 National Front skinheads went on the rampage smashing Bengali shop windows. The counter demonstrations on subsequent Sundays succeeded in temporarily driving the NF out of Brick Lane. Unfortunately, the relative lull of the 1980s was shattered in 1993, when the emergence in new force of the extreme-right, the British National Party, brought with it a marked increase in racist attacks and further confrontations at the Sunday market.

The changing ethnic make-up of Brick Lane is most clearly illustrated in the **Jamme Masjid** (Great Mosque) on the corner of Fournier Street. Established in 1743 as a Huguenot church, it became a Wesleyan chapel in 1809, the ultra-Orthodox Spitalfields Great Synagogue in 1897, and now serves as the main mosque for the area. A little further north is another example of the changing face of Brick Lane, **Christ Church primary school**, still nominally affiliated to the Church of England, though the vast majority of its pupils are Muslim; a hundred years ago they were mainly Jewish, as the Star of David on one of the drainpipes testifies. If you want to dig a bit deeper into the old Jewish presence here, phone ☎0171/247 0971 and try to arrange to see the wonderfully evocative disused **synagogue** hidden behind the Georgian facade of **19 Princelet Street**; built by Polish Jews in the 1860s, it's due to be turned into a heritage centre for the area.

Brick Lane has some of the best curry houses in London (see p.439), while for a snack there is a 24hr bagel bakery at the top end.

Truman's **Black Eagle brewery**, halfway up Brick Lane, was founded in 1666, becoming the largest brewery in the world at the turn of the century. It was closed down in 1989 and parts of it have been redeveloped as an "old-time" music hall and an art gallery, with further refurbishments planned for the future. For over a century it acted as a kind of frontier post between the immigrant population to the south, and the mostly white population to the north; today the lines are more blurred, though the predominantly Cockney and Jewish **Sunday market** is focused mainly to the north. Its nucleus is the crossroads of Brick Lane and Cheshire Street; the further east you go down Cheshire Street, the tattier the stalls and the dodgier the deals.

The bulk of the action goes on in the morning, with many people combining a visit with a browse round the lively Sunday **flower and plant market**, to the north, amid the small-scale Victorian terraces of **Columbia Road**. This open-air market is all that's left of the market that once occupied a huge cathedralesque Gothic Revival market building financed in 1869 by Baroness Burdett-Coutts, who was appalled at the dishonesty of Cockney costermongers. The Archbishop of Canterbury and the Duke of Wellington were present at the grand opening, but the high-handed philanthropy behind the scheme – the great hall was daubed with uplifting inscriptions such as "Speak everyman truth with his neighbour" – was resented by the traders; the market flopped and was handed back to the baroness within five years, after which it was let out as workshops and finally pulled down in 1960.

In the nineteenth century, the streets between Columbia Road and Bethnal Green Road formed one of the East End's most notorious slum areas, known as **"Old Nichol"** or Jago. On its northern fringe was – in the words of Engels – a "stagnant lake of thickened putrefying matter" which gave off "bubbles of pestelential exhalation". Poverty and disease were the distinguishing features of this slum, cleared away in the 1890s to make way for London's first big municipal housing development, the **Boundary Street Estate**, conceived by the newly formed London County Council. More people were displaced than were rehoused, and few of the original inhabitants could afford the new rents, but the five-storey blocks, centred around the raised garden and bandstand of **Arnold Circus**, became a model for municipal projects throughout Europe. To the modern eye, the gloomy red brickwork and poor Bengali families that now inhabit the estate make them look more like slums than ideal homes.

Whitechapel Road

Whitechapel Art Gallery is open Tues & Thurs–Sun 11am–5pm, Wed to 8pm; usually free.

Whitechapel Road – as Whitechapel High Street and the Mile End Road are collectively known – is still the East End's main street, shared by all the many races who live in the borough of Tower Hamlets. The most obvious place to start is at *Bloom's*, on the corner of Commercial Street, "the most famous kosher restaurant in Great Britain", as it proudly proclaims, though its dated 1950s interior is half-empty except on Sundays (it has a much busier branch in Golders Green). The East End institution that draws in more outsiders than any other is the **Whitechapel Art Gallery**, a little further up the High Street in a beautiful crenellated Arts and Crafts building by Charles Harrison Townsend, architect of the similarly audacious Horniman Museum (p.342). The gallery puts on some of London's most innovative exhibitions of contemporary art, as well as hosting the annual Whitechapel Open, a chance for local artists to get their work shown to a wider audience.

Like the library adjoining it, the gallery was founded by one of the East End's many Victorian philanthropists, **Samuel Barnett**, who was vicar in the worst parish in Whitechapel in the 1870s. His motives may have been dubious – "the principle of our work is that we aim at decreasing not suffering but sin," he once claimed – but the legacy of his good works is still discernible. Another of Canon Barnett's enduring foundations was **Toynbee Hall**, founded in 1884 as a residence for Oxbridge volunteers who wished to do social and educational work in the East End. The original nineteenth-century hall survives in a modern courtyard to the north of *Bloom's*; visits can be arranged by phoning ☎071/247 6943.

Barnett's wife, Henrietta, even proposed moving into one of the infamous thieves' dens and brothels to the north of Toynbee Hall. Barnett put his foot down at the suggestion, but he helped set up the **Four Per Cent Dwellings**, a scheme providing housing for the the poor while guaranteeing a four percent dividend for the wealthy

The Whitechapel Murders

In the space of just eight weeks between August and November 1888, five prostitutes were stabbed to death in and around Whitechapel; all were found with their innards removed. Few of the letters received by the press and police, which purported to come from the murderer, are thought to have been genuine, including the one which coined the nickname, **Jack the Ripper**, and to this day the murderer's identity remains a mystery. At the time, it was assumed by many that he was a Jew, probably a *shochet* (a ritual slaughterman), since the mutilations were obviously carried out with some skill. The theory gained ground when the fourth victim was discovered outside the predominantly Jewish Working Men's Club in Berner Street, and for a while it was dangerous for Jews to walk the streets at night for fear of reprisals.

Ripperologists have trawled through the little evidence there is to produce numerous other suspects, none of whom can be positively proven guilty. The most celebrated suspect is the Duke of Clarence, eldest son of Edward VII, an easy if improbable target since he was involved in a scandal involving a male brothel and was a well-known homosexual. Other famous suspects include a scholarly cousin of Virginia Woolf, who, it was rumoured, had had an affair with Clarence, and was later committed to an asylum in 1892, and the painter Walter Sickert, who exhibited an unhealthy fascination with the murders during his lifetime. Equally fanciful are the likes of George Chapman, alias Severin Klosowski, a Polish immigrant who poisoned his wife and was hanged for the crime in 1903, and Dr Pedachenko, a junior surgeon from Russia with transvestite leanings who was allegedly sent over by the Tsarist secret police to show up the defects in the British police system. The man who usually tops the lists, however, was a cricket-playing barrister named Druitt, whose body was found floating in the Thames some weeks after the last murder, though, as usual, there is no evidence linking him with any of the murders.

The one positive outcome of the murders was that they focused the attention of the rest of London on the squalor of the East End. Philanthropist Samuel Barnett, for one, used the media attention to press for improved housing, street lighting and policing to combat crime and poverty in the area. Today, the murders continue to be exploited in gory, misogynist detail by the likes of Madame Tussaud's, the London Dungeon, and the *Ten Bells* pub on Commercial Road, near where the Ripper's first victim was found, which has a painted board detailing each of the victims and the whereabouts of their bodies.

Jewish investors like the Rothschilds who backed it. The original arch survives above the entrance to the modern red-brick Flower and Dean estate, to the north of Wentworth Street, which now stands in its place.

The most visible symbol of the new Muslim presence in the East End is the Saudi-financed **East London Mosque**, an enormous red-brick building, a short walk up Whitechapel Road from the art gallery; it stands in marked contrast to the tiny little sky-blue synagogue behind the mosque in Fieldgate Street. Neither of these buildings is open to the public, but you can pay a quick visit to the small exhibition in the nearby **Whitechapel Bell Foundry**, part of which occupies the short terrace of Georgian houses on the corner of Fieldgate Street. Big Ben, the Liberty Bell and numerous English cathedral bells all hail from the foundry, established here in 1738.

Whitechapel Market is open Mon–Sat 8.30am–5.30pm, Thurs to 1pm.

Past Valance Road, the street widens at the beginning of the daily **Whitechapel market**, once one of the largest hay markets in London, now given over to the retail of everything from nectarines to net curtains, and including a large number of stalls catering for the Bengali community. At the turn of the century, this was where casual workers used to gather to be selected for work in the local sweatshops, earning it the Yiddish nickname *Hazer Mark* or "pig market". Nearby, on the other side of Valance Road, stood the Pavilion Theatre, one of several East End theatres which used to put on Yiddish shows for the thousands of newly arrived Jews. Raucous and irreverent, Yiddish theatre was frowned upon by the Anglicized Jews, the *Jewish Chronicle* stating that Yiddish was "a language we should be the last to encourage any efforts to preserve". The sole reminder of those days is the Edward VII monument at the centre of the market, erected by the local Jewish community in 1911.

Anarchists in the East End

The *Freedom Press*, a small anarchist bookshop and printing press in Angel Alley, by the side of the Whitechapel Art Gallery, is the inheritor of an East End tradition of radical politics stretching back to the late nineteenth century. In 1907 delegates to the Fifth Congress of the Russian Social Democratic Labour Party staged a meeting on the corner of Fulbourne Street, attended by Lenin, Stalin, Trostky, Gorky and Litvinov, and the Jubilee Street Anarchist Club later loaned £1700 to the Bolsheviks (paid back in full by the Soviet government after the revolution). East End anarchism found a strong following among the Jewish community, especially, and supporters of the *Arbeter Fraint* newspaper staged atheistic demonstrations outside Orthodox synagogues on the Sabbath, as well as making other gestures like ostentatiously smoking and eating ham sandwiches.

The event for which the anarchists are best remembered is the **Siege of Sidney Street**, which took place in January 1911. The first gun battle took place after a routine enquiry at the back of a jeweller's on Houndsditch, and left one Russian anarchist and three policemen dead. Over the next few weeks, all but three of the anarchist gang were arrested; and following a tip-off, they themselves were eventually cornered in a building on Sidney Street. A further gun battle ensued: a detachment of Scots Guards and two cannons were deployed, and the Home Secretary, Winston Churchill, arrived on the scene to give orders. By lunchtime the house was in flames, leaving two charred bodies in the burned-out shell. However, the ringleader, nicknamed Peter the Painter, vanished without trace, to join the likes of Jack the Ripper as an East End legend.

It was on the Mile End Road that Joseph Merrick, better known as the "**Elephant Man**", was discovered in a freak show by Dr Treves, and admitted as a patient to the **Royal London Hospital** on Whitechapel Road. He remained there, on show as a medical freak, for four years until his death from accidental suffocation in 1890, at the age of just twenty-seven. The hospital still owns his skeleton (it's not on public display), despite an offer of several million pounds from Michael Jackson.

Just before the point where Whitechapel Road turns into Mile End Road stands the old Albion Brewery (due for redevelopment), next door to the **Blind Beggar**, the East End's most famous pub since March 8, 1966, when Ronnie Kray walked into the crowded pub and shot gangland rival George Cornell for calling him a "fat poof". This murder spelled the end of the infamous Kray Twins, Ronnie and Reggie, both of whom were sentenced to life imprisonment, though their well-publicized gifts to local charities created a Robin Hood image that still persists in these parts of town.

On Saturdays, the Whitechapel market extends beyond Cambridge Heath Road onto **Mile End Waste**, which is punctuated at one end by a statue and at the other by a bust of the most famous of all the East End philanthropists, **William Booth**. It was here one late June evening in 1865 that Booth, moved by the sight of the crowds at the pubs and gin palaces, made his first impromptu public speech. Later on he set up a tent on Valance Road and began in earnest the missionary work which eventually led to the foundation of the quasi-military Salvation Army in 1878. In contrast to many Victorian philanthropists, Booth never accepted the divisive concept of the "deserving" and "undeserving" poor – "if a man was poor, he was deserving". Booth preached a simple message of "Heaven in East London for everyone", railing against the laissez-faire economic policies of his era, but he was more concerned with attending to the immediate demands of the poor, setting up soup kitchens and founding hostels, which, by the time of his death in 1912, had spread right across the globe.

William Booth is buried in Abney Park Cemetery, see p.235.

Apart from Booth's memorials, there are two unusual features worth mentioning on the Waste. The biggest surprise is the **Trinity Almshouses**, a quaint courtyard of cottages with a central chapel, built in 1695 for "Twenty-eight decay'd Masters and Commanders and the widows of such", and rebuilt after World War II as a home for the disabled. Further up, on the same side of the street, stands a large Neoclassical department store, its facade sliced in two by a small two-storey shop which used to belong to a Jewish watchmaker called **Spiegelhalter**. This architectural oddity is the result of a dispute between Spiegelhalter and his affluent Gentile neighbour, Thomas Wickham, who was forced to build his new store around the watchmaker's shop after he refused to be bought out.

East End museums and Victoria Park

The East End boasts a trio of fascinating **museums** dispersed across a wide area, all of them open to the public free of charge. The easiest one to get to, and by far the most popular, is the Museum of Childhood, with its superb collection of toys and dolls' houses; the Geffrye Museum of period interiors is housed in some of London's grandest almshouses; while the Ragged School Museum traces the philanthropic efforts of the world-famous Dr Barnardo.

Bethnal Green Museum of Childhood

The Museum of Childhood is open Mon–Thurs & Sat 10am–6pm, Sun 2.30–6pm; free; the nearest tube is Bethnal Green.

The Bethnal Green **Museum of Childhood**, a branch of the V&A, is situated just across from Bethnal Green tube station. The big open-plan hall was, in fact, part of the original V&A building designed by Paxton in 1856 and was transported here from Kensington in the late 1860s. The wide range of exhibits means that there's something here for everyone from three to ninety-three, though obviously its most frequent visitors are children; special kids' events are put on here at weekends and during school holidays.

The ground floor is flanked by antique dolls' houses dating back to 1673. Among the jumble of curiosities on the mezzanine are wooden models of carcass-hung nineteenth-century butcher shops, dolls made from found objects (including a little man made from a lobster claw), and a delicate guillotine – complete with a hacked-off head in the basket – carved by French prisoners of war after Waterloo, from the bones of their meat ration. Beyond the automata – Albert the Lion gobbling up his victim is always a firm favourite – and puppets, the museum's doll collection ranges from Native American representations of spirits, to stylish flapper dolls carried by the bright young things of the Jazz Age, and a macabre Shirley Temple. The top gallery is given over to children's books, from fragile eighteenth-century European fairy tales to the anarchic *Little Red Schoolbook*, much loved by hippy parents of the 1970s.

Geffrye Museum

The Geffrye Museum is open Tues–Sat 10am–5pm, Sun 2–5pm; free; bus #6, #22b, #55, #149 from Liverpool Street.

A quarter of a mile or so up Kingsland Road, in a none too savoury part of Hackney, is the **Geffrye Museum**, a peaceful little enclave, set back from the road in a courtyard of eighteenth-century ironmongers' almshouses. Essentially a furniture museum, the Geffrye was established in 1911 for crafts students, when Shoreditch was the centre for English cabinet-making. Today the almshouses are rigged out as period living-rooms, ranging from the oak-panelled seventeenth century through refined Georgian and cluttered Victorian to Art Deco and 1950s utility style. The museum has big ideas for the future, too, with a new extension to house its expanding twentieth-century collection planned to the south of the almshouses.

Ragged School Museum

Even further off the tourist route, the **Ragged School Museum** occupies a Victorian canalside warehouse on Mile End's bombed-out Copperfield Road. Holding more than one thousand pupils from 1877 to 1908, this was the largest of London's numerous Ragged Schools, institutions which provided free education and two free meals daily to children with no means to pay the penny a week charged by most Victorian schools. This particular Ragged School was just one of innumerable projects set up by the East End's most irrepressible philanthropist, the diminutive and devout **Dr Thomas Barnardo**, whose tireless work for the children of the East End is the subject of the ground-floor exhibition. Upstairs, there's a reconstructed Victorian schoolroom, where period-dressed teachers, cane in hand, take today's schoolkids through the rigours of a Victorian school lesson. On the top floor there are further displays on the docks and local sweatshops, plus other temporary exhibitions. As at the Geffrye Museum, there are plans to expand and renovate more of the building in the future.

The Ragged School Musuem is open Wed & Thurs 10am–5pm, first Sun of month 2–5pm; free; the nearest tube is Mile End.

Victoria Park

The Victorians were firm believers in parks as instruments of moral and physical improvement, particularly for the working classes. As "sanitary reformer" William Farr maintained, the use of parks would "diminish deaths by several thousands and add years to the lives of the entire population". **Victoria Park**, London's first public park (as opposed to royal park), was opened in the heart of the East End in 1845, after a local MP presented Queen Victoria with a petition of 30,000 signatures. The only large open space in the area, "Viccy Park" immediately became a favourite spot for political rallies: Chartists congregated here in their thousands in 1848, George Bernard Shaw and William Morris addressed demonstrations, and supporters of the East London Federation of Suffragettes (ELFS) gathered here, under the leadership of Sylvia Pankhurst, who was described by Shaw as "the most ungovernable, self-interested, blindly and deadly wilful little rapscallion-condottiera that ever imposed itself on the infra-red end of the revolutionary spectrum". As recently as 1978, over 100,000 people turned up for an open-air concert organized by the Anti-Nazi League.

The park is open daily 7am–dusk; bus #277 from Mile End tube.

The park is divided in two by Grove Road. The larger eastern section contains an extraordinarily lavish Gothic-cum-Moorish drinking fountain, paid for by Baroness Burdett-Coutts in 1861, although now closed off behind a wrought-iron fence. The Old English Garden, laid out to the northeast of the fountain, provides a nice haven of flowers and shrubs; next door there's a small animal enclosure, and a much larger children's playground.

Hackney

The borough of **Hackney** stretches from the thoroughly East End districts of Hoxton, Haggerston and Dalston in the south, to the north London suburbs of Stoke Newington and Stamford Hill. With the city's largest Afro-Carribean community after Brixton, a sizeable Orthodox Jewish community and an even greater number of Turkish/Kurdish inhabitants (its most recent arrivals), this is one of the most ethnically diverse of all London boroughs. It's hardly surprising, then, that the country's one and only black woman MP, Diane Abbott, has her constituency in Hackney, or that this was one of the infamous "loony left" councils the Thatcherite press loved to hate. The council's recent appointment of a tourist officer caused much hilarity in the press (tourist signposts have since appeared), yet the borough repays selective visits: **Ridley Road** boasts one of London's most vibrant multi-ethnic markets, the red-brick Tudor mansion of **Sutton House** hides away on the fringes of Homerton, and **Stoke Newington** is a haven of inexpensive Turkish and Indian restaurants, and trendy laid-back cafés.

Dalston and Stoke Newington

The nearest train station is Dalston Kingsland on the North London Line.

In the late 1940s **Dalston** was the scene of battles between Mosley's fascists and supporters of the 43 Club, an organization set up by Jewish ex-servicemen to combat the resurgence of fascism in Britain. Nowadays the different communities of this area have a strong enough presence not to feel threatened by the residual white racism of the borough's southern fringes. The ethnic diversity of Dalston is best expressed in the **Ridley Road market**: between the Cockney market stallholders at the high street end and the Turkish/Kurdish supermarket that marks the eastern end, you'll find West Indian grocers and fishmongers, halal butchers, and the *Ridley Bagel Bakery*, fairy lights announcing its fame as a twenty-four hour refuelling point. Another eatery of long standing is *F. Cooke*, 41 Kingsland Rd, across the road from the market, London's best preserved **eel and pie shop**, founded in 1862 by the great-grandfather of the current owner.

Of course all is not rosy in Hackney: one block north of the market is Sandringham Road, epicentre of a recent influx of crack-dealing, which has brought with it an alarming increase in shootings, stabbings and burglaries – and a sorry tale of widespread police corruption. Directly opposite Sandringham Road stands Hackney's only cinema, the Art Deco *Rio*, recently given a well-needed face-lift. In the good old days there were four cinemas on Kingsland (later, Stoke Newington) High Street alone – the northernmost of these, the Moorish *Alhambra*, has, by a judicious twist of fate, been turned into a mosque. The mosque lies at the heart of the local Turkish/Kurdish community, whose exclusively male cafés, named after Turkish football clubs, line the street. The various left-wing factions to which most of the community belong join together annually for London's largest May Day march, down the high street, while Kurdish New Year (April) is celebrated in grand style at *Halkevi*, the Turkish-Kurdish community centre housed in a disused factory built by *Simpson's* of Piccadilly.

Predominantly rural until the middle of the last century, **Stoke Newington** was something of a haven for non-Conformists, who were denied the right to live in the City, and when Bunhill Fields (see p.199) became overcrowded, **Abney Park Cemetery**, to the north of Church Street, which feeds off west from the High Street, became the "Campo Santo of English non-Conformists", in the words of the 1903 brochure. The only famous grave is that of William Booth, founder of the Salvation Army, but the romantically overrun cemetery doubles as an arboretum and is something of an inner-city wildlife reserve (not to mention a gay cruising area).

Stoke Newington is best reached on the #73 bus from Angel, King's Cross or Euston tubes.

The most famous Dissenter to live in the village was **Daniel Defoe**, who wrote *Robinson Crusoe* in a house on the corner of Defoe Road and Church Street; his gravestone is displayed in the local library opposite – stolen from Bunhill Fields in the 1870s, it was discovered in Southampton in 1940. The two local churches, both dedicated to St Mary, reflect the changes wrought on this area: the sixteenth-century village church stands on the north side of the road, opposite a more urbane structure built by Gilbert Scott in 1858, with a spire that outreached all others in London in its day.

Church Street is great for cheap ethnic eats, especially charcoal-grill Turkish joints and South Indian veggie.

This pair mark the entrance to **Clissold Park**, founded in 1899 and centred on a porticoed eighteenth-century mansion that now contains a fine vegetarian café. The clay-pits dug to make bricks for the house now serve as duckponds, and are used by a wide variety of birds, terrapins, hens and even deer. To the north, you can just make out the bizarre quasi-medieval turrets and towers of the Stoke Newington pumping station, built in 1856, closed in 1946 and currently due to be redesigned by Nicholas Grimshaw as an indoor rock climbing centre.

Clissold Park is open daily 7.30am–dusk.

Stamford Hill and the Lea Valley

Stamford Hill, the area northeast of Clissold Park, is home to a tight-knit Yiddish-speaking community of ultra-Orthodox Hassidic Jews, one of Hackney's oldest immigrant populations. The Hassidic movement originated in Poland in the eighteenth century under the charismatic leadership of Ba'al Shem Tov, who preached a message of strict adherence to the rules set down in the Torah. Their attire – frock coats and white stockings for the men, simple navy blue and white clothes for the women – is that worn by the Polish nobility of the period, but their headgear differs from sect to sect, for the Hassidim are a far from homogeneous group. Each sect takes its name from the original villages in Poland, Belarus and Hungary – for example, Lubavitch, Sadigor and Belz – from which their ancestors hailed. As such, they have more in common with their brethren in New York and Israel, than they do with their Gentile neighbours or even other less Orthodox Anglo-Jews.

The shops on Dunsmure Road and Stamford Hill are where the Hassidim buy their kosher goods, and on Sundays large families take the air at Clissold Park, and at **Springfield Park**, a beautifully landscaped park opened in 1905 "to change the habits of the people and to keep them out of the public houses". The park boasts an awesome view across the Lea Valley and the Walthamstow marshes, a valuable stretch of wetlands on which a dragonfly sanctuary has recently opened. To get to the park from Stamford Hill, walk across the remnants of Clapton Common, and down Spring Hill. En route, be sure to check out the four winged beasts (characters from *Revelations*) who sit around the base of the spire of the **Cathedral Church of the Good Shepherd**, on the corner of Rookwood Road. Six thousand people gathered outside the church in September 1902 to throw rotten tomatoes at the womanizing local vicar who had declared himself the Second Messiah.

Mare Street and Sutton House

The nearest train station is Hackney Central on the North London Line.

Hackney Museum is open Tues–Fri 10am–12.30pm & 1.30–5pm, Sat 1.30–5pm; free; there's also a tourist office here (same hours).

Sutton House is open Wed–Sun 11.30am–5pm; £1.50; NT.

The old parish of Hackney (as opposed to the modern borough) lies to the east of Dalston, around **Mare Street**, whose main claim to fame is the ornate turn-of-the-century **Hackney Empire**, one of the last surviving variety theatres in London. Opposite the *Empire* is the more austere, newly renovated Central Hall, built as a two-thousand-seater Methodist meeting place between the wars. The ground floor of the building houses the **Hackney Museum**, which displays an odd assortment of exhibits including an Anglo-Saxon log boat and Marc Bolan's leather hat from *Born to Boogie* (the elfin one was born in Stoke Newington). On the other side of the railway bridge, Mare Street is still discernibly a village high street, over-looked by the dumpy thirteenth-century tower of the parish church.

Head east across the graveyard behind the tower and down the Georgian terrace of Sutton Place and you'll come to **Sutton House**, Hackney's prime tourist attraction. In the mid-1980s this mansion was just one of the borough's numerous squats; since then it has been painstakingly restored to a state that does some justice to its status – built in 1535, it is the oldest house in the entire East End. It takes its name from Thomas Sutton, founder of Charterhouse (p.177), though it now seems likely that he lived in an adjacent building, and not in the house itself. (He is buried at Charterhouse, minus his entrails, which you've just walked over in the graveyard). The National Trust have done their best to adapt to unfamiliar surroundings and have preserved not just the exquisite Elizabethan "linenfold" wooden panelling, but also a mural left by squatters in 1986. And in addition to the rambling complex of period rooms, the house puts on contemporary art exhibitions and classical concerts, and even runs a veggie café (also open Wed & Fri evenings).

Docklands

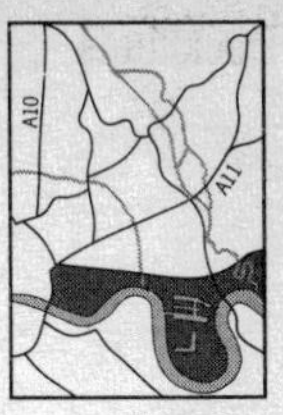

The architectural embodiment of Thatcherism, "a symbol of 1980s smash-and-grab culture" say the critics; a blueprint for inner-city regeneration say its free-market supporters – the **Docklands** redevelopment provokes reactions. Despite its catch-all name, however, Docklands is far from homogeneous. Canary Wharf, with its Manhattan-style skyscraper, is only its most visible landmark, and by no means typical of the area. Pseudo-warehouse architecture, industrial estate sheds and huge swathes of dereliction are more indicative. Wapping, the most easily accessible district, has retained and restored much of its old Victorian warehouse architecture, as has Bermondsey on the south bank (covered in Chapter Eight), while the Royal Docks, further east, and yet to be redeveloped, remain a relatively undisturbed wasteland. Travelling through on the overhead monorail, Docklands comes over as a fascinating open-air design museum, not a place one would choose to live or work – most people stationed here see it as a bleak business-orientated outpost – but a spectacular sight nevertheless.

From the sixteenth century onwards the Port of London was the key to the city's wealth. The "legal quays" – roughly the area between London Bridge and the Tower – were crowded with as many as 1400 sea-going vessels forced to wait for up to six weeks to be unloaded, with some 3500 cutters, barges and punts jostling between their hulls. It was chiefly to relieve such congestion, which worsened with the increased trade from the Empire, that from 1802 onwards London began to construct the largest enclosed cargo dock system in the world. Each dock was surrounded by forty-foot-high walls, patrolled by its own police force and geared towards a specific type of cargo. Casual dockers gathered at the dock gates each morning for the "call-on", a human scrummage to get selected for work. This mayhem was only stopped after Word War II, when the Dock Labour Scheme was introduced, and by then it was too late. Since the mid-nineteenth century, competition from the railways had been eroding the river traffic, and with the development of container ships and the movement of the port to Tilbury in the 1960s, the city docks began to close.

For almost two decades the quaysides and the surrounding areas were a wasteland, beset with high unemployment and a dwindling population, until in 1981 the London Docklands Development Corporation (LDDC) was set up, under the unfortunate slogan of "Looks like Venice, works like New York". One hundred percent tax relief on capital expenditure, no business rates for ten years and freedom from planning controls, were just some of the ploys used to kick-start the project, and the conditions which allowed Canary Wharf and the Enterprise Zone to be built. No one thought the old docks could ever be rejuvenated; the LDDC, on the other hand, predicted a resident population of over 100,000 and a working population twice that, all by the end of the milliennium. The big American property developers, Olympia & York, who had successfully converted virgin land in Canada and developed Manhattan's business quarter stepped in.

It's easy to criticize what's been achieved so far: the ad hoc approach to planning, the lack of basic amenities, of open green spaces, of civic architecture or public buildings, of consultation with the local community. The real shot in the foot though was the Tory government's negligence over basic public transport infrastructure; the government insisted it would only pay fifty percent of the costs of the new tube line extension, which has yet to materialize even now. In the end, the market-led bubble was burst by the economic reality of the recession: Olympia & York went bust, as did many other developers and projects. The end result – "a chain of highly polarized ghettoes epitomizing the gulf between the rich and poor, home-owner and tenant" as one critic aptly put it – coupled with a divisive local council run by the Liberal Democrats in Tower Hamlets helped provide conditions for the election of the first fascist councillor in British history in 1993.

Visiting Docklands

As stressed, most of Docklands is office-land, dead in the evenings and at weekends.

You can view Docklands from a distance on one of the pleasure boats that course up and down the Thames, but for a close-up you should take the driverless, monorail **Docklands Light Railway** (DLR), which sets off from Bank in the City, or from Tower Gateway close to Tower Hill tube and the Tower of London. Significantly, the service stops around 9pm from Monday to Friday, and doesn't run at all on Saturdays and Sundays. With the exception of Wapping, walking around Docklands is not really an option, since there are no pedestrian bridges linking the different quays. Despite the construction of the Limehouse Link tunnel (rumoured to be the world's most expensive piece of road), driving is a nightmare, the road system confusing, and parking well nigh impossible.

Wapping

Once famous for its boatyards and its thirty-six riverside pubs (a handful of which remain), **Wapping** changed forever with the construction of the enclosed docks in the early nineteenth century. Cut off from the rest of the East End by the high walls of the docks, its inhabitants crowded into insanitary housing, Wapping became notorious for its thieves, attracted by the opportunities of rolling drunk sailors and poorly guarded warehouses. With the demise of the docks, Wapping became an early victim of gentrification, though restoration and renovation of existing property rather than demolition and redevelopment has been the rule. Thus something of Wapping's Victorian atmosphere has been preserved, and as it lies just a short walk east of the Tower, this is one of easiest parts of Docklands to explore.

St Katharine's Dock

St Katherine's Dock was built in the late 1820s immediately east of the Tower – in the process some 11,300 people were made homeless, and the medieval foundations of St Katherine's hospital and church were demolished. Having specialized in luxury goods such as ivory, spices, carpets and cigars, St Katherine's became the first phase of the dockland renewal scheme in the early 1970s, when it was turned into a luxury yacht marina by Taylor Woodrow, who also raised the phenomenally ugly *Tower Hotel* and the neo-warehouse of the World Trade Centre, which thankfully is due to be replaced by a Richard Rogers building.

The nearest tube is Tower Hill; the nearest DLR station is Tower Gateway.

St Katherine's proximity to the Tower makes it a popular destination for tour groups, who tend to head for the eighteenth-century timber-framed *Dickens Inn*, originally a brewery warehouse situated several hundred yards east of its present site. Roughly at the centre of the docks is the ugly **Coronarium chapel**, built for Queen Elizabeth II's silver jubilee, and sited as near as possible to the old church of St Katherine's, which was itself owned by the Queen. The dock's redeeming qualities are the old swing bridges, the boats themselves and the **Ivory House** warehouses at the centre of the three basins. Built in 1854, these warehouses at their peak received over 200 tons of ivory annually (that's 4000 dead elephants), plus hippopotamus and walrus teeth and even mammoth tusks from Siberia. The silver-grey monstrosity at the eastern end of the docks is the new and ludicrously-named Thomas More shopping complex.

Wapping High Street

If you arrive on **Wapping High Street** expecting the usual parade of shops, you're in for a big surprise. Traditionally the business of Wapping took place on the river: thus tall brick-built warehouses, most now converted into yuppie flats, line the Thames-side of the street, while to the north, in a stark contrast typical of Docklands,

The nearest tube is Wapping.

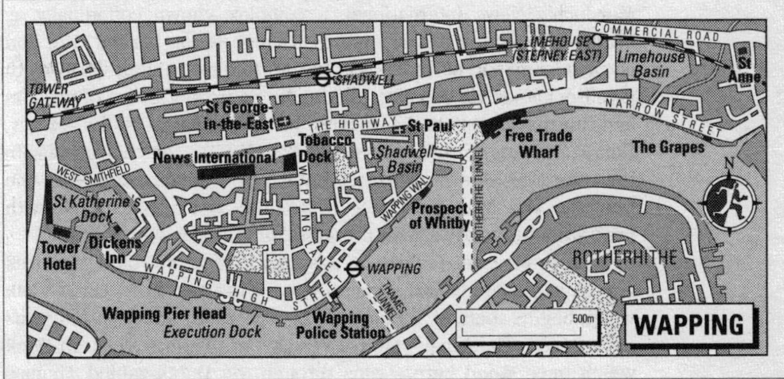

lie the council estates of the older residents. Deterred by the derelict sites in between, few tourists make it here from St Katherine's Dock, but it's only a ten-minute walk and well worth the effort.

About five minutes' walk along the high street you'll come to **Wapping Pier Head**, the former entrance to the London Docks, now grassed over but still flanked by grand Georgian terraces built for officials of the Dock Company. Further east is the unusual neo-Gothic **Oliver's Wharf**, a trail-blazing apartment conversion from 1972, with a couple of preserved overhead gangways just beyond. The nearby boatyard of **Wapping Police Station** heralds the headquarters of the world's oldest uniformed police force, the marine police, founded in the 1790s and now a subdivision of the Met. Down by the riverside here, at the low-water mark, was **Execution Dock**, where pirates and mutineers were hanged in the conventional manner, after which their bodies were left until three tides had washed over them. The most famous felon to suffer here was Captain Kidd, pirate-catcher turned pirate hung in 1701; Execution Dock's last victims were executed for murder and mutiny in 1830.

Wapping has several old riverside taverns, most famously The Prospect of Whitby *on Wapping Wall.*

Tobacco Dock to Fortress Wapping

At Wapping tube station you can either continue east to Shadwell Basin (see below) or head inland up Wapping Lane past **St Peter's Church**, a classic Victorian church worth a peek for its mock-Tudor timber-framed ceiling and red brick patterning. To the north lies **Tobacco Dock**, a huge warehouse built in 1813 and initially used to store tobacco and wine (sheepskin, cork and molasses came later). A fascinating combination of timber and early cast-iron framing, it was converted fairly sensitively into a shopping complex in the later 1980s. Dreams of the East End's answer to Covent Garden, though, evaporated within a matter of years, and the enterprise went bust. The new Kuwaiti owners have further dreams of discount warehouse shopping, the locals would probably prefer another superstore, while the rest of London wouldn't dream of making it out here.

The nearest tube and DLR station is Shadwell.

To the west of Tobacco Dock are the headquarters of Rupert Murdoch's News International, a complex known colloquially as **Fortress Wapping**, on account of its high walls, barbed wire and security cameras. Murdoch was one of the first capitalist barons to give Docklands his blessing, sacking his entire workforce of printers and journalists when he moved his newspapers – the *Times*, *Sunday Times*, *Sun* and *News of the World* – out here in 1986, thus sparking one of the most bitter trade union disputes of the Thatcher era. Mounted police engaged in violent skirmishes with protesters for nearly a year; no prizes for guessing who won.

A more pleasant feature of this area, which will take you back almost as far as St Katherine's Dock, is the tree-lined **canal walk** which begins south of Tobacco Dock, where two three-masted ships are moored. The canal – all that remains of the huge Western Dock which once stood here – runs through the Dutch-gabled Thomas

More housing estate, some of which is now council housing, a policy change which prompted legal action against the developers from some of the yuppie residents.

St George-in-the-East to Shadwell Basin

Tobacco Dock is a short distance south of Hawksmoor's church of **St George-in-the-East**, built in 1726 on the north side of the busy Highway. As bold as any of Hawksmoor's buildings, it boasts four domed towers above the nave and a hulking west-end tower topped by an octagonal lantern. Within, it comes as something of a shock to find a miniature modern church squatting in the nave, but that's all the parish could come up with following the devastation of the Blitz. Plans are afoot to redesign the place and turn part of it into rehearsal space for the Guildhall School of Music and Drama, but money has yet to be found.

Shadwell Basin, further east on the south side of the Highway, is one of the last remaining stretches of water which once comprised three interlocking docks, known simply as London Docks and first opened in 1805. Now a yachting and canoeing centre, it's enclosed on three sides by new housing finished off in primary reds and blues, a gimmicky touch characteristic of Docklands' projects. To the south is the ivy-strewn former pumping station; rising up majestically behind the houses to the north is **St Paul's Church** (closed except for services), the "sea captains' church", with a Baroque tower. Heading east towards Limehouse, the Highway is separated from the Thames by the Legoland ziggurat of **Free Trade Wharf**, a deplorable bit of speculative apartment building.

Limehouse

East of Free Trade Wharf, **Limehouse** was a major shipbuilding centre in the eighteenth and nineteenth centuries, hub of London's canal traffic and the site of the city's first Chinatown, a district sensationalized in Victorian newspapers and popular fiction as a warren of opium and gambling dens, viz Dickens: "Down by the docks the shabby undertaker's shop will bury you for next to nothing, after the Malay or Chinaman has stabbed you for nothing at all". Wartime bombing and post-war road schemes have all but obliterated Limehouse; the only remnants of the Chinese community are the street names and the *Friends* chain of Cantonese restaurants.

There is a trio of good pubs on Narrow Street, by the river.

Hawksmoor's **St Anne's Church**, on Commercial Road, is worth a visit, though its interior, which contains a superb organ built for the 1851 Exhibition, is usually only open for services. The earliest of the architect's East End churches, it's dominated by a gargantuan west tower, which boasts the highest church clock in London. In the graveyard Hawksmoor erected a strange pyramidal structure carved with masonic symbols; opposite is a war memorial with relief panels depicting the horrors of trench warfare.

The nearest DLR station is Westferry.

While you're here it's worth seeking out Newell Street, to the west, which retains several Georgian houses, while Three Colt Street, to the east, is home to the wonderful Art Nouveau **Limehouse Church Institute**, now converted into private flats.

Buildings aside, Limehouse's most recent claim to fame is as the residence of Dr David Owen (aka Dr Death), the man who split the Labour Party in the 1980s to form the short-lived Social Democratic Party. The SDP's existence and antics had little effect in themselves, but helped to ensure a decade of Thatcherism, so in a sense Docklands and its ethos is in part their memorial.

Docklands architecture

London's Docklands contains one of the worst collections of late twentieth-century architecture to be seen anywhere in the world. It is a marvel, if it were not so embarrassing, that so many very bad buildings from the same period can be found in such a comparatively small area of the city...And yet it is to Docklands you must go to find some of the best British architecture of the 1980s. The gems are few....but the concentration is high and the quality rare.

Stephanie Williams, Phaidon Architecture Guide

Williams is undoubtedly right in her judgment on Docklands' architecture, but there are a few exceptions, beyond those mentioned in our main text. You've got to be a fairly dedicated architecture buff, however, to reach most of the following buildings (all modern, save for one Victorian gem), which are mostly some distance from their nearest DLR stations.

Cascades, Westferry Road. High-rise apartments may be deeply unfashionable at the moment, but this strange, triangular wedge, erected by CZWG right by the river, remains quirky enough to pull it off. DLR Heron Quays.

Storm Water Pumping Station, Stewart Street. John Outram's boldly post-modern edifice shows just what can be done even when building what is essentially a glorified shed. DLR South Quay.

Reuters, Blackwall Yard. A bleak spot, and in some respects a disappointing building for Richard Rogers, though closer inspection reveals a few characteristic flourishes. DLR Brunswick.

Telehouse, Leamouth Road. A joint Japanese-British Telecom venture, this smart grey aluminium box is high-tech and high-security, but handsome nevertheless. DLR Preston's Road.

Financial Times Printing Works, East India Dock Road. A remarkably straightforward design by Nicholas Grimshaw, and without doubt the finest of the Docklands' many new printing presses. The giant presses can be seen clearly at night through the glass walls; tours are also possible Tues–Thurs 7.30–10.30pm; ☎0171/873 4074. DLR Preston's Road.

Abbey Mills Pumping Station, Abbey Lane. Not strictly speaking within LDDC territory, this is a glorious Victorian building just the same, a Byzantine "cathedral of cast-iron" by Bazalgette and Cooper, where the shit still hits the fan for the whole of north London. Tours possible; ☎0181/534 6717. West Ham tube.

Isle of Dogs

The Thames begins a dramatic horseshoe bend at Limehouse, thus creating the **Isle of Dogs**, a marshy peninsula on which cattle were once fattened for City banquets. The unusual name has prompted various theories as to its origin, from dead dogs washed up on the shore to old royal kennels, though the most plausible is that it's a corruption of the Flemish *dijk* (dyke). In 1802 the peninsula became an island when a canal was cut to form London's first enclosed trade dock, built to accommodate rum and sugar from the West Indies. With the opening of the Millwall Docks further south, the population rose to 21,000 by the turn of the century. The demise of the docks was slow in coming, but rapid in its conclusion: 8000 jobs in 1975 dwindled to just 600 following the closure of both docks in 1980.

The Isle of Dogs is currently the geographical and ideological heart of the new Docklands, which reaches its apotheosis in Canary Wharf, home to Britain's tallest building. The rest of the island remains surreally lifeless, an uneasy mix of drab high-rises, clapped-out housing, warehouses converted into expensive apartments, and a lot of new architecture – some of it startling, some of it crass, much of it empty. The area's long-term residents see the new developments as a threat rather than a blessing, and a section of them gave the local council a clear indication of their discontent by voting in a fascist BNP councillor in a 1993 by-election.

Canary Wharf

The nearest DLR station is Canary Wharf.

Canary Wharf – the strip of land in the middle of West India Docks, previously a destination for rum and mahogany, later bananas and tomatoes – was the brainchild of Canadian developers, Olympia & York, who were responsible for major developments in Manhattan and Toronto's financial districts. Although one of the most cohesive and complete Dockland complexes, the project is in fact only half-finished, with two more skyscrapers and a whole host of other buildings planned to the east of the landmark tower, and several more arcs to **Westferry Circus**, the double-decker roundabout park, at the western end of the long tree-lined West India Avenue. The largest development undertaken by a single developer in Europe, it proved too much for even North American purses and in 1992, Olympia & York threw in the towel, handing over to their bankers.

Canary Wharf's most famous building is Cesar Pelli's landmark tower, officially known as **One Canada Square**, which at 800ft is the highest building in Europe after Frankfurt's Messerturm. The world's first skyscraper to be clad in stainless steel, it's an undeniably impressive sight, both from a distance (with its flashing pinnacle it points the horizon from numerous points in London – and out as far as Kent) and close up. Unless you are unlucky enough to work here, however – residents include the *Daily Telegraph* and *Independent* newspapers – there is no public access except to the marble atrium.

Arriving at Canary Wharf, the monorail cuts right through the middle of the office buildings. The station platforms straddle a shopping mall: Cabot Square East is at present shopless, but features a glass-domed atrium through which you get a great view of Pelli's tower; Cabot Street West is nondescript but at least contains a few

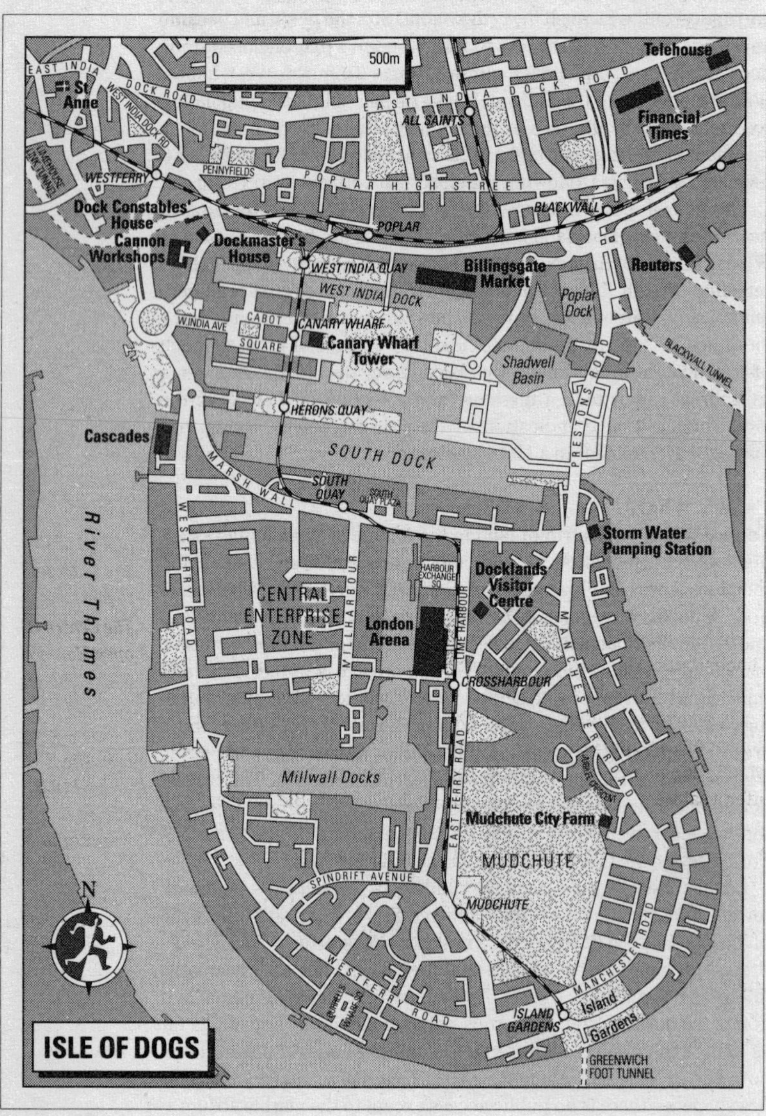

shops. Continuing west, **Cabot Square** proper, centred on a graceful fountain, is probably the most relaxing place on the Isle of Dogs.

From Fisherman's Walk, on the north side of Canary Wharf, you can see the last surviving warehouses of the **West India Docks**, the first and most successful of the nineteenth-century docks. In addition, a series of Georgian buildings survive near the old docks' entrance on West India Dock Road: the stately Dockmaster's House, with its smart white balustrade, the Ledger Building, with its equally pristine portico, and the prim row of Dock Police Cottages in Garford Street. The only finished project on West India Quay, is the new **Billingsgate fish market**, the hangar-like building visible to the east, which moved here from the City in 1989 (p.210).

Mackenzie Walk, on the south side of Cabot Square, is the best place to view **Heron Quays**, the thin slip of quayside to the south of Canary Wharf. The western section, completed in 1986, was the first major development on the Isle of Dogs, and fairly untypical of what was to follow. These inoffensive, low-rise Swedish-style clapperboard buildings always looked temporary, and are now due to be demolished to make way for rather less modest proposals.

Central Enterprise Zone and Mudchute

Symbolically enough, it was porno publishers *Northern & Shell* who were among the first to base themselves in the **Central Enterprise Zone**, the gimmicky industrial estate to the south of Heron Quays, in which shed after shed competes for the prize of most grotesque building in Docklands. These were amongst the earliest of the new Docklands buildings on the Isle of Dogs; the more substantial buildings, looking north over South Quay from Marsh Wall, are little better – cheap-looking tinted-blue glass at South Quay Plaza or ugly grey cladding at Thames Quay to the east.

The Centre is open Mon–Fri 8.30am–6pm, Sat–Sun 9.30am–5pm; free. The nearest DLR station is Crossharbour.

There's more tinted-blue glass at Harbour Exchange Square, on Limeharbour, opposite the superbly misplaced **Docklands Visitor Centre**, which doubles as a glossy museum of the docks' history and a propaganda machine for the LDDC. The centre is also the embarkation point for the LDDC **bus tours** (summer daily 9am–4pm; £6), which, depending on the guide (often a genuine East Ender), can offer a salutary overview of the area. An account of "Blood Alley", the sugar warehouse from which the workers would return each day with glassy granules of sugar embedded in their ripped skin, is a corrective to any thoughts about the good old days.

Mudchute Farm is open daily 9am–5pm; free.

One stop further south on the DLR brings you to the large grassy expanse known as **The Mudchute**, formed by silt dumped here after the dredging of Millwall Dock. In the northeastern corner of "The Muddie", as it's known locally, is **Mudchute Farm**, the most rural of all the city farms. The DLR hits its southernmost terminus at **Island Gardens**, starting point for the 1902 foot tunnel to Greenwich, and the perfect spot from which to contemplate Wren's masterpieces, the Naval Hospital and Old Royal Observatory across the river (p.346).

Lambeth and Southwark

Until well into the seventeenth century, the only reason for north bank residents to cross the Thames, to what is now **LAMBETH** and **SOUTHWARK**, was to visit the disreputable entertainment district around the south end of London Bridge, which lay outside the jurisdiction of the City. The rest of the south bank was a desolate marshland interrupted only by the odd fishing village or hamlet. During the nineteenth century, however, this land was transformed virtually overnight into a grimy jungle of warehouses, slums and overhead railways. The railways alone survive

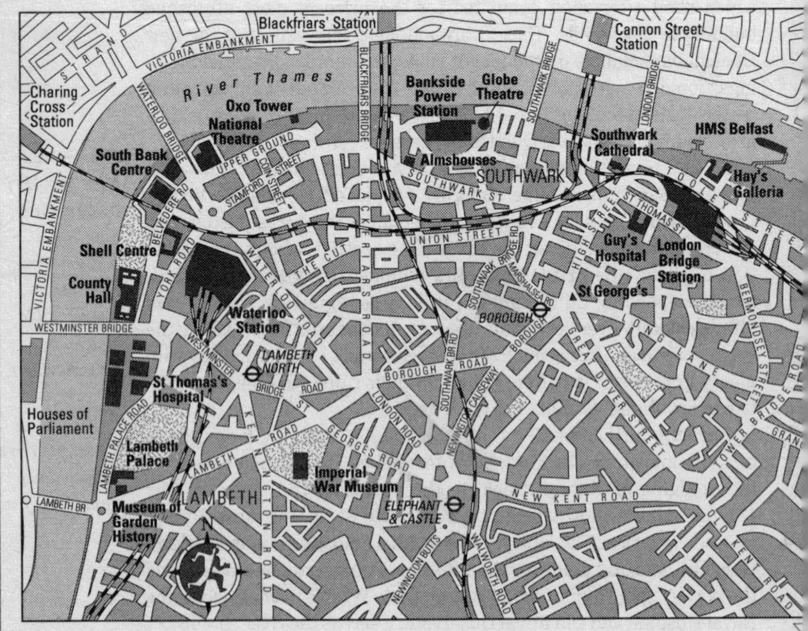

intact, the rest having either been demolished during the slum clearances or during the Blitz. But South London (a catch-all for everything south of the river) still has a reputation, among north Londoners at least, as a boring, sprawling, residential district devoid of any local culture or life.

As it turns out, this is not too far from the truth: **Lambeth**, for one, is mostly residential, but along its riverbank lie several important cultural institutions, collectively known as the **South Bank Centre**. Although a mess architecturally, these galleries, theatres and concert halls, along with the exceptional Museum of the Moving Image, draw large numbers across the river for nighttime entertainment. There are more sights further east in **Southwark**, the cradle of Elizabethan theatre, which has a range of popular museums around Tooley Street – generating a brisk daytime trade despite their inauspicious surroundings – and the wartime frigate, *HMS Belfast*, permanently moored on the Thames.

Southwark also marks the beginning of the Docklands' south bank development around **Bermondsey**, which, though less known than Canary Wharf, contains some interesting warehouse conversions, including a number of commercial art galleries and some of the developers' better stabs at new architecture. **Butler's Wharf**, in particular, is a thriving little warehouse development, centred on the

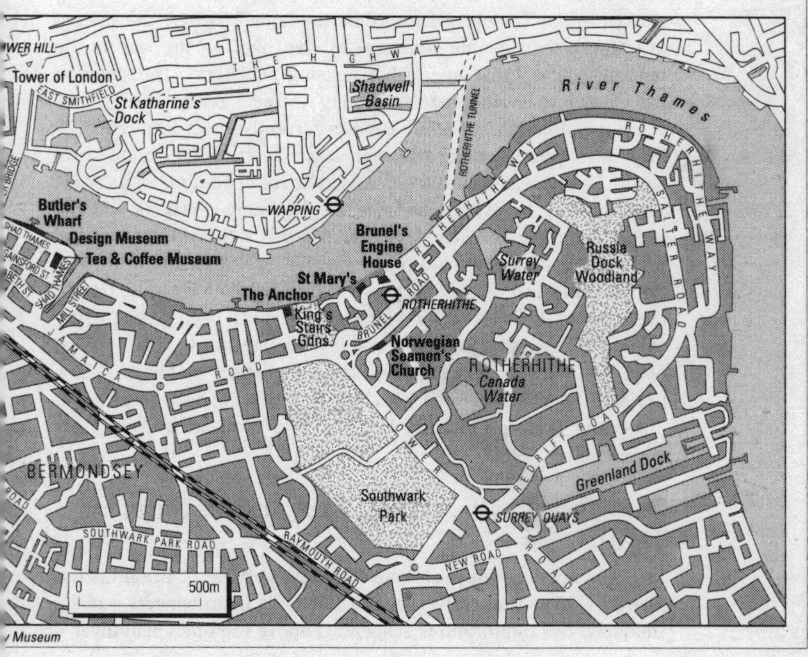

excellent **Design Museum**. Further east, **Rotherhithe** clings on to its old seafaring identity despite the demise of the nearby docks and the subsequent new housing developments.

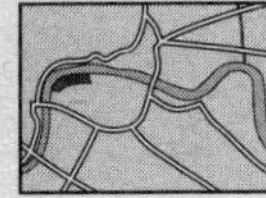

The South Bank

In 1951, the South Bank Exhibition, held on derelict land south of the Thames, formed the centrepiece of the nationwide **Festival of Britain**, an attempt to revive post-war morale by celebrating the centenary of the Great Exhibition (when Britain really did rule over half the world). The most striking features of the site were the saucer-shaped Dome of Discovery, with exhibits on exploration, and the cigar-shaped Skylon, which was held upright by wires. The great success of the festival provided the impetus for the eventual creation of the **South Bank Centre**, though it has singularly failed to capture the imagination of the public in the same way. Instead, the South Bank has become London's much unloved culture bunker, a mess of "weather-stained concrete, rain-swept walkways, urine-soaked stairs" as one critic put it.

The nearest tube is Waterloo, but the best way to approach the South Bank is via Hungerford railway bridge from Charing Cross.

The South Bank reached its nadir in the 1980s, when its concrete undercroft and the neighbouring railway arches and "Bull Ring" subway, became "**Cardboard City**", home to hundreds of homeless, sleeping out in cardboard boxes. The population of Cardboard City peaked in the Thatcher years, when the homeless were considered little more than people you have to step over on the way to the opera (to paraphrase one of her housing ministers). The situation has improved, but there are still plenty who seek refuge here.

On the plus side, the South Bank is currently under inspired artistic direction and stands very much at the heart of the capital's arts scene. Its unprepossessing appearance is softened, too, by its riverside location, its avenue of trees, its occasional buskers and the second-hand bookstalls and café outside the National Film Theatre. As for the future, there are big plans afoot to breathe new life into the area: Richard Rogers, architect of the popular Pompidou Centre in Paris and the Lloyd's Building in the City, has been given the go-ahead to redesign the entire complex, though as yet there are no plans to actually demolish any of the existing buildings. It's a project Rogers has coveted for a long time, having been rebuffed on a previous occasion by local residents over the nearby Coin Street development.

The concert halls, the Hayward and the National Theatre

The only building left over from the 1951 Festival of Britain is the **Royal Festival Hall** (RFH), one of London's main concert venues. Uniquely, the auditorium is suspended above the open-plan foyer –

its curved roof is clearly visible above the main body of the building. The interior furnishings are still appealingly Fifties, the English National Ballet put on regular seasons here, and foyer exhibitions and events are generally excellent, making this one of the most pleasant South Bank buildings to visit. You also get an excellent view from the terrace café across the Thames to the Shell-Mex building with its giant clockface, Terry Farrell's post-modern development above Charing Cross station, and the stripey brickwork and pepperpots of Gilbert Scott's New Scotland Yard.

Architecturally, the most depressing part of the South Bank Centre is the **Queen Elizabeth Hall** (QEH), and the more intimate **Purcell Room**, which share the same foyer and are built in uncompromisingly 1960s brutalist style. Events here, nonetheless, are consistently interesting. It is the same story with the **Hayward Gallery**, which sits behind and on top of all this concrete garbage, is equally repellent from the outside, but has an uncluttered gallery space that hosts major contemporary art exhibitions.

On the far side of the bridge, looking like a multi-storey car park, is Denys Lasdun's **National Theatre**, an institution first mooted in 1848 but only finally realised in 1976. It contains three separate theatres: the large open-stage Olivier (named after the famous actor, who was also the theatre's first director), the more traditional Lyttelton and the studio theatre of the Cottesloe. Again, it tends to receive flack from architectural critics, though the theatres themselves are superb, and, in fairness to Lasdun, nobody told him that the concrete exterior would receive a zero maintenance budget.

For theatre details, see Chapter 20.

The NFT and MOMI

Tucked underneath Waterloo Bridge is the **National Film Theatre**, which screens London's most esoteric films – some 2000 of them each year – alongside a variety of talks, lectures and mini-festivals. Straddling the underside of Waterloo Bridge, behind the NFT and connecting with its foyer, is the **Museum of the Moving Image**, popularly known as MOMI. This is a wonderful museum, covering an impressive amount in its somewhat cramped space, reeling through a spirited history of film and cinema, with actors on hand to enliven the proceedings. It begins with a vast array of optical toys, but the real fun starts in the following rooms, where among the memorabilia, cameras, posters and costumes, you can audition for a screen test in a 1920s-style casting session, make your own cartoons in an animation room, and watch a shoot on a Hollywood film set complete with egotistical director.

The NFT is the centre of the London Film Festival, in November.

MOMI is open daily 10am–6pm; £5.50.

There's also plenty of opportunity to watch films, often in witty settings: to see the newsreels, for example – including footage of the Hindenberg disaster, Mussolini's pompous posturing and the V-Day celebrations – you climb onto the roof of a news van, thus mimicking the logo of the Pathé newsreels. The television section, pandering rather shamelessly to twenty- and thirty-something Anglo nostalgia, leads to the bit that's most popular with children, where you get to read the television news and be interviewed by a televisual Barry Norman.

Gabriel's Wharf and beyond

Gabriel's Wharf has a small weekend crafts market.

Beyond the National Theatre, the riverside promenade takes you past another Denys Lasdun building, London Weekend Television's offices and studios, bringing you eventually to **Gabriel's Wharf**, a laid-back collection of lock-up craft shops, brasseries and bars. It's a pleasant extension to the South Bank Centre's own, rather limited facilities. Adjoining it is the landmark **OXO tower**, former HQ of the beefstock company, which has been earmarked for small-scale office and retail development.

Just beyond here stands the Seacontainers House, a grotesque 1970s speculative hotel which never came about and now serves as offices, and the similarly ugly *Doggett's Coat & Badge* pub. The latter is named after the barge race from Chelsea to London Bridge, begun by an Irish comedian called Thomas Doggett in 1715 to celebrate the beginning of the Hanoverian dynasty. The race is still run every year in late July, and the winner gets to wear a comical red Hanoverian costume as his prize.

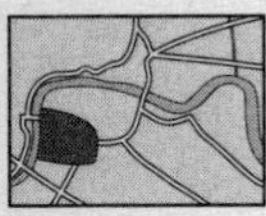

County Hall to the Imperial War Museum

The South Bank Centre stops just short of the Hungerford railway bridge; west of here stands the Stalinist-looking **Shell Centre**, and, further south still, the colonnaded crescent of **County Hall**, the only truly monumental building in this part of town. Designed to house the London County Council, it was completed in 1933 and enjoyed its greatest moment of fame as the headquarters of the GLC (Greater London Council), under the leadership of Ken Livingstone, or "Red Ken" as the Thatcherite press loved to call him. Livingstone is best remembered by Londoners for his low-fares policy that saw thousands abandon their cars and take to public transport. The Tories moved in swiftly, taking away more and more responsibilities from the GLC and finally abolishing the whole thing in 1986, leaving London as the only European city without an elected authority. Proposals to turn the empty building over to the London School of Economics were rejected in favour of a rival bid by a Japanese millionaire, Takashi Shirayama, though at the time of going to press, Shirayama himself was understood to want to pull out of the planned hotel and leisure complex and hand the building over to the Hong Kong property tycoons, the Hwang brothers.

East of County Hall, away from the riverfront, is one of London's few modern architectural triumphs, the **Waterloo International Terminal**, an astounding piece of engineering by Ove Arup, designed by Nicholas Grimshaw. Its curving glass roof shelters one of the longest railway platforms in the world, currently the main arrival and departure point for the *Eurostar* Channel Tunnel trains.

County Hall to the Imperial War Museum

Florence Nightingale Museum

On the other side of Westminster Bridge from County Hall, a series of red-brick Victorian blocks and modern accretions make up **St Thomas's Hospital**, which moved here after being ejected from its Georgian premises in 1862 when the railway came sweeping through Southwark. At the northeastern corner of the hospital, on Lambeth Palace Road, is the **Florence Nightingale Museum**, celebrating the woman who revolutionized the nursing profession by establishing the first school of nursing at St Thomas's in 1859. The exhibition hits just the right note, putting the two years she spent in the Crimea in the context of a lifetime of tireless social campaigning; exhibits include the white lantern which earned her the nickname "The Lady with the Lamp", a reconstruction of a Crimean military hospital ward, and an overlong slide show.

The museum is open Tues–Sun 10am–4pm; £2.50.

Lambeth Palace and the Museum of Garden History

To the south of St Thomas's, on the other side of the road, stands **Lambeth Palace**, London residence since 1207 of the Archbishop of Canterbury. The thirteenth-century chapel in which John Wycliffe was tried for heresy (for the second time) survives, as does much of the medieval fabric of the palace, but it is out of bounds to the public; all that you can see close-up is the imposing red-brick Tudor gateway by Lambeth Bridge.

Beside the palace gateway is the Kentish ragstone church of **St Mary-at-Lambeth**, which retains its fourteenth-century tower but is otherwise a Victorian recreation. Deconsecrated in 1972, the church now contains a café and an unpretentious little **Museum of Garden History**, which puts particular emphasis on John Tradescant, gardener to James I and Charles I. A tireless traveller in his search for new species, Tradescant set up a museum of curiosities known as "Tradescant's Ark" in Lambeth in 1629. Among the many exhibits were the "hand of a mermaid . . a natural dragon, above two inches long . . . blood that rained on the Isle of Wight . . . and the Passion of Christ carved very daintily on a plumstone"; the less fantastical pieces formed the nucleus of the Ashmolean Museum in Oxford.

The museum is open Mon–Fri 11am–3pm, Sun 10.30am –5pm; free.

A section of the graveyard has been transformed into a small and visually subdued **seventeenth-century garden**, where two interesting sarcophagi lurk among the foliage. The first, which features a sculpted eternal flame, is the resting place of **Captain Bligh**, the commander of the *Bounty* in 1787 when it set off to transport

County Hall to the Imperial War Museum

breadfruit trees from Tahiti to the West Indies for transplanting. On the way home the crew mutinied and set Bligh and eighteen others adrift in a small open boat, with no map and few provisions. Using just a sextant, Bligh navigated the craft 3600 miles to the Indonesian island of Timor, a journey of 48 days. He later became governor of New South Wales, where his subjects once again rebelled, after which he was promoted to Vice Admiral. The **Tradescant memorial** is more unusual, depicting a seven-headed griffin contemplating a skull and several crocodiles sifting through sundry ruins flanked by gnarled trees.

The Imperial War Museum

From 1815 until 1930, the domed building at the east end of Lambeth Road was the infamous lunatic asylum of Bethlehem Royal Hospital, better known as **Bedlam**. Charlie Chaplin's mother was among those confined here – the future comedian was born and spent a troubled childhood in nearby Kennington.

The museum is open daily 10am–6pm; £3.90, free after 4.30pm. The nearest tube is Lambeth North.

When the hospital was moved to Beckenham in southeast London, the wings were demolished and the central building became home to the **Imperial War Museum**, an impressively wide-ranging and sober coverage of its subject, with the main hall's display of guns, tanks, fighter planes and a giant V2 rocket offset by the lower ground floor array of documents and images attesting to the human damage of war. In addition to the static displays, a good deal of stagecraft is used to convey the misery of combat, with grim walk-through World War I trenches and a recreation of the Blitz, in which you wander from an air-raid shelter through bomb-ravaged streets accompanied by blaring sirens and human voices. Recent acquisitions include a slice of the Berlin Wall, General Schwarzkopf's Gulf War uniform and Operation Jericho, an extremely realistic flight simulator which you pay extra to play.

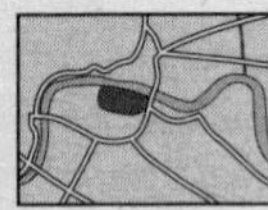

Southwark

Southwark – originally the name of the area around the southern end of London Bridge, now a vast borough reaching as far south as Dulwich – has a history as long as that of the City. It started out as a Roman red-light district, and its brothels continued to do a thriving illegal trade until 1161, when they were licensed by royal decree. This measure imposed various rules and restrictions on the prostitutes, who could now be fined three shillings for "grimacing to passers-by", but were given Sunday mornings off in order to attend church. The whores were known as "Winchester Geese", since the land was owned by the Bishops of Winchester, and the church made a small fortune out of the rent until Henry VIII closed the bawdy houses down (they returned soon after his death). Under the bishops' rule, bull- and bear-baiting, drinking, cockfighting and gambling were also rife, especially on Bankside, and although after 1556 Southwark came under the jurisdiction of the City, it was still not subject to its regulations on entertainment. So Southwark remained the pleasure quarter of Tudor and Stuart London, where brothels and other disreputable institutions banned in the City – most notably theatres – continued to flourish until the Puritan purges of the 1640s.

By the nineteenth century, warehouses and factories had occupied much of the land closest to the river, while countless houses were demolished during the construction of London Bridge and the laying of the rail tracks. As a result, little remains above ground to remind you of Southwark's most interesting pre-industrial period. The Clink Exhibition and the newly rebuilt Globe Theatre (where Shakespeare's plays had their first performances) go some way towards remedying this, as do Southwark Cathedral and the George Inn, London's last surviving galleried coaching inn.

The nearest tube is Blackfriars ten minutes' walk away on the other side of the Thames.

Bankside

Contemporary **Bankside**, running along the river east and west of Southwark Bridge, is dominated by **Bankside Power Station**, an austere, brick-built "cathedral of power", designed by Gilbert Scott after the last war. The town planners insisted the central chimney should not outreach St Paul's, a reasonable enough demand on aesthetic grounds, but which prevented the sulphurous smoke from escaping into the upper atmosphere – instead it drifted across the Thames and attacked the cathedral's exterior. Closed down in 1980, the power station is earmarked as the Tate Gallery's new museum of international modern art, due to open in the year 2000.

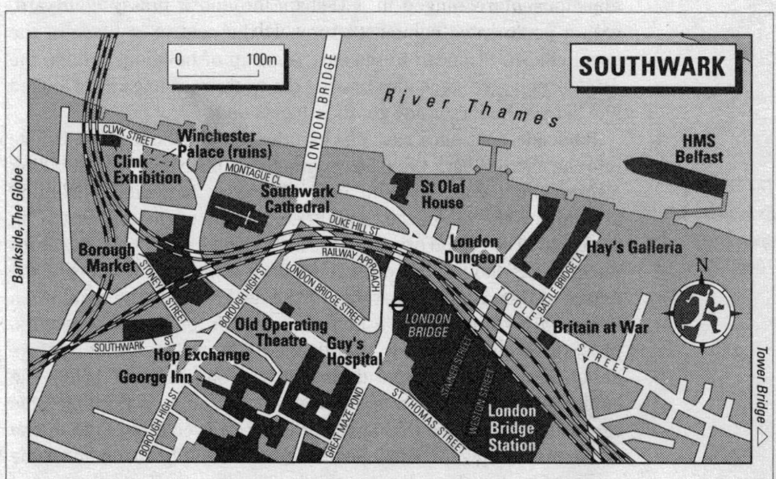

Southwark

In Elizabethan times, Bankside was the most nefarious street in London, known as "Stew's Bank" from its brothels or "stewhouses", and studded with **bull and bearpits**. Pepys recalls seeing "some good sport of the bulls tossing of the dogs; one into the very boxes", but opinion was by then inclining towards Evelyn's description of the sport as a "rude and dirty pastime" and in 1682 the last bear garden was closed down. In 1600, Bankside also boasted no fewer than four thriving **theatres**: the *Swan*, built in 1587, with Edward Alleyn (founder of Dulwich College) as the lead actor, and Christopher Marlowe as its main playwright; the *Rose*, built in 1595 and capable of seating 3000; the *Hope*, built in 1613, which doubled as a bear garden and theatre; and the *Globe*, the Burbages' theatre (originally built in Shoreditch in 1576, and later dismantled and erected on Bankside), where Shakespeare put on his greatest plays. The theatres lasted barely half a century before being closed down by the Puritans, who considered them "chapels of Satan".

The Globe is open daily 10am–5pm; £4.

Following a long campaign by the late American director and actor Sam Wanamaker, the **Globe Theatre** is now being reconstructed, using traditional materials, immediately to the east of the power station. This site was chosen because the theatre's original site, marked by a blackened plaque on a brewery wall five minutes' walk east on Park Street, lies beneath a listed Georgian terrace. The exhibition currently on the site features a makeshift exhibition of Southwark's theatrical history, and is basically a fundraising exercise, though you do get a guided tour of the work-in-progress. The project, which will include a stage, museum, exhibition space and video presentations, is due to open sometime in 1996.

On either side of these new developments are some remarkable remnants of eighteenth-century Bankside. To the west, the **Hopton almshouses** are ranged in a U-shape around a grassy courtyard, with a pedimented committee room at the centre, in place of the usual chapel. Stranded to the east, a group of buildings around the *Anchor* pub give some idea of what the waterfront must have looked like before the Victorians got their hands on it.

The Clink Exhibition is open daily 10am–6pm; £2.

Bankside continues east on the other side of Southwark Bridge into the narrow, dark Clink Street, a suitably dismal site for the **Clink Exhibition**, a small museum and – somewhat incredibly – working armoury on the site of the Clink Prison, origin of the expression "in the clink". The prison originated as a dungeon for disobedient clerics under the Bishop of Winchester's Palace – the rose window of the palace's Great Hall has survived a little further along the road; when it moved here it became a dumping ground for heretics, debtors, prostitutes and a motley assortment of Bankside lowlife, before being burnt to the ground during the Gordon Riots of 1780. The exhibition dwells less on prison history and more on pornographic reproductions of medieval brothels – there's even a red light in one of the more explicit rooms. Serious points could be made about the mores of medieval London, but this is schoolboy stuff.

Southwark Cathedral

Southwark

Continuing eastwards, Clink Street becomes Cathedral Street in the midst of new office developments, and eventually leads to **Southwark Cathedral**, built in the thirteenth and fourteenth centuries as the Augustinian priory church of St Mary Overie. It's a minor miracle that the church survived the nineteenth century, which saw the east end chapel demolished to make way for London Bridge, railways built within a few feet of the tower and some very heavy-handed Victorian restoration. As if in compensation, the church was given cathedral status in 1905, and recently it has begun to gain the upper hand – an entirely new chapter house has been built to the north, funded by a *Pizza Express* inside (Mon–Fri 10am–4.30pm).

The cathedral is open daily 8am–6pm; free; the nearest tube is London Bridge.

The cathedral's **interior**, too, has had a lot of money spent on it, and now exudes a warm honeyed hue from its walls. Of the original church, which was rebuilt after a devastating fire in 1212, only the choir and retrochoir now remain, separated by a beautiful high stone Tudor screen; they are probably the oldest Gothic structures left in London. The nave was entirely rebuilt in the nineteenth century, though several of the bosses from the original wooden ceiling are displayed against the west wall; among the most interesting are the pelican drawing blood from its breast to feed its young (a symbol of Christ's sacrifice) and the devil eating Judas Iscariot.

The cathedral contains numerous **monuments**, from a thirteenth-century oak effigy of a knight to one dedicated to the 47 people who died when the *Marchioness* pleasure boat collided with a barge on the Thames in 1989. Others include the brightly painted tomb of poet John Gower, Chaucer's contemporary, in the north aisle, his head resting on the three books he wrote, one in Latin, one in French and one in English. The quack doctor Lionel Lockyer has a humorous epitaph in the north transept, and there's an early twentieth-century memorial to Shakespeare in the south aisle, with the bard in green alabaster lounging under a stone canopy – a birthday service is held here for him each year.

The Borough

Medieval Southwark, also known as **The Borough**, was London's first suburb, clustered round the southern end of London Bridge, London's only bridge over the Thames from Roman times until 1750 and thus the only route south. Borough was the most obvious place for the Kent farmers to sell their goods to the City grocers, and there's been a thriving market here since medieval times. The present **Borough Market** is squeezed beneath the railway arches between the high street and the cathedral. It's one of the few wholesale fruit and veg markets still trading under its Victorian wrought-iron shed, which is little changed since Dickens' time (if you ignore the fork-lift trucks), and it puts on a bit of a show, with luscious

Good times to visit the market are Tuesday and Friday mornings, though there's something going on every day except Sunday.

displays to attract small shopkeepers and market traders rather than bulk buyers.

As the main road south out the City, Borough High Street was for centuries famous for its coaching inns. Chaucer's Canterbury pilgrims set off from the *Tabard* (in Talbot Yard), but by Dickens' time, "these great rambling queer old places", as he called them, were closing down. The only extant coaching inn is the **George Inn**, situated in a cobbled yard east off the high street, dating from 1677 and now owned by the National Trust. Unfortunately, the Great Northern Railway demolished two of the three original galleried fronts, but the lone survivor is an remarkable sight nevertheless.

Opposite Borough tube station, at the southernmost end of Borough High Street, is **St George the Martyr**, where Little Dorritt got married in the Dickens novel of the same name, much of which is set around The Borough. St George's has four clock faces, three white and illuminated at night, one black and pointing towards Bermondsey, whose parishioners refused to give money for the church. Beyond the church, a wall survives from the **Marshalsea**, the city's main debtors' prison, where Dickens' father was incarcerated for six months in 1824 (it, too, features in *Little Dorrit*).

The most educative and strangest of Southwark's museums is the **Old Operating Theatre Museum and Herb Garret** on St Thomas Street. Built in 1821 at the top of a church tower, where the hospital apothecary's herbs were stored, this women's operating theatre was once adjacent to the women's ward of St Thomas's Hospital, which has since moved to Lambeth. Despite being entirely gore-free, the museum is as stomach-churning as the London Dungeon (see below), for this theatre dates from the pre-anaesthetics era.

The museum is open Tues–Sun 8am–4pm; £2.

The surgeons who used this room would have concentrated on speed and accuracy (most amputations took less than a minute), but there was still a thirty percent mortality rate, many patients simply dying of shock, many more from bacterial infection, about which very little was known. This is clear from the design of the theatre itself, which has no sink and is made almost entirely of mahogany and pine, which would have harboured bacteria even after vigorous cleaning. Sawdust was sprinkled on the floor to soak up the blood and prevent it dripping onto the heads of the worshippers in the church below.

Opposite the museum stands **Guy's Hospital**, founded in 1726 by Sir Thomas Guy, a governor of St Thomas's Hospital, with the money he made on the City money markets. The hospital still occupies some of its eighteenth-century buildings, in particular the courtyard on St Thomas Street, but it is currently under threat from the Tories' health cuts. Guy's also retains its pretty little **Hospital Chapel**, built in the 1770s on the west side of the courtyard. You can wander in to admire the giant marble and alabaster tomb of the founder, who's depicted welcoming a new patient to the hospital, though in fact Guy died a year before the first patients were admitted.

The London Bridge area

Southwark

From 1651 onwards the stretch of river frontage between London Bridge and Tower Bridge was occupied by Hay's Wharf, the largest of the "suffrance wharves" that were built to ease the volume of shipping trying to dock at the "legal quays" on the north bank. So much of the city's food – in particular teas, wines, grain, butter, bacon and cheese – was stored here that the area became known as "London's Larder". Badly bombed in the Blitz, the wharf never recovered before the city's docks began to shut down in the 1960s.

However, the area's proximity to the City made this one of the first targets of the Docklands' development aimed at transforming the wharves and warehouses into a buzzing new business environment tagged "**London Bridge City**". Phase One of the complex, which went up extremely quickly in the mid-1980s, begins inauspiciously with the pink granite monstrosity of No. 1 London Bridge, a typically uncompromising piece of Big Bang architecture. Adjacent to this, emblazoned with "Hay's Wharf" in giant gold lettering, is **St Olaf House**, a 1930s Art Deco warehouse which points up the lack of imagination in its neighbour. From Tooley Street (see below), you can view the building's wonderful black and gold mosaic of the Norwegian king, Saint Olaf, who assisted Ethelred the Unready in his defence of London against the Danes.

Next comes the **Cottons Centre**, another spectacularly ugly office development, followed by **Hay's Galleria**, a new shopping precinct built over what used to be Hay's Dock. The idea of filling in the dock and covering it with curving glass and steel barrel-vaulting, while retaining the old Victorian warehouses on three sides, is an effective one, but there's still a basic lack of customers here – there's usually no one making a purchase from the pseudo market barrows, no one using the petanque terrain, no one contemplating the gimmicky kinetic sculpture, nor even anyone using the tourist-friendly red phone boxes.

After adverse criticism from the likes of Prince Charles the developers had a crisis of confidence about Phase Two, east to Tower Bridge. Eventually they plumped for John Simpson's "Venice-on-Thames", which features a grand arcaded piazza and campanile à la Saint Mark's. The one positive spin-off from all this speculative building will be the opening up of the riverside from London Bridge almost all the way to Greenwich.

London Dungeon

The vaults beneath the railway arches of London Bridge train station, on the south side of Tooley Street, are now occupied by the Gothic horrors of the **London Dungeon**, one of the city's major crowd-pleasers. The life-size waxwork tableaux include a hanging at Tyburn gallows, a rack with hideous creaking sound-effects as the victim's bones are pulled apart, and a man with a rat burrowing into his chest, the general hysteria being boosted by actors dressed as

The Dungeon is open April–Sept daily 10am–6.30pm; Oct–March closes 5.30pm; £6.95.

top-hatted Victorians pouncing out of the darkness. There are queues for the two "shows" included in the entrance fee: neither is up to much, but the thoroughly exploitative "Jack the Ripper Experience", which features an actress dressed as an East End prostitute, plus dummies and slides of the mutilated victims, has provoked sporadic protests from women's groups. You may well emerge in a similar frame of mind.

Britain at War Museum

Britain at War is open April–Sept daily 10am–5.30pm; Oct–March closes 4.30pm; £5.

A little further east still on Tooley Street is a new museum called **Winston Churchill's Britain at War**, which, despite its jingoistic name and the fact that Margaret Thatcher was one of its most enthusiastic proponents, is an illuminating insight into the stiff-upper-lip London mentality during the Blitz. It begins with a rickety elevator ride down to a mock-up of a tube air-raid shelter (minus the stale air and rats), in which a contemporary newsreel cheerily intones about "a great day for democracy" as bombs drop indiscriminately over Germany.

This is just a prelude to the museum's hundreds of sometimes bizarre wartime artefacts, such as a child's gas mask designed to look like Mickey Mouse. You can sit in an Anderson shelter beneath the chilling sound of the V1 "doodlebugs", tune in to contemporary radio broadcasts and, as a grand finale, walk through the chaos of a just-bombed street – pitch dark, noisy, smoky and chokingly hot.

HMS Belfast

HMS Belfast is open daily: summer 10am–6pm; winter to 5pm; £4.

A ferry service runs from the ship to Tower Pier from March to November.

Permanently moored opposite Southwark Crown Court, **HMS Belfast** was the largest World War II battle-cruiser in the Royal Navy. Armed with six torpedoes, and six-inch guns with a range of over fourteen miles, the Belfast spent over two years of the war in the Royal Naval shipyards, after being hit by a mine in the Firth of Forth at the beginning of hostilities. Decommissioned after the Korean War, the ship is now an outpost of the Imperial War Museum.

A series of tired-looking historical exhibitions and videos of more recent blood-letting is ranged over the ship's seven decks, which could accommodate a crew of up to 800. The fun bit is exploring the maze of cabins and scrambling up and down the vertiginous ladders. Be sure to make it down to the air-locked Boiler Room, a spaghetti of pipes and valves, from which there was no chance of escape in the event of the boat being hit.

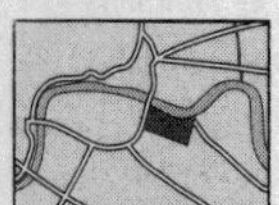

Bermondsey

Famous in the Middle Ages for its Cluniac abbey, later frequented for its pleasure gardens and spa, **Bermondsey** changed enormously in the nineteenth century. In 1836, the London and Greenwich Railway – the city's first – was built through the district, supported by 878 brick arches stretching for four miles. Teeming riverside wharves and overcrowded tenements brought some of the worst social conditions in Victorian London, as Charles Kingsley discovered: "O God! What I saw! People having no water to drink but the water of the common sewer which stagnates full of . . . dead fish, cats and dogs".

The most recent change came with the closure of the docks in the 1960s, and the area to the north of Jamaica Road is now part of the Docklands regeneration project. The **Butler's Wharf** warehouse development contains the excellent Design Museum, the area's prime attraction along with the Friday morning Bermondsey **antique market**, also known confusingly as the New Caledonian Market, since this is the ancestor of the pre-war flea market which used to take place off Islington's Caledonian Road.

Butler's Wharf and the Design Museum

The nearest tube is Tower Hill, ten minutes' walk away on the other side of the Thames.

In contrast to the brash offices of London Bridge City, the new developments to the east of Tower Bridge have attempted to retain some semblance of the historical character of the area. This is particularly true of **Butler's Wharf**, one of the densest networks of Victorian warehousing in London, which was snapped up for just £5 million by Terence Conran back in 1984. Conran's approach – restoring the old warehouses where possible while subtly enhancing the area with new modernist and post-modernist buildings – is infinitely preferable to the LDDC's scorched earth policy, and makes this one of the most enjoyable parts of Docklands to explore.

The best place to start is on Tower Bridge itself, the only place from which you can get a really good view of the old **Anchor Brewhouse**, which produced *Courage* ales from 1789 until 1982. A cheery, ad hoc sort of building, with a boilerhouse chimney at one end and malt mill tower and cupola at the other, it was sensitively converted into apartments in 1989. Next door is the original eight-storey **Butler's Wharf warehouse**, which gives its name to the surrounding area. The upper floors have again been converted into yuppie accommodation, while the ground floor shops cater for a moneyed clientele. However, the wide promenade on the riverfront is open to the public.

Butler's Wharf is a mecca for gourmands, too, with Conran's riverside restaurants, La Cantina, *the pricey* Pont de la Tour, *and the* Blueprint Café *at the Design Museum.*

Shad Thames, the street at the back of Butler's Wharf, has kept the wrought-iron overhead gangways by which the porters used to transport goods from the wharves to the warehouses further back from the river; it's one of the most atmospheric alleyways in the whole of Docklands, and was used by David Lynch as a Victorian backdrop for *The Elephant Man*. The flats around **Tower Bridge Piazza**, to the south of Shad Thames, have been successful in finding buyers, the shops on the ground floor less so. At present, the most memorable thing about the square is the central fountain –

encrusted with naked women, whose belongings are sculpted around the edge.

The Design Museum is open daily 10.30am–5.30pm; £3.50.

The big attraction of Butler's Wharf is the superb riverside **Design Museum**, at the eastern end of Shad Thames. The stylish white edifice, a Bauhaus-like conversion of an old warehouse, is the perfect showcase for an unpretentious display of mass-produced industrial design from classic cars to tupperware. The constantly evolving permanent collection is displayed on the top floor; the first floor gallery acts as a showcase for new ideas, including prototypes and failures, as well as hosting temporary exhibitions on important designers, movements or single products.

The Tea and Coffee Museum is open daily 10am–6pm; £3.

The **Bramah Tea and Coffee Museum**, housed in the crisply modernist Clove Building behind the Design Museum on Maguire Street, is not in the same league as its neighbour – it's a rambling and amateurish exhibition, and its café, bizarrely, serves a very poor cup of coffee.

St Saviour's Dock

To the east of Maguire Street, Shad Thames curves around the back of **St Saviour's Dock**, a tidal inlet overlooked by swanky new warehouse offices. Incredible though it may seem, it really is still possible to smell the spices – cinnamon, nutmeg and cloves mostly – which were once stored here, especially after a shower of rain. **New Concordia Wharf** on Mill Street, completed in 1984, was one of the first warehouse conversions in the area. Next door, stands **China Wharf**, one of the few out-and-out post-modernist buildings, with its stack of semicircular windows picked out in red. This last building, like those around St Saviour's Dock, is best viewed from the river.

The Mill Street area is dotted with small art galleries, lodging here on cheap rents and short leases. A good one is Purdy Hicks, *upstairs at Jacob Street Film Studios, on Mill Street.*

The area to the east of Mill Street was dubbed by the Victorian press as "the very capital of cholera". In 1849 *The Morning Chronicle* described it thus: "Jostling with unemployed labourers of the lowest class, ballast heavers, coal-whippers, brazen women, ragged children, and the very raff and refuse of the river, [the visitor] makes his way with difficulty along, assailed by offensive sights and smells from the narrow alleys which branch off". This was the location of Dickens' fictional Jacob's Island, where Bill Sikes met his end in *Oliver Twist*. Nowadays it lies derelict, though yet another combined business-leisure complex is promised.

The riverfront from St Saviour's Dock to Rotherhithe has yet to be attacked by the developers, thanks to some extent to Southwark Council, who backed the local residents in their battle against more yuppie residences. If you want to continue east on foot to Rotherhithe, you can follow a route alongside the river, stopping en route at the *Angel*, a fifteenth-century pub frequented by Pepys and Captain Cook, on Bermondsey Wall.

Rotherhithe

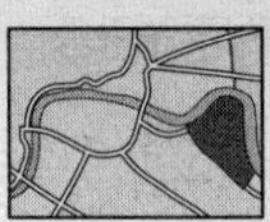

Rotherhithe, the thumb of marshy land jutting out into the Thames east of Bermondsey, has always been slightly removed from the rest of London, a separation not diminished by its current position on the obscure East London tube line. It was a thriving centre of shipbuilding even before the construction of the Surrey Commercial Docks in the nineteenth century, and remained busy until the eve of the last war. No other set of London dockyards took such a hammering in the Blitz, and the decades until their closure in 1970 were ones of inexorable decline. Most of the docks, which took up almost the entire peninsula, have now been reclaimed for new housing estates and more upmarket accommodation. The lack of any relationship between the old Rotherhithe communities, which face the street, and the new ones, which face the water, give the whole area a strange dislocated feeling that's typical of LDDC country.

Around St Mary's

The nearest tube is Rotherhithe.

The area of Rotherhithe most worth a visit is the heart of the eighteenth-century seafaring village around **St Mary's Church**, which stands in its own little grassy square not far from the tube station. The church itself is unremarkable, but it has rich maritime associations: several of the furnishings are made from the timber of the *Fighting Temeraire*, the veteran of Trafalgar which ended its days in a Rotherhithe breaker's yard (Turner's painting of its last voyage is in the National Gallery), and the master of the *Mayflower* was buried here. The *Mayflower* was pretty much Rotherhithe-owned and crewed, and set off from its mooring outside the *Mayflower* pub in 1620 to transport the Pilgrim Fathers to the New World (via Plymouth). The pub, to the north of the church, is a rickety white clapperboard building badly damaged in the last war, and a minor pilgrimage site for Americans. To the south of the church is a slip of a Georgian house, the figures of blue-coated boy and girl recalling its former use as a charity school. To squeeze the last ounce of atmosphere from Rotherhithe, check out the narrow alleyway to the northwest of the church, still flanked by old wharves featuring overhead gangways. At the western end rises the new **Princes Tower**, its whitewashed modernism harking back to Le Corbusier.

The Engine House is open first Sun of month noon–4pm; £1.50.

To the east of St Mary's, down Tunnel Street, you'll find **Brunel's Engine House**, a brick-built shed which marks the site of the Thames Tunnel, the world's first under-river tunnel. It was begun in 1825 by Marc Brunel and his more famous son, Isambard, to link Rotherhithe with Wapping, using technology which was invented by Brunel senior and whose basic principles have been used for all subsequent tunnelling. Plagued by periodic flooding, labour unrest, fatalities and lack of funds, the tunnel took eighteen years to construct and was nicknamed "The Great Bore" by the press.

The circular working shaft, which housed an engine to pump water out of the tunnel, survives to the east of the engine house, but funds ran out before the spiral ramps, which would have allowed horse-drawn vehicles to actually use the tunnel, could be built. Instead, in 1843, the tunnel was opened to pedestrians as a tourist attraction. It was visited by Queen Victoria herself, who knighted Brunel junior, but soon became the haunt of whores and "tunnel thieves". Since 1869 it has formed part of the East London Railway (now tube line) and remains the most watertight of all the rail tunnels under the Thames. Shortage of funds and Rotherhithe's dearth of tourists are responsible for the very infrequent opening hours of the engine house, but this is an interesting museum, with a short video on the tunnel and a functioning pumping engine from Chatham Docks.

The seamen's missions and the old docks

One of the more unusual legacies of Rotherhithe's seafaring past is the trio of Scandinavian seamen's missions – a reminder of the former dominance of the timber trade in the nearby Surrey Docks (see below) – which survive to the south of the tube station, around Albion Road. The most prominent is the **Norwegian Seamen's Church**, by the approach road to the Rotherhithe Tunnel, which flies the Norwegian flag and features a longboat atop its weathervane. Albion Road itself still has a Scandinavian bent – even the nearby public toilets are bilingual – and further down you'll find the well-maintained **Finnish Seamen's Mission**, built in modernist style in 1958, with a free-standing belfry that looks more like a fire station practice tower. The Swedish Seamen's Church, further south on Lower Road, completes the trio but is architecturally undistinguished.

Rotherhithe Street, which hugs the riverbanks all the way round the peninsula, may be the longest street in London, but it's not one that you're likely to want to explore, peppered as it is with derelict warehouse sites and new housing estates. This once marshy land was chosen as the site for London's first wet dock, built in 1696 to take on any extra repair work and re-fitting emanating from the Royal Dockyards in nearby Deptford. Later renamed Greenland Dock, the Rotherhithe docks became part of the network known as **Surrey Commercial Docks**. The main trade was timber, which was piled into stacks up to sixty feet high by porters nicknamed "Flying Blondins" (after the tightrope walker), who wore distinctive leather pads on their heads and shoulders to protect them from splinters. The only large expanse of water remaining is Greenland Dock itself, the rest having been reclaimed; a large tract of parkland has been created, too, with an ecological walk marked out from Lavender Pier to Greenland Dock.

You can go dinghy sailing or windsurfing in Surrey Docks; see p.535.

The Old Kent Road

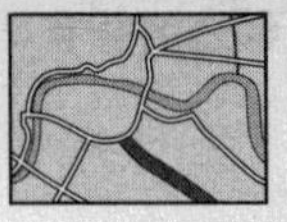

The **Old Kent Road**, the cheapest property on the Monopoly board, is still one of the most depressing roads in London. Lying along the old Roman Watling Street to Dover, it runs dead straight for more than two miles from Borough to Deptford, lined with numerous boarded-up shops and other delights such as one of the city's first drive-thru *McDonalds*.

Bus #21 runs from Borough tube; bus #53 and #63 run from Elephant & Castle tube.

The medieval Canterbury Pilgrims used to pause awhile at "St Thomas-à-Watering", now the **Thomas-á-Becket**, 320 Old Kent Road, one of several boxing pubs in the area, and for a long time a sort of unofficial museum of boxing. The gym above the pub has been graced by just about every prize fighter from Muhammed Ali to Mike Tyson, and the walls of the pub and the gym are covered with memorabilia. Both the gym and the pub are currently going through hard times, and though there are plans to relaunch the pub, the gym looks set to remain closed for some time.

The only other reason for wending your way down the Old Kent Road is the **Livesey Museum**, housed in an old Victorian library, and one of London's liveliest local museums, aimed principally to appeal to kids. There are no permanent displays as such; instead the museum puts on temporary exhibitions drawn from a wide range of other museums on topics such as dinosaurs, rubbish and robots.

The Livesey Museum is open Mon–Sat 10am–5pm; free.

Chapter 9

Hyde Park, Kensington, Chelsea and Notting Hill

Londoners tend to see their city as grimy and built-up but most visitors are amazed at how green and pleasant so much of the centre is. The three royal parks – St James's, Green Park and Hyde Park – form a continuous green that stretches for four miles. **Hyde Park**, together with its westerly extension, Kensington Gardens, is the largest of the trio, covering a distance of two miles from Speakers' Corner in the northeast to Kensington Palace in the southwest. In between, you can jog, swim, fish, sunbathe or mess about in boats on the Serpentine, cross the park on horseback or mountain bike, or view the latest in modern art at the Serpentine Gallery. At the end of your journey, you've made it to one of London's most exclusive districts, the Royal Borough of Kensington and Chelsea, which makes up the bulk of this chapter.

Other districts go in and out of fashion, but **Kensington**, to the west of Hyde Park, has been in vogue ever since royalty moved into Kensington Palace in the late seventeenth century. Aside from the shops around *Harrod's* in Knightsbridge, however, the popular tourist attractions lie in **South Kensington**, where three of London's top museums – the **Victoria & Albert**, **Science** and **Natural History museums** – stand on land bought with the proceeds of the Great Exhibition of 1851. The following half-century saw the entire borough transformed from fields, farms and private estates into street after street of ostentatious Italianate terraces, grandiose red-brick mansions and mews houses. This is prime London real estate and heartland of the so-called Sloane Rangers – the wealthy and vacuous offspring of the middle and upper classes.

Chelsea, bordering the river, also has royal connections, though these date mostly from Tudor times and have left few tangible remains. Since the nineteenth century, when artists and writers began to move here in significant numbers, Chelsea's character has been more bohemian. In the 1960s, the King's Road carved out its reputation as London's catwalk, while in the late Seventies it was the epicentre of the punk explosion. Nothing so risqué goes on in Chelsea now, though its residents like to think of themselves as rather more artistic and intellectual than the purely moneyed types of Kensington.

Once slummy, now swanky, **Bayswater and Notting Hill**, to the north of Hyde Park, were for many years the bad boys of the borough, a den of vice and crime comparable to that of Soho. Despite gentirifcation over the last twenty years, they remain the borough's most cosmopolitan districts, with a strong Arab presence and vestiges of the Afro-Caribbean community who initiated and still run the city's (and Europe's) largest street **carnival**, which takes place every August Bank Holiday.

Hyde Park and Kensington Gardens

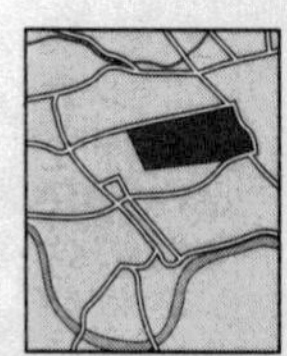

The park and gardens are open daily 5am–midnight; free.

Seized from the Church by Henry VIII to satisfy his desire for yet more hunting grounds, **Hyde Park** was first opened to the public by James I when refreshments available included "milk from a red cow". Under Charles II, the park became a fashionable gathering-place for the *beau monde*, who rode round the circular drive known as The Ring, pausing to gossip and admire each other's equipage. Its present appearance is mostly due to Queen Caroline, an enthusiast for landscape gardens, who spent a great deal of George II's money creating the park's main feature, the **Serpentine lake**.

Hangings, muggings and duels, the Great Exhibition of 1851 and numerous public events have all taken place in Hyde Park – and it is still the gathering point or destination for many political demonstrations, as well as the location of Speakers' Corner, of which more below. For most of the time, however, the park is simply a leisure ground – a wonderful open space which allows you to lose all sight of the city beyond a few persistent towerblocks.

The more tranquil half of the park, to the west of Victoria Gate and the Ring, is known as **Kensington Gardens**, and is, strictly speaking, a separate entity from Hyde Park, though you hardly notice the change. These gardens were first opened to the public in George II's reign, but only on Sundays to those in formal dress, and that didn't include sailors, soldiers or liveried servants. Unrestricted access was only granted in Victoria's reign, by which time, in the view of the Russian ambassador's wife, the park had already been "annexed as a middle-class rendezvous. Good society no longer [went] there except to drown itself."

Marble Arch and Speakers' Corner

The nearest tube is Marble Arch.

Marble Arch, located at the treeless northeastern corner of the park and the west end of Oxford Street, is the most historically

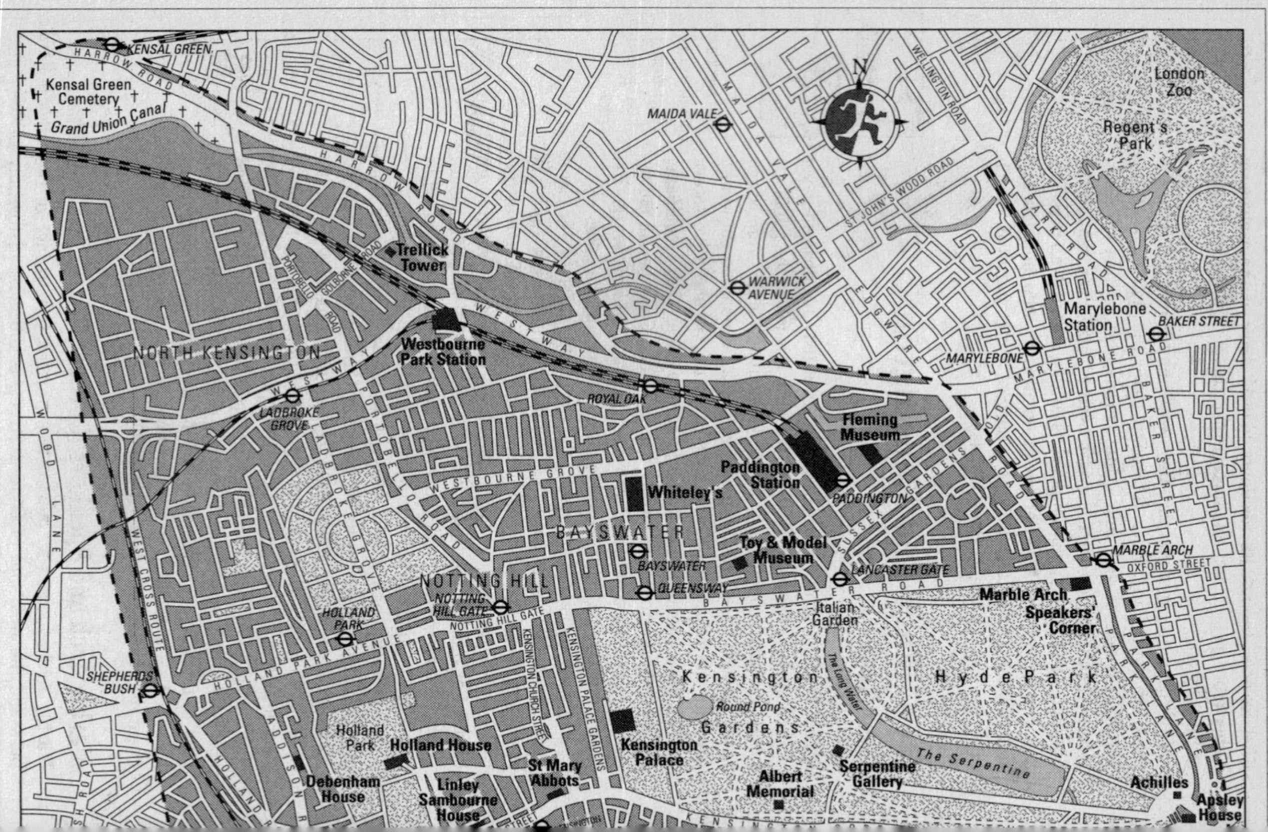

Kensal Green
Harrow Road
Kensal Green Cemetery
Grand Union Canal
N
Maida Vale
Maida Vale
Wellington Road
London Zoo
Regent's Park
St John's Wood Road
Park Road
Trellick Tower
Portobello Road
Golborne Road
Warwick Avenue
Edgware Road
Marylebone Station
Baker Street
Westway
Westbourne Park Station
North Kensington
Marylebone
Marylebone Road
Ladbroke Grove
Royal Oak
Fleming Museum
Wood Lane
Paddington Station
Baker Street
Westbourne Grove
Whiteley's
Paddington
Sussex Gardens
Ladbroke Grove
Portobello Road
Bayswater
Toy & Model Museum
Bayswater
Lancaster Gate
Marble Arch
Oxford Street
Notting Hill
Queensway
Bayswater Road
Marble Arch
Speakers' Corner
Notting Hill Gate
Notting Hill Gate
Italian Garden
Holland Park
West Cross Route
Kensington Church Street
Kensington Palace Gardens
Holland Park Avenue
Shepherds Bush
Kensington Gardens
The Long Water
Hyde Park
Park Lane
Round Pond
Holland Park
Holland House
Kensington Palace
Addison Road
Holland Road
The Serpentine
St Mary Abbots
Serpentine Gallery
Debenham House
Albert Memorial
Achilles
Linley Sambourne House
Apsley House

Olympia Station
Olympia
Leighton House
Commonwealth Institute
Orthodox Church
Royal Albert Hall
Science Museum
Natural History Museum
Victoria & Albert Museum
Brompton Oratory
Harrods
Wellington Arch
St Peter
BELGRAVIA
Holy Trinity
Royal Court
Duke of York Barracks
Michelin House
National Army Museum
Royal Hospital
Ranelagh Gardens
Chelsea Physic Garden
Carlyle's House
Chelsea Old Church
Crosby Hall
World's End
Peace Pagoda
Children's Zoo
Battersea Park
River Thames
Chelsea Harbour
Brompton Cemetery
Chelsea Football Ground
Earls Court Exhibition Hall
Fulham Palace
KENSINGTON
SOUTH KENSINGTON
EARLS COURT
CHELSEA
SLOANE STREET
CADOGAN SQUARE
SLOANE SQUARE
KNIGHTSBRIDGE
CROMWELL ROAD
GLOUCESTER ROAD
HARRINGTON GARDENS
OLD BROMPTON ROAD
THE BOLTONS
KING'S ROAD
CHELSEA EMBANKMENT
CHELSEA BRIDGE ROAD
QUEENSTOWN ROAD
BATTERSEA PARK ROAD
BATTERSEA BRIDGE ROAD
BATTERSEA BR
WARWICK ROAD
LILLIE ROAD
WEST BROMPTON
FULHAM BROADWAY
FULHAM ROAD
PARSON'S GREEN
NEW KING'S ROAD
PUTNEY BRIDGE
FULHAM PALACE ROAD
HAMMERSMITH ROAD
TALGARTH ROAD
NORTH END ROAD
SHEPHERD'S

charged spot in Hyde Park, as it marks the site of **Tyburn gallows**, the city's main public execution spot until 1783 when the action moved to Newgate (p.195). The arch itself, stranded on a ferociously busy traffic island, was designed in 1828 by Nash in imitation of the Arch of Constantine in Rome. It was originally positioned in front of Buckingham Palace, but had to be moved when it proved too narrow for the royal carriages; the equestrian statue of George IV that's now in Trafalgar Square was intended to surmount it.

Tyburn Gallows

For nearly five hundred years **Tyburn** was the capital's main public execution site, with around fifteen victims a month swinging, some of them dispatched for the most petty of crimes (there were 156 capital offences in the eighteenth century). "Hanging Matches", as they were known, usually drew huge crowds – up to 200,000 for the execution of a noted criminal – and became something of a show of working-class solidarity, with numerous side stalls and a large permanent grandstand known as "Mother Proctor's Pews". Dressed in their best clothes, the condemned were processed through the streets in a cart (the nobility were allowed to travel in their own carriage) from Newgate Prison, three miles away, often with the noose already looped in place. They received a nosegay at St Sepulchre, opposite the prison, and then at various taverns along the route they were given a free pint of ale, so that many were blind drunk by the time they arrived at the three-legged gibbet known as the "Tyburn Tree" or the "Triple Tree", which could dispatch over twenty people at one go.

The condemned were allowed to make a speech to the crowd and were attended by a chaplain, though according to one eighteenth-century spectator, he was "more the subject of ridicule than of serious attention". The same witness then goes on to describe how the executioner, who drove the cart, then tied the rope to the tree: "This done he gives the horse a lash with his whip, away goes the cart and there swings my gentleman kicking in the air. The Hangman does not give himself the trouble to put them out of their pain but some of their friends or relations do it for them. They pull the dying person by the legs and beat his breast to dispatch him as soon as possible".

Not all relatives were so fatalistic, however, and some would attempt to support the condemned in hope of a last-minute reprieve, or of reviving the victim when they were cut down. Fights frequently broke out when the body was cut down, between spectators hoping to touch the corpse in the belief it had miraculous medicinal qualities, and between relatives and surgeons who were allowed ten corpses a year for dissection. The executioner, known as "Jack Ketch" after the famous London hangman who botched the Duke of Monmouth's beheading (p.218), was allowed to take home the victim's clothes, and made further profit by selling the hanging rope inch by inch. Altogether, an estimated 50,000 were hanged at Tyburn, but following the 1780 Gordon Riots, the powers that be took fright at unruly gatherings like Tyburn and in 1783 demolished the Tyburn Tree.

Hyde Park and Kensington Gardens

In 1855 an estimated 250,000 people gathered in the section of the park directly across the road from Marble Arch to protest against the Sunday Trading Bill (Karl Marx was among the crowd and thought it was the beginning of the English Revolution), and ever since then it has been one of the most popular spots for political demos. Riots in 1866 eventually persuaded the government to license free assembly at **Speaker's Corner**, now a Sunday forum for soap-box orators, cranks and vocational hecklers. It's not serious politics but it's entertaining, nonetheless, with a peculiarly English assembly of character speakers – revolutionaries, evangelists, and always someone who regards red meat as the source of all evil.

Hyde Park Corner

The nearest tube is Hyde Park Corner.

A better place to enter the park is at **Hyde Park Corner**, the south-east corner, where **Constitution Arch** stands in the midst of another of London's busiest traffic interchanges. Designed by a youthful Decimus Burton in 1828 to commemorate Wellington's victories in the Napoleonic Wars, this arch originally formed the northern gate into Buckingham Palace grounds.

Positioned opposite Burton's delicate Hyde Park Screen, which was intended as a formal entrance into the park, the arch once formed part of a fine architectural ensemble with Apsley House, Wellington's London residence, and St George's Hospital to the west. Unfortunately the symmetry was destroyed when it was repositioned in 1883 to line up with Constitution Hill – whose name derives not from a written constitution, which England has never had, but from the "constitutional" walks which Charles II used to take there. The arch's original statue, an equestrian portrayal of the "Iron Duke", was taken down the same year, and was eventually replaced by Peace and her four-horse chariot, erected incongruously in the summer of 1914.

Known during the Iron Duke's lifetime as Number One, London, **Apsley House** was once an immensely desirable residence, but nowadays, with traffic roaring past at all hours of the day and night, it would be poor reward. The interior isn't what it used to be either, but in this case it's Wellington himself who was to blame. The house was built and exquisitely decorated by Robert Adam in 1771, but on setting up home here in 1817, the Duke had virtually all of the Adam interiors ripped out. His own replacement decor has been preserved in the house's **Wellington Museum**, which displays his personal effects, his art collection, a 400-piece dinner service decorated with scenes of Wellington's life presented by King of Prussia, and portraits of his heroes, contemporaries and adversaries, including a twice life-size nude statue of Napoleon by Canova, which was disliked by the sitter and eventually bought by the Prince Regent in 1816.

The Wellington Museum is closed for restoration at time of publication, with no date fixed for reopening.

Hyde Park and Kensington Gardens

Behind Apsley House, a pair of frothy new silvery gates – installed in 1993 as a birthday present to the Queen Mother – marks Queen Elizabeth Gate, the beginning of the park proper. Close by the entrance, overlooking the back of Apsley House, is the **Achilles statue**, a 33-ton bronze copy of a Roman original, erected in 1822 on behalf of "the women of Great Britain" to commemorate the Duke's achievements. As the country's first public nude statue it caused outrage, especially since many thought it a portrait of the Duke himself. William Wilberforce led a campaign to have the statue removed for decency's sake; a fig leaf was eventually placed in the appropriate place as a compromise.

Rotten Row and the Serpentine

At noon on Feb 6, April 21, June 2 & 10 & Aug 4, and other special occasions, the Household Cavalry wheel out cannons and the park resounds to 41-round Royal Gun Salutes.

From the Hyde Park Corner gates, two roads set off west to Kensington: South Carriage Drive, which is open to cars, and **Rotten Row**, thought to be a corruption of *route du roi*, since it was established by William III as a bridlepath linking Westminster and Kensington. William had three hundred lamps hung from the trees to try to combat the increasing number of highwaymen active in the park, thus making Rotten Row the first road in the country to be lit at night. The measure was only partly successful – George II himself was later mugged here. To the south of Rotten Row, the **Hyde Park Barracks** are difficult to miss thanks to Basil Spence's hideous high-rise design. Early in the morning, you can watch the Household Cavalry exercise in the park, and at 10.30am daily they set off for Horse Guards Building in Whitehall.

To the north of Rotten Row lies the **Serpentine Lake**, created in 1730 by damming the Westbourne, a small tributary of the Thames, in order that Queen Caroline might have a spot for the royal yachts to mess about on. A miniature re-enactment of the Battle of Trafalgar was staged here in 1814, and two years later Shelley's pregnant wife, Harriet Westbrook, drowned herself in the Serpentine after Shelley had eloped with the sixteen-year-old Mary Shelley Wollstonecraft. The popular **lido** (Whitsun–Sept daily 10am–8pm; £1.50) is situated on the south bank, alongside a utilitarian, overpriced café (Easter–Dec), though you're allowed to bring your own picnic; rowboats can be hired (March–Oct) from the boathouse on the north bank.

To the north of the lake is Jacob Epstein's **Rima monument**, whose naked goddess provoked such hostility when it was unveiled in 1925 that it was tarred and feathered on two separate occasions. The dedicatee of the monument is the naturalist W. H. Hudson, and the area around the monument is supposed to be a bird sanctuary, though its dribbling fountain and manicured lawn are not the most obvious spot for birds to seek refuge.

The nearest tube is Lancaster Gate.

The upper section of the Serpentine – beyond the bridge – is known as **Long Water**, and is by far the prettiest section of the lake.

It narrows until it reaches a group of four fountains, laid out in front of an Italianate summerhouse designed by Wren. To the east, by Victoria Gate, lies the odd little **Dog Cemetery**, begun in 1880 when the Duke of Cambridge buried his wife's pet hound here after it had been run over on Bayswater Road; two hundred other miscellaneous pets followed the pooch until burials were stopped in 1915.

There's some **outdoor sculpture** worth attention to the west of Long Water: the rough-hewn muscleman struggling with his horse is G. F. Watts's *Physical Energy*, a copy of the Rhodes memorial in Cape Town; to the north is a granite obelisk raised to John Hanning Speke, who was the first non-African to find the source of the Nile, and who died in 1864 after accidentally shooting himself rather than the partridge he was aiming at. Finally, perhaps the best known of all Hyde Park's outdoor monuments is *Peter Pan*, erected in 1912 with funds provided by its author, J. M. Barrie, who used to walk his dog in the park; fairies squirrels, rabbits, birds and mice are sculpted scampering round the pedestal.

To the south of all this statuary, on the west side of the Ring (the road that splits the park in half), stands the **Serpentine Gallery** (daily 10am–6pm; free), which hosts lively contemporary art exhibitions in its plain white galleries, and has an excellent art bookshop.

The Albert Memorial

Completed in 1876 by Sir George Gilbert Scott, the **Albert Memorial** is as much a hymn to the glorious achievements of Britain as to its subject, Queen Victoria's husband (who died of cholera in 1861), though he occupies its central canopy, clutching a catalogue for the Great Exhibition (see below). The pomp of the monument is overwhelming: the spire, inlaid with semi-precious stones and marbles, rises to 180 feet, a marble frieze around the pediment is cluttered with 169 life-size figures (all men) in high relief, depicting poets, musicians, painters, architects and sculptors from ancient Egypt onwards; the pillars are topped with bronzes of Astronomy, Chemistry, Geology and Geometry; mosaics show Poetry, Painting, Architecture and Sculpture; four outlying marble groups represent the four continents; and other statuary pays homage to Agriculture, Commerce and other aspects of imperial economics.

The Albert Hall and the museums and institutions to the south are covered on pp.274–287.

Since 1990, however, the entire memorial has been constantly obliterated by scaffolding, a fact which might have pleased Albert, who claimed that "I can say, with perfect absence of humbug, that I would rather not be made the prominent feature of such a monument . . . it would upset my equanimity to be permanently ridiculed and laughed at in effigy". The estimated £13 million restoration has only just begun for real, and is due to be completed in time for the year 2000, when Albert will be revealed gilded head to toe as he was until the outbreak of the First World War.

The Great Exhibition and the Crystal Palace

East of the Albert Memorial, opposite Prince of Wales Gate, was the site of the **Great Exhibition of the Works and Industry of All Nations**, held between May 1 and October 15, 1851. The idea originated with Henry Cole, a minor civil servant in the Record Office, and was taken up enthusiastically by Prince Albert, despite much opposition from snooty Kensington residents, who complained that it would attract an "invasion of undesirables who would ravish their silver and their serving maids". A competition to design the exhibition building produced 245 rejected versions, until Joseph Paxton, head gardener to the Duke of Devonshire, offered to build his "**Crystal Palace**", a wrought-iron and glass structure some 1848ft long and 408ft wide. The acceptance of Paxton's radical proposal was an act of faith by the exhibition organizers, since such a structure had never been built, and their faith was amply rewarded – a team of 200 workers completed the building in just four months, then more than six million people came to visit it.

The exhibition was primarily designed to show off the achievements of the British Empire but, with over a third of all the exhibits coming from outside Great Britain, it was also a unique opportunity for people to enjoy the products of other cultures. Thousands of exhibits were housed in the Crystal Palace, including the Koh-i-Noor diamond (displayed in a bird cage), an Indian ivory throne, a floating church from Philadelphia, a bed which awoke its occupant by ejecting him or her into a cold bath, false teeth designed not to be displaced when yawning, a fountain running with *eau de Cologne* and all manner of china, fabrics and glass. To everyone's surprise, the exhibition was even profit-making and the surplus was used to buy 87 acres of land to the south of Kensington Road, to create a "Museumland" where "the arts and sciences could be promoted and taught in a way which would be of practical use to industry and make Britain the leading country of the industrialized world". Much to most people's dismay, the Crystal Palace itself was dismantled after the exhibition and rebuilt in southeast London in 1854, where it served as a concert hall, theatre, menagerie and exhibition space, only to be entirely destroyed by fire in 1936. Its loss has been lamented by Londoners for decades, and there are currently two rival plans to resurrect the Palace: either a full-scale replica (with hotels and other mod cons) at Sydenham or a one-third size model in Hyde Park itself.

Kensington Palace

The nearest tube is High Street Kensington.

On the western edge of Kensington Gardens stands **Kensington Palace**, a modestly proportioned Jacobean brick mansion bought by William and Mary in 1689, because the king's asthma and bronchitis were aggravated by Whitehall's damp and fumes. Wren, Hawksmoor and later William Kent were all called in to overhaul and embellish the place, though in the end the palace was the chief royal residence for barely fifty years. The most handsome facade faces south, and stands behind a flamboyant statue of William III, given to Edward VII by the Kaiser. Most people, however, approach from the Round Pond to the east, where George I used to keep his edible turtles, and which is now overlooked by a flattering statue of Queen Victoria sculpted by her daughter, Princess Louise.

KP, as it's fondly known in royal circles, was the London residence of Charles and Di until the couple separated, Charles moving out to bachelor accommodation in St James's Palace. Today the Princess of Wales has apartments on the west side, as do Princess Margaret, Prince and Princess Michael of Kent, and the Duke and Duchess of Gloucester. On the east side, you are permitted to see a series of small, virtually unfurnished **State Apartments**, either by guided tour (should you so wish) or by wandering at will. Little of Wren's work survives here, and the most interesting rooms are mostly by Kent, in particular the *trompe l'oeil* crowds on the King's Staircase, the **Cupola Room**, whose *trompe l'oeil* fresco gives the effect of a dome, though in fact it's only three and a half inches in depth, and the **King's Gallery**, designed by Hawksmoor with an opulent ceiling painted by Kent and walls piled high with paintings by, among others, Rubens and Van Dyck. You can also view a bedroom in deep blue velvet, in which the diminutive Queen Anne died of apoplexy after overeating; the toilet on which George II died of constipation is, however, not on public view.

KP is open April–Oct Mon–Sat 9am–5pm, Sun 11am–5pm; £4.50.

On the ground floor are several rooms associated with Victoria, who was born in the North Drawing Room – a lethal colour combination of lime green and pink – in 1819. The gloomy **Red Saloon** was where the eighteen-year-old Victoria held her first Privy Council meeting, just hours after hearing of William IV's death on June 20, 1837, while the dowdy surroundings of **Victoria's Bedroom** are where she spent her dull, sad childhood, her best friends being "the black beetles" who shared the decaying palace with her. In addition to the Victoriana, the palace houses the **Queen's Court Dress Collection**, though its one-time star exhibit, Diana's wedding dress, has been rather prudishly banished.

Before you leave the palace grounds, take a look at the Sunken Garden, created to the east of the palace in 1909 in emulation of the formal gardens laid out by William and Mary. Dwarf cypresses punctuate the garden's oblong pond with terraced flowerbeds surrounding it, but the prettiest feature is the lime walk. To the north is Hawksmoor's exquisite **Orangery** (May–Sept 9.30am to one hour before dusk), built for Queen Anne as a summer dining room, where you can now enjoy expensive coffee and snacks, while taking in carving and statues by Grinling Gibbons.

Kensington Palace Gardens, the leafy avenue which runs along the edge of Kensington Gardens, was the Millionaires' Row of the Victorian period, flanked by a succession of ostentatious detached mansions set within their own grounds and built by some of the most successful architects of the day, such as Decimus Burton and Sidney Smirke. It remains a private road and an expensive piece of real estate, with most of the houses adopted as embassies or ambassadorial residences.

South Kensington: Museumland

The nearest tube is South Kensington.

To everyone's surprise, the Great Exhibition was not only an enormous success but actually yielded a profit of £186,000, with which Prince Albert and his committee bought 87 acres of land in **South Kensington**. Institutions and museums, whose purpose was to "extend the influence of Science and Art upon Productive Industry", were to be established here to form a kind of "Museumland". Albert died of typhoid in 1861 at the age of just 41, and never saw his dream fully realised, but "Albertopolis", with its remarkable cluster of **museums and colleges**, plus the vast Albert Hall, now stands as one of London's most enlightened examples of urban planning.

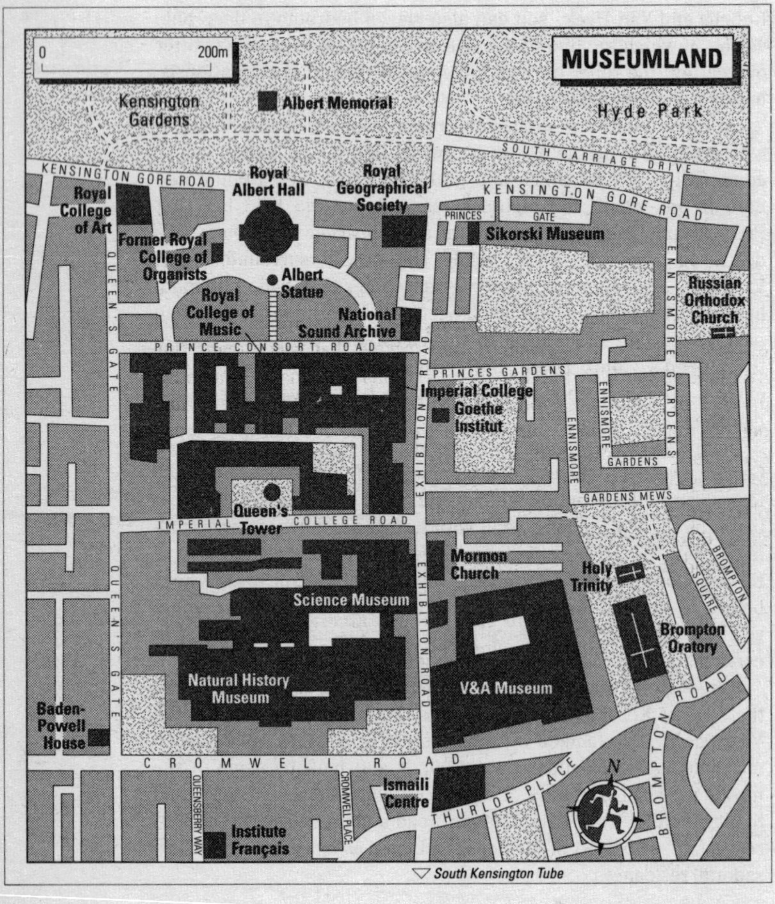

With the founding of "Museumland", the surrounding area was transformed almost overnight into one of the most fashionable in town – which it remains. The multi-storey mansions around the Albert Hall and the grand Italianate houses along Queen's Gate, and further south around Onslow Square, date from this period. South Ken has acquired further cachet thanks to its **French connections**, with a French school, crèche, bookshop and several genuine patisseries and brasseries clustered around the **Institute Français**, on Queensbury Place, which maintains an interesting programme of theatre, cinema and exhibitions. Over on nearby Exhibition Road, rival German cultural offerings emanate from the **Goethe Institute**, while the Islamic world is represented by the **Ismaili Centre**.

A further French sight – and one not to be missed while in this part of town – is the gorgeous Art Deco **Michelin House**, a short walk to the south on Fulham Road. Faced in white faience and decorated with tyres and motoring murals by French artists in 1911, its ground floors now house a shop, café, oyster bar and very trendy restaurant, all run by Terence Conran.

The Michelin House area is one of London's fashion centres, with, among others, Joseph and Issey Miyake – see p.511.

The Albert Hall and surrounding institutions

The fresh funds raised to commemorate the Prince Consort on his death in 1861 were squandered on the Albert Memorial (p.271), and it took considerable effort by Henry Cole, his collaborator on the Great Exhibition, to get funding to complete the **Royal Albert Hall**, on Kensington Gore. Plans for this splendid iron-and-glass-domed auditorium had been drawn up during the prince's lifetime, with an exterior of red brick, terracotta and marble that was already the hallmark of South Ken architecture. The hall was finally completed in 1871 by selling seats on 999-year leases – an "ownership" that persists today, though this is also the venue for Europe's most democratic music festival, the Henry Wood Promenade Concerts. Better known as the **Proms**, these top-flight classical concerts take place from July to September, with standing-only (or sit-on-the-floor) tickets for as little as £3.

See p.487 for tickets to the Proms.

Behind the hall, flanked by monumental steps, is a memorial to the Great Exhibition, once more featuring the Prince Consort. Predating the Royal Albert Hall (which Albert turns his back towards), it originally stood amid the gardens and pavilions of the Royal Horticultural Society, which were replaced in the 1880s by the colossal **Imperial Institute** building. Of this only the 280-foot **Queen's Tower** remains, stranded amid the vast Imperial College, the science faculty of London University. On the north side of this complex is the neo-Gothic **Royal College of Music** (term time Wed 2–4.30pm; £1.20), which contains a collection of nearly six hundred instruments, mostly European, dating from the fifteenth to the twentieth century.

The Sound Archive is open Mon–Fri 9am–5pm; you need to order what you want to hear in advance.

Several other educational institutions congregate near the Albert Hall, as was Albert's intention. The most striking is the former **Royal College of Organists**, to the west of the Albert Hall, a strange neo-Jacobean confection, designed for free by Henry Cole's eldest son and laced with cream, maroon and sky blue sgraffito. To the east is the **Royal Geographical Society**, a wonderful brick-built complex, which hosts exhibitions and lectures, and maintains a remarkable library, open to non-members by appointment. Opposite is another equally remarkable collection, the **National Sound Archive**, whose collections include every historic recording you can imagine and also a fabulous ethnic section.

Grouped around the west side of the Albert Hall are yet more art and science institutions, including the headquarters of the **Royal College of Art**, a seven-storey 1960s block which belies its foundation by Prince Albert; student art exhibitions are held during term time on the ground floor.

The Victoria and Albert Museum

The V&A is open Mon noon–5.50pm, Tues–Sun 10am–5.50pm; free but £4.50 donation requested.

In terms of sheer variety and scale, the **Victoria and Albert Museum** (popularly known as the V&A) is the greatest museum of applied arts in the world. The range of exhibits on display here means that, whatever your taste, there is almost bound to be something to grab your attention: the world's largest collection of Indian art outside India, plus huge Chinese, Islamic, Japanese and Korean galleries; the country's largest dress collection; a gallery of twentieth-century *objets d'art* to rival the Design Museum; more Constable paintings than the Tate; plus seven Raphael masterpieces and sizeable collections of miniatures, watercolours and medieval and Renaissance sculpture. As if all this were not enough, the V&A's temporary shows are among the best in Britain, ranging over vast areas of art, craft and technology.

Another plus for the V&A is its café and restaurant, which are excellent. Indeed, in the 1980s, it advertised itself as "A great café with a museum attached".

The V&A began life in 1852, under the directorship of Henry Cole, as the Museum of Manufactures, a gathering of objects from the Great Exhibition and a motley collection of plaster casts – it being Albert's intention to rekindle Britain's industrial dominance by inspiring factory workers, students and craftspeople with examples of excellence in applied art and design. This notion disappeared swiftly as ancient and medieval exotica poured in from other international exhibitions and from the far corners of the Empire and beyond. By the turn of the century, it was clear that Cubitt's cast-iron and glass sheds, in which the exhibits were temporarily housed, would have to be replaced with something bigger. Queen Victoria laid the foundation stone in 1899 (the last major public engagement of her life); ten years later Aston Webb's imposing main entrance, with its octagonal cupola and flying buttresses and pinnacles, was finished. The side entrance on Exhibition Road into the Henry Cole Wing, originally built in 1873 for the School of Naval Architects and more in the South Ken style, is equally ornate.

Visiting the V&A

Beautifully but haphazardly displayed across a seven-mile, four-storey maze of halls and corridors, the V&A's treasures are impossible to survey in a single visit. Floor plans from the information desks at the **main entrance** on Cromwell Road and the **side entrance** on Exhibition Road can help you decide on which areas to concentrate – we've listed some of the highlights below. Even equipped with a plan, it's easy to get lost – the room numbering is confusing and is slowly being discarded – so you may prefer to sign up for a free introductory **guided tour** (Mon noon, 12.30pm, 2pm & 3pm, Tues–Sun 11am, noon, 2pm & 3pm). If you're flagging, head for the excellent fully-licensed restaurant in the basement of the Henry Cole Wing, or the more snacky summer café in the grassy main courtyard of the Pirelli Garden.

Medieval Treasury *Ground floor room 43*

Dress Collection *Ground floor room 40*

Raphael Cartoons *Ground floor room 48a*

Nehru Gallery of Indian Art *Ground floor room 41*

Plaster Casts *Ground floor room 46a & 46b*

Morris, Gamble and Poynter Rooms *Ground floor off rooms 13–15*

Twentieth-century Galleries *First floor rooms 70–74*

Frank Lloyd Wright Gallery *Henry Cole Wing first floor rooms 202 & 203*

Glass Gallery *Second floor room 131*

Raphael, the Dress Collection and Musical Instruments

The most famous of the V&A's exhibits are the **Raphael Cartoons** (room 48a), seven vast, full-colour designs for tapestries intended for the Sistine Chapel, situated to the left of the main entrance and beyond the museum shop. These drawings, based on episodes from the *Acts of the Apostles*, were reproduced in countless tapestries and engravings in the seventeenth and eighteenth centuries, and during this period were probably more familiar and influential than any of the artist's paintings. *Room 48a*

Directly opposite the Cartoons room is the dimly lit domed hall of Costume Court, which houses the excellent **Dress Collection** (room 40). The exhibits date from as early as 1540 and come right up to date with Vivienne Westwood's giant crocodile platfom shoes, in which Naomi Campbell came a cropper on the Paris catwalk in 1993. *Room 40*

A central flight of stairs in this hall leads up to the museum's collection of **Musical Instruments**, chosen for their decorative rather than musical qualities. Among the more amazing exhibits are sixteenth-century Italian harpsichords, a three-stringed giant double bass, various lutes inlaid with ivory and shell, and a bizarre wind instrument called a serpent, a distant relative of the tuba.

India and Islam

Back on the ground floor, east of the Costume Court, there follows a string of superb Eastern galleries, kicking off with the **Nehru Gallery** *Room 41*

of Indian Art (room 41), which shows only a fraction of this world-class collection, much of it derived from the city's old East India Company Museum. The most popular exhibit, and always on display, is *Tippoo's Tiger*, a life-size wooden automaton of a tiger mauling an officer of the East India Company; the innards of the tiger feature a miniature keyboard which simulates the groans of the dying soldier. It was made for the amusement of the Sultan of Mysore, who was killed when the British took Seringapatam in 1799, and whose watch, telescope, brooch and sword are also displayed here. Other treasures at the heart of the gallery include several panels inset with *jalis* (sandstone window screens) and a display of white jade wine cups made for the Mughal emperors Shah Jahan and Jahangir.

Rooms 47a, 47b and 42

Outside the Nehru Gallery is a long corridor (rooms 47a & 47b) lined with big basalt sculptures from India and Nepal, plus copper artefacts such as a superb Nepalese mask of the wrathful Shiva, studded with skulls and snakes. Next comes the **Islamic gallery** (room 42), a dramatic gathering of vivid blue tiles, colourful earthenware and carved wooden *mimbar* (pulpits), dominated by the stupendous sixteenth-century Ardabil Persian carpet bought on the advice of William Morris, and the exquisite *Chelsea Carpet*, bought in Chelsea but of unknown origin.

Medieval Treasury, China and Japan

Room 43

The gallery straight ahead of you as you enter the museum is the darkened **Medieval Treasury** (room 43), lit through fragments of stained glass. Among the many reliquaries, sculptures and other devotional items are a hand reliquary in Flemish silver, the *Eltenburg Reliquary* (a miniature Byzantine church wrought in a mixture of bronze, oak, gilt copper, enamel and walrus ivory), and the *Gloucester Candlestick*, a Norman masterpiece of gilt bronze-work with tiny figures and animals wrapped like ivy round its stem.

Room 44

Next door the T. T. Tsui Gallery of **Chinese Art** (room 44) has been imaginatively redesigned around themes rather than in chronological sequence, with bilingual labelling and computers on hand to elucidate. The range of materials, from jade to rhino horn, lacquer to lapis lazuli, is more striking than any individual piece, though the pair of top-hatted gentlemen carved in marble stand out in the parade of Buddhas near the entrance – they are thought to represent Korean envoys.

Room 45

The most intriguing objects in the adjacent Toshiba Gallery of **Japanese Art** (room 45), standouts among a wealth of silk, lacquer and Samurai armour, are the tiny, elaborately carved, jade and marble *netsuke* (belt toggles) portraying such quirky subjects as "spider on aubergine" and "starving dog on a bed of leaves".

Fakes, Forgeries and the Cast Courts

Passing through the Korean corridor brings you to an interesting little gallery between the two cast rooms (see below); it's lined with **fakes and forgeries**, among them a "fourteenth-century" wooden oratory which the museum purchased in good faith in 1912, only to be informed by the craftsman's son that it was a fake.

Cast Courts

On either side are the two enormous **Cast Courts**. Filled with genuine fakes, as it were, they were created so that ordinary Londoners would be able to experience the glories of classical and ancient art. Still with their barrel-vaulted glass roofs and heavy Victorian decor, these little-visited rooms are an astonishing sight. In the Victorian Court, to the west, a copy of the colossal Trajan's Column from the Forum in Rome, sliced in half to fit in the room, towers over the rest of the plaster casts, which include the Brunswick Lion, Prague's St George, and a full-scale painted replica of the entire portal of the cathedral of Santiago de Compostela, set around the ill-fitting doors of Hildesheim's cathedral. In the Italian Court, opposite, a life-size replica of Michelangelo's *David* stands opposite Donatello's smaller bronze of the same subject, in the company of the pulpit of Pisa cathedral and Ghiberti's celebrated bronze doors from the Baptistery in Florence.

British sculpture and architecture

Rooms 50a and 50b

Turn right at the main information desk, and you'll reach the airy gallery of **British sculpture and architecture** (rooms 50a & 50b), with its array of funerary monuments and portrait busts. The collection is displayed "backwards", with the later stuff first, the earlier works nearest the rood loft, and, somewhat surprisingly, a load of non-British exhibits beyond. Greeting you at the entrance is a plaster model for the tomb of Victoria and Albert at Frogmore (p.393), Albert raised slightly higher than the Queen, in accordance with her wishes. The marble statue of Handel, created in 1738 by Roubiliac, caused a great stir in its day, with the composer depicted as Apollo slouching in inspired disarray, one shoe dangling from his foot. The first statue in Europe to a living artist, it originally stood in the then-fashionable Vauxhall Gardens in South London.

Rooms 62–64

The gallery's giant rood loft (from 'sHertogenbosch Cathedral) partitions the British exhibits from a collection of predominantly Italian sculpture and architectural fragments. At the centre stands Bernini's magnificent *Neptune and Triton*, initially brought to this country by Joshua Reynolds. Around the edges are bits and pieces from the churches and palaces of northern Italy, the most impressive being the towering funerary monument of the Marquis Spinetta Malaspina. Upstairs, among smaller-scale **sculpture and carvings** (rooms 62–64), concentrate on room 62, where there's a superb collection of English medieval alabaster altarpieces, a cabinet of plaster casts by Rodin, a bust of Henry VIII made out of coal, and a Prussian backgammon board inlaid with amber and decorated with scenes from Ovid.

European Art and Sculpture 1100–1900

Weaving its way around much of the ground floor is a typical V&A pot-pourri that goes under the catch-all title of **European art and sculpture** (rooms 21–24 & 1–9), with the earliest works just beyond the Medieval Treasury (see above).

Room 24

At the eastern end (room 24), there's an incredible altarpiece from Hamburg, featuring apocalyptic seven-headed beasts, frog-eating dragons and lots of slaughter and miracles. At the opposite end of the gallery, a selection of Neoclassical works by Canova stand in the half-landing (room 51) which links the main galleries with the Henry Cole Wing, while **Europe 1600–1800** (rooms 1–7) continues in the basement. The first basement room is filled with treasure cabinets in a variety of materials from Limoges enamel to ebony, walnut and bone; there's also a sixteenth-century Italian spinet inlaid with nearly two thousand precious and semi-precious stones. Beyond lies a collection of large cabinets, a painted wood-panelled room from a provincial manor house near Alençon, Meissen porcelain, gilded leather panels in "Chinese" style, exhibits reflecting the sickly tastes of the French nobility in the eighteenth century, and finally a polygonal cabinet of mirrors from Italy.

Room 51

Rooms 1–7

The chronological sequence continues on the other side of the main entrance with **Europe & America 1800–1900** (rooms 8 & 9). The first room is given over to the kind of over-the-top stuff that packed out the international exhibitions of the 1860s and 1870s – cumbersome neo-Gothic furniture and the like. The small green room at the end contains works from the 1900 Paris Exhibition, which heralded the emergence of Art Nouveau. Tiffany glassware, furniture by Adolf Loos and Otto Wagner and posters by Toulouse-Lautrec, Guimard and Mucha are thrown in for good measure.

Rooms 8 and 9

The Poynter, Gamble and Morris rooms

Whatever you do, don't miss the museum's original refreshment rooms at the back of the main galleries: the eastern **Poynter Room**, a wash of decorative blue tiling, is where *hoi polloi* ate; the dark green **Morris Room**, with its Pre-Raphaelite panels, accommodated a better class of diner; and the **Gamble Room** beyond.

These rooms lie off the L-shaped series of galleries devoted to the **Italian Renaissance** (rooms 12–20), where you'll find Michelangelo's wax model of a figure for the tomb of Pope Julius II, Giambologna's marble masterpiece, *Samson Slaying a Philistine*, and Donatello's low relief *Ascension*. Approaching from the east wing of the museum, you pass down a gallery of Northern European works, which includes a German copper tankard designed like a miniature fairy-tale castle.

Rooms 12–20

Britain 1500–1900

If you go up to the first floor from the main entrance, follow the long dark corridor of stained glass and turn left along a gallery of ironwork, you should arrive at a series of rooms covering **Britain 1500–1750** (rooms 52–58), beginning with Holbein's miniature of Anne of Cleves, and the sixteenth-century Howard Grace Cup, made from ivory and silver-gilt and crowned by a tiny St George and the Dragon. At the other end of the scale, two rooms on, is the Great Bed of Ware, a king-sized Elizabethan oak four-poster in which twenty-six butchers and their wives are said to have once spent the night. Amongst the Spitalfields silks, Huguenot silver and limewood carving by Gibbons in the following rooms (currently in the process of being redesigned) are a number of period interiors saved in their entirety from buildings which have since been demolished. These include an Elizabethan wooden-panelled room from Sizeburgh Castle in the Lake District, the Music Room from Norfolk House on St James's Square, and a pine-panelled room from Hatton Garden.

Rooms 52-58

There are more works from **Britain 1750–1900** (rooms 118–126) one more floor up, including a Chippendale four-poster made for David Garrick, Adams bookcases, and paintings by Gainsborough and Angelica Kauffman. Again, period interiors are a big feature of the collection: Adams' Venetian-red Glass Drawing Room from Northumberland House, his ceiling from Garrick's House in the Adelphi Terrace (p.163), and the fan-vaulted entrance to Lee Priory library in Kent. The largest room (118), beyond the plaster model of the Albert Memorial, is adorned with Morris wallpaper and Burne-Jones tiles, and devoted to the outpourings of the **Arts and Crafts movement**. Highlights include an almost Jazz Age piano by Baillie-Scott, a screen by Alma-Tadema, Burges' original furniture from his Tower House (p.290), Mackintosh panels from the Willow Tea Rooms and a neo-Jacobean piano by Lutyens.

Rooms 118–126

Twentieth-century Galleries

Beyond these British rooms, the attractively designed **Twentieth-century Galleries** (rooms 70–74) make a diffident attempt to address contemporary questions of art and design (the original purpose of the V&A). The collection itself is impressive, with the first and largest of the galleries taking up where the Arts and Crafts room left off. The shift into modernist gear is smoothly effected with furniture by Otto Wagner, Bauhaus and the Wiener Werkstätte co-op. Constructivist fabrics and crockery follow, alongside a range of works by Finnish modernist supremo Alvar Aalto. Irreverent hiccups are provided by the likes of Dali's pink sofa in the shape of Mae West's lips, and the whole parade ends up with a mad mélange of Olivetti typewriters, Swatch watches and a bubble-gum pink vacuum cleaner from Japan, yours in the shops for just £1000.

Rooms 70–74

The Study Collection

The remaining galleries in the main building used to be known as the **Study Collection**, a better title than the current "Materials and Techniques Collection", as these echoing suites of rooms of grimly

Rooms 103-106

unattractive display cases and minimalist labels were intended for specialist study, rather than for public consumption. With the exception of the newly redesigned Glass Gallery, that is how these rooms remain until such time as the V&A can raise the funds for redesigning. The top floor galleries of ceramics, pottery and porcelain are often closed in the summer; similarly, the twentieth-century study collection (rooms 103–106) is infrequently open.

Rooms 91–94

Despite their presentational shortcomings, the heavily guarded **Jewellery Collection** (rooms 91–93) is worth a visit, with over six thousand extremely valuable items on display, ranging from Ancient Egyptian amulets and Celtic chokers to perspex bangles from the 1960s. Another gallery of more general interest is the darkened chamber in the far northeastern corner of the museum, which is hung with precious medieval **Tapestries** (room 94), among them the famous Devonshire Hunts.

Room 131

Lastly, there's the new high-tech **Glass Gallery** (room 131) on the second floor, with touch-screen computers and a spectacular modern glass staircase and balustrade. The staggering beauty and variety of the glass on display is only slightly tarnished by the lack of any extensive twentieth-century perspective.

The Henry Cole Wing

The **Henry Cole Wing** is easily overlooked, as it's only accessible from the northwest corner of the ground floor, by the Exhibition Road entrance. Highlights here include the **Frank Lloyd Wright Gallery** (Level 2), whose centrepiece is a complete office interior created by the architect in the 1930s for a Pittsburgh department store owner – a typically organic design in luxuriant wood. Also on this floor is the **European ornamentation** room, demonstrating the influences and fashions in decoration of all kinds: antiquities, Rococo figurines and architectural plans share space with 1920s cotton hangings, inspired by Howard Carter's discovery of Tutankhamen's tomb and kitsch 1950s china ornaments.

If you're looking for a picnic spot, there are a couple of public gardens worth knowing about: Princes Gardens, to the south of Princes Gate; and further east, the grassed over graveyard of Holy Trinity church, behind Brompton Oratory.

Portrait miniatures, by Holbein, Hilliard and others, feature on Level 4, the rest of which is taken up with nineteenth-century oil paintings, densely hung in the manner of their period. The largest collection of Swiss landscape paintings outside Switzerland and sentimental Victorian genre works are of pretty specialist appeal, but persevere and you'll discover Carracciolo's *Panorama of Rome*, paintings by the Barbizon School, an Arts and Crafts piano, a Burne-Jones sideboard, and several Pre-Raphaelite works.

Level 6 is almost wholly devoted to the paintings of **John Constable**, four hundred of whose works were left to the museum by his daughter. The finished paintings include famous views of *Salisbury Cathedral* and *Dedham Mill*, and there are studies for the *Hay Wain* and *Leaping Horse*, plus a whole host of his *al fresco* cloud studies and sketches.

Season tickets

If you can see yourself making more than one visit in the coming year to either the Natural History or the Science Museum, it's worth buying a **season ticket**, which costs slightly less than the price of two tickets and allows unlimited visits within the year. There's also a combined season ticket which covers both museums and the V&A, though the latter is still nominally free.

The Science Museum

The Science Museum is open Mon–Sat 10am–6pm, Sun 11am–6pm; £4.50, free after 4.30pm.

The **Science Museum**, in Exhibition Road, is trying desperately hard to dispel the enduring image of museums devoted to its subject as boring and full of dusty glass cabinets. Sadly, though, to date, the modernization process here has been very piecemeal and the museum remains a long way from the cutting edge of technology: transparent elevators glide from floor to floor but even they don't serve all the floors, interactive computers are on hand in only a few part of the museum and the displays are very weak at explaining basic principles of science, the very purpose of the museum.

That said, the scope of the museum is impressive, filling seven floors with items drawn from every conceivable area of science, including space travel, telecommunications, time measurement, chemistry, computing, photography and medicine, and the daily demonstrations show that not all science teaching has to be deathly dry. Once you've paid your entrance fee, you can sign up for a **guided tour** on a specific subject; and it's also worth finding out the daily menu of events.

The ground floor: Power, Space and Transport

The museum unsurprisingly gives a lot of space to British innovation during the Industrial Revolution, beginning with its **Power** exhibition in the East Hall, which traces the story from James Watts' pioneering steam engines, first used in the late eighteenth century to pump water out of mine shafts, to the arrival of the combustion engine. The size of these machines is in itself quite a wonder. The largest exhibit is the bright red Burnley Mill Engine, whose enormous wheel used to drive 1700 looms and worked *in situ* until as late as 1970; you can see it working most days.

The **Synopsis Gallery** on the East Hall's mezzanine floor gives you a small-scale, manageable history of science from the Stone Age to 1914, with the help of some excellent models. Also on the mezzanine is a recreation of James Watts' garret workshop from his house in Staffordshire. And if you've ever wondered what **Foucault's Pendulum** is, check out the one by the stairs on the right-hand side.

Beyond lies the black hole of the **Space** exhibition, which follows the history of rockets from the eighteenth century, through the V1 and V2 wartime bombs and a replica of the Apollo 11 landing craft, which deposited US astronauts onto the moon in 1969, to the Space Shuttle and beyond.

The lovingly presented fire trucks, vintage cars and old steam trains of the **Transport** section in the West Hall are always popular, and include the oldest extant Rolls Royce from 1904 (still in good working order) and such iconic inventions as George Stephenson's 1813 *Puffing Billy* and his *Rocket* of 1829.

First floor

The **Launch Pad** on the first floor contains lively, hands-on displays – it's riotously popular with kids, but less successful in actually imparting any basic scientific principles. Vastly more educative is the **Food for Thought** exhibition at the far west end, past the tick-tocking of the museum's clock collection, featuring the clock from Wells Cathedral, which booms out over the West Hall every quarter of an hour. Interactive displays on nutrition, an exercise bicycle for kids who need to loose off excess energy and a series of period kitchens bring you to possibly the healthiest branch of *McDonalds* in the world (it doesn't serve food). The sponsors, *Sainsbury's*, get their plug, of course, with a reconstruction of one of their 1920s shops displayed opposite a modern supermarket scanner till.

Second floor

Much of the second floor is very heavy going – if you find yourself struggling with the **Chemistry** section, you'll need a PhD to understand the **Nuclear Physics** bit, which is sponsored by British Nuclear Fuels Limited, and is therefore less than forthcoming about the fire at Windscale in the 1950s, though it can't help but acknowledge the events at Chernobyl.

Other parts of this floor are desperately out of date: the CD-ROM-free **Computing Then and Now** stops abruptly with the behemoths of the mid-1970s, the history of **Printing** concentrates mostly on hot metal, while the interminable glass cabinets of model ocean liners in the **Ships** section hark back to the museums of old.

Third floor

The exquisitely made **eighteenth-century scientific instruments**, chiefly created by George Adams for George III, provide aesthetic relief on the third floor, especially the ornate Grand Orrery and Philosophical Table. Beyond the room occupied by the museum's radio station, GB2SM, which can pick up transmissions from all over the world (there are demonstrations daily), is another, smaller, hands-on section (by one of the cafés) called **Flight Pad**, supposedly teaching the basic principles of flight.

This, in turn, leads into the giant hangar of the **Flight** exhibition, festooned with aircraft of every description, most notably a full-size model of the flimsy contraption in which the Wright brothers made their epoch-making power-assisted flight in 1903 and the Vickers "Vimy" which completed the first transatlantic flight in 1919.

Still on the third floor, the design influence of the Wellcome Institute is evident in the excellent, high-tech **Health Matters**, which dwells on more modern medical history from the introduction of mass vaccination to the new challenge of finding a cure for HIV.

The History of Medicine

In the floor above is a much older Wellcome-sponsored gallery called **Glimpses of Medical History**, a fairly undemanding series of dioramas of medical operations, and larger mock-ups of dentists, chemists and surgeries, finishing up with the gore-free spectacle of an open-heart op, accompanied by a bleeping monitor.

The Wellcome Institute run their own museum and research centre in Euston Road, *p.158.*

The best section here – and arguably of the whole museum – is Wellcome's **Science and Art of Medicine** gallery, all too easily missed on the top floor. Using an anthropological approach, this is a visual and cerebral feast, galloping through ancient medicine, medieval and Renaissance pharmacy, alchemy, quack doctors, royal healers, astrology and military surgery. Offbeat artefacts include African fetish objects, an Egyptian mummified head, an eighteenth-century Florentine model of a female torso giving birth, George Washington's dentures, and an image of Benignus, patron saint of chilblains, crooking his outsize, strangely formed fingers.

Natural History Museum

Alfred Waterhouse's purpose-built mock-Romanesque colossus ensures the **Natural History Museum**'s status as London's most handsome museum. Its vast collections – and there is much more hidden away in the vaults – derive from a bequest by Sir Hans Sloane to the British Museum, and it was separated off here in 1860 after a huge power struggle. Darwin, notably, opposed the move, in part for the separation of science from the other arts, in part due to his hatred of the founding director, Richard Owen, an amazing figure, who arranged expeditions around the globe to provide everything from butterflies to dinosaurs for the museum's cabinets.

The Natural History Museum is open Mon–Sat 10am–5.50pm, Sun 11am–5.50pm; £5. It is free after 4.30pm Mon–Fri, after 5pm Sat & Sun.

Caught up, without huge funds, in the current enthusiasm for museum redesign and accessibility, the contents are a mish-mash of truly imaginative exhibits peppered amongst others little changed since the museum's opening in 1881. The museum is caught in a genuine conundrum, for its collections are important resources for serious zoologists, while for kids it has found itself in the 1990s with one of Britain's most marketable commodities – real dinosaurs.

The **main entrance** is in the middle of the museum's 675-foot terracotta facade; the **side entrance** on Exhibition Road leads into what used to be a separate Geology Museum. Never much of a crowd-puller, this museum is now part and parcel of the Natural History Museum, renamed the **Earth Galleries**. The old building houses the **Life Galleries**, though this division is less than clear cut, as a few rocks and minerals have sneaked in, too.

Life Galleries

The main entrance brings you straight into the **Central Hall**, which is dominated by the plaster cast of a **Diplodocus** skeleton, 26 metres in length from tip to tail. The side chapels are filled with "wonders" of the natural world – the largest egg, a model of a sabre-tooth tiger and so on – which are changed fairly regularly. It's worth pausing here to take in the architecture of this vast "nave", whose walls are decorated with moulded terracotta animals and plants: extinct ones to the west and living species to the east.

The redesigning and marketing of the new **Dinosaur** gallery, to the west of the central hall, was a stroke of a genius by the museum curators. Hour-long queues were the norm during the exhibition's first summer season, and you may still find yourself waiting in line at weekends. A raised walkway leads straight to the highlight – the grisly life-size animatronic tableau of carnivorous reptiles tearing apart a tenontosaurus, with much roaring, slurping and blood. The rest of the displays are less theatrical and more informative, with massive-jawed skeletons and models, plus a stimulating exhibition on Tyrannosaurus Rex and his pea-brained cronies.

The other firm favourite with kids is the insect room on the other side of the central hall, now known as **Creepy-crawlies** (room 33). Definitely not for arachnophobes, the gallery is filled with giant models of bugs, arachnids and crustaceans, plus real-life displays on the life cycle of the house fly and other unlovely creatures.

A small thicket of reconstructed rain forest, situated opposite the Creepy-crawlies, forms the entrance to the new **Ecology** gallery (room 32), a glass corridor, criss-crossed with overhead walkways, taking you through the basics of green politics: the food chain, recycling, the ozone layer and the greenhouse effect. It's a high-tech, child-friendly exhibition, with a serious message, only slightly marred by the fact that it's sponsored by British Petroleum.

The old-fashioned **Mammals** gallery (rooms 23 & 24), dominated by a full-size model of a Blue Whale, juxtaposed with its skeleton, is filled with stuffed animals and plastic models – it's showing its age somewhat. Upstairs, on the first floor, the story of mammals continues with an investigation into the emergence of bipeds among the primates. This, in turn, is a natural lead-in to the section on Darwin's **Origin of the Species** (room 105), which rocked the Victorian world of science shortly before this museum got off the ground.

On the same floor is the old-style **Minerals** gallery (room 102), regimented rows of glass cabinets culminating in a darkened chamber on meteorites – all of which really belongs in the Earth Galleries. If you've made it this far, don't miss the 1300-year-old slice of **Giant Sequoia**, on the second floor, a mere youngster compared to other members of the species which are still standing after more than 3200 years. While you're here, admire the view down onto the central hall and the moulded monkeys clinging to the arches.

Earth Galleries

The jazziest offering in the Earth Galleries is the **Story of the Earth** (room 73), on the ground floor, an audiovisual introduction to the solar system, tectonic plates, volcanic eruptions and other acts of God – the earthquake simulator, though popular, isn't up to much. The collection of **gemstones** (room 72), also on the ground floor, is a dazzling array of diamonds, rubies and emeralds, jades and deep blue lapis lazuli, showing just what can be done to liven up a static display. **Treasures of the Earth** (room 71) is an imaginative exploration of the use of natural materials in domestic appliances and other everyday objects, using cross-sections and cut-aways.

To get to the Earth Galleries from the central hall, head east along the wiggly "Waterhouse Way", past the stuffed birds.

Apart from the **Time Machine** (room 82), which condenses the earth's history into a one-minute video, the two upper floors hold little interest for non-geologists. There's a mercilessly technical explanation of Britain's mineral reserves and regional geology, an exhibition of British fossils, cabinets piled high with blocks of stone and minerals from around the world, plus a small exhibition on Stonehenge.

Museumland's periphery

If you still have energy after the main museums of South Ken, there are a few further sights and museums on the eastern periphery. They include an important trio of religious buildings – Brompton Oratory, the Russian Orthodox Church and the Westminster Synagogue – and a Polish museum. They stand amid an unassuming but exceedingly wealthy area of Regency terraces that makes for a pleasant stroll over to *Harrod's* and Knightsbridge.

A nearby Polish institution is the Daquise café by South Ken tube station – see p.447.

Brompton Oratory

London's most flamboyant Roman Catholic church, the **Brompton Oratory**, stands just east of the V&A. It was begun by the young and unknown Herbert Gribble in 1880 "so that those who had no opportunity of going over to Italy to see an Italian church had only to come here to see a model of one". The ornate interior contains some genuine Italian Baroque fittings – notably the seventeenth-century apostles in the nave and the main altar and reredos of the Lady Chapel – and plenty of neo-Baroque. True to its architecture, the church conducts "rigid, ritualised, smells and bells Catholicism", as one journalist put it, with a sung mass in Latin every Sunday, and some very high society weddings throughout the year.

East European connections

North of the Brompton Oratory, off Ennismore Gardens, a simple Byzantine-style church faced in warm Bath stone is now a **Russian Orthodox Church**.

Another east European connection is contained within the **Westminster Synagogue**, a couple of blocks west in Rutland Gardens. In 1964 this received 1564 Torah scrolls gathered from all over Czechoslovakia by the Nazis for their planned "Museum of an Extinct Race". Hundreds have since been restored and sent out to Jewish communities in America, Israel and throughout Europe, but the remainder are displayed here (Tues & Thurs 2–4pm).

The Sikorski Museum is open Mon–Fri 2–4pm, first Sat of month 10am–5pm; free.

The strongest connections in the area, however, are Polish, as exemplified by the **Sikorski Museum**, up towards the Albert Hall at 20 Princes Gate. This was founded after the war by disgruntled Polish exiles, many of whom had fought with the Allies against the Nazis, only to see a Soviet puppet government installed and immediately recognized by the West. The Polish contribution to the Allied cause was significant, particularly in the Air Force, and World War II militaria forms the bedrock of the museum, along with the personal effects of General Wladyslaw Sikorski, the pre-war prime minister who fled to London in 1939, only to die in a mysterious plane accident over Gibraltar in 1943. The absence of a non-Communist leader of Sikorski's standing after the war has been lamented by exiled Poles ever since.

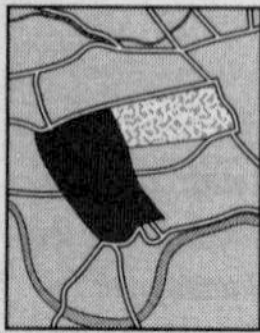

Kensington, Holland Park and Earl's Court

The nearest tube is High Street Kensington.

Despite the smattering of aristocratic mansions and the presence of royalty in Kensington Palace, **Kensington** remained little more than a village surrounded by fields until well into the nineteenth century, when the rich finally began to seek new stamping grounds away from the West End. The Great Exhibition and its legacy of museums in neighbouring Knightsbridge brought further cachet to the area and prompted a building frenzy that boosted the borough's population to over 175,000 by 1901 – a hundred years previously the figure was just 8500. The main draw nowadays are the shops (in particular the indoor clothing markets in Kensington High Street), the wooded Holland Park and the former artists' colony clustered around the exotically decorated Leighton House.

Kensington High Street and Holland Park

Shopper-thronged **Kensington High Street** is dominated architecturally by the twin presences of St Mary Abbots, whose 250-foot spire makes it London's tallest parish church, and the Art Deco colossus of *Barkers* department store.

Hyper-Hyper *and Kensington Market are both open Mon–Sat 10am–6pm.*

But what really makes High Street Ken (as the nearby tube is known) stand out from other London shopping streets are its two **clothing markets**: *Hyper Hyper* – easy to spot thanks to the kitsch caryatids at the entrance – features over seventy stalls run by young British designers, while Kensington Market, opposite, is a Gothic labyrinth of lock-up shops flogging mainly retro or just cheap clothes, interspersed with several hairdressers, a clock repair shop and much more besides.

Kensington Square

On the south side of the high street lies **Kensington Square**, an early piece of speculative building laid out in 1685. Luckily for the developers, royalty moved into Kensington Palace shortly after its construction, and the square soon became so fashionable that it was dubbed the "old court suburb".

By the nineteenth century, the courtiers had moved out and more bohemian residents had moved in: Thackeray wrote *Vanity Fair* at no. 16; the pre-Raphaelite painter Burne-Jones lived at no. 41 for a couple of years; the actress Mrs Patrick Campbell, with whom George Bernard Shaw was obsessed for most of his life, lived at no. 33; and composer Hubert Parry (of *Jerusalem* fame) gave music lessons to Vaughan Williams at no.17. John Stuart Mill, philosopher and champion of women's suffrage, lived next door, and it was here that the first volume of Thomas Carlyle's manuscript of *The French Revolution* was accidentally used by a maid to light the fire.

For more on Carlyle, see p.298.

Commonwealth Institute

Kensington's sights are mostly hidden away in the backstreets behind the high street, the one exception being the **Commonwealth Institute**, housed in a bold 1960s building on the high street – it's heralded by a forest of flagpoles. The building's exterior hasn't worn well but its tent-shaped Zambian copper roof is still a startling sight. The giant open-vaulted exhibition hall holds three floors of galleries with rather prosaic school geography lesson displays on each of the nations which, having freed themselves of colonial rule, now make up the Commonwealth; the tone is celebratory, though there's a tendency to gloss over some of the more unsavoury post-colonial political truths.

The institute is open Mon–Sat 10am–5pm, Sun 2–5pm; £1.

Despite the institute's excellent work in education, its wealth of resources, its varied programme of events and conferences and a prominent defender in the Queen, the government announced that it was withdrawing its funding as of March 1996 (a deadline later extended to 1999). The museum has responded with ambitious plans to become a kind of Disneyland, with a projected £7.5 million "Wonders of the World" ride, taking visitors through an African safari, a Caribbean hurricane, and into a volcano and ice canyon. Using virtual reality techniques, the "cars" will transform themselves into helicopters and bathyspheres. If funds are forthcoming, this should be up and running in 1996; meanwhile, the old exhibition space is likely to be closed off.

Holland Park

Two paths pass up the side of the Commonwealth Insititute towards the densely wooded **Holland Park**, a spot popular with the neighbourhood's army of nannies and au-pairs, who take their charges to the excellent adventure playground. The park is laid out in the former grounds of Holland House – only the east wing of the Jacobean mansion could be salvaged after the last war, but it gives a fairly good idea of what the place must have looked like. A youth hostel is linked to the east wing, while a concert tent to the west stages theatrical and musical performances throughout the summer months, continuing a tradition which stretches back to the first Lady Holland, who staged plays here in defiance of the puritanical laws of the Commonwealth. Several formal gardens surround the house, drifting down in terraces to the arcades, Garden Ballroom, Orangery and Ice House, which have been converted into a restaurant and art gallery complex. The newest of the formal gardens is the Kyoto Garden, a Japanese-style sanctuary to the northwest of the house, opened in 1991.

Leighton House and the artists' colony

Leighton House is open Mon–Sat 11am–5.30pm; free.

In the late nineteenth century several of the wealthier artists of the Victorian era rather self-consciously founded an artists' colony around the fringes of Holland Park, and several of their highly individual mansions are still standing. First and foremost is **Leighton House**, 12 Holland Park Road, the "House Beautiful" created by Frederic Leighton, the only artist ever to be made a peer (albeit on his death-bed), and the architect George Aitchison. The big attraction is its domed Arab Hall: based on the banqueting hall of a Moorish palace in Palermo, it has a central black marble fountain, and is decorated with Saracen tiles, gilded mosaics and woodwork drawn from all over the Islamic world. The other rooms are less spectacular but, in compensation, are hung with excellent paintings by Leighton and his pre-Raphaelite friends, Burne-Jones, Alma-Tadema and Millais. Skylights brighten the upper floor, which contains Leighton's vast studio, where his tradition of holding evening concerts continues to this day.

Leighton's neighbours included artists G. F. Watts and Holman Hunt, Marcus Stone, illustrator of Dickens, and, in the most outrageous house of all, William Burges, who designed his own medieval folly, the **Tower House**, at 29 Melbury Road. Further afield, at 8 Addison Road, is the Arts and Crafts **Peacock House**, built in 1905–07 for the millionaire Debenham family; the exterior is covered with peacock-blue and emerald-green Doulton tiles and Staffordshire bricks; the equally impressive interior can be viewed during the Craft Fair held there in December, or at other times by prior arangement (☎0171/603 6373).

Linley Sambourne House is open March–Oct Wed 10am–4pm, Sun 2–5pm; £3.

On the east side of the Commonwealth Institute, two blocks north of the high street, is **Linley Sambourne House**, 18 Stafford Terrace, where the highly successful *Punch* cartoonist lived until his death in 1910. A grand though fairly ordinary terrace house by Kensington standards, it's less a tribute to the artist (though it does contain a good selection of Sambourne's works) and more a showpiece for the Victorian Society, which was founded here in 1958 and maintains the house in all its late-Victorian excess, complete with stained glass, heavy wall-hangings, and William Morris wallpaper concealed behind works by Sambourne's arty Kensington neighbours.

Olympia, Earl's Court and Brompton Cemetery

At the western end of Kensington High Street a severe 1930s facade hides the **Olympia Exhibition Hall**, built in 1884 as the National Agricultural Hall. It later made its name as a circus venue but is now firmly established as a show centre, hosting annual events like the Ideal Home Exhibition and Cruft's Dog Show, and rock concerts by Pink Floyd and other dry-ice dinosaurs. Even larger shows, like the militaristic Royal Tournament, are put on at the **Earl's Court Exhibition Hall**, erected in 1937 to the south of Olympia, down Warwick Road. Both halls were used during the last war as internment centres for Germans and Italians, many of whom had themselves fled fascist persecution.

Earl's Court

Despite displaying the same ostentatious architecture as the rest of Kensington, **Earl's Court** itself is a less moneyed area, with many houses providing cheap bed-sits and hotels for young Australians and New Zealanders, earning it the nickname "Kangaroo Valley". In the late 1970s, Earl's Court also became the gay capital of London, a position recently challenged by trendier Soho. It's the leather crowd that predominates here, epitomized by the *Coleherne*, London's oldest leather pub on Old Brompton Road, and by its most famous former resident, **Freddie Mercury**, the flamboyant queen of Queen, whose house, Garden Lodge, 1 Logan Place, was a shrine for fans long before his AIDS-related death in 1991.

The nearest tube is Earls Court.

Brompton Cemetery

Close by the *Coleherne* (and consequently a popular cruising area) is **Brompton Cemetery**, the least overgrown of London's Victorian graveyards. It was laid out in a grid-plan in 1840 and is now overlooked by the ground of John Major's favourite football club, Chelsea – a team with a record almost as woeful as his own.

The cemetery is open daily 9am–dusk; free.

The cemetery's leafy central avenue, which leads south to an octagonal chapel, contains the most interesting graves, most notably that of Frederick Leyland, president of the National Telephone Company: designed by Burne-Jones, it's a bizarre copper-green jewel box on stilts, smothered with swirling wrought ironwork. Before you reach the chapel, eerie colonnaded catacombs, originally planned to extend the full length of the cemetery, open out into the Great Circle, a forest of tilted crosses.

Few famous corpses grace Brompton, but enthusiasts might like to seek out Suffragette leader Emmeline Pankhurst, Samuel Sotheby, who founded the auction house, Sir Henry Cole, the man behind the Great Exhibition, Fanny Brawne, the love of Keats' life, and John Snow, Queen Victoria's anaesthetist, whose chloroform fixes the monarch described as "soothing, quieting and delightful beyond measure".

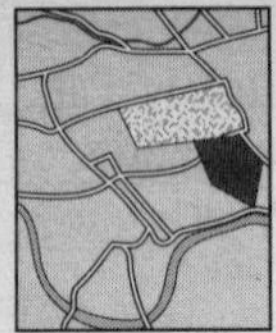

Knightsbridge and Belgravia

Knightsbridge and **Belgravia** contain some of the most expensive real estate in London. Knightsbridge is irredeemably snobbish, revelling in its reputation as the swankiest shopping area in London, largely through *Harrod's*, one of London's most popular tourist attractions. **Belgravia**, over to the east, and strategically placed behind Buckingham Palace Gardens, is embassyland, with at least twenty-five scattered amongst the grid-plan stuccoed streets.

Harrod's and Knightsbridge

Knightsbridge tube deposits you fifty yards from Harrod's; take the signposted exit.

Most people come to Knightsbridge for just one thing: to shop or gawp at **Harrod's** on Brompton Road. Without doubt the most famous department store in London, it started out as a family-run grocery store in 1849, with a staff of two. The current 1905 terracotta building, which turns into a palace of fairy lights at night, is now owned by the Egyptian Al Fayed brothers and employs over 3000 staff, including several ex-army bagpipers who perform daily in the store. The shop occupies four acres, and is made up of over 300 departments, a dozen bars and restaurants and even its own pub, spread over seven floors.

Harrod's is open Mon, Tues & Sat 10am–6pm, Wed–Fri 10am–7pm. The store has two annual sales; the Christmas one begins on Boxing Day, the Summer Sale at the end of the first week of July.

Tourists flock to *Harrod's* – it's thought to be the city's third top tourist attraction – with over 30,000 customers passing through each day. Most Londoners limit their visits to the annual sales, with over 300,000 arriving on the first day of the Christmas Sale, though the store also has its regular customers, drawn from the so-called "Tiara Triangle" of this very wealthy neighbourhood, who would think nothing of buying dog food at cordon bleu prices. To help keep out the non-purchasing riff-raff, a draconian dress code has been introduced: no shorts, no ripped jeans, no vest T-shirts and no backpacks.

In truth, much of what the shop stocks you can buy a great deal more cheaply if you can do without the Harrod's carrier bag, but the store does have a few sections that are real sights. Chief among these are the **food halls**, with their Arts and Crafts tiling and a surprisingly reasonably priced oyster counter, and the beautiful Art Deco men's hairdressers; both are on the ground floor.

Around Knightsbridge

If you want more window shopping, or you have a wallet equipped for top-range designer clothing shops, **Sloane Street**, which runs due south of Knightsbridge tube, is the obvious next stop. Right on the corner of the street, facing the tube, is *Harvey Nichols*, another palatial department store, whose reputation has spiralled in recent years. Like *Harrod's*, it has a wonderful food hall and a panoply of designer sections, while its fifth floor café-restaurant is the in lunch stop for career shoppers. Ranging down Sloane Street, the names read like a fashion directory, including *Giorgio Armani* at no. 178 and *Katherine Hamnett* at no. 20.

For the shopping-surfeited, Knightsbridge's mews and squares are good for a quick stroll. Having been built to house servants and stables, converted mews houses, like those in **Pont Street Mews** immediately behind *Harrod's*, are now among the most sought-after properties in the area. Built on a completely different scale, the red-brick four-, five- and six-storey mansions which flaunt their high Dutch gables off Pont Street gave rise to the architectural term "Pont Street Dutch". The most extreme examples of the style are in fact in **Harrington** and **Collingham Gardens**, to the west of South Kensington tube. They were built by Ernest George, who was fired up after a visit to Holland in the 1870s.

Belgravia

Despite its spacious streets of crisp, white stucco, **Belgravia** is a soulless place, and not one in which you're likely to want to spend much time. If curiosity leads you here, the best approach is to take the tube to Hyde Park Corner and walk along Grosvenor Crescent, which curves round into Belgrave Square, a grandiose nineteenth-century set-piece with detached villas positioned at three of its four corners. With royalty ensconced in nearby Buckingham Palace and Queen Victoria's mother temporarily living there in the square, the area immediately attracted exactly the sort of clientele that property developer/architect Cubitt had hoped for, with three dukes, thirteen peers and thirteen MPs in residence by 1860.

Nowadays, the place bristles with security cameras and police in bullet-proof jackets guarding the numerous embassies; few can afford whole houses here, with apartments alone fetching millions of pounds.

Chelsea, Battersea and Fulham Palace

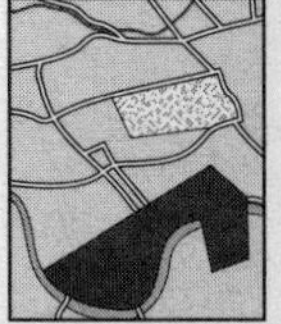

Until the sixteenth century, **Chelsea** was nothing more than a tiny fishing village on the banks of the Thames. It was Thomas More who started the upward trend by moving here in 1520, followed by members of the nobility, including Henry VIII himself. (Henry's former hunting lodge on Glebe Place is all that remains of this "Village of Palaces" today.) In the eighteenth century, Chelsea acquired its riverside houses along Cheyne Walk, which gradually attracted a posse of literary and intellectual types.

It wasn't until the latter part of the nineteenth century that Chelsea began to earn its reputation as London's very own Left Bank, a bohemianism formalized by the foundation of the *Chelsea Arts Club* in 1891 and entrenched in the 1960s, when Chelsea was at the forefront of "Swinging London", with the likes of David Bailey, Mick Jagger and George Best and the "Chelsea Set" hanging out in continental style boutiques and coffee bars. The King's Road was a fashion parade for hippies, too, and in the Jubilee Year of 1977 it witnessed the birth of punk.

These days, the area has a more subdued feel, with high rents and house prices keeping things staid, and interior design shops rather than avant-garde fashion the order of the day. The area's other aspect, oddly enough considering its Boho reputation, is a military one, with central London's main army barracks, the Royal Hospital, home of old veterans known as the Chelsea Pensioners, and the country's army museum.

Further west, Chelsea becomes rather more down-to-earth, a transition signalled by the presence of the local football ground, beyond which lies **Fulham**, whose main point of interest is Fulham Palace, at the very end of the King's Road. To the south, across the river, Chelsea aspirants have over the past decade or so colonized previously working-class **Battersea**, an area dominated by the brooding presence of the disused Battersea Power Station – familiar to many visitors from its appearance, with floating pig, on Pink Floyd's *Animals* album cover.

Sloane Square

The nearest tube is Sloane Square.

Sloane Square, a leafy nexus on the very eastern edge of Chelsea, takes its name from the wealthy eighteenth-century local doctor Sir Hans Sloane, whose "noble cabinet" of curios formed the basis of the British Museum. More recently, the square gave its name to the debutantes of the 1980s, the Sloane Rangers, whose most famous alumna was Princess Diana. Sloanes, whose natural habitat is actually further north in Kensington and Knightsbridge, are easily identifiable by their dress code: blue and white pin-striped shirts, cords and brogues for the men; blond, flick-back hair, pearls and flat shoes for the women, and waxed cotton *Barbour* jackets for all.

At the head of the square, by the tube, stands the **Royal Court Theatre**, bastion of new theatre writing since John Osborne's *Look Back in Anger* sent tremors through the establishment in 1956. At the opposite end is **Peter Jones**, a popular department store for wedding lists, housed in London's finest glass-curtain building, built in the 1930s, which curves its way seductively into King's Road. Round the corner in Sloane Street is another architectural masterpiece, the Arts and Crafts **Holy Trinity Church**, created in 1890 with Morris & Co windows designed by Burne-Jones; sadly it's only open for services.

King's Road

Bus #11, #19 and #22 run the length of the King's Road.

The **King's Road**, Chelsea's main artery, was designed as a royalty-only thoroughfare by Charles II, in order – so the story goes – to avoid carriage congestion en route to Nell Gwynne's house in Fulham, but more likely as a short cut to Hampton Court. George

III used the road to get to Kew, but lesser mortals could do so only on production of a special copper pass – it was finally opened to the public in 1830. This prompted a flurry of speculative building that produced the series of elegant, open-ended squares – Wellington, Markham, Carlyle and Paultons – which still punctuate the road.

King's Road's household fame, however, came through its role as the unofficial catwalk of the Swinging Sixties. While Carnaby Street (p.123) is still cashing in on its past, and has consequently descended into a tourist quagmire, King's Road has managed to move with the times, through the hippy era, punk and beyond. The "Saturday Parade" of fashion victims is not what it used to be, but posey cafés, boutiques (and antiques) are still what King's Road is all about. And the traditional "Chelsea Cruise", when every flash Harry in town parades his customized motor, still takes place at 8.30pm on the last Saturday of the month, though it's currently located on the Battersea side of the Chelsea Bridge.

Chelsea's split personality is evident as soon as you head off down King's Road in search of fashion and immediately come face to face with the **Duke of York's Barracks**, headquarters of the Territorial Army. A little further down on the same side is **Royal Avenue**, the first of the squares which open out onto the King's Road, where James Bond, Ian Fleming's spy hero, had his London address. Unlike the other squares off the King's Road, this one is rather like a Parisian *place*, with plane trees and gravel down the centre, and was originally laid out in the late seventeenth century, as part of William III's ambitious (and unrealized) scheme to link Kensington Palace with the Royal Hospital, to the south.

Perhaps the most famous address of all is **no. 430**, about a mile down the King's Road, where the designer Vivienne Westwood and her then-boyfriend Malcolm McLaren opened a teddy-boy revival store called *Let It Rock*, located, with a neat sense of decorum, right next door to the Chelsea Conservative Club. In 1975 they changed tack and renamed the shop *Sex*, stocking it with proto-punk fetishist gear, with simulated burnt limbs in the window. It became a magnet for the likes of John Lydon and John Simon Ritchie, better known as Johnny Rotten and Sid Vicious – the rest, as they say, is history. Now known as *World's End*, the shop, with its landmark backward-clock, continues to flog Westwood's eccentric, fashion-leading clothes.

The Royal Hospital and National Army Museum

The Royal Hospital is open Mon–Sat 10am–noon & 2–4pm, Sun 2–4pm; free.

Among the most nattily attired of all those parading down the King's Road are the scarlet or navy-blue clad Chelsea Pensioners, the army veterans who live in the nearby **Royal Hospital**, founded by Charles II in 1681. Until the Civil War, England had no standing army and therefore no need to provide for its old soldiers; by the end of

Charles' reign, all that had changed. Prompted by Nell Gwynne's encounter with a begging ex-serviceman on the King's Road, or – more likely – by Louis XIV's Hôtel des Invalides in Paris, Charles II commissioned Wren to provide a suitably grand almshouse for the veterans. The end result – plain, red-brick wings and grassy courtyards, which originally opened straight onto the river – became a blueprint for institutional and collegiate architecture all over the English-speaking world.

The **central courtyard** is centred on a bronze statue of the founder in Roman attire by Grinling Gibbons; on Oak Apple Day (May 29) the pensioners, wearing their traditional tricorn hats, festoon the statue with oak leaves to commemorate the day after the Battle of Worcester in 1651 when Charles hid in Boscobel Oak to escape his pursuers. On the north side of the courtyard, below the central lantern, a giant Tuscan portico leads to an octagonal vestibule. On one side is the austere **hospital chapel**, with a huge barrel vault and a splash of colour provided by Ricci's *Resurrection* in the apse, with Jesus patriotically bearing the flag of St George. Opposite lies the equally grand, wooden-panelled **dining hall**, where the four hundred or so pensioners still eat under portraits of the sovereigns and a vast allegorical mural of Charles II and his hospital. In the Soane-designed Secretary's Office, on the east side of the hospital, there's a small **museum** (opening times as for the hospital), with pensioners' costumes, medals and two German bombs.

The playing fields to the south, from which you get the finest view of the hospital, are the venue for the annual **Chelsea Flower Show**, which takes place during the last week of May. To the east are the last remnant of London's pleasure gardens, **Ranelagh Gardens**, now a pleasant little landscaped patch used mostly by the Chelsea pensioners, but open to the general public too. A couple of information panels in the gardens' Soane-designed shelter show what the place used to look like when Canaletto painted it in 1751. The main feature was a giant rotunda, modelled on the Pantheon in Rome, where the *beau monde* could promenade to musical accompaniment – the eight-year-old Mozart played here. Shortly after it opened in 1742, Walpole reported that "you can't set your foot without treading on a Prince or Duke". Fashion is fickle, though, and the rotunda was eventually demolished in 1805.

The Army Museum is open daily 10am–5.30pm; free.

The concrete bunker next door to the Royal Hospital, on Royal Hospital Road, houses the **National Army Museum**. The militarily obsessed are unlikely to be disappointed by the succession of uniforms and medals, but there is very little here for non-enthusiasts, beyond the skeleton of Marengo, Napoleon's charger at Waterloo, and a large model of the battlefield on which 48,000 lost their lives. The temporary exhibitions are often more critical, but otherwise you're better off visiting the infinitely superior Imperial War Museum (p.252).

Wilde about Chelsea

John Singer Sargent, Augustus John, James Whistler and Bertrand Russell all lived at one time or other in Tite Street, which runs alongside the army museum, but by far the street's most famous resident was wit and writer, **Oscar Fingall O'Flahertie Wills Wilde** (1856–1900), who moved into no. 34 with his new bride, Constance Lloyd, in 1884. It was here, in 1891, that Wilde first met the son of the Marquis of Queensbury, known to his friends as "Bosie", who was eventually to prove his downfall. At the height of Wilde's fame, just four days after the first night of *The Importance of Being Earnest*, the Marquis left a visiting card for Wilde, on which he wrote "To Oscar Wilde, posing as a somdomite" (sic). Urged on by Bosie, Wilde unsuccessfully sued Queensbury, losing his case when the Marquis produced incriminating evidence against Wilde himself. On returning to the Cadogan Hotel on Sloane Street, where Bosie had rooms, Wilde was arrested by the police, taken to Bow Street police station, charged with homosexual offences and eventually sentenced to two years' hard labour. Bankrupt, abandoned by Bosie, separated from his wife, he served his sentence in Wandsworth and later Reading gaol. On his release he fled abroad and travelled under the pseudonym of Sebastian Melmoth; he died three years later from a syphilitic infection and was buried in Paris's Père Lachaise cemetery.

Cheyne Walk

The quiet riverside locale of **Cheyne Walk** (pronounced "chainy"), with its succession of Georgian and Queen Anne houses, drew artists and writers here in great numbers during the nineteenth century. Since the building of the Embankment and the increase in the volume of traffic, however, the character of this peaceful haven has been lost. Novelist Henry James, who lived at no. 21, used to take "beguiling drives" in his wheelchair along the Embankment; today, he'd be hospitalized in the process. An older contemporary of James, Mary Ann Evans (better known under her pen name George Eliot) moved into no. 4 – the first blue plaque you come to – in December 1880, five months after marrying an American banker twenty-one years her junior. Three weeks later she was dead.

Perhaps the most famous of all Cheyne Walk's residents, however, were the bohemian trio who lived at the Queen's or Tudor House (no. 16) – painter and poet **Dante Gabriel Rossetti**, poet Algernon Charles Swinburne and writer George Meredith. Rossetti moved in shortly after the death of his first wife and model, Elizabeth Siddell, from an overdose of laudanum in 1862. The "tiny, gesticulating, dirty-minded" Swinburne, as one of his many critics described him, was habitually drunk, but it was Rossetti's back garden menagerie that really got his neighbours' backs up – an amazing array that included owls, wombats, wallabies, parrots, salamanders, a Brahmin bull, burrowing armadillo, braying jackass and screeching, belligerent peacocks. In 1872 Rossetti tried to commit suicide as his wife had done, but survived to live a progressively more debauched and withdrawn existence until his death in 1882.

The western half of Cheyne Walk, beyond Crosby Hall (see below), is no less rich in cultural associations. Mrs Gaskell was born in 1810 at no. 93, a house later inhabited by Whistler, who lived at ten different addresses in the forty-one years he spent in Chelsea. The reclusive Turner lived at no. 118 for the last six years of his life under the pseudonym Booth, and painted many a sunset over the Thames. In the 1960s, Mick Jagger and Keith Richards graced this section of Cheyne Walk with their presence, and in July 1972, the IRA and the British government met secretly at no. 96 to discuss peace, some five months after the "Bloody Sunday" massacre.

Chelsea Physic Garden

Chelsea Physic Garden is open April–Oct Wed 2–5pm & Sun 2–6pm; £2.50.

The **Chelsea Physic Garden** marks the beginning of Cheyne Walk. Founded in 1673 by the Royal Society of Apothecaries, this is the oldest botanical garden in the country after Oxford's: the first cedars grown in this country were planted here in 1683; cotton seed was sent from here to the American colonies in 1732; and the garden contains the country's oldest olive tree. At the entrance (on Swan Walk) you can pick up a map of the garden with a list of the month's most interesting flowers and shrubs, whose labels are slightly more forthcoming than the usual terse Latinate tags. A statue of Hans Sloane, who presented the Society with the freehold, stands at the centre of the garden; and behind him there's an excellent tea house, serving delicious home-made cakes and tea, with exhibitions on the floor above.

Carlyle's House and Glebe Place

Carlyle's House is open Mon–Sat 11am–5pm; NT; £2.80.

A short distance from Cheyne Walk, at 24 Cheyne Row, is **Carlyle's House**, the Queen Anne house where the historian Thomas Carlyle set up home with his wife, Jane Welsh Carlyle, having moved down from his native Scotland in 1834. Carlyle's full-blooded and colourful style, best illustrated by his account of the French Revolution, brought him great fame during his lifetime – a statue was erected to the "Sage of Chelsea" on Cheyne Walk less than year after his death in 1881, and the house became a museum just fifteen years later. That said, the intellectuals and artists who visited Carlyle – among them Dickens, Tennyson, Chopin, Mazzini, Browning and Darwin – were attracted as much by the wit of his strong-willed wife, with whom Carlyle enjoyed a famously tempestuous relationship. The house itself is a dour abode, kept much as the Carlyles would have had it: the historian's hat still hanging in the hall, his socks still in the chest of drawers – you're positively encouraged to lounge around on the sofas by the live-in curator. The top floor contains the garret study where Carlyle tried in vain to escape the din of the street and the neighbours' noisy roosters in order to complete his final *magnum opus* on Frederick the Great.

Chelsea Old Church and Crosby Hall

At the end of Cheyne Walk's gardens there's a garish, gilded statue of **Thomas More**, "Scholar, Saint, Statesman", who lived hereabouts and used to worship in nearby **Chelsea Old Church**, where he built his own private chapel in the south aisle (the hinges for the big oak doors are still visible). The church was badly bombed in the last war, but an impressive number of monuments were retrieved from the rubble and continue to adorn the church's interior. Chief amongst them is Lady Cheyne's memorial, and More's simple canopied memorial to his first wife, Jane, which is thought to contain his headless body, secretly brought here from the Tower by his daughter, Margaret Roper. (His head was buried in Canterbury.) More's second wife, Alice, is buried here too.

Though More is best known for his martyrdom in 1535, after refusing to acknowledge Henry VIII's divorce from Catherine of Aragon, he was no shy flower when it came to heretics – a few nonbelievers were tied to a tree in More's Chelsea back garden and flogged, which is perhaps one reason why the Catholic church canonized More in 1935. More would certainly have gone berserk if he had witnessed Henry's marriage to his third wife, Jane Seymour, Anne Boleyn's lady-in-waiting, which took place in secret in this church, just weeks after Anne Boleyn's execution.

More's house was destroyed in 1740 by Sir Hans Sloane, but in the 1920s **Crosby Hall**, part of a fifteenth-century wool merchant's house, once owned by More, was transferred bit by bit from Bishopsgate in the City and incorporated into the International Hostel of the British Federation of University Women, on the corner of Danvers Street, to the west of the church. Its fine hammerbeam roof and copies of Holbein portraits of More and family can usually be viewed on Saturday and Sunday afternoons. If you're wondering what the twenty-storey pagoda in the distance to the west is, it belongs to Chelsea Marina, an exclusive (in a very literal sense) marina and apartment complex completed in 1987.

Fulham Palace

The nearest tube is Putney Bridge.

One last sight worth visiting in this part of town is **Fulham Palace**, stuck at the far end of the New King's Road by Putney Bridge. Once the largest moated site in England, it was the residence of the Bishop of London – third in the Church of England hierarchy – from 704 to 1973. The oldest section of the present-day complex is the modestly scaled Tudor courtyard, patterned with black diapers; the most recent is William Butterfield's neo-Gothic chapel, which, with the other period interiors, can only be seen on guided tours, which take place at 2pm on the second Sunday of each month.

The palace museum is open April–Sept Wed–Sun 2–5pm; Oct–March 1–4pm; 50p.

At other times, you have to make do with the small **museum**, which traces the complex history of the building and displays a motley collection of archeological finds, including a mummified rat.

In the palace grounds there's a lovely herb garden, with a Tudor gateway and a maze of miniature box hedges, but sadly no sign of a moat since 1921, when it was filled in.

Battersea

In the false boom of the Thatcher years, aspiring Chelsea types began to colonize the cheaper terraces and mansions across the river in **Battersea**, which duly earned itself the nickname "South Chelsea". For the best part of this century, however, Battersea was a staunchly working-class enclave, which in the 1920s returned Shapurji Saklatvala as Britain's first coloured MP (and the only one for the next sixty years), first for the Labour Party, then as a Communist. Saklatvala was always in the news: he was banned from entry into the US and even his native India, and was the first person to be arrested during the 1926 General Strike, after a speech in Hyde Park urging soldiers not to fire on striking workers, for which he received a two-month prison sentence.

The poverty in the area was one of the main reasons behind the establishment of **Battersea Park**, the capital's second non-royal public park after Victoria Park in the East End (p.233). It is connected to Chelsea by the Albert Bridge, one of the prettiest to span the Thames, especially when lit at night. The park itself is best known nowadays for its two-tier **Peace Pagoda**, erected in 1985 by Japanese Buddhists. Made from a combination of Portland Stone and Canadian fir trees, the pagoda shelters four large gilded Buddhas in its niches. To the southeast, there's a small **Children's Zoo** (Easter–Sept daily 11am–6pm; Oct–Easter Sat & Sun 11am–3pm; 90p), established during the 1951 Festival of Britain.

Among Londoners, Battersea is known for two things: its Dogs' Home, which moved to Battersea Park Road in 1871, and **Battersea Power Station**, Giles Gilbert Scott's awesome cathedral of power. Closed in 1983, it's currently in a shocking condition, its innards ripped out, its exterior walls looking more and more precarious. The building's shameful dereliction is down to the property speculators, who, with Mrs Thatcher's forceful backing, tried to turn the place into a theme park, only to run out of money with the onset of the recession.

Bayswater and Notting Hill

It wasn't until the removal of the gallows at Tyburn (p.268) that the area to the **north of Hyde Park** began to gain respectability. The arrival of the Great Western Railway at Paddington in 1838 further encouraged development, and the gentrification of **Bayswater**, the area immediately north of the park, began with the construction of an estate called Tyburnia. These days Bayswater is mainly residential, and a focus for London's widely dispersed Arab community, who are catered for by some excellent Lebanese restaurants. For visitors, it has a couple of museums devoted to Fleming and toys.

Much more tangible attractions lie to the west in **Notting Hill**, where London's most popular market, **Portobello Road**, takes place each Saturday, and where the August Bank Holiday weekend sees West Indian London out in force for the **Notting Hill Carnival**, Europe's largest. The area is currently one of London's trendiest and most multicultural neighbourhoods. Back in the 1950s, when it was among London's poorest neighbourhoods, it was, along with Brixton in South London, settled by Caribbean immigrants, invited over to work in the public services. Gentrification in the 1980s and 90s has changed the population greatly, but there's still a significant black presence, especially in the northern fringes.

Bayswater and Paddington

The nearest tube is Paddington.

Bayswater's combination of classic urban squares, big stuccoed terraces and grand tree-lined avenues gives the district a wealthy and almost continental feel, but the volume of traffic, as usual, spoils much of the effect. The area's main focus is **Paddington Station** on Praed Street, one of the world's great early railway stations; designed by Brunel in 1851, the cathedral-scale wrought-iron sheds replaced a wooden structure which was the destination of Victoria and Albert's first railway journey. The train travelled from Slough at an average speed of 44mph, which the prince considered excessive – "Not so fast next time, Mr Conductor," he is alleged to have remarked.

The Fleming Laboratory is open Mon–Thurs 10am–1pm; £2.

One block east of Paddington is St Mary's Hospital, home of the **Fleming Laboratory**, on the corner of Norfolk Place, where the young Scottish bacteriologist Alexander Fleming accidentally discovered penicillin in 1928. A short video, a small exhibition and a reconstruction of Fleming's untidy lab tell the story of the medical discovery that has saved more lives than any other this century. Oddly enough, it aroused little interest at the time, until a group of chemists in Oxford succeeded in purifying penicillin in 1942. Desperate for good news in wartime, the media made Fleming a celebrity, and he was eventually awarded the Nobel Prize, along with several of the Oxford team.

The Toy & Model Museum is due to re-open in 1995.

Of more universal interest is the **Toy & Model Museum** which opened at 21 Craven Hill in 1982 and has been expanding slowly ever since – it should have twenty-five galleries on five floors when it re-opens. The vast collection of old toys includes a clockwork pig once owned by Stanley Baldwin, a unique 1916 Cadillac model owned by Prince Chula of Thailand and a gladiator doll from Roman times. The most popular section with younger kids, however, is the garden, which is encircled by a miniature rideable railway.

Bayswater and Notting Hill

The nearest tubes are Queensway and Bayswater.

Bayswater's main drag is **Queensway**, whose rash of cafés, clothes shops and French patisseries keeps buzzing until late in the evening. The renewed prosperity here is due, in large part, to the resurgent Arab community, but to add to the cosmopolitan atmosphere, Queensway also boasts the largest concentration of Chinese restaurants outside Soho's Chinatown, and a short distance up Moscow Road you'll find London's Greek Orthodox Cathedral.

One whole block of Queensway is taken up by **Whiteley's**, established in 1863 as the city's first real department store. The present building opened in 1912 with the boast that they could supply "anything from a pin to an elephant", and had the dubious distinction of being Hitler's favourite London building – he planned to make it his HQ once the invasion was over.

Notting Hill

The urbanization of **Notting Hill**, the area to the north of Holland Park Avenue, began in the first half of the nineteenth century, when the leafy avenues and majestic crescents of the Norland and Ladbroke estates were laid out. In those days, the area was still known as the Potteries – after the gravel pits and pottery works on Walmer Road – or the Piggeries – after the district's three-to-one ratio of pigs to people. Even forty years ago Notting Hill was described as "a massive slum, full of multi-occupied houses, crawling with rats and rubbish", and populated by offshoots of the Soho vice and crime rackets. These insalubrious dwellings – many owned by the infamous vice king and slum landlord, Peter Rachman – became home to a large contingent of Afro-Caribbean immigrants, who had to compete for jobs and living space with the area's similarly downtrodden white residents.

Colin MacInnes' novel, Absolute Beginners, *is set in Notting Hill during the race riots.*

For four days in August 1958, Pembridge Road became the epicentre of the country's first race riots, when bus-loads of whites attacked West Indian homes in the area. The **Notting Hill Carnival** began unofficially the next year as a response to the riots; in 1965 it took to the streets and has since grown into the world's biggest street festival outside Rio, with an estimated one million revellers turning up on the last weekend of August for the two-day extravaganza of parades, steel bands and deafening sound systems. Strenuous efforts have been made in recent years to ease the tension between the black community and the police, but there are still plenty of doubters among the area's wealthier and mostly white residents, most of whom switch on the alarm system and leave town for the weekend.

The rest of the year, Notting Hill is a lot quieter, though its cafés and restaurants are cool enough places to pull in media folk from all over, as well as from the various offshoots of Richard Branson's Virgin empire, which are scattered around the area. The exception, however, is Saturdays, when big crowds of Londoners and tourists alike descend on the mile-long **Portobello Road** market.

Notting Hill Carnival

When it emerged in the 1960s, the Notting Hill Carnival was little more than a few church hall events and a carnival parade, inspired by that of Trinidad – home of many of the area's immigrants. Today the carnival still belongs to West Indians (from all parts of the city), but there are participants, too, from London's Latin American and Asian communities, and, of course, everyone turns out to watch the bands and parades, and hang out.

The main sights of the carnival are the **costume parades**, known as the *mas*, which take place on the Sunday (for kids' groups) and Monday (adults) from around 10am until late afternoon. The processions consist of floats, drawn by trucks, with costume themes and steel bands – the "pans" which are one of the chief sounds of the carnival (and have their own contest on the Saturday). The parade makes its way around a three-mile route, starting at the top end of Ladbroke Grove, heading south under the Westway, then turning into Westbourne Grove, before looping north again via Chepstow Road, Great Western Road and Kensal Road.

In addition to the parades, there are three or four **stages for live music** – Portobello Green and Powis Square are regular venues – where you can catch reggae, ragga, jungle, a bit of hip-hop and maybe Caribbean soca. And everywhere you go, between Westbourne Grove and the Westway, there are **sound systems** on the street, blasting out reggae and black dance sounds. A lot of people just mull around the sound systems, dancing as the day progresses, fuelled by cans of Red Stripe, curried goat and Jamaican patties, which are sold by dozens of weekend entrepreneurs.

Over the last few years, the Carnival has been fairly relaxed, considering the huge numbers of people it attracts. However, this is not an event for you if you are at all bothered by crowds – you can be wedged stationary during the parades – and very loud music. It is worth taking more than usual care about crime, too: leave your camera and jewellery at home, and just bring enough money for the day, as pickpockets turn up from all over. As far as safety goes, don't worry unduly about the media's horror stories (a perennial feature, along with pictures of police being kissed by large Caribbean women), as you're in plentiful company. However, the carnival proper winds up at 7pm each day, and if there's going to be any trouble, it tends to come after that point, when the police look to disperse the sound systems. If you feel at all uneasy, head home early.

Getting to and from the carnival is quite an event in itself. Ladbroke Grove tube station is closed for the duration, while Notting Hill Gate and Westbourne Park are open only for incoming visitors. The nearest fully operative tube stations are Latimer Road and Royal Oak. Alternatively, there's a whole network of buses running between most points of London and Notting Hill Gate. If you attempt to drive, you'll need to park well away from the area.

Portobello Road Market

The nearest tubes are Notting Hill and Ladbroke Grove.

Portobello Road kicks off at the intersection of Chepstow Road, though this initial stretch, lined with rather junky antique stalls and classier antique shops, is geared very much to tourists and overpriced. The market gets a lot more fun and funky after a brief switch to fruit and veg around the *Electric* cinema, on the corner of Blenheim Crecent. As you emerge from this, you reach an area under the Westway flyover, where the emphasis switches to street clothes and jewellery, odd trinkets, records and books.

There are some interesting shops in a complex under the Westway, and many more in the streets around. A wander through the grid between Elgin Crecent and Lancaster Road will take you past art galleries, contemporary ceramics, old jukeboxes and all manner of exotics and essentials. Blenheim Crescent and adjoining Tablot Road are a good place to start, with the excellent *Travel Bookshop* and *Books for Cooks* on the former, and *Rough Trade* records on the latter. Don't miss *Wong Singh Jones*, at 253 Portobello Road, either; this is an amazing emporium of kitsch, and the stairs next door lead up to a great café and terrace.

Back at the market, and across the Westway, the stalls get progressively cheaper as they swing east into **Goldborne Road**, which sits in the shadow of the awesome Trellick Tower, the tallest block of flats in the country when it was built in 1973, and despite appearances still popular with its residents. Goldborne Road is a market of its own, really, with a constellation of bric-a-brac stalls, and Portuguese and Morrocan cafés and shops, giving the road some of the bohemian feel of old Notting Hill, and making it the perfect place to wind up a visit to the market.

Kensal Green Cemetery

The nearest tube and train station is Kensal Green.

Within easy walking distance from Portobello Road, on the other side of the railway tracks, gasworks and canal, is **Kensal Green Cemetery**, the first of the commercial Victorian graveyards opened in 1833 to relieve the pressure on overcrowded inner-city churchyards. It's still owned by the founding company and still a functioning cemetery, with services conducted daily in the central Greek Revival chapel.

The cemetery is open daily April–Sept until 6pm; Oct–March closes 5pm. There are guided tours Sat & Sun at 2.30pm and catacomb tours on first Sun of month.

Graves of the more famous incumbents – Thackeray, Trollope and the Brunels – are less interesting architecturally than those arranged on either side of the Centre Avenue, which leads from the easternmost entrance on Harrow Road. Vandals have left numerous headless angels and irreparably damaged the beautiful Cooke family monument. Look out, though, for Major General Casement's bier, held up by four grim-looking turbaned Indians, and circus manager Andrew Ducrow's conglomeration of beehive, sphinx and angels. Other interesting characters buried here include Emile Blondin, a famous tightrope walker, Carl Wilhelm Siemens, the German scientist who brought electric lighting to London, and "James" Barry, Inspector-General of the Army Medical Department, who, it was discovered during the embalming of the corpse, was in fact a woman. The Queen singer, Freddie Mercury, was cremated here but his ashes were scattered in Bombay.

North London: Camden, Regent's Park, Hampstead and beyond

Everything north of the Marylebone and Euston Roads was, for the most part, open countryside until the mid-nineteenth century, and is now largely residential right the way up to the "green belt", created in the immediate post-war period to try and limit the continuing urban sprawl. The area of the city covered in this **NORTH LONDON** chapter is necessarily much smaller, concentrating on just a handful of the satellite villages, now subsumed into the general mass of London. Almost all the northern suburbs are easily accessible by tube from the centre; in fact, it was the expansion of the tube which encouraged the forward march of bricks and mortar in many of the outer suburbs.

The first section of the chapter traces the route of the **Regent's Canal**, which skirts what was, at the beginning of the nineteenth century, the city's northern periphery. Along the way, the canal passes one of London's finest parks, **Regent's Park**, framed by Nash-designed architecture and the home of London Zoo. The canal forces its way into Londoners' consciousness only at **Camden**, whose weekend market is one of the city's big attractions – a warren of stalls with an alternative past still manifest in its offbeat wares, street fashion, books, records and ethnic goods.

Far fewer visitors to the capital bother to check out neighbouring **Islington**, thus missing out on one of north London's ascendant areas, endowed with its own antiques trade. The real highlights of North London, though, for visitors and residents alike, are **Hampstead** and **Highgate**, elegant, largely eighteenth-century developments which still reflect their village origins. They have the added advantage of proximity to one of London's wildest patches of greenery, **Hampstead Heath**, where you can enjoy stupendous views, kite-flying and nude bathing, as well as outdoor concerts and high art in the setting of the Neoclassical country mansion of **Kenwood House**.

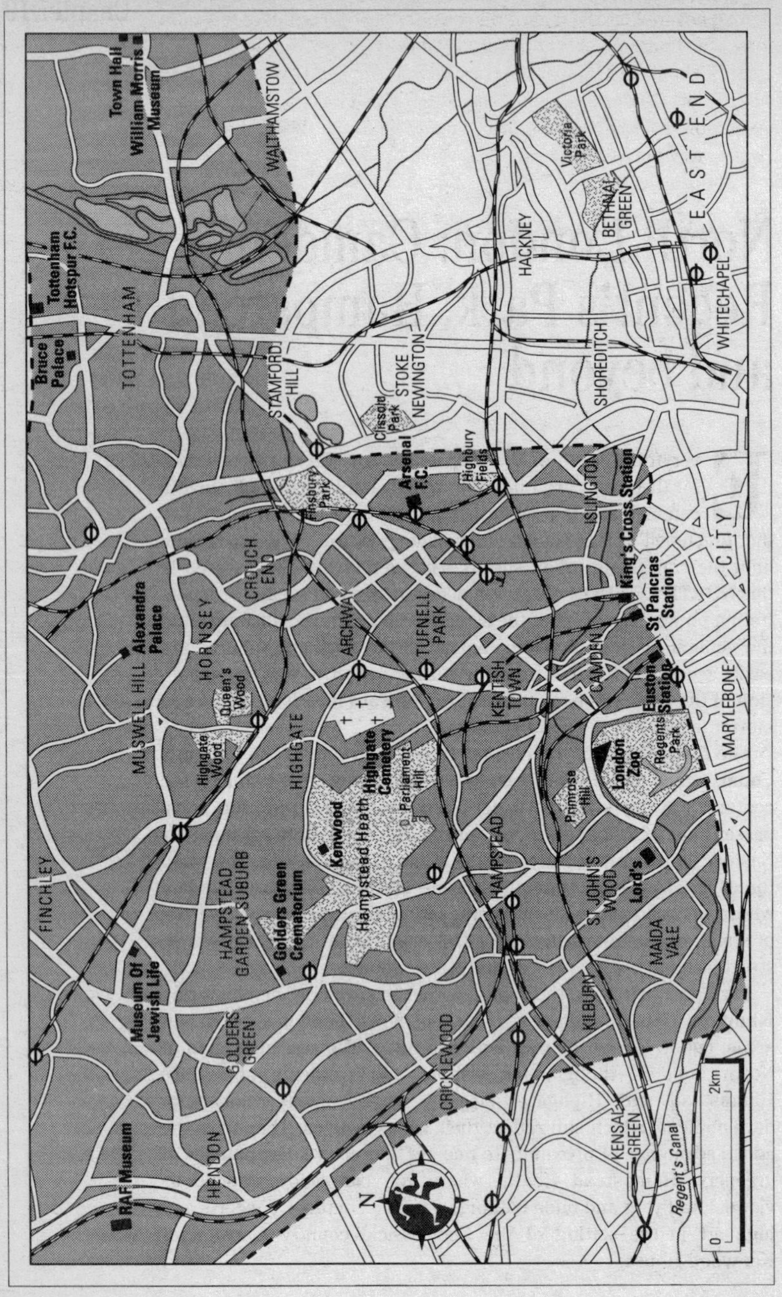
Town Hall
William Morris Museum
WALTHAMSTOW
Tottenham Hotspur F.C.
TOTTENHAM
Bruce Palace
HACKNEY
Victoria Park
BETHNAL GREEN
EAST END
WHITECHAPEL
SHOREDITCH
STAMFORD HILL
STOKE NEWINGTON
Clissold Park
Highbury Fields
Arsenal F.C.
Finsbury Park
ISLINGTON
King's Cross Station
St Pancras Station
CITY
Alexandra Palace
CROUCH END
HORNSEY
ARCHWAY
TUFNELL PARK
KENTISH TOWN
CAMDEN
Euston Station
MARYLEBONE
MUSWELL HILL
Queen's Wood
Highgate Wood
HIGHGATE
Highgate Cemetery
Parliament Hill
London Zoo
Regents Park
Primrose Hill
Kenwood
Hampstead Heath
HAMPSTEAD
FINCHLEY
HAMPSTEAD GARDEN SUBURB
Golders Green Crematorium
ST JOHN'S WOOD
Lord's
MAIDA VALE
Museum Of Jewish Life
GOLDERS GREEN
CRICKLEWOOD
KILBURN
KENSAL GREEN
Regent's Canal
RAF Museum
HENDON
N
0
2km

Also covered, at the end of this chapter, are a handful of sights in more far-flung northern suburbs. They include the nineteenth-century Utopia of **Hampstead Garden Suburb**; the Jewish Orthodox suburb of **Golder's Green**; the **RAF Museum** at Hendon; the exhibition halls of **Alexandra Palace**; and the **William Morris House**, way out of town at Walthamstow.

St John's Wood and Little Venice

The **Regent's Canal**, completed in 1820, was constructed as part of a direct link from Birmingham to the newly built London Docks. Its seemingly random meandering, from the Grand Junction Canal at Paddington to the River Thames at Limehouse, traces the fringe of London's northernmost suburbs at the time. After an initial period of heavy usage it was overtaken by the railway, and never really paid its way as its investors had hoped. By some miracle, however, it escaped being covered over or turned into a rail or road route, and its nine miles, forty-two bridges, twelve locks and two tunnels stand as a reminder of another age.

The lock-less run of the canal **between Little Venice and Camden Town** is the most attractive stretch, tunnelling through to Lisson Grove, skirting Regent's Park, slicing London Zoo in two, and passing straight through the heart of Camden Market. It's also the one section that's served all year round by narrowboat. Alternatively you can cycle or walk along the towpath.

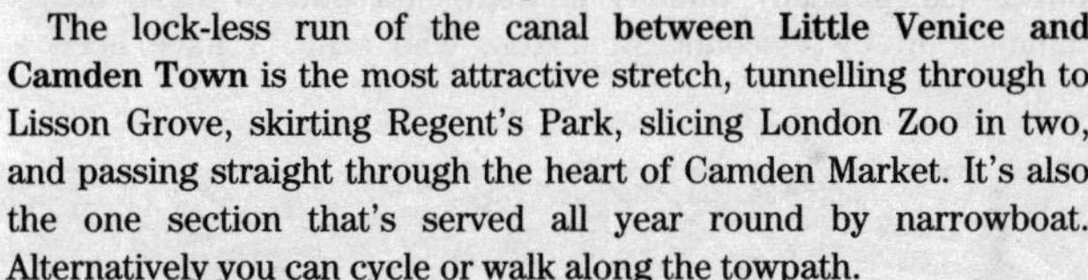

St John's Wood

The Regent's Canal starts out from the west in the smart, residential district of **St John's Wood**, which was built over in the nineteenth century by developers hoping to attract a wealthy clientele with a mixture of semi-detached Italianate villas, multi-occupancy Gothic mansions and white stucco terraces. Edwin Landseer (of Trafalgar Square lions fame), novelist George Eliot and Mrs Fitzherbert, the uncrowned wife of George IV, all lived here, while current residents include Richard Branson, Annie Lennox and Tottenham football star Jurgen Klinsmann.

The renowned **Saatchi Collection** of modern art is also based here, in a converted paint factory at 98a Boundary Rd. The gallery puts on two shows each year, and its summer event usually arouses enormous controversy – Damien Hirst displayed his famous shark in a tank of formaldehyde here. The winter show tends to feature more established names. The only de facto permanent exhibit is Richard Wilson's sump oil lake, which will continue to take up an entire room until the Saatchis can think of where else to put it.

The Saatchi Collection is open Thurs–Sun noon–6pm; £2.50, Thurs free.

To catch a canal boat to Camden through the southern borders of this neighbourhood, head for the triangular leafy basin known as

St John's Wood and Little Venice

For bookings, phone ☎ 0171/249 6876.

Little Venice, a nickname coined by one-time resident and poet Robert Browning. The title may be far-fetched, but the willow-tree island is one of the prettiest spots on the canal., and the houseboats and barges moored hereabouts are brightly painted and strewn with tubs of flowers. If you're here between October and May, be sure to catch a marionette performance on the **Puppet Theatre Barge**, moored on the Blomfield Road side of the basin, a unique and unforgettable experience; performances, for both kids and adults, take place every weekend and daily throughout the school holidays.

Lord's Cricket Ground

The building of the Regent's Canal was bad news for Thomas Lord, who had only recently been forced to shift his cricket ground due to the construction of what is now Marylebone Road. Once more he upped his stumps and relocated, this time to St John's Wood Road, where **Lord's**, as the ground is now known, remains to this day. The ground is owned by the exclusively male **MCC** (Marylebone Cricket Club), which was founded in 1787 and is the most hallowed institution in the game, boasting a twenty-eight-year waiting list (unless you're exceptionally famous or rich). Its politics were neatly summed up by Viscount Monckton, who said, "I have been a

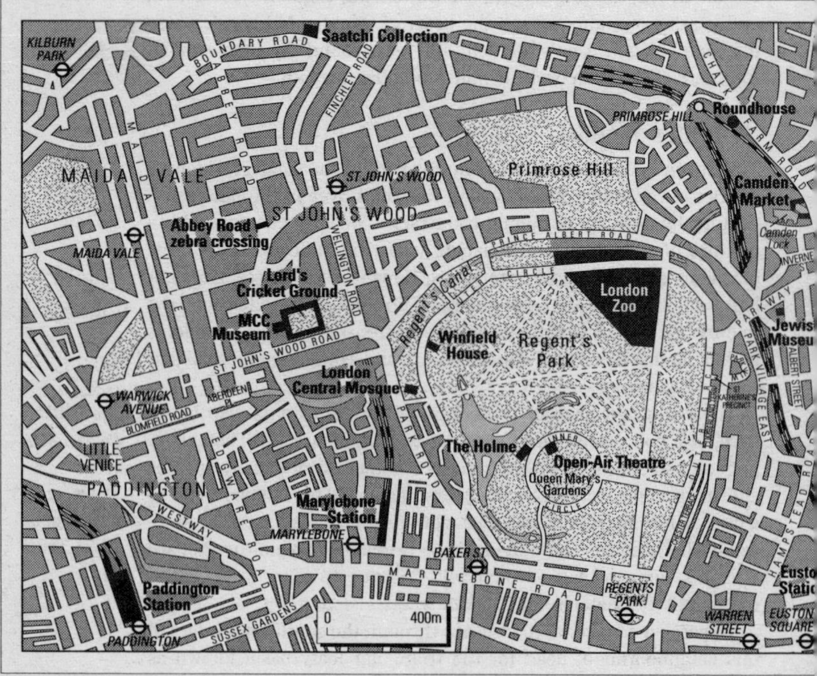

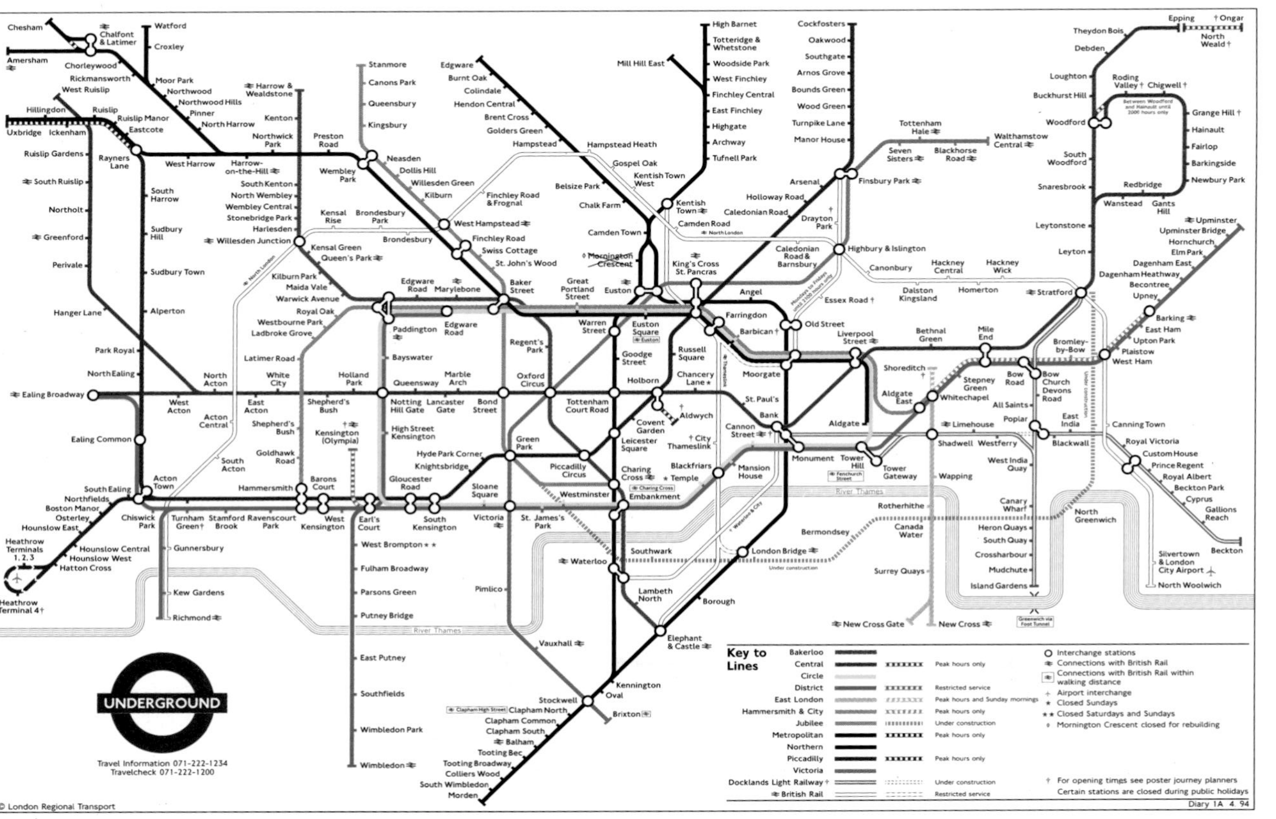

UNDERGROUND
Travel Information 071-222-1234
Travelcheck 071-222-1200
© London Regional Transport
Diary 1A 4 94
Key to Lines
Bakerloo
Central
Circle
District
East London
Hammersmith & City
Jubilee
Metropolitan
Northern
Piccadilly
Victoria
Docklands Light Railway †
British Rail
Peak hours only
Restricted service
Peak hours and Sunday mornings
Peak hours only
Under construction
Peak hours only
Peak hours only
Under construction
Restricted service
Interchange stations
Connections with British Rail
Connections with British Rail within walking distance
Airport interchange
* Closed Sundays
** Closed Saturdays and Sundays
◊ Mornington Crescent closed for rebuilding
† For opening times see poster journey planners
Certain stations are closed during public holidays
Between Woodford and Hainault until 2000 hours only
Mondays to Fridays until 2100 hours only
Under construction
River Thames
Greenwich via Foot Tunnel
Chesham
Chalfont & Latimer
Amersham
Watford
Croxley
Chorleywood
Rickmansworth
Moor Park
Northwood
Northwood Hills
Pinner
North Harrow
West Ruislip
Hillingdon
Ruislip
Ruislip Manor
Eastcote
Uxbridge
Ickenham
Ruislip Gardens
Rayners Lane
South Ruislip
Northolt
Greenford
Perivale
Hanger Lane
Park Royal
North Ealing
Ealing Broadway
Ealing Common
South Ealing
Northfields
Boston Manor
Osterley
Hounslow East
Hounslow Central
Hounslow West
Hatton Cross
Heathrow Terminals 1, 2, 3
Heathrow Terminal 4†
West Harrow
Harrow-on-the-Hill
South Harrow
Sudbury Hill
Sudbury Town
Alperton
Harrow & Wealdstone
Kenton
Northwick Park
Preston Road
Wembley Park
South Kenton
North Wembley
Wembley Central
Stonebridge Park
Harlesden
Willesden Junction
Kensal Rise
Brondesbury Park
Brondesbury
Kensal Green
Queen's Park
Kilburn Park
Maida Vale
Warwick Avenue
Royal Oak
Westbourne Park
Ladbroke Grove
Latimer Road
North Acton
West Acton
East Acton
White City
Acton Central
South Acton
Acton Town
Chiswick Park
Turnham Green†
Stamford Brook
Ravenscourt Park
Gunnersbury
Kew Gardens
Richmond
Stanmore
Canons Park
Queensbury
Kingsbury
Neasden
Dollis Hill
Willesden Green
Kilburn
West Hampstead
Finchley Road & Frognal
Finchley Road
Swiss Cottage
St. John's Wood
Edgware
Burnt Oak
Colindale
Hendon Central
Brent Cross
Golders Green
Hampstead
Hampstead Heath
Gospel Oak
Belsize Park
Chalk Farm
Camden Town
Kentish Town West
Kentish Town
Camden Road
North London
Mill Hill East
High Barnet
Totteridge & Whetstone
Woodside Park
West Finchley
Finchley Central
East Finchley
Highgate
Archway
Tufnell Park
Cockfosters
Oakwood
Southgate
Arnos Grove
Bounds Green
Wood Green
Turnpike Lane
Manor House
Finsbury Park
Arsenal
Holloway Road
Caledonian Road
Drayton Park
Highbury & Islington
Caledonian Road & Barnsbury
Canonbury
Tottenham Hale
Seven Sisters
Blackhorse Road
Walthamstow Central
Hackney Central
Hackney Wick
Dalston Kingsland
Homerton
Epping
Ongar
North Weald†
Theydon Bois
Debden
Loughton
Buckhurst Hill
Roding Valley†
Chigwell†
Grange Hill†
Hainault
Fairlop
Barkingside
Newbury Park
Woodford
South Woodford
Snaresbrook
Redbridge
Wanstead
Gants Hill
Leytonstone
Leyton
Stratford
Upminster
Upminster Bridge
Hornchurch
Elm Park
Dagenham East
Dagenham Heathway
Becontree
Upney
Barking
East Ham
Upton Park
Plaistow
West Ham
Bromley-by-Bow
Mornington Crescent
King's Cross St. Pancras
Euston
Angel
Essex Road†
Old Street
Edgware Road
Marylebone
Baker Street
Great Portland Street
Warren Street
Euston Square
Farringdon
Barbican†
Paddington
Bayswater
Regent's Park
Goodge Street
Russell Square
Moorgate
Liverpool Street
Thameslink
Holland Park
Notting Hill Gate
Queensway
Lancaster Gate
Marble Arch
Bond Street
Oxford Circus
Tottenham Court Road
Holborn
Chancery Lane*
St. Paul's
Bank
Aldgate
Aldgate East
Shoreditch†
Whitechapel
Stepney Green
Mile End
Bethnal Green
Bow Road
Bow Church
Devons Road
All Saints
Poplar
East India
Blackwall
Canning Town
Royal Victoria
Custom House
Prince Regent
Royal Albert
Beckton Park
Cyprus
Gallions Reach
Beckton
Shepherd's Bush
Kensington (Olympia)
Goldhawk Road
Hammersmith
Barons Court
West Kensington
Earl's Court
High Street Kensington
Gloucester Road
South Kensington
Hyde Park Corner
Knightsbridge
Sloane Square
Green Park
Piccadilly Circus
Leicester Square
Covent Garden
Aldwych
City Thameslink
Blackfriars
Temple
Charing Cross
Embankment
Westminster
St. James's Park
Victoria
Mansion House
Cannon Street
Monument
Tower Hill
Fenchurch Street
Tower Gateway
Limehouse
Shadwell
Westferry
Wapping
West India Quay
Canary Wharf
Heron Quays
South Quay
Crossharbour
Mudchute
Island Gardens
North Greenwich
Rotherhithe
Canada Water
Surrey Quays
New Cross Gate
New Cross
Bermondsey
London Bridge
Southwark
Waterloo
Waterloo & City
Lambeth North
Borough
Elephant & Castle
West Brompton
Fulham Broadway
Parsons Green
Putney Bridge
East Putney
Southfields
Wimbledon Park
Wimbledon
Pimlico
Vauxhall
Kennington
Oval
Stockwell
Brixton
Clapham High Street
Clapham North
Clapham Common
Clapham South
Balham
Tooting Bec
Tooting Broadway
Colliers Wood
South Wimbledon
Morden
Silvertown & London City Airport
North Woolwich

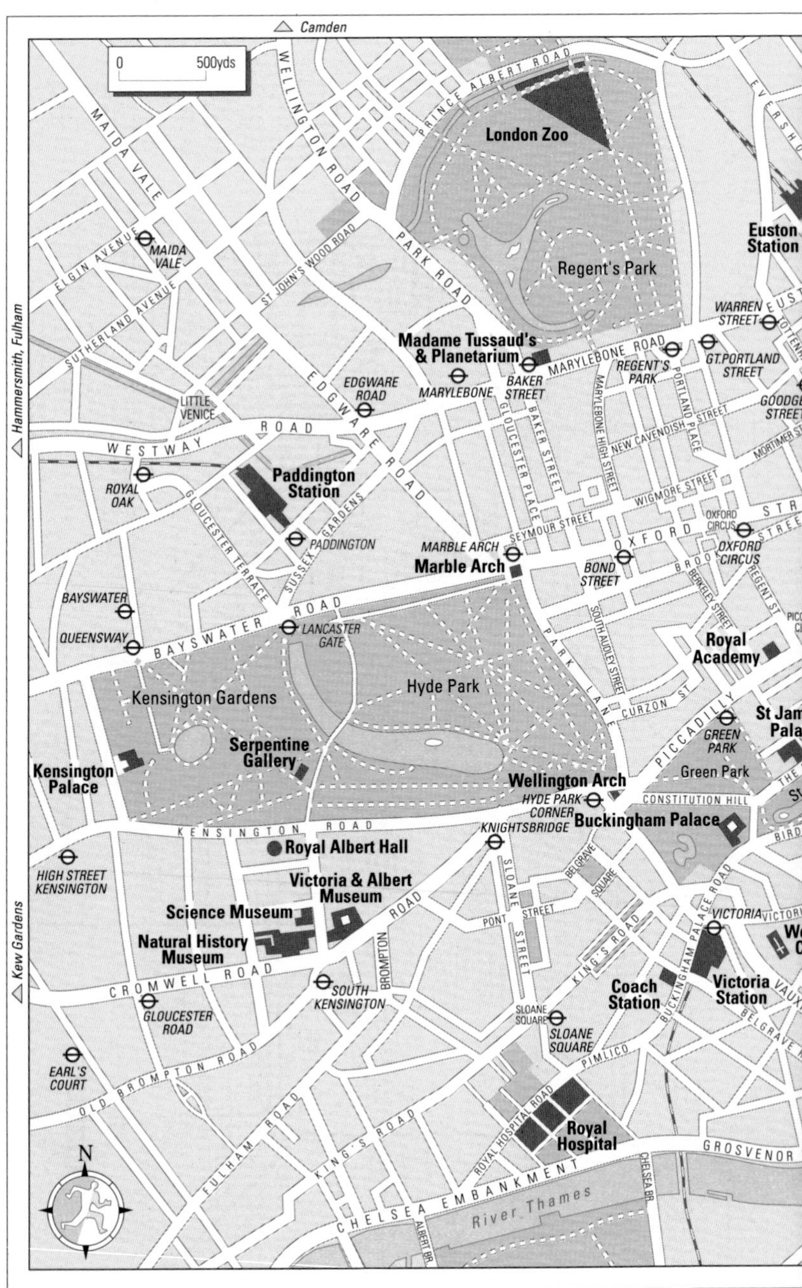
Camden
Hammersmith, Fulham
Kew Gardens
0 500yds
London Zoo
Regent's Park
Euston Station
Madame Tussaud's & Planetarium
Paddington Station
Marble Arch
Hyde Park
Kensington Gardens
Serpentine Gallery
Kensington Palace
Wellington Arch
Buckingham Palace
Green Park
Royal Academy
Royal Albert Hall
Victoria & Albert Museum
Science Museum
Natural History Museum
Coach Station
Victoria Station
Royal Hospital
River Thames
MAIDA VALE
WELLINGTON ROAD
PRINCE ALBERT ROAD
PARK ROAD
ST JOHN'S WOOD ROAD
ELGIN AVENUE
SUTHERLAND AVENUE
LITTLE VENICE
EDGWARE ROAD
MARYLEBONE
BAKER STREET
MARYLEBONE ROAD
REGENT'S PARK
WARREN STREET
GT.PORTLAND STREET
GOODGE STREET
PORTLAND PLACE
NEW CAVENDISH STREET
MARYLEBONE HIGH STREET
GLOUCESTER PLACE
WIGMORE STREET
MORTIMER ST
WESTWAY
ROAD
ROYAL OAK
GLOUCESTER TERRACE
SUSSEX GARDENS
PADDINGTON
MARBLE ARCH
SEYMOUR STREET
OXFORD CIRCUS
OXFORD
BOND STREET
BROOK
BERKELEY STREET
REGENT ST
BAYSWATER
QUEENSWAY
BAYSWATER ROAD
LANCASTER GATE
PARK LANE
SOUTH AUDLEY STREET
CURZON ST
PICCADILLY
GREEN PARK
HYDE PARK CORNER
CONSTITUTION HILL
KNIGHTSBRIDGE
KENSINGTON ROAD
HIGH STREET KENSINGTON
SLOANE STREET
BELGRAVE SQUARE
PONT STREET
VICTORIA
BUCKINGHAM PALACE ROAD
KING'S ROAD
CROMWELL ROAD
SOUTH KENSINGTON
BROMPTON ROAD
GLOUCESTER ROAD
SLOANE SQUARE
PIMLICO
EARL'S COURT
OLD BROMPTON ROAD
FULHAM ROAD
KING'S ROAD
ROYAL HOSPITAL ROAD
GROSVENOR
CHELSEA EMBANKMENT
ALBERT BR.
CHELSEA BR.
N

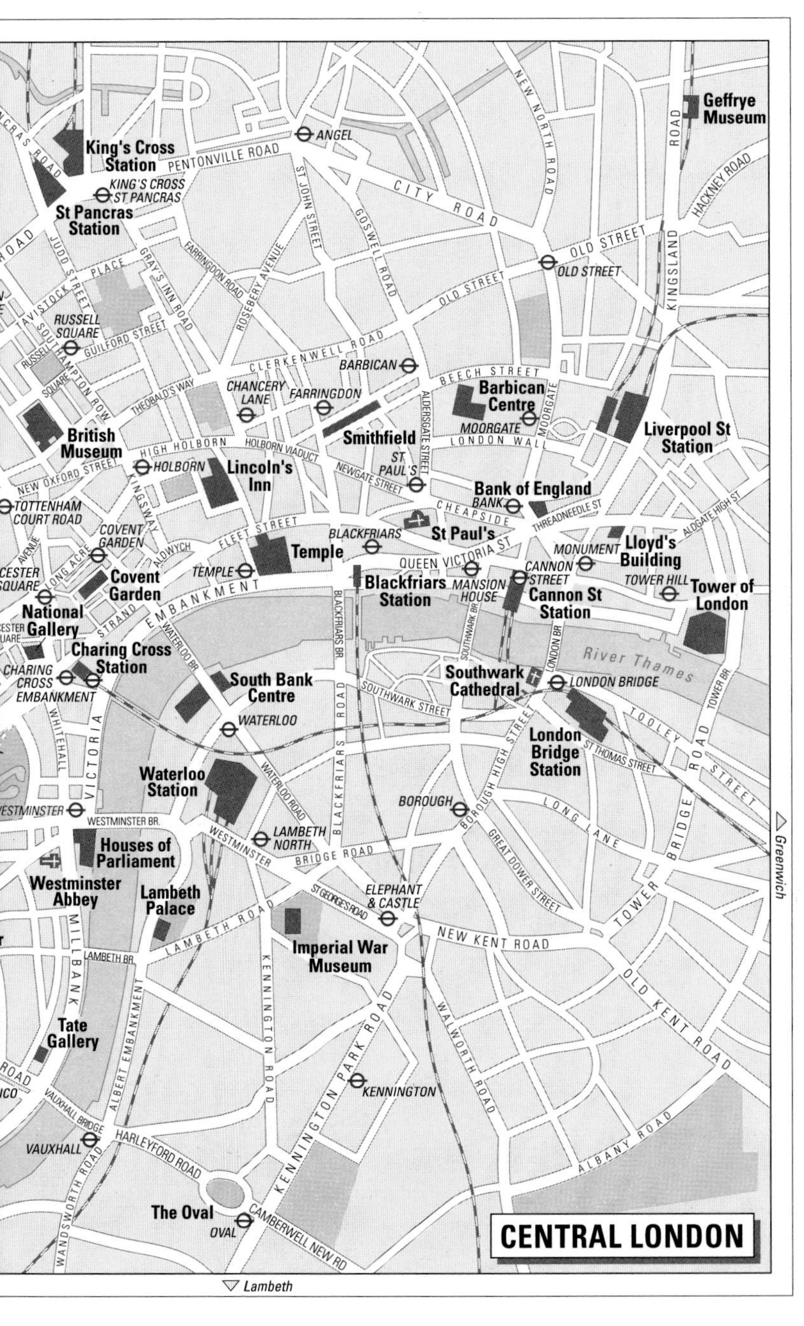
CENTRAL LONDON
King's Cross Station
St Pancras Station
KING'S CROSS ST PANCRAS
ANGEL
Geffrye Museum
British Museum
Lincoln's Inn
Smithfield
Barbican Centre
Liverpool St Station
Bank of England
St Paul's
Temple
Lloyd's Building
Covent Garden
National Gallery
Blackfriars Station
Cannon St Station
Tower of London
Charing Cross Station
South Bank Centre
Southwark Cathedral
London Bridge Station
Waterloo Station
Houses of Parliament
Westminster Abbey
Lambeth Palace
Imperial War Museum
Tate Gallery
The Oval
River Thames
Greenwich
Lambeth
PENTONVILLE ROAD
CITY ROAD
OLD STREET
NEW NORTH ROAD
KINGSLAND ROAD
HACKNEY ROAD
GOSWELL ROAD
ST JOHN STREET
CLERKENWELL ROAD
HIGH HOLBORN
NEW OXFORD STREET
FLEET STREET
STRAND
EMBANKMENT
QUEEN VICTORIA ST
CHEAPSIDE
LONDON WALL
BEECH STREET
ALDGATE HIGH ST
TOOLEY STREET
TOWER BRIDGE ROAD
LONG LANE
NEW KENT ROAD
OLD KENT ROAD
ALBANY ROAD
WALWORTH ROAD
KENNINGTON PARK ROAD
KENNINGTON ROAD
LAMBETH ROAD
WESTMINSTER BRIDGE ROAD
BLACKFRIARS ROAD
BOROUGH HIGH STREET
GREAT DOVER STREET
HARLEYFORD ROAD
CAMBERWELL NEW RD
WANDSWORTH ROAD
ALBERT EMBANKMENT
MILLBANK
VICTORIA
WHITEHALL
KINGSWAY
GRAY'S INN ROAD
FARRINGDON ROAD
ROSEBERY AVENUE
SOUTHAMPTON ROW
GUILFORD STREET
TAVISTOCK PLACE
JUDD STREET
ALDERSGATE STREET
MOORGATE
THREADNEEDLE ST
SOUTHWARK STREET
ST THOMAS STREET
HOLBORN VIADUCT
NEWGATE STREET
THEOBALD'S WAY
ALDWYCH
LONG ACRE
WATERLOO RD
SOUTHWARK BR
LONDON BR
BLACKFRIARS BR
WESTMINSTER BR.
LAMBETH BR.
VAUXHALL BRIDGE
ST GEORGE'S ROAD
BARBICAN
CHANCERY LANE
FARRINGDON
MOORGATE
ST PAUL'S
BANK
HOLBORN
TOTTENHAM COURT ROAD
COVENT GARDEN
BLACKFRIARS
MANSION HOUSE
CANNON STREET
MONUMENT
TOWER HILL
TEMPLE
LONDON BRIDGE
CHARING CROSS
EMBANKMENT
WATERLOO
BOROUGH
LAMBETH NORTH
ELEPHANT & CASTLE
KENNINGTON
VAUXHALL
OVAL
RUSSELL SQUARE

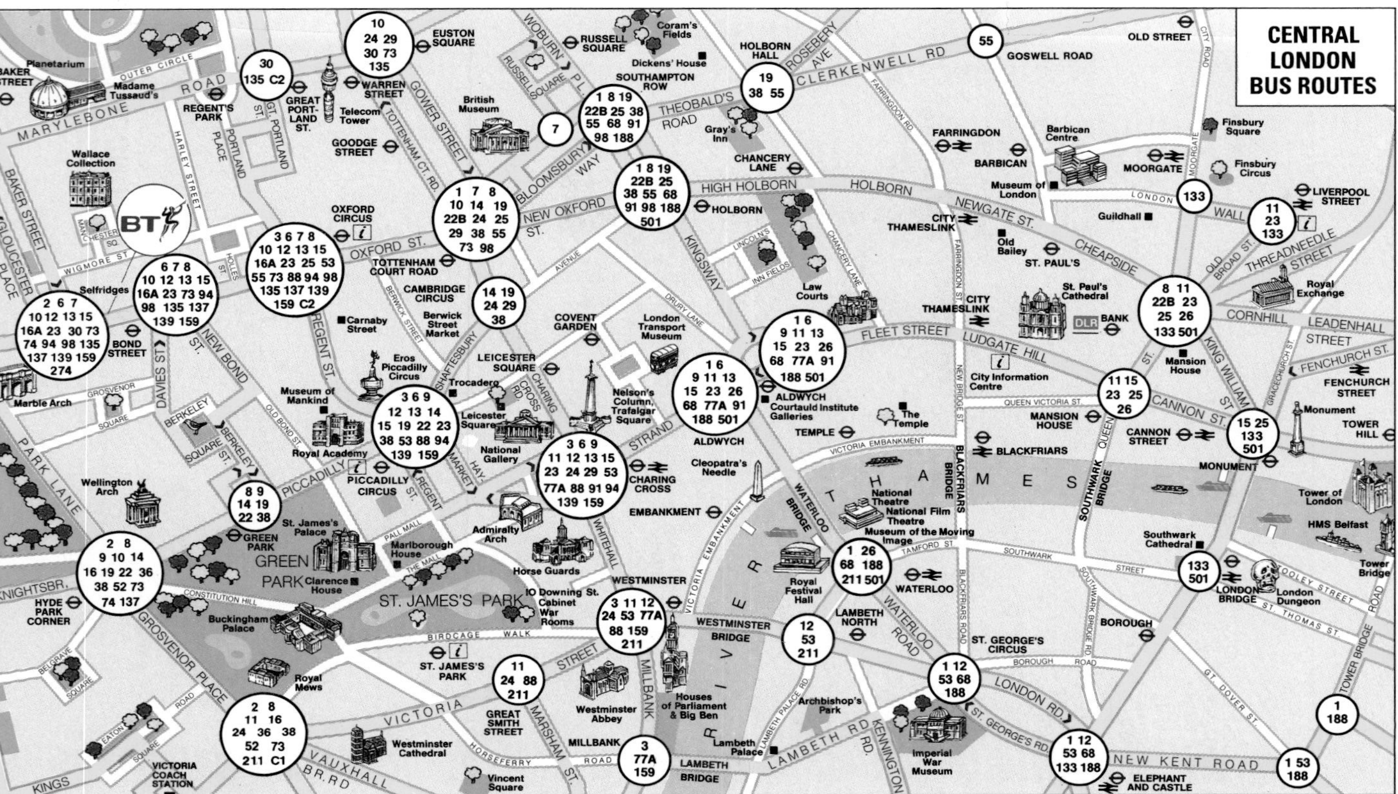
CENTRAL LONDON BUS ROUTES
BAKER STREET
Planetarium
Madame Tussaud's
MARYLEBONE ROAD
REGENT'S PARK
GREAT PORTLAND ST.
WARREN STREET
EUSTON SQUARE
RUSSELL SQUARE
Coram's Fields
Dickens' House
SOUTHAMPTON ROW
HOLBORN HALL
GOSWELL ROAD
OLD STREET
Finsbury Square
Finsbury Circus
MOORGATE
LIVERPOOL STREET
FARRINGDON
BARBICAN
Barbican Centre
Museum of London
Guildhall
CITY THAMESLINK
Old Bailey
ST. PAUL'S
St. Paul's Cathedral
BANK
Royal Exchange
Mansion House
FENCHURCH STREET
Monument
TOWER HILL
MONUMENT
Tower of London
HMS Belfast
Tower Bridge
LONDON BRIDGE
London Dungeon
Southwark Cathedral
CANNON STREET
MANSION HOUSE
BLACKFRIARS
BLACKFRIARS BRIDGE
SOUTHWARK BRIDGE
BOROUGH
ST. GEORGE'S CIRCUS
ELEPHANT AND CASTLE
Imperial War Museum
LAMBETH NORTH
WATERLOO
National Theatre
National Film Theatre
Museum of the Moving Image
Royal Festival Hall
WATERLOO BRIDGE
Archbishop's Park
Lambeth Palace
LAMBETH BRIDGE
Houses of Parliament & Big Ben
WESTMINSTER
WESTMINSTER BRIDGE
Westminster Abbey
MILLBANK
10 Downing St. Cabinet War Rooms
Horse Guards
EMBANKMENT
Cleopatra's Needle
CHARING CROSS
TEMPLE
The Temple
ALDWYCH
Courtauld Institute Galleries
Law Courts
City Information Centre
HOLBORN
CHANCERY LANE
Gray's Inn
British Museum
London Transport Museum
COVENT GARDEN
Nelson's Column, Trafalgar Square
LEICESTER SQUARE
Leicester Square
National Gallery
Trocadero
Admiralty Arch
Eros Piccadilly Circus
PICCADILLY CIRCUS
Museum of Mankind
Royal Academy
Carnaby Street
Berwick Street Market
CAMBRIDGE CIRCUS
TOTTENHAM COURT ROAD
OXFORD CIRCUS
GOODGE STREET
Telecom Tower
Wallace Collection
Selfridges
BOND STREET
Marble Arch
Wellington Arch
HYDE PARK CORNER
GREEN PARK
St. James's Palace
Marlborough House
Clarence House
ST. JAMES'S PARK
Buckingham Palace
Royal Mews
GREAT SMITH STREET
Westminster Cathedral
Vincent Square
VICTORIA COACH STATION
RIVER THAMES
BT

> **Regent's Canal by boat**
>
> **London Waterbus Company** (☎0171/482 2550). Boats to/from Little Venice to/from Camden via London Zoo; April–Sept hourly 10am–5pm; Oct–March every 1hr 30min from Little Venice 10.30am–3pm and Camden 11.15am–3.45pm; Nov–March Sat & Sun only; £3 one-way; £4 return.
>
> **Jenny Wren** (☎0171/485 4433). Boats to/from Little Venice to Camden; March–Oct 11am, 1, 2.30 & 4.30pm; £3.95 return.

member of the Committee of the MCC and of a Conservative cabinet, and by comparison with the cricketers, the Tories seem like a bunch of Commies".

A match ticket will allow you free access to the **MCC museum**, which traces the history of modern cricket, and features the minuscule pottery urn containing the Ashes (along with the complex tale of this odd trophy), numerous historic balls, bats and bails, and a sparrow which was killed by a bowler at Lord's in 1936. If you take one of the tours, you will also get to see the famous Long Room (from which the players walk onto the pitch), which is otherwise off-limits to women and non-members. The tours set off from the

The MCC Museum is open Mon–Sat 10.30am–5pm, Sun noon–5pm; guided tours daily (except match days) noon & 2pm; £4.95.

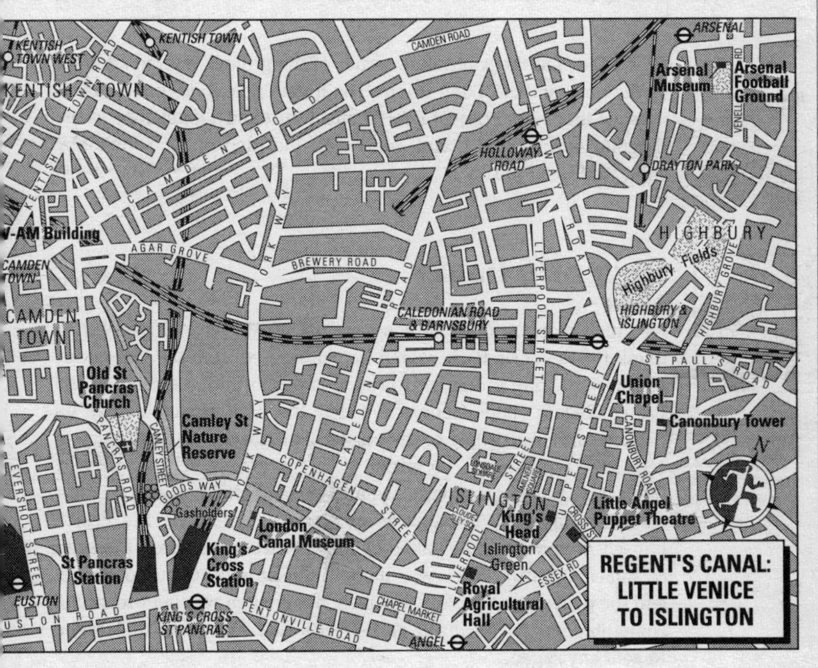

The Beatles in London

Since the Fab Four lived in London for much of the Sixties, it's hardly surprising that the capital is riddled with Beatle associations. The prime Beatles landmark is, of course, the **Abbey Road** zebra crossing, located near the EMI studios, where the group recorded most of their albums. To get there, walk up Grove End Road, which runs along the west side of Lord's cricket ground, until you come to the junction where it turns into Abbey Road – and remember to bring three other friends and someone to take the photos. Incidentally, Paul McCartney still owns the house at 7 Cavendish Avenue, two blocks east of the zebra crossing, which he bought in 1966.

One other nearby curiosity, that existed for only a brief time, was the **Apple Boutique**, opened by the Beatles at 94 Baker Street, in December 1967 as a "beautiful place where you could buy beautiful things". The psychedelic murals that covered the entire building were whitewashed over after a lawsuit by the neighbours, and eight months later the Beatles caused even more pandemonium when they gave the shop's entire stock away free in the closing down sale.

The other main Beatles location in London is the old Apple headquarters in Savile Row, where the rooftop concert took place (see p.102), while Macca has his current office on Soho Square (see p.120). Real devotees of the group, however, should get hold of a copy of *The Beatles' England* by David Heron and Norman Maslov, which covers every conceivable association. Alternatively, sign up for a Beatles tour, which is run by *The Original London Walks* (☎071/624 3978).

Grace Gates at the southwest corner of the ground, and, in addition to the museum and Long Room, you'll get endless cricketing anecdotes, a tour round Lord's Real Tennis Court and a quick look at the dazzling new Mound Stand, funded to the tune of £3.5 millionby John Paul Getty Jnr.

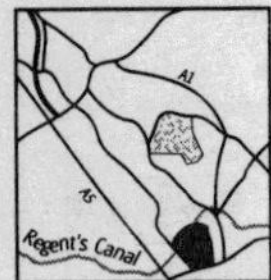

Regent's Park

As with almost all of London's royal parks, we have Henry VIII to thank for **Regent's Park**, which he confiscated from the church for yet more hunting grounds. However, it wasn't until the reign of the Prince Regent (later George IV) that the park began to take its current form. According to the masterplan, devised by John Nash in 1811, the park was to be girded by a continuous belt of terraces, blessed with two grand circuses and sprinkled with a total of fifty-six villas, including a magnificent pleasure palace for the Prince himself, which would be linked by Regent Street to Carlton House in St James's (p.86). Work was halted in 1826 due to lack of funds, and the plan was never fully realized, but enough was built to create something of the idealized garden city that Nash and the Prince Regent envisaged.

The eastern terraces

To appreciate the special quality of Regent's Park, you should take a closer look at the architecture, starting with the Nash terraces, which form a near-unbroken horseshoe of cream-coloured stucco around the Outer Circle. Each one is in a slightly different Neoclassical style, but by far the most impressive is **Cumberland Terrace**, built in 1826–28 and intended as a foil for George IV's private tea pavilion, which never materialized. Its 800-foot-long facade, hidden away on the eastern edge of the park, is punctuated by Ionic triumphal arches, peppered with classical statues and centred on a Corinthian portico with a pediment of sculptures set against a vivid sky-blue background. In 1936 an angry crowd threw bricks through the windows of no. 16, which belonged to Mrs Wallis Simpson, whose relationship with Edward VIII was seen as a national calamity.

The nearest tube is Camden Town.

Fifty-two more statues depicting British worthies were planned for the even longer facade of **Chester Terrace**, to the south, but Nash decided the ridicule they provoked was "painful to the ears of a professional man" and ditched them. Nevertheless, Chester Terrace is worth walking down if only to take in the splendid triumphal arches at each end which announce the name of the terrace in bold lettering. Still further south, facing east onto Albany Street, is Cambridge Gate, built some fifty years later in Bath stone to replace the "**Colosseum**", a rotunda built by Decimus Burton in 1829 in the style of the Pantheon. Inside, visitors were treated to a 360-degree view of London, spread out on an acre of canvas, drawn from sketches made by Thomas Hornor from the top of St Paul's Cathedral. A million visitors visited the panorama in the first year, and further attractions were added, including a hall of mirrors, stalactite caverns and even roller skating, but it fell into decline and was finally demolished in 1875.

St Katherine's Precinct and Park Village West

To the north of Cumberland Terrace, the neo-Gothic **St Katherine's Precinct** provides a respite from the Grecian surroundings, though not one Nash was at all happy with. The central church now serves the Danish community, who have erected a copy of the imposing tenth-century **Jelling Stone** in an alcove to the right. The original was erected in memory of King Gorm by his son, Harald Bluetooth, the first Danish ruler to convert to Christianity, as the colourful runic inscription and image of Christ hewn into the granite testify.

For proof that Nash could build equally well on a much more modest scale than the Regent's Park terraces, take a stroll round **Park Village West**, which lies in a secluded network of winding streets and cul-de-sacs just off Albany Street, on the other side of Gloucester Gate. The houses, Nash's last work for Regent's Park, feature copious ornamental urns and black lattice pergolas, and range from mock-Athenian cottages to Tudor and Italianate villas.

The Inner Circle and the western periphery

The nearest tubes are Regent's Park and Baker Street.

Of the numerous villas planned for the park itself, only eight were built, and of those just two have survived around the **Inner Circle**: St John's Lodge in its own private grounds to the north, and The Holme, Decimus Burton's first-ever work (he was eighteen at the time), picturesquely sited by the Boating Lake, which is fed by the waters of the Tyburn, one of London's "lost" – that is, underground – rivers. Within the Inner Circle is the Open Air Theatre, which puts on summer performances of Shakespeare, opera and ballet, and **Queen Mary's Garden**, by far the prettiest section of the park.

On the western edge of the park, the curved end wings and quirky octagonal domes of **Sussex Place** stand out amongst the other more orthodox Nash terraces. A further surprise breaks the skyline to the north – the shiny copper dome and minaret of the **London Central Mosque**, an entirely appropriate addition given the Prince Regent's taste for the orient (as expressed in Brighton Pavilion). Non-Muslim visitors are welcome to look in at the information centre, and glimpse inside the hall of worship, which is packed out with a diversity of communities for the lunchtime Friday prayers.

A little further up the Outer Circle, Quinlan Terry has added a trio of contemporary, neo-Nash villas which reflect the conservative tastes of the current Prince of Wales. On the opposite side of the road is **Winfield House**, built in the 1930s by Cary Grant and Barbara Hutton, heiress of the Woolworth chain; it's now the US ambassador's residence.

London Zoo

In the northern corner of the park, beyond acres of football pitches, lies **London Zoo**. Founded in 1826, in recent years it's been under constant threat of closure due to lack of funds, its most recent crisis being averted when the Kuwaiti government came up with a belated thank-you present for British help in the Gulf War. Since then, it has attempted to re-define itself, not altogether successfully, as an eco-conscious zoo whose prime purpose is to save species under threat of extinction.

London Zoo is open daily summer 10am–5.30pm; winter 10am–3pm; £6; the nearest tube is Camden Town.

It's not the most uplifting place for animal lovers, with far too many of the inhabitants housed in concrete and steel hovels – signs outside the cages of big cats ask you not to be distressed if you see them pacing up and down, as if such behaviour were quite normal in the wild. However, some of the enclosures seem as humane as any zoo could make them, and there are some striking architectural features here, like Lubetkin's 1930s spiral-ramped concrete penguin pool (where Penguin Books' original colophon was sketched), and the colossal tent of Lord Snowdon's Aviary, whose shape is great to look at but not so cool if you're a bird trying to fly (it's due to be rebuilt in the near future).

Kids should love London Zoo, regardless, especially the children's enclosure, where they can actually handle the animals.

Prince Albert Road and Primrose Hill

Regent's Park

Nash intended the Regent Canal to run right through the middle of the park, but potential residents objected to lower-class canal-faring families ploughing through their well-to-do neighbourhood. Instead, the canal curves its way along the northern periphery, passing right through London Zoo, with the Snowdon Aviary to one side and giraffes and camels to the other. Equally visible from the canal are the millionaire apartment buildings of **Prince Albert Road**, which boast unrivalled views across the park. The money ran out before Nash could continue his terraces along the park's north side and it was left to twentieth-century architects to fill in the gaps.

Halfway along Prince Albert Road the mansions stop to reveal the small northern extension of Regent's Park known as **Primrose Hill**, which commands a superb view from its modest summit. In the sixteenth century, Mother Shipton prophesied that "When London surrounds Primrose Hill, the streets of the Metropolis shall run with blood", and in May 1829 a Mr Wilson proposed turning the hill into a necropolis, with a lift running down the core of the hill to give access to the various levels. Neither of these calamities came about, and the most unusual thing you're likely to witness is the neo-druidic ceremony which takes place here every autumn equinox. To the east is the much sought-after residential area of Primrose Hill, which attracts successful literati and artists: H. G. Wells, W. B. Yeats, Engels, Ted Hughes and Sylvia Plath have all lived here, and you might catch the present denizens browsing the bookshops and galleries on **Regent's Park Road**.

Camden Town

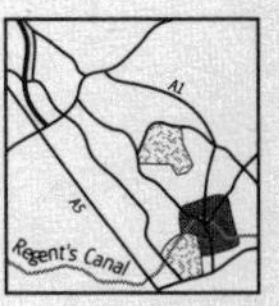

Until the canal arrived, **Camden Town** wasn't even a village, but by Victorian times it had become a notorious slum area, an image that it took most of this century to shed. Over the years, however, it has attracted a fair share of artists, most famously the Camden Town Group formed in 1911 by Walter Sickert, and more recently the likes of Lucien Freud, Frank Auerbach and Leon Kossoff. These days, despite gentrification over the last twenty years, the place retains a seedy air – it's home to Europe's largest dosshouse on Arlington Road – which is only increased by the market, the canal and the various railway lines which plough through the area. Its proximity to three main-line stations has also made it an obvious point of immigration over the years, particularly for the Irish, but also for Greek Cypriots during the 1950s.

The nearest tube is Camden Town.

Camden market and High Street

Camden Market was confined to Inverness Street until the 1970s when the focus began to shift towards the disused timber wharf and warehouses around Camden Lock. The tiny crafts market which began in the cobbled courtyard by the lock has since mushroomed out of all proportion, with everyone trying to grab a piece of the action on both sides of Camden High Street and Chalk Farm Road. More than 100,000 shoppers turn up here each weekend and parts of the market now stay open week-long, alongside a similarly-orientated crop of shops, cafés and bistros.

Camden Market

Camden market is busiest on Saturday and Sunday.

Camden's over-abundance of cheap leather, DM shoes and naff jewellery is compensated for by the sheer variety of what's on offer: from bootleg tapes to furniture and mountain bikes, along with a mass of street fashion that may or may not make the transition to mainstream stores. For all its tourist popularity, this is a market that remains a genuinely hip place.

To avoid the crowds, which can be overpowering on a summer Sunday afternoon, you'll need to come either early – before 10am – or late – say, after 4pm, when many of the stalls will be packing up to go. The oldest part of the market are the fruit and veg stalls of **Inverness Street**, which have been set up every day except Sunday since the last century. Opposite, the covered section known as **Camden Market**, which backs onto Buck Street, was rebuilt after a fire in 1994, and is now much improved; it's open Thursday to Sunday and sells mostly records and clothes.

The three-storey Victorian **Market Hall**, just past the canal bridge on the left, is home to numerous small shops, studios and stalls, which are open seven days a week. Behind the hall are the three cobbled yards of **Camden Lock**, enclosed by arty-crafty shops, most of which are open Wednesday to Sunday, and densely packed with jewellery and clothing stalls at the weekend. Further up Chalk Farm Road, the weekend clothes stalls of **The Stables** are among the cheapest in the entire market. Another adjunct to the market, which is often overlooked, is the **Electric Ballroom**, back down the High Street, a studenty club on Fridays and Saturdays, but a market for clothing and jewellery on Sundays.

Around Camden Lock

See p.309 for details of canal rides between Camden and Regent's Park/Little Venice.

If you've seen enough jangly ear-rings for one day, stand on the bowed iron footbridge by **Camden Lock** itself, and admire the flight of three locks to the east, which begin the descent to Limehouse. The castellated former lock-keeper's house, to your right, is now the **Regent's Canal Information Centre**, open very sporadically. For the boat ride down to Little Venice, you buy tickets on board; the boats leave from the lock cut, on the north side of the canal. Here too are the covered basins of the Interchange Warehouse, which in turn are linked by a disused railway line to the **Camden Catacombs**, built in the nineteenth century as stables for the pit ponies once used to shunt railway wagons.

The stabling extended as far north as the brick-built **Roundhouse**, on Chalk Farm Road, built by Robert Stephenson in 1847 to house twenty-three goods-engines arranged around a central turntable. Within fifteen years the engines had outgrown the building and it was used for storing booze. In the late 1960s, on the initiative of Arnold Wesker, the Roundhouse became a centre for political theatre and other nonconformist happenings, then through the seventies hosted legendary all-day, drug-fuelled hippy rock concerts, before being closed down in 1983. Subsequent plans to re-open the building as an arts centre for London's black community came to nothing, amid much political rivalry.

At the same time as the Roundhouse was getting off the ground, London Anti-University radicals founded **Compendium**, just by the bridge at 234 Camden High Street, which remains the best alternative bookshop in the city. The Roundhouse, Compendium, the market and **Dingwall's Dancehall** (still putting on good bands in the Camden Lock complex), all helped transform Camden from an Irish/Greek ghetto into a canalside bohemia.

Immediately to the east of Camden Lock is one of London's best-known post-modernist buildings, Terry Farrell's corrugated steel-clad **TV-AM Building**, a fairly crass attempt to brighten up a disused industrial site on Hawley Crescent. TV-AM, which was the first station to transmit breakfast television in this country, lost its franchise in 1992, so the building has new owners, though they have so far left the building's best feature, the giant blue and white egg-cups on the canal facade. Further along the canal are the technologically astonishing **canalside flats** designed by Farrell's former partner, Nicholas Grimshaw, which are built on the site of an old bakery. The upper floors feature curved aluminium vertical sliding doors which allow the dining room to become *al fresco*; the southside, by contrast, is windowless to cut out noise from the adjacent car park of the Camden Road **Sainsbury's** supermarket, another modernist structure by Grimshaw.

The Jewish Museum

The Jewish Museum has recently relocated to 129 Albert Street, just off Parkway: a somewhat surprising choice of location given the lack of Jewish connections in the area. Nonetheless, its smart, new premises here will allow much more space than its old Bloomsbury home for temporary exhibitions, as well as better facilities for displaying the museum's collection of Judaica, including treasures from London's Great Synagogue, which was burnt down by Nazi bombers in 1941. There's also a video and exhibition explaining the history of the Jewish community in Britain.

The Jewish Museum is open daily except Friday 10am–4pm; £2.50.

Old St Pancras to the King's Cross Basin

The nearest tube is King's Cross.

By tradition the first parish church built in London, **Old St Pancras Church** lies hidden and neglected behind iron railings on raised ground above Pancras Road, a few minutes' walk east of Camden High Street. Parts of the church date from the eleventh century – most notably the north and south doorways – but the rest was rebuilt in the nineteenth.

Sir John Soane's Museum is covered on p.170.

Its churchyard, which backs onto the railway lines and the Hospital for Tropical Diseases, was turned into a public garden in 1877, with the majority of graves heaped around an ash tree, though it's all now rather melancholic, with crumbling verges and cracking pathways. Only Sir John Soane's personally designed Mausoleum from 1816 – the inspiration for Giles Gilbert Scott's traditional red phone box – is still standing in its original location, to the north of the church. Also buried here was Britain's great proto-feminist, Mary Woolstonecraft Godwin, who died a few days after giving birth to her daughter, Mary. At the age of seventeen, over her mother's grave, she and the poet Shelley declared their undying love and eloped to Italy – both Marys are now buried in Bournemouth. A list of the graveyard's most prominent dead is inscribed on the monumental sundial erected by Baroness Burdett-Coutts.

If you were to continue down Pancras Road until you come to the collection of railway bridges, and then turn left, you'd come out on the desolate Goods Way, a backwater of the King's Cross red-light district. On either side of Goods Way are the brooding skeletal **King's Cross Gasholders**, framed by wrought-iron Doric pillars and embellished with red triglyphs. These Victorian monsters are still in use and hark back to an era when nothing was too lowly to be given Neoclassical decoration; they're listed buildings and are due to be carefully moved to an alternative site to make way for the new Chunnel train tracks into St Pancras.

The reserve is open summer Mon–Thurs 9.30am–5.30pm, Sat & Sun 11am–5pm.

Up Camley Street, past the gasholders, is **Camley Street nature reserve**, transformed from a rubbish dump into a canalside wildlife haven, run by the London Wildlife Trust. Pond, meadow and woodland habitats have been recreated and provide a natural environment for birds, butterflies, frogs, toads and even the odd heron, plus a rich variety of plantlife.

London Canal Museum and King's Cross Basin

A further insight into life on the canals can be gained from the **London Canal Museum**, on the other side of York Way, down New Wharf Road. Opened in 1992, this rather ad hoc museum testifies to the hard life boat families had to endure on the canal. Other exhibits relate to the building itself which was built as an ice house by Swiss-Italian entrepreneur, Carlo Gatti, London's main ice trader in the nineteenth century. Gatti single-handedly popularized ice cream in London, supplying most of the city's vendors, who became known as "Hokey-Pokey Men" – a corruption of the street cry *Ecco un poco*, "Just try a little". Also on view are a restored "butty" (an engine-less narrowboat used for extra storage), some of the unusual Measham Ware pottery that was popular with canal boat families, and a 1924 film of life on the Regent's Canal.

The Canal Museum stands alongside the **King's Cross Basin**, which is just about the end of the road if you're walking along the towpath, for under the next road bridge the canal enters the Nash-built Islington tunnel, 1000-foot long and hard work for the boatmen, who lay on their backs and pushed the boat through with their feet. In 1826, a miniature steam-boat took over the job, emerging into the light between Vincent Terrace and Noel Road, on the other side of Upper Street.

Islington

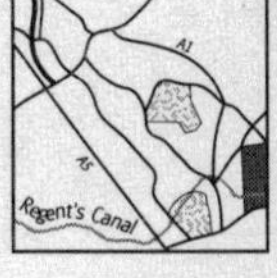

Islington has acquired something of a reputation as the home of what the British media like to call "the chattering classes" – the liberal, *Guardian*-reading middle class. Local Labour MP Chris Smith is the only member of parliament to have come out as gay and the new leader of the Labour Party, Tony Blair, also lives in the borough. Parts of Islington have certainly come a long way up the social ladder in the last twenty-odd years, since low house prices in the 1960s and 1970s encouraged a lot of arty professionals to buy and renovate the area's dilapidated Regency and early Victorian squares and terraces. In the 1980s this process was accelerated by an influx of far from left-leaning yuppies, who snapped up properties in an area attractively convenient for the City.

The impact of this gentrification has been relatively minor on the borough as a whole, which stretches as far north as Highgate Hill, and remains one of the poorest in England. Islington's main drag, Upper Street, on the other hand, has changed enormously: the arrival of its antique market, confusingly known as Camden Passage, coincided with the new influx of cash-happy customers and its trendy pubs and ethnic restaurants, from Turkish to Thai, Japanese to Lebanese, reflect the wealth of its new residents. For entertainment, there are more pub theatres in Islington than anywhere else, the oldest established being the *King's Head*, whose better productions transfer to the West End; in addition to these, there's the *Almeida*, a top fringe theatre for new writing, and several comedy and live music venues. All of which makes Islington one of the liveliest areas of North London in the evening – a kind of off-West End.

For more on London's theatre and comedy scene, see Chapter 20.

Upper Street and Liverpool Road

The nearest tube is Angel.

Looking at the traffic fighting its way along **Upper Street**, it's hard to believe that "merry Islington", as it was known, was once a spa resort to which people would flock from the City to drink the pure water and breathe the clean air. Today, Islington has fewer green spaces than any other borough – one of the few being **Islington Green**, a short distance along Upper Street from Angel tube. At the apex of the Green stands a weathered statue of Sir Hugh Myddleton, the Welsh jeweller to James I, who revolutionized London's water supply by drawing fresh water direct from springs in Hertfordshire via an aqueduct known as the New River. From 1612 until the late 1980s Myddleton's New River continued to supply most of north London with its water – the succession of ponds to the northeast of Canonbury Road is a surviving fragment of the scheme.

To the east of the Green, a black glass canopy provides shelter for the antique stalls of the **Camden Passage market** (Wed & Sat), which began in the 1960s. The antique shops in the market's narrow namesake and the surrounding streets stay open all week, as do the lock-ups in "The Mall" – in fact a converted tramshed – to the south of the passage. Since many of the locals are prepared to pay through the nose for antiques, you're unlikely to find bargains here. The perfect antidote, however, is to hand in **Chapel Street market** (Tues–Sun), a short distance up Liverpool Road, on the other side of Upper Street. Selling cheap clothes, fruit and veg and Arsenal football memorabilia, it's a salutary reminder of Islington's working-class roots.

On the other side of the Green from Camden Passage, the ugly modern glass frontage of the Business Design Centre hides the former **Royal Agricultural Hall**, built in 1862 and known locally as the "Aggie". As well as hosting annual agricultural and livestock

Orton in Islington

Playwright **Joe Orton** and his lover **Kenneth Halliwell** lived together for sixteen years, spending the last eight years of their lives in a top-floor bedsit at 25 Noel Road, to the east of Upper Street, where the Regent's Canal emerges from the Islington tunnel. It's ironic that the borough council has seen fit to erect a plaque on the house commemorating the couple, when they were instrumental in pressing for harsh prison sentences after both men were found guilty of defacing local library books in 1962. (The wittily doctored books are now among Islington Central Library's most prized possessions and can be seen by prior arrangement.)

Six months in prison worked wonders for Orton's writing, as he himself said – "Being in the nick brought detachment to my writing". It also brought him success, with irreverent comedies like *Loot*, *Entertaining Mr Sloane* and *What the Butler Saw* playing to sell-out audiences in the West End and on Broadway. Orton's meteoric fame and his sexual profligacy drove Halliwell to despair, until on August 9, 1967, he finally cracked – he beat Orton to death with a hammer and then killed himself with a drug overdose. Their ashes were mixed together and scattered over the grass at Golders Green crematorium (p.334). Apart from the local public toilets, Orton's favourite hang-out was the appropriately entitled *Island Queen* pub, at the end of Noel Road.

exhibitions, it was in many ways a precursor to the later exhibition halls of Earl's Court and Olympia, hosting the World's Fair, the Grand Military Tournament and even Cruft's Dog Show. The best view is from Liverpool Road, where two large brick towers rise up either side of the roof, rather like a Victorian railway station.

Walking along these sections of Upper Street and Liverpool Road, it's impossible not to be struck by the one of the quirky architectural features of Islington – the raised pavements which protected pedestrians from splattered mud. Such precautions were especially necessary in Islington, which was used as a convenient grazing halt for livestock en route to the City markets. The residential streets on either side of Liverpool Road, developed shortly after the completion of the Regent's Canal, are also worth exploring for their wonderful Georgian and early Victorian squares. The earliest examples, like Cloudesley Square and Myddleton Square, further south, are in plain Georgian style with early neo-Gothic churches as their centrepieces; Lonsdale Square, with its Tudor styling, and Milner Square, with its parade of giant pilasters, are slightly later Victorian variations on the same theme.

North to Highbury Fields

Back on Upper Street, past the Green, is St Mary's Church, whose churchyard opens out into Dagmar Passage, where in 1961 a former temperance hall was converted into the **Little Angel Puppet Theatre**, London's only permanent puppet theatre. The archway at the end of Dagmar Terrace brings you out onto **Cross Street**, Islington's loveliest street, with eighteenth-century houses sloping down to Essex Road and raised pavements on both sides. If you've a penchant for Deco-style buildings, head north up much less lovely Essex Road, where the former **Carlton Cinema** (now a bingo club) was built in 1929 in mock-Egyptian style, using brightly coloured Hathernware tiles.

For bookings, call ☎0171/226 1787.

The northernmost stretch of Upper Street is flanked to the east by Compton Terrace, a standard late Georgian terrace, interrupted halfway along by the fancifully extravagant **Union Chapel**, which was built in 1888 at the height of the Congregationalists' popularity. The spacious, octagonal interior is designed like a giant auditorium with raked seating and galleries capable of holding the 1600 rapt worshippers who used to come and listen to the sermons of the local pastor. The number of chapel-goers has since dwindled, and the chapel now doubles as a concert venue.

The nearest tube is Highbury & Islington.

East of Compton Terrace is Islington's most perfect Regency set-piece, **Canonbury Square**, centred on a beautifully kept flower garden but sadly blighted by traffic. In the northeast corner of the square stands the last remaining relic of Islington's bygone days as a rural retreat, the red-brick **Canonbury Tower**, originally part of a Tudor mansion and once no doubt providing a wonderful view down to the City; it's now in the hands of the Tower Theatre Company, who, on written application, will happily show visitors round the tower's three panelled Elizabethan interiors.

See p.527 for a rundown on London football clubs and tickets.

To the north of Highbury Corner, at the top of Upper Street, lies the largest open space in the entire borough, **Highbury Fields**, where over 200,000 people gathered in 1666 to escape the Great Fire. North again, and then some, midway to Finsbury Park, is **Highbury stadium**, home to **Arsenal**, the only one of London's seven premier league football clubs who ever get their hands on a trophy. They play dull defensive football in vivid contrast to their stylish but ill-defended north London rivals, **Tottenham Hotspur**, based at White Hart Lane, a few miles northeast. Both clubs maintain museums for the hopelessly committed. Tottenham has a traditional Jewish support and bagels rather than meat pies at half time.

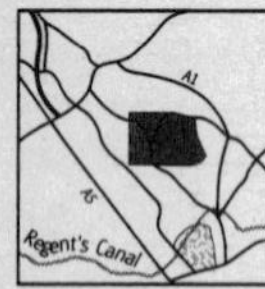

Hampstead

Perched on a hill to the west of Hampstead Heath, **Hampstead** village developed into a fashionable spa in the eighteenth century, and was not much altered thereafter. Its sloping site, which deterred Victorian property speculators and put off the railway companies, saved much of the Georgian village from destruction. Later it became one of the city's most celebrated literary *quartiers* and even now it retains its reputation – just ahead of Islington – as a bolt hole of the high-profile intelligentsia. You can get some idea of its tone from the fact that the local Labour MP is currently the actress Glenda Jackson.

Hampstead has some fine pubs, especially pleasant in summer. See p.471 for listings.

The steeply inclined High Street, lined with trendy clothes shops and arty cafés, flaunts the area's ever-increasing wealth without completely losing its picturesqueness, though the most appealing area is the precipitous network of alleyways, steps and streets north of the tube and west of Heath Street. Proximity to the Heath is, of course, the real joy of Hamsptead, for this mixture of woodland, smooth pasture and landscaped garden (see below) is quite simply the most exhilarating patch of greenery in London.

Holly Bush and Fenton House

Whichever route you take north of Hampstead tube, you will probably end up at the small triangular green on **Holly Bush Hill**, where the white weatherboarded **Romney House** stands (no admission). In 1797, painter George Romney converted the house and stables into London's first purpose-built studio house, though he spent only two years there before returning to the Lake District and the wife he had abandoned thirty years earlier.

The nearest tube is Hampstead.

Beyond wrought-iron gates on the north side of the green is the grand late seventeenth-century **Fenton House**. All three floors are decorated to eighteenth-century tastes and currently house a collection of European and Oriental ceramics bequeathed by the house's last private owner, Lady Binning. More interestingly, the house also contains the superb Benton-Fletcher collection of early musical instruments, chiefly displayed on the top floor – from which you can see right across the Heath. Among the many spinets, virginals and clavichords are the earliest extant English grand piano, an Unverdorben lute from 1580 (one of only three in the world) and a harpsichord from 1612, on which Handel played. Experienced keyboard players are occasionally let loose on some of the instruments during the day; concerts are also given in the drawing room on certain evenings, though tickets tend to sell out months in advance. The house's beautifully maintained walled gardens can be visited for free.

Fenton House is open March Sat & Sun 2–6pm; April–Oct Mon–Wed 1–5.30pm, Sat & Sun 11am–5.30pm; NT; £3.50.

Beyond Fenton House, up Hampstead Grove, is Admiral's Walk, so called after its most famous building, **Admiral's House**, a whitewashed Georgian mansion with nautical excrescences. Once painted by Constable, it was later lived in by Victorian architect Sir George Gilbert Scott, of Albert Memorial fame. Until his death in 1933 John Galsworthy lived in the adjacent cottage, Grove Lodge, where he completed *The Forsyte Saga* and received the 1932 Nobel Prize, which was presented to him here since he was too ill to travel abroad. Opposite is **The Mount**, a gently sloping street descending to Heath Street, which has changed little since it was depicted in *Work* by Pre-Raphaelite artist (and local resident) Ford Madox Brown.

St John's-at-Hampstead and Hampstead Cemetery

The Georgian terraces of **Church Row**, at the southern end of Heath Street, are the nearest Hampstead comes to an architectural set-piece and form a grand approach to the eighteenth-century church of **St John's-at-Hampstead**, less memorable for its architecture than for its romantically overgrown cemetery. John Constable is buried, in the southeastern corner; Hugh Gaitskell, the Labour Party leader from 1955 to 1963, lies in the Churchyard Extension to the northeast. If you continue up Holly Walk past the Extension, you'll come to **St Mary's Church**, whose Italianate facade is squeezed into the middle of a row of three-storey cottages. As this was one of the first Roman Catholic churches to be built in London after the Reformation, the original facade from 1816 was much less conspicuous.

Further Hampstead luminaries are buried in the rather more neatly maintained **Hampstead Cemetery**, founded in 1876 when the Churchyard Extension was full, and situated half a mile to the west, on the other side of Finchley Road. The pioneer of antiseptic surgery Joseph Lister, music hall star Marie Lloyd, children's book illustrator Kate Greenaway, Hollywood actress Lilli Palmer, and the Hungarian Laszlo Biro, who invented the ballpoint pen in 1938, are among those buried here. The full-size stone organ monument to the

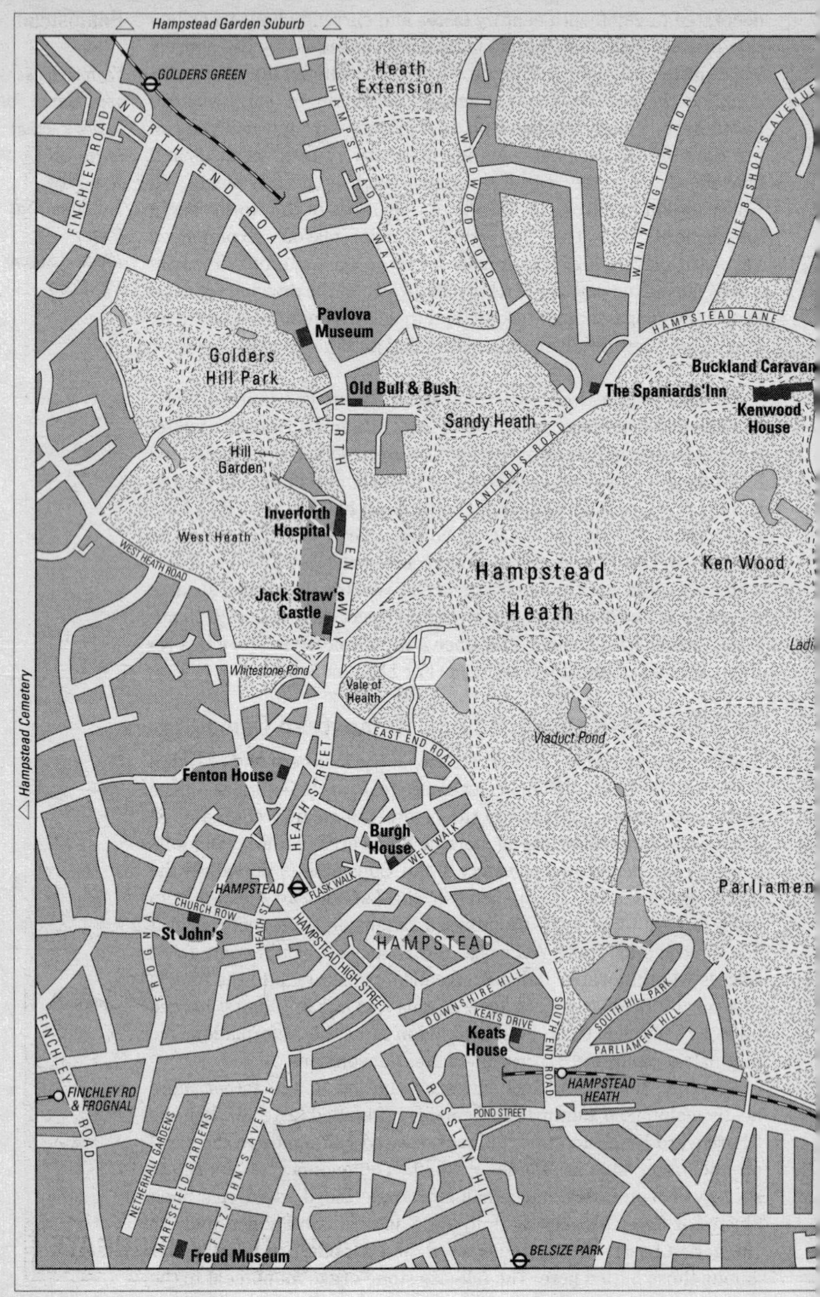

Hampstead Garden Suburb
GOLDERS GREEN
Heath Extension
FINCHLEY ROAD
NORTH END ROAD
HAMPSTEAD WAY
WILDWOOD ROAD
WINNINGTON ROAD
THE BISHOP'S AVENUE
Pavlova Museum
Golders Hill Park
HAMPSTEAD LANE
Buckland Caravan
Old Bull & Bush
The Spaniards'Inn
Kenwood House
Sandy Heath
Hill Garden
NORTH END
SPANIARDS ROAD
Inverforth Hospital
West Heath
WEST HEATH ROAD
Hampstead Heath
Ken Wood
Jack Straw's Castle
ENDWAY
Whitestone Pond
Vale of Health
Hampstead Cemetery
EAST END ROAD
Viaduct Pond
Fenton House
HEATH STREET
Burgh House
WELL WALK
HAMPSTEAD
FLASK WALK
Parliament
CHURCH ROW
St John's
HEATH ST
HAMPSTEAD HIGH STREET
HAMPSTEAD
FROGNAL
DOWNSHIRE HILL
SOUTH HILL PARK
KEATS DRIVE
Keats House
SOUTH END ROAD
PARLIAMENT HILL
FINCHLEY
FINCHLEY RD & FROGNAL
HAMPSTEAD HEATH
ROSSLYN HILL
POND STREET
ROAD
NETHERHALL GARDENS
MARESFIELD GARDENS
FITZJOHN'S AVENUE
Freud Museum
BELSIZE PARK

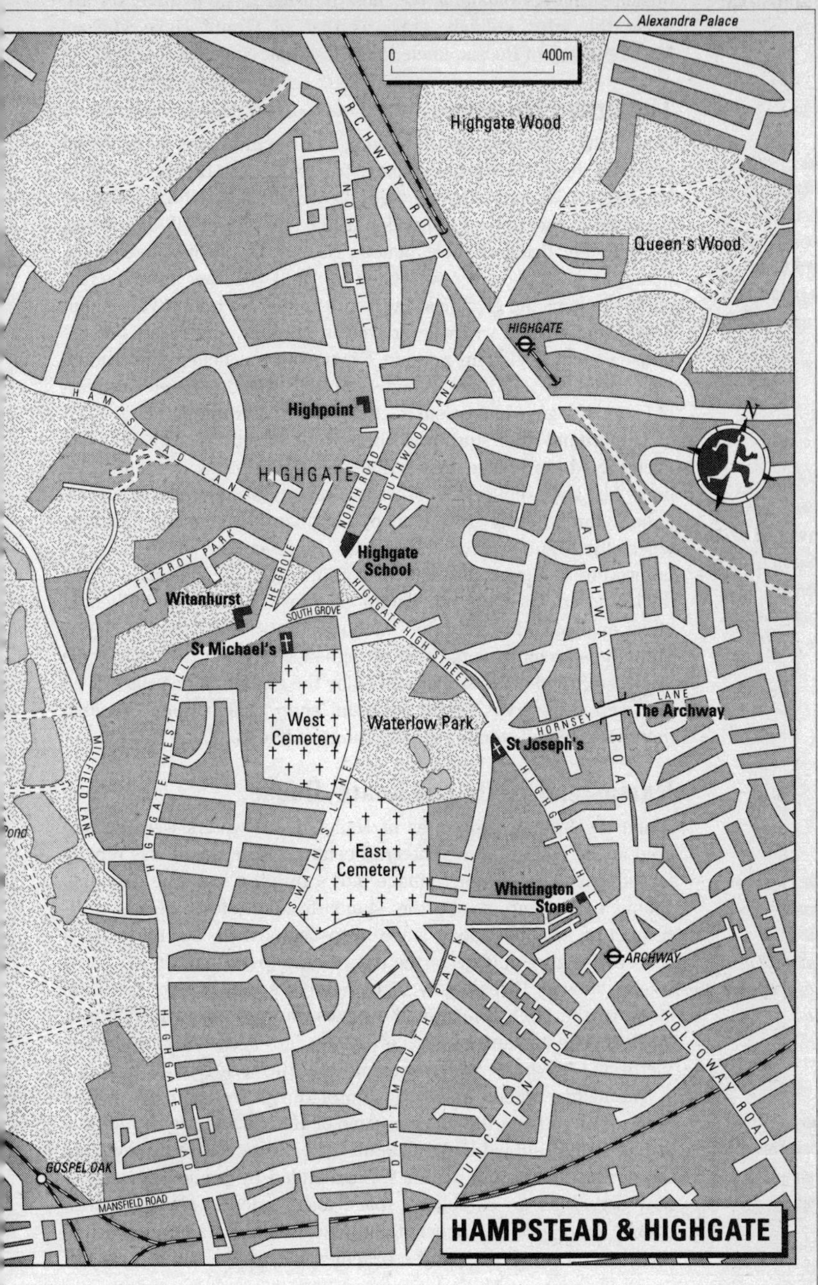
Alexandra Palace
0
400m
Highgate Wood
ARCHWAY ROAD
NORTH HILL
Queen's Wood
HIGHGATE
HAMPSTEAD LANE
Highpoint
SOUTHWOOD LANE
NORTH ROAD
HIGHGATE
Highgate School
FITZROY PARK
THE GROVE
Witanhurst
SOUTH GROVE
HIGHGATE HIGH STREET
St Michael's
ARCHWAY ROAD
HORNSEY LANE
The Archway
West Cemetery
Waterlow Park
St Joseph's
MILLFIELD LANE
HIGHGATE WEST HILL
SWAIN'S LANE
HIGHGATE HILL
Pond
East Cemetery
Whittington Stone
ARCHWAY
HIGHGATE ROAD
DARTMOUTH PARK HILL
JUNCTION ROAD
HOLLOWAY ROAD
GOSPEL OAK
MANSFIELD ROAD
HAMPSTEAD & HIGHGATE

obscure Charles Barritt is the most unusual piece of funerary art, while the most unlikely grave is that of Grand Duke Michael Michaelovitch of Russia, uncle to the last Tsar Nicholas II.

The Freud Museum

The Freud Museum is open Wed–Sun noon–5pm; £2.50; the nearest tube is Finchley Road.

One of the most poignant of London's house museums is the **Freud Museum**, hidden away in the leafy streets of south Hampstead at 20 Maresfield Gardens. Having fled Vienna after the Nazi invasion, Sigmund Freud arrived in London in the summer of 1938, and was immediately Britain's most famous Nazi exile. He had been diagnosed as having cancer way back in 1923 (he was an inveterate cigar-smoker) and given just five years to live. He lasted sixteen, but was a semi-invalid when he arrived in London, and rarely left the house except to visit his pet dog, Chun, who was held in quarantine. On September 21, 1939, Freud's doctor fulfilled their eleven-year-old pact and gave his patient a lethal dose of morphine.

Freud was cremated at the nearby Golders Green crematorium, see p.334.

The ground-floor study and library look exactly as they did when Freud lived here (they are close copies of his study in Vienna), as does his large collection of erotic antiquities and psychiatrist's couch, sumptuously draped in opulent Turkish carpets. Upstairs, where the Freud archive now resides, home movies of the doctor's family life in Vienna are shown continually, and a small room is dedicated to his favourite daughter, Anna, herself an influential child analyst, who lived in the house until her death in 1982. Sigmund's architect son, Ernst, designed a loggia at the back of the house so Freud could sit out and enjoy the garden; it has since been enclosed and serves as the museum shop, which flogs Freudian merchandise and stocks a superb range of books.

Hampstead Wells and Keats' House

The Flask, on Flask Walk, is one of Hampstead's most popular pubs.

When the healing properties of Hampstead's waters were discovered at the end of the seventeenth century, Hampstead was rapidly transformed from a quiet village into a thriving spa. The assembly rooms and pump room, the standard institutions of any self-respecting spa, have long since been demolished, but there are a few scattered reminders of the days of Hampstead Wells, as it was briefly known. Three-penny containers of spring water were sold close to the High Street in the pedestrianized alleyway of **Flask Walk** (hence its name), which opens out into **Well Walk**, where the Victorian Chalybeate Well commemorates the springs.

Burgh House is open Wed–Sun noon–5pm; free.

The nearby Queen Anne mansion of **Burgh House**, on New End Square, dates from the halcyon days of Hampstead Wells, and was at one time occupied by Dr Gibbons, the physician who discovered the spring's medicinal qualities. Surrounded by council housing, it now serves as an exhibition space and a modest museum, with special emphasis on such notable locals as Constable and Keats; there's a nice tea room in the basement. To the north, the cannon

A Hampstead Who's Who

Hampstead has more blue plaques commemorating its residents than any other London borough. Here's a by no means exhaustive selection of Hampstead figures past and present, focusing mainly on writers, artists and politicos. For full details of where everyone lived and when, check out the local history society's pamphlet, available at Hampstead bookshops.

Cecil Beaton in the 1910s
William Blake in the 1820s
Dirk Bogarde born here 1920
Richard Burton in the 1950s
John le Carré in the 1980s & 1990s
Agatha Christie in the 1940s
John Constable in the 1820s
Edward Elgar in the 1910s
Michael Foot in the 1980s & 1990s
Sigmund Freud in the 1930s
Hugh Gaitskell died here in 1963
John Galsworthy in the 1920s
Charles de Gaulle during World War II
Boy George in the 1980s & 1990s
Barbara Hepworth in the 1920s & 1930s
Gerard Manley Hopkins in the 1850s
Barry Humphries in the 1980s
John Keats in the 1820s
Oskar Kokoschka during World War II
Ramsey MacDonald in the 1920s & 1930s
A. A. Milne in the 1880s
Piet Mondrian in the 1930s
Henry Moore in the 1930s
Paul Nash in the 1930s
Ben Nicholson in the 1930s
George Orwell in the 1930s & 1940s
Peter O'Toole in the 1980s
Peter Sellers in the 1960s
Walter Sickert in the 1880s
Edith Sitwell in the 1960s
Robert Louis Stevenson in the 1870s
Twiggy in the 1960s
Sid Vicious & Johnny Rotten in the 1970s

bollards gave their name to Cannon Place and **Cannon Hall**, an early eighteenth-century house where the writer Daphne du Maurier spent her childhood. The house was used as a courtroom by the local magistrates for many years, hence the bizarre parish lock-up in the east wall of the grounds on Cannon Lane, used as a temporary prison until the 1830s.

Hampstead's most lustrous figure is celebrated at **Keats' House**, an elegant, whitewashed Regency double villa on Keats Grove, five minutes' walk southeast of Burgh House. The consumptive poet moved here in 1818 shortly after his brother Tom had died of the same illness. Inspired by the peacefulness of Hampstead and by his passion for girl-next-door Fanny Brawne (whose house is also part of the museum), Keats wrote some of his most famous works here, before leaving for Rome, where he died in 1821. In the pretty front garden, as you approach the house, you pass a deeply uninspiring plum tree which replaces a much larger specimen in whose shade

Keats' House is open Mon–Fri 2–6pm, Sat 10am–5pm, Sun 2–5pm; free.

Keats is said to have sat for two or three hours before composing *Ode to a Nightingale*. The neat, rather staid interior contains books and letters, an anatomical notebook from Keats' days as a medical student at Guy's hospital, Fanny's engagement ring and the four-poster bed in which the poet first coughed up blood, confiding to his companion, Charles Brown, "that drop of blood is my death warrant".

Hampstead Heath

The nearest tubes are Hampstead and Highgate.

Hampstead Heath, north London's "green lung", is the city's most enjoyable public park. Though it may not have much of its original heathland left, it packs in a wonderful variety of bucolic scenery from the formal gardens of The Hill and rolling green pastures of Parliament Hill to the dense woodland of West Heath and the landscaped grounds of Kenwood. As it is, the Heath was lucky to survive the nineteenth century intact, for it endured more than forty years of campaigning by the Lord of the Manor, Sir Thomas Maryon Wilson, who introduced no fewer than fifteen parliamentary bills in an attempt to build over it. It wasn't until after Wilson's death in 1871 that 220 acres of the Heath passed into public ownership. The Heath now covers over 800 acres and is currently in the relatively safe hands of the Corporation of London.

Parliament Hill and the Ponds

If you're in London for Guy Fawkes night (Nov 5), Parliament Hill is one of the best locations to watch the fireworks.

Parliament Hill, the Heath's southernmost ridge, is perhaps better known as Kite Hill, since this is north London's premier spot for kite-flying, especially busy at weekends when some serious equipment takes to the air. The parliamentary connection is explained in various ways by historians, so take your pick: a Saxon parliament is thought to have met here; Guy Fawkes and his cronies are said to have gathered here with the hope of watching the Houses of Parliament burn; the Parliamentarians placed their cannon here during the Civil War, to defend London against the Royalists; and the Middlesex parliamentary elections took place here in the seventeenth century. Whatever the reason for the name, the view over London is rivalled only by the one from Kenwood (see below).

The Heath is the source of several of London's lost rivers – the Tyburn, Westbourne and Fleet – and home to some twenty-eight natural ponds, of which the most extensive are the eight **Highgate & Kenwood Ponds**, arranged in steps along a shallow valley on the eastern edge of the Heath. The Highgate Men's Pond (daily 7am–dusk; free), second from the bottom, is a secluded sylvan spot, popular with nudists, including a strong gay contingent; two ponds up is the Kenwood Ladies Pond (times as above), with enough foliage to provide relaxed topless bathing, and similarly popular with lesbians. The Corporation is none too happy with either pond's reputation, but both are preferable to the Mixed Bathing Pond on the Hampstead side of the Heath.

To the Vale of Health

To the northwest of Parliament Hill is a fenced-off tumulus known as **Boudicca's Mound**, where, according to tradition, Queen Boudicca (Boadicea) was buried after she and 10,000 other Brits had been massacred at Battle Bridge (modern-day King's Cross). Due west lies the picturesque **Viaduct Pond**, named after the pond's red-brick bridge, also known as Wilson's Folly. It was built as part of Sir Thomas Maryon Wilson's abortive plans to drive an access road through the middle of the Heath to his projected estate of twenty-eight villas.

Below, to the west, beyond the Viaduct Pond, an isolated network of streets nestles in the **Vale of Health**, a euphemistic name tag for what was, in fact, a malarial swamp until the late eighteenth century. Literary lion Leigh Hunt moved to this quiet backwater in 1816, after serving a two-year prison sentence for libel, having called the Prince Regent "a fat Adonis of fifty", among other things. Hunt was instrumental in persuading Keats to give up medicine for poetry, and introduced him to Shelley, Byron and other members of his literary circle. Other artistic residents have included Indian poet and Nobel Prize winner, Rabindranath Tagore, who lived here in 1912, and Stanley Spencer, who stayed here with the Carline family and married their daughter Hilda in the 1920s. D. H. Lawrence spent a brief, unhappy period here in 1915: in September of that year his novel *The Rainbow* was banned for obscenity and by December Lawrence and his wife, Frieda von Richthofen, whose German origin was causing the couple immense problems with the authorities, had resolved to leave the country.

West of Spaniards Road

The section of the Heath to the northwest of the Vale of Health misses out on the wonderful views of Parliament Hill and Kenwood, but makes up for it with some of the Heath's best-kept secrets. The place to start is the busy road junction around **Whitestone Pond**, which marks the highest point in north London (440ft). This former horse pond is overlooked by the cream-coloured weatherboarding and castellations of *Jack Straw's Castle*, a pub which, despite appearances, was entirely rebuilt in the 1960s.

To the west of Whitestone Pond is **West Heath**, a densely wooded, boggy area with a thick canopy of deciduous trees, sloping down towards Childs Hill; it is a major cruising area for London gays. A track leads northwest from *Jack Straw's Castle* across West Heath to the more formal landscaped gardens of **Golders Hill Park**. The central section of the park is taken up by animal enclosures containing pygmy goats and fallow deer, and a series of aviaries, home to flamingos, cranes and other exotic birds; to the north, closer to the entrance, is a beautiful, walled garden and pond. Beside the park entrance on North End Road stands **Ivy House**, where the great Russian ballerina Anna Pavlova, lived from 1912 until her death in 1931. It now houses the College of Speech and Drama, which contains a small **Pavlova Memorial Museum** of memorabilia.

The nearest tube is Golders Green.

The Pavlova Memorial is open Sat 2–6pm; free.

Back up North End Road, past the *Old Bull & Bush* pub, there's a sign leading off to the west to **The Hill Garden**, the Heath's most secretive and romantic little gem. It was built as an extension to the grounds of nearby Hill House (now the defunct Inverforth Hospital), and the formal gardens eventually became public property in 1960. Their most startling features are the eccentric balustraded terraces, which look out over West Heath and west to Harrow-on-the Hill. All along the L-shaped terrace Doric columns support a ruinous pergola, which the Corporation is in the process of restoring, along with the bridge which Lord Lever (who bought the house in 1906) had to build over the public footpath in order to link his two gardens.

On the other side of North End Road, a rough track curves its way through another secluded patch of woodland. Halfway along you'll come across a stranded red-brick archway that leads through into **Pitt's Garden**, originally the grounds of Pitt House (destroyed in the last war), home of eighteenth-century statesman William Pitt the Elder. Pitt retreated here on several occasions, most famously in 1767, when "gout in the head", as his bouts of insanity were euphemistically called, rendered him catatonic, upon which he shut himself away and received meals through a hatch.

Past the archway, the track turns into North End Avenue, which joins up with North End, which in turn backs onto Hampstead's sole remaining farmstead, the weatherboarded seventeenth-century **Wyldes Farm**. In the first decade of this century, the adjacent farmland was bought from Eton College by Henrietta Barnett to provide land for Hampstead Garden Suburb (p.333) and also for an eighty-acre addition to the Heath, now known as the **Heath Extension**. Its origins as agricultural pastureland are evident in the surviving hedgerow boundaries, and the Corporation is considering the practicalities of re-introducing sheep, last seen here in the 1930s.

Spaniards Road runs along the eastern edge of **Sandy Heath**, a triangle of oak and beech woodland to the south of the Extension. At the northern end of Spaniards Road, cars struggle to avoid oncoming traffic as the road squeezes between the old tollhouse and the **Spaniards Inn**, an eighteenth-century coaching inn. The highwayman Dick Turpin is thought to have used this as a hiding-place and vantage point for sizing up the coaches leaving town.

Kenwood House

Kenwood House is open April–Sept daily 10am–6pm; Oct–March closes 4pm; EH; free.

The Heath's most celebrated sight is **Kenwood House**, which is most enjoyably approached via the winding path from the Highgate Ponds. Set in its own magnificently landscaped grounds, the house is seventeenth-century, but was later remodelled by Robert Adam for the Earl of Mansfield, Attorney-General, Lord Chief Justice and the most powerful jurist in the country. Mansfield, who had sent 102 people to the gallows and sentenced another 448 to transportation, was a deeply unpopular character and one of the prime targets of the Gordon rioters, who ransacked his Bloomsbury house. A crowd also made their way towards Kenwood, but they were waylaid by the canny landlord of the nearby *Spaniards Inn* (an ex-butler of Mansfield's), who plied them with free drink until soldiers arrived to disperse the mob.

Thanks to Kenwood's last private owner, the Earl of Iveagh (head of the Guinness family), the house is now open to the public and home to the **Iveagh Bequest**, a collection of seventeenth- and eighteenth-century art from the English, Dutch and French schools. You pass a whimsical Reynolds painting, *Venus Chiding Cupid for Learning to Cast Accounts*, and some good examples of Boucher's flirtatious pastoral scenes, before coming to the Dining Room, where a superb Rembrandt self-portrait shares space with Franz Hals' *Man with a Cane* and Vermeer's delicate *Guitar Player*. Works by Gainsborough, including the diaphanous *Countess Howe*, caught up in a bold, almost abstract landscape, are on show in the Music Room, alongside canvases by his more robust contemporary, Joshua Reynolds.

Of the house's period interiors, the most spectacular is Adam's sky-blue and gold **Library**, its book-filled apses separated from the central entertaining area by paired columns. The *pièce de resistance* is a tunnel-vaulted ceiling, decorated by Antonio Zucchi, who fell in love with and married Kenwood's other ceiling painter, Angelica Kauffmann. Adam was also responsible for landscaping the grounds of Kenwood, creating views across the Heath to St Paul's Cathedral and the Palace of Westminster. Trees now obscure these vistas, and a debate is raging over whether or not to restore Adam's views by axing some trees.

For ticket details for the Kenwood concerts, see p.487.

Kenwood has splendid gardens of azaleas and rhododendrons to the west, and a huge grassy amphitheatre to the south, which slopes down to a lake where outdoor **classical concerts** are held on summer evenings (Handel's *Fireworks Music* has a regular spot on July 4). The grassy lawn is also a favourite picnic spot (and a good place to catch the afternoon reheasals for free), while the provisionless can head for the excellent coach house café.

The Caravan is open Sat & Sun April–Sept 12.30–5.40pm; Oct–March 11am–3.45pm; free.

A last and little-known attraction, hidden in a purpose-built hut to the northeast of Kenwood House, is the Romany-style **Buckland Caravan**, last used in the 1920s and now beautifully restored. From the nearby sheltered viewpoint you'll get one of the finest views across the Heath to the City and West End, with the Crystal Palace TV tower on the horizon.

Highgate

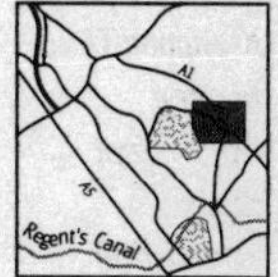

Northeast of the Heath, and fractionally lower than Hampstead (appearances notwithstanding), **Highgate** lacks the literary cachet of Hampstead, but makes up for it with London's most famous cemetery, resting place of Karl Marx. It also retains more of its village origins, especially around **The Grove**, Highgate's finest row of houses. Set back from the road in pairs overlooking the village green, they date as far back as 1685 and have been occupied by

The nearest tube is Highgate.

such luminaries as J. B. Priestley and Yehudi Menuhin. The most famous one-time resident, however, is Samuel Taylor Coleridge, who lived at no. 3 from 1819, with a certain Dr Gillman and his wife. With Gillman's help, Coleridge reduced his dosage of opium and enjoyed the healthiest, if not the happiest, period of his life.

Coleridge was initially buried in the local college chapel, but in 1961 his remains were re-buried in **St Michael's Church**, in South Grove. Its spire is a landmark but St Michael's is much less interesting architecturally than the grandiose late seventeenth-century Old Hall next door, or the two tiny ramshackle cottages opposite, which were built for the servants of one of the luxurious mansions which once characterized Highgate. Arundel House, which stood on the site of the Old Hall, was where Sir Francis Bacon, the seventeenth-century philosopher and statesman, is thought to have died, having caught a chill while trying to stuff a chicken full of ice during an early experiment in refrigeration.

One of Highgate's best pubs, The Flask, is on South Grove.

North and south of the High Street

Highgate gets its name from the tollgate – the highest in London and the oldest in the country – which stood where the *Gate House* pub now stands on **Highgate High Street**. The High Street itself, though lined with swanky Georgian shops, is marred by heavy traffic, as is its northern extension, North Road.

If you persevere with North Road, you'll pass **Highgate School**, founded in 1565 for the local poor but long established as an exclusive fee-paying public school, housed in suitably impressive Victorian buildings. Famous alumni, known as Cholmeleians after the founder, include Gerard Manley Hopkins, John Betjeman and Clive Sinclair, creator of the first mass-produced pocket calculator. Further on up North Road, on your left, are the whitewashed high-rises of **Highpoint 1 and 2**, seminal essays in modernist architecture designed by Lubetkin and his Tecton partnership in the late 1930s. The caryatids that support the entrance to Highpoint 2 are Lubetkin's little joke at the expense of his anti-modernist critics.

In the other direction, Highgate High Street slopes down into **Highgate Hill**, with still more amazing views down towards the City. The steep gradient of Highgate Hill caused enormous problems for horse-drawn vehicles, and in 1813 a tunnel was attempted through neighbouring Hornsey. It collapsed and was replaced by a stone viaduct designed by Nash, in its turn usurped by the current cast-iron **Archway** on Hornsey Lane, a favourite spot for suicide attempts. For the record, you'll find the **Whittington Stone**, which marks the spot where Dick Whittington miraculously heard the Bow Bells chime, towards the bottom of Highgate Hill (see p.192 for more on Whittington).

The other ecclesiastical landmark in Highgate is the copper dome of "Holy Joe", the Roman Catholic Church which stands on

Highgate Hill beside **Waterlow Park**. The park is named after Sir Sydney Waterlow, who donated it in 1889 as "a garden for the gardenless", and also bequeathed Lauderdale House, a much-altered sixteenth-century building which is thought to have been occupied at one time by Nell Gwynn and her infant son. The house, which backs onto the park, now puts on children's shows and other events, and contains a fine café and restaurant which spills out onto its western terraced gardens. The park itself, occupying a dramatic sloping site, is an amalgamation of several house gardens, and is one London's finest landscaped parks, providing a through route to Highgate Cemetery.

Highgate Cemetery

Ranged on both sides of Swain's Lane and receiving far more visitors than Highgate itself, **Highgate Cemetery** is London's most famous graveyard. Opened in 1839, it quickly became the preferred resting place of wealthy Victorian families, who could rub shoulders here with numerous intellectuals and artists. As long as prime plots were available, business was good and the cemetery could afford to employ as many as 28 gardeners to beautify the place. But as the cemetery filled, funds dried up and the whole place fell prey to vandals. In 1975, the old (west) cemetery was closed completely, and taken under the wing of the Friends of Highgate Cemetery. Unfortunately, the Friends see all visitors as potential vandals, allowing no unsupervised wandering – the chief joy of visiting graveyards – in this section, and they charge entry even to the still-functioning east cemetery.

West Cemetery

The old, overgrown **West Cemetery** is the ultimate Hammer-horror graveyard, and one of London's most impressive sights, with its huge vaults and stunning array of statuary. It is a shame that you have to follow a tour around it, but even so it is not to be missed, and it must be said that things were pretty seedy before the Friends took over. Wandering through you were quite likely to come across an open tomb, splashed with ketchup.

The West Cemetery is open on guided tours only Mon–Fri noon, 2pm & 3pm, Sat & Sun on the hour 10am–4pm; £3.

Among the more famous names here are Charles Chubb (of the locks), Charles Cruft (of the Dog Show), Dickens' estranged wife, and Michael Faraday, who as a member of the obscure Sandemanian sect is buried along the unconsecrated north wall. There's no guarantee your tour will cover these tombs, but you're more than likely to be shown the **Rossetti family tomb**, initiated on the death of Gabriel Rossetti, professor of Italian at King's College, London. Next in the family vault was Elizabeth Siddell, the pre-Raphaelites' favourite model and wife of Rossetti's artistic son, Dante Gabriel, who buried the only copy of his many love poems along with her. Seven years later he changed his mind and had the poems exhumed and published. The poet Christina Rossetti, Dante's sister, is also buried in the vault.

The cemetery's spookiest section is around **Egyptian Avenue**, entered through an ivy-covered portal flanked by pillars and obelisks, known as the "Gateway to the City of the Dead". Despite the restrictions of access, the tomb of the lesbian novelist Radclyffe Hall is regularly strewn with flowers and tributes (her lover, Mabel Batten is also buried here). The avenue, in turn, leads to the Circle of Lebanon, above which are the **Terrace Catacombs**, with views out across the cemetery and far beyond. Gathered together here are the most ostentatious mausoleums, some of which accommodate up to fifteen coffins; the largest – based on the tomb of Mausolus at Halicarnassos – is that of Julius Beer, one-time owner of *The Observer* newspaper.

Bram Stoker was cremated at Golders Green crematorium, *see p.334.*

This section of the cemetery provided inspiration for Bram Stoker's *Dracula*, and was at the centre of a series of bizarre incidents in the early 1970s. Graves were smashed open, cadavers strewn about, and the High Priest of the British Occult Society, Allan Farrant, was arrested here, armed with a stake and crucifix with which he hoped to destroy "the Highgate Vampire". He was eventually sentenced to four years' imprisonment, after being found guilty of damaging graves, interfering with corpses and sending death-spell dolls to two policemen.

The East Cemetery is open April–Sept daily 10am–5pm; Oct–March closes 4pm; £1.

East Cemetery

What the **East Cemetery** lacks in atmosphere is part compensated for by the fact that you can wander at will through its maze of circuitous paths. The most publicized occupant is, of course, **Karl Marx**, who spent more than half his life in London, much of it in bourgeois Hampstead. Marx himself asked for a plain and simple grave topped by a headstone, but by 1954 the Communist movement decided to move his grave to a more prominent position and erect the vulgar bronze bust which now surmounts a granite plinth bearing the words "Workers of all lands, unite", from the *Communist Manifesto*. He has been visited here by Krushchev, Brezhnev and just about every post-war Communist leader.

Buried along with Marx are his grandson, wife and housekeeper, Helene Delmuth, whom he got pregnant. Engels accepted paternity to avoid a scandal and only told Marx's daughter, Eleanor, on his deathbed in 1895. Eleanor committed suicide a few years later after discovering her common-law husband had secretly married someone else. Her ashes were put in the family vault in 1954, having been seized from the Communist Party headquarters in London by the police in 1921.

Lesser-known Communists such as Yusef Mohamed Dadoo, chairman of the South African Communist Party until his death in 1983, cluster around Marx. Not far away is **George Eliot**'s grave, and behind it that of her lover, George Henry Lewes.

Golders Green and Hendon

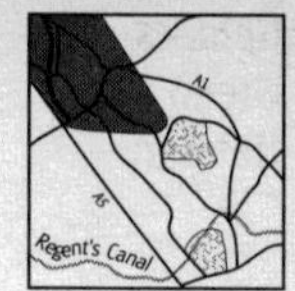

If the East End is the spiritual home of working-class Jews, **Golders Green**, to the northwest of Hampstead, is its middle-class equivalent. Less than a hundred years ago this whole area was open countryside but, like much of suburbia, it was transformed overnight by the arrival of the tube in 1907. Before and after World War II, the area was heavily colonized by Jews moving out of the old East End ghetto around Spitalfields or fleeing as refugees from Europe in the wake of the Nazis. Nowadays, Golders Green is probably the most distinctively Jewish area in London. The Orthodox community has a strong presence here: *yarmulkas* (skull-caps) are commonplace, and there's a profusion of kosher shops beyond the railway bridge on Golders Green Road, at their busiest on Sundays.

The nearest tube is Golders Green.

To the north of Golders Green, on the other side of the North Circular, the **Museum of Jewish Life**, housed within the Sternberg Centre for Judaism on East End Road, has a permanent exhibition on the history of Jews in this country, and puts on exceptionally good temporary shows on Jewish communities and issues around the world. There's an excellent Jewish bookshop within the centre. (Note that there is also a Jewish Museum in Camden, see p.310).

The museum is open Mon–Thurs 10.30am–5pm, closes 4.30pm Sun; free.

Hampstead Garden Suburb

Much of Golders Green is architecturally bland, the one exception being **Hampstead Garden Suburb**, begun in 1907 to the north of the Hamsptead Heath Extension. This model housing development was a product of the utopian dream of Henrietta Barnett, wife of the philanthropist who established Toynbee Hall in the East End (p.228). In the Barnetts' view, the only long-term solution to social reform was to create a mixed social environment where "the poor shall teach the rich, and the rich, let us hope, shall help the poor to help themselves". Yet from the start the suburb was socially segregated, with the modest artisan dwellings to the north, the middle-class houses to the west, and the wealthiest villas overlooking the Heath to the south. As a social experiment it was a failure – the area has remained a thoroughly middle-class ghetto – but as a blueprint for suburban estates it has been enormously influential.

The nearest tube is Golders Green, whence it's a fair walk.

The formal entrance to the suburb is the striking Arts and Crafts gateway of shops and flats on Finchley Road; from here ivy-strewn houses, each with its own garden encased in privet hedges, fan out eastwards along tree-lined avenues towards the deliberately "non-commercial" **Central Square**, laid out by Lutyens in a style he dubbed "Wren-aissance". (Pubs, shops, cinemas and all commercial buildings were and are still excluded from the suburb.) Lutyens also designed the square's twin churches: the Nonconformist Free

Church, sporting an octagonal dome, and the Anglican St Jude's, the finer of the two with its steeply pitched roof and spire.

East of the central green is the Lutyens designed **Institute**, now occupied by an adult education centre and Henrietta Barnett girls' school. From the square, you could walk south along cherry tree-lined Heathgate, which ends at the Heath Extension (p.328).

Golders Green Crematorium and Jewish Cemetery

Golders Green crematorium is open daily 9am–5pm.

To the east of Hampstead Garden Suburb, down Meadway and then Hoop Lane, is the **Golders Green Crematorium**, where over 250,000 Londoners have been cremated since 1902. More famous names have been scattered over the crematorium's unromantically named Dispersal Area than have been buried at any single graveyard: Anna Pavlova, T. S. Eliot, Sean O'Casey, Kipling, Shaw, Alexander Fleming, Vaughan Williams, Peter Sellers, Marc Bolan, Bram Stoker and Freud, to name but a few. Finding a particular memorial plaque among this complex of serene red-brick chapels and arcades is no easy task, and if you're keen to trace someone or wish to visit one of the columbaria, you should enquire at the office in the main courtyard. The Ernst George Columbarium is where you'll find the ashes of Anna Pavlova sealed in an urn draped with a pair of her pink ballet shoes, while Freud and his wife, Martha, are contained within one of Freud's favourite Greek urns in an adjacent room.

The cemetery is open daily except Saturday 8.30am–5pm or dusk.

On the opposite side of Hoop Lane is a **Jewish Cemetery**, founded in 1895 before the area was built up. The eastern section, to your right, is for Orthodox Sephardic Jews, whose tombs are traditionally laid flat with the deceased's feet pointing towards Jerusalem. To the left are the upright headstones of Reform Jews including the great cellist Jacqueline du Pré, who died tragically young of multiple sclerosis, and Lord Hoare-Belisha, Minister of Transport in the 1930s, who gave his name to "Belisha beacons" (the yellow flashing globes at pedestrian crossings).

The RAF Museum

The RAF Museum is open daily 10am–6pm; £5.20. The nearest tube is Colindale.

One of the most impressive collection of historic aircraft in the world is lodged at the **RAF Museum**, in a god-forsaken part of Hendon, beside the M1 motorway. In the **Main Aircraft Hall** you're greeted by a Harrier Jump Jet, the world's first vertical take-off and landing aircraft, labelled with a text extolling its role in the Falklands War. Starkly juxtaposed alongside such colossal post-war jets, and perhaps the most famous British plane of all time, the Spitfire, are flimsy biplanes from World War I and even an early triplane.

The most chilling section is the adjacent **Bomber Command Hall**, which houses Halifax and Wellington bombers, and the clinically white Valiant, the first British aircraft to carry thermonuclear bombs. To the museum's credit, the assessment of Bomber Command's wartime policy of blanket-bombing Germany into submission gives both sides of the argument. The video of the so-called "precision bombing" conducted during the Gulf War is given rather less even-handed treatment. Two other exhibits deserve special mention: the crumbling carcass of a Halifax bomber, recovered from the bottom of a Norwegian fjord, and one of the Lancaster bombers involved in Operation Upkeep, the mission immortalized in the film *The Dambusters*.

One of the most interesting sections of the museum, often overlooked, is the **Display Galleries** ranged around the edge of the Main Aircraft hall, which contain an art gallery and an exhibition on the history of flight, accompanied by replicas of some of the death-traps in which the first aviators risked their lives. Across the car park is the **Battle of Britain Hall**, an unashamedly jingoistic display of the Hurricanes and Heinkels which fought for control of the sky during the autumn of 1940.

Alexandra Palace and Walthamstow

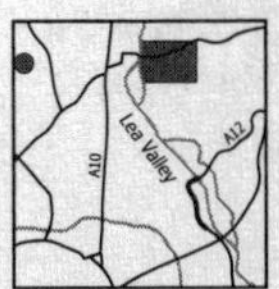

To the north of Highgate tube stretch the last two remaining slices of the Great Forest of Middlesex; **Highgate Wood**, which has an excellent café at its heart, overlooking a cricket pitch, and **Queen's Wood**, on the other side of Muswell Hill Road, which has kept rather more of its ancient woodland character. From either wood, it's a short distance to the Highgate end of the wonderful **Parkland Walk**, a disused railway line which now makes it possible to walk all the way from Highgate to the north London landmark of Alexandra Palace – a distance of around one and a half miles – without touching tarmac.

The nearest train station is Alexandra Palace, accessible from King's Cross.

Alexandra Palace

Built in 1873 on the commanding heights of Muswell Hill, **Alexandra Palace** is now the only surviving example of a Victorian "People's Palace", since its more famous rival, Crystal Palace, burned down in 1936. However, the history of "Ally Pally" is almost as tragic as that of Crystal Palace. Sixteen days after the official opening, the whole place burnt down, and despite being rebuilt within two years and boasting a theatre, a reading room, an exhibition hall and a concert room with one of the largest organs in the world, it was a commercial failure. During World War I more than 17,000 German POWs passed through its gates, and in 1936 the world's first television transmission took place here.

After another devastating fire in 1980 the palace was again rebuilt – only time will tell whether the latest round of events, exhibitions and spectacles will finally turn this splendid Victorian edifice into a profit-making venture, or whether Haringey council will end up moving in and using the place – the current reserve plan.

Walthamstow

The nearest tube is Walthamstow Central.

The northeastern suburb of **Walthamstow**, east of the River Lee, is on few tourists' itineraries, but it's somewhere you could easily spend an afternoon, especially if you've an interest in the work of William Morris, who was born here in 1834. In addition, if you come on a Thursday, Friday or Saturday, you can also visit **Walthamstow Market**, which claims to be the longest street market in the country, stretching for well over a mile along the old High Street.

The Vestry House Museum is open Mon–Fri 10am–1pm & 2–5.30pm, Sat closes 5pm; free.

From the tube, head east down Saint Mary Road, then Church End, which will take you to the heart of the old village conservation area, a surprising oasis of calm. On your right as you reach the end of Church End is the **Vestry House Museum**, built in 1730 and at one time the village workhouse. Later on, it became the police station, and a reconstructed police cell from 1861 is one of the museum's chief exhibits. The prize possession, however, is the tiny Bremer Car, Britain's first-ever car, designed in 1894 by local engineer Fred Bremer. Victorian times are comprehensively covered, but there's nothing on the area's post-war immigrants, nor yet any mention of the district's most famous sons, pop group East 17, who take their name from the area postcode. The other point of interest here is the fifteenth-century half-timbered **Ancient House**, a short walk up Church Lane.

Walthamstow's two other sights are a five-minute walk north past the concrete-encased church of St Mary's, and up The Grove/Hurst Road. First is the local **Civic Centre**, set back from Forest Road around a huge open courtyard; designed in an unusual Scandinavian style in the 1930s, it's London's grandest town hall complex. There's a touch of Stalinism about the severe classicism of the centre's central portico and in the exhortation above the adjacent Assembly Hall: "Fellowship is life and the lack of fellowship is death". Sadly, construction of the law courts which would have completed the ensemble was interrupted by the war, but this remains one of the most startling public buildings in London.

William Morris House

The William Morris House is open Tues–Sat 10am–1pm & 2–5pm & first Sun of month 10am–noon & 2–5pm; £2.

To the west of the Civic Centre, along Forest Road, stands the Georgian mansion now known as the **William Morris House**, which became the Morris family home in 1848 after the death of William Morris' father, a successful businessman in the City. Poet, artist, designer and socialist, William Morris was one of the most fascinating characters of Victorian London. He was closely associated with both the Pre-Raphaelite and Arts and Crafts movements, and went on to set up a company whose work covered all areas of applied art: glasswork, tiles, metalwork, curtains, wallpaper, furniture, calligraphy, carpets and book illumination.

The ground floor of the museum contains a modest array of every kind of work with which Morris got involved, while the upstairs rooms concentrate on his later followers and the Pre-Raphaelites – including a room of works by Burne-Jones, Holman Hunt and Rossetti. There are passing references to Morris' stormy personal life: he married Jane Burden, a working-class girl whom Rossetti picked up at the theatre in Oxford and later reclaimed as his lover. Morris also became one of the leading political figures of his day, active in the Socialist League with Eleanor Marx, and publishing several utopian tracts, most famously *News From Nowhere*, which you can buy in the bookshop for the tube journey home.

Chapter 11

Southeast London: out to Greenwich and beyond

Aside from the Royal Palace at Greenwich and the Royal Dockyards at Deptford and Woolwich, **SOUTHEAST LONDON** was a confirmed part of rural Kent until the late eighteenth century. Now largely built-up into a patchwork of Victorian terraces, one area stands head and shoulders above all the others in terms of sightseeing, and that is **Greenwich**, once home to the Tudor court. Its nautical associations are trumpeted by the likes of the Cutty Sark and the National Maritime Museum; its architecture, especially the Royal Naval College and the Queen's House, is some of the finest on the river; and its observatory is renowned throughout the world.

Boats run to Greenwich from Charing Cross and Westminster – one of the most popular and enjoyable river trips.

The rest of this chapter is really just a hotpotch of scattered suburban sights, where, given the distances involved and the dire lack of tube lines south of the river, it pays to be selective. A few sights do, however, stand out: **Dulwich**, whose public art gallery is even older than the National Gallery, and, way out on the very edge of London, the **Chislehurst Caves**.

Our accounts follow a roughly easterly and southerly direction, beginning with **Brixton** – south London's liveliest neighbourhood, with its Caribbean community and market – which pedants might claim is more southwest than southeast, though its borders actually span both postal districts.

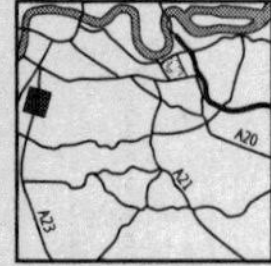

Brixton

Brixton is a classic Victorian suburb, transformed from open fields into bricks and mortar in a couple of decades following the arrival of the railways in the 1860s. The viaducts still dominate the landscape of central Brixton, with shops and arcades hidden under their arches, but it's the West Indian community, who arrived here in the 1950s and 1960s, who now define the character of the place – Notting Hill may have the Carnival but it's Brixton that has the most

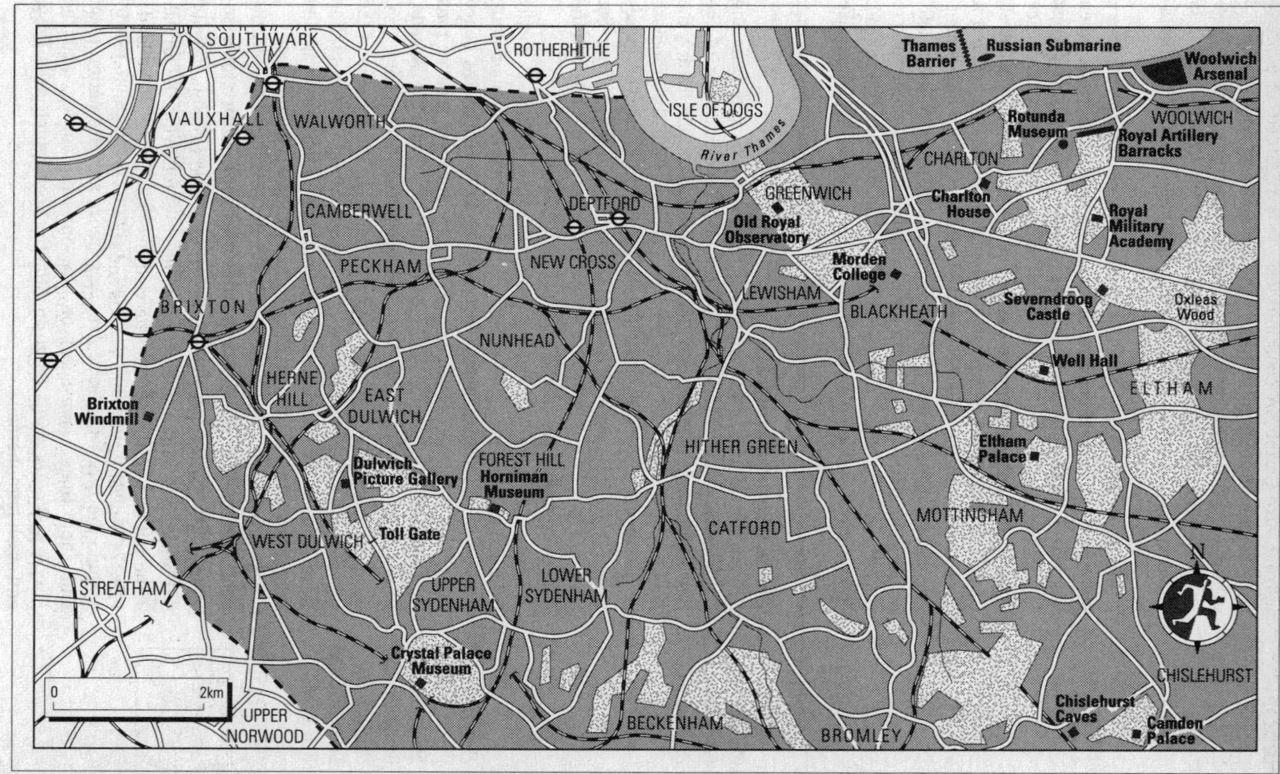

SOUTHWARK
ROTHERHITHE
ISLE OF DOGS
River Thames
Thames Barrier
Russian Submarine
Woolwich Arsenal
VAUXHALL
WALWORTH
Rotunda Museum
WOOLWICH
Royal Artillery Barracks
CHARLTON
GREENWICH
Charlton House
CAMBERWELL
DEPTFORD
Old Royal Observatory
Royal Military Academy
PECKHAM
NEW CROSS
Morden College
LEWISHAM
BLACKHEATH
Severndroog Castle
Oxleas Wood
BRIXTON
NUNHEAD
Well Hall
ELTHAM
HERNE HILL
EAST DULWICH
Brixton Windmill
HITHER GREEN
Eltham Palace
Dulwich Picture Gallery
FOREST HILL
Horniman Museum
MOTTINGHAM
CATFORD
WEST DULWICH
Toll Gate
N
UPPER SYDENHAM
LOWER SYDENHAM
STREATHAM
Crystal Palace Museum
CHISLEHURST
0
2km
UPPER NORWOOD
BECKENHAM
BROMLEY
Chislehurst Caves
Camden Palace

upfront Afro-Caribbean consciousness. It is regarded as a pretty cool neighbourhood by a large slice of white Londoners, too – youthful, media types, who like a bit of street grit in their lives. Despite popular perceptions of it as a black ghetto, the area is in fact seventy percent white, and distinctly middle class and respectable over towards Streatham.

For those who don't know the place, however, Brixton is often a bit feared, through memories of the 1981 and 1985 riots, when tensions between the police and the locals (not only the West Indians) came to a head. Various government initiatives have since attempted and failed to get to the root of the discontent – the latest, City Challenge, looks set to restore the fabric of Brixton, even if it doesn't address the real problems of racism and unemployment. The council, through much of the 1970s and 80s, had a "loony left" image second to none in Britain, which makes it all the more odd to reflect that John Major, the current Prime Minister, is a Brixton lad. He spent his childhood on Coldharbour Lane, where his father, like many other music hall and circus performers, had lodgings.

The market and around

The nearest tube station is Brixton.

Brixton's main axis is the junction of Brixton Road, Acre Lane and Coldharbour Lane, overlooked by the slender clocktower of the Edwardian town hall, the dinky neo-Renaissance public library, the *Ritzy* cinema, and the church of St Matthew, with its grandiose Doric portico. The commercial lifeblood of Brixton, however, pulses most strongly through **Brixton Market** (Mon, Tues & Thur–Sat 8am–5.30pm, Wed 8am–1pm), whose stalls spread out through the warren of streets and arcades east of Brixton Road.

Franco's pizza place in the Market Row arcade is one of the finest in London; closed Wed & Sun.

Electric Avenue, which runs behind the tube station, is solidly fruit and veg (most of it West Indian), and the market's main drag. It was one of the first London streets to be lit by electricity, hence the name. A network of appealingly shabby inter-war arcades runs parallel with the avenue, culminating in the **Granville Arcade**, where you can buy bold African and Asian fabrics, jewellery, fish, meat, amazing wigs and much more besides. On the far side of the railways tracks, the market veers eastwards along Brixton Station Road, with stalls flogging cheap second-hand clothes to rap and reggae soundtracks from *Fe Real Muzic*. Brixton is a loud place.

The crossroads of Atlantic Road and Coldharbour Lane, to the southeast of the market, marks the beginning of Brixton's so-called "**Front Line**", which, with nearby Railton Road, was the epicentre of the 1981 riots, and still has a drug-dealing reputation. The *Atlantic* pub on the corner, currently boarded up, has an especially mean reputation. Other Brixton institutions nearby include the *Black Cultural Archives* (more an information point and shop than a museum) on the opposite corner, and the *People's Weatherman Shop* on Atlantic Road which sells Rasta and stash paraphernalia.

Dulwich and Crystal Palace

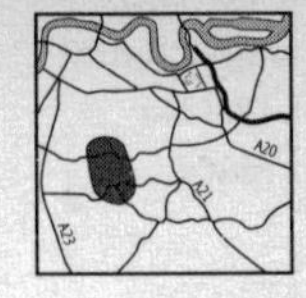

Dulwich Village is just two stops from Brixton on the (overland) railway, but light years away in every other respect. This affluent, middle-class enclave is one of southeast London's prettier patches, cut off from most of its suburban neighbours by parkland, playing fields, woods and golfing fairways. The leafy streets boast handsome Georgian houses and even a couple of weatherboarded cottages, while the Soane-designed **Picture Gallery** is one of London's finest small museums.

If it has a fault, it's the somewhat cloying self-consciousness about Dulwich's "village" status, with its rather twee little shops, rural signposts and a tollgate – the only one remaining in London. Nonetheless, it makes for a pleasant day out south of the river, and can be combined with a visit to the nearby **Horniman Museum**, an enjoyable ethnographic collection, and, for the very curious, the remants of the old **Crystal Palace**, further south.

Dulwich Village

The nearest train station is West Dulwich.

Dulwich came to prominence in the 1610s when its Lord of the Manor, actor-manager Edward Alleyn, founded the **College of God's Gift** as almshouses and a school for poor boys, on the profits of his whorehouses and bear-baiting pits on Bankside.

The college has long since outgrown its original buildings, which still stand to the northeast of the Picture Gallery, and is now housed in a fanciful Italianate complex by Charles Barry (son of the architect of the Houses of Parliament), to the south of the road confusingly called Dulwich Common; Alleyn is buried in the college chapel. The college is now a fee-paying public school, with an impressive roll-call of old boys, including Raymond Chandler, P. G. Wodehouse and World War II traitor Lord Haw-Haw, though they tend to keep quiet about the last of the trio.

Dulwich Picture Gallery

Dulwich Picture Gallery is open Tues–Fri 10am–1pm & 2–5pm, Sat 11am–5pm, Sun 2–5pm; £2.

Dulwich Picture Gallery on College Road, is the nation's oldest public art gallery. Designed by Sir John Soane in 1814, it houses, among other bequests, the collection assembled in the 1790s by the French dealer Noel Desenfans on behalf of King Stanislas of Poland, who planned to open a National Gallery in Warsaw. In 1795 Poland disappeared from the map of Europe, Stanislas was forced to abdicate and Desenfans was left with the paintings. Having failed to persuade either the British government or the Russian Tsar to purchase the collection, Desenfans proposed founding a National Gallery. In the end it was left to his friend, the landscape painter, Francis Bourgeois, and Desenfans' widow, to complete the task and open the gallery in 1817.

It's a beautifully spacious building, awash in natural light and crammed with superb paintings – elegaic landscapes by Cuyp, one of the world's finest Poussin series, and splendid works by Hogarth, Van Dyck, Canaletto and Rubens. Among the gallery's fine array of Gainsborough portraits are his famous Linley Sisters, sittings for which were interrupted by the elopement of one of them with the playwright Sheridan, and a likeness of Samuel Linley that was said to have been painted in less than an hour. Rembrandt's *Portrait of a Young Man* is probably the most valuable picture in the gallery, and has been stolen no fewer than four times in the last twenty years. At the centre of the museum is a tiny **mausoleum** designed by Soane for the sarcophagi of the Desenfans family and Francis Bourgeois. Thought to be based on an Alexandrian catacomb, it's suffused with golden light from the mausoleum's coloured glass – a characteristic Soane touch.

The Horniman Museum

The Horniman Museum is open Mon–Sat 10.30am–5.30pm, Sun 2–5.30pm; free; the nearest train station is Forest Hill, accessible from Charing Cross.

If you walk from Dulwich Picture Gallery across Dulwich Park and then turn south along busy Lordship Lane, you'll reach the wacky **Horniman Museum**, which occupies a striking edifice designed by Harrison Townsend, architect of the Whitechapel Gallery (p.228). It's about a mile's walk.

Frederick Horniman, a tea trader with a passion for collecting, financed construction of the purpose-built gallery in 1901, and the museum is principally a monument to its creator's freewheeling eclecticism. Ethnographic treasures on the ground floor include grotesque masks from Central America, a tiny mummified kitten, an Ethiopian prince's headdress, and a statue of the goddess Kali dancing on the body of Shiva. Beyond the didactic aquarium of native species (a recent addition), displays on the upper levels are even more diverse: cases of skeletons and stuffed animals (including a walrus) share space with half a fruit bat and an orang-utang's foot, while umpteen antique musical instruments cohabit with ancient puppets from Poland and Arabian shoes with flaps to scare away scorpions. There's a functional café, and some live animals in the park around the back of the museum, along with a graceful Victorian conservatory, brought here from the Horniman family's mansion in Croydon.

Concerts are given in the conservatory every Sunday afternoon.

Crystal Palace

The nearest train stations are Crystal Palace and Penge West.

In the 1850s, the **Crystal Palace** from the 1851 Great Exhibition (p.272) was re-erected on the commanding heights of Sydenham Hill, to the south of Dulwich, overlooking London, Kent and Surrey. A fantastic pleasure garden was laid out around this giant glasshouse, with a complex system of fountains, some of which reached a height of 250 feet. Exhibitions, fun fairs, ballooning, a miniature railway and a whole range of events, including, from 1894 to 1924, the FA Cup Final, were staged here. Despite its initial success, though, the Palace soon became a financial liability – then, in 1936 the entire structure burnt to the ground overnight.

All that remains now are the foundations and a small **museum** on Anerley Hill (Sun 11am–5pm; free) which tells the history of the place. The park's fountains and many of its original features have also disappeared, though the circular **Tea Maze** has recently been rebuilt and there are even plans afoot to rebuild the Palace. For the moment, though, the park is dominated by the TV transmitter, visible from all over London, and the National Sports Centre. There are further reminders of the park's heyday in and around **Lower Lake**, in the southeast corner of the park, whose islands contain a children's zoo and around thirty life-size dinosaurs lurking in the undergrowth, built out of brick and iron by Waterhouse Hawkins in the 1850s and now listed buildings.

Dulwich and Crystal Palace

Greenwich

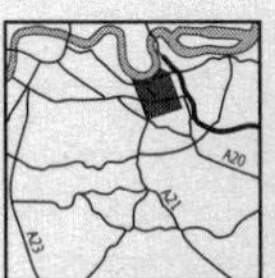

"The most delightful spot of ground in Great Britain", according to Daniel Defoe, **Greenwich** is still one of London's most beguiling spots, and the one place in southeast London that draws tourists out from the centre in considerable numbers. At its heart is the outstanding architectural set-piece of the Royal Naval College and the Queen's House, courtesy of Christopher Wren and Inigo Jones respectively. Most visitors come to see the Cutty Sark, the National Maritime Museum and the Old Royal Observatory in Greenwich Park, though Greenwich also pulls in an ever-increasing volume of Londoners in search of bargains at its Sunday market. With the added attractions of its riverside pubs and walks – with startling views across to Canary Wharf and Docklands – it makes for one of the best weekend trips in London.

The nearest train stations are Greenwich and Maze Hill, both accessible from London Bridge.

Greenwich Town Centre

Greenwich town centre, to the south of the Cutty Sark, was laid out in the 1820s, hence the Nash-style terraces of Nelson Road, College Approach and King William Walk, now a one-way system plagued

Greenwich boat trips

Greenwich is most quickly reached by rail from Charing Cross or London Bridge (every 30min), although taking a boat (every 30min) from Charing Cross, Tower or Westminster Piers is more scenic, if considerably more expensive. A third possible route takes you on the Docklands Light Railway (Mon–Fri only) from Tower Hill to Island Gardens, and where Greenwich Foot Tunnel leads under the Thames to Greenwich – the advantage of this approach being the fabulous view of the Wren buildings from across the river.

The **tourist information office** (daily 10.15am–4.45pm; ☎0181/858 6376) at 46 Greenwich Church Street should be your first port of call if you're new to Greenwich; they can answer most queries and supply maps and guides.

River boats dock right by the Cutty Sark.

Royal Greenwich

Greenwhich history is replete with royal connections. Edward I appears to be the first of the English kings to have stayed here, but it was under the Tudors that Greenwich enjoyed its royal heyday. Henry VII took over Bella Court, built in 1426 by the Duke of Gloucester, rebuilding it for his wife, Margaret of Anjou and renaming it the **Palace of Placentia** in 1500. Henry VIII, who was born in Greenwich, made this his main base, pouring even more money into it than he did at Hampton Court (p.380). He added armouries, a banqueting hall and a huge tilt-yard, hunted in the extensive grounds and kept a watchful eye over proceedings at the nearby Royal Dockyards. All three of his children were born here: Mary, Elizabeth and Edward, whose mother (Henry's third wife), Jane Seymour, died in childbirth.

Edward returned here as king in 1553 to try and restore his frail health, but died shortly afterwards. Mary came here rarely as queen, and on one of her few visits had the wall of her personal apartment blasted away by a cannonball fired in salute. For Queen Elizabeth Greenwich was her chief summer residence, and it was here in 1573 that she revived the Maundy Ceremony, washing the feet of 39 poor women (though only after three others had washed them first). The royal palace fell into disrepair during the Commonwealth, when it was turned into a biscuit factory, and was finally torn down by Charles II to make way for a new edifice, which eventually became the current Royal Naval Palace.

with heavy traffic. At the centre of these busy streets stands the old covered market, which sold mostly fruit and veg until the late 1980s; you can still see the wonderfully Victorian inscription on one of the archways: "A false balance is abomination to the Lord, but a just weight is his delight." The market and flanking stables are now part of the new **Greenwich Market** (Sat & Sun 9am–5pm), a lively antique, crafts and clothes market which has spread far beyond the perameters of its predecessor, spilling out up the High Road, Stockwell Road and Royal Hill. The best sections are the indoor second-hand book markets, flanking the Central Market on Stockwell Road; the antiques hall (actually a very mixed bag of goods), further down on Greenwich High Road; and the flea market on Thames Street.

A short distance in from the old covered market, on the opposite side of Greenwich Church Street, rises one of England's greatest Baroque churches, Hawksmoor's **St Alfege's Church**. Built in 1714 to replace a twelfth-century structure in which Henry VIII was baptized and Thomas Tallis, the "father of English church music", was buried, the church was flattened in the Blitz, but it has been magnificently repaired. Alfege is an unusual saint, in that he wasn't really martyred for his religion. As Archbishop of Canterbury he was captured in 1011 by the marauding Danes, and carried off to Greenwich, where they demanded a ransom for him. Alfege refused to allow any ransom to be paid, at which the furious Danes pelted him to death with ox bones. Thorkell the Tall, the one Dane who took pity on him, got an axe in his head for his pains.

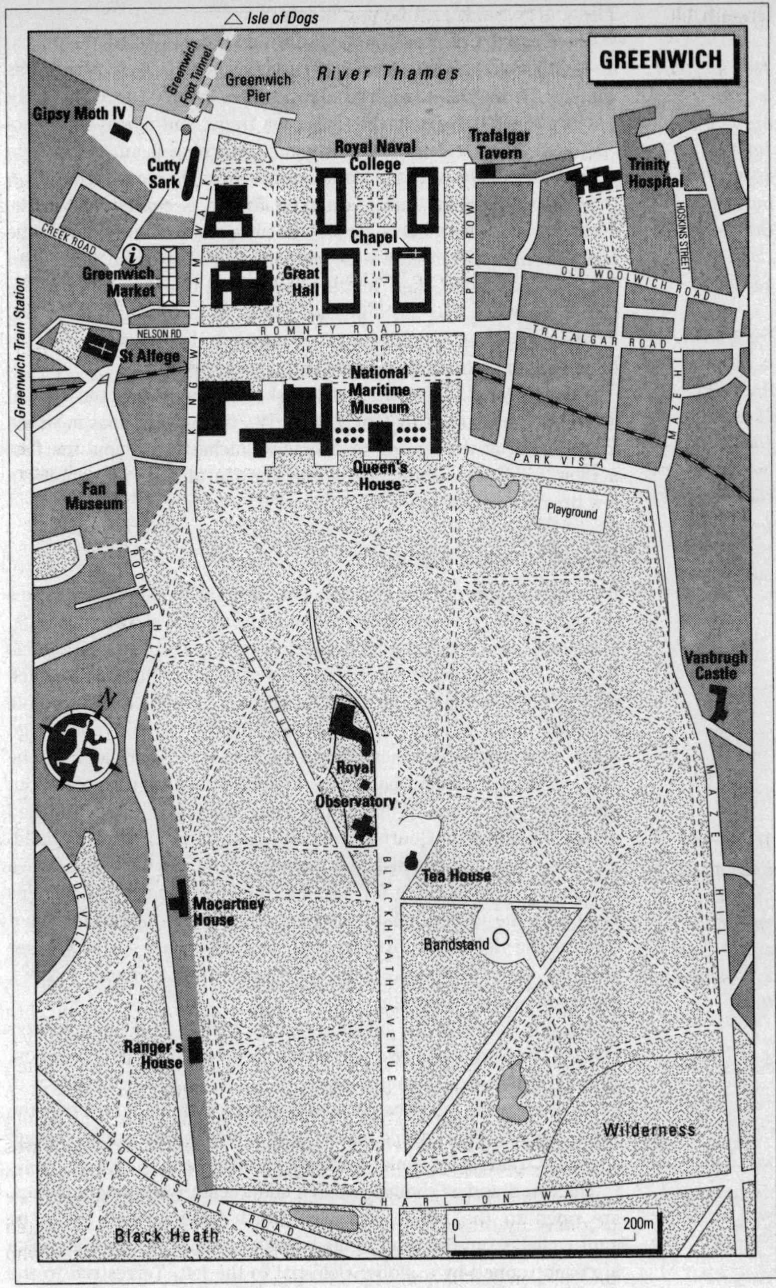
GREENWICH
Isle of Dogs
River Thames
Greenwich Foot Tunnel
Greenwich Pier
Gipsy Moth IV
Cutty Sark
Royal Naval College
Trafalgar Tavern
Trinity Hospital
HOSKINS STREET
CREEK ROAD
Chapel
PARK ROW
Greenwich Market
Great Hall
OLD WOOLWICH ROAD
NELSON RD
ROMNEY ROAD
TRAFALGAR ROAD
St Alfege
Greenwich Train Station
KING WILLIAM WALK
National Maritime Museum
MAZE HILL
Queen's House
PARK VISTA
Fan Museum
Playground
CROOM'S HILL
THE AVENUE
Vanbrugh Castle
Royal Observatory
Tea House
HYDE VALE
Macartney House
BLACKHEATH AVENUE
Bandstand
Ranger's House
Wilderness
SHOOTERS HILL ROAD
CHARLTON WAY
Black Heath
0
200m

The Cutty Sark and Gypsy Moth

The Cutty Sark is open April–Sept Mon–Sat 10am–6pm, Sun noon–6pm; Oct–March closes 5pm; £3.25.

Wedged in a dry dock to the west of King William Walk is the majestic **Cutty Sark**, the world's last surviving tea clipper, which was launched from the Clydeside shipyards in 1869. The Cutty Sark lasted just eight years in the China tea trade, and it was as a wool clipper that it actually made its name, returning from Australia in just 72 days. The vessel's name comes from Robert Burns' *Tam O'Shanter*, in which Tam, a drunken farmer, is chased by Nannie, an angry witch in a short Paisley linen dress, or "cutty sark"; the clipper's figurehead shows her clutching the hair from the tail of Tam's horse. Inside, there's little to see beyond the exhibition in the main hold which tells the ship's story from its inception to its arrival in Greenwich in 1954. Before you disembark, don't miss the colourful parade of buxom figureheads in the lower hold.

Gipsy Moth IV is open April–Oct Mon–Sat 10am–6pm, Sun noon–6pm, closed Mon–Fri 1–2pm; Oct closes 5pm; 50p.

A mast's length from the Cutty Sark, and dwarfed by the bulk of its neighbour, is the tiny **Gipsy Moth IV**, the 54-foot boat in which in 1965–66, at the age of 66, Francis Chichester became the first person to sail solo around the world. The spartan interior contains a few tired mementoes.

Royal Naval College

It's entirely appropriate that the one London building that makes the most of its riverbank location should be the **Royal Naval College**, a majestic Baroque ensemble which opens out onto the Thames. Despite the symmetry and grace of the four buildings, which perfectly frame the Queen's House beyond (see below), the whole complex has a strange and piecemeal history. John Webb, Inigo Jones' assistant and nephew, began the first of the four blocks in the 1660s as a replacement palace for Charles II, but the money ran out after just five years. William and Mary eschewed the unfinished palace for Hampton Court and decided to turn the Greenwich building into a hospital for disabled seamen, along the lines of Chelsea Hospital. Wren, working for nothing, then had his original designs vetoed by the Queen, who insisted the new development must not obscure the view of the river from the Queen's House – what you see now is Wren's revised plan, augmented by, among others, Hawksmoor and Vanbrugh.

The Painted Hall and RNC Chapel are open daily except Thurs 2.30–4.45pm; free.

The population of the hospital swelled to over 2500 in the aftermath of the Napoleonic Wars, but charges of cruelty and corruption, coupled with dwindling numbers, forced a move to new premises in 1869. Four years later the vacated buildings were taken over by the Royal Naval College, which in turn later moved to Dartmouth, though specialist training for senior officers continues here.

The two grandest rooms, situated underneath Wren's twin domes, are open to the public and well worth visiting; they must be approached from the King William Walk entrance, whose gateposts are each topped by a globe: Celestial to the left, Terrestrial to the right. The magnificent **Painted Hall**, in the west wing, is dominated by James Thornhill's gargantuan allegorical ceiling painting, which took him nineteen years to complete. It depicts William and Mary handing down Peace and Liberty to Europe, with a vanquished Louis XIV clutching a broken sword below them. Equally remarkable are Thornhill's *trompe l'oeil* fluted pilasters and decorative detailing, while on the far wall, behind the high table, Thornhill himself appears beside George I and family. Designed to be the sailors' dining hall, it was considered far too splendid for plebs and lay more or less empty and unused until Nelson's lying-in-state in 1806.

The **RNC Chapel**, in the east wing, is an altogether colder and more formal affair. The current chapel was designed by James "Athenian" Stuart (so-called becaused of his espousal of the Greek Revival style), after a fire in 1779 destroyed its predecessor. However, it is Stuart's assistant, William Newton, whom we have to thank for the chapel's exquisite pastel-shaded plasterwork and spectacular, decorative detailing, among the finest in London.

The Five-Foot Walk and Trinity Hospital

A fine vantage point for viewing the Royal Naval College is the **Five Foot Walk**, which squeezes between the college railings and the riverbank. It was here that George I landed to take the throne on September 18, 1714, though it was estimated that 57 other cousins had a better claim. His wife was not with him, having been incarcerated in a castle in Germany for thirty-two years for adultery.

If you're in need of refreshment, drop into the Regency-style *Trafalgar Tavern*, at the east end of the walk. The pub was frequented by Whig politicians and the Victorian literary set – its legendary whitebait suppers inspired Dickens to use the pub as the setting for the wedding breakfast in *Our Mutual Friend*. Just beyond the pub down Crane Street is the **Trinity Hospital**, founded in 1613 by the Earl of Northampton for 21 pensioners; the entry requirements declared the hospital would admit "no common beggar, drunkard, whore-hunter, nor unclean person . . nor any that is blind . . . nor any idiot". The mock-Gothic facade and chapel (which contains the Earl's tomb) were rebuilt in the nineteenth century but the courtyard of almshouses remains much as it was at its foundation.

Queen's House

Inigo Jones' **Queen's House**, originally built on a cramped site amidst the Tudor royal palace, is now the focal point of the Greenwich ensemble. As royal residences go, it's an unassuming little Palladian country house, "solid.....masculine and unaffected" in Jones' own words. Its significance, in terms of British architecture, however, is immense. Begun in 1616, it is the earliest example of Renaissance architecture in Britain, signifying a clear break with all that preceded it.

The Queen's House is open March–Oct Mon–Sat noon–6pm, Sun 2–6pm; Nov–Feb Mon–Sat 10am–5pm, Sun 2–5pm; same ticket as for the National Maritime Museum.

The interior, exterior and setting of the Queen's House have all changed radically since Jones' day, making it difficult to imagine the impact the building must have had when it was built. The house now forms part of the National Maritime Museum, and is linked to its neighbouring buildings by open colonnades, which were added in the early part of the nineteenth century, when the entire complex was converted into a school for the children of seamen. The colonnades follow the course of the muddy road which the H-shaped block originally straddled, thus enabling the Queen to pass from the formal gardens to the royal park without sullying her shoes.

Recent restoration has returned the **interior** to something like its appearance at the time the house was altered to provide apartments for Charles II and his queen. The main Stuart incumbent was in fact the Dowager Queen Henrietta Maria, who took up residence shortly before the Civil War and returned, for an equally brief period, following the Restoration. The painstaking reconstruction is in part based on the detailed inventory of the house made at her death in 1669.

An earphone commentary on the entire house is available from the desk in the **Great Hall**, a perfect cube, galleried and decorated with computer-enhanced copies of Gentileschi's panel paintings, which were removed to Marlborough House by the Duchess of Marlborough herself during the reign of Queen Anne. The southeastern corner of the hall leads to the beautiful **Tulip Staircase**, Britain's earliest cantilevered spiral staircase, whose name derives from the floral patterning in the ironwork balustrade.

The rest of the ground floor is given over to temporary exhibitions from the Maritime Museum; the **Royal Apartments** occupy the first floor, and have been decked out with skilful repro furniture, rush matting and damask silk wall hangings. The effect is occasionally dazzling, as in the **Queen's Presence Chamber**, which retains its ceiling decoration from the 1630s, when it was intended to be the bedchamber of Charles I and Henrietta Maria.

The National Maritime Museum

The National Maritime Museum is open March–Oct Mon–Sat noon–6pm, Sun 2–6pm; Nov–Feb Mon–Sat 10am–5pm, Sun 2–5pm; £3.75.

The west wing of the former Naval Asylum now houses the **National Maritime Museum Galleries**, which plough through seafaring history from 1450 to the present day, with scores of model ships, guns, charts, globes and many, many marine paintings. At the time of writing, the museum was in a state of disarray, which should be resolved when the long-awaited **Nelson Gallery** finally opens in the summer of 1995. The museum's collection of Nelson memorabilia includes his grog-jug, Bible and the diminutive "undress coat" worn during the Battle of Trafalgar, with a tiny bullet hole made by the musket shot that killed him. Another prize possession is Turner's *Battle of Trafalgar, 21st October, 1805*, his largest work and only royal commission, which was intended for St James's Palace.

Aside from the museum's excellent temporary exhibitions, there's an entire gallery devoted to Captain Cook's voyages of discovery, copiously illustrated by his artist-on-board, William Hodges. The **Neptune Hall**, dominated by the 1907 steam-powered paddle tug *Reliant*, traces the history of non-military vessels from prehistory to the present. Next door in the **Barge House** are four late seventeenth- and eighteenth-century river barges, including the magnificent 63-foot Royal Barge, a gilded Rococo confection designed by William Kent for Prince Frederick, the much unloved eldest son of George II. By contrast, the more recently installed **twentieth-century Seapower** gallery is disappointing, a dull parade of war artists' works, control rooms and combat footage.

Greenwich Park

Greenwich **Park** is one of the city's oldest royal parks, having been enclosed in the fifteenth century by the Duke of Gloucester, who fancied it as a hunting ground (its royal title actually came later). Henry VIII was particularly fond of the place, to which he characteristically introduced deer in 1515, as well as archery tournaments and sword-fighting contests. André le Nôtre, Louis XIV's gardener at Versailles, seems to have had a hand in redesigning the park after the Commonwealth, though he never actually set foot in Greenwich.

Greenwich Park is open daily dawn–dusk.

The park was finally opened to the public in the eighteenth century, and after the arrival of the railway in 1838 it began to attract Londoners in great numbers. In 1894 Greenwich Park witnessed one of the most bizarre incidents in London's long history of terrorism, when Martial Bourdin, a young French anarchist, was killed when the bomb he was carrying in a brown paper bag exploded. The questions of whether he was planning to blow up the observatory, and whether he was a police informer, remain unresolved. Joseph Conrad used the episode as the basis of his novel *The Secret Agent*.

The park's chief delight is the view from the steep hill crowned by the Old Royal Observatory (see below), overlooking the Canary Wharf development. The most popular place from which to take in the panorama is the statue of **General James Wolfe** (1727–59), who lived at Macartney House at the top of Croom's Hill, close to the Ranger's House (see below), and is buried in St Alfege (see above). Wolfe is famed for the audacious campaign with which he captured Québec in 1759, a battle in which he and his opposite number, the French General Montcalm, were both mortally wounded. Victory celebrations took place throughout England but were forbidden in Greenwich out of respect for Wolfe's mother, who had also lost her husband only a few months previously.

Greenwich Park is the starting point for the annual London Marathon, the world's biggest road race which takes place in mid-April.

Greenwich Park is also celebrated for its rare and ancient trees, the most famous of which, **Queen Elizabeth's Oak**, finally toppled in 1992. For over a hundred years the tree had been reduced to an ivy-covered dead stump, albeit a stump so big that the hollowed-out trunk was used as a lock-up by the park police. It was around this oak tree that Henry VIII and Anne Boleyn (whom he later accused of adultery and had beheaded) are said to have danced. Queen Elizabeth was fond of playing in the tree, and it was at a lodge gate close by that, according to tradition, Walter Ralegh earned his knighthood by gallantly throwing down his cloak for the queen to walk over.

The descendants of Henry's deer are now safely enclosed within "The Wilderness", a fenced area in the southeast corner where they laze around, in Henry James' words, "tame as children". And lastly, if you're in this part of the park, don't miss **Vanbrugh Castle**, halfway down Maze Hill, England's first mock-medieval castle, designed by the architect John Vanbrugh as his private residence in 1726.

The Old Royal Observatory

The Royal Observatory is open April–Sept Mon–Sat 10am–6pm, Sun noon–6pm; Oct–March closes 5pm; £3.75.

The **Old Royal Observatory** is the longest established scientific institution in Britain. Built on the foundations of a medieval outpost of Greenwich Palace, it was established by Charles II in 1675 to house his Astronomer Royal, John Flamsteed. Flamsteed's chief task was to study the stars in order to produce accurate navigational maps, the lack of which was causing enormous problems for the emerging British Empire. In 1884 an international convention placed Greenwich on zero longitude – signified by an illuminated strip of opaque blue glass in the main courtyard – in recognition of the observatory's pioneering work in the calibration of longitude. As a result, the entire world sets its clocks in relation to Greenwich Mean Time. Eventually the post-war smog forced the astrologers to decamp to Herstmonceux Castle and the clearer skies of Sussex (they've since moved to the Pacific), while the old observatory is now a very popular museum.

The oldest part of the observatory is **Flamsteed House**, built by Wren (himself a trained astronomer) "for the observator's habitation and a little for pompe". The northeastern turret sports a bright red Time-Ball which climbs the mast at 12.58pm and drops at 1pm precisely; it was added in 1833 to allow ships on the Thames to set their clocks. Beyond the nicely restored apartments in which the cantankerous Flamsteed lived, you reach the **Octagon Room**, containing a single eighteenth-century telescope – though, in fact, this room was never used to map the movement of the stars, acting instead as a reception room in which the king could show off.

The main galleries focus on the "Search for Longitude". A quadrant could be used to measure latitude, but before the invention of the sea-going clock which could tell travellers what time it was back home and therfore how far east or west they'd travelled, longitude was impossible to measure. The displays reveal some of the crazy ideas that were put forward in order to try and measure longitude and win the £20,000 Longitude Prize. Much the most bizarre involved stabbing a number of dogs with the same knife, then taking them off to different countries; at noon in England a man would jab the knife into a mysterious substance called "powder of sympathy", at which point, supposedly, all the dogs would bark simultaneously, thus revealing the time differentials.

The exhibition then progresses to more successful experiments, including the first precision clocks designed to tell the time at sea, designed by John Harrison, who went on to win the prize, after much skulduggery against his claims, in 1763. The downstairs rooms contain a collection of timepieces from around the world: among the more unusual are a delicate Chinese incense clock and one from the Cultural Revolution, in which the seconds tick away against a background of women waving Mao's Little Red Book.

Flamsteed carried out more than 30,000 observations – "nothing can exceed the tediousness and ennui of the life" was his dispirited description of the job – in the Quadrant House, which now forms part of the **Meridian Building**, but was originally little more than a shed in the garden. Flamsteed's meridian line is marked with pulsing red lights in the floor. Edmund Halley, who succeeded Flamsteed as Astronomer Royal in 1720, bought more sophisticated quadrants, sextants, spyglasses and telescopes, which are displayed in the Quadrangle Room. With the aid of his eight-foot iron quadrant he charted the comings and goings of the famous comet, and worked out his own version of the meridian. Next door, the Bradley Meridian Room reveals yet another meridian, standard from 1750 to 1850 and still used in Ordnance Survey maps. Finally, you reach a room that's spliced in two by the present-day Greenwich Meridian, fixed by the cross-hairs in Airy's Transit Circle, the astrological instrument that dominates the room.

The exhibition ends on a soothing note in the **Telescope Dome** of the octagonal Great Equatorial Building, built in 1857 and home to Britain's largest telescope, a Victorian 28-inch refractor which weighs over one and a half tons. The videos of space images to the accompaniment of New Age music are supplied courtesy of NASA. In addition, there are half-hourly presentations (daily except Sun; £1.50) in the **Planetarium**, housed in the adjoining South Building.

The Fan Museum and Ranger's House

The Fan Museum is open Tues–Sat 11am–4.30pm, Sun noon–4.30pm; £2.50.

Croom's Hill, the twisting road which runs along the western edge of the park, boasts some of Greenwich's finest buildings, dating from the late seventeenth and eighteenth century. At the bottom of the hill you'll find the **Fan Museum** at the end of the first terrace, at 12 Croom's Hill. It's a fascinating little place (and an extremely beautiful house), revealing the importance of the fan as a social and political document. The permanent exhibition on the ground floor traces the history of the materials employed, from peacock feathers to straw. Temporary exhibitions on the first floor explore conditions of production, the fan's link with Empire and changing fashion; outside in the garden, there's a kitsch, hand-painted Orangery.

Queen Caroline and Blackheath

Should Charles and Di ever get divorced, there is at least a precedent, though not one they would wish to repeat. In 1795 George, Prince of Wales (later to become the Prince Regent and then George IV), struck a deal with parliament that they would write off his debts in return for his marrying his cousin, Queen Caroline of Brunswick. George was already happily married to Maria Fitzherbert, a Roman Catholic widow, but the partnership was null and void in the eyes of the Royal Marriages Act of 1772.

Caroline was received on arrival at the Queen's House by another of the Prince of Wales' mistresses, Lady Jersey, and met her future husband for the first time at St James's Palace, whereupon he exclaimed "I am not well; get me a brandy". Their one and only child is thought to have been the product of a single wedding-night coupling. Shortly afterwards she moved to Montague House in Blackheath, which became her official residence for sixteen years, where she surrounded herself with a coterie of men. George had the place demolished after her death, not surprisingly, perhaps, as she used to stick pins in waxen effigies of him and throw them into the fire.

The Ranger's House is open April–Sept daily 10am–6pm; Oct–March Wed–Sun 10am–4pm; EH; £2.

Further up Croom's Hill, past Macartney House, is the **Ranger's House**, a red-brick Georgian villa which backs onto the southwest edge of Greenwich Park, facing Blackheath (see below). Built in the early eighteenth century, it was inhabited after 1749 by the Earl of Chesterfield. The largely unfurnished rooms house the Suffolk collection of paintings on the ground floor and a wide selection of antique musical instruments upstairs. The high points of the art collection are William Larkin's full-length portraits of a Jacobean wedding party, with twin bridesmaids in slashed silver brocade dresses, and the arrogant Richard Sackville, a dissolute aristocrat resplendent in pompom shoes. The Architectural Study Centre, in the courtyard, is a collection of plaques, mantels, fireplaces and chimneys saved from London's historic buildings – the spiral staircase snaking through the centre of the room was retrieved from the old Covent Garden market hall.

Blackheath

The nearest train station is Blackheath.

Immediately south of Greenwich Park lies the well-to-do suburb of **Blackheath** (so called because of the colour of the soil) whose bleak, windswept heath, crisscrossed with busy roads, couldn't be more different from the royal park. Nonetheless, with a pair of century-old pubs, the *Princess of Wales* and *Hare and Billet*, each set beside a pond (on the south side of the heath), it can be quite pleasant on a summer afternoon. The odd fair takes place here on public holidays and it's a premier kite-flying spot.

Blackheath has its historic connections, too, most famously as a plague burial ground – a role which perhaps slowed development. Lying on the main road to Dover, it was a convenient spot on which to pitch camp, as the Danes did in 1011, having kidnapped Saint Alfege. Their example was followed during the 1381 Peasants' Revolt by Wat Tyler's rebels, who were treated to a rousing revolutionary sermon by John Bull, which included the famous lines "When Adam delved and Eve span, who was then the gentleman?" The victorious Henry V was welcomed back from the Battle of Agincourt here in 1415, while Henry VII fought a pitched battle on this spot against Cornish rebels in 1497. It was at Blackheath, also, that Henry VIII was so disappointed on meeting his fourth wife, Anne of Cleves, in 1540; he didn't fancy her and filed for divorce after just six months.

The heath's chief landmark is **All Saints' Church**, which nestles in a slight depression in the south corner. Built in rugged Kentish ragstone in 1859, it's at odds with the rest of the architecture bordering the heath, which dates mostly from the area's development in the late eighteenth and early nineteenth century. One of the earliest residential developments was **The Paragon**, a crescent of four-storey Georgian mansions linked by Doric colonnades. An even earlier foundation, set in its own grounds to the east, is **Morden College**, the aristocrat of almshouses, built in 1695 not for the deserving poor but for "decayed Turkey merchants" who had lost their fortunes. The quadrangular red-brick building, built by Wren's favourite mason, possibly to a design by the master himself, reflects the lost status of its original inhabitants and is now an old people's home.

Morden College and its fine chapel are open by personal appointment only.

Woolwich

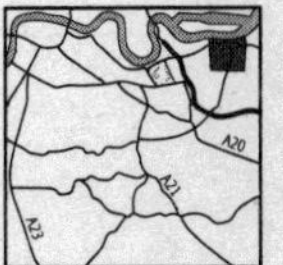

The chief reason to journey out to **Woolwich** is to visit the **Thames Barrier**, an awesome piece of modern engineering, and the largest moveable flood barrier in the world. A boat trip from Greenwich is the best way to take this in, but if you have a fascination for military history you may want to explore the arsenal and dockyards, dating from Tudor times, and the military museums and architecture.

As for the rest of Woolwich, it's difficult to disagree with the visitor who commented in 1847 that it was the "dirtiest, filthiest and most throughly mismanaged town of its size in the kingdom". With its docks and factories defunct, this is one of the poorest parts of the old Docklands – and as yet totally unregenerated. The population is also a pretty uneasy mix, with large Indian, Pakistani and Bangladeshi communities confronted by white fascists from the British National Party who have their headquarters (much to the disgust of the locals) in neighbouring Welling.

Boats run from Greenwich to the Thames Barrier 3–5 times daily; £4 return. The nearest train station is Charlton.

Thames Flood Barrier

The brief boat trip from Greenwich pier passes drab industrial landscapes before gliding towards the gleaming fins of the **Thames**

Barrier. London has been subject to flooding from surge tides since before 1236, when it was reported that in "the great Palace of Westminster men did row with wherries in the midst of the Hall". One of the worst recorded floods took place as recently as 1953, when more than 300 people were drowned in the Thames Estuary alone. A flood barrier had been advocated as far back as the 1850s, but it wasn't until global warming, rising tides and the fact that southeast England is sinking slowly into the sea made intervention imperative that the now defunct Greater London Council finally agreed to build the present barrier. Built from 1972 to 1984, it's a mind-blowing feat of engineering, with its ten movable steel gates weighing from 400 to 3700 tonnes each.

The Visitors' Centre is open Mon–Fri 10.30am–5pm, Sat–Sun 10.30am–5.30pm; £2.25.

The **Visitors' Centre**, on Unity Way, is little more than a handful of glossy models, macho videos and dull statistics, though it does explain the basic mechanism of the barrier (something which is by no means obvious from above the water). By far the most interesting way to see the Thames Barrier, however, is from the riverbank on the one day a month when it is raised for tests (call ☎081/854 1373 for dates). Alternatively, from the nearby pier there are thirty-minute cruises (£1.50) which take you much closer to the barrier gates.

The Russian Submarine is open daily 10am–6pm; £3.95.

An added attraction at the Thames Barrier is the recently acquired **Russian Submarine**, U-475 Foxtrot, moored a little way east of the Visitors' Centre, opposite the Tate & Lyle sugar factory. This matt-black Soviet sub carried nuclear weapons and could operate at a depth of 250m, making it virtually impossible to detect. Even now, the Russians will reveal little about its Cold War past, except to say that it was launched in 1967 as part of the Baltic Fleet. Life for the 75-man crew was hard, with just two toilets and one shower between the lot of them, temperatures of 50°C when the sub hit top speed, and smoking allowed only on surfacing, when a maximum of five men could ascend the conning tower. Each crew member was entitled to just one month's leave every three years, though the food on board, high wages and comradeship apparently made it an attractive enough prospect to ensure a steady stream of volunteers. Very little has been altered inside, which means visitors must be prepared to squeeze through numerous awkward circular hatches, and claustrophobes should definitely stay away.

Military Woolwich

Woolwich owes its existence to the **Royal Dockyards**, which were established here and upstream at Deptford in 1513 by Henry VIII. The great men-of-war that established England as a world naval power were built in these dockyards, starting with the *Great Harry*, the largest ship in the world when it was launched from here in 1514. Royal visits were frequent: Queen Elizabeth came to Woolwich to greet Sir Francis Drake after his voyage around the world, and Sir Walter Ralegh and Captain Cook set out on their voyages of discovery. Despite costly modernization in the early nineteenth century to enable the dockyards to build and repair steam ships, their capacities were quickly outstripped by the much larger iron-clad vessels, and they finally closed in 1869.

The Royal Arsenal

The **Royal Arsenal**, for which the area is most famous, grew up alongside the Tudor dockyards. Charles II fortified the area with a sixty-gun battery and sunk several ships in the river in preparation for an attack by the Dutch fleet which never materialized. In 1695 the Royal Laboratory for the manufacture of fireworks and gunpowder moved here, and was joined, in 1717, by the main government brass foundry. Formally entitled the Royal Arsenal in 1805, the complex grew during the following century, reaching its heyday during World War I, when it employed nearly 80,000 people. After the armistice there was a half-hearted attempt to convert the Arsenal to non-military production, paring the workforce down to just 20,000, and then another boom period during the last war. However, the ordnance factories were closed altogether in 1967 and much of the site given over to council housing.

Woolwich was the birthplace of Arsenal football club, now located in Highbury, Islington, *p.320.*

Today, the Arsenal is largely abandoned, and its fine collection of historical buildings, littered with unexploded ammunition, is slowly decaying behind a twenty-foot-high wall. The only part accessible to the public is the main **gateway**, built in 1829 on Beresford Square (currently under repair), and separated from the rest of the complex by Beresford Street/Plumstead Road. With the help of the plaque on the gateway, you can just about pick out the Royal Brass Foundry, Gun Bore Factory and Smithy, and the Model Room (all by Vanbrugh), plus later buildings by James Wyatt.

The gateway is close by Woolwich Arsenal train station.

The Royal Artillery Barracks and Museum

Britain's first two artillery regiments were founded at the Arsenal in 1716, and are now housed in the **Royal Artillery Barracks**, completed in 1802 by James Wyatt. This stands half a mile to the south of the Arsenal, up Grand Depot Road. Its three-storey Georgian facade, interrupted by stucco pavilions and a central triumphal arch, runs for an amazing 1080ft, making it one of the longest in Europe. The barracks face south onto the grassy parade ground, to the east of which lies the abandoned **Garrison Church of St George**, built in neo-Romanesque style in 1863. Gutted in the last war, it's now an attractive husk, with fragments of its colourful interior decor still surviving.

Further south still, on the other side of Woolwich Common, is Wyatt's only slightly less imposing **Old Royal Military Academy**, built in mock-Tudor style as a foil to the Royal Artillery Barracks. The 720-foot facade faces north onto a parade ground, with an imitation of the Tower of London's White Tower as its centrepiece.

Woolwich

The Royal Artillery Museum is open Mon–Fri 12.30–4.30pm; free. The Museum of Artillery is open by appointment; ☎0181/316 5402.

The Academy merged with Sandhurst (Britain's most important military academy) in 1945, and the building now houses the **Royal Artillery Museum**, which traces the history of the artillery regiments.

Of slightly broader appeal is the **Museum of Artillery** in John Nash's bizarre Chinese-style Rotunda, off Repository Road, to the west of the Royal Artillery Barracks. Originally designed for the gardens of Charlton House, the Rotunda was damaged by a gas explosion, repaired and re-erected on its present site, where it stands amidst a panoply of military hardware tracing the history of artillery from the fourteenth century to the present day.

North Woolwich

If Woolwich itself looks dismal, North Woolwich, on the north bank of the Thames, is worse – little more than an industrial wasteland. For nine hundred years it was a geographical anomaly, an island of Kent in Essex, claimed as such by the Sheriff of Kent way back in the eleventh century. The current name and the first real habitation came with the arrival of the Eastern Counties and Thames Junction Railway in 1847. In 1965 it was submerged into the East End borough of Newham, and over the next twenty years most of the area's factories closed down, as did the Royal Docks (not to be confused with the militarily-inclined Royal Dockyards, described above) which had been its life-support system. Apart from the presence of London City Airport, and the odd surviving factory, the whole area is awaiting development – and shows it.

North Woolwich Old Station is open Mon–Wed & Sat 10am–5pm, Sun 2–5pm; free.

The railway still reaches as far as North Woolwich, where a modern station serves as the terminus of the North London Line from Richmond. Meanwhile, the original station has been restored to its Victorian glory and opened as the **North Woolwich Old Station**, a museum which recounts the impact of the railways on this part of London, and displays several restored steam engines outside. To reach it you can either walk through the **Woolwich Foot Tunnel**, which opened in 1912, or take the **Woolwich Free Ferry** (Mon–Fri 6am–8.30pm, Sat 6am–8pm, Sun 11.30am–7.30pm), established in perpetuity by an act of parliament in 1889.

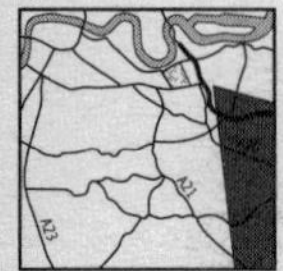

Charlton House to Chislehurst Caves

This final section is a real miscellany of sights, spread between **Charlton** and **Chislehurst**, across considerable tracts of suburbia. Unless you are driving, you'll need to be selective in your choice; top targets are the Jacobean **Charlton House** and the amazing **Chislehurst Caves**.

Charlton House to Eltham Palace

A little to the west of Woolwich, on Charlton Road, stands Charlton **House**, the finest Jacobean mansion in or around London, completed in 1612 as a "nest for his old age" by Adam Newton, tutor to the eldest son of James I, Prince Henry, who died in the same year. John Thorpe, architect of Holland House in Kensington, was the architect, though the Orangery to the north (now a public lavatory) is thought to be the work of Inigo Jones. The house as a whole is currently used as a community centre, which makes access farily easy, though little remains of the original interior beyond a few period fireplaces and strapwork ceilings.

A mile or so southeast of Charlton, up Shooters Hill, are a series of ancient woodlands, the most famous of which is the easternmost, **Oxleas Wood**, which is currently under threat from the government's road programme, despite having been declared an SSSI (Site of Special Scientific Interest). Coppicing has helped keep the woodland floor a rich floral haven, as well as home to over 200 species of fungi. Jack Wood and Castle Wood, to the west, also feature the odd bit of more formal parkland, and the one point of specific interest, **Severndroog Castle** (closed to the public), a triangular tower, erected in 1784 by Lady James of Eltham in memory of her husband, William, who once attacked a pirate stronghold in the island fortress of Severndroog, off the west coast of India.

A mile or so to the south of these woods, at the end of Court Yard, lies **Eltham Palace**, which was one of the country's foremost medieval royal residences and even a venue for parliament for some two hundred years from the reign of Edward II. All that remains of Eltham's medieval glory is the fifteenth-century bridge across the remains of the moat and the **Great Hall**, built by Edward IV in 1479, with fine hammerbeam roof hung with pendants and two fan-vaulted oriels. The rest of the complex was added in the 1930s by the Courtauld family and is closed to the public.

Bus #53 from Elephant and Castle tube (or Woolwich Arsenal) runs to Charlton House.

Eltham Palace is open Thurs & Sun 10am–6pm; winter until 4pm; free; the nearest train station is Eltham.

Red House and Chislehurst Caves

Two miles east of Oxleas Wood, in Bexleyheath, on the very outskirts of London, lies the **Red House**, a wonderful red-brick country house designed by Philip Webb in 1860 for his friend, William Morris, following his marriage to Pre-Raphaelite heart-throb, Jane Burden. The details, such as the turreted well-house and the pointed brick arches, are Gothic, but the whole enterprise stands as a landmark in English architecture and the beginning of the Arts and Crafts movement, with which Morris is most closely associated. Much of the interior has been altered beyond recognition but here and there the designs of Morris and his chief collaborator, Burne-Jones, remain.

The Red House is open Feb–Dec first Sat & Sun of month; ☎0181/303 8808; Bexleyheath train station.

The Caves are open daily 11am–4.30/5pm; £2.50 short tour; £4 long tour; the nearest train station is Chislehurst.

Finally, five miles southeast of Bexleyheath are one of London's more unusual tourist attractions, the **Chislehurst Caves**, prehistoric underground tunnels which stretch for miles and have been used over the centuries by everyone from the Romans, who set up chalk mines, to the locals, who came here to shelter from wartime bombs. You can take your pick between a short tour (45 mins) or long tour (1hr 30mins – Sunday only). Either experience is pretty spooky and claustrophobic as the caves have no lighting and you are taken around by a guide with a lamp.

Out West: Chiswick to Kew, Hampton Court and Windsor Castle

CHISWICK TO WINDSOR – a distance of some fifteen miles overland (considerably more via the river) – takes you from the traffic-clogged western suburbs of London to the heavily touristed royal outpost of Windsor Castle. In between, London and its satellites seem to continue unabated, with only fleeting glimpses of the countryside, in particular the fabulous **Kew Gardens** and the two old royal hunting parks, **Richmond** and **Bushy Park**, though as one nineteenth-century visitor observed they are "no more like the real untrimmed genuine country than a garden is like a field". Running through the chapter, and linking many of the places described, is the **River Thames**, once known as the "Great Highway of London" and still the most pleasant way to travel in these parts during the summer.

Aside from the river and the parks, the chief attractions are the numerous royal palaces and lordly mansions which pepper the riverbanks: text-book Palladian style at **Chiswick House**, unspoiled Jacobean splendour at **Ham House**, Tudor and Baroque excess (and the famous maze) at **Hampton Court**, and medieval ramparts at **Windsor** itself, which is also home to **Eton College**.

We actually kick off this chapter at **Hammersmith** – London's gateway to the west, by road or tube – which, with neighbouring **Chiswick**, and **Kew**, **Richmond** and **Twickenham** beyond, has its own appeal in its riverside walks and pubs.

River transport

Westminster Passenger Services (☎0171/930 4721) run boats between Westminster and Hampton Court daily from the Monday before Easter until the end of September, calling at Putney, Kew, Richmond and Kingston; the full trip takes between 2hr 30min and 4hr one-way.

Colliers Launches (☎0181/940 8505) run boats between Richmond and Hampton Court at weekends only from Easter to Whitsun, then daily until mid-September; the trip takes 1hr 15min one-way.

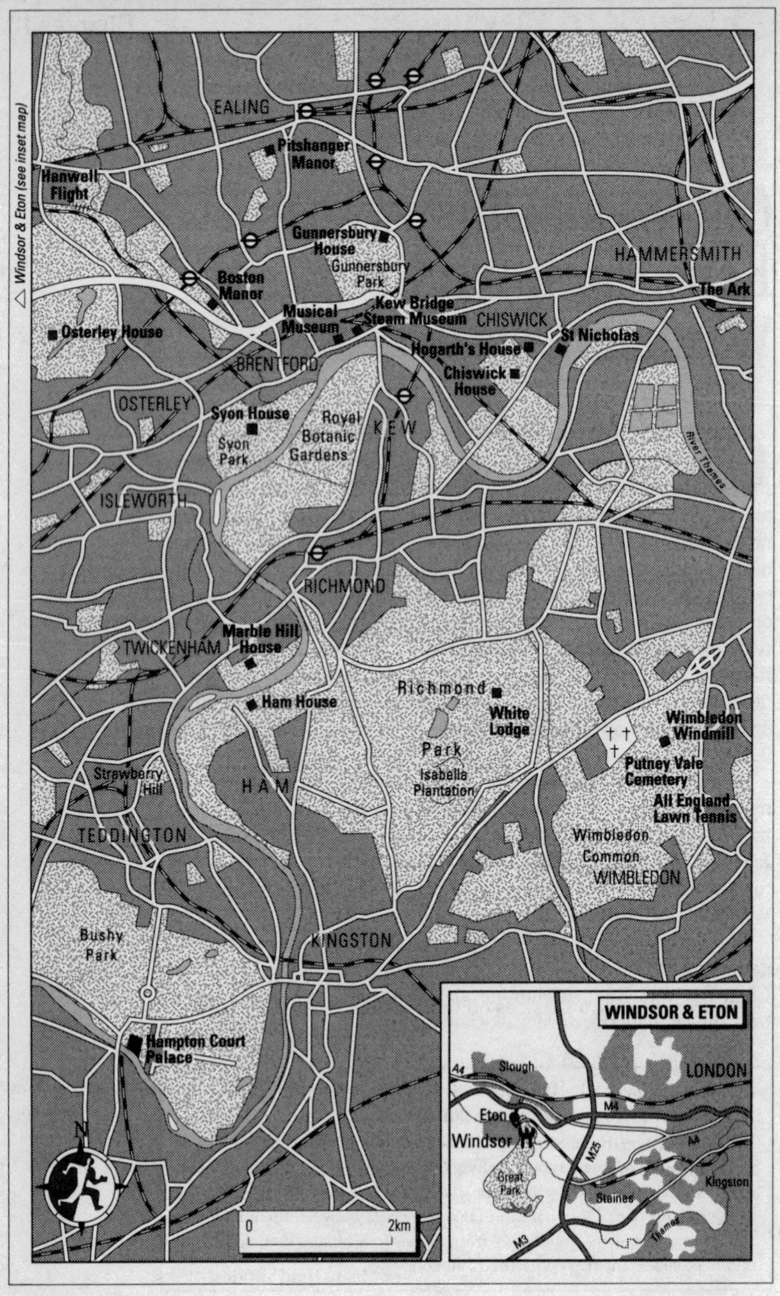
Windsor & Eton (see inset map)
EALING
Pitshanger Manor
Hanwell Flight
Gunnersbury House
Gunnersbury Park
HAMMERSMITH
Boston Manor
The Ark
Kew Bridge Steam Museum
Musical Museum
CHISWICK
Osterley House
Hogarth's House
St Nicholas
BRENTFORD
Chiswick House
OSTERLEY
Syon House
Syon Park
Royal Botanic Gardens
KEW
River Thames
ISLEWORTH
RICHMOND
Marble Hill House
TWICKENHAM
Ham House
Richmond Park
White Lodge
Wimbledon Windmill
Putney Vale Cemetery
Isabella Plantation
Strawberry Hill
HAM
All England Lawn Tennis
TEDDINGTON
Wimbledon Common
WIMBLEDON
Bushy Park
KINGSTON
Hampton Court Palace
WINDSOR & ETON
Slough
LONDON
A4
M4
Eton
Windsor
M25
A4
Great Park
Staines
Kingston
Thames
M3
N
0
2km

Chiswick to Pitshanger

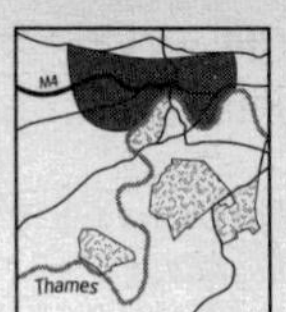

Most people experience the five-mile stretch of west London between Chiswick and Osterley en route to or from Heathrow airport, either from the confines of the tube train (which actually runs overground at this point) or from the M4, which was driven through areas of parkland in the 1960s. The sights here – former country retreats now surrounded by suburbia – are among the most neglected in this part of the city, receiving nothing like the number of visitors of Kew and Richmond, on the south bank of the Thames.

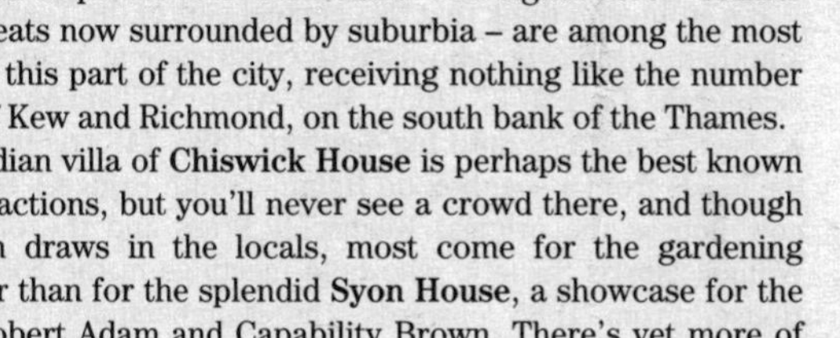

The Palladian villa of **Chiswick House** is perhaps the best known of these attractions, but you'll never see a crowd there, and though nearby Syon draws in the locals, most come for the gardening centre rather than for the splendid **Syon House**, a showcase for the talents of Robert Adam and Capability Brown. There's yet more of Adam's work at **Osterley House**, another Elizabethan conversion now owned by the National Trust, while **Pitshanger Manor** is a must for fans of Sir John Soane's architecture.

Hammersmith Bridge to Chiswick Mall

This chapter starts in the hell hole of **Hammersmith**, for two reasons: the nearby tube station and the riverside walk to Chiswick. Hammersmith's heart was ripped out in the 1960s when the Hammersmith Flyover was built to relieve congestion on the Broadway, the main shopping street. This had the simultaneous effect of making the adjacent roundabout one of the busiest traffic intersections in London, and cutting off Hammersmith from the river. The tube, which lies at the middle of the roundabout, is now enveloped on three sides by a new shopping mall and an ugly office building that's home to Coca-Cola's UK headquarters.

Squeezed between the Flyover and the railway line is another 1990s landmark, Ralph Erskine's **London Ark**, a ship-shaped office block that's been trumpeted as the city's first ecologically-sound building. Inside, the building is flooded with natural light, while triple-glazing helps to keep energy in and noise out; from the outside, the result is less laudable, particularly for local residents, as noise from the trains bounces off the building.

A riverside walk to Chiswick

This riverside walk may not be possible during very high tides.

The best aspect of Hammersmith is the **riverside walk**, which begins a short way southwest of the roundabout, down Queen Caroline Street. Passing underneath **Hammersmith Bridge**, a graceful suspension bridge from the 1880s, you can walk all the way to Chiswick along the most picturesque stretch of the riverbank in the whole of London, much of it closed to traffic.

Lower Mall, the section closest to the bridge, is a mixture of Victorian pubs, boathouses, Regency verandahs and modern flats.

Chiswick to Pitshanger

The University Boat Race, a London institution since 1845, takes place in late March/ early April; *see p.538.*

The William Morris Society is open Thurs & Sat 2–5pm; free.

An interesting array of boats huddles around the marina outside the *Dove*, a seventeenth-century riverside pub. This started out as a coffee house and has the smallest back bar in the country, copious literary associations – regulars have included Graham Greene, Ernest Hemingway and William Morris – and a canopied balcony overlooking the Thames (one of the best places from which to view the annual University Boat Race).

It's strange to think that this genteel part of the Thames was once a hotbed of radicals, who used to congregate at **Kelmscott House**, beyond the *Dove* at 26 Upper Mall, where William Morris lived and worked from 1878 until his death in 1896. (Morris used to berate the locals from a soapbox on Hammersmith Bridge.) The basement now houses the original Kelmscott Press and the offices of the William Morris Society, who hold meetings in the adjacent Coach House. From 1885 onwards, the Hammersmith Branch of the Socialist League and later the Hammersmith Socialist Society used to meet here on a Sunday evening. Keir Hardie (first leader of the parliamentary Labour Party), anarchist Prince Kropotkin, George Bernard Shaw and Fabian founders the Webbs were among the speakers, and their photos now line the walls.

A modern, pedestrianized section of the embankment connects the Upper Mall with **Hammersmith Terrace**, a line of Georgian houses built facing the river sometime before 1755. **Chiswick Mall**, which marks the end of Hammersmith, continues for another mile or so to the riverside village of Chiswick. A riotous ensemble of seventeenth- and eighteenth-century mansions lines the north side of the Mall, which cuts them off from their modest riverside gardens. Halfway along, a particularly fine trio ends with **Walpole House**, once home of Barbara Villiers, Duchess of Cleveland, Countess of Castlemaine and mistress of Charles II.

Chiswick Mall

Chiswick Mall terminates at the church of **St Nicholas**, built mostly in the last century, but retaining its original fifteenth-century ragstone tower. The church lay at the heart of the riverside village of **Chiswick** from medieval times until the nineteenth century, when the action moved north to Chiswick High Street, its modern heart. Lord Burlington and his architect friends William Kent and Colen Campbell are all buried in the graveyard, as is the aforementioned Barbara Villers, though only the painters William Hogarth and James Whistler are commemorated by gravestones, the former enclosed by wrought-iron railings.

Church Lane was the medieval village high street. Its oldest building today is the *Old Burlington*, originally a sixteenth-century inn; beyond it lies the huge *Fuller's* brewery. To continue on to Chiswick House, head across **Powell's Walk**, behind the church to Burlington Lane, which runs along the southeastern edge of the house gardens.

Chiswick House and around

Chiswick **House** is a perfect little classical villa, designed by Richard Boyle, third Earl of Burlington in the 1720s, and set in one of the most beautifully landscaped gardens in London. Like its prototype, Palladio's Villa Rotonda near Vicenza, the house was purpose-built as a "temple to the arts" – here, amid his fine art collection, Burlington used to entertain such friends as Swift, Handel and Alexander Pope, who lived in nearby Twickenham.

The nearest train station is Chiswick.

Chiswick House is open April–Sept Mon–Sat 10am–6pm; Oct–March Wed–Sun closes 4pm; EH; £2.30.

Guests and visitors (who could view the property on payment of an admission fee even in Lord Burlington's day) would originally have ascended the quadruple staircase and entered the *piano nobile* (upper floor) through the magnificent Corinthian portico. The public entrance today is via the **lower floor**, where the earl had his own private rooms and kept his extensive library. Here, you can pick up a taped commentary at the main desk, watch a short video on the house and peruse an exhibition on the history of the house and grounds, a trio of Roman statues brought back from Hadrian's villa at Tivoli and a bronze sphinx.

Entertaining took place on the **upper floor**, a series of cleverly interconnecting rooms, each enjoying a wonderful view out onto the gardens – all, that is, except the Tribunal, the domed octagonal hall at the centre of the villa, where the earl's finest paintings and sculptures would have been displayed. The Tribunal and other rooms are largely empty, but retain much of their rich, Kent-designed decor, in particular the ceilings. The most sumptuous is the Blue Velvet Room, decorated in a deep Prussian blue with eight pairs of heavy gilded brackets holding up the ceiling. The finest views onto the garden are from the Gallery, a series of interconnecting rooms, all enclosed in deference to the English climate.

The gardens

If you're a bit lost by the finer points of classical architecture, you'll probably get more pleasure from the house's extensive **gardens**, an intriguing mixture of earlier, formal elements, and more "natural" features added under Kent's direction. The gardens mark the point in the history of English gardening when the geometrical Versailles-like style flowed into the freer but equally well-orchestrated style perfected by Capability Brown.

Admission to the gardens is free: daily 8am–dusk.

On the north side of the house, under the shadow of giant cedars, a smooth carpet of grass, punctuated by urns and sphinxes, culminates in a yew hedge cut into niches harbouring lions and copies of Roman statuary. Close by is the *patte d'oie* (goose-foot), a network of narrow yew-hedge avenues, each one ending in some diminutive building or statue. The southernmost one leads to the Orange Tree Garden, a grassy amphitheatre centred on an obelisk in a pond and overlooked by an Ionic temple.

The once-straight canal which runs behind the temple was transformed into an irregular shape by Kent, and served as the prototype for other artificial lakes like the Serpentine in Hyde Park. At the far end, beyond James Wyatt's elegant stone bridge, Kent also designed England's first mock-ruin, a cascade onto which water once spurted (a feature which English Heritage are hoping to restore).

To the north of the villa stands a grand stone gateway designed by Inigo Jones (one of Burlington's heroes); it was bequeathed by Burlington's doctor, Hans Sloane, and brought here from Beaufort House in Chelsea in 1736. Beyond the gateway lies a large conservatory which looks out onto the formal **Italian Garden**, laid out in the early nineteenth century by the sixth Duke of Devonshire, who also established a zoo featuring an elephant, giraffe, elks and emus.

Hogarth's House is open April–Sept Mon & Wed–Sat 11am–6pm, Sun 2–6pm; Oct–March closes 4pm; closed first two weeks Sept & last three weeks Dec; free.

Hogarth's House

If you leave Chiswick gardens by the northernmost exit, beyond the conservatory, it's just a short walk (to the right) along the thunderous A4 road to **Hogarth's House**, where the artist spent each summer with his wife, sister and mother-in-law from 1749 until his death in 1764. Nowadays it's difficult to believe Hogarth came here for "peace and quiet", but in the eighteenth century the house was almost entirely surrounded by countryside. After Chiswick House, which epitomized everything Hogarth loathed the most, the domesticity here comes as some relief. Amongst the scores of Hogarth's engravings, you can see copies of his satirical series', *An Election*, *Marriage à la Mode*, *A Rake's Progress* and *A Harlot's Progress*, and compare the modern view from the parlour with the more idyllic scene in *Mr Ranby's House*.

The nearest tube is Acton Town.

The park is open daily 7.30am–30min before dusk. The museum is open April–Oct Mon–Fri 1–5pm, Sat & Sun 2–6pm; Nov–March closes at 4pm; free.

Gunnersbury Park

An even earlier Palladian villa, built by Inigo Jones' son-in-law, John Webb, once stood in **Gunnersbury Park**, a mile or so to the northwest of Chiswick House. In 1801 the villa was demolished and the estate divided (hence the park's two adjacent mansions), only to be reunited under the wealthy Rothschild family in the late nineteenth century. The larger of the mansions, **Gunnersbury Park House**, now serves as a **local museum**, with interesting temporary exhibitions on the local borough, and a permanent collection of historical vehicles, including a tandem tricycle and the Rothschilds' own Victorian "chariot". The park itself has been largely given over to sports pitches but overlooking the boating pond to the west of the museum there's a fine relic of the park's previous existence – a Neoclassical temple erected by George II's daughter Amelia, who used to spend her summers at the aforementioned Palladian villa. It was later used as a private synagogue by the Rothschilds.

Chiswick to Pitshanger

Adjoining the park's southeast corner is a section of **Kensington Cemetery**, which contains a black marble obelisk erected in 1976 to the 14,500 Polish POWs who went missing in 1940, when the Nazi-Soviet Pact carved up Poland. A mass grave of 4500 was later discovered by the advancing Nazis at Katyn, near Smolensk, but responsibility for the massacre was denied by the Russians until fifty years later, as a new plaque bitterly records. Fifty metres to the south is the grave of General Komorowski, leader of the Polish Home Army during the ill-fated 1944 Warsaw Uprising, who lived in exile in Britain until his death in 1966. There's no direct access to the graveyard from the park; the main entrance is 400m further south down Gunnersbury Avenue.

Kew Bridge Steam Museum and the Musical Museum

The nearest train station is Kew Bridge, or bus #237 or #267 from Gunnersbury tube.

Difficult to miss thanks to its stylish Italianate standpipe tower, yet largely overlooked as a tourist attraction, **Kew Bridge Steam Museum** occupies the former Grand Junction Water Works pumping station, on the corner of Kew Bridge Road and Green Dragon Lane, 100m west of the bridge itself. At the heart of the museum is the Steam Hall, which contains four gigantic nineteenth-century Cornish beam engines (one of which was only decommissioned in 1983), while two adjoining rooms house the pumping station's original beam engines – including the world's largest. The best time to visit is at weekends when each of the museum's industrial dinosaurs is put through its paces, and the small narrow-gauge steam railway runs round the yard.

The museum is open daily 11am–5pm; £1.70. The steam engines only run at weekends; £1 extra.

Five minutes' walk west of the Steam Museum along Brentford High Street is the little-visited **Musical Museum**, which specializes in muscial automata. Orchestrions, pianolas, barrel organs, wind-up gramophones and a self-playing Wurlitzer cinema organ are all crowded into this converted ragstone church. There are two noisy ninety-minute demonstrations each day it's open and fortnightly concerts on Saturday evenings given on the Wurlitzer.

The Musical Museum is open April–June & Sept–Oct Sat & Sun 2–5pm; July & Aug Wed–Sun 2–5pm; £3.20.

Syon House

Bus #237 or #267 from Gunnersbury tube or Kew Bridge train station.

Syon, directly across the Thames from Kew Gardens (see p.370), was one of the richest monasteries in the country. Established by Henry V after the battle of Agincourt, it was dissolved by Henry VIII, who incarcerated his fifth wife, Catherine Howard, here shortly before her execution in 1542. Half a century later Queen Elizabeth granted the **Syon House** estate to the Percys, Earls and later Dukes of Northumberland, whose family home it remains. It's a working concern these days, embracing a garden centre, a wholefood shop, a trout fishery, an aquatic club and a butterfly house, as well as the old mansion.

The House

Syon House is open April–Sept Wed–Sun 11am–5pm; Oct Sun only; £3.25.

From its rather plain Elizabethan exterior, with corner turrets and rigid castellations, you'd never guess that **Syon House** contains the most opulent eighteenth-century interior in the whole of London. The splendour of Robert Adam's refurbishment is immediately revealed, however, in the pristine **Great Hall**, an apsed double cube with a screen of Doric columns at one end and classical statuary dotted around the edges – note, too, how the monochrome marble floor cleverly mirrors the coffered ceiling. It was here – or rather, in the hall's Tudor predecessor – that Henry VIII's body lay in state en route to Windsor, and was discovered the next morning, in the process of being consumed by a pack of hounds.

From the austerity of the Great Hall you enter the lavishly decorated **Ante Room**, with its florid scagliola floor (made from a mixture of marble dust and resin) and its green-grey Ionic columns topped by brightly gilded classical statues. Here guests could mingle before entering the **Dining Room**, a compromise between the two preceding rooms, richly gilded but otherwise calm in its overall effect. The remaining rooms are warmer and softer in tone, betraying their Elizabethan origins much more than the preceding ones. The **Red Drawing Room** retains its original red silk wall-hangings from Spitalfields, upon which are hung portraits of the Stuarts by Lely, Van Dyck and others, and features a splendid ceiling studded with over two hundred roundels set within gilded hexagons.

Beyond, the **Long Gallery** – 136ft by just 14ft – stretches the entire width of the house, its monotony only slightly tempered by Adam's busy plasterwork and the sixty-two individually painted pilasters that line the room. It was in the Long Gallery that Lady Jane Grey was was formally offered the crown by her father-in-law, John Dudley, the owner of Syon at the time; nine days later they were arrested and later beheaded by "Bloody Mary". Passing through the Print Room, which contains yet more works by Lely and Van Dyck, plus a couple by Gainsborough and Reynolds, you exit via the narrow Oak Passage and West Corridor.

Syon House gardens

The gardens are open daily 10am–6pm or dusk; £2.25; combined ticket with house £4.75.

While Adam beautified Syon House, Capability Brown laid out its **gardens** around an artificial lake, surrounding it with oaks, beeches, limes and cedars, and a stretch of lawn overlooked by a statue of Flora. The gardens' highlight, though, is the crescent-shaped **Great Conservatory**, an early nineteenth-century addition which is said to have inspired Joseph Paxton, architect of the Crystal Palace; children may be more impressed by the **miniature steam train** which runs through the park at weekends from April to October.

The Butterfly House

Another plus point for kids (and adults) at Syon is the **Butterfly House**, across the car park from the house and gardens. Here, in a small mesh-covered hothouse, you can walk amid hundreds of exotic butterflies from all over the world, as they flit about amidst the foliage. The largest inhabitant is the Giant Atlas Moth, which only flies at night, but can be admired from close quarters as it sleeps. Other displays show the butterfly in its stages of metamorphosis, and an adjoining room houses a collection of iguanas, millipedes, tarantulas and giant hissing Tanzanian cockroaches.

The Butterfly House is open summer daily 10am–5pm; winter closes 3.30pm; £2.60.

Osterley House and Park

Adam redesigned another colossal Elizabethan mansion three miles northwest of Syon at **Osterley Park** – one of London's largest surviving estate parks, which still gives the impression of being in the middle of the countryside despite the presence of the M4 to the north of the house. The main approach to the house is along a splendid avenue of sweet chestnuts to the south, past the National Trust-sponsored farmhouse (whose produce you can buy all year round). From the car park, the driveway curves past the southernmost of the park's three lakes, with a Chinese pagoda at one end. Cedars planted by the Childs and oaks planted in Victorian times stand between the lake and the house, and to the north are Gresham's grandiose Tudor stables, now converted into a café.

The nearest tube is Osterley.

The park is open daily 10am–dusk.

The House

Unlike Syon, **Osterley House** was built with mercantile wealth – it was erected in 1576 by Thomas Gresham, the brains behind the City's Royal Exchange. Two hundred and fifty years later it was bought by yet another City gent, the goldsmith and banker Francis Child, who appears to have used it merely as a kind of giant safe-deposit box – it was his grandsons who employed Robert Adam to create the house as it is today.

The house is open March Sat & Sun 11am–5pm; April–Oct Wed–Fri 1–5pm, Sat & Sun 11am–5pm; NT; £3.50.

From the outside, Osterley bears some similarity to Syon, the big difference being Adam's grand entrance portico, with a broad flight of steps rising to a tall, Ionic colonnade, which gives access to the central courtyard. From here, you enter Adam's characteristically cool **Entrance Hall**, a double-apsed space decorated with grisaille paintings and classical statuary. The finest rooms are the so-called State Rooms of the south wing, where the nouveau riche Childs hoped, vainly, to entertain royalty as Gresham had once done. The **Drawing Room** is splendid, with Reynolds portraits on the damask walls and a coffered ceiling centred on a giant marigold, a theme continued in the lush carpet and elsewhere in the house. The **Tapestry Room** is hung with Boucher-designed Gobelin tapestries, while the silk-lined **State Bedchamber** features an outrageous domed bed designed by Adam. Lastly, there's the **Etruscan**

Dressing Room, in which every surface is covered in delicate painted trelliswork, sphinxes and urns, in a style Adam (and Wedgwood) dubbed "Etruscan", though it is in fact derived from Greek vases found at Pompeii.

The **Long Gallery** is much broader, taller and plainer than the one at Syon, and like much of the house, features Adam-designed furniture, as well as some fine *chinoiserie*. Sadly, the Childs' collection of Rubens, Van Dyck and Claude pictures no longer hangs here, having been transported to the family's new home in the Channel Islands (where they were destroyed by fire), and replaced instead by second-rank works from the V&A.

The north wing rooms are disappointing after the State Rooms, though the whitewashed Library is worth a quick peek. The Neoclassical **Great Staircase**, stuck rather awkwardly halfway along the north wing, has a replica Rubens ceiling painting, the original having been destroyed by fire while being removed by the last owner in 1949. Only four rooms are open on the first floor; each one pleasant enough, but by no means essential viewing.

The Hanwell Flight, Boston Manor and Pitshanger

The nearest tube is Boston Manor.

The **Grand Union Canal** skirts Osterley Park to the north, linking up with the Brent River, which in turn flows into the Thames at Brentford. You can walk along the towpath at any point, but the most interesting section is the sequence of five manually operated locks known as the **Hanwell Flight**, a mile or so up the canal from where the M4 crosses the canal near Boston Manor tube. Here, the canal drops over fifty feet in less than a quarter of a mile, and though few boats now use the canal, you're quite likely to see some action most weekends.

Boston Manor House

Boston Manor House is open June–Sept Sun 2.30–5pm; free.

To the southeast of Boston Manor tube, down Boston Gardens, is the seventeenth-century **Boston Manor House**. With their magnificent cedar trees and ornamental flowerbeds, the grounds are well worth a visit, even though the M4 cuts right through the middle. If you come on a Sunday in summer you can also visit the house, the highlight of which is the extraordinarily elaborate Jacobean ceiling of the first-floor Drawing Room.

Pitshanger Manor

Pitshanger Manor is open Tues–Sat 10am–5pm; free.

One last west London country house worth mention is **Pitshanger Manor**, a couple of miles north of Boston Manor. Built in 1770, it was later bought and remodelled by Sir John Soane, who in 1811 sold up and moved to Lincoln's Inn Fields (see p.170). In time Pitshanger became the local library, but in the late 1980s the house was superbly restored. The ballustraded main facade, though small, is magnificent, its bays divided by Ionic pillars topped by terracotta statues. As soon as you enter the narrow vestibule Soane stops you short with some spatial gymnastics, by taking a section of the ceiling up through the first floor. To the right is the now book-less Library, which features a cross-vaulted ceiling, decorated with an unusual trelliswork pattern. Soane's masterpiece, though, as at Lincoln's Inn Fields, is the **Breakfast Room**, with caryatids in the four corners and lush red porphyry and grey marbling on the walls.

The nearest tube and train station is Ealing Broadway.

An unexpected bonus is the **Martinware gallery**, a display of the idiosyncratic stoneware pottery produced around the turn of the century by the four Martin brothers from the nearby Southall Pottery. Its centrepiece is their Moorish ceramic fireplace, made for the billiard room at Buscot Park, Oxfordshire. The rest of the ware, including face mugs and bird jars, is more of an acquired taste.

The manor's south wing is all that survives from the original house by George Dance (Soane's architectural teacher), the remainder of which Soane demolished. The rooms are on a much larger scale, providing an interesting contrast to Soane's intimate and highly wrought style, while the Monk's Dining Room in the basement is the precursor of the Monk's Parlour in Lincoln's Inn Fields.

Richmond and Kew

Richmond and Kew, on the south bank of the Thames, basked for centuries in the glow of royal patronage. Plantagenet kings and Tudor monarchs frequented the riverside palace of Shene, as Richmond Palace was then called, while the Hanoverians favoured the royal estates to the north – now the **botanical gardens of Kew**, which manages to be a world-leader in botanical research and an extraordinarily beautiful park at the same time. In the eighteenth century Richmond enjoyed a brief life as a spa, and its agreeable locale began to attract City merchants, as well as successful artists, actors and writers; Pope, Gainsborough, Garrick and Reynolds are just some of the plaque-worthy names associated with the place.

Although most of the courtiers and aristocrats have gone, as has the Tudor palace on Richmond Green, Richmond is still a wealthy district, with two theatres and high-brow pretensions. In reality, though, it's been a commuter town since the arrival of the railway in the 1870s. To fully appreciate its attractions, you need to visit the old village green, walk along the riverside to one of the nearby stately homes of **Ham** or **Marble Hill**, take in the glorious view from **Richmond Hill** and pay a visit to the vast acreage of **Richmond Park**, the old royal hunting grounds, still wild and replete with deer.

Kew Gardens

Richmond and Kew

The nearest tube and train station is Kew Gardens.

The Royal Botanical Gardens started out as a pleasure garden, created in 1731 by Prince Frederick, eldest son of George II and Queen Caroline, who considered their offspring "the greatest ass, the greatest liar, the greatest canaille and the greatest beast in the whole world". But it was the widow of "Poor Fred", Princess Augusta, who established Kew's first botanical gardens in 1759, with the help of her paramour, the Earl of Bute. Some of the earliest specimens were brought back from the voyages of Captain Cook, instantly establishing Kew as a leading botanical research centre. From its original eight acres Kew has grown into a 300-acre site in

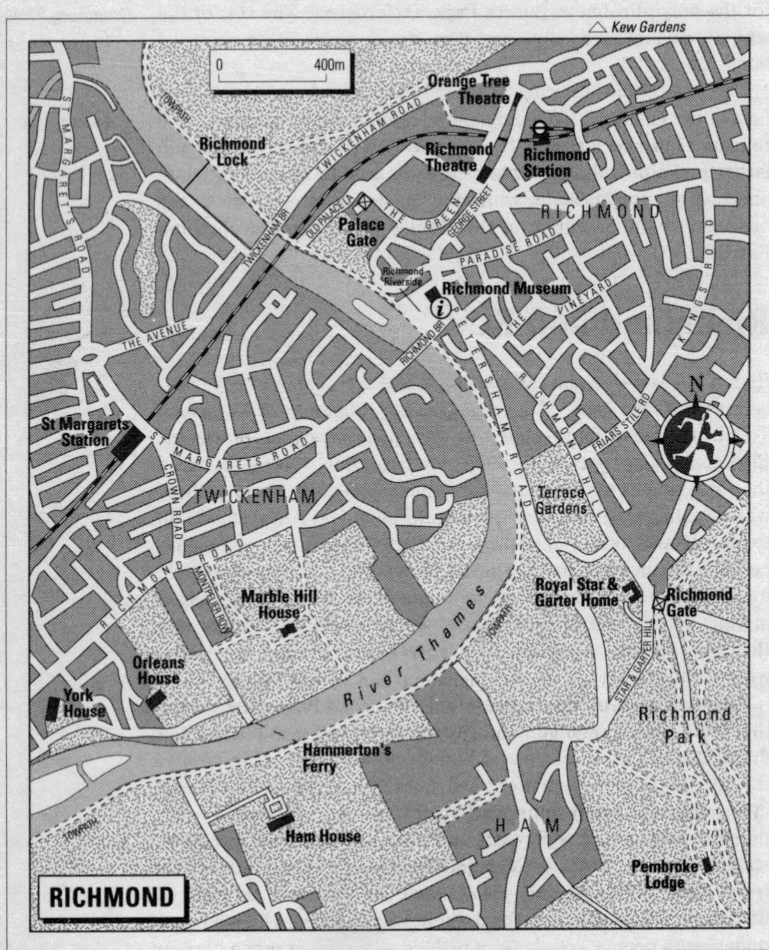

which more than 50,000 species are grown in plantations and glasshouses, a display that attracts over a million visitors every year, the vast majority of them with no specialist interest at all.

Kew Gardens are open daily 9.30am–dusk; £4, £1.50 last hour before closing.

Newens (The Maids of Honour), Kew's finest tea rooms are located opposite Victoria Gate on Kew Road; closed Sun.

The glasshouses

There are five entry points to the gardens, but the vast majority of people arrive at Kew Gardens tube and train station, a few minutes' walk east of the **Victoria Gate**, at the end of Lichfield Road. Here you'll find the main shop and visitor centre, with videos and displays about Kew. Be sure to check out the Kew Mural as you pass through – it's an unattractive piece of art, but it's made from twenty-three varieties of wood, and stands as a testimony to the one thousand trees damaged or destroyed at Kew in the 1987 storm. If at any point you're trying to find your way back to the Victoria Gate, look out for the **Campanile** which stands right next to it, and originally served as the chimney for the furnaces below the Palm House.

Beyond lies the Pond, home to a handful of black swans and two ten-ton Ming lions, and the best vantage point from which to appreciate the **Palm House**, the first and most famous of Kew's magnificent array of glasshouses. A curvaceous mound of glass and wrought-iron, the Palm House was designed by Decimus Burton in the 1840s, predating the Crystal Palace by some three years. Its drippingly humid atmosphere nurtures most of the known palm species, while in the basement there's a small but excellent aquarium. You can turn the heat up further by going to the diminutive **Waterlily House** (north of the Palm House), where a canopy of plants and creepers overhangs a circular lily pond.

To cool off, head for the **Princess of Wales Conservatory**, a rather less graceful glasshouse a little further to the north. Opened in 1987, it nurtures plants from ten distinct climatic zones, from cactus-infested desert to cloud forest. Giant koi fish swim stealthily beneath the pathways, while giant waterlilies and visitors alike benefit from intermittent artificial rainfall; an ecological slide show takes place in the underground exhibition hall.

The largest of all the glasshouses is the **Temperate House**, another of Decimus Burton's innovative structures, twice the size of the Palm House and almost forty years in the making. It contains plants from every continent, including one of the largest indoor palms in the world, the sixty-foot Chilean Wine Palm, first planted in 1846 and currently approaching the roof (and therefore the end of its life).

The eighteenth-century gardens

Almost nothing survives of William Chambers' landscape gardening at Kew, but some of the buildings he created in the 1760s for the amusement of Princess Augusta remain dotted about the gardens. The **Orangery** was one of the earliest, and the largest hothouse in the country when it was built; it now houses a restaurant and shop.

The Pagoda is closed to the public.

The most famous is his ten-storey 163-foot-high **Pagoda**, Kew's most distinctive landmark, though disappointing close up, having lost the eighty enamelled dragons which used to adorn it.

To the north of the Pagoda, you can walk through Chambers' **Ruined Arch**, purpose-built with sundry pieces of Roman masonry strewn about as if tossed there by barbarian hordes. Close by is Kew's tallest object, a 225-foot-high flagpole fashioned from a single Canadian fir tree and erected in 1959. The rest of Chambers' works are all classical temples, the most picturesque being the **Temple of Aeolus**, situated on one of Kew's few hillocks close to Cumberland Gate, surrounded by a carpet of bluebells and daffodils in the spring.

The Cottage is open April–Sept Sat–Sun 11am–5.30pm; 70p, joint ticket with Kew Palace £1.50. Kew Palace is open April–Sept daily 11am–5.30pm; £1.20.

Capability Brown's work on the gardens at Kew has proved more durable than Chambers': his lake remains a focal point of the Syon vista from the Palm House, and the **Rhododendron Dell** he devised survives to the south of it. This more thickly wooded, southwestern section of the park is the bit to head for if you want to lose the crowds, few of whom ever make it to **Queen Charlotte's Cottage**, a tiny thatched summerhouse created as a royal picnic spot.

Kew Palace

With so much natural beauty around, it's hardly surprising that the country's smallest royal residence, **Kew Palace**, to the west of the orangery, is often overlooked. A three-storey red-brick mansion measuring a mere 70ft by 50ft, it was commonly known as the "Dutch House", after its fancy Flemish-bond brickwork and its curly Dutch gables. It's the sole survivor of the three royal palaces which once stood at Kew and was bought by George II as a nursery for his umpteen children. The only king to live here, though, was George III who was confined here from 1802 onwards and subjected to the dubious attentions of two doctors who attempted to find a cure for his "madness" by straitjacketing him and applying poultices of mustard and Spanish Fly. There's nothing much inside, though you can mug up on your Hanoverian history and see the moth-eaten chair in which George III's wife, Queen Charlotte, passed away.

More enjoyable is the secluded **Queen's Garden**, to the north of the house. In contrast to much of Kew, the garden is laid out formally with a geometrical parterre of box hedges, lavender, sage and rosemary. To the west is the sunken Nosegay Garden, bordered by plaited laburnum avenues, while to the east runs a narrow walk between prim hornbeam hedges, leading to a gilded gazebo.

Kew Gardens Gallery is open the same times as the park but closed for lunch

The galleries and Kew Green

Kew also boasts two little-known art galleries, some distance from one another along the eastern edge of the gardens. **Kew Gardens Gallery**, the larger of the two, is in the northeastern corner of the gardens in Cambridge Cottage, originally the Earl of Bute's residence but rebuilt in Queen Anne style in 1867. The gallery puts on temporary exhibitions on a wide variety of horticultural themes. To the south of Victoria Gate stands the **Marianne North Gallery**, purpose-built in 1882 to house the prolific output of the self-trained artist Marianne North. Over 800 paintings, completed in fourteen years of hectic world travel, are displayed end to end, filling every single space in the gallery.

Last of all, a quick mention of Decimus Burton's majestic **Main Gates**, which fulfilled their stated function until the arrival of the railway at Kew. Beyond the gates lies **Kew Green**, which rivals Richmond's for the accolade of London's prettiest village green, lined as it is with Georgian houses and centred on the red-brick church of **St Anne**. The latter is an unusual building, sporting an ordinary polygonal clock turret at one end and a peculiar octagonal cupola at the other; the painters Gainsborough and Zoffany lie in the churchyard.

Richmond Green and Palace

On emerging from the station at **Richmond**, you'd be forgiven for wondering why you're here, but the procession of chain stores spread out along the one-way system is only half the story. To see Richmond's more interesting side, take one of the narrow pedestrianized alleyways off busy George Street, a few minutes' walk west of the station. Lined with arty shops and tea rooms, these will bring you to the wide open space of **Richmond Green**, one of the finest village greens in London, and no doubt once one of the most peaceful before it found itself on the the main flight path into Heathrow. Handsome seventeenth- and eighteenth-century houses line the southwest and southeast sides of the green, with the most striking building of all the flamboyant *Richmond Theatre*, built in terracotta and brick in 1899, on Little Green, to the northeast of its larger neighbour.

Richmond boasts another excellent venue, the Orange Tree Theatre, which puts on off-West End and fringe productions in its newly refurbished Victorian building, situated on Clarence Street, very close to the station.

On the southwest side of the green is the site of medieval **Richmond Palace**, built originally in the twelfth century (when it was known as Shene Palace) and acquired by Henry I in 1125. The first king to frequent the place was Edward III, who lay dying here in 1377 while his mistress urged the servants to prise the rings from his fingers. Seventeen years later a grief-stricken Richard II razed the place to the ground after his wife, Anne of Bohemia, died here of plague. Henry V had it restored and Edward IV held jousting tournaments on the green, but it was Henry VII, in an untypical burst of extravagance, who constructed the largest complex of all, renaming it Richmond after his Yorkshire earldom. Henry VIII was born here, and later granted the palace to his fourth wife, Anne of Cleves, as part of their surprisingly amicable divorce settlement. Mary and Philip of Spain spent part of their honeymoon here and Elizabeth I came here to die in 1603.

Very little of Richmond Palace survived the Commonwealth and even less is visible now. The most obvious relic is the unspectacular **Tudor Gateway**, on the south side of the green; to the left, the building calling itself Old Palace incorporates some of the Tudor brickwork of the outer wall. The gateway, which once led into the palace's outer courtyard, now takes you into **Old Palace Yard**, a sort of miniature village green, and Crown property even today. The palace's furnishings were once stored in the building on the left – a trio of houses known collectively as the **Wardrobe**.

Richmond Riverside

Neglected for many years, the main river frontage of **Richmond Riverside** was pedestrianized, terraced and redeveloped by Quinlan Terry, Prince Charles' favourite purveyor of ersatz classicism, in the late 1980s. To the untrained eye, the Georgian buildings initially look convincing enough, but closer inspection reveals them to be a sham: the cupolas conceal air vents, the chimneys are decorative and the facades are masks, hiding offices and flats. A few of the original Georgian and Victorian buildings do remain, though, like **Heron House**, a narrow three-storey building, where Lady Hamilton and her daughter Horatia came to live shortly after Trafalgar, the battle in which the girl's father died. Steps lead through the house's ground-level arch to the desolate space of Heron Square, which looks like a film set without any extras.

The tourist office is open Mon–Fri 10am–6pm, Sat 10am–5pm, Sun 10.15am–4.15pm; Nov–April closed Sun; ☎0181/940 7970.

The real joy of the waterfront is **Richmond Bridge** to the south – an elegant span of five arches made from Purbeck stone in 1777, and cleverly widened in the 1930s, thus preserving London's oldest extant bridge. The old town hall, set slightly back from the new development, to the north, now houses a **tourist office**, a library and, on the second floor, the **Richmond Museum**. The museum contains a small permanent exhibition on the history of the town, plus the lowdown on (and a model of) the royal palace; temporary displays tend to focus on Richmond's past luminaries.

The museum is open Tues–Sat 11am–5pm, Sun 1.30–4pm; Nov–April closed Sun; £1.

Richmond Hill

If you're still wondering what's so special about Richmond, take a hike up **Richmond Hill**. To get there, head up Hill Rise from the top of Bridge Street, passing the eighteenth-century antique shops and tea rooms on your left and the small sloping green on your right. Eventually you come to **Terrace Gardens**, which stretch right down to the river. The gardens are worth exploring but are most celebrated for the view from the top terrace out across the thickly wooded Thames valley. Turner, Reynolds, Kokoschka and countless other artists have painted this view, which takes in six counties from Windsor to the North Downs.

Richmond's wealthiest inhabitants have flocked to the hill's commanding heights over the centuries. The future George IV is alleged to have spent his honeymoon at **3 The Terrace**, after marrying Mrs Fitzherbert; twice divorced and a Catholic to boot, she was never likely to gain official approval, though she bore the prince ten children. Further along, on the opposite side of the street, William Chambers built **Wick House** in 1772 as a summer residence for the enormously successful Joshua Reynolds. The building currently houses the nurses who work at the nearby **Royal Star & Garter Home**, a rest home for war veterans built shortly after World War I and now the dominant feature of the hillside.

From April to October you can rent row boats from the nearby jetties, or take a boat trip to Hampton Court or Westminster.

Richmond Park

Richmond's greatest attraction is the enormous **Richmond Park**, at the top of Richmond Hill – over 2000 acres of undulating grassland and bracken, dotted with coppiced woodland and as wild as anything in London. Royal hunting ground since the thirteenth century (when it was known as Shene Chase), this is Europe's largest city park – eight miles across at its widest point – famous for its red and fallow deer, which roam freely here (and breed so successfully, they have to be culled twice a year) and for its ancient oaks. Though for the most part untamed, there are a couple of deliberately landscaped plantations which feature splendid springtime azaleas and rhododendrons.

The park is open March–Sept 7am–dusk; Nov–Feb 7.30am–dusk; free.

Charles I was the first to formally establish the royal park, appropriating land willy-nilly against the counsel of his advisers, and enclosing his "New Park" with a high wall nine miles long (still in existence) to keep out trespassers. Equally unpopular with the locals was **Princess Amelia**, youngest daughter of George II, who closed the park off to all but her closest friends shortly after being appointed Ranger in 1747. Local opposition, in particular from a Richmond brewer **John Lewis**, who sued the gatekeeper, Martha Gray, for assault, eventually succeeded in forcing through public access, prompting Amelia's resignation after which she moved to Gunnersbury (p.364). Lewis became a local hero, though he was bankrupted by the legal costs and the subsequent flooding of his brewery and died in poverty.

Walking or cycling are the two best ways of getting around the park. You can hire bikes from Supercycles, 219 Lower Mortlake Rd; ☎0181/940 3717.

From Richmond Gate, at the top of Richmond Hill, it's a short walk south along the crest of the hill to **Pembroke Lodge** (originally known as The Molecatcher's), enlarged in 1788 by Sir John Soane, childhood home of the philosopher Bertrand Russell, and now a teahouse with outdoor seating affording yet more spectacular views across the Thames valley. Close by, to the north, is the highest point in the park, known as **King Henry VIII's Mount**, where tradition has it the king waited for the rocket launched from the Tower of London, which signalled the execution of his second wife, Anne Boleyn, though historians believe he was in Wiltshire at the time.

For a much longer stroll through the park, head east from Pembroke Lodge into **Sidmouth Wood**, whose sweet chestnuts, oaks and beeches were planted during the nineteenth century.

Originally established as pheasant cover, the wood is now a bird sanctuary, and walkers must keep to the central path, known as the Driftway. A little further east lie the **Pen Ponds**, the largest stretches of water in the park (it's possible to fish here, if you have a permit). To the south is by far the most popular section of the park, the **Isabella Plantation**, a carefully landscaped woodland park created in 1951, with a little rivulet running through it, two small artifical ponds, and spectacular rhododendrons and azaleas in the spring. The round trip from Richmond gate is about four miles.

The two most important historic buildings in the park are sadly both closed to the public. Of the two, the **White Lodge**, to the east of the Pen Ponds, is the most attractive, a Palladian villa commissioned by George II, and frequented by his wife, Queen Caroline, and their daughter, the aforementioned Amelia. Much altered over the years, it was also the birthplace of the ill-fated Edward VIII, and home to the Duke and Duchess of York (later George VI and the Queen Mum); it currently houses the Royal Ballet School. The **Thatched House Lodge**, in the southernmost corner of the park, was built in the 1670s for the park's Rangers, and gets its name from the thatched gazebo in the garden. General Eisenhower hung out in the lodge during World War II and it's now home to Princess Alexandra and her hubby, Angus Ogilvy.

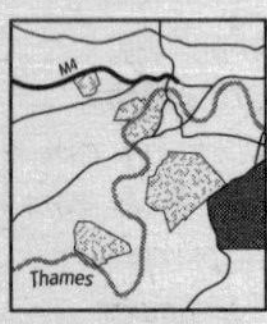

Wimbledon

Five miles southwest of Richmond, **Wimbledon** is, of course, famous for its tennis tournament, the Wimbledon Championship, held every year in the last week of June and the first week of July, on the grass courts of the All England Lawn Tennis and Croquet Club – to give the ground its official title. If you've missed the tournament itself, the next best thing for tennis fans is a quick spin around the Wimbledon Lawn Tennis Museum, featuring heaps of memorabilia, hours of vintage game footage plus a chance to see the hallowed Centre Court.

The Tennis Museum is open Tues–Sat 10.30am–5pm, Sun 2–5pm; £2; during championship daily 10.30am–7pm for ticket holders only; bus #39, #93 or #200 from Southfields tube. See p.530 for tournament details.

Wimbledon Common

There is one other reason to visit Wimbledon and that's **Wimbledon Common**, which with neighbouring Putney Heath covers an area more than three times the size of its better-known North London rival, Hampstead Heath. After Richmond Park, to the west, Wimbledon can appear rather bleak; mostly rough grass and bracken punctuated by playing fields and golf courses and cut through by the busy A3. As at Richmond, the Common has been under threat periodically from its blue-blooded landlords, most recently the Spencer family (ancestors of Princess Di), who in 1865 tried unsuccessfully to get a bill through parliament allowing them to sell off part of the Common and enclose the rest. Historically, the Common was a popular venue for duelling from at least the seventeenth century. Several Prime Ministers are recorded as having fought here, including George Canning, who was shot in the leg by another ex-minister, and William Pitt the Younger, who faced the local MP in 1798 – neither were seasoned marksmen and after two attempts and two misses, the duel was called off. The last recorded duel took place (illegally) in 1840.

The chief landmark is the **Wimbledon Windmill**, situated at the end of Windmill Road in the northern half of the Common, with a conveniently placed café nearby. Built in 1817, the mill was closed down in 1864 as part of the Spencer family's plans to sell off part of the Common, and converted into cottages, one of which was home to Baden-Powell, when he began writing his *Scouting for Boys* in 1908. The windmill has since been restored and turned into a museum, which helps to elucidate the significance of this, the last remaining hollow-post flour mill in the country; you can also climb into the first section of the wooden cap and see the giant chain wheel. The nearby pool of **Queen's Mere**, just to the west of the windmill, is one of the Common's most appealing spots, overhung with beech and oak, and home to numerous toads, coots and the odd heron.

The windmill is open April–Oct Sat & Sun 2–5pm; 50p; bus #93 from Wimbledon tube.

Ham and Twickenham

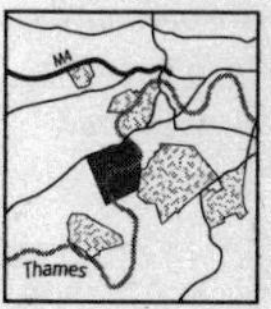

Ham and **Twickenham** lie on either side of the Thames to the south of Richmond. **Ham House**, off the beaten track and under-visited, has recently been thoroughly restored by the National Trust and the V&A, and is now one of the most appealing of all the historic houses along the river. Twickenham, best known for its rugby – there's a museum if you're really keen – also conceals a cluster of lesser-known sights close to the river, all of which repay a brief visit. The banks are connected all year round by ferry, or, weather permitting, the round trip of just over two miles from Richmond Riverside makes for a pleasant day's walk.

The Rugby Museum is open Mon–Fri 9.30am–1pm & 2.15–5pm; free. For tickets to games, see p.530.

Ham House

The best approach to **Ham House** is by foot from Richmond Riverside – heading south along the towpath which eventually leaves the rest of London far behind. On either side are the wooded banks of the Thames, to the left sheep graze on Petersham Meadows, while hidden in the woods some way beyond lies Ham House, home to the Earls of Dysart for nearly three hundred years.

The first Earl of Dysart was Charles I's childhood whipping boy (he literally received the punishment on behalf of the prince when the latter misbehaved), who was granted a peerage and the estate of Ham for his pains, but it was his ambitious daughter, Elizabeth – at one time Oliver Cromwell's lover – who is most closely associated

Ham House is open April–Sept Mon–Wed 1–5pm, Sat 1–5.30pm, Sun 11.30am–5.30pm; Nov–March Sat & Sun only; NT: £4; bus #65 from Richmond tube.

with the place. With the help of her second husband, the Earl of Lauderdale, one of the most powerful minsters to Charles II, she added numerous extra rooms, "furnished like a great Prince's" according to diarist John Evelyn, and succeeded in shocking even Restoration society with her extravagance.

Elizabeth's profligacy left the family heavily in debt, and the later Earls of Dysart could afford to make few alterations, prompting Horace Walpole (who lived across the river at Strawberry Hill) to describe Ham as a "Sleeping Beauty". Recent restoration has only enhanced this period piece, which boasts one of the finest Stuart interiors in the country. The Great Staircase, to the east of the central hall, is stupendously ornate, featuring huge bowls of fruit at the newel posts and trophies of war carved into the balustrade. The rest of the house is equally sumptuous, with lavish plasterwork, silverwork and parquet flooring, Verrio ceiling paintings and rich hangings, tapestries, silk damasks and cut velvets. The Long Gallery, in the west wing, features six "Court Beauties" by Peter Lely and elsewhere there are works by Van Dyck and Reynolds.

The gardens are open daily 10.30am–6pm or dusk; free.

Another bonus are the formal seventeenth-century **gardens**, recently restored to something like their former glory. The first feature to be appreciated on entering the grounds from the river are the stone pineapples (looking more like pine cones) set at intervals along the railings. To the east lies the Cherry Garden, laid out with a pungent lavender parterre, surrounded by yew hedges and pleached hornbeam arbours. To the south, there's a "Wilderness", where the Lauderdales would display their orange trees, considered the height of luxury at the time. Finally, to the west, you'll find the original kitchen garden, now a rose garden, overlooked by the orangery (which currently serves as a tea room).

Marble Hill, Orleans House and York House

Hammerton's ferry can take you across the Thames between Easter–Oct daily on demand; Nov–Easter Sat & Sun only.

On the Twickenham side of the river, not far from Hammerton's Ferry, is **Marble Hill House**, a stuccoed Palladian villa set in rolling green parkland. Unlike Chiswick, this is no architectural exercise, but a real house, built in 1729 for the Countess of Suffolk, mistress of George II for some twenty years and, conveniently perhaps, also a lady-in-waiting to his wife, Queen Caroline. Her wit and intelligence (though not her beauty) were renowned and she entertained literary figures of the day such as Alexander Pope, John Gay and Horace Walpole Another royal mistress, Mrs Fitzherbert, the Prince Regent's unofficial wife, later occupied the house in 1795.

Nothing remains of the original furnishings, alas, and though some period furniture has taken its place, the house feels barren. The principal room is the Great Room on the *piano nobile*, a perfect cube whose coved ceiling carries on up into the top floor apartments. Copies of Van Dyck decorate the walls as they did in Lady Suffolk's day and a further splash of colour is provided by Panini's Roman landscapes above each of the five doors (two of which are purely decorative to complete the symmetery). The other highlight is Lady Suffolk's Bedchamber, which features an Ionic columned recess – a classic Palladian device.

Marble Hill House is open April–Oct daily 10am–6pm; Nov–March Wed–Sun 10am–4pm; free.

Set in a small adjacent wood to the west of Marble Hill House is **Orleans House**, a villa built in 1710 for James Johnston, occupied by the exiled Duc d'Orléans in 1815–17, and subsequently all but entirely demolished in 1926 – all, that is, except for the **Octagon**. Designed by James Gibbs in 1720 as a garden pavilion, it was added to the original house by Johnston in honour of a visit by the aforementioned Queen Caroline. Though the gallery puts on interesting exhibitions in the modern extension, it's the Octagon that steals the limelight, with its masterly Italian stucco decoration.

The Orleans House Gallery is open April–Sept Tues–Sat 1–5.30pm, Sun 2.30–4.30pm; Oct–March closes 4.30pm; free.

A little further west, towards Twickenham town centre, is **York House**, an early seventeenth-century mansion which now belongs to the local council, though the gardens, laid out by the last private owner, the Indian prince Sir Ratan Tata, are open to the public. The bit to head for is the riverside section – which lies on the other side of the delicate arched bridge spanning the road; here you'll find the house's celebrated "naked ladies", eight marble nymphs frolicking in the waters of an Italian fountain.

Strawberry Hill

One last Twickenham oddity well worth making the effort to visit is Strawberry Hill, the Gothick fantasy home of writer, wit and fashion queen, Horace Walpole, youngest son of the Prime Minister, Sir Robert Walpole. In 1747 Walpole bought this "little play-thing house . . . the prettiest bauble you ever saw . . . set in enamelled meadows, with filigree hedges", renamed it Strawberry Hill and set about inventing the most influential building in the Gothic Revival. Walpole appointed a "Committee of Taste" to embellish his project with details from other Gothic buildings: screens from Old St Paul's and Rouen Cathedral, and fan vaulting from Henry VII's Chapel in Westminster Abbey.

Strawberry Hill is open April–Oct Sun 2–4.30pm; rest of the year by appointment; ☎0181/892 0051.

The house quickly became the talk of London, a place of pilgrimage for royalty and foreign dignitaries alike. Walpole was forced to issue tickets to cut down the number of visitors, whom he used to greet dressed in a lavender suit and silver embroidered waistcoat, sporting a cravat carved in wood by Grinling Gibbons and an enormous pair of gloves which once belonged to James I. When he died in 1797, he left the house to his friend the sculptor Anne Damer, who continued to entertain in the same spirit, giving lavish garden parties dressed in a man's coat, hat and shoes. The house is now owned and carefully maintained by St Mary's Roman Catholic Training College.

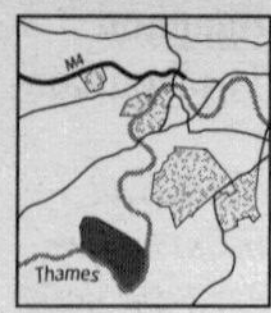

Hampton Court Palace

Hampton Court Palace is open March–Oct Mon 10.15am–6pm, Tues–Sun 9.30am–6pm; Oct–March Mon closes 4.30pm, other hours the same; £7 including maze.

The nearest train station is Hampton Court, accessible direct from Waterloo; see p.359 for boats from Richmond, Kew and Westminster piers.

Hampton Court Palace, a sprawling red-brick ensemble on the banks of the Thames, thirteen miles southwest of London, is the finest of England's royal abodes. It began life, however, as an ecclesiastical palace, built in 1516 by the upwardly mobile **Cardinal Wolsey**, Henry VIII's high-powered, fast-living Lord Chancellor. The good times which rolled at Hampton prompted Henry to enquire why the cardinal had built such an extravagant home for himself. Wolsey, in a vain attempt to win back the king's favour, made the fatal reply "to show how noble a palace a subject may offer to his sovereign". In 1529, when Wolsey failed to secure a papal annulment for Henry's marriage to Catherine of Aragon, Henry took him at his word, sacked him and moved into Hampton Court.

Like Wolsey, **Henry VIII** spent enormous sums of money on the palace, enlarging the kitchens, rebuilding the chapel and altering the rooms to suit the tastes of the last five of his six wives. Under Elizabeth I and James I Hampton Court became renowned for its masques, plays and balls; during the Civil War, it was a refuge and then a prison for Charles I. The palace was put up for sale during the Commonwealth, but with no buyers forthcoming, Cromwell decided to move in and lived here until his death in 1658. Charles II laid out the gardens, inspired by what he had seen at Versailles, but it was **William and Mary** who made the most radical alterations, hiring Christopher Wren to remodel the buildings. Wren intended to tear down the whole palace and build a new Versailles, but contented himself with rebuilding the east and south wings, adding the Banqueting House on the river, and completing the chapel for Queen Anne.

George III eschewed the place, apparently because he associated it with the beatings he received here from his grandfather, George II. Instead, he established grace-and-favour residencies for indigent members of the royal household, premises which still occupy parts of the palace not opened to the public by Queen Victoria in 1838. In March 1986, extensive damage was sustained in a fire started by one such elderly grace-and-favour resident, Lady Gale, who ignited the silk hangings with a bedside candle and died in the blaze.

The palace

From the train station, it's a short walk across the river to the **Trophy Gates**, designed for William III as the main approach to the palace, but not completed until the reign of George II, when the frisky-looking lion and unicorn were added. The ticket office and main shop are housed in the former Cavalry Barracks on the left. Ahead lies the Tudor west front, no longer moated but prickling with turrets, castellations, chimneypots and pinnacles. The **Great Gatehouse**, the main entrance to the palace courtyards, would have been twice its present height in Wolsey's day.

Before you get stuck into the royal apartments, it's worth getting your bearings by walking through the three main courtyards. The first and largest quadrangle, **Base Court**, is reminiscent of an Oxbridge college and features another Tudor gateway known as Anne Boleyn's Gateway, though it too dates from the time of Wolsey. Beyond lies **Clock Court**, which has none of the uniformity of the other two courtyards: to the north rises the Tudor Great Hall (see below), to the south Wren's colonnade, announcing the new state apartments, and to the east a fairly convincing mock-Tudor gateway by William Kent. Originally centred on a large fountain

Hampton Court Palace

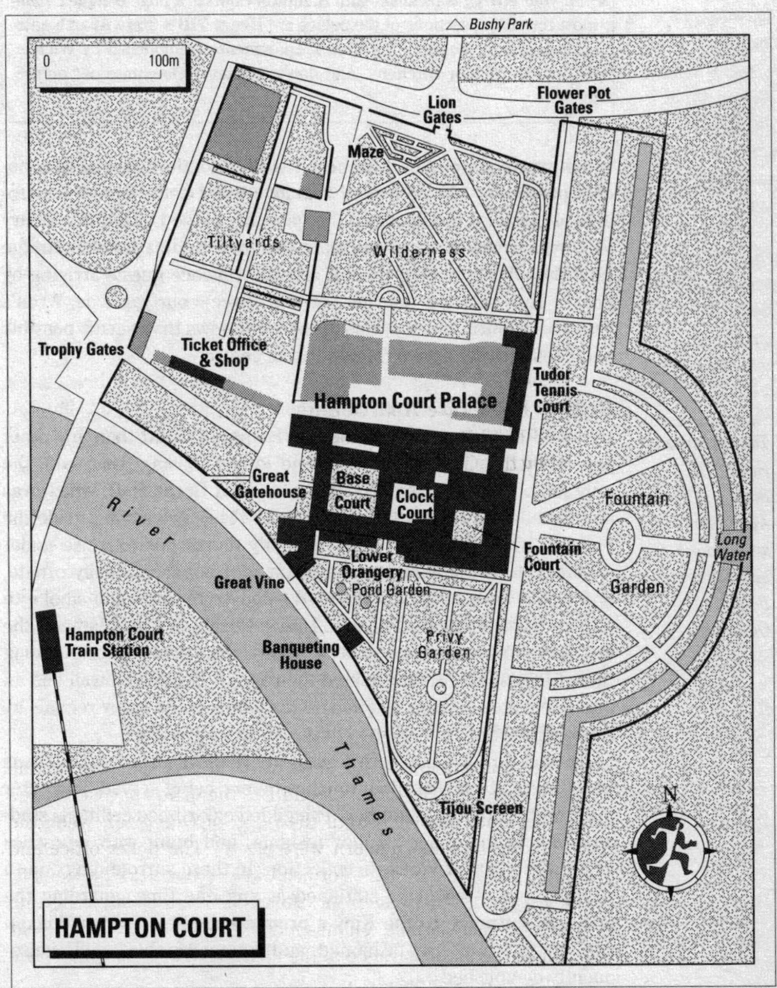

Visiting the royal apartments

The royal apartments are divided into six thematic walking tours, which are numbered and colour-coded. Guided tours, each lasting forty-five minutes, are available at no extra charge for Henry VIII's, the King's and (in summer) the Queen's apartments; all are led by period-costumed historians, who do a fine job of bringing the place to life. In addition, the King's Apartments and the Tudor Kitchens are served by audio tours, available (again at no extra charge), from either of the pick-up points in the northwest corner of Clock Court and the south wing of Fountain Court. The audio tours have no fast forward button, and take forty-five and twenty-five minutes respectively.

If your energy is lacking – and Hampton Court is a huge complex – the most rewarding sections of the palace are **Henry VIII's State Apartments** (aka the Tudor Rooms), the **King's Apartments** (remodelled by William III) and the **Tudor Kitchens**. And don't, whatever else, miss out on the **maze**.

which was equipped by Elizabeth I with a nozzle that soaked innocent passers-by, the courtyard gets its current name from the astrological clock on the inside of the gateway, made in 1540 for Henry VIII, which was used to calculate the high tide at London Bridge (and thus the estimated time of arrival of palace guests arriving by boat). The last and smallest of the three courtyards is Wren's **Fountain Court**, which crams in more windows than seems possible and does actually have a fountain at its centre.

Henry VIII's State Apartments

The entrance to Henry VIII's State Apartments is situated beneath Anne Boleyn's Gateway.

Henry VIII lavished more money on Hampton Court than any other palace except Greenwich (which no longer exists). That said, the only major survival from Tudor times is his **Great Hall**, which was completed with remarkable speed in 1534, Henry having made the builders work day and night – a highly dangerous exercise under candlelight. The double hammerbeam roof is exceptionally ornate, and would have originally featured a louvre to allow the smoke to escape from the central hearth. Under Elizabeth I and James I the hall served as the palace theatre, where theatrical troupes, among them Shakespeare's, entertained the royalty. Even Cromwell had an organ installed here so that he and his family could enjoy recitals by John Milton, an accomplished musician as well as poet.

Passing through the Horn Room, where dishes from the kitchens below were given their final touches before being served, you enter the **Great Watching Chamber**. The gilded oak-ribbed ceiling is studded with leather-maché Tudor insignia, and hung with tapestries which were part of Wolsey's collection. In these surroundings up to eighty yeomen would be stationed at any one time, guarding the principal entrance to the King's private chambers, which William and Mary found "old-fashioned and uncomfortable" and consequently demolished.

From here you come to the **Haunted Gallery**, built by Wolsey to connect his apartments to the chapel, and home to the ghost of Henry's fifth wife, nineteen-year-old Catherine Howard. The night before her arrest for high treason in November 1541, Catherine is alleged to have run down the gallery in an attempt to make a final plea for mercy to the King, who was praying in the chapel. Henry refused to see her and she was dragged kicking and screaming back to her chambers – or so the story goes, for it's been proved that Catherine could not, in fact, have reached the chapel from her rooms via the gallery.

The Haunted Gallery leads into the Royal Pew in the chapel gallery, which was decorated for Queen Mary but has been a feature since Wolsey's day – it was here that Henry VIII was passed the note alleging that Catherine Howard was not in fact a virgin when he married her. From here, you can look down on the **Chapel Royal**, and admire the colourful false timber vaulting wrought in plaster, heavy with pendants of gilded music-making cherubs – one of the most memorable sights in the whole palace.

The Queen's Apartments

The Queen's Apartments were intended for Queen Mary II, but completed some years after her death in 1694. The main approach is via the grandiose **Queen's Staircase**, splendidly decorated with *trompe l'oeil* reliefs and a coffered dome by William Kent. This, in turn, leads to the **Queen's Guard Chamber**, where life-size marble yeomen guard the main chimneypiece.

The entrance to the Queen's Apartments is situated in the passageway between Clock and Fountain Courts.

The Queen's state rooms continue in the east wing of Fountain Court, overlooking Fountain Garden and Long Water. One of the finest is the **Queen's Drawing Room**, decorated top to bottom with paintings depicting Queen Anne's husband, George of Denmark – in heroic naval guise, and also, on the south wall, riding naked on the back of a dolphin. Queen Anne takes centre stage on the ceiling as Justice, somewhat inappropriate given her habit of not paying her craftsmen, including Verrio, the painter of this room. After Anne's death in 1714, the Prince and Princess of Wales (later George II and Queen Caroline) took over the Queen's apartments, until they fell out with the King in 1717 and moved to Kew. The ceiling painting in the **Queen's Bedroom** by James Thornhill pre-dates the quarrel, with a seemingly happy Hanoverian family portrait in the coving.

The **Queen's Gallery** features one of the finest marble fireplaces in the palace – originally intended for the King's Bedchamber – with putti, doves and Venus frolicking above the mantelpiece. The walls are hung with Gobelins tapestries depicting Alexander the Great's exploits, and there are a few tulip vases and china pagodas from William and Mary's vast collection of Delft ware. This route ends with **Queen Mary's Closet**, so-called because the walls were once hung with needlework by the queen and her ladies, though Mary herself never set foot in the place.

The entrance to the Georgian Rooms is situated on the east side of Fountain Court.

The Georgian Rooms

The **Georgian Rooms** route begins with the ascent of the Caithness Staircase, which leads to the **Queen's Private Chapel**, completed for Queen Caroline in 1728 – it's one of the few windowless rooms, hence the octagonal dome and skylight. Apart from a couple of marble wall basins and the Gibbons' overmantle in the King's Private Chamber, the rooms prior to the Cartoon Gallery contain little of interest.

The **Cartoon Gallery** itself, designed by Wren for the Raphael cartoons now in the V&A (see p.276), was at the heart of the 1986 fire. By a stroke of luck, the Brussels tapestries which are now hanging here, some of which were made from the cartoons, were elsewhere on the night of the disaster. Next is the **Communication Gallery**, constructed to link the King's and Queen's apartments, now lined with Lely's flattering portraits of the mistresses of Charles II.

Beyond here you'll find the tiny **Wolsey Closet**, the only remnant of Wolsey's apartments, and a tantalizing glimpse of the splendour of the original palace. It's a jewel of a room, though easy to miss as it's just 12ft square, with brightly coloured fifteenth-century paintings set above exquisite linenfold panelling and a fantastic gilded ceiling of interlaced octagons.

Last of all you enter the three small rooms of the **Cumberland Suite**, lived in by George II before his accession, then by his eldest son Prince Frederick, and lastly by Frederick's brother, the Duke of Cumberland, better known as "Butcher Cumberland" for his ruthless suppression of the Jacobites in Scotland. The rooms were decorated by Kent, who added Gothick touches to the first two rooms and a grandiose Neoclassical alcove in the bedchamber.

The entrance to the King's Apartments is situated in the south wing of Clock Court.

The King's Apartments

William III's state apartments are approached via the **King's Staircase**, the grandest of the lot thanks chiefly to Verrio's busy *trompe l'oeil* paintings glorifying the King, depicted here as Alexander the Great. The **King's Guard Chamber** is notable chiefly for its 3000-piece display of arms, arranged as they were laid out in the time of William III. William's rather modest throne still stands in the **King's Presence Chamber**, under a canopy of crimson damask. The magnificent sixteenth-century Brussels tapestries in the room were originally commissioned by Henry VIII for Whitehall Palace.

The rest of the rooms on this floor feature furnishings similar to those in the corresponding apartments for the Queen (see above) – most notably woodwork by Gibbons and ceiling paintings by Verrio. They are gradually being put back to their original state, following damage in the 1986 fire. Ground floor highlights include the only room in the palace lockable solely from the inside (a tryst room – highly unusual for the royals' very public life), a splendidly throne-like velvet toilet and the **Orangery**, built to house the King's orange trees during the winter. Past here is the **King's Private Dining Room**, its table laden with pyramids of meringues and fruit. Its chief interest is a series of eight full-length portraits of Queen Mary's favourite ladies-in-waiting (known as the "Hampton Court Beauties") for which the German-born painter Godfrey Kneller received a knighthood. Several of these rooms are frequented by the costumed guides, who can expound on related anecdotes.

The entrance to the Wolsey Rooms is situated in the southeastern corner of Clock Court.

The Wolsey Rooms and the Renaissance Picture Gallery

The **Wolsey Rooms** comprise three early Tudor rooms, where the only reminder of Wolsey's day is the linenfold panelling of the walls. The suite now houses the palace's **Renaissance Picture Gallery** which is chock-full of treasures from the vast private collection of the current monarch. Among the finest are a Raphael self-portrait presented to George III in 1781, Bronzino's *Portrait of a Lady in Green*, a soft-focus depiction of an aristocrat from the court of Pesaro and Lotto's portrait of the art collector Andrea Odoni, surrounded by artefacts. Pieter Breugel the Elder's *Massacre of the Innocents* looks more like a village fete, though it was intended as an allegory for the contemporary atrocities committed by the Spanish troops of the Duke of Alba in Holland. Other paintings include Daniel Myrtens' *Charles I and Henrietta Maria*, which displeased the king so much it had to be repainted, using a more flattering portrait of the queen by Van Dyck as a model. The final two **Victorian Rooms** are examples of grace-and-favour apartments of the period.

The Tudor Kitchens

After a surfeit of opulent interiors, the workaday **Tudor Kitchens** come as something of a relief. Henry VIII quadrupled the size of the kitchens, large sections of which have survived to this day and have recently been restored and embellished with historical reconstructions. To make the most of this route, you really do need to use the audio tour guide which helps to evoke the scene with contemporary accounts. Past the Boiling Room and Flesh Larder (not for squeamish vegetarians) you come to the **Great Kitchen**, one of three which Henry built to cope with the prodigious consumption of the royal court – six oxen, forty sheep and a thousand or more larks, pheasants, pigeons and partridges were an average daily total.

The tour ends in Henry's vast **Wine Cellar**, where the palace's Rhineland wine was stored. At each main meal, the King and his special guests would be supplied with eight pints of wine; courtiers had to make do with three gallons of beer, which was very weak and drunk as a subsitute for what was then a very dodgy water supply.

The gardens

The palace gardens are open daily 7am–dusk; free.

The 669-acre **palace gardens** were largely the creation of three monarchs: Henry VIII, Charles II and William III. The last's **Fountain Garden** – a grand, semicircular parterre fanning out from the Broad Walk, which runs along Wren's austere east front – is the most distinctive section. In William's day the lawns featured box hedges and thirteen fountains, and the dwarf yew trees were pruned to look like obelisks. These "black pyramids", as Virginia Woolf called them, have been reduced to chubby cone shapes, while a solitary pool stands in place of the fountains and the box hedges have become plain lawns. A semicircular canal separates the Fountain Garden from the Home Park beyond, its waters feeding Charles II's **Long Water**, Hampton Court's most Versaillean feature, which splices the Home Park in two.

To the south of the palace lies the **Privy Garden**, much altered over the centuries and last laid out by William III. It is currently being restored – all that actually survives from William's day are twelve magnificent wrought-iron panels at the river end of the garden, the work of Jean Tijou. The **Pond Gardens**, further west, were originally constructed as ornamental fishponds stocked with freshwater fish for the kitchens, and feature some of the gardens' most spectacularly colourful flowerbeds. Beyond the gardens, beside the river is William III's dinky little red-brick **Banqueting House**, built for intimate riverside soirées, with castellations and mouldings by Gibbons and paintings by Verrio.

The Banqueting House is open Easter–Oct Mon 10.15am–6pm, Tues–Sun 9.30am–6pm.

To the west of the Pond Gardens are the scented Tudor-style Knot and Herb Gardens and the palace's celebrated **Great Vine**, grown from a cutting in 1768 by Capability Brown and averaging about seven hundred bunches of Black Hamburg grapes per year. (The grapes are sold each year at the palace in September.) Close by stands the **Lower Orangery**, built for William and Mary by Wren and used as a gallery for Andrea Mantegna's heroic canvases, *The Triumphs of Caesar*, bought by Charles I in 1629 and kept here ever since. Painted around 1486 for the Ducal Palace in Mantua, Mantegna's home town, these nine vast paintings are among his best works, characterized by his obsessive interest in archeological and historical accuracy.

The Lower Orangery is open as for the Banqueting House.

Before setting off into the grounds, make sure you walk along the magnificent **Broad Walk** which runs for half a mile from the Thames past the palace's east front to the *putti*-encrusted Flower Pot Gate, and is lined with some of the country's finest herbaceous borders. En route you can visit the indoor **Tudor Tennis Court**, established here by Henry VIII (a keen player of Real Tennis himself), but extensively restored by Charles II – you might even catch a game of this arcane precursor of modern tennis.

The maze

To the north of the palace, Henry VIII laid out a **Tiltyard** with five towers for watching jousting tournaments, one of which survives near the garden restaurant. William III transformed the tiltyard into a "**Wilderness**" – a formal garden of evergreens – which now contains the most famous feature of the palace gardens, the deceptively tricky **Maze**, laid out in 1714.

Mazes, or labyrinths as they were called at the time, were all the rage among the eighteenth-century nobility, though their origins lie in the Middle Ages, when they were used by pilgrims who used to crawl along on hands and knees reciting prayers, as penance for not making a pilgrimage to the Holy Land. On the north side of the Maze stand the Wren's **Lion Gates**, built as a new grand approach to Wren's planned north front which was never realized.

Bushy Park

Beyond the Lion Gates, and across Hampton Court Road, lies **Bushy Park**, the palace's semi-wild enclosure of over a thousand acres, which sustains copious herds of fallow and red deer. Wren's mile-long royal road, Chestnut Avenue, cuts through the park and is at its best in May when the horse chesnuts are in blossom. The main architectural feature of the park is the **Diana Fountain**, situated a third of the way along the avenue to help break the monotony. The statue – which, in fact, depicts Arethusa – was commissioned by Charles II from Francesco Fanelli and originally graced the Privy Garden; stranded in the centre of this vast pond, she looks ill-proportioned and rather isolated.

Off to the west, a little further up the avenue, you'll come upon the **Waterhouse Woodland Gardens**, created in 1949, and at their most colourful each spring when the rhododendrons, azaleas and camellias are in bloom. The crowds are fairly thin even here, compared with the crush around the palace, but if you really want to seek out some of the park's abundant wildlife, head for the wilder western section of the park where few visitors venture.

Windsor and Eton

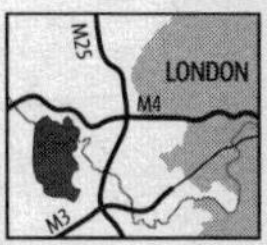

Every weekend trains from Waterloo and Paddington are packed with people off on the trail to **Windsor**, the royal enclave twenty-one miles west of London, where they join a human conveyor belt round Windsor Castle. Towering above the town on a steep chalk bluff, the castle is an undeniably awesome sight, its chilly grey walls, punctuated by mighty medieval bastions, continuing as far as the eye can see. Once there, the small selection of state rooms open to the public are unexciting, though the magnificent St George's Chapel and the chance to see another small selection of the Queen's private art collection make the trip worthwhile. On a fine day, it pays to put aside some time for exploring Windsor Great Park, which stretches for several miles to the south of the castle.

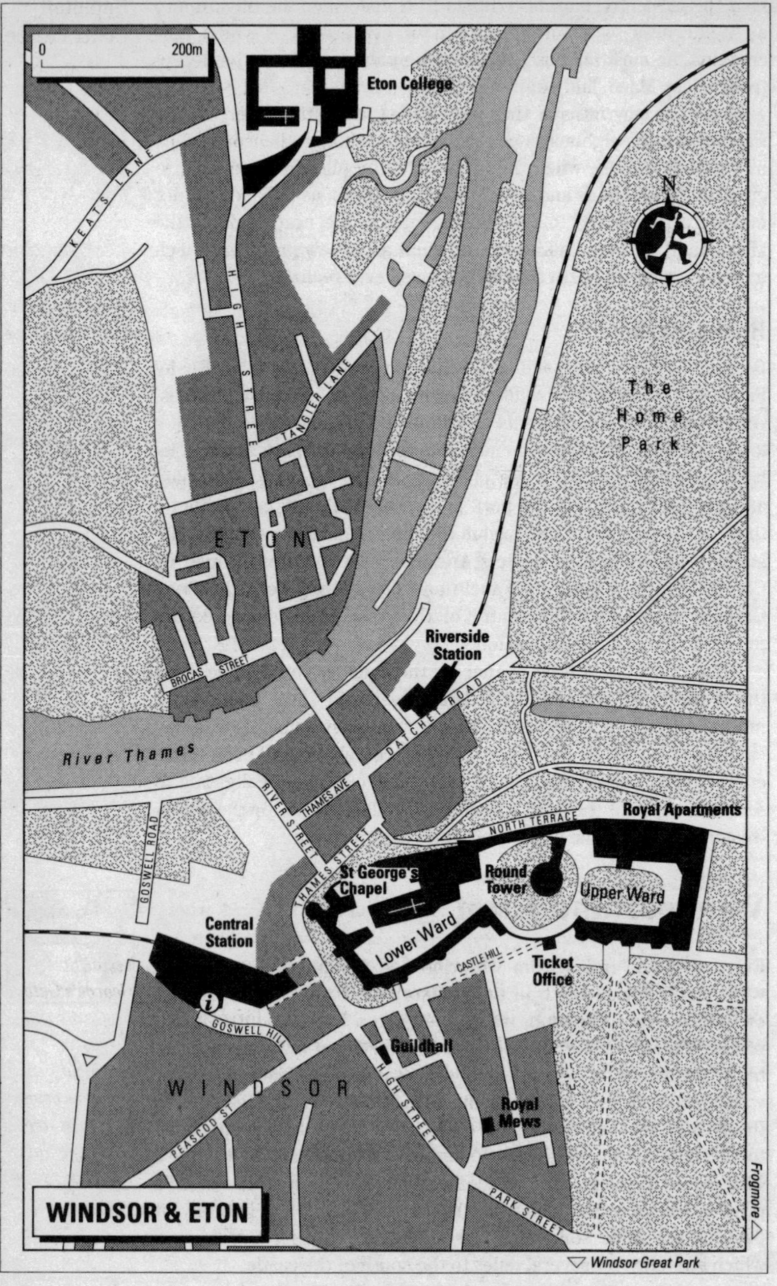
0
200m
Eton College
KEATS LANE
HIGH STREET
TANGIER LANE
The Home Park
ETON
Riverside Station
BROCAS STREET
DATCHET ROAD
River Thames
RIVER STREET
THAMES AVE
GOSWELL ROAD
THAMES STREET
NORTH TERRACE
Royal Apartments
St George's Chapel
Round Tower
Upper Ward
Lower Ward
Central Station
CASTLE HILL
Ticket Office
GOSWELL HILL
Guildhall
WINDSOR
HIGH STREET
Royal Mews
PEASCOD ST
PARK STREET
Frogmore
WINDSOR & ETON
Windsor Great Park

Windsor travel details

Windsor has two **train stations**, both very close to the centre, with trains from Waterloo arriving at **Windsor & Eton Riverside**, five minutes' walk from the centre, and trains from Paddington arriving at **Windsor & Eton Central**, directly opposite the castle. The **tourist information office** (Mon–Sat 9.30am–5pm, Sun 10am–4pm; open longer hours in summer; ☎0753/852010) is in the latter and can deal with most enquiries.

Though almost as famous as Windsor, **Eton**, the exclusive and inexcusably powerful school founded by Henry VI in 1440 directly across the river from the castle, receives a mere fraction of the tourists. True, there's not so much to see here, but the guided tours give an eye-opening glimpse of life as lived by the offspring of Britain's upper classes, and the Gothic chapel is definitely worth a visit.

Windsor Castle

Windsor **Castle** began its life as a wooden keep built by William the Conqueror, and numerous later monarchs had a hand in its evolution. Henry II tore down the wooden buildings and rebuilt the castle in stone, much as you see it today – in plan at least – though George IV was mainly responsible for today's rather over-restored appearance.

The castle is open March–Oct daily 10am–5pm; Nov–Feb 10am–4pm; £8; if any part of castle is closed £5.

The most significent event which has befallen the castle in recent years was the devastating **fire** of November 20, 1992, which gutted a good number of the state apartments, many of which are still closed for restoration. Having ignored the advice of various fire officers, and failed to insure the place, the royal family found itself faced with a repair bill of £50 million – or rather, the taxpayers did. In an attempt to assuage public opinion, the Queen subsequently offered to foot half the bill, and set about raising some of the money by upping the entry charges here and letting the public into a tiny portion of Buckingham Palace for a similarly exorbitant fee.

For more on the royals' finances, see p.58.

The Middle and Upper Wards

Leaving the ticket office, you find yourself in the **Middle Ward**, where the flagpole of the **Round Tower** flies the Royal Standard when the Queen is in residence, and the Union Flag at other times. Constructed out of Caen stone in 1170 and heightened thirty feet by George IV, the tower is the direct descendent of William the Conqueror's fortress and stands on the original motte-hill; despite its name, the moat below the tower has never held water, as its chalky soil is highly porous.

The ticket office is situated beside St George's Gate, up Castle Hill.

The Moat Gardens below the tower are open Aug Sat & Sun only; £1.

It's best to head straight for the state apartments before the tour groups get into their stride – to do so, walk round the Round Tower and pass under the **Norman Tower**. Three kings have been imprisoned in the prisonhouse above the gate: David of Scotland, John of France and James I of Scotland, whose only compensation for his eleven years' imprisonment was a glimpse of his future wife, Jane Beaufort, from his cell window.

From here you enter the **Upper Ward** or Quadrangle, where an equestrian statue of Charles II looks across the manicured stretch of lawn where the **Changing of the Guard** takes place when the Queen is at home. The south and east wings contain the Queen's private apartments, where she still hangs out at the weekend, at Easter and during the Ascot horse races. The State Apartments lie to the north: the official State entrance is immediately to your left, but plebs must trot down the passageway and enter from the North Terrace, after admiring the splendid view across to Eton College Chapel, the Mars chocolate factory at Slough and the Chiltern Hills beyond.

The State Apartments

The State Apartments are closed Easter, June & Dec.

Despite the fire, around half of the **State Apartments** – originally created for Charles II and his wife, Catherine of Braganza, but much altered since then – are still open to the public. Visitors enter via the **Grand Staircase**, a quasi-medieval stairwell lit by a polygonal lantern – until the 1820s this area was an open courtyard which once served as the herb garden. To the east lies George III's **Grand Vestibule**, featuring a smaller octagonal lantern, pseudo-Gothic fan vaulting and Victorian showcases, which display such treasures as the bullet which killed Nelson at Trafalgar and some wonderful armoury siezed from Tipu Sultan of Mysore when the British took Seringapatam in 1799.

The **Waterloo Chamber**, the largest of the rooms currently open, is lined with dull portraits of Napoleonic War worthies and royals. More interesting is the seamless Indian carpet woven in Agra for the Empress of India, Queen Victoria. The rest of the state rooms, with just one or two exceptions, are devastatingly dull, for all their gilded grandeur. The highlights are the paintings from the Queen's private collection, among them a series of works by Rubens in the **King's Drawing Room** and Van Dyck's triple portrait of Charles I, plus works by Dürer and Rembrandt, in the **King's Dressing Room**.

A couple of pieces of furniture stand out: the French eighteenth-century domed bed in the **King's Bedchamber**, and the superb seventeenth-century ebony-veneered cabinet in the **Queen's Drawing Room**. Only three of of Verrio's thirteen ceiling paintings have survived the whims of the royals, the finest of which is the *Banquet of the Kings* in the **King's Dining Room**, which has fish and fruit hanging from the coving. From the Queen's Guard Chamber you can look into the fire-damaged **St George's Hall**, in which monarchs from Edward III onwards held banquets for the Knights of the Garter. Before the blaze its Victorian neo-Gothic appearance inspired Sir Hugh Casson to call it "the most boring room in Europe"; with a typically British fear of innovation it is to be restored in identical fashion.

The Gallery and Queen Mary's Doll's House

Before you leave the vicinity of the State Apartments, it's worth paying a quick visit to the **Gallery**, to the left of the main entrance, where you can see exhibitions of prints and drawings culled from Windsor's slice of the royal art collection (which includes the world's finest collection of sketches and notebooks by Leonardo da Vinci). You should also pay a visit to **Queen Mary's Dolls' House**, a palatial micro-residence designed by the eminent architect Edwin Lutyens for the wife of George V and situated in a dimly-lit chamber beneath the royal apartments. The three-storey Neoclassical house features a fully plumbed-in toilet and working electric lights, and contains paintings by eminent artists and hand-written books by Kipling, Hardy and Conan Doyle.

There's an additional entrance fee of £1.50 for the Doll's House.

The Lower Ward and St George's Chapel

You leave the castle via the sloping **Lower Ward**, site of **St George's Chapel**, a glorious Perpendicular structure ranking with Henry VII's Chapel in Westminster Abbey (see p.72), and the second most important resting place for royal corpses after the Abbey. The chapel was founded by Edward III in 1348 as the spiritual centre for the Order of the Knights of the Garter, the chivalric elite established in the same year; the present edifice was begun by Edward IV but not completed until 1528. If you're interested in visiting only the chapel, you can enter free of charge for the daily services; the 5.15pm evensong is particularly atmospheric thanks to the chapel's excellent boys' choir.

The chapel is open Mon–Sat 10am–4pm, Sun 2–4pm; closed Jan.

At the entrance the church staff will hand you a leaflet with a plan of the significant tombs; a one-way system operates. What strikes you at once is the superb fan vaulting of the chapel ceiling, the final flowering of English Gothic architecture. The first tomb you come to is that of **Prince Napoleon** (son of Napoleon III), who was speared to death in 1879 during the Zulu War, at the age of just twenty-three. In the Unswick Chantry in the north aisle is the extravagant marble monument to George IV's only child, **Princess Charlotte**, who died giving birth to her stillborn son in 1817; nearby is a statue of her husband, Leopold, a particularly vile colonial monarch after his accession as King of Belgium. **George V** and **George VI** are both buried in the north aisle, the latter in his own memorial chapel with a space ready and waiting for his wife, the Queen Mother.

Continuing up the north choir aisle, it's worth peeking into the tiny **Hastings Chantry**, decorated with brightly coloured sixteenth-century paintings of Saint Stephen's martyrdom. More architectural glories lie within the choir itself, with its intricate fifteenth-century three-tier stalls and two exquisite oriel windows side by side: the Gothic **Royal Gallery**, built in wood for Catherine of Aragon, the other Renaissance and carved in stone. Underneath the floor of the choir is the **Queen's Closet**, built for the burial of Jane Seymour, Henry VIII's third wife, who died giving birth to Edward VI; it also contains Henry himself, Charles I and one of the children born to Queen Anne. Edward IV, Henry VI and Edward VII lie either side of the high altar.

There are more tombs in the **Albert Memorial Chapel**, which adjoins St George's Chapel to the east, but is currently closed for restoration. Built by Henry VII as a burial place for Henry VI, and completed by Wolsey as a burial place for himself, it was eventually converted for

Queen Victoria into a memorial to her husband, Prince Albert (who was later moved to Frogmore, see below). Also buried here is "Eddy", the Duke of Clarence and eldest son of Edward VII, who was as dissolute as his father but differed in his sexual preference; he died in 1892, officially from pneumonia, probably from syphilis. Beneath the chapel lies the **Royal Vault**, where George III and Queen Charlotte are buried along with six of their sons, including George IV and William IV.

The Changing of the Guard takes place at 11am daily May to mid-Aug; alternate days the rest of the year.

The foot of the Lower Ward is occupied by the Guard Room, where the Changing of the Guard takes place when the Queen is not in residence. More interesting is the **Horseshoe Cloister**, hidden away to the west of the chapel. These medieval timber-framed houses form an arresting piece of domestic architecture in the otherwise frigid surroundings of the castle, and provide accommodation for members of the chapel choir. When you leave the Lower Ward, be sure to admire the **King Henry VIII Gate**, the castle's main gate; built in 1511, it's decorated on the outer arch with a panel carved with the Tudor rose and the pomegranate of Henry's first wife, Catherine of Aragon.

Windsor town and Windsor Great Park

Once you've seen the castle, you've seen just about everything worth seeing in Windsor, with the exception of the park (see below). The small network of cobbled streets to the south of the castle are too busy scrambling for every tourist pound to retain any quaintness. More appealing is the town's **Guildhall**, with a delicate arcaded loggia designed by Wren. The story goes that the town authorities insisted that Wren's initial version, which was supported by only one line of columns, was unstable, so Wren duly added the central row, but placed a one-inch gap at the tops of the columns to prove his point.

The Royal Mews are open daily 10am–4pm: £1.70.

In St Albans Street you'll find Burford House, built in the 1670s by Charles II for Nell Gwynn, and the adjacent **Royal Mews**, part of which contains a very small sample of the incredible presents that the Queen receives during her royal tours. It's a compelling extravaganza of bad taste – try picturing the Duke of Edinburgh in his white Mexican sombrero and Texan cowboy boots with "Philip" and "Prince" emblazoned in gold up the side (okay – it's not hard). Next door a covered courtyard houses several old carriages, including the Scottish State Coach, used for the fateful 1981 marriage between Charles and Di.

Windsor Great Park

Windsor Great Park is open daily 10am–6pm or dusk.

Most tourists are put off going to **Windsor Great Park** by its sheer scale. Covering nearly five thousand acres, fifteen miles in circumference and accessible only via the three-mile long Long Walk, it's, in fact, a mere fraction of the whole estate, since the Home Park, nearer to the castle, is off limits to the public.

At the far end of the Long Walk stands the gargantuan equestrian statue of George III, known as the **Copper Horse**, sculpted by Westmacott and erected by George IV. It was here at Windsor that

George III lived out his last years, racked by "madness", subsequently diagnosed as porphyria, a rare metabolic disorder, which gets its name from the port-coloured urine which characterizes it. It was during one of his attacks at Windsor that George famously leapt from his carriage and addressed an oak tree, believing it to be the King of Prussia.

If you need a focus for your wandering, head for **Savill Garden**, a thirty-five acre patch of woodland on the park's southeastern boundary. Begun in 1932, this is one of the finest floral displays in and around London, with magnolias, rhododendrons and camellias galore, plus many other more unusual trees and shrubs.

Savill Garden is open daily 10am–6pm or sunset; £3.20.

Finally, there's **Frogmore**, the extravagant Romanesque royal mausoleum built in Windsor Home Park, to the southeast of the castle, by Queen Victoria as a shrine to her husband, Albert, whose life was cut short by typhoid at the age of just forty-two. Centre stage is Carlo Marochetti's double monument of Victoria and Albert (both depicted at the time of Albert's death in 1861). Also commemorated with appropriately florid monuments are Princess Charlotte, heir to the throne until her death in 1817; Victoria's daughter Princess Alice and Alice's four-year old daughter Mary, both of whom died of diptheria in 1878 and Victoria's grandson, Christian Victor, who died of malaria during the Boer War in 1900. The Duke and Duchess of Windsor (Edward VIII and Mrs Simpson) are also buried here.

Frogmore is open in May only – on at least three days, including the Wed closest to Queen Victoria's birthday (May 23).

Eton College

Crossing the footbridge at the end of Thames Avenue in Windsor brings you to **Eton**, a one-street village lined with bookshops and antique dealers, but famous all over the world for **Eton College**, a ten-minute walk from the river. When this, Britain's most aristocratic public school, was founded in 1440 by Henry VI, its aim was to give free education to seventy poor scholars and choristers – how times have changed. It would be easier to list Establishment figures who haven't been to Eton than vice versa – Percy Bysshe Shelley, George Orwell and Tony Benn are rare rebels in the roll call. This is the old school of half the current Conservative cabinet (and of most before them), and it is shortly due to receive Wills and Harry, Diana's sons.

The college and chapel are open Easter, July & Aug daily 10.30am–4.30pm; Easter–June, Sept & Nov daily 2–4.30pm; £2.20; guided tours daily 2.15 & 3.15pm £3.20.

Within the rarefied complex, the original fifteenth-century **schoolroom**, gnarled with centuries of graffiti, survives to the north of the first courtyard, but the real highlight is the **College Chapel**, a wonderful example of English Perpendicular architecture completed in 1482. The fan vaulting, which was destroyed in the last war, has been completely reconstructed in concrete (though you'd never know looking at it), but the most remarkable feature of the place is its medieval *grisaille* wall paintings, the finest in the country, which were whitewashed over by the Victorians and only uncovered in 1923.

The small self-congratulatory **Museum of Eton Life** is well worth missing unless you have a fascination with flogging, fagging and bragging about the school's facilities and alumni.

7
ROW (K) SEAT 15

London: Listings

Accommodation

At the top end of the **hotel** market, London can compete with any city in the world, and such elegant institutions as *Claridge's*, *The Dorchester* and *The Connaught* have long-established reputations that ensure a constant stream of guests willing to pay up to £300 per luxurious night. However, London has far too many hotels charging four-star prices for accommodation that really isn't anything special, and the costs of running a business in the middle of the city mean that even the most fair-minded hoteliers have problems offering rooms with all mod cons for under £100 a night.

That said, there are bargains to be found, especially in the capital's numerous **B&Bs**, unpretentious small-scale places providing homely accommodation and breakfast from around £40 for a double room (or from £50 for a room with a private bathroom). Moreover, the sheer size of London means that there is little chance of failing to find a room even in midsummer, and the underground network makes accommodation in most of the satellite boroughs a feasible option. The capital also has plenty of **hostel** space, in YHA properties, independent hostels and student halls, although all these can be booked up months in advance in summer. Inveterate **campers** can pitch their shelters at one of a clutch of peripheral sites.

We've given phone numbers and faxes where available for all our listed accommodation, but if you fail to find a bed in any of the places we've recommended you could turn to one of the various **accommodation agencies**. All the LTB offices listed on p.32 operate a room booking service, for which they charge £5 (£1.50 for hostels), and take fifteen percent of the first night's room fee in advance; credit card holders can also book through the LTB by phone (☎0171/824 8844).

In addition, **Thomas Cook** has accommodation desks at Gatwick airport (☎01293/529 372), Victoria train station (☎0171/828 4646), King's Cross (☎0171/837 5681), Paddington (☎0171/723 0184) and Earl's Court (☎0171/244 0908). Most of these are open daily 7am till 11pm, and will book anything from youth hostels through to five-star hotels for a £4 fee.

There are also **British Hotel Reservation Centre** (*BHRC*) desks at both the Heathrow underground stations (☎0181/564 8808–8211), at Stansted Airport (☎01279/662929), Victoria train station (☎0171/828 1027), Victoria coach station (☎0171/824 8232) and 10 Buckingham Palace Rd (☎0171/828 2425). The Victoria train station office, open daily from 6am to 11.30pm, has the longest opening hours; all offer their services free of charge.

Hotels and B&Bs

London has a huge range of **hotels** from palatial establishments patronized by royalty, statesmen and other celebrities to budget-bracket B&Bs. The recommended **hotels and B&Bs** have been grouped by location, starting in the Victoria area and following the order set out below; the

Accommodation

hyper-expensive places have been creamed off and placed in the special section on pp.405–06.

The roads south and west of **Victoria station** harbour dozens of inexpensive B&Bs – notably along Belgrave Road and Ebury Street. This area is pretty deadly in the evening – unlike the other nucleus of budget places, Earl's Court (see below), but on the other hand, it's within easy striking distance of the West End, and is very convenient for Continental arrivals by rail and bus departures up country.

Adjoining Victoria to the west, the fashionable areas of **Belgravia**, **Knightsbridge** and **Kensington** are full of hotels catering for the sort of customers who can afford to shop in *Harrods* and other local stores, but there is a scattering of small, independentl hotels offering good value for this exclusive neighbourhood. Average prices are slightly lower in **South Kensington** (site of the Victoria and Albert, the Natural History, and the Science museums), and tariffs take a drastic dive to the west of Kensington in **Earl's Court**, a network of Victorian-terraced streets that's become a recognized backpackers' ghetto. Here you'll find a huge concentration of bottom-end B&Bs, some offering dormitory-style accommodation (see p.412). Earl's Court Road, which bisects this area, is full of late-night supermarkets, cheap cafés and fast-food joints, money exchange booths and laundries.

North of here prices rise again in **Holland Park**, with its well-preserved early Victorian residential squares and crescents. Neighbouring **Notting Hill** offers architecture from a similar era (albeit a little worse for wear) and harbours a faintly Bohemian community, as exemplified by the Portobello Road market. Proximity to Hyde Park is an added bonus for the B&Bs and hotels in this area. Similarily close to Hyde Park, but with less intrinsic appeal, are the **Paddington** and **Bayswater** areas, east of Notting Hill. There's a lot of inexpensive accommodation here, especially along Sussex Gardens and in Norfolk Square, where small hotels and B&Bs outnumber residential homes. Slightly pricier places are ranged along the busy Gloucester Place, a convenient location between Regent's Park and Oxford Street.

An extended stay in the majority of **West End** hotels is out of most people's price range, but you might be tempted to try a taste of hedonism for a night or two. The recession of the late 1980s hit these places hard and the consequent spirit of competition has seen a welcome sharpening of standards. We've included what we consider to be the best of these plush hotels, and you shouldn't necessarily be deterred by their advertised rates. During quiet weeks it is possible to negotiate discounts (as it is with hotels in all price categories) and because these top-class hotels tend to make their money from

HOTEL PRICES

All hotel accommodation has been graded on a scale of 1–9 according to the minimum nightly charge you can expect to pay for a double room in high season (breakfast is generally included in the price). The prices signified by these categories are as follows:

① = under £40	④= £60–70	⑦ = £90–100
② = £40–50	⑤ = £70–80	⑧ = £100–200
③ = £50–60	⑥= £80–90	⑨= over £200.

With each entry we've given the name of the nearest tube station (or other public transport details if no tube exists), and a list of the credit and charge cards accepted by the establishment, using the following abbreviations:

Amex = American Express　　MC = Mastercard/Access

V = Visa　　D = Diners Club

All cards = all the above.

corporate clients who are in town from Monday to Friday, most of them provide "Weekend Breaks" throughout the year. You can expect these special deals to offer at least twenty percent discount, and in some instances you might even get half price. As a general rule, West End prices are highest in **Mayfair** and **St James's**, while the belt of the city from the eastern half of **Oxford Street** through **Covent Garden** to the **Strand** harbours a few more modest places.

Gower Street, in the heart of **Bloomsbury**, has a terrace of reasonably priced B&Bs, and is handy for the British Museum and the West End – Oxford Street and Covent Garden are no more than ten minutes' walk away. Cartwright Gardens, a short distance east of Gower Street, also offers a selection of inexpensive accommodation in a more residential, villagey atmosphere. Note that with the exception of the few we've listed, nearly all the hotels in the seedy neighbourhood opposite **King's Cross station**, north of Bloomsbury, cater for the homeless on welfare (signified by "DSS welcome"). We've rounded off with a few attractive places in the City and the farther-flung areas of Clapham (south London) and Hampstead (north).

Victoria and Pimlico

Brindle House Hotel, 1 Warwick Place North, SW1 ☎0171/828 0057. Quaint, diminutive mews house B&B; no private bathrooms. All cards. ②.

Cartef House, 129 Ebury St, SW1 ☎0171/730 6176. Run by the owners of *James House* opposite, but with a greater selection of en suite rooms with TVs. V; MC. ③.

Cherry Court Hotel, 23 Hugh St, SW1 ☎0171/828 2840. Run-down, small but inexpensive rooms with TVs and washbasins, but with other facilities shared. Continental breakfast is served in rooms. All cards. ①.

Collin House, 104 Ebury St, SW1 ☎0171/730 8031. Has some of the most spacious rooms offered by the twenty-odd B&Bs along this road. V; MC. ③.

Dover Hotel, 44 Belgrave Rd, SW1 ☎0171/821 9085; fax 0171/845 2331. Among the best B&Bs of the many in this area. All rooms are well equipped with a shower and toilet, telephone and TV. All cards. ③.

Easton Hotel, 36–40 Belgrave Rd ☎0171/834 5938. Small rooms past their prime but this B&B is close to the train station and has en suite rooms at a reasonable price, plus a pleasant garden. All cards. ②.

Elizabeth Hotel, 37 Eccleston Square, SW1 ☎0171/828 6812; fax 0171/828 6814. Comfortable and elegantly furnished hotel, very close to train and coach stations and providing en suite and more basic rooms at a decent price. Large TV lounge, and the gardens and tennis courts of Eccleston Square are available for use by hotel residents. Apartments from £200 a week are also available for up to three months' let. All cards. ⑤.

The Goring, 17 Beeston Place, SW1 ☎0171/396 9000; fax 0171/834 4393. Owned and run by the Goring family for three generations, the *Goring* succeeds in creating an atmosphere of elegance and tranquillity despite its position amid busy roads between Victoria train station and Buckingham Palace. Elegantly furnished communal areas and spacious corridors lead to the comfortable and fully equipped rooms (twins/doubles from £150), some of which look over the delightful private gardens. Afternoon tea served on the garden terrace in fine weather. V; MC. ⑧.

Leicester Hotel, 18–24 Belgrave Rd, SW1 ☎0171/233 6636; fax 0171/932 0538. Good B&B conveniently situated between train and coach stations, offering English breakfast; popular with young travellers. V; MC. ②.

Limegrove Hotel, 101 Warwick Way, SW1 ☎0171/828 0458. Just about the cheapest decent rooms with washbasins and TVs in this area. Showers and toilets are shared; English breakfast is served in the rooms. No cards. ①.

Accommodation

Except where indicated otherwise, Victoria is the nearest tube station to all the hotels in this section.

Accommodation

Except where indicated otherwise, Knightsbridge is the nearest tube station to all the hotels in the Knightsbridge & Belgravia section.

Lime Tree Hotel, 135–137 Ebury Street, SW1 ☎0171/730 8191; fax 0171/730 7865. A bigger than average B&B with TVs and telephones in all rooms and access to a pretty, secluded garden. All cards. ④.

Luna & Simone Hotel, 47–49 Belgrave Rd, SW1 ☎0171/834 5897. Inexpensive B&B with en suite facilities, TVs and telephones in all rooms. No cards. ②.

Melbourne House, 79 Belgrave Rd, SW1 ☎0171/828 3516; fax 0171/828 7120. One of two good B&Bs along Belgrave Road: totally refurbished, offering clean and bright rooms, excellent communal areas, and friendly family service. Victoria or Pimlico tube. V; MC. ③.

Oak House, 29 Hugh St, SW1 ☎0171/834 7151. Friendly service and rock-bottom prices for tiny rooms; no breakfast, but a TV in each room. No cards. ①.

Oxford House, 92–94 Cambridge St, SW1 ☎0171/834 6467. Good value B&B situated in a quiet backstreet a few minutes' walk from the coach and train stations; washbasins but no other private facilities. Reduction for stays of more than one night. V; MC; Amex. ①.

St James Court, 41 Buckingham Gate, SW1 ☎0171/834 6655; fax 0171/630 7587. Superbly renovated 400-room Edwardian hotel, popular with business travellers. Large twin rooms overlooking the peaceful fountained courtyard from £170. There is a health club and gym in the basement, and Provençal and Chinese restaurants on the ground floor. All cards. ⑧.

Scandic Crown Victoria, 2 Bridge Place, SW1 ☎0171/834 8123; fax 0171/828 1099. Right next to Victoria train station, a well-equipped and unfussy high-quality hotel with large, comfortable rooms from £145. Guests have use of a health club and pool; the restaurant serves Swedish cuisine. All cards. ⑧.

Topham's Ebury Court Hotel, 26 Ebury St, SW1 ☎0171/730 8147; fax 0171/823 5966. Charming family-owned hotel in the English country-house style, just a couple of minutes' walk from the Victoria stations. Sumptuously furnished en suite twins or doubles from £115, including full English breakfast. All cards. ⑧.

Winchester Hotel, 17 Belgrave Rd, SW1 ☎0171/828 2972; fax 0171/828 5191. Exemplary B&B, one of the best low-cost places in Victoria. All rooms have en suite facilities and TV, and are freshly decorated. No cards. ③.

Windsor Guest House, 36 Alderney St, SW1 ☎0171/828 7922. B&B set in a quiet street about five minutes' walk from Victoria train and coach stations. All rooms have a TV, most have a washbasin, and some have showers – toilets are shared. English breakfast is included. No cards. ①.

Knightsbridge and Belgravia

Basil Street Hotel, 8 Basil St, SW3 ☎0171/581 3311; fax 0171/581 3693. Welcoming privately-owned hotel in the heart of Knightsbridge, boasting a variety of idiosyncratically decorated rooms; from £165, with long-stay and weekend deals available. The women-only *Parrot Club* is a welcome riposte to the stuffy masculine bars of many traditional-style hotels. All cards. ⑧.

The Cadogan, 75 Sloane St, SW1 ☎0171/235 7141; fax 0171/245 0994. The *Cadogan* has a touch more charisma than many similar establishments in Knightsbridge – it was the former home of Edward VII's mistress Lillie Langtry, and site of Oscar Wilde's arrest. At £145 for doubles, rooms are good value too, with "Special Break" deals up to half price. Guests can use the private garden and tennis courts opposite the hotel. All cards. ⑧.

The Claverley, 13–14 Beaufort Gardens, SW3 ☎0171/589 8541; fax 0171/584 3410. Situated in a quiet cul-de-sac off Brompton Road, this B&B offers twins and doubles from £95, all prettily furnished with floral fabrics and other homely touches. A full English breakfast is included. All cards. ⑦.

The Fenja, 69 Cadogan Gardens, SW3 ☎0171/589 7333; fax 0171/581 4958. Charming, 14-room luxury hotel; *The Fenja*'s personal service and elegant, antique-studded interiors will appeal to those looking for a quiet, exclusive environment. Breakfast, not included in the tariff, is served in the rooms, which are named after prominent writers rather than numbered. Prices start from £130. Sloane Square tube. All cards. ⑧.

L'Hôtel, 28 Basil St, SW3 ☎0171/589 6286; fax 0171 225 0011. An upmarket B&B with plain but immaculate rooms from £125. Continental breakfast is served in the rooms; there is a wine bar downstairs and the restaurants and bars of the adjacent *Capital* are open to guests. All cards. ⑧.

Parkes Hotel, 41 Beaufort Gardens, SW3 ☎0171/581 9944; fax 0171/581 1999. Hotel in a quiet cul-de-sac, with a handful of double rooms but mostly offering self-catering suites sleeping two to eight people, costing from £40 per person. All rooms are very well equipped (satellite TV, hair dryers, trousers presses, etc), and English breakfast is included. V; MC; Amex. ⑦.

Kensington

Abbey House Hotel, 11 Vicarage Gate, W8 ☎0171/727 2594. Inexpensive B&B in a quiet street just north of Kensington High Street, maintained to a very high standard by its especially attentive owners. Rooms are large and bright – prices are kept down by sharing facilities rather than fitting the usual cramped bathroom unit. Full English breakfast, with free tea and coffee available all day. High Street Kensington tube. All cards. ③.

Annandale House Hotel, 39 Sloane Gardens, SW1 ☎0171/730 6291. Long established B&B in leafy residential street, close to trendy Kings Road. Some rooms are large and all have TVs and hair dryers. The genuinely "full" breakfast menu is varied daily. Sloane Square tube. V; MC; Amex. ⑤.

Aster House House, 3 Sumner Place, SW7 ☎0171/581 5888; fax 0171/584 4925. Pleasant, small, non-smoking B&B in a quiet street; light breakfast is served in the conservatory. South Kensington tube. V; MC. ⑦.

Blakes Hotel, 33 Roland Gardens, SW7 ☎0171/370 6701; fax 0171/373 0442. *Blakes'* dramatically designed interior and glamorous suites have long attracted visiting celebs. A faintly *Raffles*-esque flavour pervades, with bamboo furniture and old travelling trunks mixing with unusual *objets*, tapestries and prints. Doubles from £125 are smart but small; fully equipped suites are spectacular, as they should be for £235. The restaurant and bar are excellent, and service is of a very high standard. Gloucester Road tube. All cards. ⑧.

The Franklin Hotel, 28 Egerton Gardens, SW3 ☎0171/584 5533; fax 0171/584 5449. Small secluded hotel offering air conditioned rooms (from £175) outfitted in Olde-English style – including four-poster beds. South Kensington tube. All cards. ⑧.

The Gallery Hotel, 8–10 Queensberry Place, SW7 ☎0171/915 0000; fax 0171/915 4400. Elegantly and tastefully restored pair of spacious Georgian houses with doubles from £115 and roomy suites at £175. Traditionally decorated and furnished to a luxurious standard. South Kensington tube. All cards. ⑧.

The Gore, 189 Queen's Gate, SW7 ☎0171/584 6601; fax 0171/589 8217. Popular, privately owned century-old hotel, awash with oriental rugs, rich mahogany and walnut panelling, and other Victoriana. Rooms from £140. An award-winning restaurant adds to its allure. Gloucester Road tube. All cards. ⑧

Hotel 167, 167 Old Brompton Rd, SW5 ☎0171/373 0672; fax 0171/373 3360. More stylish than most B&Bs in this price range. All rooms have en suite facilites, double glazing and a fridge. Breakfast is a continental-style buffet. Gloucester Road tube. All cards. ④.

Leicester Court Hotel, 41 Queen's Gate Gardens, SW7 ☎0171/584 0512; fax 0171/584 0246. Huge old hotel close to the Kensington museums, past its prime but a bargain for this area. Basic twins with shared facilities are £10 less than en suites. Gloucester Road tube. All cards. ④.

The Pelham, 15 Cromwell Place, SW7 ☎0171/589 8288; fax 0171/584 8444. Small hotel luxuriously appointed in the English-country-house style, with each room (doubles from £145) individually decorated; ask for the photographic portfolio at reception and choose your favourite. South Kensington tube. All cards. ⑧.

Accommodation

Periquito Hotel Queens Gate, 68–69 Queens Gate, SW7 ☎0171/370 6111; fax 0171/370 0932. Part of a fast-growing budget hotel chain catering for business and leisure clients. Rooms (sleeping up to four) are small and brightly furnished, and there's a bistro and bar on the ground floor. Rates drop by ten per cent at weekends. Gloucester Road tube. All cards. ③.

Sorbonne Hotel, 39 Cromwell Rd, SW7 ☎0171/589 6636. Very good value small B&B on a busy road, offering good-sized basic or en suite rooms: better than you might expect for its price and location – right opposite the museums. No children under ten. Continental breakfast. V; MC. South Kensington tube. ③.

South Kensington Guest House, 13 Cranley Place, SW7 ☎0171/589 0021; fax 0171/723 0727. A plainly furnished B&B in a salubrious residential street, with very reasonable prices for basic or en suite rooms. South Kensington tube. V; MC; Amex. ③.

Vicarage Private Hotel, 10 Vicarage Gate, W8 ☎0171/229 4030. Much the same as the adjacent *Abbey House* B&B, with shared facilities and a full English breakfast. High Street Kensington tube. No cards. ③.

Earl's Court

All hotels in this section are close to Earl's Court tube.

Amsterdam Hotel, 7 Trebovir Rd, SW5 ☎0171/370 5084; fax 0171/244 7608. Just off Earl's Court Road, this presentable B&B has bright, clean rooms (with TV) and a continental breakfast. V; MC; Amex. ③.

Boka Hotel, 33–35 Eardley Crescent, SW5 ☎0171/373 2844; fax 0171/589 6412. Most rooms share facilities, but breakfast is included and guests have use of a tiny kitchen. Popular with Australians and South Africans. All cards. ①.

Half Moon, 10 Earl's Court Square, SW5 ☎0171/373 9956. Small, friendly B&B with clean en suite rooms at very keen prices. V; MC; Amex. ②.

Henley House, 30 Barkston Gardens, SW5 ☎0171/370 4111; fax 0171/370 0026. Nicer than average B&B, with fully-equipped en suite rooms and a pleasant lounge. Continental breakfast. All cards. ④.

Kensington Court Hotel, 33 Nevern Place SW5 ☎0171/370 5151; fax 0171/370 3499. Situated near a quiet square, this fine hotel offers comfortable rooms with satellite TV, as well as an attractive lounge/bar area. Dinners can be provided if pre-booked and the breakfast is English. There's also a small car park. All cards. ④.

Kensington International Hotel, 4 Templeton Place, SW5 ☎0171/370 4333; fax 0171/244 7873. The drab grey colour scheme in the public areas is misleading, as the rooms feature Oriental, Deco and Tudor decor, and are very well equipped (satellite TV, hair dryers, trouser presses). There's also a bar, inclusive continental breakfast and discounts at local restaurants. All cards. ⑥.

Lord Jim Hotel, 23–25 Penywern Rd, SW5 ☎0171/370 6071; fax 0171/373 8919. Rooms are small, but the doubles (either basic or with en suite facilities) are among the cheapest bearable ones around. V; MC; Amex. ①.

Manor Hotel, 23 Nevern Place, SW5 ☎0171/370 6018; fax 0171/244 6610. B&B offering inexpensive rooms and continental breakfast. All cards. ②.

Merlyn Court Hotel, 2 Barkston Gardens, SW5 ☎0171/370 1640; fax 0171/370 1531. Well appointed and popular B&B in a quiet street close to the tube. Most rooms feature en suite facilities and an English breakfast is included. V; MC; Amex. ③.

Nevern Hotel, 31 Nevern Place, SW5 ☎0171/244 8366. Another good B&B near the Exhibition Centre. Most rooms are en suite with TV, continental breakfast is included, and guests can relax in the large residential lounge. The *Nevern* offers weekly rates as well as reductions of twenty per cent from October to March. V; MC; Amex. ③.

Oxford Hotel, 24 Penywern Rd, SW5 ☎0171/370 1161; fax 0171/373 8256. One of the better B&Bs along this popular road; all rooms have en suite facilities, and there is a large garden. V; MC; Amex. ②.

Philbeach Hotel, 30–31 Philbeach Gardens, SW5 ☎0171/373 1244; fax

0171/244 0149. Friendly gay hotel, with basic and en suite rooms, a pleasant TV lounge area and popular *Wilde About Oscar* garden restaurant. All cards. ④.

Rushmore Hotel, 11 Trebovir Rd, SW5 ☎0171/370 3839; fax 0171/370 0274. With its colourful murals and imaginative room decor, the *Rushmore* is a cut above the average in this often dreary area. The attic rooms are especially spacious and comfortable. Breakfast is "full continental". All cards. ③.

Terstan Hotel, 30 Nevern Square, SW5 ☎0171/244 6466; fax 0171/373 9268. Clean and mostly en suite rooms with TV. Full English breakfast included, and there's also a bar and a pool table. V; MC. ③.

White House Hotel, 12 Earl's Court Square, SW5 ☎0171/373 5903. Budget-price B&B in quiet square, providing some rooms with en suite facilities, a TV lounge and a small kitchen for guests' use. V; MC. ②.

York House, 28 Philbeach Gardens, SW5 ☎0171/373 7519; fax 0171/370 4641. B&B in quiet crescent right next to the Exhibition Centre; has a mixture of en suite rooms and more basic alternatives, all with English breakfast. V; MC; Amex. ③.

Notting Hill and Holland Park

Demetriou Guest House, 9 Strathmore Gardens, W8 ☎0171/229 6709. Small, family-run guest house tucked in a quiet cul-de-sac just off Notting Hill Gate; good value rooms, with English breakfast included in the tariff. V; MC. ③.

Holland Park Hotel, 6 Ladbroke Terrace, W11 ☎0171/792 0216; fax 0171/727 8166. Tastefully converted Victorian town-house in a quiet street. Most rooms are en suite and all have a TV; there's also a nice lounge with a real fire, and a lovely garden. Holland Park tube. All cards. ④.

Leinster Hotel, 7–12 Leinster Square, W2 ☎0171/229 9641; fax 0171/229 8671. Budget hotel with not-quite-hostel feel, offering en suite doubles, shared rooms, and a special rate of around £50 per week with breakfast and dinner – call for details. All cards. ④.

Pembridge Court Hotel, 34 Pembridge Gardens, W2 ☎0171/229 9977; fax 0171/727 4982. Attractively converted townhouse close to Portobello market (hence the Victoriana), with cosy, fully equipped rooms from £110. Two cats add to the homely feel, as does the *Caps Restaurant and Bar*. All cards. ⑧.

The Portobello Hotel, 22 Stanley Gardens, W11 ☎0171/727 2777; fax 0171/792 9641. Victorian hotel with rooms ranging from fairly ordinary doubles to a couple of splendid Special Rooms (£180) overlooking the private gardens. Breakfast is included and there is a restaurant and 24-hr bar. All cards. ⑧.

Paddington and Bayswater

Ashley Hotel, 15 Norfolk Square, W2 ☎0171/723 3375; fax 0171/723 0173. Three long-established hotels joined into one, just a couple of minutes' walk from Paddington station. Rooms with handbasins or with en suite facilities; English breakfast included. Paddington tube. V; MC. ③.

Continental Hotel, 40 Norfolk Square, W2 ☎0171/723 3926; fax 0171/262 0238. Among the cheapest rooms in Paddington, either with shared or private facilities – and offering seven nights for the price of six. Very basic. Paddington tube. No cards. ①.

Europa House Hotel, 151 Sussex Gardens, W2 ☎0171/723 7343; fax 0171/224 9331. Dependable and recently refurbished B&B, with all rooms en suite. Paddington tube. V; MC, ④.

Garden Court Hotel, 30–31 Kensington Garden Square, W2 ☎0171/229 2553; fax 0171/727 2749. Presentable, family-run B&B close to Portobello market; less expensive rooms with shared facilities also available. English breakfast included. Bayswater tube. All cards. ③.

The Gresham Hotel, 116 Sussex Gardens, W2, ☎0171 402 2920; fax 0171 402 3137. Recently restored B&B with a touch more class than many in the area. Rooms are small but tastefully kitted out, and all have TV. Continental breakfast included. Paddington tube. All cards. ⑤.

Accommodation

Except where indicated otherwise, Notting Hill Gate is the nearest tube station to all the hotels in the Notting Hill & Holland Park section.

Accommodation

Hyde Park House, 48 St Petersburg Place, W2 ☎0171/229 1687. Small, inexpensive, homely and very popular B&B in a pleasant street. Rooms are basic, with shared facilities, and the price includes a continental breakfast. There's also a kitchen for making hot drinks, and a small lounge. Queensway tube. No cards. ①.

Inverness Court Hotel, 1 Inverness Terrace ☎0171/229 1444; fax 0171/706 4240. Late Victorian facade, reception area, bar and lounges lend a charmingly downbeat Grand Hotel ambience to the *Inverness*, even if most of the bedrooms are in an undistinguished modern style. Continental breakfast included in price; restaurant on the premises too. Bayswater tube. All cards. ②.

London's top hotels

What follows is by no means an exhaustive list of the city's plushest accommodation – there are scores of other establishments in which corporate high-fliers could easily rack up a £300 expenses claim for a night's stay. The places listed below are a mix of the most famous, the most distinctive and the most luxurious (not necessarily the same thing); if any astronomically expensive hotels could be said to make you feel that you've had value for money, these are the ones.

Knightsbridge and Belgravia

The Berkeley, Wilton Place, SW1 ☎0171/235 6000; fax 0171/235 4330. A purpose-built hotel decorated in a conservative classic style; rooms, from £266, are notably bigger than most, and decorated with a flair commensurate with the price. A rooftop fitness and beauty centre has a small pool and sauna; the ground floor has two restaurants – the formal, astronomically expensive *Restaurant*, and more casual *Perroquet*. Knightsbridge tube. All cards. ⑨.

The Halkin, 5 Halkin St, SW1 ☎0171/333 1000; fax 0171/333 1100. A luxury hotel that spurns the chintzy country-house theme: elegant, Italian-influenced minimalism prevails in each of the 41 rooms, which cost from £230. The contemporary Italian theme is continued in the cuisine of the restaurant, which overlooks a private garden. Hyde Park Corner tube. All cards. ⑨.

The Hyatt Carlton Tower, Cadogan Place, SW1 ☎0171/235 1234; fax 0171/245 6570. Huge, 244-room establishment just couple of minutes from *Harrods*. Comprehensive five-star facilities from rooftop health club to a range of lavish eating and drinking venues. Twins or doubles cost from £250 with no charge for under-18s sharing their parents' room. Knightsbridge tube. All cards. ⑨.

The Hyde Park Hotel, 66 Knightsbridge, SW1 ☎0171/235 2000; fax 0171/235 4552. With its imposing Edwardian frontage and matching interior, the *Hyde Park* is a convincingly elegant re-creation of the post-Victorian era. Fine views over the park from north-facing rooms, which cost from around £284. Knightsbridge tube. All cards. ⑨.

The Lanesborough, Hyde Park Corner, SW1 ☎0171/259 5599; fax 0171/259 5606. A former hospital, this early nineteenth-century building has been meticulously restored in the style of that era, with all mod-cons discreetly hidden amid the ornate decor. Rooms cost from £280. Service is formal and the overall ambience conservative, in keeping with the tone of the diplomatic neighbourhood which it borders. Hyde Park Corner tube. All cards. ⑨.

Holland Park

The Halcyon, 81 Holland Park, W11 ☎0171/ 727 7288; fax 0171/229 8516. This small and discreet hideaway is popular with paparazzi-dodging stars and anyone else with £235 or more to spare for a room. For your money you get the best of personal service, lavish classical decor equal to London's best and cuisine to match. Holland Park tube. All cards. ⑨.

London's top hotels contd.

MAYFAIR AND ST JAMES'S

The Athenaeum, 116 Piccadilly, W1 ☎0171/499 3464; fax 0171/493 1860. Overlooking Green Park, the *Athenæum* offers a variety of very well-appointed rooms and apartments, all with little touches that set it apart from the competition – a mini bar here really is a small bar rather than a fridge full of miniature gins and tinned orange juice. Doubles start from around £215 and include hi-fi and videos. Public areas include the traditionally club-styled Windsor Lounge, the cosy Malt Bar (with a vast range of whiskys), and the Health Spa with a gym, sauna and jacuzzi. Green Park tube. All cards. ⑨.

Brown's Hotel, 30–34 Albemarle St, W1 ☎0171/493 6020; fax 0171/493 9381. An ever-popular, traditionally English hotel dating from the coronation of Queen Victoria, *Brown's* is renowned as one of the best in its class. Rosewood, antiques, stained glass and other fine period details set the tone, and the rooms are individually and warmly decorated (without air conditioning). Nothing under £225. Green Park tube. All cards. ⑨.

Claridge's, Brook St, W1 ☎0171/629 8860; fax 0171/499 2210. This famous and glamorous Mayfair hotel is the chosen abode of visiting heads of state and media megastars. Twins or doubles cost nearly £300 – among the priciest in London – but for this you get wardrobes bigger than most bathrooms, showerheads the size of dinnerplates and decor as plush as any vacationing potentate could wish for. Bond Street tube. All cards. ⑨.

The Connaught, Carlos Place, W1 ☎0171/499 7070; fax 0171/495 3262. Providing the acme of traditional English service – unobtrustive, formal and discreet – the *Connaught* has a clientele of regular visitors who value this small, club-like hotel's impeccable standards and low-key approach. Rooms are in country-house style, and at £272 and upwards they match the standards of any in London. Bond Street tube. All cards. ⑨.

The Dorchester, Park Lane, W1 ☎0171/629 8888; fax 0171/409 0114. Following a complete refurbishment, the sixty-five-year-old *Dorchester* returns as one of the capital's finest hotels. Facing west onto Hyde Park, rooms cost from £270, for which you get luxuries such as individual buzzers for valet, waiter or maid, and huge bathrooms. Superb European cuisine in the *Grill Room* and the *Terrace*, with the *Oriental* restaurant featuring Thai, Chinese and Indian food, and the *Bar* providing light Italian meals, cocktails and jazz in the evenings. There is also a fabulously equipped spa and gym. Hyde Park Corner tube. All cards. ⑨.

The London Hilton, 22 Park Lane, W1 ☎0171/493 8000; fax 0171/493 4957. From the outside the *Hilton* may look dated, but the quality of the service, decor and furnishings makes it clear that the hotel is not sitting on its five-star laurels. The *Hilton* boasts the finest views in Mayfair – especially from the *Windows* restaurant on the 28th floor. Rooms cost from around £240; those prefering a more intimate, town-house setting could stay at the popular *Hilton Mews* behind the main building in Stanhope Row (☎0171/493 7222; fax 0171/629 9423), where rooms start at around £170. Green Park tube. All cards. ⑨.

The Ritz, 150 Piccadilly, W1 ☎0171/493 8181; fax 0171/493 2687. In a class of its own among London's hotels, the *Ritz* is a tourist attraction in its own right, with its extravagant Louis XVI interiors and overall air of decadent luxury. Rooms maintain the opulent French theme and cost from £230, with the west-facing accommodation, overlooking Green Park, in greatest demand. Weekend packages, including breakfast and champagne, are available throughout the year from £220. Green Park tube. All cards. ⑨.

Accommodation

London's top hotels contd.

The Stafford, St James's Place, SW1 ☎0171/493 0111; fax 0171 493 7121. Tucked in a quiet backstreet off St James's Street, with views of Green Park, the *Stafford* provides high-class rooms in the main building from around £200, with more expensive accommodation in the unique Carriage House, a row of eighteenth-century stables luxuriously converted to large guest rooms. The hotel also offers the usual refined dining rooms, while the sporty *American Bar* and its courtyard terrace make a welcome change from the gentlemens'-club norm. Green Park tube. All cards. ⑨.

OXFORD STREET AND MARYLEBONE

The Langham Hilton, 1 Regent St, W1 ☎0171/636 1000; fax 0171/323 2340. Built in 1865 as London's first grand hotel, the *Langham* has rejoined the elite following a refurbishment that has painstakingly re-created the Victorian atmosphere of well-padded luxury. Standard twins are available from £235, but weekend breaks are available for around £176 per day. Oxford Circus tube. All cards. ⑨.

The Montcalm, Great Cumberland Place, W1 ☎0171/402 4288; fax 0171/724 9180. Japanese-owned hotel situated in an attractive crescent just off Marble Arch. Its stylish Georgian interior creates an air of tranquillity that's augmented by the courteous staff. Rooms come in various sizes and shapes, but all are finely furnished and decorated. Standard twin rooms start from £212, with promotional rates and packages offered throughout the year. Marble Arch tube. All cards. ⑨.

The Regent London, 222 Marylebone Rd, NW1 ☎0171/631 8000; fax 0171/631 8080. The location is hardly fashionable, but this superbly refurbished hotel can stand comparison with almost any luxury establishment in London. Once inside the magnificently bright atrium, with its huge cast-iron pillars (a great spot for afternoon teas), all external distractions can be forgotten. The rooms are notably bigger than average, and cost from around £220 for the least expensive of the three grades. In addition to bars and restaurants, the *Regent* has a fitness centre and pool. Marylebone tube. All cards. ⑨.

THE STRAND

The Savoy, Strand, WC2 ☎0171/836 4343; fax 0171/240 6040. Popular with businesspeople and politicians, the *Savoy* is a byword for luxury and service, though in some respects the charisma of the place is what keeps it ahead of many of its rivals. Rooms are decorated in the Deco style of the hotel's heyday or in a more classical vein, and cost from £220 – a river view will set you back an extra £100. Guests have the use of the new Fitness Gallery and small pool on the third floor. *The Grill* is justly famed for its excellent cuisine, while the *American Bar* has jazz most evenings. Breakfasts and afternoon teas are served on the *Thames Foyer*, which peers through trees onto the river. Charing Cross tube. All cards. ⑨.

Mitre House Hotel, 178–184 Sussex Gardens, W2 ☎0171/723 8040; fax 0171/402 0990. The rooms in this large hotel aren't tremendously spacious, and the street-facing ones may be a bit noisy, but the hotel has the enormous advantage of free off-street parking. English breakfast included. Paddington tube. All cards. ⑤.

Mornington Hotel, 12 Lancaster Gate, W2 ☎0171/262 7361; fax 0171/706 1028. Large Swedish-owned hotel with rooms decorated in Scandinavian style. Swedish buffet breakfast is included, and there's a sauna in the basement. The exception to the Nordic theme is the bar/lounge, fitted out like a gentlemen's club with book-crammed shelving. Lancaster Gate tube. ⑥.

Rhodes House, 195 Sussex Gardens, W2 ☎0171/262 5617; fax 0171/723 4054. Recently refurbished in Greekish style; most rooms have private facilities and breakfast is continental. Paddington tube. V; MC. ④.

Ruddiman's Hotel, 160 Sussex Gardens, W2 ☎0171/723 1026; fax 0171/262 2983. A couple of minutes from Paddington station, offering basic or en suite rooms. English breakfast is included and prices are negotiable for longer stays or during quiet periods. Paddington tube. No cards. ②.

Saint David's Hotel, 16 Norfolk Square, W2 ☎0171/723 4963; fax 0171/402 9061. A friendly welcome from George at this inexpensive B&B, famed for its substantial English breakfast. Paddington tube. All cards. ②.

Sass House, 10–11 Craven Terrace, W2 ☎0171/262 2325. Small, recently refurbished B&B, with basic and en suite rooms. Well situated in a street with cafés and a couple of pubs. Lancaster Gate or Paddington tube. V; MC. ②.

Westpoint and Abbey Court, 170 Sussex Gardens, W2 ☎0171/402 0281; fax 0171/224 9114. Not the best rooms in this area, but these twinned hotels are open to deals for longer stays. Breakfast is continental, with English for £2 extra. Paddington tube. All cards. ②.

Mayfair and St James

Flemings Mayfair, Half Moon St ☎0171/499 2964; fax 0171 499 1817. Situated just off Piccadilly and offering excellent value for this part of London, privately owned *Flemings* consists of five connected Georgian houses, each room having its own configuration and style of decor. Prices start at £140, although all rates are flexible for longer visits and drop by up to fifty per cent on most weekends. The hotel also offers luxury apartments from £1350 per week. Green Park tube. All cards. ⑧.

22 Jermyn Street, 22 Jermyn St, SW1 ☎0171/734 2353; fax 0171/734 0750. Discreet hotel just off Piccadilly, winner of an "Urban Sanctuary" award and providing well appointed and traditionally decorated studios (from £190) or suites (from £253). Small enough to offer a genuine personal service, although there is no bar or dining room – breakfast is served in the rooms. Piccadilly Circus tube. All cards. ⑧.

Oxford Street and Marylebone

Berners Park Plaza, 10 Berners St, W1 ☎0171/636 1629; fax 0171/580 3972. Though it's situated at Oxford Street's less fashionable eastern end, this is a sumptuous hotel, and at £140 for a standard double room it represents excellent value in this four-star category. Tottenham Court Road tube. All cards. ⑧.

Cumberland Hotel, Marble Arch, W1 ☎0171/262 1234; fax 0171/724 4621. Huge hotel (nearly 900 beds) standing at one of London's focal points. South-facing rooms on the upper floors provide great views across Hyde Park to Knightsbridge and beyond, and all rooms (from £125) are tastefully furnished and well equipped. Ground-floor restaurants include a carvery that does a lunchtime all-you-can-eat buffet for around £16. Very popular with tour groups. Marble Arch tube. All cards. ⑧.

Dorset Square Hotel, 30–40 Dorset Square, NW1 ☎0171/723 7874; fax 0171/724 3328. Beautifully appointed and relaxing hotel with chintz-wrapped rooms and communal areas designed in Regency townhouse style. Comfortable doubles from £121. A chauffeur-driven Bentley is at the disposal of guests, and there's a fine restaurant in the basement. Marylebone tube. All cards. ⑧.

Kenwood House Hotel, 114 Gloucester Place, W1 ☎0171/935 3473; fax 0171/224 0582. Superior B&B, with low-cost singles and five en suite doubles. Situated on a busy road but with street-facing rooms double-glazed. Popular with families (babysitting arranged) and just a few minutes' walk from *Madame Tussaud's* and Regents Park. Baker Street tube. V; MC; Amex. ③.

Hotel La Place, 17 Nottingham Place, W1 ☎0171/486 2323; fax 0171/486 4335. Just off the busy Marylebone Road, this is

Accommodation

Accommodation

a small, good-value place; rooms are equipped with all the gadgets usually found in grander establishments and are comfortably furnished. Baker St tube. V; MC; ④.

Lincoln House Hotel, 33 Gloucester Place, W1 ☎0171/486 7630; fax 0171 486 0166. One of the best of the numerous B&Bs along this busy Georgian terraced street. Rooms all en suite and all well equipped. Marble Arch or Baker Street tube. V; MC; Amex. ④.

London Continental Hotel, 88 Gloucester Place, W1 ☎0171/486 8670; fax ☎0171/486 8671. Not to be confused with the similarly named four-star establishment on Park Lane, this B&B makes a handy low-cost central London base. Ten percent discount for stays over one week. Baker Street or Marble Arch tube. V; MC; Amex. ③.

Palace Hotel, 31 Great Cumberland Place, W1 ☎0171/262 5585; fax 0171/706 2427. Small but luxurious hotel which oozes class from the hand-painted friezes of the staircase to the four-poster beds in many of the rooms. From £110, breakfast included. Marble Arch tube. All cards. ⑧.

The Selfridge, Orchard St, W1 ☎0171/408 2080; fax 0171/629 8849. Old-fashioned four-star establishment adjacent to the famous department store of the same name. Classical English decor of dark wood panelling and plush furnishings in public areas and bedrooms, which start at around £160. Bond Street tube. All cards. ⑧.

Wigmore Court Hotel, 23 Gloucester Place, W1 ☎0171/935 0928; fax 0171/487 4254. Better than average B&B, boasting a high tally of repeat clients. Comfortable rooms all with en suite facilities and, unusually, a laundry and basic kitchen for guests' use. Marble Arch or Baker Street tube. V; MC. ④.

Soho, Covent Garden and the Strand

The Fielding Hotel, 4 Broad Court, Bow St, WC2 ☎0171/836 8305; fax 0171/497 0064. Quietly situated on a traffic-free and gas-lit court, this excellent hotel is one of Covent Gardens undiscovered gems. Recently refurbished, the Fielding offers some of the best value accommodation in this ideal location, just a few yards from the Royal Opera House, Covent Garden market and numerous fine restaurants. Covent Garden tube. All cards. ⑤.

Hazlitt's, 6 Frith St, W1 ☎0171/434 1771; fax 0171/439 1524. Located off the south side of Soho Square, this early eighteenth-century building is a hotel of real character and charm, offering en suite rooms (from £150) decorated and furnished in a style as close to that period's as convenience and comfort allow. *Hazlitt's* has no dining room (although some of London's best restaurants and coffee bars are a stone's throw away), so continental breakfast (£7 extra) is served in the rooms. Tottenham Court Road tube. All cards. ⑧.

The Howard Hotel, Temple Place, Strand, WC2 ☎0171/836 3555; fax 0171/379 4547. A top-hatted doorman and an ornate foyer set the tone for one of London's few five-star riverfront hotels. Rather sober and expensive – rooms generally cost from £233, though week-end breaks are available from £148. Temple tube. All cards. ⑧.

Manzi's, 1–2 Leicester St, WC2 ☎0171/734 0224; fax 0171/437 4864. Set over the Italian and seafood restaurant of the same name, *Manzi's* is one of very few West End hotels in this price range, although noise might prove to be a nuisance. A continental breakfast included in the price. Leicester Square tube. All cards. ④.

The Mountbatten, Monmouth St, WC2 ☎0171/836 4300; fax 0171/240 3540. Celebrating Earl Mountbatten with memorabilia, oriental decor and antiques from the countries in which he served, this elegant hotel is situated a short walk from the West End's cinemas and theatres. Rooms (from £180) are rather small but immaculately outfitted, and the hotel restaurant and bar maintain the gracious ambience. Leicester Square or Covent Garden tube. All cards. ⑧.

Strand Continental Hotel, 143 Strand, WC2 ☎0171/836 4880. Tucked unobtrusively between such notables as the *Waldorf* and the *Savoy*, this tiny hotel offers basic rooms with shared facilities, plus continental breakfast, at a very competitive price. Long overdue for a facelift but an unbeatable central London bargain. Temple or Covent Garden tube. ①.

The Strand Palace Hotel, Strand, WC2 ☎0171/836 8080; fax 0171/836 2077. Following a complete facelift both inside and out, the huge *Strand Palace* is an ideal base for a binge on London's theatres. Rooms cost from around £120, representing very good value by West End standards. Charing Cross tube. All cards. ⑧.

The Waldorf, Aldwych, WC2 ☎0171/836 2400; fax 0171/836 7244. A stay in the serenely luxurious Edwardian-era *Waldorf* is a memorable experience. The rooms, priced from £180, match the standards of rivals charging £100 more, and the attentive service is as good as any in London. Covent Garden or Aldwych tubes. All cards. ⑧.

Bloomsbury and King's Cross

Arran House Hotel, 77–79 Gower St, WC1 ☎0171/636 2186. Hospitable, family-run B&B, with more efficient soundproofing than most on this busy street. All rooms have TVs, and there's also a TV lounge with a small library, a laundry and a garden. Goodge St tube. V; MC. ③.

Avalon Hotel, 46–47 Cartwright Gardens, WC1 ☎0171/387 2366; fax 0171/387 5810. One of several attractive and inexpensive hotels in this pleasant and well-preserved Georgian crescent, whose spacious buildings lend themselves well to hotel conversion. All rooms have washbasin and TV, some are en suite, and English breakfast is included. As is the case with all hotels on this street, guests can use the Cartwright Gardens tennis courts. Euston or Russell Square tube. ③.

Crescent Hotel, 49–50 Cartwright Gardens, WC1 ☎0171/387 1515; fax 0171/383 2054. Superior B&B; some rooms have en suite facilities, all have TV. Euston or Russell Square tube. V; MC. ④.

Euro & George Hotels, 51–53 Cartwright Gardens, WC1 ☎0171/387 8777; fax 0171/383 5044. A pair of decent co-managed hotels; the former has rooms with shared facilities, while the latter has en suite rooms. All rooms have TV. Euston or Russell Square tube. V; MC; Amex. ② & ③.

Forte Crest Bloomsbury, Coram St, WC1 ☎0171/837 1200/ fax 0171/837 5374. Smart, modern hotel looks much better inside than out and caters mostly for business clients, although good-value weekend deals during early summer and autumn are also offered. All rooms, starting from £130, are comfortable and well equipped, and the hotel has a few rooms designed for solitary women travellers. Russell Square tube. All cards. ⑧.

Garth Hotel, 69 Gower St, WC1 ☎0171/636 5761; fax 0171/637 4854. Another good B&B along this busy Georgian terraced street. Rooms are narrow but well equipped with colour TV and washbasins, and some en suite rooms are available. A traditional Japanese breakfast is offered as an alternative to the indigenous version. Goodge Street tube. V; MC. ③.

Great Northern Hotel, Euston Rd, NW1 ☎0171/837 5454; fax 0171/278 5270. This purpose-built hotel opened in 1854 opposite the newly completed King's Cross train terminus. Pre-dating the truly grand late Victorian hotels, the *Great Northern* caters primarily for business types, with several meeting rooms of various sizes. All rooms are en suite and well equipped; full English breakfast included. King's Cross tube. All cards. ⑥.

Gresham Hotel, 36 Bloomsbury St, WC1 ☎0171/580 4232; fax 0171/436 6341. Popular Italian-owned B&B at the southern end of Gower Street; all rooms have TV, and some have en suite facilities – but make sure you get one of the quieter back rooms. Large English breakfast included. Tottenham Court Road tube. All cards. ④.

Harlingford Hotel, 61–63 Cartwright Gardens, WC1 ☎0171/387 1551; fax 0171/387 4616. Another good option in this fine Georgian crescent. All rooms are en suite with TV, and breakfast is included. Russell Square or Euston tube. V; MC; Amex. ④.

Accommodation

Accommodation

Imperial Hotel, Russell Square, WC1 ☎0171/837 3655; fax 0171/837 4653. Unappealing concrete exterior and communal areas, but the higher rooms offer a pleasing view, and all are fully equipped with satellite TV, minibar, etc. Low on panache, but good value. Russell Square tube. All cards. ⑤.

Jesmond Hotel, 63 Gower St, WC1 ☎0171/636 3199. Friendly and inexpensive family-run B&B, within a short walk of the West End and the British Museum. Goodge St tube. V; MC. ②.

Jesmond Dene Hotel, 27 Argyle St, WC1 ☎0171/837 4654. Hospitable and bright family-run B&B hotel in what is otherwise a seedy district. Some rooms are better than others but all represent good value and all have TV. Deals offered for longer stays. Note that most other hotels in this immediate area cater for the homeless on welfare rather than for tourists. King's Cross tube. No cards. ②.

Mabledon Court Hotel, 10–11 Mabledon Place, WC1 ☎0171/388 3866; fax 0171/387 5688. Nicely converted former student hostel with small en suite rooms and continental or English breakfast included. Euston tube. V; MC; Amex. ④.

Morgan Hotel, 24 Bloomsbury St, WC1 ☎0171/636 3735. Good-value rooms (all en suite) with an added touch of class in the decor and fittings; air conditioning and soundproofing in the streetside rooms. Full English breakfast is served in the oak-panelled dining room. Tottenham Court Road tube. No cards. ④.

Ridgemount Hotel, 65–67 Gower St, WC1 ☎0171/636 1141. Recently extended into the former hotel next door but still offering bargain rates; has a garden, free hot drinks machine and a laundry. Goodge St tube. No cards. ②.

Ruskin Hotel, 23–24 Montague St, WC1 ☎0171/636 7388; fax 0171/323 1662. Central, family-run B&B right opposite the British Museum. Rooms are fairly plain, most with shared facilities and all with TV. Russell Square tube. V; MC. ④.

Hotel Russell, Russell Square, WC1 ☎0171/837 6470; fax 0171/837 2857. From its grand exterior to its opulent interiors of marble, wood and crystal, this late Victorian landmark fully retains its period atmosphere. No two rooms are identical in size or facilities but all are well appointed and decorated in a homely manner. Rooms usually cost from around £130 (with buffet breakfast), but half-price weekend deals are available. Russell Square tube. All cards. ⑧.

St Margaret's Hotel, 26 Bedford Place, WC1 ☎0171/636 4277; fax 0171/323 3066. Friendly B&B in good central location, with small but clean rooms. Russell Square tube. V; MC. ③.

City

The Great Eastern Hotel, Liverpool St , EC2 ☎0171/283 4363; fax 0171/283 4897. Close to the City's core and adjacent to Liverpool Street station, this old hotel is geared mainly to business travellers. The tariff includes an English breakfast and a newspaper of your choice. Liverpool St tube. All cards. ⑦.

Tower Thistle Hotel, St Katherine's Way, E1 ☎0171/481 2575; fax 0171/488 4106. Strikingly situated by St Katherine's Dock, the Tower of London and Tower Bridge, this modern hotel is popular with tour groups as well as business types. All rooms are air conditioned, with standard doubles costing £144. The hotel has three restaurants, two bars and a nightclub as well as facilities for conferences. Tower Hill tube. All cards. ⑧.

Clapham

The Windmill, Clapham Common Southside, SW4 ☎0181/673 4578; fax 0181/675 1486. Newly opened hotel adjoining an established pub in an easy-to-find detached situation on the edge of Clapham Common. Continental breakfast served in your room, or you can have English breakfast downstairs in the restaurant. Lower rates Friday–Sunday. Clapham Common tube. All cards. ④.

Accommodation

Hampstead

La Gaffe, 107–111 Heath St, NW3 ☎0171/435 4941; fax 0171/794 7592. Small, warren-like hotel situated over a restaurant and bar in the heart of Hampstead village. All rooms are en suite and there's a roof terrace for use in fine weather. Parking is a problem close to the hotel. Hampstead tube. All cards. ④.

Hampstead Village Guesthouse, 2 Kemplay Rd, NW3 ☎0171/435 8679; fax 0171/794 0254. Lovely B&B in an old house set in a quiet backstreet between Hampstead village and the Heath. Rooms (some en suite, all non-smoking) have "lived-in" clutter which makes a change from anodyne hotels and spartan B&Bs. Meals to order. Hampstead tube. V; MC; Amex. ③.

Hostels, student halls and camping

Most of London's seven **Youth Hostel Association hostels** are significantly superior to their provincial counterparts and their independent competitors in the capital. Buildings have been properly converted, are spotlessly clean and provide spacious modern facilities, but at a price around fifty percent greater than most private hostels. While curfews and character-building daily chores have been abolished in the capital's hostels they still exude an institutionalized wholesomeness that isn't to everyone's taste: dorms are segregated and drinking and smoking are forbidden or discouraged. Nevertheless, if you value excellent locations and amenities over atmosphere, the metropolitan YHA hostels won't disappoint. Note that in summer you'll have to book way ahead to stand a chance of getting a room (especially in the Oxford Street hostel) and long-term stays are not encouraged. Members of any IYHF-affiliated association have automatic membership of the YHA; non-members can join at any of the hostels or at the **YHA Adventure Shop**, 14 Southampton St, Covent Garden, WC2 (☎ 0171/836 1036).

At best, **independent hostels** offer facilities commensurate with those of YHA places at a lower price and in a less constricted atmosphere. However, many of these hostels are located in run-down former hotels, and make their money by over-cramming their rooms with beds. Kitchens are often inadequate or non-existent and washing facilities can be similarly poor. That said, a lot of people find the freedom to smoke, drink and chat-up fellow travellers is ample compensation for the less than salubrious environment. Rooms in the city's **YMCA** and **YWCA** hostels are only attractive if you're staying for at least a week, in which case you can get discounts on rates that otherwise are no better than than many budget B&Bs.

Outside term time, hostel-style accommodation is offered by **student halls of residence**. Prices are reasonable and some locations are very attractive, although rooms tend to be fairly basic and get booked out quickly. Rooms are offered on a B&B or self-catering basis, which can provide inexpensive lodgings for families.

Finally, London's campsites are all out on the perimeters of the city and for committed campers only. Pitches cost around £4, plus a fee of around £3 per person per night, with reductions for children and during the low season.

YHA hostels

City of London, 36 Carter Lane, EC4 ☎0171/236 4965; fax 0171/236 7681. 200-bed hostel right opposite St Paul's Cathedral; 4- and 5-bed dorms for £18.90, larger ones for £14. There are also private rooms for £22 and a few twins for around £44. St Paul's tube.

Earl's Court, 38 Bolton Gardens, SW5 ☎0171/373 7083; fax 0171/835 2034. Better than a lot of accommodation in Earl's Court, but only offering dorms of 4–16 beds, and the triple-bunk layout of some of them may take some getting used to. Kitchen is just about adequate and the restaurant offers inexpensive evening meals. Breakfast is included and there is a large garden. £16.90. Earl's Court tube.

Accommodation

Hampstead Heath, 4 Wellgarth Rd, NW11 ☎0181/458 9054; fax 0181/209 0546. One of the biggest and best appointed YHA hostels, near the wilds of Hampstead Heath. Rooms with 3–6 beds cost £13.90. Golders Green tube. V; MC.

Highgate Village, 84 Highgate West Hill, N6 ☎0181/340 1831; fax 0181/341 0376. Very pleasant setting in Highgate Village makes up for the long walk to the tube station, although bus #214 from King's Cross stops five minutes from the hostel. Rooms have 4–16 beds (with one very popular twin room), and all beds cost £11.75. Archway tube. V; MC.

Holland House, Holland Walk, W8 ☎0171/937 0748; fax 0171/376 0667. Idyllically situated in the wooded expanse of Holland Park and fairly convenient for the centre, this extensive hostel offers a decent kitchen and inexpensive restaurant but tends to be popular with school groups. £16.90. Holland Park or High Street Kensington tube. All cards.

Oxford St, 14 Noel St, W1 ☎0171/734 1618; fax 0171/734 1657. Its unbeatable West End location and modest size (90 beds in rooms of 2, 3 and 4 beds) mean that this hostel tends to remain full even out of the high season. £16.50. Oxford Circus or Tottenham Court Rd tube. V; MC.

Rotherhithe, Island Yard, Salter Rd, SE16 ☎0171/232 2114; fax 0171 237 2919. Specially built for the YHA, London's largest hostel is located in a redeveloped area that has little going for it compared to the location of other London YHAs, but is only a 20-minute tube ride from the West End and is rarely full. Rooms have 2, 4, 5 or 10 beds, costing £14–30 per person. Rotherhithe tube.

Private hostels

Albion Court Hotel, 1 Trebovir Rd, SW5 ☎0171/373 0833. Shared rooms (5 beds maximum) for £12 per person, and en suite twins for under £40, breakfast included. Lively hostel atmosphere, with a club and bar downstairs and access to a large garden. Earl's Court tube. V; MC. Amex.

Chelsea Hotel, 33–41 Earl's Court Square, SW5 ☎0171/244 6892; fax 0171/244 6891. 260-bed hotel offering dorm beds for as little as £9, and twins with own bathroom for £25, breakfast included. There is no kitchen but there's a TV lounge, restaurant, bar with pool table and a laundry. Popular with backpackers. Earl's Court tube. V; MC; Amex.

Curzon House Hotel, 158 Courtfield Gardens, SW5 ☎0171/581 216; fax 0171/835 1319. Shared rooms from just £13 in summer and £10 in winter, including continental breakfast and use of a small kitchen and TV lounge. Doubles are available for around £38, but no rooms have private facilities. Gloucester Road tube. V; MC.

Maree Hotel, 25 Gower St, WC1 ☎0171/636 4868. The *Maree* may be past its prime, but with dorm beds from as little as £10, plus access to a garden, TV lounge/library and laundry, this is one of the West End's better deals. Goodge St tube. V; MC.

Museum Inn Hostel, 27 Montague St, WC1 ☎0171/580 5360; fax 0171/636 7948. Excellent central position, with 4- to 10-bed mixed dorms (under £15) and no curfew, but a little cramped when it comes to cooking arrangements. Lively atmosphere at the price of a somewhat grubby interior. Tottenham Court Road tube. V; MC.

Quest Hotel, 45 Queensborough Terrace, W2 ☎0171/229 7782; fax 0171/727 8106. Small, well-worn but lively hostel, very popular with young travellers. 4 or 5 beds per room, costing from £11 per person, including breakfast. Kitchen is fine for the hostel's capacity and there's a TV lounge. Queensway tube. V; MC.

Hotel Saint Simeon, 38 Harrington Gardens, SW7 ☎0171/373 0505. Budget accommodation close to the big Kensington museums; shared rooms from £10 per person, doubles around £22, breakfast included. Gloucester Road tube. All cards.

YMCA City, Luwum House, 8 Errol St, EC1 ☎0171/628 8832; fax 0171/628 4080. Smaller of the two City YMCAs, with just a few single rooms (from £25) for short-term visitors. Very good weekly rate of £129.50 with breakfast and evening meal. Old Street, Moorgate or Barbican tube. V; MC.

Accommodation

YMCA Barbican, Fann St, EC2 ☎0171/628 0697; fax 0171 638 2420. Huge, 16-storey towerblock with a few short-term singles (£22) and doubles (£40). Barbican tube. V; MC.

Student halls

Carr Saunders Hall, 18–24 Fitzroy St, W1 ☎0171/323 9712; fax 0171/580 4718 (Warren St tube). The London School of Economics offers singles and twins here from £18 per person including breakfast. Similar LSE accommodation at **Rosebery Avenue Hall**, EC1 (☎0171/278 3251; fax 0171/278 2068; Angel tube), and self-catering flats from £238 per week for two people in **Butlers Wharf Residences**, Gainsford Steet SE1 (☎0171/407 7164; fax 0171/403 0847; London Bridge tube) and Fitzroy Street (see above). Open late March to late April, and July to late Sept.

Goldsmiths' College ☎ 0181/692 7171, ext 2279; fax 0181 694 2234. Several attractive halls of residence available in the New Cross, Deptford and Greenwich areas of southeast London from £16.45 per night for bed only or £35.25 full-board. Open two weeks in mid-April and early June to mid-Sept.

International Student House, 229 Great Portland St, NW1 ☎0171/631 3223; fax 0171/631 8315. Hundreds of beds in a vast complex at the southern end of Regent's Park. Singles at £23.40, doubles £19.75 per person. Open all year. Great Portland Street or Regent's Park tube.

John Adams Hall, 15–23 Endsleigh St, WC1 ☎0171/387 4086. Singles £21 per person (£19 for students and for stays of six or more nights); doubles £37 for room (£33 for students or long stays). Open Jan, March, April, July–Sept, Dec. Euston Square tube.

King's Campus Vacation Bureau, 552 King's Rd, SW10 ☎0171/351 6011; fax 0171/352 7376. King's College has a range of accommodation from July to September, mostly in the Kensington, Chelsea and Westminster areas, with some cheaper alternatives in outlying Hampstead, Wandsworth and Denmark Hill. Singles £14–22, twin rooms £22.60–33.50, all prices including breakfast.

Linstead Hall, Watts Way, Prince's Gardens, SW7 ☎0171/594 9507; fax 0171/594 9505. Single (£24.75) and twin room (£38.50) B&B accommodation offered by Imperial College from late March to late April and July to late September, with ten percent reduction for stays over a week. South Kensington tube.

Passfield Hall, 1 Endsleigh Place, WC1 ☎0171/387 7743; fax 0171/387 0419. Singles £18–19, doubles £30, including breakfast. Open March, April, July–Sept. Euston Square tube.

Ramsay Hall, 20 Maple St, W1 ☎0171/387 4537. Fairly central and comfortable, with over 400 beds, mostly singles. £19 per person or £18 for stays of a week or longer, including breakfast. Open Jan, March, April, June–Sept, Dec. Warren St or King's Cross tube.

Walter Sickert Hall, Graham St, N1 ☎0171/477 8822; fax 0171/477 8823. Over 200 en suite single rooms available July to late Sept for £30, with breakfast. Angel tube.

Campsites

Abbey Wood, Federation Road, Abbey Wood, SE2 ☎0181/310 2233. Enormous year-round site, ten miles east of central London. Mainline train from Charing Cross to Abbey Wood.

Crystal Palace, Crystal Palace Parade, SE19 ☎0181/778 7155. All-year site, with maximum one-week stay in summer, two weeks in winter. Mainline train from London Bridge to Crystal Palace or bus #2 or #3.

Hackney Camping, Millfields Rd, Hackney Marshes, E5 ☎0181/ 985 7656. Big but very inconvenient, way over in the east of the city with poor tube connections. Bus #38 or #55 from Victoria to Hackney Central, then #236 or #276. Open June–Aug.

Tent City Summer Tourist Hostel, Old Oak Common Lane, W3 ☎0181/743 5708. The cheapest beds in London: dorm accommodation in 14 large tents (single sex and mixed) for £5 per night, or you can pitch your own tent for the same price. Open June–Sept. East Acton tube.

Cafés and snacks

Other quick or cheap meals can be had at many of our restaurant listings in the following chapter. Try, especially, the pizza and pasta joints, Chinese dim sum, and the city's ever -expanding ranks of French bistros.

This short chapter covers **cafés, coffee bars, ice-cream parlours and tea rooms**, all of which you'll find open during the day for light snacks or just a drink. Some of them also provide full evening meals, and, as they make no pretense to being restaurants, you can use them for an inexpensive or quick bite before going out to a theatre, cinema or club.

The listings here cover the range, from unreconstructed British caffs, where you can get traditional **British** breakfasts (usually up until 11am), fish and chips, pies and other calorific treats, to the refined salons of London's top hotels, good for a tea-time splurge.

We have divided the listings into two: "Snacks, sandwiches, cakes and coffee", and "Lunches and quick meals". Also featured are boxes on "Afternoon tea" and a check list of the best museum cafés and restaurants – some of which are almost worth a trip in their own right.

Snacks, sandwiches, cakes and coffee

The establishments listed below will just serve you a coffee if that's all you want. However, you'd be missing out to do so, as our selection criterion lies in the quality of their cakes, sandwiches or snacks.

London-wide chains

Aroma: branches at 168 Piccadilly, W1 (Green Park tube; ☎0171/495 6995); West One Centre, 381 Oxford St, W1 (Bond St tube; ☎0171/495 6945); 273 Regent St, W1 (Oxford Circus tube; ☎0171/495 4911); 1b Dean St, W1 (Leicester Square tube; ☎0171/287 1633); 36a St Martin's Lane, WC2 (Charing Cross tube; ☎0171/836 5110). Typical of the new wave of London coffee shops – bright Aztec colours, designer sandwiches on Italian bread and good coffee in varying strengths. The groovy crockery is on sale, too. *Aroma* is now moving into bookshops, North American-style – the first such operation is at *Books etc* on Charing Cross Rd (Tottenham Court Rd tube). *Varied hours but usually open Mon–Fri 8am–8pm, Sat & Sun 9am–8pm.*

Häagen-Dazs: branches at 14 Leicester Square, WC2 (Leicester Square tube; ☎0171/287 9577); Covent Garden Market, WC2 (Covent Garden tube; ☎0171/240 0436); 138 King's Rd, SW3 (Sloane Square tube; ☎0171/823 9326); 75 Hampstead High St, NW3 (Hampstead tube; ☎0171/794 0646). More ice-cream flavours than you can shake a stick at; cakes, sundaes, shakes and coffee served, too. Long queues at peak hours in Leicester Square. *Varied hours; the Leicester Square branch is open Mon–Thurs & Sun 10am–midnight, Fri & Sat 10am–1am.*

Pret à Manger: branches at 77–78 St Martin's Lane, WC2 (Leicester Square tube; ☎0171/379 5335); 54–56 Oxford St, W1 (Tottenham Court Rd tube; ☎0171/636 5750); 12 Kingsgate Rd, Victoria St, SW1 (St James's Park tube; ☎0171/828 1559); 23 Fleet St, EC4

(Blackfriars tube; ☎0171/353 2332). Rapidly expanding chain of designer snack bars serving a selection of ready-made sandwiches, as well as imaginative salads, hot stuffed croissants and even *sushi* selections. Good coffee, too, and speedy service. *Varied hours, but most open from 8am to 6pm, with the St Martin's Lane branch open until 10pm.*

Central London

Bar Italia, 22 Frith St, W1 ☎0171/437 4520. A tiny café that's a Soho institution, serving coffee, croissants and sandwiches around the clock – as it has been for nigh on forty years. Popular with late-night clubbers and those here to watch the Italian league soccer on the giant screen. *Leicester Square tube. Daily 24hr.*

Bonne Bouche, 2 Thayer St, W1 ☎0171/935 3502. Coffee and French cakes; outdoor seating, too. *Baker St or Bond St tube. Mon–Sat 8.30am–7pm, Sun 10am–6pm.*

The Box, 32 Monmouth St, WC2 ☎0171/240 5828. Cool, licensed café that becomes a humming gay bar at night. Great big sandwiches, salads, veggie specials and live jazz on Sundays. *Leicester Square tube. Mon–Sat 11am–11pm, Sun noon–10.30pm.*

Caffé Nero, 43 Frith St, W1 ☎0171/434 3887. Terrific coffee in various guises, a range of cakes to die for, and pasta, calzone and pizza to fill the holes. The outdoor seats – opposite the *Bar Italia* – are among the hottest tickets in Soho; if you get one, stick to it like glue. There's a second branch in Covent Garden, 28–29 Southampton St (opposite the *YHA* shop). *Leicester Square tube. Mon–Fri 8am–2am, Sat 9am–2am, Sun 9am–1.30am.*

Canadian Muffin Company, 9 Brewer St, W1 (Piccadilly Circus tube; ☎0171/287 3555) and 5 King St, WC2 (Covent Garden tube; ☎0171/379 1525). Top-notch sweet and savoury muffins, reliable coffee and frozen yoghurt. *Mon–Fri 8am–7.30pm, Sat 9am–7.30pm, Sun 10am–7pm.*

Cyberia, 39 Whitfield St, W1 ☎0171/209 0983. Coffee and croissants for refuelling, but the real business here is cybersurfing on the internet, on one of a stack of computers lined up for their netizens. Internet access is £2.50 per half-hour (£1.90 for students). *Goodge St tube. Sun & Mon 11am–6pm, Tues–Fri 11am–10pm, Sat 11am–9pm.*

Espresso Bar, Cranbourn St, WC2. Stand-up corner coffee bar, at the edge of Leicester Square, with outdoor tables looking onto the action. Good coffee and pizza slices at a pound or so a go. *Leicester Square tube. Daily 9am–1am.*

The Fountain, *Fortnum & Mason*, 181 Piccadilly, W1 ☎0171/734 8040. Highly civilized department store café with snacks, sandwiches, ice cream, or a full High Tea for shopped-out visitors. It's open at night, too, for "suppers". *Green Park tube. Mon–Sat 7.30am–11pm.*

Kowloon, 21 Gerrard St ☎0171/437 0148. Popular Chinatown stop for tea and cakes, particularly on Sundays when queues form for their *char siu bau* (pork buns) and custard tarts. Eat in or take-away. *Leicester Square tube. Tea served daily 11am–6.30pm.*

Maison Bertaux, 28 Greek St, W1 ☎0171/437 6007. Long-standing, old-fashioned, downbeat Soho patisserie, with tables on two floors (and one or two outside) and a loyal clientele that keeps them busy. You'll be tempted in by the window-full of elaborate cakes. *Leicester Square tube. Daily 9am–8pm.*

Maison Sagne, 105 Marylebone High St, W1 ☎0171/935 6240. Belle Epoque decor, great cakes and pastries from the *Patisserie Valerie*, as well as breakfasts and quick meals. Bond St tube. Mon–Fri 8am–7pm, Sat 8am–6pm, Sun 9am–6pm.

MJ Bradley's, 9 King St, WC2 ☎0171/240 5178. You'd have to go a long way to find designer sandwiches as good as these. Seats inside and out; takeaway, too. *Covent Garden tube. Mon–Fri 8am–8.30pm, Sat 11am–8pm, Sun 11am–7pm.*

Monmouth Coffee House, 27 Monmouth St, WC2 ☎0171/836 5272. The marvellous aroma's the first thing you notice while the cramped wooden booths and

Cafés and snacks

daily newspapers on hand evoke an eighteenth-century coffee house atmosphere – pick and mix your coffee from a fine selection (or buy the beans to take home) and soak it up with Sally Clarke's fancy goods. *Leicester Square tube. Mon–Sat 9.30am–6pm, Sun 11am–5pm.*

Patisserie Valerie, 44 Old Compton St, W1 ☎0171/437 3466. Popular coffee, croissant and cake emporium dating from the 1920s and attracting a loud-talking, arty, people-watching, Soho crowd. *Leicester Square tube. Mon–Fri 8am–6pm, Sat 8am–7pm, Sun 10am–6pm.*

East London

Brick Lane Beigel Bake, 159 Brick Lane, E1 ☎0171/729 0616. Classic 24-hour bagel takeaway shop in the heart of the East End – unbelieveably cheap, even when stuffed with laks and cream cheese. *Whitechapel tube. Daily 24hr.*

Jones Dairy Café, 23 Ezra St, E2 (no phone). The nicest of the many cafés around the popular Columbia Road flower market – filled bagels and sandwiches, snacks and drinks. *Shoreditch tube. Fri–Sun 7am–3pm.*

West London

Cullens Patisserie: branches at 108 Holland Park Avenue, W11 (Holland Park tube; ☎0171/221 3598); 28a Kensington Church St, W8 (High St Kensington tube; ☎0171/938 2880). Tip-top cakes, croissants and chocolates in tip-top areas. *Mon–Fri 8am–8pm, Sat & Sun 8am–7pm.*

Kaffe Opera, 315 King's Rd, SW3 ☎0171/352 9854. Coffee, sandwiches and a few hot dishes in a comfy little place that encourages lingering with its games and unobtrusive music. *Sloane Square tube. Mon–Sat 9am–11pm, Sun 10am–11pm.*

Lisboa Patisserie, 57 Golborne Rd, W10 ☎0181/968 5242. Authentic Portuguese *pastelaria*, with the best custard tarts this side of Lisbon – also, coffee, cakes and a friendly atmosphere. The *Oporto* at no. 62a (closed Mon) is a similar draw for the local Portuguese community. *Ladbroke Grove tube. Daily 8am–8pm.*

The Muffin Man, 12 Wrights Lane, W8 ☎0171/937 6652. Cream teas, sandwiches and snacks in frilly, Miss-Marple-like surroundings. *High St Kensington tube. Mon–Sat 8am–5.30pm.*

Southwest London

Coin de Paris, Red Lion St, Richmond ☎0181/332 6348. North African-run café offering superb French-style cakes, baguettes and sandwiches. Very small but with a nice upstairs room, and located a short way from the river. *Richmond tube. Mon–Sat 9am–5pm.*

The Gallery Tearooms, 103 Lavender Hill, SW11 ☎0171/350 2564. A camp kitsch extravaganza with soft toys, baroque furnishings, mix-and-match cups and plates and a bar lit up like a night sky. If you can keep your eyes on the breakfasts, brunches, teas and cakes, you'll find them rather good, and you can walk it off across nearby Clapham Common. *Clapham Common tube. Mon–Thurs 11am–11pm, Fri & Sat 11am–11.30pm, Sun 11am–6.30pm.*

Maids of Honour, 288 Kew Rd, Richmond ☎0181/940 2752. Famous old tearoom serving cream teas and wondrous cakes including the eponymous "maids of honour" tart. Oddly, and annoyingly, it's not open on Sunday. *Kew Gardens tube. Mon 9.30am–12.30pm, Tues–Sat 9.30am–5.30pm.*

Stravinsky's Russian Tea House, 6 Fulham High St, SW6 ☎0171/371 0001. Speciality teas served with breakfast, lunch or early dinner – sandwiches and heftier eastern European dishes are on the menu, as is (surprisingly inexpensive) caviar. *Putney Bridge tube. Mon–Sat 10am–9pm, Sun 11am–9pm.*

North London

Blue Legume, 101 Stoke Newington Church St, N16 ☎0171/923 1303. Buzzy atmosphere, arty decor and mosaic tables, and delicious chocolate cakes, teas and coffee. Good breakfasts too – smoked fish, wild mushrooms on toast., and such. *Bus #73. Tues–Fri 9.30am–6.30pm, Sat & Sun 10.30am–6.30pm.*

Huff's, Southend Rd, NW3 (no phone). Cakes, coffee and newspapers for the punters – a short trot from Parliament Hill. A good place for a lazy Sunday. *Belsize Park tube. Daily 11am–7pm.*

Louis Patisserie, 32 Heath St, NW3 ☎0171/435 9908. Popular central European tearoom serving sticky cakes to a mix of heath-bound hordes and elderly locals. *Hampstead tube. Daily 9.30am–6pm.*

Manhattan Bagel Bakery, 31 Seven Sisters Rd, N7 ☎0171/263 9007. Great bagels and fillings, served until late. *Finsbury Park tube. Daily 7am–midnight.*

Marine Ices, 8 Haverstock Hill, NW3 ☎0171/485 3132. Splendid old-fashioned ice-cream parlour with a reputation for ices that spreads far and wide; pizza and pasta served in the adjacent restaurant. *Chalk Farm tube. Mon–Sat 10.30am–11pm, Sun 11.30am–10pm.*

Patisserie Bliss, 428 St John St, EC1 ☎0171/837 3720. A friendly little place best known for its gooey, fragrant almond croissants, though it also serves creative savoury snacks and splendid coffee. Best in summer, when you can sit outside. Sundays are very popular. *Angel tube. Mon–Fri 8am–7pm, Sat & Sun 9am–6pm.*

World Café, 130 Crouch Hill, N8 ☎0181/340 5635. Pounding salsa and African beats, good healthy breakfasts (served up until 2.30pm), Portuguese cakes and home-made lemonade. *Archway or Finsbury Park tube. Mon–Sat 9.30am–11pm, Sun 9.30am–10.30pm.*

Breakfasts, lunches and quick meals

There are cafés and small, basic restaurants all over London that can rustle up an inexpensive meal. You should be able to fill up at all of the places listed in this section for a little over £5, including tea, coffee or a soft drink. A few are licensed, in which case the price might rise to around £10 a head.

Most of these cafés here feature big English breakfasts, served most often till 11am – though a few offer breakfast all day – then move over to pies, fish and chips, and the like. Some cafés, and many of the Italian places listed here, are also open in the evening but the turnover is fast, so don't expect to linger. They are best seen as fuel stops before – or in a few cases, after – a night out elsewhere.

What's not listed here (nor in the restaurants chapter that follows) are pizza, steak and burger chains – *McDonalds, Burger King, Pizza Hut*, and the like. You'll need no help to find the nearest branch of any of these – every tourist destination in the city has a full selection within walking distance. Keep in mind, however, that their fare doesn't neccessarily come cheaper than the far tastier meals served in many of the places below.

Cafés and snacks

London-wide

Crank's: branches at 17 Great Newport St, WC2 (Leicester Square tube; ☎0171/836 5226); 9 Tottenham St, W1 (Goodge St tube; ☎0171/631 3912); 8 Marshall St, W1 (Oxford Circus tube; ☎0171/437 9431); 23 Barrett St, W1 (Bond St tube; ☎0171/495 1340); 11 The Market, WC2 (Covent Garden tube; ☎0171/379 6508); 5 Cowcross St, EC1 (Farringdon tube; ☎0171/490 4870). The veggie (and vegan) eating house that spawned a thousand imitators with its wholemeal decor, keen staff, lentil bakes, exotic fruit juices and no-smoking policy. Several useful locations, but food that is too often a bit bland – and a bit pricey. *Varied hours, but usually Mon–Fri 8am–10pm, Sat 9am–10pm, Sun noon–9pm.*

Dino's: branches at 33 North Audley St, W1 (Marble Arch tube; ☎0171//629 7070); 242 Earl's Court Rd, SW5 (Earl's Court tube; ☎0171/373 3767); 1 Pelham St (South Kensington tube; ☎0171/589 3511); 127 King's Rd, SW3 (Sloane Square tube; ☎0171/362 4921); 117 Gloucester Rd, SW7 (Gloucester Road tube; ☎0171/373 3678); 16 Kensington Church St, W8 (High St Kensington tube; ☎0171/937 3896). Cheery Italian diners, with tables packed so closely together

Cafés and snacks

that you'll not get out after your plate of pasta. The daily specials are good value, and wine and beer is served. *Varied hours, but usually daily 7am–11pm.*

Ed's Easy Diner: branches at 12 Moor St, W1 (Leicester Square tube; ☎0171/439 1955); 362 King's Rd, SW3 (Sloane Square tube; ☎0171/352 1956); 335 Fulham Rd, SW10 (Fulham Broadway tube; ☎0171/352 1952); 16 Hampstead High St, NW3 (Hampstead tube; ☎0171/431 1958). Bright, good-time Fifties theme diners (check out the last four digits of the phone numbers), dishing up some of the city's best burgers and fries for middling prices. At busy times you'll have to wait in line – it's strictly eat and go. *Mon–Thurs 9am–midnight, Fri & Sat 9am–1am, Sun 9am–11pm.*

Stockpot: branches at 18 Old Compton St, W1 (Leicester Square tube; ☎0171/287 1066); 40 Panton St, SW1 (Piccadilly Circus tube; ☎0171/839 5142) and 6 Basil St, SW3 (Knightsbridge tube; ☎0171/589 8267). Big portions at rock-bottom prices – tables are cramped, and style isn't an ingredient in much use in the kitchen, but if you want a roast lunch, spaghetti, omelette or grill and you've only got a fiver, this is the business. Cheap wine, too. *Varied hours, but Panton St opens earliest, at 8am, while all branches open Mon–Sat until at least 11pm, Sun 10pm.*

Central: Soho and Piccadilly Area

Bar du Marché, 19 Berwick St, W1 ☎0171/734 4606. A weird find in the middle of raucous Berwick St market – quick French snacks and meals, fried breakfasts and a licensed bar. Dig into lunch and then pop over the road to the sausage shop for the best bangers in the country. *Tottenham Court Rd tube. Mon–Sat 8am–11pm, Sun noon–8pm.*

Bonbonnière, 36 Great Marlborough St, W1 ☎0171/437 2562. A good find in the Oxford Circus neighbourhood – cheap, plain fry-ups and Italian dishes, served in a no-nonsense dining room. Wine served

Afternoon Tea

The classic **afternoon tea** – assorted sandwiches, scones and cream, cakes and tarts and, of course, lashings of tea – is available all over London. Best venues are the capital's top hotels and most fashionable department stores; a selection of the best is picked out below. Expect to spend £10–15 a head, and leave your jeans at home – most hotels will expect a jacket and tie for men.

Brown's, 33–34 Albermarle St, W1 ☎0171/493 6020. *Green Park tube. All cards. Daily 3–6pm.*

Claridge's, Brook St, W1 ☎0171 629 8860. *Bond St tube. All cards. Daily 3–5pm.*

The Criterion, 224 Piccadilly, W1 ☎0171/925 0909. *Piccadilly Circus tube. All cards. Mon–Sat 2.30–5.30pm, Sun 3–5.30pm.*

The Dorchester, Park Lane, W1 ☎0171/629 8888. *Hyde Park Corner tube. All cards. Daily 3–6pm.*

Fortnum & Mason's, 4th Floor, 181 Piccadilly, W1 ☎0171/734 8040. *Green Park tube. All cards. Mon–Sat 3–5.30pm.*

Harvey Nichols, Fifth Floor Café, Knightsbridge, SW1 ☎0171/235 5000. *Knightsbridge tube. All cards. Mon–Sat 3–6pm.*

Park Lane, Piccadilly, W1 ☎0171/499 6321. *Green Park tube. All cards. Daily 3–6pm.*

Ritz, Piccadilly, W1 ☎0171/493 8181. *Piccadilly Circus tube. All cards. Daily 3–5pm.*

Savoy, The Strand, WC2 ☎0171/836 4343. *Charing Cross tube. All cards. Daily 3–5.30pm.*

Waldorf, Aldwych, WC2 ☎0171/836 2400. *Aldwych tube. All cards. Daily 3.30–6pm; also weekly tea dances.*

by the carafe. *Oxford Circus tube. Mon–Sat 7.30am–7pm.*

Centrale, 16 Moor St, W1 ☎0171/437 5513. Tiny Italian café that serves up huge plates of steaming, garlicky pasta (*rigatoni Alfredo* and *spaghetti vongole* the clear winners), as well as omelettes, chicken and chops. You'll almost certainly have to wait for – or share – a table. Bring your own booze; there's a corkage charge. *Leicester Square tube. Daily noon–9.30pm.*

China China, 3 Gerrard St. ☎0171/439 7502. Best Chinatown bet for a quick plate of noodles – bright, efficient and even reasonably friendly. Try the spicy Singapore-style noodles, or the *ho fun* (flat noodles) with beef and black bean sauce, either of which will fill a yawning hole. *Leicester Square tube. Daily noon–midnight.*

Marché Mövenpick, Swiss Centre, Leicester Square, WC2 ☎0171/734 1291. Pick-your-own food centre with meat, fish, veg and salads – there's fondue, too, though this is slightly more expensive than the self-service choices. *Leicester Square tube. Mon–Sat 8am–midnight, Sun 9am–midnight.*

Mediterranean Barbecue, 8 Irving St, WC2 ☎0171/930 4519. Cubby-hole felafel and kebab joint, off Leicester Square. The felafels are very tasty, the chilli sauce a killer, and there are a couple of tables if you don't want to eat on the hoof. *Daily 11am–9pm. Leicester Square tube.*

Pho, 2 Lisle St, WC2 (no phone). Vietnamese fast-food café in Chinatown; big bowls of noodle soup are the speciality, and there's a great vegetarian selection, too, of noodles, curries and stir-fries. *Leicester Square tube. Daily noon–11pm.*

Pollo, 20 Old Compton St, W1 ☎0171/734 5917. This place has a reputation – some say unjustified – for the best-value Italian food in town, which means that even though there are two floors, you'll either have to wait in line or share a table. The queues move quickly, though, and it's a friendly, buzzing place – even if the food is workmanlike at times. Alcohol is served. *Leicester Square tube. Mon–Sat 11.30am–11pm.*

Rabin's, 39 Great Windmill St, W1 ☎ no phone. Great sandwiches – the salt beef and pastrami are famous – and soups and bagels, too, in a caff known as the "Nosh Bar". It's changed little since the 1950s – red leatherette stools and red-checked tablecloths. *Piccadilly Circus tube. Mon–Sat 11am–8pm.*

Star Café, 22 Great Chapel St, W1 ☎0171/437 8778. Soho café tucked away off Oxford St, run for years by Mario and his team. Breakfasts, grills. Good daily specials that show a spark of imagination pull in the arty punters at lunchtime. Wine served with meals. *Tottenham Court Rd tube. Mon–Fri 7am–4pm.*

Tai Ka Lok, 18 Gerrard St ☎0171/437 2354. One of the best places in Chinatown for a simple plate of cooked meat and rice – roast pork or duck, steamed chicken or spare ribs, all dangling in the window awaiting the axeman. Wash it down with a fish-head-and-bean-curd soup and you'll be in good local company. *Leicester Square tube. Daily noon–11.45pm.*

Wren at St James's, 197 Piccadilly – next to the church, SW1 ☎0171/437 9419. Vegetarian and wholefood café with outdoor courtyard seating in summer. *Piccadilly Circus tube. Mon–Sat 8am–7pm, Sun 10am–5pm.*

Central: Covent Garden Area

Café in the Crypt, St Martin-in-the-Fields church, Duncannon St, WC2 ☎0171/839 4342. Below the church, in the crypt, the good-quality buffet food – including veggie dishes – makes this an ideal spot to fill up before hitting the West End. *Charing Cross tube. Mon–Sat 10am–8pm, Sun noon–6pm.*

Diana's Diner, 39 Endell St, WC2 ☎0171/242 0272. Cramped wooden benches, a friendly welcome for regulars and improbably large plates of home-made pies, omelettes, grills and chips. A favourite with local office workers. *Covent Garden tube. Mon–Sat 7am–8pm, Sun 8am–6pm.*

Cafés and snacks

Cafés and snacks

Ecology Centre Café, 45 Shelton St, WC2 ☎0171/379 4324. Relaxing café with vegetarian/vegan snacks, soups and sandwiches; bookshop and information centre, too. *Covent Garden tube. Mon–Sat 10am–6pm.*

Fatboy's Diner, 21–22 Maiden Lane, WC2 ☎0171/240 1902. A 1940s' trailer transplanted from the US to a Covent Garden backstreet, where it continues to serve decent burgers, hot dogs, excellent fries and shakes. Take some change for the tableside jukebox. *Covent Garden tube. Mon–Sat 11am–11pm, Sun 11am–10.30pm.*

Food for Thought, 31 Neal St, WC2 ☎0171/836 9072. A sympatico veggie restaurant and takeaway counter – the food is good, with daily changing specials, and vegan and wheat-free options. Expect to queue at peak times, when there's a £1.50 minimum charge. *Covent Garden tube. Mon–Sat 9.30am–8pm, Sun 10.30am–4pm.*

Frank's Cafe, 52 Neal St, WC2 ☎0171/836 6345. Italian café/sandwich bar with easy-going service. All-day breakfasts, plates of pasta and omelettes on offer; come either side of lunch to make sure of a table. *Covent Garden tube. Mon–Sat 8am–8.30pm.*

Gaby's, 30 Charing Cross Rd, WC2 ☎0171/836 4233. Jewish café and takeaway joint serving a wide range of home-cooked veggie and Middle Eastern specialities. Hard to beat for value, choice or long hours. It's licensed, too. *Leicester Square tube. Mon–Sat 8am–midnight, Sun noon–10pm.*

Neal's Yard Dining Room, 14 Neal's Yard, WC2 ☎0171/379 0298. First floor veggie café that comes into its own in summer, when the windows are flung open and you can gaze down upon trendy humanity as you tuck into tasty dishes from all corners of the globe. Bring your own booze, or stick to the fruit juices. *Covent Garden tube. Mon, Tues & Thurs–Sat noon–5pm, Wed noon–8pm.*

Porky's Place, 49 Chandos Place, WC2 ☎0171/836 0967. Cracking little early-opening diner/sandwich bar tucked behind Charing Cross post office, with all-day breakfasts or super fry-ups for well under a fiver. *Charing Cross tube. Mon–Sat 6am–5.30pm.*

North London

Alfredo's, 4–6 Essex Rd, N1 ☎0171/226 3496. An unusually elegant neighbourhood diner with Art Deco fittings – all mirrors and chrome – big portions and low prices. *Angel tube. Mon–Fri 7am–2.30pm, Sun 7.30am–4pm.*

Bar Room Bar, 48 Rosslyn Hill, NW3 ☎0171/435 0808. Airy converted pub with decent lunches (noon–3.30pm); there's an oyster bar on Tuesday nights. Handy for the heath. *Hampstead tube. Daily 11am–11pm.*

Manze's, 74 Chapel Market, N1 (no phone). Traditional Cockney food – meat pies, mashed potato, jellied/stewed eels – in traditional caff surroundings. You'll be pushed to spend a fiver. *Angel tube. Tues–Sat 10am–5pm, Sun 10am–2pm.*

The City and East End

Al's Café Bar, 11–13 Exmouth Market, EC1 ☎0171/837 4821. This is a trendy little spot – a glorified greasy spoon with a media-luvvie clientele, who are served up Italian breads, Mediterranean dishes, nachos, decent coffee and good soups alongside the chips and grills. *Angel or Farringdon tube. Tues 7am–8pm, Wed–Fri 7am–11pm, Sat & Sun 7am–8pm.*

F. Cooke, 41 Kingsland High St, E8 ☎0171/254 2878. Eels, pies and mash in one of London's most elaborately decorated caffs – tiles that yuppies would die for, in place since 1910. *Dalston Kingsland BR. Mon–Thurs 10am–7pm, Fri & Sat 10am–10pm.*

Diana's Dining Room, 30 St Cross St, EC1 ☎0171/831 72 61. Middle Eastern and Jewish specials that work out a bit more expensive than most of the places in this section, but the service is friendy and the portions large – the salt beef is good, and there's a filling vegetarian meze dish. *Farringdon tube. Mon–Fri 8am–3.30pm.*

Museum Cafés

Most museums in London have a café of some description. Some are terrible, but others are worth planning your visiting times around. The best of the bunch include:

Design Museum (p.260)	**National Gallery** (p.43)
ICA (p.56)	**Tate Gallery** (p.77)
Museum of Mankind (p.101)	**Victoria and Albert Museum** (p.276)

Cafés and snacks

East West Centre, 188 Old St, EC1 ☎0171/608 0300. Macrobiotic and wholefood meals in a centre devoted to "alternative lifestyles". *Old St tube. Mon–Sat 10.30am–10.30pm, Sun 10.30am–5pm.*

Fox & Anchor, 115 Charterhouse St, EC1 ☎0171/253 4838. Smithfield market pub with unbeatable breakfasts – there's a veggie option, too – and traditional British pies. If you're interested by the fact that you can get a beer at 7.30am, you've either just finished clubbing or are a sick person. *Farringdon tube. Meals served Mon–Fri 7.30–10am & noon–2.15pm, Sat 8–10.30am.*

The Place Below, St Mary-le-Bow, Cheapside, EC2 ☎0171/329 0789. Dine in the Norman crypt on a predominantly vegetarian menu. The food is fine, if slightly pricey, and you can bring your own bottle on Thursday and Friday evening when dinner is served. *St Paul's tube. Mon–Wed 7.30am–2.30pm, Thurs & Fri 7.30am–2.30pm & 6.30–9.30pm.*

Victoria & Knightsbridge

Chelsea Kitchen, 98 King's Rd, SW3 ☎0171/589 1330. Bargain-basement international dishes – stews, egg dishes pastas, etc – served to the impecunious young since the 1960s. Even the house wine is as cheap as it gets in London. *Sloane Square tube. Mon–Sat 8am–11.45pm, Sun 10am–11.45pm.*

King's Road Café, *Habitat*, 208 King's Rd, SW3 ☎0171/351 1211. Soups, sandwiches – with an Italian twist – and salads in perfectly stylish surroundings. Mainly vegetarian. *Sloane Square tube. Mon–Fri 10am–6pm, Sat & Sun noon–5.30pm.*

The Well, 2 Eccleston Place, SW1 ☎0171/730 7303. In a location handy for the Victoria bus and train stations, this serves good-value café food throughout the working day. *Victoria tube. Mon–Sat 9.30am–5pm.*

West

Café Grove, 253a Portobello Rd, W11 ☎0171/243 1094. Very popular first-floor terrace café with a nice line in omelettes, pasta, salads and all-day breakfasts. *Ladbroke Grove tube. Mon–Fri 9am–11pm, Sat 9am–6.30pm, Sun 10.30am–5.30pm.*

Chapter 15

Restaurants

London in the 1990s is a great place to eat – not yet a rival for New York or Paris, perhaps, but well on the way. You can sample more or less any kind of cuisine here, and – wherever you come from – you sould find something new and possible unique. Our listings take in everything from classic French and Italian cooking, through Chinese, Thai, Malaysian, Indian and Bengali, to Lebanese, Greek, Turkish and Russian. Not forgetting, of course, British cooking – a tradition greatly revitalized over the past decade.

There are plenty of places to eat around the main tourist drags of the West End – **Soho** has long been renowned for its eclectic and fashionable restaurants, while **Chinatown**, on the other side of Shaftesbury Avenue, offers value-for-money eating right in the centre of town. Upmarket areas like **Kensington** and **Chelsea**, too, feature many haute-cuisine restaurants.

A checklist of restaurants, area by area, appears on p.453.

To sample the full range of possibilities, however, it is well worth taking time to explore quarters away from the core of the city. Try the Indian, Pakistani and Bangladeshi restaurants of **Brick Lane** in the East End and **Drummond Street** near Euston, for example, or the bistros and brasseries of **Camden** and **Islington**, a short tube ride away to the north. You can often eat much better, and much cheaper, in these more local neighbourhoods.

Not that the **prices** are so outrageous. The recession forced many restaurants, both good and bad, to the wall, and those that remain, as well as most new ventures, are making a conscious effort to attract diners with keenly priced set meals or special promotions such as pre-theatre menus and all-you-can-eat buffets.

Inevitably, some cuisines are far better represented than others. If you're used to North American quality and portion size, you're not going to be impressed by London's American, Mexican or Tex-Mex establishments, few of which show any imagination and all of which are overpriced. With a few honourable exceptions, you're also likely to feel shortchanged after a meal in one of London's Japanese restaurants, though here, admittedly, the problem is more one of having to pay for shockingly expensive ingredients.

But the list of positive recommendations is wide and ever-expanding. London is home to some of the best **Cantonese** restaurants in the whole of Europe, is a noted centre for **Indian and Bangladeshi** food, and has numerous French, Greek, Italian, Spanish and Thai restaurants. And within all these cuisines you can choose anything from simple meals to gourmet spreads.

Traditional **British** food is available all over town, and some of the best venues are reviewed below. However, many of the capital's hottest young chefs are cooking up a storm in a developing style known, for want of a better description, as **modern British**. The setting might be a barebones café or a plush hotel, but the food will be characterized by fresh ingredients, inspired combinations of

Restaurants

Category Index

Credit Cards

The following abbreviations are used in the reviews:
Amex: American Express
Diners: Diners' Club
MC: Mastercard/Access
V: Visa
All cards: all of the above are accepted.

flavours, and a mixture of traditional and trendy techniques: in a modern British restaurant you're as likely to be served preservative-free bangers and mash as char-grilled tuna with salsa.

Most of the restaurants we've listed will be busy on most nights of the week, particularly on Friday and Saturday. You're best advised to **reserve a table** wherever you're headed, and with the most renowned places you'll probably be disappointed if you don't plan at least a week ahead. At these, too, don't be surprised to be asked for a contact number and for your table reservation to be confirmed by the restaurant nearer the date. If you can't make your reservation, let the restaurant know.

We've given the **opening hours** for all the restaurants listed in this chapter, but it's always worth calling to check, as things change and some proprietors have a creative attitude towards timekeeping.

As far as payment goes, we've noted where possible whether an establishment takes **credit cards** or not, and which ones (see box above). At most places, **service** is discretionary, but restaurants tend to take no chances, emblazoning their bills with reminders that "Service is NOT included", or even rounding up the bill to show you how much it would be if you paid the recommended 10, or 12 (or even 15) percent. Normally you should, of course, pay service – it's how most of the staff make up their wages – but check the bill to ensure you're not paying twice, as at some restaurants there's a compulsory service charge (which has to be announced on the menu by law).

In addition, if you're paying by credit card and service *is* already included, check that the "total" box in the card slip is not left blank, thereby encouraging you to leave another tip. If this happens, complain to the management.

Restaurants

African/Caribbean

Beewees, 96 Stroud Green Rd, N4 ☎0171/263 4004. Long-established Caribbean restaurant, with downbeat, front-room decor, good meat and prawn curries, rice and peas and other staples. Curried goat is a favourite. *Finsbury Park tube. Tues–Sat noon–midnight, Sun 5–9.30pm. No cards. Inexpensive.*

Brixtonian, 11 Dorrell Place, SW9 ☎0171/978 8870. The stylish *Brixtonian* has a pleasant bar and more expensive upstairs restaurant. *Brixton tube. Bar: Sun & Mon 5pm–midnight, Tues & Wed noon–midnight, Thurs–Sat noon–1am. Restaurant: Tues–Sat 7–11pm. Amex, MC, V. Inexpensive (bar) to Moderate (restaurant).*

Calabash, Africa Centre, 38 King St, WC2 ☎0171/836 1976. Attractive, laid-back basement restaurant serving hearty quantities of (sometimes stodgy) food from various African countries. The *aloco* (spicy plantain) starter blows heads off; the heady Zimbawean red wine doesn't mess about either. Note that last orders is at 10.30pm. *Covent Garden tube. Mon–Fri 12.30–3pm & 6pm–midnight, Sat 6pm–midnight. All cards. Inexpensive.*

Cotton's, 55 Chalk Farm Rd, NW1 ☎0171/482 1096. Caribbean restaurant with loud reggae and dishes to fill your boots – rice and peas, Camden-style. *Chalk Farm tube. Daily noon–11.45pm. All cards. Inexpensive to Moderate.*

Smokey Joe's Diner, 131 Wandsworth High St, SW18 ☎0181/871 1785. Rave reviews for this bargain neighbourhood restaurant serving mountainous portions of Caribbean specials. Take your own booze and undo your belt a notch. *East Putney tube or Wandsworth Town BR from Victoria or Waterloo. Mon–Fri noon–3pm & 6–11pm, Sat noon–midnight, Sun 3–10pm. No cards. Inexpensive.*

American

See also Mexican / Tex-Mex, *p.446.*

Christopher's, 18 Wellington St, WC2 ☎0171/240 4222. Massively hyped and lusciously decorated, this modern American place is good for grills (terrific strip steak), though not so hot on value for money. Eating in the café, rather than the restaurant, is one way to keep the price down, the other is to come for the excellent Sunday brunch. *Covent Garden tube. Café: Mon–Sat 11am–11pm, Sun noon–3.30pm. Restaurant: Mon–Fri noon–3pm & 6–11.30pm, Sat 6–11.30pm. All cards. Moderate (café) to Expensive (restaurant).*

Hard Rock Café, 150 Old Park Lane, W1 ☎0171/629 0382. The original "Hard Rock" and the best-known burger joint in town, with permanent queue, loud music and an interior awash with rock memorabilia. Food and drinks are pricey, and quality is questionable, but no one seems to care. *Hyde Park Corner tube. Mon–Thurs & Sun 11.30am–12.30am, Fri & Sat 11.30am–1am. Amex, MC, V. Moderate.*

Joe Allen, 13 Exeter St, WC2 ☎0171/836 0651. Rather anonymous from outside, this buzzing, media-people, basement restaurant has a rowdy bar-room atmosphere. The burgers are excellent, but you have to ask for them – they are not on the menu. What is listed is contemporary Cal-Ital cooking of extreme competence, with dishes that change daily. *Covent Garden tube. Mon–Sat noon–12.45am, Sun noon–11pm. No cards. Expensive.*

Kenny's, 2a Pond Place, SW3 ☎0171/225 2916. Highly-regarded southern US/Cajun restaurant, serving up blackened fish, jambalaya, ribs and splendid appetizers – try the crab cakes. A revelation after the burger theme bar antics of West End American restaurants. *South Kensington tube. Mon–Sat noon–midnight, Sun 11am–10.30pm. All cards. Moderate.*

Budget: under £8
Inexpensive: £8–15
Moderate: £15–20
Expensive: £20–30
Very Expensive: over £30
These are per person prices for a three-course meal (or equivalent), excluding drinks and service.

Planet Hollywood, 13 Coventry St, W1 ☎0171/287 1000. The latest in celebrity theme restaurants, its muscled investors – Sly, Arnie and Bruce – reputedly coming up with some of the recipes (variations on a burger) as well as the movie-time decor. If you enjoyed waiting in line at the *Hard Rock* you'll like it here, too. *Piccadilly Circus tube. Daily 11am–1am. All cards. Moderate.*

Rock Garden, The Piazza, Covent Garden, WC2 ☎0171/836 4052. Eat here and you get in free to the gig (live music nightly from rock bands you've never heard of). Outdoor seating on the piazza is the other main draw. *Covent Garden tube. Mon–Sat noon–3am, Sun noon–1am Amex, MC, V. Moderate.*

Rock Island Diner, London Pavilion, Piccadilly Circus, W1 ☎0171/287 5500. Its proximity to the *Rock Circus* ensures a steady supply of kids, who thrill to the sparkly chrome, Fifties' music, dancing waiters and (distinctly average) chilli, burgers, shakes and fries. Cheaper than most of the other nearby American theme restaurants – and you get a free kid's meal with every adult meal at weekends until 5pm. *Piccadilly Circus tube. Daily noon–11pm. All cards. Inexpensive.*

Sticky Fingers, 1a Phillimore Gardens, W8 ☎0171/938 5338. Bill Wyman-backed restaurant with standard diner food, cocktails and the Rolling Stones on its mind. More hard rock than *Hard Rock*, but not bad for all that. *High Street Kensington tube. Mon–Sat 2–11.30pm, Sun 2–11pm. All cards. Moderate.*

TGI Friday's, 6 Bedford St, WC2 ☎0171/379 0585. Office parties determined to live up to the name (**T**hank **G**od **I**t's. . .) set the tone here – the Tex-Mex food, burgers, steaks and salads are all pretty good but come a distinct second to the intention to down as many cocktails as possible by closing time. If you've never danced on a table, you may. Note that you have to be 21 to drink at the bar. There's a second central London branch on Coventry Street, near Piccadilly Circus. *Charing Cross tube. Daily noon–11pm. Amex, MV, V. Moderate.*

Argentinian

Gaucho Grill, 19 Swallow St, W1 ☎0171/734 4040. New restaurant getting rave reviews for the quality of its steaks – flown in from Argentina and cooked to perfection. It's not worth coming unless you're going to indulge; other dishes are uninspired. *Piccadilly Circus tube. Mon–Fri noon–3pm & 5pm–midnight, Sat & Sun noon–midnight. All cards. Expensive.*

El Gaucho, Chelsea Farmer's Market, 125 Sydney St, SW3 ☎0171/376 8514. A great place in summer when you can sit outside and chew on steak (again flown in from home) or chicken, with minimal vegetable accompaniment. *South Kensington tube. Tues–Sun noon–3pm & 7–11pm. No cards. Moderate.*

Belgian

Belgo, 72 Chalk Farm Rd, NW1 ☎0171/267 0718. Monastic life was never so much fun – the roughed up, rope-and plaster entrance gives way to a hugely popular basement diner-restaurant (with suitably ascetic chairs), where eager waiters in monks' habits dish up mussels, *frites* and Belgian beer. The various price deals are hard to beat – including lunch for a fiver and all-the-mussels-and-frites you can eat (Mon–Fri lunch & 6–7pm) for around £8. A winner – you'll need to book several days in advance. A massive second branch, *Belgo Centraal*, occupies the corner site on Neal St, Covent Garden, WC2. *Chalk Farm tube. Mon–Fri noon–3pm & 6–11.30pm, Sat noon–11.30pm, Sun noon–10.30pm. Amex, MC, V. Inexpensive to Moderate.*

Brazilian

Amazonas, 75 Westbourne Grove, W11 ☎0171/243 0090. Good, bright, lively night-time venue for authentic Brazilian tastes. There's a set dinner if you want someone else to make the choices. *Notting Hill Gate tube. Mon–Sat noon–2pm & 7–11.30pm, Sun 7–10.30pm. All cards. Moderate.*

Paulo's, 30 Greyhound Rd, W6 ☎0171/385 9264. Among the oldest of London's South American restaurants, the draw

Restaurants

here is the £10 all-you-can-eat buffet, with a variety of stews, rices and salads, some of which are decidedly more interesting than others. Wicked *caipirinhas*, friendly service and cheerful surroundings add up to a decent night out. *Baron's Court or Hammersmith tube. Mon–Sat 7.30–10.30pm. No cards. Moderate.*

Sabor de Brasil, 36 Highgate Hill, N19 ☎0171/263 9066. The £10 set buffet provides a variety of Brazilian tastes in welcoming surroundings. Take your own booze. *Archway tube. Tues–Sun 1–3pm & 7–11pm. No cards. Inexpensive.*

British

For more British food, see: "Lunches and quick meals", *p.417 and* "Fish and Chips", *p.434.*

Alfred, 245 Shaftesbury Avenue, WC2 ☎0171/240 2566. Stylish new restaurant using traditional ingredients to conjure up dishes like mussels in Stilton sauce and desserts with lavender custard. Staff are wonderfully amiable and drinks are a welcome surprise, too, with British wines, beers and spirits to the fore. *Tottenham Court Rd tube. Mon–Sat noon–3.30pm & 6–11.45pm. All cards. Expensive.*

Butlers Wharf Chop House, Butlers Wharf Building, Shad Thames, SE21 ☎0171/403 3403. High prices but perfectly judged cooking in this Conran-owned restaurant. Excellent traditional British food and Tower Bridge views; you can't reserve the terrace tables but try and book ahead for a window seat. Set lunch (around £20) and Sunday brunch (£13–15) keep the prices down a bit. *Tower Hill or London Bridge tube. Mon–Fri & Sun noon–3pm & 6–11pm, Sat 6–11pm. All cards. Expensive.*

Foxtrot Oscar, 79 Royal Hospital Rd, SW3 ☎0171/352 7179. Stylish bistro serving big portions of British food, from proletarian mushroom and kidney pie to luscious smoked goose – choose from the dishes chalked up on the blackboard. *Sloane Square tube. Mon–Fri 12.30–2.30pm & 7.30–11.30pm, Sat 12.30–3.30pm & 7.30–11.30pm, Sun 12.30–3.30pm & 7.30–10.30pm. Amex, MC, V. Moderate.*

Porters, 17 Henrietta St, WC2 ☎0171/836 6466. The pies are famous here – steak and mushroom, chicken and broccoli, lamb and apricot, even vegetarian – though there's also roast beef, bubble and squeak and steamed desserts. Not the greatest food in the world, but reasonably priced and served in fair-sized portions. Decor is pseudo-Victorian, all polished brass and burnished wood. *Covent Garden tube. Mon–Sat noon–11.30pm, Sun noon–10.30pm. All cards. Inexpensive.*

Quality Chop-House, 94 Farringdon Rd, EC1 ☎0171/837 5093. Big plates of high-quality English food – roasts, fish cakes, sausages and mash, sticky puddings – served to ranks of pinewood booths. "Quality, Civility" reads the business card. *Farringdon tube. Mon–Fri noon–3pm & 6.30pm–midnight, Sat 6.30pm–midnight, Sun noon–4pm & 7–11.30pm. No cards. Moderate.*

Rules, 35 Maiden Lane, WC2 ☎0171/836 5314. London's oldest restaurant oozes traditional, Edwardian charm and sports a menu that's strong on game and desserts. If you want to know what dining in a gentleman's club is like, look no further and dress up (jacket and tie compulsory for men). Offers a pre-theatre menu (Mon–Fri) and a (tie-less!) weekend set lunch. *Covent Garden tube. Mon–Sat noon–11.30pm, Sun noon–10.30pm. Amex, MC, V. Expensive.*

The Savoy Grill, *Savoy Hotel*, The Strand, WC2 ☎0171/836 4343. Dignified British dining at extremely serious prices, just about worth paying for the glorious surroundings and fine service. The pre-theatre dinner is a price category down, but you'll have to eat early (6–7.30pm); otherwise expect your grills, fish pie and

Budget: under £8
Inexpensive: £8–15
Moderate: £15–20
Expensive: £20–30
Very Expensive: over £30
These are per person prices for a three-course meal (or equivalent), excluding drinks and service.

sensational desserts to form part of a dinner costing upwards of £50. *Charing Cross tube. Mon–Sat 12.30–2.30pm & 6–11pm. All cards. Very Expensive.*

Simpson's in the Strand, 100 The Strand ☎0171/836 9112. Well-known for its "Great British Breakfast" – £11–13 depending on what you have (fried eggs to lamb's liver) – *Simpson's* also excels at heavy-duty British lunches and dinners. Just the place for oysters or quail's eggs, followed by a roast or high-class sausages and mash. *Charing Cross tube. Breakfast Mon–Fri 7am–noon; meals Mon–Sat noon–2.30pm & 6–11pm, Sun noon–2.30pm & 6–9pm.. All cards. Expensive.*

Ye Olde Cheshire Cheese, Wine Office Court, off Fleet St, EC4 ☎0171/353 6170. Age-old Fleet St pub with a decent sideline in traditional British lunches and dinners – fish cakes and pies to steaks and fish and chips. Squeeze onto the wooden benches and tuck in. *Chancery Lane tube. Food served daily noon–2.30pm & Mon–Sat 6–9.30pm. All cards. Moderate.*

Modern British

Central London

Alastair Little, 49 Frith St, W1 ☎0171/734 5183. Austere (some say uncomfortable) decor but magnificently inventive cooking, with an ever-changing menu drawing ideas from the Mediterranean, Japan and China. Its troupe of affluent regulars rate this London's finest restaurant, delighted by the informal but knowledgeable service. If the prices horrify, it's worth knowing there's a set lunch for around £25. *Leicester Square tube. Mon–Fri noon–3pm & 6–11.30pm, Sat 6–11.30pm. Amex, MC, V. Very Expensive.*

Andrew Edmunds, 46 Lexington St, W1 ☎0171/437 5708. There aren't many bargains like this: intimate, candlelit Soho dining from a modern British menu that changes daily. Book ahead since it's very small and very popular. *Piccadilly Circus tube. Mon–Sat 12.30–3pm & 6–11pm, Sun 1–3pm & 6–11pm. MC, V. Inexpensive to Moderate.*

Atlantic Bar and Grill, 20 Glasshouse St, W1 ☎0171/734 4888. The chic Art Nouveau decor and seriously cool, late-opening cocktail bar have proved a hit with the moneyed punters. The food's good, too, if hard to pin down – meze/tapas-style platters, seafood, and traditional Brit dishes with mash. Booking and designer togs a must. *Piccadilly Circus tube. Mon–Fri noon–3pm & 7pm–12.30am, Sat 7pm–12.30am, Sun 6–10.30pm; bar open daily noon–2am. Amex, MC, V. Expensive.*

Le Caprice, Arlington House, Arlington St, SW1 ☎0171/629 2239. Classy internationalist menu, weighted in favour of Italian-Med dishes. Some people feel the prices reflect its social cachet more than the quality of the food, but on a good day *Le Caprice* takes some beating. Sunday brunch is more democratically priced. *Green Park tube. Mon–Sat noon–3pm & 6pm–midnight, Sun noon–3.30pm & 6pm–midnight. All cards. Expensive.*

The Criterion, 224 Piccadilly, W1 ☎0171/925 0909. One of the city's most beautiful restaurants, right by Piccadilly Circus. Refurbishment has made the huge dining room sparkle, and the food – various fish dishes, steaks, salads and variable Cal-Ital creations – is generally fine. The £10 set meal is very good value, though pricey drinks push the cost up. *Piccadilly Circus tube. Mon–Sat noon–11.30pm; Sun noon–5.30pm. All cards. Moderate to Expensive.*

dell'Ugo, 56 Frith St, W1 ☎0171/734 8300. Mediterranean flavours prevail both in the ground-floor café and in the double-decker restaurant above. A hit with Soho pacesetters, who don't mind the occasionally slow service – budget-watchers should seek out the set meals in the ground-floor café. You can't book for the café; you'll need to for the upstairs rooms. *Leicester Square tube. Mon–Fri noon–3pm & 7pm–midnight, Sat 7pm–midnight; café Mon–Sat 11am–11.30pm. Amex, MC, V. Inexpensive (in the café) to Expensive (upstairs).*

Restaurants

For more on the history of the French House *pub, see p.120.*

Fire Station, 150 Waterloo Rd, SE1 ☎0171/620 2226. The old fire station premises mean plenty of room, but tables are still at a premium in this horrendously noisy bar-restaurant. Unless you book, you'll have to queue, but there's an echoing front bar where you can knock back glasses from the fine wine list while pondering the blackboard menu. *Waterloo tube. Mon–Sat 12.30–2.30pm & 6.30–11.30pm, Sun 12.30–2.30pm, bar open Mon–Sat noon–11pm. All cards. Inexpensive.*

French House, 49 Dean St, W1 ☎0171/437 2477. Dining room above the pub of the same name turns out interesting and hearty dishes – from roast partridge to salt cod – to a fashionable Soho clientele enjoying the lower than average prices for this part of town. It's very small – booking is essential. *Leicester Square tube. Mon–Sat 12.30–3pm & 6.30–11.30pm, Sun 12.30–3pm & 6.30–10.30pm. All cards. Moderate.*

The Ivy, 1 West St, WC2 ☎0171/836 4751. The mock Art Deco setting is a favourite for media power-lunches and celeb interviews. Up-to-the-minute and invariably excellent British food, with influences culled from all corners of the world. *Leicester Square tube. Mon–Sat noon–3pm & 5.30pm–midnight, Sun noon–3.30pm & 5.30pm–midnight. All cards. Expensive.*

Museum Street Café, 47 Museum St, WC1 ☎0171/405 3211. Very good-value set-price lunches and dinners, short on choice but high on quality, with char-grilled meat and fish to the fore. Desserts are a strong point. Booking essential at lunchtime. *Russell Square or Tottenham Court Rd tube. Mon–Fri 12.30–2.30pm & 7.15–9.15pm. Moderate to Expensive.*

Quaglino's, 16 Bury St, SW1 ☎0171/930 6767. Huge 1930s ballroom revived by Terence Conran as one of the capital's busiest and most fashionable eating spots. Tourists are more in evidence than the glitterati these days but you still need to book well in advance. Dishes don't always work but the splendid surroundings and an unmistakeable buzz are the reward. You can snack (expensively) in the bar, too. *Green Park or Piccadilly Circus tube. Daily noon–3pm & 5.30pm–midnight, until 1am Fri & Sat, 11pm Sun; bar open Mon–Thurs & Sun 11.30am–1am, Fri & Sat 11.30am–2am. All cards. Moderate (bar) to Expensive (restaurant).*

Stephen Bull, 5–7 Blandford St, W1 ☎0171/486 9696. The decor won't appeal to those without Bauhaus leanings and the food won't please fans of gastronomic complexity, but the food here – especially the fish dishes and desserts – has plenty of foodie admirers. Reasonably priced set lunches are a bonus; otherwise prices are right at the top of this category. *Baker St or Marble Arch tube. Mon–Fri 12.15–2pm & 6.30–10.30pm, Sat 6.30–10.30pm. Amex, MC, V. Expensive.*

Kensington and Knightsbridge

Bibendum, Michelin House, 81 Fulham Rd, SW3 ☎0171/581 5817. Magnificent eclectic dishes are served in the upstairs restaurant, courtesy of one of Britain's brightest talents, Simon Hopkinson; champagne and exorbitant molluscs are consumed in quantities in the downstairs oyster bar. You're looking at upwards of £60 a head, but it's one of the few places in Britain that are worth it. *South Kensington tube. Mon–Sat 12.30–2.30pm & 7–11.30pm, Sun 12.30–3pm & 7–10.30pm. Amex, MC, V. Very Expensive.*

Boyd's, 135 Kensington Church St, W8 ☎0171/727 5452. This nouveau-British restaurant is one of the pacesetters in the gourmet's ghetto of Kensington Church Street. Char-grilling is much in evidence; there are wonderful desserts and wine

Budget: under £8
Inexpensive: £8–15
Moderate: £15–20
Expensive: £20–30
Very Expensive: over £30
These are per person prices for a three-course meal (or equivalent), excluding drinks and service.

list, and a decent value set lunch. *Notting Hill Gate tube. Mon–Sat 12.30–2.30pm & 7–11pm. All cards. Expensive.*

Clarke's, 124 Kensington Church St, W8 ☎0171/221 9225. Californian-influenced international menu, with the emphasis on simple techniques and interesting combinations of the freshest ingredients; Sally Clarke's bread is famous and sold at various outlets in town. No-choice set menu in the evenings will cost around £40 per person; it's worth every penny. *Notting Hill Gate tube. Mon–Fri 12.30–2pm & 7–10pm, Sat & Sun 12.30–2pm. MC, V. Expensive (lunch) to Very Expensive (dinner).*

Kensington Place, 201 Kensington Church St, W8 ☎071/727 3184. Busy, happening, neo-internationalist restaurant that's a touch less pricey than many of its rivals. The bargain set lunch is popular and while dining here is never exactly relaxing, you feel you've been well served in terms of food and style. *Notting Hill Gate tube. Mon–Fri noon–3pm & 6.30–11.45pm, Sat noon–3.30pm & 6.30–11.45pm, Sun noon–3.30pm & 6.30–10.15pm. MC, V. Expensive.*

The Restaurant, *Hyde Park Hotel*, 66 Knightsbridge, SW1 ☎0171/259 5380. British kitchen brat-pack leader Marco Pierre White knocks out hotel dinners of spectacular skill at £70 a head, with the wine at another twenty quid or so a bottle. Clearly a night out for lottery winners, but at the sharp end of modern British cooking. *Knightsbridge tube. Mon–Fri noon–2.30pm & 7–11pm, Sat 7–11pm. All cards. Very Expensive.*

192, 192 Kensington Park Rd, W11 ☎0171/229 0482. Excellent modern-English restaurant, popular with a music media crowd (the Virgin companies are local). The changing daily menu runs the gamut from fish and chips to the latest international fad. Call in for a one-course lunch or make an evening of it, but just make sure you look your best – staff and clientele are among the most fashionable in London. *Ladbroke Grove tube. Daily 12.30–3pm & 6.30–11.30pm. Amex, MC, V. Moderate to Expensive.*

City

Stephen Bull's Bistro and Bar, 71 St John St, EC1 ☎0171/490 1750. Bargain city outlet for Stephen Bull's talents, which show themselves off here in a short menu that draws from France and the Med. Few frills, just good food from a constantly changing menu, and a decent choice of wine by the glass. *Barbican or Farringdon tube. Mon–Sat noon–2pm & 6–10.45pm, closed Sat lunch. All cards. Moderate to Expensive.*

North

Odette's, 130 Regent's Park Rd, NW1 ☎0171/586 5486. Wide-ranging *cordon bleu* menu, merging Italian, French and even Japanese ideas. Garden at the back and pavement tables in summer. Good wine list, too, and a less pricey wine bar downstairs. *Chalk Farm tube. Mon–Fri 12.30–2.30pm & 7–11pm, Sat 7–11pm. All cards. Expensive.*

West

Brackenbury, 129–131 Brackenbury Rd, W6 ☎0181/748 0107. High-quality food (with French-Med-Oriental influences) at a cost that undercuts almost every comparable place in central London. *Goldhawk Rd tube. Mon 7–10.45pm, Tues–Fri 12.30–2.45pm & 7–10.45pm, Sat 7–10.45pm, Sun 12.30–2.45pm. Amex, MC, V. Moderate.*

Chinese

Chinatown and Around

China City, White Bear Yard, 25 Lisle St, WC2 ☎0171/734 3388. New restaurant tucked into a little courtyard off Lisle St; fresh and bright, with *dim sum* that's up there with the best and a menu with eminently reasonable prices. *Leicester Square tube. Mon–Sat noon–11.45pm, Sun 11am–11pm. All cards. Inexpensive.*

Chuen Cheng Ku, 17 Wardour St, W1 ☎0171/437 1398. Big Cantonese restaurant that's one of the closest in spirit to Hong Kong's cavernous diners. There's a massive range of dishes, the best dishes on the Chinese-only menu – ask for the

Restaurants

At restaurants serving dim sum *(usually 11am–5pm or so) you'll be able to eat for around £6–8 per person, including tea. It's busiest on Sundays, when you can expect to queue if you go between noon and 3pm.*

Restaurants

day's special. Authentic *dim sum*, too, served from circulating trolleys until 6pm. *Leicester Square tube. All cards. Daily 11am–midnight. Moderate.*

Friendly Inn, 47 Gerrard St, W1 (no phone). No-frills café with a jolly proprietress. The menu is extremely limited, and rarely rises above the sweet-and-sour pork level, but it's cheap, filling and late-opening. *Leicester Square tube. Mon–Thurs & Sun 5pm–1am, Fri & Sat 5pm–2am. No cards. Budget to Inexpensive.*

Fung Shing, 15 Lisle St, WC2 ☎0171/437 1539. Smart decor, consistently high standards and some unusual dishes make this a top-ranking Cantonese – the staples are cooked better here than at most places and if you want to experiment, the staff aren't too discouraging. *Leicester Square tube. Daily noon–11pm. All cards. Moderate to Expensive.*

Hong Kong, 6–7 Lisle St, WC2 ☎0171/287 0352. One of Chinatown's best vegetarian choices, and with excellent *dim sum* during the day, ordered from cards. *Leicester Square tube. Daily noon–11.30pm. Amex, MC, V. Moderate.*

Jade Garden, 15 Wardour St, W1 ☎0171/439 7851. Welcoming double-decker Cantonese restaurant, offering some of the best, freshest *dim sum* in town – the plump paper-wrapped prawns are a joy, and ask for the mysteries of the Chinese menu to be explained. It's worth booking for one of the upstairs tables. *Leicester Square tube. Mon–Fri noon–11pm, Sat 11.30am–11.30pm, Sun 11.30am–11pm. Amex, MC, V. Moderate.*

Man Fu Kung, 29 Leicester Square, WC2 ☎0171/839 4146. There's a touching uncertainty in the boast that it's "probably the largest Chinese restaurant" in Europe, but the fact is that (except for Sunday lunch, when you'll have to queue), you'll always find a table for decent *dim sum*, served from trolleys. The main menu is a bit disappointing, though cheaper than most in the area. *Leicester Square tube. Daily noon–midnight. MC, V. Inexpensive.*

Mayflower, 68–70 Shaftesbury Ave, W1 ☎0171/734 9207. Not the most stylish restaurant in the West End, and the service occasionally borders on the hostile, but the nightly presence of scores of Taiwanese says much for its authenticity and its late hours are a boon. Be adventurous in your ordering to get the best out of the menu – steer clear of the set meals and try the "pot" dishes. *Piccadilly Circus tube. Daily 5pm–4am. All cards. Moderate.*

Mr Kong, 21 Lisle St, WC2 ☎0171/437 7341. One of Chinatown's finest, with a chef-owner who pioneered many of the modern Cantonese dishes now on menus all over town. You may have to be firm with staff if you want the more unusual dishes – order from the Cantonese "specials" menu and don't miss the mussels in black bean sauce. If you want to avoid the rather grungy basement, book ahead. *Leicester Square tube. Daily noon–1.30am. All cards. Moderate.*

New Loon Fung, 39 Gerrard St, W1 ☎0171/437 6232. Friendlier-than-average restaurant on several floors, next to Chinatown's best supermarket. The smart interior is a good place to try *dim sum* – otherwise, there's a fairly standard Cantonese/Szechuan/Peking hybrid menu. *Leicester Square tube. Daily noon–11.30pm. All cards. Moderate.*

New World, 1 Gerrard Place, W1 ☎0171/734 0396. Another reasonable stab at an overblown Hong Kong dining palace – all red, gold and dragons – best deal here is the lunchtime *dim sum*, served by indefatigable trolley-pushers. The restaurant featured in the film of *Soursweet*, adapted from Timothy Mo's book. *Leicester Square tube. Mon–Sat 11am–midnight, Sun 10.45am–10.45pm. All cards. Moderate.*

Budget: under £8
Inexpensive: £8–15
Moderate: £15–20
Expensive: £20–30
Very Expensive: over £30
These are per person prices for a three-course meal (or equivalent), excluding drinks and service.

Panda Si Chuen, 56 Old Compton St, W1 ☎0171/437 2069. Rare Szechuan restaurant amid the Cantonese domination of Chinatown, though there's a crossover of dishes as you might expect. Still, the Szechuan food is good and spicy, service friendlier than usual and prices fair. Try the beancurd with pork. *Leicester Square or Piccadilly Circus tube. Open Mon–Sat noon–11.30pm. All cards. Moderate.*

Poons, 4 Leicester St, WC2 ☎0171/437 1528; and 27 Lisle St, WC2 ☎0171/437 4549. The Lisle St branch, the original *Poons*, has had a face-lift, but still resembles Old Mother Hubbard's house as you rise through the rickety floors, and still remains cheap and authentic – its wind-dried meats are a speciality. There's a slightly more refined air (and marginally higher prices) at the smarter Leicester St branch, around the corner. Either is a great bet for a decent, inexpensive meal out. For the flagship branch, see overleaf. *Leicester Square tube. Daily noon–11.30pm. No cards. Inexpensive to Moderate.*

Tai Wing Wah, 7–9 Newport Place, WC2 ☎0171/287 2702. A relatively new arrival in Chinatown, already with a good reputation for *dim sum* and politer than average service. *Leicester Square tube. Mon–Thurs noon–11.30pm, Fri & Sat noon–midnight, Sun 11am–5pm. Amex, MC, V. Moderate.*

Wong Kei, 41–43 Wardour St, W1 ☎0171/437 6833. Legendarily rude waiters serve up very inexpensive, if not entirely convincing, Cantonese food for cash only. If you're looking to linger over a meal, you'll soon discover you're in the wrong place. *Leicester Square tube. Daily noon–11.30pm. No cards. Budget to Inexpensive.*

Yung's, 23 Wardour St, W1 ☎0171/437 4986. A step away from *Wong Kei*, and a world away in ambience – a quiet, three-storey Cantonese serving food with thought. Seafood and hotpot dishes are recommended; the waiters are usually good for recommendations, too. *Leicester Square tube. Daily noon–4.30am. All cards. Moderate.*

Covent Garden

Happy Wok, 52 Floral St, WC2 ☎0171/836 3696. Small, welcoming restaurant with a few Shanghainese dishes on the predominantly Cantonese/Szechuan menu. *Covent Garden tube. Mon–Fri noon–2.30pm & 5.30–11.30pm, Sat 5.30pm–midnight. All cards. Moderate.*

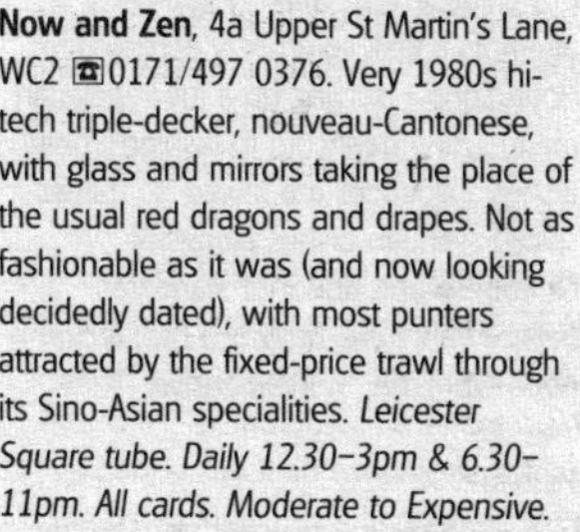

Now and Zen, 4a Upper St Martin's Lane, WC2 ☎0171/497 0376. Very 1980s hi-tech triple-decker, nouveau-Cantonese, with glass and mirrors taking the place of the usual red dragons and drapes. Not as fashionable as it was (and now looking decidedly dated), with most punters attracted by the fixed-price trawl through its Sino-Asian specialities. *Leicester Square tube. Daily 12.30–3pm & 6.30–11pm. All cards. Moderate to Expensive.*

North

Cheng Du, 9 Parkway, NW1 ☎0171/485 8058. Probably London's best Szechuan restaurant, full of Camden trendies soaking up the spices in a most un-Chinese-restaurant-like environment. *Camden Town tube. Daily noon–2.30pm & 6.30–11.30pm. Amex, MC, V. Expensive.*

Feng Shang, Cumberland Basin, opposite 15 Prince Albert Rd, NW1 ☎0171/485 8137. Double-decker floating restaurant on Regent's Canal with food not quite good enough to justify the high prices. But it makes for a different night out, and there's a fine vegetarian choice. Book in advance. *Camden Town tube. Mon–Fri noon–2pm & 6–11pm, Sat & Sun noon–2pm. All cards. Expensive.*

Good Earth, 143 The Broadway, NW7 ☎0181/959 7011. Terrific choice of Chinese vegetarian dishes – upmarket dining and good service. A mite far for a simple meal, but worth considering for a veggie blow-out. *Mill Hill East tube. Mon–Sat noon–2.30pm & 6–11pm, Sun 12.30–3pm & 6–10.45pm. All cards. Expensive.*

New Culture Revolution, 42 Duncan St, N1 ☎0171/833 9083. Great name, great concept – big bowls of freshly cooked noodles in sauce or soup, dumplings and rice dishes, all offering a one-stop meal at

Restaurants

bargain prices in simple, minimalist surroundings. To plump for the carrot juice is probably taking things too far. *Angel tube. Mon–Fri noon–2.30pm & 6–10.30pm, Sat 1–11pm. MC, V. Budget to Inexpensive.*

Vegetarian Cottage, 91 Haverstock Hill, NW3 ☎0171/586 1257. Rare for London, this Chinese vegetarian restaurant attempts a task commonly achieved in Hong Kong – serving up a full vegetarian menu, using beancurd to fashion "meat" dishes. Influences are mixed, so there's spicy Szechuan dishes alongside Cantonese and Buddhist standards. *Belsize Park tube. Daily 6–11pm & Sun noon–3pm. MC, V. Inexpensive.*

Victoria

Hunan, 51 Pimlico Rd, SW1 ☎0171/730 5712. Probably England's only restaurant serving Hunan food, a relative to Szechuan food with the same spicy kick to most dishes, and a fair wallop of pepper in those that aren't actively riddled with chillis. The £20 set dinner lets the chef show what he can do. *Sloane Square tube. Mon–Sat noon–2.30pm & 6.30–11pm, Sun 6.30–11pm. Amex, MC, V. Moderate to Expensive.*

Memories of China, 67–69 Ebury St, SW1 ☎0171/730 7734. Owner Kenneth Lo has written more books on Chinese cookery than anyone else – odd then that there's so little that's different about the dishes here. However, both cooking and service excel. *Sloane Square or Victoria tube. Mon–Sat noon–3pm & 7–11pm, Sun 7–11pm. All cards. Expensive.*

Mayfair

Oriental, *The Dorchester Hotel*, 55 Park Lane, W1 ☎0171/629 8888. Simply the best Chinese restaurant in London, but you'll have to don jacket and tie to taste it and bring large amounts of money. You don't *have to* spend £60 a head here (there's a £20 *dim sum* lunch for example), but the kitchen only really comes into its own once the financial gloves are off. *Hyde Park Corner tube. Mon–Fri noon–2.30pm & 7pm–midnight, Sat 7pm–midnight. All cards. Very Expensive.*

City

Imperial City, Royal Exchange, Cornhill, EC3 ☎0171/626 3437. Sensational modern Hong Kong cooking from a menu laid down by the prolific Ken Hom – no MSG and plenty of surprises. The surroundings are impressive, too, though the limited city hours and braying clientele are off-putting. *Bank tube. Mon–Fri 11.30am–8.30pm. All cards. Moderate.*

Poons in the City, 2 Minster Pavement, Minster Court, Mincing Lane, EC3 ☎0171/626 0126. Flagship restaurant of the small *Poons* chain, with a spread of dishes taken from all over China served to a keen city clientele (hence the weekend closing). *Monument tube. Mon–Fri 11am–10.30pm. All cards. Expensive.*

Bayswater

Four Seasons, 84 Queensway, W2 ☎0171/229 4320. This slightly more reasonably priced alternative to the *Mandarin Kitchen* (below) is very popular with the local Bayswater Chinese community, so you can be confident that you're getting the goods. *Bayswater tube. Daily noon–11.15pm. Amex, MC, V. Moderate.*

Mandarin Kitchen, 14–16 Queensway, W2 ☎0171/727 9012. In this western outpost of Chinatown, this large and very classy Cantonese is renowned for its fish and seafood, all of which are sparklingly fresh. Service can be brittle, though. *Bayswater tube. Daily noon–11.30pm. All cards. Moderate to Expensive.*

Budget: under £8
Inexpensive: £8–15
Moderate: £15–20
Expensive: £20–30
Very Expensive: over £30
These are per person prices for a three-course meal (or equivalent), excluding drinks and service.

Southeast

Gracelands Palace, 881–883 Old Kent Rd, SE15 ☎0171/639 3961. A Chinese Elvis impersonator hosts one of London's more bizarre evenings out. Mainstream Cantonese food and Las Vegas-era Elvis cabaret on Fri & Sat at 11.30pm. Booking essential, at least a week in advance. *Bus #53. Mon–Thurs noon–2pm & 5.30pm–midnight, Fri & Sat 5.30pm–1am, Diners, MC, V. Moderate.*

Czech

Czech Club, 74 West End Lane, NW6 ☎0171/372 5251. Meat- and dumpling-dominated meals of Schwarzenegger-like dimensions, in a restaurant set in a lovely house and garden. Very popular with Czech expats – book ahead if you want to come for Sunday lunch. *West Hampstead tube. Mon–Fri 6–10.30pm, Sat & Sun noon–3pm & 6–10.30pm. Amex. Inexpensive.*

Fish

Bentley's, 11–15 Swallow St, W1 ☎0171/734 4756. Creative modern fish cookery in the upstairs restaurant, a simpler (and more entertaining) oyster bar downstairs – half a dozen of the beasts for around £8. Splendid surroundings, matched by the quality of the food. Choose carefully and you'll escape with a bill in the lower category. *Piccadilly Circus tube. Mon–Fri noon–2.30pm & 6–11pm, Sat 6–11pm. All cards. Expensive to Very Expensive.*

Café Fish, 39 Panton St, SW1 ☎0171/930 3999. Fishy French-style restaurant (tiger prawns to shark) and wine bar (*moules*, fish pie, fish and chips) which opens out onto the pavement in summer. Always busy with a West End crowd; check out the dishes of the day for unusual ideas; vegetarian dishes, too. *Piccadilly tube. Restaurant: Mon–Fri noon–3pm & 5.45–11.30pm, Sat 5.45–11.30pm. Wine bar Mon–Sat 11.30am–11pm. All cards. Inexpensive (wine bar) to Moderate (restaurant).*

Chez Liline, 101 Stroud Green Rd, N4 ☎0171/263 6550. Splendid neighbourhood fish restaurant, with dishes heavily influenced by Mauritian cooking styles – which means plenty of spices and sauces, and creamy fish soups. A great spot in an unlikely part of London and affordable prices for this kind of cuisine provided you tread carefully. Good for a special occasion – but book in advance. *Finsbury Park tube. Mon–Sat 12.30–2.30pm & 6.30–10.30pm, Sun 12.30–2.30pm. MC, V. Moderate.*

Grahame's, 38 Poland St, W1 ☎0171/437 3788. Traditional, kosher fish restaurant with chopped herring and gefilte fish starters, followed by fresh fish in various guises – fried, grilled or sauced. It's a great lunch spot, when you could escape for under a tenner all in; closes early at night. *Oxford Circus tube. Mon–Sat noon–2.45pm & 5.30–9pm (8pm Fri & Sat). All cards. Inexpensive to Moderate.*

Lobster Pot, 3 Kennington Lane, SE11 ☎0171/582 5556. All that's humanly possible is done to help you forget you're at the deeply unattractive Elephant and Castle – a warm welcome, recorded seagull noises, a splendidly fishy-kitschy interior, excellent bouillabaisse and the best *assiette des fruits de mers* in town. Book in advance. *Elephant & Castle or Kennington tube. Tues–Sat noon–2.30pm & 7–11pm. All cards. Expensive.*

Manzi's, 1–2 Leicester St, WC2 ☎0171/734 0224. Bustling red-checked-tablecloth joint off Leicester Square, swarming with old-school waiters dishing up excellently cooked fish to an odd mix of in-the-know tourists, the twin-set-and-pearls brigade and expense accounters. After the fish, everything else is a bit of a disappointment – vegetables aren't all they could be, but the chips are fine. *Leicester Square tube. Mon–Sat noon–2.30pm & 5.30–11.30pm, Sun 6–11pm. All cards. Expensive.*

Wheeler's: branches all over London; central branch at 19 Old Compton St, W1 ☎0171/437 2706. Old-established seafood restaurant with reliable standards., from cod and chips and a fish mixed grill to poached Dover sole. The Soho branch is one of the smarter venues and offers an

Restaurants

early bird dinner that won't break the bank. *Leicester Square tube. Mon–Sat 12.30–2.30pm & 6–11.15pm, Sun 12.30–2.30pm & 7–10.30pm. All cards. Expensive.*

Fish and Chips

Alpha One Fish Bar, 43 Old Compton St, W1 ☎0171/437 7344. Soho takeaway with a few tables inside serving decent fish and chips; eat here, and then go over the road for coffee. *Leicester Square tube. Mon–Thurs & Sun 11.30am–1am, Fri & Sat 11.30am–2am. No cards. Budget.*

The Golden Hind, 73 Marylebone Lane, W1 ☎0171/486 3644. Fish-and-chip restaurant with a lot of admirers and very reasonable prices. *Bond St or Baker St tube. Mon–Fri 11.30am–2.30pm & 5.30–10pm, Sat 5.30–10pm. No cards. Budget.*

North Sea Fish Restaurant, 7–8 Leigh St, WC1 ☎0171/387 5892. Top-notch fish and chips – a dozen kinds, fried or grilled – in a licensed restaurant heavy on the nineteenth-century furnishings. *Russell Square tube. Mon–Sat noon–2.30pm & 5.30–10.30pm. All cards. Inexpensive.*

Rock & Sole Plaice, 47 Endell St, WC2 ☎0171/836 3785. Not the most prepossessing of diners, but reliable fish and chips in a handy, central location are hard to find. You can sit ouside in summer. *Covent Garden tube. Daily 11.30am–10.30pm. No cards. Budget.*

Sea-Shell, 49–51 Lisson Grove, NW1 ☎0171/723 8703. Already on the tourist circuit, fish and chips don't come much better than this. But add starters (prawn cocktail and the like) and house wine and you'll spend more than you'd think. *Marylebone tube. Mon–Fri noon–2pm & 5.15–10.30pm, Sat noon–2pm. All cards. Inexpensive to Moderate.*

Upper Street Fish Shop, 324 Upper St, N1 ☎0171/359 1401. Classy, yuppie-ish sit-down fish and chip restaurant in the heart of trendy Islington. Bring your own booze, and if you have room, dive into the heavy-duty puddings. *Angel tube. Mon 5.30–10pm, Tues–Fri noon–2pm & 5.30–10pm, Sat 5.30–10pm. No cards. Budget to Inexpensive.*

French restaurants, brasseries and bistros

London-wide

Café Flo: eight branches including 51 St Martin's Lane, WC2 (Charing Cross tube; ☎0171/836 8289); 676 Fulham Rd, SW6 (Parson's Green tube; ☎0171/371 9673); 127–129 Kensington Church St, W8 (Notting Hill Gate tube; ☎0171/727 8142); 334 Upper St, N1 (Angel tube; ☎0171/226 7916); and 205 Haverstock Hill, NW3 (Chalk Farm tube; ☎0171/435 6744). Brightest and best of the brasserie chains, serving breakfasts, fixed-price menus, French classics and coffee. Meals are rarely spectacular, but hard to beat for price and atmosphere. *Daily 9am–11.30pm. Amex, MC, V. Moderate.*

Soho

Bistrot Bruno, 63 Frith St, W1 ☎0171/734 4545. A new venture for superchef Bruno Loubet, who occasionally takes time off from his day-job at the *Four Seasons Hotel* to wield the spoons and spatulas here. The food shows a mix of the classic and curious; the resolutely utilitarian layout keeps prices down. You'll have to book. *Leicester Square tube. Mon–Fri 12.15–2.30pm & Sat 6.15–11.30pm. All cards. Expensive.*

L'Escargot, 48 Greek St, W1 ☎0171/437 2679. Long fashionable with media and publishing types, *L'Escargot* has a comfortable New York-style brasserie downstairs and an elegant French restaurant above. Service is unobtrusively first-rate and the perfectly cooked food deserves the accolades. *Leicester Square tube. Mon–Fri 12.15–2.15pm & 6–11pm, Sat 6–11pm. All cards. Expensive.*

Budget: under £8
Inexpensive: £8–15
Moderate: £15–20
Expensive: £20–30
Very Expensive: over £30
These are per person prices for a three-course meal (or equivalent), excluding drinks and service.

Restaurants

Soho Soho, 11–13 Frith St, W1 ☎0171/494 3491. Likeable bar-rotisserie-brasserie downstairs, with high-volume media clientele and drowned-out pianist; more expensive, less boisterous restaurant upstairs. Both have Soho street views and reliable food – mainly French with a Med twist. *Tottenham Court Rd tube. Rotisserie: Mon–Sat noon–1am; restaurant: Mon–Fri noon–3pm & 6pm–midnight, Sat 6pm–midnight. All cards. Moderate (rotisserie) to Expensive (restaurant).*

Le Tire Bouchon, 6 Upper James St, W1 ☎0171/437 5348. Small, friendly, workaday bistro just off Soho's Golden Square – choose from the ever-changing *carte* or dig into the cheaper set menu. *Piccadilly Circus tube. Mon–Fri 8am–midnight. Amex, MC, V. Moderate.*

Covent Garden

Café des Amis du Vin, 11–14 Hanover Place, WC2 ☎0171/379 3444. Roomy, mainstream brasserie, with good-value lunches and pre-theatre set dinner. *Covent Garden tube. Mon–Sat 11.30am–11.30pm. All cards. Moderate.*

Café Pelican, 45 St Martin's Lane, WC2 ☎0171/379 0309. Popular brasserie with a particularly convincing Parisian-style bar – again, the set meals (from £10) offer the best value. Otherwise, it's steak, *confit de canard* and steamed fish. Busiest at night – and open later than most. *Charing Cross tube. Mon–Sat 11am–1am, Sun 11am–10.30pm. All cards. Expensive.*

L'Estaminet, 14 Garrick St, WC2 ☎0171/379 1432. Central brick-walled bistro that does the business without ever sparkling. Lunch for a tenner is a good buy, though. *Covent Garden or Leicester Square tube. Mon–Sat noon–2.30pm & 6–11.30pm. Amex, MC, V. Moderate to Expensive.*

Mon Plaisir, 21 Monmouth St, WC2 ☎0171/836 7243. One of London's best imitations of a Parisian bistro. The set lunch is a bargain at £13.95; otherwise pay up for some of the most pleasing French food in town. *Covent Garden tube. Mon–Fri noon–2pm & 6–11.15pm, Sat 6–11.15pm. All cards. Expensive.*

Le Palais du Jardin, 136 Long Acre, WC2 ☎0171/379 5353. Call in for a drink and a quick meal at the front tables (open onto the street in summer); or walk through to the spacious brasserie behind the bar and enjoy the elegant surroundings. Service is occasionally with attitude, but the seafood is great – oysters, lobster and *fruits de mer* are all good value while cheaper meals are provided by the cuisine *grand-mère* section of the menu (fish cakes, *coq au vin*, or French sausages and mash). *Covent Garden tube. Mon–Sat noon–3.30pm & 5.30pm–midnight, Sun noon–3.30pm; bar open Mon–Sat 10am–midnight, Sun noon–11pm. All cards. Moderate.*

Tuttons Brasserie, 11–12 Russell St, WC2 ☎0171/836 4141. Reasonable French/international food from breakfast to dinner – no surprises, but budget set meals, windows onto Covent Garden's piazza and a few outdoor seats in summer. *Covent Garden tube. Mon–Thurs & Sun 9.30am–11.30pm, Fri & Sat 9.30am–midnight. All cards. Inexpensive.*

Mayfair

Chez Nico, *Grosvenor House Hotel*, 90 Park Lane, W1 ☎0171/409 1290. Nico Ladenis' lair is one of London's foodie shrines, though you'll have to be prepared to spend at least £70 a head to worship here. For this, you will receive perfectly presented dishes of the highest quality, served by frighteningly competent staff. Lunch at £25 seems a giveaway by comparison. Booking is essential. *Hyde Park Corner tube. Mon–Fri noon–2pm & 7–11pm, Sat 7–11pm. All cards. Very Expensive.*

Holland Park

Chez Moi, 1 Addison Avenue, W11 ☎0171/603 8267. High-class local restaurant that's been going for a quarter of century, a fair indication of its consistent standards. *Holland Park tube. Mon–Fri 12.30–2pm & 7–11pm, Sat 7–11pm. All cards. Expensive.*

Restaurants

Victoria

Simply Nico, 48a Rochester Row, SW1 ☎0171/630 8061. The master himself has moved on (see "Mayfair" above), which means you can probably ask for the salt without being chucked out, but standards remain high and costs surprisingly low. For well under £30 (more like £25 at lunch) you're served assured, classic French dishes in soothing surroundings. *St James's Park or Victoria tube. Mon–Fri noon–2pm & 7–11pm, Sat 7–11pm. All cards. Expensive.*

Waterloo and London Bridge

RSJ, 13a Coin St, SE1 ☎0171/928 4554. Regularly high standards of Anglo-French cooking make this a good spot for a meal after an evening at a South Bank theatre or concert hall. Good brasserie in the basement, which is cheaper and, generally, more popular – though the restaurant-only set meal has its fans. *Waterloo tube. Mon–Fri noon–2pm & 6–11pm, Sat 6–11pm. Amex, MC, V. Moderate (brasserie) to Expensive (restaurant).*

Truffe Noire, 29 Tooley St, SE1 ☎0171/378 0621. Yuppie bolthole amid the warehouses of Tooley Street; you can eat from a fine "brasserie" menu in the bar; or there's an excellent fixed-price lunch and dinner menu in the more formal restaurant. Straying into the *à la carte* soon puts you in expense-acccount territory. *London Bridge tube. Mon–Fri noon–3pm & 6.30–11.30pm. All cards. Expensive.*

Kensington and Chelsea

Aubergine, 11 Park Walk, SW10 ☎0171/352 3449. Heavily feted newcomer with food as awesome as the prices. Imaginative modern French cuisine from a chef (Gordon Ramsay) who did a cooking-and-shouting stint with Marco Pierre White. Set lunches are a bargain £20 or so; set dinners are £30–36, plus drinks. *Sloane Square tube. Mon–Fri noon–2.30pm & 7–11pm, Sat 7–11pm. Very Expensive.*

Bistrot 190, 190 Queen's Gate, SW7 ☎0171/581 5666. Part of the Anthony Worral Thompson empire, this serves brasserie classics with great panache and a hefty price tag. Very popular, but no telephone booking, so expect to queue at the weekend. *South Kensington tube. Mon–Sat noon–12.30am, Sun noon–11.30pm. All cards. Expensive.*

Canteen, Unit G4, Harbour Yard, Chelsea Harbour, SW10 ☎0171/351 7330. Marco Pierre White and Michael Caine co-own this establishment; that, and the conservatory tables looking out over the Chelsea Harbour development, have kept the *Canteen* busy since it opened. The top-quality cooking takes in brasserie favourites and trendy newcomers; decor is decidedly not canteen-style. *Fulham Broadway tube and #C3 bus. Mon–Sat noon–3pm & 6.30pm–midnight, Sun 12.30–3.30pm & 7–11pm. MC, V. Expensive.*

Cote à Cote, 74–75 Battersea Bridge Rd, SW11 ☎0171/738 0198. Converted, candlelit pub which packs in partying punters for its bargain menu – three courses of serviceable though never electrifying French bistro food for under £7. Come in a group and sit in the suspended rowboats; watch the alcohol consumption – at prices like these, that's where the profit is made. Book ahead for dinner. *South Kensington or Sloane Square tube. Daily noon–midnight.. No cards. Budget.*

Rotisserie Jules, 6–8 Bute St, SW7 ☎0171/584 0600. Friendly joint where grilled chicken and frites are the speciality, served speedily. Bring your own booze. *South Kensington tube. Daily 11.30am–11.30pm. No cards. Inexpensive.*

Budget: under £8
Inexpensive: £8–15
Moderate: £15–20
Expensive: £20–30
Very Expensive: over £30
These are per person prices for a three-course meal (or equivalent), excluding drinks and service.

St Quentin, 243 Brompton Rd, SW3 ☎0171/581 5131. Handy for the South Kensington museums, this bistro-ish French restaurant serves good set-price lunches and dinners. Otherwise, it can be pricey, but it is authentic. *South Kensington tube. Mon–Sat noon–3pm & 7–11.30pm, Sun noon–3.30pm & 6.30–11pm. All cards. Expensive.*

La Tante Claire, 68 Royal Hospital Rd, SW3 ☎0171/352 6045. The *Tante Claire* is very formal (jacket & tie compulsory, menu entirely in French), and you'll get no change from £50 per person at dinner, but it is very, very good – no one would argue with the Michelin stars awarded to chef Pierre Koffmann. For £25 you can sample his virtuosity with the set lunch. *Sloane Square tube. Mon–Fri 12.30–2pm & 7–11pm. All cards. Very Expensive.*

North: Camden

Café Delancey, 3 Delancey St, NW1 ☎0171/387 1985. Spacious Camden brasserie that's always buzzing. Great for breakfast (served all day) and snacks – after dark it transforms into a romantic, candlelit rendezvous. All the confidence of a place that knows it's got the formula right. *Camden Town tube. Daily 8am–midnight. MC, V. Moderate.*

Camden Brasserie, 216 Camden High St, NW1 ☎0171/482 2114. Ever-popular north London brasserie (with basement café), serving reliable char-grilled specials, pasta and French-Med favourites. *Camden Town tube. Mon–Sat noon–3pm & 6–11.30pm, Sun noon–4.30pm & 5.30–10.30pm. MC, V. Moderate.*

Greek

Café Grec, 18 Charlotte St, W1 ☎0171/436 7411. Perhaps the best of the Charlotte Street Greek restaurants, with friendly service and good meze – which also come as a set lunch or dinner. There are streetside tables in the summer – book in advance for these. *Tottenham Court Rd tube. Mon–Fri noon–2.30pm & 6–11pm, Sat 6–11pm. All cards. Inexpensive to Moderate.*

Daphne, 83 Bayham St, NW1 ☎0171/267 7322. Long-established and reliable Camden Town taverna. Stick to the specials and you won't go far wrong. Very popular – book ahead. *Camden Town tube. Mon–Sat noon–2.30pm & 6–11.30pm. MC, V. Moderate.*

Jimmy's, 23 Frith St, W1 ☎0171/437 9521. Basement Greek restaurant that's long been part of the Soho cheap eating scene – mammoth portions of serviceable Greek-Cypriot food with chips. *Leicester Square tube. Mon–Sat 12.30–3pm & 5.30–11pm. No cards. Budget to Inexpensive.*

Lemonia, 89 Regent's Park Rd, NW1 ☎0171/586 7454. Spirited Greek taverna, doing all the basics well, especially the charcoal-grilled meats and fish – the fish meze is splendid. It's extremely popular, so book ahead, though if you can't get in, try the associated *Limani* at no. 154 (☎0171/483 4492), with similarly fine food at roughly the same prices. *Chalk Farm tube. Mon–Fri noon–3pm & 6–11.30pm, Sat 6–11.30pm, Sun noon–3pm. MC, V. Inexpensive.*

Mega-Kalamaras, 76–78 Inverness Mews, W2 ☎0171/727 9122. Arguably the best Greek restaurant in London, serving dishes you won't come across at most others. The menu is in Greek only, though the waiters provide translations. There's a smaller, cheaper and slightly less refined branch, *Micro-Kalamaras*, at no. 66 (☎0171/727 5082) in the same street, which is unlicensed so take your own booze. *Bayswater tube. Mon–Sat 7pm–midnight. All cards. Moderate.*

Nontas, 14–16 Camden High St, NW1 ☎0171/387 4579. Very good, slightly upmarket Camden Town Greek restaurant with a deservedly popular bar. *Camden Town tube. Mon–Sat noon–2.30pm & 6–11.30pm. All cards. Inexpensive.*

Rodos, 59 St Giles High St, WC2 ☎0171/836 3177. Very near Centre Point, this hidden-away taverna has all the usual dishes, but rates highly for its personal service, resident cat and reasonable prices.. *Tottenham Court Rd tube. Mon–Sat noon–3pm & 6–11pm. No cards. Inexpensive.*

White Tower, 1 Percy St, W1 ☎0171/636 8141. Historic house (see p.124) with literary connections and clientele, fabulous food and slick service. You may baulk at the prices – expect to pay £40 a head – but it's a world away from the plate-smashing party places. *Tottenham Court Rd tube. Mon–Fri 12.30–2.30pm & 6.30–10.30pm, Sat 6.30–10.30pm. All cards. Very Expensive.*

Hungarian

Gay Hussar, 2 Greek St, W1 ☎0171/437 0973. Nominally Hungarian, but in fact gathering its ideas from all of central Europe, this restaurant has been a Soho institution for years, and claims a regular clientele of politicians and journalists, happy to soak up the timeworn atmosphere, cherry soup and fiery palenka digestifs. *Tottenham Court Rd tube. Mon–Sat 12.30–2.30pm & 5.30–10.30pm. All cards. Expensive.*

Indian, Bangladeshi and Nepalese

West End

Akash, 14–15 Irving St, WC2 ☎0171/930 0744. A surprising find so close to Leicester Square. There's a warm welcome from the elderly white-coated doorman, slick service in a comfortable old-style dining room and very reasonably priced food – Punjabi specialities to boot. *Leicester Square tube. Daily noon–midnight. All cards. Moderate.*

Gopal's of Soho, 12 Bateman St, W1 ☎0171/434 0840. Unusual nouvelle Indian food of the highest quality in a small, backstreet Soho restaurant full of class. *Piccadilly Circus tube. Daily noon–3pm & 6–11.30pm. All cards. Moderate to Expensive.*

India Club, 143 Strand, WC2 ☎0171/836 0650. Unlicensed upstairs restaurant (above the Strand Palce hotel) that serves authentic Indian food in faded, utilitarian canteen surroundings – try the excellent *dosas* or the masochistic deep-fried whole green chillis. Service with a smile from friendly, white-coated waiters. Take your own booze or pay a small membership fee to use the private hotel bar. *Aldwych tube. Mon–Sat 6–10pm, Sun 6–8pm. No cards. Inexpensive.*

Mandeer, 21 Hanway Place, W1 ☎0171/323 0660. Well-known central vegetarian restaurant with a menu that often sounds more interesting than the final result. Still, it's a nice, low-key place for dinner and there's a good-value buffet lunch that attracts the local workers. *Tottenham Court Rd tube. Mon–Sat noon–3pm & 5.30–10pm. All cards. Inexpensive to Moderate.*

Red Fort, 77 Dean St, W1 ☎0171/437 2525. Renowned Bangladeshi restaurant, where the excellent service and refined decor compensate for sometimes unexceptional food. *Leicester Square tube. Daily noon–2.45pm & 6–11.30pm. All cards. Expensive.*

Ragam, 57 Cleveland St, W1 ☎0171/636 9098. Classy south Indian food, though the dining room is so constricted that you may not get the best out of it. A great place for vegetarians, nonetheless. *Goodge St tube. Daily noon–4.30pm & 6–11.15pm. All cards. Inexpensive.*

Strand Tandoori, 45 Bedford St, WC2 ☎0171/240 1333. An unreconstructed curry house of the old school, between Covent Garden and The Strand. Reliable tandoori food served to tourists who daren't stray further east, local office workers and sporting icons Gary Lineker and Bob Willis, both of whom drop in from time to time. *Charing Cross tube. Mon–Wed & Sat noon–3pm & 6pm–midnight, Thurs & Fri noon–midnight, Sun noon–3pm & 6–11.30pm. All cards. Inexpensive to Moderate..*

Veeraswamy, 99–101 Regent St, W1 ☎0171/734 1401. London's oldest Indian restaurant (founded 1927), attracting tourists and well-heeled local business-people in search of dining formality. More surprises

Budget: under £8
Inexpensive: £8–15
Moderate: £15–20
Expensive: £20–30
Very Expensive: over £30
These are per person prices for a three-course meal (or equivalent), excluding drinks and service.

on the menu than in a mainstream curry house, but not special enough to warrant the high prices – the *thalis* and set lunches offer best value. *Piccadilly Circus tube. Mon–Sat noon–2.30pm & 6–11.30pm. All cards. Expensive.*

Woodlands, 37 Panton St, SW1 ☎0171/839 7258. Central vegetarian restaurant (part of an international chain) serving classic south Indian dishes – including several kinds of *dosa* and the intriguingly decribed *uthappam* ("lentil pizza"), actually a lentil-and-flour pancake with a spicy topping. A nice place, with Indian art on the pastel-green walls. There's another branch ar 77 Marylebone Lane, W1. *Piccadilly Circus tube. Daily noon–2.45pm & 5.30–10.45pm. All cards. Inexpensive.*

Drummond Street and Around

Ravi Shankar, 133–135 Drummond St, NW1 ☎0171/388 6458. One of the best of a number of bargain south Indian restaurants on this street, renowned for its *dosas*. It's gone a bit more upmarket in recent years, but is still pretty good value, as is the associated *Chutneys* at no. 124 (☎0171/388 0604), which is worth a punt if you can't get in here. *Euston tube. Daily noon–11pm. MC, V. Inexpensive.*

Diwnana Bhel Poori House, 121 Drummond St, NW1 ☎0171/387 5556. Unlicensed, south Indian restaurant, specializing in *dosas, bhel poori* and vegetarian *thalis*. Not a place for a night out, but food and prices that usually manage to please. *Euston tube. Daily noon–11.30pm. All cards. Inexpensive.*

Great Nepalese, 48 Eversholt St, NW1 ☎0171/388 6737. One of very few places in London serving genuine spicy Nepalese dishes. *Euston tube. Daily noon–2.30pm & 6–11.45pm. All cards. Moderate.*

Haandi, 161 Drummond St, NW1 ☎0171/383 4557. South Indian vegetarian food is the dominant tendency in this street; the *Haandi* is a first-rate carnivorous exception. *Warren St tube. Mon–Sat noon–2.30pm & 6–11.30pm. All cards. Inexpensive.*

Indian YMCA, 41 Fitzroy Square, W1 ☎0171/387 0411. Canteen full of Indian students eating food you'll not see at this price anywhere else. Institutional surroundings, large portions – a place to fill up and go. *Warren St tube. Daily 8–9am, 12.30–1.30pm & 7–8pm. No cards. Budget.*

East End

Clifton, 126 Brick Lane, E1 ☎0171/247 2364. One of the classiest and priciest of the Brick Lane Bangladeshi restaurants, featuring a wide-ranging menu of diverse influence. *Aldgate East tube. Daily noon–1am. All cards. Moderate.*

Kundan Karahi, 108 Brick Lane, E1 ☎0171/247 8685. Kebab and tandoori-food specialist gaining a reputation for the quality of its dishes. The nan bread is great. *Aldgate East tube. Daily 11am–11pm. MC, V. Budget.*

Lahore Kebab House, 4 Umberston St, E1 ☎0171/481 9738. Splendid tandoori specialities in fairly basic surroundings (though the upstairs restaurant offers a bit more room). *Whitechapel tube. Daily noon–midnight. No cards. Inexpensive.*

Namaste, 30 Alie St, E1 ☎0171/488 9242. An award-winning chef has secured the popularity of this East End Indian, where the menu is a touch more varied than in many of its rivals – Goan dishes are often included, and you're as likely to find squid or potato cakes as your usual favourites. *Aldgate East tube. Mon–Fri noon–3pm & 6–11pm, Sat 7–10pm. All cards. Moderate.*

Nazrul, 130 Brick Lane, E1 ☎0171/247 2505. The unlicensed *Nazrul* is among the cheapest of the Brick Lane cafés, drawing a student crowd. *Aldgate East tube. Daily noon–3pm & 5.30pm–midnight, Fri & Sat until 1am. No cards. Budget.*

Shampan, 79 Brick Lane, E1 ☎0171/375 0475. Quickly established as one of the more refined Bangladeshi eateries, the *Shampan* has a menu that takes in most of the more familar curry-house dishes. You can't beat the Bangladeshi

Restaurants

specialities, though, and you shouldn't try. *Aldgate East tube. Daily noon–3pm & 6pm–midnight. All cards. Inexpensive to Moderate.*

West

Khan's, 13–15 Westbourne Grove, W2 ☎0171/727 5420. Long-established, huge and crowded Indian restaurant, with its palms, pillars and pastel blues – unexceptional food, often lousy service, but great atmosphere. *Bayswater or Queensway tube. Daily noon–3pm & 6–11.45pm. All cards. Inexpensive.*

South

Kastoori, 188 Upper Tooting Rd, SW17 ☎0181/767 7027. You're not exactly going to be passing through the area, but it's worth braving the Northern Line's more remote outposts for the *Kastoori*'s splendidly inventive Gujerati food – the *thali* gives you a taste of most things. *Tooting Broadway tube. Mon & Tues 6–10.30pm, Wed–Sun 12.30–2.30pm & 6–10.30pm. MC, V. Moderate.*

Maharani, 117 Clapham High St, SW4 ☎0171/622 2530. One of the longest survivors on what was once the Clapham curry strip. The other Indian restaurants here became tapas bars and pizzerias – the *Maharani* continues to cook high-quality north Indian food at above-average prices for an affluent Clapham crowd. The *kormas* are reliable, the mixed grill pricey but good. *Clapham Common tube. Mon–Sat noon–2.30pm & 6–11pm. Sun noon–3pm & 6–10.30pm. All cards. Moderate to Expensive.*

Southwest

Bombay Brasserie, Courtfield Close, Courtfield Rd, SW7 ☎0171/370 4040. Seriously expensive Bombay-style cooking in glam surroundings. Every dish isn't the winner it should be at these prices, but as a dining-out experience, it's one of the best. *Gloucester Rd tube. Daily noon–3pm & 7.30pm–midnight. Diners, MC, V. Expensive to Very Expensive.*

Chutney Mary, 535 King's Rd, SW10 ☎0171/351 3113. Raj-style cooking, which means a menu mixing regional Indian dishes with western ideas. It's a successful venture and has a nice conservatory. You'll need to book. *Fulham Broadway tube. Mon–Sat 12.30–2.30pm & 7–11pm, Sun 12.30–2.30pm & 7–10.30pm. All cards. Expensive.*

Ma Goa, 244 Upper Richmond Rd, SW15 ☎0181/780 1767. Specialist Goan restaurant, good on fish and seafood, and with fine desserts. *East Putney tube. Tues–Fri noon–2.30pm & 7–11pm, Sat 7–11pm. All cards. Inexpensive.*

Planet Poppadom, 366 King's Rd, SW3 ☎0171/823 3369. Trendy balti house-brasserie bringing good, quick meals to the King's Road. Choose your ingredients, and the heat you want it, and you're away. *Sloane Square tube. Mon–Wed 4pm–midnight, Thurs–Sun noon–midnight. Diners, MC, V. Inexpensive.*

North and Northeast

Indian Veg Bhel Poori House, 92–93 Chapel Market, N1 ☎0171/837 4607. One of London's culinary bargains, with buffet lunches and dinners for under £4. The clever choices, though, are from the menu or daily specials – great *thalis* and other delights. Avoid the house wine – stick to beer – and you'll be as happy as the people in the photos on the wall. *Angel tube. Daily noon–3pm & 6–11pm. MC, V. Budget.*

Jai Krishna, 161 Stroud Green Rd, N4 ☎0171/272 1680. Very popular neighbourhood café with good veggie food (mostly south Indian) at unbeatable prices. It's unlicensed, but you can take

Budget: under £8
Inexpensive: £8–15
Moderate: £15–20
Expensive: £20–30
Very Expensive: over £30
These are per person prices for a three-course meal (or equivalent), excluding drinks and service.

your own drink. *Finsbury Park tube. Mon–Sat noon–2pm & 5.30–10.30pm. No cards. Budget.*

Rani, 7 Long Lane, N3 ☎0181/349 4386. Family-run vegetarian Indian restaurant, with fine food and very welcoming people. Vegans could eat here happily, too. *Finchley Central tube. Tues–Fri noon–3pm & 6–10.30pm, Sat 6–11pm, Sun noon–3pm & 6–10.30pm. Amex, MC, V. Moderate.*

Rasa, 55 Stoke Newington Church St, N16 ☎0171/249 0344. Splendid new South Indian vegetarian restaurant with unusual, delicate dishes and staff that take the time to explain what's what. *Stoke Newington BR. Daily noon–2.30pm & 6pm–midnight. All cards. Inexpensive.*

Sabras, 263 Willesden High Rd, NW10 ☎0181/459 0340. A long, long way out of central London and rather austere in its surroundings, but considered to be among the best Indian vegetarian restaurants in the capital, with awards from just about anyone who matters. It's certainly doing something right – it's been in business for over twenty years. Try the *thalis*. *Dollis Hill tube. Tues–Sun 12.30–3.30pm & 6.30–10.30pm. No cards. Inexpensive.*

Suruchi, 82 Mildmay Park, N1 ☎0171/241 5213. Mainly south Indian vegetarian cooking (with seafood dishes on offer, too), served in elegant, roomy, untypical surroundings – jazz rather than sitars and even a few outdoor tables in summer. *Bus #73. Daily noon–2.30pm & 6–11.30pm. Diners, MC, V. Moderate.*

Italian restaurants

Restaurants: Central

Amalfi, 29–31 Old Compton St, W1 ☎0171/437 7284. Bright and good-value Soho eatery that's been around for years – whether you want pasta, pizza, meat and fish, or coffee and a cake at a pavement table, there'll be something to tempt you. *Leicester Square tube. Mon–Sat 9am–11pm, Sun 9am–10pm. All cards. Inexpensive.*

Arts Theatre Café, 6 Great Newport St, WC2 ☎0171/497 8014. Excellent jazz- and blues-washed North Italian café-restaurant in the dimly-lit theatre basement, serving a set-price three-course menu (£12.50) that's one of central London's culinary bargains. Best to book, though you could just pop in for a glass of wine and an *antipasto* dish. *Leicester Square tube. Mon–Fri noon–11pm, Sat 6–11pm. No cards. Inexpensive.*

Bertorelli's, 44a Floral St, WC2 ☎0171/836 3969. Neither the prices nor the staff are as intimidating as might be suggested by this place's reputation and locale (opposite the Opera House), and the modern Italian food – squid, polenta and rustic sausages, among other dishes – is often outstanding. Cheaper downstairs section for superior pizza and pasta. Book in advance. *Covent Garden tube. Mon–Sat noon–3pm & 5.30–11.30pm. All cards. Expensive.*

Italian Graffiti, 163–165 Wardour St, W1 ☎0171/439 4668. Handy Soho trattoria mixing pasta, pizza and meat and fish dishes – no surprises here, but reliable enough and decently priced for the area. *Tottenham Court Rd tube. Mon–Fri noon–3pm & 6–11.45pm, Sat noon–11.45pm. All cards. Moderate.*

Neal Street Restaurant, 26 Neal St, WC2 ☎0171/836 8368. Antonio Carluccio's London base (his fantastic deli is next door). The somewhat ludicrous prices here don't deter keen wild mushroom fans – a Carluccio speciality – or those with the money to indulge themselves in a thoroughly stylish Italian job. Contemporary art on the walls, contemporary Italian dinners in the tum. A good £45 a head and counting. *Covent Garden tube. Mon–Sat 12.30–2.30pm & 7.30–11pm. All cards. Very Expensive.*

Orso, 27 Wellington St, WC2 ☎0171/240 5269. Ultra-trendy new-wave Italian; too self-satisfied for some tastes, but others think it has maintained an edge on its imitators. The menu changes daily, but you'll always find various pizzas, pasta and grilled specials. *Covent Garden tube. Daily noon–midnight. No cards. Expensive.*

Restaurants

La Quercia d'Oro, 16a Endell St, WC2 ☎0171/379 5108. Shabby, cheerful, basic trattoria, with big rustic portions and a loud, boisterous crowd. The daily specials on the blackboard are the things to go for – and expect quantity, and not always quality. *Covent Garden tube. Mon–Fri noon–2.45pm & 6–11.30pm, Sat 6–11.30pm. Amex, MC, V. Moderate.*

Sol e Luna, Thomas Neal's Centre, 22 Shorts Gardens, WC2 ☎0171/379 3336. Located downstairs in this Covent Garden shopping centre, the fine wood-fired pizzas and main courses (exotic pastas and *bresaola* are specialities) all cost around the same here, which makes it pricey for a pizzeria but not bad value if you're looking to mix it with London's media people. *Covent Garden tube. Daily noon–midnight. All cards. Moderate.*

Villa Carlotta, 33 Charlotte St, W1 ☎0171/636 6011. The *Villa Carlotta* was always a place out-of-towners came when they wanted a "real" Italian meal. Its mock rusticity and trad pasta, meat and fish meals appear a bit dated now, but there's nothing wrong with the food, service or atmosphere. *Goodge St tube. Mon–Thurs noon–3pm & 6–11pm. Fri & Sat noon–3pm & 6–11.30pm.* All cards. *Moderate to Expensive.*

Restaurants: Clerkenwell

Eagle, 159 Farringdon Rd, EC1 ☎0171/837 1353. Technically a pub, frequented by a loyal crowd of journos (the *Observer* and *Guardian* are down the road) and vocal Soho types on an away-day tucking into authentic regional Italian food; the day's dishes are chalked up on the board, and vary according to what was available at the market. Grab a seat if you can, pick a wine off the other board and enjoy. Plenty of wine by the glass, and no need to have the full three courses means you can escape lightly. *Farringdon tube. Mon–Fri 12.30–2.30pm & 6.30–10.30pm. No cards. Inexpensive.*

Peasant, 240 St John St, EC1 ☎0171/336 7726. The second of this area's Cinderella pubs that's forsaken traditional drinking and concentrates on serving up quality Italian food (by fine chef Carla Tomasi) at decent prices. Unlike the nearby *Eagle*, you can book tables, too. *Angel or Farringdon tube. Mon–Fri noon–2.30pm & 5.30–11pm, Sat 5.30–11pm. Diners, MC, V. Moderate.*

Restaurants: Islington

Casale Franco, 134–137 Upper St, N1 ☎0171/226 8994. Up a side alley just off Upper Street, fashionable Islington and its leftish literati and politerati dine here on big pizzas and traditional and modern Italian dishes. There are two floors of cramped tables, but since there's no booking (except at lunch), you might have to stand outside and queue. It's worth it. Note: there's no pizza at lunch; and no pizza-only meals at dinner. *Angel tube. Tues–Sun 6.30–11.30pm. Fri–Sun 12.30–2.30pm. MC, V. Moderate to Expensive.*

Restaurants: Southeast

Caffè Italia, 107 Humber Rd, SE3 ☎0181/858 7577. Marvellous Italian restaurant out in a residential part of Greenwich. First-rate ever-changing fixed menu and just about the friendliest owners in London – the whole menu is explained and it all tastes fab. *Westcombe Park BR. Tues–Sat 7.30–9.30pm. MC, V. Expensive.*

Cantina del Ponte, Butlers Wharf Building, 36c Shad Thames, SE1 ☎0171/403 5403. More designerdom from Terence Conran, this time Italian – food from all regions, with pizzas alongside meat and fish. Great views from the south bank at Tower Bridge, too, with outdoor seats in summer. *Tower Hill or London Bridge tube. Mon–Sat noon–3pm & 6–11pm, Sun noon–3pm. All cards. Expensive.*

Budget: under £8
Inexpensive: £8–15
Moderate: £15–20
Expensive: £20–30
Very Expensive: over £30
These are per person prices for a three-course meal (or equivalent), excluding drinks and service.

Restaurants

Del Buongustaio, 283 Putney Bridge Rd, SW15 ☎0181/780 9361. Worth the trip out to Putney for modish northern Italian food, a wine list that isn't afraid to roam outside Italy and very decent desserts. *East Putney tube. Mon–Fri noon–3pm & 6.30–11.30pm, Sat 6.30–11.30pm. Amex, MC, V. Expensive.*

Osteria Antica Bologna, 23 Northcote Rd, SW11 ☎0171/978 4771. Unpretentious and very popular neighbourhood restaurant with regional Italian food, washed down with jugs of Sicilian wine. Decor seems the result of someone having looked up the word "rustic" in the dictionary. Not a great location, but you'll still need to book in advance, especially for the weekend. *Clapham Junction BR. Mon–Fri noon–3pm & 6–11pm, Sat noon–11pm, Sun 12.30–10.30pm. Amex, MC, V. Moderate.*

River Café, Rainville Rd, W6 ☎0171/381 8824. Superb modern Italian food, packed with flavour. Prices are high, but so is the quality, while the designer surroundings hold the eye. *Hammersmith tube. Mon–Sat 12.30–2.30pm & 7.30–9.30pm, Sun 1–2.30pm. MC, V. Expensive.*

Pizzas

Central

Chicago Pizza Pie Company, 17 Hanover Square, W1 ☎0171/629 2669. Seriously deep-pan, American-style pizzas in a good-time restaurant. Kids like it here and are well looked after – adults get to eat till they drop. *Oxford Circus tube. Mon–Sat 11.45am–11.30pm, Sun noon–10.30pm. Amex, MC, V. Inexpensive.*

Gourmet Pizza Company: branches at Gabriel's Wharf, 56 Upper Ground, SE1 (Waterloo tube; ☎0171/928 3188); and 42 New Oxford St, WC1 (Tottenham Court Rd tube; ☎0171/580 9521). The weirdest pizza toppings in London – Chinese duck and plum sauce, or cajun chicken are typical – but accompanied by good salads and a decent wine list. At the South Bank venue you can eat outside in the summer. *Mon–Sat noon–11pm, Sun noon–11.30pm. Amex, MC, V. Inexpensive.*

Kettner's, 29 Romilly St, W1 ☎0171/734 6112. Grand old place with high ceilings, private rooms, brass-and-mirror-laden bathrooms and a pianist, yet part of the *Pizza Express* chain and consequently cheaper than you'd expect from the ambience. You can't book and might be forced to hang out a while in the noisy *Champagne Bar* – no great hardship. *Leicester Square tube. Mon–Sat 11am–11pm. All cards. Inexpensive to Moderate.*

Lorelei, 21 Bateman St, W1 ☎0171/734 0954. Tiny, dingy but welcoming unlicensed pizza restaurant offering Soho's cheapest route to a full stomach. The pizzas aren't huge – if you need filling up, the house *antipasto* does the trick. *Tottenham Court Rd tube. Mon–Sat noon–11pm. No cards. Inexpensive.*

Pizza Express, 10 Dean St, W1 (Tottenham Court Rd tube; ☎0171/437 9595); 30 Coptic St, WC1 (Tottenham Court Rd tube; ☎0171/636 3232); and numerous other branches all over London. Easily the best of the pizza chains, doing a good line in (admittedly small) thin-crust pizzas and great house red wine – there's nothing much else to choose. The Dean Street branch has regular live jazz in the basement; the Coptic Street one is sited in a former dairy. *Daily noon–midnight. Amex, MC, V. Inexpensive.*

Pizzeria Condotti, 4 Mill St, W1 ☎0171/499 1308. Another *Pizza Express* offshoot, serving some of the capital's best pizzas in upscale surroundings. Book at lunchtime, when the office crowd is in. *Oxford Circus tube. Mon–Sat 11.30am–midnight. All cards. Moderate.*

North

Calzone, 66 Heath St, NW3 ☎0171/794 6775. Handily located for heath trippers, with smallish pizzas prepared promptly and a few pasta dishes, too. *Hampstead tube. Daily noon–11.30pm. No cards. Inexpensive.*

Parkway Pizzeria, 64 Parkway, NW1 ☎0171/485 0678. Fashionable, crowded, Art Deco Camden pizza joint – book at weekends. *Camden Town tube. Daily noon–midnight. No cards. Inexpensive.*

Restaurants

South

Eco, 162 Clapham High St, SW4 ☎0171/978 1108. Ludicrously popular Clapham haunt – book well in advance – with splendidly inventive new-wave pizzas that spill over the edge of the plate; the seafood calzone is a favourite. The uncomfortable designer wood-and-wire interior doesn't encourage any hanging around – but they'll want your table quick in any case. *Clapham Common tube. Daily 11.30am–3.30pm & 6.30–11pm. MC, V. Inexpensive.*

Pizzeria Castello, 20 Walworth Rd, SE1 ☎0171/703 2556. Highly regarded local pizzeria that's well worth the short trip on the tube, though it's admittedly an unsavoury locale. Stick to the pizzas and unless you've booked, expect to wait ages for a table. If you get stuck downstairs, you're in for sing-along-a-"Lying' Eyes" with the office party crowd. *Elephant & Castle tube. Mon–Fri noon–11pm, Sat 5–11pm. Amex, MC, V. Inexpensive.*

Pizzeria Franco, 4 Market Row, Electric Lane, SW9 ☎0171/738 3021. A great favourite – superb pizzas served in a tiny caff in the middle of Brixton market. Lunch in south London at its best – note that pizzas aren't served until noon or so. *Brixton tube. Mon, Tues & Thurs–Sat 8am–5pm. No cards. Inexpensive.*

Pasta

Bella Pasta: branches London-wide including 22 Leicester Square, WC2 (Leicester Square tube; ☎0171/321 0016); 30 Henrietta St, WC2 (Covent Garden tube; ☎0171/836 8396); 116 Baker St, W1 (Baker St tube; ☎0171/224 3334); 70 St Martin's Lane, WC2 (Charing Cross tube; ☎0171/836 0484); 152 Victoria St, SW1 (Victoria tube; ☎0171/828 7664); 60 Old Brompton Rd, SW7 (South Kensington tube; ☎0171/584 4028); and 155 Earl's Court Rd, SW5 (Earl's Court tube; ☎0171/244 8320). The *Bella Pasta* chain provides standardized pasta dishes at tourist hotspots all over London – the food is never brilliant, but you can sit outside at the Leicester Square branch. *Varied opening hours, but usually daily noon–midnight.. MC, V. Inexpensive.*

Palms, 39 King St, WC2 ☎0171/240 2939. Covent Garden pasta joint popular with the after-office crowd. A new Mediterranean menu also offers grills, salads and risotto. Big servings, no-nonsense service, decent prices; second branch at 3–5 Campden Hill Rd, W8 (High St Kensington tube; ☎0171/938 1830). *Covent Garden tube. Daily noon–midnight. MC, V. Inexpensive.*

Spaghetti House: 20 branches, including 30 St Martin's Lane, WC2 (Charing Cross tube; ☎0171/836 1626); 15 Goodge St, W1 (Goodge St tube; ☎0171/636 6582). London-wide chain of bustling trattorias that serve varied, reliable pasta dishes (as starters or main courses) and more substantial dishes – beef, chicken and fish – for reasonable prices. *Mon–Thurs noon–11pm, Fri & Sat noon–11.30pm, Sun 5.30–10.30pm. All cards. Inexpensive.*

Japanese

Benkei, 19 Lower Marsh, SE1 ☎0171/401 2343. Bargain backstreet diner with a short menu of classics. Great-value set lunches, too. *Waterloo tube. Mon–Fri noon–3pm & 6–10.30pm, Sat 5–10.30pm. Amex. Inexpensive.*

Café Sogo, 39–45 Haymarket, SW1 ☎0171/333 9000. Ground-floor department store café with picture windows onto Haymarket and speedily delivered *sushi* and *sashimi* sets at prices mere mortal shoppers can afford. Drink *Kirin* beer or green tea. *Piccadilly Circus tube. Mon–Sat 10am–9pm, Sun 11am–5pm. All cards. Inexpensive.*

Budget: under £8
Inexpensive: £8–15
Moderate: £15–20
Expensive: £20–30
Very Expensive: over £30
These are per person prices for a three-course meal (or equivalent), excluding drinks and service.

Ikkyu, 67 Tottenham Court Rd, W1 ☎0171/436 6169. Basement Japanese restaurant, good enough for a quick lunch (set meals run £5–10) or a more elaborate dinner. Either way, prices are infinitely more reasonable than elsewhere in the capital, and the food is tasty and authentic. *Goodge St tube. Mon–Fri 12.30–2.30pm & 6–10.30pm, Sun 6–10.30pm. All cards. Inexpensive to Moderate.*

Suntory, 72 St James's St, SW1 ☎0171/409 0201. Grit your teeth and the set lunches are just about affordable (around £20–30 for a full meal); otherwise you're talking telephone numbers for dinner in one of London's most famous Japanese restaurants. Expense account holders only. *Green Park tube. Mon–Sat noon–2pm & 6–10pm. All cards. Very Expensive.*

Tokyo Diner, 2 Newport Place, WC2 ☎0171/287 8777. Brilliant Japanese diner on the edge of Chinatown serving authentic food at a fraction of the cost of its rivals. Try one of the *bento* meals – an entire meal in a little box. Perfect service; tips not accepted. *Leicester Square tube. Daily noon–midnight. No cards. Inexpensive.*

Wagamama, 4 Streatham St, WC1 ☎0171/323 9223. An austerely hi-tech setting – and probably the only restaurant in London where the waiters take your orders on hand-held computers. Share long benches and slurp up the huge bowls of noodle soup or stir-fried plates – vegetarians will do well here, too. You'll have to queue, but it moves quickly, though the rapid turnover means it's not a place to consider for a long, romantic dinner. *Tottenham Court Rd tube. Mon–Fri noon–2.30pm & 6–11pm, Sat 1–3.30pm & 6–11pm. No cards. Budget to Inexpensive.*

Yaohan Plaza Food Court, Yaohan Plaza, 399 Edgware Rd, NW9 ☎0181/200 0009 A hike from the centre, but worth it to shop at the massive Japanese *Yaohan* department store – there's a superb supermarket and a games arcade for the kids. The *Food Court* lets you mix and match Japanese snack food from the various counters. *Colindale tube. Daily 10am–7pm. No cards. Budget.*

Jewish

Bloom's, 90 Whitechapel High St, E1 ☎0171/247 6001. London's most famous kosher restaurant serving stomach-defeating portions. Note the early closing hours. *Aldgate East tube. Mon–Thurs & Sun 11am–9pm, Fri 11am–2pm. All cards. Inexpensive.*

Korean

Busan, 43 Holloway Rd, N7 ☎0171/607 8264. Very friendly neighbourhood restaurant that serves exquisite Korean food in unpretentious surroundings. It gets packed, too, so think about booking in advance. *Highbury and Islington tube. Mon–Fri noon–2.30pm & 6–11pm, Sat & Sun 6–11pm. V. Moderate.*

Cho Won, 27 Romilly St, W1 ☎0171/437 2262. Cheap, central, family-run Korean with a short, but good menu. *Leicester Square tube. Daily noon–3pm & 6–11pm. All cards. Moderate.*

Jin, 16 Bateman St, W1 ☎0171/734 0908. Absolutely authentic Korean food, including great *bulgogi* – marinaded strips of beef – grilled at a barbecue in the centre of your table. Set meals are pretty good value, but you needn't be frightened by the menu – friendly staff steer first-timers through the intricacies. *Leicester Square tube. Mon–Sat noon–3pm & 6–11pm. All cards. Moderate.*

Min Sok Chon, 33 Pratt St, NW1 ☎0171/485 7899. Cramped local restaurant with a nice line in noodles and superb-value set dinners. Book on Friday and Saturday nights. *Camden Town tube. Mon–Sat 6–11pm. All cards. Inexpensive.*

Malaysian/Indonesian

Central

Jakarta, 150 Shaftesbury Avenue, WC2 ☎0171/836 2644. All the usual Indonesian and Malaysian dishes at decent prices – the fish and seafood dishes are particularly good. Set lunches ar a fiver or so are worth knowing about. *Tottenham Court Rd tube. Mon–Sat 6–11.30pm, Sun 5.30–10.30pm. Amex, MC, V. Moderate.*

Restaurants

For more Jewish/kosher food, see the entries on Brick Lane Beigel Bake, Manhattan Bagel Bakery *and* Rabin's *(Chapter 14), and* Grahame's *(p.433).*

Restaurants

Malaysia Hall, 46 Bryanston Square, W1 ☎0171/723 9484. This student canteen dishes up strictly authentic Malaysian meals (including breakfast) at rock-bottom prices. It's not to everyone's taste (and it's certainly not a place for a night out), but you can't beat the prices. *Marble Arch tube. Daily 8–10am, noon–3pm & 5–9pm. No cards. Budget.*

Melati, 21 Great Windmill St, W1 ☎0171 734 6964. One of the best places in the centre for Malaysian/Indonesian food, with excellent prawn or meat satays and a few more unusual dishes you don't often see – ask the waiter for recommendations or plump for the fish-head curry. Book for dinner if you don't want to wait in line. *Piccadilly Circus tube. Mon–Thurs & Sun noon–11.30pm, Sat & Sun noon–12.30am. All cards. Moderate.*

Minang, 11 Greek St, W1 ☎0171/287 1408. Top-notch cooking at prices a little over the odds, especially for the more adventurous Indonesian specialities. Set-price lunches and evening meals provide some budgetary comfort. *Tottenham Court Rd tube. Mon–Sat noon–3pm & 5.30–11.30pm. All cards. Moderate.*

Satay Stick, 6 Dering St, W1 ☎0171/629 1346. There's only one thing to have with a name like this, and it's the best reason to come – the succulent satay is terrific. This place attracts a lunchtime Malaysian crowd, so it's very much the real thing, but if you start diving wildly into the menu you can easily spend more than you think. *Oxford Circus tube. Mon–Fri noon–3pm & 6–10pm, Sat noon–9pm. Amex, MC, V. Moderate.*

West

Mawar, 175a Edgware Rd, W2 ☎0171/262 1663. One of London's most authentic Malaysian experiences: come for the café buffet or eat in a little more comfort in the restaurant; either way, try the fish-head curry, or the rice and chicken. *Edgware Rd tube. Café: daily noon–10.30pm; restaurant: daily noon–3pm & 6–10.30pm. Amex, MC, V. Budget (café) to Inexpensive (restaurant).*

North

Bintang, 93 Kentish Town Rd, NW1 ☎0171/284 1640. Malaysian/Indonesian food that rarely reaches the heights, but served in gloriously overdone decor by friendly staff at eminently reasonable prices; three out of four ain't bad. *Camden Town tube. Daily 6–11.30pm. MC, V. Inexpensive.*

Southwest

Nancy Lam's, 56 Lavender Hill, SW11 ☎0171/924 3148. Popular, cheek-by-jowl Battersea neighbourhood restaurant presided over by the voluble Nancy. The food's great – a tried and tested menu of Malaysian, Singaporean and Indonesian classics – and Nancy keeps things ticking along with some judicious teasing and jousting with the customers. Booking essential. *Bus #77 or 77a. Mon–Sat 7.30–10.30pm. Amex, MC, V. Moderate.*

Mexican/Tex-Mex

Arizona, 2a Jamestown Rd, NW1 ☎0171/284 4730. A useful pit-stop for market shoppers, this Wild Western outfit dishes up tacos, enchiladas and all the usual suspects. More of a bar at night; roof terrace open in summer. *Camden Town tube. Mon–Sat noon–midnight, Sun noon–11pm. Amex, MC, V. Inexpensive.*

Break for the Border, 5 Goslett Yard, off Charing Cross Rd WC2 ☎0171/437 8595. However you like your Tex-Mex food, you have to like your R&B loud to come here – the nightly bands take no prisoners; neither do the tequila-slammer "girls" who virtually force-feed you the stuff. Given that the food's a secondary consideration, it's not bad. *Tottenham Court Rd*

Budget: under £8
Inexpensive: £8–15
Moderate: £15–20
Expensive: £20–30
Very Expensive: over £30
These are per person prices for a three-course meal (or equivalent), excluding drinks and service.

tube. Mon & Tues noon–midnight, Wed–Sat noon–1am, Sun 5.30–11.30pm. Amex, MC, V. Moderate.

Café Pacifico, 5 Langley St, WC2 ☎0171/379 7728. Rated as the best Mexican restaurant in central London, though that isn't much of a title. Fairly quiet during the day, unbelievably noisy in the evening; you'll have to book. Stoke up at the long bar before digging into hefty portions – the *fajita* specials are good. *Covent Garden tube. Mon–Sat noon–11.45pm, Sun noon–10.45pm. Amex, MC, V. Moderate.*

Down Mexico Way, 25 Swallow St, W1 ☎0171/437 9895. Best-looking and most refined of the city's Mexican eateries, with superb tiling, stained glass and wood panelling throughout. Take the opportunity to roam gastronomically for a change – traditional poultry in chocolate sauce makes an appearance, as do other less challenging but equally interesting dishes. Book ahead (and note that the bar stays open until 3am). *Piccadilly Circus tube. Mon–Sat noon–midnight, Sun noon–10.30pm. All cards. Moderate.*

Salsa!, 96 Charing Cross Rd, WC2 ☎0171/379 3277. A newish arrival that is quickly making friends with its better-than-average food, good cocktails and regular Latin bands – including the odd big Cuban name. You need to book for gigs at weekends when the late-night drinking pulls in the punters. *Leicester Square tube. Mon–Wed 5.30pm–midnight, Thurs–Sat 5.30pm–1am. Amex, MC, V. Moderate.*

Middle Eastern

Adams Café, 77 Askew Rd, W12 ☎0181/743 0572. What started off as a greasy spoon, miraculously transformed at night into an enthusiastically run Tunisian restaurant, has gone from strength to strength. New decor, but still great couscous, tasty starters and Tunisian and Moroccan wine. Only drawback is location, but the eminently reasonable prices make it worth the hike. *Hammersmith tube and bus #266. Mon–Sat 7.30–10.30pm. No cards. Moderate.*

Al Alysse, 134 Upper St, N1 ☎0171/226 0122. Intimate Lebanese restaurant, offering a bargain buffet lunch and very reasonable evening meals, including a good-value meze meal. *Angel tube. Mon 6.30–11.30pm, Tues–Fri noon–3pm & 6.30–11.30pm, Sat 6.30–11.30pm. All cards. Moderate.*

Al Hamra, 31–33 Shepherd Market, W1 ☎0171/493 1954. Long-standing Lebanese restaurant in the raffish surroundings of Shepherd Market. The meze are much the best reason to come, with three dozen different dishes on offer, hot and cold; grilled meats predominate otherwise. If you go the whole hog, you'll easily push into the upper price range. *Green Park tube. Daily noon–midnight. All cards. Moderate to Expensive.*

Olive Tree, 11 Wardour St, W1 ☎0171/734 0808. Cheap West End venue for mainstream Middle Eastern/Mediterranean food – couscous, falafels, houmous and kebabs. Not a bad vegetarian choice, either. *Leicester Square tube. Daily 11am–10.30pm. Diners, MC, V. Inexpensive.*

Osmani, 46 Inverness St, NW1 ☎0171/267 4682. Titchy North African restaurant with engaging staff and great food – the starters alone have most purring with delight. Booking is essential. *Camden Town tube. Mon–Fri 12.30–2.30pm & 7–11.30pm, Sat & Sun 7–11.30pm. Amex. Moderate.*

La Reash Cous-Cous House, 23–24 Greek St, W1 ☎0171/439 1063. Friendly Soho restaurant, where you can often get a table when others are full; mainly Moroccan, but with a choice of Middle Eastern meze dishes. Huge portions of couscous, both meat and vegetarian – the *royale* is a monster. *Leicester Square tube. Daily noon–midnight. Amex, MC, V. Inexpensive to Moderate.*

Polish

Daquise, 20 Thurloe St, SW7 ☎0171/589 6117. Something of a cult, with its gloomy Eastern Bloc decor, long-suffering staff and heartily utilitarian Polish food.

Restaurants

Good place for a quick bite and a shot of vodka after the South Kensington museums. *South Kensington tube. Daily 10am–11.30pm. No cards. Inexpensive.*

Magical Buska, 32 Crouch Hill, N4 ☎0171/281 7448. Traditional food served in friendly surroundings – chicken soup, stews and savoury pancakes at middling prices. *Finsbury Park tube. Tues–Sun 6.30–11pm. Inexpensive.*

The Pilot, 14 Collingham Gardens, SW5 ☎0171/370 1229. Big, meaty meals, vodkas and beer in the irresistibly offbeat premises of the Polish Air Forces Club. *Earl's Court tube. Tues–Sat noon–2.30pm & 6–10.30pm, Sun noon–2.30pm & 7–10pm. MC, V. Inexpensive.*

Wódka, 12 St Alban's Grove, W8 ☎0171/937 6513. With food cooked with a little imagination, the smart *Wódka* is perhaps the best choice if you want to experience the best that Polish cuisine has to offer. It's not cheap, though, especially once you start ladling out the ice-cold flavoured vodkas. *High St Kensington tube. Mon–Fri noon–2.30pm & 7–11pm, Sat & Sun 7–11pm. All cards. Expensive.*

Portuguese

Café Portugal, 6a Victoria House, South Lambeth Rd, SW8 ☎0171/587 1962. This combines a rough and ready basment restaurant and a lighter café, both of which serve some of the best-value Portuguese food in London to half the city's Portuguese population who live in the neighbourhood. Great snacks, cakes and ice cream in the café; heavier stews and salt-cod dishes in the restaurant. *Vauxhall tube. Mon–Tues & Thurs–Sun noon–3.30pm & 7–10.30pm; café open same days 10am–11pm. MC, V. Inexpensive.*

Caravela, 39 Beauchamp Place, SW3 ☎0171/581 2366. Live music encourages a party atmosphere; the food is good, if unadventurous. *Knightsbridge or South Kensington tube. Mon–Sat noon–3pm & 7pm–1am, Sun noon–3pm & 7pm–midnight. All cards. Moderate.*

Churrasqueira, 168 Old Lambeth Rd, SW8 ☎0171/793 0744. Crusty Portuguese grill-house that's a treat for meat-eaters; there's a great range of ports and Portuguese brandies, too. *Vauxhall tube. Daily noon–3pm & 6pm–midnight. MC, V.. Inexpensive.*

O Fado, 49 Beauchamp Place, SW3 ☎0171/589 3002. Probably the oldest Portuguese restaurant in London, which speaks volumes for its authenticity. It can get rowdy when the family parties are in, but that's half the enjoyment. You'll need to reserve a table. *Knightsbridge or South Kensington tube. Mon–Sat noon–3pm & 6.30pm–12.30am, Sun noon–3pm & 6.30–11.30pm. Amex, MC, V. Moderate.*

Russian

Borshtch 'n Tears, 46 Beauchamp Place, SW3 ☎0171/589 5003. If you didn't know much about Russian food before you went, don't expect a great deal of enlightenment after a night out here. Serious vodka-drinking venue where the food is secondary to shouting and singing loudly. *Knightsbridge tube. Daily 6pm–2am. MC, V. Moderate.*

Kaspia, 18 Bruton Place, W1 ☎0171/493 2612. Devastatingly expensive haunt of the rich and famous. It's a lovely room in which to eat (caviar, naturally, is celebrated here), but you won't enjoy it if you're worried about meeting the bill – the set menus would be one way to go, but even those start at £30 a head. Booking essential. *Bond St tube. Mon–Sat noon–3pm & 7–11.30pm. All cards. Very Expensive.*

Luba's Place, 164 Essex Rd, N1 ☎0171/704 2775. Hybrid menu but one which has enough Russian dishes to satisfy – portions are huge (ie, Russian) and prices low. *Essex Rd BR. Tues–Sun 10am–midnight. No cards. Inexpensive.*

Budget: under £8
Inexpensive: £8–15
Moderate: £15–20
Expensive: £20–30
Very Expensive: over £30
These are per person prices for a three-course meal (or equivalent), excluding drinks and service.

Restaurants

Spanish

Albero & Grana, Chelsea Cloisters, 89 Sloane Avenue, SW3 ☎0171/225 1048. New-wave Spanish cuisine at inflated prices, though many swear this to be among the best restaurants in London. Hang out at the cool tapas bar up front and then slip inside for some highly imaginative food, culling influences from all over Spain; it's going to cost a good £40 a head. *Sloane Square tube. Mon–Sat noon–2.30pm & 7.30–11.30pm; bar Mon–Sat 12.30–3.30pm & 6–11pm, Sun 7–10.30pm. All cards. Moderate (bar) to Very Expensive (restaurant).*

Bar Gansa, 2 Inverness St, NW1 ☎0171/267 8909. Busy, buzzy Camden tapas bar with above-average food and no chance of a table on weekend evenings. *Camden Town tube. Mon–Sat noon–midnight, Sun 10.30am–11pm. MC, V. Inexpensive.*

Costa Dorada, 47–55 Hanway St, W1 ☎0171/636 7139. Boisterous, late-night flamenco party venue – go in a group, don't expect gourmet cooking and don't be surprised if the bar bill exceeds the charge for food. There's a separate tapas bar and restaurant. *Tottenham Court Rd tube. Mon–Sat 7pm–3am. All cards. Moderate (tapas bar) to Expensive (restaurant).*

Galicia, 323 Portobello Rd, W10 ☎0181/969 3539. Groovy Notting Hill tapas bar-restaurant, specializing in Galician (north-west Spanish) dishes – octopus is a favourite. *Ladbroke Grove tube. Tues–Sun noon–2.30pm & 7–11pm; tapas bar Tues–Sun noon–11.30pm. Diners, MC, V. Inexpensive to Moderate.*

Méson Bilbao, 33 Malvern Rd, NW6 ☎0171/328 1744. Top-quality Basque cooking, specializing in fish and seafood. A nice place where you can either tuck into tapas or eat from a good-value set menu. *Maida Vale tube. Mon–Fri & Sun 11am–3pm & 6pm–midnight, Sat 6pm–midnight. Diners, MC, V. Inexpensive.*

Méson Don Felipe, 53 The Cut, SE1 ☎0171/928 3237. Long, thin tapas bar which gets uncomfortably crowded at times – and in summer, it's a sweatbox. But the food's good, and the Spanish guitarists keep things swinging. *Waterloo tube. Mon–Sat noon–11.30pm. MC, V. Inexpensive.*

Rebato's, 169 South Lambeth Rd, SW8 ☎0171/735 6388. One of south London's best. Fronted by an atmospheric (always crowded) tapas bar, with an array of toothsome food, this enjoyable Spanish restaurant offers an excellent-value set meal for around £15. Very popular with parties, so book ahead and be prepared for congas. *Vauxhall or Stockwell tube. Mon–Fri noon–2.30pm & 7–11pm, Sat 7–11pm; bar opens 5.30pm Mon–Fri. Amex, MC, V. Inexpensive.*

La Rueda, 66–68 Clapham High St, SW4 ☎0171/627 2173. Another premier south London party night venue: mobbed tapas bar to one side, with tables like gold dust, more refined restaurant the other – the twain meet on the postage-stamp-sized dancefloor at weekends. The tapas dishes are surprisingly good. There's more of the same at a second branch at 624 King's Rd, SW6 (Fulham Broadway tube; ☎0171/384 2684). *Clapham Common tube. Mon–Fri 11am–3pm & 6–11.30pm, Sat noon–11.30pm. Amex, MC, V. Moderate.*

Sevilla Mia, 22 Hanway St, W1 ☎0171/637 3756. Hard-to-find basement bar (opposite the *Costa Dorada*) which throbs most nights with Spaniards and their flamenco singing and dancing buddies. The tapas is almost a side issue – and if you come after 8pm or so there'll be nowhere to sit anyway – but it's actually very good. *Tottenham Court Rd tube. Mon–Sat 6pm–1am, Sun 7pm–midnight. No cards. Budget.*

Swedish

Anna's Place, 90 Mildmay Park, N1 ☎0171/249 9379. London's most renowned Scandinavian restaurant, a homely place with traditional Swedish cooking and an effusive un-Nordic welcome. Seasonal dishes are worth investigating, but you can't beat the *gravadlax*. Garden tables in summer. *Canonbury BR. Tues–Sat 12.15–2.15pm & 7.15–10.45pm. No cards. Expensive.*

Restaurants

See p.104 for more on Claridge's.

The Causerie, *Claridge's Hotel*, Brook St, W1 ☎0171/629 8860. Not exactly a secret, but not many would think of swanning into one of London's premier hotels for the set meal – which here, just happens to be a sensational *smörgasbord*. A bottle of wine virtually doubles the price, but you can go back for more as often as you like. *Bond St tube. Mon–Fri noon–3pm & 5.30–10.30pm, Sat noon–3pm. All cards. Moderate.*

Garlic & Shots, 14 Frith St, W1 ☎0171/734 9505. Go with a very good friend – everything (starters, main courses, desserts, drinks) is laced with garlic. Try the vodka. Good in summer, when you can sit in the courtyard out back. *Leicester Square tube. Mon–Sat 5pm–midnight, Sun 5–11pm. MC, V. Inexpensive.*

Swiss

St Moritz, 161 Wardour St, W1 ☎0171/734 3324. Great fondues – cheese or meat – in a dining room decorated by someone who once went on a skiing holiday; Swiss kitsch at its worst, but friendly enough. *Piccadilly Circus tube. Mon–Fri noon–3pm & 6–11.30pm, Sat 6–11.30pm. All cards. Moderate.*

Thai

Central

Bahn Thai, 21a Frith St, W1 ☎0171/437 8504. Rather depressing decor belies the quality of the food in this long-established – and rather overpriced – Thai restaurant. However, there's a large and interesting menu, with some particularly good vegetarian choices, and the cooking is undeniably accomplished. *Leicester Square tube. Mon–Sat noon–2.30pm & 6–11.15pm, Sun 12.30–2.30pm & 6.30–10.30pm. All cards. Expensive.*

Chiang Mai, 48 Frith St, W1 ☎0171/437 7444. The main Soho alternative to the *Bahn Thai*, specializing in northern Thai food, and although not as authentic an experience in terms of the dishes and ingredients on offer, probably a more pleasant ambience. *Leicester Square tube. Mon–Sat noon–3pm & 6–11pm, Sun 6–10.30pm. Amex, MC, V. Expensive.*

Pu's Brasserie, 10 Gate St, W2 ☎0171/404 2132. Bustling and informal Thai restaurant tucked away down an alleyway just off Lincoln's Inn Fields. Service is prompt and pleasant, the food a standard blend of coconut-based curries and noodles. Low prices make it a good place for lunch, but it's just as rewarding in the evening too. *Holborn tube. Mon–Thurs noon–3pm & 5–10pm, Fri & Sat noon–3pm & 5.30–9.30pm. MC, V. Inexpensive.*

Sri Siam, 14 Old Compton St, W1 ☎0171/434 3544. Nicely furnished Thai restaurant, with an unusually extensive list of vegetarian options. It is also – for Soho at least – not too expensive. *Leicester Square tube. Mon–Sat noon–3pm & 6–11pm, Sun 6–10.30pm. All cards. Moderate.*

North

Tuk Tuk, 330 Upper St, N1 ☎0171/266 0837. Gothic-Oriental Islington favourite, with more hits than misses – clay-pot curries, grilled baby chicken and fish cakes are all excellent. *Angel tube. Daily 6pm–midnight. MC, V. Inexpensive to Moderate.*

Yum Yum, 26 Stoke Newington Church St, N16 ☎0171/254 6751. Trendy new Thai restaurant – always busy – with a reasonably priced, wide-ranging menu strong on vegetarian dishes. The one-plate set lunches are a particular bargain. *Stoke Newington BR. Daily noon–2.30pm & 6pm–midnight. All cards. Moderate.*

West

Ben's Thai, *Warrington Hotel*, 93 Warrington Crescent, W9 ☎0171/266 3134. Worth the trudge from the tube

Budget: under £8
Inexpensive: £8–15
Moderate: £15–20
Expensive: £20–30
Very Expensive: over £30
These are per person prices for a three-course meal (or equivalent), excluding drinks and service.

station, as this serves tasty Thai food at bargain prices, above a highly attractive pub. Go for the specials – generally better than the standard menu offerings. *Maida Vale tube. Mon–Sat noon–2.30pm & 6–10pm, Sun noon–2.30pm & 7–9.30pm. MC, V. Inexpensive to Moderate.*

Southwest

Bedlington Cafe, 24 Fauconberg Rd, W4 ☎0181/994 1965. Another of the capital's "caff-by-day-restaurant-by-night" operations, this time Thai, fairly long-established and deserved popular. Good value, reasonably authentic cooking, with meals served in squashed surroundings. Book well in advance and take your own booze. *Chiswick Park or Turnham Green tube. Mon–Sat noon–2pm & 6.30–10pm, Sun 6.30–9pm. No cards. Inexpensive.*

Blue Elephant, 4–6 Fulham Broadway, SW6 ☎0171/385 6595. Thai restaurant as theme park, which means an unfailingly popular Fulham night out amid the pools, grottos and palms of this enormous restaurant. The cooking doesn't always sparkle, but there's a fair old choice (including good veggie dishes) – shame about the high prices, which can easily lead to bills of £40 a head. *Fulham Broadway tube. Mon–Fri noon–2.30pm & 7pm–12.30am, Sat 7pm–12.30am, Sun noon–2.30pm & 7–10.30pm. All cards. Very Expensive.*

East

Thai Garden, 249 Globe Rd, E2 ☎0181/981 5748. Thai vegetarian and fish restaurant that's a firm local favourite: *tom yum* soup is always good, and there are vegetarian satays (with mushroom), whole fried fish and other delights. Set lunches and dinners, too, for those who can't decide. Book in advance. *Bethnal Green tube. Mon–Sat noon–2.45pm & 6–10.45pm. MC, V. Moderate.*

Southeast

Thailand, 15 Lewisham Way, SE14 ☎0181/691 4040. Fabulous Laotian-Thai dishes, with fish and seafood, particularly, presented splendidly. Fairly high prices, and you don't get much say in what you're served, but this is quality cooking. Booking essential, as there are very few tables. *New Cross Gate tube or New Cross BR from Charing Cross. Tues–Sat 6–10.30pm. Amex, MC, V. Expensive.*

Turkish

Efes, 80 Great Titchfield St, W1 ☎0171/636 1953. Vast Turkish kebab restaurant – a reliable and friendly place, with doner and shish kebabs big enough to sink a battleship, and some great starters. There's another branch, *Efes II*, round the corner at 175 Great Portland St – it's not quite as good, but is open on Sundays. *Oxford Circus or Great Portland St tube. Mon–Sat noon–11.30pm. All cards. Moderate.*

Istanbul Iskembecisi, 9 Stoke Newington Rd, N16 ☎0171/254 7291. Tripe specialist (try it as a soup) that's popular with local Turks, though there's plenty here for the constitutionally delicate, too, including fine kebabs. It's licensed, unlike many in the neighbourhood, and open extremely late – worth knowing about. *Dalton Kingsland BR. Mon–Sat 5pm–5am, Sun 2pm–5am. All cards. Inexpensive.*

Mangal, 10 Arcola St, E8 ☎0171/275 8981. One of the best and cheapest places in so-called Little Turkey, specializing in char-grilled meats. Choose from the counter, and the meal comes with great fresh bread and a salad. Bring your own booze if you want to drink. *Dalton Kingsland BR. Daily noon–midnight. No cards. Inexpensive.*

Sofra, 36 Tavistock St, WC2 ☎0171/240 3773. Good central spot with a bargain set meal and meze assortment. Choosing from the menu is more expensive, but the food's good and there's plenty of room to enjoy it – even a conservatory upstairs. The original Mayfair branch (18 Shepherd St, W1; Green Park tube; ☎0171/493 3320) is even better, though pricier. *Covent Garden tube. Daily noon–midnight. All cards. Moderate.*

Restaurants

For vegetarian cafés – mostly open during the day, and unlicensed – see "Lunches and quick meals", *p.417. For other specifically vegetarian options, see the relevant entries in* "Indian" *(p.438) and* "Chinese" *(p.429) sections.*

Vegetarian

Blah Blah Blah, 78 Goldhawk Rd, W12 ☎0181/746 1337. Food from four continents, decent prices, cosmic decor and a local clientele – what more could you want? A better name probably. Take your own booze. *Goldhawk Rd tube. Mon–Sat noon–3pm & 7.30–11pm. No cards. Inexpensive.*

Fungus Mungus, 264 Battersea Park Rd, SW11 ☎0171/924 5578. Another triumph for the Rotten Name Committee. Ramshackle hippy-dippy restaurant, with service to match, where the mainly Mediterranean food usually comes up to scratch. Book before you cross the river; growing a pointy beard is optional. *Battersea Park BR or bus #45a. Mon–Fri 6–11.30pm, Sat noon–11.30pm, Sun noon–10.30pm. No cards. Inexpensive.*

The Gate, 51 Queen Caroline St, W6 ☎0181/748 6932. Thoughtful cooking and cool, appealing surroundings make this a firm favourite with Hammersmith meat-avoiders. There's live jazz and blues at the weekend, and tables in the courtyard in summer – a good neighbourhood find. *Hammersmith tube. Mon 6–10.45pm, Tues–Fri noon–3pm & 6–10.45pm, Sat 6–10.45pm. Amex, MC, V. Inexpensive to Moderate.*

Leith's, 92 Kensington Park Rd, W11 ☎0171/229 4481. Vegetarian haute cuisine at a Michelin-starred restaurant; there's a superb, ever-changing set veggie menu (around £25 without drinks) alongside the usual carte, so you can even go with a meat-eater – at least one of you will have to have shoals of cash, though. Booking essential. *Notting Hill Gate tube. Daily 7.30–11.30pm. All cards. Expensive to Very Expensive.*

Mildred's, 58 Greek St, W1 ☎0171/494 1634. Busy, central vegetarian café-restaurant, which attracts plaudits for its varied cooking, utilizing Oriental and Mediterranean influences. It serves alcohol, vegan dishes and a decent range of desserts, too. *Tottenham Court Rd tube. Mon–Sat noon–11pm. No cards. Inexpensive.*

Vietnamese

Golden Triangle, 15 Great Newport St, WC2 ☎0171/379 6330. Pleasant, plant-strewn central Vietnamese place with amenable staff and, usually, tables to spare. The menu twists and turns from familiar items – spring rolls, deep-fried squid balls and noodles – through to more interesting Vietnamese specialities. Seafood soup "from our part of world" doesn't give away too much but it's great. *Leicester Square tube. Daily noon–3pm & 5–11pm. All cards. Inexpensive.*

Nam Bistro, 326 Upper St, N1 ☎0171/354 0851. Welcoming Islington restaurant with tasty dishes from all over Vietnam. You'll need to book on Friday and Saturday nights – the prices and late hours are popular with the local trendies. *Angel tube. Tues–Sun noon–3pm & 6pm–1am. Amex, MC, V. Inexpensive.*

Saigon, 45 Frith St, W1 ☎0171/437 7109. The Soho location means higher prices than you might feel comfortable paying, but the food is pretty good. *Leicester Square tube. Mon–Sat noon–11.30pm. All cards. Moderate to Expensive.*

Vietnamese, 34 Wardour St, W1 ☎0171/494 2592. Cheap and cheerful restaurant where your money gets you quickly delivered dishes that don't always smack of authenticity (a good half of the menu is Cantonese). You can't go far wrong with the big portions of noodle soups, though. *Leicester Square tube. Mon–Sat 11.30am–11.30pm, Sun 11am–11pm. All cards. Inexpensive.*

Budget: under £8
Inexpensive: £8–15
Moderate: £15–20
Expensive: £20–30
Very Expensive: over £30
These are per person prices for a three-course meal (or equivalent), excluding drinks and service.

RESTAURANT DIRECTORY

What follows is a directory of all the restaurants listed in this chapter, arranged by area; the areas are listed in an order that's close to the order followed in the main part of the guide. To find the review of each restaurant, just refer back to the relevant cuisine section.

Places marked ❍ are open after midnight most days of the week.

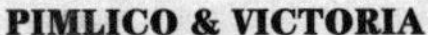

PIMLICO & VICTORIA

Chinese

Hunan, 51 Pimlico Rd.
Memories of China, 67–69 Ebury St.

French

Simply Nico, 48a Rochester Row.

Pasta

Bella Pasta, 152 Victoria St.

LEICESTER SQUARE, PICCADILLY & ST JAMES'S

American

Planet Hollywood, 13 Coventry St. ❍
Rock Island Diner, London Pavilion, Piccadilly Circus.
TGI Friday's, 22–24 Coventry St.

Argentinian

Gaucho Grill, 19 Swallow St.

Chinese

Man Fu Kung, 29 Leicester Square.

Fish

Bentley's, 11–15 Swallow St.
Cafe Fish, 39 Panton St.

Indian, Bangladeshi and Nepalese

Akash, 14–15 Irving St.
Veeraswamy, 99–101 Regent St.
Woodlands, 37 Panton St.

Japanese

Café Sogo, 39–45 Haymarket.
Suntory, 72 St James's St.

Mexican/Tex-Mex

Down Mexico Way, 25 Swallow St.

Modern British

Atlantic Bar and Grill, 20 Glasshouse St. ❍
Le Caprice, Arlington House, Arlington St.
The Criterion, 224 Piccadilly.
Quaglino's, 16 Bury St.

Pasta

Bella Pasta, 22 Leicester Square.

MAYFAIR

American

Hard Rock Café, 150 Old Park Lane. ❍

Chinese

Oriental, *The Dorchester Hotel*, 55 Park Lane.

French

Chez Nico, *Grosvenor House Hotel*, 90 Park Lane.

Malaysian/Indonesian

Satay Stick, 6 Dering St.

Middle Eastern

Al Hamra, 31–33 Shepherd Market.

Pizza

Chicago Pizza Pie Company, 17 Hanover Square.
Pizzeria Condotti, 4 Mill St.

Russian

Kaspia, 18 Bruton Place.

Swedish

The Causerie, *Claridge's Hotel*, Brook St.

Turkish

Sofra, 8 Shepherd St.

CHARLOTTE STREET/ FITZROVIA

Greek

Café Grec, 18 Charlotte St.
White Tower, 1 Percy St.

Indian, Bangladeshi and Nepalese

Mandeer, 21 Hanway Place.
Ragam, 57 Cleveland St.

Italian

Villa Carlotta, 33 Charlotte St.

Japanese

Ikkyu, 67 Tottenham Court Rd.

Pasta

Spaghetti House, 15 Goodge St.

RESTAURANT DIRECTORY continued

Spanish

Costa Dorada, 47–55 Hanway St. ❍

Sevilla Mia, 22 Hanway St.

Turkish

Efes, 80 Great Titchfield St.

Efes II, 175 Great Portland St (see *Efes* entry).

EUSTON

Indian, Bangladeshi and Nepalese

Chutneys, 124 Drummond St (see *Ravi Shankar* entry).

Ravi Shankar, 133–135 Drummond St.

Diwnana Bhel Poori House, 121 Drummond St.

Great Nepalese, 48 Eversholt St.

Haandi, 161 Drummond St.

Indian YMCA, 41 Fitzroy Square.

MARYLEBONE

Fish and chips

The Golden Hind, 73 Marylebone Lane.

Sea-Shell, 49–51 Lisson Grove.

Indian, Bangladeshi and Nepalese

Woodlands, 77 Marylebone Lane.

Malaysian/Indonesian

Malaysia Hall, 46 Bryanston Square.

Modern British

Stephen Bull, 5–7 Blandford St.

Pasta

Bella Pasta, 116 Baker St.

BLOOMSBURY

Fish and chips

North Sea Fish Restaurant, 7–8 Leigh St.

Japanese

Wagamama, 4 Streatham St.

Modern British

Museum Street Café, 47 Museum St.

Pizza

Gourmet Pizza Company, 42 New Oxford St.

Pizza Express, 30 Coptic St.

SOHO

Chinese

Panda Si Chuen, 56 Old Compton St.

Fish

Graham's, 38 Poland St.

Wheeler's 19 Old Compton St.

Fish and chips

Alpha One Fish Bar, 43 Old Compton St. ❍

French

Bistrot Bruno, 63 Frith St,.

L'Escargot, 48 Greek St.

Soho Soho, 11–13 Frith St. ❍

Le Tire Bouchon, 6 Upper James St.

Greek

Jimmy's, 23 Frith St.

Hungarian

Gay Hussar, 2 Greek St.

Indian, Bangladeshi and Nepalese

Gopal's of Soho, 12 Bateman St.

Red Fort, 77 Dean St.

Italian

Amalfi, 29–31 Old Compton St.

Italian Graffiti, 163–165 Wardour St.

Korean

Cho Won, 27 Romilly St.

Jin, 16 Bateman St.

Malaysian/Indonesian

Melati, 21 Great Windmill St.

Minang, 11 Greek St.

Middle Eastern

Olive Tree, 11 Wardour St.

La Reash Cous-Cous House, 23–24 Greek St.

Modern British

Alastair Little, 49 Frith St.

Andrew Edmunds, 46 Lexington St.

dell'Ugo, 56 Frith St.

French House, 49 Dean St.

Pizza

Kettner's, 29 Romilly St.

Lorelei, 21 Bateman St.

Pizza Express, 10 Dean St.

Swedish

Garlic & Shots, 14 Frith St.

St Moritz, 161 Wardour St.

Thai

Bahn Thai, 21a Frith St.
Chiang Mai, 48 Frith St.
Sri Siam, 14 Old Compton St.

Vegetarian

Mildred's, 58 Greek St.

CHINATOWN

Chinese

China City, White Bear Yard, 25 Lisle St.
Chuen Cheng Ku, 17 Wardour St.
Friendly Inn, 47 Gerrard St. ❍
Fung Shing, 15 Lisle St.
Hong Kong, 6–7 Lisle St,.
Jade Garden, 15 Wardour St.
Mayflower, 68–70 Shaftesbury Ave. ❍
Mr Kong, 21 Lisle St. ❍
New Loon Fung, 39 Gerrard St.
New World, 1 Gerrard Place.
Poons, 4 Leicester St & 27 Lisle St.
Tai Wing Wah, 7–9 Newport Place.
Wong Kei, 41–43 Wardour St.
Yung's, 23 Wardour St. ❍

Fish

Manzi's, 1–2 Leicester St, WC2.

Japanese

Tokyo Diner, 2 Newport Place.

Mexican/Tex-Mex

Break for the Border, 5 Goslett Yard.

Vietnamese

Saigon, 45 Frith St.
Vietnamese, 34 Wardour St.

COVENT GARDEN

African/Caribbean

Calabash, Africa Centre, 38 King St.

American

Christopher's, 18 Wellington St.
Joe Allen, 13 Exeter St. ❍
Rock Garden, The Piazza, Covent Garden. ❍
TGI Friday's, 6 Bedford St.

Belgian

Belgo Centraal, Neal St.

British

Alfred, 245 Shaftesbury Ave.
Porters, 17 Henrietta St.
Rules, 35 Maiden Lane.

Chinese

Happy Wok, 52 Floral St.
Now and Zen, 4a Upper St Martin's Lane.

Fish and chips

Rock & Sole Plaice, 47 Endell St.

French

Café des Amis du Vin, 11–14 Hanover Place.
Café Flo, 51 St Martin's Lane.
Café Pelican, 45 St Martin's Lane. ❍
L'Estaminet, 14 Garrick St.
Mon Plaisir, 21 Monmouth St.
Le Palais du Jardin, 136 Long Acre.
Tuttons Brasserie, 11–12 Russell St.

Greek

Rodos, 59 St Giles High St.

Indian, Bangladeshi and Nepalese

Strand Tandoori, 45 Bedford St.

Italian

Arts Theatre Café, 6 Great Newport St.
Bertorelli's, 44a Floral St.
Neal Street Restaurant, 26 Neal St.
Orso, 27 Wellington St.
La Quercia d'Oro, 16a Endell St.
Sol e Luna, Thomas Neal's Centre, 22 Short's Gardens.

Malaysian/Indonesian

Jakarta, 150 Shaftesbury Ave.

Mexican/Tex-Mex

Café Pacifico, 5 Langley St.
Salsa!, 96 Charing Cross Rd.❍

Modern British

The Ivy, 1 West St.

Pasta

Bella Pasta, 30 Henrietta St & 70 St Martin's Lane.
Palms, 39 King St.
Spaghetti House, 30 St Martin's Lane.

Turkish

Sofra, 36 Tavistock St.

Vietnamese

Golden Triangle, 15 Great Newport St.

RESTAURANT DIRECTORY continued

STRAND & FLEET STREET

British

The Savoy Grill, *Savoy Hotel*, The Strand.

Simpson's in the Strand, 100 The Strand.

Ye Olde Cheshire Cheese, Wine Office Court.

Indian, Bangladeshi and Nepalese

India Club, 143 Strand.

HOLBORN & CLERKENWELL

British

Quality Chop-House, 94 Farringdon Rd.

Italian

Eagle, 159 Farringdon Rd.

Peasant, 240 St John St.

Modern British

Stephen Bull's Bistro and Bar, 71 St John St.

Thai

Pu's Brasserie, 10 Gate St.

THE CITY

Chinese

Imperial City, Royal Exchange, Cornhill.

Poons in the City, 2 Minster Pavement, Mincing Lane.

EAST END

Indian and Bangladeshi

Clifton, 126 Brick Lane. ❍

Kundan Karahi, 108 Brick Lane.

Lahore Kebab House, 4 Umberston St.

Namaste, 30 Alie St.

Nazrul, 130 Brick Lane.

Shampan, 79 Brick Lane.

Jewish

Bloom's, 90 Whitechapel High St.

Thai

Thai Garden, 249 Globe Rd.

SOUTH BANK TO TOWER BRIDGE

British

Butlers Wharf Chop House, Butlers Wharf Building, Shad Thames.

French

RSJ, 13a Coin St.

Truffe Noire, 29 Tooley St.

Indian, Bangladeshi and Nepalese

Bombay Brasserie, Courtfield Close, Courtfield Rd.

Italian

Cantina del Ponte, Butlers Wharf Building, 36c Shad Thames.

Japanese

Benkei, 19 Lower Marsh.

Modern British

Fire Station, 150 Waterloo Rd.

Pizza

Gourmet Pizza Company, Gabriel's Wharf, 56 Upper Ground.

Pizzeria Castello, 20 Walworth Rd.

Spanish

Méson Don Felipe, 53 The Cut.

SOUTH KENSINGTON, KNIGHTSBRIDGE & EARL'S COURT

American

Kenny's, 2a Pond Place.

Argentinian

El Gaucho, Chelsea Farmer's Market, 125 Sydney St.

French

Bistrot 190, 190 Queen's Gate.

Cote à Cote, 74–75 Battersea Bridge Rd.

Rotisserie Jules, 6–8 Bute St.

St Quentin, 243 Brompton Rd.

Modern British

Bibendum, Michelin House, 81 Fulham Rd.

The Restaurant, *Hyde Park Hotel*, 66 Knightsbridge.

Pasta

Bella Pasta, 60 Old Brompton Rd and 155 Earl's Court Rd.

Polish

Daquise, 20 Thurloe St.

The Pilot, 14 Collingham Gardens.

Portuguese

Caravela, 39 Beauchamp Place. ❍

O Fado, 49 Beauchamp Place. ❍

Russian
Borshtch 'n Tears, 46 Beauchamp Place. ❍

Spanish
Albero & Grana, Chelsea Cloisters, 89 Sloane Ave.

KENSINGTON & HOLLAND PARK

American
Sticky Fingers, 1a Phillimore Gardens.

French
Café Flo, 127–129 Kensington Church St
Chez Moi, 1 Addison Ave.

Modern British
Boyd's, 135 Kensington Church St.
Clarke's, 124 Kensington Church St.
Kensington Place, 201 Kensington Church St.
192, 192 Kensington Park Rd.

Pasta
Palms, 3–5 Campden Hill Rd.

Polish
Wódka, 12 St Alban's Grove.

CHELSEA & FULHAM

British
Foxtrot Oscar, 79 Royal Hospital Rd.

French
Aubergine, 11 Park Walk.
Café Flo, 676 Fulham Rd.
Canteen, Unit G4, Harbour Yard, Chelsea Harbour.
La Tante Claire, 68 Royal Hospital Rd.

Indian, Bangladeshi and Nepalese
Chutney Mary, 535 King's Rd.
Planet Poppadom, 366 King's Rd.

Spanish
La Rueda, 624 King's Rd.

Thai
Blue Elephant, 4–6 Fulham Broadway. ❍

BATTERSEA, CLAPHAM & SOUTHWEST LONDON

African/Caribbean
Smokey Joe's Diner, 131 Wandsworth High St.

Indian, Bangladeshi and Nepalese
Kastoori, 188 Upper Tooting Rd.
Maharani, 117 Clapham High St.
Ma Goa, 244 Upper Richmond Rd.

Italian
Del Buongustaio, 283 Putney Bridge Rd.
Osteria Antica Bologna, 23 Northcote Rd.

Malaysian/Indonesian
Nancy Lam's, 56 Lavender Hill.

Pizza
Eco, 162 Clapham High St.

Spanish
La Rueda, 66–68 Clapham High St.

Vegetarian
Fungus Mungus, 264 Battersea Park Rd.

NOTTING HILL & BAYSWATER

Brazilian
Amazonas, 75 Westbourne Grove.

Chinese
Four Seasons, 84 Queensway.
Mandarin Kitchen, 14–16 Queensway.

Greek
Mega-Kalamaras, 76–78 Inverness Mews.
Micro-Kalamaras, 66 Inverness Mews (see entry for *Mega-Kalamaras*).

Indian, Bangladeshi and Nepalese
Khan's, 13–15 Westbourne Rd.

Japanese
Yaohan Plaza Food Court, Yaohan Plaza, 399 Edgware Rd.

Malaysian/Indonesian
Mawar, 175a Edgware Rd.

Spanish
Galicia, 323 Portobello Rd.
Méson Bilbao, 33 Malvern Rd.

Thai
Ben's Thai, *Warrington Hotel*, 93 Warrington Crescent.

RESTAURANT DIRECTORY continued

CAMDEN

African/Caribbean
Cotton's, 55 Chalk Farm Rd.

Belgian
Belgo, 72 Chalk Farm Rd.

Chinese
Cheng Du, 9 Parkway.
Feng Shang, Cumberland Basin.

French
Café Delancey, 3 Delancey St.
Camden Brasserie, 216 Camden High St.

Greek
Daphne, 83 Bayham St.
Lemonia, 89 Regent's Park Rd.
Limani, 154 Regent's Park Rd (see entry for *Lemonia*).
Nontas, 14–16 Camden High St.

Korean
Min Sok Chon, 33 Pratt St.

Malaysian/Indonesian
Bintang, 93 Kentish Town Rd.

Mexican/Tex-Mex
Arizona, 2a Jamestown Rd.

Middle Eastern
Osmani, 46 Inverness St.

Modern British
Odette's, 130 Regent's Park Rd.

Pizza
Parkway Pizzeria, 64 Parkway.

Spanish
Bar Gansa, 2 Inverness St.

HIGHBURY & ISLINGTON

Chinese
New Culture Revolution, 42 Duncan St.

Fish and chips
Upper Street Fish Shop, 324 Upper St.

French
Café Flo, 334 Upper St.

Indian, Bangladeshi and Nepalese
Indian Veg Bhel Poori House, 92–93 Chapel Market.

Italian
Casale Franco, 134–137 Upper St.

Korean
Busan, 43 Holloway Rd.

Middle Eastern
Al Alysse, 134 Upper St.

Russian
Luba's Place, 164 Essex Rd.

Thai
Tuk Tuk, 330 Upper St.

Vietnamese
Nam Bistro, 326 Upper St. ❍

HAMPSTEAD & HIGHGATE

Brazilian
Sabor do Brasil, 36 Highgate Hill.

Chinese
Vegetarian Cottage, 91 Haverstock Hill.

Czech
Czech Club, 74 West End Lane.

French
Café Flo, 205 Haverstock Hill.

Pizza
Calzone, 66 Heath St.

HACKNEY & STOKE NEWINGTON

Indian, Bangladeshi and Nepalese
Rasa, 55 Stoke Newington Church St.
Suruchi, 82 Mildmay Park.

Swedish
Anna's Place, 90 Mildmay Park.

Thai
Yum Yum, 26 Stoke Newington Church St.

Turkish
Istanbul Iskembecisi, 9 Stoke Newington Rd. ❍
Mangal, 10 Arcola St.

WAY OUT NORTH

African/Caribbean
Beewees, 96 Stroud Green Rd.

Fish
Chez Liline, 101 Stroud Green Rd.

Indian, Bangladeshi and Nepalese
Jai Krishna, 161 Stroud Green Rd.
Rani, 7 Long Lane.

RESTAURANT DIRECTORY continued

Sabras, 263 Willesden High Rd.

Polish

Magical Buska, 32 Crouch Hill.

STOCKWELL, BRIXTON & SOUTHEAST LONDON

African/Caribbean

Brixtonian, 11 Dorrell Place.

Chinese

Gracelands Palace, 881–883 Old Kent Rd.

Fish

Lobster Pot, 3 Kennington Lane.

Italian

Caffè Italia, 107 Humber Rd.

Pizza

Pizzeria Franco, 4 Market Row, Electric Lane.

Portuguese

Café Portugal, 6a Victoria House, South Lambeth Rd.

Churrasqueira, 168 Old Lambeth Rd.

Spanish

Rebato's, 169 South Lambeth Rd.

Thai

Thailand, 15 Lewisham Way.

WEST LONDON

Brazilian

Paulo's, 30 Greyhound Rd.

Chinese

Good Earth, 143 The Broadway.

Italian

River Café, Rainville Rd.

Middle Eastern

Adams Café, 77 Askew Rd.

Modern British

Brackenbury, 129–131 Brackenbury Rd.

Thai

Bedlington Cafe, 24 Fauconberg Rd.

Vegetarian

Blah Blah Blah, 78 Goldhawk Rd.

The Gate, 51 Queen Caroline St.

Pubs and Bars

Pubs & Bars

A pint costs anything from £1.50 to £2, depending on the brew and the locale of the pub.

This chapter covers pubs, bars and wine bars that are good for drinking – and, sometimes, eating – in. It doesn't include pubs and bars that are primarily music venues, which you'll find in Chapter 17, nor gay pubs and bars, which are covered in Chapter 18.

Pubs and wine bars

Pubs are one of England's great social institutions. Originating as wayfarers' hostelries and coaching inns, they have outlived the church and marketplace as the focal points of communities – London's fringe theatre, alternative comedy and live music scene is largely pub-based. At their best they can be as welcoming as the full name, "public house", suggests, offering a fine range of "real ales" and filling and inexpensive food. At their worst, they're dismal rooms with surly bar staff and rotten snacks. It pays to be picky – especially in the West End.

The great period of pub building in London was the Victorian era, to which many newly refurbished pubs also pay homage. Older style inns, with oak-beams, open fires and polished brass fittings survive here and there, but they're not a great feature of London. Nor, these days, are the old inward-looking traditions, with areas divided along class and sex lines: a "spit and sawdust" public bar for working men to bond over a pint or two, and a plusher saloon or lounge bar for couples, the middle classes and unaccompanied women. Most pubs have transformed their image over the past twenty years, welcoming a broad mix of custom to all areas.

Despite a government effort to end their monopoly, a large number of pubs are owned by, or "tied" to, the large breweries, and sell mainly their own brand of **beers** and **lagers**, along with a few "guest beers", all dispensed by the pint or half-pint.

From a beer-drinking point of view, the most interesting places are "free houses", pubs that are unattached to breweries and free to sell whatever beers they like, often including a good range of real ales (see box); they are often more characterful places, too. **Wines** sold in pubs are generally appalling and if you're after a decent bottle, you're nearly always better off in a brasserie or wine bar (covered in our *Snacks* and *Restaurants* chapters).

Pub food, on the whole, is a lunchtime affair, although pubs which put effort into their cooking are increasingly offering meals in the evening, too. The traditional image of London pub food is dire – pseudo "ploughman's lunches" of bread and cheese, or murky-looking pies and chips – but the last ten years has seen a lot of change for the better. At almost all pubs listed in this chapter you can get a palatable lunchtime meal, and at a few of them you're looking at cooking worthy of high restaurant praise. The latest fad, unthinkable a few years back, is for serving Thai food, which is suprisingly well complemented by good bitter.

Pubs & Bars

Late-night bars

For drinking beyond the standard 11pm last orders at a pub, London has a rather paltry number of **late-night drinking bars**, chiefly in Soho, Covent Garden and Notting Hill. These are very different places to your average pub, catering to a young, often somewhat cliquey crowd, with designer interiors and drinks; they're also expensive, often levying an entry charge after 11pm. We've listed the more enjoyable – while leaving the clubs, and dance places for the "Music and Nightlife" chapter, following.

The Listings

Listings below are divided according to area, following the chapters in this book, so you can tie in sights and pubs (which sometimes coincide). Each of our sections leads off with pub recommendations, followed by bars, when there are any worth a call.

Whitehall and Westminster

Adam & Eve, 81 Petty France, SW1 ☎0171/222 4575. Nice real ale pub run by *Scottish & Newcastle*, a short hike from Buckingham Palace. *St James's Park tube. Theakstons, Courage.*

Albert, 52 Victoria St, SW1 ☎0171/222 5577. Roomy High Victorian pub serving good food, including hearty breakfasts in the upstairs restaurant (Mon–Fri 7.45–10.30am). *St James's Park tube. Ruddles, Websters, Courage, Wadworth.*

Orange Brewery, 37 Pimlico Rd, SW1 ☎0171/730 5984. Pimlico may be posh, but this is a fairly down-to-earth boozer with its very own micro-brewery. *Pimlico tube.*

Paviour's Arms, Page St, SW1 ☎0171/834 2150. Untouched Art Deco pub, close to the Tate Gallery and offering Thai food. *Pimlico tube. Mon–Sat 11am–11pm, Sun 11am–4pm. Fullers and guests.*

Westminster Arms, 9 Storey's Gate, SW1 ☎0171/222 8520. Big Victorian pub, convenient for Westminster Abbey and Parliament. Popular with MPs who are called to votes by a division bell in the bar. *Westminster or St James's Park tube. Adnams, Bass, Brakspear, Theakston, Wadworth.*

Standard pub opening hours are Mon–Sat 11am–11pm and Sun 11.30am–3pm & 7–10.30pm. Our listings specify only the exceptions.

Beers

The classic English beer is **bitter**, an uncarbonated and dark beverage that should be pumped by hand from the cellar and served at room temperature. In recent years, boosted by aggressive advertising, **lager** overtook bitter in popularity, and every pub will have at least two draught lagers on offer, plus innumerable foreign bottled brands, which go in and out of fashion extremely quickly. Current favourites include *Sol* from Mexico, *Sapporo* and *Kirin* from Japan, and *Hoegaaden* from Belgium.

English beer drinkers go almost exclusively for bitter, and take the various brews extremely seriously. A moving force in this camp is **CAMRA** – the Campaign for Real Ale – who worked hard to stop local beers from death amid the big brewery takeovers of the 1970s. Some of the beer touted as good English ale is nothing of the sort (if the stuff comes out of an electric pump, it isn't the real thing), but these days even the big breweries distribute some very good beers – for example, *Directors*, produced by the giant Courage group, is a very classy strong bitter. (*Guinness*, a very dark, creamy Irish stout, is also on sale virtually everywhere, and is an exception to the high-minded objection to electrically pumped beers – though purists will tell you that the stuff the English drink does not compare with the home variety.)

Smaller operations whose fine ales are available over a wide area include *Young's* and *Fuller's* – the two main London breweries – *Wadworth's*, *Adnams*, *Greene King*, *Flowers* and *Tetley's.* Regional concoctions from other independent breweries are frequently available, too, at "free houses", and London also has a number of brewpubs, which produce their own peculiar brand on the premises, the most famous being the Firkin chain.

Wherever there are real ales available, we've listed them at the end of the entry.

Pubs & Bars

BARS

ICA Bar, 12 Carlton House Terrace (The Mall), SW1 ☎0171/930 0493. You have to be a member to drink at the ICA bar – but anyone can join, at £1.50 a day. It's a cool drinking venue, with a *noir* dress code observed by the arty crowd and cute bar staff. *Charing Cross tube. Mon noon–11pm, Tues–Sat noon–1am, Sun noon–3pm & 7–10.30pm.*

St James's, Mayfair and Marylebone

Audley, 41 Mount St, W1 ☎0171/499 1843. A grand Mayfair pub, with original Victorian burgundy plaster ceiling, chandeliers and clocks. *Green Park/Hyde Park Corner/Marble Arch tube. Courage, John Smith's.*

Barley Mow, 8 Dorset St, W1 ☎0171/935 7318. A local tucked away in the backstreets of Marylebone, it has pine, pawnbrokers' booths and serves a range of real ales. *Baker St tube. Mon–Sat 11am–11pm. Brakspear, Adnams, Tetley, Wadworth.*

Cock & Lion, 62 Wigmore St, W1 ☎0171/935 8727. Congenial pub with an old-fashioned restaurant upstairs serving

Hotel Bars

All of the larger hotels have bars open to non-residents, and many of them are spectacular (if expensive) places to sit over a cocktail. Some require a jacket and tie for men (which they will usually loan), and most have a strictly no jeans and sneakers policy. Officially, hotels can only serve drinks to non-residents during normal pub hours; at other times you may be asked (in the nicest possible way) to abstain from alcoholic beverages, or buy some food (which again won't come cheap).

Pick of the bunch – most of them in and around Mayfair – include:

Claridges, Brook St, W1 ☎0171/629 8860. The Foyer Bar is high colonial Art Deco, with Terribly English waiters, and splendid, very costly cocktails. *Bond St tube. Mon–Sat noon–11pm, Sun 11am–3pm & 7–10.30pm.*

Dorchester, Park Lane, W1 ☎0171/629 8888. You may wear the shades for the Dorchester's bar: wildly over-the-top decor, re-gilt to the highest specs for new owner, the Sultan of Brunei. Jolly good champagne cocktails at £9 a hit. *Hyde Park Corner tube. Mon–Sat 11am–midnight, Sun noon–10.30pm.*

Langham Hilton, 1 Portland Place, W1 ☎0171/636 1000. This fantastically ornate nineteenth-century hotel harbours *The Russian Bar*, a favoured BBC watering hole, replete with over 100 vodkas. *Oxford Circus tube. Mon–Thurs noon–midnight, Fri noon–1am, Sat 6pm–1am, closed Sun.*

London Hilton, Park Lane, W1 ☎0171/493 7586. The lure here is *Trader Vic's*, decked out like a film set from "South Pacific" – and that includes the waitresses. Cocktails go from £4.50. *Hyde Park Corner tube. Mon–Sat 5.30pm–1am, Sun 5.30–10.30pm.*

Hotel Russell, Russell Square, WC1 ☎0171/837 6470. This is a lot less posh – and more fun. Head for the wood-panelled *King's* or "weird" *Benjamin* bar. *Charing Cross/Embankment tube. Mon–Sat 10am–1am, Sun noon–2pm & 7–10.30pm.*

The Savoy, Strand, WC2 ☎0171/836 4343. The Art Deco Savoy hotel's American Bar is renowned for its cocktails, as it should be since you're paying upwards of £6 a throw. There's a pianist from 7 to 10pm. *Charing Cross or Embankment tube. Mon–Sat 11am–3pm & 5.30–11pm, Sun noon–3pm & 7–10.30pm.*

Waldorf Astoria, Aldwych, WC2 ☎0171/836 2400. The place to drink here is the gorgeous Palm Court – don't stop by mistake in their horrid streetside bar. The decor is a dream, there's a ritzy pianist, a (fairly) relaxed dress code (no ties needed), and nice, un-stuffy Filipino waiters. *Covent Garden tube. Daily 6–11pm.*

wholesome English food. *Oxford Circus tube. Mon–Sat noon–11pm, Sun noon–3pm & 7–10.30pm. Courage, John Smith's, Theakston.*

Ye Grapes, 16 Shepherd Market. W1 ☎0171/499 1563. Victorian free house, with good selection of beers and a real fire. George Best., the greatest footballer ever to grace these shores, is a regular. *Green Park/Hyde Park Corner tube. Boddingtons, Brakspear, Flowers, Wethered.*

Mulligans, 4 Cork St, W1 ☎0171/409 1370. A fine Irish pub with an odd mix of clientele – Cork St gallery staff and Irish lads – and the best Guinness in London. Also has a high class restaurant downstairs, with a fine Modern British cook. *Green Park/Piccadilly tube. Mon–Sat noon–11pm, Sun noon–3pm & 7–10.30pm.*

Red Lion, Duke of York St, SW1 ☎0171/930 2030. Popular little gin palace, which has preserved its classic Victorian decor. *Green Park/Piccadilly Circus tube. Mon–Sat noon–11pm. Burton, Bass, Greene King, Tetley's.*

Soho, Fitzrovia and Covent Garden

SOHO PUBS

Argyll Arms, 18 Argyll St, W1 ☎0171/734 6117. One of the pleasanter places in the immediate orbit of Oxford St, with original etched glass partitions and wood fittings. *Oxford Circus tube. Mon–Sat 11am–11pm. Everards, Greene King, Marston, Tetley's, Wadworth.*

Blue Posts, 28 Rupert St, W1 ☎0171/437 1415. A fine central Soho drinking spot, where you can usually get a seat in the upstairs bar. *Piccadilly Circus tube. Boddingtons, Flowers, Marston.*

Clachan, 34 Kingly St ☎0171/734 2659. Another good-sized pub in which to escape from the torment of Oxford St, it has a vaguely Scottish theme. *Oxford Circus tube. Mon–Sat 11am–11pm. Adnams, Bass, Greene King, Marstons, Tetley's, Wadworth.*

Coach & Horses, 29 Greek St, W1 ☎0171/437 5920. Long-standing – and, for once, little-changed – haunt of the ghosts of old Soho, *Private Eye*, nightclubbers and art students from nearby St Martin's college. Run by Norman Balon, who claims to be the rudest landlord in London. *Leicester Square tube. Burton, Dorchester, Tetley's.*

Dog & Duck, 18 Bateman St, W1 (no phone). Tiny Soho pub that retains much of its old character, beautiful Victorian tiling and mosaics, and a loyal clientele that often includes jazz musicians from nearby *Ronnie Scott's* club. *Leicester Square or Tottenham Court Rd tube.*

French House, 49 Dean St, W1 ☎0171/437 2799. The tiny French pub has been a Soho institution since Belgian Victor Berlemont bought the place shortly before the First World War. Free French and literary associations galore (p.120), half pints only at the bar (no real ale) and a fine little restaurant upstairs. *Leicester Square tube. Mon–Sat noon–11pm, Sun noon–3pm & 7–10.30pm.*

Star & Garter, Poland St, W1 (no phone). Old-fashioned pub with new-fashioned clientele, full of media types bitching about the companies they work for. *Oxford Circus tube.*

SOHO BARS

Café Boheme, 13–17 Old Compton St, W1 ☎0171/437 1503. A fairly convincing French import, with a very useful late licence. *Leicester Square tube, Mon–Sat 8am–3am, Sun 11am–11pm. Charge after 10.30pm.*

Riki-Tik, 23–24 Bateman St, W1 ☎0171/437 1977. Very trendy bar with futuristic decor and friendly staff. *Tottenham Court Rd tube. Mon–Sat 11am–1am. Charge after 11pm.*

The Edge, 11 Soho Square, W1 ☎0171/439 1313. A smartly dressed gay and straight crowd hang out at this newly expanded Soho drinking hole. *Tottenham Court Rd tube. Mon–Sat 10am–1am, Sun noon–10.30pm.*

IT Bar, 3 Panton St, SW1 ☎0171/925 0779. Small, minimalist bar, popular with Soho's clubbing crowd. *Piccadilly Circus tube. Mon–Sat noon–1am, Sun 7–11pm.*

Pubs & Bars

O Bar, 83–85 Wardour St, W1 ☎0171/437 3490. A young hetero crowd pack this place out, posing and sipping from cocktail jugs. *Piccadilly Circus tube. Mon–Sat noon–11pm, Sun 7–10.30pm.*

FITZROVIA PUBS

Bricklayers Arms, 31 Gresse St, W1 ☎0171/636 5593. Tucked away among the harsh modern buildings just off Tottenham Court Rd, this is a real gem, with a neighbourhood feel and good food. *Tottenham Court Road tube. Sam Smith's.*

Hope, 15 Tottenham St, W1 ☎0171/637 0896. Chiefly remarkbale for its sausage (veggie ones included), mash and bean lunches, provided by *Simply Sausages. Goodge St tube. Flowers, Wadsworth.*

FITZROVIA BARS

Bradley's Spanish Bar, 48 Hanway St, W1 ☎0171/636 0359. Appealingly unpretentious backstreet bar with a bizarre but faithful clientele. *Tottenham Court Rd tube. Mon–Sat 11am–11pm, closed Sun.*

Sevilla Mia, 22 Hanway St, W1 ☎0171/637 3756. Another Fitzrovia Spanish bar, and often more fun, with impromptu flamenco and a good range of tapas. *Tottenham Court Rd tube. Mon–Sat 11am–11pm, closed Sun.*

COVENT GARDEN PUBS

The Angel, 61 St Giles High St, WC2 ☎0171/240 2876. A friendly local in the centre of town. Small garden, open fires and a loyal crowd. *Tottenham Court Rd tube. Courage, Theakston, Wadworth.*

Lamb & Flag, 33 Rose St, WC2 ☎0171/497 9504. Busy and highly atmospheric pub, tucked away down an alley between Garrick Street and Floral Street, where John Dryden was attacked in 1679. *Leicester Square tube. Courage, John Smith's, Wadworth.*

Punch & Judy, 40 The Market, WC2 ☎0171/379 0923. Horribly mobbed and expensive, but unbeatable location with a balcony overlooking the Piazza – and a nice cellar bar. *Covent Garden tube. Mon–Sat 11.30am–11pm, Sun noon–3pm & 7–10.30pm. Courage, John Smith's, Theakstons.*

Round House, 1 Garrick St, WC2 ☎0171/836 9838. Popular corner pub, with drinkers happily spilling out onto the pavement in the summer months. *Leicester Square/Covent Garden tube. Marstons, Theakstons, Youngers.*

Salisbury, 90 St Martin's Lane, WC2 ☎0171/836 5863. This is one of the most beautifully preserved Victorian pubs in the capital, with cut, etched and engraved windows, bronze figures, and lincrusta ceiling. Overzealous doormen and overcrowding the only drawbacks. *Leicester Square tube. Burton, Theakston, Tetley's.*

Sun, 66 Long Acre, WC2 ☎0171/836 4520. Another reasonable Covent Garden choice, with a bustling atmosphere and fair pub grub. *Covent Garden tube. Courage, John Smith's, Ruddles, Websters.*

COVENT GARDEN BARS

Africa Centre, 38 King St, WC2 ☎0171/836 1976. Noisy, convivial basement bar, attracting Africans and Africa-philes. The beer's awful but that's missing the point. *Covent Garden tube. Mon–Sat 5.30–11pm.*

Bar Gritte, 46 The Piazza, WC2 ☎0171/240 286. Bottled beer, decent wine list and great (if cramped) roof terrace. *Covent Garden tube. Mon–Sat 11.30am–2am, Sun 11.30am–10.30pm.*

Freuds, 198 Shaftesbury Ave, WC2 ☎0171/240 9933. Designer-minimalist basement dive with pricey bottled beers and tasty bar snacks. *Tottenham Court Rd/Covent Garden tube. Mon–Sat 11am–11pm, Sun noon–11pm.*

Mars, 59 Endell St, WC2 ☎0171/240 8077. Gaudi meets Gauguin in this wonderful little designer-squat bar. It's run in very relaxed fashion and features weird bottled beers, flavoured vodkas, a mighty fine menu, and a couple of tables outside in summer. *Covent Garden tube. June–Aug Mon–Sat 5pm–midnight Sept–May Mon–Sat noon–midnight.*

Pubs & Bars

The Spot, 29 Maiden Lane, WC2 ☎0171/379 5900. Basement bar short of seats, strong on soul and jazz. *Covent Garden/Charing Cross tube. Mon–Thurs noon–midnight, Fri & Sat noon–1am, Sun noon–11pm.*

Bloomsbury

Lamb, 94 Lamb's Conduit St, WC1 ☎0171/405 0713. Pleasant pub with a marvellously well-preserved Victorian interior of mirrors, old wood and "snob" screens. *Russell Square tube. Young's.*

Museum Tavern, 49 Great Russell St, WC1 ☎0171/242 8987. Large and characterful old pub, right opposite the main entrance to the British Museum. *Tottenham Court Road/Russell Square tube. Brakspear, Courage, Greene King, John Smith's, Theakston.*

Princess Louise, 208 High Holborn, WC1 ☎0171/405 8816. Old-fashioned place, with high plasterwork ceilings, lots of glass, brass and mahogany, and a good range of real ales. *Holborn tube. Brakspear, Bass, Greene King, Theakston, Wadworth plus guest ales.*

Sun, 63 Lamb's Conduit St, WC1 ☎0171/405 8278. This place once boasted by far the widest choice of draught real ales in the entire capital. At the start of 1995 it changed hands, however, and initial reports of the refit are not encouraging. Still might be worth checking out though. *Russell Square tube.*

The Strand, Holborn and Clerkenwell

Castle, 34 Cowcross St, EC1 ☎0171/253 2892. The only pub in the country with a pawnbroker's licence. Also features delicious Thai food at lunchtimes. *Farringdon tube. Mon–Fri 11am–11pm. Bass, Young's.*

Cittie of York, 22 High Holborn, WC1 ☎0171/242 7670. Upstairs is the grand quasi-medieval wine hall, with cubicles once the preserve of lawyers and their clients; below is the cellar, perfect for savouring the distinctive Yorkshire bitter. *Chancery Lane tube. Mon–Fri 11.30am–11pm, Sat 11.30am–3pm & 5.30–11pm. Sam Smith's.*

Coal Hole, 91 Strand, WC1 ☎0171/836 7503. Former coalheavers' hang-out, next to the *Savoy* hotel. There's a nice gallery upstairs and a cellar bar down. *Charing Cross/Covent Garden tube. Mon–Sat 11am–11pm. Brakspear, Bass, Tetley's, Wadworth.*

George, 213 Strand, WC2 ☎0171/353 9238. Half-timbered inn opposite the High Court. Mood of the clientele tends to reflect how their cases are going across the road. *Temple tube. Mon–Fri 11am–11pm, Sat (summer only) 11am–2.30pm. Bass, Young's.*

Lyceum Tavern, 354 Strand, WC2 ☎0171/836 7155. A convenient place to go before and after the theatre, though it gets a few lads from across the river, too. *Charing Cross tube. Sam Smith's.*

Seckforde Arms, 34 Seckforde St, EC1 ☎0171/253 3251. A peaceful backstreet local in Clerkenwell, not far from the Green. *Farringdon tube. Mon–Sat 11am–11pm, Sun noon–4pm. Young's.*

Wellington, 351 Strand, WC2 ☎0171/836 0513. Favourite with the after-show crowds; bottled beers served at cut price during the early evening. *Covent Garden/Temple tube. Boddingtons, Courage.*

Ye Olde Mitre Tavern, 1 Ely Court, Ely Place, EC1 ☎0171/405 4751. Ancient two-bar pub, popular with City wage-slaves. Minimal pub food. *Farringdon tube. Open Mon–Fri 11am–11pm. Burtons, Tetley's.*

BARS

Gordon's, Villiers St, WC2 ☎0171/930 1408. Cave-like wine bar specializing in ports, right next door to Charing Cross station. The excellent and varied wine list, decent buffet food and genial atmosphere have made it a favourite with the local office workers. *Charing Cross/Embankment tube. Mon–Fri 11am–11pm.*

The City

FLEET STREET

Ye Olde Cheshire Cheese, Wine Office Court, off Fleet St, EC4 ☎0171/353 6170. A famous seventeenth-century watering hole, with several snug, dark panelled

Pubs & Bars

bars and real fires. Popular with tourists, but by no means exclusively so. *Temple/Blackfriars tube. Mon–Sat 11.30am–11pm, Sun noon–3pm. Sam Smith's.*

Clachan, Mitre Court, off Fleet St, EC4 ☎0171/936 2294. A small bar at ground level with largish dining hall downstairs. Stifling on hot days but you can drink outside. *Temple/Blackfriars tube. Mon–Fri 11am–11pm. Youngers.*

Old Bell Tavern, 95 Fleet St, EC4 ☎0171/583 0070. Built in 1678 by Wren as his masons' local boozer, and for years the printers' favourite. Now a listed building with characteristic triangular oak stools. *Temple/Blackfriars tube. Mon–Fri 11am–11pm. Brakspears, Marstons, Tetley's, Wadworth.* .

Ye Olde Cock Tavern, 22 Fleet St EC4. ☎0171/353 8570. A very old pub, much refurbished after an extensive fire. T. S. Eliot held regular editorial meetings for the *Criterion* here in the 1920s. It is now a legal watering hole. *Temple tube. Mon–Fri 11am–11pm. Courage.*

THE REST OF THE CITY

Blackfriar, 174 Queen Victoria St, EC4. ☎0171/236 5650. A gorgeous, utterly original pub, with Art Nouveau marble friezes of boozy monks. Handy for the City sights. *Blackfriars tube. Mon & Tues 11.30am–10pm, Wed–Fri 11.30am–11pm.*

Fox & Anchor, 115 Charterhouse St, EC1 ☎0171/253 4838. Smithfield market pub famous for its early opening hours and huge breakfasts served from 7–10.30am. *Farringdon tube. Mon–Fri 7am–8pm, Sat 8am–11pm, closed Sun. Nicholsons, Tetley's, Wadworth.*

Hamilton Hall, Liverpool St Station, EC2 ☎0171/247 3579. Cavernous, gilded, former ballroom of Great Eastern Hotel, adorned with nudes and chandeliers. Packed out with City commuters tanking up before the train home, but a great place nonetheless. *Theakstons, Younger, Courage.*

Jamaica Wine House, St Michael's Alley, EC3 ☎0171/626 9496. An old City institution tucked away down a narrow alleyway. Despite the name, this is really just a pub, divided into four large "snugs' by high wooden-panelled partitions. *Bank tube. Mon–Fri 11am–10pm. Whitbread.*

Lamb, Leadenhall Market, EC3 ☎0171/626 2454. A great pub right in the middle of Leadenhall Market, with pricey, but excellent roast beef sandwiches. *Liverpool St tube and train station. Mon–Fri 11am–9pm. Young's.*

Old King Lud, 78 Ludgate Circus, EC4 ☎0171/329 8517. A real (male) beer drinkers' pub, with 20 cask-conditioned ales on tap – try the *Old Speckled Hen. Blackfriars tube. Too many beers to mention.*

Pavilion End, 23 Watling St, EC4 ☎0171/236 6719. Creamy weatherboarding and cricket theme make for a bright and airy pub with a pleasant sun-trap terrace out back. *Mansion House tube. Mon–Fri 11.30am–10.30pm. Bass, Courage, Tetley's, Worthington.*

Pump House, 82 Fenchurch St, EC3 ☎0171/481 1163. The bar is downstairs – mind how you go – and packed with City types. Beers and food very good. *Fenchurch Street tube. Mon–Wed 11am–10.30pm, Thurs & Fri 11am–11.30pm. Bass, Hancock, Young's plus guests.*

Sea Horse, 64 Queen Victoria St, EC4 ☎0171/248 5275. Cosy pub which proclaims itself "One of the nicest pubs in the City." Judge for yourself. *Mansion House tube. Mon 11am–10pm, Tues–Fri 11am–11pm. Courage, John Smiths, Theakston.*

Viaduct Tavern, 126 Newgate St, EC1 ☎0171/606 8476. Glorious gin palace built in 1869 opposite what was then Newgate Prison and is now the Old Bailey, its walls adorned with oils of faded ladies representing Commerce, Agriculture and the Arts. *St Paul's tube. Mon–Fri 11am–11pm, Sat noon–3pm & 7–11pm, Sun noon–3pm & 7–10.30pm.*

Ye Olde Watling, 29 Watling St, EC4 ☎0171/248 6235. Low oak-beamed ceiling and dark wooden-panelled interior, rebuilt by Wren as an office and inn for the St Paul's workmen. *Mansion House tube. Mon–Fri 11am–10pm. Greene King, Wadworth, Young's.*

The East End and Docklands

WHITECHAPEL/MILE END

Hoop & Grapes, 47 Aldgate High St, EC3 ☎0171/480 5739. A very old pub before the developers got at it, but the beer is good, the food is quite passable, and it's roomy. *Aldgate tube. Mon–Wed 11am–10pm, Thurs & Fri 11am–11pm, Sun noon–3pm. Bass.*

Lord Rodney's Head, 285 Whitechapel Rd ☎0171/247 9795. Well placed in the middle of Whitechapel Market, this is a surprisingly pleasant East End pub. *Whitechapel tube.*

Royal Cricketers, 211 Old Ford Rd, E2 ☎0181/980 3259. Eighteenth-century canalside pub overlooking Victoria Park. *Bus #277.* Mon–Fri 11am–3pm & 5.30–11pm, Sat 11am–3pm & 7–11pm, Sun noon–3pm & 7–10.30pm. *Boddingtons, Wethered.*

HACKNEY/STOKE NEWINGTON

Dove, 24 Broadway Market, E8 ☎0171/275 7617. A pub almost worth venturing into Hackney for: friendly publicans, great food, satellite TV, board games and even a café out back. *Bus #6, #55, #106, #236, #253. Flowers, Boddingtons, Budvar, Theakston.*

Falcon & Firkin, 360 Victoria Park Rd, E9 ☎0181/985 0693. Another Firkin great pub (as they say) on the edge of Victoria Park, with a children's play area indoors and its own Hackney brew. *Bus #6, #30, #277. Mon–Sat noon–11pm, Sun noon–3pm & 7–10.30pm. Firkin beers.*

Magpie & Stump, 132 Stoke Newington Church St, N16 ☎0171/254 0959. The best pub on Church St – good pub meals downstairs and a superlative restaurant up top. *Bus #73. Mon–Sat noon–11pm, Sun noon–3pm & 7–10.30pm. Fuller's, Ruddles.*

Prince George, 40 Parkholme Rd, E8 ☎0171/254 6060. One of Hackney's finest pubs, tucked away in the back streets off Dalston Lane. Great Sunday lunches and prawns at the bar. *Bus #38. Boddingtons, Brakspears, Flowers, Greene King, Marstons, Young's.*

DOCKLANDS

Barley Mow, Narrow St, E14 ☎0171/265 8931. Decor and food are entirely unremarkable but the riverside position is hard to beat, right on a U-bend in the Thames. *Limehouse DLR.. Tetley's.*

Dickens Inn, St Katherine's Way, E1 ☎0171/488 1226. Eighteenth-century timber-framed warehouse transported on wheels from its original site. A remarkable building, but very firmly on the tourist trail. *Tower Hill tube. Adnams, Courage, Wadworth.*

Grapes, 76 Narrow St, E13 ☎0171/987 4396. The Grapes' fame is assured thanks to a mention in Dickens' *Our Mutual Friend*; it has a riverside balcony out back and fine fish in the restaurant upstairs. *Westferry DLR. Burton, Tetley's.*

Henry Addington, 20–28 MacKenzie Walk, E14 ☎0171/512 9022. Named after the Prime Minister who sanctioned the original Canary Wharf, this is a pub built on almost as grand a scale as the present office developments; it has a nice dockside terrace. *Canary Wharf DLR. Bass, Fuller's, Stones, Speckled Hen.*

The House They Left Behind, 27 Ropemakers Fields, E14 ☎0171/538 5102. Lacking the river views of its nearby competitors, this Victorian relic makes up for it with a homely feel and friendly bar staff. *Westferry DLR. Bass, Websters, Courage.*

Prospect of Whitby, 57 Wapping Wall, E1 ☎0171/481 1317. Flagstone floor, cobbled courtyard and river views. *Wapping tube. Mon–Sat 11.30am–3pm & 5.30–11pm, Sun noon–3pm & 7–10.30pm. Ruddles, Courage, Websters.*

Town of Ramsgate, Wapping High St, E1 ☎0171/488 2685. Dark, narrow medieval pub located by Wapping Old Stairs which once led down to Execution Dock. Captain Blood was discovered here with the crown jewels under his cloak, "Hanging" Judge Jeffreys was arrested trying to flee, and Admiral Bligh and Fletcher Christian were regular drinking partners in pre-mutiny days. *Wapping tube. Bass, Young's plus guests.*

Pubs & Bars

Riverside, canalside and dockland pubs

In summer, the most popular pubs in London are those with a **riverside, canalside or dockland view**. You can sit outside at any of the places listed below; see main text for reviews. Another option is to drink on one of the old **naval and merchant boats**, moored on the north bank of the Thames between Westminster and Blackfriars bridges: there's little to distinguish these, so stroll down and take your pick.

East End and Docklands
Barley Mow
Grapes
Herny Addington
Prospect of Whitby
Royal Cricketers
Town of Ramsgate

Lambeth and Southwark
Anchor
Angel
Founders Arms
Mayflower

Greenwich
Cutty Sark
Trafalgar Tavern

Chiswick to Hammersmith
Black Lion
Blue Anchor
Dove

Richmond and Twickenham
Barmy Arms
Fox and Grapes
Slug and Lettuce
White Cross Hotel

Lambeth and Southwark

WATERLOO

Founders Arms, 52 Hopton St, SE1 ☎0171/928 2899. A modern pub but right by the river, and with outside tables and great views across to the City. *Blackfriars tube. Young's.*

Hole in the Wall, 5 Mepham St, SE1 ☎0171/928 6196. Underneath the arches near Waterloo station, with good pub grub and a wide range of ales from *Godson-Chudley. Waterloo tube/Waterloo East train station. Ruddles, Young's and guest beers.*

National Film Theatre Bar, South Bank, SE1 ☎0171/928 3535. The only riverfront bar on the South Bank between Westminster and Blackfriars bridges – which is a scandal, really, considering the views. Lots of outside seating and a congenial crowd. *Waterloo tube.*

Wellington Tavern, 81–83 Waterloo Rd, SE1 ☎0171/928 6083. Perfectly ordinary real ale pub, convenient for South Bank, but chiefly remarkable every other Friday when deaf drinkers from all over meet up for a raucous evening of sign language. *Waterloo tube. Adnams, Boddingtons, Ruddles, Young's plus guests.*

SOUTHWARK & BERMONDSEY

Anchor, 1 Bankside, SE1 ☎0171/407 1577. Large, yuppified old pub (with restaurant) in the heart of the old warehouse area near Southwark Bridge. Good for outside drinking by the river. *London Bridge tube/train station. Adnams, Courage, John Smith's, Ruddles.*

Anchor Tap, Horseleydown Lane, SE21 ☎0171/403 0105. The former tap (workers' pub) of the old Anchor brewery – itself now converted to yuppie flats. A nice place, though, and with a surprisingly un-yuppie clientele for these parts. *Tower Hill tube. Sam Smith's.*

Angel, 101 Bermondsey Wall East, SE16 ☎0171/237 3608. Ancient and enjoyable riverside inn, stranded in no-man's-land between Bermondsey and Rotherhithe. Bob Hoskins got blown up here in "The Long Good Friday". *Rotherhithe tube. Mon–Sat 11am–3pm & 5.30–11pm, Sun 12.30–3pm & 7–10.30pm. Courage, Websters.*

Pubs & Bars

George Inn, 77 Borough High St, SE1 ☎0171/407 2056. London's only surviving coaching inn, dating from the seventeenth century and now owned by the National Trust. *Borough/London Bridge tube. Boddingtons, Flowers.*

Market Porter, 9 Stoney St, SE1 ☎0171/407 2495. Busy semicircular pub with early opening hours for workers at the Borough Market and a goodly range of ales. *London Bridge tube. Boddingtons, Greene King, Young's.*

Mayflower, 117 Rotherhithe St, SE16 ☎0171/237 4088. Steeped in history (no prizes for guessing why) in the heart of old Rotherhithe, with a good view out onto the Thames. *Rotherhithe tube. Greene King, Bass.*

Hyde Park, Kensington, Chelsea and Notting Hill

BELGRAVIA

Antelope, 22 Eaton Terrace, SW1 ☎0171/730 7781. Old-fashioned posh pub that predates Belgravia itself; high-class pub food downstairs, real restaurant upstairs. *Sloane Square tube. Adnams, Tetley's plus guests.*

Grenadier, 18 Wilton Row, SW1 ☎0171/235 3074. Wellington's local (his horse block survives outside) and his officers' mess; the original pewter bar survives, the Bloody Marys are special. *Hyde Park Corner tube. Mon–Sat noon–3pm & 5–11pm, Sun noon–3pm & 7–10.30pm. Courage, John Smith's.*

Star Tavern, 6 Belgrave Mews West, SW1 ☎0171/235 3019. Two-storey mews pub, built for the large local servant population. Fine *Fuller's* beer and very classy food. *Knightsbridge tube. Mon–Thurs 11.30am–3pm & 5–11pm, Fri & Sat 11am–11pm, Sun noon–3pm & 7–10.30pm. Fuller's.*

SOUTH KENSINGTON & CHELSEA

Bunch of Grapes, 207 Brompton Rd, SW3 ☎0171/589 4944. This High Victorian pub, complete with snob screens, is the perfect place for a post-museum pint. *Knightsbridge/South Kensington tube. Courage, John Smith's.*

Chelsea Potter, 119 King's Rd, SW3 ☎0171/352 9479. This is the only remotely decent pub actually on the King's Rd, and it has tables outside in summer. *Sloane Square tube.*

Enterprise, 35 Walton St, SW3 ☎0171/584 3148. In keeping with the neighbourhood, this is no ordinary pub – white tablecloths, fresh flowers, ruched curtains, expensive drink and very posh food. Even Princess Di has been known to sink a half here. *South Kensington/Knightsbridge tube. Mon–Sat noon–3.30pm & 5.30–11pm, Sun noon–3pm & 7–10.30pm.*

Front Page, 35 Old Church St, SW3 ☎0171/352 2908. Centre of boho Chelsea and infinitely preferable to anything on offer on the King's Rd. *Sloane Square tube. Mon–Sat 11am–3pm & 5.30–11pm, Sun noon–3pm & 7–10pm. Boddingtons, John Smith's, Ruddles, Wadworth.*

NOTTING HILL PUBS

Churchill Arms, 119 Kensington Church St, W8 ☎0171/727 4242. A fine local with excellent Thai food served (except Mon) in the butterfly-bedecked conservatory. *Notting Hill Gate tube. Fuller's.*

Duke of Wellington (Finch's), 179 Portobello Rd, W11 ☎0171/727 6727. One of Henry Hobson Finch's wonderful chain of Victorian pubs, all now owned by Young's, but still known locally as Finch's. *Ladbroke Grove tube. Young's.*

Frog and Firkin, 41 Tavistock Crescent ☎0171/727 9250. Another of the excellent Firkin chain of pubs; it is handy for Portobello Market and is decorated with an impressive array of hats. *Westbourne Park tube. Firkin beers.*

Windsor Castle, 114 Campden Hill Rd, W8 ☎0171/727 8491. Posh, snug, eighteenth-century "country pub" with low ceilings and posh nosh, and a small garden out back. *Notting Hill Gate tube. Adnams, Bass.*

NOTTING HILL BARS

Beach Blanket Babylon, 45 Ledbury Rd, W11 ☎0171/229 2907. Worth a visit if only for the freaked-out decor and the

Pubs & Bars

beautiful W11 types who frequent it. *Notting Hill tube. Daily noon–11pm.*

Ground Floor, 186 Portobello Rd, W11 ☎0171/243 8701. Another funked-out freaked-out Portobello pub conversion, with DJs, a dance floor and very few seats. *Ladbroke Grove tube. Mon–Sat noon–11pm, Sun 7–10.30pm.*

Market Bar, 24a Portobello Rd, W11 ☎0171/229 6472. Pub converted by BBB (see above) into a bar/restaurant, with gilded mirrors and weird *objets* – all very Notting Hill. Ladbroke Grove tube. *Mon–Thurs noon–11pm, Fri–Sun 11am–midnight.*

Mas Café, 6 All Saints' Rd, W11 ☎0171/243 0969. Laid-back, licensed and located on Notting Hill's "front line", a pre-clubbing classic. *Ladbroke Grove tube. Mon–Sat 6pm–1am, Sun 7pm–11pm.*

Paradise by Way of Kensal Green, 19 Kilburn Lane, W10 ☎0181/969 0098. Out-of-the-way Bohemian bar, convenient for the local *Virgin Records* crowd, stuffed full of art, and not far from Kensal Green cemetery. *Kensal Green tube/Kensal Rise train station. Mon–Thurs 5–11pm, Fri–Sun 5pm–midnight.*

North London

LITTLE VENICE & ST JOHN'S WOOD

Crocker's Folly, 24 Aberdeen Place, NW8 ☎0171/286 6608. Gloriously over-the-top Victorian pub with oodles of marble and mahogany and coffered ceilings, built as a railway hotel by Frank Crocker, who committed suicide when an alternative location was announced for Marylebone Station. *Warwick Avenue/Edgware Road tube. Adnams, Brakspear, Bass, Courage, Greene King, Theakston, Wadworth.*

Prince Alfred, Formosa Street, W9 ☎0171/286 3027. Another fantastic period-piece Victorian pub with all its original 1862 fittings intact, right down to the glazed partitions, once a common feature of all pubs. *Warwick Avenue tube. Mon–Sat noon–11pm, Sun noon–3pm & 7–10.30pm. Burton, Tetley's, Young's.*

Warrington, 93 Warrington Crescent, W9 ☎0171/286 2929. Yet another architectural gem – this time flamboyant Art Nouveau – in an area replete with them. Excellent Thai restaurant upstairs. *Warwick Avenue/Maida Vale tube. Brakspear, Fullers, Ruddles, Young's.*

CAMDEN

Crown & Goose, 100 Arlington St, NW1 ☎0171/485 2342. Laid-back cross between a pub and a wine bar, a block away from the High Street and not too badly mobbed even during the market. Food's a bit special, too. *Camden Town tube. Fullers, Websters.*

Fusilier & Firkin, 7–8 Chalk Farm Rd, NW1 ☎0171/485 7858. Another Firkin pub, right opposite Camden Lock market. Live music on Sat afternoon, and heaving with people all weekend. *Camden Town tube. Mon–Thurs noon–11pm, Fri noon–midnight, Sat 11am–midnight, Sun noon–3pm & 4–10.30pm. Firkin beers.*

Hawley Arms, 2 Castlehaven Rd, NW1 ☎0171/485 2855. A bare-boards favourite with Camden stallholders, crusties and bikers. *Camden Town tube. Mon 6–11pm, Tues–Sat noon–11pm, Sun noon–3pm & 7–10.30pm.*

Lansdowne, 90 Gloucester Ave, NW1 ☎0171/483 0409. Big, bare-boarded minimalist pub with comfy sofas, over towards elegant Primrose Hill. Pricey, tasty food. *Chalk Farm tube. Closed Mon lunch. Bass, Tolly Cobbold.*

ISLINGTON

Camden Head, 2 Camden Walk, N1 ☎0171/359 0851. Confusingly not in Camden at all, but in the midst of Islington's antique market. The pub itself is something of an antique, with engraved glass fittings and mirrors. *Angel tube. Theakston, Younger.*

Island Queen, 87 Noel Rd, N1 ☎0171/226 5507. Appropriately enough this was Joe Orton's local. It's a lot stranger now thanks to the giant papier-maché figures suspended from the ceiling. *Angel tube. Mon–Thurs noon–3pm & 5–11pm, Fri & Sat noon–11pm, Sun noon–3pm & 7–10.30pm. Bass, Young's.*

Pubs & Bars

King's Head, 115 Upper St, N1 ☎0171/226 1916. Busy theatre pub in the heart of Islington with regular live music, a useful late licence, and a bizarre affectation of quoting prices in pre-decimal money. *Angel tube. Mon–Sat 11am–midnight, Sun noon–3pm & 7–10.30pm. Adnams, Burton, Benskins.*

Minogue's, 80 Liverpool Rd, N1 ☎0171/354 4440. One of North London's most enjoyable Irish pubs, with faultless Guinness and live music at weekends. Decent bar food and a pricier restaurant if you want the full business. *Angel tube. Mon–Sat noon–11pm, Sun noon–3pm & 7–10.30pm. Courage, Fuller's.*

Old Queen's Head, 44 Essex Road, N1 ☎0171/354 9273. Currently *the* trendy pub in Islington, with cool minimalist decor and an original Elizabethan fireplace. Go there for lunch for the excellent Med/Thai food, or early evening before the crowds. *Angel tube. Mon–Sat noon–11pm, Sun normal hours. Courage, Budvar.*

Old Red Lion, 418 St John St, EC1 ☎0171/837 7816. Cosy plush red theatre pub and a useful pre-Sadlers Wells watering hole. *Angel tube. Mon–Fri 11.30am–3pm & 5.30–11pm, Sat 11am–3pm & 7–11pm, Sun noon–3pm & 7–10.30pm. Bass, Flowers.*

HAMPSTEAD & HIGHGATE

Flask, 14 Flask Walk, NW3 ☎0171/435 4580. Convivial Hampstead local, which retains its original Victorian snob screen, serving good food and real ale. *Hampstead tube. Young's.*

Flask, 77 Highgate West Hill, N6 ☎0181/340 7260. Idyllically situated at the heart of Highgate village green, with a rambling low-ceilinged interior and a summer terrace. *Highgate tube. Young's, Burton, Tetley's.*

Holly Bush, 22 Holy Mount, NW3 ☎0171/435 2892. A lovely old gas-lit pub, tucked away in the steep backstreets of Hampstead Village. *Hampstead tube. Mon–Fri 11am–3pm & 5.30–11pm, Sat 6–11pm, Sun noon–3pm & 7–10.30pm. Benskins, Burtons, Tetley's.*

Jack Straw's Castle, North End Way, NW3 ☎0171/435 8885. Named after the Peasants' Revolt leader who was executed outside the pub, the present building is a 1960 pastiche, popular with heath-walking types. *Hampstead tube. Bass, Fuller's.*

Old Bull & Bush, North End Rd, NW3 ☎0181/455 3685. Described by Gainsborough as "a delightful little snuggery", made famous by the music hall song, but sadly less remarkable nowadays. *Golders Green tube. Burton, Tetley's.*

Spaniard's Inn, Spaniards Rd, NW3 ☎0181/455 3276. Big sixteenth-century coaching inn, frequented by everyone from Dick Turpin to John Keats. Aviary, pergola and roses in the garden. *Hampstead/Golders Green tube. Bass, Fuller's, Worthington.*

Brixton and Southeast London

BRIXTON

Hope & Anchor, 123 Acre Lane, SW2 ☎0171/274 1787. A very pleasant local (not a phrase you'd use about most pubs in central Brixton), with great beer and food and a kids' play area in the back garden. *Brixton tube. Bass, Fuller's.*

Prince Albert, 418 Coldharbour Lane, SW9 ☎0171/274 3771. Just around the corner from the Ritzy cinema. Effortlessly hip, full of bright young things on their way to The Fridge nightclub across the way. *Brixton tube. Boddingtons, Flowers, Wethered.*

Trinity Arms, Trinity Gardens, SW2 ☎0171/274 4544. Brixton's most attractive pub, hidden in the backstreets off Acre Lane. Crowds spill out into the nearby square in summer. *Brixton tube. Young's.*

DULWICH

Crown & Greyhound, 73 Dulwich Village, SE21 ☎0181/693 2466. Grandiose Victorian pub with ornate plasterwork ceiling and a nice summer beer garden. Dead convenient for the Picture Gallery. *North Dulwich train station. Mon–Thurs 11am–3.30pm & 5.30–11pm, Fri & Sat 11am–11pm, Sun noon–3pm & 7–10.30pm. Burton, Tetley's, Young's.*

Pubs & Bars

GREENWICH

Cutty Sark, Lassell St, SE10 ☎0181/858 3146. The nicest riverside pub in Greenwich – a sixteenth-century building, yet much less touristy than the *Trafalgar Tavern* (it's a couple of minutes walk further on, following the river). *Maze Hill train station. Bass, Charrington, Worthington.*

Richard I, Royal Hill, SE10 ☎0181/692 2996. Popular Greenwich local tucked away off the main drag. Good beer and a garden make it an ideal post-market retreat – and if it's too crowded the *Fox & Hounds* next door is good too. *Greenwich train station. Young's.*

Trafalgar Tavern, Park Row, SE10 ☎0181/858 2437. Great riverside position and a mention in Dickens' *Mutual Friend* have made this Regency-style inn a firm tourist favourite. Good whitebait and other snacks. *Maze Hill train station. Courage, John Smith's, Ruddles.*

BLACKHEATH

Hare & Billet, 1a Eliot Cottages, SE3 ☎0181/852 2352. A small heathside pub with drinkers drifting outside in summer and cut-price four-pint jugs on offer. *Blackheath BR. Too many beers to mention.*

Princess of Wales, 1a Montpelier Row, SE3 ☎0181/852 6881. Another old heathside pub, on a fine Georgian terrace. Extremely popular in summer when it's hard to move on the grass outside. *Blackheath BR. Bass, Fuller's, Wadworth.*

Chiswick to Windsor

HAMMERSMITH AND CHISWICK

Black Lion, 2 South Black Lion Lane, W6 ☎0181/748 7056. Slightly set back from the river, with an indoor skittle alley, and a bouncy castle in summer. *Stamford Brook/ Ravenscourt Pk tube. Theakstons, Courage.*

Blue Anchor, 13 Lower Mall, W6 ☎0181/ 748 5774. First of Hammersmith's riverside pubs, with a boaty theme and a beautiful pewter bar; most people sit outside and enjoy the river though. *Hammersmith tube. Wadworth.*

Dove, 19 Upper Mall, W6 ☎0181/748 5405. Old, old riverside pub with literary associations (see p.362) and the smallest back bar in the UK (4ft x 7ft). *Ravenscourt Pk tube. Fuller's.*

WIMBLEDON

Fox & Grapes, Camp Rd, SW19 ☎0181/ 946 5599. Right on the edge of Wimbledon Common, great in summer when you can sit outside on the grass. *Wimbledon tube. Courage, John Smith's.*

RICHMOND AND TWICKENHAM

Barmy Arms, Riverside, Twickenham ☎0181/892 0863. A converted fifteenth-century school building overlooking Eel Pie Island. *Twickenham train station. Courage.*

Slug & Lettuce, Water Lane, Richmond ☎0181/948 7733. Less character, but much better food than its rivals on the Richmond Riverside. *Richmond tube. Courage.*

White Cross Hotel, Water Lane, Richmond ☎0181/940 6844. Closer to the river than its rivals, with a garden out back and average pub food. *Richmond tube. Young's.*

Live Music and Clubs

On any night of the week London offers a bewildering range of places to go after dark – to hear bands, dance or generally club. The live **music** scene is amazingly diverse, encompassing all variations of **rock music**, from big names on tour at the city's main venues, through to a network of indie and pub bands in more immediate surroundings. There's a fair slice of **world music**, too, especially African, Latin and Caribbean bands, many of whom are based in London, and a scattering of clubs and pubs devoted to **Irish music** and **English roots**. London's **jazz clubs** aren't on a par with the big American cities but there's a highly individual scene of home-based artists, which is supplemented by top-name visiting players.

The rise of danceable **ambient and techno** sounds has meant that many venues once exclusively used by performing bands now pepper the week with club nights, and you often find dance sessions starting as soon as the band's stopped playing, to make the most of the extended drinking hours granted to clubs. Bear in mind, then, that there's an overlap between "live music venues" and "clubs" in the listings below; we've indicated which places serve a double function.

The dance and club scene is, of course, in pretty much constant flux, with the hottest items remaining so for just a brief season. The **listings magazine** *Time Out* gives details of prices and access, plus previews and reviews, but many of the best club events are one-offs that rely on word-of-mouth or mailing lists for publicity. If you want to know what's happening, before it happens, check dance magazines such as *DJ* or *Mixmag*, and pick up the flyers that litter the counters of Soho record shops such as *Black Market* at 25 D'Arblay Street, *Downtown* at 94 Dean Street or *Quaff* at 2 Silver Place.

Note that exclusively gay clubs and discos are covered in Chapter 18.

Live music

Major bands on world tours always stop off in London, despite there being no decent venue for the biggest names to play: Wembley Arena and Earl's Court have all the atmosphere of a shopping mall, while the Royal Albert Hall is far too decorous. But London is hard to beat for its musical mix: whether you're into **jazz**, **indie rock**, **R&B**, **blues or world music** you'll find something worth hearing on almost any night of the week. Entry prices for gigs run from a couple of pounds for an unknown band thrashing it out in a pub to around £30 for the likes of U2, but £10–15 is the average price for a good night out – not counting expenses at the bar.

The mega-venues

Earl's Court, Warwick Rd, SW5 ☎0171/385 1200. Bands like Pink Floyd play here on their world tours; most smaller outfits would have difficulty filling this soulless hall. *Earl's Court tube.*

Live Music and Clubs

Hammersmith Apollo, Queen Caroline Street, W6 ☎0181/741 4868. A cavernous, theatre-style venue which tends to put on safe mainstream bands. *Hammersmith tube.*

Royal Albert Hall, Kensington Gore, SW7 ☎0171/589 8212. Colosssal Victorian concert hall, visited by the likes of Eric Clapton and Luther Vandross from time to time. *South Kensington tube.*

Wembley Arena, Empire Way, Middlesex ☎0181/900 1234. The main indoor venue for megabands. Rip-off ticket, snack and souvenir prices, poor sound quality and a severe shortage of atmosphere make for a generally disappointing experience. *Wembley Park or Wembley Central tube.*

Wembley Stadium, Empire Way, Middlesex ☎0181/900 1234. Some of the world's most famous bands have played this massive football stadium, but it's not much fun for the punter – the tickets cost a fortune, the band is a distant speck, the sound disappears into the sky, and there's a good chance of getting wet and cold. *Wembley Park or Wembley Central tube.*

Cooler general venues

Academy, 211 Stockwell Rd, SW9 ☎0171/924 9999. This refurbished Victorian hall can hold 4000 and usually does, but manages to seem small and friendly, probably because no one is forced to sit down. Hosts mainly mid-league bands, and has great club nights too. *Brixton tube.*

Astoria, 157 Charing Cross Rd, W1 ☎0171/434 0403. One of London's best venues – a large, balconied one-time theatre that has bands usually from Monday to Thursday. More adventurous than most other big venues. *Tottenham Court Road tube.*

The Forum, 9–17 Highgate Rd, NW5 ☎0171/284 2200. Formerly the much-loved Town & Country Club, this is perhaps the capital's best medium-sized venue – large enough to attract established bands, but also a prime spot for newer talent. *Kentish Town tube.*

The Grand, Clapham Junction, St Johns Hill, SW11 ☎0171/738 9000. Another grand old theatre, now exclusively a rock venue. Good acoustics and not so big that the band gets lost. *Clapham Junction BR from Waterloo or Victoria.*

London Palladium, 8 Argyll St, W1 ☎0171/494 5020. Crowd-pulling acts (Lou Reed, Elvis Costello) very occasionally play here. *Oxford Circus tube.*

The Marquee, 105 Charing Cross Rd, WC2 ☎0171/437 6603. Though relocated from the Wardour Street site where the Rolling Stones and innumerable others made their names, this is still one of London's top venues for up-and-coming rock and indie bands. Also holds club nights. *Leicester Square or Tottenham Court Road tube.*

Rock and blues clubs and pubs

Amersham Arms, 388 New Cross Rd, SE14 ☎0181/694 8992. Students from nearby Goldsmith's College pack out this indie-oriented venue. *New Cross tube.*

Borderline, Orange Yard, off Manette Street, W1 ☎0171/734 2095. Intimate basement joint with diverse musical policy. Good place to catch new bands, although big ones (REM on one occasion) sometimes turn up under a pseudonym. Also has club nights. *Tottenham Court Road tube.*

Bull & Gate, 389 Kentish Town Rd, NW5 ☎0171/485 5358. Basic pub venue for obscure indie bands. *Kentish Town tube.*

Dover Street Wine Bar, 8–9 Dover St, W1 ☎0171/629 9813. An enjoyable, central brasserie with blues, R&B, jazz and soul bands. *Green Park tube.*

Dublin Castle, 94 Parkway, NW1 ☎0171/485 1773. Music pub with a diverse booking policy. *Camden Town tube.*

The Falcon, 234 Royal College St, NW1 ☎0171/485 3834. Grubby pub showcasing loud indie bands. *Camden Town tube.*

Fusilier and Firkin, 7–8 Chalk Farm Rd, NW1 ☎0171/485 7858. Chock-full on Camden market days, this is often good for R&B. *Chalk Farm tube.*

Live Music and Clubs

The Garage, 20 Highbury Corner, N1 ☎0171/ 607 1818. Mainly rock bands, but with the occasional excursion into jazz. *Highbury & Islington tube.*

Half Moon Putney, 93 Lower Richmond Rd, SW15 ☎0181/780 9383. Well-respected pub venue – good for blues and rock. *Putney Bridge tube.*

The Mean Fiddler, 24–28a Harlesden High St, NW10 ☎0181/961 5490. An excellent if rather distant small venue with a main hall and smaller acoustic room. The music veers from rock to world to folk to soul (and even, occasionally, gospel). Good sound. *Willesden Junction tube.*

Powerhaus, 1 Liverpool Rd, N1 ☎0171/ 837 3218. Under a variety of names this has been a venue for small and rising acts for over a decade. Indie bands every night followed by a club. *Angel tube.*

Roadhouse, Jubilee Hall, 35 The Piazza, Covent Garden, WC2 ☎0171/240 6001. American food, fifties American decor and a line-up of mainly blues and rock'n'roll bands performing to an older, nostalgic crowd. *Covent Garden tube.*

Robey, 240 Seven Sisters Road, N4 ☎0171/263 4581. Cavernous, dingy pub-club; something of a North London institution, but with an atmosphere that's a bit aggressive for some tastes. *Finsbury Park tube.*

Station Tavern, 41 Bramley Rd, W10 ☎0171/727 4053. Arguably London's best blues venue. *Latimer Road tube.*

Swan, 1 Fulham Broadway, SW6 ☎0171/ 385 1840. Rock'n'roll pub. *Fulham Broadway tube.*

Underworld, 174 Camden High St, NW1 ☎0171/482 1932. This labyrinthine venue is good for new bands and has sporadic club nights. *Camden Town tube.*

The Venue, 2a Clifton Rise, New Cross, SE14 ☎0181/692 4077. Indie bands on a tiny stage, with a club afterwards. *New Cross tube or BR from Charing Cross.*

Jazz

Bass Clef, 35 Coronet St, off Hoxton Square, N1 ☎0171/729 2440 or 2476. Sweaty venue with excellent live jazz, plus African and Latin nights. *Old Street tube.*

Bull's Head Barnes, Barnes Bridge, SW13 ☎0181/876 5241. This riverside alehouse attracts Britain's finest jazz musicians. It's way out of town, but worth it. *Hammersmith tube, then bus #9, or Barnes Bridge BR from Waterloo.*

Café Club, 62 Union St, SE1 ☎0171/378 1988. A small but immensely popular place with a sliding scale of entry charges; you pay less if you don't actually want the band in your line of vision. *London Bridge or Borough tube.*

Dingwalls (Camden Jongleurs), Camden Lock, NW1 ☎0171/267 1999. This comedy venue becomes a top-ranking jazz club on Mondays and Wednesdays. *Camden Town tube.*

Jazz Café, 5 Parkway, NW1 ☎0171/916 6000. Slick modern venue with an adventurous booking policy exploring Latin, rap and other unlikely avenues. Die-hard trad jazz fans won't be happy. *Camden Town tube.*

The Orange, 3 North End Crescent, W14 ☎0171/371 4317. Pub-like venue for serious-minded jazz-funkers. There are also club nights. *West Kensington tube.*

Pizza Express, 10 Dean St, W1 ☎0171/437 9595. Enjoy a good pizza, then listen to the resident band or highly skilled guest players. *Tottenham Court Road tube.*

Pizza On the Park, 11 Knightsbridge, Hyde Park Corner, SW1 ☎0171/235 5273. Spacious restaurant with upmarket ambience and mainstream jazz acts. *Hyde Park Corner tube.*

Ronnie Scott's, 47 Frith St, W1V ☎0171/ 439 0747. The most famous jazz club in London: small, smoky and you have to endure Ronnie's jokes (the same ones, each night). Nonetheless, it's still the place for top-line names, who play two sets – one at around 10pm, the other after midnight. Book a table, or you'll have to stand. *Leicester Square tube.*

South Bank Centre (see World Music, below). Hosts an annual jazz festival, as well as big names like Keith Jarrett.

Live Music and Clubs

Vortex, Stoke Newington Church Street, N16 ☎0171/254 6516. Cheap, cheerful and hugely enjoyable jazz club. Often showcases local and up-and-coming musicians. *Stoke Newington BR from Liverpool Street or bus #73.*

100 Club, 100 Oxford St, W1 ☎0171/636 0933. After a brief spell as a stage for punk bands, the *100 Club* is once again an unpretentious and inexpensive jazz venue. *Tottenham Court Road tube.*

606 Club, 90 Lots Rd, SW10 ☎0171/352 5953. London's newest all-jazz venue, located off the untrendy end of the King's Road. *Fulham Broadway tube.*

World music and roots

Africa Centre, 38 King St, WC2 ☎0171/ 836 1973. African bands perform here in a packed old hall. The atmosphere is usually great, as much of the audience are London-based Africans. *Covent Garden tube.*

Cecil Sharp House, 2 Regent's Park Rd, NW1 ☎0171/485 2206. A centre for British folk music: singing, dancing and a folk music shop. *Camden Town tube.*

Club Azul at The Landor, Landor Rd, Clapham, SW9 ☎0171/358 1140. Flamenco, Latin and other roots events. *Clapham North tube.*

Halfway House, 142 The Broadway, West Ealing, W5 ☎0181/567 0236. Regular roots bands, from Cajun music to Irish folk. *Ealing Broadway tube, then bus #207.*

Jazz Café (see Jazz, above). Hosts regular Latin and world acts.

The Mean Fiddler (see Rock and Blues, above). Good for Irish and other roots bands.

South Bank Centre, SE1 ☎0171/928 8800. The all-seater Queen Elizabeth Hall, Purcell Rooms and Royal Festival Hall feature an imaginative programme of world music and jazz acts, as well as classical music concerts. *Waterloo tube.*

Swan, 215 Clapham Rd, SW9 ☎0171/978 9778. Live Irish music. *Stockwell tube.*

Union Chapel, Compton Avenue, N1 ☎0171/226 1686. A wonderful organization called Muti-Culti put on an array of world fusions at this fabulous old chapel. Dress up warm for winter gigs. *Highbury and Islington tube.*

Weavers Arms, 98 Newington Green Rd, N1 ☎0171/226 6911. Intimate pub venue with folk, blues or country bands nightly. *Highbury & Islington tube.*

Clubs and discos

Recession might have taken its toll, but London is still a seven-nights-a-week party town, maintaining its status as Europe's **dance capital** – and a port of call for DJs from around the world. Recent relaxations in attitudes towards late-night licensing have allowed many venues to keep serving drink until 6am or even later, accelerating the move from illegal warehouse parties to purpose-renovated legitimate venues – just in time, in light of the 1994 Criminal Justice Act, which makes raves and other spontaneous gatherings illegal.

In the last couple of years club music has become ever-more fragmented – house still dominates, but the term now covers anything from US garage and deep house, through European trance-techno to the home-grown styles of hard house and the super-fast hardcore/jungle (a reggae offshoot). The jazz and acid jazz scene still thrives, too, and in addition to dance-hall reggae and ragga, the US-led fusion of swingbeat and hip hop is gaining ground with young black kids. Latin, African and world music fans have their own clubs, too, some of them (like the itinerant *Whirl-y-gig*) veering off into ambient-ethno and chill-out sounds.

Nearly all **dance clubs** open their doors between 10pm and midnight, with most favouring the 11pm slot. Some are open six or seven nights each week, some keep irregular days, others just open at the weekend – and very often a venue will host a different club on each night of the week. Check *Time Out*, or phone ahead, if you want to be sure of what you're getting. Admission **charges** vary enormously, with small midweek nights starting at around £3 and large weekend events charging as much as £25; around £10 is the average for a Saturday night, but bear in mind that profit margins at the bar are even more wicked than at live music venues.

Club venues

Astoria, 157 Charing Cross Rd, W1 ☎0171/434 0403. Massive dancefloor packed full of young and raucous ravers on its Friday and Saturday club nights. *Tottenham Court Road tube.*

Bagley's, King's Cross Goods Yard, off York Way, King's Cross, N1 (no phone). Vast warehouse-style venue. The perfect place for enormous raves, with a different DJ or atmosphere in each room. *King's Cross tube.*

Bar Rumba, 36 Shaftesbury Avenue, W1 ☎0171/287 2715. New West End venue with a programme of Latin, jazz-based and funk dance music. *Piccadilly Circus tube.*

The Big Chill at Union Chapel, Compton Avenue, N1 ☎0171/226 1686. This once monthly event (currently the second or third Sunday) features a chill-out disco in a church, with live acts, tarot and shiatsu massage. *Highbury and Islington tube.*

Café de Paris, 3 Coventry St, W1 ☎0171/287 3602. Following several dark years the elegant *Café* ballroom has been restored to its former glory and reopened for the city's trendy set. *Leicester Square tube.*

Camden Palace, 1 Camden High St, NW1 ☎0171/387 0428. A key venue for the New Romantics back in the Eighties; great lights, great sound, heaving crowds. *Mornington Crescent tube.*

Club Latinos, 7 Islington Green, N1 ☎0171/359 6416. If you're into Latin dance, it's hard to beat this club. The London School of Salsa gives salsa classes from 7.30–9.30pm, then you can try out your steps on the dancefloor. Salsa on Tues, Thur & Sat, tango on Wed. *Angel tube.*

Cuba, 11–13 Kensington High St, W8 ☎0171/938 4137. Small bar/café with basement club nights ranging from Latin to disco and garage. *High Street Kensington tube.*

Electric Ballroom, 184 Camden High St, NW1 ☎0171/485 9006. Attracts a mixed crowd with a wide range of sounds: from rock to hip-hop, from jazz to house. *Camden Town tube.*

Equinox, Leicester Place, WC2 ☎0171/437 1446. Seventies glamour takes to the floor at this palace of high-camp hedonism. Hosts assorted drinks promotion events, student shindigs and so on. *Leicester Square tube.*

Flamingo Club, 9 Hanover St, W1 ☎0171/493 0689. What used to be *Club Industria* is now the resplendently refurbished *Flamingo*. House speciality is urban funk with a splash of salsa. *Oxford Circus tube.*

Fridge, Town Hall Parade, Brixton Hill, SW2 ☎0171/326 5100. South London's big night out, with a musical policy running from funk to garage. Great gay nights – only *Heaven* (see below) runs it close. *Brixton tube.*

Gardening Club, 4 Covent Garden Piazza, WC2 ☎0171/497 3154. Small, trendy and nearly always reliable for a good night's clubbing. Open till the dawn chorus. *Covent Garden tube.*

Gossips, 69 Dean St, W1 ☎0171/434 4480. Cave-like basement club that seems to have been around forever. A different sound each night of the week. *Tottenham Court Road tube.*

Hanover Grand, 6 Hanover St, W1 ☎0171/499 7977. How can you resist a danceclub in an old Masonic hall? Opened at the end of 1994, this is a cool and extravagant new club, with a hundred grand of lights and sound system, a fine dancefloor, lots of alcoves – and air conditioning. Open Thurs–Sat. *Tottenham Court Road tube.*

Heaven, The Arches, Villiers Street, WC2 ☎0171/839 3863. Gigantic and justly famous gay club with supremely good sound and lights. Watch out for the great one-off *Megatripolis* dance extravaganzas, which are often held here. *Embankment or Charing Cross tube.*

Hippodrome, Charing Cross Rd, WC2H ☎0171/437 4311. London's leading

Live Music and Clubs

neon pleasure house and a byword for tackiness. An atmosphere-free zone. *Leicester Square tube.*

HQs, West Yard, Camden Lock, NW1 ☎0171/485 6044. Smallish venue by the canal with a range of nights, although the emphasis is on funky vibes. *Camden Town tube.*

Iceni, 11 White Horse St, W1 ☎0171/495 5333. Newish, three-floor club patronized by a slightly older, self-consciously stylish crowd. Music ranges from funk and rap to house, but is always the last word in drop-dead cool. *Green Park tube.*

LA2, 157 Charing Cross Rd ☎0171/734 6963. Disco with gay and straight nights. *Tottenham Court Road tube.*

Legends, 29 Old Burlington St, W1 ☎0171/437 9933. Weekend house nights are a star attraction at this style-conscious club. The dancefloor is populated by some very nifty movers. *Green Park or Oxford Circus tube.*

The Leisure Lounge, 121 Holborn, EC1 ☎0171/242 1345. Popular punk/rock/funk night on Fridays, and an all-night house session on Saturdays. *Chancery Lane tube.*

Limelight, 136 Shaftesbury Ave, WC2 ☎0171/434 0572. Housed in a high-tech converted church; super-trendy when it opened a few years back, now overpriced, though with the odd good night. *Leicester Square tube.*

Loughborough Hotel, corner of Loughborough & Evandale roads, SW9 (no phone). Massively popular jazz/funk/roots venue which is more about having a good time than worrying about what label you're flashing. On Friday nights it becomes the ever-wonderful *Mambo Inn*, with scalding hot Latin and world sounds. *Brixton tube or #3/#159 bus.*

Maximus, 14 Leicester Square, W1 ☎0171/734 4111. Once a supremely tacky disco, now playing host to hip club nights. *Leicester Square tube.*

Ministry of Sound, 103 Gaunt St, SE1 ☎0171/378 6528. A vast, state of the art club based on New York's legendary Paradise Garage. Has an exceptional sound system. Fabulously hip in the very recent past – though now nobody is quite so sure. Open Fri & Sat only. *Elephant & Castle tube.*

Ormonds, 6 Ormonds Yard, off Duke of York St, W1 ☎0171/930 2842. An older-than-usual crowd soaks up the plush ambience of this relaxed, glossily chic club. *Piccadilly Circus tube.*

RAW, 112a Great Russell St, WC1 (no phone). Very clubby and kitsch. Billion Dollar Babes is always a sell-out on Saturdays, then there's indie on Thursday and funky numbers on Fridays. Bizarre dress advised. *Tottenham Court Road tube.*

The Rocket, Holloway Road, N7 ☎0171/700 2421. This is part of North London University so it has a studenty edge, and some good and inexpensive raves. *Holloway Road tube.*

The Sound Shaft, Hungerford Lane, off Craven Street, WC2 (no phone). Small underground dance club, with a heavily populated dancefloor. *Charing Cross tube.*

Stringfellow's, 16 Upper St Martin's Lane, WC2 ☎0171/240 5534. Possibly the most famous club in the city, but far from the best; the photos of suntanned minor celebs on display outside will give you the basic customer profile. *Covent Garden tube.*

Subterania, 12 Acklam Rd, W10 ☎0181/960 4590. In the heart of trendy Notting Hill, worth a visit for its diverse (if dressy) club nights on Fridays and Saturdays. Notoriously choosy door staff. *Ladbroke Grove tube.*

SW1, 191 Victoria St, SW1 ☎0171/828 7455. Serious clubbers congregate at this Edwardian oak-panelled dance hall for some hard house. *Victoria tube.*

Turnmills, 63 Clerkenwell Rd, EC1 ☎0171/250 3409. Coffee bar upstairs, alcohol and dancing below; frequented by grown-up, dressed-up, mostly gay clubbers. *Farringdon tube.*

United Kingdom, Buckhold Road, SW18 ☎0181/877 0110. More often known as *Club UK*, this is one of the newest big clubs in town, despite its entombment in an ugly shopping centre stuck out in the sticks. Cutting-edge British DJs, but the young clubbers have way too much attitude. *Wandsworth Town BR from Waterloo.*

Velvet Underground, 143 Charing Cross Rd, WC2 ☎0171/439 4655. Very cool velvet-dripping interior design; happy, housey tunes. *Tottenham Court Road tube.*

Vox, 9 Brighton Terrace, SW9 ☎0171/737 2095. Good, if basic, venue on two floors, with one-offs from ragga to techno, house to garage. *Brixton tube.*

The Wag Club, 35 Wardour St, W1 ☎0171/437 5534. A hot spot in the mid-Eighties, this famous space is in need of an overhaul but is still going strong with two floors of dance sounds. *Leicester Square or Piccadilly Circus tube.*

Lesbian and Gay London

It's ironic that the infamous Clause 28 – now Section 28 of the 1988 Local Government Act – played a large part in making lesbian and gay London what it is today. This draconian legislation, outlawing the "promotion" of homosexuality in schools and council-run establishments, politicized the lesbian and gay community to an unprecedented degree, as tens of thousands took to the streets to voice their anger at a measure that was bound to entrench prejudice. The protests failed but the campaign brought gay men and lesbians into a new political unison, and the energy of that period has been maintained, as action groups such as OutRage! and Stonewall continue to keep homosexual issues in the national spotlight.

In parallel with these developments, London's lesbian and gay scene has become one of the liveliest in Europe, with Soho evolving into the country's most vibrant "gay village". Walking along Old Compton Street, the core of Soho, you might think that its bars are exclusively male. This isn't quite the case, as most of the venues consider themselves mixed, but gay men do predominate here and they enjoy the best permanent facilities London-wide. The lesbian scene tends to be more fragmented, with far fewer dedicated venues, although mixed bars and clubs often have women-only nights.

As for special events, the year's big summer diary date is **Lesbian and Gay Pride** in June (see p.540), while the colder months are spiced up by November's **Winter Pride**, an indoor festival usually held at the Union Building of the University of London, with stalls, discos, live music, cabaret and all-day bars. Information on both is available from The Pride Committee on ☎0171/738 7644. The National Film Theatre (see p.499) also holds a lesbian and gay film festival every March .

Details of most events appear in *Time Out*, but you should check the up-to-the-minute listings in *Capital Gay* and *The Pink Paper*, free weekly newspapers available at many of the places listed below. Another excellent source of information is the London Lesbian and Gay Switchboard which operates around the clock; details of this and other services are given on p.483.

Clubs

Clubs are listed according to clientele: mixed first (including both bars that are mixed straight/gay/lesbian and those which have specific gay or lesbian nights), followed by those places which are specifically for lesbians, and those specifically for gay men. Because the club scene is so fast-moving, we haven't detailed nights and times – but they are listed in the gay newspapers (see above). Entry prices start at £3 and rise to around £20 for special events, like New Year's Eve parties. Some clubs, especially the men's, stipulate dress codes – mainly leather, rubber, uniform and other bootboy paraphernalia. We've specified such sartorial regulations, but again, things change fast, so it's best to check before setting out for a costumed night on the town.

Lesbian and Gay London: Clubs

Clubs tend to get going after 11pm. Be aware that many of them operate for different clienteles on different nights.

Many of the venues listed under "Bars and cafés" – see overpage – also have disco nights, generally lower-key than those listed in this section.

Mixed clubs

The Fridge, Town Hall Parade, Brixton Hill, SW1 ☎0171/326 5100. Huge dancefloor, house music and the wildest, most popular mixed gay nights – *Ciao Baby* and *Love Muscle* – in London. *Brixton tube.*

Gardening Club, 4 Covent Garden Piazza, WC2 ☎0171/497 3153. On Sunday nights this hosts the fabulous Queer Nation, when a dressed-up, danced-up gay and lesbian crowd ensures the finest in clubbing. *Covent Garden tube.*

Heaven, The Arches, Villiers St, WC2 ☎0171/839 3852. Lurking under Charing Cross station, this mammoth three-floor venue is the UK's most popular gay club, especially with the boys, although the mixed nights attract their fair share of women. *Charing Cross or Embankment tube.*

LA2, 157 Charing Cross Rd, WC2 ☎0171/734 6963. Big nights out for smiley happy gay boys and girls, primarily the former. More about fun than fashion, with mainstream disco tunes keeping the massive dancefloor steaming. *Tottenham Court Road tube.*

Madame Jo Jo's, 8–10 Brewer St, W1 ☎0171/734 2473. High-camp drag-based entertainment as popular with hooting hen-nighters as with gay punters. Vegas-style glamour in opulent surroundings. *Piccadilly Circus tube.*

RAW, 112a Great Russell St, WC1 (no phone). Very kitsch weekly mixed gay night with an easy-on-the-ear blend of disco classics, chart monsters, indie and house. A dancing queen's dream. *Tottenham Court Road.*

The Site Club, 196 Piccadilly, W1 ☎0171/439 1245. Weekly gay night draws in a funky mixed crowd of disco-fiends. *Piccadilly Circus tube.*

Substation, 5 Falconberg Court W1 ☎0171/287 9608. Cheap beer and a full floor at a gay club that's mixed from Monday to Friday, exclusively male on a Saturday and just for girls on a Sunday. *Tottenham Court Road tube.*

Turnmills, 63b Clerkenwell Rd, EC1 ☎0171/250 3409. Two major late-late weekend clubs – *Trade* and *ff* – attract dedicated gay clubbers of both genders to Turnmills. While *ff* winds up at the comparatively respectable hour of 5am, *Trade* keeps on grooving until 12.30pm on Sunday, with breakfast served from 6am. *Farringdon tube.*

Velvet Underground, 143 Charing Cross Rd, WC2 ☎0171/439 4655. High-fashion, low-inhibition gay nights twice a week. Lots of men on a Sunday. Not many lesbians anytime. *Tottenham Court Road tube.*

Way-Out Club, 143 Knightsbridge, SW1 ☎0181/363 0948. A drag club for transvestites, transsexuals, gay and straight people. Alternative glamour culture is celebrated behind these doors and, although there's no dress code, you're positively encouraged to dress up to the nines. There are changing facilities, so you don't have to risk harassment getting there. *Knightsbridge tube.*

Lesbian clubs

Ace of Clubs, 52 Piccadilly, W1 ☎0171/408 4457. Though perhaps not quite at the cutting edge, this club is nonetheless a relaxed, friendly and very popular venue for women of all ages and sartorial leanings. *Green Park tube.*

Club Tiempo, 64 Wilton Rd, SW1 ☎0171/834 5620. Once a week, women dance cheek-to-cheek at the intimate *Diva Dive. Victoria tube.*

The Garage, 20 Highbury Corner, N5 ☎0171/607 1818. Jazz, soul, funk, hip-hop, reggae and ragga at Saturday's *Rumpus* club. There's a chill-out room for those who can't take the heat. It's a night for the girls, but gay men are welcome as guests. *Highbury & Islington tube.*

The Site Club, 196 Piccadilly, W1 ☎0171/439 1245. Held on the first Thursday of every month, the legendary *Venus Rising* has fun-loving disco dykes flocking from

Lesbian and Gay London: Clubs

all over Britain and even the Continent. Perhaps Europe's biggest and best women-only night. *Piccadilly Circus or Green Park tube.*

Gay men's clubs

The Anvil, The Shipwright Arms, 88 Tooley St, SE1 ☎0171/407 0371. A leather, rubber and denim dress code ensures that it's wall-to-wall testosterone seven nights a week. *London Bridge tube.*

The Block, 1–5 Parkfield St, N1 ☎0171/226 7453. Dress codes don't come much stricter than *The Block*'s: uniform, leather, kilts, PVC, western and lycra. Absolutely no trainers at any time. *Angel tube.*

Central Station, 37 Wharfdale Rd, N1 ☎0171/278 3294. Fun-filled complex on three floors, one of them non-smoking. There's a pub space at ground level and a club down below. Women are rare visitors but aren't turned away. *King's Cross tube.*

Club 180, 180 Earl's Court Rd, SW5 ☎0171/835 1826. Comfortable, atmospheric gay men's club, formerly known as the *Club Copa*. *Earl's Court tube.*

Bars and cafés

Most of these cafés and bars have free admission, though a few levy a small charge for the evening session.

There are loads of lesbian and gay watering holes in London, many of them operating as cafés by day and transforming into drinking dens at night. Lots have disco nights and are open until the early hours, making them a fine alternative to the more expensive clubs. Whether it's air-kissing artiness you're after or an honest-to-goodness, spit-and-sawdust backstreet bar, you'll find your niche somewhere in the places listed below.

Mixed bars and cafés

Angel, 65 Graham St, N1 (no phone). Relaxed, stylish lesbian and gay café/bar, attracting a youngish crowd. Good music, pleasant surroundings and charming staff make this one of the most popular venues in London. *Angel tube.*

Balans, 60 Old Compton St, W1 ☎0171/437 5212. This relaxed café-bar is at the heart of the Soho scene, hugely popular, with a singer or cabaret after 10.30pm. Open late. *Leicester Square tube.*

The Bell, 257–259 Pentonville Rd, N1 ☎0171/837 5617. Long-established pub, attracting a mixed, trendy young crowd with its nightly discos, frequent tea dances and general spirit of bonhomie. Open late. *King's Cross tube.*

The Black Cap, 171 Camden High St, NW1 ☎0171/485 1742. North London cabaret institution – a big venue on the drag scene, with live acts almost every night. A friendly mixed crowd joins in the fun on two floors. *Camden Town tube.*

The Box, 32–34 Monmouth St, WC2 ☎0171/240 5828. Bright, gay-owned café/bar which is predominantly patronized by gay customers. The *Girl Bar* on Sunday nights packs the place out with lipstick-wearing, label-flaunting lesbians. *Leicester Square tube.*

Brixtonian Backayard, 4 Neal's Yard, off Shorts Gardens, WC2 ☎0171/240 2769. A good-looking venue to which good-looking people flock in their droves. Mixed-gay night on Wednesday and a determinedly attractive, enormously popular women's night – the *Wow Bar* – on Saturday. Funky music, the odd live act and a Caribbean restaurant upstairs. *Covent Garden tube.*

Edge, 11 Soho Square, W1 ☎0171/439 1223. Style-conscious café/bar which attracts pretty faces both gay and straight. *Tottenham Court Road tube.*

Fanny's, 305a North End Rd, W14 ☎0171/385 9359. Mixed, bisexual and TV/TS nights, lesbian *Blind Date* and assorted outbreaks of frivolity. The punters are predominantly female. *West Kensington tube.*

First Out, 52 St Giles High St, WC2 ☎0171/240 8042. Fashionable and popular café/bar. There's a women-only pre-club session on Friday night; men are admitted as guests. *Tottenham Court Road tube.*

Freedom, 60–66 Wardour St, W1 ☎0171/734 0071. Extremely stylish, occasionally excessively busy café/bar, popular with drinkers across the sexual

Lesbian and Gay London: Bars and Cafés

Helplines and information

All the following services provide information, advice and counselling, but the **Lesbian & Gay Switchboard** is perhaps the one to turn to first; its volunteers have details on all the capital's resources and can point you in the direction of specific organizations and community or support groups.

Beaumont Society ☎0171/730 7453. Tues & Thurs 7–10pm. Helpline offering support and information for transvestites and transsexuals.

Lesbian & Gay Switchboard ☎0171/837 7324. Daily 24hr.

Lesbian Line ☎0171/251 6911. Mon–Thurs 7–10pm, Fri 2–10pm.

London Friend ☎0171/837 3337. Daily 7.30–10pm. Counselling for lesbians and gay men; there's a women-only service on ☎0171/837 2782. Sun–Tues 7.30–10pm.

National AIDS Helpline ☎0800/567 123. Daily 24hr (freephone).

Terrence Higgins Trust ☎0171/242 1010. Daily noon–10pm. AIDS information and advice offered from this pioneering charitable organization.

Campaigning organizations

OutRage! ☎0171/439 2381. A broad-based group of lesbians and gay men committed to the pursuit of non-violent direct action to fight homophobia and discrimination.

Stonewall ☎0171/222 9007. A lobbying group established in response to Section 28's passage through Parliament, *Stonewall* works with politicians to campaign for legal and social equality for lesbians and gay men. Its most famous member is Sir Ian McKellen, who in 1991 became the first openly gay person to hold formal talks on gay discrimination issues with the Prime Minister.

Publications

The past few years have witnessed a boom in the availability and diversity of lesbian and gay publications, which were once restricted to the odd underground freesheet or porno mag lurking on the top shelf. The papers and magazines listed below can be picked up at most major newsagent's, in many bookshops (gay and straight), and in the cafés and bars of Soho. We've concentrated on the ones that provide up-to-date information not just on the the club and pub scene, but also on current political events and cultural issues. In addition to these, consumerist freesheets like *Boyz*, *Shebang* and *QX* abound, but they are pretty vacuous. Details of gay bookshops appear on p.519.

Capital Gay. Informative London publication with news, features, listings and reviews. The articles are wide-ranging, often provocative and have been known to cause offence. Aimed at men, but doesn't ignore women. Weekly, free.

Diva. National lifestyle magazine for lesbians. A midbrow range of features, news pieces and reviews, with exhaustive listings of London women's venues. Bi-monthly, £2.

Gay Times. Long-established national glossy magazine, incorporating *Gay News*. Authoritative news stories and well-written articles, plus listings, reviews and other community information. Aimed primarily at gay men, but also read by lesbians. The leader in the field. Monthly, £2.

The Pink Paper. Respected free national newspaper for lesbians and gay men. Big on news stories and information, and often used as a forum for community debate. Extensive "personals" section. Weekly.

Lesbian and Gay London: Bars and Cafés

spectrum. Fashionably health-conscious beverages complement the more decadent liquids on offer. There's a theatre space downstairs which can be hired for private parties. Some intriguing art installations, too. *Leicester Square tube.*

King William IV, 77 Hampstead High St, NW2 ☎0171/435 5747. Relaxed, unpretentious and friendly mixed gay pub. Punters are so cordial, in fact, that they occasionally go off on coach trips together. There are cream teas on a Sunday. *Hampstead tube.*

Kudos, 10 Adelaide St, WC2 ☎0171/379 4573. Predominantly a men's venue, but gradually attracting more women and keen to keep doing so. Only the ground-floor café is open during daylight hours; come nightfall the boys throng the basement bar. On Saturday nights, there's a free bus service to *The Fridge. Charing Cross tube.*

Market Tavern, Market Towers, 1 Nine Elms Lane, SW8 ☎0171/622 5655. Once a strictly male space, this south London drinking establishment and disco is now more mixed. Wednesday night, however, is for leather lads only. *Vauxhall tube.*

Royal Vauxhall Tavern, 372 Kennington Lane, SE11 ☎0171/582 0833. This pub is a predominantly male venue, at its most lively on Sunday afternoons. It also has a women-only night – *Vixens at the Vauxhall* – on Fridays. *Vauxhall tube.*

The Village Soho, 81 Wardour St ☎0171/434 2124. Elegant bi-level café/bar in the "gay village", the haunt of many a gay celebrity. Attracts more men than women, but is striving to redress the balance. *Leicester Square tube.*

The White Swan (BJ's), 556 Commercial Rd, E14 ☎0171/791 0747. A mainly male venue, especially at the weekend, but more mixed during the week. Country dancing lessons are among the attractions. *Limehouse BR from Fenchurch Street, or Limehouse DLR, or buses #15 or #D11.*

The Yard, 57 Rupert St, W1 ☎0171/437 2652. An attractive café/bar making full use of its courtyard and loft areas. It's a lesbian and gay venue, but heterosexuals are welcome. *Piccadilly Circus tube.*

Lesbian bars and cafés

Drill Hall Arts Centre, 16 Chenies St, WC1 ☎0171/637 8270. Relaxed arts centre venue whose bar, restaurant and workshops are women-only on Monday nights. *Goodge Street tube.*

Duke of Clarence, 140 Rotherfield St, N1 ☎0171/226 6526. A down-to-earth women's bar with pool tables and a beer garden. *Angel or Highbury & Islington tube.*

The Eliza Doolittle, 3 Ossulston St, NW1 ☎0171/387 0836. Hosts *Eliza's* at the weekend, a women-only bar with pool-playing, music and an easy-going ambience. Not for the label-conscious. *Euston or King's Cross tube.*

Rosanna's, 17 Strutton Ground, SW1 ☎0171/233 1701. Friendly café/bar which is women-only on Wednesdays, Thursdays and Fridays. *St James's Park tube.*

Gay men's bars and cafés

Brief Encounter, 43 St Martin's Lane, WC2 ☎0171/240 2221. Two loud, hectic bars – one bright, one dim. A popular pre-*Heaven* or post-opera hang-out (it's next door to the Coliseum). *Leicester Square tube.*

Brompton's, 294 Old Brompton Rd, SW5 ☎0171/370 1344. Long-established and newly refurbished gay men's bar; a new cocktail bar has added to its already immense popularity with a wide range of males. *Earl's Court tube.*

The Coleherne, 261 Old Brompton Rd, SW5 ☎0171/373 9859. Crowded, long-established leather/SM bar. Heaving with brutish-looking types flexing their pecs. *Earl's Court tube.*

Compton's of Soho, 53 Old Compton St, W1 ☎0171/437 4445. Very busy men's bar central to the London gay scene. A relaxed place in which to drink, cruise and chat. Lesbians are a rare, but not unwelcome, sight. *Leicester Square or Piccadilly Circus tube.*

Crews, 14 Upper St Martin's Lane, WC2 ☎0171/379 4880. Hot and sweaty bar-cum-club that's men-only during the early part of the week, but admits women from Thursday to Sunday. *Leicester Square tube.*

King's Arms, 23 Poland St, W1 ☎0171/734 5907. Friendly men's bar in Soho, with both frenetic and relaxed drinking spaces. *Oxford Circus tube.*

London Apprentice, 333 Old St, EC1 ☎0171/739 5949. One of the best-known gay pubs in town. Busy, fairly cruisy, with a small dancefloor downstairs. *Old Street tube.*

Lesbian and Gay London: Bars and Cafés

Classical Music, Opera and Dance

With the South Bank, the Barbican and the Wigmore Hall offering year-round appearances by generally first-rank musicians, and numerous smaller venues providing a stage for less established or more specialized performers, London should satisfy most devotees of **classical music**. True, things would be better if the programming of the big halls were less reliant on a diet of Mahler, Beethoven and Brahms, but more radical stuff does get exposure from time to time, and the Promenade Concerts – a three-month season of concerts at bargain prices – are one of Europe's greatest, most democratic music festivals. And if the Royal Opera House is an expensive luxury by most people's standards, the English National Opera has done a lot to demolish the elitist stereotypes that the Royal Opera seems determined to uphold, while the Spitalfields Market Opera is one of the most enterprising recent developments on the London arts scene.

The more modest economics of **dance** mean that you'll often find ambitious work on offer, with several adventurous companies appearing sporadically, while fans of classicism can revel in the Royal Ballet, as accomplished a company as any in Europe.

Classical music

London's orchestras might not quite possess the charisma of the Vienna and Berlin ensembles, but on a good night they can match the standards of any, and in terms of the sheer number of bands on the circuit, London is very impressive. On most days you'll be able to catch a concert by either the London Symphony Orchestra, the London Philharmonic, the Royal Philharmonic, the Philharmonia or the BBC Symphony Orchestra, or a smaller-scale concert from the English Chamber Orchestra or the Academy of St-Martin-in-the Fields. Except when a glamorous guest conductor is wielding the baton, or when one of the world's high-profile orchestras is giving a performance, a full house is a rarity (most of London's orchestras are dependent on parsimonious government funding), so even at the biggest concert halls you should be able to pick up a ticket for around £12 (the full range is about £6–30).

The Proms provide a feast of music at bargain basement prices (see box below), and from Monday to Friday there are **free lunchtime concerts** in many of London's **churches**, with performances of chamber music or solo works from students or professionals. Look out also for performances at the Royal College of Music and the Royal Academy of Music – the standard is amazingly high, the choice of work is a lot riskier than the commercial venues can manage, and the prices are low.

Concert venues

Barbican Centre, Silk Street, EC2 ☎0171/638 8891. Home to the London Symphony Orchestra and the English Chamber Orchestra and the regular haunt of big-name soloists. However, programmes are too often pitched squarely at a corporate audience – you won't hear much music from the post-war years or obscure repertoire from earlier generations. *Barbican or Moorgate tube.*

Blackheath Concert Halls, 23 Lee Rd, SE3 ☎0181/318 9758. Often a venue for excellent solo recitals – even top-of-the-bill performers from the Met have sung here. *Blackheath BR from Charing Cross.*

British Music Information Centre, 10 Stratford Place, W1 ☎0171/499 8567. Free recitals most Tuesdays and Thursdays, usually of freshly minted British music. *Bond Street tube.*

Fenton House, Hampstead Grove, NW3 ☎0171/435 3471. Recitals of Baroque music on period instruments, most Wednesdays between May and September. *Hampstead tube.*

Classical Music, Opera and Dance

Classical music festivals

The BBC Henry Wood Promenade Concerts, Royal Albert Hall, Kensington Gore, SW7 ☎0171/589 8212. The BBC Henry Wood Promenade Concerts – known to Brits solely as The Proms – tend to be associated primarily with the raucous Last Night, when the flag-waving audience sings its patriotic heart out. This jingoistic nonsense completely mispresents the Proms, which from July to September feature at least one concert daily in an exhilarating melange of favourites and new or recondite works. You can book a seat for a Prom as you would for any other concert, but that would be to miss the essence of the Proms, for which the stalls are removed to create hundreds of standing places costing just £3. The upper gallery is similarly packed with people sitting on the floor or standing, and tickets there are even cheaper. The acoustics aren't the world's best, but the performers are usually outstanding, the atmosphere is great, and the hall is so vast that only megastars like Jessye Norman can pack it out, so the likelihood of being turned away if you turn up on the night is slim. The annual *Proms Guide*, available at most bookshops from May, gives information on every concert. *South Kensington tube.*

Greenwich Festival, various venues, Greenwich, SE3 ☎0181/317 8687. Classical music plays its part in this combined arts festival in June, housed in venues ranging from the Royal Naval College Chapel to nearby pubs. *Greenwich or Maze Hill BR from Charing Cross.*

Kenwood Lakeside Concerts, Kenwood House, Hampstead Lane, NW3 ☎0171/973 3427. The grassy amphitheatre in front of Kenwood House is the venue for alfresco classical concerts every Saturday from June to September. The programme is conservative and crowd-pleasing, but executed with real panache. On July 4, Handel's *Fireworks Music* is accompanied by a firework show to celebrate America's Independence Day. *Hampstead or Highgate tube.*

Meltdown, South Bank Centre, SE1 ☎0171/928 8800. A festival of avant-garde offerings, held in various parts of the South Bank complex in June and July. This is one of the most stimulating musical events on the London calendar, but in view of the conservatism of British musical audiences, the festival's continuation is by no means certain. *Waterloo tube.*

Spitalfields Festival, Christ Church, Spitalfields, E1 ☎0171/377 0287. Classical music recitals in Hawksmoor's mighty Christ Church, during the area's June arts shindig. *Shoreditch, Aldgate or Aldgate East tube.*

Classical Music, Opera and Dance

Purcell Room, South Bank Centre, SE1 ☎0171/928 8800. The South Bank Centre's most intimate venue; excellent for chamber music and solo recitals by future star instrumentalists and singers. *Waterloo tube.*

Queen Elizabeth Hall, South Bank Centre, SE1 ☎0171/928 8800. Housed in the concrete conurbation of the South Bank Centre, this is a prime venue for chamber orchestras and big-name soloists. Offers more specialized programmes than its larger neighbour, the Royal Festival Hall. *Waterloo tube.*

Royal Festival Hall, South Bank Centre, SE1 ☎0171/928 8800. Gargantuan space tailor-made for large-scale choral and orchestral works. It plays host to some soloists as well, though only quasi-legendary figures such as Maurizio Pollini can fill the hall nowadays. *Waterloo tube.*

St John's, Smith Square, SW1 ☎0171/222/1061. This charming deconsecrated church, horribly close to the Conservative Party HQ, presents a musical menu dominated by chamber music. Its high reputation is partly maintained by the live broadcasting of its Monday concerts on Radio Three. *Westminster tube.*

Wigmore Hall, 36 Wigmore St, W1 ☎0171/935 2141. The refurbished Wigmore, with its nigh-perfect acoustics, is a favourite with artists and audiences alike. An exceptional venue for chamber music, it is renowned for its song recitals by the world's very best singers and performances by rising young instrumentalists. Holds very popular mid-morning concerts on a Sunday. *Bond Street tube.*

Free lunchtime concerts

St Anne and St Agnes, Gresham Street, EC2 ☎0171/373 5566. As well as lunchtime recitals, this Lutheran place of worship is big on Bach as part of its Sunday service. *St Paul's tube.*

St Giles Cripplegate, Barbican, EC2 ☎0171/606 3630. Lurking in the midst of the Barbican, this church provides the complex with an extra performance space. *Barbican or Moorgate tube.*

St James's Church, Piccadilly, W1 ☎0171/734 5053. The emphasis is on Baroque music in this beautiful Wren church. *Piccadilly Circus tube.*

St Lawrence Jewry, Guildhall, EC2 ☎071/600 9478. Piano recitals on Mondays and organ-playing on Thursdays. *Bank or St Paul's tube.*

St Margaret, Lothbury, EC2 ☎0171/606 8330. Wednesday lunchtime recitals make great play of the nearly two-hundred-year-old church organ. *Bank tube.*

St Martin-in-the-Fields, Trafalgar Square, WC2 ☎0171/930 0089. Lunchtime recitals two or three times a week, plus a few fee-charging concerts in the evenings, sometimes featuring the top-notch Academy of St Martin-in-the-Fields. Has a good café in the crypt too. *Charing Cross tube.*

St Martin-within-Ludgate, Ludgate Hill, EC4 ☎0171/248 6504. A fantastically-spired Wren church with a varied recital programme. *St Paul's or Blackfriars tube.*

St-Mary-le-Bow Church, Cheapside, EC2 ☎0171/248 5139. An excellent Thursday programme of medieval and Renaissance recitals. *St Paul's tube.*

St Michael's, Cornhill, EC3 ☎0171/626 8841. Organ recitals lift the spirits of wage slaves every Monday. *Bank tube.*

St Olave's, Hart Street, EC3 ☎0171/488 4318. Chamber pieces on Wednesday and Thursday. *Tower Hill tube.*

St Sepulchre-without-Newgate, Holborn Viaduct, EC1 ☎0171/248 1660. The so-called "Musicians' Church" holds frequent piano recitals. *Chancery Lane or St Paul's tube.*

Opera

Opera has enjoyed a surge in popularity in London over the last few years, largely owing to the efforts of the **English National Opera** at the London Colisseum, a company that's worked hard to bring exciting, entertaining opera to the masses. Smaller halls give Londoners the chance to see innovative productions by touring companies such as **Opera Factory** and **Opera North**, both of which play to packed houses annually. Only at the **Royal Opera House** do seat prices climb to inexcusable heights, and even at this most exclusive of venues there are ways of getting into a show without breaking the bank, as long as you don't mind a spot of queueing.

Opera companies and venues

English National Opera, Colisseum, St Martin's Lane, WC2 ☎0171/632 8300. Home of the English National Opera, the Colisseum has more radical producers, a more ambitious programme and way more democratic prices than its Royal Opera House rival – they begin at £8, and unsold seats are usually released after 10am on the day of the performance at a maximum price of £28. All works are sung in English and are of a generally high standard, though singers tend to forsake the Colisseum once they can command the stratospheric fees of Europe's bigger houses. *Leicester Square or Charing Cross tube.*

Royal Opera House, Bow St, Covent Garden, WC2 ☎0171/240 1066. London's premier opera house has a deserved reputation for snobbery, conservative productions, over-reliance on star names and ludicrous seat prices – if Placido Domingo is in the cast, the ROP will be demanding £120 for a lot of its seats. Despite the expense, performances are often sold out (corporate clients take blocks of seats), although 65 less expensive seats (ie under £30) are held back for sale on the day from 10am – they are restricted to one per person and you need to get there by 8am for popular shows. Standing places are also sometimes available for otherwise sold-out shows. All operas are performed in the original language but are discreetly surtitled. *Covent Garden tube.*

Almeida Theatre, Almeida Street, N1 ☎0171/359 4404. The summer Almeida Opera festival, a showcase for new works, is a highlight of the music year in London. *Angel or Highbury & Islington tube.*

Holland Park, Holland Park, Kensington High Street, W8 ☎0171/602 7856. Opera, as well and dance and theatre, takes to the great outdoors in green and pleasant Holland Park during the summer months. There's a canopy to cover you in case of rain. *High Street Kensington tube.*

Queen Elizabeth Hall, South Bank Centre, South Bank, SE1 ☎0171/928 8800. A regular venue for productions by touring opera companies and the resident Opera Factory, known for its stripped-down versions of classic operas. *Waterloo tube.*

Spitalfields Market Opera, 4–5 Lamb St, E1 ☎0171/247 2558. Founded in 1995, this excellent venue offers a year-round programme of chamber operas. Average ticket price is just £12, and standby tickets, on sale on the day of the performance, cost just half that. *Aldgate or Aldgate East tube.*

Dance

From the time-honoured showpieces of the **Royal Ballet** to the offbeat acts of kinetic surrealism on show at the **ICA**, there's always a **dance performance** of some species afoot in London. The Royal Ballet is the only major company with a permanent base at which they dance regularly, but the calendar is punctuated by brief seasons from talented peripatetic groups, such as the renowned Rambert company, and London has a good reputation for international dance festivals showcasing the work of a spread of ensembles. The biggest of these annual events is the **Dance Umbrella** (information ☎0181/741 4040), a six-week season (Oct–Nov) of new work from bright young choreographers and performance artists at venues across the city.

Dance companies and venues

Chisenhale Dance Space, 64 Chisenhale Rd, E3 ☎0181/981 6617. Showcases the work of new choreographers and student performers. *Mile End tube.*

Coliseum, St Martin's Lane, WC2 ☎0171/632 8300. The English National Ballet becomes resident at this beautiful venue for a fortnight in the summer. *Charing Cross tube.*

Classical Music, Opera and Dance

ICA, The Mall, SW1 ☎0171/930 3647. Performance-cum-dance shows dominate at the Institute of Contemporary Arts. *Piccadilly Circus or Charing Cross tube.*

The Place, 17 Duke's Rd, WC1 ☎0171/387 0031. The London Contemporary Dance School has its base here, and the theatre also plays host to the finest in performance art and contemporary dance from across the globe. *Euston tube.*

Riverside Studios, Crisp Road, W6 ☎0181/748 3354. Two performance spaces used for small-scale productions, often on the border between dance and performance art. *Hammersmith tube.*

Royal Opera House, Bow St, Covent Garden, WC2 ☎0171/240 1066. The Royal Ballet is one of the world's finest classical companies, but the repertoire isn't all tutus and swans. Star dancers such as Darcey Bussell, Sylvie Guillem, Irek Mukhamedov and Jonathan Cope have also demonstrated that classicists can do modern dance with unequalled panache – the Royal Ballet's production of William Forsythe's pelvis-cracking *In the middle, somewhat elevated* was the cult success of recent years. As with the opera productions, sell-outs are frequent – for details of ticket availability, see Royal Opera House listing above. Prices are considerably lower for the ballet than for the opera – for most productions you should be able to get tickets for around £25 if you act quickly. *Covent Garden tube.*

Sadler's Wells Theatre, Rosebery Avenue, EC1 ☎0171/278 8916. Major British and international companies grace the stage of this historic theatre, while its recently opened Lillian Baylis Theatre, round the back on Arlington Way, offers smaller-scale shows at lower prices. *Angel tube.*

South Bank Centre, South Bank, SE1 ☎0171/928 8800. Company in residence is the English National Ballet, which performs *The Nutcracker* to capacity audiences every winter and has a three- to six-week summer season in the Royal Festival Hall. The smaller Queen Elizabeth Hall and Purcell Room also regularly host dance performances, featuring some of Europe's most adventurous groups. *Waterloo tube.*

Theatre, Cabaret and Cinema

London has enjoyed a reputation for quality **theatre** since the time of Shakespeare, and despite the increasing prevalence of fail-safe blockbuster musicals and revenue-spinning star vehicles, the city still provides a platform for innovation. From the Victorian splendour of the major West End theatres to the stark modernism of the South Bank Centre, London has a plethora of major stages to play host to the cream of home-grown and international talent, while the more experimental fringe circuit makes use of a vast array of buildings all over the city.

Comedy, too, is big on the London stages – although more in clubs and pubs than in theatres. A little confusingly, almost everything on offer, no matter what the status of the comedian, is referred to as "alternative" comedy, a genre that emerged and boomed in the 1980s as young stand-up acts provided an alternative to the old seaside smut. The comedy and cabaret circuit has disgorged a stream of fast-thinking young wits, and some cabaret-type venues also command a devoted following for their **poetry** readings.

Cinema is rather less healthy, for London's repertory screens are a dying breed, edged out by the multiplex complexes, which show mainstream Hollywood fare some months behind America and most of the rest of Europe. There are a few excellent independent cinemas, though, including the National Film Theatre, which is the focus of the richly varied **London International Film Festival**, in November.

Current details of what's on in all these areas can be found in a number of publications, the most comprehensive being the weekly *Time Out*. The *Guardian*'s *Review* section (free with the paper on Saturdays) and Friday's *Evening Standard* are other good sources.

Theatre

At first glance it might seem that London's **theatreland** has become a province of the Andrew Lloyd Webber global empire, but in fact few cities in the world can match the variety of the London scene. The government-subsidized **Royal Shakespeare Company** and the **National Theatre** (or Royal National Theatre as it has rather foolishly dubbed itself) ensure that the masterpieces of the mainstream tradition remain in circulation, often in productions of startling originality. Many of the West End's **commercial theatres** have been hijacked by long-running musicals or similarly unchallenging shows (see box) but others offer more intriguing productions. London's **fringe theatres**, whether they be cosy pub venues or converted warehouses, offer a good spread of classic and contemporary work, while some of the most exciting work is mounted by various small **theatre**

Theatre, Cabaret and Cinema

The Globe Theatre, a replica of Shakespeare's original performance space in Southwark, is due to open in 1995 (see p.254).

companies which have no permanent base – we've listed the best of them as well.

Unfortunately, theatre-going doesn't come cheap in this city. **Tickets** under £10 are very thin on the ground for any of the major theatres; the box-office average is close to £15, with £30 the usual top whack. Furthermore, tickets for the durable musicals and well-reviewed plays are like gold dust.

If the box office turns you away, however, several measures are still open to you. The ticket booth operated by the *Society of West End Theatres* in Leicester Square (Mon–Sat noon for matinees, 2.30–6.30pm for evening performances) sells **half-price** tickets for that day's performances of all the West End shows, but they specialize in the top end of the price range. Tickets are limited to four per person, are sold for cash only and carry a service charge of up to £1.50 per ticket. If they have sold out, you could turn to *Ticketmaster* (☎0171/344 4444) or *First Call* (☎0171/497 9977), who can get seats for all West End shows (even ones that are technically "sold out"), but a hefty booking fee is charged. There are plenty of other, less reputable agencies in the West End, with mark-ups as high as two hundred percent – and often on very poor seats. Touts' profit margins are even more outrageous, and there's no guarantee that the tickets aren't fakes: beware.

Students, senior citizens and the unemployed can get concessionary rates on tickets for many shows, and nearly all theatres offer reductions on standby tickets (ie tickets unsold on the day of performance) to all these groups.

The venues

What follows is a list of those West End theatres which offer a changing roster of good plays, along with the most consistent of the small-scale venues. This by no means represents the full tally of London's stages, as there are scores of fringe places that present work on an intermittent basis – check *Time Out* if you want a detailed up-to-the-minute survey.

Almeida, Almeida Street, N1 ☎0171/359 4404. A deservedly popular venue which premieres excellent new plays and excitingly reworked classics. *Angel or Highbury & Islington tube.*

Battersea Arts Centre, Old Town Hall, Lavender Hill, SW11 ☎0171/223 2223. The BAC is a triple-stage building, known for comedy and cabaret as well as straight plays. *Clapham Junction BR from Victoria or Waterloo.*

Barbican Centre, Silk Street, EC2 (box office ☎0171/638 8891; information ☎0171/628 2295). After a season in the company's HQ at Stratford, Royal Shakespeare Company productions move to one of the Barbican's two venues: the excellently designed Barbican Theatre and the much smaller Pit. A wide range of work is produced, though the writings of the Bard predominate. *Barbican or Moorgate tube.*

Bush, Shepherd's Bush Green, W12 ☎0181/743 3388. This minuscule above-pub theatre specializes in new writing, a policy that has turned up some real crackers. *Goldhawk Road or Shepherd's Bush tube.*

Donmar Warehouse, Thomas Neal's, Earlham St, WC2 ☎0171/867 1150. This recently renovated performance space is noted for new plays and top-quality reappraisals of the classics – it's even managed to make Noel Coward look radical. *Covent Garden tube.*

Drill Hall, 16 Chenies St, WC1 ☎0171/637 8270. This studio-style venue specializes in gay, lesbian, feminist and all-round politically correct new work. *Goodge Street tube.*

Finborough, The Finborough Arms, 118 Finborough Rd, SW10 ☎0171/373 3842. A pub venue presenting a challenging range of high-minded new pieces. *Earl's Court tube.*

Gate, The Prince Albert, 11 Pembridge Rd, W11 ☎0171 229 0706. A small pub theatre notable for its excellent revivals of neglected European classics. *Notting Hill Gate tube.*

Hampstead Theatre, Swiss Cottage Centre, Avenue Rd, NW3 ☎0171/722 9301. A shed-like but comfortable theatre whose productions often move on to the West End. Such is its prestige that the likes of John Malkovitch have been enticed into performing here. *Swiss Cottage tube.*

Theatre, Cabaret and Cinema

London's long-runners

Most overseas visitors to the West End theatres come to see one of the city's big musicals, which have been so successful in recent years that serious theatre has all but been squeezed off these stages. On any given night in the West End there are more people watching musicals than all other forms of theatre put together, and the trend shows no sign of abating, despite a few well-publicized flops. Below is a list of the established songfests, along with the two plays that have attained comparable landmark status.

Blood Brothers, Phoenix Theatre, Charing Cross Rd, WC2 ☎0171/867 1044 or 1111. Willy Russell and Bob Thomson's sentimental, decade-old musical about Scouse (Liverpool) twins separated at birth. *Tottenham Court Road or Leicester Square tube.*

Buddy, Victoria Palace Theatre, Victoria St, SW1 ☎0171/834 1317. All the old favourites resurrected in the story of Buddy's brief life. *Victoria tube.*

Cats, New London Theatre, Drury Lane,WC2 ☎0171/405 0072 or 404 4079. Lloyd Webber's most popular musical, and London's longest-running, with all-singing, all-dancing feline favourites from T. S. Eliot's *Old Possum's Book of Cats*. *Holborn or Covent Garden tube.*

Five Guys Named Moe, Lyric Theatre, Shaftesbury Ave, W1 ☎0171/494 5045. Jazz numbers galore in this jumpin' musical tribute to Louis Jordan. *Piccadilly Circus tube.*

Grease, Dominion Theatre, Tottenham Court Rd, W1 ☎0171/416 6060. Along the same lines as the film – lots of energy, teen heartache and bad jokes – but lacking the charisma of John Travolta and Olivia Newton-Squirrel. *Tottenham Court Road tube.*

Les Misérables, Palace Theatre, Shaftesbury Ave, W1 ☎0171/434 0909. Trevor Nunn's sanitized adaptation of Victor Hugo's classic. Alluring peasants, vicious villains and heart-wrenching musical numbers. *Leicester Square tube.*

Miss Saigon, Theatre Royal Drury Lane, Catherine St, WC2 ☎0171/494 5001. Lavish adaptation of *Madame Butterfly*, tracing a GI's tragic affair with a Vietnamese prostitute in 1975 Saigon. The theatre itself is one of London's most historic, designed in 1812 by Benjamin Wyatt. *Covent Garden tube.*

The Mousetrap, St Martin's, West St, WC2 ☎0171/836 1443. Run-of-the-mill Agatha Christie mystery that's been running for nearly 50 years, a world record. *Leicester Square tube.*

The Phantom of the Opera, Her Majesty's Theatre, Haymarket, SW1 ☎0171/494 5400. Extravagant Lloyd Webber production about a physiognomically-challenged subterranean who falls for a beautiful young opera singer. *Piccadilly Circus tube.*

Starlight Express, Apollo Victoria Theatre, Wilton Road, SW1 ☎0171/416 6042. Lloyd Webber on wheels. Fast-moving, roller-skating extravaganza, with an innovative set circling the audience above and below. *Victoria tube.*

Sunset Boulevard, Adelphi Theatre, Strand, WC2 ☎0171/344 0055. Lightweight adaptation of Billy Wilder's film, with music by Lloyd Webber, direction by Trevor Nunn. The rococo sets are awesome. *Charing Cross tube.*

The Woman in Black, Fortune Theatre, Russell St, WC2 ☎0171/836 2238. Susan Hill's ghost tale is the longest-running play in this theatre's history. *Covent Garden tube.*

Theatre, Cabaret and Cinema

ICA, The Mall, SW1 ☎0171/930 3647. The Institute of Contemporary Arts attracts the most innovative practitioners in all areas of performance. It also attracts a fair quantity of modish junk, but the hits generally outweigh the misses. *Piccadilly Circus or Charing Cross tube.*

King's Head, 115 Upper St, N1 ☎0171/226 1916 or 8561. The oldest and probably most famous of London's thriving pub theatres. Adventurous performances in a pint-sized room. *Angel or Highbury & Islington tube.*

National Theatre, South Bank Centre, South Bank, SE1 (box office ☎0171/928 2252; information ☎0171/633 0880). The National consists of three separate theatres: the 1100-seater Olivier, the proscenium-arched Lyttelton and the experimental Cottesloe. Standards set by the late Larry Olivier, founding artistic director, are maintained by the country's top actors and directors in a programme running the gamut from *Wind in the Willows* to Arthur Miller. Many of the National's productions sell out months in advance but a few discount tickets go on sale on the morning of each performance – get there by 8am for the popular shows. *Waterloo tube.*

New End Theatre, 27 New End, NW3 ☎0171/794 0022. Comparable to Islington's Almeida, this cosy neighbourhood venue in literary-minded Hampstead offers a reliable programme of fringe-like fare. *Hampstead tube.*

Old Vic, Waterloo Road, SE1 ☎0171/928 7616. Classic revivals and new plays are shown in this beautifully refurbished Victorian theatre, once the home of the National Theatre. *Waterloo tube.*

Open Air Theatre, Regent's Park, Inner Circle, NW1 ☎0171/486 2431 or 1933. If the weather's good there's nothing quite like a dose of alfresco playgoing. This beautiful space hosts a summer programme of Shakespeare, musicals and plays. *Baker Street tube.*

Queens, Shaftesbury Ave, W1 ☎0171/494 5040. Of all the Shaftesbury Avenue theatres, this is the one most likely to be offering a meaty production of Ibsen, Chekhov or Shakespeare, usually with a starry cast. *Piccadilly Circus tube.*

Richmond Theatre, The Green, Richmond, Surrey ☎0181/940 0220. Suburban theatre with an excellent record of classic dramas, from Aristophanes to the present century. *Richmond tube or BR from Waterloo.*

Royal Court, Sloane Square, SW1 ☎0171/730 1745. The Royal Court has a long tradition of presenting the finest in new writing – George Bernard Shaw, John Osborne, Samuel Beckett and Edward Bond have all had British premieres here. Smaller-scale and often more radical work gets its chance in the Theatre Upstairs. *Sloane Square tube.*

Theatre Royal Stratford East, Gerry Raffles Square, E15 ☎081/534 0310. This decaying Victorian theatre, in one of London's most grotty areas, was made famous back in the Sixties by the pioneering Joan Littlewood. Nowadays it's not the force it was then, but it still boasts a good track record. *Stratford tube.*

Tricycle, 269 Kilburn High Rd, NW6 ☎0171/328 1000. One of London's most dynamic fringe venues, showcasing a mixed bag of new plays and international productions of the core repertoire. *Kilburn tube.*

Young Vic, 66 The Cut, SE1 ☎0171/928 6363. A large, in-the-round space, perfect for Shakespeare, which is something of a speciality. Big names have trodden these boards – such as Vanessa Redgrave in a near-legendary version of Ibsen's *Ghosts. Waterloo tube.*

Independent theatre companies

Several of Britain's most exciting **theatre companies** are rootless collectives which periodically take occupancy of a London stage for a brief season. The list below is a selection of the best current practitioners – keep an eye out for them.

Cheek by Jowl ☎0171/793 0153. Best known for tackling the world's classics in offbeat ways.

Paine's Plough ☎0171/284 4483. A company that presents nothing but new work.

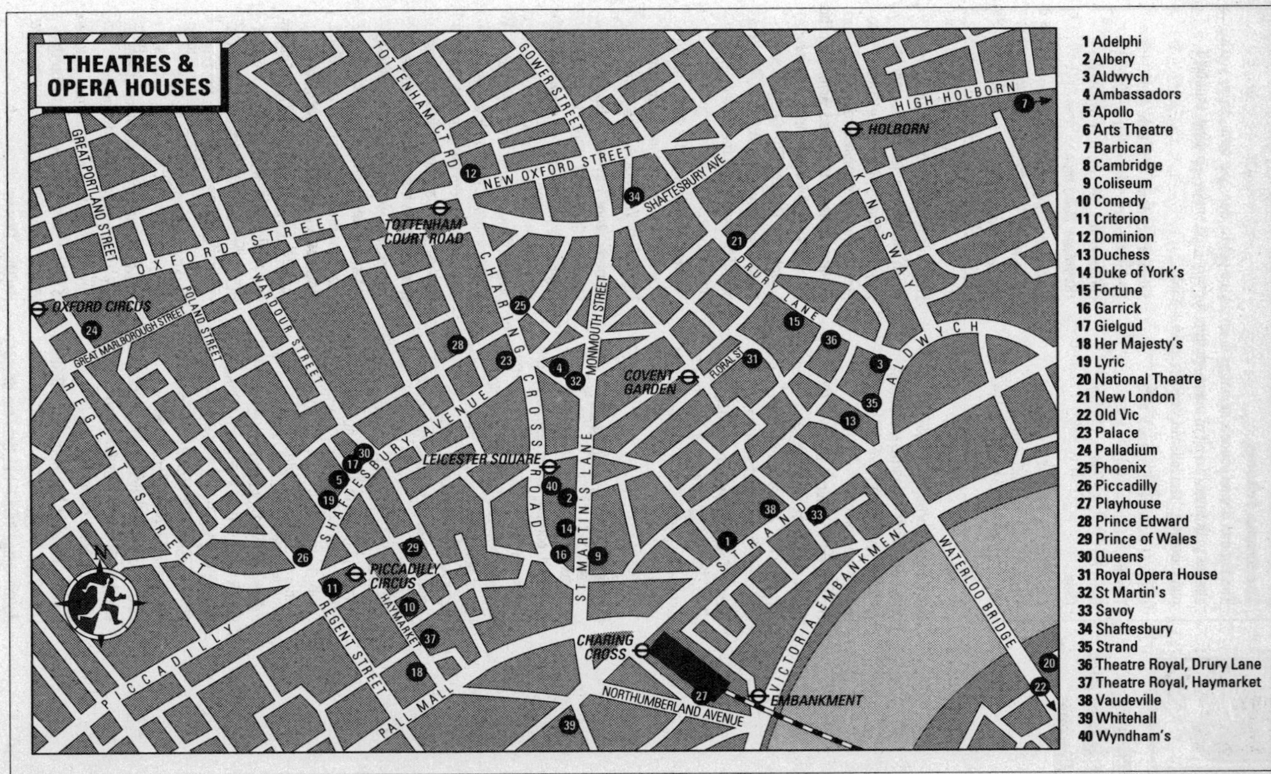
THEATRES & OPERA HOUSES
1 Adelphi
2 Albery
3 Aldwych
4 Ambassadors
5 Apollo
6 Arts Theatre
7 Barbican
8 Cambridge
9 Coliseum
10 Comedy
11 Criterion
12 Dominion
13 Duchess
14 Duke of York's
15 Fortune
16 Garrick
17 Gielgud
18 Her Majesty's
19 Lyric
20 National Theatre
21 New London
22 Old Vic
23 Palace
24 Palladium
25 Phoenix
26 Piccadilly
27 Playhouse
28 Prince Edward
29 Prince of Wales
30 Queens
31 Royal Opera House
32 St Martin's
33 Savoy
34 Shaftesbury
35 Strand
36 Theatre Royal, Drury Lane
37 Theatre Royal, Haymarket
38 Vaudeville
39 Whitehall
40 Wyndham's
HIGH HOLBORN
HOLBORN
KINGSWAY
ALDWYCH
WATERLOO BRIDGE
VICTORIA EMBANKMENT
EMBANKMENT
STRAND
DRURY LANE
FLORAL ST
COVENT GARDEN
SHAFTESBURY AVE
NEW OXFORD STREET
GOWER STREET
MONMOUTH STREET
ST MARTIN'S LANE
CHARING CROSS ROAD
LEICESTER SQUARE
CHARING CROSS
NORTHUMBERLAND AVENUE
TOTTENHAM CT RD
TOTTENHAM COURT ROAD
SHAFTESBURY AVENUE
PICCADILLY CIRCUS
HAYMARKET
PALL MALL
REGENT STREET
WARDOUR STREET
OXFORD STREET
POLAND STREET
GREAT MARLBOROUGH STREET
OXFORD CIRCUS
GREAT PORTLAND STREET
PICCADILLY
N

Theatre, Cabaret and Cinema

The drama schools

The London drama schools mount as many as ten productions per term, giving you a chance to indulge in a bit of talent-spotting for very little outlay – indeed, Guildhall plays are free. The following are the main schools.

Central School of Speech and Drama, 64 Eton Avenue, NW3 ☎0171/722 8183. *Swiss Cottage tube.*

Guildhall School of Music and Drama, Silk St, Barbican, EC2 ☎0171/628 2571. *Moorgate tube.*

London Academy of Music and Dramatic Art, Tower House, 226 Cromwell Rd, SW5 ☎0171/373 9883. *Gloucester Road tube.*

Royal Academy of Dramatic Art, 62–64 Gower St, WC1 ☎0171/636 7076. *Goodge Street tube.*

The People Show ☎0171/729 1841. A nutty, doggedly experimental bunch whose shows don't have titles but are always memorable.

Theatre de Complicité ☎0171/700 0233. The outstanding, energetic work of this company has cemented its place at the forefront of British performance.

Trestle Theatre Company ☎0181/441 0349. The UK's premier masked theatre company, specializing in mordant social critiques.

Comedy and cabaret

As a hundred media pundits have remarked, comedy is the new rock'n'roll on the London scene, with the leading stand-up funnypersons commanding the sort of adoration that was previously the preserve of pretty-boy singers. The **Comedy Store** is the best known venue on the circuit, but even in the lowliest suburbs you can often find a local pub giving a platform to young hopefuls (*Time Out* gives full listings). Note that many venues operate only on Friday and Saturday nights, and that August is a lean month, as much of London's talent then heads north for the Edinburgh Festival. **Tickets** vary in price, but average around £5. The painfully shy should be warned that audience participation and/or humiliation is a mandatory element of many stand-up acts and thus front row seats are not always desirable.

Banana Cabaret, The Bedford, 77 Bedford Hill, SW12 ☎0181/673 8904. This double-stage venue has become one of London's finest comedy venues – well worth the trip out from the centre of town. Fri–Sun. *Balham tube.* (There's also an enormously popular Friday night *Acton Banana*, at the King's Head, Acton High St, W3 ☎0181/673 8904; *Acton Town tube.*)

Canal Café Theatre, The Bridge House, Delamere Terrace, W2 ☎0171/289 6054 or 6056. Perched on the water's edge in Little Venice, this venue is good for improvisation acts and is home to the *Newsrevue* team of topical gagsters. Thurs–Sun. *Warwick Avenue tube.*

Comedy Store, Haymarket House, Oxendon Street, W1 ☎0171 344 4444. Feted as the birthplace of alternative comedy, the *Comedy Store* has catapulted many a comic onto prime time TV. There's improvisation on Wednesdays and Sundays from the Comedy Store Players, Thursday night offers a try-out spot for those brave enough to handle the hecklers, while Friday and Saturday are the busiest nights – as much for the late-night drinking as for the comedians. Closed Mon. *Piccadilly Circus tube.*

Downstairs at the King's Head, 2 Crouch End Hill, N8 ☎0181/340 1028. A well-run club which secures excellent acts. Sat & Sun. *Finsbury Park tube, then W7 bus.*

Hackney Empire, 291 Mare St, E8 ☎0171/739 5706. Famous and well-loved old variety theatre which stages a diverse programme of cabaret and comedy on Saturday nights from October to Easter. Star-name solo acts crop up from time to time. *Hackney Central or Hackney Downs BR.*

Hurricane Club, The Black Horse, 6 Rathbone Place, W1 ☎0171/580 0666. The in-house team performs a Saturday night stand-up and improvisation act. *Tottenham Court Road tube.*

Jongleurs Battersea, The Cornet, 49 Lavender Gardens, SW11 (*Clapham Junction tube & 45 bus*) and **Jongleurs Camden Lock**, Dingwalls Building, Middle Yard, Camden Lock, NW1 (*Camden Town tube*); ☎0171/924 2766 for both venues. Twin top-ranking venues on opposite sides of the city. The Camden club has a spot of post-revelry disco-dancing included in the ticket price. Book well in advance for either venue. Fri & Sat.

Red Rose Club, 129 Seven Sisters Rd, N7 ☎0171/281 3051. Half the price of the *Comedy Store* but with an equally strong line-up and a livelier audience. Fri & Sat. *Finsbury Park or Holloway Road tube.*

Poetry

In recent years poetry readings in London have become a thriving outpost of the performing arts. In response to burgeoning demand, several music and theatre venues now host extremely popular poetry nights, many of which are free; a selection of the best long-standing poetry groups is given below, but performances can be sporadic, so always call the venue for dates. Good sources of information about readings and poetry-related events are the Poetry Society, 22 Betterton St, WC2 (☎0171 240 4810; *Covent Garden tube*), and the ICA (see "Theatres" above), which occasionally plays host to eminent writers. *Time Out* also lists the week's readings and performances.

Apples & Snakes, Battersea Arts Centre, Old Town Hall, Lavender Hill, SW11 ☎0171/223 2223. Fortnightly performances of poetry of sound political persuasion, from the longest-running group in London. *Clapham Junction BR from Waterloo or Victoria.*

Chelsea Poets Society, Café Opera, 315 King's Rd, SW3 ☎0171/352 9854. This long-established poetry club sticks to unaccompanied recitations, with a bit of a cappella singing thrown in. *Sloane Square tube.*

Poetry Of My Shoulders, Samuel Pepys Theatre Bar, 289 Mare St, E8 ☎0171/372 0418. Boisterous off-the-wall verse, free of charge. *Hackney Central or Hackney Downs BR from Liverpool Street.*

Pull My Daisy, The Paradise, Kilburn Lane, W10 ☎0181/969 0098. Poems from stylish young blades with a social conscience. *Kensal Green tube.*

Subvoicive, The Three Cups, 21 Sandland St, Holborn, WC1☎0171/831 4302. Very avant-garde performance poetry, and free to boot. *Chancery Lane or Holborn tube.*

Vertical Images, The Victoria, Mornington Place, NW1 ☎0181/340 5807. Sunday night slot (weekly or twice-weekly) for a poetry performance-cum-workshop, with contributions from the floor invited. *Camden Town tube.*

Voice Box, Royal Festival Hall, South Bank Centre, South Bank, SE1 ☎0171/921 0906. Established names and newer talent enjoy the spotlight at the South Bank Centre, which presents a wide range of contemporary, generally published, poetry. Drop into the excellent Poetry Library while you're here – it's the country's largest archive of twentieth-century verse. *Waterloo tube.*

World Oyster Club, Bunjie's Café, 27 Litchfield St, WC2 ☎0181/808 6595. A mixed bag of poets – funny, sensitive, very angry – perform to an equally mixed audience. An open floor spot gives would-be wordsmiths a stab at fame. *Leicester Square tube.*

Cinema

If you walk round the West End, across Leicester Square and down Haymarket or up Charing Cross Road to Oxford Street, you'll pass a lot of cinemas. Unfortunately, the number of cinemas does not correspond to the variety of films on offer and there are all too many pocket-sized multiplexes. Nonetheless, there are some good places committed to European art-house movies, and a few repertory cinemas programme serious films from the back-catalogue. November's **London Film Festival**, which occupies half

Theatre, Cabaret and Cinema

a dozen West End cinemas, is an increasingly important occasion, too, and so popular that most of the films sell out within a couple of days of the publication of the festival's plans.

Seats tend to **cost** upwards of £7 at the West End major screens, although afternoon shows are usually discounted. The suburban screens run by the big companies (see *Time Out* for full listings) tend to be a couple of pounds cheaper, as do independent cinemas. Students, senior citizens and the unemployed can get concessionary rates for some shows at virtually all cinemas: reductions are usually available either for all screenings on an off-peak day (Monday as a rule), or for off-peak screenings on all weekdays (ie first show, or first and second shows at the biggest places).

First-run cinemas

The dozen cinemas here are the pick of the bunch for first-run movies, with decent-sized screens and/or interesting programming.

Chelsea Cinema, 206 King's Rd, SW3 ☎0171/351 3742. Aesthetically impressive cinema with an equally attractive programme of art-house offerings. *Sloane Square tube.*

Curzon West End, Shaftesbury Ave, W1 ☎0171/369 1722. Big screen venue with a preference for international features and the quirkier American films. *Green Park tube.*

Empire, Leicester Square, WC2 ☎0171/437 1234. Huge, expensive hi-tech, big-screen cinema – blockbusters open here. *Leicester Square tube.*

Lumière, 42 St Martin's Lane, WC2 ☎0171/836 0691. One of London's plushest cinemas, screening major, arty movies – Jane Campion, Kieslowski, Woody Allen and the like open here. *Leicester Square tube.*

Metro, 11 Rupert St, W1 ☎0171/437 0757. A fine, two-screen cinema, especially good for offbeat US films and for Asian and Chinese features. *Piccadilly Circus or Leicester Square tube.*

MGM Shaftesbury Avenue, 135 Shaftesbury Ave, W1 ☎0171/836 6279. Best of the West End MGMs. Favours the classier end of the Hollywood catalogue – *Pulp Fiction, Geronimo*, etc. *Leicester Square or Tottenham Court Road tube.*

Minema, 45 Knightsbridge, SW1 ☎0171/235 4225. Tiny independent cinema, favouring upmarket films. *Knightsbridge or Hyde Park Corner tube.*

Odeon Leicester Square, 28–30 Leicester Square, WC2 ☎01426/915 683. London's largest cinema, and thus a favourite for celeb-packed premieres. There's just one screen here, but the adjacent Odeon Mezzanine crushes five screens into a far smaller space (one reason why it's been voted London's worst). *Leicester Square or Piccadilly Circus tube.*

Odeon Marble Arch, 10 Edgware Rd, W2 ☎01426/914501. Blockbuster specialist, on account of possessing the city's biggest screen, with a sound system to match. *Marble Arch tube.*

Renoir, Brunswick Centre, Brunswick Square, WC1 ☎0171/837 8402. Highly regarded foreign films make this place popular with cinéastes. *Russell Square tube.*

Screen on the Green, 83 Upper St, N1 ☎0171/226 3520. Gorgeous old cinema in the heart of trendy Islington, usually showing the more challenging latest releases. *Angel tube.*

Screen on the Hill, 203 Haverstock Hill, NW3 ☎0171/435 3366. Artistically inclined cinema. *Belsize Park tube.*

Repertory

These are the places you're most likely to catch back catalogue and foreign movies, often as part of a themed programme lasting a week or more.

Barbican, Barbican Centre, Silk Street, EC2 ☎0171/638 8891. The Barbican's Screen Two specializes in revivals, often as part of a themed season. *Barbican or Moorgate tube.*

Electric Cinema, 191 Portobello Rd, W11 ☎0171/792 2020. London's first purpose-built cinema, eking out a precarious existence through adventurous schedules. *Ladbroke Grove or Notting Hill Gate tube.*

Everyman, Hollybush Vale, NW3 ☎0171/435 1525. The city's oldest repertory cinema and still one of its best, with strong programmes of classics, cultish crowd-magnets and directors' seasons. Very hot in summer. *Hampstead tube.*

French Institute, 17 Queensberry Place, SW7 ☎0171/589 6211. French films both old and new. *South Kensington tube.*

Goethe Institute, 50 Princes Gate, Exhibition Road, SW7 ☎0171/411 3400. Sporadic showings of German cinematic masterpieces. *South Kensington tube.*

ICA Cinemathèque, Nash House, The Mall, SW1 ☎0171/930 3647. Varied programme of vintage and undergound movies shown on a tiny screen. *Piccadilly Circus tube.*

National Film Theatre, South Bank, SE1 ☎0171/928 3232. For people who take cinema seriously. Attentive audiences and a great eclectic programme, including directors' seasons and thematic series. Around six films daily shown in the vast NFT1, the smaller NFT2 and the cinema of the adjoining Museum of the Moving Image. *Waterloo tube.*

Prince Charles, 2–7 Leicester Place, WC2 ☎0171/437 8181. The bargain basement of London's cinematic society (many shows at £1.99), with a programme of new movies, classics and cult favourites – *Reservoir Dogs* and *Rocky Horror Picture Show* are regulars. *Leicester Square or Piccadilly Circus tube.*

Rio, 107 Kingsland High St, E8 ☎0171/249 2722. Shabby but charismatic old cinema, specializing in art-house double-bills, and at bargain prices (adult £2.50, child £1.50). *Dalston Kingsland BR from Highbury & Islington tube, or buses #67, #76, #149 or #243.*

Riverside Studios, Crisp Rd, W6 ☎0181/748 3354. There's often very good work on show in this converted film studio (usually a different film each day), but it's a bit far from the centre of town. *Hammersmith tube.*

Theatre, Cabaret and Cinema

Galleries

The vast collections of the **National Gallery** and the **Tate**, the fascinating miscellanies of the Victoria and Albert Museum, and the select holdings of such institutions as the Courtauld and the Wallace Collection make London one of the world's great repositories of western art. However, the city is also a dynamic creative centre, with young artists such as Helen Chadwick and *enfant terrible* Damien Hirst maintaining the momentum established by the likes of Hockney, Caro, Auerbach, Freud and Caulfield. In the environs of Cork Street, behind the Royal Academy, you'll find various **commercial galleries** showing the best of what's being produced in the studios of Britain and further afield, while numerous other private showcases are scattered all over London, from the superb Saatchi gallery in St John's Wood to the consistently challenging place run by Angela Flowers over in the East End.

In only one respect does London fail to compete with Berlin, Paris and New York – it doesn't have a special **exhibition space** good enough to handle the sort of blockbuster shows that regularly pack them at the Grand Palais or MOMA. Even the major spaces, such as the National Gallery, the Hayward, the Royal Academy and the Tate, are **cramped** by comparison, and it's become routine for the massive touring shows to miss out Britain altogether, or at best to arrive here in pared-down versions. On the other hand, at any time of the year London's public galleries will be offering at least one absorbing exhibition, on anything from ancient Mexican art to the latest angst-ridden neo-Expressionist outpourings.

Annual fixtures include the **Royal Academy's Summer Exhibition**, when hordes of amateur artists enter their efforts for sale, and November's controversial **Turner Prize**, which is preceded by a month-long display of work by the shortlisted artists at the Tate. More exciting than these, however, are the art school **degree shows** in late May and June, when the current crop of student talent puts its work on display. The Royal College, the Royal Academy, Slade and St Martin's are all good, but Goldsmith's, which has produced some of the most celebrated artists of the last ten years, is the one likeliest to thrill devotees of the avant-garde. Pick up a copy of *Time Out* in mid-May for the times and locations of the student shows.

Public art galleries

The following galleries are generally open Monday to Saturday from around 10am to 5 or 6pm, plus Sunday from around noon to 5 or 6pm. However, hours tend to change from show to show, so it's always best to check *Time Out* or ring the gallery before setting off. Expect to pay in the region of £6 for entry to one of the big exhibitions at the Barbican or Hayward. Similar prices are charged for special shows at the National Gallery, Tate, Royal Academy and V&A (see box above). Students, senior citizens and the unemployed are eligible for concessionary rates.

Galleries

Barbican Art Gallery, Level 8, Barbican Centre, Silk Street, EC2 ☎0171/588 9023. The Barbican's two-floor gallery is badly designed, but its thematic exhibitions –ranging from African bush art to the latest photography – are often well worth the entrance fee. *Barbican or Moorgate tube.*

Camden Arts Centre, Arkwright Road, corner of Finchley Road, NW1 ☎0171/435 2643. Showcases the work of both new and established artists. Finchley Road tube.

Hayward Gallery, South Bank Centre, Belvedere Road, SE1 ☎0171/261 0127. Part of the huge South Bank arts complex, the Hayward is one of London's most prestigious venues for major touring exhibitions, with the bias towards twentieth-century work. *Waterloo tube.*

ICA Gallery, The Mall, SW1 ☎0171/930 6393. The Institute of Contemporary Arts

Permanent collections

Below is a list of London's principal permanent art collections, with a brief summary of their strengths and a cross-reference to the page of the guide where each is covered in more detail.

British Museum, Great Russell St, WC1 ☎0171/636 1555. The BM owns a stupendous collection of drawings and prints, part of which is always on show; it also has excellent one-off exhibitions, often free. *Russell Square tube. See p.135.*

Courtauld Institute, Somerset House, Strand, WC2 ☎0171/873 2526. Excellent collection of Impressionists and post-Impressionists – especially good Cézannes. *Covent Garden or Embankment tube. See p.164.*

Dulwich Picture Gallery, College Road, SE21 ☎0181/693 8000. London's first public art gallery; small but high-quality selection – notable work from Poussin, Gainsborough and Rembrandt. *West Dulwich BR from Victoria. See p.341.*

Iveagh Bequest, Kenwood House, Hampstead Lane, NW3 ☎0181/348 8000. Best known for its pictures by Rembrandt, Gainsborough, Reynolds and Vermeer. *Highgate or Archway tube. See p.328.*

Leighton House, 12 Holland Park, W14 ☎0171/602 3316. Work from Frederic Leighton and his Pre-Raphaelite cohorts. *High Street Kensington tube. See p.290.*

National Gallery, Trafalgar Square, WC2 ☎0171/839 3321. The country's premier collection; difficult to think of a major artist born between 1300 and 1850 who isn't on show here. *Charing Cross tube. See p.43.*

National Portrait Gallery, 2 St Martin's Place, WC2 ☎0171/306 0055. Interesting faces, but few works of art to match those on display in the neighbouring National Gallery. *Leicester Square or Charing Cross tube. See p.54.*

Queen's Gallery, Buckingham Palace, Buckingham Palace Road, SW1 ☎0171/930 4832. Frequently changing displays from the royal hoard of Old Masters. *St James's Park or Victoria tube. See p.59.*

Tate Gallery, Millbank, SW11 ☎0171/887 8000. The country's main array of British and international modern art. *Pimlico or Vauxhall tube. See p.77.*

Victoria & Albert Museum, Cromwell Rd, SW7 ☎0171/938 8500. A scattering of European painting and sculpture, a fine collection of English statuary, two remarkable rooms of casts, Raphael's famous tapestry cartoons, and occasional special shows of prints, watercolours and photography, though applied arts are the V&A's speciality. *South Kensington tube. See p.276.*

Wallace Collection, Hertford House, Manchester Square, W1 ☎0171/935 0687. Small, eclectic collection; fine paintings by Rembrandt, Velásquez, Hals, Gainsborough and Delacroix. *Bond Street tube. See p.106.*

has two gallery spaces (it's easy to miss the upstairs Nash Rooms), in which it displays works that are invariably characterized as "challenging" or "provocative". Sometimes they are. To visit, you must be a member of the ICA; a day's membership costs £1.50. *Piccadilly Circus or Charing Cross Road tube.*

Riverside Studios, Crisp Road, W6 ☎0181/741 2251. A wide range of exciting new work is shown at this multifunctional arts centre. *Hammersmith tube.*

Royal Academy of Arts, Burlington House, Piccadilly, W1 ☎0171/439 7438. The Royal Academy has a small permanent collection (see p.98), but is mainly known for its major one-off exhibitions – Monet, Picasso and Goya have all been subjects of recent single-artist shows, and the RA has staged some brilliant surveys of entire periods, such as Venice in the sixteenth century, Italian art in the twentieth century and modern figurative painting. The award-winning Sackler Galleries, designed by Norman Foster and opened in 1991, often have a smaller show in parallel to the exhibition in the RA's main suite of rooms – you have to pay for the two shows separately, but usually get a discount if buying tickets for both. From early June to mid-August the RA stages its Summer Exhibition, when the public can submit work to be displayed (and sold) alongside the work of Academicians. Tasteful landscapes, interiors and nudes tend to predominate, but there's the odd splash of experimentation.

Whatever the show, crowds are a problem at the Royal Academy, as the rooms are not enormous. For the most popular shows a timed ticketing system has been introduced, limiting the number of people allowed into the building in a given hour; for these you're best advised to pre-book a ticket for a weekday morning if possible. For other shows, avoid weekends and the midday period during the week. *Green Park or Piccadilly Circus tube.*

Serpentine Gallery, Kensington Gardens, Hyde Park, W2 ☎0171/402 0343. Formerly the Kensington Gardens tearooms, this fine gallery displays dynamic work by new and established modern artists, sometimes acting as an adjunct to exhibitions at the Hayward. Hosts interesting Sunday afternoon lectures, and a performance art festival in the summer. It's free, too. *Lancaster Gate or South Kensington tube.*

Whitechapel Gallery, Whitechapel High Street, E1 ☎0171/522 7888. The Whitechapel is a consistently excellent champion of contemporary art, housing major shows by living or not-long-dead artists. It's also the focal point of the Whitechapel Open, an annual summer survey of the work of artists living in the vicinity of the gallery; the show spreads into several local studios too. *Aldgate East tube.*

Private and commercial galleries

The galleries listed below are at the hub of London's modern art market. This is not to say that you'll see price tags on everything on display in these galleries, or indeed that everything hanging on their walls is for sale, but rather that their owners make their money promoting new names and selling their work behind the scenes. Most are open Monday to Friday 10am to 6pm plus a few hours on Saturday morning, but you'd be best advised to ring to check the latest hours, as rehangings or private viewings often interrupt the normal pattern of business. Some of these places can seem as intimidating as designer clothes shops, but all are free except the Saatchi, the showcase for the collection of the most powerful mover on the British art scene.

Anderson O'Day, 225 Portobello Rd, W11 ☎0171/221 7592. An impressive array of contemporary painting and sculpture, with a particularly strong selection of prints. Young up-and-coming artists often have their work displayed here. *Ladbroke Grove tube.*

Annely Juda, 23 Dering St, W1 ☎0171/629 7578. One of the city's best modernist galleries; strong on abstract painting and sculpture. *Green Park or Bond Street tube.*

Galleries

Anthony d'Offay, 9, 21 & 23 Dering St, W1 ☎0171/499 4100. Three excellent galleries devoted to the work of international contemporary artists. One of the real powerbrokers in the world of art politics. *Green Park or Bond Street tube.*

Anthony Reynolds, 5 Dering St, W1 ☎0171/491 0621. British and foreign contemporary art; stages challenging group shows. *Oxford Circus or Bond Street tube.*

Bernard Jacobsen Gallery, 14a Clifford St, off Savile Row, W1 ☎0171/495 8575. This gallery's reputation is based on its backing for contemporary British figurative artists. *Green Park or Piccadilly Circus tube.*

Edward Totah, First Floor, 13 Old Burlington St, W1 ☎0171/734 0343. Set atop a tailor's, this three-floor gallery shows an attractive range of minimalist/conceptualist art. *Green Park or Piccadilly Circus tube.*

Flowers East, 199–205 & 282 Richmond Rd, E8 ☎0181/985 3333. This outstanding, ever-expanding gallery complex in the East End shows a huge variety of work, generally by young British artists. *London Fields BR from Liverpool Street.*

Frith Street, 60 Frith St, W1 ☎0171/494 1550. Good shows are held six times per year in this fine old Soho building. *Tottenham Court Road tube.*

Karsten Schubert, 41–42 Foley St, W1 ☎0171/631 0031. Exciting and often influential new work, predominantly from Britain, Germany and the States, is displayed at this exceptionally good two-floor gallery. Many cognoscenti of the avant-garde rate this as the city's best gallery. *Goodge Street tube.*

Lisson, 67 Lisson St, NW1 ☎0171/724 2739. An extremely important gallery whose regularly exhibited sculptors – among them Anish Kapoor and Richard Deacon – are hugely respected on the international circuit. *Edgware Road tube.*

Marlborough Fine Art, 6 Albermarle St, W1 ☎0171/629 5161. This is where you'll find the latest work of many of Britain's most celebrated artists, many in one-person shows. Essential viewing for anyone interested in modern British art. *Green Park tube.*

Paton, 282 Richmond Rd, E8 ☎0181/986 3409. Relocated from the ruinously expensive West End site he occupied for years, Graham Paton now has far more space in which to display his bright young (generally figurative) artists. *London Fields BR from Liverpool Street.*

Raab, 9 Cork St, W1 ☎0171/734 6444. Exceptional work by figurative artists, with a pan-European scope. *Green Park tube.*

Saatchi Collection, 98a Boundary Rd, NW8 ☎0171/624 8299. First-rate exhibition space owned by Charles Saatchi, the Mr Big of Britain's art (and advertising) world. Shows change twice-yearly, and a couple of Saatchi's youngsters always hit the headlines straight afer the opening. Damien Hirst's notorious shark was shown here, as was Marc Quinn's self-portrait in frozen blood. Thurs–Sun, free on Thurs, £2.50 other days. *St John's Wood tube.*

Todd Gallery, 1–5 Needham Rd, W11 ☎0171/792 1404. This attractive purpose-built space focuses chiefly on the work of young abstract painters, not exclusively British. *Notting Hill Gate tube.*

Victoria Miro, 21 Cork St, W1 ☎0171/437 8611. Spartan gallery with a penchant for minimalist abstraction. *Green Park tube.*

Waddington's, 5, 11, 12 & 34 Cork St, W1 ☎0171/437 8611. No. 12 is the largest of four Cork Street premises owned by Leslie Waddington, and tends to concentrate on the established greats of the twentieth century – this is where to pick up your modest Picasso print or Mirò sketch. At the others you'll find newer international stars and even younger artists whose fame will probably spread beyond these shores now that Waddington is backing them. *Green Park tube.*

Photography

The Barbican, Hayward and V&A all host photographic exhibitions from time to time. The galleries listed below are the only spaces that always have photos on show.

Galleries

Hamilton's, 13 Carlos Place, W1 ☎499 9493. Classy exhibition space for the most famous contemporary photographers. Loads of prints for sale as well, if you fancy dropping a few hundred quid on an Irving Penn fashion shot. *Bond Street or Green Park tube.*

National Portrait Gallery, 2 St Martin's Place, WC2 ☎0171/306 0055. The NPG has several fine photos in its permanent collection, and also regularly holds special (fee-charging) exhibitions on internationally famous photo-portraitists. *Leicester Square or Charing Cross tube.*

Photographer's Gallery, 5 & 8 Great Newport St, WC2 ☎0171/831 1772. The capital's premier photography gallery shows work by new and established British and international photographers, often with a couple of exhibitions running concurrently. The prints are often for sale. *Leicester Square tube.*

Zelda Cheatle Gallery, 8 Cecil Court, WC2 ☎0171/836 0506. A good little gallery with shows by names and unknowns alike; specially strong on documentary and landscape work. *Leicester Square tube.*

Zwemmer Fine Photographs, First Floor, 28 Denmark St, WC2 ☎0171/379 6248. Part of the Zwemmer group, which publishes and retails books on the arts, this gallery features photographic art both modern and classic. *Tottenham Court Road tube.*

Shops and Markets

As you'd expect from the capital city of what Napoleon termed "a nation of shop-keepers", London is a consumerist delight. Whatever your resources or tastes, the city offers plenty of temptations, from *Harrods* and its neighbouring monuments to Mammon, through the showcase branches of the nationwide chainstores, to oddball stores and street fashion, to the seething streetmarkets of the East End. In the sections that follow, we've classified the shops according to what they sell; for a few indicators as to the character of London's main commercial zones, check out the box below.

Opening hours for central London shops are generally Monday to Saturday 9.30am to 6pm, though several stores stay open an hour or two later, especially on Thursdays and in the month leading up to Christmas, and supermarkets and many shops near weekend markets are open on Sundays. For chain stores, we've given the **main branch** opening hours of each store listed; other branches are usually open slightly different hours, so you should phone for details if you're worried you might turn up to find the store shut.

The lengthy British recession has resulted in special **discount** offers at various times of the year (*Time Out*'s "Sell Out" section offers an up-to-date list of one-off sales), but the best times to snap up a bargain are the two annual **sale seasons**, centred on January and July, when prices are routinely slashed by between twenty and fifty percent. The winter sale is the bigger event, and the New Year news bulletins invariably feature a report on the hardy bargain-hounds who have spent the Christmas period camping outside *Harrods* in order to be at the head of the stampede.

To pay, **credit cards** are almost universally accepted by shops (notable exceptions being *Marks & Spencer* and *John Lewis*, the latter of which accepts certain debit cards), and department stores and chain stores often run their own credit schemes as well. **Traveller's cheques**, whether in sterling or other currency, are not commonly accepted as payment. Market stalls tend to accept cash only, or cheques for more expensive items. It's always worth keeping receipts, which are useful if you want to return **faulty goods** – whatever the shop may say, the law allows a full refund or replacement on purchases that turn out to be imperfect. If you just decide that you don't like something, most retailers will offer a credit note, but they are not legally obliged to.

Finally, foreigners can sometimes claim back the **value added tax** (VAT) that applies to most goods in British shops, although you probably won't get anything if you spend under £100. On request, participating stores will issue you with a form which you should hand in to Customs on your way out of the country. There's a six-week wait for reimbursement.

London's shopping districts

Almost every district of London has a shopping character that is in some way

Shops and Markets

Shopping Categories

distinctive. This is a very basic resumé of the busiest and most characterful.

OXFORD STREET AND AROUND

Oxford Street This is the most frantic shopping area in the city. Chain stores dominate, many of them bland but a few of them – notably *Selfridge's* and the Marble Arch *Marks & Spencer* – well worth investigation. As a rule of thumb, the shops are tackier on the eastern half of Oxford Street, where cheap jeans outlets and souvenir shops jostle with giants like *HMV* and *Next*. The tone alters to the west of Oxford Circus, and the upmarket drift is especially strong in the tributaries to the north and south of this section of Oxford Street: Christopher Place (north side) is chock-full of designer outlets, as is South Molton Street (south side), while Bond Street/New Bond Street is the preserve of very expensive clothes shops, jewellers and the like.

Regent Street Formerly a lot more expensive than Oxford Street, but now becoming more mainstream with inroads from *The Gap* and other worldwide outlets. It still retains more upmarket pockets than Oxford Street (it has *Garrards*, the royal jewellers), and in *Hamleys*, the world-famous toyshop, boasts one of the city's great feelgood stores.

PICCADILLY AREA

Piccadilly Piccadilly Circus is a maelstrom of traffic, overlooked by the hideous consumerist warren of the Trocadero (a hive of small outlets of major chainstores) and a colossal *Tower Records*. To the west, Piccadilly itself is fairly sparse as a shopping street, but you'll find some illustrious names here – notably *Fortnum & Mason* and *Simpson's*, two of the gentry's favourite department stores.

St James's On the south side of Piccadilly, the streets of St James's – notably Jermyn

Street – harbour some quintessentially English small shops, most of them dedicated to the grooming of the English male.

SOHO AND COVENT GARDEN

Soho A staunchly off-beat zone, full of specialist stores stocking everything from Italian olives to the lastest indie record releases, plus of course the porno and sex goods for which Soho has long been notorious.

Charing Cross Road Dividing Soho from Covent Garden, this street has long been the focus of the book trade, both new and second-hand.

Covent Garden This is more mainstream by the month but still has a remarkable concentration of small, idiosyncratic shops. The former market has been colonized chiefly by nationwide stores, with a bias towards clothes and household items, while the surrounding streets – especially Floral Street – have become known for designer clothes. To the north of the market, Neal Street is synonymous with well-heeled "alternative" types – wholefood, books, design and clubwear take up a fair amount of space.

KNIGHTSBRIDGE, KENSINGTON AND CHELSEA

Knightsbridge/Brompton Road You need serious money for a spending spree round here. On Knightsbridge itself you've got *Harrods*, set amid a plethora of pricy jewellers and shoe shops; from there, Brompton Road heads east to Brompton Cross, a focal point of the fashion scene, with the *Joseph* flagship presiding over a cluster of choice designer shops.

Sloane Street Smaller-scale version of the above, with glitzy department store *Harvey Nichols* standing at the head of a line of plush clothes shops, among them *Armani* and another large *Joseph* branch.

King's Road At its southern end Sloane Street runs into Sloane Square, from where the King's Road heads west into Chelsea. Formerly the coolest street in the city, King's Road is less characterful than it was (most of its shops are smaller branches of places you'll find in the West End), but it still has a good range of fashion and design shops, and a more laid-back feel than rival areas.

NOTTING HILL

Portobello Road area The market and hip natives have helped to spawn dozens of specialist and wacky shops off Portobello Road, which itself is lined with antique dealers. Off Portobello, Blenheim Crescent/Talbot Road and Elgin Crecent are worth exploring for all kinds of books, music, design and ethnic goods.

CAMDEN

Camden High Street/Chalk Farm Road It's a similar story around Camden Market, with oriental tiles, antiques and alternative pursuits, including London's most switched-on bookshop, *Compendium*.

Department stores

In *Harrods* London has a department store so glamorous that it ranks as a tourist attraction in its own right, and the city centre boasts plenty of other similarly upmarket emporia, many of them with a pedigree equally as impressive as that of the Knightsbridge flagship. For all but the wealthiest, however, a visit to one of these intimidating establishments is more an exercise in social observation than a serious shopping expedition. Viewed in terms of general appeal and economic turnover, London's most successful department stores are the mid-range megastores of the Oxford Street area, the best of which is *Marks & Spencer*, a chain that has become synonymous with high quality at moderate cost.

Fortnum & Mason, 181 Piccadilly, W1 ☎0171/734 8040. London's most interesting-looking department store – golden cherubs, fountains, wondrous displays and eccentric staff who seem to have been there forever. Fine food is the main attraction: kitsch packaging makes the biscuits, jams and teas irresistible, despite the inflated prices. *Green Park or Piccadilly Circus tube. Mon–Sat 9.30am–6pm.*

Harrods, Knightsbridge, SW1 ☎0171/730 1234. *Harrods* is so proud of itself that it

Shops and Markets

actually has a dress code – even pop stars have been unceremoniously turfed out for wearing shorts. The snobbery may be appalling but this is the best-stocked shop in London, and just as spectacle it's worth checking out the exquisitely tiled food hall and the children's department, where filthy-rich infants whizz around in miniature sports cars. The January sale sees decorum thrown to the wind in a riot of snatching fingernails and credit cards; July's bargain time is rather less frenzied. *Knightsbridge tube. Mon, Tues & Sat 10am–6pm, Wed–Fri 10am–7pm.*

Harvey Nichols, 109–125 Knightsbridge, SW1 ☎0171/235 5000. This is where London's svelte young aristos stock up on the new season's designer frocks, nipping downstairs to pick up a bit of jewellery and make-up. The cosmetics section is the best in London – "Harvey Nicks" is the city's sole purveyor of the exclusive MAC range, so you can't move for aspiring models. For a glimpse of how the other half lives, pop into the café on a Saturday afternoon – if you're not drinking champagne you shouldn't really be there – and take a look at the food hall, which runs *Harrods* close for quality and taste. On the design front, there is a menswear section, but essentially this is *Vogue*-readers' territory. *Knightsbridge tube. Mon–Tues & Thurs–Fri 10am–7pm, Wed 10am–8pm, Sat 10am–6pm.*

Laura Ashley, 256–258 Regent St, W1 ☎0171/437 9760 (Oxford Circus tube) and many other branches. One of the great British commercial successes of recent decades, *Laura Ashley* is the look that launched a thousand Home Counties weddings. In recent years the company has produced attractively simple coats and dresses, but floral prints, lacy collars, puff sleeves and long skirts still prevail. *Mon & Tues 10am–6.30pm, Wed & Fri 10am–7pm, Thurs 10am–8pm, Sat 9.30–7pm.*

John Lewis, Oxford Street, W1 ☎0171/629 7711. A real London institution: John Lewis specializes in well-made homeware from saucepans to duvet covers and furniture, and, in the words of its slogan, is never knowingly undersold. *Bodum* coffee pots are about as innovative and exciting as the goods get, but for dependability it can't be beaten. *Oxford Circus tube. Mon–Wed & Fri 9am–6pm, Thurs 10am–8pm, Sat 9am–6pm.*

Liberty, 210–222 Great Marlborough St, W1 ☎0171/734 1234. At one time the pseudo-Tudor exterior of this high-class landmark store perfectly encapsulated its cosy values; nowadays *Liberty* is a lot more adventurous, and you'll find some fantastic designer clothes amid the shop's trademark print fabrics, ethnic jewellery and rugs, ceramics, and so on. *Oxford Circus tube. Mon–Tues & Fri–Sat 9.30am–6pm,* Wed *10am–6pm, Thurs 9.30am–7.30pm.*

Lillywhites, Piccadilly Circus, W1 ☎0171/930 3181. The capital's largest and most stylish sports store. Pricier than most but hunt around and you'll always come upon some special offers. *Piccadilly Circus tube. Mon–Sat 9.30am–6pm, Thurs till 7pm.*

Marks & Spencer, 458 Oxford St, W1 ☎0171/935 7954 (Marble Arch tube). There are branches of the ever-reliable *M&S* all over Britain and beyond – but this one is the biggest, with many clothes not stocked by the chain's other outlets. Each year *M&S* clones that season's must-have designer items, and often only a trained eye can tell the difference between the overpriced original and the cut-price copy. If you find the crush too much (and on Saturday the Marble Arch *M&S* can be purgatorial), try the large branch not far away at 173 Oxford St ☎0171/437 7722 (Oxford Circus tube). The food halls of these two stores are good sources of on-the-hoof snacks as well. *The Marble Arch store is open Mon–Wed & Sat 9am–7pm, Thurs & Fri 9am–8pm.*

Selfridge's, Oxford Street, W1 ☎0171/629 1234. London's first great department store, *Selfridge's* still exudes sophistication, but its prices have none of the Knightsbridge exclusivity. This old-style department store will refund the difference on any goods you find cheaper elsewhere – and the building is superb, too. *Bond Street tube. Mon–Wed & Fri–Sat 9.30am–7pm, Thurs 9.30am–8pm.*

Clothes and accessories

London might have lost some of its gloss since the Sixties, when Carnaby Street was the centre of the fashion world, but there's still a decent crop of home-grown talent to be unearthed in the trendy shops of Kensington, Knightsbridge, Chelsea, Bond Street, Covent Garden and Soho – not to mention the roster of big international names.

If you're after a designer label, don't forget to check out the department stores listed above – especially *Harvey Nichols*. If your budget doesn't run to these extremes, the **high-street stores** offer a good line in high-fashion facsimiles – the durability might be limited, but the expense is far less painful. Alternatively, check out the **market stalls** (especially Camden – see p.525), for London has the best street fashion in Europe – Jean-Paul Gaultier, enfant terrible of the Parisian catwalks, regularly nips across the Channel to spy on the city's pacesetting young clubbers.

High-street chains

Esprit, 6 Sloane St, SW1 ☎0171/245 9139 (Knightsbridge tube) and other branches. A chain specializing in simple, colourful and youthful clothes in natural fabrics. The shop itself is a radical design by Norman Foster. *Mon–Tues & Fri–Sat 10am–6.30pm, Wed 10am–7pm.*

French Connection, 249–251 Regent St, W1 ☎0171/493 3124 (Oxford Circus tube) and many other branches. Budget-range fashion, particularly good on knitwear. The place to go if you like Nicole Farhi but can't afford her stuff. *Mon–Wed & Sat 10am–6.30pm, Thurs 10am–8pm, Fri 10am–7pm.*

Hobbs, 47 South Molton St, W1 ☎0171/629 0750 (Bond Street tube), Unit 17, Covent Garden Market, WC2 ☎0171/836 9168 (Covent Garden tube), and many other branches. Sensibly styled and well-priced clothing, plus a good selection of shoes. *The South Molton Street store is open Mon–Wed & Fri–Sat 10am–6pm, Thurs 10.30am–7.30pm; the Covent Garden store is open Mon–Wed & Fri–Sat 10.30am–6.30pm, Thurs 10.30am–7.30pm, Sun noon–5pm.*

Jigsaw, 31 Brompton Rd, SW3 ☎0171/584 6226 (Knightsbridge tube), 65 Kensington High St, W8 ☎0171/937 3573 (High Street Kensington tube) and numerous other branches. Has a very good reputation for stylish, moderate-priced casual women's wear, and is now diversifying rather cautiously into menswear – stocked in its Floral St (Covent Garden) branch, close to the women-only *Jigsaw* on Long Acre. *The Brompton Road store is open Mon–Tues & Thurs–Sat 10am–7pm, Wed 10am–8pm; the Kensington High Street store is open Mon–Wed & Fri–Sat 9.30am–7pm, Thurs 9.30am–7.30pm.*

Miss Selfridge, 40 Duke St, W1☎0171/629 1234 (Bond Street tube). This is the largest branch, tacked on to the side of *Selfridge's* – you'll find smaller versions all over the place. Passable versions of the latest fashions at rock-bottom prices, with clothes for everyone from spotty teenagers to poverty-stricken forty-somethings. *Mon–Wed & Fri–Sat 9.30am–7pm, Thurs 9.30am–8pm.*

Monsoon, 264 Oxford Street, W1 ☎0171/499 2578 (Oxford Circus tube), 5 James St, WC2 ☎0171/379 3623 (Covent Garden tube) and many other branches. Started as an outlet for floaty, quasi-ethnic tie-dyes, now more like a funkier *Laura Ashley*. *The Oxford Street store is open Mon–Wed & Fri–Sat 9.30am–6.30pm, Thurs 9.30am–8pm; the James Street store is open Mon–Sat 10am–8pm, Sun 11am–6pm.*

Next, 327–329 Oxford St, W1 ☎0171/409 2746 (Bond Street tube). With around thirty branches in London (there are two more on Oxford Street alone) and scores scattered all over the country, *Next* is now a national byword for reasonably stylish, reasonably well-made clothing. *Mon–Wed & Fri 10am–6.30pm, Thurs 10am–8pm, Sat 10am–7pm, Sun noon–6pm.*

Oasis, 85–86 Regent St, WC2 ☎0171/323 5978, and lots of other branches. Budget-priced up-to-the-minute separates and flashy jewellery. *Oxford Circus tube. Mon–Wed & Fri–Sat 9.30am–6.30pm, Thurs 9.30am–8pm.*

Shops and Markets

Top Shop/Top Man, 214 Oxford St, W1 ☎0171/636 7700. A godsend for the financially embarrassed follower of fashion. The clothes may not last much beyond the journey home, but you can't complain about the price. The Oxford Circus branch is the HQ, but smaller establishments abound. *Oxford Circus tube. Mon–Wed & Fri–Sat 10am–7pm, Thurs 10am–8pm.*

Warehouse, 19–21 Argyll St, W1 ☎0171/734 5096 (Oxford Circus tube) and numerous other branches. *Warehouse* offers inexpensive versions of the plainer and more wearable catwalk collections. Especially good for taller women who normally find that high-street stuff flaps about the ankles. *Mon–Wed & Fri–Sat 10am–7pm, Thurs 10am–8pm, Sun noon–6pm.*

Whistles, 12 St Christopher's Place, W1 ☎0171/487 4484 (Bond Street tube), 27 Sloane Square, SW1 ☎0171/730 9819 (Sloane Square tube) and other branches. Mix of designer wear (with slight French bias) and own-label clothes at lower prices. Small range, but well chosen – *Whistles* regularly turns up on the "top tip" fashion pages. *The St Christopher Place store is open Mon–Wed & Fri–Sat 10am–6pm, Thurs 10am–7pm.*

Streetwear/New Designers

American Retro, 35 Old Compton St, W1 ☎0171/734 3477 John Smedley knitwear and other chic accoutrements. *Leicester Square tube. Mon–Sat 10.15am–7pm.*

Boxfresh, 2 Short's Gardens, WC2 ☎0171/240 4742. Cool casuals and clubwear – jeans, jackets and T-shirts – for funksters. *Covent Garden tube. Mon–Wed 11am–6.30pm, Thurs–Sat 11am–7pm.*

The Dispensary, 25 Pembridge Rd, W11 ☎0171/221 9290. Club fashion from labels like Hysteric Glamour. *Notting Hill Gate tube. Mon–Sat 11am–7pm.*

Duffer of St George, 27 D'Arblay St, W1 ☎0171/439 0996. Very successful hybrid of mainstream English casuals and snappy street styles. *Tottenham Court Road tube. Mon–Wed & Fri–Sat 10am–6pm, Thurs 10am–7pm.*

Four Star General, 4 Camden Rd, NW1 ☎0171/267 8610. If you already wear a baseball cap back-to-front, you should find what you're after here – including Ewing sneakers and Karl Kani jeans. *Camden tube. Daily 10.30am–6.30pm.*

Have A Nice Day, 45 Pembridge Rd, W11 ☎0171/727 6306. Hip, street fashion T-shirts for ravers. *Notting Hill Gate tube. Mon–Fri 11am–6.30pm, Sat 9.30am–7pm.*

Hyper Hyper, 26–40 Kensington High St, W8 ☎0171/938 4343. A counter-culture institution with a variety of small shops run by young, sometimes up-and-coming designers. *High Street Kensington tube. Mon–Tues & Thurs–Sat 10am–6pm, Wed 10am–7pm.*

Jane Kahn, 4 Pembridge Rd, W11 ☎0171/792 2616. Cutting-edge women's wear from a designer who made her name at Hyper Hyper. *Notting Hill Gate tube. Mon–Fri 10am–7.30pm, Sat 10am–7pm.*

Libido, 83 Parkway, NW1 ☎0171/485 0414. The slogan is "Hot Clothes for Cool Women", and the emphasis is firmly on rubber and leather. Latex knickers, anyone? *Camden tube. Mon–Sat 11am–7pm.*

Nothing, 230 Portobello Rd, W11 ☎0171/221 2910. Ten young designers show their wares here, sharing a street/club sense of fashion. *Notting Hill Gate tube. Mon–Sat 11am–6pm.*

Sign of the Times, 15 Short's Gardens, WC2 ☎0171/240 6694. You want to blend in for a night's clubbing? It's easy – just get yourself some trash down here. Ultra hot. *Covent Garden tube. Mon–Sat 10.30am–6.30pm.*

Big Name Designers

Ally Capellino, 95 Wardour St, W1 ☎0171/494 0768. Classic women's clothes with a twist in the detailing. *Leicester Square tube. Mon–Fri 11am–6pm, Sat 10.30am–6pm.*

Browns, 23–27 South Molton St, W1 ☎0171/491 7833 (Bond Street tube) and 6c Sloane St, SW1 ☎0171/493 4232 (Knightsbridge tube). London's biggest range of designer clothes, for both women and men, featuring Rifat Ozbek, Jil Sander,

Isaac Mizrahi and a host of modish names. If you don't look a seriously rich fashion victim, the staff will probably treat you with disdain. Last season's lines are sold at large reductions at *Labels for Less*, on the first floor of the *G-Gigli* shop at no. 38. *The South Molton Street store is open Mon–Wed & Fri–Sat 10am–6pm, Thurs 10am–7pm; the Sloane Street store is open Mon–Tues & Thurs–Sat 10am–6pm, Wed 10am–7pm.*

Burberry's, 18–22 Haymarket ☎0171/930 3343 and 165 Regent St, SW1 ☎0171/734 5928 (both Piccadilly Circus tube). A very British institution, best known for their classic *Burberry* trenchcoat, though they sell everything you need for a high-class wet-weather ensemble. You can buy the same goods, with minor blemishes, at heavily discounted prices at **Burberry's Factory Shop**, 29–53 Chatham Place, E9 ☎0181/985 3344 (Hackney Central BR). *The Haymarket store is open Mon–Wed & Fri–Sat 10am–6pm, Thurs 10am–7pm; the Regent Street store is open Mon–Fri 10am–7pm, Sat 9am–6.30pm; the Factory Shop is open Mon–Fri noon–6pm, Sat 9am–3pm.*

Comme des Garçons, 59 Brook St, W1 ☎0171/493 1258. The brains behind *Comme* is Rei Kawakubo, Japan's most successful designer. Her outfits tend to be monochromatic and severe, with bizarre detailing – jackets that look as if the arms have been torn off, dresses with unfinished hems and so on. Wildly expensive. *Bond Street tube. Mon–Wed & Fri–Sat 10am–6pm, Thurs 10am–7pm.*

Emporio Armani, 187–191 Brompton Rd, SW3 ☎0171/823 8818 (Knightsbridge tube), 57–59 Long Acre, WC2 ☎0171/917 6882 (Covent Garden tube). The "budget" wing of the Armani empire – the Brompton Road is the flagship, with a very good café on the first floor. *The Brompton Road store is open Mon–Tues & Thurs–Sat 10am–6pm, Wed 10am–7pm; the Long Acre store is open Mon–Wed & Fri–Sat 10am–6.30pm, Thurs 10am–7.30pm, Sun 11.30am–5.30pm.*

Equipment, 26 Brook St, W1☎0171/491 3130 (Bond Street tube) and 21 Sloane St, SW1 ☎0171/235 9868 (Knightsbridge tube). Small, unisex range of top-quality silk and cotton shirts in a delicious range of colours. *The Brook Street store is open Mon–Wed & Fri–Sat 10am–6.30pm, Thurs 10am–7pm; the Sloane Street store is open Mon–Tues & Thurs–Sat 10am–6.30pm, Wed 10am–7pm.*

G-Gigli, 38 South Molton St, W1 ☎0171/629 0666 (Bond Street tube). Romeo Gigli's budget/youth line is always a gorgeous riot of colour – strong on jackets, waistcoats and fabulous sunglasses for both women and men. For stronger wallets, or sale time visits, **Romeo Gigli** has his own namesake shop down the road at no. 62. *Both stores are open Mon–Wed & Fri–Sat 10am–6pm, Thurs 10am–7pm.*

Hackett, 137 Sloane St, SW1 ☎0171/730 3331 and other branches. Quintessential high-quality English men's casuals; too tweedy for many tastes, but the height of style in some quarters. *Piccadilly Circus tube. Mon–Tues & Thurs–Sat 9am–6pm, Wed 9am–7pm.*

Issey Miyake, 270 Brompton Rd, SW1 ☎0171/581 3760. Sculptured designs, extraordinarily fine pleating and unbelievably sensuous fabrics are all Miyake hallmarks, as are heart-stopping prices. The shop itself is the last word in sensuous sparseness. Men and women. *South Kensington tube. Mon–Sat 10am–6pm.*

Jean-Paul Gaultier, 171 Draycott Ave, SW3 ☎0171/584 4648. Gorgeously histrionic clothes for both sexes, sold by staff as wacky and charming as Jean-Paul himself. The mid-price *JPG* range is sold here as well. *South Kensington tube. Mon–Tues & Thurs–Sat 10am–6pm, Wed 10am–7pm.*

Jones, 13–15 Floral St, WC2 ☎0171/240 8312. The wilder shores of fashion – Gaultier, Mugler, Galliano et al (men's at 13, women's at 15). The favourite shop of clubland's high-income denizens. *Covent Garden tube. Mon–Sat 10am–6.30pm, Sun 1–5pm.*

Joseph, 77 Fulham Rd, SW3 ☎0171/823 9500 (South Kensington tube), 28 Brook St, W1☎0171/629 6077 (Bond Street tube), 26 Sloane St, SW1 ☎0171/235

Shops and Markets

Hairdressers

If you want a stylish crop to go with your new outfit, any of the places listed below will be glad to oblige. Few of them will be able to fit you in if you just turn up on spec – it's best to make an appointment a week or so in advance. All cater for both women and men.

Antenna, 27a Kensington Church St, W8 ☎0171/938 1866. The baby of Simon Forbes, inventor of mono-fibre hair extensions, *Antenna* was once the trendiest name in town, with a client list including the likes of Boy George and Jean-Paul Gaultier. Still commands the loyalty of a phalanx of fashionables who think nothing of paying a minimum £28 for a cut. *High Street Kensington tube. Mon–Fri 10am–7pm, Sat 10am–5pm.*

Base Cuts, 252 Portobello Rd, W11 ☎0171/727 7068. State-of-clubland cuts – £16 for men, £19 for women. Not the place for a regular perm. *Notting Hill tube. Mon–Sat 10am–6pm.*

Cuts, 39 Frith St, W1 ☎0171/734 2171. Both boys and girls can get a sleek, sharp, angular haircut for £18 at a salon which steers studiously clear of perms, colouring and other fripperies. The barbers tend to talk about clubbing a lot. *Leicester Square or Tottenham Court Road tube. Mon–Fri 11am–6.30pm, Sat 10am–around 5.30pm.*

Daniel Field, 8–12 Broadwick St, W1 ☎0171/439 8223. For an utterly oatmeal experience, *Daniel Field* uses only organic and mineral products – such as spring water shampoo – on its globally conscious clients. Haircuts by mid-range stylists hover around the £35 mark. *Piccadilly Circus tube. Mon & Wed 10am–5.30pm, Tues & Thurs 10am–8pm, Fri 10am–7pm, Sat 9am–4pm.*

Fish Hairdressing Company, 30 D'Arblay St, W1 ☎0171/494 2398. Once a fishmonger's, now a high-fashion hair emporium and the toast of *le tout* Soho. Basic cuts cost £20 for men and £24 for

5470(Knightsbridge tube) and other branches. Less wide-ranging than *Browns*, but more discriminating. Alaïa, Tatsuno, Helmut Lang, Dolce e Gabbana and other such luminaries, displayed alongside Joseph's own-label clothing – Joseph Tricot knitwear is especially covetable, and not too pricey by London standards. The Brook Street branch is women only; the others cater for both sexes. *The Fulham Road store is open Mon–Tues & Thurs–Fri 10am–6.30pm, Wed 10am–7pm, Sat 9.30am–6pm, Sun noon–5pm.*

Katharine Hamnett, 20 Sloane St, SW1 ☎0171/823 1002. The woman responsible for big slogans on big T-shirts, now specializing in sequinned jeans and other attention-monopolizing clobber. Worth a visit just to check out the boudoir-like interior, which is fronted by a multi-storey fishtank. Mostly for women. *Knightsbridge tube. Mon–Tues & Thurs–Fri 10am–6.30pm, Wed 10am–7pm, Sat 10am–6pm.*

Nicole Farhi, 158 Bond St, W1 ☎0171/499 8368 (Bond Street tube), 12 Floral St, WC2 ☎0171/497 8713 (Covent Garden tube), 25–26 St Christopher's Place, W1 ☎0171/486 3416 (Oxford Circus tube), Hampstead High St, NW3 ☎0171/435 0866 (Hampstead tube), and 193 Sloane St, SW1 ☎0171/235 0877 (Sloane Street tube). England's answer to the classic Milanese stylists, Fahri's designs are sober and soft-hued, sometimes to the point of somnolence. Menswear stocked only at the Hampstead and flagship Bond Street branches. *The Bond Street store is open Mon–Wed & Fri–Sat 10am–6pm, Thurs 10am–7pm.*

Paul Smith, 41–44 Floral St, WC2 ☎0171/836 7828 (Covent Garden tube). Financially Britain's most successful designer, Smith made his name producing classic menswear with the odd humorous twist, but now turns out women's and kids' lines as well. Good for shoes as well as suits. Massively women. *Tottenham Court Road tube. Mon–Wed & Fri 10am–7pm, Thurs 10am–8pm, Sat 10am–5pm.*

Rox, 49 Old Compton St, WC2 ☎0171/287 0666. *Rox* snips the locks of those for whom Old Compton Street is essentially a catwalk with kerbs. A basic men's cut starts at £22; girls have to stump up at least £26. *Leicester Square tube. Mon–Sat 10am–10pm, Sun noon–8pm.*

Vidal Sassoon, 45a Monmouth St, WC2 ☎0171/240 6635 (Covent Garden tube), 130 Sloane St, SW1 ☎0171/730 7288 (Sloane Square tube), 60 South Molton St, W1 ☎0171/491 8848 (Bond Street tube) and other branches. The inventor of the bob has lost his elitist edge but still charges prices to make your hair stand on end – at least £34.50 for women. For a more modestly priced restyle, you can attend a staff training session or visit the Sassoon Academy (ring Monmouth St for details): the first option lets you choose the style but can place you in the hands of a nervous first-year student; the second is the province of visiting professionals, and they tend to dictate the style you'll have. Costing as little as £9.50 it's a bargain. Call any of the branches for details. *The Monmouth Street salon is open Mon–Fri 10am–7.45pm, Sat 8.30am–5.45pm.*

Trevor Sorbie 10 Russell St, WC2 ☎0171/379 6901. Consummate professionals who pay close attention to a client's wishes. Prices for both men and women start at £36. *Covent Garden tube. Mon–Tues 9am–6pm, Wed 9am–7pm, Thurs–Fri 9am–7.40, Sat 9am–5pm.*

Toni & Guy, 49 Sloane St, SW1 ☎0171/730 8113 (Sloane Square tube), 34 Southampton St, WC2 ☎0171/240 7342 (Covent Garden tube), 10–12 Davis St, W1 ☎0171/629 8348 (Bond Street tube), Kensington Barracks, 28 Kensington Church St, W8 (High Street Kensington tube) and other branches. Reputable chain of high-fashion hairdressers. Cuts cost upwards of £33 for women and a little bit less for men. *The Sloane Street salon is open Mon & Thurs–Fri 10am–7.30pm, Tues & Wed 10am–6.30pm, Sat 9.30–5.30pm.*

Shops and Markets

discounted old stock is sold at the *Smith Sale Shop*, 23 Avery Row, W1 ☎0171/493 1287 (Bond Street tube). *The Floral Street store is open Mon–Wed & Fri–Sat 10.30am–6.30pm, Thurs 10.30am–7pm, Sat 10am–6.30pm; the Avery Row store is open Mon–Wed & Fri 10.30am–6.30pm, Thurs 10.30am–7pm, Sat 10am–6pm.*

Vivienne Westwood, 6 Davies St, W1 ☎0171/629 3757 (Bond Street tube), and at World's End, 430 King's Rd, SW3 ☎0171/352 6551 (Sloane Square tube). Possibly the most influential designer in Britain, regarded at home as a screwball but revered by the Continental cognoscenti. "Red Label" confections, utterly desirable items at a fraction of the cost of their "Gold Label" counterparts, can be snapped up at 44 Conduit St, W1 ☎0171/439 1109 (Oxford Circus tube). Mostly for women. *The Davies Street store is open Mon–Wed & Fri–Sat 10.30am–6pm, Thurs 10.30am–7pm.*

Discount and second-hand

Amazon, 1–3, 7a, 7b & 19–22 Kensington Church St, W8 ☎0171/376 0630. The posse of neighbouring locations says much for the success of this shop, which buys up designer seconds and discontinued lines (for women only) and sells them at a fraction of the intended prices. *Kensington High St tube. Mon–Wed & Fri 10am–6pm, Thurs 10am–7pm, Sat 9.30am–6pm.*

Designer Sale & Exchange Shop, 61d Lancaster Rd, W11 ☎0171/243 2396. Bargain-priced, top-range design – second-hand and samples – from Rifat Ozbek, Vivienne Westwood and the like. Mainly for women. *Notting Hill tube. Mon noon–6pm, Tue–Sat 10am–6pm.*

Designers Sale Studio, 241 King's Rd, SW3 ☎0171/351 4171. More end-of-line bargains, mainly from Italian labels, and for both sexes. *Sloane Square tube. Mon–Sat 10am–6.30pm.*

See also Camden Market (p.525; Sat/Sun), whose hundreds of stalls have the best selection of second-hand and young designer gear in London. Portobello Road also has designer and used clothing stalls, especially under the tent at the Westway (p.526; Sat only).

Shops and Markets

Flip, 125 Long Acre, WC2 ☎0171/836 4688. Used American clothes, with a largely wacky bent, but including worn-in Levis and leathers. *Covent Garden tube. Mon–Wed & Fri–Sat 10am–7pm, Thurs 10am–8pm, Sun noon–6pm.*

Kensington Market, 49–53 Kensington High St, W8. Dozens of stalls, good for used jeans, army surplus gear and the like. *High Street Kensington tube. Mon–Sat 10am–6pm.*

Merchant of Europe, 232 Portobello Rd, W11 ☎0171/221 4203. Vintage clothes for men and women, from the turn of the century to the 1970s. If you ever thought glitter flares might have suited you, check out the theory here. You can hire as well as buy. *Notting Hill tube. Mon–Fri 10.30am–6pm, Sat 10.30am–6pm.*

70, 70 Lamb's Conduit St, WC1 ☎0171/430 1533. Big name designers at up to 70 percent discount; mainly for men. *Covent Garden tube. Mon–Wed & Fri–Sat 10am–7pm, Thurs 10am–8pm, Sun noon–6pm.*

Westaway & Westaway, 65 & 92 Great Russell St, WC1 ☎0171/405 4479. Not strictly a discount shop – but the best value woollen goods you'll find in London: Shetland jumpers, tartans and so on, at half the price you'll see them in Piccadilly and Bond Street stores. *Tottenham Court Road tube. Mon–Sat 9am–5.30pm.*

Jeans

Sonico, 47 Oxford St, W1 ☎0171/734 7958; and other branches. Levis and other big names at the best discount prices in town. *Tottenham Court Road tube. Mon–Sat 9am–6.30pm, Thurs till 8pm.*

Shoes

Church's, 58–59 Burlington Arcade, W1 ☎0171/493 0502. In Italy, brogues are known as "Churches", which gives a sense of this manufacturer's status. You'll need £150–180 to spare, but it's an investment that can last forever. Mainly men's shoes, but also a limited women's range. *Piccadilly tube. Mon–Sat 9.30am–6pm.*

Dr Martens Department Store, 1–4 King St, WC2 ☎0171/497 1460. DMs are an enduring part of London's street fashion, worn by boys and girls alike for style and statement (the higher the boots the more of both); they are also amazingly comfortable due to the good doctor's patent air-cushioned sole. This vast new shop has the biggest ever selection, plus amusing accessories. *Covent Garden tube. Mon–Sat 10am–7pm, Sun 11am–5pm.*

Emma Hope, 33 Amwell St, EC1 ☎0171/833 2367. Hand-made foot fashions for dandies of either gender. *Angel tube. Mon–Wed & Fri–Sat 10am–6pm, Thurs 10am–7pm.*

Jones The Bootmakers, 15 Foubert's Place, W1 ☎0171/283 6595 (Oxford Circus tube), 16 New Row, WC2 ☎0171/836 2207 (Leicester Square tube) and other branches. Good-value own-brand shoes and boots, plus a small range of trendy, no-nonsense footwear – *Caterpillars* and the like. *The Foubert's Place branch is open Mon–Wed & Fri–Sat 10am–6.30pm, Thurs 10am–7.30pm.*

Natural Shoe Store, 21 Neal St, WC2 ☎0171/836 5254 (Covent Garden tube) and 325 King's Rd, SW3 ☎0171/351 3721 (Sloane Square tube). From Birkenstock sandals and Dexter deck shoes to classic Grenson brogues and Chelsea boots – it's all very well made and pretty good value. *The Neal Street store is open Mon–Tues 10am–6pm, Wed–Fri 10am–7pm, Sat 10am–6.30pm, Sun noon–5.30pm; the King's Road store is open Mon–Sat 10am–6pm.*

Patrick Cox, 8 Symons St, SW3 ☎0171/730 6504. Cox made his name working for Vivienne Westwood, and is now established in his own right as one of the classiest designers in town. *Sloane Square tube. Mon–Tues & Thurs–Sat 10am–6pm, Wed 10am–7pm.*

Pied à Terre, 14 Sloane St, SW1 ☎0171/235 0564 (Knightsbridge tube), 19 South Molton St, W1 ☎0171/493 3637 (Bond Street tube) and many other branches. Stylish shoes at moderate prices. *The Sloane Street store is open Mon–Tues & Thurs–Sat 10am–6.30pm, Wed 10am–7pm.*

Plumline, 55 Neal St, WC2 ☎0171/379 7856. A choice selection of well-made shoes and boots, ranging from No Name stacked plimsolls to Sweeney brogues. *Covent Garden tube. Mon–Tues 10am–6pm, Wed–Fri 10am–7pm, Sat 10am–6.30pm.*

Red or Dead, 33 Neal St ☎0171/379 7571, Thomas Neal's Centre, Earlham St, WC2 ☎0171/240 5576 (Covent Garden tube), 49–53 Kensington High St, W8 ☎0171/937 3137 (High Street Kensington tube) and 186 Camden High St, NW1☎ 0171/482 4423 (Camden Town tube). Gimmicky clubbers' clogs; the Earlham Street and Kensington High Street branches can also supply outrageous upper-body kit to match. *The Neal Street store is open Mon–Tues & Thurs–Fri 10am–6.30pm, 10am–7pm, Sun 12.30–6pm.*

Robot, 37 Floral St, WC2 ☎0171/836 6156. Very silly and very trendy shoes. *Covent Garden tube. Mon–Wed 10am–6.30pm, Thurs 10am–7pm, Fri noon–5pm.*

R. Soles, 109a & 178a King's Rd, SW3 ☎0171/351 5520. The weirdest cowboy boots money can buy. *Sloane Square tube. Mon–Wed & Fri–Sat 10am–6.30pm, Thurs 10am–7pm, Sun noon–5.30pm.*

Shellys, 266–270 Regent St, W1 ☎0171/287 0939 (Oxford Circus tube), 159 Oxford St, W1☎0171/437 5842 (Tottenham Court Road tube), 14 Neal St, WC2 ☎0171/240 3726 (Covent Garden tube) and elsewhere. Instant street cred at bargain prices – mutant Doc Martens and wacky footwear from the likes of Katharine Hamnett and John Richmond. *The Regent Street store is open Mon–Wed & Fri–Sat 9.15am–6.15pm, Thurs 9.15am–7.15pm.*

Accessories

Acessorize, 293 Oxford St, W1 ☎0171/629 0038 (Oxford Circus tube), Unit 22, The Market, Covent Garden, WC2 ☎0171/240 2107 (Covent Garden tube), and other branches. Hats, costume jewellery and other medium-priced but high-fashion items. *Mon–Wed & Sat 10am–7pm, Thurs 10am–8pm.*

Bates the Hatter, 21a Jermyn St, SW1 ☎0171/734 2722. Old-fashioned, characterful men's hat shop – handy for the tropics and for reassuring those with abnormally sized craniums ("Sir's head is not a problem"). *Piccadilly tube. Mon–Fri 9am–5.30pm, Sat 9.30am–4pm.*

Butler & Wilson, 189 Fulham Rd, SW3 ☎0171/352 3045 (South Kensington tube), and 20 South Molton St, W1 ☎0171/409 2955 (Bond Street tube). Wonderful costume jewellery at reasonable prices. *The Fulham Road store is open Mon–Tues & Thurs–Sat 10am–6pm, Wed 10am–7pm; the South Molton Street store is open Mon–Wed & Fri–Sat 10am–6pm, Thurs 10am–7pm.*

Gohil's, 246 Camden High St, NW1 ☎0171/485 9195. Belts, belts and more belts, all made on the premises – you can even have one tooled to your very own specifications. *Camden Town tube. Tues–Sun 10am–6pm.*

The Great Frog, 51 Carnaby St, W1 ☎0171/734 1900 and 10 Ganton St, W1 ☎0171/439 9357. Offbeat jewellery shop which has been in once-swinging Carnaby Street longer than any of its neighbours. The other branch is just around the corner. *Oxford Circus tube. Mon–Sat 10am–6.30pm.*

The Hat Shop, 58 Neal St, WC2 ☎0171/836 6718 (Covent Garden tube), and 8 South Molton St, W1 ☎0171/495 5727 (Bond Street tube). Small shops but their stock runs the gamut from simple berets to Ascot-style extravaganzas. *The Neal Street store is open Mon–Wed & Fri–Sat 10am–6pm, Thurs 10am–7pm; the South Molton Street store closes 30min earlier on Sat.*

Janet Fitch, 25 Old Compton St, W1 ☎0171/287 3789. Contemporary jewellery from a couple of dozen stylish exponents. *Tottenham Court Rd tube. Mon–Sat 11am–7pm.*

Jess James, 3 Newburgh St, W1 ☎0171/437 0199. Modern designer jewellery; ultra-chic but not outrageously expensive. *Oxford Circus tube. Mon–Fri 10.30am–7pm, Sat 10.30am–6pm.*

Kodo, 133 King's Rd, SW3 ☎0171/376 5082. Hats, bags, belts and hi-tech accessories for the chronically trendy. Worth a look-in for the imaginatively placed displays alone. *Sloane Square tube. Mon–Sat 10am–6.30pm.*

Shops and Markets

Swaine & Adeney, 185 Piccadilly, W1 ☎0171/734 4277. The finest umbrellas in the world. *Green Park tube. Mon–Wed & Fri–Sat 9.30am–6pm, Thurs 9.30am–7pm.*

Design and oddball shops

This section is basically devoted to objects you might put in your home – or other peoples. It ranges through state of the art design goods and offbeat ethnic wares, through to the wilder shores of kitsch.

For design enthusiasts, Chelsea (Fulham Rd/King's Rd), Notting Hill (Portobello area), Covent Garden (Neal St area) and Camden (Chalk Farm Rd) are all rewarding territory. For **antiques**, at relatively affordable prices, you're best off at one or other of the markets detailed on p.525; there are concentrations of antique shops, as well as stalls, in the market areas of Portobello Road, Camden and Church Street.

Design and crafts

Ceramica Blue, 10 Blenheim Crescent, W11 ☎0171/727 0288. A brilliant array of African, British and Italian ceramics at a wild mix of prices. *Notting Hill Gate tube. Tue–Fri 10am–6pm; Sat 10am–4pm.*

Conran Shop, 81 Fulham Rd, SW3 ☎0171/589 7401. Terence Conran re-introduced the British to style in the 1960s, through his Habitat stores and designs. This was where he moved on to, among other ventures: a superstore of adventurous and classic design, from furniture to food. It's worth a call, if only to admire the Art Deco foyer of Michelin House, the rear of which it occupies. *South Kensington tube. Mon & Wed–Sat 9.30am–6pm, Tue 10am–6pm, Sun noon–5pm.*

Contemporary Applied Arts, 43 Earlham St/corner of Neal St, WC2 ☎0171/836 6993. Ceramics, jewellery, glass, wood and other creations from a fairly adventurous group of British artists and designers. *Covent Garden tube. Mon–Wed & Fri–Sat 10am–6pm, Thurs 10am–7pm.*

Designers Guild, 271 & 277 Kings Rd, SW4 ☎0171/351 5775. Bright Mediterranean colours are the trademark of this enormously successful interior design chain. Their London showroom is stacked with luscious hangings and furniture, as well as Mexican and Egyptian ceramics, and gifts. *Sloane Square tube. Mon–Tues & Thurs–Fri 9.30am–5.30pm, Wed & Sat 10am–5.30pm.*

Design Museum, Shad Thames, SE1 ☎0171/403 6933. A superb selection of design classics and innovations. *Tower Hill or London Bridge tube. Mon–Fri 11.30am–6pm, Sat & Sun noon–6pm.*

Muji, 26 Great Marlborough St, W1 ☎0171/494 1197 (Oxford Circus tube), 39 Shelton St, WC2 ☎0171/379 1331 (Covent Garden tube) and 157 Kensington High St, W8 ☎0171/376 2484 (High Street Kensington tube). Japanese micro department store, selling no-label clothes, kitchenware, stationery – even bicycles. The self-consciously austere packaging comes at a price, but the distinctive Muji look has a lot of admirers. *The Great Marlborough Street store is open Mon, Tues & Sat 10am–6.30pm, Wed 10.15am–6.30pm, Thurs & Fri 10am–7pm.*

Oggetti, 135 & 143 Fulham Rd, SW3 ☎0171/581 8088. An extensive, expensive, highly covetable array of household wares, gadgets and gizmos. The no. 143 branch stocks exclusively Alessi goods. *South Kensington tube. Mon–Sat 9.30am–6pm.*

Space, 28 All Saint's Rd, W11 ☎0171/727 0134. An ultra-contemporary international design showcase opened by avant-garde chair designer Tom Dixon; everything from vases to the tables to put them on. *Notting Hill Gate tube. Mon–Sat 11am–6pm.*

Ethnic

African Escape, 127 Portobello Rd, W11 ☎0171/221 6650. The best-selected African goods you'll find in London – beautiful and reasonably priced. *Notting Hill Gate tube. Mon–Fri 10.30am–5.30pm, Sat 9am–6pm.*

Kasbah, 8 Southampton St, WC2 ☎0171/379 5230. Moroccan emporium where you can buy everything from a door to a shrub-toothpick, and indulge in mint tea and pastries while you're about it. *Covent Garden tube. Mon–Wed & Fri–Sat 10am–7pm, Thurs 10am–8pm.*

Neal Street East, 5 Neal St, WC2 ☎0171/240 0135. A rambling store, packed with crafts, books, coverings and artefacts of all kinds from a loosely defined Orient. There's an excellent kids' section downstairs, full of cheap and diverting gifts. *Covent Garden tube. Mon–Sat 10am–7pm, Sun noon–6pm.*

Tibet Shop, 10 Bloomsbury Way, WC2 ☎0171/405 5284. Crafts, clothing, books and posters supplied by Tibetan exiles – and with all profits devoted to the Tibetan foundation. *Holborn tube. Mon–Sat 11am–6pm.*

Tumi, 23 Chalk Farm Rd, NW1 ☎0171/485 4152. Long-established importer of Latin American crafts, clothing and music (including releases on its own record label). *Camden tube. Daily 10am–6pm.*

Wong Singh Jones, 235 Portobello Rd, W11 ☎0171/221 1906. A true original. Where else in London (or anywhere else, for that matter) will you find Jamaican air-fresheners, Mexican gear knobs, bead-curtains from Singapore, and much, much more (half of it for £5 or less), under one roof? The owner, Paul Spencer, describes it as "a kind of hardware shop – a place that, if Mr Wong from Shanghai, Mr Singh from Calcutta and Mr Jones from Hartlepool had met on holiday in Torremolinos, they might have decided to open". And why not? *Notting Hill Gate tube. Mon–Sat 9.30am–6.30pm.*

Oddballs

Anything Left-Handed, 65 Beak St, W1 ☎0171/437 3910. Essentials, gadgets and gizmos, from pens to potato peelers. *Leicester Square tube. Mon–Fri 9.30am–5pm, Sat 10.30am–5pm.*

Just Games, 71 Brewer St, W1 ☎0171/734 6124. A wonderful selection of games – from chess to computers. *Leicester Square tube. Mon–Fri 9.30am–6pm, Sat 9am–5.30pm.*

Kite Store, 48 Neal St, WC2 ☎0171/836 1666. Kites from around a tenner to well into three figures, sold with professional advice. Good spots to fly them are Greenwich/Blackheath and Parliament Hill. *Covent Garden tube. Mon–Sat 10.30am–6pm.*

Knutz, 1 Russell St, WC2 ☎0171/836 3117. A nasty little den of practical jokes, smack opposite the British Museum. *Tottenham Court Road tube. Mon–Sat 11am–8pm.*

Museum Store, 37 The Market, WC2 ☎0171/240 5760. Museum goods and replicas from across Britain, Europe and America. Highlights include an inflatable Edvard Munch *Scream* figure. *Covent Garden tube. Mon–Sat 10.30am–6.30pm, Sun 11am–5pm.*

Oddball Juggling Company, 323 Upper St, N1 ☎0171/354 5660 (Angel tube) and Unit 2, Camden Lock Place (market), NW1 ☎0171/284 2460 (Camden tube). Balls, batons and frisbees. *The Upper Street store is open Mon–Wed & Fri–Sat 10am–6pm, Thurs 10am–8pm; the Camden market stall is open Tue–Sun 10am–6pm.*

Radio Days, 87 Lower Marsh St, SE1 ☎0171/928 0800. Attic treasures from the 1920s to 1950s – china and bakelite, clocks and watches, magazines and all. *Waterloo tube. Mon–Fri 10.30am–5pm, Sat 11am–4pm.*

Smith's Snuff Shop, 74 Charing Cross Rd, WC2 ☎0171/836 7422. Fancy a new

Shops and Markets

The Museum Shops

All of London's major **museums** have shops selling books relating to each collection as well as a range of gifts and interesting souvenirs. The **British Museum**, for example, sells some very impressive (and not overpriced) replicas of its star exhibits, from tiny Egyptian amulets to life-size horse's heads from the Parthenon, and the South Ken **Natural History**, **Science** and **V&A** museums have particularly good ranges of educational games and toys.

Shops and Markets

The shops listed under "General interest" also have some foreign-language books in stock – Foyles and the Gower St branch of Dillons are best.

carcinogenic addiction? Snuff could just be what you're looking for – and Smith"s is the place to purchase, with over fifty aromatic varieties. They do a nice range of tobaccos, cigarettes and cigars, too. *Leicester Square tube. Mon–Fri 8.30am–6pm, Sat 9am–5.45pm.*

Soccer Scene, 30–31 Great Marlborough St/corner of Carnaby St, W1 ☎0171/439 0778. You just happened to see Raith Rovers in the Scottish FA Cup – and you fell in love with their away strip? A sad fate, perhaps, but this is the place to track it down. *Tottenham Court Rd tube. Mon–Sat 9.30am–6pm.*

Vinyl Experience, 18 Hanway St, W1 ☎0171/636 1281. This is London's main outlet for rock memorabilia. They acquire everything from John Lennon's old wash-basins to celebrity-trashed guitars to kitsch fan-produce – oh and even some vinyl, too, so long as it's scarce. The prices may deter anything beyond sightseeing. *Tottenham Court tube. Mon–Sat 10am–6.30pm.*

Books

The London (and British) bookselling trade is dominated by a trio of chains – *Books Etc, Dillons, Waterstone's* – and by the ubiquitous *W.H. Smith* bookshop/newsagent outlets. The flagship branches of these chains, listed below, are real megastores, and obvious ports of call for browsers. For specialist interests, however, there are superb independent bookshops, many of them concentrated around the Charing Cross Road area, the book trade's traditional home for much of this century.

At time of publication, the Net Book Agreement obliges booksellers to offer all net published books at the publisher's marked price. A few self-serving publishers have recently left this scheme (which helps to maintain small bookshops and prevent monopoly trading), but for most new books you'll find that prices remain uniform across the stores.

General interest

Books Etc, 120 Charing Cross Rd, WC2 ☎0171/379 6838 and other branches. A relaxed, airy, state-of-the-art shop, with a coffee bar up the front. Especially good on fiction and US imports. *Tottenham Court Road tube. Mon–Sat 9.30am–8pm, Sun noon–6pm.*

Compendium, 234 Camden High St, NW1 ☎0171/485 8944. This is a great bookshop, worth a trip to Camden in its own right. Set up in the 1960s, it has long been London's main "alternative" general bookstore, covering everything from underground poetry and fiction through Althusserian Marxism to New Age psychology. Especially strong on small imprints and US imports, women's, gay and New Age books. *Camden Town tube. Mon–Sat 10am–6pm, Sun noon–6pm.*

Dillons, 82 Gower St, WC1 ☎0171/636 1577 (Goodge Street tube) and other branches. The main supplier to the University of London, with a quarter of a million books on the shelves. Stock is among the best in the city, and the staff are more knowledgeable than most. *Mon–Fri 9am–7pm, Sat 9.30am–6pm, Sun noon–6pm.*

Elgin Books, 6 Elgin Crescent, W11 ☎0171/229 2186. Fine general bookshop, offering the sort of personal service that's rarely encountered in the chain bookstores. *Ladbroke Grove tube. Tues–Sat 10am–6pm.*

Foyles, 119 Charing Cross Rd, WC2 ☎0171/437 5660. Awesomely enormous and famously chaotic, with notoriously offhand staff and an archaic paying system which forces you to queue twice – once to part with the cash and once to pick up the book. *Tottenham Court Road tube. Mon–Wed & Fri–Sat 9am–6pm, Thurs 9am–7pm.*

John Sandoe, 10 Blacklands Terrace, SW3 ☎0171/589 9473. Just off the top end of the King's Road, this is one of the city's best independent literary booksellers. *Sloane Square tube. Mon–Sat 9.30am–5.30pm; open till 7.30pm on Wed.*

Waterstones, 121–129 Charing Cross Rd, WC2 ☎0171/434 4291 (Tottenham Court Road tube) and other branches. Well-organized and capacious shop, with very good fiction and biography sections. *Mon–Sat 9.30am–9pm, Sun noon–6pm.*

Shops and Markets

Art and photography

Dillons Arts Bookshop, 8 Long Acre, WC2 ☎0171/836 1359. Fairly good stock of books, though nothing esoteric; a lot of its customers come here for the selection of postcards and calendars. *Leicester Square tube. Mon–Sat 9.30am–10pm, Sun noon–7pm.*

Shipley, 70 Charing Cross Rd, WC2 ☎0171/836 4872. New and second-hand titles covering art, architecture, fashion and much more. Helpful staff. *Leicester Square tube. Mon–Sat 10am–6pm.*

Zwemmer, 24 Litchfield St, WC2 ☎0171/240 4158 and 80 Charing Cross Rd, WC2 ☎0171/240 1559. Top-class art books to inspire the students of nearby St Martin's School of Art. The branch on Charing Cross Road specializes in film and photography. *Leicester Square tube. Mon–Fri 9.30am–6pm, Sat 10am–6pm.*

Cinema, theatre and dance

Cinema Bookshop, 13–14 Great Russell St, WC1 ☎0171/637 0206. Huge range of movie writings – plus posters, cards and knick-knacks. *Tottenham Court Road tube. Mon–Sat 10.30am–5.30pm.*

Dance Books, 9 Cecil Court, WC2 ☎0171/836 2314. Best specialist shop in the city. Leicester Square tube. *Mon–Sat 11am–7pm.*

Dress Circle, 57–59 Monmouth St, WC2 ☎0171/240 2227. High-camp purveyor of books – plus CDs, tapes, T-shirts and mugs – on every West End and Broadway musical you can think of. Hoofer heaven. *Covent Garden tube. Mon–Sat 10am–7pm.*

French's Theatre Bookshop, 52 Fitzroy St, W1 ☎0171/387 9373. Celebrated shop-cum-publisher, with books on all aspects of board-treading, plus thousands of texts and a sound effects collection. *Warren Street or Goodge Street tube. Mon–Fri 9.30am–5.30pm*

National Film Theatre Bookshop, South Bank Centre, WC2 ☎0171/928 3535. Cineaste's bookshop, installed in the foyer of the city's major repertory cinema. *Waterloo tube. Daily 12.30–9pm.*

Comics

Comic Showcase, 76 Neal St, WC2 ☎0171/ 240 3664. Small shop run by real connoisseurs; up-to-the-minute graphics from all over the world. *Covent Garden tube. Mon–Wed 10am–6pm, Thurs–Fri 10am–7pm, Sat 2–6pm, Sun 10am–6pm.*

Forbidden Planet, 71 New Oxford St, WC1 ☎0171/836 4170 or 379 6042. From Tintin to Tank Girl and beyond. Comics, annuals, cards, novels, T-shirts and assorted sci-fi ephemera on two generously stocked floors. *Tottenham Court Road tube. Mon–Wed & Sat 10am–6pm, Thurs–Fri 10am–7pm.*

Cookery

Books for Cooks, 4 Blenheim Crescent ☎0171/ 221 1992. Mouth-watering cookbooks, new and old, and occasional offerings from the recipe-test kitchen behind. *Notting Hill Gate tube. Mon–Sat 9.30am–6.30pm.*

Crime

Murder One, 71–73 Charing Cross Rd, WC2 ☎0171/734 3485. Enough to keep any armchair detective busy for life. *Leicester Square or Tottenham Court Road tube. Mon–Wed 10am–7pm, Thurs–Sat 10am–8pm.*

Gay and lesbian

Gay's the Word Bookshop, 66 Marchmont St, WC1 ☎0171/278 7654. Gay and lesbian bookshop selling a comprehensive selection of new and second-hand books, plus magazines, videos and cards. *Russell Square tube. Mon–Wed & Fri–Sat 10am–6pm, Thurs 10am–7pm, Sun 2–6pm.*

Language and foreign-language literature

Africa Book Centre, Africa Centre, 38 King St, WC2 ☎0171/ 240 6649. The centre's first floor bookshop has a good selection of fiction and non-fiction titles, plus books in African languages. *Covent Garden tube. Mon–Fri 10.30am–5.30pm.*

Shops and Markets

Books From India, 45 Museum St, WC1 ☎0171/405 7226. A staggering 20,000 books on all things Indian occupy three floors at this specialist outlet. *Tottenham Court Road tube. Mon–Fri 10am–5.30pm, Sat 10am–5pm.*

European Bookshop, 4 Regent Place and 5 Warwick St, both W1, both ☎0171/734 5259. The former branch specializes in language books and learning materials, while the latter has a more general library of foreign-language titles. *Piccadilly Circus tube. Mon–Wed & Fri–Sat 9.30am–6pm, Thurs 9.30am–7.30pm.*

Grant & Cutler, 55–57 Great Marlborough St, W1 ☎0171/734 2012. London's best general stock of European literature, some in translation, but most in the original. Also stocks language books. *Oxford Circus tube. Mon–Wed & Fri–Sat 9.30am–5.30pm, Thurs 9.30am–7pm.*

Zwemmer, 28 Denmark St, WC2 ☎0171/379 6253. Specialist Russian and Eastern European bookshop, with a fine selection of literature, phrasebooks, travel guides and historical, cultural and political works. *Tottenham Court Road tube. Mon–Fri 9.30am–6pm, Sat 10am–6pm.*

Second-hand and remaindered

Any Amount of Books, 56 & 62 Charing Cross Road, WC2 ☎0171/836 3697. Any amount indeed, as this excellent store stocks a vast range of titles. Particularly strong on fiction and the arts. *Leicester Square. Daily 10.30am–9.30pm.*

Book Warehouse, 46 Shaftesbury Ave, W1 ☎0171/287 2414, and other branches. Discounted books appear on the shelves of this chain around three months after publication. Especially good reductions on art books. *Leicester Square or Piccadilly Circus tube. Mon–Sat 10am–midnight, Sun 11am–11pm.*

Henry Pordes, 58–60 Charing Cross Rd, WC2 ☎0171/836 9031. With books from as little as 50p, this is one of the city's best second-hand and remainder book stores. *Leicester Square tube. Mon–Sat 10am–7pm.*

Quinto, 48a Charing Cross Rd, WC2 ☎0171/379 7669. Pick a book, any book – the chances are it will be on these shelves. Prices are ridiculously low, starting at 50p. *Leicester Square tube. Mon–Sat 9am–9pm, Sun noon–8pm.*

Cecil Court, an alley off the lower end of Charing Cross Road, is a centre for specialist and second-hand bookshops.

Serious book sleuths should pick up a copy of Drif's Guide, the most bizarre and entertaining of all guidebooks.

Skoob, 15 Sicilian Ave, Southampton Row, WC1 ☎0171/404 3063. Good-quality second-hand books, geared to a student/academic market. *Holborn tube. Mon–Sat 10.30am–6.30pm.*

The Two Jays, 14 Whitchurch Lane, Edgeware ☎0181/952 1349. A long way out, so for bookhounds only, who are rewarded with the best general selection in the city – arranged in vast piles, and scowled at mainly by dealers. *Canons Park tube. Tues–Wed & Fri–Sat 9am–5pm.*

Ulysses, 31 & 40 Museum St, WC1 ☎0171/637 5862. The best of a cluster of bookshops around the British Museum; it specializes in modern first editions, art and travel. *Tottenham Court Rd tube. Mon–Sat 10.30am–6pm, Sun noon–6pm.*

Sport

Sportspages, Caxton Walk, 94–96 Charing Cross Rd, WC2 ☎0171/240 9604. From football fanzines (Britain's largest collection) to baseball biogs – every sport that's been written about is represented here. *Leicester Square or Tottenham Court Road tube. Mon–Sat 9.30am–7pm.*

Travel

Daunt, 83 Marylebone High St, W1 ☎0171/224 2295. A beautiful, galleried shop, with careful selections of world fiction and other literature dovetailing with its travel sections. *Marylebone or Baker Street tube. Mon–Sat 9am–7.30pm.*

Stanford's, 12–14 Long Acre, WC2 ☎0171/836 1321. The world's largest specialist travel bookshop; the map stock is especially vast and includes customized survey maps of any part of Britain. *Leicester Square or Covent Garden tube. Mon & Sat 10am–6pm, Tues–Fri 9am–7pm.*

Travel Bookshop, 13 Blenheim Crescent, W11 ☎0171/229 5260. Travel guides, travel writing and travel fiction in new and second-hand versions. *Ladbroke Grove or Notting Hill tube. Mon–Sat 10am–6pm.*

Shops and Markets

Travellers' Bookshop, 25 Cecil Court, WC2 ☎0171/836 9132. Small but well-stocked shop in London's most attractive bookselling street; sells travel books and guides both old and new, including a huge range of old Baedekers. *Leicester Square tube. Mon–Fri 11am–7pm, Sat 11am–6.30pm.*

Women

Silver Moon Women's Bookshop, 64–68 Charing Cross Rd, WC2 ☎0171/836 7906. Vast stock of feminist and lesbian books. *Leicester Square tube. Mon–Wed & Fri–Sat 10am–6.30pm, Thurs 10am–8pm.*

Music

London is crawling with record shops – from megastores down to specialists so specialized that most people would have no idea what it is they're selling. CDs have pretty much taken over on new purchases, though vinyl is alive and kicking in the second-hand shops – and at the many record stalls at Camden market.

Megastores

HMV, 150 Oxford St, W1 ☎0171/631 3423. Largest branch of this nationwide chain, stocking a daunting backlist. The world music and classical sections are particularly comprehensive, and there's always something in the bargain bins. *Oxford Circus or Tottenham Court Road tube. Mon–Wed & Fri–Sat 9.30am–7pm, Thurs 9.30am–8pm.*

Tower Records, 1 Piccadilly Circus, W1 ☎0171/439 2500. London's showpiece Tower store, unbeatable for rock music, with a strong indie section, and good jazz, folk and world selections upstairs. *Piccadilly Circus tube. Mon–Sat 9am–midnight, Sun noon–6pm.*

Virgin Megastore, 14–30 Oxford St, W1 ☎0171/631 1234. Good for mainstream rock, plus a huge range of T-shirts, posters, games and videos. *Tottenham Court Road tube. Mon–Sat 9.30am–8pm, Sun noon–6pm.*

Rock and stuff

Black Market, 25 D'Arblay St, W1 ☎0171/437 0478. Hip-hop, rap and other funky sounds. *Tottenham Court Road tube. Mon–Sat 10.30am–7pm.*

Daddy Kool, 12 Berwick St, W1 ☎0171/437 3535. Number one for hard to find vintage West Indian music – and the place to pick up the latest ragga and jungle. *Piccadilly Circus tube. Mon–Sat 10.30am–7.30pm.*

Downtown, 94 Dean St, W1 ☎0171/494 0208. Primarily techno, house and rap. *Oxford Circus tube. Mon–Wed & Fri–Sat 11am–7pm, Thurs 11am–8pm.*

Rough Trade, 16 Neal's Yard, WC2 ☎0171/240 0105 (Covent Garden tube) and 130 Talbot Rd, W11 ☎0171/229 8541 (Ladbroke Grove or Westbourne Park tube). London's top indie specialist – staffed by those that know. *Mon–Sat 10am–6.30pm.*

Stern's, 116 Whitfield St, NW1 ☎0171/387 5550. World-famous African and Latin music store, with superb range of stock (including other world sounds) and highly knowledgeable staff. *Euston tube. Mon–Sat 10.30am–6.30pm.*

Jazz

Honest Jon's, 278 Portobello Rd, W10 ☎0181/969 9822. A fine, very knowledgeable store, packed with new, second-hand, rare and import jazz, reggae, soul, funk and a few corners of rock. *Notting Hill tube. Mon–Sat 10am–6pm, Sun 11am–5pm.*

Mole Jazz, 291 Pentonville Rd, N1 ☎0171/278 8623. The discerning jazzer's favourite, loaded with fresh imports and second-hand classics. *King's Cross tube. Mon–Thurs & Sat 10am–6pm, Fri 10am–8pm.*

Classical

Covent Garden Records, 84 Charing Cross Rd, WC2 ☎0171/379 7635. Classical music specialists, selling CDs at around ten percent less than the big chains. *Leicester Square or Tottenham Court Road tube. Mon–Sat 10.30am–7.30pm.*

Music Discount Centre, 437 The Strand, WC2 ☎0171/240 2157. Bargains always available on classical labels at this, the

Shops and Markets

largest of London's five Music Discount Centres. Especially good for rare imports. *Charing Cross tube. Mon–Fri 9.30am–7.30pm, Sat 9.30am–7pm.*

Templar Records, 9a Irving St, WC2 ☎0171/930 3579. London's best discounts on classical sounds. *Leicester Square tube. Mon–Fri 9am–6pm, Sat 9.30am–6pm.*

Shows and soundtracks

58 Dean Street Records, 58 Dean St, W1 ☎0171/734 8777. Movie soundtracks, TV theme music, big showtunes and other kitsch delights. *Piccadilly Circus tube. Mon–Sat 10am–6.30pm.*

Second-hand

Music & Video Exchange, 23 & 30 Pembridge Rd, and around the corner at 36 & 38 Notting Hill Gate, W11 ☎0171/221 1444 (Notting Hill Gate tube); also at 229 Camden High St, NW1 ☎0171/267 1898 (Camden Town tube). Truckloads of second-hand rock, pop, soul, reggae and jazz CDs, vinyl, tapes and videos, marshalled by some of the most knowledgeable staff in the city. Rarities are at the 30 Pembridge Rd branch. *Daily 10am–8pm.*

Reckless Records, 30 Berwick St, W1 ☎0171/437 4271 (Charing Cross tube); and at 79 Upper St, N1 ☎0171/359 0501 (Angel tube). Huge CD and vinyl selections of rock (indies, included), soul, dance and jazz. *Mon–Fri 9.30am–7.30pm, Sat 9.30am–7pm.*

Food and drink

London's food stores more than merit a shopping section. Soho and Covent Garden in particular are a gourmand delight, the former replete with Chinese supermarkets and Italian delicatessens, the latter harbouring Neal's Yard, a haven of all that's best in health-conscious nutrition. The upmarket department stores – specifically *Fortnum & Mason* and *Harrods* (see p.507) – are also good sources of fine foods.

For less refined requirements there are numerous supermarkets in the high streets of London's outer reaches. *Safeway, Tesco, Sainsbury* and *Waitrose* are the biggest, with the last pair projecting a slightly posher image and, in the case of *Sainsbury*, a taste for new architecture – check out the one on Camden Road (see p.315). *Tesco Metro* shops (there's one in Covent Garden and another on Oxford Street) and the *Waitrose* store on the King's Road are the only branches of the big four supermarkets you'll find in the centre of town, where their chief rivals are the food halls of the larger branches of *Marks & Spencer*. Other than these, you'll only find small supermarkets which stay open late and charge a lot – *Europa Food and Wine*, 178 Wardour St, W1, is your best bet in the centre.

General gourmet shops

Cullens, 95–97 Baker St, W1 ☎0171/224 2772 (Baker Street tube) and elsewhere. Upmarket groceries, great bread and deli goods. *Mon–Sat 7.30am–midnight, Sun 8am–midnight.*

Mortimer & Bennett, Unit 14, Thomas Neal's, Short's Gardens, WC2 ☎0171 240 6277 (Covent Garden tube) and 33 Turnham Green Terrace, W4 ☎0181/742 3068 (Turnham Green tube). Vast array of quality food items. *The Short's Gardens store is open Mon–Fri 11am–7pm, Sat 11am–6.30pm, Sun 1–6pm; the Turnham Green Terrace store is open Mon–Fri 8.30am–7pm, Sat 8.30am–5.30pm.*

Neal's Yard Wholefood Warehouse, 23 Short's Gardens, WC2 ☎0171/379 8553. Pricey, but if it's Japanese seaweed or any other esoteric health food you're after, it'll be here alongside the usual load of lentils. *Covent Garden tube. Mon–Wed & Fri 9am–7pm, Thurs 9am–7.30pm, Sat 9am–6.30pm, Sun 10am–5.30pm.*

Le Pont de la Tour Food Store, 36b Shad Thames, SE1 ☎0171/403 4030. The retail unit of Terence Conran's high-class "gastrodrome", selling the best fresh fruit and veg, herbs and spices, olive oils, smoked salmon and so on. There's a separate crustacean shop. *London Bridge tube. Mon–Fri 10am–8.30pm, Sat–Sun 10am–6pm.*

Cheese and dairy

International Cheese Centre, 21 Goodge St, W1 ☎0171/631 4191 (Goodge Street tube) and Liverpool Street Station, EC2 ☎0171/628 6637 (Liverpool Street tube). Take your pick from over 350 cheeses. *The Goodge Street store is open Mon–Fri 9am–6.30pm, Sat 9.30am–6.30pm; the Liverpool Street Station store is open Mon–Tues 7am–7.30pm, Wed–Fri 7am–8.30pm, Sat 11am–7.30pm.*

Neal's Yard Dairy, 17 Short's Gardens, WC2 ☎0171/379 7646. A fine (mainly English) cheese shop with around 40–50 varieties in stock at any time. *Covent Garden tube. Mon–Sat 9am–7pm, Sun 11am–5pm.*

Paxton & Whitfield, 93 Jermyn St, SW1 ☎0171/930 0259. Very British outlet, established in 1797, with over 250 cheeses from the UK and Continent. *Green Park or Piccadilly tube. Mon–Sat 9am–5.30pm.*

Chinese

Loon Fung, 41 & 42 Gerrard St, W1 ☎0171/437 1922. Excellent Chinatown food store. *Piccadilly Circus tube. Daily 10am–8.30pm.*

Loon Moon, 9a Gerrard St, W1 ☎0171/734 9940. Another large Chinatown food shop – with the *Loon Fung* the best of the numerous places in this area. *Piccadilly Circus tube. Daily 10.30am–8pm.*

French

Bagatelle, 44 Harrington Rd, SW7 ☎0171/581 1551. Traditional Parisian patisserie. Wave goodbye to your waistline. *South Kensington tube. Mon–Sat 8am–8pm, Sun 8am–6pm.*

Randall & Aubin, 16 Brewer St, W1 ☎0171/437 3507. Wonderful French foods in impressive displays – cheeses, patés, bread and other delights to take away. *Piccadilly Circus tube. Mon–Fri 7.30am–6.30pm, Sat 7.30am–6pm.*

Italian

Carluccio's, 28a Neal St, WC2 ☎0171/240 1487. The most delicious Italian foodstuffs at somewhat excessive prices. *Covent Garden tube. Mon–Thurs 11am–7pm, Fri 10am–7pm, Sat 10am–6pm.*

Fratelli Camisa, 1a Berwick St, W1 ☎0171/734 5456 (Piccadilly Circus tube) and 53 Charlotte St ☎0171/255 1240 (Goodge Street tube), both W1. Old-style Italian delis. *Mon–Sat 8.30am–6pm.*

I Camisa & Son, 61 Old Compton St, WC2 ☎0171/437 7610. Salamis, pastas, oils, fine wines, etc, packed into this small and busy Soho favourite. *Leicester Square or Piccadilly Circus tube. Mon–Sat 9am–6pm.*

Confectionery

Bendicks, 7 Aldwych, WC2 ☎0171/836 1846 and other branches. Great chocolate shop, famous for its bitter mints. *Covent Garden tube. Mon–Fri 9.30am–7.30pm, Sat 10.30am–7pm.*

Charbonnel et Walker, 1 Royal Arcade, 28 Old Bond St, W1 ☎0171/491 0939. English chocolate shop dating from 1875 with beautifully presented sweets. *Green Park or Piccadilly Circus tube. Mon–Fri 9am–6pm, Sat 10am–5pm.*

Godiva, 247 Regent St, W1 ☎0171/495 2845. Perhaps Europe's finest chocolate truffles. *Oxford Circus tube. Mon–Wed & Fri–Sat 9.30am–6pm, Thurs 9.30am–7pm.*

Coffee and tea

Algerian Coffee Stores, 52 Old Compton St, WC2 ☎0171/437 2480. From strawberry pick-me-ups to Colombia's finest. *Leicester Square tube. Mon–Sat 9am–7pm.*

Monmouth Coffee House, 27 Monmouth St, WC2 ☎0171/836 5272. Range of top-quality coffees, roasted on the premises. *Leicester Square tube. Mon–Fri 9am–6.30pm, Sat 11am–5pm.*

The Tea House, 15 Neal St, WC2 ☎0171/240 7539. Bizarre teapots and a large selection of teas. *Covent Garden tube. Mon–Sat 10am–7pm, Sun noon–6pm.*

Wine and beer

The specialist **beer and wine outlets** listed below are the pick of central London's numerous retailers, but you'll also find an ever-improving range in the main supermarkets, for whom budget-

Shops and Markets

range wine is a highly competitive area. All outlets have to observe the same ridiculous licensing laws, which mean you can't buy take-home alcohol on a Sunday except between noon–3pm and 7–9pm.

The Beer Shop, 8 Pitfield St, N1 ☎0171/739 3701. Beers from all over the world in bottles and barrels. *Old Street tube. Mon–Fri 11am–7pm, Sat 10am–4pm.*

Berry Bros & Rudd, 3 St James's St, SW1 ☎0171/396 9600. Helpful and expert wine merchants, still occupying their original Dickensian premises. *Green Park tube. Mon–Fri 9am–5.30pm.*

The Bloomsbury Wine and Spirit Company, 3 Bloomsbury St, WC1 ☎0171/436 4763. The place to head for Scottish malt whiskies – boasting over 175 varieties. *Tottenham Court Road tube. Mon–Fri 9.30am–6pm, Sat 10.30am–3.30pm.*

Oddbins, Earlham Street, WC2 ☎0171/836 6331 (Leicester Square or Covent Garden tube), and some fifty other branches, including Brewer Street in Soho, W1 ☎0171/437 6371 (Piccadilly tube) and on the Strand, WC2 ☎0171/240 3008 (Charing Cross tube). Britain's best high-street wine retailer, especially strong on New World wines, and with an interesting range of beers from around the world. *The Earlham Street store is open Mon–Fri 10am–9pm, Sat 10.30am–9.30pm, Sun noon–3pm & 7–9pm.*

The Vintage House, 42 Old Compton St, WC2 ☎0171/437 2592. Superb selection of wines, and more than 180 whiskies. *Leicester Square or Piccadilly tube. Mon–Sat 9.15am–11pm, Sun noon–2pm & 7–10pm.*

Pharmacies and cosmetics

As well as dispensing a large range of over-the-counter drugs, **London's pharmacies** are major retailers of cosmetics and perfumes – indeed *Boots* (the main chain and found all over London) accounts for the lion's share of UK cosmetics sales. For the best range, check outlets below and also the big department stores – *Harvey Nichols, Selfridge's* and *Harrods* are especially good.

Bliss, 5 Marble Arch, W1 ☎0171/723 6116. This central branch of a three-outlet chain is the only pharmacy in London open from 9am till midnight seven days a week. *Marble Arch tube.*

Body Shop, 64 Long Acre, WC2 ☎0171/836 4901 (Covent Garden tube) and all over London – there are three branches on Oxford Street alone. An Eighties success story, the *Body Shop* has colonized almost every British high street, thanks to a combination of simple packaging, frequently changing stock and an eco-friendly image. The apricot lip balm and white musk body lotions continue to sell in bucketloads. *Mon–Fri 10am–midnight, Sat 10am–6.30pm, Sun noon–6pm.*

Boots, 44 Regent St, W1☎0171/734 6126 (Piccadilly Circus tube) and numerous other branches. As with most central London *Boots'*, this store stocks loads of cosmetics and photographic equipment as well as a big range of pharmaceuticals. It's one of the largest branches and is open slightly longer than most. *Mon–Fri 8.30am–8pm, Sat 9am–8pm, Sun noon–6pm.*

Crabtree & Evelyn, 30 James St, WC2 ☎0171/379 0964 (Covent Garden tube), 239 Regent St, W1 ☎0171/409 1603 (Oxford Circus tube), 134 King's Rd, SW3 ☎0171/589 6263 (Sloane Street tube) and 6 Kensington Church St, W8 ☎0171/937 5029 (High Street Kensington tube). Soaps and scents in pretty packages – the cosmetic equivalent of *Laura Ashley. The James Street store is open Mon–Sat 10am–8pm, Sun 11am–5pm.*

Culpeper Herbalists, 21 Bruton St, W1 ☎0171/629 4559 (Bond Street tube) and 8 Covent Garden Market, WC2 ☎0171/379 6698 (Covent Garden tube). Herbal remedies and scents. *The Bruton Street store is open Mon–Fri 9.30am–6pm, Sat 10am–5pm; the Covent Garden store is open Mon–Fri 10am–8pm, Sun 10am–6pm.*

Floris, 89 Jermyn St, SW1 ☎0171/930 2885. Traditional "English garden" toiletries – suppliers to the royals (and the Reagans). *Piccadilly Circus tube. Mon–Fri 9.30am–5.30pm, Sat 10am–5pm.*

Neal's Yard Remedies, 14 Neal's Yard, WC2 ☎0171/284 2039 and other branches. Stylish blue bottles of eco-friendly lotions, plus homeopathic "cures" for all ailments. *Covent Garden tube. Mon–Sat 10am–6pm, Sun noon–6pm.*

Penhaligon's, 41 Wellington St, WC2 ☎0171/836 2150 (Covent Garden tube), 16 Burlington Arcade, W1 ☎0171/629 1416 (Piccadilly or Green Park tube), 20a Brook St, W1 ☎0171/493 0002 (Bond St tube) and 5 Royal Exchange, EC3 ☎0171/283 0711 (Bank tube). Posh old-style perfumery, with a wonderful range of unique colognes and powders. *The Wellington Street store is open Mon–Sat 9.30am–5.30pm.*

Markets

London's **markets** are more than just a cheap alternative to high-street shopping: many of them are significant remnants of communities endangered by the heedless expansion of the city. You haven't really got to grips with London until you've rummaged through the junk at Brick Lane or haggled for a jacket at Camden, but whichever market you sample, keep an eye out for pickpockets – the weekend crowds provide them with easy pickings .

Clothes, antiques and junk

Bermondsey (New Caledonian) Market, Bermondsey Square, SE1. An enormous array of silverware, paintings, furniture and the like. There's always a bargain or an eccentric gift in there somewhere, but the experts arrive at dawn to grab the real delights. *Borough or London Bridge tube. Fri 5am–2pm.*

Brick Lane, Brick Lane, E1. Cheaper and more authentically East End than the nearby market in Petticoat Lane (see below), and also, on its fringes, more desperate. Its nucleus is the crossroads of Brick Lane and Cheshire Street, where fruit and veg, clothes and household goods are sold; the further east you go down Cheshire Street, the tattier the stalls and the dodgier the deals. *Aldgate East or Shoreditch tube. Sun 5am–2pm.* *See p.226.*

Camden, Camden High Street to Chalk Farm Rd, NW1. Famed above all for its jewellery, ceramics and street fashion, but far more extensive than most people realize. The oldest parts of the market are the fruit and veg stalls of Inverness Street, which have been set up every day except Sunday since the last century. Opposite, the covered section known as Camden Market, which backs onto Buck Street, is open Thursday to Sunday and sells mostly records and clothes. The three-storey Victorian Market Hall, just past the canal bridge on the left, is home to numerous small shops, studios and stalls open seven days a week. Behind the hall are the three cobbled yards of Camden Lock, lined with arty-crafty shops (most open Wed–Sun), and densely packed with jewellery and clothing stalls at the weekend. Further up Chalk Farm Road, the weekend stalls of The Stables are among the cheapest in the entire market. Another adjunct to the market is the Electric Ballroom (back down Camden High Street), a market for clothing and jewellery on Sundays. *Camden Town tube.* *See p.314.*

Church Street, Edgware, W2. This is one of London's best antiques markets, and flanked by plenty of permanent shops – including a good number of buildings with multiple stalls (*Alfie's Antiques Centre* at 13–25 Church St is the biggest, and has a rooftop restaurant). The market actually takes in fruit and veg and hardware, too, at the Edgware Road end, becoming more focussed on antiques towards Lisson Grove. *Edgware Road tube. Daily.*

Covent Garden, Covent Garden, WC2. The old fruit and veg market has crafts stalls daily, except for Mondays when "antiques" take over, both here, and in the Jubilee Market and outdoor market (which normally sell clothes), to either side. The tone can be a bit twee but it's an enjoyable area to wander around, with street performers doing their thing. *Covent Garden tube. Daily.* *See p.126.*

Gabriel's Wharf, Gabriel's Wharf, SE1. A small crafts and clothes market. Nearby,

Shops and Markets

by the National Film Theatre, there is a second-hand books market. *Waterloo tube. Sat & Sun 9am–5pm. See p.250.*

Greenwich, Market Square, SE3. The main market hall is an arty-crafty market, good for cheap, hippy-ish clothes. In other sections, across the road, there are not-quite-antiques, furniture and a hall of second-hand booksellers. *Greenwich BR from Charing Cross. Sat & Sun 9am–5pm. See p.343.*

Kensington, 49–53 Kensington High St, W8. Once an outlet for trendy but inexpensive clothes, now a bit seedy and rather in the shadow of *Hyper Hyper* across the road. Still good for army surplus and second-hand jeans. *High Street Kensington tube. Daily. See p.288.*

Petticoat Lane, Middlesex Street, E1. Very famous and thus with rather inflated prices, but it's good fun and worth a look for leather goods and bizarre bric-a-brac. *Aldgate, Aldgate East or Liverpool Street tube. Sun 9am–2pm. See p.223.*

Piccadilly Crafts Market, Courtyard of St James's Church, Piccadilly, W1. Low-key crafts market. *Green Park or Piccadilly tube. Thurs–Sat 10am–5pm. See p.96.*

Portobello Road, Portobello Rd, W11. This enormously popular, mile-long street market kicks off at Westbourne Grove, site of numerous antique shops, switching to fruit and veg around the *Electric* cinema, then giving way to second-hand clothes and jewellery under Westway. The stalls get progressively less expensive as the market swings east into Golborne Road. Friday is the day to go if you're looking for for the best quality stuff; Saturday is far busier. *Ladbroke Grove or Notting Hill Gate tube. Fri & Sat 9am–5pm. See p.303.*

St Martin-in-the-Fields, Courtyard of St Martin-in-the-Fields Church, Trafalgar Square, WC2. A few stalls selling clothes, jewellery and crafts in the shadow of the church. *Charing Cross tube. Mon–Sat 11am–5pm, Sun noon–5pm. See p.42.*

Food

Spitalfields, Spitalfields, E1. Sunday organic food market, with clothes, jewellery and foodie stalls, kids' rides, a miniature railway and a troupe of animals from the local city farm. *Aldgate East or Shoreditch tube. See p.225.*

Berwick Street Market, Berwick Street to Rupert Street, W1. Down-to-earth fruit and veg market in the heart of Soho. *Piccadilly Circus tube. Mon–Sat 9am–6pm. See p.121.*

Flowers

Columbia Road Market, Columbia Road (east of Ravenswood Street), E2. Superb flower market in pretty Victorian street. *Shoreditch or Old Street tube. Sun 8am–12.30pm. See p.227.*

Wild Bunch, Earlham St, WC2. Central London's best source of cut flowers, on the edge of the Covent Garden area. *Leicester Square tube. Mon–Sat 9am–6pm.*

Sport

As a quick glance at the national press will tell you, **sport** in Britain is a serious matter, with each defeat being taken as an index of the country's slide down the scale of world powers. Many of the crucial international fixtures of the **football, rugby and cricket** seasons take place in the capital, and London also hosts one of the world's greatest tennis tournaments, the **Wimbledon** championship, as well as top-flight athletics at **Crystal Palace**. On the domestic front, the city's football (soccer) teams might lack the star quality of northern England's best sides, but every Saturday there's a chance to see Premier League action here, and the calendar is chock-full of other quality sports events, ranging from the sedate pleasures of **county cricket** to the thrills of **horse racing** on Epsom Downs.

For those who'd rather compete than spectate, London offers all the facilities you'd expect from a city of this size. Council-run leisure centres and parks provide inexpensive access to **swimming pools**, **gyms**, **aerobic classes**, **tennis courts** and so forth, while a host of private establishments cater for everyone from the pool-hall shark to the amateur canoeist.

For up-to-the-minute details of sporting events in London, check the *Evening Standard* or *Time Out*, or ring the London Sportsline on ☎0171/222 8000. For exhaustive listings of the capital's sports facilities, get hold of a copy of the Sports Council's *Directory of Sport in London* – just send an SAE, A4 envelope and 61p postage to PO Box 480, CPNSC, London, SE19 2BQ.

Spectator sports

In this section we've listed details of each of the main **spectator sports** in London, including a run-through of venues and ticket prices. For the top international events it can be almost impossible to track down a ticket without resorting to the services of a grossly overcharging ticket agency, but for many fixtures you can make credit-card bookings by ringing the numbers we've given.

Should you be thwarted in your attempts to gain admission, you can often fall back on **TV or radio coverage**. BBC Radio 5 has live commentaries on major sporting events, while BBC TV always carries live transmission of the big international rugby and cricket matches. To watch Premier League (and some international) football, you'll need to find a set that has the Sky satellite station – many pubs offer Sky games (sometimes on big screens) to draw in custom.

Football

English football is passionate, and if you have the slightest interest in the game, then catching a **league** or **FA Cup** fixture is a must. The season runs from mid-August to early May, when the FA Cup Final at Wembley (for which tickets are almost impossible to obtain) rounds things off. There are four league divisons: one, two, three, and, at the top of the pyramid, the twenty-club Premier League.

Sport

Currently, this is dominated by the big northern clubs – Manchester United, Liverpool, Newcastle, Blackburn – but London clubs (at time of writing) make up seven of the twenty.

The team everyone wants to see (and beat) is **Manchester United**, led by their sublime Frenchman, Eric Cantona; tickets for United games in London are gold-dust, but well worth the hunt. It's easy enough to get tickets, if booked in advance, for most other London Premier League games, unless two London sides are playing each other. The biggest of these "derby" fixtures are the meetings of North London rivals, **Tottenham Hotspur** (Spurs) and **Arsenal** (the Gunners), whose styles – beauty and the beast – show much of what's good and bad about the English game.

We've listed the ticket office numbers for all the main London clubs; if they give you no joy, you could try one of the capital's ticket agencies, or just resign yourself to watching the highlights of the day's best games on BBC's *Match of the Day*, on Saturday night. Most Premier fixtures kick-off at 3pm on Saturday, though there are always a few mid-week games (usually 7.30pm on Wednesday), and one each Sunday (kick-off between 2 and 4pm) and Monday (kick-off at 8pm) broadcast live on Sky TV.

Since the introduction of all-seater Premiership stadiums in 1994, top-flight games have lost their reputation for tribal violence, and there's been a striking increase in the number of women and children watching the "beautiful game". Nonetheless, it's an intense business, with a lot of foul language, and being stuck in the middle of a few thousand West Ham supporters as their team goes down is not one of life's most uplifting experiences.

Premier football stadiums and clubs

Wembley Stadium, Wembley Way, Middlesex ☎0181/900 1234. Tickets for international matches £12–40. *Wembley Park or Wembley Central tube.*

Arsenal, Highbury Stadium, Avenell Rd, N5 ☎0171/359 0131. Tickets £10–23 *Arsenal tube.*

Crystal Palace, Selhurst Park, Whitehorse Lane, SE25 ☎0181/771 8841. Tickets £16–20. *Selhurst BR from Victoria.*

Chelsea, Stamford Bridge, Fulham Rd, SW6 ☎0171/386 7799. Tickets £10–30. *Fulham Broadway tube.*

Queens Park Rangers, South Africa Rd, W12 ☎0181/749 5744. Tickets £11–25. *Shepherd's Bush, Hammersmith or White City tube.*

Tottenham Hotspur, White Hart Lane Stadium, 748 High St, N17 ☎0181/365 5000. Tickets £15–40. *Seven Sisters tube or White Hart Lane BR from Liverpool Street.*

West Ham United, Green St, E13 ☎0181/548 2700. Tickets £11–20. *Upton Park tube or Stratford BR from Liverpool Street, then bus #104.*

Wimbledon, Selhurst Park, Whitehorse Lane, SE25 ☎0181/771 8841. (Wimbledon share Crystal Palace's ground, playing alternate weeks.) Tickets £13–20. *Selhurst BR from Victoria.*

Cricket

In the glory days of Empire the English took cricket to the colonies as a means of instilling the gentlemanly values of fair play while administering a sound thrashing to the natives. These days the former colonies, such as Australia, the West Indies and India, all beat England on a regular basis, so to see the game at its best you should try to get into one of the **Test matches** between England and the summer's touring team. These international matches are played in the middle of the cricket season, which runs from April to September. Two of the matches are played in London: the second is always played at Lords, the home of English cricket, and the last is held at The Oval in Kennington. In tandem with the full-blown five-day Tests, there's also a series of one-day internationals, two of which are again usually held in London.

Getting to see England play one of the big teams can be difficult unless you book months in advance. If you can't wangle your way into a Test, you could watch it live on BBC (the Test series is always televised), or settle down to an inter-county match, either in the **county championship** (these are four-day games) or in one of the three fast and furious one-day competitions: the **Benson and Hedges Cup** and the **Nat West Trophy** (both knock-out competitions), or the **AXA Equity and Law** Sunday league. Of the sixteen county teams in the championship, two are based in London – **Middlesex**, who play at Lord's, and **Surrey**, who play at The Oval.

Cricket grounds

Lord's, St Johns Wood, NW8 ☎0171/289 1611. Tickets: Test matches £15–30 per day; one-day internationals, £20–40; county games from £6 per day. *St John's Wood tube.*

The Oval, Kennington, SE11 ☎0171/582 6660. Tickets: Test matches £21–36 per day; one-day internationals £25–45; county games start at around £7 per day. *Oval tube.*

Rugby

Rugby (or rugger) gets its name from Rugby public school, where the game mutated from football (soccer) in the nineteenth century. A rugby match may at times look like a bunch of weightlifters grappling each other in the mud – as the

Sport

The rules of cricket

The laws of cricket are so complex that the official rule book runs to some twenty pages. The basics, however, are by no mean as Byzantine as the game's detractors make out. There are two teams of eleven players. A team wins by scoring more runs than the other team and dismissing all the opposition – in other words, a team could score many runs more than the opposition, but still not win if the last enemy batsman doggedly stays in (hence ensuring a draw). The match is divided into innings, when one team bats and the other fields. The number of innings varies depending on the type of competition; one-day matches have one per team, Test matches and county championship matches have two.

The aim of the fielding side is to limit the runs scored and get the batsmen "out". Two players from the batting side are on the pitch at any one time. The bowling side has a bowler, a wicket keeper and nine fielders. Two umpires, one standing behind the stumps at the bowler's end and one square on to the play, are responsible for adjudicating if a batsman is out. Each innings is divided into **overs**, consisting of six deliveries, after which the wicket keeper changes ends, the bowler is changed and the fielders move positions.

The batsmen score runs either by running up and down from wicket to wicket (one length = one run), or by hitting the ball over the boundary rope, scoring four runs if it crosses the boundary having touched the ground, and six runs if it flies over. The main ways a batsman can be dismissed are: by being "clean bowled", where the bowler dislodges the bails of the wicket (the horizontal pieces of wood resting on top of the stumps); by being "run out", which is when one of the fielding side dislodges the bails with the ball while the batsman is running between the wickets; by being caught, which is when any of the fielding side catches the ball after the batsman has hit it and before it touches the ground; or "LBW" (leg before wicket), where the batsman blocks with his leg a delivery that would otherwise have hit his stumps.

These are the bare rudiments of a game whose beauty lies in the subtlety of its skills and tactics. The captain, for example, chooses which bowler to play and where to position his fielders to counter the strengths of the batsman, the condition of the pitch and a dozen other variables. Cricket also has a beauty in its esoteric language, used to describe such things as fielding positions ("silly mid-off", "cover point", etc) and the various types of bowling delivery ("googly", "yorker", etc). For beginners, some enlightenment may be gained by listening to the detailed commentary on BBC Test Match Special on Radio 4, watching the TV coverage, or befriending a spectator – cricket fans tend to be congenial types, eager to introduce newcomers to the mysteries of the true faith.

Sport

old joke goes, rugby is a hooligan's game played by gentleman, while football is a gentleman's game played by hooligans – but it is in reality a highly tactical and athletic game. What's more, England's rugby teams have represented the country with rather more success in the last few years than the cricket squad, even if they can't quite match the power and attacking panache of the New Zealand side.

There are two types of rugby played in Britain: fifteen-a-side **Rugby Union**, which has retained its upper-class associations by maintaining amateur status (though the game is also very strong in working-class Wales); and thirteen-a-side **Rugby League**, which is a professional game played almost exclusively in the north of England (though the final of its knock-out trophy is played at Wembley).

In London all rugby clubs play Rugby Union. The two big local teams are the **Harlequins** and the **Wasps**, who often challenge such giants as Bath and Leicester at the top of the championship. Excellent rugby is also played by London clubs in the lower divisions, notably Blackheath, London Irish, London Scottish, Richmond, Rosslyn Park and Saracens.

The season runs from September 1 until the end of April, finishing off with the **Pilkington Cup**, rugby's equivalent of the FA Cup. The Pilkington Cup final, international Test matches and some games in the Five Nations Cup (a round-robin tournament between England, Scotland, Wales, Ireland and France) are played at Twickenham stadium in west London. Unless you are affiliated to one of the 2000 clubs of the Rugby Union, or willing to pay well over-the-odds at a ticket agency, it is tough to get a ticket for one of these big Twickenham games. A better bet is to go and see a Harlequins or Wasps league game, where there's bound to be an international player or two or display.

Rugby stadiums and clubs

Twickenham Stadium, Whitton Rd, Twickenham ☎0181/892 8161. *Twickenham BR from Waterloo.*

Blackheath, Rectory Field, Charlton Road, SE8 ☎0181/858 1578. Tickets £5. *Blackheath or Westcombe Park BR from Charing Cross.*

Harlequins, Stoop Memorial Ground, Craneford Way, Twickenham ☎0181/892 0822. Tickets: standing £8; seats £10. *Twickenham BR from Waterloo.*

London Irish, The Avenue, Sunbury-on-Thames ☎01932/783 034. Tickets: standing £5; seats from £7. *Sunbury BR from Waterloo.*

London Scottish, Athletic Ground, Kew Foot Road, Richmond ☎0181/332 2473. Tickets £5–7. *Richmond tube or BR from Waterloo.*

Richmond, Athletic Ground, Kew Foot Rd, Richmond ☎0181/332 7112. Tickets £5–7. *Richmond tube or BR from Waterloo.*

Saracens, Green Rd, off Chaseside, Southgate, N14 ☎0181/449 3770. Tickets £5–7. *Oakwood or Southgate tube.*

Wasps, Repton Avenue, Sudbury, Middlesex ☎0181/902 4220. Tickets: standing £8; seats £10. *Sudbury Town tube, or North Wembley tube/BR from Euston, or Sudbury & Harrow Road BR from Marylebone.*

Tennis

Tennis in England is synonymous with **Wimbledon**, the only Grand Slam tournament to be played on grass, and for many players the ultimate goal of their careers. The Wimbledon championship lasts a fortnight, in the last week of June and the first week of July. Most of the tickets, especially those with seats for the main show courts (Centre and No. 1), are allocated in advance to Wimbledon's members, other tennis clubs and corporate "sponsors" – as well as by public ballot (see below) – and by the time these have taken their slice there's not a lot left for the general public.

It is possible, however, to turn up on the day and buy tickets, and if you're rich enough you could buy through ticket agencies (although these sales are technically illegal). On tournament days, queues (lines) start to form around dawn and if you arrive by around 7am you have a reasonable chance of securing the limited number of Centre and No. 1 court tickets held back for sale on the day. If you're there by around 9am, you should get admission to the outside courts (where you'll catch some top players in the first week of the tournament). Either way, you then have a long wait until play commences at noon – and if it rains you don't get your money back.

If you want to see big-name players in London, an easier opportunity is the **Stella Artois** championship at **Queen's Club** in Hammersmith, which finishes a week before Wimbledon. Many of the stars use this tournament to acclimatize themselves to British grass-court conditions. As with Wimbledon, you have to apply for tickets in advance (see below), although there is a limited number of returns on sale at 10am each day.

For the unlucky, there's the consolation of TV coverage, which is pretty all-consuming for Wimbledon.

Tennis clubs

All England Lawn Tennis and Croquet Club, Church Road, Wimbledon SW19 5AE. ☎0181/946 2244. Seats £20–50; ground admission £7–8. For public ballot tickets, you have to send a stamped addressed envelope to the club for an application form (available from Sept preceding the championship) and return it by Jan 31st. *Southfields or Wimbledon Park tube.*

Queens Club, Palliser Road, W14 9EQ ☎0171/385 3421. Seats £14–37; ground admission £8. For public ballot tickets to the Stella Artois, send a stamped addressed envelope to the club for an application form, and return it by Sept 30. *Baron's Court tube.*

Horse Racing

There are five horse racecourses within easy reach of London: **Ascot**, **Epsom**, **Kempton Park**, **Sandown** and **Windsor**. The last three hold top-quality races on the flat (April–Sept) and over jumps (Aug–April), but the first two are the real glamour courses, hosting major races of the flat-racing season every June.

Thousands of Londoners have a day out at Epsom on Derby Day, which takes place on the first or second Saturday in June. **The Derby**, a mile-and-a-half race for three-year-old thoroughbreds, is the most prestigious of the five classics of the English flat season (April–Sept), and is preceded by another classic, **the Oaks**, which is for fillies only. The three-day Derby meeting is as much a social ritual as a sporting event, but for sheer snobbery nothing can match the **Royal Ascot** week in mid-June, when the Queen and selected members of the royal family are in attendance, along with half the nation's bluebloods. As with the Derby, the best seats are the preserve of the gentry, but the rabble are allowed into the public enclosure for a mere £5, and can get considerably closer to the action for around £25, providing they dress smartly.

Racecourses

Ascot Racecourse, High St, Ascot, Berkshire ☎01344/22211. Royal Ascot tickets £5–25. *Ascot BR from Waterloo.*

Epsom Downs, Epsom, Surrey ☎01372/470 047. Tickets £10–50. *Epsom Downs BR from Waterloo, Charing Cross and Victoria.*

Kempton Park, Staines Road East, Sunbury-on-Thames ☎01932/782 292. Tickets £5–15. *Kempton Park BR from Waterloo.*

Sandown Park, The Racecourse, Esher Station Rd, Esher ☎01372/463 072. Tickets £4–25. *Esher BR from Waterloo.*

Windsor, Maidenhead Rd, Windsor ☎01753/865 234. Tickets £4–12. *Windsor and Eton Riverside BR from Waterloo or Paddington.*

Greyhound Racing

A night out at the dogs is an increasingly popular pursuit in London. What was once a lower-class substitute for horse racing has now acquired a cult following among younger sophisticates. It's an inexpensive, cheerful and comfortable spectacle: a grandstand seat costs less

Sport

than £5 and all five London stadiums – Catford in southeast London, Wembley in the north, Walthamstow and Hackney in east London, and Wimbledon in the southwest – have one or more restaurants, some surprisingly good. Indeed, so popular has the sport become that you'd be best advised to book in advance if you want to watch the races from a restaurant table, particularly around Christmas. Discounts on entrance fee are often offered to groups planning to eat at the stadium – at Hackney, for example, entrance is free if you book a meal.

Meetings usually start around 7.30pm and finish at 10.30pm, although Hackney also has racing on Tuesday afternoons and Saturday mornings.

Greyhound tracks

Catford, Adenmore Rd, SE26 ☎0181/690 2261. Tickets £2.50–3.50. *Catford Bridge BR from Charing Cross.*

Hackney, Waterden Rd, E15 ☎0181/986 3511. Tickets £3.50 plus £1 for race programme. *Stratford tube, then taxi or bus #308.*

Wimbledon, Plough Lane, SW17 ☎0181/946 5361. Tickets £2.50–4.50. *Tooting Broadway tube, then taxi.*

Walthamstow, Chingford Rd, E14 ☎0181/531 4255. Tickets £2–4. *Walthamstow tube.*

Wembley Stadium, Wembley Way, Middlesex ☎0181/902 8833. Tickets £2.50–4.50. *Wembley Park or Wembley Central tube.*

Athletics

In the age of multiple sponsorships, zillion-dollar TV deals and huge appearance fees, Britain is beginning to lag behind in the ranks of athletics venues, for all the achievements of stars such as Linford Christie, Colin Jackson and Sally Gunnell. Of the half-dozen international athletic meetings held annually in Britain, the two biggest both take place at the **Crystal Palace National Sports Centre**. The first is usually held in June or July (booking starts in April), the other in August (booking from May or June). If you want to be there, don't leave it too late to apply for a ticket – the pulling power of these meetings is such that as many as 6000 extra seats have to be added to the stadium's 17,000 permanent capacity.

Crystal Palace, Ledrington Road, off Anerley Hill, Upper Norwood, SE19. ☎0181 778 0131. Tickets £7–27. *Crystal Palace BR from Victoria, or bus #3.*

Motorsport

The only forms of motorsport in London itself are stock car and banger races at Wimbledon stadium (see "Greyhound Racing", above), held every Sunday

Betting

Most of the money spent by Britain's gamblers is blown on the horses, though only a small minority of punters actually goes to the races. At the course itself you can place a bet with one of the independent trackside book-keepers (or "tic-tac men" as they are known, from the bizarre sign language with which they signal the odds), or with the state-run **Tote**, a system by which the total money placed on a race is divided among the winners.

Competing with Tote and the small bookies are the representatives of the big nationwide betting organizations, such as Ladbrokes and William Hill, who make their money by taking wagers on anything from the result of the 4.15 at Epsom to the name of the rider who will finish fourth in the Tour de France or the identity of the next Prime Minister.

Anyone aged eighteen or over can place a bet, and an eight percent tax is levied on every wager – you can have it deducted either from the stake or from your hypothetical winnings.

Sport

except during June and July. The nearest track for top-class motorsport is **Brands Hatch** in Kent, which holds about eighteen big meetings between February and December, usually on Sundays and bank holidays. Brands Hatch hasn't held a Formula One race since 1986 and is unlikely to do so in future, as the regulations appear to have ruled the circuit out of contention. The circuit is, however, host to motorbike races and three rounds of the **British Touring Car Championships**, which attracts crowds of some 35,000, second only to the British Grand Prix at Silverstone (near Northampton).

Brands Hatch, Fawkham, Longfield, Kent ☎01474 872 331 or Ticketmaster on ☎01474/872 367. Tickets £1–16. *BR to Dartford or Swanlea from Charing Cross, then taxi.*

Participating

The following section lists most of the **sporting activities** possible in the capital. As a rule, the most reasonably priced facilities are provided by council-run leisure and sports centres, all of which have membership schemes which give discounts to regular users. A year's membership tends to cost around £30, a bargain for Londoners (private clubs charge around twenty times more), but if you're only here for a short time it's unlikely to be a sensible investment unless you intend using the gym or swimming pool twice every day.

Ice-skating

London has three ice rinks, two indoor plus the new outdoor Broadgate rink – located in the heart of the City near Liverpool Street station, this is London's answer to the Rockefeller centre in New York.

Broadgate Ice Rink, Eldon St, EC2 ☎0171/588 6565. A little circle of ice open from early November through to March. Adults £5 plus £2 for skate hire, children £3 plus £1. Mon–Thurs noon–2.30pm & 3.30–6pm, Fri noon–2.30pm, 3.30–6pm & 7–10.30pm, Sat & Sun 11am–1pm, 2–4pm & 5–7pm. *Liverpool Street tube.*

Queens Ice Skating Club, 17 Queensway, W2 ☎0171/229 0172. The whole family can strap on its skates at this well-known rink, which has ice-discos on Fri–Sun evenings. Adults £5, children £3.50 (or £5 for discos), skate rental £1.50. Mon–Fri 10am–4.30pm & 7.30–10pm, Sat–Sun 10am–5pm & 7.30–10pm. *Queensway or Bayswater tube.*

Streatham Ice Rink, 386 Streatham High Rd, SW16 ☎0181/769 7771. £3.70 for adults, £2.70 for children. Skate rental £1.30. Mon–Fri 10am–4.30pm & 7.30–10.30pm, Sat & Sun 11.45am–4.45pm & 7.30–10.30pm. *Streatham BR from Charing Cross.*

Jogging and running

All over London middle-aged executives trying to stave off stress-related coronaries can be seen pounding the streets in their lunch hour. If you prefer a more scenic jog, the best locales in central London are **Hyde Park** and **Regent's Park**, and there's even more space out in **Richmond** or up on **Hampstead Heath**.

The numbers of joggers on display increases in the months leading up to the **London Marathon** in April, which draws a field of around 35,000. The course runs from Greenwich to Westminster Bridge, a route lined with tens of thousands of Londoners shouting encouragement. If you'd like to take part, you must apply between April and September for the following April's race; for details contact the marathon hotline on ☎0891/334 450.

Pool and snooker

Pool has replaced darts as the most popular pub sport in London. There are scores of pubs offering small-scale pool tables, even in the centre of the city, where space is at a premium. In some places you may find it hard to get a game, as the regulars tend to monopolize the tables, but in theory the way to get a game is to lay down the fee, usually 50p, on the side of the table, and then wait your turn. Some pubs operate a "winner stays on" policy, which generally means you end up paying for the privilege of being slaughtered by the local champ.

Sport

Generally more pleasurable would be a session in one of the capital's **snooker halls**. Real **American pool**, played on a larger table than pub pool, is moving into halls once dedicated to **snooker**, the equivalent British game. In the London *Yellow Pages* phonebook you'll find numerous pool/snooker clubs – we've picked out a famously friendly pool hall, plus a couple of establishments where the subtle skills of snooker still prevail. If none of these is convenient, you could ring the head office of *New World Snooker Clubs*, the country's largest organization, and ask them for details of their nearest hall (☎0171/228 0934 after 6pm).

Camden Snooker Centre, 16 Delancey St, NW1 ☎0171/485 6094. Camden Town snooker hall where aspiring Stephen Hendrys hone their skills throughout the night. No alcohol, but soft drinks and snacks are available. Although a members club, the management will let you in for a £1.50 fee if the place isn't full. Tables £4.20 per hour. Mon–Fri 11am–6am, Sat & Sun 10am–6am. *Camden Town tube.*

Connaught Health and Snooker Club, 61–65 Great Queen St, Holborn, WC2 ☎0171/405 5303. An upmarket club, used mainly by lawyers from the nearby Inns of Court. £5 for day membership, then a further £5.40 per hour. There is a bar, and snacks are available. Mon–Fri 10am–midnight. *Holborn or Covent Garden tube.*

Ritzy's Pool Shack, 16 Semley House, Semley Place, SW1 ☎0171/823 5817. One of the city's trendiest pool clubs (it has a cocktail bar and American style diner), *Ritzy's* used to be exclusively a snooker hall but has now added 17 pool tables to its facilities. Day membership for the downstairs snooker club is £5; for pool you just pay the £3–8 fee per table per hour – the later the hour the pricier it gets. Daily 11am–11pm. *Victoria tube.*

Horse riding

Strange though it might seem, there are places in the metropolis where you can saddle up, though at quite a price – £25 per hour is the average. It is usually possible to borrow a hard hat, but you must wear shoes or boots with a heel.

Hyde Park Riding Centre, 8 Bathhurst Mews, W2 ☎0171/262 3791. The only riding outlet in central London, open Mon–Fri 7am–dusk, Sat & Sun 10am–dusk. An hour's ride or lesson in a group costs £25, or you can pay £30 for a private lesson. *Lancaster Gate tube.*

Suzanne's Riding School, Brooks Hill Drive, Harrow Weald, Middlesex ☎0181/954 3618. Only 12 miles from the West End, *Suzanne's* has 200 acres of grassland to hack over, as well as three all-weather arenas and an indoor school. There is a showjumping course and a cross-country course if you wish to polish your skills. Prices from £15 for an hour-long group hack or lesson, £21 for a private lesson. *Harrow and Wealdstone BR from Euston.*

Wimbledon Village Stables, 24 High St, SW19 ☎0181/946 8579. Hack over the wilds of Wimbledon Common and Richmond Park for £20 per hour. Private lessons available from British Horse Society approved instructors at £27 per hour. Mon–Fri 10am–3pm, Sat & Sun 9am–3pm. *Wimbledon tube.*

Softball

A domesticated version of baseball, **softball** has recently taken off in London. Every major London company seems to have a softball team, and semi-serious league games take place all over London's bigger parks on summer evenings. Alongside these matches you'll find more casual games, which strangers are welcome to join in – all you have to do is ask. If you'd rather know exactly what's going on where, ring the Greater London branch of the National Softball Federation, which is based in Malvern, in the Midlands (☎0886/884 203).

Boating and watersports

Although the Thames is a dangerously tidal river, and an unappealingly dirty one at that, the city does offer a few opportunities for messing around on the water. Quite close to the centre of town there are non-tidal basins in the former docks, and you'll find calm river waters upstream at Richmond. Local parks with lakes, such as Hyde Park and Battersea Park, also rent out small boats during the summer.

Richmond Boathouse, 13 Richmond Bridge Boathouses ☎0181/948 8270. Rowing boats can be hired all year round, but the prices vary according to season: the lowest rate is £2.50 per person per hour in the winter. Motorboats are available from March to September. *Richmond tube or BR from Waterloo.*

Royal Docks Waterski Club, Gate 16, King George V Dock, Woolwich Manor Way, E16 ☎0171/511 2000. The only place you can waterski in London. Open daily March–Nov, weather permitting. *Mon–Fri Docklands Light Railway to Gallion's Reach, then #101 bus; Sat & Sun East Ham tube, then bus #101.*

The Serpentine, Hyde Park, W2 (no phone). Between March and October you can rent a pedalo or a rowing boat for £6 per hour. *Lancaster Gate tube.*

Surrey Docks Watersports Centre, Greenland Dock, Rope St, off Plough Way, SE16 ☎0181/940 5550. Greenland Dock is a non-tidal basin, which makes it perfectly safe for beginners. A two-hour windsurfing session with an instructor costs £7, including equipment. Accompanied canoeing and dinghy sailing cost the same, but if you want to sail the single-handed dinghies you'll need proficiency certificates. Open daily 9am–6pm, later in the summer depending on the daylight. *Surrey Quays tube.*

Tennis Courts

The most reasonably priced tennis courts in London are those in the council-run parks, which should cost around £4.50 an hour, the downside being that they are rarely maintained to perfect standard. If you want to book a court in advance, you usually have to join the local borough's registration scheme, which is priced between £10 and £20 per year; we've given the phone numbers relating to the courts and registration schemes of the main central London parks. However, during the day, it is generally possible to simply turn up and get a court within half an hour or so, except during July and August, when the Wimbledon tournament spurs a mass of couch potatoes into ill-advised activity. For those who want a better class of facilities, or to keep on playing when the rain pours, there are a few private indoor tennis centres which grant admission to the public.

Sport

Council courts

Battersea Park, and other courts in Wandsworth ☎0181/871 7542.

Bishop's Park, and other courts in Hammersmith and Fulham ☎0171/736 1735.

Holland Park, and other courts in Kensington and Chelsea ☎0171/602 2226.

Hyde Park ☎0171/262 3474. *Lancaster Gate tube.*

Paddington Recreation Ground, and other courts in Westminster ☎0171/798 3642.

Regent's Park ☎0171/486 7905. *Regent's Park or Baker Street tube.*

Private courts

Islington Tennis Centre, Market Rd, N7 ☎0171/700 1370. Indoor tennis courts Sept–May, £13 per hour; outdoor courts all year at £4.50. *Caledonian Road tube.*

Market Sports, 65 Brushfield Street, Spitalfields, EC1 ☎0171/377 1300. Three indoor courts, £10–20 per hour. *Liverpool Street tube.*

Westway Sports Centre, 1 Crowthorne Rd, W10 ☎0181/969 0992. Four indoor courts daily 9am–10pm, £9–13 per hour. Outdoor courts May–Sept, £4.50. *Latimer Road tube.*

Swimming pools, gyms and fitness centres

Below is a selection of the best-equipped, most central and most reasonably priced of London's multi-purpose fitness centres. We haven't given the addresses of the city's many council-run swimming pools, virtually all of which now have fitness classes and gyms; you'll find details of them in the London Business and Services phonebook, under the names of the local council.

Sport

Marshall Street Leisure Centre 14 Marshall St, W1 ☎0171/287 1022. A charming Victorian pool in the heart of Soho, with a gym and rooms for exercise classes. The pool is open Mon 7.15am–7pm, Tues–Fri 7.15am–9pm, Sat 8.30am–7pm & Sun 9am–noon. A swim will set you back £2.50; before you can use the gym you have to take an induction course, which costs £6.75 for two hours. The aerobics studio has classes from £4.20 per hour. *Oxford Circus or Piccadilly tube.*

Oasis Sports Centre 32 Endell St, WC2 ☎0171/831 1804. The Oasis has two pools, one of which is the only heated outdoor pool in central London; the pools are open Mon–Fri 7.30am–10pm, Sat & Sun 9.30am–6pm, and a swim costs £2.40. Other facilities include the Mirage Fitness Studio (induction sessions £15), women-only gym sessions (Tues & Thurs), a health suite with sauna and sunbed (women-only sessions Tues, Thurs, Fri & Sat), massage, and badminton and squash courts (which have to be booked one week in advance. *Covent Garden tube.*

If you fancy an alfresco dip, Hampstead Heath is your place – *see p.326.*

Porchester Spa, 225 Queensway, W2 ☎0171/792 3980. Built in 1926, the *Porchester* is one of only two Turkish baths in central London, and is well worth a visit for the Art Deco tiling alone. There are separate bathing sessions for men and women (women Tues, Thurs, Fri 10am–8pm & Sun 10am–4pm, mixed couples Sun 4–10pm, men Mon, Wed & Sat 10am–8pm), and the £15.40 admission entitles you to use the saunas, steam rooms, plunge pool, Jacuzzi and swimming pool. If you want to splash out you can also have massages or beauty treatments, and there is a snack bar serving light meals and soft drinks. *Bayswater or Queensway tube.*

The Sanctuary, 11 Floral St, WC2 ☎0171/240 9635. For a serious day of self indulgence this women-only club in Covent Garden is a real treat: the interior is filled with lush tropical plants and you can swim naked in the pool. It's an investment at £39.50 a day, or £27.50 for 5–10pm, but your money gets you unlimited use of the pool, Jacuzzi and sauna, plus one sunbed session. You can pay extra for beauty treatments. Open Mon, Tues, Sat & Sun 10am–6pm, and Wed–Fri 10am–10pm. *Covent Garden tube.*

Dance classes

London's dance studios offer an extensive range of classes, ranging from Brazilian capoeira through classical ballet and tap to Pilates – a currently in-fashion style which was devised in the 1930s for dancers with injuries. At all the places listed below you can expect to find concessionary rates for students, Equity members and the unemployed.

Club Latinos, 7 Islington Green, N1 ☎0171/359 6416. If you're into Latin dance, it's hard to beat this club. The London School of Salsa gives salsa classes from 7.30–9.30pm, then try out your steps on the dancefloor. Salsa on Tues, Thur & Sat, tango on Wed. *Angel tube.*

Dance Attic, 368 North End Rd, SW6 ☎0171/610 2055. *Dance Attic* has various kinds of membership, starting at a daily pass for £1.50, and classes cost an average of £3. Courses include tap, lambada, rock & roll, belly dancing, flamenco and Pilates. Open Mon–Fri 9am–10pm, Sat & Sun 10am–5pm. *Fulham Broadway tube.*

Danceworks, 16 Balderton St, W1 ☎0171/629 6183. Membership £4 per day or £22 per month; classes from £4 per hour. Courses include jazz, ballet, capoeira, contemporary and tap, as well as martial arts. There is also a clinic offering every kind of massage and natural therapy. Open Mon–Fri 8am–10.30pm, Sat & Sun 10am–6pm. *Bond Street tube.*

Pineapple Dance Studio, 7 Langley St, WC2 ☎0171 836 4004 (Covent Garden tube) & 38 Harrington Rd, SW7 ☎0171 581 0466 (South Kensington tube). *Pineapple* is the best-known dance studio in London, and its Covent Garden branch is often hired out for auditions, rehearsals and video shoots, so you might be rubbing shoulders with the famous. Daily membership is £4; classes cost around £4 per hour. Open Mon–Fri 9am–8.45pm, Sat 9.30am–6pm & Sun noon–3.30pm.

Chapter 24

Festivals and Special Events

This chapter is simply a run-down on the principal festivals and one-off events in the capital, ranging from the upper-caste rituals of Royal Ascot to the sassy street party of the Notting Hill Carnival, plus a few oddities like the Cart Marking ceremony. Our listings cover a pretty wide spread of interests, but they are by no means exhaustive; London has an almost endless roll-call of ceremonials and special shows and for daily information, it's well worth checking in *Time Out* and the *Evening Standard.*

Regular displays of pageantry like the Ceremony of the Keys (see p.217) and the Changing of the Guard (see p.61) are covered in the main part of the guide, while the chapters on music, dance, sport, art and so on give details of additional events and fixtures in those areas, plus fuller details on the ones referred to here. What follows is essentially a calendar of those London attractions that most people might want to make a special effort to see.

January 1
London Parade
To kick off the new year, a procession of floats, marching bands, clowns, American cheerleaders and classic cars wends its way through the centre of London, from Westminster Bridge to Berkeley Square, collecting money for charity from around one million spectators en route.
Information ☎ 0181/566 8586. Admission £10 for grandstand seats in Whitehall, otherwise free.

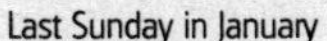
Last Sunday in January
Commemoration of Charles the Martyr
In a ceremony marking the execution of Charles I in 1649, a platoon of ardent royalists in period costume retraces the monarch's final steps from St James's Palace to Banqueting House, placing a wreath on the spot once occupied by the scaffold.
Information ☎ 0171/836 3205.

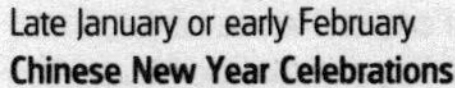
Late January or early February
Chinese New Year Celebrations
The streets of Soho's Chinatown explode in a riot of dancing dragons and firecrackers on the night of this vibrant annual celebration. The restaurants are packed out too.
Information ☎ 0171/437 5256.

Shrove Tuesday (late February or early March)
Soho Pancake Day Race
Carnaby Street, erstwhile heart of Swinging London, is the arena for this annual bout of absurd athleticism, when anyone armed with frying pan and pancakes is allowed to run the street's short but frantic course.
Information ☎ 0171/375 0441.

Festivals and Special Events

Easter Sunday and Monday (March or April)

Battersea Easter Show

Floats, funfairs and all-round family entertainment in and around Battersea Park. *Information ☎ 0181/871 6363.*

Easter

Kite Festival

An army of kite flyers fills the sky above on Blackheath in southeast London, usually with a three-day funfair close by. *Information ☎ 0181/808 1280.*

Late March or early April

Oxford and Cambridge Boat Race

Since 1845 the rowing teams of Oxford and Cambridge universities have battled it out on a four-mile, upstream course on the Thames, from Putney to Mortlake. It's as much a social as sporting event, and the pubs at prime vantage points pack out early. Alternatively you can catch it on TV. *Information ☎ 0171/730 3488.*

Second week in April

Chaucer Festival

Geoffrey Chaucer's *Canterbury Tales* tells of a group of pilgrims who journey from Southwark's Tabard Inn to the Canterbury shrine of Thomas à Becket, telling stories as they travel. Every year, a band of latter-day imitators traverses the somewhat shorter distance between Southwark Cathedral and the Tower of London, where they hold a hearty medieval fair. *Information ☎ 0171/229 0635.*

Third week in April

London Marathon

The world's most popular marathon, with some 35,000 masochists sweating the 26.2 miles from Greenwich Park to Westminster Bridge. Only a handful of world-class athletes enter each year; most of the competitors are club runners and obsessive flab-fighters. There's always someone dressed up as a gorilla and you can generally spot a fundraising celebrity or two. *Information ☎ 0171/620 4117.*

Early May

May Fayre and Puppet Festival

The garden of St Paul's church, Covent Garden, is taken over by puppet booths to commemorate the first recorded sighting of a Punch and Judy show, by diarist Samuel Pepys in 1662. *Information ☎ 0171/375 0441.*

Mid-May

FA Cup Final

This is the culmination of the football year: the premier domestic knock-out competition, played to a packed house at Wembley Stadium. Tickets are pretty much impossible to obtain if you're not an affiliated supporter of one of the two competing clubs, though they are often available at inflated prices on the black market. The game is shown live on both the BBC and independent TV, and at least half the male population of England tunes in for it. *Information ☎ 0171/262 4542.*

Third or fourth week in May

Chelsea Flower Show

The world's finest horticultural event transforms the normally tranquil grounds of the Royal Hospital in Chelsea with a daily inundation of up to 50,000 gardening gurus and amateurs. Organized by the Royal Horticultural Society, it's a solidly bourgeois event, admitting the public only for the closing stages, and charging an exorbitant fee for the privilege. Nonetheless, all forms of flowers and plants are displayed, many of them rare and some of them brand-new hybrids, and there's a chance to buy some of the exhibits on the last day of the four days. Elaborately ornate gardens are planted for the occasion, the best of which are awarded a Gold Medal. *Information ☎ 0171/834 4333. Admission £20–23.*

End of May

Festival of Mind, Body and Spirit

New Agers and the cosmically inclined gather at the Royal Horticultural Halls for this hippy happening. Massage, aromatherapy, Chinese medicine, Tarot readings

and masses of other alternative options are on offer.
Information ☎ 0171/938 3788. Admission £5.

June
Spitalfields Festival
Classical music recitals in Hawksmoor's Christ Church, the parish church of Spitalfields.
Information ☎ 0171/377 0287.

June to September
Kenwood Lakeside Concerts
Classical concerts every Saturday from June to September, held in the grounds of Kenwood House.
Information ☎ 0171/973 3427. (See p.487)

First or second Saturday in June
Derby Day
The Derby, run at the Epsom racecourse in Surrey, is the country's premier flat race – the beast that gets its snout over the line first is instantly worth millions. Admission prices reflect proximity to the horses and to the watching nobility. The race is always shown live on TV.
Information ☎ 01372/726 311. Admission £10–120.

Early June
Beating the Retreat
This annual display on Horse Guards Parade marks the old military custom of drumming the troops back to base at dusk. Soldiers on foot and horseback provide a colourful, very British ceremony which precedes a flood-lit performance by the Massed Bands of the Queen's Household Division.
Information ☎ 0171/930 4466. Admission £3–12.

Early June to mid-August
Royal Academy Summer Exhibition
Thousands of prints, paintings, sculptures and sketches, most by amateurs and nearly all of them for sale, are displayed at one of the city's finest galleries.
Information ☎ 0171/439 7438. Admission about £4. (See p.501)

Around June 11
Trooping of the Colour
This celebration of the Queen's official birthday (her real one is in April) features massed bands, gun salutes, fly-pasts and crowds of tourists and patriotic Britons paying homage. The ceremony originates in the battlefield practice of identifying a regiment by its raised colours.

Tickets for the ceremony itself (limited to two per person) must be applied for in writing, by the end of February, from: The Brigade Major (Trooping the Colour), HQ, Household Division, Horse Guards, Chelsea Barracks, London SW3. Otherwise, the royal procession along the Mall lets you glimpse the nobility for free – though stake your place early.
Information ☎ 0171/930 4466. Admission about £12.

Mid-June
Royal Ascot
A highlight of the society year, held at the Ascot racecourse in Berkshire, this high-profile meeting has the Queen and sundry royals completing a crowd-pleasing lap of the track in open carriages prior to the opening races. The event is otherwise famed for its fashion statements; a female TV commentator is always landed with the job of discussing the more extravagant headgear of attention-courting race-goers.
Information ☎ 01344/22211. Admission from £22.

June
Greenwich Festival
Music, dance, theatre, art and spectacle at various Greenwich venues.
Information ☎ 0181/317 8687.

June
Fleadh
A raucous, rollicking Irish music festival in Finsbury Park, north London. Van Morrison has pitched up here on a few occasions. *Information ☎ 0171/284 4111. Admission around £20.*

Festivals and Special Events

Mid- or late June

Lesbian and Gay Pride

This huge event gets bigger by the year, attracting gay men, lesbians, bisexuals and straight supporters from all over Europe. A circuitous march through London is followed by a day-long party in a London park (Brixton's Brockwell Park, in recent years), with bands, comedians, disco tents, a fairground and stalls.
Information ☎ 0171/738 7644.

Last week in June and first week in July

Wimbledon Lawn Tennis Championships

This major international tournament attracts the cream of the world's professionals and is one of the highlights of the sporting and social calendar. Tickets are hard to get hold of, but as they are valid for the whole day you could always hang around outside in the hope of gleaning an early leaver's cast-off. Don't buy off touts, even if you can afford to, as the tickets may well be fakes.
Information ☎ 0181/944 1066. Admission from £7 for a ground pass to £50 for a centre court ticket. (See p.530)

July–August

Test Cricket matches

The English cricket team plays a series of five international Test matches at home over the summer, and the second match always takes place at Lord's, in north London. The match is most exciting – and most crowded – when either Australia or the West Indies are playing. The best views are from the award-winning Mound Stand, but this is generally the domain of blazer-wearing MCC (Marylebone Cricket Club) members; the less decorous, more entertaining enthusiasts tend to occupy the open stands. The other four Tests take place at a variety of venues – the Oval, in south London, is often used. There's always live TV coverage of all five Tests.
Information: Lords ☎ 0171/289 1611; Oval ☎ 0171/582 6660. Admission £15–35. (See p.528)

Early to late July

City of London Festival

Churches (including St Paul's), halls and corporate buildings play host to musicians, theatre companies and other guest performers.
Information ☎ 0171/377 0540. Admission free–£25.

Mid- to late July

Royal Tournament

A testosterone-rich show of strength by the armed forces at Earl's Court. Booming cannons, deafening military bands and various displays of gung-ho bravado.
Information ☎ 0171/799 2323. Admission £5–24.

Mid-July to mid-September

BBC Henry Wood Promenade Concerts

Commonly known as the **Proms**, this series of classical concerts at the Royal Albert Hall is a well-loved British institution.
Information ☎ 0171/927 4296. Admission from £2. (See p.487)

Early August

Cart Marking

Marking a 1681 Act which restricted to 421 the number of horse-drawn carts allowed in the city, this arcane ceremony involves vintage vehicles congregating in Guildhall Yard in a branding ceremony organized by the Worshipful Company of Car Men.
Information ☎ 0171/489 8287.

Early August

Great British Beer Festival

A five-day binge at Olympia hosted by the Campaign for Real Ale. With 500 brews to sample, the entrance fee is a small price to pay to drink yourself silly.
Information ☎ 01727/867 201. Admission around £3.

Last weekend of August (Summer Bank Holiday)

Notting Hill Carnival

The two-day free festival in Notting Hill Gate is the longest-running, best-known and biggest street party in Europe. Dating

back almost thirty years, the Caribbean community's carnival is a tumult of imaginatively decorated floats, eye-catching costumes, thumping sound systems, live bands, irresistible food and big, big crowds. Its reputation for trouble is largely the product of press scaremongering.
Information ☎ 0800/300 332. (See p.303)

Second and third weeks in September
Festival of Street Theatre
Covent Garden's Piazza's usual compliment of jugglers, mime artists, didgeridoo players and unicyclists are annually outshone by large-scale shows of trapeze acrobatics, circus performances, sword fighting displays and other outdoor theatricals.
Information ☎ 0171/836 9136.

Third or fourth Sunday in September
Horseman's Sunday
In an eccentric ceremony at the Hyde Park church of St John & St Michael, a vicar on horseback blesses a hundred or so horses; the newly consecrated beasts then parade around the neighbourhood before galloping off through the park.
Information ☎ 0171/262 1732.

First Sunday in October
Costermongers' Pearly Harvest Festival Service
It's "Gawd bless the Queen Mum" and suchlike at this Cockney fruit and vegetable festival at the church of St Martin-in-the-Fields. Of most interest to the onlooker are the Pearly Kings and Queens in their traditional pearl-button studded outfits.
Information ☎ 0171/930 0089. (See p.43)

Early October
Horse of the Year Show
Dressage, fence-jumping and other equine exercises whip a genteel audience into a frenzy at this Wembley Arena event. Tickets need to be booked well in advance.
Information ☎ 0181/900 1234. Admission £10–30.

November 5
Guy Fawkes/Bonfire Night
In memory of Guy Fawkes, executed for his role in the 1605 Gunpowder Plot to blow up King James I and the Houses of Parliament, effigies of the hapless Mr Fawkes are burned on bonfires all over Britain. There are council-run fires and fireworks right across the capital, the biggest being the one in Battersea Park. Parliament Hill in Hampstead is a nice place to watch over proceedings.
Information on major displays ☎ 0171/ 971 0026. Admission usually free.

First Sunday in November
London to Brighton Veteran Car Run
In 1896 Parliament abolished the Act that required all cars to crawl along at 2mph behind someone waving a red flag. Such was the euphoria in the motoring community that a rally was promptly set up to mark the occasion, and a century later it's still going strong. Classic cars built before 1905 travel the 58 miles from Hyde Park along the A23 to Brighton at the heady maximum speed of 20mph. The vehicles all turn out in gleamingly beautiful condition and many of the owners dress themselves up in period garb to match their cars' vintage.
Information ☎ 01753/681 736.

Second Saturday in November
Lord Mayor's Show
The newly appointed Lord Mayor begins his or her day of investiture at Westminster, leaving there at around 9am, heading for Guildhall. At 11.10am the vast ceremonial procession, headed by the 1756 State Coach, begins its journey from Guildhall to the Law Courts, where the oath of office is taken at 11.50am. From there the coach and its train of 140-odd floats make their way back towards Guildhall, arriving at 2.20pm. Later in the day there's a firework display from a barge tethered between Waterloo and Blackfriars bridges, and a small funfair on Paternoster Square, by St Paul's Cathedral.
Information ☎ 0171/606 3030.

Festivals and Special Events

Nearest Sunday to November 11
Remembrance Sunday
A day of nationwide commemorative ceremonies for the dead and wounded of the two world wars and other conflicts. The principal ceremony, attended by the Queen, various other royals and the prime minister, takes place at the Cenotaph in Whitehall, beginning with a march-past of veterans and building to a one-minute silence at the stroke of 11am.
Information ☎ 0171/730 3488.

November
London Film Festival
A three-week cinematic season with scores of new international films screened at the National Film Theatre and some West End venues.
Information ☎ 0171/928 3232. Admission £6–8.

Mid-November to early December
Christmas lights
Assorted celebrities flick the switches, and Bond, Oxford and Regent streets are bathed in festive illumination from dusk to midnight until January 6. The lights along Oxford Street are invariably tacky but Regent Street usually puts on a tasteful show, and there are other, less ostentatious displays in St Christopher's Place, Kensington High Street and Carnaby Street. Shop windows are dressed up for the occasion, too, with the automated displays of the biggest stores, such as *Selfridge's*, a major seasonal attraction.

Each year since the end of World War II, Norway has acknowledged its gratitude to the country that helped liberate it from the Nazis with a gift: the mighty spruce tree that appears in Trafalgar Square in early December. Decorated with lights, it becomes the venue for carol singing each evening until Christmas Eve.

December 31
New Year's Eve
The New Year is welcomed en masse in Trafalgar Square as thousands of inebriated revellers stagger about and slur along to *Auld Lang Syne* at midnight. In recent years the crowds have become dangerously large (there have been fatalities), and unless you're pathologically gregarious, you'll have a better time at a pub or club, scores of which stay open very late for the occasion. London Transport runs free public transport all night, sponsored by various public-spirited breweries.

Kids' London

On first sight London seems a hostile place for children, with its crowds, incessant noise and intimidating traffic. English attitudes can be discouraging as well, particularly if you've experienced the more indulgent approach of the French or Italians – London's restaurateurs, for example, tend to regard children as if they were one step up the evolutionary scale from rats. Yet if you pick your place carefully, even central London can be a delight for the pint-sized, and it needn't overly strain the parental pocket. **Covent Garden**'s buskers and jugglers provide no-cost entertainment in a car-free setting, and there's always the chance of being plucked from the crowd to help out with a trick. Right in the thick of the action you'll find plentiful green spaces such as **Hyde Park** and **Battersea Park**, providing playgrounds and ample room for general mayhem, as well as a diverting array of city wildlife. If you want something more unusual than ducks and squirrels, head for one of London's several **city farms**, which provide urbanites with a taste of country life.

Don't underestimate the value of London's **public transport** as a source of fun either. The mere idea of an underground train gives a buzz to a lot of kids, and you can get your bearings while entertaining your offspring by installing them on the panoramic top deck of a red double-decker bus. The number 11, for instance, will trundle you past the Houses of Parliament, Trafalgar Square and the Strand on its way to St Paul's Cathedral for around 50p per child – about one eighth of what you'd pay for a ride on one of the capital's tour buses, and you don't have to endure a mind-numbing commentary either.

Museums are another, more obvious diversion. Some of the more engrossing ones may now charge for admission, but the high-tech, hands-on sections of the **Science Museum** and the **Natural History Museum** in particular will keep the young things busy for hours, and they'll learn while they're at it. There are museums, too, devoted to childhood and toys – while horror fans will, of course, demand the **London Dungeon** and **Madame Tussaud's** Chamber of Horrors.

The spread of **shows** on offer – from puppet performances to specially commissioned plays – is at its best during school holidays, when even the biggest theatres often stage family entertainments. This is especially the case at Christmas, when there's a glut of traditional British pantomimes, stage shows based on folk stories or fairytales, invariably featuring a showbiz star or two, and often with an undercurrent of innuendo aimed at the adults. If that's too passive for you, there are plenty of venues providing more strenuous amusement, from go-kart racing to laser-gun warfare.

Lastly, be warned that London is pretty hot on **toyshops**. The panoply is headed by *Hamleys*, the world's top toy shop, while other stores cater for kids of all temperaments and ages, from the studious to the computer-addicted.

Time Out has weekly listings of kids' events. Kidsline (Mon–Fri 4–6pm; ☎0171/222 8070) also gives details of shows, films, exhibitions, workshops, courses and sports.

The Main Attractions

The following list gives the London museums, galleries and other attractions that are at least partly geared towards entertaining and/or educating children, and are covered in detail in the main part of our guide. Most offer child-oriented programmes of workshops, educational story trails, special shows and suchlike during the school holidays.

Barbican Arts Centre, ☎0171/638 4141. See p.198.

Bethnal Green Museum of Childhood, ☎0181/980 2415, 3204 or 4315. See p.232.

Cabaret Mechanical Theatre, ☎0171/379 7961. See p.130.

Commonwealth Institute, ☎0171/603 4535. See p.289.

Guinness World of Records, ☎0171/439 7331. See p.94.

Horniman Museum, ☎0181/699 1872. See p.342.

Kew Bridge Steam Museum, ☎0181/568 4757. See p.365.

Livesey Museum, ☎0171/639 5604. See p.263.

London Butterfly House, ☎0181/560 7272. See p.367.

London Dungeon, ☎0171/403 0606. See p.257.

London Planetarium, ☎0171/486 1121. See p.110.

London Toy and Model Museum, ☎0171/262 7905. See p.301.

London Transport Museum, ☎0171/379 6344. See p.129.

London Zoo, ☎0171/722 3333. See p.312.

Madame Tussaud's, ☎0171/935 6861. See p.109.

Museum of the Moving Image (MOMI), ☎0171/928 3535. See p.249.

National Maritime Museum, ☎0181/858 4422. See p.348.

Natural History Museum, ☎0171/938 9123. See p.285.

Science Museum, ☎0171/938 8000. See p.283.

Tower of London, ☎0171/709 0765. See p.212.

Parks and city farms

Battersea Park, Albert Bridge Rd, SW11 ☎0181/871 7540 (zoo) or ☎0181/871 7539 (playground). A children's zoo (daily summer 11am–6pm; winter 11am–3pm; adults 90p, children 30p), free adventure playground (term time Tues–Fri 3.30–7pm; holidays & weekends 11am–6pm) and lots of open space. Every August the free "Teddy Bears' Picnic" draws thousands of children and their plush pals. *Battersea Park or Queenstown Road BR from Victoria.*

Coram's Fields City Farm, 93 Guildford St, WC1 ☎0171/837 6138. Ducks, sheep, rabbits, goats and chickens. Adults admitted only if accompanied by a child. *Russell Square tube. Daily 9.30am–4.30pm; free.*

Crystal Palace Farm, Crystal Palace Park, Anerley Hill, SE19 ☎0181/778 4487. Small zoo with exotic animals and birds. *Crystal Palace BR from Victoria or bus #3. Daily 11am–3.30pm; adults £1, children 50p, under-3s free.*

Hampstead Heath, Hampstead, NW3 (no phone). Acres of grassland and woodland, with superb views of the city. Excellent kite-flying potential too. *Hampstead tube.*

Highbury Fields, Highbury, N5 (no phone). A large free playground with sandpit, climbing frames, slides and swings. There's a paddling pool in summer and a nearby indoor pool for winter bathing. *Highbury & Islington tube.*

Holland Park, Abbotsbury Rd, W11 (information on playgroups ☎0171/603 2838). Much-loved park with a one o' clock club for under-eights and a playgroup for under-fives; the former is a free drop-in facility, but you must register in advance for the latter and it costs £3.50 per week. *Holland Park tube. One O'clock Club Mon–Fri 12.30–4pm, playgroup Mon–Fri 9.45am–12.15pm.*

Hyde Park/Kensington Gardens, W8 ☎0171/724 2826. Hyde Park is central London's main open space; in Kensington Gardens, adjoining its western side, the famous Peter Pan statue stands close to a playground and a pond that's perfect for toy boat sailing. *High Street Kensington or Lancaster Gate tube. Daily dawn–dusk; free.*

Kentish Town City Farm, 1 Cresfield Close, Grafton Rd, NW5 ☎0171/916 5421. Five acres of farmland with horses, cows, sheep, goats and chickens. *Chalk Farm or Kentish Town tube. Tues–Sun 9.30am–5.30pm; free.*

Mudchute City Farm, Pier Street, E14 ☎0171/515 5901. Covering some 35 acres, this is London's largest city farm, with barnyard animals, an orchard, study centre and café. *Mudchute or Island Gardens DLR. Daily 9am–5pm; free.*

Richmond Park, Richmond, Surrey ☎0181/948 3209. A fabulous stretch of countryside, with opportunities for duck-feeding and deer-spotting. *Richmond tube or BR from Waterloo. Daily 7.30am–4pm; free.*

Surrey Docks Farm, Rotherhithe St, SE16 ☎0171/231 1010. A corner of southeast London set aside for goats, sheep, chickens, pigs, ducks and bees in hives. *Surrey Quays tube. Tues–Fri 10am–5pm, Sat & Sun 10am–1pm & 2pm–5pm; free.*

Shops

Benjamin Pollock's Toy Shop, 44 Covent Garden Market, WC2 ☎0171/379 7866. An old-fashioned outlet selling puppets, traditional teddies and dolls, as well as charming model theatres complete with cut-out sets, props and tiny actors. *Covent Garden tube. Mon–Sat 10.30am–6pm.*

Children's Book Centre, 237 Kensington High St, W8 ☎0171/937 7497. Immense bookstore just for kids, where classic yarns nestle alongside the best in contemporary adolescent fiction. *Kensington High Street tube. Mon, Wed & Fri–Sat 9.30am–6.30pm, Tues 9.30am–6pm, Thurs 9.30am–7pm.*

Davenport's Magic Shop, Charing Cross Shopping Arcade, WC2 ☎0171/836 0408. London's oldest magic shop sells tricks for the professional and the infant amateur. *Charing Cross or Embankment tube. Mon–Fri 10.15am–5.30pm, Sat 10.15am–4.30pm.*

The Disney Store, 140–141 Regent St, W1 ☎0171/287 6558. Walt-inspired merchandise from teapots to stuffed mice. *Oxford Circus tube. Mon–Sat 9.30am–8pm, Sun noon–6pm.*

Dorling Kindersley Bookshop, 10–13 King St, WC2 ☎0171/836 2015. Dazzling illustrated children's books direct from the publisher. *Covent Garden or Leicester Square tube.*

Early Learning Centre, 36 King's Rd, W3 ☎0171/581 5764 (Sloane Square tube), 225 Kensington High St, W8 ☎0171/937 0419 (High Street Kensington tube) and other branches. No Barbie dolls or plastic weaponry – instead masses of toys, puzzles and books to educate and entertain. *The King's Road store is open Mon–Tues & Fri–Sat 9am–6.30pm, Wed 9am–7pm; Kensington High Street is open Mon–Sat 9am–6pm.*

Eric Snook's Toyshop, 32 Covent Garden Market, WC2 ☎0171/379 7681. Eschewing movie merchandise and cheap tat, this shop sells only the most tasteful, meticulously crafted playthings. *Covent Garden tube. Mon–Sat 10am–7pm, Sun 11am–6pm.*

Frog Hollow, 15 Victoria Grove, W8 ☎0171/581 5493. Winsome amphibians and other soft toys, plus a great range of child-budget items. *High Street Kensington tube. Mon–Fri 8.30am–5.30pm, Sat 9am-5.30pm.*

Future Zone Games Centre, 100 Oxford St ☎0171/637 7911. All the latest computer games to excite the goggle-eyed enthusiast, plus more traditional board games. *Tottenham Court Rd tube. Mon–Wed & Fri–Sat 9.30am–7pm, Thurs 9.30am–8pm, Sun 11am–4pm.*

Hamleys, 188 Regent St, W1 ☎0171/734 3161. The most celebrated toy shop on the planet, multi-storey *Hamleys* is bursting with childish delights – from the humble Slinky to scaled-down petrol-driven Porsches. A smaller branch in the

Kids' London

Covent Garden Piazza gives a taste of the treats on offer at the real thing. *Oxford Circus or Piccadilly Circus tube. Mon–Wed & Fri 10am–6.30pm, Thurs 10am–8pm, Sat 9.30am–6.30pm.*

The Kite Store, 69 Neal St, WC2 ☎0171/836 1666. Kites of all kinds for beginner and stunt master alike. *Covent Garden tube. Mon–Sat 10am–6pm.*

Skate Attack, 95 Highgate Rd, NW5 ☎0171/267 6961. Europe's largest retailer of roller skates and equipment. Skate rental, with protective equipment, is £10 a day or £20 a week, plus £100 deposit. *Tufnell Park tube. Mon–Fri 10am–6pm, Sat 9am–6pm.*

Slam City Skates, 16 Neal's Yard, WC2 ☎0171/240 0928. The latest skates, boards and associated clobber. *Covent Garden tube. Mon–Sat 10am–6.15pm, Sun noon–5pm.*

Warner Studio Store, 178–182 Regent St, W1 ☎0171/434 3334. Cuddly versions of Bugs Bunny and pals at this cartoon-lover's toy store, which stocks everything associated with the Warner Brothers stable. *Oxford Circus or Piccadilly Circus tube. Mon–Wed & Fri 10am–7pm, Thurs 10am–8pm, Sat 9am–8pm, Sun noon–6pm.*

Plays, puppets and films

Barbican Children's Cinema Club, Cinema 1, Barbican Centre, EC2 ☎0171/638 8891. Films for kids at 2.30pm on a Saturday; children must become members which costs £3 a year and entitles them to bring up to three guests. £2.50. *Barbican or Moorgate tube.*

Battersea Arts Centre, Old Town Hall, Lavender Hill, SW11 ☎0171/223 8413. Children's theatre shows at 2.30pm on Saturdays. Adults £3.50, children £1.75, group (two adults, two children) £8. *Clapham Common tube or Clapham Junction BR from Waterloo or Victoria.*

Little Angel Marionette Theatre, 14 Dagmar Passage, off Cross Street, N1 ☎0171/226 1787. London's only permanent puppet theatre, with shows on Saturdays and Sundays at 11am and 3pm; the mornings are for three- to six-year-olds; the afternoons are for older kids. Additional shows during the holidays and occasionally in the evenings. Adults £5–6.50, children £4–5. *Angel or Highbury & Islington tube.*

Lyric Theatre Hammersmith, King St, W6 ☎0181/741 2311. Children's shows at 11am and 1pm on Saturdays – plays, puppetry, clowns and more. Advance booking essential; children and adults £3. *Hammersmith tube.*

National Film Theatre, South Bank, SE1 ☎0171/928 3232. Children's matinées at around 3–4pm on Saturday and Sunday. Adults £3.95, children £2.75. *Waterloo tube.*

Nomad Puppet Studio, 37 Upper Tooting Rd, SW17 ☎0181/767 4005. Short puppet shows for the under-fives on Sundays at 11.30am and 2.30pm. Adults and children £2.50, including soft drink and biscuits. Booking essential. *Closed mid-July to August. Tooting Bec tube.*

Polka Theatre for Children, 240 The Broadway, SW19 ☎0181/543 4888. A specially designed junior arts centre, with two theatres, a playground, a café and a toy shop. Storytellers, puppeteers and mimes make regular appearances. Aimed at kids aged up to around twelve; tickets £3.50–8 for children and adults alike. *Wimbledon or South Wimbledon tube.*

Puppet Theatre Barge, Little Venice, W2 ☎0171/249 6876. Wonderfully imaginative puppet shows on a 50-seater barge moored in Little Venice from November to May, then at various points on the Thames. Shows usually start at 3pm at weekends and in the holidays. Adults £5, children £4.50. *Warwick Avenue tube.*

Rio Cinema, 107 Kingsland High St, E8 ☎0171/249 2722. Movies for minors at 11am on Saturdays. Adults £2.50, children £1.50. *Dalston Kingsland BR from Euston, or buses #67, #76, #149 or #243.*

Tricycle Theatre, 269 Kilburn High Rd, NW6 ☎0171/328 1000. High-quality children's shows most Saturdays at 11.30am and 2pm. Budding thespians can also attend drama and dance workshops after school and during the holidays. Tickets £2.25 in advance, £2.75 on the day. *Kilburn tube.*

Unicorn Theatre, 6–7 Great Newport St, WC2 ☎0171/836 3334. The oldest professional children's theatre in London. Shows run the gamut from mime and puppetry to traditional plays. Performances Sat & Sun 11.30am & 2.30pm, with additional shows during school holidays, usually at 2.30pm. Tickets for performances £5–8.50 for kids and adults. *Leicester Square tube.*

Activities and sports

Alien War, Trocadero, Coventry St, W1 ☎0171/437 2678. Get chased by aliens through a maze of tunnels in the bowels of the Trocadero Centre. Too scary for small kids, and for many adults. Adults £7.95, children £5.95. *Piccadilly Circus tube. Mon–Fri & Sun 11am–11pm, Sat 10.30am–11pm.*

Brass Rubbing Centre, crypt of St Martin-in-the-Fields, Trafalgar Square, WC2 ☎0171/437 6023. Children (and adults) can make rubbings from copies of ancient church brasses, paying £1.50–11.50, depending on the size of the brass. *Charing Cross tube. Mon–Sat 10am–6pm, Sun noon–6pm.*

Britannia Leisure Centre, 40 Hyde Rd, N1 ☎0171/729 4485. Water chutes, wave machine, fountains and more for splash-happy striplings. Adults £2.50, children £1.25, under-fives free. *Old Street tube. Mon–Fri 9am–8.45pm, Sat–Sun 9am–5.45pm.*

Broadgate Ice Rink, Eldon St, EC2 ☎0171/588 6565. A little circle of ice, open from early November through to March, provides London's only opportunity for outdoor skating. Adults £5 plus £2 for skate hire, children £3 plus £1. *Liverpool Street tube. Mon–Thurs noon–2.30pm & 3.30–6pm, Fri noon–2.30pm, 3.30–6pm & 7–10.30pm, Sat & Sun 11am–1pm, 2–4pm & 5–7pm.*

The Circus Space, Coronet St, N1 ☎0171/613 4141. After-school circus courses for children; an eleven-week block costs around £50, while an intensive two-week summer holiday course is priced around £75. *Old Street tube. Mon–Thurs 10am–10pm, Fri 10am–9.30pm, Sun 7am–10pm.*

Playscape, Clapham Kart Raceway, Triangle Place, SW4 ☎0171/498 0916. Go-karting track offering training and racing for daredevils over eight. £30 an hour (£18 per half-hour), but this includes supervision and protective gear. *Clapham Common tube. Daily 10am–10pm.*

Quasar, Trocadero Centre, Coventry St, W1 ☎0171/734 8151. A futuristic fantasy in which you zap your friends and relatives with laser guns. Adults and children £7. *Piccadilly Circus tube. Mon–Thurs & Sun 10am–11pm, Fri–Sat 10am–midnight.*

Queens Ice Skating Club, 17 Queensway, W2 ☎0171/229 0172. Well-known rink, which has roller-discos on Fri–Sun evenings. Adults £5, children £3.50 (or £5 for discos), skate rental £1.50. *Queensway or Bayswater tube. Mon–Fri 10am–4.30pm & 7.30–10pm, Sat–Sun 10am–5pm & 7.30–10pm.*

Kids' London

For more on sport, see p.527.

Babysitting services

The following organizations offer babysitting services at £3–5 an hour, excluding travel expenses and agency fees. Should you find them all booked solid (which you will if you don't call at least one day in advance), you can find other agencies in the *Yellow Pages*. Nearly all hotels are also able to arrange childcare, but their rates are likely to be considerably higher.

Childminders, 9 Paddington St, W1 ☎0171/935 2049. *Baker Street tube.*

Koala Nannies, 22 Craven Terrace, W2 ☎0171/402 4224. *Lancaster Gate tube.*

Pippa Pop-ins, 430 Fulham Rd ☎0171/385 2458. A crèche, nursery and children's hotel as well as a babysitting service. *Parsons Green tube.*

Universal Aunts, PO Box 304, SW4 ☎0171/738 8937.

Part 4

The Contexts

A Brief History

Two thousand years of compressed history – featuring riots and revolutions, plagues, fires, slum clearances, lashings of gin, Mrs Thatcher and the London people.

Roman Londinium

There is evidence of scattered **Celtic settlements** along the Thames, but no firm proof that central London was permanently settled by the Celts before the arrival of the Romans. That process began in 55 and 54 BC, when Julius Caesar led several small cross-Channel incursions; the Celts used the Thames as their main line of defence.

Britain's rumoured mineral wealth was a primary motive behind the Roman raids, but the immediate spur to the eventual conquest nearly a century later was the dangerous collaboration between British Celts and the fiercely anti-Roman tribes of France, and the need of the emperor Claudius, who owed his power to the army, for a great military triumph. The death of Cunobelin, king of the Catuvellauni (and the original of Shakespeare's Cymbeline) offered the opportunity Claudius required, and in **August 43 AD,** an army of 40,000 landed in Kent.

Once more the Celts used the Thames as their main defensive line, and once again they were overwhelmed. The Romans built a bridge some fifty metres east of today's London Bridge, where the river was easily fordable, and within ten years had established a permanent military presence at the port of Londinium. The site was chosen partly for navigable reasons, partly due to the solid soil, which could support a wooden bridge. It was not, however, the Romans' principal settlement, which was at **Camulodunum** (modern Colchester) to the east.

In 61 AD, the East Anglian people known as the Iceni, under their queen **Boudicca** (or Boadicea), rose up against the invaders, sacked Camulodunum, and made their way to the ill-defended port of Londinium. According to Tacitus, the inhabitants were "massacred, hanged, burned and crucified", but the Iceni were eventually defeated and Boudicca committed suicide. In the aftermath, **Londinium** emerged as the new commercial and political capital of Britannia, and was endowed with an imposing basilica and forum, temples, bathhouses and an amphitheatre. To protect against further attacks, fortifications were built, three miles long, fifteen feet high and eight feet thick, with a fortress near today's Museum of London.

Although only fragments of Roman London survive – mostly foundations and the odd patch of wall – Londinium was a prosperous imperial outpost, which evolved into the empire's fifth largest city north of the Alps, with an estimated population of 30,000 by the fourth century AD. In 410 AD, however, the emperor Honorius withdrew the last Roman troops, leaving the country and its chief city at the mercy of the marauding Saxon pirates who had been making increasingly persistent raids on the coast since the middle of the previous century.

Saxon Lundenwic and the Danes

Roman London appears to have been more or less abandoned in the decades following the troops' withdrawal, and the next phase of permanent settlement dates from the sixth century, by which time the **Anglo-Saxons** controlled most of England. Recent archeological finds suggest that they had little interest in the Roman city and instead colonized the area immediately to the west of the Roman walls. On the conversion of the local Saxons to Christianity in 604, their city of **Lundenwic** was considered important enough to be granted a bishopric, though it was Canterbury, not London, that was chosen as the seat of the Primate of England. Nevertheless, trade flourished once more during this period, as attested by the Venerable Bede who wrote of London in 730 as "the mart of many nations resorting to it by land and sea".

In 834, 841 and 851 London suffered Danish Viking attacks which left the city in ruins. In 871 the **Danes** were confident enough to establish London as their winter base, but in 886 Alfred the Great, King of Wessex, recaptured the city, rebuilt the walls and formally re-established London as a fortified town. After a lull, the Danes returned once more in the late tenth century, attacking unsuccessfully in 984 and 994, but eventually taking the city again in 1013. Three years later, the Danish leader Cnut (or Canute) became King of All England, and made London the national capital (in preference to the Wessex base of Winchester), a position it has held ever since.

On the return of the House of Wessex to the English throne under **Edward the Confessor**, the court and church moved upstream to Thorney Island (or the Isle of Brambles). Here, Edward built a splendid new palace so that he could oversee construction of his "West Minster" (later to become Westminster Abbey). Edward was too weak to attend the official consecration and died just ten days later: he is buried in the great cathedral he founded, where his shrine has been a place of pilgrimage for centuries. Of greater political and social significance was his geographical separation of power, with royal government based in **Westminster**, while the City of London remained the commercial centre.

1066 and all that

On the death of the celibate Edward in 1066, several rivals claimed the throne. Having defeated his brother Tostig (who was in cahoots with the Norwegians), King Harold – the nation's choice – was himself defeated by **William of Normandy** (aka William the Conqueror) and his invading army at the Battle of Hastings. On Christmas Day of 1066, William crowned himself king in Westminster Abbey, thus establishing a tradition which continues to this day. Elsewhere in England, the Normans ruthlessly suppressed all opposition, but in London William granted the City a charter guaranteeing to preserve the privileges it had enjoyed under Edward. However, as an insurance policy, William also built three forts in the city, of which the sole remnant is the White Tower, now the nucleus of the **Tower of London**. As a further precaution, he also established another castle, a day's march away at **Windsor**, and based the court at Westminster.

Neither the later Normans nor their successors, the Plantagenets, succeeded in diluting the City's autonomy, a status embodied in the personage of the **Mayor**, an office established some time around 1200. Though the monarchs struggled to subdue the City, successive kings needed the City's money and support in times of crisis, and were regularly forced to back off and grant further concessions instead. Financial considerations were the primary motive behind the invitations extended to Jewish immigrants by William the Conqueror and others. Other foreign merchants were also drawn to London, where large profits could be made in the export of wool. All foreigners were subject to occasional outbreaks of violence by the local population, and in particular the Jews, whose coffers Edward I bled dry. They were finally expelled in 1290.

From the Black Death to the Wars of the Roses.

The Europe-wide plague outbreak known as the **Black Death** arrived in England in 1348 and in the following two years wiped out something like half the capital's population. Other plagues followed in 1361, 1369 and 1375 and created a volatile economic situation which was worsened by the introduction of the Poll Tax, a head tax imposed on all men regardless of means.

During the ensuing **Peasants' Revolt** of 1381, London's citizens opened the City gates to Wat Tyler's Kentish rebels and joined in the lynching of the archbishop, plus countless rich merchants and clerics. Tyler was then lured to meet the boy-king Richard II at Smithfield, just outside the City, where he was murdered by Mayor Walworth, who was subsequently knighted for his treachery. Tyler's supporters were fobbed off with promises of political changes that never came, as Richard unleashed a wave of repression and retribution.

Parallel with this social unrest were the demands for clerical reforms made by the scholar and heretic **John Wycliffe**, whose ideas were keenly taken up by Londoners. His followers, known as **Lollards**, made the first translation of the Bible into English in 1380. Another sign of the elevation of the common language was the success enjoyed by **Geoffrey Chaucer** (c.1340–1400), a London wine merchant's son, whose *Canterbury Tales* was the first major work written in vernacular English and one of the first books to be printed.

The so-called Wars of the Roses, the name now given to the strife between the rival noble houses of Lancaster and York, left London relatively untouched. As far as the city was concerned, the only serious disturbance of the period was **Jack Cade's Revolt**, which took place in 1450, a decade before the Yorkist king Edward IV overthrew the mad Henry VI, thereby precipitating the war. An army of 20,000 rebels – including gentry, clergy and craftsmen – defeated the king's forces at Sevenoaks, and reached Southwark in early July. Once more the citizens of London opened the gates to the insurgents, who spent three days wreaking vengeance on their enemies before being dispersed with yet more false promises. The reprisals, which became known as the "harvest of heads" were as harsh as before.

Tudor London

The **Tudor** family, which with the coronation of **Henry VII** emerged triumphant from the mayhem of the Wars of the Roses, reinforced London's pre-eminence during the sixteenth century, when the Tower of London and the **royal palaces** of Whitehall, St James's, Richmond, Greenwich, Hampton Court and Windsor provided the backdrop for the most momentous events of the period.

One of the crucial developments of the century was the English **Reformation**, the separation of the English church from Rome, a split initially prompted not by doctrinal issues, but by the failure of Henry VIII's first wife, Catherine of Aragon, to produce a male heir. The subsequent **Dissolution of the Monasteries**, a programme commenced in 1536, changed the entire fabric of the city. Previously dominated by its religious institutions, London's property market was suddenly flooded with confiscated estates, which were quickly snapped up and redeveloped by the Tudor nobility. The violence of this schism was at its most extreme in London, where the citizens embraced enthusiastically the teachings of Protestantism, desecrating churches and monasteries with great abandon.

The Tudor economy boomed, reaching its height in the reign of **Elizabeth I**, when the piratical exploits of seafarers Walter Ralegh, Francis Drake, Martin Frobisher and John Hawkins, helped to map out the world for English commerce. London's commercial success was epitomized by the millionaire merchant Thomas Gresham, who erected the **Royal Exchange**, establishing London as the premier world trade market. At the same time the population soared, spilling over into outlying districts and reaching 200,000 by the end of the century, making London one of the five largest cities in Europe.

The forty-five years of Elizabeth's reign also witnessed the efflorescence of a specifically **English Renaissance**, especially in the field of literature, which reached its apogee in the brilliant careers of **Christopher Marlowe**, **Ben Jonson** and **William Shakespeare**. The presses of **Fleet Street**, established a century earlier by William Caxton's apprentice Wynkyn de Worde, ensured London's position as a centre for the printed word. Beyond the jurisdiction of the City censors, in the entertainment district of Southwark, whorehouses, animal-baiting pits and theatres flourished. The carpenter-cum-actor, James Burbage, designed the first purpose-built playhouse in 1574, eventually rebuilding it south of the river as the Globe Theatre, where Shakespeare premiered many of his works (the theatre is currently being reconstructed).

From Gunpowder Plot to Civil War

On Elizabeth's death in 1603, James VI of Scotland became **James I** of England, thereby uniting the two crowns and marking the beginning of the **Stuart dynasty**. His intention of exercising religious tolerance after the anti-Catholicism of Elizabeth's reign was thwarted by the reaction which followed the **Gunpowder Plot** of 1605, when Guy Fawkes and a group of Catholic conspirators were discovered attempting to blow up the king at the state opening of Parliament. James, who clung to the medieval notion of the divine right of kings, inevitably clashed with the landed gentry who dominated parliament, too, and tensions between Crown and Parliament were worsened by his persecution of the Puritans, an extreme but increasingly powerful Protestant group.

Under James's successor, **Charles I**, the animosity between Crown and Parliament came to a head. From 1629 to 1640 Charles ruled without the services of Parliament, but was forced to recall it when he ran into problems in Scotland, where he was attempting to subdue the Presbyterians. Faced with extremely antagonistic MPs, Charles attempted unsuccessfully to arrest several of their number, who, acting on a tip-off, fled by river to the City, which sided with Parliament. Charles withdrew to Nottingham where he raised his standard, the opening military act of the **Civil War**.

London was the key to victory for both sides, and as a Parliamentarian stronghold it came under attack almost immediately from Royalist forces. Having defeated the Parliamentary troops to the west of London at Brentford in November 1642, the way was open for Charles to take the capital. Londoners turned out in numbers to defend their city, some 24,000 assembling at Turnham Green. Charles hesitated and in the end withdrew to Reading, thus missing his greatest chance of victory. A complex system of fortifications was thrown up around London, but never put to the test. In the end the capital remained intact throughout the war, which culminated in the execution of the king outside Whitehall's Banqueting House in January 1649.

For the next eleven years England was a **Commonwealth** – at first a true republic, then, after 1653, a Protectorate under **Oliver Cromwell**, who was ultimately as impatient of Parliament and as arbitrary as Charles had been. London found itself in the grip of the **Puritans**' zealous laws, which closed down all theatres, enforced observance of the Sabbath, and banned the celebration of Christmas, which was considered a papist superstition.

Plague and Fire

Just as London proved Charles I's undoing, so its ecstatic reception for **Charles II** helped ease the **Restoration** of the monarchy in 1660. The "Merry Monarch" immediately caught the mood of the public by opening up the theatres, and he encouraged the sciences by helping the establishment of the **Royal Society** for Improving Natural Knowledge, whose founder members included **Christopher Wren**, **Isaac Newton** and **John Evelyn**.

The good times which rolled in the early period of Charles' reign came to an abrupt end with the onset of the **Great Plague** of 1665. Epidemics of bubonic plague, carried by the fleas which lived on black rats, were nothing new to London – there had been major outbreaks in 1593, 1603, 1625, 1636 and 1647 – but the combination of a warm summer and the chronic overcrowding which was a feature of the city, proved calamitous in this instance. Those with money left the city (the court moved to Oxford) while the poorer districts outside the City were the hardest hit. The extermination of the city's dog and cat population – believed to be the source of the epidemic – only exacerbated the situation. In September, the death toll peaked at 12,000 a week, and in total an estimated 100,000 lost their lives.

A cold snap in November extinguished the plague, but the following year London had to contend with yet another disaster, the **Great Fire** of 1666. As with the plague, outbreaks of fire were fairly commonplace in London, whose buildings were predominantly timber-framed, and whose streets were narrow, allowing fires to spread rapidly. So it was that between September 2 and September 5 some eighty percent of the City was razed to the ground, including 87 churches, 44 livery company halls, and 13,200 houses; the death toll didn't even reach double figures, but over 100,000 were left homeless.

Within five years, 9000 houses had been rebuilt with bricks and mortar (timber was banned), and fifty years later **Christopher Wren** had almost single-handedly rebuilt all the City churches and completed the world's first Protestant cathedral, **St Paul's**. Medieval London was no more, though the grandiose masterplans of Wren and other architects had to be rejected due to the legal intricacies of property rights within the City. The **Great Rebuilding**, as it was known, was one of London's remarkable achievements – and this despite a chronic lack of funds, a series of very severe winters, continuing wars against the Dutch, the Monmouth Rebellion of 1685, and the disruption of the "Glorious Revolution" of 1688, which brought the Dutch king William of Orange to the throne.

William and his wife, **Mary**, daughter of James II, were made joint sovereigns, having agreed to a Bill of Rights defining the limitations of the monarch's power and the rights of his or her subjects. This, together with the Act of Settlement of 1701 – which among other things, barred Catholics or anyone married to one from succession to the throne – made Britain the first country in the world to be governed by a

constitutional monarchy, in which the roles of legislature and executive were separate and interdependent. A further development during the reign of **Anne**, second daughter of James II, was the Act of Union of 1707, which united the English and Scottish parliaments.

Georgian London

When Queen Anne died childless in 1714 (despite having given birth seventeen times), the Stuart line ended, though pro-Stuart or Jacobite rebellions continued on and off until 1745. In accordance with the Act of Settlement, the succession passed to a non-English-speaking German, the Duke of Hanover, who became **George I** of England. As power leaked from the monarchy, the king ceased to attend cabinet meetings (which the new king couldn't understand anyway), his place being taken by his chief minister. Most prominent among these chief ministers was **Robert Walpole**, the first politician to live at **10 Downing Street**, and effective ruler of the country from 1721 to 1742.

Meanwhile, London's expansion continued unabated. The shops of the newly developed **West End** stocked the most fashionable goods in the country, the volume of trade more than tripled, and the city's growing population created a huge market for food and other produce, as well as fuelling a building boom. In the City, the **Bank of England** – founded in 1694 to raise funds to conduct war against France – was providing a sound foundation for the economy. It could not, however, prevent the mania for financial speculation, which resulted in the fiasco of the **South Sea Company**, which in 1720 sold shares in its monopoly of trade in the Pacific and along the east coast of South America. The "bubble" burst when the shareholders took fright at the extent of their own investments and the value of the shares dropped to nothing, reducing many to penury and almost wrecking the government, which was saved only by the astute intervention of Walpole.

Wealthy though London was, it was also experiencing the worst mortality rates since records began in the reign of Henry VIII. Disease was rife in the overcrowded immigrant quarter of the East End and other slum districts, but the real killer during this period was **gin**. It's difficult to exaggerate the effects of the gin-drinking orgy which took place among the poorer sections of London's population between 1720 and 1751. At its height, gin consumption was averaging two pints a week for every man, woman and child, and the burial rate exceeded the baptism rate by more than 2:1. Its origins lay in the country's enormous surplus of corn, which had to sold in some form or another to keep the landowners happy. Deregulation of the distilling trade was Parliament's answer, thereby flooding the urban market with cheap, intoxicating liquor, which resulted in an enormous increase in crime, prostitution, child mortality and general misery amongst the poor. Eventually, in the face of huge vested interests, the government was forced to pass an act in 1751 that restricted gin retailing and brought the epidemic to a halt.

Policing the metropolis was an increasing preoccupation for the government. It was proving a task far beyond the city's 3000 beadles, constables and nightwatchmen, who were, in any case, "old men chosen from the dregs of the people who have no other arms but a lantern and a pole", according to one French visitor. As a result, crime continued unabated throughout the eighteenth century, so that, in the words of Horace Walpole, one was "forced to travel even at noon as if one was going into battle". The government imposed draconian measures. The prison population swelled, transportations began, and 1200 Londoners were hanged at Tyburn's gallows, mostly for petty offences.

Despite such measures, and the passing of the Riot Act in 1715, rioting remained a popular pastime among the poorer classes in London. Anti-Irish riots had taken place in 1736; the 1743 Gin Act had provoked a riot in defence of cheap liquor; and in the 1760s there were more organized mobilizations by supporters of the great agitator **John Wilkes**, calling for political reform. The most serious insurrection of the lot, however, was the **Gordon Riots** of 1780, when up to 50,000 Londoners went on a five-day rampage through the city. Although anti-Catholicism was the spark that lit the fire, the majority of the rioters' targets were chosen not for their religion but for their wealth. The most dramatic incidents took place at Newgate Prison, where thousands of inmates were freed, and at the Bank of England, which was saved only by the intervention of the military – and John Wilkes, of all people. The death toll was in excess of 300, twenty-five rioters were subsequently hanged, and further calls were made in Parliament for the establishment of a proper police force.

Nineteenth-century London

The nineteenth century witnessed the emergence of London as the capital of an empire that stretched across the globe. The world's largest enclosed **dock system** was built in the marshes to the east of the City, Tory reformer **Robert Peel** established the world's first civilian **police force**, and the world's first public transport network was created, with horse buses, trains, trams and an underground railway.

The city's population grew from just over one million in 1801 (the first official census) to nearly seven million by 1901. **Industrialization** brought pollution and overcrowding, especially in the slums of the East End. Smallpox, measles, whooping cough and scarlet fever killed thousands of working-class families, as did the cholera outbreaks of 1832 and 1848–49. The **Poor Law** of 1834 formalized **workhouses** for the destitute, but failed to alleviate their problems – in the end becoming little more than hospitals for the penniless. It is this era of slum-life, and huge social divides, that Dickens evoked in his novels.

Architecturally, London was changing rapidly. **George IV**, who became Prince Regent in 1811 during the declining years of his father, George III, instigated several grandiose projects that survive to this day. With the architect **John Nash** he laid out London's first planned processional route, Regent's Street, and a prototype garden city around **Regent's Park**. The Regent's Canal was driven through the northern fringe of the city, and Trafalgar Square began to take shape. The city already boasted the first public museum in the world, the **British Museum**, and in 1814 London's first public art gallery opened in the suburb of Dulwich, followed shortly afterwards by the National Gallery, which was founded in 1824. London finally got its own university, too, in 1826.

1837 saw the accession of **Queen Victoria**, who, reigning though a period in which the country's international standing reached unprecedented heights, came to be as much a national icon as Elizabeth I had been. Though the intellectual achievements of Victoria's reign were immense – typified by the publication of Darwin's *The Origin of Species* in 1859 – the country saw itself above all as an imperial power founded on industrial and commercial prowess. Its spirit was perhaps best embodied by the great engineering feats of Isambard Kingdom Brunel, such as the Thames Tunnel, and by the **Great Exhibition** of 1851, a display of manufacturing achievements from all over the world, which took place in the Crystal Palace erected in Hyde Park.

Despite being more than twice the size of Paris, London did not experience the political upheavals of the French capital – the terrorists who planned to wipe out the cabinet in the 1820 Cato Street Conspiracy were the exception. The 1832 Reform Act, which acknowledged the principle of popular representation (though most men and all women still had no vote), left London relatively untouched: its administration remained dominated by the City oligarchy, and the **Chartist movement**, which campaigned for universal male suffrage (among other things), was much stronger in the industrialized north than in the capital.

Nevertheless, when the Chartists planned a mass demonstration in London in the revolutionary year of 1848, the government panicked. Thousands of "special constables" were drafted in to boost the capital's 4000 police officers, and troops were garrisoned around all public buildings. In the end the march passed off peacefully, and there was little home-grown militancy in London until the emergence of trade unionism in the 1880s.

The birth of local government

The first tentative steps towards a cohesive form of metropolitan government were taken in 1855 with the establishment of the **Metropolitan Board of Works** (MBW). Its inital remit only covered sewerage, lighting and street maintenance, but it was soon extended to include gas, fire services, public parks and slum clerance. The achievements of the MBW – and in particular, those of its chief engineer, Joseph Bazalgette – were immense, creating an underground sewer system (much of it still in use), improving transport routes and wiping out some of the city's more notorious slums. However, vested interests and resistance to reform from the City hampered the efforts of the MBW, which was also found to be involved in widespread malpractice.

In 1888 the **London County Council** (LCC) was established. It was the first directly elected London-wide government, though as ever the City held on jealously to its independence. Its arrival coincided with an increase in working-class militancy within the capital. In 1884 120,000 gathered in Hyde Park to support the ultimately unsuccessful London Government Bill. A demonstration held in 1886 in Trafalgar Square in protest against unemployment ended in a riot through St James's. The following year the government banned any further demos, and the resultant protest brought even larger numbers to Trafalgar Square. The brutality of the police in breaking up this last demonstration led to its becoming known as "Bloody Sunday". In 1888 the Bryant & May matchgirls won their landmark strike action over working conditions, a victory followed up the next year by further successful strikes by the gasworkers and dockers.

Charles Booth published his seventeen-volume *Life and Labour of the People of London* in 1890, providing the first clear picture of the social fabric of the city, and shaming the council into action. In the face of powerful vested interests – landlords, factory owners and private utility companies – the LCC's Liberal leadership attempted to tackle the enormous problems, partly by taking gas, water, electricity and transport into municipal ownership – a process that took several more decades to achieve. The LCC's ambitious housing programme was beset with problems, too. Slum clearances only exacerbated overcrowding, and the new dwellings were too expensive for those in greatest need. Rehousing the poor in the suburbs also proved unpopular, since there was a policy of excluding public houses, traditionally the social centre of working-class communities, from these developments.

While half of London struggled to make ends meet, the other half enjoyed the fruits of the richest nation in the world. Luxury establishments such *The Ritz* and *Harrod's* belong to this period, which was personified by the dissolute and complacent Prince of Wales, later **Edward VII**. For the masses, too, there were new entertainments to be enjoyed: music halls boomed, public houses prospered and the circulation of populist newspapers such as the *Daily Mirror* topped one million. The first "Test" cricket match between England and Australia took place in 1880 at the Kennington Oval in front of 20,000 spectators, and during the following twenty-five years nearly all of London's professional **football clubs** were founded.

From World War I to World War II

Public patriotism peaked at the outbreak of **World War** I, with crowds cheering the troops off from Victoria and Waterloo stations, convinced the fighting would all be over by Christmas. In the course of the next four years London experienced its first aerial attacks, with Zeppelin raids leaving some 650 dead, but these were minor casualties in the context of a war that destroyed millions of lives and eradicated whatever remained of the majority's respect for the ruling classes.

At the war's end in 1918, the country's social fabric was changed drastically as the voting franchise was extended to all men aged twenty-one and over and to women of thirty or over. The tardy liberalization of women's rights – largely due to the radical **Suffragette** movement led by Emmeline Pankhurst and her daughters – was not completed until 1928, the year of Emmeline's death, when women were at last granted the vote on equal terms with men.

Between the wars, London's population increased dramatically, reaching close to nine million by 1939, representing one fifth of the country's population. In contrast to the nineteenth century, however, there was a marked shift in population out into the **suburbs**. Some took advantage of the new "model dwellings" of LCC estates in places such as Dagenham in the east, though far more settled in "Metroland", the sprawling new suburban districts which followed the extension of the underground out into north London.

In 1924 the British Empire Exhibition was held, with the intention of emulating the success of the Great Exhibition. Some 27 million people visited the show, but its success couldn't hide the tensions that had been simmering since the end of the war. In 1926 a wage dispute between the miners' unions and their bosses developed into the **General Strike**. For nine days, more than half a million workers stayed away from work, until the government called in the army and thousands of volunteers to break the strike.

The economic situation deteriorated even further after the crash of the New York Stock Exchange in 1929, with unemployment in Britain reaching over three million in 1931. The Jarrow March, the most famous protest of the Depression years, shocked London in 1936, the year in which thousands of British fascists tried to march through the predominantly Jewish East

End, only to be stopped in the so-called **Battle of Cable Street**. The end of the year brought a crisis within the royal family, too, when Edward VIII abdicated, following his decision to marry Wallis Simpson, a twice-divorced American. His brother, **George VI**, took over.

There were few public displays of patriotism with the outbreak of **World War II, and** even fewer preparations were made against the likelihood of aerial bombardment. The most significant step was the evacuation of 600,000 of London's most vulnerable citizens (mostly children), and around half that number had drifted back to the capital by the Christmas of 1939, the mid-point of the "phoney war". The Luftwaffe's bombing campaign, known as the **Blitz**, began on September 7, 1940, when in one night alone some 430 Londoners lost their lives, and over 1600 were seriously injured. For 57 consecutive nights the Nazis bombed the capital until the last raid on May 10, 1941. Further carnage was caused towards the end of the war by the pilotless V1 "doodlebugs" and V2 rockets, which caused another 20,000 casualties. In total, 30,000 civilians lost their lives in the bombing of London, with 50,000 injured and some 130,000 houses destroyed.

Post-war London

The end of the war in 1945 was followed by a general election, which brought a landslide victory for the Labour Party under **Clement Atlee**. The Atlee government created the **welfare state**, and initiated a radical programme of **nationalization**, which brought the gas, electricity, coal, steel and iron industries under state control, along with the inland transport services. London itself was left with a severe accommodation crisis, with some eighty percent of the housing stock damaged to some degree. In response, pre-fabricated houses were erected all over the city, some of which were to remain occupied for well over forty years. The LCC also began building huge housing estates on many of the city's numerous bomb sites, an often misconceived strategy which ran in tandem with the equally disastrous New Towns policy of central government.

To lift the country out of its gloom the **Festival of Britain** was staged in 1951 on derelict land on the south bank of the Thames, a site that was eventually transformed into the **South Bank Arts Centre**. Londoners turned up at this technological funfair in their thousands, but at the same time many were abandoning the city for good, the start of a process that in the 1960s saw the population decline by half a million. The ensuing labour shortage was made good by mass **immigration** from the former colonies, in particular the **Indian sub-continent** and the **West Indies**. The newcomers were given small welcome, and in 1958 violence broke out in the Notting Hill race riots.

Things picked up for Londoners, however, during the following decade. In the so-called **Swinging Sixties** London became the hippest city on the planet, thanks to the likes of the Beatles, the Rolling Stones, Twiggy and innumerable other habitués of Carnaby Street. Less groovily, in the middle of the decade London's local government was reorganized, the LCC being supplanted by the **Greater London Council** (GLC), whose jurisdiction covered a much wider area, including many Tory-dominated suburbs. As a result, the Conservatives gained power in the capital for the first time since 1934, and one of their first acts was to support a huge urban motorway scheme which would have displaced as many people as did the railway boom of the Victorian period. Luckily for London, Labour won control of the GLC in 1973 and halted the plans. The Labour victory also ensured that the Covent Garden building was saved for posterity, but it was against the grain. Elsewhere whole swathes of the city were pulled down and redeveloped, and many of London's worst tower blocks were built.

Thatcher and after

In 1979 **Margaret Thatcher** won the general election for the Conservatives, and the country and the capital would never be quite the same again. Thatcher went on to win three general elections, steering the country into a period of ever greater social polarization. While taxation policies and easy credit fuelled a consumer boom for the professional classes (the yuppies of the 1980s), the erosion of manufacturing industry and weakening of the welfare state created a calamitous number of people trapped in long-term unemployment, which topped three million in the early 1980s. The Brixton riots of 1981 and 1985 were reminders of the price of such divisive policies.

Nationally the Labour Party went into sharp decline, but in London the party won a narrow victory in the GLC elections on a radical manifesto which was implemented by its new leader **Ken Livingstone**, or "Red Ken" as the tabloids dubbed him. Under Livingstone the GLC poured money into projects among London's ethnic minorities, into the arts, and most famously into a subsidized fares policy which saw thousands abandon their cars in favour of inexpensive public transport. Such schemes endeared Livingstone to the hearts of many Londoners, but his popular brand of socialism was too much for the Thatcher government, who in 1986 abolished the GLC, leaving London as the only European capital without a directly elected body to represent it.

Abolition exacerbated tensions between the poorer and richer districts of the city. Rich Tory councils like Westminster proceeded to slash public services and sell off council houses to boost Tory support in marginal wards – a practice exposed by the district auditor in 1994 and currently under investigation. Meanwhile in impoverished Labour-held Lambeth, millions were being squandered by corrupt council employees. **Homelessness** returned to London in a big way for the first time since Victorian times, and the underside of Waterloo Bridge was transformed into a "Cardboard City", sheltering up to 2000 vagrants on any one night. In the face of government spending cuts, London council building programmes produced a pitiful 320 new homes in 1990.

The **Docklands** development was the one great Thatcherite experiment in the capital. Aimed at creating a new business quarter in the derelict docks of the East End, Docklands was hampered from the start by the Tories' blind faith in "market forces" and refusal to fund even transport links. Unable to find tenants for more than fifty percent of the available office space in the Canary Wharf development, the Canadian group Olympia & York found itself facing costs of some £38 million a day, and inevitably the receivers moved in. Docklands is still under-occupied and only tenuously connected to the rest of the city by the much-derided Docklands Light Railway.

In 1987, a year after the brief boom that followed deregulation of the stock exchange (the Big Bang), London's money market crashed, ushering in a recession which has still not been left behind. After Thatcher was deposed as Prime Minister by John Major, the Conservatives were re-elected, but London, in particular, is counting the cost of the Thatcher years. Riches were undoubtedly created: the middle classes, so long as they kept their jobs, did well, and their ranks grew. But the tax-cutting, which ensured their self-interested re-election of Thatcher and Major, had all too predictable consequences. The infrastructure of the city – indeed of Britain as a whole – has been left untended for the past twenty years, and the cracks are becoming craters.

As with the city, so with the people. Crime has soared amid the mass unemployment and poverty, and the city's residents have again been voting with their feet, moving out of London at a rate of 350,000 a year, to be replaced by just 250,000 newcomers from overseas and the provinces. With the ineffective John Major continuing with Thatcherite policies (the latest folly is to sell off the railways, antagonizing the most loyal commuters), even the Royal Family has joined in with protests: Prince Charles speaks out for compassionate liberalism while his estranged wife Diana sallies forth to meet the homeless in their cardboard shelters.

In the face of radical conservatism, dissident politics has become increasingly radicalized. The Thatcher years saw huge **demonstrations** in London: half a million for nuclear disarmament and a full-blooded riot against the new **Poll Tax** in 1990. Major, astonishingly, trumped even his predecessor with the dim-witted **Criminal Justice Act**, which targeted the young and vulnerable, making it virtually illegal for any group of people to gather in a manner that was not to the liking of the police. As it passed into law at the end of 1994, a series of demonstrations once more escalated into violence.

Such notes sound apocalyptic, but London will surely bounce back as the next millennium approaches. There is enough wealth around to sort out the problems, given the political will and a little imagination. There is certainly a pool of labour to fix the collapsing sewers and some of the semi-derelict tube stations. And there are signs already of a consensus that building new roads is not an answer to the city's impending gridlock. If, as looks likely, the Labour Party is elected in the next few years, London seems at least set to regain a properly elected governing body. It has to be hoped that it is given the power to reverse the last decades' decline.

An Architectural Chronology

Date	Buildings and architects (Buildings are listed by date of commencement)	*Main historical events*
50 AD		*43 Roman invasion*
100	First London Bridge (destroyed)	
190–220	Roman forum (destroyed)	
second century	Roman wall (ruins remain)	
	Temple of Mithras (ruins remain)	*410 Romans leave Britain*
		605 Bishopric of London established
1078	Tower of London	*1066 Battle of Hastings*
1106	Southwark Cathedral	*1086 Domesday Book*
1120	St Margaret Westminster	
1123	St Bartholomew the Great	
1160	Temple Church	
1205	St Helen's Bishopsgate	*1215 Magna Carta*
1245	present Westminster Abbey begun	*1216 First Parliament*
1297	Lambeth Palace	
1300	St Etheldreda	
"	Eltham Palace	
1350	Temple Church	*1348–49 Black Death*
1390	Westminster Abbey nave finished	*1381 Peasants' Revolt*
1394	Westminster Hall	
1400	Lincoln's Inn	
1410	Bishop's Palace, Fulham	
1411	Guildhall	*1415 Battle of Agincourt*
1492	Lincoln's Inn – Old Hall and Gatehouse	*1492 Columbus*
1503	Henry VII's Chapel, Westminster Abbey	*"discovers" America*
1514	Hampton Court Palace	*1509–47 Henry VIII*
1520	St Andrew Undershaft	
1530	St James's Palace	*1558–1603 Elizabeth I*
1586	Staple Inn	*1588 Spanish Armada*
1590	Holland House	*1603–25 James I*
1607	Charlton House	
1616	Queen's House, Greenwich (Inigo Jones)	
1619	Banqueting House, Whitehall (ditto)	
"	Lincoln's Inn Chapel	
1623	Queen's Chapel (Inigo Jones)	
1631	St Paul's Covent Garden & the Piazza (ditto)	

Date	Buildings and architects	*Main historical events*
1640	Lincoln's Inn Fields	
"	Lindsey House (Inigo Jones)	*1645–49 Civil War*
1661	Kensington Palace (Christopher Wren)	*1649–60 Commonwealth*
1665	Greenwich Palace (John Webb)	*1665 Great Plague*
1670	St Michael Cornhill (Christopher Wren)	*1666 Fire of London*
"	St Lawrence Jewry (ditto)	
"	St Mary-at-Hill (ditto)	
"	St Bride, Fleet Street (ditto)	
"	St Mary-le-Bow (ditto)	
1671	St Magnus (ditto)	
1672	Monument (Robert Hooke)	
1674	St Stephen Walbrook (Christopher Wren)	
1675	St James Garlickhithe (ditto)	
1676	St Paul's Cathedral (ditto)	
1677	St James's Piccadilly (ditto)	
"	St Anne and St Agnes (ditto)	
"	Christ Church, Newgate Street (ditto)	
1681	St Martin, Ludgate Hill (ditto)	
"	St Mary Abchurch (ditto)	
1682	Royal Hospital Chelsea (ditto)	
1683	St Mary Aldermary (ditto)	
1685	St Clement Eastcheap (ditto)	
1689	St Andrew by the Wardrobe (ditto)	
1695	Hampton Court Palace, East Wing (ditto)	*1689–1702 William & Mary*
"	King's Gallery & Orangery, Kensington (Nicholas Hawksmoor)	
1696	Royal Naval Hospital Greenwich (Wren)	*1702–14 Anne*
1709	Marlborough House (ditto)	*1707 Union with Scotland*
1712	St Alfege Greenwich (Hawksmoor)	*1714–27 George I*
1714	St George in the East (ditto)	
"	St Anne Limehouse (ditto)	
"	Christ Church, Spitalfields (ditto)	
"	St John, Smith Square (Thomas Archer)	
"	St Mary-le-Strand (James Gibbs)	
1715	Burlington House (Lord Burlington)	
1716	St Mary Woolnoth (Hawksmoor)	
"	St George Bloomsbury (ditto)	
1717	Woolwich Arsenal (John Vanbrugh)	
"	Vanbrugh Castle (ditto)	
1721	St Martin-in-the-Fields (James Gibbs)	
1725	Chiswick House (Lord Burlington)	
1731	St Giles in the Fields (Henry Flitcroft)	*1727–60 George II*
1733	Treasury Building (William Kent)	
1736	St Leonard Shoreditch (George Dance the Elder)	

Date	Buildings and architects	*Main historical events*
1739	Mansion House (ditto)	
1741	St Botolph Aldgate (ditto)	
1745	Horse Guards (William Kent)	
1746	Strawberry Hill (Horace Walpole)	
1761	Orangery & Pagoda, Kew (William Chambers)	*1760–1820 George III*
"	Syon House (Robert Adam)	
1763	Osterley Park (ditto)	
1764	Kenwood House (ditto)	*1764 Watt's steam engine*
1765	All Hallows, London Wall (George Dance the Younger)	
1776	Somerset House (William Chambers)	*1776 US Declaration of Independence*
1800	Pitshanger Manor (John Soane)	
1807	Royal Mint (Robert Smirke)	*1789 French Revolution*
1811	Dulwich Picture Gallery (John Soane)	
1816	Royal Opera House (John Nash)	*1815 Battle of Waterloo*
1822	All Soul's Langham Place (ditto)	
1823	British Museum (Robert Smirke)	
1825	Hyde Park Corner Screen & Arch (Decimus Burton)	
1826	Holy Trinity Cloudesley Square (Charles Barry)	
1827	Carlton House Terrace (John Nash)	
"	University College (William Wilkins)	
"	St George's Hospital (ditto)	
1831	Theatre Royal Haymarket (John Nash)	
1832	National Gallery (William Wilkins)	
1835	Houses of Parliament (Charles Barry & A. W. Pugin)	
1837	Reform Club (Charles Barry)	*1837–1901 Victoria*
1844	Palm House, Kew (Decimus Burton)	
1848	All Saints Margaret Street (William Butterfield)	*1851 Great Exhibition*
1859	Red House (Philip Webb)	
1863	Albert Memorial (George Gilbert Scott)	*1863 First London Underground line*
1868	St Pancras Station (ditto)	
1873	Natural History Museum (Alfred Waterhouse)	
"	Royal Geographical Society (R Norman Shaw)	
1874	Royal Courts of Justice (George Edmund Street)	
1879	Albert Hall Mansions (R Norman Shaw)	
1886	New Scotland Yard (ditto)	
1896	Horniman Museum (C. H. Townsend)	
1897	Whitechapel Art Gallery (ditto)	

Date	Buildings and architects	*Main historical events*
1899	Victoria and Albert Museum (Aston Webb)	
1901	Admiralty Arch (ditto)	
1906	Ritz Hotel (Arthur Davies)	*1901–10 Edward VII*
1908	Royal Automobile Club (ditto)	
1909	Hampstead Garden Suburb (Edwin Lutyens)	
1912	Buckingham Palace facade (Aston Webb)	*1914–18 World War I*
1919	Cenotaph (Edwin Lutyens)	
1924	Wembley Stadium (J. W. Simpson)	
1935	Reuters Building (Edwin Lutyens)	
1929	Battersea Power Station (Giles Gilbert Scott)	
1930	Olympia (Joseph Emberton)	
1932	Daily Express Building (Owen Williams)	
"	Senate House (Charles Holden)	
1933	Highpoint 1 & 2 (Berthold Lubetkin)	
"	Penguin Pool, Regent's Park Zoo (ditto)	
1935	Simpsons, Piccadilly (Joseph Emberton)	
1939	Waterloo Bridge (Giles Gilbert Scott)	*1939–45 World War II*
1951	Royal Festival Hall (LCC Architects)	*1951 Festival of Britain*
"	Heathrow Airport (Frederick Gibberd)	*1952– Elizabeth II*
1959	Barbican Estate (Chamberlin, Powell & Bon)	
1963	Centre Point (Richard Seifert)	
1964	Queen Elizabeth Hall & Hayward Gallery (LCC Architects)	
"	Economist Building (Alison & Peter Smithson)	
1967	National Theatre (Denys Lasdun)	
1977	Regent's Park Mosque (Frederick Gibberd)	*1973 Britain joins EEC*
1979	Tate Gallery Extension (James Stirling)	*1979 Thatcher government elected*
"	Lloyds Building (Richard Rogers)	
1981	National Westminster Tower (Richard Seifert)	
1983	TV-AM Building (Terry Farrell)	
1984	Broadgate complex (various architects)	*1986 GLC abolished*
1987	Embankment Place (Terry Farrell)	
1988	Canary Wharf Tower (Cesar Pelli)	
"	Richmond Riverside (Quinlan Terry)	
"	Sainsbury Wing, National Gallery (Robert Venturi & Denise Scott-Brown)	
1991	The London Ark (Ralph Erskine)	*1990 Poll Tax riot*
"	Waterloo International Terminal (Nicholas Grimshaw)	

London in Film

As early as 1889 Wordsworth Donisthorpe made a primitive moving film of Trafalgar Square. Since then, countless films have used a London setting, though it has to be admitted that the cinema has not always reflected the city's diversity. Location shooting became common only in the post-war period – until then, London-set films tended to be made in studios on the suburban edges, in places such as Elstree or Shepperton. Yet some fascinating films have been set in a semi-mythical London created on a studio soundstage, and part of their appeal is the very distance between London as it was portrayed and London as it was lived. The following list picks out the significant landmarks, and some of the differing versions, of London on film.

Broken Blossoms (D. W. Griffith, 1919). Limehouse melodrama about a peace-loving Chinese immigrant (Richard Bathelemess), the girl who loves him (Lilian Gish), and her brutal prize-fighter father (Donald Crisp). Remarkable for its display of Griffith's technique and Gish's incandescent performance.

The Lodger (Alfred Hitchcock, 1926). "The first true 'Hitchcock movie'" (according to Hitchcock), and one of the first of many variations on a Jack-the-Ripper theme, here given the "wrong man" twist much favoured by the director.

Piccadilly (E. A. Dupont, 1929). British pot-boiler made with Germanic style, featuring Anna May Wong caught in the East-West divide as she moves from Chinatown poverty to clubland luxury.

Underground (Anthony Asquith, 1929). Technically innovative pre-talkie set on and around the Northern Line, and culminating with a fight in Battersea Power Station.

Dr Jekyll and Mr Hyde (Rouben Mamoulian, 1931). Still the best version of this often-filmed story, with Frederic March in the title parts. Set in Paramount's chiaroscuro recreation of a repressive Victorian London, and made with an assured cinematic style.

Die Dreigroschenoper (G.W. Pabst, 1931). An un-Brechtian treatment of Brecht and Weill's update of *The Beggar's Opera*, placing the legendary Lotte Lenya in a stylized recreation of turn-of-the-century London. The film retained enough political bite to be banned on its initial British release.

Death at Broadcasting House (Reginald Denham, 1934). A conventional but clever whodunit given curiosity value by being set at the heart of the BBC.

The Man Who Knew Too Much (Alfred Hitchcock, 1934). Witty and pacy thriller about assassination-plotting anarchists, with Peter Lorre in fine villainous form, and a nice use of setting (an East End mission house, the Royal Albert Hall). Hitchcock directed a glossier remake in 1956.

Drôle de Drame (Marcel Carné, 1936). The great French director attempts to poke fun at the British love of detective stories, setting the action in a peculiar London designed by art director Alexander Trauner. Also known, appropriately enough, as *Bizarre, Bizarre*.

They Drive by Night (Arthur Woods, 1938). An atmospheric quota-quickie set in a world of Soho clubs and Great North Road transport caffs. Emlyn Williams stars as a petty thief on the run, Ernest Thesiger excels as a sinister sex-murderer.

The Adventures of Sherlock Holmes (Alfred Werker, 1939). The Baker Street detective has made countless screen appearances, but Basil Rathbone was the most convincing incarnation.

Here he and Nigel Bruce (Dr Watson) are pitted against Moriarty (George Zucco), out to steal the Crown Jewels.

Dark Eyes of London (Walter Summers, 1939). Moody British chiller from an Edgar Wallace story, with Bela Lugosi orchestrating a series of murders at a home for the blind, and disposing of the bodies in the Thames.

Fires Were Started (Humphrey Jennings, 1942). A recreation of a day in a firefighter's life during the Blitz. One of several vivid and highly individual films documenting English life in wartime made by Jennings in his too brief career.

This Happy Breed (David Lean, 1944). Inter-war saga of Clapham life, taken from Noel Coward's play, with the emphasis on community values and ordinary British decency. Enormously popular in its day.

Waterloo Road (Sidney Gilliat, 1944). Worried about his wife's infidelity a soldier goes AWOL. South-of-the-river melodrama with realist touches, and John Mills and Steward Grainger literally fighting out their differences.

Hangover Square (John Brahm, 1945). Not an address listed in the streetfinder, and having next to nothing to do with the Patrick Hamilton novel it was nominally based on, but an atmospheric Hollywood thriller, in which Laird Cregar plays a schizophrenic composer living in gas-lit Chelsea.

London Town (Wesley Ruggles, 1946). A big-budget technicolour musical that brought music hall comedian Sid Field to the screen and aimed to bring Hollywood style to post-war Britain. It ended up as a commercial and critical disaster.

Hue and Cry (Charles Crichton, 1947). Boys' Own adventure yarn featuring Jack Warner as a dubious Covent Garden trader, Alistair Sim as a timid writer of blood-and-thunder stories, and hordes of juvenile crime-fighters. Good use is made of the bomb-damaged locations.

It Always Rains on Sunday (Robert Hamer, 1947). An escaped convict (John McCallum) hides out in the Bethnal Green home of his former girlfriend (Googie Withers). Fatalistic and tense drama with a strong sense of place.

Oliver Twist (David Lean, 1948). An effective distillation of the Dickens novel, featuring Alec Guinness as a caricaturist's Fagin, and a stylized recreation of early nineteenth-century London from art director John Bryan.

Passport to Pimlico (Henry Cornelius, 1948). The quintessential Ealing Comedy, in which the inhabitants of Pimlico, discovering that they are actually part of Burgundy, abolish rationing and closing time. Full of all the usual eccentrics, among them Margaret Rutherford in particularly fine form as an excitable history don.

Spring in Park Lane (Herbert Wilcox, 1948). One of a series of refined romances directed by Wilcox, and pairing his real-life wife Anna Neagle (austerity Britain's most popular star) with Michael Wilding, here playing an impoverished nobleman who takes a job as a footman.

The Blue Lamp (Basil Dearden, 1949). Metropolitan police drama introducing genial P.C. Dixon (Jack Warner) and charting the hunt for his killer (bad boy Dirk Bogarde). Now seems to come from another world, but its location photography was groundbreaking.

Dance Hall (Charles Crichton, 1950). An evocative melodrama centred on the life and loves of four working-class women, who spend their Saturday nights at the Chiswick Palais, dancing to the sound of Ted Heath and his music.

Night and the City (Jules Dassin, 1950). London-set film noir, with Richard Widmark as a hustler on the run in an expressionistic city. Made when Dassin was himself escaping from McCarthyite America, and probably his best film.

Seven Days to Noon (Robert Boulting, 1950). Nightmares about the arms race lead a scientist (Barry Jones) to threaten to blow up London. Tense Cold War drama that gives an eerie view of the evacuated city.

Limelight (Charles Chaplin, 1952). Chaplin's final American film – a sentimental recreation of poverty and music hall life – was a return to his London roots. With Claire Bloom as the ballerina whose career is promoted by Calvero (Chaplin), and a cameo from Buster Keaton.

The Ladykillers (Alexander Mackendrick, 1955). Delightfully black comedy set somewhere at the back of King's Cross, with Katie Johnson as the nice old lady getting the better of Alec Guiness, Peter Sellars and assorted other crooks.

Every Day Except Christmas (Lindsay Anderson, 1957). Short, lyrical and somewhat idealized documentary about work and the workers at Covent Garden.

Nice Time (Claude Goretta, Alain Tanner, 1957). Short impressionistic view of Piccadilly Circus on a Saturday night, made by two Swiss film-makers and released like Anderson's film under the banner of "Free Cinema".

Expresso Bongo (Val Guest, 1959). A musical "comedy" in which smooth-talking agent Johnny Jackson (Laurence Harvey) takes "Bongo Herbert" (Cliff Richard) all the way from the coffee bars of Soho to the dizzy heights of fame.

Sapphire (Basil Dearden, 1959). A body discovered on Hampstead Heath is revealed to be that of a black woman passing for white. A worthy but fascinating "problem picture" that takes on rather more (black sub-culture, white racism and sexual repression) than it can deal with.

Beat Girl (Edmond T. Gréville, 1960). Also known as *Wild for Kicks*, this hilariously dated drama of teen rebellion marks Adam Faith's film debut and contains an early glimpse of Oliver Reed's smouldering skills. Notable for a wild party scene in Chislehurst Caves.

Peeping Tom (Michael Powell, 1960). A timid London cameraman (Carl Boehm) films women as he murders them. A discomforting look at voyeurism, sadism and movie-watching; reviled on its original release, but latterly recognised as one of the key works of British cinema.

The Day the Earth Caught Fire (Val Guest, 1961). London swelters as the earth edges towards the sun following nuclear tests. A solidly British science-fiction film based around the then Fleet Street headquarters of the Daily Express.

Gorgo (Eugene Lourii, 1961). A creature from the ocean floor is exhibited at Battersea Funfair, until its mother comes to take it home, knocking down assorted London monuments on her way. An enjoyably tacky variation on the old monster-in-the-city theme.

One Hundred and One Dalmatians (Wolfgang Reitherman, Hamilton S. Luske, Clyde Geromini, 1961). Disney's classic of animal liberation, in which the eponymous dogs do Scotland Yard's work, unmasking a plot to turn puppies into fur coats. Villainess Cruella de Vil still manages to steal the show.

It Happened Here (Kevin Brownlow, Andrew Mollo, 1963). A shoestring production, filmed in and around London, that imagines Britain in 1944 after a successful German invasion. An anti-fascist film that refused to see people in terms of simple heroes and villains.

The Pumpkin Eater (Jack Clayton, 1964). Pinter-scripted story of middle-class, mid-life crisis unravelling in St John's Wood, Regent's Park Zoo, and *Harrods*. Anne Bancroft is excellent as the mother of eight cracking under the strain.

Bunny Lake is Missing (Otto Preminger, 1965). Laurence Olivier plays a policeman trying to ascertain the whereabouts of Carol Lynley's daughter. An accomplished, psychological thriller set in an off-beat London. Creepy cameo by Noël Coward.

Four in the Morning (Anthony Simmons, 1965). This film started out as a documentary about the Thames, but evolved into a low-key yet affecting drama of a night in the life of two couples.

The Ipcress File (Sidney J. Furie, 1965). An attempt to create a more down-to-earth variety of spy thriller, with Michael Caine as bespectacled Harry Palmer, stuck in a London of offices and warehouses rather than the exotic locations of the Bond films.

Repulsion (Roman Polanski, 1965). A study of the sexual fears and mental disintegration of a young Belgian woman left alone in a Kensington flat. Polanski's direction and Catherine Deneuve's performance draw the audience into the claustrophobic nightmares of the central character.

Alfie (Lewis Gilbert, 1966). Cockney wide-boy Alfie Elkins (Michael Caine) has assorted affairs, and talks about them straight to the camera. An un-feminist comedy taken from Bill Naughton's play.

Blow-Up (Michelangelo Antonioni, 1966). Swinging London and some less obvious backgrounds (notably Maryon Park, Charlton) feature in this metaphysical mystery about a fashion photographer (David Hemmings) who may unwittingly have photographed evidence of a murder.

The Deadly Affair (Sidney Lumet, 1966). Downbeat adaptation of a John Le Carré novel concerning an investigation into the supposed suicide of a Foreign Office diplomat. One of a number of thrillers portraying London as a city of repressed secrets.

Georgy Girl (Silvio Narizzano, 1966). A comedy of mismatched couples enlivened by excellent performances from Lynne Redgrave (as plain but loveable Georgy) and Charlotte Rampling (as her beautiful but cold flatmate).

Morgan, A Suitable Case for Treatment (Karel Reisz, 1966). A schizophrenic artist (David

Warner) with a gorilla fixation attempts to win back his divorced wife (Vanessa Redgrave). The "madman as hero" message is rather swamped by the modish Sixties humour.

Tonite Let's All Make Love in London (Peter Whitehead, 1967). Documentary on the "Swinging London" phenomenon, including music from The Animals, an interview with Allen Ginsberg, and a happening at Alexander Palace. Very much of its time.

Up the Junction (Peter Collinson, 1967). Middle-class Polly (Suzy Kendall) moves from Chelsea to ungentrified Battersea. Adapted from Nell Dunn's novel, this well-intentioned attempt to put working-class London on the big screen lacked the commitment and vitality of Ken Loach's earlier television version.

One Plus One (Jean-Luc Godard, 1968). A deliberately disconnected mix of footage of the Rolling Stones, assorted Black Power militants in a Battersea junkyard, and "Eve Democracy" talking about culture and revolution. Also released as *Sympathy for the Devil*, with a complete version of the Stone's number; Godard wasn't pleased.

The Strange Affair (David Greene, 1968). Made at the sour end of the Sixties, and set in a landscape of office blocks and multi-storey car parks, this effectively gloomy police thriller stars Michael York as an innocent policeman in a corrupt world.

Leo the Last (John Boorman, 1969). Whimsical, sometimes striking, fantasy set in a crumbling Notting Hill terrace, where stateless prince Marcello Mastroianni gradually begins to identify with his neighbours.

Performance (Nicholas Roeg, Donald Cammell, 1969). A sadistic gangster (James Fox) finds shelter and begins to lose his identity in another Notting Hill residence, this one belonging to a reclusive rock star (Mick Jagger). An authentic piece of psychedelia, and a cult movie that just about lives up to its reputation.

Deep End (Jerzy Skolimowski, 1970). At the public baths a naive teenager (John Moulder-Brown) becomes obsessed by his older workmate (Jane Asher). Excellent bleak comedy, set in an unglamorous London, made by a Polish director and mainly shot in Munich.

Death Line (Gary Sherman, 1972). Effectively seedy horror film about cannibalistic ex-navvies lurking in the tunnels around Russell Square underground station. Most of the sympathy is reserved for the monsters.

Frenzy (Alfred Hitchcock, 1972). Hitchcock's final return to London, adapted from the novel *Goodbye Piccadilly, Farewell Leicester Square*, and filmed in and around Covent Garden. Displays all his old preoccupations (violence, sex, food . . .), with added graphic detail.

The Satanic Rites of Dracula (Alan Gibson, 1973). At one point known as *Dracula is Alive and Well and Living in London*, this Hammer horror uses the neat premise of a vampire property developer, but is otherwise unremarkable.

Punk in London (Wolfgang Büld, 1977). An earnest piece of German anthropology, featuring performances and interviews with the likes of The Sex Pistols, The Jam and X-Ray Specs.

Jubilee (Derek Jarman, 1978). Jarman's angry punk collage, in which Elizabeth I finds herself transported to the urban decay of late twentieth-century Deptford. Features Jordan as Amyl Nitrate, Little Nell as Crabs, Adam Ant as Kid and Jenny Runacre as the Queen.

The Long Good Friday (John Mackenzie, 1979). An East End gang boss (Bob Hoskins) has plans for the Docklands but finds himself fighting the IRA. A violent, contemporary thriller, looking towards the Thatcherite Eighties.

Babylon (Franco Rosso, 1980). Attempting to win a sound-system contest, Blue (Brinsley Forde) finds himself up against street crime, racism and police brutality. A sharp, South London drama with a fine reggae soundtrack.

The Falls (Peter Greenaway, 1980). Long, strange, ornithologically-obsessed pseudo-documentary, supposedly setting out to provide 92 biographies for the latest edition of the Standard Dictionary of the Violent Unexplained Event. The locations include Goldhawk Road and Birdcage Walk.

The Elephant Man (David Lynch, 1980). The story of John Merrick (John Hurt), exhibited as a fairground freak before being lionized by society. Freddie Francis's black-and-white photography brings out the beauty and horror of Victorian London. Much of it was shot in Shad Thames, on the south side of Tower Bridge.

An American Werewolf in London (John Landis, 1981). Comic horror movie with state-of-the-art special effects, about an innocent abroad who gets bitten. Required viewing for all American backpackers.

Dance with a Stranger (Mike Newell, 1984). A well-groomed recreation of Britain in the repressive Fifties, carried by Miranda Richardson's intense impersonation of Soho nightclub hostess Ruth Ellis, the last woman to be hanged.

Defence of the Realm (David Drury, 1985). Political thriller about state secrecy and newspaper ethics. With Gabriel Byrne, the always excellent Denholm Elliot, and some atmospheric London locations.

My Beautiful Laundrette (Stephen Frears, 1985). A surreal comedy of Thatcher's London, offering the unlikely combination of an entrepreneurial Asian, his ex-National Front boyfriend, and a laundrette called "Powders". Frears and scriptwriter Hanif Kureshi worked together again on *Sammy and Rosie Get Laid* (1987); set in riot-torn Ladbroke Grove, it lacked the magic of their first collaboration, but was at least better than *London Kills Me* (1991), which Kureshi directed.

Absolute Beginners (Julien Temple, 1986). Musical version of the Colin MacInnes book, attempting to create a bold, stylized version of late Fifties' Soho and Napoli (Notting Hill), but ending up as a confused mix of pastiche and pop promo.

Mona Lisa (Neil Jordan, 1986). A small-time crook (Bob Hoskins) falls for a high-class call-girl (Cathy Tyson) and helps search for her missing friend. Strikingly realized story of vice and betrayal, with great performances from the leads, and a view of King's Cross at its most infernal.

Hidden City (Stephen Poliakoff, 1987). Interesting piece of paranoia about an ill-matched couple (Charles Dance and Cassie Stuart) literally delving beneath the surface of the city. The plot treads fairly familiar territory but the subterranean locations reveal a decidedly unfamiliar aspect of London.

Little Dorritt (Christine Edzard, 1987). Two-part adaptation (running to six hours in total) of Dickens' novel of Victorian greed and deprivation. Faithful to the complexities of the original, but put together with almost too much care.

Dealers (Colin Buckley, 1989). A risk-taking city trader with a private plane discovers that there's more to life than making money. A film as slick and empty as the characters it portrays.

Melancholia (Andi Engel, 1989). Intelligent thriller about a London-based German art critic (Jeroen Krabbe) whose radical past is brought back to him when he's asked to assassinate a Chilean torturer. Effective portrait of urban angst.

Queen of Hearts (Jon Amiel, 1989). Family life and troubles in Little Italy, London. This genial mix of fantasy and realism comes complete with a talking pig, a beautifully shiny espresso coffee machine, and a jumbled sense of time and place.

I Hired a Contract Killer (Aki Kaurismäki, 1990). Jean-Paul Léaud decides to end it all by hiring a hit man, and then changes his mind. A typically wry film from this Finnish director, featuring such lesser-known landmarks as the Honolulu (a Docklands bar) and Vic's Café (in Hampstead Cemetery).

The Krays (Peter Medak, 1990). A chronicle of the life of Bethnal Green's gangland twins (Gary and Martin Kemp) that portrays them both as violent anti-heroes and damaged mother's boys. With Billie Whitelaw as the strong-willed mother.

Life is Sweet (Mike Leigh, 1990). Comic, poignant and acutely observed picture of suburban life and eating habits, with Leigh's semi-improvisational approach drawing fine performances from Alison Steadman, Jim Broadbent and just about everyone else.

Riff-Raff (Ken Loach, 1990). A young Glaswegian works on a dodgy East End building site and shares a squat with a hopeful singer from Belfast. Less didactic and more comic than much of the director's work, Loach's film is good at conveying the camaraderie of the workers, but less convincing in its story of love found and lost.

Naked (Mike Leigh, 1993). David Thewlis is brilliant as the disaffected and garrulous misogynist who goes on a tour through the underside of what he calls "the big shitty" – life is anything but sweet in Leigh's darkest and most substantial film.

London (Patrick Keillor, 1994). Paul Schofield is the sardonic narrator of this "fictional documentary", describing three pilgrimages to little-visited London sights: the first to Strawberry Hill, Twickenham; the second in search of Edgar Allan Poe's old school in Stoke Newington; and the third along the river Brent. A witty and original film essay that looks at both London's literary past and the city's political present.

Guy Barefoot

Books

Given the enormous number of books on London, the list below is necessarily a highly selective one. Most of the recommendations we've made are in print and in paperback – those that are out of print (o/p) should be fairly easy to track down in second-hand bookshops (see p.520). Publishers are detailed with the British publisher first, separated by an oblique slash from the US publisher, in cases where both exist. Where books are published in only one of these countries, UK or US follows the publisher's name; where the book is published by the same company in both countries, the name of the company appears just once. UP designates University Press.

Travel and Journals

James Boswell, *London Journal* (Penguin). Boswell's diary, written in the year following his arrival in London, is remarkably candid about his frequent dealings with the city's prostitutes, and a fascinating insight into eighteenth-century life.

John Betjeman, *Betjeman's London* (John Murray). A selection of writings and poems by the Poet Laureate, who spearheaded the campaign to save London's architectural heritage in the 1960s.

Gustave Doré & Blanchard Jerrold, *London: A Pilgrimage* (Dover). This travel sketchbook by the French duo was first published in 1872; it includes over 180 superb illustrations by Doré alongside text by Jerrold, taking you through every stratum of Victorian London.

John Evelyn, *The Diary of John Evelyn* (Oxford UP). In contrast to Pepys, his contemporary, Evelyn gives away very little of his personal life but his diaries cover a much greater period of English history and a much wider range of topics.

Daniel Farson, *Soho in the Fifties* (Pimlico, UK). Rose-tinted reminiscences of boho life in Soho and Fitzrovia by a writer who hung out at the *Colony* club with the likes of Jeffrey Bernard, Colin MacInnes, Francis Bacon and Lucien Freud.

George Orwell, *Down and Out in Paris and London* (Penguin). Orwell's tramp's-eye view of the 1930s, written from first-hand experience. The London section is particularly harrowing.

Samuel Pepys, *The Shorter Pepys* (Penguin); *The Illustrated Pepys* (Unwin/University of California). Pepys kept a voluminous diary while he was living in London from 1660 until 1669, recording the fall of the Commonwealth, the Restoration, the Great Plague and the Great Fire, as well as describing the daily life of the nation's capital. The unabridged version is published in eleven volumes; Penguin's *Shorter Pepys* is abridged (though still massive); Unwin's is made up of just the choicest extracts accompanied by contemporary illustrations.

V. S. Pritchett, *London Perceived* (Hogarth/Harcourt Brace). An extended soliloquy by a London-based writer who lived in the city through both wars and much more besides. First published in 1962.

Andrew Saint & Gillian Darley, *The Chronicles of London* (Weidenfeld & Nicolson/St Martin's Press). Selection of first-hand accounts of the city, chronologically laid out – from Tacitus to 1960s Labour politician Richard Crossman – and beautifully illustrated.

Peter Vansittart, *London: A Literary Companion* (John Murray/Trafalgar). A rambling guide to the city, sprinkled with large chunks of literary quotes from everyone from Marx to P. G. Wodehouse.

A. N. Wilson, *The Faber Book of London/The Norton Book of London* (Faber/Norton). A voluminous collection of writings on all aspects of the capital by writers as diverse as Dostoyevsky and Joe Orton.

History, Society and Politics

Francoise Barret-Ducrocq, *Love in the Time of Victoria* (Penguin). An extraordinary insight into the sexual mores of the London working-class, reaped mostly from the archives of the Thomas Coram Foundling Hospital.

E. J. Burford, *The Bishop's Brothels; Wits, Wenchers and Wantons; London: The Synfulle Citie* (all Hale, UK). Burford has written numerous somewhat prurient books on the sexual practices of Londoners through the ages. *The Bishop's Brothels* discusses the medieval whorehouses of Southwark, while *Wits, Wenchers and Wantons* is a bawdy history of post-Restoration Covent Garden. *London: The Synfulle Citie* covers the capital's bumping and grinding from Roman times to the eighteenth century.

Angus Calder, *The Myth of the Blitz* (Pimlico, UK). A timely antidote to the backs-against-the-wall, "London can take it" tone of most books on this period. Calder dwells instead on the capital's internees – Communists, conscientious objectors and "enemy aliens" – and the myth-making processes of the media of the day.

Kellow Chesney, *Victorian Underworld* (Penguin). Lively trawl through the low-life of nineteenth-century London, its prison-houses, slums and criminal fraternity.

Hugh Clout *London History Atlas* (Times Books/ Harper Collins). This history atlas is packed full of illustrations and maps, which accompany a detailed account of the city's development from Londinium to Docklands.

William J. Fishman & Nicholas Breach, *The Streets of East London* (Duckworth, UK). Eminently readable social history of the East End from Victorian times to the present day by a Jewish East Ender and scholar, accompanied by black-and-white photos, old and new.

Peter Linebaugh, *The London Hanged* (Penguin). Superb Marxist analysis of crime and punishment in the eighteenth century, drawing on the history of those hanged at Tyburn.

Henry Mayhew, *London Labour and the London Poor* (Penguin). Mayhew's pioneering study of Victorian London, based on research carried out in the 1840s and 1850s.

Nick Merriman (ed), *The Peopling of London* (Museum of London, UK). A large illustrated history of immigration to the capital from the French Huguenots to the Somalis of the 1990s, with a separate section tracing the progress of each community.

George Theodore Wilkinson, *The Newgate Calendar* (Cardinal, UK). Grim and gory account of the most famous London criminals of the day – Captain Kidd, Jack Sheppherd, Dick Turpin – with potted biographies of each victim, ending with an account of his execution. First published in 1828, it was second in popularity only to the Bible at the time of publication.

Roy Porter, *London: A Social History* (Hamish Hamilton). Published in 1994, this immensely readable history is one of the best books on London published since the war. It is particularly strong on the continuing saga of London's local government and includes an impassioned critique of the damage done by Mrs Thatcher.

Donald Rumbelow, *The Complete Jack the Ripper* (Penguin/Berkley UP). Of all the books exploiting this sordid tale of misogyny, Rumbelow's stands head and shoulders above the rest, trashing most previous accounts as sensationalist, and concluding that there is insufficient evidence to pin the crime on any suspect.

Gareth Stedman-Jones, *Outcast London* (Penguin). A superb and scholarly Marxist critique of class conflict in Victorian London.

John Stow, *A Survey of London* (Alan Sutton, UK). Stow, a retired tailor, set himself the unenviable task of writing the first ever account of the city in 1598, for which he is now revered, though at the time the task forced him into penury.

Richard Tames, *A Traveller's History of London* (Windrush Press/Interlink). A useful and compact introduction.

Andy Thornley (ed), *The Crisis of London* (Routledge). Collection of academic essays on contemporary issues facing London as it approaches the next millennium.

Judith R. Walkowitz, *City of Dreadful Delight: Narratives of Sexual Danger in Late-Victorian London* (Virago/Chicago UP). Weighty feminist tract on issues such as child prostitution and the Ripper murders, giving a powerful overview of the image of women in the fiction and media of the day.

Gavin Weightman, *London River* (Collins & Brown/Trafalgar). A well-illustrated account of the history of the Thames, once London's main thoroughfare and source of (not so fresh) water.

Ben Weinreb & Christopher Hibbert, *The London Encyclopaedia* (MacMillan/St Martin's Press). More than 1000 pages of concisely presented information on London past and present, accompanied by the odd illustration. The most fascinating book on the capital.

Art, Architecture and Archeology

Ken Allinson & Victoria Thornton, *A Guide to London's Contemporary Architecture* (Butterworth/ Heinemann). Comprehensive gazetteer to the new buildings, great and small, erected all over Greater London in the 1980s and 1990s, with a black-and-white photo for each entry.

Felix Barker & Ralph Hyde, *London As It Might Have Been* (John Murray, UK). A richly illustrated book on the weird and wonderful plans which never quite made it from the drawing board.

Felix Barker & Peter Jackson, *The History of London in Maps* (Barrie & Jenkins/Abbeville Press). A beautiful volume of maps, from the earliest surviving chart of 1558 to the new Docklands, with accompanying text explaining the history of the city and its cartography.

John Betjeman, *Victorian and Edwardian London from Old Photographs* (Batsford, UK). Self-explanatory title, dating back to the very earliest days of British photography, recording the building of much of the city we see today.

Bill Brandt, *London in the Thirties* (Gordon Fraser, UK). Brandt's superb black-and-white photos pay witness to a London lost in the Blitz.

Robert Cowan, *London After Dark* (Phaidon/ Chronicle). Unusual, arty and highly atmospheric black-and-white photos of the city at night.

Joe Friedman, *Inside London* (Prentice Hall). Beautiful colour illustrations of London's most ostentatious and opulent interors, many of which are out of bounds to the public, though details of accessibility appear at the end of the book.

Elaine Harwood & Andrew Saint, *London* (HMSO, UK). Part of the excellent series, *Exploring England's Heritage*, sponsored by English Heritage. It's highly selective, though each building is discussed at some length and well illustrated.

Samantha Hardingham, *London: A Guide to Recent Architecture* (Artemis, UK). Wonderful pocket guide to the architecture of the last ten years or so, with a knowledgeable, critical text and plenty of black-and-white photos.

Howgego, *London in the Twenties and Thirties* (Fitzhouse, UK). Collection of black-and-white photos of inter-war London.

Hawkes & Barker, *London from the Air* (Ebury Press/Trafalgar). The best of the aerial photo albums, with some intriguing arty shots of the city's more unusual landscapes.

Edward Jones & Christopher Woodward, *A Guide to the Architecture of London* (Weidenfeld & Nicolson/Thames & Hudson). Straightforward illustrated catalogue of London's buildings, each one accompanied by a black-and-white photo, and with useful maps at the beginning of each chapter.

Steven Parissien, *Regency Style*; *Adam Style* (both Phaidon/Preservation Press); *Palladian Style* (Phaidon/Chronicle). Glossy coffee-table books with arty photographic illustrations. The Regency volume is particularly strong on Sir John Soane's work.

Niklaus Pevsner and others, *The Buildings of London* (Penguin, 3 vols). Magisterial series, covering just about every structure in the capital. This project was initially a one-man show, but later authors have revised Pevsner's text, inserting newer buildings but generally respecting the founder's personal tone. So far three of four projected London volumes have been published, with just Northeast London still to come.

Phillips & Phillips, *Notting Hill in the 1960s* (Lawrence & Wishart/Humanities). A unique snapshot of Notting Hill in its slum years when it was home to thousands of newly arrived West Indian immigrants.

Richard Rogers & Mark Fisher, *A New London* (Penguin, UK). A blueprint for London in the next millennium by the architect of the Lloyd's building.

Ann Saunders, *The Art and Architecture of London* (Phaidon, UK). Weighty, well-illustrated and clearly-presented run-down of just about every significant building in and around the capital.

John Schofield, *The Building of London* (British Museum Press, UK). A copiously illustrated architecural and archeological guide to pre-Fire London, stretching from the Norman Conquest to the Great Fire.

John Summerson, *Georgian London* (Penguin/ Trafalgar). Scholarly treatise on the architecture of the capital between 1714 and 1830 which still predominates in areas like Mayfair, Marylebone and Bloomsbury. The Trafalgar volume is richly illustrated.

Richard Trench & Ellis Hillman, *London under London* (John Murray/Trafalgar). Fascinating book revealing the secrets of every aspect of the capital's subterranean history, from the lost rivers of the underground to the gas and water systems.

Stephanie Williams, *Docklands* (Phaidon/Van Nos Reinhold). Useful pocket-size architectural guide to the good, bad, old and new in the Docklands area, with photos of the vast majority of edifices and strong views on all of them.

Literature

Peter Ackroyd, *English Music* (Penguin/Ballantine), *Hawksmoor* (Penguin, UK), *The House of Doctor Dee* (Penguin, UK), *The Great Fire of London* (Penguin/Chicago UP) and *Dan Leno and the Limehouse Golem* (Sinclair Stevenson, UK). Ackroyd's novels are all based on arcane aspects of London, wrapped into thriller-like narratives, and conjuring up kaleidoscopic visions of various ages of English culture. *Hawskmoor*, about the great church architect, is the most popular and enjoyable.

Martin Amis, *London Fields* (Penguin/Random House). "Ferociously witty, scabrously scatological and balefully satirical," it says on the back cover, though many regard Amis Jnr's observation of low-life London as pretentious drivel.

J. G. Ballard, *Concrete Island* (Vintage/Farrar Strauss Giroux) and *High Rise* (Vintage/Carroll & Graf). Wild stuff. In *Concrete Island*, a car crashes on the Westway, leaving its driver stranded on the central reservation, unable to flag down passing cars; in *High Rise* the residents of a high-rise block of flats in East London go slowly mad.

Samuel Beckett, *Murphy* (Jupiter, UK). Nihilistic, dark-humoured vision of the city, written in 1938, and told through the eyes of anti-hero Murphy.

James Boswell, *Life of Samuel Johnson* (Penguin). London's most famous man of letters has his engagingly low-life Scottish biographer, thiry years his junior, to thank for the longevity of his reputation.

Elizabeth Bowen, *The Heat of the Day* (Penguin). Bowen worked for the Ministry of Information during the war, and witnessed the Blitz first-hand from her Marylebone flat; this novel perfectly captures the dislocation and rootlessness of wartime London.

Anthony Burgess, *A Dead Man in Deptford* (Vintage, UK). Playwright Christopher Marlowe's unexplained murder in a tavern in Deptford provides the background for this historical novel, which brims over with Elizabethan life.

G. K. Chesterton, *The Napoleon of Notting Hill* (Oxford UP). Written in 1904 but set eighty years in the future, in a London divided into squabbling independent boroughs – something prophetic there – and ruled by royalty selected on a rotational basis.

Joseph Conrad, *The Secret Agent* (Penguin). Conrad's wonderful spy story based on the botched Anarchist bombing of Greenwich Observatory in 1894, exposing the hypocricies of both the police and the Anarchists.

Buchi Emecheta, *Second Class Citizen* (Heinemann, UK). A fine novel whose heroine follows her husband to London from Lagos.

Daniel Defoe, *Journal of the Plague Year* (Penguin). An account of the Great Plague seen through the eyes of an East End saddler, written some sixty years after the event.

Charles Dickens, *Bleak House, A Christmas Tale, Little Dorritt, Oliver Twist* (Penguin). The descriptions in Dickens' London-based novels have become the clichés of the Victorian city: the fog, the slums and the stinking river. *Little Dorritt* is set mostly in the Borough and contains some of his most trenchant pieces of social analysis; much of *Bleak House* is set around the Inns of Court that Dickens knew so well.

Farrukh Dhondy, *East End at Your Feet* (Macmillan, UK). Short stories on Asian life in the East End.

Alison Fell, *Every Move You Make* (o/p). Bleak low-life vision of London in the 1970s, viewed from a squat in the seedy King's Cross district.

Monica Grant, *The Ragga and the Royal* (The X Press, UK). Princess Di discovers what raggamuffins are really like, as she gets involved with a Jungle DJ. Wicked.

Henry Green, *Caught* (Collins Harvill/Kelley). In the claustrophobic atmosphere of the "phoney war" of late 1939, auxiliary firemen re-live painful memories which are finally exorcized by the fire of the Blitz.

Graham Greene, *The Human Factor, It's a Battlefield, The Ministry of Fear, The End of the Affair* (all Penguin). Greene's London novels are all fairly bleak, ranging from *The Human Factor*, which probes the underworld of the city's spies, to *The Ministry of Fear*, which is set during the Blitz.

Patrick Hamilton, *20,000 Streets Under the Sky* (Hogarth/Trafalgar). Trilogy completed in 1935 focusing on the interconnected lives of three people who frequent a Fitzrovia pub.

Helene Hanff, *84 Charing Cross.* (Warner/Moyer Bell). A touching novel of letters between the author and a now defunct Charing Cross Road bookshop.

Russell Hoban, *The Lion of Boaz-Jachin and Jachin-Boaz* (Picador, UK). Hoban's hugely enjoyable grail-novel begins in front of the Assyrian sculptures of the British Museum, and ranges through the London Underground.

Maxim Jakubowski, *London Noir* (Serpent's Tail, UK). A selection of contemporary crime writings based around the capital.

Henry James, *The Awkward Age* (Penguin). Light, ironic portrayal of London high society at the turn of the century.

P. D. James, *Original Sin* (Faber). James's latest crime novel is not one of her best, though the locations – London's Docklands – are atmospheric.

Hanif Kureishi, *The Buddha of Suburbia* (Faber). Raunchy account of life as an Anglo-Asian in late Sixties' suburbia, and the art scene in the Seventies.

Rosamund Lehmann, *The Weather in the Streets* (Virago/Trafalgar). Tragic sequel to *Invitation to the Waltz*, in which the heroine, Olivia Curtis, finds herself in boho London trying to breathe life into a doomed love affair.

Jack London *The People of the Abyss* (Journeyman/L. Hill Books). London's classic London novel.

Colin MacInnes, *Absolute Beginners* (Allison & Busby, UK). MacInnes' story of life in Soho and Notting Hill in the 1950s (much influenced by Selvon – see below) is infinitely better than the film of the same name.

Somerset Maugham, *Liza of Lambeth* (Mandarin/Penguin). Maugham considered himself a "second-rater" but this book on Cockney low-life is packed with vivid local colour.

Timothy Mo, *Sour Sweet* (Vintage/Random House). Very funny and very sad story of a newly arrived Chinese family struggling to understand the English way of life, written with great insight by Mo, who is himself of mixed parentage.

Michael Moorcock, *Mother London* (o/p). A magnificent rambling novel by a once-fashionable but now very much underrated writer.

Thomas Pynchon, *Gravity's Rainbow* (Picador/Penguin). Pynchon's great novel features sporadic V2-directed scenes in wartime London, not to mention a wonderful description of British boiled sweets, and a rooftop banana breakfast.

Thomas de Quincey, *Confessions of an English Opium Eater* (Penguin). Tripping out with the most famous literary drug-taker after Coleridge, and one of the greatest of all English prose stylists.

Derek Raymond, *Not till the Red Fog Rises* (Little Brown). A book which "reeks with the pervasive stench of excrement," as Ian Sinclair (see below) put it, this is a low-life spectacular set in the seediest sections of the capital.

Will Self, *The Quantity Theory of Insanity* and *My Idea of Fun* (both Penguin). Along with Martin Amis, Self is the current darling of the London literary world. Incisive social commentator or self-indulgent smart-arse? Judge for yourself.

Samuel Selvon, *The Lonely Londoners* (Longman, UK). "Gives us the smell and feel of this rather horrifying life. Not for the squeamish," ran the quote from the *Evening Standard* on the original cover. This is, in fact, a wry and witty account of the Afro-Carribean experience in London in the 1950s.

Ian Sinclair, *White Chapell, Scarlet Tracings; Down River* (both Paladin/Random House); *Radon Daughters* (Cape/Random House). Sinclair's idiosyncratic and richly textured novels are a strange mix of Hogarthian caricature, New Age mysticism and conspiracy-theory rant. Deeply offensive and highly recommended.

Stevie Smith, *Novel on Yellow Paper* (Virago/New Directions). Poet Stevie Smith's first novel takes place in the publishing world of 1930s' London.

John Sommerfield, *May Day* (o/p). Set in the revolutionary fervour of the 1930s, this is a novel "as if *Mrs Dalloway* was written by a Communist Party bus driver" in the words of one reviewer.

Paul Theroux, *The London Embassy* (Penguin). Not Theroux at his best, though enthusiasts for *The Consul's File* may be interested in the hero's posting to London of the 1980s.

Izaak Walton, *Compleat Angler* (Oxford UP). Light-hearted seventeenth-century fishing guide set on London's River Lea, sprinkled with poems and songs. It has gone through more reprints than any other book apart from the Bible.

H. G. Wells, *Tono-Bungay* (Everyman/C.E. Tuttle). A failed London pharmacist makes a valueless best-selling medicine – and a lot of money.

Patrick White, *The Living and the Dead* (Penguin). Novel set in 1930s' London by the Australian Nobel Prize winner.

P. G. Wodehouse, *Jeeves Omnibus* (Penguin). Bertie Wooster and his stalwart butler, Jeeves, were based in Mayfair, and many of their exploits take place with London showgirls, and in the Drones gentlemen's club.

Virginia Woolf, *Mrs Dalloway* (Penguin). Woolf's novel relates the thoughts of a London society hostess and a shell-shocked war veteran, with her "stream of consciousness" style in full flow.

Specialist Guides

Felix Barker & Denise Silvester-Carr, *The Black Plaque Guide to London* (Constable, UK). An alternative to the official Blue Plaque Guide (see below), cataloguing dens of vice, abodes of love and the homes of the disreputable.

Asa Briggs, *Marx in London* (o/p). Slim volume detailing the whereabouts of Karl Marx during his thirty-four-year exile in London, with photos and practical info; there is a small postcript on Lenin's visits, too.

Peter Bushell, *London's Secret History* (Constable, UK). Esoteric romp through London, focusing on the most eccentric and mischievous former inhabitants of each area.

Jennifer Clarke, *In Our Grandmothers' Footsteps* (Virago/Macmillan). Biographical A–Z of London's most illustrious women, from royal mistresses such as Nell Gwynne to out-and-out feminists like Mary Wollstonecraft.

Judi Culbertson & Tom Randall, *Permanent Londoners* (Robson Books/Chelsea Green). An illustrated guide to the finest of London's cemeteries, from Westminster Abbey and St Paul's to the Victorian splendours of Highgate and Kensal Green. Very good on biographical histories of the deceased, too.

Caroline Dakers, *The Blue Plaque Guide to London* (Macmillan, UK). Potted biographies of the famous (and not so famous) people commemorated by blue plaques across London.

Michael Elliman & Frederiock Roll, *Pink Plaque Guide to London* (GMP, UK). A–Z of gay and lesbian residents from the famous – Oscar Wilde, Vita Sackville-West and E. M. Forster – to the not so well-known.

Bob Gilbert, *The Green London Way* (Lawrence & Wishart, UK). This hundred-mile walk (also cyclable) circles the capital, taking in favourites like Greenwich and Kew Gardens, but also covering more unusual urban landscapes such as the Northern Outfall Sewerway. Politically astute and ecologically sound text, too.

Fran Hazelton, *London's American Past* (Macmillan, UK). A twelve-mile walk tracing the city's long-standing American connections from Bejamin Franklin to General Eisenhower.

Kay Mann, *London: The German Connection* (KT Publishing, UK). Fun anecdotal run-down of our very German royal family from the Hanovers to Prince Albert himself, plus sections on the likes of Handel, Heine, Holbein and Marx.

Ian McAuley, *Guide to Ethnic London* (Butler & Tanner/Saint Mut). A fine, accessible outline of the major ethnic communities in present-day London, with useful practical tips and a good all-round bibliography.

Luree Miller, *Literary Villages of London* (Starrhill Press/Elliott & Clark). Pocket-sized anecdotal guide to the literary inhabitants of old in the City, Bloomsbury, Chelsea and Hampstead.

Main Index

C

D

H

I

J

K

L

O

P

Q

R

Index of Museums

Help Us Update

We've gone to a lot of effort to ensure that this first edition of *The Rough Guide to London* is up-to-date and accurate. However, London information changes fast: new bars and clubs appear and disappear, museums alter their displays and opening hours, restaurants and hotels change prices and standards. If you feel there are places we've under-praised or overrated, omitted or ought to omit, please let us know. All suggestions, comments or corrections are much appreciated and we'll send a copy of the next edition (or any other Rough Guide if you prefer) for the best letters.

Please mark letters "Rough Guide London Update" and send to:

The Rough Guides, 1 Mercer Street, London WC2H 9QJ, or

The Rough Guides, 375 Hudson Street, 3rd Floor, New York NY 10014.

DIRECT ORDERS IN THE USA

Title	ISBN	Price
Amsterdam	1858280869	$13.59
Andalucia	185828094X	$14.95
Australia	1858280354	$18.95
Barcelona & Catalunya	1858281067	$17.99
Berlin	1858280338	$13.99
Brazil	1858281024	$15.95
Brittany & Normandy	1858281261	$14.95
Bulgaria	1858280478	$14.99
California	1858280907	$14.95
Canada	185828130X	$14.95
Classical Music on CD	185828113X	$19.95
Corsica	1858280893	$14.95
Crete	1858281326	$14.95
Cyprus	185828032X	$13.99
Czech & Slovak Republics	185828029X	$14.95
Egypt	1858280753	$17.95
England	1858280788	$16.95
Europe	185828077X	$18.95
Florida	1858280109	$14.95
France	1858281245	$16.95
Germany	1858281288	$17.95
Greece	1858281318	$16.95
Greek Islands	1858281636	$14.95
Guatemala & Belize	1858280451	$14.95
Holland, Belgium & Luxembourg	1858280877	$15.95
Hong Kong & Macau	1858280664	$13.95
Hungary	1858281237	$14.95
India	1858281040	$22.95
Ireland	1858280958	$16.95
Italy	1858280311	$17.95
Kenya	1858280435	$15.95
London	1858291172	$12.95
Mediterranean Wildlife	0747100993	$15.95
Malaysia, Singapore & Brunei	1858281032	$16.95
Morocco	1858280400	$16.95
Nepal	185828046X	$13.95
New York	1858280583	$13.95
Nothing Ventured	0747102082	$19.95
Pacific Northwest	1858280923	$14.95
Paris	1858281253	$12.95
Poland	1858280346	$16.95
Portugal	1858280842	$15.95
Prague	1858281229	$14.95
Provence & the Côte d'Azur	1858280230	$14.95
Pyrenees	1858280931	$15.95
St Petersburg	1858281334	$14.95
San Francisco	1858280826	$13.95
Scandinavia	1858280397	$16.99
Scotland	1858280834	$14.95
Sicily	1858280370	$14.99
Spain	1858280818	$16.95
Thailand	1858280168	$15.95
Tunisia	1858280656	$15.95
Turkey	1858280885	$16.95
Tuscany & Umbria	1858280915	$15.95
USA	185828080X	$18.95
Venice	1858280362	$13.99
Wales	1858280966	$14.95
West Africa	1858280141	$24.95
More Women Travel	1858280982	$14.95
World Music	1858280176	$19.95
Zimbabwe & Botswana	1858280419	$16.95
Rough Guide Phrasebooks		
Czech	1858281482	$5.00
French	185828144X	$5.00
German	1858281466	$5.00
Greek	1858281458	$5.00
Italian	1858281431	$5.00
Spanish	1858281474	$5.00

Rough Guides are available from all good bookstores, but can be obtained directly in the USA and Worldwide (except the UK*) from Penguin:

Charge your order by Master Card or Visa (US$15.00 minimum order): call 1-800-253-6476; or send orders, with complete name, address and zip code, and list price, plus $2.00 shipping and handling per order to: Consumer Sales, Penguin USA, PO Box 999 – Dept #17109, Bergenfield, NJ 07621. No COD. Prepay foreign orders by international money order, a cheque drawn on a US bank, or US currency. No postage stamps are accepted. All orders are subject to stock availability at the time they are processed. Refunds will be made for books not available at that time. Please allow a minimum of four weeks for delivery.

The availability and published prices quoted are correct at the time of going to press but are subject to alteration without prior notice. Titles currently not available outside the UK will be available by July 1995. Call to check.

* For UK orders, see separate price list